BENGAL
AND
ASSAM BEHAR AND ORISSA

BENGAL
AND
ASSAM BEHAR AND ORISSA

Their History, People, Commerce, and Industrial Resources

COMPILED BY
SOMERSET PLAYNE, F.R.G.S.

ASSISTED BY J. W. BOND

EDITED BY ARNOLD WRIGHT

GYAN

Published by

GYAN

Gyan Publishing House
5, Ansari Road
Daryaganj, New Delhi-110002
Phone: 011-47034999, 9811692060
E-mail: books@gyanbooks.com

Distribution Network
gyanbooks.com
India, USA, Canada, UK, Australia, France

ISBN : 978-81-212-3145-9 (PB)
First Published, 1917

2nd Impression 2020

Printed at: Gyan Press, Delhi.

BENGAL AND ASSAM BEHAR AND ORISSA

Their History, People, Commerce, and Industrial Resources

COMPILED BY

SOMERSET PLAYNE, F.R.G.S.

ASSISTED BY J. W. BOND

EDITED BY ARNOLD WRIGHT

THE FOREIGN AND COLONIAL COMPILING AND PUBLISHING CO.

27 PILGRIM STREET, LONDON, E.C.

1917

PREFACE

THE issue of this volume to the public at the present juncture, when the problem of the future of the Empire is receiving the special attention of Imperial statesmen, calls for no apology. Never was there a time when the fullest information in regard to all component parts of the vast territories that owe allegiance to the British Crown was more needed; never was there an occasion which more insistently called for the production of the amplest material which may throw a light on the complex questions of commercial polity, the supreme importance of which has been so abundantly demonstrated in the Great War. We are at the parting of the ways in Imperial policy, and upon the decisions taken will depend the future destinies of all the great communities of the far-flung British possessions. As an aid to that "thinking Imperially" which is the first essential to a successful handling of the questions which are now clamouring for settlement, this volume may reasonably claim to have a distinct purpose. It is one of a series of publications commenced some years ago with the object of supplying the British public with a picture—complete as far as literary and pictorial effort could make it—of the several different parts of the Empire. In turn the compilers have prepared volumes dealing with British East Africa and Uganda, Cape Colony and the Orange-Free State, New Zealand and Southern India, and now in this work they have essayed a survey of Bengal and Assam, Behar and Orissa.

In the present book, as in the companion volume dealing with Southern India, the aim kept in view has been to compile a work on broad and independent lines. While it embodies material of a character commonly associated with the admirable works issued from time to time under official auspices, it also embraces literary and popular features not found in those productions, and it has, besides, an immense amount of information relative to the purely commercial aspects of life, which are not touched either in official works or in the volumes descriptive of India which have a popular character. Moreover, the pages are illustrated by a wealth of pictorial matter absolutely without precedent in any literary undertaking dealing with the Indian Empire. These features, literary, artistic and utilitarian, it is believed from the experience gained elsewhere, and from the extremely favourable reception accorded to "Southern India," will ensure for it a friendly welcome from the Indian public, and ultimately a recognized place in the bibliography of that great Dependency.

This prefatory note would not be complete without a reference to the valuable assistance which the compiler has received from all classes—official and unofficial—in the territory covered by his operations. Without the aid so freely and generously extended it would have been impossible to produce the work in anything approaching the completeness which it is hoped now characterizes it. In another part of the volume special acknowledgment is made of the assistance rendered in individual cases in India itself, but the opportunity offered by these opening sentences cannot be allowed to pass without paying a tribute to the kindness of the

PREFACE

India Council in permitting a reproduction of a selection of pictures from the unique collection at the India Office. These works, as our readers will be able to note, are of great artistic and antiquarian value, and give glimpses of bygone days in India that are extremely fascinating. The processes of reproduction, necessarily elaborate and protracted, were greatly facilitated by the arrangements made by Mr. F. W. Thomas, the librarian, whose kindly assistance on this and other occasions the editor desires to acknowledge.

A final sentence or two must be devoted to the difficulties under which the work has been produced. The Great War has had its influence on India as on other parts of the Empire, and the work of the compilers' staff has been impeded at many points by the exigencies of the war period. The delays and obstructions encountered in India have had their counterpart in the exceptional conditions prevailing at home owing to the war. Not only was the printing of the book made extraordinarily difficult by the enormous depletion of the staff of the printers by the war, but the problem of providing paper was a most serious one for a time. Happily it was ultimately possible to overcome all these obstacles, and to produce the book in a manner equal to the high artistic standard established in earlier works of the series. The delay in the publication will, it is hoped, be overlooked as the inevitable outcome of a period of unexampled strain and difficulty.

CONTENTS

CONTENTS

H.E. THE RIGHT HON. BARON CARMICHAEL, OF SKIRLING, G.C.I.E., K.C.M.G., GOVERNOR OF BENGAL, 1912–1917.

Photo by Johnston & Hoffmann, Calcutta.

HER EXCELLENCY LADY CARMICHAEL.

Photo by Bourne & Shepherd, India.

BENGAL AND ASSAM, BEHAR AND ORISSA

THEIR HISTORY, PEOPLE, COMMERCE, AND INDUSTRIAL RESOURCES

BENGAL—EARLY HISTORY

By ARNOLD WRIGHT

CHAPTER I

Hindu and Mahommedan Ascendancy

Origins of the population—Early dynasties—The Buddhist kings—Supplanted by the Sen line of Hindu monarchs—Rise of Mahommedan influence—Mahommedan dynasty established independent of Delhi—Sher Shah's conquest of Bengal—Annexation of Bengal by Akbar—Bengal under governors appointed by the Mogul emperors.

BENGAL shares to a very large extent in the historical traditions of the northern parts of India. The movements of population which settled the ethnological characteristics of those areas largely affected the province, and it was conspicuously associated with the great religious developments which so profoundly influenced the life history of the people. Generally speaking, the population of Bengal is of Dravidian and Aryan origin, though on the eastern side there are marked Mongoloid elements, pointing to a close association of those tracts with the stream of immigration which settled the character of Burma and the other parts of Further India. The Aryan immigration is that which has left its deepest mark upon the life and literature of Bengal.

A heavy mist obscures the early dynastic history of Bengal. It seems probable that for a good many centuries the province consisted of a number of independent and mutually warring States. In the earliest period of the Christian era North and East Bengal with Assam formed the important kingdom of Pragjyotisha, or Kamapura, as it was subsequently called. This territory was ruled over by a succession of Mongoloid princes, whose line was still powerful when Hiuen Tsiang, the Chinese pilgrim, visited the country in the seventh century. Another early kingdom was Pundra, or Paundravardhana, the country of the Pods, which is thought to have given the name to the modern Pabna. References to it are found in Hiuen Tsiang's work, and as late as the eleventh century we read of it as a place of pilgrimage. The other dynastic features of early Bengal were Banga or Samatata, a kingdom east of Bhagirathi, the home of the modern Chandals; Karna Suvarna (Burdwan, Bankura, Murshidabad, and Hooghly), associated with Sasanka or Narendra, famed in Hindu history as the last of the Guptas—the monarch whose fanatical zeal on behalf of Hinduism prompted him to invade Magadha in the seventh century and cut down the sacred Bodhi tree; and, finally, the kingdom of Tamralipta, or Suhma, a country which comprised what are now the districts of Midnapur and Howrah.

In the ninth century the history of Bengal becomes more clearly outlined with the accession of the Pal dynasty, which, rising to power in the country originally styled Anga, finally extended its sway over the whole of Behar and North Bengal. Buddhist in religion, these kings exercised a very benevolent sway over the population, and left a distinct mark on the country, both as regards place-names and the traditions of the people. The rising tide of Hinduism overwhelmed them in the eleventh century, when they were ousted by the Sen dynasty, which had placed itself well abreast of the Hindu movement, and by its influence had established itself in East and deltaic Bengal in the previous century. This dynasty gradually drew to itself all the authority in Bengal proper, from the Mahánanda and the Bhagirathi on the west to Karatoya and the old

Brahmaputra on the east. It was in its day a great power in Hinduism. To one of its kings, Ballal Sen, belongs the fame of having reorganized the caste system and introduced Kulinism among the Brahmans, Baidyas, and Kayasths. The line survived until the period of the Mahommedan invasion in the twelfth century, and in a severely reduced form even lingered on 150 years later in East Bengal, with Bikrampur, in the Dacca district, as the capital.

The Mahommedan influence in Bengal dates back to the twelfth century, when, in common with the adjacent areas, the country was subjected to the inroads of the Turki hordes. One of the adventurers, Muhammad-i-Bakhtyar Khilji, after conquering Behar in about 1199, took possession of Gaur and Nabadwip, and the former became the seat of a line of potentates who ruled the country sometimes with, and sometimes without, the overruling authority of the Delhi emperors. For two hundred years, from the fourteenth to the sixteenth century, Bengal was under the sway of successive lines of independent kings of a mixed origin. Some were Pathans, others were Turkis, others, again, were Abyssinian eunuchs, and in one instance the ruler was a Hindu. In 1539 a new and powerful ruler appeared upon the scene in the person of Sher Shah, the famous Afghan adventurer, who was to become one of the greatest of the early line of emperors of Delhi. Sher Shah, in the first years of the reign of the Mogul Humayun at Delhi, carved out for himself an independent position on the borders of Bengal, with Chunar as his headquarters. Humayun becoming jealous of his power, six years after his accession, marched against him, and besieged and took his fortress of Chunar. Sher Shah himself, however, evaded the emperor's attacks, and retired to Rohtasgarh, in Bengal, which he had wrested from its owners. Here he successfully withstood a siege, and when, at the expiration of six months, Humayun retired discomfited to Delhi, he ousted the Mogul governor who was resident at Gaur, and proclaimed himself King of Bengal and Orissa. This was a prelude to a still greater triumph in the defeat of Humayun at Kanauj and Sher Shah's occupation of the Imperial throne, from which he had evicted the defeated monarch. After Sher Shah's death Humayun was able to restore his authority at Delhi, but the position in Bengal remained unchanged, a series of Afghan governors upholding the authority which Sher Shah had established. In 1568 Orissa was conquered by Raju, better known as Kala Pahar, the general of Sulaiman Kararani, a prince who was really independent, but who acknowledged the authority of Akbar. Sulaiman's son Daud, when he came into authority, followed his father's example, and gave in his adhesion to Delhi, but he subsequently rebelled, and Akbar, seizing an opportunity for which he had been waiting, definitely annexed Bengal to his empire. Henceforward, until the British assumed power, the country was under Mogul rule.

The authority now devolved upon a succession of governors and viceroys, who wielded authority with varying degrees of success. At an early period, owing to the incursions of defeated Afghans who had taken refuge in Orissa, the capital, which had usually been established at Gaur or the neigbouring towns of Pandua and Rajmahal, was transferred to Dacca, and here it continued for a hundred years, at the expiration of which, under the viceroyalty of Ismael Khan, the centre of government was again removed, this time to Murshidabad. The province shared in the vicissitudes of the Imperial throne. When Shah Jehan revolted against his father, the Emperor Jehangir, in 1621, he seized Bengal, and held it for two years with the aid of Afghan adventurers. Eventually he was defeated and compelled to relinquish his conquest. When later he came to the throne he established his son, Sultan Shuja, as Governor of Bengal. This prince, following the evil precedent of the Imperial house, fought against his brother Aurangzebe, and being defeated by his general, Mir Jumla, was compelled to fly to Arakan, where he died in obscurity. As a reward for his services Mir Jumla was appointed to Sultan Shuja's place, and made an admirable ruler. Mir Jumla died near Dacca on March 30, 1663, after an arduous campaign in Cooch Behar and Assam, in which he had suffered great exposure. His successor was Shayista Khan, the premier prince of the empire. Later, on Aurangzebe's death, the governorship of Bengal was conferred upon Murshid Kuli Khan, a Brahman convert to Islam, who had worked his way into favour by his commanding talents. This worthy, profiting by the weak and divided condition of the Imperial family, took to himself a considerable amount of power, and eventually made himself practically independent. Thereafter the authority of Delhi was of the smallest, the Governors of Bengal being all but in name sovereign princes.

CHAPTER II

Rise of European Influence

The Portuguese in Eastern India—Their settlement at Chittagong—Portuguese piracies—Shah Jehan destroys the Portuguese settlement at Hooghly—Appearance of the Dutch in Bengal—Their factories at Pipli and Chinsurah—Early English trading expeditions—Balasar becomes the English headquarters—English factory established at Hooghly—The East India Company dispatch a special commission to Bengal—Disputes between the Company's officials and the Mogul authorities—Sir Edward Winter advocates an energetic policy—Growth of Bengal trade—Establishment of the Bengal Pilot Service—Streynsham Master visits Bengal—He reorganizes the English establishments with Hooghly as the head quarters.

BEFORE the Mahommedan domination of Bengal had been firmly established a new influence had made its appearance, which was destined in course of centuries to produce a revolutionary change in the government and the commercial life of the country as of the rest of India. This was the European factor, brought into existence by Vasco da Gama's epoch-making achievement of doubling the Cape in 1498. The Portuguese, as the pioneers of the new movement, reaped all the early advantages that attached to the discovery of the sea route to India. For a century they enjoyed a practical monopoly of the trade, with all that their position of splendid isolation implied in the way of political power. Though their territorial conquests were mainly on the western coast, with Goa as a splendid capital, Portuguese emissaries penetrated to almost every part of the peninsula then open to outside influence. As early as 1530 they began to frequent Bengal, and they were not slow to grasp the immense potentialities which its trade offered. They established themselves firmly at Chittagong and Saptagram or Satgaon, the foundation of the latter settlement, which was in the neighbourhood of the modern town of Hooghly, anticipating by nearly two centuries the decision of the English East India Company to fix their headquarters there, and so to form the beginnings of the great city of Calcutta. An immense trade was rapidly created under Portuguese auspices, with Satgaon, or Porto Piqueno, as it was known, as its chief centre on one bank of the river, and Betor, near Sabpur, on the other. Chittagong also shared in large measure in the oversea trading operations initiated by the Portuguese, but in course of years this port became the refuge of numerous adventurers from Goa and other settlements in the west, and their piracies became infamous throughout India, largely tending to neutralize the success of the legitimate commerce which their more orderly countrymen carried on. From time to time efforts were made by the Mogul Government to deal with these desperadoes. They managed, however, by their knowledge of the sea and their superior military talent to evade the punishment they so richly deserved until 1632, when Shah Jehan, enraged beyond endurance at the crimes perpetrated, sent a big force against the Portuguese settlement at Hooghly, and when the town had been captured caused all its Portuguese inhabitants to be transferred to Agra as slaves. The disaster practically sealed the fate of the Portuguese trade in this part of India. With some of the outer settlements at the mouth of the river fitful relations were maintained by Portuguese from Calicut and elsewhere on the Coromandel coast, but the days of ascendancy and even of equality of effort were gone never to return.

The downfall of the Portuguese was hastened, if it was not actually caused, by the action of the Dutch. From the outset of their intervention in Eastern trade the Hollanders had constituted themselves bitter foes of the Portuguese. In the Malayan region and in the Eastern Archipelago, as well as in Ceylon and Southern India, before the destruction of Hooghly by Shah Jehan, they had fought an unrelenting fight, driving the descendants of Albuquerque from one settlement after another, until their power was a mere shadow of its old self. In Bengal the Dutch made their first appearance in 1625, establishing themselves at Pipli and Chinsurah. They were at the time too much occupied with the task of consolidating their positions in other regions of the East to give much attention to the trade of Eastern India, but their records show that they grasped its importance, and that if the exigencies of their policy had admitted they would have made a much stronger bid for supremacy in Bengal than they did. Not, however, that they were an insignificant element in this early struggle for commercial predominance. They made a great display with their ships, and by the masterful way in which they handled local problems supplied an example which their more timid English rivals were constrained in the end to follow.

The early essays of the English representatives of the East India Company in Bengal were certainly neither heroic nor well planned. They were traders pure and simple, and the influence of the ledger was ever present in their transactions. Even as traders they left a great deal to be desired, since we find them taking with them as suitable articles of merchandise the stout English broadcloths, which could have no possible market in a sweltering climate such as that of the Gangetic delta is. Nevertheless, as the first of their race to establish themselves in Eastern India, they are entitled to the respectful notice of the historian. We may think lightly of their acumen and cast stones at their morals, but we cannot forget that they were the banner-bearers of a Power which was destined profoundly to influence the course of history in this part of Asia.

The first appearance of the English as traders in the Bay of Bengal was in 1633. In that year a small expedition, composed of eight Englishmen, led by Ralph Cartwright, voyaging in a country boat, proceeded from Masulipatam to the mouth of the Patua in Orissa, and thence to Cuttack and the Court of Malcandy, or Mukund Deo, the last of the line of independent Hindoo kings in that province. Friendly relations were established with the native power, and under the authority given by the king factories were set up at Hariharapur and Balasar in the same year. This initial effort to create trade relations with the rich provinces bordering on the Bay of Bengal was but feebly supported, and after an inglorious existence the Hariharapur factory fell into utter decay. The Balasar establishment, however, survived, and after various vicissitudes it was constituted the headquarters of the English trading operations in this part of India. It so remained until 1650, when, acting on the advice of Gabriel Broughton, a surgeon in the employ of the East India Company, who had won favour with Shah Shuja, the Mogul Governor of Bengal, by his skill in treating a member of that prince's family, the Company dispatched the ship *Lyoness* to Bengal with the object of establishing a factory inland up the Ganges. The *Lyoness* did not proceed beyond Balasar, and it was from that port that the Company's representatives, James Bridgeman and Edward Stephens, with two assistants named Blake and Tayler, started on the mission which took the form of a design to secure powers for the starting of a factory at Hooghly. There is some doubt as to what really happened after this, but the generally accepted view is that, probably owing to Broughton's influence, though this is by no means clear, a *nishan*, or authority, was procured for Rs. 3,000 from Shah Shuja in 1651 or 1652, giving the English the right to trade in Bengal without payment of custom dues. The factory established at Hooghly under this grant suffered under the same disabilities which had nullified the efforts of the

THE GAME OF CHAWGAR (AN INDIAN POLO).

From an Indian drawing in the Johnson Collection at the India Office.

earlier expedition at Hariharapur. It had, in fact, barely been brought into existence before the Council at Madras came to the conclusion that the enterprise must be abandoned. This decision was come to in 1657, but before there was time to give it effect the condition of the Company's affairs at home, with the amalgamation of Courtin's Company with the original Company and the renewal of the latter's charter by Cromwell, had so greatly improved that a new forward policy was deemed politic, and under this an arrangement was concluded for the dispatch of a special commission to Bengal, with the object of removing abuses and strengthening the Company's position in that quarter. A large new staff was appointed to equip the factory at Hooghly as well as provide for subordinate agencies at Balasar, Kasimbazar, and Patna. It is to be noted that one of the junior officers thus appointed was Job Charnock, who was to become famous some years later in connection with the founding of Calcutta.

A new era in the connection of the English with Bengal was opened with the dispatch of the commission referred to in the foregoing paragraph. Hitherto the efforts of the Company to create a position in Bengal had been spasmodic and disconnected. Their agents had been men of inferior status, and lacking in the support which was needed in a situation such as then existed, with exigent native authorities on the one hand, and aggressive rivals, Dutch and Portuguese, on the other. Now there was a regular organization, with a proper system of control, and possessing authority to consolidate and extend the Company's influence in the vast region comprehended in the sphere of the Hooghly factory's operations. Unfortunately the introduction of the new system coincided with one of those dynastic upheavals which from time to time convulsed India. The Emperor Shah Jehan falling seriously ill in 1657, his third son, Aurangzebe, went into rebellion, and after imprisoning his father and defeating his elder brothers, seated himself upon the Imperial throne. These changes for a time reacted disastrously upon the English position. Disputes immediately arose relative to the payment of the annual sum of Rs. 3,000, and the new native officials vexatiously hampered trade. At length the Company's agent at Hooghly retaliated by seizing a native vessel in the river. This brought down upon the English the wrath of Mir Jumlah, the Mogul Governor of Bengal, who threatened to destroy the Company's factories and expel their servants from Bengal if the vessel was not returned. Alarmed at the turn that affairs had taken, the Company's officials made their peace with the irate governor by restoring the vessel and paying a fine by way of indemnity. Their action was a humiliating confession of weakness, which served to accentuate the arrogance and extortion of native officialdom. Sir Edward Winter, who, under the new charter of the Company issued by Charles II in 1661, had been sent out to India as President of Fort St. George,

"BABER PADSHAH."

From an original Indian drawing in the Johnson Collection at the India Office.

with full control of the Bengal factories, was greatly in favour of the adoption of a more energetic policy. His view was that the only suitable argument for use in discussion with the native Government was sea power, and that this should be energetically employed so as to convince them that the English were as strong on the water as the Mogul power was on the land. His theory had much to commend it, as the subsequent course of events clearly demonstrated, but the times were not suitable for the adoption of thoroughgoing measures. The home authorities, imbued with the idea that trade and aggressive action, even for purposes of defence, were incompatible, took strong exception to Winter's policy, and in order that they should not be committed too far by him, sent out a new agent in the person of George Foxcroft to supersede him. Winter openly opposed these measures, seizing Foxcroft and casting him into prison, and continuing to exercise official authority in spite of protests, until, three years later, a commission was sent out from home with powers which he could not disregard.

Winter's *coup d'état* belongs more to the history of Madras than to that of Bengal, but it, nevertheless, was not without its influence on the course of events in the latter territory, where development was delayed by the fierce official feud waged at headquarters over the prostrate body of Foxcroft. The trouble was the more unfortunate as the Bengal trade at this juncture was proving its value. A great export was growing up in Bengal silk, and such was the demand for the beautiful muslins and other light fabrics of Bengal that in 1668 the Company had authorized the establishment of an agency at Dacca, then the capital of the province.

It was in this year that the famous Bengal Pilot Service was formed. The Company's ships had found the difficulties of navigating the river so serious that they had up to 1662 landed their cargoes at Balasar, a practice which seriously militated against the profits of the voyages, owing to the necessity of transhipment and the incidental expenses. As the large Dutch ships were able to get up to Chinsurah in safety, the Court of Directors determined to grapple with the problem of navigating the difficult channels of the river by giving special orders to their captains to have a survey of the waterway made. The instructions were very definite, and in order that some permanence should be given to the system, six young men were appointed as apprentices to be trained in survey work. Admirable work was done by these youthful pioneers. To one of their number—George Herron—belongs the credit of producing the first chart of the river which was of any scientific value. It was, however, not until 1679, when Captain Stafford made the passage to Hooghly in the *Falcon*, that their labours reached fruition.

No change of any moment occurred in the position of the English in Bengal until 1676, when the Company introduced an improved system of administration, and sent out Streynsham Master, one of its ablest servants, to inaugurate the new regime in Eastern India. Master, in his well-known "Diary," has left a record of his mission—or missions, for he paid two separate visits to the Bay of Bengal—which is one of the classics of Indian official literature. Besides being a clever official, he was a man of considerable culture, and his writings have a literary quality which is not often found in the Company's records of that period. He gives us a graphic picture of the life of the English factories in Bengal as they then existed, and also tells us a great deal about the conditions of trade and the openings offered for enterprise in the rich Gangetic delta. His visits resulted in a marked extension of the Company's activities. The existing factories were reorganized, with Hooghly as more definitely the headquarters of the Bengal agencies, and a new factory was started at Malda, bringing the number of the Company's agencies up to six, the other centres being Hooghly, Balasor, Dacca, Patna, Kasimbazar, and Singhiya. A considerable extension of the Company's investments followed upon the completion of these arrangements. The trade was a very lucrative one, so much so that in 1677 it is noted in the records that the year's transactions on the east coast were greater than in any other period of the Company's commerce.

CHAPTER III

Growth of English Influence

Authority to trade given by Aurangzebe—Native exactions—William Hedges, the chief factor at Hooghly, recommends the adoption of a strong policy—Expedition to the Bay of Bengal—Mogul troops assume the offensive at Hooghly—Job Charnock successfully attacks the Moguls, and the English sack Hooghly—Shayista Khan, the Mogul Governor of Bengal declares war against the English—The English take refuge at Hijili—Precarious position of the English—English reinforcements arrive and save the situation—Occupation of Sutanuti, the modern Calcutta.

HOOGHLY, though a far more desirable centre for the Company's headquarters than Balasor, had many and serious disadvantages. Some of these were inherent in the situation; others were the product of the short-sightedness of the founders of the factory, who chose for its site a position hemmed in by native houses and open to attack from the land as well as the river. As the Company's trade grew the drawbacks of the position were accentuated. Powerless to resist the native exactions, the Company's agents more and more fell under the evil influence of the system, which made their operations the sport of avaricious officials. In 1680 an authority to trade without payment of any dues other than the $3\frac{1}{2}$ per cent. tax imposed at Surat was obtained from Aurangzebe, but, owing to the obscure wording of the rescript, the Bengal officials repudiated the exemption claimed by the Company's agents, and enforced their exactions as of yore. In vain William Hedges, who had been sent out as agent and governor in Bengal, appealed to the Mogul Governor, Shayista Khan, to have the impediments to the Company's trade removed. Shayista Khan was conciliatory, and even promised to procure a new *farman* from the Emperor, and to compel the obnoxious officials to make restitution. But, in spite of all, the old abuses continued, and even assumed an aggravated form. It became more than ever obvious that if the Company wished to enjoy real freedom in its trading operations it must have a fortified position, with power in the background to protect its interests when they were unfairly assailed. Hedges in his dispatches home strongly recommended the adoption of a forward policy of this kind, but, as in the case of Winter before him, the directors were indisposed to acknowledge the soundness of their servant's logic. They thought that strong measures would defeat their own ends,

THE EMPEROR SHAH JEHAN.
From an original Indian drawing in the Johnson Collection at the India Office.

and that, in any event, if they were to be resorted to, the pressure could be more effectively applied in Bombay than in Bengal. Their opposition, however, was not long proof against the evidence which accumulated year by year indicative of the serious effects produced upon the Company's trade by the unrestrained violence of the local officials. In 1686, having obtained permission from James I to make war on the Mogul, the Court made arrangements for a vigorous campaign on both coasts of India. On the western side the Company's officials had orders to withdraw from Surat and seize every Mogul ship that was encountered at sea. To Eastern India a large fleet was despatched, with instructions to rendezvous at Balasor, and from thence proceed to Chittagong, which port was to be seized and held for the Company, with Job Charnock in the position of governor.

The expedition to the Bay of Bengal was for that period an imposing force. It consisted of three men-of-war—the *Beaufort*, the *Nathaniel*, and the *Rochester*—mounting altogether 185 guns and manned by 600 seamen, and three small frigates, each mounting 12 guns and having a crew of 20. In addition to this force, there was at the disposal of the local officials a number of river craft and a miscellaneous contingent of troops made up of English soldiers and Portuguese or native Christian fighting men—the latter "very sorry fellows," according to the official statement. It was a sufficiently large force, if used with judgment, to effect much as matters then stood, but the arrangements for the concentration of the various elements of the expedition were ill-conceived, and before they were completed the native authority assumed the offensive, and sent a considerable body of troops, including artillery, to occupy Hooghly. Hostilities commenced on October 28, 1686, when three English soldiers were set upon, and, after being badly beaten, taken prisoners. A company of soldiers were sent out from the factory with orders to rescue the captives. They made a gallant attempt to execute their instructions, but were met by a largely superior force of the enemy, and were compelled to retreat with the loss of seven men killed or wounded. Following up their success, the Moguls fired the houses adjacent to the factory and opened fire with their artillery on the Company's ships in the river. Alarmed at the turn that affairs had taken, Charnock, who was in charge of the factory, sent to Chandernagore for some English troops that were quartered there. These in due course arrived, and, ably led by Captain Arbuthnot, attacked and captured the enemy's battery, and, having spiked and dismounted the guns, pushed on to the Mogul Governor's house, driving all before them. The Mogul Governor, fearing for his safety in the presence of this impetuous onslaught, incontinently fled, leaving the English in undisputed possession of the field. In order that the lesson they had given might lack nothing in point, the English later opened fire from their ships on the native settlement, "and kept firing and battering most part of the night and next day, and making frequent sallies on shore, burning and plundering all they met with." Impressed by this vigorous assertion of power, the Mogul Governor, through the Dutch, sought to effect an accommodation. Charnock, who was in no condition to continue the fight indefinitely, and was anxious to gain time for the completion of his plans for the removal of the Company's property to a more secure position, gladly accepted these overtures.

A "sort of peace" now followed, the English actively employing themselves with their loading operations, and meanwhile conducting negotiations for an Imperial authority to trade. But they had reckoned without Shayista Khan, who was not the type of functionary to sit down meekly under such a heavy rebuff, as the defeat of the Mogul troops undoubtedly was, to the supreme power. The Mogul Viceroy almost immediately took steps to avenge the Hooghly attack. Rejecting with contempt the demand for a new authority to trade, he issued orders for the seizure of the Company's property and the imprisonment of their servants at Dacca, and he followed this up with the issue of orders to the subordinate governors of Bengal to collect all the forces they could get together with the purpose of driving the English out of Bengal never to return. Charnock now realized that it was to be open war. He promptly took the initiative by burning the King's salt houses and assaulting the forts at Thana or Garden Reach. When the latter had been demolished the English agent loaded the ships with the Company's property and records and went off downstream to the island of Hijili.

Charnock so far had shown himself a shrewd and resourceful leader in a time of emergency, but the choice of Hijili as a place of refuge was an unfortunate one. The island was naturally a swamp, and malarious to a degree which has passed into a proverb. Its gravest defect, however, was that it was not a spot on which a good defence could be made. The serious disadvantages of the situation were revealed ere the new colony had been in being many weeks. As the hot season approached the English soldiers and seamen sickened in alarming numbers. Simultaneously the Mogul forces became stronger and more menacing. By the middle of May 1687 two hundred of the English troops had succumbed to the climate, and Charnock, with his sadly diminished force, was called upon to meet the attacks of twelve thousand well-equipped Mogul troops. Desperate almost as the position was, Charnock never lost heart. When on a day at the end of May the Moguls surprised one of his outposts and penetrated into the town, threatening his communications with the ships in the river, he concentrated his attenuated forces in a small masonry building midway between the town and the landing-place, and successfully, in that position of advantage, repulsed the enemy's attacks. On the 1st of June the gallant defenders were greatly heartened by the arrival on the scene of a reinforcement of seventy men fresh from Europe. Skilfully utilizing these new troops, Charnock so impressed the Mogul general that on June 4th he sent in an intimation that he desired peace. Ultimately an arrangement was come to by which the English were able to march out with all the honours of war. Charnock was promised by the Mogul general a consideration of his demands for freedom of trade and a site for a factory. But, as had often happened before, these pledges proved altogether illusory. The utmost that Shayista Khan would concede was permission to continue trading from Hooghly and to create a factory at another point on the river, Ulubaria, whither the English had gone after leaving Hooghly. Charnock was under no misconception as to the uselessness of the concessions made, and as soon as Shayista Khan's intentions were fully disclosed he made up his mind to abandon Ulubaria and take all the ships up the river to Sutanuti, the site of the modern Calcutta. The agent had by this time a clearer vision of what was really needed, and his skilled eye saw in the geographical position of the little

1. HINDOO PAGODAS BELOW BARRACKPORE. 2. HINDOO GHAUT ON THE GANGES.
3. HINDOO VILLAGE ON THE GANGES, NEAR AMBROAH.
Illustrations from Lieut.-Col. Forrest's "Picturesque Tour on the Ganges and Jumna" (1824).

village of Sutanuti strategical advantages such as were not readily to be secured at any other available spot. In due course the new haven of refuge was reached, and a settlement of rude mat huts was formed, which was destined to live in history as the embryo of the greatest of Indian cities.

CHAPTER IV

The English driven from Bengal

Charnock's able conduct of affairs—His supersession by Heath—Evacuation of Sutanuti—English attack on Balasor—Subsequent abortive expedition to Chittagong—Departure of the English for Madras—Aurangzebe invites the English to return to Bengal—The invitation accepted—Reoccupation of Sutanuti—New authority to trade received.

CHARNOCK so far had played an able and even a brilliant part in the transactions with the Moguls. With a ridiculously small contingent he had for months held at bay the formidable forces of the native Government, and had implanted in their minds such a lively sense of English prowess that he had been able to make a not unfavourable composition with the Mogul Governor. In all his dealings with the enemy he had shown himself a clever diplomatist, and had revealed a knowledge of native character of a very uncommon kind. His services, it might have been supposed, would have commended him to his superiors. But the Court at home had conceived a violent prejudice against Charnock, and at the very moment when his policy was reaching successful development they were dispatching an envoy out charged with the execution of a design which ran counter to the agent's idea of establishing a settlement up the river. This was the plan previously alluded to for the capture of Chittagong. The directors had long been in favour of a settlement at Chittagong, and their predilection for that port was strengthened by the earlier accounts of the difficulties encountered by Charnock after the evacuation of Hooghly. In sending out a special representative in the person of Captain William Heath, the commander of the Company's ship *Defence*, the Court were thinking more of the desirability of settling at Chittagong than of the expediency of reversing Charnock's policy. But in dispatches they had bitterly impugned his judgment in the Hijili affair, and his supersession was doubtless regarded as a measure of wisdom in view of his supposed deficiencies. However that may be, Heath was given a pretty free hand, and he was not slow to use his power, with disastrous results to the carefully laid schemes of Charnock.

Heath was a man of ill-balanced mind, reckless to a dangerous degree, and, what perhaps was even worse in such a position as that in which he was placed, strongly self-opinionated. He went out to India with the idea that the way to peace was through war, and he would tolerate no suggestion that the English might get all they wanted if they remained at Sutanuti, or Calcutta as we may now call it, as Shayista Khan was no longer in power, and his successor, Bahadur Khan, had shown himself well disposed to the English. His orders were that the local officials should wind up the Company's affairs with a view of the transfer of the whole establishment to Chittagong. In due course the orders were carried out, and, much to the astonishment of the native officials, who could not comprehend the meaning of the move, the whole staff set sail on November 8th for the Bay. Eight days later the flotilla dropped anchor off Balasor. At this port a very considerable English force was gathered, reinforced by two captured French frigates, which had been seized by the fleet a short time previously. Heath parleyed with the native authorities for some days without effect, and then, on November 29th, landed a force, which attacked and put to flight the Mogul troops, and temporarily occupied the town. The easily purchased victory availed nothing so far as the demands on the Mogul Government were concerned. If it had any effect it was to stiffen the local opposition, and make Bahadur Khan more indisposed than he had been to grant facilities to the English.

Finding that nothing further was to be accomplished at Balasor, Heath at the close of the year proceeded to Chittagong to execute the plan formed by the Court for a settlement there. On arrival at that port it was very apparent that the position was far too strong to be susceptible to effective attack by so small a force as that under Heath's command. Heath, however, was not disposed to relinquish his task without an effort. He consequently opened up negotiations with the local king, who was at war with the Moguls, offering the services of his force. As Heath had before made a similar offer unsuccessfully to Bahadur Khan, and the fact was probably well known in Chittagong, the overtures were treated with scant respect. Enraged at the rebuff, Heath decided to quit a scene in which his generous impulses appeared to have so little play. Weighing anchor on February 17, 1688, he steered south, and a short time later appeared off Fort St. George. Here the Bengal staff found a temporary resting-place after their six months' wanderings.

It now seemed that the star of the Company's destiny in Bengal had finally set. Their factories razed, their agents all either prisoners or fugitives, and their ships without a friendly anchorage to resort to, the prospect was gloomy indeed. But proverbially it is the darkest hour before the dawn. Ere the peripatetic officials had barely settled down in Madras, measures were afoot for their reinstatement in Bengal under promising conditions. The truth is that the native authorities did not want to lose them. They required their trade, which was very helpful to the local revenue, and they wanted the immunity for Mogul shipping which a contented and friendly English connection brought. Even the great Aurangzebe was constrained to intervene to secure a reversal of the English policy of evacuating Bengal. "You must understand," he wrote to the Nawab of Bengal, "that it has been the good fortune of the English to repent them of their irregular past proceedings and their not being in their former greatness, have by their attornies petitioned for their lives and a pardon for their faults, which, out of my extraordinary favour towards them, I have accordingly granted. Therefore, upon receipt here of my order you must not create them any further trouble, but let them trade in your government as formerly, and this order I expect you see strictly observed."

The conversion of Aurangzebe to the rôle of a friend of the English was so sudden that Charnock was at first disposed to distrust the motive of the overtures. He replied to the summons from Ibrahim Khan, who had replaced Bahadur Khan in the viceroyalty, by demanding a specific warrant stating on what terms trade would be permitted. Ibrahim Khan, in reply, intimated that he had applied to the Emperor for the warrant, but pointed out that it would probably be some months before the instrument could be arranged, and urged the English to proceed to Bengal without delay. Charnock thought that the prospect was sufficiently good to justify whatever risk there might be in the acceptance of the offer. He therefore made arrangements for the return of the staff to their posts in Bengal. The decision, as events proved, was a wise one. On arrival in the river in August the returned merchants were received in friendly fashion, and by the end of the month they were once more in occupation of their quarters, or what remained of them, at Sutanuti and Hooghly. Afterwards the relations with the native officials were established on a more friendly base than they had ever been previously. Aurangzebe was genuinely anxious to see the English trade continued, and Ibrahim Khan was, by disposition as well as policy, disposed to befriend them. It was, however, not until February 10, 1691, that the desired authority to trade was received. On that date an Imperial rescript was signed allowing the English to prosecute their operations in Bengal on payment of Rs. 3,000 annually in lieu of all dues. This official recognition of the English right to trade in Bengal was the herald of a new dispensation, in which the Company's power was consolidated and strengthened until it became the most powerful foreign influence that was exerted in Eastern India.

CHAPTER V

The Founding of Calcutta

Charnock's administration of the settlement—His death—Condemnation of Charnock by Sir John Goldsborough, the Company's Commissary-General—Reforms instituted—Steady progress of the settlement—Charles Eyre's administration—Bengal created a separate Presidency—Fort William completed—John Beard's administration—The Rotation Government—Aurangzebe's death—Shah Alum threatens to attack Calcutta—New authority to trade procured—Growth of the settlement.

CERTAIN events mark the historic progress of the British Empire. The founding of Calcutta is one of these. It constitutes a distinct dividing line between the early India in which the English were struggling for a footing in the guise of humble traders, and the later India in which the British power by gradual stages gained a paramount position as an administrative force. As far as Bengal is concerned there was still much to be accomplished after the establishment of the settlement at Calcutta ere the position was made secure even against local tyranny, but the undoubted turning-point in the British connection with Eastern India was when Job Charnock, with his little band of merchants and writers, settled down on the swampy banks of the river and sought to make there a home and a habitation for themselves as free as might be from tiresome Mogul interference.

Charnock was the right man for a task such as this, calling not only for energy and foresight but for the possession of a wide experience of the country and its people. As we have seen, he was an old officer of the Company, one who had for years held responsible positions in its hierarchy. He was not a man of great education or of high intellectual power. But he knew Bengal like a book, and this profound knowledge of local conditions stood him in good stead in the continuous struggle he had to wage to obtain for the Company in Eastern India its "place in the sun." Many things to his disadvantage were said at the time by his fellow-countrymen. The directors, too, were his stern critics. But we can only judge him by his public acts, and these, as far as we can estimate things, show him as a highly capable official, and one who had the gift of true statesmanship.

It is doubtless true that Charnock in the later years of his life displayed qualities which were not compatible with full efficiency. Long residence in India had dulled his faculties, and he was too prone to ease. Furthermore, he was open to the charge of favouritism and of taking an active part in quarrels when he should have maintained a rigid impartiality. So the record of his association with Calcutta is rather blurred and spotted. It was the rounding off of a strenuous and chequered life in a certain squalor. Circumstances, general as well as local, were against him, and he was content to float in a muddy stream and knock against the shoals rather than to exert himself and get into clear and deep water.

In point of fact Charnock's opportunity came too late in his life. He died on January 10, 1693, less than three years from the time of the landing of the old chief and his council after their sojourn in Madras. In the interval England had become involved in warlike operations with France, and the commercial activities of the Company had been seriously hampered by the hostilities conducted between the rival naval forces in Indian waters. Added to this grave disability—doubly felt in the case of a settlement just struggling into existence—was the mischievous influence of personal animosities, which divided the community and prevented anything in the nature of healthy progress. In the circumstances it is not remarkable that when Sir John Goldsborough, Commissary-General and Chief Governor of the Company's settlements, arrived at Calcutta in the August following Charnock's death, he should have found the settlement in a very disorganized condition. His report upon it is coloured by a strong prejudice against Charnock, who is held responsible for the unsatisfactory condition of affairs, but in the main we may accept it as a faithful picture of what this early Calcutta was like. No place, we are told, had been marked out for a factory, and people had been allowed to enclose lands, dig tanks, and build houses where and how they pleased. The moral atmosphere of the place was bad. One of the leading officials—Hill by name—had been "allowed to keep a punch-house and billiard-table gratis while others paid for it." There were other abuses associated with the Company's trade which could not be reconciled with an efficient administration. Using the authority with which he was invested, Goldsborough instituted sweeping reforms in the settlement. Hill was summarily dismissed and packed off to Madras, and Ellis, the official who had succeeded Charnock, was superseded by Charles Eyre, one of the few officials who appeared to possess ability and character. At the same time the military establishment was reduced and other retrenchments made, the net effect of which was a saving of Rs. 4,000 a year. On the constructive side Goldsborough was equally energetic. Arrangements were made for the erection of a factory as soon as permission for the undertaking of the work could be obtained from the native authorities. Goldsborough also interested himself in the religious condition of the community. Finding that the merchants and factors were marrying native wives and coming too much under the influence of the Augustinian friars, he turned the priests out of the settlement and pulled down their church. His zeal for reform, as he regarded it, might have carried him a good deal farther had not he been seized with illness and carried off in November ere it had been possible to secure formal approval of his plans.

Charles Eyre, Goldsborough's nominee for the chief office, after some delay assumed control of the settlement, and justified the faith reposed in him by the Commissary-General. He is, perhaps, best remembered in this day as the husband of Charnock's daughter, Mary, and the builder of the massive mausoleum to that worthy which still stands in St. John's Churchyard.

Under the improved system of administration which Goldsborough introduced the Calcutta settlement made steady progress, but it was not until 1696 that it was possible to commence to make it the fortified position which the Company had always contemplated it should be. The opportunity for completing its equipment in the manner desired came through some local troubles in which a Hindoo landowner named Cubha Singha played the leading part. Cubha Singha raised a rebellion, and, joining forces with Rahim Khan, an Afghan chief, soon became a menace to the peace of the country. As the Mogul authority took no active steps to crush the revolt, the heads of the European settlements sought and obtained from the Nawab Ibrahim Khan permission to raise troops to deal with the disturbers of the peace. Acting on the authority given, the English set to work to fortify their factory. They made good progress with the operations, and by the middle of 1698 had erected a substantial structure of brick and mud, which in due course developed into the first Fort William. A more important advance towards the creation of a stable position for the Company even than this essay in fortification was made in July of the same year, when, for a sum of Rs. 16,000, the Company obtained letters patent from Azimu-sh-Shan, who had succeeded Ibrahim Khan as Nawab of Bengal, allowing them to purchase from the existing holders the right of renting the three villages of Calcutta, Sutanuti, and Govindpur, a permit which gave the English a firm foothold on the territory which they required for their settlement.

Eyre returned home in 1699, and the Company, in gratitude for his services in securing the grant from the Nawab, used its influence and obtained for him the honour of knighthood. As Sir Charles Eyre he returned to Calcutta at the end of the year to superintend the important changes which had been made in the administration by the Court of Directors, under which Bengal was created a separate Presidency. Eyre carried with him instructions to complete the fortifications of the factory, which, it was arranged, should, in compliment to the King, be called Fort William. The newly-created knight arrived in Calcutta on May 26, 1700, but within the year he returned to England "on urgent private affairs"—in point of fact to contract a marriage which he had set his heart on. The reins of power fell from his hands into those of John Beard, an old servant of the Company, who had first come out to India about twenty years previously with his father, in the company of Governor Hedges, at this period a leading figure in the official world, whose "Diary" vies with that of Streynsham Master in historic interest. Beard took up office at a somewhat important juncture in the affairs of the English in India. Not long after his assumption of office Aurangzebe issued an edict directing the arrest of all Europeans in India because of the depredations of pirates, who had robbed Mogul ships in the Eastern seas and maltreated Mahommedans on the way to and from the pilgrimage to Mecca. Beard showed conspicuous courage and ability in meeting the situation which arose in Bengal in this crisis. By a combination of finesse and firmness he prevented the Mogul officials from doing any mischief. On one occasion, when a Mogul officer ordered the Company's goods at Calcutta to be seized, Beard mounted additional guns and drafted men from the ships to work them, his reasoning being that it was better to spend money on powder and shot than "to be always giving to every little rascal" who thought he could do the Company some injury.

Beard's career of usefulness was cut short, or at all events seriously disturbed, by the arrangements which were made in 1703 for the union of the old East India Company with its newer rival, which had for years been a thorn in the official flesh in Eastern India. Under the plan adopted the office of governor was abolished, and the general affairs of the settlement placed under the control of a joint council composed of members of the local staff of each council, and with as its heads Mr. Robert Hedges and Mr. Ralph Sheldon, who presided over the council in alternate weeks. Beard did not long survive his supersession. Falling ill in 1704, he proceeded to Madras for change of air, and, after lingering for some months, died there on July 7th. Meanwhile his rival, Sir Edward Littleton, who had managed the affairs of the new Company in the years prior to the union, got into disgrace for making too free with the Company's cash. He was ultimately dismissed from his office, and died under a heavy cloud on October 24, 1707.

The Rotation Government, as it came to be known, was a makeshift, and it was not more successful than makeshifts usually are. Its dual character led to many difficulties, not the least perplexing of which was the impossibility of making the native authorities believe that the two rival Companies were now really only one, and that unity implied but a single contribution to the Mogul exchequer. While the council were haggling with the local governor over the question of the amount of the contribution, news was received of the death of Aurangzebe. Immediate steps were taken to prepare for the emergency which it was clearly seen would arise owing to the conflicting claims of the dead emperor's sons to the throne. The council called in their Company's representatives from the outstations and strengthened the defences of the fort. Meanwhile they broke off the negotiations for a payment to the Imperial treasury, and steadily refused to consider a demand for a special levy towards the support of the forces of Shah Alum, the victorious aspirant to the Imperial succession. An attack was threatened on the settlement about the middle of 1708, and was only averted by the spirited measures adopted to ward off any aggression.

At length the negotiations for a contribution to the Imperial funds were resumed, and after many vicissitudes, were carried to a successful conclusion in 1709, when, in consideration of a payment of Rs. 45,000, the Company obtained an order giving them freedom of trade in Bengal, Behar, and Orissa. This arrangement placed the affairs of the Company in Eastern India in a more satisfactory position, and a considerable extension of trade followed. Simultaneously extensive building operations were carried on in the settlement, and Calcutta gradually but surely assumed the character of a centre of social life as well as of commerce. In 1710 the Rotation Government disappeared from the scene, and, dying in anything but the odour of sanctity, gave place to a unified administration, in which Sir Anthony Weltden figured as President of the Council and Governor.

CHAPTER VI

The Eclipse of English Power in Bengal

Murshid Kuli Khan, better known as Jafar Khan, the Governor of Bengal—His great power—Unsatisfactory relations with the English—Mission to Delhi—The Emperor Farrukhsiyar grants to the Company important privileges—Improvement of trade—Death of

1. VILLAGE AND PAGODA BELOW PATNA, AZIMABAD. 2. THE FAKEER'S ROCK AT JANGUIRA, NEAR SULTANGUNJ.
3. PART OF THE CITY OF MOORSHEDABAD.

Illustrations from Lieut.-Col. Forrest's "Picturesque Tour Along the Ganges and Jumna" (1824).

BENGAL AND ASSAM, BEHAR AND ORISSA

Jafar Khan—His successors—The Ostend Company establishes a factory at Bankipore—English and Dutch opposition—The Germans driven out—The Mahratta Ditch — Suraj-ud-Dowlah attains to power — The tragedy of the Black Hole of Calcutta.

AFTER Aurangzebe's death the power in Bengal was largely concentrated in the hands of Murshid Kuli Khan, the Nawab or Governor, with whom the English Council had negotiated for a licence to trade. This worthy was one of those remarkable men in Eastern history who through force of character raise themselves from comparatively obscure positions to the height of worldly power. A Brahman by birth, he was early sold into slavery in Persia, and there assumed the Mahommedan faith. He was taken into the Imperial service, and his conspicuous talents, supplemented by his natural gift of intrigue, secured him steady advancement, until he was associated by Aurangzebe with Azimu-sh-Shan in the government of Bengal in the position of Imperial Treasurer. The princely Governor, who at the time was thinking a good deal more of the succession to the Mogul throne than of his charge in Eastern India, left the government very much under Murshid Kuli Khan's control. Making the best of his opportunity, the crafty treasurer gradually got all the reins of power into his hands, and eventually became in name as well as fact Governor of Bengal. Nor was he content to be merely a servant of an Imperial master. As the Mogul power, under the influence of the mortal disease with which it was stricken, became less and less a reality, the Governor of Bengal arrogated to himself to an increasing extent the rights of a sovereign ruler. Transferring the seat of government from Dacca, where it had long been, to Murshidabad, he established a Court to which representatives of the principal trading nations of Europe resorted on the frequent occasions when they required concessions or had to complain of grievances or protest against exactions. The intercourse was the more intimate as the Governor's Court was in close proximity to Kasimbazar, which had long been a centre of commercial importance to the European traders, and which at the beginning of the eighteenth century contained factories belonging to the French and the Dutch as well as the English.

Murshid Kuli Khan, though he disliked Europeans and was at no pains at times to conceal his aversion, had a very intelligent conception of the advantages that European trade brought, and he left the East India Company to pursue its trade with only occasional checks. The position nevertheless, was not altogether satisfactory, owing to the vagueness of the terms of the authority which had been conferred upon the Company, and it was not until some years after the establishment of the new régime that a definite legal status was secured.

The first step of importance taken to secure a permanent status after Aurangzebe's death was the dispatch in 1714 from Calcutta to the Court of Farrukhsiyar, the new Emperor, of an embassy headed by Mr. John Surman, one of the Company's experienced officials. As the first English diplomatic mission which had been sent to the Mogul's Court since Sir William Norris's unfortunate embassy, the event excited much interest at the time, and every effort was made to invest it with importance. Surman carried with him presents of the value of £30,000, and his train was an imposing one. He, however, was ignorant of the intricate politics of the Delhi Court of that day, and only a favourable chance probably saved the mission from failure. This was the successful medical treatment of the Emperor by William Hamilton, the surgeon attached to the mission. Farrukhsiyar was to have been married to the daughter of Raja Ajit Singh, one of the Rajput princes, but the wedding had been postponed because the Emperor was suffering from a complaint which his own physicians had been unable to cure. Hamilton, by a skilful operation, restored the Imperial patient to health, and by so doing won his fervent gratitude. Any reward that he cared to ask for might have been obtained by the young Scotch surgeon, but with rare self-denial and fidelity to his employers he merely stipulated for the granting of their petition for trading rights. Farrukhsiyar was well disposed towards the appeal, and referred the matter to his leading officials. In so doing he gave an opening for intrigue, of which Jafar Khan, as Murshid Kuli Khan was now known, was not slow to take advantage. The sand which that worthy now put into the Imperial machine caused the negotiations to drag inordinately. It was only after repeated efforts and elaborate bribery that Surman was able, two years after his arrival, to depart, carrying with him the sealed compact which gave to the English greatly increased powers. The principal of these were a right to have handed over to the Company for trial all Europeans or natives who might be accountable to the Company, and a concession of the lordship of thirty-eight towns in the vicinity of Calcutta, with the same rights as were attached to the Company's existing possessions.

Jafar Khan was incensed at the success of the English mission, and he took instant measures to nullify the grant of new territory by prohibiting the local landowners from parting with their rights to the English on pain of severe punishment. In other respects, however, the wily Nawab saw fit to accept the situation, and the Company's representatives, realizing now that they had to deal with Jafar Khan as the real power in Bengal, lost no opportunity of conciliating him with valuable presents. This prudent policy secured for Calcutta a lease of vigorous life. Trade grew enormously in volume, and the streets of the settlement hummed with life. Farrukhsiyar's death in 1719 by the hand of an assassin, and the further degradation of the Imperial power by sordid parricidal warfare, enabled Jafar Khan to consolidate his position. The Nawab was a man of great strength of character, and he established a rule in Bengal which was, regarded by Oriental standards, both firm and just. Dying in 1725, he left instructions for the succession to the Nawabship of his grandson, Serferaz Khan. This arrangement was set aside in favour of one in which Serferaz Khan's father, Shuja Adem Khan, was made Nawab and Serferaz Khan was Dewan.

Shuja Adem Khan early in his career gave evidence of his jealousy of the power of the English, and he availed himself of every opening which presented for thwarting and prejudicing their trade. It was this spirit that prompted him in 1724 to give the Ostend Company, which a short time previously had been floated under the auspices of the Court of Vienna, a concession for a factory at Bankipore.

Neither the English nor the Dutch relished the prospect of competition which the introduction of this new rival into their midst threatened, and they set to work immediately to oust the intruder. Their labours were not very fruitful at first, because Jafar Khan for his own ends threw the mantle of his powerful protection over the newcomers, and refused to entertain any proposals for their eviction. When, however, Jafar Khan disappeared from the scene, the opposition to the Ostend Company was more suc-

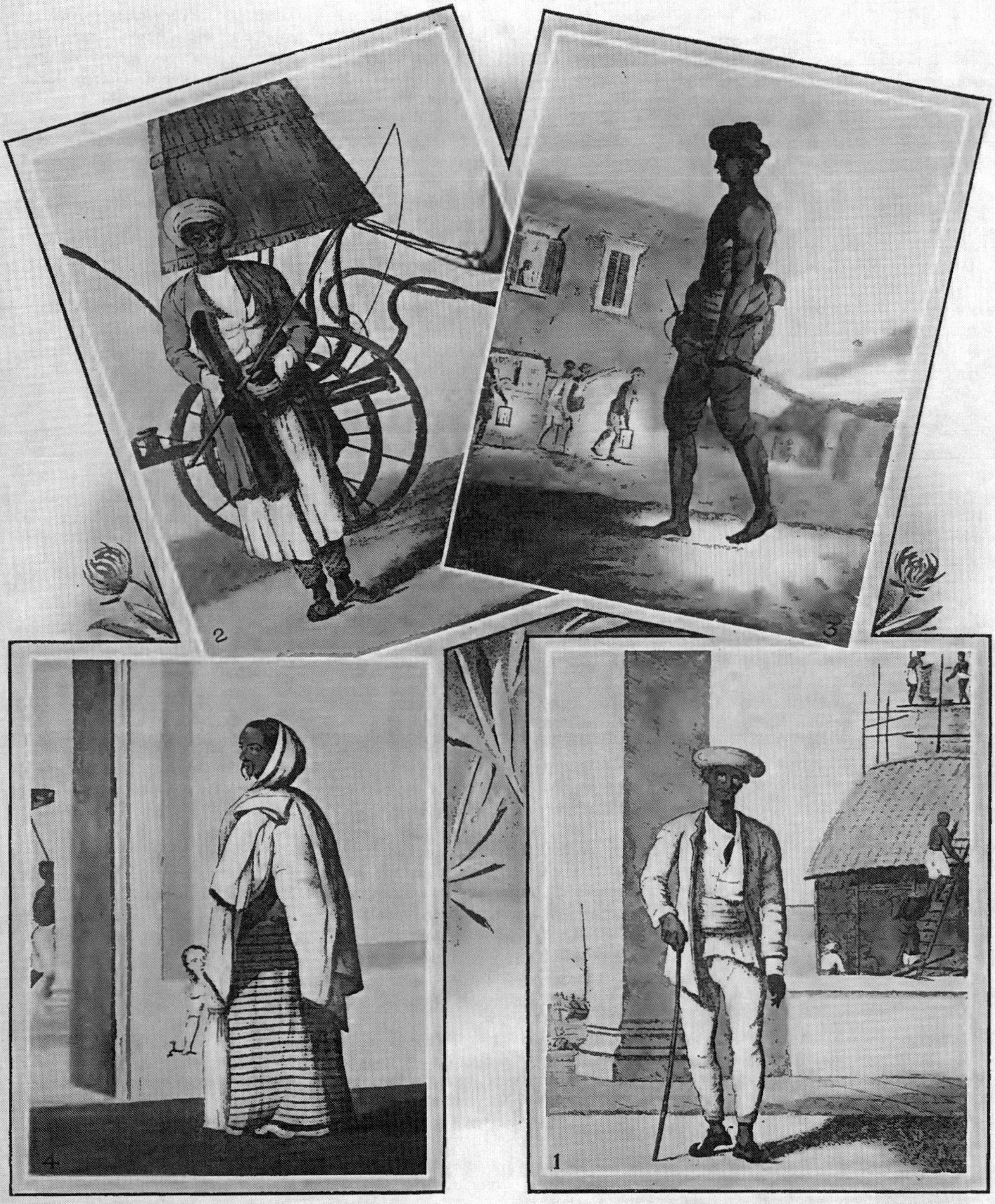

1. KHELASSY. 2. COACHMAN. 3. MUSHAULJEE LINK BOY. 4. AYAH.

Illustrations from Solvyn's "Les Hindous." Published in Paris, 1812.

cessful. In 1733, acting on the instigation of the English and Dutch Council, the Mahommedan Governor of Hooghly attacked the German settlement, and forced the defenders, after a stiff fight, to capitulate. Thereafter the whole of the Ostend Company's staff embarked for Europe, bringing to a close one of the most interesting essays in European trading in the East of that day. A second attempt on the part of the Germans to gain a foothold in India was made under the patronage of Frederick the Great in 1750. It was even less successful than the earlier essay. After abortive efforts to trade the company was wound up.

The elimination of this important rival from the path of the East India Company in Bengal had scarcely been effected than another and more serious danger arose to menace not merely the trade of its settlements but the whole prosperity of Bengal. This was the Mahratta peril. Falling more and more into decrepitude as the eighteenth century wore on, the Mogul Empire became a mark for the attentions of the virile Hindoo race of Western India, which the genius of Sivaji had disciplined into a formidable power for offensive, or, more properly speaking, destructive warfare. Sweeping across the plains of India, these light horsemen shook to the very foundations the crazy structure of Mogul rule. They penetrated into Bengal, and threatened to appear even at the gates of Calcutta itself. Alarmed at the increasing boldness of the Mahratta forays, the Bengal Council sought and secured from the Nawab of Bengal permission to construct an outlying line of fortification to keep off the intruding hordes. Thus came into existence the Mahratta Ditch, a familiar place-name in the Calcutta of to-day.

The Nawab who sanctioned the Mahratta Ditch was Ali Varda Khan, an adventurer who in 1740 had wrested from the feeble hands of Jafar Khan's descendant the power to rule Bengal. Ali Varda Khan continued to exercise authority until his death in 1756, when the succession devolved upon his son, Suraj-ud-Dowlah of infamous memory. Suraj-ud-Dowlah was a youth of eighteen of vicious instincts and despotic temperament. Ere he had been long on the throne he came into collision with the British power over a member of his family who had fled to Calcutta to escape his vengeance. Collecting a great army, Suraj-ud-Dowlah placed himself at its head and marched on Calcutta. The local officials of the Company pursued the worst possible course that could have been adopted in such an emergency. Instead of taking all the measures they could to make a stout defence of the settlement, the Governor and leading functionaries took refuge on board ships in the river, leaving the difficult task of opposing Suraj-ud-Dowlah's force to their dispirited and disorganized subordinates. A show of resistance was offered by the little band of Englishmen, but in the end they had to capitulate. When the fort had fallen the Nawab ordered the prisoners to be brought before him in the principal hall of the factory. He assumed towards them an arrogant bearing, but promised to spare their lives. They were then handed over to the tender mercies of their guards to undergo that terrible ordeal which lives in English memory as one of the foulest and darkest crimes that have stained the pages of British Indian history.

Many accounts have been written (on the basis of the narrative of Holwell, who was one of the prisoners) of the tragedy of the Black Hole of Calcutta, but nothing has ever brought the scene of that fateful night more vividly home to the present-day Briton than Macaulay's brilliant pen-picture in his essay on Clive. "The English captives," says Macaulay, "were left to the mercy of the guards, and the guards determined to secure them for the night in the prison of the garrison, a chamber known by the fearful name of the 'Black Hole.' Even for a single European malefactor the dungeon would in such a climate have been too close and narrow. The space was only 20 ft. square. The air-holes were small and obstructed. It was the summer solstice, the season when the fierce heat of Bengal can scarcely be rendered tolerable to natives of England by lofty halls and the constant waving of fans. The number of prisoners was 146. When they were ordered to enter the cell they imagined that the soldiers were joking; and, being in high spirits on account of the promise of the Nabob to spare their lives, they laughed and jested at the absurdity of the notion. They soon discovered their mistake. They expostulated, they entreated, but in vain. The guards threatened to cut down all who hesitated. The captives were driven into the cell at the point of the sword, and the door was instantly shut and locked on them. . . . They cried for mercy. They strove to burst the door. Holwell, who even in that extremity retained some presence of mind, offered large bribes to the gaolers. But the answer was that nothing could be done without the Nabob's orders, and that the Nabob was asleep, and that he would be angry if anybody woke him. Then the prisoners went mad with despair. They trampled each other down, fought for the places at the windows, fought for the pittance of water with which the cruel mercy of the murderers mocked their agonies, raved, prayed, blasphemed, implored the guards to fire among them. The gaolers in the meantime held lights to the bars, and shouted with laughter at the frantic struggles of their victims. At length the tumult died away in low gaspings and moanings. The day broke. The Nabob had slept off his debauch, and permitted the door to be opened. But it was some time before the soldiers could make a lane for the survivors by piling up on each side the heaps of corpses on which the burning climate had already begun to do its loathsome work. When at length a passage was made twenty-three ghastly figures, such as their own mothers would not have known, staggered one by one out of the charnel house. A pit was instantly dug. The dead bodies, 123 in number, were flung into it promiscuously and covered up."

After the terrible night in the "Black Hole" Holwell and the other male survivors were dispatched up country in irons, and the sole Englishwoman who escaped the ordeal was sent to Murshidabad to grace the Nawab's harem. Practically the little English community in Bengal had ceased to exist when the tyrannical Nawab had completed his operations. In fancied security he issued edicts designed to secure that the power which he hated should never again rear its head in Bengal. He even went so far as to re-name Calcutta Alinapore—the city of God. But he had reckoned without the growing sense that once helpless English traders possessed of their superiority in arms, and he had particularly left out of his estimate one of the greatest soldier-statesmen that England ever possessed—Robert Clive, the obscure writer in the Company's service, who a few years previously in Southern India had laid the foundations of his great reputation by a memorable campaign in which the French domination in India received a mortal blow.

1. GOVERNMENT HOUSE, CALCUTTA, IN 1837. 2. KIDDERPORE BRIDGE, CALCUTTA, IN 1837.
3. BURRA BAZAAR, CALCUTTA.

Illustrations from "Views in Calcutta,' by Capt. R. Jump, H.C.S. Published n 1837.

BENGAL AND ASSAM, BEHAR AND ORISSA

CHAPTER VII

The Battle of Plassey

Robert Clive entrusted with the command of an expedition to Bengal—Reoccupation of Calcutta and sacking of Hooghly—Suraj-ud-Dowlah sues for peace—Chandernagore attacked and occupied by the British—Clive and Mir Jafar—British army marches to attack Suraj-ud-Dowlah—Complete defeat of the latter at Plassey—Mir Jafar installed by Clive as Nawab of Bengal, Behar and Orissa—Profound effect of the Battle of Plassey—Enormous wealth acquired by Clive and his associates—The Company's share of the spoil.

CLIVE was in Madras at the time that the news was received of Suraj-ud-Dowlah's attack on Calcutta with its lamentable sequel. He was immediately entrusted with the leadership of an expedition to avenge the disaster. Under his command were placed nine hundred British troops and fifteen hundred sepoys. Admiral Watson, who fortunately also was in Madras at the time with his fleet of well-found ships, was sent to support the expedition with the naval power which had previously proved so valuable in Bengal. Contrary winds delayed the passage of the expedition, and it was not until December, several months after the Black Hole tragedy, that Bengal was reached. But once within the sphere of action the combined force speedily asserted its power. Calcutta was attacked and occupied without much difficulty, and Hooghly was stormed and sacked. The Nawab, thoroughly alarmed at the energetic operations of the invaders, sought an accommodation. Clive was for disregarding the overtures and continuing the war until more substantial victories had been obtained. But his ardent spirit was kept in check by the civilian council, who were eager to grasp the immediate advantages that a composition with their arch-enemy and persecutor held out. A peace was, therefore, concluded on the understanding that the factory should be restored to the British and that compensation should be paid for the losses sustained by Suraj-ud-Dowlah's aggression.

Before the negotiations for peace were terminated the shadow of a new trouble had arisen in the outbreak of war between Great Britain and France. Suraj-ud-Dowlah, smarting under the humiliations which Clive had inflicted upon him, opened up an intrigue with the French, whose support he invited for a new campaign against the British. Clive, obtaining knowledge of this move, and setting little store by the arrangement which he had by this time concluded with his wily enemy, resolved to anticipate the coalition of hostile forces by acting as the aggressor against the French. With the valuable support afforded by Watson's ships, Clive directed a successful attack against the French settlement at Chandernagore. The fort was surrendered to him, and with it its garrison of five hundred Frenchmen. It was a brilliant feat of arms, and did much to re-establish British prestige. Suraj-ud-Dowlah recognized in it a deadly blow at his own power, and was torn with alternate gusts of passion and fear as he sought a means of checking this insolent power which had so demonstratively crossed his path. The significance of the events had not been lost upon the Nawab's subjects, who had little love for him. But he was still able to command powerful resources, and in a short period he had in the field a great army ready to drive the audacious Englishmen into the sea.

Clive was under no delusions as to the magnitude of the task before him at this critical juncture of affairs. But he faced the situation with the cool determination which he ever showed in moments of danger. One of his first steps was to get into communication with the disaffected element in Suraj-ud-Dowlah's dominions and complete an arrangement with Mir Jafar, a rival aspirant to the throne, for mutual aid. When his plans were completed he marched out at the head of his little army of 1,000 Europeans, 2,000 sepoys, and 8 pieces of artillery, to meet the Nawab's army, which consisted of 35,000 foot, 15,000 horse, and 50 cannon. An essential part of the arrangement with Mir Jafar was that that worthy should at the appropriate moment join forces with the British, and that a combined attack should be delivered. But Clive advanced as far as Kasimbazar without any sign of an intention on the part of Mir Jafar to honour his part of the contract. Attempts made to elicit his intentions resulted in evasive replies, which only served to deepen the natural distrust which had been aroused by his inaction.

Clive was now in a very difficult position. He had gone too far to retreat without danger, and to advance appeared almost suicidal, seeing how formidable were the forces opposed to his little contingent. In his perplexity Clive called a council of war, with the result proverbially attributed to such councils, that a decision was come to not to fight. But Clive, after mature thought, elected to disregard the view of the majority of his military colleagues, and deliver an attack at the earliest possible moment. His army was immediately set in motion, and when night fell on June 22, 1757, he camped in a grove of mango-trees near the village of Plassey, about seventy miles north of Calcutta. Here he was so close to the Nawab's army that his sleep was disturbed by the noise of the drums and cymbals with which the enemy forces were celebrating in advance the easy victory that they expected to win over the hated infidel. When morning broke the Nawab attacked with his entire force of artillery. The guns were badly served and nearly all the shots went wide. The little force of British artillery responded with considerable effect on the serried masses of the enemy. The battle continued until noon, when the Nawab's army retired to an entrenched camp for their midday meal. Clive seized this opportunity to deliver an attack on one of the enemy's advanced posts. His men drove in the Nawab's forces, and, carrying everything before them, effected a lodgment in an angle of the camp. So impetuous was their onset that a panic seized the enemy, and they fled in confusion, leaving Clive in possession of the position, with the guns and baggage and the entire impedimenta of Suraj-ud-Dowlah's great army. The Nawab himself fled from the field on a camel to Murshidabad, from whence, after a brief sojourn, he proceeded in disguise to Patna. Meanwhile Mir Jafar, finding how completely fortune had favoured the British, had made his peace with Clive and had been saluted by him as Nawab of Bengal, Behar, and Orissa. The actual ceremony of installation took place amid much pomp at Murshidabad, whither Clive had proceeded immediately after the battle with an imposing escort.

The Battle of Plassey was one of the most notable victories ever won in Asia. From it dates the real foundation of the British Empire in India. Hitherto the British had been mere traders, living a precarious existence on sufferance. Henceforward they were to take an ever-increasing part as administrators and rulers in directing the destinies of the country. It was, perhaps, the cheapest triumph ever won by British arms, for the total loss sustained by Clive's force in the battle was only twenty killed and fifty wounded, casualties no greater than those of many a street fight. But it was, no doubt, quite as much due to diplomatic as to military qualities that

1. HINDOO TEMPLES AT AGOUREE, ON THE RIVER SOANE, BEHAR.

2. THE SACRED TREE OF THE HINDOOS AT GYA, BEHAR. 3. CITY OF PATNA.

Illustrations from "Oriental Scenery," by Thomas Daniell (1795).

the vengeance wreaked on Suraj-ud-Dowlah was so complete. Clive was a statesman as well as a soldier, and he turned his military advantages to the fullest account. History has reproached him severely for some of his dealings in this momentous period in his career, and it would be idle to assert that his actions will all bear the full light of day. But the credit belongs to him that he dared greatly, and that by his calm courage and prescience he opened up a path which led his country directly to the summit of Imperial greatness.

The immediate result of the Battle of Plassey was the pouring of a great stream of wealth into the coffers of the Company and into the pockets of all who had been prominent on the British side in the operations which terminated in the battle and Mir Jafar's elevation to the throne. Macaulay in his picturesque way describes the apportionment of the spoils of victory. "A sum of £800,000 sterling in coined silver," he says, "was sent down the river from Moorshidabad to Fort William. The fleet which conveyed this treasure consisted of a hundred boats, and performed its triumphal voyage with flags flying and music playing. Calcutta, which a few months before had been desolate, was now more prosperous than ever. Trade revived, and signs of affluence appeared in every English house. As to Clive, there was no limit to his acquisitions but his own moderation. The treasury of Bengal was thrown open to him. There were piled up, after the usage of Indian princes, immense masses of coin, among which might not seldom be detected the florins and byzants with which, before any European ship had turned the Cape of Good Hope, the Venetians purchased the stuffs and spices of the East. Clive walked between heaps of gold and silver, crowned with rubies and diamonds, and was at liberty to help himself. He accepted between £200,000 and £300,000." Nor were these payments in solid coin the sole rewards reaped for the victory. The Company obtained the grant of the *zamindari*, or landholder's rights, over an extensive tract of country round Calcutta known as the District of the Twenty-four Parganas, and Clive somewhat later was given as a *jagir*, or military fief, the quit rent of these lands, amounting in value to nearly £30,000 a year. In after years these transactions became the subject of heated criticism and prolonged inquiry in England, and it was then that Clive, defending his action before a Parliamentary Committee, uttered his historic exclamation, "My God, Mr. Chairman, at this moment I stand astonished at my own moderation!" That remark is a pregnant estimate of the situation as it existed in the period following the battle. The flow of wealth knew no limit so far as the principal actor in the scene was concerned. The native powers that then existed were only too ready to purchase his invaluable support at any price he might demand. It was a demoralizing position, which in due course produced its inevitable fruit in the disorganization of the public service, and Clive cannot be entirely acquitted of responsibility for the results. But in fairness we must bear in mind that the traditions of the Company's service in those days were not exalted, and that the acquisition of wealth by irregular means was encouraged by the miserably low scale of official remuneration.

CHAPTER VIII

After Plassey

Clive's great reputation—He is created Governor of Bengal—Sends to Madras an army to fight the French—Shah Alum and the Nawab of Oudh march against Mir Jafar—Clive defeats the movement—Mir Jafar intrigues with the Dutch against the English—Clive attacks and captures the Dutch station of Chinsurah—Clive returns to England—Demoralization in Bengal—The massacre of Patna—The Battle of Baxar—Clive proceeds to India for the last time—His reforms—Warren Hastings appointed Governor of Bengal.

THE effect of Clive's success on the home public was tremendous. They dimly saw in it the realization of a dream of Indian conquest which had long fascinated them, but which after the Black Hole tragedy seemed more fanciful than ever. The East India Company, in their joy at the wonderful transformation effected in their affairs by brilliant and courageous leadership, constituted Clive Governor of Bengal, with the highest honours that it was possible for them to confer. This dignity was so natural a corollary of the achievements of the young soldier-statesman in the field that even before the Company's instructions arrived he had, by the general request and desire of the Council, assumed the supreme position. Nothing, indeed, could surpass the prestige that Clive enjoyed on this morrow of his great triumph. He was courted and feared by every one. The whole Indian world, with Mir Jafar at its head, was at his feet, ready to do his instant bidding.

Not without justification was the trust reposed in Clive. His greatness was not limited to ability to lead in the field. He possessed all the qualities which make the successful statesman—sound judgment, foresight, tact, and ability to take quick decisions. He had wide knowledge of India, and had that instinct for getting into the Indian mind which all our great administrators in the East have possessed in a greater or less degree as an essential part of their mental equipment. Knowing what he knew of the then existing conditions in India, and understanding, as he well did, that the British could not rest on the laurels of Plassey, Clive from the outset of his career as head of the Bengal Government pursued an energetic policy. When the call came from Madras for support in the campaign against the French under Lally and Bussy, he sent south a considerable body of troops, and in that way assisted materially to secure the ultimate predominance of Britain in that theatre.

While the bulk of Clive's army was still away fighting in Southern India a serious crisis arose in Bengal itself owing to the rebellion of Shah Alum, the Shahzada, or Imperial Prince. Shah Alum, supported by the Nawab of Oudh, marched with forty thousand men with the object of dethroning Mir Jafar and securing for himself a vantage ground for his larger designs. He got as far as Patna, and invested the city, greatly to the terror of Mir Jafar. Clive, whose advice was sought, strongly urged his protégé to deal boldly with the position. He promised his powerful support if the course he recommended was followed. Mir Jafar, gladly acquiescing in the proposed resistance, gave Clive the cue for the advance which he had seen to be inevitable from the first. The British commander could only muster a force of under 3,000 soldiers, of whom only 450 were Europeans. But such was the glamour of his name that when Shah Alum heard of his approach he abandoned his investment of Patna and precipitately fled, leaving his huge army to disperse in the absence of leadership.

Relieved of a great danger, Mir Jafar overwhelmed his benefactor with attentions, but his gratitude was not more lasting than that of a despot rescued from threatened peril usually is. Jealousy of Clive's power soon made itself conspicuous in his policy. In his desire to emancipate himself from what had become a galling thraldom the Nawab opened up an intrigue with the Dutch, who were then the only European Power

1. MOSQUE ON THE BOORAGUNGA BRANCH OF THE GANGES.
2. PART OF THE INTERIOR OF THE CITY OF DACCA.
3. THE FORT AND GATEWAY OF THE GREAT KUTHA, DACCA.
4. THE SMALL KUTHA WITH ITS ENCLOSED MOSQUE, DACCA.

Illustrations from "Antiquities of Dacca." Published in 1817.

in India capable of being an effective ally against the English. The Dutch, who had long conceived designs for establishing their supremacy in Eastern India, responded to the overtures made to them, and the Batavia Government dispatched an expedition composed of seven well-found ships to co-operate with Mir Jafar against the British. Clive, still heavily handicapped by the absence of a large part of his force in Madras, was now confronted with a situation of great peril. But he never hesitated as to the policy that he must pursue in the emergency. He clearly perceived that he must attack the Dutch before they could form a junction with the Nawab if the situation was to be saved. Acting with characteristic energy, he made a combined water and land attack on the Hollanders. Although the Dutch were superior in numbers they were unable to withstand the onset of Clive's disciplined forces, and a great victory for British arms was the result. It gave the last blow to Dutch pretensions to dominion in India. Henceforward the Dutch settlement at Chinsurah was under strict regulation and existed on sufferance. In other parts, notably in Southern India, a semblance of power was maintained for some time longer, but the humiliating terms which Clive wrung from the factors of Chinsurah were the real death warrant of Dutch ambitions in India.

When Clive had made the British position in Bengal secure in this fashion he proceeded to England on a well-earned holiday. For five years he remained in England, dazzling the fashionable world with a display of riches which seemed fabulous. In the meantime the conduct of affairs in Bengal fell into the hands of men who had been raised to high position under the corrupting influences of the reign of profusion and extravagance which the Battle of Plassey ushered in. The natural consequences followed in a degradation of the whole system of administration. Extortion was practised as a fine art, and the principal end which almost every official had in view was the accumulation of a private fortune which would enable him to figure as a man of fashion at home. Following these principles of conduct, the Bengal Council soon saw fit, in 1761, to remove Mir Jafar from the throne and place upon it a creature of their own, Mir Kasim. Substantial rewards were paid to his sponsors by the new Nawab for his honour, and his generous recognition of the power that elevated him also took the form of the grant to the Company of the three districts of Bardwan, Midnapur, and Chittagong. But Mir Kasim did not long remain in the favour of his patrons. They expected more of him than he would or could give, and he, on his part, was irritated at the effective way in which the Company squeezed the sponge before he himself had an opportunity of trying his hand at the operation. Eventually he went off from Murshidabad to Monghyr, where he took up a strong position ready to cross swords with the British if a favourable opportunity offered. He had not long to wait for his opening. In 1763 a dispute in reference to claims made by the servants of the Company to carry on their private trade without the payment of local dues led to a rupture. In the course of its passage up the river an English boat was fired upon by the Nawab's officials. Immediately the whole province became aflame. Mir Kasim, who had carefully laid his plans, attacked and practically annihilated a force of about two thousand sepoys at Patna, and at the same time instituted a vendetta against all Englishmen in the province.

The Bengal Council took energetic measures to meet the formidable situation which had arisen. A series of well-organized movements led to successive defeats of the Nawab's troops, first on the banks of the Adjee River, on July 17th, then, two days later, at Kutwah; again, on August 2nd, at Gheeriah, and finally, on August 11th, at Oodeynulla. These reverses aroused the fanatical rage of the Nawab to such an extent that he determined to wreak his vengeance on the comparatively large force—numbering over two hundred—of European officials and soldiers he had in his power as a result of the earlier operations at Patna. Orders given to his native generals for the execution of his shameful plan elicited from them a noble refusal, accompanied by the remark that they were soldiers and not assassins. But Mir Kasim had at his elbow a pliant tool for the dark work in hand in Dyce Sombre, a foreign adventurer, probably of Germanic origin, from Strassburg, who had come out to India as a carpenter, and, like many other men of his class, had found an easy road to fortune in native military employ. Sombre, without the least qualms of pity, took up the rejected commission, and proceeded to execute it with an energy that seemed to indicate a real zest for villainy. On October 5th, having surrounded the building in which the prisoners were interned, he sent for the three leading civilians of the party—Ellis, Hay, and Lushington. No sooner had they approached than they and the party accompanying them were attacked and killed, their mutilated bodies afterwards being cast into an adjacent well. Subsequently, a body of sepoys, under Sombre's orders, mounted the roof of the house and poured down a deadly fire upon the unfortunate prisoners who were in the yard below. Some who escaped the murderous volleys took refuge in an inner chamber, where they desperately defended themselves against the parties of sepoys sent against them. The sepoys, struck by the heroism shown, sought to be excused from proceeding further with the massacre. But Sombre would accept nothing short of a full tale of slaughtered victims, and, by energetically exercising his authority, ultimately achieved his vile purpose. So complete was the holocaust that even Mr. Ellis's infant child was murdered by Sombre's directions. Altogether, more than fifty civil and military officers and over one hundred European soldiers perished on the occasion.

An immediate effect of this terrible massacre was to lead to a concentration of English power against the Nawab and the double-dyed villain his accomplice. By a swift march Patna was taken on November 6th and Mir Kasim forced to retreat to the territory of the Nawab Vizier of Oudh. A demand that the fugitive should be handed over being rejected, the Bengal Council took measures to enforce their views. This led to a coalition of the forces of Shah Alum, who was now Emperor, and of the Nawab of Oudh against the British. The danger, formidable enough of itself, was, as time wore on, intensified in 1764 by a mutiny of sepoys. Major (afterwards Sir) Hector Munro, who was in command, took prompt action to suppress this rising, and by dealing out stern punishment to the ringleaders ultimately restored discipline. Major Munro afterwards, at the Battle of Baxar, showed that the *moral* of his force had not been permanently affected by events by winning a great victory, which placed Oudh at his mercy and made the Mogul Emperor a creature of British policy.

The events which had been passing in Bengal in these years following Clive's departure had a powerful reflex action in England. Not without good reason

1. DANCING BOYS. 2. DANCING GIRLS. 3. GROUP OF MENDICANTS.

Illustrations from Mrs Belnos' "Manners in Bengal." Published in 1832.

the directors became seriously alarmed at the evidence that almost every ship brought of the increasing anarchy into which Bengal was falling under the influence of incompetent administration. The cry went up that Clive alone could evolve order out of the chaos that had been created, and, bowing to the universal demand, the great soldier-statesman (now Baron Clive of Plassey in the peerage of the United Kingdom) went once more to India. On landing at Calcutta in May 1765 he found that the machinery of government was terribly disorganized. The discoveries he made had a profound effect on him. "Alas!" he said in a communication home, "how is the English name sunk! I could not avoid paying the tribute of a few tears to the departed and lost fame of the British nation—irrecoverably so, I fear. However, I do declare, by that great Being who is the searcher of all hearts, and to whom we must be accountable if there be a hereafter, that I am come out with a mind superior to all corruption, and that I am determined to destroy these great and growing evils or perish in the attempt." Clive was as good as his word. Before he left India, at the end of an eighteen months' sojourn, he had laid solidly the foundations of an edifice of administration which left no effective opening for the evils which so rankly flourished at the time. Besides this work of official reorganization, Clive carried out a great scheme of territorial adjustment, which may be said to have settled the lines of British domination in India. Preserving still the fiction of Mogul overlordship, he entered into arrangements with the Nawab of Oudh by which that province was handed back in consideration of a payment of £500,000 towards the cost of the war, and he agreed to yield up the provinces of Allahabad and Kora to the Emperor Shah Alum in return for the grant to the Company of the *diwani*, or fiscal administration, of Bengal, Behar, and Orissa, with the jurisdiction of the Northern Circars. An essential part of the arrangement in regard to Bengal was that the Nawabship should be maintained, and that an allowance of £600,000 should be paid for its maintenance out of the revenues of the province.

In this fashion Clive rounded off his official career in India. Ere he had disappeared from the scene the great name of Warren Hastings, which is indissolubly associated with his in the foundation of the British Empire in India, had come to the front as that of an official of great promise. When Clive quitted India for the last time in 1767 Hastings had already served nearly sixteen years in Bengal. He had advanced by successive stages in the official hierarchy, until in 1769 he had reached the dignified position of Member of Council at Madras. He remained at the Southern Presidency until 1772, when his conspicuous talents and long service marked him out for promotion to the still higher office of Governor of Bengal. With his assumption of this appointment opened the most important period of his life, and with it was ushered in a new epoch in the government of India.

CHAPTER IX

Consolidation of the British Power

Hastings institutes reforms abolishing the dual system of control—The Company "stand forth as Dewan"—Passage of the Regulating Act creating a supreme government in Bengal—The new administration torn by faction—Hastings's great measures—His return to England—Lord Cornwallis's administration—The permanent settlement of Bengal—Consolidation of British power—Financial difficulties.

When Hastings arrived in Calcutta he bore with him instructions to initiate a series of reforms in the administration which experience had shown to be necessary. The dual system of control which Clive had established had not borne the test of actual experience. "There was," says Kaye in his "History of the Administration of the East India Company," "no responsibility and no control. The strong preyed upon the weak—and the weak had none to look up to for protection. Misgovernment brought its wonted bitter fruit, and the revenue began to decline. So, in 1769, European advisers were appointed as a check to the native functionaries. The most elaborate instructions were issued to them. It is hard to say what they were not expected to do; but still the double government continued to work grievously. And there were those who thought that the supervisors only made confusion worse confounded and corruption more corrupt." It was Hastings's special mission to change all this by initiating an entirely new system, under which the entire control of the administration was to be vested in British officials. To adopt the words of the historic proclamation of May 11, 1772, announcing the reform, the Company was from that time forward to "stand forth publicly in the character of Dewan." "This," as Kaye observes, "was the greatest step in the progress of Anglo-Indian administration ever made by the Company—the greatest administrative revolution, perhaps, to which Bengal had ever been subjected."

A task so tremendously important as that which was embodied in the Company's instructions was not to be quickly discharged, and Hastings spent many busy and eventful years in organizing the government on the new basis. If he had been left to himself to carry out the change unaided, with the unrivalled knowledge that he possessed of India, all might have been well. But Parliament in 1773 had passed an important measure, known in history as the Regulating Act, under which great constitutional changes were effected in India. By the provisions of this Act a Governor and Council, consisting of four members, was appointed to Bengal, with supreme authority over all the Presidencies of India, and a Supreme Court of Judicature was created, with its seat at Calcutta. The appointment of the four members of the Supreme Council, as well as of the judges, was vested in the Crown, and the right of choice as regards the Members of Council was exercised by the dispatch to India of General Clavering, Colonel Monson, and Mr. Philip Francis, not one of whom had had any prior experience of India. Mr. Barlow, the fourth member, was an experienced servant of the Company, and might in favourable circumstances have redressed the balance which weighed so heavily against experience. But, unhappily, almost from the first a cabal was organized against Hastings, with the object of concentrating in the hands of the trio of inexperienced members all the governing power. Ably led by Francis, who is known to literary fame from his association with the controversy as to the authorship of "The Letters of Junius," this majority of the Council speedily made Hastings's authority to a large extent a nullity. The story of that remarkable conflict, with its tragic sequel in the execution of the Brahman Nuncoomar on a charge of forgery, is told by Macaulay, with many and gross inaccuracies in points of detail, in his well-known essay on Hastings. It is not necessary to dwell upon it here further than to say that the enmities then aroused were largely responsible for the subsequent impeachment of Hastings, which lives among the most absorbing features of British history in the eighteenth century.

The changes introduced by Hastings were of a far-reaching description.

1. VIEW IN CLIVE STREET. 2. CHURCH ENTRANCE TO THE DHURAMTOLLA.
3. CALCUTTA FROM THE OLD HOUSE. 4. CHOWRINGHEE ROAD FROM THE ESPLANADE.

From Sir Charles D'Oyley's "Town and Port of Calcutta." Published 1840.

Bengal was divided into fourteen districts, and over each was appointed a European official, termed a collector, who was charged with the duty of collecting the public revenue and of presiding over the Diwani Adalat, or civil courts. It was also the collector's business to keep an eye on the Faujdari Adalat, or criminal courts, which were still presided over by the Mahommedan officials. Appeals from the local civil and criminal courts were allowed to two superior courts in Calcutta. Subsequently this system was changed by the substitution for the collectorates of six provincial councils at Calcutta, Burdwan, Dacca, Murshidabad, Dinajpur, and Patna. But later still, in Lord Cornwallis's time, the Hastings's plan was revived in a somewhat extended form, the collector under the new régime filling the position of civil judge and magistrate.

Now that Hastings's work in India can be seen in its true perspective, free from the distorting mediums of personal animosity and political prejudice, it is impossible not to yield to it the meed of our highest admiration. With patient statesmanship, illumined by the resources of a mind stored with the rich experience of nearly a quarter century's contact with Indian problems, the great man gradually evolved the complete machinery of a system of internal administration. It is largely upon his measures that the present official organization of Bengal is based. If he had accomplished nothing else he would have won an indisputable title to enduring fame. But side by side with his work of domestic reform he conducted a diplomacy of the most far-reaching kind ; he made and unmade potentates and he directed the movement of great armies, all his operations tending to the aggrandisement of the power of his native country. That he perpetrated some bad moral blunders from the standpoint of British integrity and fair dealing is not seriously to be denied. But it is impossible to separate him from the system of which he was a part—a system in which successful administration was judged by the extent of the exactions that could be squeezed out of the unfortunate population. Hastings in this matter was the good servant of a bad cause. Driven forward by the inexorable demands from home for financial results, he acted injudiciously, and even tyrannically, but rarely had failure to be written on any of his projects.

In 1781, when Hastings retired from India, the foundations had been laid of a stable system of government and a foreign policy which extended to almost every part of the continent. It now remained for others to rear upon the base of his far-seeing measures an enduring superstructure. Fortunately at this juncture there was nominated as the head of the Government of India a nobleman of high moral purpose and good attainments in the person of Lord Cornwallis. The new Governor-General, the first of a long line of aristocratic proconsuls who have ruled India, addressed himself to the work of administrative construction with a zeal and judgment which bore fruit in a code of written laws and regulations which gave luminous expression to the aspiration of the British nation to make the government of India worthy of them. Under his official auspices criminal jurisdiction was first entrusted to Europeans, and the Nizamat Sadr Adalat, or Court of Criminal Jurisdiction, at Calcutta was established. Another of his measures was the separation of the jurisdiction of the district collector and judge. But the most important of his reforms was the Permanent Settlement of the Land Revenue of Bengal. This great scheme, introduced in its final form in 1793, gave rise to a fierce controversy, which extended over many years, and even still has an academic interest for land reformers. It had, no doubt, many defects, not the least serious of which was that it did not sufficiently protect the rights of the occupying tenants. In later years many attempts were made by legislation to remedy the defects in the system, and something like an equipoise was established between the propertied rights of the zamindar, or landowner, on the one hand, and the interests of the ryot, or tenant, on the other. But it is open to serious question whether it has been possible entirely to recover what was lost by the enforcement of the one-sided conception of the landed rights of Bengal embodied in Lord Cornwallis's settlement. Its greatest value, perhaps, is that it established for the first time a system of revenue collection on a scientific basis. The native population, instead of being subjected to the evils of frequent and arbitrary changes in the method of collection, knew exactly where it stood, and was able to conduct its life accordingly.

The end of the eighteenth century found the British power well consolidated from the mouths of the Ganges to Benares. It became the duty of Lord Wellesley, who succeeded Lord Cornwallis, after an interim of five years filled by the colourless régime of Sir John Shore, to carry the British flag farther, so as to make it the supreme authority throughout the country, and so safeguard the position already secured in the three Presidencies, but most conspicuously in Bengal. This glorious chapter in British Indian annals belongs to the general history of India, and need not be touched upon here further than to say that in consequence of the brilliant victories secured over Tipu Sahib in the South and the Mahrattas in Western and Central India, the centre of government in Calcutta attained a new splendour. It was in this period that some of the most important of the city's institutions—Government House amongst them—were erected, and it is from the same spacious age that dates the inception of the Presidency banking system. Calcutta life grew in splendour with the steady march of the British arms ; but the times were not entirely free from anxiety. The great Napoleonic war was then opening, and Britain, as in our day, was face to face with a struggle in which its very existence as a nation was threatened. How well her sons comported themselves, whether in the homeland or in exile, the records of the time show. In India a great wave of patriotism swept over the European communities, and large sums were contributed to the support of the national cause. In Calcutta volunteer forces were formed, and the *Maidan* every morning resounded with military words of command addressed to miscellaneous bodies of civilians who had banded themselves together for the aid of authority in the event of a not unexpected raid by "the little Corporal."

Financial difficulties arising out of the state of war that existed in Europe and in India itself occupied a large share of the attention of the Supreme Government in the early years of the new century. It is an interesting fact, and one which enables us to realize how enormously British credit in India has enhanced in the past century, that the Government borrowings in Calcutta at that period carried interest at the rate of 12 per cent., and that in 1801 this 12 per cent. paper—Treasury notes payable in the ensuing autumn—was selling at a discount of 3 or 4 per cent. The crisis was weathered in due time, but the financial stress left its mark for a long period on the administration.

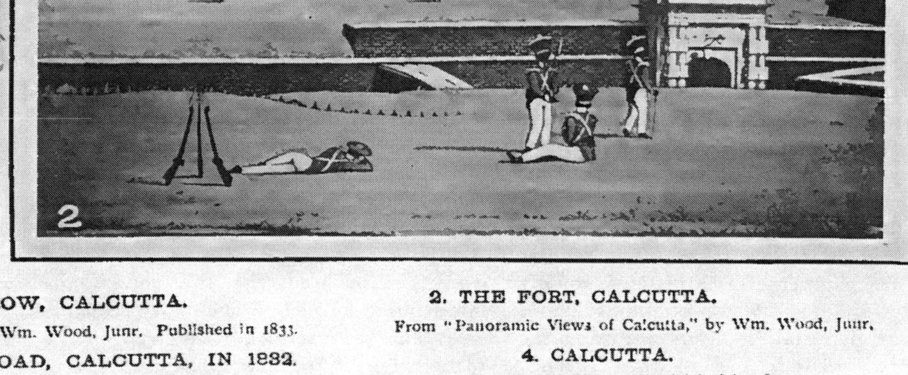

1. ESPLANADE ROW, CALCUTTA.

From "Panoramic Views of Calcutta," by Wm. Wood, Junr. Published in 1833.

3. CHOWRINGHEE ROAD, CALCUTTA, IN 1832.

From "Panoramic Views of Calcutta," by Wm. Wood, Junr.

2. THE FORT, CALCUTTA.

From "Panoramic Views of Calcutta," by Wm. Wood, Junr.

4. CALCUTTA.

From "Salt's Views." Published in 1809.

BENGAL AND ASSAM, BEHAR AND ORISSA

CHAPTER X

A Century of Progress

North-West Provinces government formed—The liberty of the Press granted by Metcalfe—The first Burmese War—Annexation of Assam—Land reform—The first Lieutenant-Governor appointed—The Mutiny of 1857—An era of peaceful progress—The partition of Bengal—The coronation Durbar changes—Conclusion.

WITH the lapse of years and the growth of the activities of the administration, increasing difficulty was found in effectively governing the huge area which was included in the Province of Bengal. As early as 1808 a proposal was made that a separate system of government should be established in the North-West Provinces. Nothing came of the scheme then, but the question was revived in 1829, when the division was strongly recommended by a Finance Committee appointed by the Supreme Government. Lord William Bentinck, the then Governor-General, was opposed to the separation of authority, and held that if a change was to be made it should be the removal of the Supreme Government to the North-West Provinces and the delegation of Bengal business to local authorities in Calcutta. The influences at home in favour of the creation of the new Government were, however, too strong to be resisted, and when the Bill for the renewal of the Company's Charter was passed in 1833 it embodied a scheme for the establishment of a fourth Presidency with its seat at Agra. Eventually the project was revised, and in the place of the larger Government designed in the Charter Act, a subordinate administration, with a Lieutenant-Governor at its head, came into being.

The period during which this change was being discussed witnessed also a prolonged and acrimonious discussion in regard to the liberty of the Press in India, and more especially in Bengal. In its earliest days the Calcutta Press, like that of every Indian centre, had reprehensible features. It dealt largely in scurrility, and showed an entire lack of responsibility. Gradually as Calcutta grew in importance the character of its newspapers improved, but the old taint clung to the Press, and when the war broke out with France at the end of the eighteenth century Lord Wellesley had no difficulty in finding reasons for establishing a rigorous censorship. The regulations framed were very drastic, involving the suppression of the offending paper and the deportation of its editor in the event of infringement of them. They were probably a necessary provision for the state of war which existed at the time, but they were incompatible with the era of peace which followed, and when the Marquess of Hastings proceeded to India in 1814, he caused the restrictions to be relaxed to a very large extent, in spite of the protests of the local officials. On Lord Hastings's departure in 1823 the supreme office was held temporarily by Mr. John Adam, one of the old oligarchy of Calcutta who had objected to the policy of gentle dealing with the Press, and that gentleman took upon himself to re-enforce the Press restrictions. The weight of his authority fell upon Mr. J. Silk Buckingham, a journalist of some standing, whose name has become famous in connection with the struggles of the Press for freedom. Mr. Buckingham was seized and deported to England, and his property in Calcutta was rendered worthless. Afterwards the East India Company had to pay dearly for the arbitrariness of their servant, but meanwhile the Indian Press was put under the lash of a new set of regulations of a most stringent kind, issued on March 14th and April 15, 1823. These ill-considered proposals added fuel to the fire of the resentment excited by Buckingham's deportation, but the forces of reaction were for the time being too strong to permit of a change of policy being made. During Lord Amherst's Governor-Generalship, and still more during that of his successor, Lord William Bentinck, the regulations were allowed to fall into disuse. But it was not until Sir Charles (afterwards Lord) Metcalfe filled the office of Governor-General temporarily in 1835 that the Indian Press was actually freed. In April of that year he caused to be passed a law repealing the Press regulations throughout India, and substituting for them a new enactment of a mild and unexceptionable character. Thereafter until quite modern times the Bengal Press, in common with Indian journalism, generally went its way unshackled, to the infinite advantage not only of the Press itself but of the interests of the country.

As the lines of British rule in India broadened the military operations necessitated from time to time by political exigencies, though, of course, directed by the Supreme Government, became less directly associated with the Bengal administration as such. The province, however, was very seriously involved in the prosecution of the first Burmese War in 1824, and sent out two of the three expeditions which formed the army of invasion. One of these proceeded up the Brahmaputra into Assam, and the other took the land route through Arakan to Chittagong. Some initial reverses on the frontier, and notably the cutting up of a small British force in Assam, created for the time a most unpleasant impression in Calcutta, and special measures were taken in view of what seemed to the fevered imaginations of the local public an imminent Burmese invasion. But in due course the might of British arms was asserted, and Assam, Cachar, and other territory passed under the Company's rule.

In spite of the persistent demands made upon the Bengal Army during the wars of the nineteenth century, domestic rather than military problems engaged the attention of the Government during the earlier decades of that period. The land settlement was a continuous source of unrest and heated controversy. As has been noted, the settlement made by Lord Cornwallis took too little account of the cultivator's rights, and the partiality shown for the landlord had been aggravated by stringent regulations passed in 1799 and 1812, which placed the tenants at the mercy of rack-renting landlords. After prolonged discussion the question was seriously taken up in 1859, when a Land Law was passed which greatly curtailed the landlord's powers of enhancing rent in certain cases. Even this legislation was found in practice to be inadequate to remove the admitted grievances of the cultivators, and it was not until 1885 that finality was reached by the carrying of legislation embodying the recommendations of a Commission which sat in 1879 to inquire into the land system of the province.

Before this great reform had reached fruition the entire administrative system of Bengal had undergone a striking change by the creation of a definitely local executive with a Lieutenant-Governor at its head. The old arrangement by which the Supreme Government was responsible for the working of the administrative machinery in the province served very well for the time when the British power was in its infancy, but with the growth of the vast interests beyond the confines of Bengal which flowed from the various extensions of British territory on the continent, consequent upon the overthrow of the Mogul and the Mahratta power, the need came to be felt for a system which left the control of local

1. THE SILK AND CLOTH MERCHANT.
2. ABLUTIONS OF A YOUNG HINDOO WOMAN OF RANK ON THE BANKS OF THE GANGES.
3. THE VILLAGE GOSSIPS.
Illustrations from Mrs. Belnos' "Manners In Bengal." Published in 1832.

affairs in the hands of officials specially appointed to deal with Bengal affairs. Sir Frederick Halliday was the first of the series of Lieutenant-Governors. Since his day a long series of able men, drawn from the ranks of the Covenanted Civil Service, have filled the office.

The great Mutiny of 1857, which for a time shook the foundations of British power in India, deeply involved Bengal, whose native army supplied the principal material to the forces of the rebels. But apart from the famous incident at Barrackpore, which gave the signal for the rising, and such episodes as the disturbances at Dacca and the heroic defence maintained by a handful of civilians and Sikhs at Arrah, the province did not become the scene of any notable conflicts. An enormous amount of demoralization, however, was caused by the loosening of the ties of discipline which followed upon the successive mutinies of the native regiments in Lower Bengal, and a considerable time elapsed after the crushing of the revolt in Northern and Central India before normal conditions were restored.

The noble Proclamation of Queen Victoria, announcing the transfer of the government of India to the Crown, which was read at a great durbar at Allahabad on November 1, 1858, by Lord Canning, ushered in for Bengal, as for the rest of India, an era of peace and progress. A vigorous policy of public works construction was inaugurated on lines which the past troubles had shown to be desirable. In particular the construction of railways was actively promoted, and nowhere in India was the need for this means of communication greater at this time than in Bengal. Before the Mutiny broke out the entire railway system of the province consisted of a short section of what is now the East India Railway, starting from Calcutta. This had proved of great service to the military during the Mutiny, and the work was now pushed on energetically. Other lines were projected, and in due course the magnificent system of communication now seen came into being. Meanwhile trade developed enormously, bringing into existence thriving centres of commerce in regions which had hitherto been mere jungle. These activities are treated at length in other sections of this volume, and call for no further reference here. Nor is it necessary in this historical survey to do more than record briefly the measures associated with the Partition of Bengal introduced during Lord Curzon's Viceroyalty in 1905. The scheme then introduced, based on a long-entertained desire to make the government of Bengal more effective by dividing the province, cut off the eastern districts of the old Presidency, and, combining these with Assam, constituted a new province with the designation of Eastern Bengal. Though at the time no very serious opposition was offered to the project, it was afterwards bitterly assailed, and a formidable agitation was promoted in favour of the reversal of the policy of partition. Grave disorders, incited by an anarchical propaganda which was conducted in more or less open association with the constitutional movement, arose in various parts of the Presidency, and were a source of much anxiety to the Government. The King's visit to India in connection with the Coronation ceremonies at the end of 1911 brought a welcome reaction from the turbulence of the period of political discontent which had preceded it, and the memorable proclamation of State changes which was made at the great Delhi Durbar on December 12, 1911, opened the way to a new era of peace and reconciliation. Amongst the measures announced by His Majesty was the removal of the capital of India from Calcutta to Delhi and the substitution for the partition scheme of 1905 of a new arrangement by which Bengal, with the districts in the east which had been separated from it, was created a single entity under the rule of a Governor, while Behar, Chota Nagpur, and Orissa was constituted a new province, presided over by a Lieutenant-Governor, Assam being left, as before, under a Chief Commissioner. The visit of the King and Queen to Calcutta after the great Delhi function set the seal upon this compromise. Their Majesties were received with extraordinary enthusiasm, and any doubts that were entertained as to the wisdom of some portions of the plan—notably that which deposed Calcutta from its position as capital—were drowned in the chorus of loyal gratification at the auspicious circumstance which brought the Sovereign and his Consort to the banks of the Hooghly.

Though from time to time episodes occur which indicate that the virus of anarchy implanted in the Bengal body politic by maleficent agitators is still working, the condition of the province as a whole is satisfactory. Absorbed in the work of building up a commercial and industrial fabric which is ever increasing in strength and magnificence, the great masses of the people are only anxious to live their lives in peace. The more influential classes recognize the value of the protection of the Paramount Power, and are content to work out their destinies under its shadow; the lower grades of the inhabitants, the cultivators and those engaged in the humbler walks of industry, are little prone to disorder, and with their modest needs ensured and safeguarded by a firm and just administration, may be trusted to rest contentedly under the *Pax Britannica*. The Great War has happily passed so far without directly touching their lives or in any serious degree adversely affecting their interests. But it has not been without its influence in strengthening in Bengal, as in other parts of India, the sentiment of loyalty to the Crown, which in recent times has been so markedly and beneficially developed. Thus we may hope that in due time, when the stupendous World War has been followed by the Great Peace, Bengal will play a noble part in the work of economic regeneration which will be a leading, if not the chief, concern of our Imperial statesmanship.

LATER HISTORY

IF it be true that happiness attends a country that has no history, that country is doubly favoured if it has no recent history; for, of course, it is the events of to-day and yesterday that really count, rather than those of centuries ago. Judged by the poet's exacting standard, Bengal should at the present time be in a very lugubrious mood. In common with the rest of India, it has experienced the thrills of the Great War; in association with the rest of the Empire, it has taken a part, and a noble one, in the memorable struggle for the world's freedom. But this, unfortunately, is not the only side of the picture that this great Province has exhibited in later days. Sedition has reared its ugly head in a fashion which has caused the gravest official anxiety. Fed from outside sources, the character of which it is not now difficult to determine, an anarchical movement has alternately smouldered and burst into flame, producing unrest in wide areas in which the agents of disorder operated. There are many who think that the trouble has to a very considerable extent been created by past supineness in dealing with disorder. But whether so or not, it is beyond question that the criminals have shown an audacity and contempt for the law without parallel in the modern history of India.

Some of the worst phases of this orgy of organized crime were experienced in the tenure of office of Lord Carmichael, who was the first statesman to fill the office of Governor created under the new arrangements for the ruling of the Province. A man of high distinction in Home politics, Lord Carmichael took to his new position more than a common share of the exalted Liberal aspirations in regard to India which were prevalent at that time. His desire was to rule by kindness and persuasion rather than by force, and at the outset he was subjected to strong criticism because he did not more thoroughly apply the forces of the law to the work of extirpating the conspiracy. But the stern logic of events in the end compelled him to show that, as Gladstone said on a famous occasion when he was faced with Irish troubles, the resources of civilization were not exhausted. After a careful investigation, conducted by his instructions by Mr. John Cumming, had disclosed the existence of a widespread conspiracy against British rule, he put into execution the powers conferred by the Defence of the Realm Act, causing a number of suspected persons to be interned. His action was fiercely criticized by a section of the public who did not adequately realize either the extremely dangerous character of the movement or the perilous character of the times in which we live. In plain truth, Lord Carmichael did no more than was done in liberty-loving England without any serious protest. Constitutional government is a very precious thing, and not lightly to be thrust on one side, but there are times when it would be madness to allow a pedantic interpretation of the laws of government to restrain the administration from suppressing organized crime, and this assuredly is one of them.

Lord Carmichael, at all events, had no difficulty when, at the closing durbar of his administration he addressed the assembled notables of Bengal, in justifying the policy which he had followed. Step by step in his speech on that occasion he took his hearers through the developments of the subject, showing how he had come to the conclusion that there existed "a well-organized conspiracy, whose aim is to weaken the present form of government and, if possible, to overthrow it by means which are criminal"; how, faced by the insidious ramifications of the movement, the deliberate corruption of the young, side by side with the more overt acts of disorder such as organized gang robbery, the authorities had to adopt severe measures; and how such measures of necessity took an exceptional form owing to the special characteristics of the conspiracy and the gravity of the times in which we live. He went on to claim that the Government measures had been amply justified by results. Not only, he declared, had crime been diminished by direct measures, but the administration of the Defence of the Realm Act had been a great indirect factor in the prevention of crime by the discoveries which it brought to light in the course of its operations. At the same time, Lord Carmichael did not disguise from himself the fact that executive action alone would never eradicate the evils of anarchy. A healthy public sentiment antagonistic to the criminals was, as he properly pointed out, by far the best safeguard that the Province could have from the disorders which it had experienced in recent times.

It was an admirable speech with which to round off a career which will be gratefully remembered hereafter when the harvest of this first Bengal Governorship comes to be reaped. In what form events will shape themselves no one can say, but, as the retiring Governor in his valedictory remarks pointed out, the war has worked a wonderful transformation in all Imperial affairs—to use his exact words, "the war has taught us to realize more clearly than we ever did before that if the British Empire is to continue as the greatest Power in the world for good, every part of that Empire, India no less than any other, must be allowed, and, if need be, helped, to develop to the full all that its people feel themselves capable of doing for the mutual welfare of the whole." There will be changes, no doubt, but they will be on constitutional lines, and they will be helped or retarded according to the degree to which the anarchical conspiracy is successfully grappled with.

It is a curious fact, and a significant one, that in spite of unrest within and war without, Bengal in the past few years has been remarkably prosperous. Economic development has made wonderful strides in the Province of late, and has now reached dimensions which show, in a very impressive way, the vast future that lies ahead for India as a producer. This movement commenced long anterior to the war, and on the outbreak of hostilities there were fears that a grave check would be given to commercial and industrial activities. For a time a serious influence was exercised on the course of trade. But as the war proceeded and it was seen that few of India's material interests would be adversely affected, and that in certain directions she would actually profit by the war, the situation became stable. Some industries, notably jute, underwent enormous expansion owing to demands for war purposes, and there was for a time in Calcutta in 1916 a wild speculation in shares, the value of which in some instances increased by 600 per cent. on the pre-war figure. Coal and tea also, though not to the same extent, profited by the war, the heavy orders made on Government account stimulating business in spite of the severe handicaps imposed by the war conditions. The satisfactory character of trade generally is clearly revealed in the official statistics, which show that in 1916 a more valuable trade was done than in any preceding year save 1912 and 1913. As far as Bengal is concerned, imports during the year increased 13 per cent. and exports nearly 14 per cent. To a considerable extent, no doubt, the increase represents the enhancement of values which the war has caused; but even allowing for that, it is a remarkable testimony to the strength of the Indian commercial position that these results should be possible after two years of war. It can hardly be expected, perhaps, that future returns will be so favourable. The shortage of tonnage, due to submarine warfare, and difficulties of finance arising out of the stoppage of the sale of Treasury Bills towards the end of 1916, have given a check to business, and this may continue. Such handicaps as those indicated, however, can have little influence on the steady march of economic development, which is, perhaps, the most striking feature of modern India. Indeed, it may confidently be anticipated that here, as in the United Kingdom, the invigorating effects of war activities—the making of munitions, the production of all kinds of war material and the improvisation of transport machinery—will be felt long after the war has ceased, and that out of the welter of this terrible death-struggle may arise a new and improved system of industry which will be of enormous permanent value.

By a happy conjuncture of events, the destinies of Bengal at this most interesting period are entrusted to a public man of considerable distinction in the person of Lord Ronaldshay. This peer, who assumed office in the early part of 1917, on Lord Carmichael's departure, has had a somewhat arduous apprenticeship in Home affairs, and possessing as he does broad sympathies and the invaluable quality of tact, he can scarcely fail to make his administration a success. It will be his duty, in all human probability, to supervise the work, political as well as industrial, which will follow the war. No more difficult task, probably, has been imposed upon any modern administrator of Bengal, for the forces of disloyalty have still to be finally reckoned with. In Bengal, as elsewhere in India, however, there has been an increasing disposition to realize that in the gradual development of Indian institutions under the shadow of the Empire lies the best hopes of future peace and happiness, and this feeling may doubtless be relied on to smooth the path of the Government. Advancing on lines of peaceful progress, Bengal has a future more splendid than that of any other part of India. Nowhere else, probably, will be found such flourishing industries, such noble public institutions, or such a high state of intellectual development. Her old premiership of the Indian Presidencies will have received a new endorsement, and, in a deeper sense, Calcutta will be the capital of India.

GENERAL VIEW OF CALCUTTA AT THE BEGINNING OF THE NINETEENTH CENTURY.
From an old print.

VIEW OF DACCA, SHOWING THE RUINS OF THE FORT AND PALACE OF THE NAWABS OF DACCA, CALLED LAL BAG.

From "Panorama of the City of Dacca." Published about 1847.

NATIVE RACES

By L. S. S. O'MALLEY, I.C.S., Fellow of the Royal Anthropological Institute

THE peoples of Bengal and Assam, Behar and Orissa, number a little under 92 millions, or three-tenths of the total population of India. They include many distinct races at widely different stages of civilization. Some are still primitive semi-savage tribes, ignorant of the use of the plough, whose weapons are the axe, the spear, and the bow and arrow. Others attained a high degree of civilization at a time when the Britons painted themselves with woad, and they have not lagged behind in modern times. Not to multiply instances, a living Bengali poet (Sir Rabindra Nath Tagore) has a European reputation and the rare distinction of being a Nobel prizeman. To give more homely illustrations, bicycles and sewing-machines, gramophones and the cinematograph are popular, while Association football is a game that has thousands of devotees of no mean skill. In spite of all this diversity, some national characteristics can be distinguished.

The Bengalis, in particular, have certain peculiarities which mark them off from all other races of India. Living in a humid, relaxing climate, in a country of which a large part is a network of rivers and swamps, and subsisting mainly on a diet of fish and watery rice, they are a slenderly built, small-boned race. Although, however, they are not robust, they are capable of long and continuous rather than arduous labour, and are able to stand exposure better than hardier races not acclimatized to Bengal. The great mass are tillers of the soil, passionately attached to their land and their homes. "The *ryot's* main property," says the Bengali littérateur Mr. R. C. Dutt, in "The Peasantry of Bengal," "the means of his livelihood, the ground of all his hopes, is the little bit of land he cultivates. His most dearly cherished hope points to nothing higher than a good harvest ; his greatest fear is lest his produce is decreased or his rent increased. Abuse him and the *ryot* will not complain, beat him and he will not bend, but increase the rent and he can bear no more."

Largely on account of this home-loving spirit, and also because the natural fertility of the soil brings in abundant harvests, which put the cultivator beyond the fear of want, Bengal contains a dense, settled population with little mobility. A small area produces sufficient for the cultivator and his family, so that there is little emigration, and the Bengali is content to allow immigrants to furnish the bulk of the labour force of the modern factory industries and commercial undertakings in and around Calcutta. There is but little concentration in towns, and the people are spread over a multitude of villages, mostly consisting of scattered homesteads buried in thickets of bamboos, fruit-trees, and undergrowth, which secure the seclusion and privacy which the Bengali likes for his home. They have not, however, the homely wits of home-keeping youth, but possess alert and subtle intellects. The higher classes, who are known as *bhadra-lok*, in particular, are a clever, keen, and excitable people. Their natural bent is not so much to commerce and industries as to professional pursuits. Here the Bengali shines. "In the field of law his success has been fully admitted. In literature his high standard of excellence has long been known to students of Indian letters, and has begun to gain the acknowledgment of the Western world. In arts and science also he is winning his way to recognition." Education is almost a passion with them, and private enterprise has spread English education broadcast; one in every seven of those able to read and write has a knowledge of English. It has well been said that the difference between the Bengali *bhadra-lok* and the middle classes of other Provinces of Upper India is that the former are more enterprising, more intelligent, and far more ready to put their hands into their pockets to secure educational advantages. It has regretfully to be admitted that one advanced section have found vent for a discontented and refractory spirit in an anarchical movement, professing to aim at self-government, the outcome of which has been a number of murders perpetrated with bombs and revolvers.

A little over half of the Bengalis are Mahommedans, who, with a strength of 24 millions, outnumber the whole Mahommedan population of Turkey, Persia, and

Afghanistan. The great majority of them are descendants of Bengali Hindu converts; the minority are of foreign stock, the descendants of immigrants from North-West India, e.g. noblemen and their *entourage*, or soldiers of the Moghul army. Thus, one will find Mahommedans whose robust body, high stature, Semitic nose, and luxuriant beard contrast strongly with the features of their slim and meagre, flat-faced, and almost beardless co-religionists. In Chittagong, where Arab traders and sailors resorted, the high cheek-bones, hook noses, and narrow faces of many Mahommedans proclaim their Arab origin; while others, who are muscular, bull-necked, and thick-bearded, are equally clearly the descendants of foreign soldiers.

The Beharis, living in a less enervating climate than that of the humid delta of Bengal, are a more manly, robust, and vigorous people, whom the Bengalis themselves are glad to employ in posts requiring physical strength, courage, or endurance. They furnished a large number of recruits to the Sepoy army in pre-Mutiny days, and during the Mutiny the forces that besieged the little Arrah House mainly consisted of Behari levies. They are a nation of industrious and thrifty cultivators, but when social or religious ceremonies, such as marriages and funerals, occur, their thrift gives place to lavish expenditure; the savings of a lifetime disappear, and the peasant will incur a crushing load of debt. When the crops are off the land they migrate to Bengal in hundreds of thousands and find employment on the roads and railways, in the fields and factories, of that rich and fertile Province, returning a few months later with their savings to resume the cultivation of their land.

A MANIPURI DANCING-GIRL.

Photo by G. C. Ghoshal, Jorhat

The Assamese are an amalgam of races, the fertile valley of the Brahmaputra having been overrun by successive waves of invaders from India on the one side and from China, Tibet, and Burma on the other, each of which has left its traces on the physique of the inhabitants. The aborigines of the country, the autochthones, so far as can be traced, are believed to be the Bodos, of whom several branches still survive. The most easterly are the Dimasas—a name meaning the great river people—who were driven out of the Brahmaputra Valley and became masters of the tract known as Cachar (Kachar). North-west of them, in a long, narrow belt of country to the north of the Brahmaputra, live a kindred tribe, called Kacharis after that district, who are described as a cheerful and smiling people, the most innocent and kindly of semi-savage races. To the west, in the Garo Hills and the plains of Goalpara at their foot, are the Garos, once a savage race of head-hunters, of whom a description will be found later; while to the south-west are the Tiparas, in the Hill Tippera State of Bengal. Under the name of the Chutiyas, the Bodos, or Kacharis, established a powerful kingdom in the east of Assam, from which they were ousted in the thirteenth century by the Ahoms, a Shan race from the upper portion of the Irrawaddy Valley, who held sway for many centuries and gave their name to the Province. In the valleys the conquerors fused with the aboriginal inhabitants, and the descendants of fierce and warlike invaders, softened by centuries of peace and settled life in a somewhat enervating climate, are a race of quiet and somewhat indolent cultivators. While the main stock of the valley population is Indo-Chinese, Hinduism is the predominant religion, and the language is almost entirely Indian, Bengali being spoken by half the population of the Province, and Assamese, which is very similar to Bengali, by nearly one-fourth. In the hills, however, which formed a refuge against the hordes of invaders, there are still many aboriginal races, with long traditions of war and rapine, who have clung to their primitive customs and beliefs, have maintained their purity of race, and still adhere to the religion and speech of their forefathers. It is on this account that Assam has

1. TIBETAN WOMAN. 2. A PAHARI LADY. *Photo by H. Sain.* 3. A LADY FROM NEPAL. *Photo by Himalayan Art Studio.* 4. A YOUNG ASSAMESE GIRL. *Photo by D. C. Ghoshal, Jorhat.*

5. LUSHAI WOMAN. 6. YOUNG KHASI GIRL. *Photos by D. C. Ghoshal, Jorhat.* 7. WIDOW COUNTING BEADS, EASTERN BENGAL.

8. KOOKI WOMEN, ASSAM. *Photo by D. C. Ghoshal, Jorhat.* 9. BHUTIAS. *Photo by H. Sain.* 10. NEPALESE WOMAN. *Photo by Vanderlowen.*

been aptly described as "a museum of nationalities." In modern times the tea industry has introduced yet another foreign element in the heterogeneous population, the tea gardens importing a

KHASI COOLIES.
Photo by Ghoshal Bros., Shillong.

large labour force of Dravidian descent from the plateau of Chota Nagpur.

The Oriyas are a quiet, law-abiding and conservative people, Orissa having till quite recently been so isolated that it was a kind of "sleepy hollow." They are intensely religious, and adhere to the old Hindu system, with its rigid restrictions and rules of ceremonial purity. So strong is immemorial tradition that the lowest castes must build their houses on the outskirts of the village; their children till recently were not allowed inside the village schools, and even now must, in some places, sit apart from other Hindu boys; they may not draw water from the village tanks; the village barber will not shave them, and the village washerman will not wash their clothes. The Oriyas are devout Vaishnavas, whose greatest festival is the annual car festival of Jagannath. On this occasion the image of the god rides in procession on a car, 45 feet in height, with 16 wheels, through a huge concourse of people. The cases of self-immolation under the wheels of the car which used to take place, as well as accidental deaths, have given rise to a well-known expression in the English language, though the god Jagannath is often confused with the car.

A striking contrast to the slim, slender, and somewhat listless Oriya is afforded by the Himalayan races to the north of Bengal. Here the Nepalese predominate, a squat, sturdy people with characteristic Mongolian features—a bullet head, a flat face, almond eyes, high cheek-bones, and almost hairless chins. Energetic and resourceful, they are ready to turn their hands to almost any task. They have a cheerful, merry temper, a zeal for work, and a wiry strength, which enables them to carry up the steepest hills loads weighing as much as 80 lb.; the loads rest on the back, and are suspended by a band passed over the head. They are not true Gurkhas, but immigrants or descendants of immigrants from the east of Nepal, and are divided into several tribes, each of which is bilingual, speaking the tribal language as well as Naipali Hindi, the *lingua franca* of the hills. Other immigrants are the Bhotias, stalwart mountaineers, burly rather than tall, whose original home was Tibet, as, indeed, their name implies, Bhot being merely an Indian form of Tibet, which is a corruption of the Mongolian Thubot. The real aboriginals are the Lepchas of Sikkim, a peaceful, timid people of effeminate appearance; it is often difficult to distinguish men from women (both wearing pigtails), except from their dress. They dwell in the valleys, and are true men of the woods. Forest fruits, fungi, and roots enter largely into their dietary: more than 100 different kinds are eaten by them. They have separate names for practically every bird, orchid, and butterfly, and, with training, make excellent naturalists and entomologists.

Both the Bhotias and Lepchas are Buddhists, who revere the Dalai Lama of Tibet, not only as an arch-pontiff, but also as an incarnation of the deity. There is a hierarchy of priests called Lamas, who live in monasteries, and in their temples observe a ceremonial reminiscent of the Roman Catholic Church. Mitres and vestments are worn, incense is burnt, bells are rung, and the priests prostrate themselves before altars on which are images and burning lamps. An ingenious method of prayer is followed by the people. Prayers are printed on strips of cotton, which are attached to bamboo poles and aptly named "horses of the wind," for as they flutter in the breeze the petitions are borne to the gods. Another device consists of enclosing rolls of printed prayers or pious passages in cylinders, great and small. Some of these, about the size of a round cigarette-tin, are carried in the hand, and revolve with a twist of the wrist. Others are huge barrels, which are turned by water-power like the wheels of a mill. With each turn the prayers are borne to the gods without any personal exertion of the worshipper. Demonolatry enters largely into their religion, but its terrors are relieved by the cheerful outlook on life that so many of the hillmen have. A typical instance of this came recently to the writer's notice. A Lama had been engaged to drive out a devil that was thought to have taken possession of a house. In answer to an inquiry how long the operation would take, it was explained with a hearty laugh that the Lama would stay in the house till the devil was expelled, and that it would probably take a long time as the good woman of the house kept a good table.

To the ethnologist the most interesting races are the Mongoloid tribes of Assam and the Dravidians, who are found in Chota Nagpur, the Santal Parganas, and the hilly hinterland lying between the coast districts of Orissa and the Central Provinces. They follow that primitive form of religion known as Animism that peoples the valleys, the hills, and the streams with spirits, chiefly malignant, which have to be propitiated with offerings and sacrifices. It is scarcely to be distinguished from demonolatry, and finds practical expression in a rooted belief in the powers of exorcism. Sickness, for instance, is not due to insanitary surroundings, but to the anger or malice of an evil spirit. Many have a faint belief in a Creator, but he is a *roi fainéant*, and does not trouble himself with the petty affairs of men. Many of their customs and superstitions are weird, and some are repulsive. The Sauria Paharias of the Santal Parganas imagine that epidemics of disease are due to evil spirits, which come by train. The remedy is found in making a rude model of a train, which they wheel into the forest. Thus the demon of disease is expelled from the village. The Oraons of Chota Nagpur believe in a spirit called Murkuri, i.e. "the thumper," which is thought to exercise its power if a European slaps a man on the back. The result is fever or illness, to cure which the spirit has to be exorcised. Among the Khasis of Assam there is an order of men called Thlens, who are said to have sprung from a gigantic and ravenous snake. It is believed that, like their ancestor, they have a craving for human blood. This ghastly superstition leads to cold-blooded murders, the offerings to the Thlen being some of the victim's blood, hair, and the tips of the fingers. Equally strange are the beliefs regarding the future state and the customs observed at death. According to the Lushais of Assam, the soul is born again in the shape of a hornet, which is eventually transformed into water. If it falls as dew upon a man, the soul is born again in his son. One Naga tribe smoke their dead and place the body in a bamboo coffin, which is kept in the house for some weeks before it is taken to the village cemetery. A similar insanitary practice is followed when wealthy Lushais die. The corpse is placed in a hollow tree trunk, with a lid carefully plastered with mud. This strange coffin is kept beside a fire inside the house for three months, after which the bones are taken out and kept in a basket. One section of the Lushais smear a preservative grease over the corpse, dress it up, and pour rice-beer down the throat, while the people dance round it every evening, sometimes for months together.

The most warlike and independent of the aboriginal tribes are found in the hills of Assam. From time immemorial they have indulged in rapine, and some of their names are grim reminders of their old marauding life. One of the Aka tribes, for instance, is called "the devourers of a thousand homes." Another bears the sobriquet of "the thieves who lurk in the cotton fields." Their ferocity has led to many a raid on the peaceful villages of the plains, the motive being sometimes the desire to carry off plunder, women, or slaves, and sometimes a murderous thirst for blood, their incursions being simply head-hunting expeditions. The necessity for maintaining the *pax Britannica* against these savage caterans has caused several punitive expeditions and small frontier campaigns, such as the Lushai Hills Expedition of 1871-2, the Garo Hills Expedition of 1872, the Naga Hills Expedition of 1879-80, the Aka Expedition of 1883-4, the Chin-Lushai Expedition of 1889-90, the Lushai (Lalbura) Expedition of 1892, and the Abor Expedition of 1911-12. To this list should be added the Manipur Expedition of 1891, which was due to the cold-blooded murder of the Chief Commissioner and other officers by a claimant of the chieftainship. The Manipuris, though of Mongolian descent, are not, however, wild primitive people like those above mentioned. They are best known for the zeal with which they play polo, which is, indeed, thought to have been introduced into Europe from this remote corner of India. The niceties of the game are not regarded; there are often no goal-posts, and the rush of a Manipuri team sweeping down the field, careless of rules about crossing and fouling, has been likened to the shock tactics of a cavalry regiment.

The Nagas are, perhaps, the most primitive of these Mongolian races, and the least affected by outside influences. Their villages are typical of a gladiatorial type of life, being built on the tops of hills and strongly fortified with a stockade and a moat filled with bamboo caltrops. Until brought under British rule they were bloodthirsty head-hunters. No head came amiss, whatever the age or sex, and whether taken in fair fight or by treachery. One Naga, who afterwards became an interpreter in a British Court of Justice, is said to have taken eighteen heads in his younger days. The same savage custom still obtains among the Nagas living beyond the frontier, who are also addicted to human sacrifices, which, they believe, ensure good harvests. Scanty clothing is the fashion, and the men of one or two tribes are often stark naked except for a small bone ring, through which the foreskin is drawn. It has been said that the Naga is three-parts a savage, and that if you judge savagery

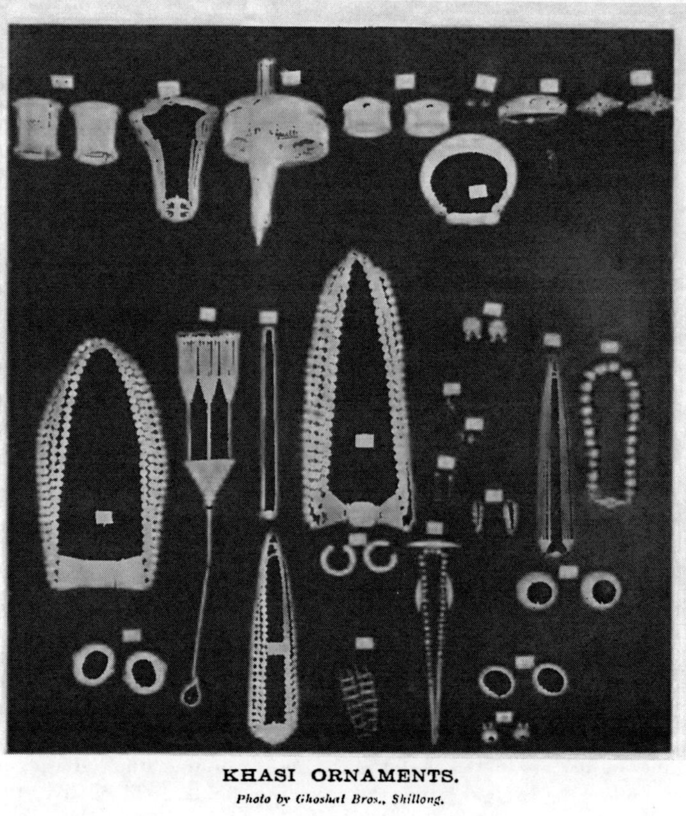

KHASI ORNAMENTS.

Photo by Ghoshal Bros., Shillong.

by the superficial area of a man's nakedness the fraction that is not savage would be small indeed! They have, however, a real standard of decency, a code of morals which is by no means low, a regular social organization, and considerable intelligence. They love ornaments, and their ear-rings are extraordinary, the lobe being pierced and distended to such an extent that it will hold bulky articles; even a shaving-soap cylinder will find a place in it!

The costume of the Garos is also as scanty as is compatible with decency, and they have an equal love of ornaments. The women wear masses of brass-wire ear-rings; fifty brass rings weighing 1 lb. to 2 lb. will sometimes be seen hanging from the lobe of each ear. The lobes often break under the weight, and the rings are then supported by a double string over the head. The system of matriarchy prevails among the Garos, descent being traced through the mother, while inheritance is restricted to the female line. A man may not inherit property, and can only possess what he has acquired by his own labour. Gongs are a highly valued form of property, a man's social status being often gauged by the number he possesses. A man's corpse is laid out on rows of gongs before cremation, and old gongs fetch fancy prices out of all proportion to their real value, Rs. 100 being sometimes paid, though the value of the metal may be only Rs. 10. When a man dies it is a common practice for a hole to be made in one of his gongs, which is then put on a stick close to his memorial-post. The top of the latter is carved into the likeness of a human face intended to represent the deceased, and is dressed up in some of his clothes. Close to it is another post, on which are placed the horns of the buffalo which is sacrificed at the time of cremation. The Garos have, as a rule, two houses—one in the village and another in the fields. They live in the latter during the cultivating season, so as to be near their crops and protect them from wild animals. Sometimes the field houses are perched in the tops of trees, 20 or 30 feet above the ground, so as to be safe from the attacks of wild animals, and access is obtained by means of a bamboo ladder. The houses in the villages are built on piles, and often exceed 100 feet in length. In every village there is a bachelors' house, for young unmarried men may not live with their parents. The bachelors' houses are built on higher platforms than the ordinary houses, and the young men climb up by rude staircases made of notched logs of wood, often assisted by lengths of cane suspended from an overhanging beam.

The Khasis, who live in the Khasi and Jaintia Hills, are a race totally distinct from the neighbouring hill tribes, and are certainly of different origin. Their speech is intimately connected with the languages of the Mon-Khmer group of Burma and the Malay Peninsula, while they are decidedly Malay in appearance. The Khasi language has also affinities with that of the Hos and Mundas of Chota Nagpur, and there is a further sign of connection between these widely separated tribes in the common practice of erecting memorial stones. These are megalithic monuments dedicated to the spirits of the dead. The groups of menhirs, or vertical monoliths, dolmens, or table stones, and cromlechs, or cairns, which are met with throughout their country, are strangely reminiscent of those which are a familiar

1. KHASI WOMEN'S DANCE. **2. KHASI DANCE.** *Photos by Ghoshal Bros., Shillong.* **3. KHASI WOMEN'S DANCE.** *Photo by D. C. Ghoshal, Jorhat.*

sight in Brittany. Ancestor-worship is a marked feature of their religion, and goes on side by side with the propitiation

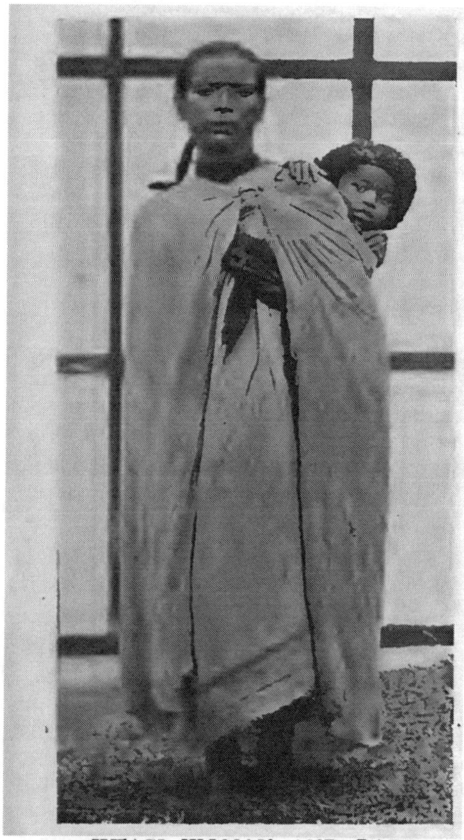

KHASI WOMAN AND BABY.
Photo by Ghoshal Bros., Shillong.

of other spirits. They obtain auguries by examining the entrails of animals and birds, like the Romans. Another form of divination, which was also practised by the Romans, is the breaking of eggs, the events of the future being discerned from the position of the fragments of the broken egg-shells. So firm is the belief in the efficacy of divination by eggs that a Khasi will undertake nothing of importance—e.g. building a house and taking a journey—until he has broken some eggs and found whether the venture will be lucky or not. The Khasis, like the Garos, observe the matriarchal system under which women inherit property. A national saying is, "From the woman sprang the clan." This institution has far-reaching effects on the social organization. Even the property which a man acquires before marriage is held to belong to his mother. The husband can take no part in the rites and ceremonies of his wife's family. After death his ashes are deposited in the cromlech of his mother's kin, and can, with few exceptions, find no place in the wife's family tomb. Ceremonial religion is conducted by women, especially in the home, and male priests are merely their deputies. The ancestress of the tribe receives special veneration, and the spirits of sickness and death, who are most frequently worshipped, are female. In one Khasi State a woman is both spiritual and temporal head of the people; her regal functions are, in practice, delegated to a son or nephew, but her sacerdotal supremacy is not transferred. The order of succession to this post of queen and arch-pontiff is typical of female primogeniture. She is succeeded by the eldest surviving daughter; failing daughters, by the eldest daughter of the eldest daughter; failing the latter, by the eldest daughter of her second daughter, and so on. If there are no daughters or granddaughters in the female line, she is succeeded by her eldest sister, and if she

NEPALI WOMEN.
Photo by D. C. Ghoshal, Jorhat.

has no sister, by the eldest daughter of her mother's eldest sister, and so on.

Another tribe with whom the British have recently come into conflict is the Abor, whose land was until recently almost a *terra incognita*, while their name, meaning "unknown savage," is significant. The men are pale and hairless; most have large goitres on their neck; and some are tattooed on the face with a sign resembling a cross. The natural ugliness of the woman is enhanced by blue lines tattooed on the face, which gives their features a curious twisted expression; their wedding-ring consists of a spiral gaiter of thin twisted bark bound round the calf of the leg. They have a high opinion of their own strength and importance, but when, after their murder of a Political Officer and a doctor, a punitive expedition was sent aganist them, in 1911-12, they put up a poor fight. Their tactics consisted of sniping with poisoned arrows, discharging great boulders and tree trunks from booby-traps, and making a short stand behind stockades. The fines then levied on the villages show how rudimentary is their currency, being paid in arrows, the jungle knives called *daos*, and semi-domesticated bisons and pigs.

The other great and distinctive group

TIBETANS.

Photo by Himalayan Art Studio.

of aboriginal tribes consists of the Dravidian races, whose home is in Chota Nagpur, the Santal Parganas, and the Orissa States. Of these the largest and most representative are the Santals, Mundas, Hos, Oraons, and Khonds, or Kandhs. Their main physical characteristics are a long head, a broad, bridgeless nose, a low, narrow forehead, thick, protruding lips, hair inclined to be woolly, a low stature, and long arms. Huxley surmised that they might be related to the aborigines of Australia, but the latest conclusion of ethnologists is that they are autochthonous, the earliest inhabitants of India of whom we have knowledge. It has, indeed, been suggested that the tiny huts in which some live, with low doors so small that the owner has to crawl in on all fours, are an indication that originally they were troglodyte cave-dwellers. In the huts of the Oraons, which are only about 7 feet in height, a hole, $4\frac{1}{2}$ feet high, serves as an entrance; it is kept from falling in by a log above, which is aptly called the *kaparphora*, or "forehead-breaker." "The huts of the Juangs," wrote Colonel Dalton, "are about the smallest that human beings ever deliberately constructed as dwellings. They measure about 6 feet by 8 feet, and are very low, with doors so small as to preclude the idea of a corpulent householder. The paterfamilias and all his belongings of the female sex huddle together in this one stall, not much larger than a dog-kennel. For the boys there is a separate dormitory."

The village "dormitory" system also obtains among other tribes, and is the result of the houses being too small to contain large families. Among the Khonds, for instance, the youths of a village sleep in one dormitory, and the grown-up girls in another, under the charge of an old woman. The same custom is observed by the Oraons. Before admission to the bachelor hall the boys have to be branded on the arm, the scars being the mark by which, after death, they will be recognized as Oraons by other Oraon spirits. Once admitted, they form a close fraternity, bound down to secrecy about all that goes on inside. It is known, however, that there is a regular system of "fagging," the small boys serving the elder, and being punished for slackness. It is also known that the girls slip off at night to the bachelors' hall, sexual intercourse before marriage being common.

One and all of these races have the greatest attachment to their land, combined with a dislike of foreigners, and especially of foreign landlords. The land, in their view, belongs solely to the descendants of the men who cleared and reclaimed it from the forest—a belief which clearly shows their rôle as pioneers in forest tracts. Not all have been able to retain their land, and a large proportion of these landless men have had to migrate and earn their bread by the sweat of the brow in distant countries. Nearly half a million are found in Bengal and a quarter of a million in Assam. "Labour," writes Sir Herbert Risley, "is the birthright of the pure Dravidian, and as a coolie he is in great demand wherever one meets him. Whether hoeing tea in Assam, the Duars, and Ceylon, planting sugar-cane in far Fiji, cutting rice in the swamps of Eastern Bengal, or doing scavenger's work in the streets of Calcutta, Rangoon, and Singapore, he is recognizable at a glance by his black skin, his squat figure, and the negro-like proportions of his nose."

This love of the land plays a great part in their history, and has led to more than one rising. The loss of the fields which the Santals of the Santal Parganas had cleared, but from which they were ousted by Hindu landlords and money-lenders, led to the Santal War of 1855. The Santals rose with the idea of avenging themselves on the land-jobbers and usurers who oppressed them, and, to their surprise, found themselves at war with the British, with whom, as they said, they had no quarrel. When a Hindu money-lender was captured, they treated him with a grim and ghastly humour. First they cut off his feet, saying, "That is four annas in the rupee"; next they lopped off his legs, shouting, "Eight annas have been paid"; and then they cut through his body at the waist to make up another four annas. Finally he was beheaded, to the accompaniment of yells that his bill was paid in full. To the English they often acted in a spirit of chivalry. Notice, for instance, was sent to some indigo-planters that, as they cultivated the land like the Santals themselves, they would not be molested if they stayed at home and gave the Santals supplies. On another occasion they sent a message to a town they intended to attack, viz. a branch bearing three leaves, to show that they would attack in three days and that the inhabitants had three days' warning. It is also significant that, though it is their custom to use poisoned arrows in the chase, they never used them against the troops.

More recently, in 1899, there was an *émeute* among the Mundas of Chota Nagpur, who rose under a semi-religious leader called Birsa, who proclaimed, among other things, their ancient rights over the land and forests. All land was to be rent-free, all foreigners were to be slain or driven out, and the people would have their Utopia. A similar spirit has led to a more salutary movement among the Khonds, who some years ago took a vow to become teetotallers. Drunkenness, they said, led to wife-beating, poverty, and—worst of all—the loss of their lands. A still stranger movement sprang up in 1915-16 among the Oraons of Chota Nagpur, and spread to their brethren in the Duars of Bengal. The original inspiring idea appears to have had a twofold basis. The object was partly to expel from the Oraon country the evil spirits who were believed to be responsible for bad crops and high prices, and partly to raise the social position of the Oraons to the higher level occupied by Christian and Hindu converts of the race. The former object was to be attained by the recitation of certain powerful spells (*mantras*), the latter by the abandonment of degrading practices such as the keeping and eating of pigs and fowls and the use of intoxicants. The excitement was aggravated by the general atmosphere of unrest caused by the war, and an invocation of the German Kaiser crept into the *mantras*. The drafting of extra police into the chief centres of unrest had a reassuring effect, and with the harvesting of the winter crops, which were unusually good, the movement began to subside. It did not, however, die out altogether, for the people thought that the expulsion of evil spirits from one village resulted in their transfer to others. The movement accordingly continued with a campaign of witch-hunting, in which the whole populace, and not merely the *sokhas*, or special witch-hunters, took part, and several brutal murders of supposed witches occurred.

The belief in the mischief done by witches and in the power of wizards, who, like the African medicine-men, can "smell out" witches, is common to all these tribes. A similar campaign took place in 1857, when the Hos of Singhbhum took the opportunity of the temporary breakdown of law and authority during the Mutiny to make a clean sweep of all women suspected of witchcraft. Even now among the Santals not a year passes without some woman being killed, frequently by being beaten to death, for the mysterious mischief she is believed to have done. A simple and efficacious way of stopping this practice was employed by a magistrate many years ago. When he heard that a woman had been denounced as a witch, he called the villagers together and produced a galvanic battery. The woman was told to hold the handles and the current was disconnected. Then her accuser did the same and the current was turned on. He got a galvanic shock, and was unable to release his hands till he acknowledged that he had made a mistake.

1. ORIYA GIRL, ORISSA. 2. A SANTAL GIRL, ORISSA. 3. HILL TRIBES, ORISSA.

Photos by Van Ierlowen.

BENGAL AND ASSAM, BEHAR AND ORISSA

The Khonds believe that witches have power to take the shape of tigers, leopards, and wolves, and put down to them the deaths of cattle and human beings from wild animals. Old women and men are often declared to be evil spirits in human form or metamorphosed tigers. If a death occurs and some one is definitely suspected of causing it, a fowl is taken and its legs are plunged into boiling water and rapidly withdrawn. If the skin peels off the suspected person is held to be guilty, and he is turned out of the village unless he undertakes to undergo the ordeal by fire. For this purpose a long, narrow trench is dug and filled with burning embers. The legs of the accused are smeared with *ghi* (clarified butter), and he is made to walk twice through the trench. If he is burned it is a proof of his guilt. If no one in particular is suspected, the ordeal by iron is resorted to. A bar of iron is put into the blacksmith's furnace, the witch-finder working the bellows. The names of the villagers are called out one after another, and the person at whose name the iron melts is held to be guilty.

The Khonds are particularly afraid of the spirits of pregnant women. Their bodies are buried far away from the village across a stream, the idea being that no spirit can cross water; as a further precaution, pieces of iron are driven into the leg and a perforated iron spoon is placed inside the breast. The same belief that women who die in pregnancy become evil spirits is common to other tribes, and has caused the ghastly practice of the womb being ripped open and the fœtus extracted. The husband himself is charged with this sickening task. The Bhuiyas of the Orissa States, who usually burn their dead, bury the embryo and the woman's body on opposite sides of a stream, because they think that the mother will be unable to become an evil spirit without union with her child, and that the water will be an impassable barrier. Again, when a pregnant Oraon woman dies her ankles are broken and her feet wrenched backwards to prevent her spirit walking; and, to make doubly sure, a heavy stone and a bundle of thorns are placed over the grave to prevent her spirit getting out.

Another belief is that souls return to animate human forms in families in which they were first born. The Gonds think that the soul of a man comes back to the house on the fifth day after death. His relations go to the side of a river or stream and call him by name, after which they catch a fish or an insect and take it home. There they either place it in a room reserved for the spirits of dead ancestors or eat it in the belief that the dead man will again be born in the family.

The Hos have a similar idea that the spirits of the dead return to the house, and seven days after death the spirit is solemnly recalled. Ashes are spread on the floor of the house, a woman sitting at each corner, while the family and their guests sit outside. Two go out and call to the *bongas*, or evil spirits, praying that if any have taken the deceased they will allow him to come back. The house is kept dark, and suddenly the women cry out, "The spirit has come!" They then light a lamp and look for the marks the spirit has left on the ashes. Some spirits leave the footprints of birds, some of snakes or cats, others of dogs. These footmarks show whether the spirit is happy or not. The greatest happiness is indicated by the footprints of birds, then of cats, and then of dogs, but the mark of a snake shows that the spirit is in great misery. After this, the spirit is supposed to remain in an invisible form in the house, and a space is set aside for him in the inner room, which no one but members of the family may enter.

The Khonds are convinced that the souls of deceased persons return to animate human bodies, but such persons must have been married, or at least have had sexual intercourse, during their lifetime. The souls of unmarried persons cannot enter the circle of family spirits, but are malevolent spirits, causing fever, ague, apoplexy, and other ailments. The spirits of married people animate the fœtus as soon as it is fully formed. This belief was formerly the cause of female infanticide, which was so common that in many villages there was not a single female child. Girls were killed immediately after birth by exposure in the jungle ravines, because the Khonds, who ardently desire male offspring, thought that this was an effectual way of reducing the number of females which would be reborn.

The Khonds also used to practise human sacrifice. The victims, who were called Meriahs, were purchased, as an ancient ordinance lay down that they must be bought with a price. The purveyors were a servile race called Pans, who in their turn bought up children or kidnapped them. The sacrifice was made to propitiate the earth-goddess and ensure good crops, the flesh of the victims being buried in the fields. In whatever way the rite was performed, it was invariably accompanied by the most revolting cruelty. One method was to tie the victim—who had previously been stupefied—by his hair to a stout wooden post on the ground. His arms and legs were then seized by four men and the body was held out horizontally from the post, face downwards. The priest took the sacrificial knife and, amid the yells of the victim, commenced hacking him on the back of the neck, shouting in his ear, "We bought you with a price; no sin rests on us." Once the blood flowed the Khonds rushed in, intoxicated and wildly excited, every man's object being to cut a morsel from the living victim to bury in his fields. At times, when the gathering was large and it was feared that the blood and flesh of the victim would not go round, a disappointed Khond would, it is said, as the next best thing, slice off a piece from another Khond who was hacking at the victim.

Another method was to dig a shallow pit long enough to contain the victim. Into this was poured the blood of a freshly slaughtered hog. The victim, bound hand and foot, was suffocated by having his face pressed down in the blood. Still another method was to drag the living victim over the fields, followed by drunken and excited Khonds, who cut pieces from him, taking care to avoid the head and bowels in order not to kill him outright.

This hideous practice has long since been given up, and the sacrifice of buffaloes, which has been substituted for it, is found to produce just as good harvests as the immolation of human beings. In the rites many of the old Meriah customs are preserved. The buffalo is smeared with oil and garlanded, and the people dance before it to the deafening noise of drums and cymbals. The Meriah songs are chanted in its ears, and the invocations are the same as those which used to be made at the human sacrifice. Everybody tries to induce the animal to eat a portion of the offering he has brought, and after touching its anointed body they smear the oil on their foreheads. The victim is driven round the boundaries of the village, or the pole to which it has been bound is carried round it, accompanied by a band of Pan musicians. It is then led to the sacred grove, on the outskirts of the village, where a pit has been previously dug and filled with the blood of a pig. The priest cuts off a small piece of the flesh from the back of the head and buries it at the shrine of the goddess. The poor animal is immediately borne to the ground, and is partially flayed alive for the purpose of collecting its blood, while the assembled people hack off lumps of its flesh, which they carry away in great haste and bury with much ceremony at the shrine of the goddess and on the boundaries of their villages. The remains of the victim, with the unmutilated head, are buried in the bloody pit. A great feast and a bout of heavy drinking, in which both men and women join, close the sacrifice.

1. WRESTLING BY RAJPUTS.
Photo by D. C. Ghoshal, Jorhat.

2. LUTHA NAGAS, FROM THE NAGA HILLS.
Photo by Ghoshal Bros.

PALM AVENUE, BOTANICAL GARDENS, CALCUTTA.

Photo by Johnston & Hoffmann.

THE VEGETATION OF BENGAL, ASSAM, BEHAR AND ORISSA

BY HUMPHREY G. CARTER, M.B., CH.B., OFFICIATING DIRECTOR, BOTANICAL SURVEY OF INDIA

PLANTS usually live in communities of sufficient bulk and extent to determine the landscape of vast tracts of country. For this reason the botany of a district may be looked upon from points of view from which its zoology cannot be studied.

A fauna of a country is a list of the animals in it and a flora a list of its plants. But the vegetation of a district is something quite distinct from its flora; each, moreover, is determined by separate climatic factors.

As we shall here deal chiefly with vegetation, let us at once make clear the difference between it and flora.

Now the woodland, let us say, of Upper Assam belongs essentially to the same type of vegetation as an English oakwood, but the flora of the two is entirely different. The two woodlands among their conspicuous plants have no two species in common.

Further the flora of each of these *woodlands* is made up of trees, shrubs, and herbs. It would be conceivable that either of these floras, by reducing the number of trees and shrubs and multiplying the herbs and grasses, might make up a totally different type of vegetation, namely, *grassland*.

In general, the factor determining the vegetation of a district is rainfall; that determining its flora is temperature. Assam and England have the same type of vegetation, chiefly because they both have wet climates. Their floras differ chiefly because the climate of Assam is hot while that of England is cold.

The three chief types of vegetation are: (1) Woodland, often called forest, dominated by trees; (2) Grassland, made up chiefly of grasses and sedges; and (3) Desert, containing only scattered and stunted shrubs and herbs. *Woodland* occurs where much rain falls; *grassland* occurs where the rainfall is insufficient for woodland but is evenly distributed throughout the year; *desert* occurs where rain is deficient for the needs of either woodland or grassland.

Woodland of one type or another is probably the characteristic vegetation of our area. In India, chiefly owing to the wet monsoon, alternating with a long, dry season, typical grassland does not occur,[1] but all transitions are seen from the most luxuriantly developed woodland to desert. The reason that woodland needs heavy rainfall is that trees with their heavy crowns of leaves evaporate much water, and this loss must be made good. The roots of trees penetrate so deeply into the ground that they are not, like grasses, dependent on constant rain. Furthermore, the heavier the rainfall the more luxurious the woodland. This is well seen where we leave the plains to go up the hills.

As one ascends, the temperature falls. But at the foot of the hills the first slight fall of temperature, while still insufficient

[1] There are large tracts of swamp within our area, and these tracts support a vegetation which often consists largely of grasses. These swamp associations are very unstable, and are not to be connected with the "grass land" of, let us say, South America.

1. WOODLAND IN UPPER ASSAM. (THE TALL STRAIGHT-STEMMED TREES ARE "DIPTEROCARPUS PILOSUS," ROXB.).
2. SHILLONG, SHOWING EXAMPLES OF "PINUS KHASYA." 3. BENGAL PLAINS. 4. A BENGAL ROADSIDE.
5. A JHEEL, SHOWING FLOATING MASSES OF "EICHHORNIA CRASSIPES."
6. A REED SWAMP, OR "TYPHA AUGUSTATA."

Photos by D. N. Carter.

to affect the flora, brings about a great increase of rainfall. This determines woodland, or larger and better woodland.

WOODLAND SCENERY, NEAR SHILLONG.

Photo by Chotalal Bros.

Let us take for example the journey between Siliguri and Darjeeling. In this region the plains are much cultivated, but doubtless their primitive vegetation would be a poor type of woodland.

A slight rise brings us into a region of increased rainfall, hence of better woodland. It is here (about 1,000 feet) that the sal (*Shorea robusta*) becomes gregarious and covers large areas. Higher up still the woodland becomes much better developed and shows a magnificent confusion of huge trees, tangled creepers, and shrubs and herbs, which not only bedeck the ground but often cover the branches of the trees. At this altitude (2,000 to 3,000 feet) the flora is practically that of the plains serried and massed together to form a different kind of vegetation.

At Darjeeling (about 7,000 feet) the rainfall, owing to the low air pressure, has begun to decrease, and a corresponding decline is seen in the luxuriance of the forest. The temperature is much lower and is beginning to affect the flora. Whereas the flora of the plains and of the forests at the base of the hills is tropical, at the altitude of Darjeeling the temperate element becomes evident in the flora.

Many British genera are at once recognized: *Quercus* (oak), *Alnus* (alder), *Potentilla acer* (maple), *Epilobium* (willow herb), *Heracteum* (hog-weed), *Viburnum ajuga* (bugle), *Scutellaria* (skull-cap), occur to one at once as British genera easily recognized by non-botanical Britishers in Darjeeling.

Much the same changes are seen in going up the Khasya Hills. At Shillong (5,000 feet) most of the above genera are present, and in addition to them the woodland is dominated by a pine (*Pinus Khasya*, Royle). In the Darjeeling part of the Himalayas, conifers begin at about 9,000 feet, which carries us over the political boundary of Bengal. The conifer which is so conspicuous at Darjeeling is a Japanese tree, *Cryptomeria japonica*, which has been planted there.

In the hilly district of Chutia Nagpur the rainfall is much less than it is in the lower Himalayas and Assamese hills, and the forest is of a much less luxuriant type.

At the base of all these hills there is often a swampy zone covered by tall grasses, tamarix, and scattered trees, a kind of vegetation similar to that which often flanks our rivers and also occurs in the Sunderbans.

In general the landscape of the plains is the result of agriculture and not of natural vegetation. Woodland, especially in Assam, covers large areas and in Assam, too, wide expanses of sandy soil by the Brahmaputra are clad with a kind of savannah of tall grasses and scattered trees alternating with large tracts of Tamarix. But a great part of the plains has been cultivated for many centuries, and even many of the trees which diversify their landscape are introduced plants. Four palms are everywhere in evidence. The coco-nut palm (*Cocos nucifera*) is found chiefly near the sea; it has a smooth stem which seldom stands quite straight and a crown of feather-leaves. *Phœnix sylvestris* has straight stems which are clad in an armour plating of leaf bases so that the actual surface of the stem is not seen. It, too, has feather-leaves. The Palmyra palm (*Borassus flabellifer*) has a straight, smooth stem surmounted by a handsome crown of fan leaves. *Areca catechu* which yields the betel-nut which Indians love to chew may be known by its very slender stems, which Sir Joseph Hooker compared to "arrows shot down from heaven." It is often planted in groups near houses.

Other common trees seen, especially about villages, are *Artocarpus integrifolius* (the jack fruit), *Nephelium litchi* (the litchi), *Mangifera indica* (the mango), *Terminalia catappa* (the country almond), *Bombax malabaricum*, and many species of *Ficus*, of which perhaps the best known are *Ficus benalensis* (the banyan) and *Ficus religiosa* (the pipal).

The banana (*Musa sapientum*) is always seen near habitations, and clumps of bamboos are ubiquitous.

The "jheels" or swamp-lakes of the plains show natural vegetation. Plants which live partially or entirely in water have many peculiarities. Structural changes are present, some of which are connected with the fact that the roots live in mud, which is deficient in oxygen. Such plants have in their stems hollow channels which, connecting with similar channels in their roots, form a regular system of air canals. Some plants have some of their leaves submerged, and these leaves are very different from those which are born in the air. The submerged leaves are often finely divided as in *Cardanthera*. Other plants, as the water-lilies, have floating leaves. Others, again, are *floating plants*, whose roots instead of being fast in the mud are free in the water. Such plants are *Pistia stratoides*, an aroid common on all jheels, and *Eichhornia crassipes* (water hyacinth), an American plant which is spreading rapidly over watery tracts in India and Burma.

Allied to the "jheel" vegetation are the communities of *Typha, Phragmites*, etc., which often cover wet, low-lying ground on the plains.

Throughout the plains, and especially in Bengal, one is struck by the vast host of alien plants to be seen. They bulk so large in the flora that one wonders what the land looked like before they came. Brühl in 1908 wrote an account of two hundred and thirty-four "recent plant immigrants," and others have got a footing since then.

Our area abuts on the sea and we must say something about its sea-shore vegetation. The sea, chiefly owing to the salt it contains, has a profound effect on plants. Sandy foreshores are almost devoid of vegetation. What plant can root itself in sand firmly enough to ĕnable it to stand the scour of the tide and the thrashing of the waves on the Puri beach? Above high-water mark, however, plants get a hold.

The commonest seashore plant in our area, and perhaps in all tropical regions, is *Ipomœa biloba*, Forsk, called by Linnæus *Convolvulus pes-Capræ*, from a fancied likeness of its leaves to goats' cloven hoofs. Its stems form great tangled masses which bind the sand so admirably that persons whose houses are near the beach welcome it in their gardens. All who have ever seen a tropical sea-beach must know its purple trumpet flowers. In our area *Hydrophylax maritima* and *Cyperus arenarius* also are very common. All these plants have extensively growing stems which can carry the growing point quickly through shifting masses of sand to bring it up to the light. The stems of *Ipomœa* and *Hydrophylax* spread in all directions, those of *Cyperus arenarius* travel in straight lines so that the sedge tufts of this plant are seen ranged on the beach in long rows as if they had been planted out with a tape.

These plants play an important rôle in the formation of "dunes." The drifting sand becomes heaped up on the side of the plant and threatens to bury it; the plant grows to keep pace with the encumbrance. More sand becomes heaped up, the plant grows more, and the larger the sand heap the more sand is it able to stop. A large sand hill or dune is eventually formed in which the stems and roots of the dune plant ramify in all directions. On the more sheltered parts of this dune other plants are able to get footing. These plants living and dying bind the sand and make humus on which grasses and other herbs can grow. In this way, out of sandy waste good pastures are eventually formed. These processes can be seen going on at Puri.

Before leaving the Puri dunes mention must be made of *Spinifex squarrosus*, L., a curious grass very common there. Its fruits are arranged on stiff rays which make up balls about the size of a child's head. When the fruit is ripe the head falls off, and bounding and dancing about on its rays ensures dispersal for its seeds. All visitors to Puri must have seen these independent, toy-like objects racing along the beach.

Salt water makes its effects felt in situations more sheltered than dunes and beaches. Sluggish tropical estuaries are inhabited by a kind of vegetation totally distinct from anything else in the world. This "mangrove vegetation," as it is called, occurs in the tropics where "salt marsh" would occur in temperate regions. In our area it is extensively developed about the delta of the Ganges in the low, swampy region called the Sundribuns.

TAPPING DATE TREES.

Photo by Ghoshal Bros.

Mangrove-trees, though they belong to

various families, resemble one another closely. The seeds of these plants germinate while the fruit is still attached to the tree and continue to grow until the young roots hang down, sometimes attaining more than a foot in length. The young roots are thickened towards the end so that when the fruit drops the root sticks fast in the mud. It is by this curious contrivance that the seedlings are able to get a hold in the tidal wash.

Mangrove-trees belonging to the family *Rhizophoraceæ* develop early in their life history a remarkable scaffolding of roots which grow out from their main stem obliquely down into the mud, branching as they go. Eventually the base of the main stem dies away and the tree appears to be growing on a frame of basket-work.

In *Sonneratia* (Sonneratiaceæ), *Bruguiera* (Rhizophoraceæ), and *Avicennia* (Verbenaceæ), peculiar roots of another kind are present. These rise vertically out of the mud; it is their function to carry oxygen to the normally situated roots embedded as they are in unaerated mud.

Heritiera minor, Roxb. (Sterculiaceæ) is one of the most abundant mangrove-trees in our area, and it is from the vernacular name of this tree (Sundri) that the Sundribuns derive their name.

Those interested in the vegetation of the district and desirous of making a thorough investigation of the subject, will find more detailed information in the following books:—

Brühl, P., "Recent Plant Immigrants" (Journ. As. Soc. Beng., pp. 603-656, December 1908); Gamie, G. A., Report on a Botanical Tour in the Lakhimpur District, Assam (Records, Bot. Surv. Ind., 1895, vol. i., No. 5, pp. 61-88); Haines, H. H., "A Forest Flora of Chota Nagpur, including Gangpur and the Santal-Parganah"; Prain, D., "Bengal Plants" (unfortunately out of print); "Flora of the Sundribuns" (Records, Bot. Surv. Ind., vol. ii., No. 4, 1903); "The Vegetation of the Districts of Hughly-Howrah and the Twenty-four Pergunnahs" (Records, Bot. Surv. Ind., vol. iii., No. 2, 1905).

1. A FINE FLOWERING MASS OF PHRAGMITES (ON RIGHT).
2. A SMALL SAND-DUNE ON PURI BEACH, SHOWING "HYDROPHYLAX MARITIMA."
Photos by D. N. Carter.
3. MANGROVE VEGETATION. "AVICENNIA OFFICINALIS," SHOWING THE ERECT AERATING ROOTS.
Photo by F. W. Graveley

CHOWRINGHEE AND THE MAIDAN, CALCUTTA.

Photo by Johnston & Hoffmann Calcutta.

THE CITY OF CALCUTTA

CALCUTTA is one of those cities whose histories are synonymous with the making of empires; their birth has in many instances been ushered in to the accompaniment of turmoil and conflict between opposing military forces; attempts to develop them socially, industrially, and politically have been frustrated again and again by the jealousy and subsequent invasions of foreign foes; and it has only been after continuous struggles on the part of the founders of these places that solid commercial foundations were eventually obtained, upon which imposing superstructures have subsequently been raised. Such cities, however, are monuments to-day of the indomitable energy of those who had sufficient confidence in their own ideas to resist all opposition to their schemes, and they are now found in nearly every country of the world, standing as examples of the steady progress made in private and public life. "Mushroom" cities which have sprung up in a night are not of the above-mentioned class, and these notes are concerned only with Calcutta, one of many Eastern cities which have centuries of history behind them.

Calcutta, in common with many other Eastern cities, has its legend, which, according to the late Dr. C. R. Wilson, in "The Early Annals of the English in Bengal," is as follows: "Long, long ago, in the age of truth, Daksha, one of the Hindu Patriarchs, made a sacrifice to obtain a son, but he omitted to invite the god Siva to attend. Now, Sati, the daughter of Daksha, was married to Siva, and she was indignant that so great an insult should have been offered to her divine husband, and deeply grieved that such a slight should have passed upon him through her kindred. In vain did she expostulate with her father. 'Why,' she asked, 'is my husband not invited? Why are no offerings to be made to him?' 'Thy husband,' was the reply, 'wears a necklace of skulls; how can he be invited to a sacrifice?' Then in grief and indignation she shrieked out, 'This father of mine is a villain; what profit have I in this carcass sprung from him?' She puts an end to her life; and Siva, 'drunk with loss,' transfixed her dead body on the point of his trident and rushed hither and thither through the realms of Nature. The whole world was threatened with destruction, but Vishnu, the Preserver, came to the rescue. He flung his disk at the body of Sati and broke it into pieces, when it fell scattered over the earth. Every place where any of the ornaments of Sati fell became a sanctuary, a sacred spot full of the divine spirit of Sati. The names of these sacred places are preserved in the garlands of sanctuaries. Some of them are well-known places of pilgrimage, others are obscure and forgotten; but to-day the most celebrated of them is in Calcutta (or Kalighat), the spot which received the toes of the right foot of Sati, that is Kali."

It will be unnecessary here to refer at length to historical events connected with the rise of Calcutta, as they are fully dealt with on another page; but some particulars may be given as to the establishment of commercial relationships between the native population and visiting traders.

Direct trading between England and Bengal appears to have been firmly established in or about the year 1645, and the English flag was first hoisted in 1690, by one Job Charnock, on the spot where the Royal Mint now stands at Nimtollah, at the northern end of the Strand Road, and practically on the eastern bank of the River Hooghly.

The site of Calcutta was selected after several attempts had been made to establish a port and city in other places on or near the Hooghly, and the decision was arrived at because the spot chosen was the highest point at which the river was navigable for sea-going vessels. There is an ancient fallacy that the site

1. THE BENGAL CLUB, CALCUTTA. 3. CLIVE STREET, CALCUTTA, LOOKING NORTH.
2. DALHOUSIE SQUARE, EAST, AND TANK, SHOWING ST. ANDREW'S CHURCH, CALCUTTA.

Photos by Johnston & Hoffmann, Calcutta.

THE CITY OF CALCUTTA

was chosen by chance on account of a midday halt by Charnock, but nothing could be farther from the truth than this.

Kipling, in his "Departmental Ditties," makes an ignominious splash in this sea of error when he says :—

"Thus the mid-day heat of Charnock, more's the pity,
Grew a city ;
As the fungus sprouts chaotic from its bed,
So it spread ;
Chance-directed, chance-erected, laid and built,
On the silt.
Palace, byre, hovel—poverty and pride,
Side by side ;
And above the packed and pestilential town,
Death looked down."

Calcutta, the second city in the British Empire as regards population, extends for several miles on the east bank of the River Hooghly—an arm of the mighty Ganges—and the approaches, either by river or railway, present a striking variety of pleasing effects. The eighty miles journey by passenger steamer from the Sunderbunds—the delta of the Ganges, Brahmaputra, and Hooghly—will enable the visitor to appreciate to some extent the great difficulties, owing to the large number of shoals, which confront the skippers of sea-going vessels. These treacherous banks have been the cause of destruction of a large number of ships, and this river has been frequently described by mariners as the most difficult in the world for navigators.

When nearing Calcutta by steamer, attention will be drawn to the beautiful Botanical Gardens on the west bank of the river, while on the opposite side is Garden Reach, now occupied by tidal docks and the extensive wharf accommodation for which the port is famous, the arsenal, the Maidan, with its beautiful drives, and the Eden Gardens, with their tropical plants and trees. Still sailing in a northerly direction, one notices the magnificent pile of Government House buildings, erected in 1802 ; while on either side of the river are ghats, docks, shipbuilding yards, foundries, mills of all kinds, timber yards, goods sheds, landing stations for large steamers, warehouses, and other buildings, which are continued past the Howrah pontoon bridge for a distance of about two miles.

The entrance to the city, too, by the railway systems or roads, affords a view of extensive warehouses, factories with chimney-stacks emitting volumes of smoke, and yards in which passenger and cargo steamers, launches, and other craft are being constructed ; while the large thoroughfares and narrower streets through which one drives are teeming with inhabitants on business bent.

The city of Calcutta is a curious mixture of magnificent buildings of imposing architectural designs on the one hand and of squalid tenements on the other. Nothing could be finer than the palatial commercial houses of the Esplanade, Old Court House Street, Clive Street, or Chowringhee ; nor could anything be more unsightly than the insanitary, unstable, and primitive dens—constructed

SITE OF THE BLACK HOLE, CALCUTTA.

Photo by Johnston & Hoffmann, Calcutta.

chiefly of mud, bamboo, and matting—which may be seen in numberless streets and lanes. Families are huddled together, and the absence of the barest necessities which make for cleanliness and health is a blot upon twentieth-century civilization. One might point to some of these abominations in Harrison Road, Chitpore, and the northern portion of the city generally, to portions of Free School Street, Market Street, Corporation Street, Upper and Lower Circular Road, and in the alleys—distinguished as a rule by the word "lanes"—and it is doubtful if anything less salutary than a fierce fire in these quarters will ever purge them of the countless millions of germs with which they must be infested.

Many of the principal thoroughfares, however, are of considerable width, and are usually kept in good order. These include Government Place East, West, and North ; Chowringhee, the Esplanade, Mayo and Outram Roads, Camac Street, Loudon Street, Park Street, Old Court House Street, Council House Street, Clive Street, Wellesley Street, Auckland Road, and several others ; and it will be observed that many of these are named after noted Englishmen who have been connected with the earlier history of India. The narrower streets and bazaars, in which the native element reigns supreme, are anything but attractive ; yet they are full of interest to the Westerner who gazes for the first time upon Oriental faces, customs, dress, and methods of conducting business.

The number of separate residences for persons of the so-called "middle" class is amazingly small, and entirely out of proportion to the vast number of families for whom a private residence is so desirable. The consequence is that these people are compelled to live in flats, or suites of apartments—a most unsatisfactory arrangement to those who are blessed with children.

There are, of course, many very handsome private residences belonging to the wealthy classes, which have been substantially erected in spacious compounds, where the luxuriant vegetation of the East is seen in the richest profusion. The majority of these are in the neighbourhood of Chowringhee, as, for instance, in Lower Circular Road, Theatre Road,

Camac Street, Wood Street, Park Street, Loudon Street, and others. Somewhat farther afield, however, there are private palatial residences of great architectural beauty, and of immensely valuable contents, whose owners occupy an honoured position among the nobility of India. The majority of these have been erected in comparatively recent years, and while English designs in architecture have been followed to a very large extent, the builders have not overlooked the fact that certain alterations were necessary in order that the structures should be suitable for the Indian climate. One of these is the handsome palace of the Maharaja Bahadur Sir Jotindra Mohun Tagore, K.C.S.I., which is situated on the left-hand side of Chitpore Road, between Lal Bazar Street and Beadon Square, in Calcutta. Entry is gained under a massive portico with six Corinthian columns supporting a pediment in which is a representation of the Star of India in *bas relief*. The mansion is luxuriously furnished throughout, and on every hand one sees priceless old pictures, statuary, and other artistic contents. Opposite the palace is Tagore Castle, built in the year 1886 at a cost, including furniture, of more than 11 lakhs of rupees. A very finely polished granite floor is laid in the entrance hall, while all around is a fine collection of old armour, busts, and paintings. The library is a most attractive room upholstered in dark blue leather, and crammed with volumes of a general historic character, political law, and a miscellaneous host of good readable literature of a general character. The truly artistic and æsthetic tastes of its owner are manifested in the architectural beauties of this feudal-like castle, with its battlements, towers, and other emblems of a bygone age.

COMFORTS FOR THE TROOPS BEING DISPATCHED BY LADY CARMICHAEL'S BENGAL WOMEN'S WAR FUND, CALCUTTA.

Photo by T. P. Sen.

"Emerald Bower," the country seat of the Maharaja of Tagore, is situated on the Barrackpore Road, on the north-eastern border of Calcutta, and is one of the "show" places of Bengal. The grounds are beautifully laid out, and the interior of the residence is sumptuously furnished; but many visitors will be attracted chiefly by the magnificent collection of about seven hundred valuable paintings, than which there is no finer in India. Van Dyck, Murillo, Ribara, Moltino, Daniel, Rubens, and other noted masters are represented; but the gem is a work by Sir John Opie, R.A., which was formerly in the possession of His late Majesty King George IV, and is believed to have cost no less than £12,000.

No more gorgeously furnished palace in Calcutta can be found than the marble one in Mooktaram Babu's street belonging to the ancient Mullick family, who belong to the *Subornobanik* (or banker) caste of Bengal, and are justly renowned for their enterprise, wealth, and great liberality. Thirteen generations ago their ancestor Jadab Sil was honoured by the Mahommedan Government of the day with the hereditary title of Mullick, but the name of Sil is retained for use in religious and matrimonial ceremonies. The mansion is approached through exceedingly massive gates, and from entering to leaving this mansion visitors will be deeply interested in the priceless collection of paintings and art treasures of great variety.

In attempting a description of the principal buildings, mention must be made first of all of Government House, a handsome building constructed at the beginning of the nineteenth century and modelled upon the designs of Keddleston Hall, in the county of Derby, England. The Throne Room—so called from the fact that it contains the throne of Sultan Tipu Tib—is an exceedingly noble apartment, containing portraits of their late Majesties Queen Victoria, King George III, and Queen Charlotte, and of Sir Arthur Wellesley and others; while the Council Room is adorned with portraits of viceroys and notabilities, including the Earl of Minto, Lord Hardinge, Sir Eyre Coote, Lord Cornwallis, Warren Hastings, the Earl of Auckland, the Marquis of Wellesley, Lord Clive, and Lord William Bentinck. There are many objects of great historical interest both in the house and the grounds, among them being subsidiary treaties of Hyderabad, Mysore, and Seringapatam relating to the years 1798 and 1799; several guns captured during the wars with Hyder Ali and his warlike son Tipu; on the south side is a fine brass 32-pounder taken at Aliwal in 1846, and on the north is a huge iron gun with carriage representing a dragon.

The State entrance is approached by a grand flight of 33 steps, 100 feet in width at the bottom and 67 feet at the top, where there is a noble portico with pillars 45 feet in height, of the Ionic order. The portico opens on to the first floor, where may be seen the vestibule, used as a breakfast-room, and the Grand Durbar Hall with beautifully polished marble floor. This apartment is known as the "Hall of the Cæsars," from the 12 marble busts (believed to have been taken from a French vessel by Admiral Watson in 1757) which adorn the side circles. The public drawing-room is one of the finest in the building, and from it is obtained a lovely view of the Maidan and Fort William.

1. GOVERNMENT HOUSE, CALCUTTA. 2. THE RED ROAD, CALCUTTA. 3. WRITER'S BUILDINGS, CALCUTTA.

Photos by Johnston & Hoffmann, Calcutta.

The Town Hall, on the western side of Government House, is Doric in style of architecture, and it is the home of fine statues and paintings of (*inter alia*) Warren Hastings, Lord Cornwallis, Lord Gough, Bishop Wilson, and Sir C. Metcalfe. Old Post Office Street separates this building from the High Court, which is a most imposing structure erected in the year 1872, somewhat after the style of the Town Hall of Ypres, in Belgium. Accommodation has been found for seven courts, libraries for judges and the Bar, and numerous other rooms which are occupied by officials. The exterior of the building is worthy of close attention, as it presents a most pleasing effect of the combination of Western and Eastern ideas; but the interesting collection of portraits of judges and other celebrities in the various rooms should not be overlooked. It has a tower, 180 feet in height, from which very extensive views are obtained.

A walk of five minutes will take the visitor to St. John's Church. This is one of the most interesting buildings in Calcutta, and dates from the year 1788. Its construction was due very largely to the personal influence of Warren Hastings, and while the eastern and western entrances have a noble appearance with their perfect Corinthian columns, the interior offers an infinity of attractions. There are a number of valuable paintings, but the tablets and tombs will be the chief attraction to the historian; and conspicuous among the latter are the resting-places of Admiral Watson, who assisted Clive in retaking Calcutta from Suraj-ud-Daulah, Nawab of Bengal, at the battle of Plassey in 1757, and of Job Charnock, the founder of Calcutta.

One cannot gaze at the General Post Office—facing Dalhousie Square—without being reminded of the terrible horrors of the massacre of more than 120 British subjects in what is known in history as the "Black Hole of Calcutta," a spot within the precincts of the Old Fort William, now included in the area of the Post Office premises and denoted by a mural tablet erected by one of the few survivors to the memory of those who perished. The modern portion of the present Post Office, distinguished by its fine Corinthian pillars, was completed in the year 1870 at a cost of Rs. 6,30,000. Within a radius of two or three hundred yards of the Post Office are the handsome new structures of the Telegraph Department, the Royal Exchange, Writers' Buildings or the Bengal Secretariat, and the magnificent premises belonging to practically all the banking companies in Calcutta. It would be a great oversight if one were at this juncture to omit reference to the "Old Mission Church"—situated in Mission Row, a street on the eastern side of Dalhousie Square—the building of which was commenced in the year 1767 by a Swedish missionary named Keirnander. Financial troubles overtook this gentleman at a later date, and his creditors took possession of the edifice, although it was afterwards redeemed at a cost of Rs. 10,000 by Mr. Charles Grant, father of Lord Glenelg. While in this portion of the city, a visit should be paid to the Imperial Library at the corner of Strand Road and Hare Street, which contains a large number of very valuable works; special notice should be taken of the collection of ancient prints hanging on the walls of the principal staircase.

The foundations of the Royal Mint were laid in the year 1824, and the construction

1. HIGH COURT, CALCUTTA **2. CLIVE STREET, CALCUTTA, LOOKING SOUTH.**

Photos by Johnston & Hoffmann, Calcutta.

of the central portico, which is a copy of the Temple of Minerva at Athens, covered a period of six years. While in this neighbourhood, a visit should be paid to the floating pontoon bridge which unites Calcutta with the Municipality of Howrah. It is 1,530 feet in length between abutments, and the width (including wood pavements and roadway) is about 75 feet. The vehicular and pedestrian traffic is exceedingly great from early morn until nearly midnight, and as it provides the only means of crossing the Hooghly—excepting by ferry steamers—for several miles from the city in either direction, it is not surprising that the authorities have decided to replace the pontoon by a permanent structure. Elaborate designs have been prepared, and it is expected that the work of construction will be put in hand in due course. On the Howrah side of the bridge are the passenger station and terminus of the systems of the Bengal-Nagpur and East Indian Railway Companies, but this is referred to elsewhere.

The entrance to Sealdah Station, the city terminus of the Eastern Bengal Railway Company, abuts upon Lower Circular Road, in which there are not any buildings of particular importance; but proceeding in a westerly direction through Dhurrumtollah, one arrives at the splendid thoroughfare known as Chowringhee Road, in which the leading clubs, hotels, and shops are situated. On the western side of this fine road is the splendid Maidan, while on the opposite side may be seen the very extensive business premises of Messrs. Leslie & Co., Whiteaway, Laidlaw & Co., Ltd., Messrs. G. F. Kellner & Co., Ltd., Messrs. Hall and Anderson, Ltd., the Continental and Grand Hotels, the Theatre Royal, the Young Men's Christian Association, the Indian Museum (housing zoological, anthropological, industrial, art, and archæological collections; and also a fine collection of minerals, fossils, and antiquities, among which are Buddhist remains believed to be more than 2,000 years of age), the United Service and Bengal Clubs, the Army and Navy Stores, and the Bishop's Palace.

St. Paul's Cathedral is situated between Chowringhee and Cathedral Road, and is a very handsome building, mainly in the Gothic style, but with certain deviations calculated to suit the exigencies of the Indian climate. The chief attraction for visitors will be the western window, which was erected in the year 1880 as a memorial to Lord Mayo, a former Viceroy. An historian has written: "The library is perhaps the oldest in India. In the transept will be seen Chantrey's colossal statue of Bishop Heber, also a black marble tablet to the memory of sixteen officers who fell during the Indian Mutiny. It is ornamented with sixteen bronze medallions representing the blowing-up of the Cashmir Gate by Lieutenant Salkeld at the siege of Delhi. Near to the tablet is one to the memory of fifteen officers who fell in the Bhutan Campaign, and adjoining this is a peculiar and elaborate monument of John Paxton Norman, Officiating Chief Justice of Bengal, who was assassinated on the steps of the Town Hall, Calcutta, on September 20, 1871."

THE HOWRAH BRIDGE, CALCUTTA.

Photo by Johnston & Hoffmann, Calcutta.

The Victoria Memorial Hall.—If there is an incident in the modern history of British India, other than the magnificent support given to Great Britain in the bloodiest war the world has ever seen, which commenced in August 1914, it is the unexampled outburst of loyalty and devotion to the Throne of England manifested in the hearty co-operation of Europeans and Indians of all castes and creeds, from princes to peasants, who have contributed of their wealth towards the erection of a permanent memorial in honour of Her late Majesty Queen Victoria, Empress of India, which will, as Lord Curzon, Viceroy of India, said in a speech delivered in Calcutta in February 1901, afford India an opportunity "not merely to express its devotion to the late Queen's memory, but also to demonstrate to the world in some striking manner the truth of that Imperial unity which was so largely the creation of her personality and reign."

A VIEW OF OLD COURT-HOUSE STREET IN THE NINETIES.
Photo by Johnston & Hoffmann, Calcutta.

The proposal for the erection of a Memorial assumed concrete form by the appointment of a large and representative committee upon which every portion of India was represented, and donations forthwith began to flow in from all quarters.

The question of a suitable site was discussed at a number of meetings, but the feeling was practically unanimous that it should be erected at Calcutta, as the then capital of India, and that it should stand on that part of the Maidan west of the cathedral where the unsightly jail then stood. It was intended that there should be a beautiful and spacious park, in the middle of which would rise the glittering marble structure, standing upon a terrace of white marble and facing northwards across the parade-ground, with its central dome of 160 feet in height, and visible from every part of the river and the Maidan.

Designs for the building were obtained from Sir William Emerson, the President at the time of the Royal Institute of British Architects; and the plans eventually accepted, which followed the Italian Renaissance style, blended with a suggestion of Oriental feeling in some details, provided for: (1) a Hall of Sculpture; (2) a Hall of Paintings; (3) the Hall of Princes, to be devoted to collections presented or lent by Indian Chiefs; (4) a Hall of Arms; (5) galleries or apartments to be devoted to the exhibition of minor objects; and (6) a Durbar Hall for investitures or public meetings. The contents will include statuary and sculpture, paintings, engravings, prints, miniatures, photographs, maps, documents, manuscripts, letters, treaties, flags, models, and personal relics and mementoes appertaining particularly to British rule in India up to the end of Queen Victoria's reign. The whole of the beautiful white marble used in construction is being obtained from the Makrana quarries, in the State of H.H. the Maharaja of Jodhpur, in Rajputana, and about a mile distant from the railway station at Makrana. His late Majesty King Edward VII was the first patron of and donor to the proposed Memorial, and his personal gifts included a number of oil paintings depicting scenes in the life of the "Good Queen," and these will ultimately be hung in the vestibule of the Central Hall—which will be called the Queen's Vestibule—and will be set apart for memorials personal to herself.

An immense number of objects have already (November 1916) been presented to or acquired by the Trustees of the Hall, and among the names of other donors of arts, treasures, and relics, many of which are priceless, are His Majesty King George V and Her Majesty Queen Mary, Lord Curzon—who has been indefatigable in his exertions to further the project—and the leading Rulers and nobility in India, exclusive of many persons in England, some of whose ancestors have been closely identified with the making of political and commercial history in the East.

The total cost of the Memorial is expected to be between £300,000 and £400,000; and although an undertaking of this character must necessarily extend over many years, the Trustees have every reason to be highly satisfied with the progress of the work and with the handsome manner in which donations in money and kind have been received or promised.

The Secretary to the Trustees is Mr. C. B. Bayley, C.V.O.

On the south side of Lower Circular Road is Belvedere House, at Alipore, near to the Calcutta racecourse, in whose grounds was fought the duel between Warren Hastings and Sir Philip Francis. This noble mansion was the residence of the Lieutenant-Governors of Bengal until that portion of India was converted into a Presidency with a Governor of its own. The rooms are now used as a temporary home for the exhibits, which will be transferred to the Victoria Memorial Hall upon its completion.

Not far from Belvedere is Hastings House, originally the country seat of Warren Hastings, the first Governor-General of Fort William in Bengal during the years 1774-85; and within a few minutes' drive in Thackeray Road is "Magistrate's House," where the famous novelist lived when a child.

Returning citywards, one notices the Presidency General and the Military Hospitals. The original General Hospital was the property of the East India Com-

1. CHOWRINGHEE, ALCUTTA, FROM PARK STREET. 2. GOVERNMENT HOUSE, BARRACKPORE. 3. BELVEDERE, CALCUTTA.
4. HASTINGS HOUSE, ALIPORE, CALCUTTA.

Photos by Johnston & Hoffmann, Calcutta.

pany, and was situated at the north-east corner of and adjoining what is now St. John's Churchyard. Concerning it, Hamilton, who wrote in 1717, says: "The Company have a pretty good Hospital at Calcutta where many go to undergo the grievance of physic, but few come out to give an account of its operation." Another satire, probably of the same period, ran :—

"In a very few days you're released from all cares,
If the Padre's asleep Mr. Oldham reads prayers:
To the grave you're let down with a sweet, pleasant thump,
And there you may lie till you hear the last trump."

It may be mentioned that Mr. Oldham was Calcutta's first recognized undertaker.

The new hospital is near to the southern end of Chowringhee, and is a handsome red-brick building with very large airy wards and private rooms. It is 555 feet in length, with an extreme width in the centre of 69 feet; and it was opened in the year 1901 by Sir John Woodburn, then Lieutenant-Governor of Bengal.

Turning to the north, with the racecourse on the left hand, Fort William—the largest fortress in India—next claims one's notice. Its construction was commenced in the year 1757, but completion did not take place until the year 1781. One of the first buildings to be seen on entering by the Chowringhee Gate is a massively constructed warehouse, which bears upon one of its walls a tablet with the following inscription: "This building contains 51,258 *máns* of rice and 20,023½ *máns* of paddy, which were deposited by order of the Governor-General and Council, under the charge of John Belli, agent for providing victualling stores to the garrison, in the months of March, April, and May 1782." Visitors should also find time to see St. Peter's Church, which is an exceedingly pretty building; and, by permission, they may inspect the armoury and arsenal.

One of the sights of the city is undoubtedly the Sir Stuart Hogg Market, situated between Lindsay and Free School Streets and Corporation Place, and not more than 100 yards distant from the principal business section of Chowringhee. The building is most substantially built of good red bricks, and neatly arranged stalls, in avenues running at right angles, are crammed with goods of all descriptions, ranging from fish, meat, and vegetables for the kitchen to ornamental articles for the drawing-room, and from a packet of needles to a com-

THE CATHEDRAL, INTERIOR, CALCUTTA.
Photo by Johnston & Hoffmann, Calcutta.

THE CITY OF CALCUTTA

JAIN TEMPLE, CALCUTTA.
Photo by Johnston & Hoffmann, Calcutta.

plete costume or suit of clothing. The market is under the control of a Superintendent appointed by the Calcutta Municipality.

Calcutta is remarkably well provided with open spaces and squares, and few cities in the East can boast of such a magnificent area for sporting and recreation purposes as is furnished by the Maidan, which is four square miles in extent. It was dense jungle until the year 1757, when the work of clearing was commenced; but now it provides ample accommodation for the racecourse of the Calcutta Turf Club, golf links, and grounds for numerous cricket, football, and tennis clubs; while several well-kept roads are thronged every evening from about 5.30 to 7.30 with stylish carriages, motor-cars, and cycles. Further than this, there are thousands of individuals of all ages who take advantage of the quiet of the day in order to enjoy the ever-green turf and the welcome shade of a large number of noble trees, which were reprieved when the felling-axe opened out this delightful breathing-spot.

The Eden Gardens, situated at the north-west corner of the Maidan and separated by the Strand Road from the River Hooghly, contain a rare variety of tropical and other trees and plants, together with artificial lakes and a finely carved pagoda, which was brought from Burma in the year 1856. The bandstand is occupied by a detachment of the City Volunteers, which plays selections of music from six to seven o'clock each evening; and the surrounding lawns are the nightly rendezvous of the belles of Calcutta and their gallant swains. Dalhousie, Wellington, Wellesley, Beadon, Rawdon, and Auckland Squares, situated in thickly populated districts of the city, are veritable oases in the wilderness of streets, and the inhabitants are not slow in taking advantage of these pleasant retreats.

The Botanical Gardens are situated on the west bank of the River Hooghly, and they may be reached by ferry steamer from the principal landing-stages or by driving through Howrah. Several hours may be passed enjoyably in these beautiful grounds, but visitors should make a point of seeing the Herbarium, the finest in the East, which contains about 40,000 choice specimens. Then the famous banyan-tree must be inspected; it is about 235 years of age; the girth of the trunk is 52 feet, the height is 85 feet, and the circumference at the crown is nearly 1,000 feet.

The development of India under British rule is associated with the names of illustrious men, whose records are ineffaceably written on the pages of history; but the memory of many of these statesmen, soldiers, and others is perpetuated by a

E*

number of statues which have been erected in various parts of Calcutta, but chiefly on the Maidan. These include monuments dedicated to Lords Canning, Mayo, Lansdowne, Auckland, Roberts, Dufferin, Dalhousie, and Kitchener, together with an excellent one representing Her Majesty the late Queen Victoria ; while on the eastern side of the Maidan there is a very fine obelisk—165 feet in height—in honour of Sir David Ochterlony, who was largely responsible for the termination of the Nepal War in 1814-16, and who was British Resident in Rajputana in the year 1823.

The Zoological Gardens are situated within five minutes' walk from the Kidderpore Bridge, which can be reached by tram from any part of the city, and they were opened in 1876 by His Majesty the late King Edward VII when Prince of Wales. The gardens are very prettily laid out, and the collection of animals, birds, fish, and snakes contains many remarkably fine specimens. Excellent accommodation is provided for beasts and birds alike ; the mammoth rhinoceros revels in his boggy paddock; deer, antelopes, wallabies, and others roam about in spacious turf-covered arenas ; lions, tigers, leopards, and other *feræ naturæ* are comfortably housed in quarters provided with ample space for exercise ; and monkeys, birds, and reptiles appear as happy in confinement—and probably happier—than their uncaged fellows.

Not far from these gardens is the celebrated temple at Kalighat, which was built on the bank of Tolly's Nullah in honour of Kali, the wife of Siva. During the *Durga Puja* festival in the month of October a very large number of pilgrims assemble to take part in the religious proceedings which are conducted then. There are other shrines of the goddess Kali in Bowbazar Street and elsewhere in the city, but none of them are of great importance.

One must not, however, forget to mention the Mahommedan mosque at the corner of Bentinck and Dhurrumtollah Streets, which was endowed in 1842 by Prince Gholam Muhammad, son of the famous Sultan Tipu Tib. An inscription upon it reads as follows : "This *Musjid* was erected during the Government of Lord Auckland by the Prince Gholam Muhammad, son of the late Tipu Sultan, in gratitude to God and in commemoration of the Honourable Court of Directors granting him the arrears of his stipend in 1840."

UNIVERSITY HALL, CALCUTTA.

Photo by Johnston & Hoffmann Calcutta.

One of the most beautiful temples in Calcutta is the celebrated one near Halsi Bagan Road, which branches off from Upper Circular Road. It is in the Jain style of architecture, and was founded in 1867 by Rai Budree Dass Bahadur, Mookim and Court Jeweller to the Government of India. The whole building, from ground to ceiling, consists of pure white marble and mosaic work. The temple is dedicated to one of the Jain prophets, whose image is placed in the innermost portion of the sanctuary. The grounds in front of the temple are very picturesque in character, and it is worthy of notice that this most restful garden, with its fountains and statuary, is thrown open to the public during the greater part of each day.

The Municipal Offices of Calcutta are situated in a handsome red-brick building, with frontages on Corporation, Hogg, and Fenwick Bazar Streets and Corporation Place. The officials include a Chairman, Vice-Chairman, and twenty-five Ward Commissioners, together with Executive Officers in the following Departments : Secretary's, Engineer's, Medical Officers of Health, Drainage, Accounts, Provident Fund Accounts, Assessors, City Architect and Surveyor's, Collection, Licences, Hackney Carriage and Carts, Treasury, and Waterworks. The Health Department, it may be mentioned, has, in a city like Calcutta, which contains so many unsavoury localities, and in which so large a proportion of the population exhibit supreme indifference to the primary laws of sanitary science and hygiene, a good deal of responsibility on its hands; but the Chief Health Officer and his assistants are fighting bravely against the stubborn foes of disease—overcrowding, uncleanliness, and wilful carelessness as to the disposal of decaying garbage. The various branches of this department, staffed by competent officials, comprise experts in analytical work, medical, sanitary, food, and Disinfecting Inspectors, and midwives. Other departments are concerned with the burning ghat, burial-grounds, and lighting of streets.

The High Court of Judicature of Bengal, situated in Esplanade West, is presided over by the Chief Justice, the Honourable Sir Lancelot Sanderson, Kt., K.C., who is assisted by seventeen Puisne Judges. The Court of Small Causes has its headquarters at 3, Bankshall Street, but there is a suburban court at 136, Lower Circular Road. There are about half a dozen judges, who sit in their respective courts, and the chief judge is Dr. T. Thornhill, LL.D.

Manufacturing and industrial enterprises have increased rapidly during the past half-century, since the opening of railways in the interior of Bengal and other Provinces has provided greater facilities for the transfer of raw materials and produce to commercial centres, and has given increased opportunities to merchants for the consignment of merchandise to markets. The manufacture of jute is the most valuable industrial concern in Calcutta, and a history of the cultivation of this plant and the subsequent treatment of fibre in the mills on the Hooghly is the subject-matter of special notes on another page. Other important concerns in or near to the city include mills and factories for crushing bones, spinning cotton, the manufacture of flour, sugar, ice, pottery tiles, bricks, and ropes, and the crushing of oil-seeds, together with shipbuilding and iron and brass foundries.

The Calcutta Tramways Company, Ltd., was registered in England in December 1880, having obtained a "running" concession for twenty-one years, and operations were commenced in certain portions of the city with a service of steam trams and horse cars. Two years before the expiry of that period, however, an agreement was entered into with the Calcutta Corporation, under which the company was granted a "new concession for thirty years, dating from January 1, 1901, in consideration of the system being converted from steam- and horse-power to electric traction within three years."

The installation of electric motive power—conveyed to cars by an overhead trolley system—was commenced in the year 1900, and the whole of the work was completed for regular service in November 1902. The company have from time to time linked the central portions of the city with rising suburbs, and at the present time (November 1916) the routes cover a distance of 30½ miles of double-track lines, inclusive of the system in the town of Howrah, in which there are nearly five miles of permanent way. First- and second-class cars (the latter "trailers") are run on every trip on all sections, and the convenience of the travelling public has been further considered by the issue of transfer tickets, which are available for one change of cars on a journey involving travel on two distinct sections, of which there are eleven in Calcutta and three in Howrah.

The service is, on the whole, a satisfactory one, and punctuality is observed in the running of the cars. During the summer months the cars start from their respective stations at five o'clock in the morning, and in winter the time is 5.30, but they continue to run until 11.30 p.m. throughout the whole of the year.

Hackney carriages and taxis can be engaged at appointed places in nearly all the principal streets, while private vehicles and saddle-horses may be obtained from a number of first-class livery stables.

Very enjoyable trips can be made in ferry steamers on the Hooghly, and among the interesting places to be visited are: Matiabrooze, 40 minutes' journey; Rajabagan, noted for its shipbuilding yards and factories; Rajgunge, centre of fishing and coconut industries; and Cossipore, where there is a gun factory, in addition to a sugar factory and a number of jute presses. These and a few other places can be reached in less than an hour, but longer trips may be made to Chandernagore, a French settlement, 21 miles distant from Calcutta; Hooghly, founded by the Portuguese in 1457; Chinsurah, formerly belonging to the Dutch, and containing quaint old specimens of architecture; Ooloobcrria, 20 miles, and Fultah, 36 miles, both in the direction of the outlet of the river into the Bay of Bengal.

The majority of the suburbs of Calcutta are situated in the districts in which busy native bazaars predominate, but a brief reference may be made to the following:—

Howrah, which might almost be taken as a part of Calcutta, is the chief town in the district of Howrah, which extends for a distance of about eight miles along the right bank of the River Hooghly. It is a municipal borough with a population of about 180,000 inhabitants, a large proportion of whom are engaged in the busy shipbuilding yards, foundries, and factories on the Hooghly.

Various schemes for the improvement of streets and other highly necessary works have repeatedly been placed before the citizens, but there appear to be many urgent reasons for the pigeon-holing of the proposals for a practically indefinite period.

Garden Reach, also on the Hooghly, was formerly the principal residential quarter of the fashionable inhabitants of Calcutta; but almost the whole area—including a very beautiful house and grounds occupied about the year 1856 by a former king of Oudh—is now a busy commercial centre, in which are jute and cotton mills, soap-works, coolie lines, and the Army Remount Department. The palatial offices of the Bengal-Nagpur Railway Company are situated here, and the Kidderpore Docks are entered from Garden Reach Road. Proceeding in a northwardly direction past Calcutta, but within a distance of four and a half miles from the city, is Dum-Dum, a cantonment with station on the Eastern Bengal Railway system. There is a small-arms ammunition factory here, which gives employment to a large number of hands. Here are also several attractive bungalows with gardens and grounds, which are used largely by picnic parties from Calcutta.

THE BAKR-ID FESTIVAL: MAHOMMEDANS AT PRAYER ON THE CALCUTTA MAIDAN.

Photo by T. P. Sen.

Tollygunge is one of those well-timbered beauty-spots, with scores of acres of velvety sward, which are never too numerous in the vicinity of largely populated towns and cities. It is within half an hour's drive from Calcutta, along a road which is being widened and improved. Upon arrival one notices a fine open stretch of park-like grounds, flanked by beautiful trees of all kinds; and in the distance is a large building known as the Club House, which is the headquarters for members who indulge in racing, golf, archery, polo, tennis, and other games.

Three miles from Calcutta is Lillooah, the headquarters, with offices and workshops of the carriage and wagon department of the East Indian Railway Company. It is with pardonable pride that the officials of this company are able to point to exceedingly superior workmanship manifested here in the construction of a most luxuriantly furnished broad-gauge State railway train of ten bogie vehicles, for the use of their Imperial Majesties on the occusion of the Coronation Durbar in 1911-12. The total weight of the train was 428 tons, and it had an extreme length of 700 feet. The workshops cover an area of about 95 acres, and upwards of 5,000 men are employed in construction and maintenance work. An idea of the importance of the establishment is conveyed by the statement that the output of new work at the shops is equivalent to one carriage and five wagons daily throughout the year.

1. GENERAL POST OFFICE, CALCUTTA. 2. PAGODA, EDEN GARDENS, CALCUTTA. 3. KALI TEMPLE, CALCUTTA.

Chief among the suburbs within five miles from Calcutta, and situated in easterly and north-easterly directions, are Entally, Shambazar, Chitpore, Baghbazar, Jorabagan, Manicktollah, and Belgatchia; but all of these are business centres, with little of importance to recommend them as visiting-places for tourists.

F. ACERBONI & CO.

The manufacture of "Excelsior" mosaic walling, laid plastically, and proof against damp, is a special feature of the business enterprise of Messrs. F. Acerboni & Co., of 2 Watkins Lane, Howrah, near Calcutta. The firm was established more than fifty years ago by Mr. F. Acerboni, and he was succeeded by Mr. C. Albertini, who was sole proprietor until 1915, when his manager, Mr. A. Prati, became owner.

The firm are dealers in Italian marble tiles of all descriptions, slabs, flooring tiles, tables, and pillars, and they undertake any kind of work in "Excelsior" mosaic or patent stone, among which may be mentioned: ordinary patent stone for floors, footpaths, roads, kerbs, channels, and balustrades; reinforced ferro-concrete for walls, railway sleepers, cargo boats, pontoons, and roofing; red patent stone polished for floors and walls; white polished imitation marble for floors and walls; imitation coloured marble for walls, pillars, and ornamental works; mosaic stone polished in any colour laid down plastically, and also supplied in tiles for floors, pillars, basins, and dissecting and other tables; and polished white cement plastering.

Messrs. Acerboni & Co. carried out the greater portion of the marble and mosaic work at Government House, Calcutta, at a number of Government buildings, for the Calcutta Port Commissioners, and at several stations on the principal railway systems in India; and they are contractors to the Government of Bengal, the Public Works Department, railway authorities, and the Howrah Municipality.

A gold medal and a first-class certificate for excellence of works were awarded to this firm at the Calcutta Industrial and Agricultural Exhibition held in 1906-7.

Very fine marble and "Excelsior" mosaic works have been done at many of the principal buildings in India, including the Presidency General Hospital, Medical College Hospital, Lady Dufferin's Victoria Hospital, Eden Hospital, Campbell Hospital, Imperial Library, the Foreign and Military Offices, the palace of the Lord Bishop of the Diocese, the General Post Office, High Court, Paper Currency Office, His Majesty's Mint, the palaces of H.H. the Governor of Bengal and H.H. the Maharaja of Nattore, Writers' Building in Calcutta, Pilgrim Hospital at Puri, the Curzon Hall at Dacca, the palaces of the Bettiah Raj at Bettiah, the palace at Dacca of the late Governor of Eastern Bengal, General Hospital at Howrah, East Indian Railway stations, and at the Bengal-Nagpur Railway new station at Howrah.

A large supply of marble is kept in stock at the firm's workshops, godowns, and showrooms in Watkins Lane, and the daily output of their well-known manufactures has reached very large dimensions, owing to the first-class quality of materials and to the exceedingly satisfactory manner in which commissions are executed.

The telegraphic address is "Acerboni, Watkins Lane, Howrah."

F. ACERBONI & CO.

1. THE FACTORY AT HOWRAH. 2. MOSAIC WALLING BY F. ACERBONI & CO. AT DUNCAN BROS. & CO.'S BUILDING, CLIVE STREET, CALCUTTA.

AHMUTY & CO.

"The original ship-chandlers of the East" is the designation by which the old-established and reputable firm of Messrs. Ahmuty & Co., of 6 Church Lane, Calcutta, is widely known. The title is pregnant with meaning when it is remembered that the firm have been in existence since the memorable year of Waterloo, and that in those days sailing ships, after long and tedious voyages from England by way of the Cape, depended largely upon Calcutta for stores, and occasionally equipment, before they could set forth on their return journeys.

Imperial troops were being conveyed to the Old Country about this time, and contracts for provisioning the men were entrusted to Messrs. Ahmuty & Co., who forthwith established a bakery and distillery for the supply of biscuits and rum respectively, and the factories were known by the name of "The Albion Works."

What a history is wrapped up in these hundred years! "Wind-jammers" are rarely seen to-day; Calcutta is now a huge city with extensive dock accommodation, and not a mere settlement on the muddy banks of the Hooghly as it was then; and the small ship-chandlery store opened by Messrs. Ahmuty & Co. has grown into one of the most important trading establishments in India.

The firm had the valuable support of the East India Company, which was a substantial asset to a newly started business, and from that time to the present (April 1916) the transactions of the century reveal a record of uninterrupted progress.

Briefly, Messrs. Ahmuty & Co. may now be described as engineers, machinery, metal, and hardware merchants, Government and railway contractors, ships' chandlers, general storekeepers, suppliers of rum, spirits of wine, and Indian condiments, and contractors to His Majesty's Royal Indian Marine Dockyard, the Ordnance Department, Arsenals, Indian Government factories, the Supply and Transport Departments, State railways, steamship companies, jute, cotton, and saw-mills, and tea and indigo factories.

A special feature is made of the supply of manila, coir, cotton, and wire ropes, paulins, ships' composition, waterproof and rot-proof canvas, paints, oils, fine varnishes, enamels, cement, signal lamps, rockets, blue lights, fog-signals, wood-working machinery, lathes, drilling machines, and practically all engineering requirements.

The agencies held by the firm are of a very important character, and include: The Silicate Paint Company and Messrs. Colthurst and Harding, of London, for varnishes and paints; Messrs. Storry, Smithson & Co., Ltd., of Hull, for protective compositions for the bottoms of ships; Messrs. Hamilton & Co., of London, for paint brushes and sash tools; Messrs. W. B. Brown & Co., of Liverpool, for steel wire ropes for hauling or mining purposes; Messrs. Platts and Lowther, London, for packings; Messrs. Crawshaw & Sons, Dewsbury, for belting for mills; the Willesden Paper and Canvas Works, Ltd., London, Messrs. Samuel Wills & Co., Ltd., Bristol, Messrs. Pinchin, Johnson & Co., London, for paints and enamels; and Messrs. John Pickles & Son, Hebden Bridge, England, for saw-mill and wood-working machinery.

The manager, Mr. C. F. Jordan, has

AHMUTY & CO. (THE SHALIMAR ROPEWORKS).

1. The Head Office. 2. A Portion of the Shalimar Ropeworks. 3. House-Rope Machine Room.

AHMUTY & CO. (THE SHALIMAR ROPEWORKS).

1. THE ROPE WALK. 2. SPINNING ROOM. 3. PREPARING DEPARTMENT. 4. ENGINE ROOM. 5. COIR OPENING.

been connected with Messrs. Ahmuty & Co. for a very lengthy period, and his practical experience, combined with personal attention, is an ample guarantee that the requirements of customers will receive the utmost consideration.

THE SHALIMAR ROPE WORKS

It is somewhat curious to notice that many important firms in Calcutta are unable to produce authentic records of their early history when Calcutta was "in the making," but this is no fault of the proprietors, as there have been two deadly enemies at work, namely, fire and white ants. The Shalimar Rope Works, as a case in point, were established many decades ago, but old documents and books were destroyed, and definite information can only be obtained from the time when Messrs. Ahmuty & Co., of 6 Church Lane, Calcutta, came into possession of them, about the year 1850.

The ropery is situated at Howrah, on the western bank of the River Hooghly, near to the beautiful Botanical Gardens. Between the years 1905 and 1906 the premises were entirely rebuilt and refitted with modern rope-making plant, and new engines and boilers of the latest type, which were obtained from the well-known firm of Messrs. Fairburn, Lawson, Coombe, Barbour, Ltd., of Leeds and Belfast. With such an equipment as this the proprietors are justified in their contention that one of the largest and most complete roperies in the East is to be found at the Shalimar Works.

Nearly all the ropes manufactured in Calcutta are made from Manila, New Zealand, or country-grown hemp, from sisal or aloe fibre, and from coir, and each rope when completed is coiled neatly, packed, and then sent to the weighing-room to be scaled, and subsequently dispatched to its destination.

Some interesting figures may be given here as to the breaking strains of Manila cordage: a rope having a circumference of 2 in. yields to a pull of 1 ton 4 cwt., and a 10 in. one withstands 30 tons; while a 16-in. cable will not snap under 76 tons.

Contracts are held for the annual supply of Manila and country hemp, coir and wire ropes and lines to the Indian Government Dockyard, the Ordnance and Supply and Transport Departments, to Arsenals and the Indian Government factories, State railways, and steamship and other companies; but products are also consigned to Burma, the Straits Settlements, Siam, Java, Borneo, Sumatra, Hong Kong, the Philippine Islands, Karachi, Bushire, Aden, Australia, New Zealand, and South and East Africa.

The paulin factory, situated on the premises of the rope works, has for many years supplied goods to Government departments, State railways, and factories and steamship and other companies, but there is a very large demand from private firms in the principal cities and towns of India. English canvas is used for these covers, which are dressed with a patent preparation in black, blue, green, khaki, or red colours, which are guaranteed to be free from adhesiveness in sunshine or rain, and also from any matter likely to cause spontaneous combustion. Tar was formerly used to render such sheets waterproof, but that substance was discarded owing to its viscid qualities, and the composition just referred to was substituted.

Other products of the factory are tents, awnings, boat and wagon covers, *purdahs*, and screens.

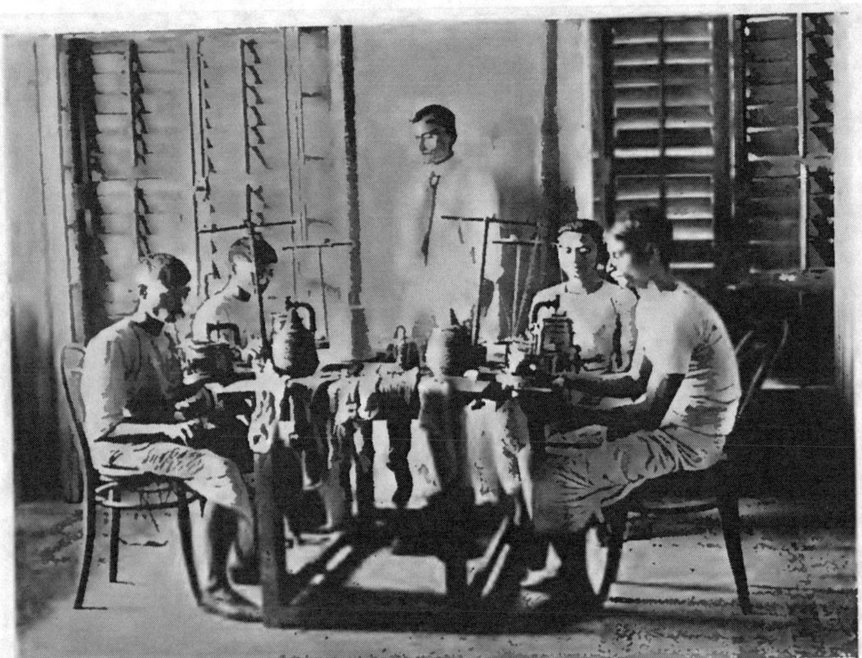

THE ALL-INDIA HOSIERY CO. (F. L. HARCOURT).
WORKING ON HAND MACHINES.

THE ALL-INDIA HOSIERY MANUFACTURING COMPANY

It is an undoubted fact that India has throughout a long period of years been importing necessaries as well as luxuries when she herself might have manufactured them from the wealth of raw material within her own borders, and it is satisfactory to note that interest has lately been aroused in the promotion of industries which will present good investments for capitalists, and will find profitable occupation for thousands of her population.

What are known as "cottage" industries have had a distinct check placed upon them by the introduction of machinery, but on the other hand it has been shown that it is possible for families to produce practically everything required for their own homes and thus become self-supporting.

The manufacture of hosiery and underwear is an imported industry, but special machines have been introduced into India for use in factories and schools and in private houses, with the result that a very large number of articles are now being knitted and placed upon the Indian market where ready sales are effected. The All-India Hosiery Manufacturing Company, of 11/1 and 11/2 Lindsay Street, Calcutta, have introduced very efficient hand-knitting machines, and they have supplied more than a thousand of these in various parts of the country from Tinnevelly to Peshawar.

During the year 1916 more than 500,000 pairs of socks were manufactured for the company on those machines, while thousands of other pairs were disposed of to local traders. The company keep a large number of these machines on their premises, and they are prepared, at a moment's notice, to send out trained workmen for the equipment of large or small factories. The hand machines are so simple that even children can quickly learn the art of knitting, and it may be added that a number of them are now in use in schools for the deaf and dumb and blind in Calcutta and other cities. Expert knitters can in their own homes earn Rs. 50 or Rs. 60 monthly, while capitalists may secure a good return upon their investments from the manufacture of all kinds of underwear, *banians*, sweaters, neckties, gas mantles, and other articles.

The company are agents in India for general goods of all kinds, including agricultural and other machinery and implements, electrical goods, hardware, metals, windmills, lamps, fans, motor-cars and cycles, leather goods, harness, saddles, wearing apparel, clocks, watches, musical instruments, and boots and shoes.

The telegraphic address of the company is "Bobbins," Calcutta.

THE ALLIANCE JUTE MILLS COMPANY, LTD. (BEGG, DUNLOP & CO.).
1. SOUTH MILL ENGINE, 2,200 H.P. 2. OVERHEAD-TANK FOR FILTERING DRINKING WATER.

ALLIANCE JUTE MILLS COMPANY, LTD.

This company was formed towards the end of 1895 by Messrs. Begg, Dunlop & Co., of 12 Mission Row, Calcutta, who conduct the affairs of the company as its managing agents.

The original mill, containing a full complement of all classes of preparing and finishing machinery and three hundred looms, was built during 1896, and completed in time to allow manufacturing to be commenced in May 1897. Subsequent extensions and the building of a second mill in 1904 have brought the property up to a spinning power of 22,459 spindles and 1,073 looms, with buildings capable of accommodating 200 more looms and other necessary machinery. The daily out-turn of the mill is 100 tons of manufactured cloth, equalling 270,000 yards, with sewing machines equal to the production of 120,000 bags per day.

The power for driving the machinery is generated by three compound condensing steam engines developing 4,400 i.h.p., and the steam is raised by two batteries of ten and nine boilers respectively. There is electric lighting throughout, the company having its own generating plant.

The repair shops are well equipped with up-to-date tools, including gear-cutting and milling machines, power hammer, and other plant, and there is also a foundry with a cupola capacity of 4 tons of molten metal per hour. The mill buildings and warehouses are protected against fire by a complete installation of "Grinnell" automatic sprinklers, chemical extincteurs, and the necessary buckets to meet the requirements of the fire insurance offices. A hydrant service of eighty-one stand-pipes surrounds the mill buildings, and is fed by three large steam pumps, drawing a practically unlimited supply from the mill tanks, which can be readily replenished from the River Hooghly. In addition twenty-four hydrants are distributed in the coolie lines.

The warehouses for carrying stocks of raw jute have a capacity of 3,678,375 cub. ft., and there are also two large warehouses, fitted with travelling cranes, for accommodating bales of manufactured goods awaiting shipment.

THE ALLIANCE JUTE MILLS COMPANY, LTD. (BEGG, DUNLOP & CO.).

1. OFFICE. 2. NORTH FACTORY. 3. AVENUE.

THE ALLIANCE JUTE MILLS COMPANY, LTD. (BEGG, DUNLOP & CO.).

1. Yarn Pressing. 2. Looms. 3. Hydraulic Press, also War Bags and Trusses, each containing 250 British War Bags. 4. Sewing Shed, with War Bags.

A water filter plant of 40,000 gallons per hour capacity supplies the residents in the compound, the coolie lines, and the immediate neighbourhood with a plentiful supply of pure drinking water.

A dispensary, free to all workers, is under the charge of a qualified medical officer and compounder, and there is an operating theatre where first aid can be given in cases of accidents, while sanitary arrangements are provided in four large septic tank latrines, the filters of the installations being automatically fed by revolving spreaders.

Other buildings consist of a central office, dwellings for the European staff, a block of houses for Indian clerks, and 1,025 brick-built huts for mill coolies. The Indian establishment consists of over 6,400 workers.

The property consists of 61 acres of land abutting on the River Hooghly at Jagatdal, Shamnagar, in the District of Twenty-four Pergannas, Bengal, and is 22 miles distant by road from the city of Calcutta. Two railway sidings connect the property with the main line of the Eastern Bengal Railway, by which route all coal required and the greater part of the mills' requirements in raw jute come forward, while, owing to inter-railway running, a direct route is available for the dispatch of goods to any part of India served by a railway system. For the dispatch of goods for export from Calcutta the company has two loading berths on the river, and they own a fleet of sixteen 50-ton cargo boats and a powerful steam tug for conveying the goods by river to the side of the export vessel. Raw jute is also transported by the river routes.

The managing agents are assisted in the conduct of the company's business by a staff of Scotsmen, consisting of a commercial manager and assistant, a mill manager, two assistant managers, three clerks, two engineers, and eighteen departmental overseers and mechanics.

It may be incidentally mentioned that this company have been largely employed in the manufacture of sand and other bags for the Allied Governments during the prosecution of the great European War.

ALLEN, BERRY & CO.

The history of this firm, who commenced business some years ago as general engineers at Behala, a suburb of Calcutta, is a record of consistent development, due to the impetus given to mechanical enterprises by the firm grip which the motor industry has obtained in commercial circles throughout the world. Motor-cars and cycles are seen in increasing numbers in our streets, and their advent has changed the whole character of the majority of the engineering workshops in this and other countries.

Mr. P. Gibson became proprietor of the concern in 1910, and he removed the factory to Ballygunge, where repairs to motor vehicles were made a special feature, although a commodious garage was at the same time opened in Wellesley Street, Calcutta. It was subsequently found that the latter site possessed superior advantages for the conduct of business, and the owner thereupon enlarged the garage, and removed all his machinery and plant to the city premises. During the next three years progress was so rapid that greater building accommodation became a necessity, and a large depot was accordingly secured in Free School Street, where additional machinery and a complete oxy-acetylene welding plant were installed.

About the close of the year 1913 Mr. Gibson keenly felt the enormous responsibilities which he had to bear, and, with the view of a division of the burden, he admitted into partnership Mr. J. A. Thomson, who had been connected with the Dunlop Motor Company, of Kilmarnock, Scotland.

A very extensive repairing connection was then established, and, in response to repeated inquiries for new cars, it was decided to open showrooms in a central portion of the city. Suitable premises were therefore erected on a prominent position in Park Street in the year 1914, and the firm then became agents for the Hillman Motor Car Company, Ltd., of Coventry, the Palladium Autocars, Ltd., of London, the Cadillac Motor Company, Ltd., of Detroit, the James Motor Cycle Company, of Birmingham, and the Saxon Motor Company, of Detroit, who build comparatively low-priced two-seater cars, which, with their special qualifications of cantilever springing and high ground clearance, have proved to be particularly suitable for the apologies for roads in the mofussil.

These agencies necessitated a further extension of the Park Street building, and accommodation was also found for a separate department for painting and coach repairs, which had hitherto been done by sub-contractors.

The workshops—and especially the repairs branch—are under the direct supervision of thoroughly trained European motor engineers, and it is believed that the firm have as large a percentage of competent overseers as any other firm in the East.

Towards the close of the year 1914 the oxy-acetylene welding branch had grown to such an extent that it was made a separate concern by the formation of a private limited liability company, the shareholders comprising the partners of the firm and a few personal friends.

Since the establishment of the Oxy-Acetylene Welding and Metal Cutting Company, Ltd., a large number of important cutting and welding contracts have been entered into, among which may be mentioned the work done for the Lower Ganges bridge at Sara.

Special attention is devoted to repairs to broken machine parts, including intricate castings, such as motor-car cylinders and aluminium crank-cases, and, in order that repairs to boilers and ships may be undertaken, the services of a competent European welder have been obtained.

Owners of mills and factories now realize that, by the aid of oxy-acetylene blowpipes, broken machinery can be repaired at a fraction of the cost of a new part, and with the saving of an enormous amount of valuable time.

A considerable business is done by the firm in the importation of carbide of calcium for oxy-acetylene welding and lighting purposes.

ANDERSON WRIGHT & CO.

This firm of general merchants and agents, with offices at 22 Strand Road, Calcutta, carry on an extensive inland and foreign trade in the export of general merchandise and produce of India, and in the importation of various descriptions of hard and soft goods from Europe.

They are managing agents for the Khardal Coal Company, Ltd., Bokaro and Ramgur, Ltd., and the Central Kurkend Company, Ltd., and are agents for the Alliance Assurance Co., Ltd., the Commercial Union Assurance Company, Ltd. (marine department), the West Presses, Sulkea, and the Natal Direct Line of steamers.

Their correspondents in London are Messrs. Clarke, Wilson & Co.

THE ANGLO-SWISS WATCH COMPANY

The most remarkable success has attended the efforts of Mr. E. O. Gam-

ALLEN, BERRY & CO.

1. PARK STREET SHOWROOMS. 2. INTERIOR, PARK STREET SHOWROOMS. 3. THE WORKSHOPS, FREE SCHOOL STREET.
4. INTERIOR VIEW OF WORKSHOPS, FREE SCHOOL STREET.

meter, the proprietor of the Anglo-Swiss Watch Company since he commenced business at 4 Dalhousie Square, Calcutta, in the month of October 1909. Little more than seven years ago he occupied one small room, and being fortunately well-equipped with necessary tools and up-to-date appliances for the watchmaking trade, and possessing an indomitable spirit enabling him to overcome difficulties, he soon proved himself to be a man who was confident that his practical experience in his own line of business would eventually be widely recognized by the inhabitants of the city.

Four assistants provided all the help that Mr. Gammeter required in those days, but no better proof can be given of the immense expansion of the business than to point to the fact that employment is now found for about fifty Indian workmen and clerks and some ten European assistants.

All employees are of the highest ability in their respective grades, and expert Europeans supervise all work carried out on the premises, whether it be the oiling and cleaning of an ordinary timekeeper or the manufacture of a wheel or some other intricate piece of mechanism of the most delicately made watch. The watch-making department is fitted with up-to-date labour-saving appliances, and that important work, as well as the execution of repairs, is either personally executed or is controlled by highly qualified Europeans who hold diplomas for conspicuous skill in both theoretical and practical knowledge.

The company's claim to be the largest importers of watches and clocks in the East is not difficult to be understood when one sees the huge stock of all classes of goods which they always maintain, and is, further, made acquainted with the very wide area of the firm's activities.

As wholesale watchmakers and jewellers they supply more than five hundred European and Indian firms in the trade with their requirements, while their business connections extend throughout the whole of India, as well as in Burma, Ceylon, the Straits Settlements, Java, Sumatra, and even as far as British East Africa.

A special feature is made of the "Cavalry" lever wrist watch, which has made a coveted name for itself in the East as a reliable, durable, accurate, and distinctly serviceable timekeeper. These watches have recently been provided with "Tropical" non-oxidising silver cases, guaranteed not to become black, even in India, where the climate plays havoc with the best silver of the ordinary kind. The company are patentees and sole manufacturers of the "Novelty," "Simplex," and "Saddle Novelty" wrist watch bands.

The jewellery manufacturing department is a comparatively new venture, but it is already full of promise of success, and the most intricate and frail pieces of plain gold and gem-set jewellery (hitherto obtained from Birmingham or the Continent of Europe) is being manufactured by the company in their workshops by highly skilled Indian workmen under the supervision of a European lapidarist.

The company have been compelled to enlarge their accommodation from time to time, and although the floor space occu-

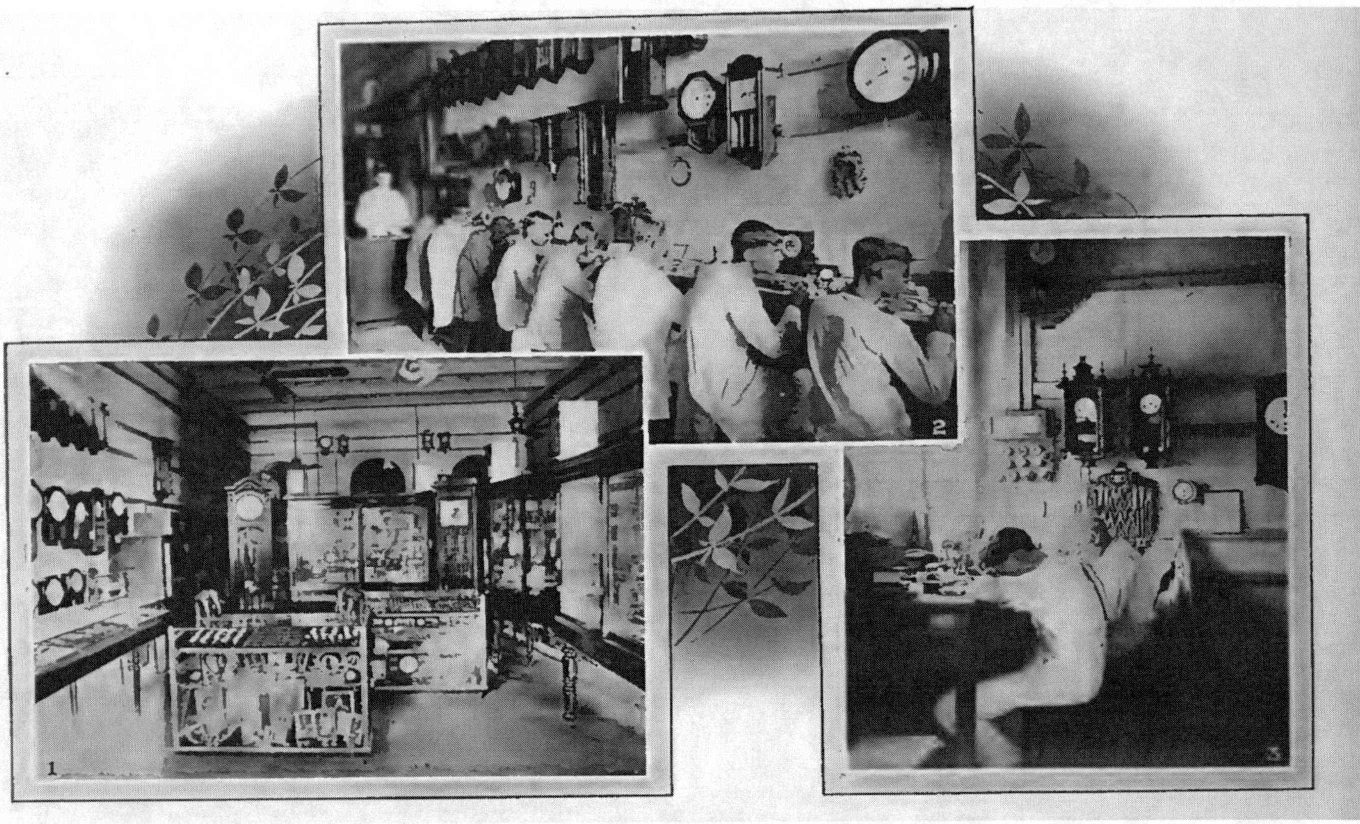

THE ANGLO-SWISS WATCH COMPANY.

1. A Portion of the Showroom. 2. A Corner of the Indian Watchmaking Section.
3. Where the most Frail Parts of a Watch can be Manufactured.

pied by offices, show, and workrooms to-day is fully twelve times greater than in 1909, the need for further room is keenly felt by the proprietor, and it cannot be long before he will be under the necessity of meeting this deficiency.

The home offices and factory of the company are at Quartier de l'Industrie, Soleure, Switzerland.

GEO. BEAVER & CO.

This firm was established in Calcutta in the year 1899 by Mr. Geo. Beaver and Mr. J. N. Vinall, who commenced trading as importers of every description of india-rubber goods for mechanical purposes, hoses, tubings, packings, beltings, and railway, shipping, colliery, mills, and general engineering requisites. Mr. Beaver retired from the firm in 1910, and the business was continued by Mr. Vinall and Mr. D. A. Dalling until the death of the former in March 1914, since which date Mr. Dalling has been sole proprietor.

The firm are the largest independent importers of rubber goods in Calcutta, and their reputation is such that their regular customers now include various Government departments in India and Burma, the principal railway systems, shell and arms factories, jute and other mills, collieries, municipalities, and district boards.

Messrs. Beaver & Co. have been nearly twenty years in the Indian market, and they have made the best possible use of their experience, with the result that the quality of their wares is such that the peculiarly trying climatic conditions of the East have no deteriorating effect upon them.

A special feature is made of vulcanized indiarubber and canvas hose, air and water valves, and "Karmal" high-pressure packing for steam power service from 80 to 120 lb. The firm's stores and godowns, situated behind their offices, carry a very large stock of imported goods, and a cursory inspection reveals a marvellous display of manufactures of first-class quality.

One notices concentric ring springs, wagon, Board of Trade regulation and other buffers; solid indiarubber mats for hotels, mansions, public buildings, steamships, railway saloons, carriages, and cabs; matting for staircases; specially hardened solid rubber tyres; tubing for acids and other chemicals; armoured and plain delivery hose, seamless woven canvas hose for use in mills, brass hose fittings, including branches, taps, cones, couplings, and rings; sheet indiarubber; and asbestos millboard, gaskets, fibre, block packing, woven tape, and thread and cord.

A brief reference should be made to the "Karmal" engine packing, which withstands the highest pressure of steam, and, being a self-lubricating substance, it does not require oil, tallow, or any other kind of grease.

Messrs. Beaver & Co. also supply best English leather belting, oak tanned and well shrunk, woven hair, cotton, laminated and other beltings suitable for jute mills, brattice cloth, and cast-steel hooks and eyes.

One must not overlook Bishop's adamant gauge glasses, which will resist the highest steam pressure, the greatest

GEORGE BEAVER & CO.

1. Exterior of the Premises. 2. A Portion of the Warehouse.

THE BENGAL TELEPHONE COMPANY, LTD.

1. Operators' Retiring Room. 2. Exchange. 3. Test Room.

heat, and all variations of temperature. Testimonials as to their superiority over all others have been given by the Admiralty authorities at the Royal Dockyard, Portsmouth, Messrs. Vickers Sons & Maxim, Ltd., and by several commanders and engineers of the leading shipping companies of the world.

Mr. Dalling has the management of the business in his own hands, and he employs three European assistants and a large number of Indian labourers.

THE BENGAL TELEPHONE COMPANY, LTD.

The Bengal Telephone Company, Ltd., was formed in the year 1883, with registered offices at 7 Council House Street, Calcutta. The paid-up capital at that time was Rs. 8,80,000, but in 1911 this was increased by the issue of new shares to Rs. 10,00,000, and, in addition, debenture loans amounting to Rs. 7,50,000 have been issued. The authorized capital was enlarged in 1914 to the extent of Rs. 10,00,000, of which sum one-half was issued to members of the company. The whole of the company's plant has been selected with the greatest care, and there is nothing of a modern character in connection with cables, fittings, and other appliances which has not been secured, provided it is suitable for Indian requirements. The service is metallic circuit underground, and the efficiency with which it has been laid is proved by the fact that the system is being largely extended in order to meet the ever-increasing demand by residents in suburban districts for telephonic connection with the city.

In order to illustrate this growth it may be said that on June 30, 1915, there were 4,607 exchange and private lines in operation, whereas in the year 1901 the number was only 800. The company are holders of a new licence for a period of sixty years, which was granted by the Government of India on April 1, 1903.

In addition to the very large number of installations in private and public buildings which have been undertaken by the company, it may be added that they have also provided and maintain the police and fire alarm systems in and around Calcutta.

The directors are Mr. Shirley Tremearne (chairman), Messrs. S. C. Berridge, A. E. Mitchell, and J. B. Saunders.

BIRKMYRE BROTHERS (HASTINGS JUTE MILLS)

These mills, situated at Rishra, near Calcutta, of which Birkmyre Brothers, 6 Clive Row, Calcutta, are the proprietors, were established in 1874 by Messrs. William and Adam Birkmyre. They had owned a small jute works, called the Greenock Sacking Company, in Lyndoch Street, Greenock, driven by a water turbine. Foreseeing the development and future importance of the jute manufacturing industry in Bengal, they decided to dismantle the works and transfer their entire machinery to Calcutta for re-erection on the banks of the Hooghly.

The machinery of the Greenock Sacking Company was therefore installed in the buildings prepared at Rishra, and the new works were named the Hastings Jute Mills from the circumstance of the land having formerly belonged to Warren Hastings, as evidenced by two leases, forming part of the title-deeds, which bear his signature and seal in a perfect state of preservation.

Messrs. William and Adam Birkmyre associated with them, in the new undertaking, their brothers Henry and John, and founded in Calcutta, simultaneously with the starting of the new jute mills, the now well-known firm of Birkmyre Brothers.

The Hastings Jute Mills prospered from the start. In 1893 the plant had been increased to over 500 looms, with other machinery in proportion. Electric lighting was in that year installed, and from 1894 to 1904 the works were run at night by artificial light, the average working time being about 22 hours per diem. It was the first Indian jute mill to have electric lighting introduced, and the only one that attempted working at night, but labour difficulties occurring in 1904 compelled the cessation of this practice.

The proprietors of the Hastings Jute Mills then proceeded further to enlarge the mill and factory, at the same time discarding the old steam-power engines, replacing them by electric generators driven by steam turbines, giving about 4,000 h.p. There is, at date, a perfectly equipped factory of 1,050 looms, with the relative preparing, spinning, and finishing machinery, all electrically driven.

There is in addition to the manufacture of jute, a separate department at Hastings Mill for making up all descriptions of canvas and waterproof paulins, kit bags, and other military equipment, the well-known Birkmyre patent waterproof canvas being now extensively used by the Indian Government for military, postal, and other purposes.

Connected with this department there is special machinery for weaving and preparing the "Hastings" camel-hair and cotton-belting, which commands a ready and steadily increasing sale throughout India.

In the Calcutta office, Messrs. Birkmyre Brothers, in addition to managing the Hastings Jute Mills, direct jute buying agencies in Naraingunge, Sharishabari, Northern Bengal, Purnea, and Jessore, for the purchase of the raw material for the Hastings mills. There are also the canvas and belting, the gunny export, and the piece goods departments, which have been established for some years. Recently Messrs. Birkmyre Brothers have given their attention to the baling of their own marks of jute for export to Dundee and the Continent, and they have already been successful in introducing these to the favourable notice of spinners.

The telegraphic address of the firm is "Birkmyres," Calcutta.

BIRD & CO.

This firm, which was originally founded some sixty years ago by the late Mr. Samuel Bird, associated later with his brother, Mr. Paul Bird, may justly claim to have taken a prominent part in the development of local industries on the eastern side of India. The present partners are Sir Ernest Cable, Mr. W. A. Ironside, Mr. B. A. White, Mr. J. Bell-Robertson, Mr. H. M. Peat, and Mr. H. F. Wheeler.

For several years after its establishment the firm's main business was the supply of labour, but later, and notably since 1885, many other and various enterprises have been progressively taken up and pushed until the present time, when its management and operations extend to the following concerns and businesses: Contractors for the supply of labour for the loading and unloading of goods at docks, railways, and warehouses; controlling agencies of collieries, with an annual output of 1,500,000 tons; controlling agencies of jute mills, aggregating 5,981 looms and 122,021 spindles, with a daily output of 450 tons, or 1,500,000 yards; jute baling, raw jute exports, manufactured jute exports, raw hides and skins exports and semi-tanned leather exports, general produce exports, timber import and exports, woollen manufacture, metal-

THE BENGAL TELEPHONE COMPANY, LTD.

1. Portion of Main Distributing Frame. 2. Repair Shop. 3. Workshop.

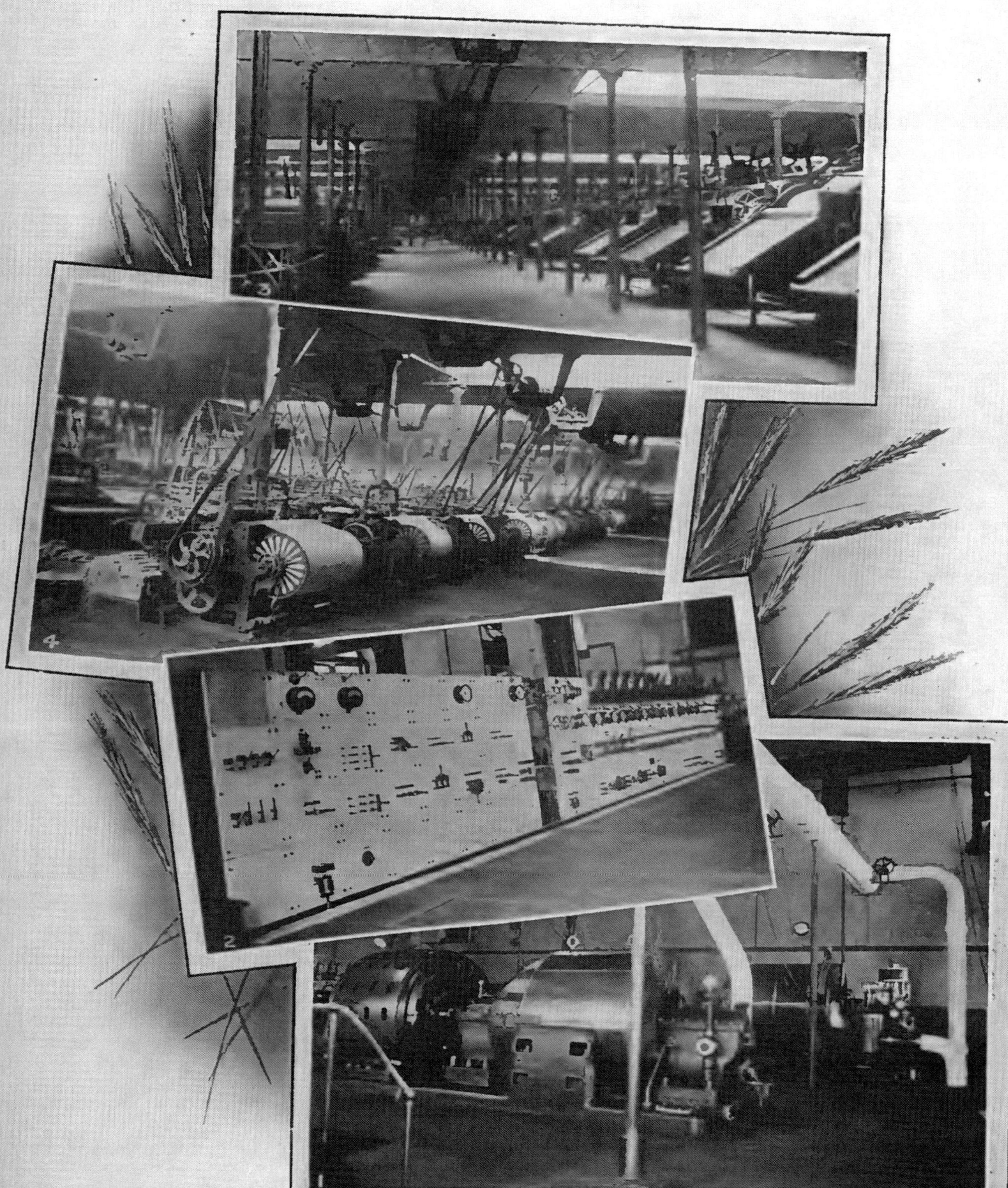

BIRKMYRE BROTHERS.

1. Nos. 1 and 2, Turbo Generators. 2. Main Switchboard. 3. Batching and Preparing. 4. Weaving Department.

BIRD & CO. (INDIAN PATENT STONE COMPANY, LTD.).

1. General View. 2. Oscillating Tables and Concrete Mixer. 3. Crushing Mills. 4. Armoured Tubular Flooring (Tube Department). 5. Reinforced Concrete (Stone Department).

BIRD & CO. (CROWN WOOLLEN MILLS).

1. Crown Woollen Mills. 2. Carding and Weaving Room. 3. Spinning Room.

BIRD & CO. (LAWRENCE JUTE MILL).

THE LAWRENCE JUTE MILL.

liferous mining, engineering works, electric power supply, regenerative coke oven and by-product manufacture, pottery, etc., manufacture, artificial stone and ferro-concrete construction works, sanitary engineering, sawmills and veneer timber factories, limestone quarries and lime-kilns, oil mills, graphite mines, sugar factories, insurance company agencies, etc.

INDIAN PATENT STONE COMPANY

This concern, which is under the control of Messrs. Bird & Co., Calcutta, is engaged in the manufacture of artificial stone floors and floorwork in every form of moulded and concrete construction, much used in modern Calcutta dwelling-houses and mercantile premises. About 400 hands are employed, and about 1,000,000 square feet of artificial stone flooring alone is laid every year, whilst several hundred miles of pavement in Calcutta testify to its general and extensive use.

CROWN WOOLLEN MILLS

This concern is under the control of Messrs. Bird & Co., and is at present solely engaged upon the manufacture of blankets and cloth for military purposes.

LAWRENCE JUTE MILLS

One of the extensive group of mills under the control of Messrs. Bird & Co., Calcutta.

BURN & CO., LTD.

"This building was the town residence of Warren Hastings, Governor-General of Fort William in Bengal 1774-85."

These words are inscribed on a mural tablet on the offices of the well-known firm of Messrs. Burn & Co., Ltd., in Hastings Street, Calcutta, and in Blechynden's work on "Calcutta Past and Present" the following paragraph occurs: "Mrs. Hastings, whose 'Town House,' which she had occupied in earlier years as Mrs. Imhoff, was at No. 7 Hastings Street, where some ancient *punkahs,* quaintly painted in crimson and gold, still remain, stranded waifs of the tide of fashion which once filled the old house with its flood."

The historic residence, seen to-day, carries one's thoughts back to the period when English and French struggled strenuously for supremacy in India; it brings to mind the attack on Calcutta made in June 1756 by Suraj-ud-daulah, Nawab of Bengal; it throws on the screen the tragedy of the "Black Hole," the Battle of Plassey in 1757 when Clive avenged that disaster; and it also directs one's thoughts to the time when the firm but wise policy of Hastings contributed very largely to the ultimate peaceful state of the country. Would it be drawing too much on the imagination to suggest that these associations with a period so pregnant with possibilities for the future of India have had a stimulating effect upon those who have been engaged in that very house in the building up of the colossal enterprise now controlled by Messrs. Burn & Co.?

The founder of the business was Colonel Archibald Swinton, who, in the year 1781, established an iron foundry and other works at Howrah, which at that time was a mere settlement on the west side of the River Hooghly, immediately opposite the site which had been selected by Job Charnock, about a hundred years previously, as the place where the town of Calcutta should be built. It is unfortunate that the early records of the progress of the concern are not as complete as one would wish, but they show that the name of "Burn" appears for the first time in 1799, when Mr. Alexander Burn became chief partner, with a Mr. Currie as his colleague. The business grew at a remarkably rapid rate during following years, and many changes took place in the *personnel* of the partnership owing to death or retirement, but like the banyan-tree, which spreads by striking fresh roots, so the firm enlarged their operations by increasing the number of their activities.

The development of the agricultural and industrial resources of India was most marked in the early nineties of last century; railways were being projected; rivers had to be bridged; manufacturers required machinery of a more modern character; new ventures had to be fitted with up-to-date plant; and this firm, who had already gained a great reputation in the world of iron and steel, and determining to keep in the van in meeting these demands, formed a joint stock company in the year 1895.

The concern with which the company is most closely identified is the Howrah Ironworks, which comprise the following departments: (1) metals, machinery, and engineering stores; (2) ship-yard; (3) forge and smithy; (4) roof and light structural iron works; (5) girder shops; (6) wagon shops; (7) engine shops; (8) conservancy shop; (9) general office and accounts; and (10) costs branch. In order that an account of the magnitude of the operations of the company may be made as intelligible as possible, it will perhaps be advisable to refer to each of the above ten sections in the order in which they are placed above.

The stores and the yard connected therewith claim attention on passing through the main entrance, and the first thing to be noticed is the extensive floor area, which covers 64,800 sq. ft., and is devoted entirely to a large stock of angle bars, rounds and squares, cast iron and lap-welded steel spigot and socket pipes, while a covered rack is provided for gas and steam pipes and boring tubes. A very fine godown on the left-hand side of the stores, 220 ft. in length and 90 ft. in width, contains portable engines, oil engines, pumps, sinking and centrifugal pumps, hand pumps in endless variety, colliery winding engines of sizes from a 9-in. diameter cylinder by 18-in. stroke up to 20-in. diameter cylinder by 44-in. stroke, locomotive and vertical boilers, disintegrators, horizontal steam engines, saw benches, ice-making machines, lathes, pulley blocks, shafting, coupling, plumber-blocks, steam fittings, piles, and a sundry assortment of other manufactures too numerous to mention. Hard by is the rolled steam beam store-yard, measuring 386 ft. by 120 ft., which contains a stock of about 4,000 tons of joists, and adjoining is the store in which plates of varying lengths and thicknesses are kept. The company have special facilities for the quick dispatch of goods from this section, consisting of an electric gantry crane with a clear span of 120 ft., which runs the entire length of the yard, together with a large number of extra strong bullock carts for service between the works and railway stations.

The ship-yard has a frontage upon the River Hooghly of 750 ft., and there is ample water at high tides for the launching of vessels of very considerable tonnage, made up of all classes of steamers, launches, barges, flats, tugs, pontoons, landing stages, wagon ferries, and yachts and boats of every description, in addition to tanks, well curbs, caissons, and oil tanks. The machinery, which is thoroughly up to date in every respect, is fixed in a large shed 325 ft. in length and 100 ft. in width, and the greater portion of it is driven separately by its own engine, although other parts

BURN & CO.

1. Part of an Order for 500 Jute Wagons built for the Eastern Bengal State Railway. 2. Sitting-room of Broad Gauge Saloon Coach built for H.H. The Maharaja of Benares. 3. Bedroom, Broad Gauge Saloon Carriage built for H.H. The Maharaja of Benares. 4. Private Dining Saloon (68 ft.), Broad Gauge Bogie. Built for H.H. The Maharaja of Mysore.

BURN & CO.

1. Interior View of Carriage Repair Shop, Eastern Bengal State Railway, Kanchrapara. 2. Three-track Railway Bridge, Eastern Bengal State Railway. 3. Twin-Screw Passenger Steamer. 4. Paddle Steamer for Assam.

are grouped together and derive their motive power from a compound horizontal engine, the steam being obtained from four Lancashire boilers. As an illustration of the variety of the excellent work turned out by the company, mention may be made of some important contracts which have been carried out in this department in recent years. A large dock caisson of exceptionally strong design and of heavy scantlings has been completed for the Calcutta Port Commissioners to suit the entrance lock of the Kidderpore Docks. A pontoon 280 ft. in length and 40 ft. in width and 10 ft. in depth was built for the Bengal-Nagpur Railway Company, and this was used at first for floating heavy bridge girders into position on their piers, but after several additions had been made it became one of the landing stages of that company's wagon ferry at Calcutta. Landing stages composed of pontoons 10 ft. in width by 5 ft. in depth, and varying in length from 40 ft. to 59 ft., have been built for the Rangoon Port Commissioners, and each of the stages is connected with the shore by two bridges of 150 ft. span and a width of 12 ft. Messrs. Burn & Co. earned an enviable reputation by their construction of a number of first-class paddle steamers, among which are the ***Bassein***, 190 ft. in length, 45 ft. in breadth, and drawing 8 ft. 2 in. of water; the ***Buckland*** and ***Howrah*** (built for the Port Commissioners), designed to carry 1,200 passengers, and specially constructed with bow and stern rudders so that they can be navigated from either end; also the ***Barbara*** and ***Marjorie***, built for the Assam Bengal Railway for ferry service between Bhairab and Azimgunge. A large contract carried out successfully for the Burma Railway Company was for the building of the Henzada Wagon Ferry, which comprised four barges, two landing stages, and two pontoon bridges, together with all the shore connections, trolley girders, and other adjuncts for uniting the railway lines to the stages.

The stages and barges within a period of twelve months were built, launched, and towed by tug to Rangoon and successfully installed at Henzada, a distance of more than 800 miles. Other large wagon ferries have since been designed and constructed. These include standard and metre gauge ferries for the Eastern Bengal Railway, metre gauge ferry for the Assam Bengal Railway, 2 ft. 6 in. gauge ferry for the North-Western Railway.

There are very large tracts of land in Eastern Bengal and Assam yielding crops of jute, tea, and other produce which are many miles distant from any railway, and whose sole means of communication with the outer world is by means of numerous rivers and canals. Here, again, Messrs. Burn & Co. led the way in constructing steamers, barges, and flats for transport purposes, cargo flats, varying in length from 130 ft. to 200 ft., being towed by specially constructed twin-screw steamers along the numerous waterways and creeks. A special feature, too, is made of strongly built steam launches, in which Government officials occasionally spend some weeks when their duties call them into outlying districts, and of harbour tugs, which may be seen in nearly all Indian ports. It will be understood that, with the immense number of sea-going vessels which call at Calcutta, there must necessarily be repairs of all kinds to be effected, and Messrs Burn & Co. have been entrusted with a large number of important contracts in this line. Among these which have been successfully carried out were the repairing of the bow of the P. & O. steamer *Somali*, which was seriously damaged in collision with the s.s. *Delta* at Colombo.

Leaving the ship-yard we enter the forge and smithy. The building containing the forge and smithy is 460 ft. in length and 182 ft. in width, and it comprises more than a hundred smiths' hearths, forge, oil and coke furnaces, plate and angle furnaces, steam hammers of all sizes up to 25 cwt., Pilkington's pneumatic and hydraulic hammers, batteries of Bretts' drop stamps ranging from 7 to 30 cwt., a 15 cwt. Massey stamp, power trimming and hydraulic presses, hot saw tyre benders, steam strikers, and welding and other machines. Great attention has been paid in recent years to railway wagon forgings, and the smithy can now turn out 1,200 sets of these in a year. In this branch there is an almost endless variety of forgings for ship, engine, railway, army transport, commissariat, contractors, and irrigation work, boring tools, gates, railways, tree guards, doors, windows, lightning conductors, and other necessaries in constructional or building enterprises.

The roof and light structural department is in a building measuring 100 ft. in length and 600 ft. in width, and it is equipped with radial drills, saws, shears, and all other requisite plant and tools for securing well finished work. Messrs. Burn & Co. can point with some pride to several most important structures which have been erected by them in various parts of India, but mention need only be made of eleven roofs for the Ischapore rifle factory, the platform roofs for the remodelling of the Delhi railway station, the Manipur Durbar hall, and the immense roof over the Gautama, a reclining figure sacred to the Burmese at Pegu in Burma. Tanks for waterworks and oil installations have been erected for the Umballa, Howrah, Bhandra, Benares, and Amritsar waterworks; and oil storage tanks (with a capacity of more than four million gallons) for the Standard Oil Company and the Burma Oil Company at their Budge Budge depots.

The girder shops, which compare most favourably with similar ones in Great Britain or America, have a covered area of more than two acres, and here the visitor may observe a constant supply of raw material being landed from boats on the river, while there is at the other end of the buildings a never-ceasing output of finished constructional work which is being loaded into railway trucks for dispatch to all parts of India. Powerful cranes remove steel plates and bars from country boats and place them at the various machines. The three principal shops have twelve 10-ton electric cranes, radial drills, hydraulic portable riveters, cold saws, plate-edge planers, butting machines, and machines for notching ends of joists to fit into each other. The firm is in a position to deal with inquiries of any nature, and to give expert technical advice on the building of bridges spanning 6 ft. to 450 ft. The Diroontah suspension bridge may be mentioned to illustrate the difficult problems which have at times to be faced. This was the first steel rope suspension bridge to be erected in Afghanistan, and it spans the Kabul River at the mouth of the Diroontah Gorge, about seven miles distant from Jellalabad. This structure has a span of 306 ft., and as it is 10 ft. in width between the centres of the towers and the roadway it is suitable for light cart traffic. Other recent contracts for constructional work at Howrah include the Ganges Mill, 974 ft. in length, consisting of 3,000 tons of material; the East Indian Railway's riverside warehouse, 650 ft. in length, with 3,000 tons; the Buckland Bridge, Howrah, East Indian Railway, having spans of 75 ft., with 2,500 tons; together with truss bridges, carriage and wagon shops, piers, boiler shops, steel tube syphons, and foundry sheds and other work of a similar description.

The wagon shops have lately been remodelled, and now consist of a machine shop capable of dealing with a large number of complete sets of wagon materials per month, an underframe erection shop connected up to the machine shop by overhead electric cranes, a panel shop where all plate work is dealt with, and the wagon erection and riveting shop, painting shop, and finishing and inspection shop. The carriage shops are arranged in close proximity to the wagon department, and consist of a wood-machining shop, all the machines being electrically driven; alongside the machine shop is the finishing shop, where all work is completed on the separate parts before they are assembled.

The carriage erection shop contains space for twenty standard gauge coaches to be laid down at once. An electrically worked traverser is used for removing the coaches from the erecting shop to the painting and varnishing shop.

The output of the wagon departments consists mainly of standard gauge wagons for the State and company-owned lines. In the carriage shops besides work for State and company-owned lines very well equipped private saloons have been designed and built for the Maharaja of Mysore, Maharaja of Rewah, and the Maharaja of Benares.

From the wagon shops the visitor is conducted to the engine shops. These include the iron and brass foundries, pattern shops, smithy, turning and fitting shops. The iron foundry has three separate moulding shops, and here one sees a general class of work going through, such as bed-plates for winding engines, road rollers (5 tons in weight), engine cylinders, rope and bell pulleys, ornamental railings, water and steam pipes, and rainwater gutters. The brass foundry is a brick building fitted with all necessary tools for moulding engine and wagon bearing brasses, hydraulic ram plungers, pump valves, and other sundries. The smithy for engine shop work is equipped with steam hammers, forging furnaces, hydraulic presses and other machinery. Castings and forgings are received at the western end of the new engine shops, and after they have been marked off they are passed through the various machines towards the eastern end, where the fitting department resolves them into jute presses, winding engines, mill gearing, and other plant. A wing extends along the northern side of the shops, and this is divided on the ground floor into brass stores, tool-making shop, and offices for foremen. These shops cover an area of 52,000 sq. ft., and are the finest and most up to date of their kind in India.

The conservancy branch deals solely with the manufacture of sanitary and municipal requirements, and it is responsible for the output of a very large number of carts for night-soil, water, refuse, and other purposes, incinerators, and latrine and other fittings.

The general office is the oldest structure in the works, and many years ago it was occupied as a bungalow by some of the partners. Drawing and costs offices have been erected round the above bungalow, the whole block now covering an area of 1,480 sq. ft. The drawing office is divided into four main sections, namely, structural, mechanical, shipbuilding, and railways, and each of these sections is primarily controlled by a manager, who is also in charge of the shops to which the particular work belongs. There are about 25 European and more than 60 Indian expert draughtsmen who have specialized in their several departments, while the accounts office employs 2 Europeans and nearly 60 Indians. It will be seen from the above notes that Messrs. Burn & Co. are thorough masters of every detail of work undertaken in the Howrah Works, and are as well prepared to supply a steamer, a bridge, or a warehouse, as to hand to a purchaser a steel nut or rivet.

A reference to another section in this volume contains an account of the famous Raneegunge Pottery Works, owned by Messrs. Burn & Co., which are the most important of their kind in the East.

THE CHARTERED BANK OF INDIA, AUSTRALIA, AND CHINA

The practice of securing a Royal Charter on the establishment of banking businesses was quite a common event in the days when financial institutions of importance were rapidly coming into existence, and a certain amount of definite control of the management of their internal affairs gave confidence to investors and clients generally.

The Chartered Bank now under notice obtained Royal assent upon its foundation in the year 1853, and its headquarters were at that time situated in Hatton Court, London. The original prospectus stated that the bank was "established chiefly in order to extend the legitimate facilities of banking to the vast and rapidly extending trade between the Australian colonies, British East India, China, and other parts of the Eastern Archipelago, a field at present wholly unoccupied by any similar institution. The objects of the company will, however, also embrace in connection therewith the extension of banking accommodation to the direct trade of British India, China, and Australia with this country (England), at present so inadequately provided for." The promoters regarded this as "an ambitious programme," but it may be observed that, with the exception of the three Presidency banks, there were then only three other similar institutions in India, namely, the Commercial Bank of Bombay, the Oriental Bank Corporation, and the Agra and United Services Bank.

Initial difficulties were experienced by the Chartered Bank, partly owing to certain exacting conditions in the Charter, and in part with regard to the subscription of the necessary capital, but actual business was commenced in 1857, and in the same year offices were opened in Calcutta, Bombay, and Shanghai.

The early history of the bank is a record of unexampled prosperity, and other branches in various parts of the world were established in order to cope with the rapid advancement made in those days. These places include Amritsar, Bangkok, Batavia, Canton, Cebu, Colombo, Delhi, Foochow, Haiphong, Hankow, Hongkong, Ilo-ilo, Ipoh, and Klang (in the Federated Malay States), Karachi, Kobe, Kuala Lumpur, Madras, Malacca, Manila, Medan (Sumatra), New York, Penang, Puket, Rangoon, Saigon, Seremban (Federated Malay States), Singapore, Sourabaya, Taiping, Tientsin, and Yokohama. It will be seen from this list that India, China, the Straits, Siam, the Dutch East Indies, and Japan are brought within the sphere of the bank's operations, and as each new agency has been formed a considerable growth in business has been the result.

Banking experiences in India have not by any means been a bed of roses, as there have been financial crises which brought about the downfall of many institutions which had hitherto borne an

THE CHARTERED BANK OF INDIA, AUSTRALIA, AND CHINA.
THE CALCUTTA AGENCY.

unquestionable reputation for stability. One might mention the financial upheaval between the years 1865 and 1866 which caused six Calcutta banks to close their doors. In this disastrous period the Chartered Bank weathered the storm, although the whole of its reserve fund was swept away during the next few years. The depreciation in silver which occurred about the year 1869 was even more serious in several aspects, as undebased coinage in several countries was reduced in value by 30 or 40 per cent.

Mr. John Howard Gwyther became manager of the Chartered Bank in 1870, and by the exercise of strict economy he succeeded in paying a fair dividend two years later, and in establishing a substantial reserve fund on a new basis. The latter was built up out of profits, and not by means of premiums on new issues, a practice which was very largely indulged in by other financial institutions.

The directors exercised the greatest caution during these troublous times, and they limited all dividends to 8 per cent. until the reserve had reached an amount equivalent to half of the paid-up capital, and even 10 per cent. was not paid until the capital was equalled by the reserve. Periodical balance sheets show that returning prosperity has been gradual but sure; earnings have been increasing year by year; and so secure are the foundations upon which the bank constructed its business that it occupies at the present time a most honourable position among the leading financial institutions of the world.

A report of the directors and statements of accounts were presented at the sixty-first ordinary general meeting of shareholders held on March 31, 1915, and the following particulars have been extracted therefrom:—

The net profit, after providing for bad and doubtful debts, was £492,333, inclusive of £120,253 brought forward from the previous year. An interim dividend at the rate of 12 per cent. per annum, paid in the previous September, absorbed £72,000; £24,000 had been appropriated as a bonus to the staff; and the directors proposed to deal with the available balance of £396,333 as follows: To pay a final dividend at the rate of 16 per cent. per annum (making 14 per cent. for the year), to place £150,000 to a special fund to meet contingencies, to write off premises account the sum of £25,000, and to carry forward an amount of £125,333. The report was adopted unanimously, and the proposals of the directors were concurred in heartily.

The paid-up capital of £1,200,000 consists of 60,000 shares of £20 each, the reserve fund stands at £1,800,000, and the reserve liability account of the proprietors amounts to £1,200,000.

Fixed deposits are received by the bank for twelve months, or shorter periods, upon terms which may be ascertained on application at any of the offices. Drafts are granted payable at any of the agencies or branches, approved bills of exchange are purchased or are received for collection, letters of credit are issued, and Indian Government and other securities are bought or held in safe custody.

The London offices were some time ago found to be much too small, and a remarkably fine building was erected on the site of the once famous Crosby Hall, 38 Bishopsgate, E.C. It is situated in the centre of a large number of the leading banking houses of the metropolis, and it is not less pleasing in its general appearance or less commodious in its internal arrangements than those by which it is surrounded. It is in the Italian Renaissance style of architecture, and the Corinthian pilasters above the ground floor form a distinctive feature of its design, while the whole of the frontage is built in Portland stone with a base of Aberdeen granite. The banking hall is lofty and not less than 23 ft. in height, while an abundance of light is obtained from windows of exceptional size. This room measures 56 by 68 ft., the walls are of white marble relieved by columns and pilasters of Pavanazzo marble, and the dado consists of Vertantico marble with a black marble plinth. The security of bullion and documents is assured in the strong-room, which is not excelled by any other in London. Within this chamber is the "inner treasury," which is said by experts to be proof against any efforts of the modern burglar in the space of time that could be gained by him for his adventurous attack. The twentieth-century marauder makes use of oxy-acetylene plant for forcing his way through doors and walls, but it has been proved by the makers of this powerful apparatus that "intersected" steel (which has been used in the treasury chamber) is able to resist the severest forms in which midnight visitors prosecute their dangerous avocations.

The Chartered Bank building in Clive Street, Calcutta, is one of the most imposing structures in the East. It dominates the principal business quarter of the city, being immediately opposite the Royal Exchange.

The bankers of the company are the Bank of England, the London, City, and Midland Bank, Ltd., the London County and Westminster Bank, Ltd., the National Provincial Bank of England, Ltd., and the National Bank of Scotland, Ltd. Corresponding agents have been appointed as follows: The Bank of Australasia, the Bank of New South Wales, the Bank of Victoria, Ltd., the Colonial Bank of Australasia, Ltd., the Commercial Bank of Australia, Ltd., the Commercial Banking Company of Sydney, Ltd., the English, Scottish, and Australian Bank, Ltd., the London Bank of Australia, Ltd., the Union Bank of Australia, Ltd., the Bank of New Zealand, and the National Bank of New Zealand, Ltd.

The court of directors is composed of Sir Montagu Cornish Turner (chairman), Sir Henry S. Cunningham, K.C.I.E., Mr. Thomas Cuthbertson, Sir Henry Dent, K.C.M.G., Mr. William Henry Neville Goschen, the Right Hon. Lord George Hamilton, G.C.S.I., Mr. William Foot Mitchell, and Mr. Lewis Alexander Wallace. Messrs. T. H. Whitehead and T. Fraser are joint general managers, and Mr. H. Harris is the agent of the Calcutta branch.

CONTINENTAL HOTEL

Calcutta is not overburdened with first-class residential hotels, but there is a consensus of opinion that the premier city in India is fortunate indeed in having such an extremely comfortable and well-appointed one as the "Continental," which is situated in one of the best positions in Chowringhee, the leading thoroughfare in the city.

It has a very extensive frontage upon the *maidan*, a fine open space of nearly 3,000 acres of grass land beautifully timbered with magnificent old trees, and from its front windows excellent views are obtained of Government House, of the Curzon Gardens, of a portion of the Esplanade, of Fort William with its bastions and mounted guns, of the "Rotten Row" of Calcutta, of the charming Eden Gardens (where an efficient band plays nightly), while a long stretch of the River Hooghly with its incessant flotilla of merchant and passenger steamers and native craft of all descriptions is plainly visible.

The "Continental" practically adjoins

the principal theatres and picture houses, and carriages, cabs and taxis may be engaged on the stand immediately opposite the chief entrance.

The hotel, established in the year 1874 by Mr. F. Boscolo, was recently purchased by Mr. Makertich John, and during the short period of his tenure he has caused the house to be widely known throughout the East as one in which the owner's personal supervision and thoroughly practical experience are constantly being manifested in order to secure the entire approval of his numerous patrons.

It is a common experience of travellers in all parts of the world that railway and other guide books frequently refer to certain hotels as being unparalleled for comfort, cleanliness, exceptional cuisine, and civility of servants, while the practical experience of visitors goes to show that in the majority of instances these much-belauded houses do not offer any entertainment which can by a liberal stretch of the imagination be said to coincide with the rosy descriptions given of them.

The "Continental" at Calcutta, however, does not come in the category of those failures; Mr. Makertich John is an ideal host, the comfort of his visitors is his first consideration, and he is astute enough to know that the most reputable purveyors and the best servants are in constant need of the keenest watchfulness.

The hotel has accommodation for 140 guests, and all the rooms are elegantly furnished with modern appointments, including electric lighting and fans. Special mention should be made of a very large drawing-room, an upstairs dining-room for permanent residents, another one on the ground floor for casual visitors (these having seating room for a hundred and fifty and a hundred guests respectively), a commodious lounge suitable for receptions, public and private bars, and a billiard-room with two Burroughes and Watts tables.

Excellent arrangements are made for catering in a thoroughly up-to-date manner for picnic and wedding-parties, Lodge dinners, and banquets, while the "Continental" mid-day lunches are very rightly considered to be unsurpassed in Calcutta.

It is worthy of note that the immense frontage of the building has enabled the architect to arrange for a very large number of the bedrooms to have a full view of the *maidan* and other places of interest which have already been mentioned, and each of these rooms is provided with an electric bell, and has a separate bathroom, which is fitted with complete sanitary appliances.

Hotel runners meet all trains and steamers and visitors are attended to by a large staff of well-trained servants, who are most assiduous in their attentions.

CONTINENTAL HOTEL.

1. Continental Hotel. 2. The Café Royal.

CRAWFORD & CO.

It is not more than seven years since the firm of Messrs. Crawford & Co., general merchants, engineers, contractors, and stevedores, was established by Mr. A. F. Newell in Calcutta, but they have already become widely known on account of the large variety of the machinery, implements, hardware, and other goods supplied by them, which for sterling quality and reasonable prices cannot easily be excelled. The principal offices

CRAWFORD & CO.

1 AND 2. GOVERNMENT TURPENTINE DISTILLERY, BHOWALI. 3. A PORTION OF CRAWFORD & CO.'S CALCUTTA WAREHOUSE.

of the firm are in Clive Buildings, Clive Street, and very commodious godowns have been secured at No. 87A in the same street.

Contracts are undertaken for the building of steam launches, tugs, and barges, and most favourable quotations may always be depended upon for structural steel and ironwork of every description. Messrs. Crawford & Co. are sole agents for Messrs. James & John G. Scott, paint manufacturers, Glasgow; Messrs. Loudon Brothers, Ltd., makers of engines, boilers, and machine tools; Messrs. John Ferguson & Sons, manufacturers of painting brushes; Messrs. Binks Brothers, London, wire rope manufacturers; Messrs. Hamilton & Co., Chemical Works, Glasgow; Messrs. J. and R. Wilson & Co., Ship Stores and Export Merchants, London; and the British Anti-Fouling Composition and Paint Company, Ltd. The firm have recently secured the sole agency for Bengal and surrounding territory of the Indian Government Turpentine and Rosin Distillery, Bhowali, and hold large stocks of their manufactures in Calcutta. It would be impossible to specify even a thousandth part of the hardware and other goods which may be obtained from this firm, but reference may be made to some which are in constant demand in agricultural, shipping, and commercial centres in India.

Such a list should include traction, portable, horizontal, and other engines, bridges, cranes, Lancashire and vertical boilers, jute presses, steam excavators, iron fencing, hydraulic jacks, drilling machines, saw benches, sugar, rice, and flour mills, pontoons, steam and petrol pumps, manila, coir, and wire ropes, shafting, wrought iron tanks, weighing machines, winches, paulins, canvas, sailcloth, and numerous other sundries.

A word or two might perhaps be added with regard to the firm's agency for "Crown" brand paints of brilliant and permanent shades, which are suitable for steamers, bridges, railways, and iron and wooden buildings. The "Corona" distemper paint, too, is a most effective and durable preparation for any class of work, and it is guaranteed that it will not blister or peel off, even though brought into contact with lime.

All work undertaken by the firm is entrusted only to fully qualified artisans, and Mr. Newell gives strict personal attention to the requirements of customers.

Gunny bags, Hessian cloth, and other Indian produce are among the principal exports, and consignees may always rely upon the most favourable rates being obtained for the shipment of their goods.

S. CURLENDER & CO.
VIEW OF THE BONE MILLS.

S. CURLENDER & CO.

The use of bones for fertilizing soils has now become almost universal, and there is scarcely a single crop of cereals or legumes which does not derive very considerable benefit from a liberal dressing of this manure.

The Bengal Bone Mills, which is a private concern, was founded in Calcutta in 1897 by Messrs. S. Curlender & Co., who are the sole proprietors and who personally manage the works.

There are two separate mills with up-to-date steam-driven machinery They stand upon the bank of the company's waterway, which is an outlet from the Belliaghatta Circular Canal. One mill is used entirely for steamed and sterilized bone meal which is shipped chiefly to New Zealand and Japan, while the other is used for crushed bones and unsteamed bone meal. The crushed bones are shipped to Europe and America for manufacturing purposes, and the bone meal is used for manuring soils. The monthly output of the mills is now about 1,500 tons of crushed bones and 750 tons of meal, and constant employment is found for some three hundred hands.

CROMPTON & CO., LTD.

Electricity as a means for lighting and other purposes was practically unknown in India up to about twenty years ago when the well-known firm in England of Messrs. Crompton & Co., Ltd., established a business in Calcutta which has been instrumental in fitting up many electric installations, plant, and other appliances in the principal cities in the country. They were the first to introduce hydro-electric alternating plant, and to commence the lighting of jute and other mills by electricity; they inaugurated in India the present type of ceiling fan; and, without unnecessarily prolonging this list, it may, in a word, be said that Messrs. Crompton & Co. were pioneers with regard to electricty in this continent. Inhabitants of cities and towns clamoured for the new brilliant illuminant to supersede the gas and oil which had served them for so long in their streets and dwelling houses; factories required an improved light at looms and benches; and manufacturers recognized the fact that the cumbrous and old-fashioned machinery then in use could—with advantage to themselves—be replaced by electrically driven plant of more modern designs. Numerous contracts were taken

CROMPTON & CO., LTD.

1. Typical Generating Plant for Lighting, Traction, and Power Purposes. 2. Typical Generating Plant for Lighting, Traction, and Power Purposes. 3. Typical Central Station Switchboard. 4. Motors for Driving Rice-hulling and Polishing Machines introduced by Crompton & Co., Ltd.

in hand by the firm, and among the earlier ones were the electrification of Calcutta, Madras, Nagpur, Karachi, and Cawnpore, while they are now (1916) engaged upon similar works at Lucknow, Allahabad, and Agra. It is deserving of notice that the hydro-electric alternating plant which was put down by Messrs. Crompton & Co. at Darjeeling in the year 1903 has been in continuous work ever since.

Among other important enterprises manufactured at their workshops at Chelmsford in Essex, England. The premises of the firm at 6 and 7 Clive Street, Calcutta, have been occupied by them since the year 1910, and here they have a large staff of competent European engineers and Indian *mistries*. Other branches have been established at Bombay and Madras, but agencies have been opened in every part of the world. The head offices are at Salisbury House, London Wall, E.C.

was established in the year 1900 by Mr. R. A. Dickie, who commenced business as an importer of hardware, milling plant, and ironware of every description, but the most important branch to-day is the sole agency held for Messrs. Bullivant & Co., Ltd., of London, who are recognized throughout the world as the leading marine engineers and makers of wire ropes. This noted company are inventors and manufacturers of flexible steel wire ropes for ships' hawsers, cables, running

R. A. DICKIE & CO.

1. Head Office. 2. Bullivant's Wire Ropes being dispatched from Godown.

which have been successfully completed are: the electrification of Government rifle and ammunition factories at Ishapore and Dum Dum respectively, of several Hindu temples, of the Bengal Iron and Steel works at Kulti, in the district of Burdwan, of a completed plant at the Government gun and shell factory at Cossipore, of arc lamps on the Howrah bridge, and of the principal theatres in Calcutta. The firm have extensive godowns in which all kinds of machinery and accessories are stored, and, in fact, they keep on hand spare parts of everything connected with electric plant which may possibly be needed, all of which are

Messrs. Crompton & Co. are contractors to the Calcutta Electric Supply Corporation, the Karachi Electric Supply Corporation, Ltd., the Madras Electric Supply Corporation, Ltd., and the Nagpur Electric Light and Power Company, Ltd.

The managing agents in Calcutta are Messrs. Martin & Co., 6 and 7 Clive Street, and Mr. W. Bent, A.M.I.M.E., A.M.I.E.E., is manager.

R. A. DICKIE & CO.

This firm, whose headquarters are at Canning House, Clive Street, Calcutta, and salvage ropes, cranes, lifts, hoists, derricks, collieries, suspension bridges, cable tramways, and aerial ropeways, and they are also makers of blocks, pulleys, crab-winches, and wire rope cutting and other machineries. Bullivant's system of protecting vessels from the attack of torpedoes was invented and patented by this company, and they are, further, contractors to the Admiralty, the War and India Offices in London, the Crown Agents for the Colonies, and other British and foreign Government departments. Several of the largest vessels afloat, including H.M.S. *Thunderer* and the White Star liner *Olympic*, have been launched by Bullivant's ropes; and among many gigantic undertakings carried out by that firm the following may be mentioned : the dry dock "Dewey" was towed by means of this company's hawsers from Baltimore to the Philippine Islands; the successful salving of H.M.S. *Gladiator* in the Solent in 1908 was attributed mainly to the excellent quality of their galvanized extra flexible steel wire ropes; and the dredger *Octopus* was raised after being sunk near Bombay.

Messrs. Dickie & Co. are, further, sole agents for Messrs. Campbell, Achnach & Co., of the "Thistle" Rubber Works, Glasgow, who are manufacturers of sheet rubber asbestos packings, rubber insertions, and jointings, and a large stock of these and other goods of a similar character is always kept on hand.

"Victor" motor cycles, tyres, and other accessories are always procurable, and regular shipments from England enable the firm to compete on favourable terms with any other garage and repairing and outfitting shops in Calcutta.

Messrs. Dickie & Co. have extensive business connections with practically every engineering and milling company in Eastern Bengal, and in further pursuance of their increasing trade they have recently opened a branch establishment at 58 West Regent Street, Glasgow.

The present managing proprietor is Mr. H. Hartopp.

THOMAS DUFF & CO., LTD.

This company was formed and registered in Scotland in the year 1883, for the purpose of carrying on the business of managing agents of jute mills in India. At the present time it has under its control all the mills—seven in number—belonging to the Samnuggur Jute Factory Company, Ltd., the Titaghur Jute Factory Company, Ltd., and the Victoria Jute Company, Ltd.

The process of manufacture is practically identical in all the mills belonging to these companies, the raw material, which is chiefly obtained from Eastern Bengal, being brought down by boat or rail to the mills, where, after a careful process, it emerges in the shape of Hessian cloth, bags, and sacking goods. The produce is sent to all parts of the world, and at the present time very large quantities of British, French, and Russian bags are being turned out by these mills and delivered to the order of the British Government at a material discount on current market rates. The average output from the mills of the above three concerns is over 10,000 tons per month. Thoroughly up-to-date machinery has been installed in the mills, and some idea of the magnitude of these industrial concerns may be gathered from the fact that the monthly consumption of coal in the three mills is between 9,000 and 10,000 tons, and that more than 100 European and 31,000 native labourers are employed constantly. Each mill has its own private railway siding and its own steam-launch and fleet of boats for transport purposes, the latter being used for conveying the manufactured goods to ocean-going steamers at Calcutta.

The managing agents pay careful attention to the welfare of their employees, each mill being provided with a dispensary in charge of Indian medical officers, together with quarters for workers, with efficient sanitary arrangements, including a filtered water supply.

Each mill is within the limits of a municipality, and the children within the several areas receive free instruction in the primary schools.

The Samnuggur Company own three mills, two of which are on the left bank and one on the right bank of the River Hooghly, about 21 miles from Calcutta, and containing altogether 1,572 looms.

The company held its Forty-third Annual Ordinary General Meeting of Shareholders on March 16, 1916, when the report of the directors and statement of accounts were presented. The directors reported that the year ending December 31, 1915, opened with a healthy demand for all classes of goods, and orders continued plentiful. Although the average price per ton of the manufactured article was under the average of the preceding three years, the results were much in excess of any previous year, this being due chiefly to favourable purchases of the raw material, of which the company hold large stocks at cost prices considerably lower than current market values.

The capital consists of £300,000 in ordinary shares of £10, each fully paid, and £150,000 in 5 per cent. cumulative preference shares of £10, each fully paid. The profit for the year, including a credit balance brought forward from the previous 12 months, was £313,753. After placing £45,000 to the Reserve Fund, £30,683 towards depreciation on plant, £100,000 to Suspense Account to meet contingencies, writing off £2,818 for special replacements, and the payment of a dividend at the rate of 30 per cent. on the ordinary shares and 5 per cent. on preference shares for the year, a balance of £37,752 was carried forward.

The Titaghur Company own two large mills situated at Titaghur, about 14 miles from Calcutta, and containing altogether 1,718 looms. This company held its Thirty-third Annual Ordinary General Meeting of Shareholders on March 16, 1916, when the directors' report was submitted in terms similar to that of Samnuggur above detailed.

The capital consists of £300,000 in ordinary shares of £10, each fully paid, and £150,000 in 5 per cent. cumulative preference shares of £10, each fully paid. The profit for the year, including a credit balance brought forward, was £340,575. After placing £30,000 to depreciation on plant, £50,000 to Reserve Fund, and £100,000 to Suspense Account to meet contingencies, writing off £770 for special replacements, and the payment of a dividend at the rate of 30 per cent. on the ordinary shares and 5 per cent. on the preference shares for the year, a balance of £52,305 was carried forward.

The Victoria Company own two mills, situated at Telinipara, about 21 miles from Calcutta, and containing altogether 1,053 looms. The Thirty-third Annual Ordinary General Meeting of the Shareholders was held on March 17, 1916, when the directors' report and statement of accounts were presented.

The capital of the company consists of £200,000 in ordinary shares of £10, each fully paid, and £150,000 in 5 per cent. cumulative preference shares of £10, each fully paid. The statement of accounts showed a balance at credit of Profit and Loss of £205,181. After writing off £323 from Steam Launch and Boats Accounts, and placing £20,000 to Depreciation Account and Reserve Fund respectively, and paying a dividend of 30 per cent. on the ordinary shares and 5 per cent. on preference shares, a balance of £97,357 was carried forward.

From the foregoing particulars it will be seen that these companies, in common with other jute concerns, are enjoying the benefits of increasing and more profitable trade returns between India and other parts of the world.

THE DUNLOP RUBBER COMPANY, LTD.

Travelling in the days of our grandparents was a very different matter from taking a journey almost at the close of

THOMAS DUFF & CO., LTD.—TITAGHUR NO. 2 JUTE MILL.

1. Preparing Department. 2. Spinning Department. 3. Factory Department. 4. Sewing Department.

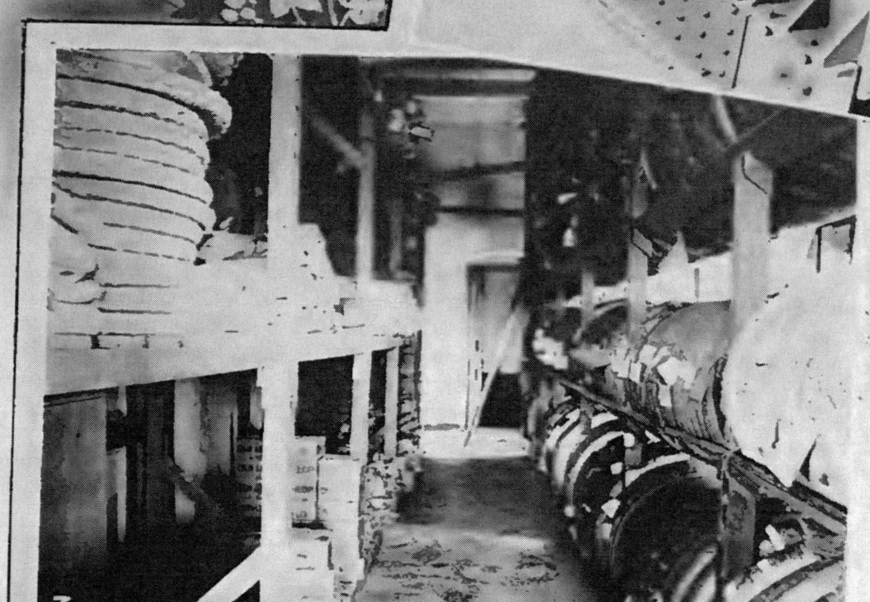

THE DUNLOP RUBBER COMPANY, LTD.

1. Exterior. 2. Solid Tyre Press. 3. Main Motor-tyre Godown.

the second decade of the twentieth century. It is perfectly safe to say that those ancestors possessed the same characteristic which is found to-day in the well-balanced minds of practically all individuals of the civilized world, namely, a desire for as much comfort as possible, but they had fewer facilities, and scarcely any of the luxuries which are now associated with trips by land or sea. The lumbering old mail or family coaches which were objects of the special attention of intrepid knights of the road, gave place to lighter-made vehicles of various descriptions, but even these conveyances were wonderfully improved about the 'eighties of last century by the fixing of india-rubber tyres on wood or iron wheels. The days of rough jolting over badly constructed thoroughfares came to an end, and the credit for perfecting, manufacturing, and inaugurating the use of pneumatic tyres for nearly every kind of vehicle is due to the Dunlop Rubber Company, Ltd.

The registered offices of the company are at 150 and 152 Clerkenwell Road, London, E.C., their works are at the Para Mills, Aston Cross, and Manor Mills, Salford Street, Aston, both in Birmingham, and at Alma Street, Coventry; and they have branch depots at Nottingham, Manchester, Newcastle-on-Tyne, Glasgow, Dublin, Belfast, Bristol, Leeds, Norwich, and Liverpool. The head offices in India are at Bombay, while branch depots have been opened at Calcutta, Delhi, Madras, and Colombo, in Ceylon.

The company are manufacturers of pneumatic and solid Dunlop cycle, motor-cycle, and aeroplane tyres, of solid band tyres, of Dunlop detachable wire wheels, steel and wooden motor wheels, rims, valves, inflators, golf balls, and sundry other goods.

The company were the founders of the pneumatic tyre industry in the year 1888, and the name "Dunlop" is inseparably connected with tyres for motor-cars or cycles of all kinds. The chief factor in the amazing progress of the company is the fact that the utmost care is always exercised throughout the whole process of manufacture in order to ensure that all products shall be free from any defect, and shall be in every way suitable for the purposes for which they are intended. The very best materials procurable are used in the works, and highly qualified employees are engaged in every branch.

A special feature is made by the company of the Dunlop grooved tyre, which was the forerunner of all the present non-skidding patterns. It is claimed that this tyre provides a cut-resisting and very durable tread, which, apart from its superiority over a plain tread in the prevention or mitigation of lateral skidding, provides a fore and aft non-skid of a very real character, as well as an extra thickness of rubber. It secures a thorough grip of roads, and this is of peculiar advantage when surfaces are greasy or when vehicles are climbing hills. The Dunlop plain tyre also commands an enormous sale, and it represents the highest grade of tyre in its least expensive form, and while it has not the special features of the grooved one, it is an excellent cover for those who do not experience the necessity for anything more than it gives. The Dunlop "Limousine" tyre, manufactured in either a grooved or plain style, is made in various sizes and of extra strength, and it is exceptionally suitable for heavy cars.

The company manufacture all descriptions of accessories, and a large stock of them is kept at their works as well as at their branches. These include forked levers, tyre manipulators, security bolts, wing nuts, leather and metal washers, spare parts of large or small valves, pump tubing and adaptors, tyre pumps and jacks, repair outfits containing every-requisite to cope with breakdowns, "Sure-patch" solutions, patches, canvas repair rolls, vulcanising material and outfit, tyre testers, cover bags, and numerous other articles.

The company have a large hydraulic press by which solid band tyres are rigidly fixed on wheels for motor lorries and other vehicles.

The directors of the Dunlop Company have always been alive to the fact that an apparently perfect tyre may, owing to new discoveries or improved methods of manufacture, be excelled in some particular, and, having acted on this principle, the goods offered by them may be guaranteed to be up-to-date in every respect.

That which has already been said in favour of the high-class tyres and accessories for motor-cars might with equal truth be applied to motor and ordinary cycle tyres and sundries. In this branch the company manufacture Dunlop "Magnum," "Roadster," "Juvenile," auto-wheel, rubber-studded, three-ribbed, side-car, combination and ribbed racing tyres, all of which are thoroughly efficient as regards anti-slipping qualities and resiliency, while experiments directed towards obtaining an extremely high degree of resistance to wear have been crowned with conspicuous success.

Spare parts and sundries, similar to those prepared for motor-cars, are also manufactured.

Re-treading and repairs of all kinds are promptly attended to by skilled artisans under thoroughly efficient supervision.

Dunlop golf balls have justly earned the highest reputation among players, and it would be difficult to find an exponent of the game who is not aware of the practically unchallenged preference for them.

It should be added that the Dunlop Company have, during the past two or three years, supplied an immense quantity of goods of all descriptions for war requirements, and although this exceptional strain has fallen with some force upon the Calcutta establishment, motor and cycle owners in Bengal have had little reason to complain that their orders have not been executed with that promptness for which the company have earned so great a reputation.

The company occupy extensive offices, store rooms, warehouses, and godowns, at 3 and 3/1 Mangoe Lane, Calcutta.

DYKES & CO., LTD.

One cannot be in the streets of Calcutta for even an hour without being impressed by the immense number of motor-cars which are seen flying along in all directions, and the mind naturally reverts to those days when—according to history—the only means of transport for either human beings or goods were of the most primitive description. From the very beginning of things, the coolie has, in India and other similar countries, been the ordinary beast of burden, and he can still hold his own in places where no wheeled vehicle could possibly travel.

Even in the year 1773 when the well-known firm of Dykes & Co., Ltd., of Calcutta, was formed by Mr. Robert Dykes, there were no carriages on the roads, and any one desiring to go on a journey of two miles or twenty had to make his choice between the box-like *palki* or the clumsy and most uncomfortable bullock cart. The first attempt to produce anything which had the slightest claim to be called an improvement was made a few years later by a Mr. Brownberry, an assistant in this firm, who designed a four-wheeled carriage which came to be known as the "Brownberry," or "office juan," and these useful, if un-

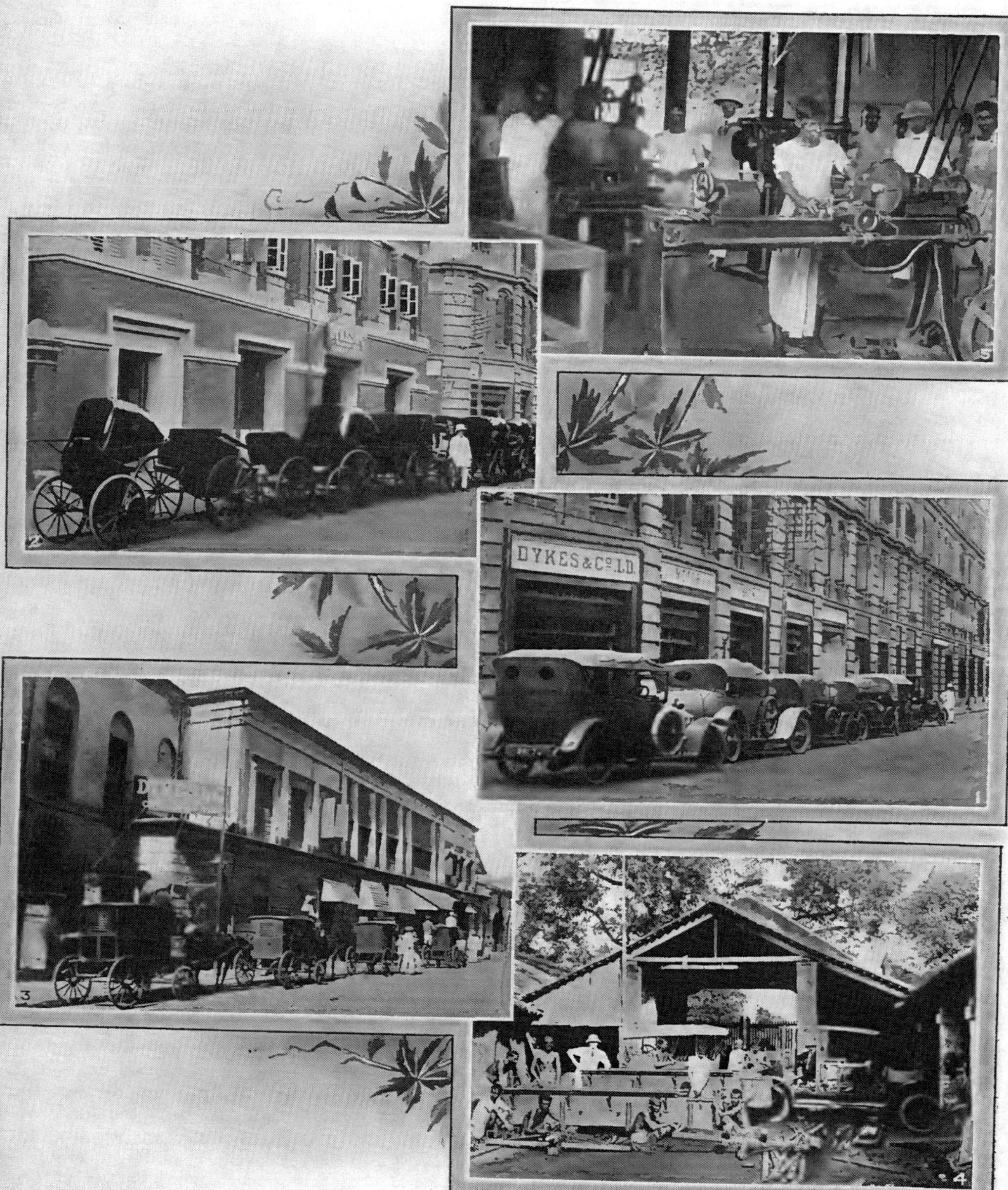

DYKES & CO., LTD.

1. Exterior of Motor Showroom. 2. Exterior of Carriage Showroom. 3. Exterior of Carriage and Motor Shop. 4. Body-building Shop. 5. Motor Engineering Shop.

attractive vehicles appear to be unlikely for some time to lose favour in Bengal.

Messrs. Dykes & Co. engaged in the building of carriages of all descriptions for a considerable number of years, new styles being introduced from time to time, and they were in the van in connection with the importation and manufacture of broughams, landaus, victorias, barouches, and phaetons, in addition to two-wheeled carts and cars such as the Norfolk, Ralli, and many others. In the year 1897, when motor-cars were first imported into Calcutta, it was suggested to Mr. Newing (since deceased), who was then head of the firm, that he should seriously take into consideration the question of entering into the motor business, but that gentleman scoffed at the idea, and said that "motors would never take the place of carriages in this country." Very few cars (and they were far from being perfect) were imported during the next six or seven years, but about the time of Mr. Newing's retirement in 1905 it was evident to intelligent men of business that, while horse vehicles would always have a place in India, motor-cars were gaining in popularity and were destined to play an important part as a means of conveyance for individuals or in the transport of merchandise. The senior partner at that time, Mr. Coward, clearly recognized the change that was taking place, and, during the time that he was on leave in England, he purchased a few reliable cars which, on their arrival at Calcutta, very quickly found customers.

One would imagine that these transactions furnished abundant proof that motor-cars had now really got a hold upon the wealthy classes of Calcutta, but one and all seemed to be imbued with the ultra-conservatism of India, and they appeared to be unwilling to give up their carriages in favour of a somewhat costly vehicle of whose management they were entirely ignorant.

About three years later, that is in 1908, Mr. Coward left India, and he was succeeded by Mr. Ferris, a keen motorist, who accepted on behalf of the firm a number of agencies for motor-cars of repute, among them being the world-renowned "Wolseley," several hundreds of which have been sold by Messrs. Dykes & Co.

A stroll through the very extensive works of the firm reveals the fact that while the carriage-building and repairing industry is still an exceedingly busy and important branch, the motor department has grown to enormous dimensions, the employees numbering some hundreds of men.

After passing through the boiler and engine houses one notices smiths, fitters and others busy as bees in their respective places, but all of them evidently keenly alive to the fact that careful and not slipshod work is expected from them.

In one shed there was a row of "Brownberrys" in various stages of construction, and, pointing to them, Mr. James, the energetic and courteous manager of the firm, said: "I do not think these carriages will ever go out of fashion in Calcutta." Farther along there were broughams, victorias, and other European types, beautifully finished and simply marvellous in the luxuriance of their appointments.

Messrs. Dykes & Co. make motor-car bodies for any description of chassis, and every detail of work, from the commencement in the engineering shops to the final touch of upholstering, is carried out on the firm's premises by thoroughly skilled workmen. A stock of 150 cars may usually be seen in the large garages and stores in Waterloo Street, and these include motors belonging to clients, in addition to a number of "Wolseley," "Vinot," "Arrol-Johnston," "Stellite," "Swift," and "Buick" cars, for all of which the firm are agents in Bengal, Bihar, and Assam.

It should be mentioned that Messrs. Dykes & Co. have supplied a large number of motor vehicles of various kinds for use in the present European War, but particular reference should be made to a wagon designed for use in the transport of munitions and stores along roads, but which forms a pontoon for the crossing of rivers as soon as the wheels have been removed and a few other slight alterations have been made.

All kinds of repairs to carriages and motor vehicles are executed by fully qualified artisans, and accessories and fittings of every description are always kept in stock.

The firm constructed a particularly beautiful royal carriage for the use of His Majesty King George V, on the occasion of the Coronation Durbar at Delhi in 1911, and the Royal Coat of Arms over the entrance to the works proclaims the fact of the patronage of the King-Emperor. The firm also hold appointments from the late Viceroy, Baron Hardinge of Penshurst, and the Governors of the several Provinces and the predecessors of these officials for many years past also conferred similar honours.

Messrs. Dykes & Co. are now a private limited liability company whose directors are Messrs. W. T. Coward, G. T. Horton, and W. Ferris, while Mr. P. James is Secretary and General Manager.

The firm have very large engineering shops in Circular Road, Calcutta, while the Waterloo Street premises are in the very heart of the city, near to Government House, and surrounded by all the leading banking and other companies.

The telegraphic address is "Dykesanko," Calcutta.

THE EAST BENGAL ENGINEERING WORKS

From time immemorial the vast waterways of Bengal have been largely used for the transfer of agricultural produce and general merchandise between Calcutta and towns and villages in the interior, and many barges, junks, and flats which were in use nearly a century ago were prototypes of some of those seen to-day, but the development of the land and of milling and other industries has necessitated the construction of larger and faster craft.

Shipbuilding yards, with their complement of iron and brass foundries and timber-sawing mills, have sprung into existence on the banks of the Hooghly in and near to Calcutta, and at the close of the year 1916 there are remarkable evidences of activity in all that concerns the supply of steam, motor, and other vessels for the conveyance of both passengers and goods.

One of these yards is owned by the East Bengal Engineering Works, who have engineering workshops, a slipway for the drawing up of boats from the river, and a thriving shipbuilding business on the Rustomjee Parsi Road, at Cossipore, some four miles from Calcutta.

The works were built in the year 1907 by Messrs. Raja Sreenath Roy and Bros., of Sova Bazar Street, Calcutta, who are the managing agents, while Mr. G. S. Thompson has held the position of superintending engineer since 1911. The shipbuilding yard is designed for the construction of all classes of river craft, including steam and motor launches and boats, cargo flats, and other vessels suitable for the very heavy traffic now carried on upon the waters of the great rivers hereinbefore mentioned.

EAST BENGAL ENGINEERING WORKS.

1. Entrance to Slipway.
2. Twin-screw Steamer, 110 ft. × 17 ft., and Cargo-flat, 150 ft. × 26 ft., under Construction on Slipway.
3. Steamer on Carriage Ready for Launching.

The workshops comprise iron and brass foundries, shops for blacksmiths, carpenters, and pattern-makers ; and the machinery—driven by steam from a boiler of 40 h.p.—consists of lathes, planes, drills, gear-cutters, shearers, grinders, punches, hammers, and other plant of the usual character.

Component parts of all kinds of structural work are manufactured in the shops, while a portion of the premises is set apart for general repairs, not only to boats, but also to machinery, motor-cars, and other steam or petrol driven vehicles. This workshop is conveniently situated in the midst of several jute presses and other factories, and has every facility for dealing with their heavy and urgent repairs.

Iron is imported from England and worked up in the foundry, and brass castings and fittings are entirely made by skilled artificers at Cossipore. Between 250 and 300 hands are in constant employment.

Enterprising companies, such as the one now under notice, have, by the conveniences they afford, rendered very great assistance by enabling agriculturists to obtain good markets for their produce by providing Calcutta and other merchants with the means of forwarding goods of all kinds to various places in the interior.

THE EASTERN BANK, LTD.

1. Exterior. 2. Interior.

THE EASTERN BANK, LTD.

The most important feature connected with this bank is the remarkable progress which has been made during the five years of its existence, and it is believed that such an advance made in so short a period is unparalleled in the history of Indian banks. The company is, without doubt, fortunate in having on its directorate several exceedingly well-known men in financial circles in England and on the continent of Europe, who, not content with being mere figure-heads, take an intelligent and active interest in concerns in which they invest capital. The chairman is the Right Hon. Lord Balfour of Burleigh, K.T., and his colleagues are Sir Jacob E. Sassoon, Bart., Messrs. G. Bromley-Martin, J. C. Georges Bouillat, Emile Francqui, J. S. Haskell, and J. Leigh Wood, C.M.G. The bank was incorporated in England, and its head offices are at 4 Crosby Square, London, E.C., with branches at Calcutta, Bombay, Bagdad, and Basra.

The fifth annual general meeting of the shareholders of the bank was held in London on March 18, 1915, when the report of the directors and the balance-sheet for the year ending December 31, 1914, were duly presented. Lord Balfour of Burleigh, in moving the adoption of the report, pointed out that the profits of the bank for the first six months of the year were most satisfactory, but that on the outbreak of war in Europe the directors and other officials had a most anxious time, as a considerable amount of produce upon which money had been advanced was shipped in German and Austrian vessels, the majority of which had either been captured by the British Navy or had been compelled to enter neutral ports, thus making it difficult to obtain delivery of cargoes. The outlook as regards the release of this temporarily locked-up capital proved to be more favourable at the date of the meeting, and the chairman added that both imports and exports had greatly improved, and he looked forward with some confidence to a period of prosperity, owing, in part, to the prospect of a record wheat crop in India between May and December 1915—estimated at from three to six million tons—which, with the high prices prevailing in Europe for grain, might be expected to benefit agriculture to such an extent that the bank would eventually participate therein. A net profit for the year of £45,123 6s. 2d. (including £8,152 8s. 11d. brought forward from the previous year) was declared, and the board, feeling that a policy of extreme caution was necessary owing to the density of the war-cloud, had placed £15,000 to a reserve fund for contingencies. After carrying forward a sum of £6,477 9s. 6d., a dividend at the rate of 5 per cent. per annum was proposed by the chairman, and subsequent speakers, in supporting the motion, expressed the opinion that the result of the year's working reflected the greatest credit on the entire management of the bank.

Current deposit accounts are opened at the head office or at any of the branches, and interest is allowed at 2 per cent. per annum on daily balances between Rs. 1,000 and Rs. 1,00,000, provided that the interest for the half year is not less than Rs. 5. Fixed deposits are received for one year at 4½ per cent., but special rates for shorter periods may be obtained on application. British and foreign stocks and bills of exchange are purchased or sold, and dividends are collected on behalf of clients.

General banking and exchange business is carried on, and loans and credits are granted on approved security. The authorized capital of the company is £1,500,000 (in shares of £10), the amount called up is £600,000, the reserve liability of shareholders is £900,000, and the reserve fund stands at £55,000.

The bankers of the company are the Bank of England, the Bank of Scotland, the London Joint Stock Bank, Ltd., the County and Westminster Bank, Ltd., the National Provincial Bank of England, Ltd., and the London and South-Western Bank, Ltd.

The Calcutta branch is situated at 9 Clive Street.

THE FRENCH MOTOR-CAR AND ELECTRIC COMPANY, LTD.

Not many years have elapsed since the first motor-car was placed upon the streets as an established form of transport, but the rate of progress which has been made in perfecting it to the standard of excellence of the present day is nothing less than remarkable. Prejudice against horseless vehicles on town and country roads was exceedingly strong and active, and motor pioneers had to run the gauntlet of biassed criticisms which were as unreasonable as they were untrue. Many persons will call to mind a drawing in the "London Charivari," or *Punch*, in which were depicted the anguish of mind, and a kind of "I-wish-I-were-anywhere-else-but-here" feeling of a motorist whose car had broken down and was being ignominiously towed along by a couple of proud-looking farm-horses in the centre of a crowd of jeering yokels. Accidents happen to the motor-car even now, as they do to the railway train, the four-in-hand, or the costermonger's barrow, but practical experience, backed up by improved scientific methods, have greatly reduced the number of casualties. When speed, comfort, and a certain amount of reliability had been secured, India at once availed itself of the opportunity of relieving horses and oxen of a tremendous quantity of hard work in a tropical sun, and agencies for the sale of continental cars by the best makers were soon opened in the principal centres of the country.

The city of Calcutta was in the van in this enterprise, but it was found that there were many features in imported cars which were not suitable for the climate of India; there were individual preferences for pattern of body, colour, upholstery, and mechanism; and the consequence was that customers were not always supplied with the kind of vehicle most in accordance with their tastes and requirements.

It was in April 1905 that the French Motor-Car and Electric Company, Ltd., came upon the scene in Calcutta, and commenced business at 55 Bentinck Street as motor-car importers and repairers, coach-builders, electrical engineers, contractors, and general merchants. They began in quite a modest way with about twenty workmen, a stock of ten cars, and floor space of only 2,500 sq. ft., but as they quickly realized that "bodies" made in Europe were unsuited to India, they began manufacturing them in their works from teakwood and then having them attached to selected imported chassis, thus obtaining for the company premier position in the coach-building trade in India.

This use of indigenous timber was fully appreciated by motorists in Calcutta, and very rapid expansion of business compelled the company to obtain further larger premises at 35 and 36 Ripon Street and 3 Sharriff Lane.

The workshops—which occupy a floor space of 62,000 sq. ft., and yet are too small for present requirements—are models of their kind, and they are equipped with all up-to-date and labour-saving machinery and appliances.

The company opened a branch in Bombay in the year 1910, in order to keep in touch with the increasing circle of their customers, and in the two cities already mentioned they now employ seven hundred workmen, as well as over fifty assistants and six European engineers, and keep a stock of some ninety cars of all descriptions.

Agencies are held for Automobiles Berliet, Lyons, France; Automobiles Mors, Ltd., France; Automobile Clement Bayard, France; Minerva Motors, Ltd., Belgium; Vulcan cars, London; Automobiles Panhard, France; Automobiles Bianchi, Milan; Philip's metal filament lamps, Holland; Ercole Marelli, Ltd., Milan; Mawdsleys, Ltd., Dursley, England; Electric motors and dynamos and the Westinghouse Brake Company, Ltd., London.

The company is incorporated in Belgium, and its principal offices and garages are: Calcutta, 55 Bentinck Street; Bombay, New Queen's Road, Girgaum; and Paris, 56 Rue Lafayette.

J. C. GALSTAUN

The manufacture of shellac is an industry which is practically confined to the East, where the raw material for the factory is somewhat extensively produced. In the year 1886, the production of this valuable commodity was commenced by Mr. J. C. Galstaun of Calcutta at the same time as he opened up his business as a general merchant.

Lac is obtained in a crude form from Assam, the Central and North-Western Provinces, and Nagpur, and, after it has been crushed into seed, it is washed, boiled, and subsequently rolled into "garnet" or thin sheets, the product being known as shellac. Four crops are obtained in the course of a year; one, found in the Central Province and North-Western Provinces, arrives in April and

THE FRENCH MOTOR-CAR AND ELECTRIC COMPANY, LTD.

1. Head Office, Calcutta. 2. Showroom. 3. Motor Repair Shop. 4. Machine Shop. 5. Coach-building Shop. 6. Motor Repair Shop.

J. C. GALSTAUN (SHELLAC DEPARTMENT).

1. MANAGER'S QUARTERS. 2. SHELLAC MANUFACTURING. 3. EXTERIOR OF FACTORY.

OCTAVIUS STEEL & CO. (GENERAL ELECTRIC COMPANY (INDIA), LTD.).

1. 250-Kilowatt Set at H.M. Mint, Calcutta.
2. 100-H.P. Motor Driving Set at H.M. Mint, Calcutta.
3. 500-Kilowatt Set Erected for the Port Commissioners, Calcutta.
4. Small 10-Kilowatt Lighting Set.
5. 250-Kilowatt Set Installed for the Royal Durbar at Delhi.

May; *rungeen*, and a small yield of *jetu* of superior quality, come in the month of August; while *kusmee* is produced in November and December, and, as the last named is the most valuable of the series, it is made up entirely by hand and is afterwards consigned to purchasers in the United States of America. Statistics recently published show that all the exports of shellac from India—amounting to 250,000 cases annually—are shipped at the port of Calcutta, and of this total, Mr. Galstaun is responsible for from 12,000 to 15,000 cases.

The factory is situated at Ultadinghi, near Calcutta, and it contains first class steam-driven machinery which is capable of manufacturing about five tons of shellac daily. About 150 hands are constantly employed on the premises, and it is worthy of note that if the proprietor had to depend upon manual labour alone, he would require at least one thousand employees.

Mr. Galstaun is the owner of a considerable quantity of landed and other property, in and around Calcutta, and one building, the warehouse occupied by Messrs. Ralli Brothers, in Lall Bazar, is the largest of its kind in the city. His offices are situated at 58 Radha Bazar Street.

THE GENERAL ELECTRIC COMPANY (INDIA) LTD. (OCTAVIUS STEEL & CO.)

The pioneers of the electric installation work in Bengal were Messrs. Octavius Steel & Co., 14 Old Court House Street, Calcutta, who twenty-five years ago (i.e. 1890) introduced the now universal lighting system into the second city of the British Empire by installing plant for the electric lighting of the Kidderpore Docks and Howrah Bridge for the Calcutta Port Commissioners; Harrison Road was undertaken next, and plant was afterwards fixed in the station yard at Howrah for the East Indian Railway Company.

Subsequently very many important contracts were carried out—chiefly for the Government—including the electrification of Meerut Cantonment, His Majesty's Mint, Calcutta, and installations in numerous Native States, jute mills, and other industrial concerns.

With the development of the business, the firm entered into an arrangement with the General Electric Company, London, in order that they might secure the latest design and manufacture of every class of electrical plant, fittings, and accessories as soon as they were placed on the market, and so rapidly did this venture progress in India that Messrs. Octavius Steel & Co. were successful in executing contracts for every class of electric power and light installations from one end of India to the other. The great expansion thus created led to the formation in 1911 of the General Electric Company (India), Ltd., which acquired the whole of the business, but Messrs. Octavius Steel & Co. retained the position of managing agents of the concern. The new company was at the same time affiliated with the parent company, The General Electric Company, London, which is known all over the world as the "G.E.C."

The G. E. C. (India), Ltd., holds the largest stock in the East of everything of an electrical character connected with electric power and lighting in central power stations, towns, industrial concerns, palaces, residences, and offices—in a word, from a power-house to a bell-push, not to mention the numerous labour-saving and comfort-affording devices such as the "Swan" ceiling and "Freezor" desk fans, and electric heating and cooking apparatus.

The showrooms and extensive godowns at 14 Old Court House Street, contain a most comprehensive and unique assortment of every class of electrical requisite, of which reference may be made to the display of electric light fittings, "Magnet" electric heating and cooking apparatus, switchgear, radiators, telephones, bells, instruments, and the world-famous "Osram" drawn-wire filament lamp, which has many imitators, but no equal.

It would be impossible in this brief note to give a full list of all the important work carried out by this interesting concern, but the following may be taken as typical enterprises: (1) His Majesty's Mint—three 250-kw. Belliss and Morcom G.E.C. steam dynamos with boiler-house equipment complete, also numerous motors from 5 to 150 h.p. (2) 500 kw. set direct coupled to G.E.C. generator with Belliss and Morcom engine, also boilers, for the Port Commissioners, Kidderpore; (3) a similar combination, but for 250 kw., for the Delhi Durbar, and (4) 16 jib electric cranes for the East Indian Railway, Howrah.

The General Electric Company, London, of which the Indian company may be considered an adjunct, has enormous engineering works at Witton, near Birmingham, where also are situated carbon, conduit, switchgear, and "Arc" lamp works. The fittings works are in Birmingham, the telephone and instrument works in Salford, the "Osram" lamp, and Robertson carbon filament lamp works at Hammersmith, London, and the general accessories works are at Southwark, while the Pirelli general cable works are at Southampton. More than ten thousand hands are employed in these establishments.

There are branches in all the principal cities throughout the British and other chief centres in Europe, Asia, Australasia, Canada, and South America, and these are in the hands of the General Electric Companies of France, Spain, Belgium, and other European countries. The General Electric Company (India), Ltd., The General Electric Company (China), The British General Electric Company, South Africa, The British General Electric Company, Australia, and the British General Electric Company, Canada.

The manager of the General Electric Company (India), Ltd., is Mr. Francis Holt, and the telegraphic address is "Kilowatt," Calcutta or Madras.

P. E. GUZDAR & CO.

The merchant—or "middle man," as he is frequently termed—who purchases agricultural produce from growers and then either deals with it himself or sells to mill-owners, is an absolute necessity in nearly every country in the world, but he is especially indispensable in India, where the majority of the landholders are cultivators of exceedingly small areas. The fields of paddy, jute, wheat, and other cereals are frequently many miles from a centre touched by railway or river, and it would be impossible for small consignments to be transported to market or factory excepting at a ruinous cost to the producer.

Here it is that the middle-man steps in, who can afford to clear the countryside of small lots and then send them collectively to such places as he may desire. It is therefore of the utmost importance that these merchants should be men of strict integrity in order that *ryots* may obtain a fair price for their crops, and it is satisfactory to note that here in Bengal there are hundreds of such buyers who have gained the entire confidence of dwellers upon the soil.

Among those who enjoy this highly desirable reputation is the firm whose name appears at the commencement of these notes, and it is no mere figure of speech to say that the partners are fully

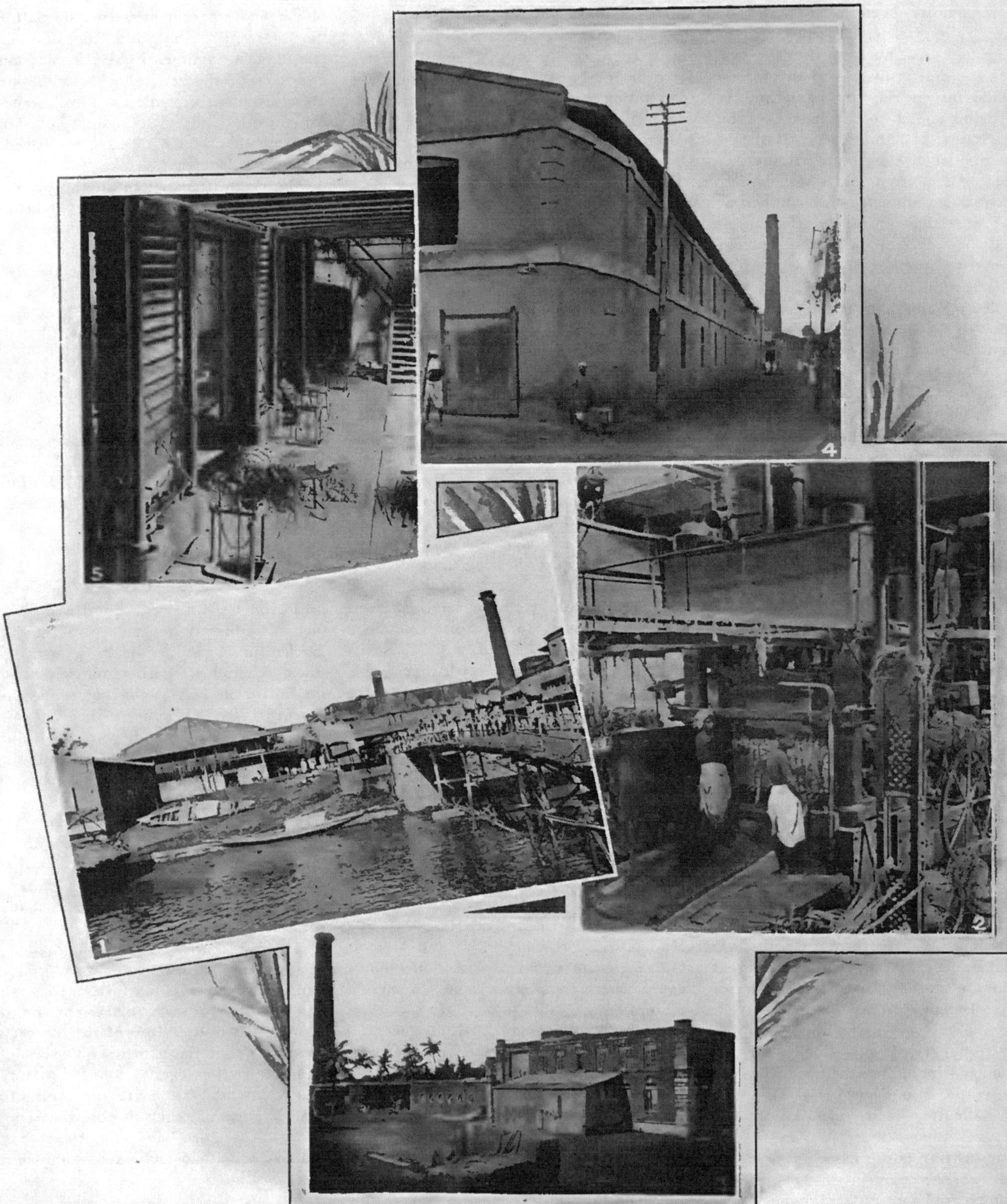

P. E. GUZDAR & CO.

1. The Guzdar Ghoosery Jute Press House. 2. Jute Presses. 3. Victoria Cotton Mills. 4. The Howrah Hydraulic Press. 5. Jute Presses.

P. E. GUZDAR & CO.

1. Blow Room. 2. Carding Department. 3. Spinning Department. 4. Reeling Department. 5. Bundling and Baling Department.

entitled to the highest credit for the honourable position which they have attained.

Messrs. Guzdar & Co. are not only purchasers of large quantities of agricultural and general produce, but they are proprietors of the Victoria Cotton Mills and the Ghoosery and Howrah Jute Presses, all of which are on the banks of the River Hooghly in Calcutta.

The firm was established in the year 1865 by Messrs. P. E. and C. E. Guzdar, who were concerned chiefly in the export of rice, *pucca* jute bales, and other commodities.

Their business connections increased gradually but surely, and in 1886 they established a jute press, which, owing to greater accommodation which has since been provided, is now capable of turning out some two thousand bales in a working day of twelve hours.

This venture proved to be such a success that two years later the firm erected a cotton-mill containing 12,000 spindles, and which gives constant employment to about 520 labourers. Full of energy and with a laudable desire to enlarge their environment, they purchased in the year 1904 the Howrah Hydraulic Press, which is able to send forth, day by day, no fewer than 1,200 bales of jute.

The activities of the partners did not, however, rest with cotton and jute-mills; they recognized the fact that there was a great future in industrial enterprise in India in the mining of coal which had not, twenty or thirty years ago, assumed that degree of importance which the extent of payable seams and the accessibility of the fields appeared to warrant. They therefore in the year 1908 formed the Kajora Coal Company for the working of a colliery in the Raneegunge district, and when the machinery is employed constantly the average monthly yield of very good second-class coal is not less than 6,000 tons.

The present partners are Messrs. C. E., E. P., and M. C. Guzdar, and their offices are situated at 44 Ezra Street, Calcutta.

J. H. R. HARLEY & CO.

Old China Bazar Street in Calcutta is not by any means a pretentious-looking thoroughfare and as it is situated in a densely populated portion of the city, in which the majority of the buildings have no imposing exteriors, one is all the more surprised to find such commodious and well-arranged business premises as those occupied at 87 by Messrs. J. H. R. Harley & Co., manufacturers of paulins and waterproof canvas, Government contractors, and general merchants.

The firm was founded in the early eighties of last century by Mr. J. H. R. Harley, and the proprietor's name soon became a household word throughout the East in connection with the making of paulins for all commercial purposes.

The present European war has made enormous claims upon the resources of manufacturers of machinery and goods of all descriptions, ranging from aeroplanes and heavy guns to the most common-place article of domestic use, and Messrs. Harley & Co., who have had the honour of being one of the selected firms to receive Government contracts, have been entrusted with the largest single order given by the Government of India for canvas waterproofed locally, this being for no fewer than 60,000 yards of that substance. The major portion of this material is required for use in the commissariat departments of the various expeditions, chiefly as covers for mules and other transport animals. Apart from the war, however, Messrs. Harley & Co. have purchasers for their waterproofed goods throughout the whole of the East, although India and Burma contain the most important markets. The firm's waterproofing factory is situated in the Grand Trunk Road, Howrah, near Calcutta, and the extensive premises cover an area of about 400 sq. yds. The number of daily labourers constantly employed is about one hundred.

Mr. J. H. R. Harley died in the year 1911, and he was succeeded by his son, Mr. W. S. G. Harley, who is now sole proprietor.

The latter established the "Harlequin" printing press on the property in China Bazar Street in the year 1913, and he undertakes all kinds of job and artistic printing, book-binding, and other similar works.

Messrs. Harley & Co. have agencies for the sale of their paulins in Burma and in the Province of Madras, while they are representatives in India of Messrs. David Corsair and Sons, Ltd., of Arbroath, Scotland, for their waterproof canvas, and for the Swiss Silk Bolting Cloth Manufacturing Company, of Zurich, Switzerland.

Mr. Harley gives personal supervision in every department, and he is assisted by several reliable foremen.

The London correspondents of the firm are Messrs. Henry W. Bush & Co., Ltd., and the local telegraphic address is "Harlequin," Calcutta.

W. H. HARTON & CO.

Rope was manufactured by hand in Calcutta very many years ago, and it is not surprising that this was the case seeing that sisal, Manila hemp, aloe, cotton, country hemp, jute, various descriptions of fibre, and other raw produce are found in luxurious abundance in the East. Another contributing cause was the extremely plentiful supply of cheap labour, and thus an industry was started which has largely increased the revenue of the State and has indirectly been the means of providing improved conditions of living for thousands of workers.

The Ghoosery Rope Works are the oldest of the kind in India. They were established in the year 1780 by Mr. W. H. Harton, upon an area of about 68 acres on the west bank of the River Hooghly, within the municipality of Howrah. They have a frontage upon the river of 1,977 ft., and the property extends inland for a distance of some 700 ft., the municipal main road dividing the works into two parts. A building, which tradition says was a church during the period of the Danish settlement, is still standing on the premises, and is now used for the storage of yarn, hemp, and other goods.

The business was commenced and is still being carried on under the name of W. H. Harton & Co., but the proprietor, Mr. J. C. Stalkaart, is a grandson of Marmaduke Stalkaart (Naval Architect to King George III), who joined the firm in 1812.

"Harton's" ropes are looked upon as representing the standard of excellence in every part of the civilized world, and their reputation for sterling quality and strength is unsurpassed by any other make: "Heave me a Harton" cries the skipper as he approaches the wharf, and when he has one of the Ghoosery cables firmly secured to his stanchions he defies all sorts of weather, and all resistance too.

Manila hemp is imported in bales from the Philippine Islands, and it is used for making high-class ropes, while paulins are made from specially prepared canvas and composition. The hemp is passed through spinning, heckling, and softing machines, and the whole of the plant con-

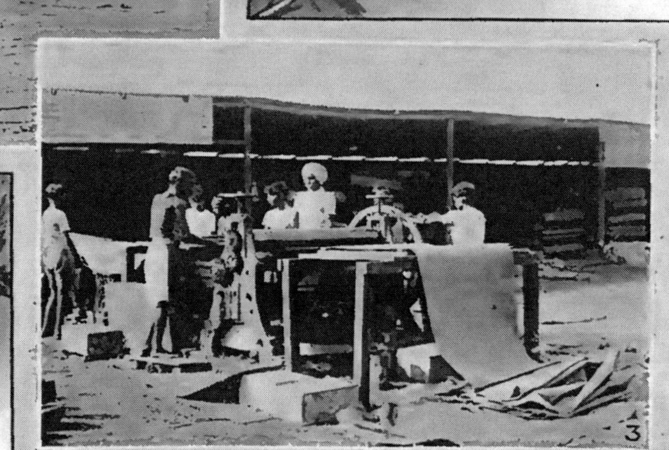

J. H. HARLEY & CO.

1. The Older Method of Hand Labour. 2. Machine and Labourers. 3. Closer View of Machine at Work. 4. In the Printing Department

W. H. HARTON & CO.

1. Exhibit, Paris Exhibition, 1900: the Largest Rope ever Made. 2. A General View.

W. H. HARTON & CO.

1. Spinning Manilla. 2. Coir Shed. 3. Wire Rope Making. 4. Rope Making.

W. H. HARTON & CO.

1. House. 2. Fernery. 3. Lawn and Grounds.

nected with these premises is driven by steam. Women engaged in spinning are paid according to the quantity turned out, but all other labour is engaged at a daily rate of remuneration.

Country hemp is used for small lines of all descriptions, such as lead and log lines, signal halyards, house-lines, and others of a similar diameter, while tow from Central Provinces hemp is made into oakum.

Messrs. Harton & Co. were pioneers in the importation of coir yarn from the convict settlements in the Andaman Islands, but at the same time large quantities are received from Calicut and other places on the western coast of India. The yarn arrives in lengths of from 80 ft. to 90 ft. being knotted up to 1,400 ft., and after it has been shaped like a ball, it is subsequently made into ropes.

The extent of these works is of the great advantage, as it has been possible to arrange for five rope-walks (each of which is a quarter of a mile in length). So spacious are the premises that they can, without undue trouble, be utilized for turning out a single rope measuring 1,800 ft. from end to end.

Ordinary ropes range from 1 in. to 26 in. in circumference, but, at the last exhibition in Paris in the year 1900, the firm had a magnificent display of rope products which included a rope of 16 in. in diameter, this being the largest size that the commercial or shipping world has ever seen. First-class machinery has been installed for the making of flexible steel ropes varying in size from 1 to 6 in. in circumference.

The plant in the works is of modern design and includes twenty-four spinning and four heckling and softing machines, and the steam engine and boiler which have been fixed are available also for the carpenters', fitting, and engineering shops.

A special feature is made of coir cables, from 12 in. to 26 in., which are supplied to the Harbour Boards in New Zealand, San Francisco, Seattle, Manchester Ship Canal, and to a considerable number of South African ports.

A system of rollers has been adopted for the transport of rope from the works to barges on the river, and the output of the various products is now so great that weekly shipments are made to nearly every country in the world.

Messrs. Harton & Co. are contractors to H.M. arsenals in India, to the Royal Indian Marine, the Port Commissioners, and Government railways in India and Burma, to leading firms in Calcutta, and to the following steamship companies: The British India Steam Navigation Company, Ltd., the Asiatic Steamship Company, the River Steam Navigation Company, and to the services of Messrs. Donald Currie, Apcar, McIlwraith, McEachern & Co., of Melbourne, and other owners trading to Calcutta. Sole agencies for Bengal are held for Suter Hartmann's Red Hand Brand of anti-corrosive and anti-fouling compositions, for the bottoms of ships; for anti-corrosive paints mixed ready for use; and for the famous Lacvelva enamel.

If further proof were needed as to the high position in the world's markets held by Messrs. Harton's ropes, it may be gained from the fact that the following—among other awards of merit—have been received: bronze and gold medals at the Calcutta Exhibition of 1882; four gold and two silver medals at the Calcutta International Exhibition, 1883-4; a gold medal at Amsterdam in 1883; a bronze medal at the Colonial and Indian Exhibition held in London in 1886; and the never-to-be-forgotten bronze medal of the République Française of 1900.

Mr. Stalkaart's private residence is a dream of luxury combined with that comfort which is only obtainable in a well-appointed house. It stands in the midst of spacious and beautifully kept lawns; and the tanks—of which there are seven—are nearly all full of fish.

HEATLY AND GRESHAM, LTD.

The history of railways in India is an interesting one; and closely bound up with the various devices to secure the safe working of them which have been introduced upon them during the last quarter of a century, the name of Heatly and Gresham, Ltd., railway engineers and specialists, of Calcutta and Bombay, has come to be familiarly known.

This company had its inception at the time when comparative trials were conducted in India to determine the relative advantages of the vacuum and the Westinghouse brake. The representatives sent out on behalf of the former company were Mr. H. Heatly and Mr. S. T. Gresham, who subsequently formed the company which forms the subject of this article.

The battle of the brakes in India is now old history, and it is sufficient to say in connection with it that it resulted in the universal adoption of the vacuum brake which has now been made "standard" and is exclusively employed on every broad, metre, and narrow-gauge railway system throughout the country, while its adoption for feeder lines is being rapidly proceeded with.

The efforts of the new company were originally and primarily directed towards the exploitation and proper maintenance of the vacuum brake in India, but this was supplemented by an extension to other branches of railway engineering, embracing improvements to cover the requirements of the engineering, locomotive, and carriage and wagon departments of the Indian railways; in short, Messrs. Heatly and Gresham became pioneers in the supply of railway equipment, and, with the experience they possessed, were successful in introducing improvements that have withstood the most severe tests as to efficiency, in addition to which, their expert advice has always been greatly valued by departmental officials.

Another branch of railway engineering to which the company turned their attention was the provision of efficient signalling and interlocking equipment to the Indian railways, and in this connection they were entrusted with the agency, and, later, the managing agency of Messrs. Saxby and Farmer (India), Ltd., the well-known firm of railway signal engineers. They are also agents for the Vaughan rail anchor, which has long passed the experimental stage and is now in regular use on many of the Indian railways.

Attention was early devoted to the better lighting and equipment of railway coaching stock and Messrs. Heatly and Gresham took up the agency, which they still hold, of the patent Lighting Company, who for many years past have devoted special attention to the illumination of railway carriages by compressed oil gas, and, later, interested themselves specially in the lighting and ventilation of coaching stock by electricity. In addition to railway carriage lighting, the Patent Lighting Company have for many years past specialized in coast and harbour lighting, and here again Messrs. Heatly and Gresham have rendered valuable service in improvements which had for their object the better lighting of the various ports, harbours, and river approaches around the coast of India.

In the field of locomotive engineering, the name of this firm has for many years been a household word. As representa-

HEATLY & GRESHAM, LTD.

1. VIEW OF THE WORKS. 2. MACHINE SHOP. 3. GALVANIZING SHOP.

tives for the Vulcan Foundry, Ltd., the well-known locomotive builders of Newton-le-Willows, Lancashire, they have been able to keep in touch with the latest developments in locomotive designs and practice.

Foremost among locomotive cab fittings, in which they specialize, is the well-known Gresham and Craven injector, for which they have been agents from the date of the company's inception. This particular injector is now practically a standard requirement on all Indian railways.

Still dealing with the subject of engine equipment, mention must be made of the Wakefield mechanical lubricator, which Messrs. Heatly and Gresham have successfully exploited for several years past and which has attained as much favour in India as it has on the railways at home. The same may be said of the "Robinson" locomotive superheater, the agency for which has been placed with the same firm in whose hands it has made considerable progress, and has now been made the "standard" for Indian railways.

Then, too, there are the manufacturers of Messrs. Taylor Brothers & Co., Ltd., steel manufacturers, who for many years past have specialized in high tonnage tyres and axles for locomotive, carriage, and wagon stock, and in solid rolled steel wheel disc centres, for which Messrs. Heatly and Gresham are representatives also; while in connection with the Economical Boiler Company, Ltd., they have been instrumental in arranging for the installation of several large plants, that are now in satisfactory operation, for the automatic washing-out of locomotive boilers.

At the same time the Hasler Telegraph Works have, through Messrs. Heatly and Gresham, been successful in placing a large number of their speed recorders on the Indian railways; while the requirements of boiler lagging, or covering, are catered for by the company who represent the Keasbey and Mattison Company, Messrs. Newalls Insulation Company, and Messrs. J. Dampney & Co., for their boiler-washing compound.

Turning to the fields of carriage and wagon building, there are considerable improvements and progress to be reported, for the standard type of bogie carriage now turned out by Indian railway workshops compares favourably, both in design and construction, with the output of the leading railways in England.

The easy riding, so noticeable a feature on India coaching stock, is explained to a large extent by the employment of bolster bogies patented by Mr. Alex. Spencer, of the well-known firm of Messrs. George Spencer, Moulton & Co., Ltd. This company also specialize in railway carriage springs, produced of the highest grade of rubber, large quantities of which have for many years past been supplied to the Indian railways through the agency of the firm at present under review.

The avoidance of hot boxes on coaching and wagon stock is accounted for by the employment of the Armstrong oiler, which Messrs. Heatly and Gresham have been instrumental in introducing on many of the principal Indian railways, on several of which no other form of axle-box lubrication is now employed.

Artistic carriage furnishing is also a matter to which Messrs. Heatly and Gresham have devoted special attention.

In connection with this branch of their business, they have identified themselves with such well-known firms as the General Seating Company, Ltd., Messrs. Jas. McIlwraith & Co., Ltd., for carriage roofing; Messrs. Jas. Beresford & Son, Ltd., for carriage fittings; Messrs. Mead, McLean & Co., for patent ventilators; and Messrs. Lewis Berger & Sons, Ltd., for paint and varnishes; while their efforts have been largely instrumental in the adoption of the patent Watson-Jones coupler, which is to-day practically the standard coupling for metre and narrow gauge stock in India. In addition to this coupler, the A.B.C. Coupler Company, the makers of the Patent Watson-Jones coupling, have also, through this firm, supplied many sets of the automatic A.B.C. coupler both to broad and narrow-gauge lines.

To the proper equipment of the locomotive and carriage and wagon workshop, Messrs. Heatly and Gresham have also devoted special attention, being representatives in this country for such well-known firms as Messrs. Brett's Patent Lifter Company, power drop stamps; the Howard Pneumatic Engineering Company, Ltd., for pneumatic tools and accessories; Messrs. H. W. Ward & Co., Ltd.; Messrs. Webster and Bennett, Ltd., for machine tools; Messrs. Kynoch, Ltd., for gas engines; Messrs. Broom and Wade, for air compressors; and Electromotors, Ltd., the well-known makers of motors and dynamos.

The connection that Messrs. Heatly and Gresham have built up with Indian railways for the supply of material and fittings has led them to turn their attention to the development of feeder lines, in the survey of several of which they are at present interested, and a further earnest of their enterprise is afforded by the flotation of a company with a factory in Calcutta for the manufacture of galvanized iron utensils of all descriptions. The articles now being produced by the Indian Galvanizing Company, Ltd., are as good in point of strength, quality, and galvanizing as those previously imported into this country from English makers. The success of the project has been so marked that arrangements are at present being made for the installation of further machinery with a view of obtaining a greater output.

Although essentially railway engineers, specializing in the supply and equipment of fittings for all branches of railway requirements, Messrs. Heatly and Gresham, Ltd., have within recent years been extending their sphere of operations to general engineering, being representatives in this country for such firms as Engineering and Arc Lamps, Ltd., the New Phonopore Telephone Company (patentees and manufacturers of the long-distance telephone which bears their name), the Silent Electric Clock Company (of which several installations are now fitted up throughout India), the Ironite Company, Ltd., who have successfully interested themselves in a waterproofing composition which is largely employed for the covering of roofs and for station platforms, the Langdon Davies Motor Company, and the Asbestos Manufactures Company, Ltd., in connection with which Messrs. Heatly and Gresham were the pioneers and original introducers into the Indian market of asbestos cement corrugated sheeting, very large quantities of which are now employed for the covering of engine shed roofs, workshops, and other buildings, and which is also rapidly replacing galvanized corrugated iron on account of its heat-resisting properties and its practically indefinite length of life.

The care and upkeep of roads have also received Messrs. Heatly and Gresham's attention, they having supplied a number of Messrs. Clayton and Shuttleworth's steam wagons for the transport of stores on the North-West Frontier, to municipalities and to private contractors; while their connection with Hill's Patent Vacuum Road Cleanser, Ltd., places them in a position to render expert advice on the maintenance of roads in a clean and dustless condition.

The firm under notice have a branch in Bombay, where matters in connection with railways on the western side of India are given every attention. Extensive stocks of railway and other fittings are also held in that city, in which the offices of the company are located at 75 Hornby Road. These premises were opened in 1909 with a view of extending operations in that portion of India, and their establishment has fully justified the venture.

HOLMES, WILSON & CO.

1. STAR FOUNDRY AT LILOOAH. 2. BRITANNIA FOUNDRY AT BHOWNIPORE, CALCUTTA.

HOLMES, WILSON & CO.

This firm was established by Mr. Charles H. Holmes, at 15 Canning Street, Calcutta, on January 1, 1915, in conjunction with Mr. A. D. Wilson, of 101 Leadenhall Street, London, E.C., who acts as the representative and correspondent of the firm in England.

Shortly after their establishment, Mr. Holmes and Mr. Wilson purchased the goodwill and trade marks of the business of Messrs. J. H. Elliott & Co., Ltd., of Birmingham, who for many years had been trading as merchants in India with branch offices and connections in the principal trade centres in that country.

In addition to trading as import metal and hardware merchants, Messrs. Holmes, Wilson & Co. carry on an extensive local trade, principally with railways, tea gardens, and collieries. They also act as managing agents for the Star Foundry Company, of Lillooah, who have a large business in cast and wrought-iron work of all descriptions.

In 1916, Mr. Holmes, in conjunction with Mr. J. H. Simpson and Babu Mahendra Nath Dutt, initiated the Britannia Brass Foundry at 5, Bhowanipore Road, Calcutta, for the manufacture of all kinds of brass articles, specializing particularly in art brass and copper work.

The company, although in its infancy, has already carried out some important art brass work for the Alliance Bank of Simla, the Government House at Bankipore, and other establishments.

The telegraphic address of the firm is "Benelliott," Cālcutta.

THE HONGKONG AND SHANGHAI BANKING CORPORATION

The headquarters of this corporation are at Hongkong, but branches or agencies have been established at Amoy, Bangkok, Batavia, Bombay, Calcutta, Canton, Colombo, Foochow, Hamburg, Hankow, Hongkew (Shanghai), Harbin (Manchuria), Ilo-ilo, Ipoh, Johore, Kobe, Kuala Lumpur, London, Lyons, Malacca, Manila, Nagasaki, New York, Pekin, Penang, Rangoon, Saigon, San Francisco, Shanghai, Singapore, Sourabaya, Tientsin, Taipeh, Tsingtau, and Yokohama. Every description of banking and exchange business is carried on, including the negotiation and collection of bills, the issue of letters of credit for the accommodation of clients who travel in various parts of the world, the payment of interest on fixed deposits, and the safe custody of title-deeds, shares, and other securities. Credits are granted on approved securities, and interest is allowed on daily balance of current accounts. The ninety-ninth report of the directors and a statement of accounts for the half year ending on December 31, 1914, were presented to a general meeting of shareholders held at Hongkong on the 20th of February, and it was shown that the net profits for that period, including a balance brought forward, and after paying all charges, deducting interest paid and due, and making provision for had and doubtful accounts and contingencies, amounted to $5,894,227. After deducting the remuneration to directors, there remained a sum sufficient for the payment of a dividend of £2 3s. and a bonus of 5s. per share, leaving a balance of $2,607,274 to be carried to new profit and loss accounts. In order to effect adjustments caused by the writing down of Consols, and to enable the reserve fund to be maintained at the sum of £1,500,000, war loan 3½ per cent. stock was purchased, and this left the amount of "other sterling securities" at £371,100. The whole of this expenditure was provided for out of the earnings of the half year.

The London bankers of the corporation are the London, County, and Westminster Bank, Ltd.

The accounts, which were audited in Hongkong in the month of February 1915, were signed by Messrs. David Landale, W. L. Pattenden, and P. H. Holyoak, directors, and by Mr. N. J. Stabb, the chief manager.

GEO. F. JAMES & CO.

Only a few months before the preparation of this notice, Mr. George F. James established a business under the style of George F. James & Co., the firm commencing to trade as motor, mechanical, and electrical engineers. Premises were secured at 14 Wellesley Street, in Calcutta, with a staff, including the manager, of not more than twelve persons, but the sound practical experience of Mr. James, who has been connected with automobilism

HONG KONG AND SHANGHAI BANKING CORPORATION.

1. The Present Premises. 2. Proposed New Building in Dalhousie Square.

since its introduction into India, caused the business to expand so rapidly that within a few weeks it became necessary to obtain a building with more accommodation, and that was secured at 46 Wellesley Street. The firm began well by adopting as their motto "promptitude and diligence," and by coupling with it a determination to give careful personal attention to the wishes of clients, their name soon became a household word in all matters pertaining to motor and electrical engineering.

The business, firmly established on a sound basis, continued to grow, and once again the firm are compelled to look for considerably larger premises in order to provide space for the additional machinery which is about to be erected, and to meet the abnormal demands which are made upon them.

There is as yet no particular type of motor which can claim a monopoly of popularity, and therefore the firm, by keeping in touch with leading manufacturers, may be relied upon, with all possible dispatch, to supply a car of any recognized build in its normal style, or in any other form to suit the diversified tastes of their patrons. Special attention is given to ensure quality in all materials employed, as it is common knowledge that "tinkering" is practised by many unscrupulous traders, but Messrs. James & Co. point with pride to the names of their regular customers as evidence of the thorough manner in which they execute all orders entrusted to them.

The extensive warehouses occupied by the firm are replete with a valuable stock of accessories of every description, and by forethought the management have been able to anticipate an adequate supply for a constant and continuous demand.

An idea of the extent to which the business has progressed may be gathered from the fact that the staff, which originally consisted of a dozen persons, now numbers nearly a hundred.

GEO. F. JAMES & CO.

1. Premises. 2. Garage. 3. Workshop.

JARDINE, SKINNER & CO.

Among the many keen and progressive men of business who left the Old Country for India for the purpose of establishing a commercial house in Calcutta in the early forties of the nineteenth century was Mr. David Jardine, the founder of the firm of Messrs. Jardine, Skinner & Co. That gentleman commenced trading in 1843 as a general merchant and commission agent, and in January 1845 he admitted Mr. Charles Binny Skinner into partnership, the title of the firm being Jardine, Skinner & Co.

The present partners of the firm are: Messrs. F. G. Steuart, R. Jardine Paterson, and W. A. Bankier (residing in Europe), and Messrs. J. A. Horne, F. E. Phillips, and P. W. Newson, of Calcutta, and their offices at 4 Clive Row, in that city, are situated in a substantial block of buildings specially erected for them in the year 1869.

By reason of the large number of managing and general agencies for companies held by the firm, it follows that the businesses in which they are concerned are of an exceedingly varied character, and that the area over which their activities extend is an exceedingly wide one.

In commencing with jute, which is the special product of the Bengal Presidency,

JARDINE, SKINNER & CO.

1. East Indian Coal Co., Ltd.—Bararee Pits. 2. East Indian Coal Co., Ltd.—South Bulliaree Pits. 3. Indo-China S.N. Co., Ltd.—s.s. "Lai Sang." 4. 4 Clive Row, Calcutta. 5. Bengal Timber Trading Co., Ltd.—Sawing Sleepers.

JARDINE, SKINNER & CO.

1, Kamarhatty Mill—Traveller. 2. Kamarhatty Mill—Weaving. 3. Kanknarrah Mill—Finishing 4. Kanknarrah Mill—Spinning.

the Kamarhatty Company, Ltd., may be mentioned as their mill was the first one to be erected after the industry had been well nigh extinguished owing to the abnormal increase of factories between the years 1872 and 1875. In that period several companies were compelled to close their doors, while all the others had a terrible struggle with the most adverse circumstances which had arisen.

The Kamarhatty Company was registered in Calcutta in the year 1877, and the mill at Kamarhatty on the Hooghly River had at that time 320 looms. Twenty years later these had been increased to 500; in 1904 a new mill was erected with 300 looms; and at the close of the year 1916 the two factories contained a total of 1,710 looms and 32,632 spindles.

The Kanknarrah Company, Ltd., was started in 1882, when the mill at Bhatpara in the district of the Twenty-four Pergannas, near Calcutta, had not more than 250 looms, although there was accommodation for 420. The capital, which originally stood at Rs. 14,00,000, has at various times been increased to the present sum of Rs. 40,00,000. A second mill has been erected, necessitating additional looms, and the last-named have increased in number simultaneously with other extensions, until there is now a total of 1,521, together with 27,720 spindles. The two above-mentioned companies (for whom Messrs. Jardine, Skinner & Co. are managing agents) have also jute-buying and baling agencies at Naraingunge and Chandpore working in connection with their mills.

Tea is the next commodity to be dealt with, and the firm now under notice are managing agents for the following eight companies:—

The Bengal United Tea Company, Ltd., was registered in London in 1897, upon the amalgamation of several small companies, and owns tea estates in the district of Darjeeling, and in Cachar and elsewhere in Assam.

The Cachar and Dooars Tea Company, Ltd., registered in London in the year 1895, are owners of tea estates in the district of the Dooars, and Cachar, in Assam.

The Rydak Tea Syndicate, Ltd., acquired their two gardens, Rydak and Kartik, in the Dooars, in 1897, and the company was registered in Calcutta in the following year. The whole estate comprises about 2,300 acres, of which nearly 1,300 acres are under cultivation for tea.

The Ballacherra Tea Company, Ltd., formed in 1910, have gardens at Ballacherra, Narencherra, Heroncherra, and Panicherra, in the Surma Valley districts of Cachar, comprising a gross area of 7,500 acres, about 491 of which are under tea.

The Baradighi Tea Company, Ltd., are owners of a tea garden of about 850 acres at Baradighi in the Dooars. Registration took place in Calcutta in 1893.

The Central Cachar Tea Company, Ltd., was formed in 1863 for the purpose of taking over the tea estates of Burnie Braes, Mohunpore, Serispore, and Rattakandi belonging to the old Assam company, and comprising 1,457 acres.

The Chandypore Tea Company, Ltd., was registered in Calcutta in the year 1867, and in this instance there was an amalgamation of the gardens known as Chandypore, Ballykandy, and Ferdinandpore in Cachar. The estate is about 8,000 acres in extent, of which 734 acres are under tea.

The Kallinugger and Khoreel Tea Company, Ltd., have gardens at Kallinugger, Khoreel, Massempore, and Kina Tillah, in Cachar, comprising about 640 acres.

Messrs. Jardine, Skinner & Co. are, further, managing agents for the Bengal Timber Trading Company, Ltd., which was registered in 1897, upon the acquisition of the undertakings of the old Bengal Timber Trading Company, Ltd., and the Nagra Timber Company, Ltd. The company have large forest concessions over an extensive area stretching in a northerly direction from near Panposh in Gangpur, one of the feudatory States in Northern Orissa, to and along the *terai* of the Ranchi plateau, and their rights include the extraction of *sal* for the making of railway sleepers. In addition to the forest concessions the company deal largely in imported timbers such as teak, pine, *padouk*, and others.

The coal-mining industry has for a number of years claimed the attention of Messrs. Jardine, Skinner & Co., and they are managing agents for three important coal companies.

The East Indian Coal Company, Ltd., registered in England in 1893, have collieries in the centre of the famous Jherria fields in the district of Manbhum, in the Province of Behar and Orissa, which include those known as Kendwadih, Khoira, Dheriajoba, Kurkend, Brahmanbararee, Bhulanbararee, Jealgorah, South Bulliaree, and Pandra. The output of the company's collieries for some time reached a total of nearly 40,000 tons a month, but when in full work they are capable of raising no less than 60,000 tons.

The Sutkidih Coal Company, Ltd., are owners of mines of first-class coal in the Jherria fields which have an annual output of from 60,000 to 80,000 tons. The company was registered in Calcutta in 1908.

The Bansdeopur Coal Company, Ltd., was registered in Calcutta at the commencement of the present year, 1917, and the Bansdeopur Colliery, also situated in Jherria, raises from 60,000 to 80,000 tons of steam coal per annum.

Messrs. Jardine, Skinner & Co. have for a number of years been agents in Calcutta for a regular service of ships to China, their records going back as far as the year 1869; this line is now the Indo-China Steam Navigation Company, Ltd., and the firm are its agents. A joint mail service is worked with the Apcar Line, whose steamers were formerly owned by Messrs. Apcar & Co., but now belong to the British Indian Steam Navigation Company, Ltd. The service was a few years ago extended to Japanese ports.

Agencies are also held for the Pacific lines of the Royal Mail Steam Packet Company, the "Glen" Line, and the Toyo Kisen Kaisha, and the firm are also secretaries in Calcutta for the Calcutta-Trans-Pacific Conference.

The firm are largely interested in fire and marine insurance, being managing agents for the Triton Insurance Company, Ltd.—the result of a combination in 1905 of the Triton Insurance Company and the Eastern Insurance Company, Ltd.—and agents for the Manchester Assurance Company, Ltd. (incorporated with the Atlas Assurance Company, Ltd.), the Canton Insurance Office, Ltd., the Hongkong Fire Insurance Company, Ltd., and the South British Insurance Company, Ltd.

The firm are importers on an extensive scale of Manchester piece goods, while the chief exports consist of gunnies and tea.

Messrs. Jardine, Skinner & Co.'s London agents are Messrs. Matheson & Co., Ltd., of 3 Lombard Street, E.C., and their telegraphic address is "Jardines," Calcutta. Their China agents are Messrs. Jardine, Matheson & Co., Ltd.

G. F. KELLNER & CO.

It is probable that no greater change in any branch of industry has been more noticeable during the past forty or fifty years than that which has been manifested in the manner in which articles of food

G. F. KELLNER & CO.

1. THE PREMISES. 2. SHOWROOM. 3. BONDED WAREHOUSE. 4. COLLECTION OF KELLNER'S SPECIALITIES.
5 REFRESHMENT ROOM AT HOWRAH (CALCUTTA) STATION.

and drink have been prepared and served to the general public. This is the outcome of a truer conception of the laws of hygiene and sanitation; and applied science has, through its multifarious channels, been called to the aid of law-makers for the enforcement of medical inspection not only of the buildings in which food is handled, but also of the goods which are intended for the public market.

Prominent among merchants in the East who have been successful in removing all causes of complaint as to the manner in which tinned goods were prepared some years ago, are Messrs. G. F. Kellner & Co., of Chowringhee Road in the city of Calcutta. They went to the root of the evil, and determined that at all costs they would completely remodel the various processes of selection, preparation, preservation, and packing which had previously been in vogue. Absolute purity of food was insisted upon, and the highest scientific skill was displayed in manufacturing the goods, in packing, and in hermetically sealing the cans or tins before they were allowed to be offered for sale. As a result of this extreme care, Messrs. Kellner & Co. now have the supreme satisfaction of seeing that their efforts have enabled them to place before the public, in a perfectly fresh and palatable condition, certain delicacies, as well as the more solid foods, of the leading countries of the world. Public opinion—an unerring guide—has voted solidly for "Kellners," and as a consequence the trade of the firm in this particular branch has increased to such an extent that they are justified in saying that they have gained the confidence of their customers in a manner unparalleled by any other firm in India.

Messrs. Kellner & Co. are, further, widely known as proprietors of and caterers for refreshment-rooms and cars on the East Indian, Delhi-Umbala-Kalka, and Simla-Kalka Railways. It must not be forgotten that the responsibility of providing meals and refreshments in trains in Europe is child's-play compared to similar duties in India. In this country there is a tropical climate to contend with; there are endless worries inseparable from the employment of native servants, and there are innumerable difficulties connected with the obtaining of fresh food during long journeys, but Messrs Kellner & Co. spare neither pains nor expense in order to make this department equally as efficient as that upon any other railway system in the world, and in this they have succeeded admirably.

It should be added that the resources of this firm as caterers are not by any means limited to dining-cars or refreshment-rooms, as they have been entrusted with some of the most important contracts in India, among which the following may be instanced. They were contractors for the camp, in the Nepal jungles, of H.M. the King-Emperor, when he visited India as Prince of Wales; and they supplied several other camps at the Delhi Durbar; while one undertaking which is specially deserving of mention was the "Princes Restaurant" at the Minto fête at Calcutta, when dinners were served nightly to more than two hundred of the élite of that city, including the Viceregal party and Lord Kitchener.

Another branch of this important commercial establishment in the "city of palaces" is the importation of wines and spirits, and let it be at once understood that nothing less than lengthy practical experience, and sound judgment in blending, maturing, and bottling would have enabled Messrs. Kellner & Co. to reach the proud position which they occupy to-day as the leading firm of wine and spirit merchants in Eastern India.

Wines, such as port, sherry, and Madeira, are imported in bulk, and as during the voyage they obtain an increased maturity equivalent to about 50 per cent. of their original value, they can be bottled in the firm's godowns as required, with the assurance that freshness and quality cannot be surpassed.

The firm's bonded warehouses in Calcutta contain an enormous reserve of a variety of Highland malt and other whiskies, and their sixty years of experience place them in a unique position with regard to blending and bottling in a manner suited to the Indian climate. The last two-mentioned processes are carried out under the immediate supervision of expert Europeans, and each cask is submitted to a thorough test before any of the spirit is withdrawn for consumption. Some of the favourite brands issued by Messrs. Kellner are: "O.H.M.S.," "Green Seal," "Red Seal," and "White Seal," and as a proof of their popularity it may be said that the quantity of whisky imported by this firm is three times greater than that of their nearest competitor.

Agencies are held for the following well-known shippers: Pommery, Et Greno, Ayala & Co., St. Marceaux & Co., Lalande et Cie, Bordeaux; Marie et Fils, Beaune; Mackenzie & Co., Jerez de la Frontera; Mackenzie Driscoll & Co., Oporto; Blandy Brothers, Madeira; the Distillers Company, Ltd., Edinburgh; Bass & Co., Burton-on-Trent; and many others.

THE KINNISON JUTE MILLS COMPANY, LTD.

This company, for whom Messrs. F. W. Heilgers & Co., of Chartered Bank Buildings, Calcutta, are managing agents, was incorporated on September 14, 1899, with an authorized capital of Rs. 15,00,000, divided into 10,000 ordinary shares and 5,000 preference shares, each of Rs. 100.

All kinds of sacking and hessian cloth are manufactured in two mills situated side by side on the left bank of the River Hooghly at Titaghur, on the Eastern Bengal State Railway, and about 14 miles distant from Calcutta. The original mill, which may be called No. 1, was started in the year 1899, while the foundations of No. 2 were laid on September 7, 1912, and work was commenced about eleven months later.

Referring to the whole block, it may be said that the buildings have been constructed in a very substantial manner; they are fitted with the most modern type of jute machinery and plant, driven by engines of 4,600 h.p., constructed by Messrs. Carmichael & Co., of Dundee, Scotland. There are no fewer than 1,220 looms; there is a complete up-to-date installation of electric light, and a private fire service consisting of modern appliances, in addition to patent "Grinnell" sprinklers, which have been provided by Messrs. Mather and Platt, Ltd., of London and Calcutta.

Messrs. Heilgers & Co. have their own launches and lighters between the mills and Calcutta, whence consignments are shipped for export to the world's consuming markets; and great saving in time and expense is secured owing to the fact that the mills are connected with the River Hooghly by a private jetty, and with the Eastern Bengal State Railway by a branch siding, these two auxiliaries facilitating the removal of raw material into the mills and the transfer of the products of the looms to the river boats. The daily average number of labourers is 7,500.

Mill No. 1 had about 360 looms in full work at the close of the year 1901, but such steady progress was made that this

F. W. HEILGERS & CO.

1. Kinnison Jute Mills, Titaghur. 2. Naihati Jute Mills.

F. W. HEILGERS & CO.

1. No. 1 Mill, Titaghur Paper Mills. 2. Beater House, No. 2 Mill, Titaghur Paper Mills. 3. No. 4 Machine, No. 1 Mill, Titaghur Paper Mills.

number had to be increased from time to time, until the end of 1915 there were about 750. The first ordinary dividend, declared for the year ended on September 30, 1901, was at the rate of Rs. 10 per share, and this amount was paid during the four following years. It should be mentioned that the increase in the number of looms just referred to necessitated the expenditure of considerable sums of money, and that the greater portion of such amounts was paid out of revenue. During the following years the dividend was Rs. 12 a share, and in 1912 it was Rs. 15. The capital of the company was increased in November 1912 (owing to the building of mill No. 2) to Rs. 30,00,000, divided into 15,000 ordinary and a similar number of preference shares, each of Rs. 100.

The balance-sheets of that date give the following satisfactory particulars: On September 30, 1913, a sum of Rs. 25 per share was paid on the old ordinary share capital of Rs. 10,00,000, and on the new issue of Rs. 5,00,000 a dividend was paid of Rs. 10 per share for the half-year ending on March 31, 1914 (equal to 20 per cent. per annum); a similar amount was declared six months later; and on March 31, 1915, there was another payment of Rs. 10 per share, together with a bonus, at the same rate, on all ordinary shares, while another Rs. 30 per share has just been declared for the half-year ending September 30, 1915, making a total distribution of Rs. 50 per share on the ordinary share capital for the year ending on that date.

During the whole of this period a very considerable amount has been transferred annually to depreciation and reserve fund accounts, and these payments are a sure indication of the prosperous condition of the company's affairs.

The directors of the company, whose registered offices are at Chartered Bank Buildings, Calcutta, are Sir Allan Arthur, Mr. T. E. T. Upton, and Mr. W. L. Carey.

THE NAIHATI JUTE MILLS COMPANY, LTD.

The mills owned by this company are situated at Hajeenuggar, near Naihati, a station on the Eastern Bengal State Railway, and 24 miles distant from Calcutta.

The capital (issued) consists of ordinary and preference shares amounting respectively to Rs. 6,00,000 and Rs. 7,50,000, making a total of Rs. 13,50,000, and ordinary dividends have been paid as follows: for half-year ended December 31, 1907, the sum of Rs. 3 per share, similar amounts on June 30 and December 31, 1908 and 1909, Rs. 5 on December 31, 1914, and Rs. 5 on June 30, 1915.

The mill was erected in 1905, and in the following year work was commenced with 350 looms, but the excellent and up-to-date plant now consists of 430 looms and 8,544 spindles.

The managing agents are Messrs. F. W. Heilgers & Co., and they have had the buildings fitted with all modern improvements (similar to the Kinnison mills), including electric lighting apparatus and a private fire service; and as the mill is situated on a bank of the River Hooghly and practically adjoins the railway, it has the benefit of being secured, in the movement of produce, by a jetty connecting with barges and by a branch railway siding.

Steam is the motive power of the machinery, among which is an engine (by Carmichael, of Dundee) of 1,800 h.p.; and some 12,000 tons of sacking and hessian goods are manufactured annually.

About 3,800 labourers are employed constantly. The registered offices of the company are at Chartered Bank Buildings, Calcutta, and the directors are Messrs. Shirley Tremearne, H. F. Yeoman, and W. L. Carey.

THE TITAGHUR PAPER MILLS COMPANY, LTD.

Industrial concerns in India using indigenous raw materials for consumption, and depending almost wholly upon local markets for the disposal of their products, are remarkably few in number in comparison with the vast material wealth of the country.

Development has taken place in certain directions since the middle of the nineteenth century, but much remains to be done, especially with regard to the manufacture of articles necessary for domestic purposes.

Printing, wrapping, writing, and other papers are required in business houses, offices, and private residences every day throughout the year; but large quantities are being imported from Europe, although the necessity for this should not arise, seeing that an abundance of suitable fibres are available in this country. It is therefore refreshing to witness the activities of the Titaghur Paper Mills Company, Ltd., which is one of the largest concerns of its kind in the British Empire, and which depends entirely upon local sources for its supplies.

The company are owners of two mills, situated at Titaghur and Kankinara, which are 14 miles and 25 miles distant from Calcutta respectively, and each of these has four paper-making machines.

The first-named mill was started in July 1884 with one machine; a second and third were added in 1886 and 1893; while the other mill, having three machines, was constructed in the year 1893 by the Imperial Paper Mills Company, who went into liquidation in 1903, when the property was acquired by the Titaghur Company.

Three years later the Bally Paper Mills—the oldest in Bengal—were in the market, and, with the view of controlling production and of restricting competition, the Titaghur directors purchased the undertaking and removed its two manufacturing machines to Titaghur and Kankinara.

The machinery at Titaghur is now driven by electricity, the power being derived from steam turbines, while at Kankinara the main drive is accomplished by one triple-expansion 1,100 h.p. engine with rope drives throughout. There are four Lancashire boilers working at a pressure of 100 lb., three others at 120 lb., and four at 160 lb. The mills not only have the advantage of an unfailing supply of water from the River Hooghly, upon whose bank they are erected, but they have, further, sidings upon the Eastern Bengal Railway system and river jetties to facilitate the dispatch of goods.

Each property has excellent workshops for mechanics, blacksmiths, joiners, and plumbers; the shops contain an unlimited supply of tools of the latest approved pattern, and the staff of trained workpeople are under the constant supervision of four European superintendents.

The annual output of the two mills is about 19,000 tons, and the products, which are of admirable quality, comprise papers known as engine and tub-sized cream wove, cream laid, bank posts, azure laid, white and toned printing, coloured printing, white and brown cartridges, Badami, Manila, and glazed art. All the raw materials are obtained locally, and they consist chiefly of Sabai grass, hemp, and cotton and jute rags; but when the price of sulphite wood is suitable certain quantities are imported, though the mills are in no way dependent upon this supply.

The labour question here is not the same serious difficulty as it is in many parts of India, and even in Bengal, hence it is that the company have no trouble in obtaining a sufficient number of intelligent workmen who readily adapt themselves to all the processes of manufacture. Climatic conditions naturally have a somewhat prejudicial effect upon the physical powers of the average Indian labourer, and thus it is found that three natives are required at Titaghur to accomplish the same amount of work as would be done by one operative in an English factory.

The European staff—consisting of married and single men—have been provided by the company with comfortably furnished dwelling-houses, and they reciprocate the thoughtful care of the directors by vieing with one another in making their quarters as neat and attractive as possible.

Each mill has a soda-recovery plant on the multiple evaporator principle, and a thoroughly efficient fire service gives the utmost protection to employees as well as to the premises and their contents, while ample accommodation in the shape of godowns is provided for the storage of raw materials, chemicals, and products of the mills. In short, the whole concern compares most favourably with others of its kind in Europe or elsewhere.

The Titaghur Paper Mills Company, Ltd., with head offices at Chartered Bank Buildings, in Calcutta (the managing agents being Messrs. F. W. Heilgers & Co.), was registered in the year 1882, the local directors being Mr. Guy Shorrock, the Hon. J. C. Shorrock, Mr. R. H. A. Gresson, Mr. Shirley Tremearne, and a member of the firm. The general manager at the mills is Mr. William Bryce.

EDWARD KEVENTER

Dairying is not, and it is doubtful if it ever can be, carried on in India as it is in New Zealand, Australia, the British Isles, and in many other countries of Europe where this exceedingly profitable industry is conducted on truly scientific principles.

There are many conditions existing in India which seem to preclude all possibility of its becoming a payable branch of agriculture, and in the forefront of unfavourable features is the climate of this vast country. There are huge tracts where the intense heat dries up all vegetation, and animals are in consequence reduced to starvation; then there are monsoons which turn thousands of acres into huge lakes, or they form roaring torrents of water which sweep away herds, flocks, and studs; and finally the indigenous cattle consist very largely of animals which are unable to yield returns of greater value than the cost of their keep. It must be remembered that dairying is largely a question of feeding, and in order that a cow may give a large quantity of milk, rich in butter fat, it must have good food. Dairying as an industry is inseparable from scientific agriculture, and with agricultural methods such as are commonly practised in India it is obviously impossible to expect great things at present.

Then again, there is an unusually large proportion of small holdings—plots they are in reality, but called "holdings" by courtesy, upon which it would be nothing short of a miracle for a single cow to be reared. At the same time it is admitted that one does occasionally see a dairy farm conducted on modern principles, but they are few and far between, a leading directory stating that there are not more than about eighty in the whole of India.

One of the principal dairy farmers in India is Mr. Edward Keventer, of the Aligarh Dairy Farm in the United Provinces of Agra and Oudh, who has similar concerns at Ballygunge, in the municipality of Tollygunge, near Calcutta, and at Delhi, Simla, Karachi, and Darjeeling.

Mr. Keventer experienced the greatest difficulty in obtaining land for a farm near Calcutta, but eventually he succeeded in purchasing about fifteen acres of land at Ballygunge, about five miles from the city, and as the area is so small it can only be regarded as a kind of exercising place for the cattle. A small quantity of artificial food is produced, but the major portion is purchased elsewhere.

There are about a hundred cows in full milk, the majority of which are of the Montgomery or Hissar strains, and the whole of the milk is sent twice daily to the proprietor's retail shop in Lindsay Street, Calcutta. A couple of fine bulls are kept on the farm, but Mr. Keventer draws largely upon his stud property at Aligarh for newly calved cows to fill vacancies at Ballygunge.

An imported Ayrshire bull was used, as an experiment, at Tara Devi Farm, Simla, and the heifers resulting from the cross give great promise of becoming very valuable cows for dairy purposes.

The dairy is a model of cleanliness; there is an abundance of fresh air, and the cemented floors are constantly washed with a plentiful supply of water. All pails, bottles, tins, and other utensils are thoroughly cleansed twice daily; they are first rinsed out with clean water, then they are placed in a tub containing water with an admixture of soda, in which the interiors are steamed three times; that operation is followed by a washing with a solution of Condy's fluid, then they are carefully brushed out with fresh water, and finally they are sterilized.

Few dairies can boast of such complete processes of purification, and this fact—coupled with the extremely satisfactory quality of the milk—accounts for the fact that Mr. Keventer always has a long list of names of persons waiting to become regular customers.

A steam boiler is used for providing a sufficient supply of hot water, and an oil engine is employed for cutting fodder and crushing grain.

Mr. Keventer realizes that the most profitable cow is very rarely the heaviest milker, and that the only method of ascertaining whether an animal is paying its way is to keep careful records of the tests made of its daily yield. The milk of each cow is weighed as soon as it is given, and a discrepancy between the yields of successive days is followed by a strict examination of the manner in which the servants perform the operation of milking. When the process of testing reveals the fact that there is a diminution in the percentage of butter fat, a change of diet may be tried, but the more usual plan is to replace the cow by a newly calved animal.

Mr. Keventer exercises the greatest care in the selection of his breeding stock, and bulls as well as cows must give evidence that they belong to good milking strains.

The large shed which is used at milking and feeding times consists of a corrugated iron roof supported on substantial brick pillars, and the cows are chained on either side of a cemented double manger which runs the whole length of the building, while the floor and drainage channels are also of brickwork.

There is another shed of smaller dimensions, together with a few well-constructed separate enclosures, or loose boxes, which are occupied by about sixty calves and young heifers. The floors of all buildings are kept scrupulously clean by washing and scrubbing, and all superfluous water is quickly removed along the numerous excellent channels which have been constructed.

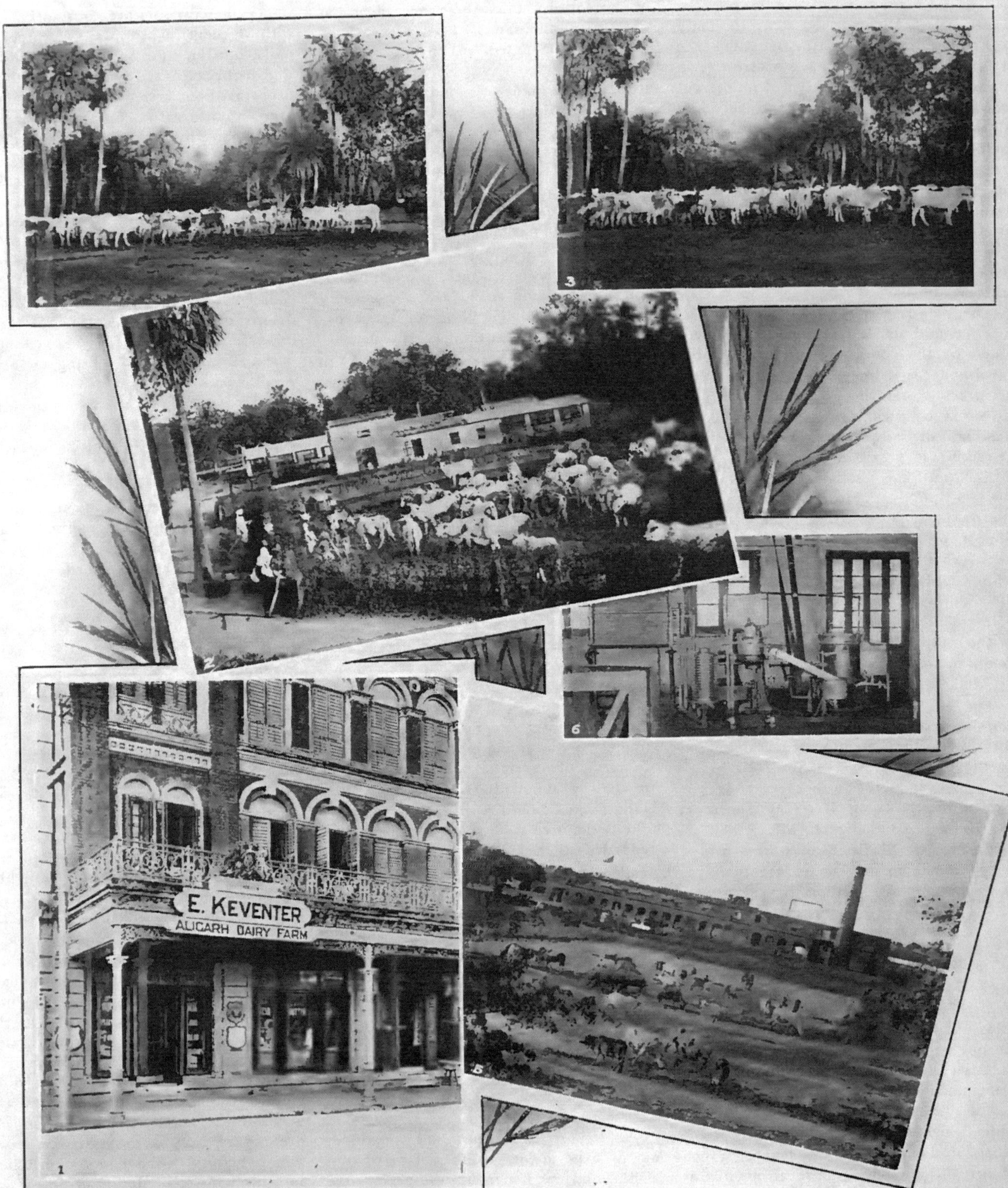

EDWARD KEVENTER.

1. The Calcutta Shop (Lindsay Street). 2. Ballygunge Farm. 3. Ballygunge Farm Cattle. 4. Ballygunge Farm Cattle. 5. Headquarters, Aligarh, U.P. 6. In the Dairy.

Few farm servants can boast of finer or more airy quarters, with brick walls, corrugated iron roofs, and cemented floors, than those here provided, but Mr. Keventer believes in doing things thoroughly, and he has no sympathy with primitive bamboo or grass huts with ordinary mud floors.

The farm, which is ably managed by Mr. R. Wernlund, is connected by telephone with the retail stores in Calcutta.

Mr. Keventer's dairy stores in Calcutta are situated at 6 Lindsay Street, a busy thoroughfare in the centre of the city and almost adjoining the Sir Stewart Hogg market.

The fresh milk yielded at Ballygunge is sent twice daily to the stores for dispatch to the owner's regular customers, while daily supplies of sterilized milk, fresh butter in packets and tins, and of cream and cream cheese are received from Aligarh. Ice chests are kept in the shop for the storage of butter, cheese, and cream, and a large number of bottles of sterilized milk are always on hand in order that extra demands may be fully met.

A very extensive connection has been established between the stores and shipping authorities, the principal hotels, restaurants, clubs, and scholastic and other institutions, while dozens of bottles of sterilized milk are—in normal times—supplied to persons who are taking young children to European and other countries.

Mr. Keventer is agent for the Dairy Supply Company, Ltd., of London, and keeps in stock a large quantity of dairy appliances, such as "Alfa-Laval" cream separators, pasteurizers, coolers, milk and cream vessels of all descriptions, milk-testing appliances and other sundries, while he is also agent for the well-known Darjeeling tea obtained from the Lopchu Estate belonging to Messrs. Langmore Brothers.

Mustard oil for cooking, medical, and other purposes (manufactured at the Aligarh farm) is also kept for sale in the stores.

Scores of medals and certificates have been awarded to Mr. Keventer's produce at exhibitions, and the proprietor has had the honour of receiving appointments as purveyor to His Majesty the King-Emperor, King George V, the Right Hon. Baron Hardinge of Penshurst, G.C.I.E., G.C.S.I., the Right Hon. the Earl of Elgin, P.C., the Right Hon. the Earl of Minto, P.C., and a number of other notable personages.

The manager of the stores is Mr. A. Shepherd.

KILBURN & CO.

The premises at 4 Fairlie Place, Calcutta, occupied by Messrs. Kilburn & Co., general merchants and agents, were in existence when Calcutta was in the making, when the mud-stained waters of the Hooghly were free from intrusions by ocean-going cargo or passenger steamers, and when the pioneers of industrial enterprise in Bengal were few in number. The very walls must be saturated with history, and if it were possible to glean secrets from them there would be revealed many stories of mercantile enterprise and of vicissitudes in commercial life; but as far as Messrs. Kilburn & Co.'s property is concerned there can be no more soul-stirring episode than that which occurred during the Mutiny, when a meeting of merchants was held in the old drawing-room to consider the question of defence, with the result that Mr. Edward Dunbar Kilburn was instrumental in enrolling the Calcutta Volunteer Cavalry for service in case of necessity.

The firm was founded in the year 1842 by Mr. C. E. Schoene, who opened offices at 4 Garstin's Place, business premises at 4 Fairlie Place, and godowns at the last-named address and in Clive Street. Mr. E. D. Kilburn commenced his business career in London with his uncle, who was trading in silk and silk piece goods, and on his arrival in India, in 1847, he at once entered into commercial relationships with Mr. Schoene, who admitted him as partner a couple of years later, the style of the firm being Schoene, Kilburn & Co.

The partners confined their early business transactions to commission agencies, and to orders for produce and sales of imported goods.

With regard to indigo, the firm employed an expert during the summer months, who visited continental merchants dealing in this substance in order to ascertain their probable requirements, and the latter were met by Messrs. Schoene and Kilburn purchasing the necessary quantity at the autumn sales in Calcutta.

Silk and silk piece goods were purchased respectively in France and England, cotton was shipped against orders from Liverpool, and rice was sent to Melbourne and to Colombo. Orders for jute were obtained by an agent in Dundee, under cover of credit with London bankers; shellac, lac-dye, safflower, and other produce were shipped in small quantities; hides were consigned to London and the continent of Europe; and opium was sent upon instructions from firms of merchants in Shanghai.

The goods imported and sold on commission about this time included cotton goods and yarns, French wines and brandies in large quantities, occasional copper consignments from Melbourne, and silk filatures from Messrs. Springfield Son and Nephew, London. The business of the firm expanded very rapidly during the first 20 years of the partnership, and it is noted that in the year 1865 Messrs. Schoene, Kilburn & Co. shipped in Calcutta a greater quantity of indigo than any other firm.

It was in or about that year, too, that the firm opened a branch establishment at Manchester, in England, under the management of Mr. Tolputt, who had been connected with the Calcutta house for a number of years, and this step had a very far-reaching effect upon the turnover of the firm. Advance in one direction led to a corresponding movement in another, as the firm opened up a trade in the mofussil which has, in its growth, exceeded all expectations.

Indigo planters were at this time making huge annual profits, and many of them, confident in the security of their invested capital, resided in England, leaving the supervision of their concerns to managers whose names are still held in the highest esteem, especially in Behar and Orissa. Parenthetically, it should be mentioned here that this prosperity continued, with few interruptions, until the year 1899, when the discovery of synthetic dye temporarily checked the cultivation of indigo and caused planters to resort to the manufacture of sugar. The export of this dye continued to be one of the most important branches of the firm's business, although consignments of general produce, including Bengal silk, cotton, hides, and tobacco, were sent more frequently and in larger quantities to Europe.

In the earlier years of the firm's existence, shipping matters generally played an important part in general commercial enterprise, and Messrs. Schoene, Kilburn & Co. became representatives of the then famous East Indiamen frigate-built ships, among which were the ***Hotspur*** and ***St. Lawrence*** (commanded respectively by those well-known mariners Captains Henry and Joseph Toynbee), the ***Lord***

Warden (Captain Smith), the *Superb* (Captain Jones), the *Winchester, Essex*, and many others. Further, the firm had the honour of receiving in Calcutta waters, in the year 1870, the first steamers of the Blue Cross Line which made the voyage to India by way of the Suez Canal.

The earliest direct agencies undertaken by the firm were the Durrung Tea Company, Ltd., in the year 1865, and the Assam Company, in 1867; while now (1916) they are managing agents for the India General Navigation and Railway Company, Ltd., which issues bookings on steamships and railways between Calcutta and Eastern Bengal, Assam, Cachar, and the Ganges; the Raneegunge Coal Association, Ltd.; the Indian Collieries Syndicate, Ltd.; the Bansra Coal Company, Ltd.; the Darjeeling Tea and Cinchona Association, Ltd.; the Kuturi Tea Company Ltd.; the Kornauli Association, Ltd.; Kodala, Ltd.; the Pashok Tea Company, Ltd.; Oodaleah, Ltd.; the Pahargoomiah Tea Association, Ltd.; the Rampore Tea Estate, Ltd.; the Sylhet Lime Company, Ltd.; the Russa Engineering Works, Ltd.; the Assam Company; the Lopchu Tea Estate; the New Terai Association, Ltd.; the Maulvie Tea Estate; the Norwich Union Fire Insurance Society, Ltd.; the Commercial Union Assurance Company, Ltd.; the Diamond Drill Syndicate; Messrs. H. Bull & Co., Ltd.; and the Crushed Limestone Syndicate; while they are general agents and supervising engineers of the Indian Electric Supply and Traction Company, Ltd.

The changes in the personnel of the partnership have been numerous during the three-quarters of a century of the firm's history, and the following references have been obtained from private documents. Mr. C. E. Schoene commenced business in 1842; he admitted Mr. Edward Dunbar Kilburn as a partner on May 1, 1849, and the latter retired in 1900. Messrs. George Adie and R. L. Eglinton joined the firm after the retirement of Mr. F. A. Jung in 1863; Mr. Robert Brown Mackay and Henry Tolputt were given shares in the business in 1865; Mr. Henry Francis Brown held interests from May 1866 until his retirement in April 1911; Messrs. W. R. Brown and Charles Kilburn were admitted in May 1873; Messrs. John Macfadyen and Alfred Simson followed in 1883; Mr. William Henry Cheetham in 1889; Messrs. W. D. Kilburn and Charles Conning Kilburn in May 1893; Sir Ralph P. Ashton in 1900; Messrs. Charles John Elton and Seton George Legge Eustace in 1911; while the partners at the present time are Messrs. A. Simson, W. H. Cheetham, C. C. Kilburn, Sir R. P. Ashton, Kt., C. J. Elton (London), S. G. L. Eustace, and E. P. J. de B. Oakley (Calcutta).

Mr. Edward Dunbar Kilburn, who played a most important part in the establishment and the subsequent activities of the firm now under notice, had an almost inexhaustible fund of historical incidents relating to the early days of Calcutta, but he will be best remembered for the spirit of intense loyalty which he exhibited during the troublous days leading up to the Mutiny. Mr. Kilburn went on a business visit to China in the year 1856, and upon hearing, on his return, of the disaffection which was spreading in certain parts of India, he called upon Lord Canning at Government House and offered his personal services, and any other help which he might be able to obtain, in order to protect the lives of peaceable and law-abiding citizens. The result of the interview was that Mr. Kilburn, with characteristic enthusiasm, summoned a meeting of leading commercial men, and the old drawing-room in Fairlie Place witnessed the formation of the Calcutta Volunteer Cavalry, of which Mr. Kilburn was gazetted captain. This gentleman lavishly spent both time and money in assisting the Government to suppress disloyalty, and the services rendered by him were so highly appreciated by the Viceroy that the latter decided to recommend Mr. Kilburn for the distinguished honour of a Companionship of the Bath. Lord Canning, however, died before effect could be given to his desire, and thus a patriotic and devoted servant of the Crown was denied that official recognition which his meritorious conduct richly deserved.

THE RUSSA ENGINEERING WORKS, LTD.

The Russa Engineering Works, Ltd., was founded as a private company in 1904, but it may be described as a branch of the engineering department of Messrs. Kilburn & Co., of 4 Fairlie Place, Calcutta, who are now the managing agents of the concern.

Originally the bulk of the work undertaken consisted of contracts for electric installations in mills and factories throughout India, and Messrs. Kilburn & Co. were the pioneers of electric enterprises in the Indian Empire. In about the year 1898 they obtained the concession for the public supply of electricity in Calcutta, and they floated and were the first managing agents of the Calcutta Electric Supply Corporation, Ltd. The installation of electric lights and fans in Calcutta was an important branch of their business, and this branch is continued, coupled with the work of complete electric installations in the collieries of Bengal and in jute and cotton mills.

The advent of the motor-car necessitated the building of workshops, and the mechanical engineering side of the Russa Engineering Works started operations with a small plant consisting of three machines. The work turned out gave such satisfaction to clients that extensions of the premises soon became necessary. These were duly carried out prior to the year 1906, when the original company was formed into a limited liability company, with a capital of Rs. 3,25,000, and from that date the works have steadily increased in size and prosperity. In 1912 the works consisted of 8 bays, three of which were occupied by the machine-shop, holding 22 machine tools of various types, and the remainder of the buildings were devoted to motor-car repair work.

At this date there was a large tank on the west side of the actual buildings, but this was filled up in order to provide ground for further extensions; and at the end of 1915 the premises consisted of 13 bays, arrangements having been made for large stores and car body building and painting departments. In this department there are two universal wood-working machines, circular and band saws, and all types of motor-car bodies are now being made and completed throughout under expert European supervision.

A special type of body has been adopted for fitting to the standard Ford model chassis, and a large demand has been met for high-class body-work of this description. Platform and charabanc bodies are also under construction for fitting to commercial cars' chassis, and this business, too, shows an ever-increasing growth throughout India. During the year 1915 the machine-shop had been expanded to four bays, and further provision having been found necessary for repairs to motor-cars and lorries (particularly the latter), a new

THE RUSSA ENGINEERING WORKS (KILBURN & CO.).

1. GENERAL VIEW OF WORKS FROM ROADWAY. 2. MOTOR-CAR REPAIR SHOP. 3. VIEW OF MACHINE SHOP. 4. VIEW OF MACHINE SHOP.

erecting and testing shed was added to the buildings early in 1916. This shed measures 150 feet by 50 feet, with height of 40 feet, and is probably the largest building in India devoted to the special purpose of testing and overhauling cars. The works also comprise a large blacksmith's shop with pneumatic-power hammer, as well as an up-to-date foundry, which deals with all the castings required by the machine-shop, whether in cast iron, brass, or gun-metal. It should be noted that very special attention is given in this foundry to high-class castings for gear wheels used in jute-mill machinery.

One might observe here that it is a matter of general interest to note the increased size and output of the machine-shop of the Russa Engineering Works, Ltd. Primarily the machine-shop was opened to meet the demands of the motor-car repairing department for spare parts of cars, and it was therefore equipped with the latest type of machine tools and gear-cutting plant, the number of machines in work in 1911 being 20. About this time the question of manufacturing spares for jute-mill machinery was taken in hand, and the result of the first move in this direction was an immediate and ever-growing demand for spares, such as necks and step bearings, spinning spindles, cop spindles, faller bars, roving spindles, roving necks, sack sewing-machine gears (worm and bevel), mangle pinions, and other accessories. This demand was met by the introduction of new machinery of the very latest types, comprising turret and engine lathes, also universal milling machines and grinding plant, and the machine-shop has now the most up-to-date and complete plant for light, accurate machine work in India.

The following machinery has been erected: engine lathes, 22; turret lathes, 11; machines for milling, 4; gear cutting, 3; drilling, 5; grinding, 8; woodworking, 4; slotting, 1; hand-tapping, 2; hand-milling, 2; power metal saws, 2; straightening presses, 2; hardening furnaces, 2. The latest methods have also been adopted for hardening gears by the use of gas-fired furnaces, controlled by electrical pyrometers, and a very high reputation has been gained for gear cutting of all types. Motor-car gears naturally predominate, but worm gears for lifts, collieries, and heavy duties generally are now part of the regular output of the shops. Oxy-acetylene plant has also been installed, and is largely used for repairing broken castings in cast iron and aluminium.

Owing to the special facilities afforded by this machine-shop, the car-repairing department has also steadily increased its output, and holds a very high reputation all over India. The ever-increasing demand for motor-cars in Calcutta during the past five years has been met by the Russa Engineering Works taking up agencies for such well-known cars as the Siddeley-Deasy, the Rover, the Humber, the Briton, the Autocarrier, and the Singer cars from England, and the Hudson, the Jeffery, the Regal, and the all-popular Ford car from America. The sales of this last make of car have now reached an average of 30 per month.

Commercial cars have also not been overlooked, and the firm hold the agency for the famous Albion lorries, which are so highly appreciated by the War Office in England that the factory is solely engaged in supplying their requirements, and are unable to accept orders for shipment to India. The Chase motor-lorry is also being imported from America in the 1-ton, 2-ton, and $3\frac{1}{2}$-ton models, and many sales have been effected of these useful cars. In general, it can be said that the Russa Engineering Works, Ltd., have kept in touch with all the latest movements in the motor engineering world.

Reference has already been made to the very fine machine-shop installed at the works, and since February 1915 the major portion of its plant has been solely engaged on munition work. A night shift has been in operation since July 1915, and a steadily increasing output is given to the Government authorities. Primarily the plant is engaged in manufacturing fuse needle holders for shrapnel shell, and at a recent date large orders have been received from the Gun Carriage Factory, Jubbulpore, for elevating gear for gun-carriages, which work involves the utmost accuracy in screw cutting, gear making, and other operations. A larger output on munitions work has been engaging the attention of the directors for some time past, but the management is unfortunately much handicapped by the shortage of skilled native labour at the present time in Calcutta.

Agencies have been established at Lahore, Karachi, and Dibrugarh, thus affording facilities for the numerous clients of the company who live at a distance from the capital city.

The managing agents of the company are Messrs. Kilburn & Co.

W. LESLIE & CO.

Chowringhee Road, Calcutta, contains some remarkably fine residential mansions and business establishments, and prominent among the latter are the two capacious buildings, 3 and 5, occupied as shops and storerooms by Messrs. W. Leslie & Co., hardware and metal merchants, mechanical engineers, Government contractors, and agents for motor-cars and cycles. Their works are situated at 60 Dhurrumtollah Street, and the shops for blacksmiths, fitters, turners, foundrymen, and plumbers are fitted with thoroughly up-to-date machinery, which is controlled by European engineers. The firm's godowns in Mati Sil Street are connected with the premises, 3 Chowringhee Road, and they are literally packed from roof to floor with an almost endless quantity of hardware goods of all descriptions, of which Messrs. Leslie & Co. are said to be the largest importers in Calcutta.

The business, established in the year 1890, has increased with great rapidity, and, in addition to the magnitude of their trade relationships in every district in India, the firm are now supplying immense quantities of stores for the military and railway authorities. It is only recently that the British Government ordered piping, many miles in length, for war purposes in Mesopotamia, but this is only an individual item culled from a lengthy list of orders for goods of a similar character.

It is extremely difficult to know where to commence in attempting to give even a brief description of the mass of the contents of Messrs. Leslie & Co.'s premises. They supply portable, fixed, vertical, and horizontal steam engines, vertical and other boilers, oil engines, saw benches, screw-cutting lathes, pneumatic-power hammers, and Morgans' crucibles and furnaces. The motor department comprises Scripps, Booth, Singer, Belsize, Delage, Hotchkiss, Rudge-Multi, and other motor-cycles, auto-wheels, oil and acetylene lamps, tyres, saddles, and, in fact, numerous accessories for motor-cars. A special feature is made of the sale of tools for carpenters, blacksmiths, platelayers, tinsmiths, and boilermakers, and they are agents for Messrs. Cammell, Laird & Co.'s files, Sir Joseph Jonas and Colver's files and steel sets of engineering

W. LESLIE & CO.

1. Exterior. 2. Showroom (Furnishing). 3. Showroom (Motor-cars, Bicycles, and Typewriters). 4. Metals and Timber Store. 5. Machine Tool Department.

and carpenters' tools. Household furnishings and appointments include writing and roll-top desks, silver and electroplated goods, chairs, tables, brackets, lamps, cutlery, ice-chests, churns, glassware, bedsteads, mattresses, matting, and cooking utensils of all descriptions. The requirements of planters, contractors, and agriculturists have been fully considered, and one can select the best types of weighing machines, axes, bellows, belting, benches, cement, chains, forges, hammers, tea sieves (imported from Japan), pruning knives, lawn-mowers, *kodallies*, jacks, crushing-mills, rice-hullers, hoes, spades, and almost every description of machinery. The godowns contain a very large quantity of bolts and nuts, the largest stock of wire nails in India, more than 100 tons of paint, iron rods, wire for fencing, barbed wire, iron hooping for tea chests, pumps, cisterns, files, and a miscellaneous assortment of hardware goods.

Messrs. W. Leslie & Co. are agents in Calcutta for the famous "Underwood" and "Bijou" typewriters, each of which has become exceedingly popular in its own sphere of work. The foolscap model (No. 5) of the first-named machine takes a sheet of paper 10 in. in width, and it is found in nearly all Government offices in India as well as in many other countries. Other sizes are kept in stock, and one of these will write a single line not less than 24 in. in length. Grand and gold medals, prizes, and diplomas have been awarded to the manufacturers during the past fifteen or twenty years at exhibitions held at places situated so widely apart as Paris, Buffalo, Venice, Rome, St. Louis, Jamestown, Oregon, Petrograd, Philadelphia, Buenos Ayres, Barcelona, Glasgow, and London.

The "Bijou" machine, weighing about 8 lb., is a great boon to the traveller, as its bulk can be so reduced that it can be fitted into a neat and compact leather travelling case, similar to a handbag, and when folded it measures only 10½ by 5 by 8 in. More than sixteen thousand of these typewriters have been sold in the course of twelve months.

One might extend this list almost indefinitely, but sufficient has been said to show that Messrs. W. Leslie & Co. have built up a very large and prosperous connection with customers in all parts of India, and the fact that a very large number of their patrons have supported them continuously for a number of years is abundant evidence of the sterling worth of the goods sold by the firm, and of the careful and expeditious manner with which all commissions are executed.

The proprietor of the concern is Mr. W. Leslie, who is assisted by his partners, Mr. M. J. Leslie and Mr. J. F. Greig.

About 500 hands are employed in the engineering works in Dhurrumtollah Street, and about 150 in the shops and stores in Chowringhee Road.

THE LINDE BRITISH REFRIGERATION COMPANY, LTD.

This company, whose head offices are at 35 Queen Victoria Street, London, E.C., had works in England, at Shadwell and Birmingham, before establishing their first factory in India in 1901, at 138 Balliaghatta Road, Calcutta, when a Linde Refrigerating Plant on the ammonia system was installed to produce 26 to 27 tons of ice daily and with, in addition, refrigerated stores for about 800 tons of ice. In this plant two single-acting horizontal compressors were driven direct from the crank-shaft of a marine type inverted, triple-expansion, jet-condensing engine, working with steam at 160 lb. pressure from two "Economic" boilers fitted with return tubes. The ice was manufactured on the "can system" in blocks of 250 lb. and 18 of these cans or, 2 tons, constituted one lift, or about one hour's working from the ice tank.

In 1903 it was found that increasing business demanded extension of plant, and a second unit, almost exactly similar to the first, was installed, thus raising the ice production to 52 or 54 tons per day.

Ten years later a third extension was made bringing the out-turn of ice up to more than 80 tons daily, but instead of using steam in this last unit, two Diesel engines were fitted, one operating the ammonia compressor through a rope drive, and the other coupled direct to a dynamo generating the electric current for driving the auxiliary gear, the electric ice-lifting crane, and other machinery. The compressors, condensers, and ice tank evaporators of the three units are so arranged as to allow the different compressors to be used in conjunction with any of the ice tanks or condensers. The ice produced is very clear and hard and is of a readily marketable size for all purposes, the blocks being 43 in. by 24 in. by 8 in., and are easily cut to suit smaller requirements.

In 1912 the Linde Company opened an ice factory at Byculla Bridge, Bombay, where the most modern ice-making plant in India was installed. This was on the "plate system," whereby absolutely transparent blocks of ice 12 in. in thickness and weighing about 5 tons each are made. The Bombay works can produce a daily quantity of 70 tons, and they also have refrigerated storage capacity for a stock of about 700 tons. Plans are already out for a duplication of this plant. Internal combustion engines are employed to drive the ammonia compressors and auxiliaries, and the engine-room is well laid out and ranks with the finest in India.

In addition to ice-producing plants, the Linde Company have, at the same addresses in Calcutta and Bombay, separate factories wherein oxygen of high purity is mechanically produced from liquid air. The first of these works (and the first to be established in India) was started in 1912, and for some time the Calcutta works forwarded supplies to Bombay, but as the demands for oxygen gas by engineering firms and shipyards in the latter city increased, an oxygen factory was built at Byculla Bridge, Bombay, in 1914. The air and oxygen compressors and auxiliaries are, in both places, driven by internal combustion engines, and these works undoubtedly established the use of oxygen for welding and metal-cutting in India and developed its employment for other purposes, as, prior to their erection, all the oxygen for India was imported from England or the continent of Europe, and the freight and charges prohibited it from being employed to any extent. Oxygen is supplied in cylinders containing 20, 40, 100, and 200 cub. ft. at a pressure of 120 atmospheres, the two smaller sizes being used for medical and limelight work, and the two larger for welding and metal cutting. Describing the process of manufacture of the gas, notes in a Journal of Proceedings of the Institution of Mechanical Engineers, dated Calcutta 1912-13, say that "the plant depends upon a method by which a moderate amount of refrigeration, produced by the expansion of a gas which has been previously cooled, may be accumulated and intensified until it reaches the point at which the gas becomes liquid, at, or slightly above, atmospheric pressure. The expanded gas is directed over coils which contain the compressed gas, and a much lower temperature is the result. The intensification of cooling continues, and the effect is so powerful that even the small amount of cooling, due to the free expansion of gas through a

THE LINDE BRITISH REFRIGERATOR COMPANY, LTD.

1. The Ice Factory in Calcutta. 2. Oxygen Factory in Calcutta. 3. Some of the Machinery in the Ice Factory Engine-room. 4. General View of Machinery in the Oxygen Factory. 5. Native Mistry Welding by the Oxy-Acetylene Process.

throttle valve, may be made to liquefy air without using any other refrigeration. After passing through lime purifiers, atmospheric air enters the first stage of the air compressor, and is delivered through water-cooled coils before entering the second stage. When the compressor is first started, the final pressure is 2,000 lb. to the sq. in., but, after liquefaction has taken place, the normal working pressure during the actual separation of the oxygen and nitrogen falls to about 720 lb. per sq. in."

The oxygen gas is drawn by a three-stage compressor from a large gas-holder, and is compressed into steel cylinders to a pressure of 120 atmospheres (1,800 lb.) to the sq. in.

Air contains about 79·1 per cent. of nitrogen, and 20·9 per cent. of oxygen, and a healthy person consumes about 20 ft. of the latter in the course of 24 hours. An individual may suffer through the presence of noxious gases in the atmosphere, or through enfeebled respiration, and as the inhalation of oxygen is then of vital importance, it will be understood that the company have, by providing this chemically pure gas (compressed into cylinders so as to be readily transported), furnished the medical profession with a therapeutic agent of which they have not been slow to avail themselves. Oxygen is now used with signal success in cases of asphyxia, in the treatment of wounds and sores, or for many maladies not connected with the respiratory organs, and it is gratifying to know that many lives have been saved by the prompt administration of gas. The company are in a position to supply, together with the oxygen, the necessary india-rubber tubing, nipples, adjustment valves, and other accessories in order that the gas may be inhaled direct from the cylinder. These can be obtained from the works in Calcutta or Bombay.

We now come to the consideration of the use of oxygen in welding joints and cutting metals by the oxy-acetylene blowpipe process, but before entering into details upon this point it may be observed that among the purposes to which this practice may be advantageously employed are (says the Mechanical Engineer's Journal above referred to): the manufacture of iron or steel bolts as a substitute for rivets; the repair of steam boilers *in situ*; the manufacture of safes; the fusion welding of all joints in metallic casks or drums; as a substitute for rivets in their sheet-iron work; for adding metal to worn parts; the fusion welding of tanks and hot-water boilers; the welding of hospital furniture as a substitute for joints and rivets; for artistic iron work; in welding new teeth in broken gear wheels; and the repairing of differential and other gear boxes. In the year 1899 it was demonstrated that, after heating an iron plate to incandescence by means of the oxygen and coal-gas flame obtained with a blowpipe, it was possible, by largely increasing the supply of oxygen, to "fuse" holes in the plate. These investigations paved the way for a general use of the blowpipe for welding purposes, and engineers are now discovering innumerable ways in which it can be used in construction work as well as in general repairs. The Linde Company assert that autogenous welds can be effected by means of the oxy-acetylene blowpipe without any injurious effect upon the metal, and it is now fully established that defects or breakages in machinery or plant can be remedied, and thus the scrap-heap is robbed of further additions. Engineers have repeatedly shown their approval of this rapid and effective system of welding, and the extraordinary demand from all parts of the world for blowpipes is a striking testimony to their worth. The Linde Company are not makers of dissolved acetylene, but they are in a position to supply cylinders of this agent in quantities varying from 100 to 200 cub. ft.

It will naturally occur to many persons to ask questions as to the possible strength of an oxy-acetylene blowpipe joint, and the answer would be that bars of Staffordshire iron, fused together by this system, have given tests of more than 29 tons per sq. in. at the joint, and plates of iron and steel varying in thickness from 20 gauge upwards, when thus welded together, have proved stronger at the joint than in the body of the plate.

In cutting through metal, an ordinary blowpipe, with an additional passage through which an independent and separately-controlled stream of oxygen is supplied at the discretion of the operator, is employed, and this gas may be discharged through the centre of the blowpipe, or the supply may be brought into a passage immediately behind the heating flame.

The Linde Company keep a large stock of seamless steel oxygen cylinders, gas pressure gauges, automatic regulators, "Universal" blowpipes with welding range on mild steel-plate, hydraulic back-pressure valves, self-adjusting cylinder stands for use in hospitals, and oxygen respirating apparatus for working in noxious or irrespirable gases, together with an extensive and varied assortment of accessories.

Experienced workmen are sent to give demonstrations and instruction in the event of an installation of plant being contemplated, and visitors to the company's works are courteously received and are permitted to witness the welding of joints and the cutting of metal or any other work which the blowpipe may be called upon to perform.

The company are also large suppliers of refrigerating machinery for all purposes and accessories and stores for same. Machines constructed according to the Linde system may be seen at work in Delhi, Lahore, Peshawar, Allahabad, Lucknow, Agra, Cawnpore, Gwalior, Hyderabad, Meerut, Fyzabad, Mysore, Sealkot, Ambala, Aligarh, Simla, Bareilly, Moradabad, Jhansi, Malabar, Poona, Ludhiana, Surat, Chittagong, Madras, Rangoon, and many other places.

The telegraphic addresses of the company are: "Lindfrost" Calcutta and "Lindeice" Bombay.

LLEWELYN & CO.

In the year 1800 a certain Rajah in Northern India brought across the seas one Jenkin Llewelyn, a Welsh artist and sculptor, for the purpose of utilizing his services in the production of a number of paintings and statuary work, and, on the termination of this engagement in the year 1804, Mr. Llewelyn removed to Calcutta and began to practise his art on his own account in a building in Bentinck Street, which is now occupied by the Savoy Hotel. A special feature was made of monumental masonry, but progress was so disappointingly slow that two years later he entered into partnership with an undertaker named Simpson, who was then occupying premises (immediately opposite his own place of business), which from that time to this day have been in the hands of Llewelyn & Co.

Incidentally it may be mentioned that the building tenanted by the partners had previously been the residence of Governors of Bengal, and even to-day (1916) one can see the old throne and other rooms which were used by their Excellencies during meetings of council.

The style of the new firm was "Simpson and Llewelyn," and unmistakable proof of the excellent quality of their work is found in the fact that memorial stones prepared by them more than a hundred years ago are still in a sound condition and may be inspected in the Old Park Street and numerous other burial-grounds. Mr. Simpson, unfortunately, died in 1812, and the surviving partner continued the business under the style of Llewelyn & Co. Mr. Llewelyn subsequently admitted two of his brothers, and, at a later date, two of his sons, into the concern, and a member of the family was associated with the firm until the death of Mr. John Griffith Llewelyn in 1880, when Mr. J. H. Herbert became sole proprietor. Several other changes took place prior to the latter part of the year 1914, when Mr. James Reid, the present owner, whose connection with the firm dates from the early part of the year 1911, entered into sole possession.

Messrs. Llewelyn & Co. (whose firm was one of the oldest members of the Calcutta Trades Association) import the choicest marble direct from the quarries, and an enviable reputation has been gained by them for the quality of the materials used and for the first-class manner in which all work is carried out. The firm's showrooms contain an exceedingly large quantity of decorative statuary and memorial stones in marble, granite, and stone, and their workshops—the largest in the trade in Calcutta—are the only ones of their kind in the city which contain machinery driven by electricity.

The importance of the undertaking and funeral furnishing department is manifested by the punctilious care which is exercised in carrying out the desires of the firm's patrons, and Mr. Reid's personal supervision of arrangements is a guarantee that all duties will be satisfactorily performed.

LLEWELYN & CO.

1. THE HEAD OFFICE. 2. INTERIOR, SHOWING STONEMASONS AT WORK. 3. INTERIOR—POLISHERS AT WORK.

WALTER LOCKE & CO., LTD.

It is not a difficult matter, after strolling through the extensive premises in Esplanade East, Calcutta, occupied by Messrs. Walter Locke & Co., Ltd., to realize the correctness of their claim that theirs is "the largest concern in India dealing purely in sporting goods."

The business was commenced in the year 1888 at the present address, in a very fine building situated near to the handsome block erected by the Government for the Foreign Office and Military Departments, and the firm began with the importation and handling of guns and sporting goods generally.

The history of the firm may be summed up in the one word "progress"; their business having increased steadily and rapidly to the present time, when they are rightly regarded as being in the van of commercial enterprises in Calcutta.

Messrs. Walter Locke & Co. are dealers in every description of sporting gear, guns, rifles, and ammunition, and in appliances for cricket, lawn tennis, bowls, fencing, rackets, hockey, Badminton, golf, cycling, football, croquet, boxing, polo, and other amusements.

The firm are agents in India for Messrs. Holland and Holland, Westley-Richards, and Cogswell and Harrison for guns and rifles; and for Messrs. Kynoch, Eleys Ltd., and Curtis and Harvey, Ltd.,

WALTER LOCKE & CO., LTD.

1. The Head Office, Calcutta. 2. Fleet of Machine-gun Sidecars, Manufactured Entirely by Walter Locke & Co. for Government. Fitted to "Ariel" Motor Cycles. 3. Opening up a Shipment of "Indian" Machines at the Garage.

for sporting ammunition. Guns and rifles recommended by the firm include: The H. and R. Arms Company single-barrel automatic ejector shot-gun, an ideal weapon for a *shikari*; the Locke "Wonder" gun, 12 bore, of best English manufacture; the Locke "Improved Marvel" double-barrel breech-loading gun in 12, 16, or 20 bores, specially bored for long range and great penetration; Locke's hammerless ejector, a handsome double-barrel gun with latest improvements; the Westley-Richards special model high-grade hammerless ejector gun; the famous Ross high velocity rifle, noted for its great killing power; the Westley-Richards ·318 accelerated express magazine rifle; Jaffrey's "Mauser" magazine-action rifle ·334 and ·404 bores; and Winchester and other first-class weapons. The firm carry a large stock of English and American revolvers by Webley, Colt, Ivor Johnson, Harrington, and Richardson, and they supply all kinds of cartridges, gun cases, bullets, and accessories. Other sporting requisites comprise (*inter alia*) bullet moulds, cleaning rods, decoy ducks, game carriers, hog spears, hunting-knives, powder-flasks, shooting seats, and a host of other sundries.

Messrs. Walter Locke & Co. held the first agency in India for Messrs. Slazenger & Co.'s tennis rackets and balls; and it may be mentioned here that the latter were used for the twelfth successive year for the World's Championship meeting in 1913. Many other varieties of rackets are kept in stock, such as "The Spalding Gold Medal," "The Doherty," "The Phenomenon," "The Riseley," "The Demon," and others.

This department of sporting goods of a general character is so well stocked that an accomplished athlete or the boy or girl emerging from the nursery would have little difficulty in finding exactly what was fancied for the development of already hardened muscles or for mere amusement during hours of cessation from studies.

The six-foot "blue" might look with pleasant recollections of 'Varsity days at a grand selection of boxing and batting gloves; cricket bats by well-known makers would remind him of centuries made at Lord's or the Oval; and he would gaze with keen delight upon fencing foils, horizontal bars, polo sticks, or Indian clubs; while the youngsters would be seized with a desire to charter a Pickford van to carry away a load of boxes of games, skipping ropes, cricket and croquet sets, footballs, and numerous other attractions.

At this juncture one is reminded that when the boom in motor cycling commenced in India Messrs. Walter Locke were early in the field with agencies for several of the leading manufacturers in England, and they are now agents for the "Triumph," and sole agents on the eastern side of India for the famous "Indian," the "Lea Francis," the "Ariel," the "Levis," and many other machines of the highest quality. They are the largest importers of, and specialize in, motor-cycles. The "Indian," a leading cycle on the market to-day, is supplied in six different models, and it has stood many remarkably severe tests as to durability, speed, and ease in running. At the time of writing (April 1916) the firm have seventy-five of these machines on the sea *en route* for Calcutta. Again, riders of "Ariel" machines won the team prize in the Scottish and English six days' trials in 1913, thus beating all records. No fewer than eight gold medals were awarded during these contests. Spare parts and accessories are kept in stock, and repairs of all kinds are attended to by thoroughly skilled workmen serving under European motor engineers.

Messrs. Walter Locke & Co. are, further, agents in India for Messrs. Elkington & Co., Ltd., the well-known manufacturing jewellers, gold and silversmiths, and originators of electro-plating, who are specialists in medals in bronze, gold, and silver, cups, bowls, trophies, shields, and prizes for every branch of sport, jewels, watches, clocks, silverware, "Elkington" plate cutlery, and other articles of a similar nature.

Reference must be made before closing to the "True Life Targets," for which this firm have been appointed sole agents in India. These targets approach as nearly as possible to the shape, colour of uniforms, and movements of soldiers, and they present such unexampled opportunities for practice in rifle shooting that they have been approved by the Hythe School of Musketry and various Government departments in England.

The South African War, and now the tremendous conflict in Europe, have shown that ordinary targets are practically out of date for instruction purposes in modern warfare, but the inventions just referred to give a reality to the object of the firing by depicting a supposed enemy in uniforms corresponding in colour to trees, bare land, rocks, roadways, or buildings, and thus a soldier in training gains a very vivid representation of scenes with which he will be confronted on active service.

It should be added that the firm have a garage at 14 British Indian Street, Calcutta, and this building not only provides ample space for the storage of motor-cars and cycles, but it also contains extensive workshops where these machines can be refitted or repaired—however badly damaged—in the shortest possible time.

The firm are sole agents in Bengal, Bihar and Orissa, Assam, the United Provinces, and the Punjab for the Lister-Bruston Automatic Electric Lighting and Pumping Installation, and the special feature of this patent system is that it generates electricity automatically immediately it is required for lighting or any other purpose, and thus removes the necessity for expensive storage batteries.

Other important agencies are those for direct-current motors supplied by the Rhodes Motors, Ltd., of Doncaster, England, and of Hart's celebrated storage batteries, which are designed more particularly for motor-cars, boats, automobiles, small plating work, and other light loads.

The "Locke" electric ceiling fan possesses three distinct features: (1) reliability, as it has a minimum of separate parts, and consequently a minimum of risk of disorder; (2) accessibility, it being unnecessary to take the fan to pieces in order to get at the commutator and brushes; and (3) simplicity, because there are no loose ornamental castings to cause noise or to harbour dust. The firm's electric cooking apparatus is highly appreciated wherever it has been introduced, and it includes combined grill and toaster, electric irons, saucepans, frying-pans, hot-water jugs, cooker, kettles, and sundry other articles.

Many important contracts for electric work have been carried out for the Governments of India and Bengal, for several hospitals, the Treasury buildings, the Telegraph Office, the Presidency College, and other buildings, as well as for leading business houses in Calcutta.

The firm retain a staff of highly qualified electrical engineers who were trained in the Old Country, although two of these have received commissions since the outbreak of war.

Messrs. Walter Locke & Co. have

branches at Lahore and Delhi, and the managing director is Mr. W. J. Bradshaw, who has for many years past taken an active part in the administration of local affairs in Calcutta. He was President of the Market Committee when important additions were made to the Stewart Hogg Market Buildings; he has served on the Port Trust as the representative of the Calcutta Trades Association, and he has been a municipal commissioner for many years, and was the first elected representative of the Calcutta Trades Association on the Bengal Council.

The telegraphic address of the firm is "Waltlocke," Calcutta.

H. P. MAITRA & CO.

The sole proprietor of this firm, Mr. H. P. Maitra, was formerly financially interested in certain commercial concerns in Calcutta, but in the year 1906 he commenced business on his own account, trading as H. P. Maitra & Co., as a general merchant and commission agent, dealing in stone lime, coal, timber, and Manchester piece and other goods.

The premises are situated at the junction of Clive Row with Clive Street, two of the busiest thoroughfares in Calcutta, and within a couple of minutes' walk of the Royal Exchange and the principal banks of the city.

The firm are managing agents for the Gonesh Cotton Mills Company, Ltd., and for the Maitra Stone and Lime Company, Ltd., whose kilns, built in 1912, are situated at Maihar, on the East Indian Railway, about 96 miles distant from the important junction of Jubbulpore and 637 miles from Calcutta. The Maihar lime is one of the very best stone limes of India, and is extensively used by the Government Public Works Department, District Boards, railways, municipalities, and other public bodies, as well as by the most eminent architects, builders, and contractors of Bengal and the United Provinces. It is also used largely upon tea gardens and indigo and sugar estates for manuring purposes, and it constitutes one of the principal ingredients in the manufacture of the different manures and fertilizers.

Coal, which is obtained from collieries in the Jherria fields (for which the firm are managing agents), is sold chiefly in wholesale quantities to the Government and to mills, and imported timber is disposed of to the Ordnance and Public Works Departments, to the Calcutta and other Municipalities, some of the District Boards, and also to the principal contractors and shipbuilders.

Messrs. Maitra & Co. are, further, proprietors of the Bay Fishery at Balugaon, on the Chilkah Lake, in the Province of Orissa. Motor-boats are used in fishing, and the catches are packed in ice and forwarded by rail to Calcutta and other places, where they are sold wholesale only to merchants in the fish markets. They also prepare cured, dried, and salted fish for the Burma and Straits markets and for export to other countries.

The firm have a very valuable asset in the monopoly which they enjoy for the sale of cigarettes in the Independent Kingdom of Nepal. They purchase a certain brand from the manufacturers in India, and the latter, according to agreement with Messrs. Maitra & Co., are precluded from making any of the same kind for any other firm.

Mr. Maitra undertakes personal management of the business, and he usually employs altogether about 250 hands in his different businesses.

The telegraphic address is "Maitraph, Calcutta," and the London correspondents are Messrs. Alfred Young & Co.

MARSHALL, SONS & CO., LTD.

It is believed that fully 80 per cent. of the steam engines in India have been manufactured by Messrs. Marshall, Sons & Co., Ltd., of the Britannia Works, Gainsborough, in England, where they established themselves in the year 1848. Their premises in that Lincolnshire town, abutting on the banks of the River Trent, cover an area of nearly 40 acres, and about five thousand skilled workmen and labourers are constantly employed; or, in other words, one-quarter of the total population of the town are found in the Britannia workshops, yards, and offices.

The firm are amongst the largest makers of industrial and agricultural machinery in the world, and they were pioneers in India with their well-known steam threshing machines. Their Calcutta branch was opened in Lal Bazar in the year 1889, and about seven years later they removed to their present commodious quarters at 99 Clive Street, where they occupy extremely well-appointed offices, together with extensive godowns, in which is stored a large and varied selection of the productions of the Gainsborough factories.

The firm are manufacturers of (*inter alia*) high-class horizontal engines up to 2,000 h.p.; Lancashire, Cornish, locomotive multi-tubular, vertical, and other boilers; portable and semi-portable engines; oil and electric light engines; road rollers; traction engines; steam and oil tractors; threshing, grinding, and sawing machinery; disintegrators; pumps of all descriptions; and, in fact, almost everything in the way of mechanical plant known to modern engineers.

One of the most important economic questions in India at the present time is the regulating of the supply of labour not only for mills, factories, foundries, and other similar works, but also for agricultural development.

Labour-saving appliances are only now beginning to receive the recognition which they deserve, but as the supply of labourers in India is becoming more and more unreliable, economists realize that the only remedy is in the increase of power plants in the country.

Messrs. Marshall have devoted careful thought to this question, and their lengthy experience has enabled them to come to the assistance of agriculturists, spinners, weavers, millers, and other leaders of industrial concerns.

A reference is called for to their steam threshing machinery, which has received the following, among other, awards: First prize of £40 at the Royal Agricultural Society's Show at Cardiff, the only first prize and special mention at the New Zealand International Exhibition, the only first prize at the Sydney International Exhibition, a special first prize and gold medal at the Tasmanian International Exhibition, five gold medals and three silver ones at the Calcutta International Exhibitions, and gold and silver medals at the Omsk-Siberian Exhibition. This threshing machinery—including the engines—is constructed and equipped to meet the requirements of the country in which it is to be used, and the firm are always alert to discover and supply any manifest improvement.

Special mention should be made of the thoroughly up-to-date machinery—designed by the well-known inventor, Mr. William Jackson—for the drying, rolling, fanning, sifting, equalizing, and packing of tea, all of which is manufactured only by Messrs. Marshall. This plant is made of first-class materials, and tea-planters in Bengal, Assam, Ceylon, and elsewhere

H. P. MAITRA & CO.

1 AND 2. FISHING IN THE CHILKA LAKE. 3. LIME WORKS AT MAIHAR. 4. LIMESTONE QUARRY AT MAIHAR.

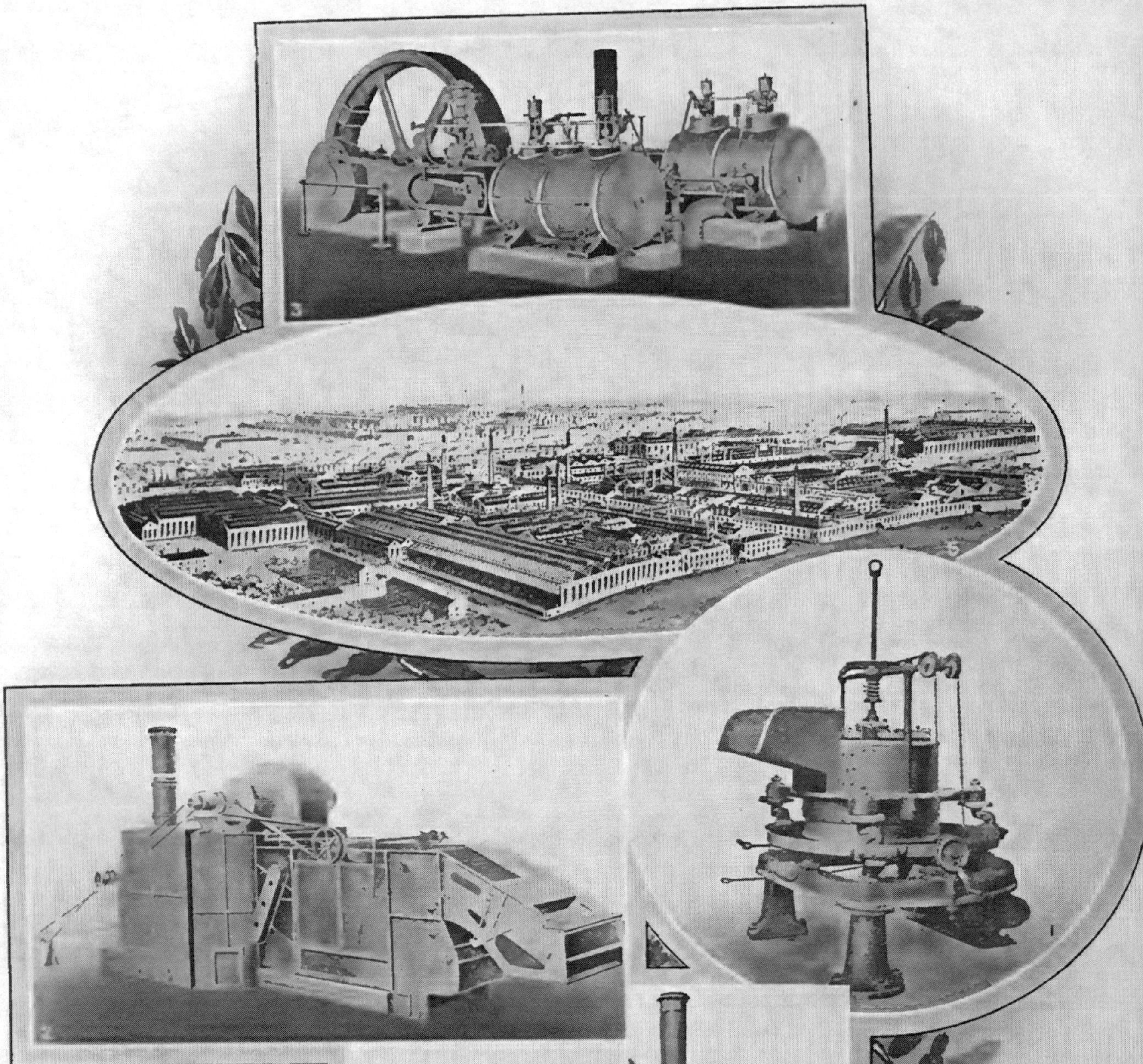

MARSHALL, SONS & CO., LTD.

1. Tea-leaf Rolling Machine. 2. Empire Tea-drying Machine. 3. Cross Compound Engine, Class "L". 4. Compound Road Roller. 5. View of the Works, Gainsborough, England.

MARTIN & CO.

1. The Alliance Bank of Simla, Ltd., Calcutta. 2. Esplanade Mansions, Calcutta. 3. Calcutta Club. 4. Residence, Patna Capital.

have shown their appreciation of the firm's action in placing such valuable tea factory requirements within their reach.

Messrs. Marshall have branches in Bombay, Lahore, Bezwada, and Madras, but their agencies are found in nearly all the principal cities and towns of the civilized world.

During the past half century, in open competition with other manufacturers, Messrs. Marshall have received more than five hundred awards for the excellence of their productions, these distinctions including grand prix, diplomas of honour, and gold and silver medals.

The London offices and showrooms of the firm are at Marshalls' Buildings, 79 Farringdon Road, E.C., while the general manager for India is Mr. J. Harper.

MARTIN & CO.

India provides a grand field for contractors and engineers, and among many firms of note that of Messrs. Martin & Co., of 6 and 7 Clive Street, Calcutta, stands out most prominently in the van. During the past thirty or forty years there have been few undertakings of any magnitude—whether in the construction of systems of waterworks, light railways, Government buildings, rajah's palaces, private mansions, or other contract work —with which Messrs. Martin & Co. have not been connected in some way or other. If they have not actually prepared designs and specifications, they have probably built the buildings, or, failing that, they may have supplied iron and steel fittings, or bricks, or coals, with the result that investors and others, on hearing of any new venture to-day, immediately ask the question, "Are Martins in it?" and if Martins *are* in it, then the confidence of the public is manifested towards a firm whose name is synonymous with sound and honest work in straightforward concerns.

The firm was founded in the year 1875 by the late Sir Acquin Martin, Kt., and the partners now (1916) are Sir Rajendra Mookerjee, K.C.I.E., Mr. Harold Martin, Mr. C. W. Walsh, and Mr. Oswald Martin.

Messrs. Martin & Co. have carried out most important contracts for the supply of water and drainage schemes and other public works in all parts of India, from north to south and east to west, and among the principal waterwork systems which have been completed are those at Allahabad, Agra, Arrah, Aurungabad, Benares (drainage also), Berhampore, Bhagalpore, Bombay (Tansa duct), Calcutta (also drainage), Cawnpore, Cossipore, Delhi, Dum Dum, Hooghly-Chinsurah, Khandwa, Lucknow, Meerut, Mirzapur, Monghyr, Muttra, Naini-Tal, Srinagar, and Serampore.

Messrs. Martin & Co. are deserving of the highest credit for their pioneer work in introducing light railways, which are usually constructed on district roads, and which have proved to be of immense benefit in connecting outlying areas, rich in agricultural produce, with main lines of railways, and they have financed and constructed, and are now managing, the following: the Howrah-Amta, Howrah-Sheakhala, Ranaghat-Krishnagar (acquired by Government), Bukhtiarpur-Bihar, Baraset-Basirhat, Shahdara-Saharampur, and the Arrah-Sasaram sections.

Not the least important branch of the many activities in which Messrs. Martin are engaged is that of architecture, and the firm have a large staff of highly trained architects, whose skill is manifested in some of the handsomest buildings in Calcutta. A striking feature in these edifices is the happy combination of utility with beauty of outline, and the adaptation of certain characteristics of the West which harmonize with the graceful and artistic work of the East. The firm have constructed the following among other completed works: a palace built for His Highness the Maharajah of Tippera; the Bank of Bengal buildings at Allahabad, Benares, and Lahore; the Government Secretariat Buildings at Dacca; the Government Agricultural College at Bhagalpore; the Royal Insurance, South British Insurance, Chartered Bank, and Alliance Bank premises; the head offices of the Bengal-Nagpur Railways; the Sir Stuart Hogg Market; and the Park, Esplanade, Harrington, and Alexandra Mansions.

A particularly beautiful specimen of the firm's work is the Mysore Memorial at Kalighat, Calcutta, which was erected on the precise spot on the banks of Tolly's Nullah on which the body of a Maharajah of Mysore (who died in Calcutta in 1897) was cremated. The buildings include a Dravidian temple, *ghat*, and pavilion designed by the firm's chief architect, Mr. Edward Thornton, F.R.I.B.A., and the work is typical of the best traditions of the East. The commercial section of Calcutta is indebted to Messrs. Martin for the erection of a large number of jute mills, including the Auckland, Clive, Dalhousie, Kelvin, Kharda, Lawrence, Northbrook, Standard, and Union factories.

The firm have, further, been entrusted by the Government of Bihar and Orissa with the construction of the buildings at the new capital of Bankipur, comprising the High Court, Government House, Secretariat Buildings, Post and Telegraph Offices, and residences for officials, and these works, now in progress, are estimated to cost about Rs. 55 lakhs, while the new Government European Asylum at Ranchi was designed, and has just been completed, by them.

Important as are the above-mentioned contracts, they are eclipsed by one which confers upon Messrs. Martin & Co. the honour of erecting on the *maidan* in Calcutta the "All-India Victoria Memorial Hall," which was designed by Sir William Emerson, at an estimated cost of about Rs. 70 lakhs. Some 200,000 cub. ft. of marble are required for this work, and this quantity is being obtained from Makrana, in Rajputana, where the firm have, under expert European supervision, opened quarries and erected a large factory, which is equipped with the latest type of marble-working machinery, including frame, rip, wire, and diamond saws, rubbing beds, milling machines, lathes, and plainers. It is expected that the Hall will be completed by the end of the year 1921.

Messrs. Martin make all their own bricks, and the extent of their building operations may be gauged from the fact that during the season 1914-15 they made at their six brickfields more than sixty millions of bricks for their own construction works.

The firm are now managing agents for the Satpukuria and Asansol, the Samla-Kendra, the Kosoonda and Nyadee, and the Ghusick and Muslia collieries, the Indian Manganese Company, Ltd., the Hooghly Docking and Engineering Company, Ltd., the National Indian Life Insurance Company, Ltd., Messrs. Crompton & Co., Ltd., the well-known electrical engineers, and the Bengal Iron and Steel Company, Ltd., which is referred to at length hereafter. The firm have also been appointed managing agents for the following companies which have been floated recently, namely, the Futwah-Islampur Light Railway Company (which is being constructed with Messrs. Martin & Co. as consulting engineers),

MARTIN & CO.

1. Howrah-Amata Light Railway. 2. Dry Dock. 3. Machine Shop.

MARTIN & CO.

1. Government House, Patna Capital. 2. Residences for Officials, Patna Capital. 3. Post and Telegraph Office, Patna Capital. 4. High Court, Patna Capital. 5. Secretariat Offices, Patna Capital.

the Chaparmukh-Silghat Railway Company, Ltd., and the United Provinces Electric Supply Company, Ltd.

Messrs. Martin & Co. are, in all probability, the leading importers of engineering tools and plant, and they hold several very important agencies from English manufacturers, including the Frodingham Iron and Steel Company, Ltd., for joists and sections; Messrs. Laycocks, Ltd., for railway carriages and rolling stock; the Bells United Asbestos Company, Ltd., for "Poilite" roofing; Messrs. Tuck & Co., Ltd., for engine packing, belting, and rubber goods; Messrs. Robert Hudson, Ltd., for light railway plant; Messrs. Ruston, Proctor & Co., Ltd., for road rollers, boilers, portable, fixed, and gas engines; the Silent Machine and Engineering Company, Ltd., for specialities in foundry requisites; the Peerless Lock-woven Wire Fence Company for fencing; Messrs. William Cumming & Co. for moulders' requisites; Messrs. Walkers, Ltd., for disinfectants; the Cails Bitmo Company, Ltd., for anti-corrosive paints; Messrs. Locke, Lancaster & Co., Ltd., for pig lead and lead yarn; and Messrs. Williamson, Ltd., for paints and varnishes. The unique position held by Messrs. Martin & Co. in the engineering world is proved by the fact that their monthly metal price list and market report is accepted as a standard guide, and its circle of readers comprises the entire engineering community of India. The firm have always loyally supported local industries, and their stock includes the Tata Iron and Steel Company's sections, together with Portland cement from the Katni Cement and Industrial Company, for whom they are agents for Eastern India.

Their London offices are at Vestry House, Laurence Pountney Hill, E.C.

THE BENGAL IRON AND STEEL COMPANY, LTD.*

It would be far too modest an estimate of the value of this company to regard it merely as a commercial undertaking producing satisfactory dividends upon invested capital, as it has been the means of bringing to light one of the richest fields of iron ore in India, if not in the world. The property belonged originally to the Burrakur Iron Works Company, but it was acquired by the present company in the year 1889.

The works are situated at Kulti, on the East Indian railway system, about 142 miles distant from Calcutta, and they comprise blast furnaces, iron foundries, engineering shops, by-product coke ovens, collieries, iron ore mines, and sulphuric acid plant.

The blast furnace plant consists of four furnaces, 60 ft. in height, and having a daily capacity of 300 tons, connected with which are thirteen "Cowper" stoves for heating the blast, the stoves being from 60 to 75 ft. in height, with a diameter 21 ft. Five blowing engines are connected with the furnaces, with a total power capacity of 5,050 h.p. Two of these are vertical engines, and three are Parsons' turbines with condensers. Two batteries of twenty-six Lancashire boilers supply steam to the blowing engines, the boilers being fired by waste gas from the blast furnaces. Iron ore, coke, and limestone are delivered from railway wagons at the back of the furnaces, and then raised by three electric hoists to the charging hoppers.

The furnace plant is able to turn out 300 tons of pig-iron daily, and the product, marked with the brand "Bengal," is made from selected ores, and compares favourably in quality with the best Middlesbrough foundry iron. The company has recently put on the market several special kinds of iron, some of which are known by the names Manharpur, Burrakur, high manganese, high phosphorus, and low silicon. The pig-iron is supplied to all the principal railways and iron foundries in India, and, in addition, the iron is exported to Ceylon, the Straits Settlements, Australia, New Zealand, Japan, and South America.

All the iron ores used in the works are obtained from the company's own properties in the district of Singhbhoom. A new deposit of high-grade ore has recently been opened up in an area which is connected with the Bengal-Nagpur Railway by a light line, 16 miles in length, constructed by the company, the ore being loaded in trucks by an aerial ropeway 5,000 ft. in length. With the high-class ores now at the disposal of the company it is possible to supply pig-iron of almost any analysis, excepting only hematite iron.

The coke plant consists of two batteries of thirty-four Simon Carves' by-product ovens, which are able to turn out 100,000 tons yearly. The coal is discharged from the railway wagons into hoppers, whence it is elevated to the storage bunkers, which have a capacity of 600 tons, and is then transferred to the compressor, where it is pressed under the stampers into a cake to be placed in the ovens. The waste gases from the ovens, after the by-products of coal-tar and sulphate of ammonia have been extracted, pass to the battery of boilers, where they are utilized for raising steam for the generation of electric power for the whole works, while the crusher, elevators, and compressor are operated by electric power.

The sulphuric acid plant has been installed for the purpose of manufacturing the acid required for the recovery of sulphate of ammonia, and the annual output of 2,500 tons allows an ample margin for future extensions or outside orders.

The foundries comprise those for pipes, railway sleepers, and chairs, general castings, and brass, and they cover an area of 160,000 sq. ft.

There are two plants for the manufacture of cast-iron pipes made in dry sand moulds and cast vertically, and they are respectively fitted with hydraulic and electric power. All pipes are coated with Dr. Angus Smith's solution, and are tested to any hydrostatic pressure required, while very large numbers of flanged pipes of all sizes suitable for steam or water mains are constantly being made at the works.

Another section of the foundries is fitted with moulding machines for making cast-iron railway sleepers—either plate or bowl designs—and railway chairs of any type or size, while in the general foundry (which measures 500 by 100 ft.) all kinds of castings, up to 25 tons in weight, are made, including columns for public buildings and mills, straining posts and sockets for railway fencing, mortar-mills, road rollers, ornamental columns, lamp posts, railing and machinery castings for engineers.

The brass foundry is able to supply every description of castings which may be required in engineering works. The annual collective output of the foundries is from 50,000 to 60,000 tons of castings, as follows: pipes, 8,000 tons; sleepers and chairs, 40,000 to 45,000 tons; and general castings, from 6,000 to 7,000 tons.

Messrs. Martin & Co. always keep a large stock of engineering requisites of all kinds, including more than 3,000 tons of cast-iron pipes from 2 to 12 in. bore, with planed, turned, and bored or double-flanged joints, in addition to a large quantity of "I.S.R." fencing sockets,

* For illustration see page 757.

MANTON & CO.

1. Calcutta Premises. 2. Showroom. 3. Portion of Workshops.

straining posts, railway chairs, and other sundries.

The engineering department embraces machine shop (290 by 90 ft.), smiths' shops, and riveting and erecting yards, and all these buildings are fully equipped with up-to-date appliances for general work and repairs.

The company's collieries are situated at Ramnagore, in the Raneegunge field, and at Noonoodih and Jeetpore in the Jherria coal-producing area, and supplies are drawn from them for the company's requirements and for disposal to railway authorities and private consumers. About 150,000 tons of first-class coal are raised annually.

Excellent facilities for the dispatch of goods to any part of India have been provided by private sidings between the works and the East Indian and Bengal-Nagpur Railways.

MANTON & CO.

The founder of the well-known firm of Messrs. Manton & Co., of Old Court House Street, Calcutta—the premier gunmakers in the East—was one Joe Manton, who was regarded by sportsmen of his day as "the greatest artist in firearms that the world has ever produced." A contributor to *Land and Water* wrote years ago that "if asked who were the fathers of modern shooters and gunmakers, ninety-nine out of every hundred men qualified to express an opinion would name Colonel Hawker and Joe Manton." The latter originated and perfected more inventions in small arms than any other maker in England, and it was commonly said that if Joe Manton had expressed approval of a weapon there was nothing wrong with it.

This pioneer maker of all kinds of guns sent his nephew, Frederick Manton, to India in the year 1820, and the latter commenced a business which is still known as Manton & Co., and which, since its foundation, has been the means of supplying firearms and other sporting requisites to thousands of sportsmen in India. The uncle died in the month of June 1835, and his chief friend and supporter, Colonel Hawker, wrote of him that "an everlasting monument to his unrivalled genius is already established in every quarter of the globe by his celebrity as the founder and father of the modern gun trade, and as a most scientific inventor in other departments."

The business of Manton & Co. in Calcutta was, in 1847, purchased by William Robert Wallis (and is still held by his relatives), who, after some thirty years of most successful trading, retired in favour of his sons. In the year 1850 Mr. W. R. Wallis acquired the goodwill of the very old-established business of Samuel Nock, of Regent Circus, London (gunmaker by Royal Warrant to Her late Majesty Queen Victoria, 1838), now the property of Messrs. Manton & Co.

The original premises of the firm were situated in that portion of Calcutta now called Bentinck Street (formerly known as Cossitollah), but the extensive building now occupied by Messrs. Manton & Co. is situated in a most commanding position in Old Court House Street and Mangoe Lane, in Calcutta; and it is stocked with an immense quantity of rifles, shot-guns, revolvers, pistols, ammunition, and all kinds of sporting requisites and accessories for every outdoor game enjoyed by man or woman.

Messrs. Manton & Co. make a special feature of the manufacture of their "Standard" cartridges, which are the best sporting ammunition in India. An immense amount of time and money has been expended in making these cartridges as perfect as possible, and too much importance cannot be attached to the necessity for absolute accuracy in measurements of cases and in the quality and quantity of powder and shot. With regard to the cases, which are manufactured by the famous firm of Eley Brothers, Ltd., of London, the principal conditions to which a perfectly made shot-gun case must conform are: (*a*) superiority in the quality of paper used in the manufacture of the tube, enabling it to resist, as far as possible, climatic influences; (*b*) the lining of the head of the case and a considerable portion of the inside of the tube with metal; (*c*) the selection of a suitable cap which may be relied upon on ignition to give a regular flash; and (*d*) conformation of all component parts of the case to the standard measurements. Space will not permit any detailed reference to the whole process of manufacture, but the utmost care is taken to use powder which possesses the maximum stability, to place the loading of the cases under strict European supervision, to have the shotting, wadding, and ramming machines in correct working order, and to give the minutest attention to all detail work to ensure the continued support of their very large and influential *clientèle*.

The repairs department is an exceedingly important branch in a business which annually receives hundreds of weapons requiring attention, and skilled artisans who have been specially trained on the firm's own premises for a number of years are constantly employed upon this work.

Any one unacquainted with the component parts of, say, a shot-gun or rifle would be astounded to see the delicate nature of the mechanism and the precision with which the various fittings are placed in position, but after such an inspection he would realize that a very high degree of skill was necessary to manufacture or even to repair a firearm of modern construction.

In the repairing workshops one sees men employed in rejointing or tightening action and barrels, replacing broken springs, regulating ejectors, fitting new hammers and strikers, correcting a faulty pull-off, removing dents from barrels, adjusting sights, and a quantity of other mechanical work too bewildering for a novice to understand. Messrs. Manton & Co. never allow a rifle or gun to leave their workshops until it has been tested, sighted, and regulated at their private range, which is provided with fixed and disappearing targets of all kinds.

The firm holds warrants of appointment to the following Viceroys of India: Lord Northbrook, 1872-6; Lord Lytton, 1876-80; Marquis of Ripon, 1880-84; Earl of Dufferin, 1884-8; Marquis of Lansdowne, 1888-94; Earl of Elgin, 1894-9; Earl Curzon of Kedleston, 1899-1905; Earl of Minto, 1905-10; and Baron Hardinge of Penshurst, 1911-16; and also to the undermentioned Commanders-in-Chief, namely: General Sir William Lockhart, 1898-1900; General Viscount Kitchener of Khartoum, 1902-9; and General Sir O'Moore Creagh in 1909.

At the Calcutta International Exhibition held in 1883-4, Messrs. Manton & Co. were awarded three silver medals for local and other manufactures, while a bronze medal and diploma were gained at the Indian and Colonial Exhibition in London in 1886.

MATHER AND PLATT, LTD.

This firm, whose head offices for India are situated in Wallace House, 5 Bankshall Street, Calcutta, are a branch of the well-known house which was established in Salford, Manchester, early in the last century by the grandfather of the present chairman, Sir William Mather. They were at first chiefly concerned in the manufacture of machinery for bleaching, dyeing, printing, and finishing textile materials. It was not until many years afterwards that their energies were directed into new channels, and the first departure was the establishment of the electrical engineering department, which has subsequently developed into a very important branch.

The firm's next undertaking was to specialize in hydraulic plant, including the manufacture of water filters (both pressure and gravity), of sewage distribution plant, well-boring apparatus, and almost every known description of pump; and here they were pioneers, in that they were the first to introduce and manufacture the turbine high-lift pump.

Pursuing their progressive policy, the firm next turned their attention (and it is now thirty years since they did so) to the all-important problem of fire protection—a question which then commenced to loom very large owing to the enormous losses that were being sustained by the insurance companies, more especially through fires in textile mills, which had raised the rates of premium to such an extent that they became a heavy burden on industries. These losses to the individual, as well as to the community, led to a demand for some drastic improvement in the means of extinguishing fire, and Messrs. Mather and Platt were first in the field with the "Grinnell" sprinkler, which has since won for itself so world-wide a reputation, and may be said to have revolutionized fire insurance.

In 1900 the whole of the available space on the old site at Salford had become quite exhausted, and as there was no room for extension except in an upward direction, it was then decided to secure fresh land on which to build works more suited to the advancing requirements of the business.

The question of where these were to be placed exercised the mind of the board for a long time, many sites being inspected, and ultimately a fine block of land at Park, Manchester, almost level, surrounded by roads, and bounded on one side by a canal and on the other by three railways, and comprising 50 acres, was acquired by the company, and was destined to be the site of one of the finest machine shops of modern times.

One by one the various departments were transferred to the new works at Park; in 1909 it was finally decided to make provision for the removal of all remaining branches from Salford; and in 1910 seven more shops were constructed. Subsequently various other buildings were added, including a large foundry.

A summary of the production of the various departments of the new works will probably be of interest.

Textile Department.—In this section is undertaken the equipment of complete works for bleaching, calico printing, dyeing, and finishing, including power plant with large gas engines or electric motors. No engineering firm has had more practical experience than Messrs. Mather and Platt in arranging and equipping throughout such works, and the new extensive machine shops, replete with every modern appliance, are capable of producing the highest class of manufacture. Some specialities are as follows: Gas-singeing machine, Mather kiers, open-width bleaching machinery, duplex and intermittent printing machines, high-speed stentering and beetling machines, open soaping and mercerizing ranges, dyeing machines for cops, cheeses, raw cotton, and other articles, spray damping machines, calendars for all purposes, and warp stop motion for looms. In the "Vortex" automatic self-cleansing system of humidification and ventilation for moistening and cooling the atmosphere of textile workrooms, the humid conditions are produced by the diffusion of "atomized" water, thus ensuring great economy in working charges and in maintaining pleasant working conditions during the hot months of the year. Numerous textile mills in India have been equipped with the various specialities turned out by this department.

Electrical Department. — Messrs. Mather and Platt's long experience (over thirty years) in the manufacture and installation of electrical machinery enables them to give expert advice on all matters relating to economical electric driving. Electrical plant of every description is manufactured for the complete electrification of collieries and mines, paper-mills, bleaching and finishing works, and spinning, weaving, and other mills. The products of the electrical shops comprise direct current and alternating current generating plants and motors, dynamos for chemical and welding processes, and train lighting equipments. In the latter field the firm's patent system is being used by a considerable number of railways in India, Ceylon, Great Britain, and in other parts of the world, and because of its simplicity and robustness is giving every satisfaction. Many mills and factories in India are equipped throughout with electrical drive apparatus manufactured by Messrs. Mather and Platt.

Hydraulic Department.—High-lift turbine pumps are supplied for collieries, mines, and water supply (high and low pressure services). The practical results of a very wide experience of the construction of high and low-lift turbine pumps are embodied in the modern pumps made by Messrs. Mather and Platt (the original makers of the turbine pump). In the latest type there are no thrust bearings of any kind, and all end thrust is avoided by an effectual hydraulic balancing arrangement. The special features of the pumps are absence of thrust bearings, automatic differential hydraulic balance, high efficiency, low first cost, and accessibility and adaptability for increased or decreased number of chambers. These pumps can be made for any conceivable duty. Patent centrifugal pumps for low lifts, which possess the following special merits as compared with all other makes: efficiency, greater simplicity, less total weight, smaller dimensions (the pumps combine the advantages of the volute and turbine designs). Patent mechanical filters for town supplies and all industrial purposes. For many years the firm have been engaged in the construction of mechanical filters and auxiliary plant. They have tested the merits of numerous processes of filtration, and these have led to their putting on the market their patent filter, which embodies many points of superiority over others. Water softening and purification are obtained by the Archbutt-Deeley process for municipal supplies, boiler feeding, and any other purpose for which a soft and pure water is required.

In regard to the working of this department, many electrically-driven turbine pumping sets are at work in the colliery district of Bengal and in mills and factories in and around Calcutta. Several installations of these pumps are now being erected for municipal water supply schemes in connection with tube well supplies, which are now being so prominently adopted in the United Provinces and elsewhere.

A typical gravity type mechanical

MATHER & PLATT, LTD.

1. AUTOMATIC SEWAGE DISTRIBUTOR AS ADOPTED FOR DISPOSAL OF EFFLUENT AT MILLS AND FACTORIES IN BENGAL. 2. PARTIAL VIEW OF MATHER & PLATT'S MECHANICAL FILTER INSTALLATION IN A JUTE MILL NEAR CALCUTTA. 3. BIRD'S-EYE VIEW OF MATHER & PLATT'S NEW WORKS, MANCHESTER. 4. GOVERNMENT STAMP AND STATIONERY BUILDINGS, CALCUTTA; PROTECTED AGAINST FIRE BY "GRINNELL" AUTOMATIC SPRINKLERS. 5. ELECTRICALLY-DRIVEN HIGH-LIFT TURBINE PUMP, AS SUPPLIED TO MANY COLLIERIES, MILLS, AND FACTORIES IN BENGAL.

filter plant, supplied and erected by Messrs. Mather and Platt, is that which has been working since 1914 at the Alliance Jute Mills, near Calcutta. This plant is dealing with water from the River Hooghly, which is undoubtedly one of the most difficult waters to treat in an efficient manner, but the results which have been obtained have shown that with a properly designed scheme and appliances such as have been put in by the firm the treatment is a very simple matter. Further, the results obtained with this plant show a higher degree of bacteriological as well as chemical purification than has been obtained previously on this river.

The important question of the satisfactory disposal of latrine effluent as well as of town's sewage, particularly in Bengal, has been dealt with by the adoption of the open-type filter-beds (oxidization process), fitted with Messrs. Mather and Platt's patent automatic rotary sewage distributors.

Fire Department.—Messrs. Mather and Platt are manufacturers of the "Grinnell" automatic sprinkler and fire alarm, which absolutely prevents serious fires. This sprinkler has been adopted extensively in every part of the world, and reports of fires successfully extinguished come in daily. More than 50,000 buildings are now protected, and it has operated in over 17,000 actual fires, has never failed, and the average amount of damage is under £60 per fire. All insurance companies accept risks upon premises protected with "Grinnell" sprinklers at greatly reduced premiums, which are sufficient in many cases to pay the whole cost of the installation in a few years. Sprinkler installations are supplied by water from town mains, elevated tanks, pressure tanks, electrical and steam fire pumps, and they are fitted in accordance with insurance regulations. All sizes of standard cast-iron tanks can be supplied from stock, and these are made up of a series of tank units of high-grade quality, machined true to within a thousandth of an inch, from which tanks of almost every size and shape may be constructed. Plates 2 ft. and 2 ft. 6 in. square respectively are used for the most part, and no heavy hoisting tackle is required for erection. "Underwriter" steam fire pumps, fire hydrants, hose and appliances, and "Simplex" chemical fire extinguishers. Self-closing armoured fire doors, fitted with Messrs. Mather and Platt's apparatus for self-closing in case of fire, form the best possible means of preventing an outbreak from spreading from one building to another.

It is interesting to note that, in the Calcutta mill district alone, there are installations of "Grinnell" sprinklers numbering 150,000 heads. More than half of the jute-mills in Bengal, and their respective godowns, are protected against fire by this system, in addition to a considerable quantity of Government property, flour, cotton, and other mills.

All these various departments in Calcutta are efficiently represented by a fully technical and commercial staff. A large stock of materials is held in the firm's godowns, which are fitted with the most modern tools and appliances for the cutting and screwing of pipes and fittings for use in sprinkler equipments, in "Vortex" humidifier installations, and in the manufacture of fire doors. One of the latest pattern patent "Diamond" mechanical filters, specially suitable for use on tea and rubber estates, can be inspected at work in the godowns,—and a large number of standardized cast-iron tank plates (2 ft. square), from which almost any size of tank can be constructed without difficulty, are always available.

Messrs. Mather and Platt also have an office in Bombay at 10 Forbes Street, where all departments are efficiently represented, as in Calcutta, by a large technical and commercial staff.

MACNEILL & CO.

The original founders of this firm were Messrs. Duncan Macneill and John Mackinnon, who established themselves in Strand Road, Calcutta, in the year 1872, and traded as general merchants and agents under the title of Macneill & Co. Head offices were opened at Winchester House, London, E.C., under the style of Duncan Macneill & Co., and a very extensive business has been built up by the energy and foresight of the various partners. The firm are very largely interested in the management of a number of tea gardens, in coal mines, in the manufacture of ropes and lines, the weaving of cloth and sacks from jute, in controlling inland navigation and railway companies, and in general agency work. Special reference is made on other pages in this volume to several of the above-named branches of industry, and it will be seen that the firm have, by the magnitude of trade which passes through their hands, assisted greatly in building up that immense commercial fabric which places India in such a favourable position among British dependencies and colonies.

The present partners are managing agents for nearly 40 tea gardens in Assam and Eastern Bengal, which are yielding an annual crop of nearly 180,000 maunds. They control the work of the Ganges Rope Company, which has a very large output of ropes and lines of all kinds; they are agents for the River Steam Navigation Company, Ltd., whose splendid steamers for passenger and freight traffic ply between Calcutta, Assam, and Cachar, as well as on the Ganges and on all the rivers and creeks in the delta of Bengal; they are the representatives in Calcutta for the old-established and renowned Atlas Assurance Company; and they own saw-mills in Cachar, in which chests are made for the tea which is grown on the plantations in which they are concerned. They are also largely interested in coal mining.

Mr. Duncan Macneill, one of the founders, died in 1892, and Mr. Mackinnon became senior partner until his death in 1908, when the business was continued by his trustees. In the year 1914 Lord Inchcape took over the interests of the latter, and he is now senior partner, the remaining members of the firm being Mr. D. F. Mackenzie, Mr. George Lyell, Mr. Dan Currie, Mr. Alexander Topping, Mr. John Taylor, Mr. J. Mackenzie, Mr. Duncan Mackinnon, jun., Mr. W. Mackinnon, and the Hon. Kenneth Mackay.

The premises now occupied by the firm are at 2 Clive Ghat Street, Calcutta.

THE GANGES ROPE COMPANY, LTD.

Although there does not appear to be any definite information as to the time when the rope-making industry was commenced in India, there is no doubt that it must have been at a very early period; and as the raw materials are grown so largely in the East, it is not surprising that the manufacture of all kinds of ropes, lines, twines, and paulins should have become such a prosperous undertaking, and especially near Calcutta, where shipping-masters and others are ready purchasers of the finished products.

The Ganges Rope Company, Ltd., was established in 1904, and Messrs. Macneill & Co., of 2 Clive Ghat Street, Calcutta, who were appointed managing agents, were confident that there was a promising

MACNEILL & CO.

1. The Ganges Rope Company, Ltd. 2. Jute Weaving Department (Ganges Manufacturing Company, Ltd.). 3. Jute Preparing Department (Ganges Manufacturing Company, Ltd.). 4. Narainpore Tea Estate Bungalow. 5. Dilkhoosh Ghat Crossing, Barak River. 6. Narainpore Bhil Garden, Cachar.

future for the making of ropes, provided that the old system of manual labour was superseded by machinery which would materially increase the output and save much valuable time. A ropewalk was therefore opened, which is 1,250 feet from end to end, and therefore is sufficiently large to allow the spinning of lines to a length of about a quarter of a mile, and of any circumference, without their being spliced in any way. The preparing and spinning plant was supplied by Messrs. Lawson and Sons, of Leeds, and the ropewalk machinery was obtained from Messrs. Coombe, Barbour & Co.; and the works, which cover an area of 12 acres, are undoubtedly the largest and the most modern of their kind in the whole of Asia.

Ropes are made from manila-hemp, sisal, aloe, cotton, country hemps, jute, and various descriptions of coir fibres, and the company guarantee their manila ropes to be made entirely from the hemp of that district. Other products of the factory include aloe and coir ropes (the latter being dry or oiled), ratlines, tarred bolt ropes, hand lead lines, deep-sea lead lines, signal halyards, seizing and log lines, spun yarn, manila and hemp sash cords, tarred hambrolines, house lines, marlines, fishing lines, superior jute, gasketings, iron wire seizings, rope and cork fenders, green and white prepared canvas; dressed paulins in black or any other colour, hatch covers, awnings, and sundry other articles.

It may be well to observe at this juncture that the owners of Indian rope manufactories have a distinct advantage over European makers, inasmuch as the former are practically on the ground where the raw material is produced, and further, that the cost of labour and freightage is considerably less than that which the Westerner is called upon to pay. The question might naturally occur as to whether the Eastern manufactures are, price for price, equal in quality to others on the market, but this doubt can be removed very quickly by observing that the Ganges Company are, at the present time, exporting a considerable quantity of their goods to England. Shipowners are the largest customers, but large orders are received from timber-yard proprietors in Burmah, and from all the leading shipping, railway, and milling companies in the East, while contracts are held for supplying His Majesty's dockyard authorities and Government arsenals and factories.

The average daily output is about 12 tons, and some 600 hands are employed.

The Twenty-fifth Ordinary General Meeting of the shareholders of the company was held at Calcutta on June 14, 1915, and a report and statements of accounts for the half-year ended on April 30th preceding were then submitted. The directors have had an uphill battle to fight owing to the heavy cost of land, buildings, and machinery, and on account of the exceedingly severe competition which had to be faced in the early days of the company; but at this meeting they were able to show that preliminary difficulties had been overcome, that trade was increasing by leaps and bounds, and that the finances were in a far more satisfactory state than at any previous time. All the buildings and machinery were said to be in a thorough state of repair, and the future of the company was full of promise.

The accounts showed a balance of Rs. 1,06,637 to the credit of the trading account, as compared with Rs. 70,826 for the corresponding period of the previous year. After providing for depreciation and other charges, the profit and loss account presented a credit balance of Rs. 57,889 (including Rs. 19,588 brought forward), which the directors recommended should be dealt with as follows: dividend at the rate of 6 per cent. per annum, equivalent to Rs. 3 per share, amounting to Rs. 21,000; transfer to Debenture Redemption Fund, Rs. 20,000; and a balance of Rs. 16,889 to be carried forward.

The accounts had been duly audited, and they were signed by J. Mackenzie, D. Carmichael, and L. Warlow Harry, directors, and by Messrs. Macneill & Co. as managing agents.

THE GANGES MANUFACTURING COMPANY, LTD.

This company—of which Messrs. Macneill & Co., of 2, Clive Ghat Street, Calcutta, are managing agents—was established in the year 1876, and a mill and factory were opened at Seebpore, on the right bank of the Hooghly River, in the same year. The first directors were Messrs. W. Mackinnon, J. Macdonald, Eli Lees, A. R. Young, W. Haworth, and D. Macneill.

The mill started with 200 looms, and this number has been gradually increased until it now stands at 568, but in 1908 a new mill was erected on about 30 acres of land adjoining the original premises. The machinery in the new building was set in motion towards the close of 1909, and it now contains 726 looms. Steam power is used in each mill, with engines of 2,000 h.p. and 2,500 h.p. respectively, and the wages-roll contains the names of about 8,300 hands.

Specialities are a feature of the products of this mill, and among these are twill cloth for the making of cement bags, articles chiefly exported to London, and hop pocketing, the greater portion of which is sent to San Francisco. Other products are gunny bags of all descriptions; Hessian cloth, the chief markets for which are North and South America; and wool sheets for Australia, New Zealand, and South Africa. During the year 1914 about 30,000 tons of raw jute were used, to the value of £463,000, and the manufactured output for the same was of the value of £800,000.

The company have a private railway siding to the mills, in addition to two jetties upon the River Hooghly, but practically all finished goods are sent away by water.

The present directors are the Right Hon. Lord Inchcape, G.C.M.G., K.C.S.I., K.C.I.E., Messrs. George Lyell, Dan Currie, and Donald F. Mackenzie, and the registered offices of the company are at Winchester House, Old Broad Street, London.

Jute is one of the largest crops of Eastern Bengal, and the manufacture of fabrics therefrom is one of the most prosperous industries in India, as it gives employment to many thousands of persons in the numerous mills which have been erected in close proximity to the Hooghly River, every facility being afforded thereby for the transport of the raw material to the mills and for the shipment of products to the United Kingdom, America, and other countries.

The rapidity with which this industry has grown is nothing short of marvellous, and it may be interesting to illustrate this advance by the following figures, taken from returns published for the decade between the years 1900 and 1910. In the former year there were 8,727 sacking looms and 6,609 Hessian looms, and the output of the mills was 257,000,000 bags and 380,000,000 yards of Hessian cloth; while the statistics for 1910 show 13,992 and 18,719 of the two kinds of looms, and a production of 464,000,000 bags and 1,005,000,000 yards of cloth. The latest available particulars are as follows: For the year ended December 1915 the actual clearances of jute fabrics from Calcutta were 734,000,000 bags and 1,148,000,000 yards of Hessian cloth.

A glance at the exports and at the consumption of raw jute in local mills during the same period will perhaps give a clearer idea of the enormous trade which has sprung up. From 1900 to 1901 the bales, each weighing 400 lb., consigned to the United Kingdom, numbered 1,512,662; those sent to the continent of Europe, 1,479,299; to America, 523,495; and to other countries, 16,173; giving a total of 3,531,629 bales; but to these must be added 2,415,000 and 300,000 bales used locally and in country mills respectively, thus bringing the aggregate number of bales of raw material to 6,246,629. For the twelve months from July 1914 to June 1915 there were 30 lakhs of bales exported, and the mills consumption was about 48 lakhs, to which must be added 500,000 for country consumption.

A. AND J. MAIN & CO., LTD.

This firm is an offshoot of the widely known establishment of Messrs. A. and J. Main & Co., Ltd., of Glasgow and London, and the history of its connection with India begins with the year 1873, when Mr. J. A. R. Main, one of the original founders of the company, opened an agency in Calcutta, under the management of Messrs. Duncan Brothers. Ten years later, at the time of the Calcutta Exhibition, the agency was taken over by Messrs. McLeod & Co., whose representative was Mr. Alistair McNiven, and the business was conducted by the last-named gentleman until his death in 1900.

Up to this date nearly all work undertaken by the firm was in connection with the tea industry, and Main's leaf and tea houses may be seen to-day in all districts in which this plant is cultivated.

It was, of course, inevitable that other manufacturing firms should enter the field in which Messrs. Main & Co.'s enterprise had been so successful, but the fact remains that this company were the pioneers in structural work in the tea gardens and factories of India, and the improvement that is noticeable in buildings erected in more recent years is to a very large extent due to the manner in which this firm adapted designs to meet the changed requirements of planters.

The company's workshops at Sealdah were soon found to be altogether inadequate for the increasing volume of trade, and in 1907 new works were opened at Shalimar, on the western bank of the River Hooghly, and about four miles distant from Calcutta.

The first contract to be executed under the new conditions was the superstructure of the North-Western Railway carriage and wagon shops at Lahore, a work which required about 7,000 tons of steel.

Other steel works of importance erected by the company include an extensive range of buildings for the Tata Iron and Steel Company at Sakchi; workshops for the Bengal-Nagpur Railway Company at Khargpur, having a covered area of 500,000 sq. ft.; the Grand Oriental

A. & J. MAIN & CO., LTD.
INTERIOR, NEW SMITH SHOP, BENGAL-NAGPUR RAILWAY, KHARGPUR.

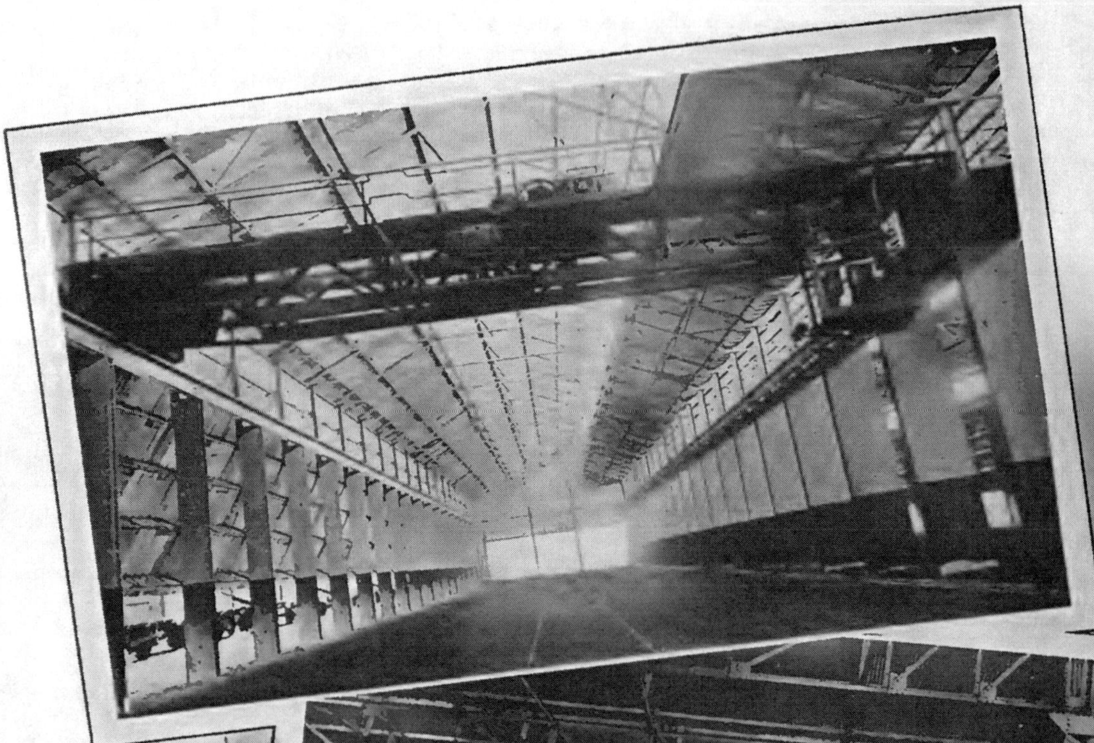

A. & J. MAIN & CO., LTD.

1. Interior, New Wagon-lifting Shop, Bengal-Nagpur Railway, Khargpur. 2. New Wagon Shop, Bengal-Nagpur Railway, Khargpur. 3. Sealdah Station, North, Eastern Bengal Railway.

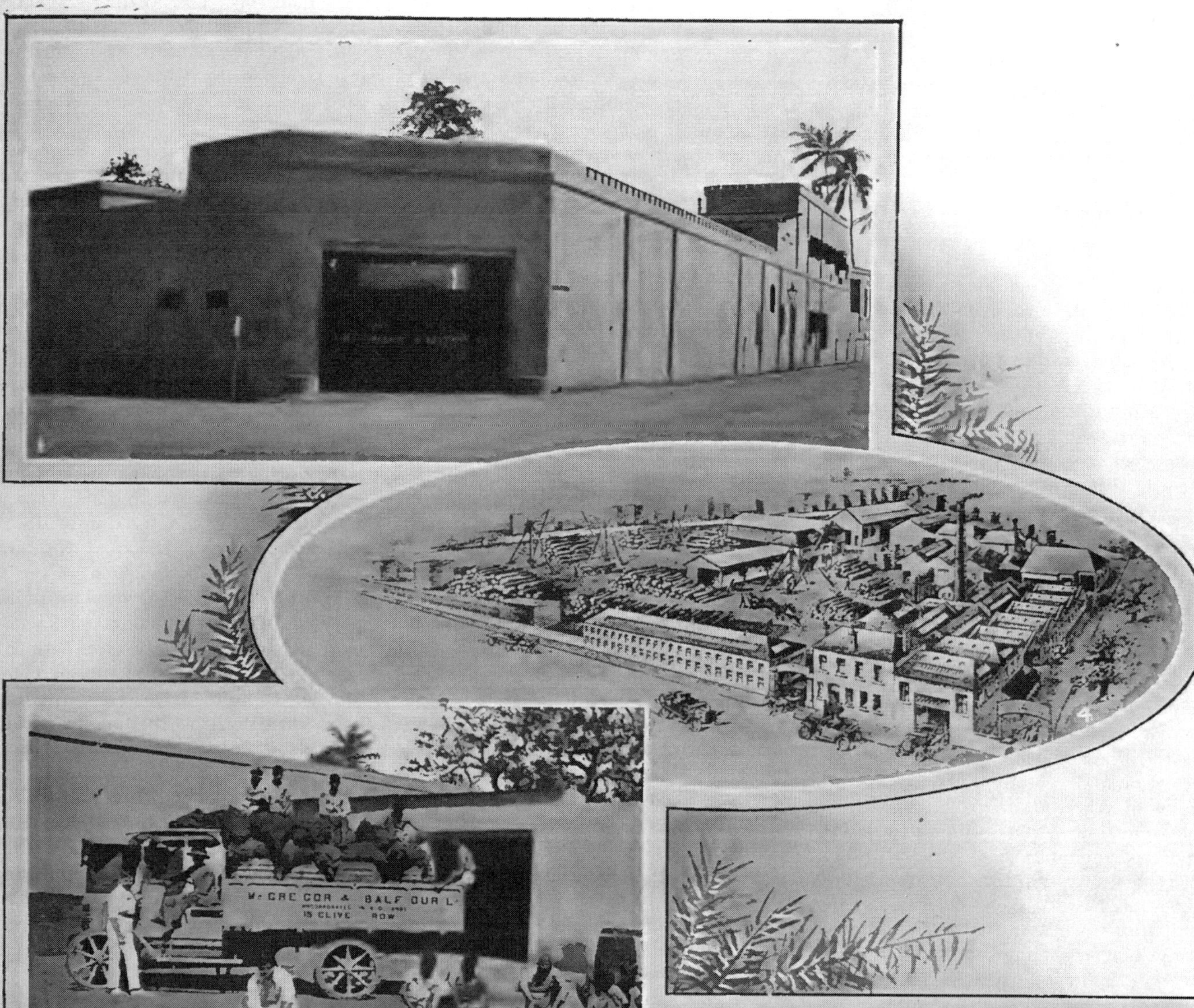

McGREGOR & BALFOUR, LTD.

1. Calcutta Premises. 2. Workshop. 3. Motor Lorry. 4. Headquarters Establishment.

Hotel, Colombo, for which 2,500 tons of steel were supplied; a suspension bridge, with a clear span of 630 ft., for the Burma Oil Company, Rangoon; the Sealdah Station, Calcutta, for the Eastern Bengal Railway Company; the Howrah Station, Calcutta, for the East Indian and Bengal-Nagpur Railway systems; and a large number of bridges for railway crossings, rivers, and roads.

Although the firm occupy a leading position in supplying steel roofing for all purposes, they have built up a very extensive fencing business, and it is no exaggeration to say that a very large proportion of the fencing and railing used in India by railway and other enterprises is manufactured by this firm.

The company have recently extended their activities to Bombay and other important parts of India, and a local business that was primarily established to meet the requirements of the tea industry is expanding rapidly, and now promises to create for the firm as enviable a reputation in the East as that which they enjoy in Great Britain.

It should be added that designs and estimates are specially prepared on receipt of particulars of all kinds of roofs, bridges, fencing, and other structural work, and quotations are given upon designs of other engineers.

Messrs. Main & Co.—with whom is incorporated the business of Arrol's Bridge and Roof Company, Ltd.—are proprietors of the Clydesdale Iron Works, Possilpark; the Germiston Works, Glasgow; and the Calcutta Bridge and Roof Works, Calcutta; and they have extensive offices at 10-15 Canning Street, Calcutta.

Their local telegraphic address is "Mainco," Calcutta or Bombay.

McGREGOR AND BALFOUR, LTD.

This well-known firm, proprietors of the North Tay Works, Dundee, Scotland, was established in the year 1853, and one is perfectly justified in saying that its history of commercial progress is on parallel lines with the rise and growth of the jute manufacturing industry in that city and in India, as there is nothing in the way of requisites and accessories for the machinery and plant in the mills which cannot be supplied by this firm.

The weaving of jute fibre by handlooms into clothing and other articles has been known in India for many centuries, but it was as late as the thirties of last century that Dundee spinners became convinced of the value of Indian fibre, and by its use upon their looms a vast amount of wealth poured into that city. It was not, however, until the year 1855 that spinning machinery was brought to Calcutta from Dundee, and the first jute-mill in India was thereupon erected on the bank of the Hooghly River upon land formerly owned by Warren Hastings.

As soon as the pioneer jute-mills were erected a demand arose for the thousand-and-one separate parts required for running them, and Messrs. McGregor and Balfour, Ltd., established the North Tay Works in Dundee, and prepared themselves to meet the need which was manifested. They can supply the machinery itself, and they manufacture sectional parts such as picking arms, bobbins and ends, planetree rollers, shuttles, beech, persimmon, and birch box backs, reeds and cambs, lathe races, spools, swell woods, springs, and any other similar furnishings of a well-equipped mill.

A limited liability company was formed in 1897, when the business had grown to such an extent that further capital and increased accommodation became necessary, and in 1904 a branch office was opened in Calcutta, together with godowns and workshops at 49 South Road, Entally. Reeds and cambs are manufactured at the last-mentioned works, where a large stock is kept in hand of the company's lines made in Dundee and of goods of the firms they represent, such as dyes, leather, hair, and cotton belting, hoops and buckles, canvas hose, canvas, felt cloths, flax twine, hydraulic hides, rubber goods, pickers, picking bands, iron and steel bars, plates and sectional material, and numerous other sundries.

The company are leather factors, mill, factory, and engineers' furnishers, fish and whale oil merchants, and commission agents. They are representatives in the eastern portion of India of Messrs. Geo. Angus & Co., Ltd., of St. John's Works, Newcastle-on-Tyne, and the Woven Hose and Belting Works, Bentham, Lancaster, who are the largest manufacturers in England of all kinds of leather goods, indiarubber and asbestos goods, canvas hose, textile beltings, and similar goods required for jute, rice, cotton, and other mills.

The company are agents for Messrs. Hunter, Doig, and Palmer, brassfounders, Dundee, who make fittings of every description connected with steam, water, heating, fire, in gunmetal, brass, and iron. The company are, further, agents for Messrs. Halley Brothers, Ltd., Dundee, who make hackles, gills, wood-card covering, steel-faced card covering, hackle gill, card pins, gill rivets, and other accessories.

Mr. W. B. Edward is manager of the Calcutta branch, and he is assisted by Messrs. F. M. Petrie, C. G. Ferrier, and C. A. Crews. The Calcutta office is at 15 Clive Row, and the telegraphic addresses of the company is "Shuttle, Dundee," and "Warpbobbin," Calcutta, the public codes used being A.B.C., 4th and 5th edition.

McLEOD & CO.

The story of the selection of the settlement on the eastern bank of the Hooghly River, which has grown into the city of Calcutta, of the construction of dock and wharfage accommodation at Kidderpore, and of the rapid expansion of the shipping trade between the newly established port and the principal countries of the world is told at length elsewhere in this volume, and it only remains here for an allusion to be made to the spirited action of mercantile firms, hailing from Europe and elsewhere, who laid the foundation of the commercial prestige of the port of Calcutta. These immigrants brought with them a stock-in-trade of ability, forcefulness, and keen business instincts, and they soon founded establishments whose ramifications have extended to all parts of the East.

European goods were brought to India and exchanged for country produce, and in course of time extensive interests were developed in the cultivation of rice, jute, indigo, tea, coal, and sugar. At the present time plantations and concerns of the last-mentioned six commodities are very largely in the hands of Calcutta merchants who act as managing agents, and thus it happens that many firms have the control of quite a number of these enterprises.

A case in point is that of Messrs. McLeod & Co., of 31 Dalhousie Square, Calcutta, who have been for many years interested in the jute trade, and are exporters of considerable quantities of both the raw and manufactured article, their first essay in the jute-mill industry occurring in 1907, when they took over the agency of the Soorah Jute Mill, a small sacking factory of only 175 looms. The plant was by no means modern, and a comprehensive scheme of

McLEOD & CO. (EMPIRE JUTE MILLS).

1. General View of Empire Jute Mill, showing House. 2. Preparing Department. 3. Another View of the Empire Mill.

reconstruction and extension had to be undertaken, the results of which are now being evidenced in reports which for some time past, show a steady 10 per cent. per annum to the shareholders, despite the fact that this concern is handicapped by the absence of any machinery for producing hessian fabrics.

Very soon after their initial venture, Messrs. McLeod & Co. floated the Kelvin Jute Company, Ltd., which, originally designed as a 400-loom mill, has now been extended to 600 looms, and the success of this enlargement is amply verified by the popularity of its fabrics on the market, no less than by the fact that the last dividend paid to its shareholders was at the rate of 60 per cent. per annum.

While this mill forms one of the best representatives of its type on the Hooghly, Messrs. McLeod & Co. made a further advance in 1912, when they floated the Empire Jute Mill, which is electrically driven throughout, the power being generated by steam turbines, the whole plant exemplifying the last word to date in jute-mill design. Although this mill only started running in the early part of 1914, its success has been so marked that the latest distribution on the ordinary shares was at the rate of 30 per cent. per annum, while reserves to the extent of Rs. 5,00,000 had already been accumulated.

Altogether, Messrs. McLeod & Co. now control 1,175 looms, consuming more than 9 lakhs of maunds of raw jute and producing 34,750 tons of manufactured goods per annum. Their concerns give employment to 25 European overseers and some 8,000 Indian workers, while the capital invested amounts to about Rs. 40,00,000.

THE MERCANTILE BANK OF INDIA, LTD.

The original name of this bank was the Chartered Mercantile Bank of India, London, and China, and the institution was formed at Bombay on November 30, 1853, the first notice of commencement of operations being in the nature of an advertisement which appeared in the *Telegraph and Courier* of that city, stating that the offices would be opened for business on January 3, 1854. A schedule was added in which were shown the rates of interest on deposits repayable respectively on demand, or at three, six, or twelve months, and reference was, further, made to the rate of discount on bills varying in duration from fifteen days to four months, and to cash credits being granted (on approved security) for sums between Rs. 5,000 and Rs. 30,000.

Records of important events connected with the early history of the bank have been found in files of old newspapers and in minute and other books, and these have been supplemented by personal reminiscences of individuals who have a distinct recollection of the transactions of those days. For much of the information thus collated we are indebted to Vol. II, No. 5, of the *Mercantile War Cry*, the "magazine of the assistants in the Calcutta branch of the Mercantile Bank of India, Limited," this being the imposing title on the cover.

Very soon after the opening of the bank there were highly coloured reports as to the rich nature of the ore in newly discovered goldfields in Ceylon, and the directors, ready to take advantage of every opportunity to extend business, opened branches at Colombo and Kandy in March and April 1854. Before the close of that year proposals were made by the directors of the Chartered Bank of Asia with a view to the amalgamation of the two institutions. The journal above mentioned says in connection with this matter that "a proposition was made by dissentient shareholders of the Bank of Asia to wind up the business, and at this juncture Mr. Flower and Mr. Mecke, representing the Mercantile Bank, offered to purchase at par the interest of all shareholders who wished to retire from the concern, and having thereby obtained £60,000 out of the subscribed capital of £100,000, they held the charter of the Bank of Asia at the command of the Mercantile Bank, and the amalgamation was accordingly carried into effect." Other branches were formed in 1855 at Canton, Shanghai, Calcutta, and London, and by the close of the year 1860 Madras, Singapore, Hongkong, Mauritius, and Penang had been added to the list.

It appears that on November 26, 1857, "a deed for winding up the Mercantile Bank of India, London, and China was signed by the parties concerned, and a new deed was executed by the shareholders of the Bank of Asia and the Mercantile Bank for the establishment of a new incorporated company to be called the Chartered Mercantile Bank of India, London, and China."

As the present volume relates very largely to the Province of Bengal, one may mention that the Calcutta branch was heralded by an advertisement in the *Eastern Star* of January 27, 1855, which stated that business would be commenced on the 1st of February following, with Mr. D. T. Robertson as manager. The offices at that time were at 1 Writers' Buildings, immediately opposite St. Andrew's Church, and the current accounts were about fifty in number; the next few years witnessed such a large increase of business that more extensive and convenient premises were secured in Council House Street; and at the present time (September 1915) the officials are housed in a handsome building at 8 Clive Street.

Owing to serious losses following on the closing of the Indian Mints to the free coinage of silver, to great depression in the Straits Settlements and Mauritius, and to the downfall of coffee-planting in Southern India and Ceylon, caused by blight, it was decided to close several of the branches and to reconstruct the business. This was done, and the new institution was named the Mercantile Bank of India, Ltd.

The twenty-second annual general meeting of the shareholders of this bank was held at Winchester House, Old Broad Street, London, E.C., on March 30, 1915, when resolutions, expressive of the deepest gratitude, were unanimously passed to the chairman, directors, chief manager, and the staff of the bank for their work during the year ending December 31, 1914. The report of the directors, signed by Mr. P. Mould, chief manager, referred to the fact that the net profits for the year, after making the customary allowance for bad and doubtful debts, and including a sum of £34,604 brought forward, amounted to £136,224. An interim dividend of 4 per cent. on "A" and "B" shares, amounting to £22,500, had been paid on June 30, 1914; the sum of £35,000 was added to the reserve fund (raising it to £500,000); the officers' pension fund had benefited by £4,000; and £5,000 had been written off the freehold banking premises account. After payment of a further dividend on the "A" and "B" shares of 4 per cent. for the second half of the year (making 8 per cent. for the year), and allowing for the above deductions, a balance of £47,224 would be carried forward.

The chairman, in submitting the report and statement of accounts, referred to the "almost overwhelming problems with which finance and commerce were sud-

THE MERCANTILE BANK OF INDIA, LTD.

1. Entrance. 2. General Banking Hall from the Entrance. 3. Another View of the Banking Hall. 4. Section of General Office.

denly faced in August 1914 by the outbreak of hostilities on the continent of Europe," and he added that the greatest praise was due to the Government of the day for the very prompt and effective manner in which relief was given by emergency legislation, thus restoring confidence, and saving the credit of the country. A feature of the speech, which was received in the heartiest fashion by the meeting, was the statement that more than 25 per cent. of the home staff, in addition to a few of the foreign officers of the bank, were then serving their country in the field, and the directors had undertaken to keep open the appointments for these volunteers. The chairman concluded his remarks by saying that the directors had reason to be satisfied with the result of the work during such an abnormal and exceptional year.

The bank was registered in London, under the Companies Acts of 1862 to 1890, on December 2, 1892, its present offices being at 15 Gracechurch Street, E.C.

The authorized capital is £1,500,000, of which the sum of £1,125,000 has been subscribed; the paid-up capital is £562,500; and the reserve fund amounts to £500,000.

The board of directors consists of Mr. R. J. Black (chairman), Mr. James Campbell, Mr. J. M. Ryrie, Mr. H. Melvill Simons, and Sir David Yule. The London bankers are the Bank of England and the London Joint Stock Bank, Ltd., while in Scotland the agents are Messrs. R. and E. Scott, Queen Street, Edinburgh.

The following are the branches and agencies: Bombay, Calcutta, Howrah, Delhi, Madras, Karachi, Rangoon, Colombo, Kandy, Galle, Singapore, Penang, Kota Bharu, Kuala Lumpur, Batavia, Hongkong, and Shanghai.

The manager of the Calcutta branch is Mr. A. Scott Smith.

A. MILTON & CO.

The telegraphic code word "Equus" is an admirable one for such a firm as Messrs. A. Milton & Co., as they are recognized throughout India, Burma, the Straits, Australia, and New Zealand as being in the forefront of those who purchase, sell, train, or keep at livery, horses of every description, from the handy pony to the thoroughbred racer. These activities, however, do not exhaust the list of Messrs. Milton & Co.'s operations, for they also enjoy a large and influential practice as veterinary surgeons, and are contractors for forage, grain, and condiments. The business was established in the year 1880 by the late Mr. Richard Morgan, M.D., M.R.C.V.S., and the present proprietor, Mr. A. M. Milton, and the extensive premises at 156 Dhurrumtollah Street, in Calcutta (which have accommodation for about two hundred animals), are known as being one of the most famous and best equipped repositories in the East. The firm have regular consignments of horses from Australia and New Zealand, and these comprise racers, steeplechasers, hunters, polo and race ponies, chargers, hacks, and trappers, together with animals suitable for forming teams or pairs. The Indian horse is not overlooked, however, as some really excellent ponies, many of them by English or Arab sires, are obtained from the north-west and the Punjab, and although these show an average height of only about 14 hands 1 in., they are extremely hardy and sure-footed. The majority of the occupants of the stables and paddocks are sold privately, but clients who are unable to pay a personal visit to Calcutta may always rely upon the sound judgment and care of the firm when supplying their wants. It is an old saying, but a very true one, that a purchaser of a horse should always appraise the seller equally as well as the animal, but Messrs. Milton & Co. are fortunate in possessing a well-established reputation for the straightforward manner in which their business is conducted, and they have thus been able to give unbounded satisfaction to customers.

A most important step was taken when the firm secured about 20 acres of land at Ballygunge, near Calcutta, as they have provided paddocks in which sick or overworked horses are turned out to graze, and where youngsters are put through a most complete course of breaking and training, either harness or saddle. Further than this, there is a special track where horses are schooled over a series of jumps, and when they have finished their lessons they may be looked upon as safe fencers. One of the fields is set apart as a segregation camp, in which animals suffering from any contagious or infectious disease can be kept under treatment, either in the open air or in well-ventilated stables. Green barley, oats, paddy, guinea grass, and lucerne are cultivated at Ballygunge, and trees for shelter and shade purposes have been extensively planted.

The hack department is a great boon to the inhabitants of Calcutta, as hirers can always obtain very stylish broughams or landaus (with smart pairs of horses), comfortable *gharries*, phaetons, and other vehicles, and these are turned out in the most attractive manner.

Another branch of the business is the importation and sale of light Australian iron-tyred sulkies, hooded buggies, (rubber tyres), American four-wheel buggies, and hickory gigs, together with English harness and stable requisites of all kinds.

The firm are contractors for every description of forage for horses or cattle, and they keep a large stock of oats, gram, barley, bran, linseed, compressed hay, crushed and mixed grain, chaff, hay, straw, and prepared foods for milch cows and poultry.

Special reference should be made to the firm's "XL condition mixture" for horses, which is not a chemical preparation, but is a pure, wholesome food of great efficacy in its invigorating and muscle-forming properties; it excels as a digestive ingredient; and its sustaining qualities have withstood the severest of all tests. But this preparation is not merely an appetizing adjunct, as it possesses certain medicinal qualities which expel worms, tends to cure coughs and colds, rouse the sluggish liver, and to keep the horse in a bright and naturally healthy condition. This condiment is the result of years of patient study of the constitutional ailments common to horseflesh, and since it was placed upon the market it has proved to be superior to all existing foods of a similar character. Thousands of unsolicited testimonials have been received from clients throughout India and the Far East, and these letters of appreciation of "XL" have been penned after actual tests as to its value have been made.

Messrs. Milton & Co. not only supply double and single harness, saddles, bridles, and other leather requisites, but they are patentees of a preservative (specially manufactured in Australia) which renders all these goods absolutely impervious to water, and it is guaranteed to keep them perfectly flexible during several months of continual hard use.

Policies of insurance against the death of all classes of horses from disease, or from accidents on land or sea, during hunting, steeplechasing, or ordinary

A. MILTON & CO.

1. GARAGE. 2. YARD. 3. FLEET OF MOTOR LORRIES SUPPLIED TO THE GOVERNMENT. 4. PADDOCKS.

work, or owing to surgical operations of an intricate character, are issued by the firm at the lowest possible rates.

As the veterinary department is in the capable hands of Mr. Norman Gilford, M.R.C.V.S., it goes without saying that greater skill or more careful attention in the various phases of complicated maladies could not be offered by any other practitioners.

Although the above branches of Messrs. Milton & Co.'s extensive business have been growing rapidly since their formation, the firm have gladly yielded to the wishes of their numerous clients by establishing a motor department, and they are now sole agents for Fiat, Crossley, Maxwell, Dennis, Alldays motors, motor lorries, ambulances, and Kerry-Abingdon motor cycles.

The premises, which extend from Dhurrumtollah Street to Princep Street, contain airy stables, loose boxes, coach-houses, harness-rooms, carriage-building shops, stores, shoeing forge, garage, offices, surgery, and other accommodation, and special attention is now being devoted to the repairs and adjustment of engines, and coach and wheel work, together with enamelling and upholstering.

Mr. A. Milton and Mr. M. B. Milton bestow personal supervision over all matters, and they have five European assistants and about 250 natives in their employ.

THE NATIONAL BANK OF INDIA, LTD.

The Calcutta City Banking Corporation, Ltd., was established at Calcutta on September 29, 1863, but the name was altered to the National Bank of India, Ltd., on March 2, 1864. The original premises were in Council House Street, and although the staff was largely increased in number from time to time owing to the exceedingly rapid growth of business, it was not until the year 1902 that the company obtained further accommodation by removing to their property at 104 Clive Street. This building, however, soon proved to be too small for the requirements of the bank, and it was enlarged to its present size in the year 1914. Abundance of room is now available for each of the numerous departments, and the exceedingly fine banking hall has a floor area of 23,300 sq. ft.

The company was registered in London under the Companies Act of 1862 on March 23, 1866, its head offices being at 26 Bishopsgate Street, E.C. Branches have been established at Calcutta, Bombay, Madras, Karachi, Chittagong, Amritsar, Cawnpore, Delhi, Lahore, Tuticorin, Cochin, Rangoon, Mandalay, Colombo, Kandy, Newera Eliya, Aden, Steamer Point, Aden; at Zanzibar, Mombasa, Nairobi, Nakura, and Kisumu in British East Africa; and at Entebbe, Kampala, and Jinja in Uganda. The ninety-fifth report of the directors (together with a statement of accounts to December 31, 1914) was submitted to the shareholders at the annual meeting, held in London on March 23, 1915, and, notwithstanding the crippling effect upon commerce caused by the European war, the very satisfactory position of the bank was shown by the fact that the net profits for the previous year, after providing for bad and doubtful debts,

THE NATIONAL BANK OF INDIA, LTD.
THE BANKING HALL. *Photo by E. Lorenz.*

THE NATIONAL BANK OF INDIA, LTD.

Photo by E. Lorenz.

amounted to £347,995 13s. 4d., inclusive of a balance brought forward of £78,625 2s. 4d. An *ad interim* dividend at the rate of 12 per cent. per annum, free of income tax, and amounting to £60,000, had been paid for the half year ending on June 30, 1914, and the directors then recommended a further dividend at the rate of 16 per cent. per annum, and a bonus of 2 per cent., making 16 per cent. for the whole year. They further proposed to add £75,000 to the reserve fund, raising it to £1,175,000, to write off £10,000 from the house property account, and to add £10,000 to the officers' pension fund, leaving a balance of £92,995 13s. 4d. to be carried forward. The amount of the subscribed capital is £2,000,000, of which the sum of £1,000,000 has been paid up by 1,231 shareholders. Interest is allowed by the bank on current deposit accounts at the rate of 2 per cent. per annum on balances from Rs. 1,000 to Rs. 1,00,000, and fixed deposits are received for definite periods on terms which are obtainable at any of the company's offices. General banking business is carried on, and stocks, shares, and other securities are purchased, sold, or kept in safe custody.

The board of directors consists of Mr. Robert Campbell, chairman, Mr. Robert Williamson, deputy chairman, and Mr. A. V. Dunlop Best, Sir John P. Hewett, G.C.S.I., C.I.E., Mr. Robert Miller, Mr. Alfred Simson, Mr. J. N. Stuart, Mr. J. A. Toomey. The bankers of the company are the Bank of England, the National Provincial Bank of England, Ltd., and the National Bank of Scotland, Ltd., while the manager of the Calcutta branch is Mr. W. J. K. Hegarty.

THE BRITISH COMMERCIAL BANK, LTD.

This enterprising institution was originally started as an adjunct to Reuter's Telegraphic Agency Company, but its area of operations extended so widely and with such rapidity that it now conducts exchange and general banking business with England (through its head office at 43 Coleman Street, London), South Africa, and Australia. The premises of the company in Calcutta occupy an unrivalled position at 26-27 Dalhousie Square, immediately opposite the General Post Office, and practically in the centre of the leading mercantile houses and the other exchange banks.

Fixed deposits are received upon favourable terms, which may be ascertained from the managers. Indian Government securities, stocks, and shares, are purchased or sold, and bills payable in Europe, Africa, Australia, India, and in other countries are negotiated or collected. Interest, salaries, and pensions, are collected, and the safe custody of valuable documents is undertaken Current accounts are opened free of charge and interest is allowed at usual rates on daily balances of Rs. 500.

The capital of the company is £1,000,000, made up of 100,000 shares of £10, of which the sum of £500,000 has been fully paid.

The directors, well-known financial men in the city of London, are Mr. Gerald Williams (chairman), the Hon. Mark F.

BRITISH COMMERCIAL BANK, LTD.

1. Portion of Office. 2. Exterior View.

Napier, Mr. George Grinnell Milne, and the Hon. Edmund W. Parker.

FEDERICO PELITI

Calcutta and many other Eastern cities situated within a few degrees from the tropics would not be so endurable were it not for those havens of rest and refreshment, in the form of high-class restaurants, which have come into prominence during the past thirty or forty years. Their elegant but comfortably furnished rooms, sheltered from the heat of an Indian sun and cooled by the use of electric fans, present the most fascinating opportunities for young and old alike to enjoy those periods of relaxation which occasion offers, while at the same time they are served, in the best European style, with delicacies of the most delectable character, manufactured by princes in the art of confectionery. How tongues wag and teaspoons rattle at Peliti's in Calcutta (every one knows Peliti's), which is one of the most famous restaurants in the Eastern hemisphere !

The present proprietors may perhaps tell of the days when Mr. Federico Peliti, the founder of the firm, left Italy to enter the service of the Earl of Mayo—a former Viceroy—as chief confectioner, this being the first appointment of the kind in Government House; they will refer to the assassination of the Viceroy at Port St. Blair, and then one may hear how their predecessor commenced business on his own account in Calcutta in the year 1869.

This was a bold step, involving serious difficulties, as luxuries such as Mr. Peliti wished to place before the public were absolutely unknown in India, and further, there were no chances of his obtaining skilled makers of such goods in the whole of the country. He persevered, however, practically single-handed, for a number of years, and eventually he was compelled by the increasing size of the business to obtain qualified assistants from Italy.

A very notable expansion in the turnover followed very rapidly, and it was not long before extensive premises were secured at 11 Government Place, and immediately opposite Government House. Attention was then directed to hotel accommodation and catering on a much larger scale, and the founder's two sons, Edoardo and Federico Peliti, are now owners of the splendid restaurant building in Calcutta and of the Grand Hotel at Simla.

A very large business is now carried on in the manufacture of wedding and other cakes, chocolates, an endless variety of sweets, and pastry of all kinds, while the stores used and exhibited for sale in the restaurant are made in Carignano, in Italy, and are imported specially for the partners.

Catering is undertaken for wedding parties, entertainments, and picnics; the firm are caterers by Royal Appointment to His Majesty the King-Emperor, in addition to holding similar warrants from all the Viceroys of India and Governors of Bengal since the time of Lord Mayo; they are official restaurateurs to the Turf and other clubs in Calcutta; and they enter into important contracts for the supply of all refreshments to Indian chiefs on special occasions, such as the visits of Viceroys and Governors, and for tiger-shooting parties.

Gold medals were awarded to Messrs. Peliti at Exhibitions held in Paris, Turin, and Calcutta, and they possess quite a collection of warrants of appointment and testimonials.

There are a spacious tearoom and shop on the ground floor, and a fine restaurant and balcony tearoom on the first floor, the last named being one of the most popular resorts in the city.

The partners give direct personal supervision over a numerous and fully trained staff of attendants.

THE PLANTERS' STORES AND AGENCY COMPANY, LTD.

The Planters' Stores Company, Ltd., formed in the year 1872 by a number of influential tea-planters in the district of Dibrugarh of the Province of Assam, was, six years later, incorporated in England under the title at the heading of these notes, and its business concerns have developed with such rapidity and to such an extent, that important branches or agencies are now opened not only at 11 Clive Street, Calcutta, but also at Chittagong, and practically throughout Bengal, Assam, and the Federated Malay States.

The company are managing or selling agents for about twenty-five tea estates, for several coal, stone, and lime works, and some rubber and other companies; but they have for a number of years made a special feature of, and have been working up a virtual monopoly for, "Sirocco" tea machinery and fans for all the tea-planting districts of Assam and Northern India generally. No name is better known in connection with machinery used in all the processes of the manufacture of tea than that of "Sirocco," the trade-mark distinguishing the machinery made by Messrs. Davidson & Co., Ltd., of Belfast, for whom the Planters' Stores and Agency Company, Ltd., are sole representatives in Northern India.

In former days it was the usual practice in tea-drying machinery to draw the hot air through the drying chamber by suction, but in the "Sirocco" endless chain pressure driers this principle is reversed, the air being forced through under pressure, a new departure marking a distinct advance, in that the hot air presses down upon the upper surfaces of the leaves, and dries them almost as rapidly as the lower surfaces. These driers require no brickwork in their erection, and they comprise three distinct parts—the heater, the fan, and the drying chamber.

Many improvements have during recent years been added to the heater of the multitubular type, all of these tending to convenience in working, to economy in fuel consumption, and durability. The products of consumption pass from the furnace to the right and left into two chambers at the back of the heater, thence through the top groups of tubes into the front chambers, and then through the bottom groups to the lower back chambers, which communicate with the chimney.

All multitubular air heaters which are used in conjunction with the endless chain pressure driers, can now be supplied with a mechanical stoker of the latest improved type, and using forced draught. This form of stoking possesses two chief advantages, as it effects economy both in fuel consumption and in labour. The consumption of coal is reduced on account of the complete and smokeless combustion of the fuel, which produces a uniformly high furnace temperature, with a bright, incandescent fire, and ensures that the gases are burnt before entering the tubes, whilst the amount of labour required is much less than with hand-firing, as the attendant has only to fill the coal hopper at fairly long intervals, and the fire has to be cleaned about twice a day only.

The "stoker" works on the underfeed principle; that is to say, the fresh fuel is supplied continuously from below, and is advanced upwards towards the zone of combustion. The coal is emptied into the hopper, the base of which communi-

F. PELITI.

1. Restaurant and Confectionery Premises, Government Place, Calcutta.
2. Interior of Restaurant.
3. Refreshment Pavilion at the Zoological Gardens, Calcutta.
4. Wedding Cake made by F. Peliti.

THE PLANTERS' STORES AND AGENCY COMPANY, LTD.

1. SONE STONE AND LIME WORKS. 2. NO. 12 SIROCCO HEATER WITH STOKER. 3. SIROCCO ENDLESS CHAIN DRIER (LATEST TYPE). 4. INTERIOR OF OFFICE. 5. MAIN PIT—CENTRAL DHARMABAND COLLIERY.

cates with the horizontal trough or combustion retort within the furnace of the heater. This trough contains a tapered screw, or worm conveyer, which is actuated by gearing connected with a countershaft placed above the heater, and by rotation of the worm the fuel is advanced from the hopper into the retort, and overflows in a rounded mound on to the sloping firebars, where the coal is coked, i.e. deprived of its volatile gases. The latter, being mixed with air introduced at this point, and escape being only possible by rising through the glowing coke above, are heated to such a high temperature that they are completely consumed without smoke, while the combustion of the fixed carbon of the coal is completed by the air introduced through the apertures between the firebars. In this manner a clear, bright surface of incandescent fuel is always obtained, without the inevitable fluctuations of temperature in the furnace consequent upon firing by hand. The ashes and slack (of which the quantity is usually very small) pass down the sloping firebars to each side of the furnace, whence they can be periodically raked out through the two doors in the front of the furnace.

Mr. Richard Rowe has acted as chairman of the company since 1904, and it is largely due to his enterprise and shrewd common sense that the expansion of the business has been maintained so steadily. The company occupied premises in Mission Row, Calcutta, in earlier days, but they removed to their present quarters in a very fine new building in Clive Street in the year 1913.

The London offices of the company are at 17 St. Helen's Place, E.C., and the telegraphic address is "Planters."

T. R. PRATT

The history of the present age is a record of progress in all directions, but in engineering matters (which are being dealt with at the moment) one need not go far afield to witness the astounding advance which has been made.

The old-fashioned trek-wagons of Africa and the palanquins, the pack bullocks, and the coolie carriers of India, would long ago have been swept into oblivion if those countries had been developed to such an extent that good metalled roads were a possibility. But in the traffic of our cities and towns one sees daily numbers of motor-lorries conveying huge loads of merchandise from place to place in an incredibly short space of time, thus displacing the horse or mule carts for transport service, which are almost as rare as 10-rupee notes on the green sward of the *maidan*.

The greatest revolution, however, is noticeable in the present-day facilities for business or pleasure purposes afforded by the luxurious motor-cars which are in constant use by professional and commercial men, or by private persons who are only too glad to turn their backs upon evil-smelling streets scorched by high temperatures and rendered unpleasant by dust of roads and smoke from chimneys. The motor vehicles of 1916 are wondrously fast in speed, and, by their luxurious furnishings and fittings, extend invitations, which one finds it impossible to refuse, to partake of the intense enjoyment to be derived from a spin of 40 or 50 miles amid gorgeous scenery in various parts of the globe.

One of the leading motor establishments in Bengal where one can obtain magnificent cars with all modern improvements and trolleys for heavy goods, together with all kinds of accessories and fittings required in the rebuilding or repair of any kind of petrol-driven vehicles, is that of Mr. T. R. Pratt, of 301-2 Bowbazar Street, in Calcutta.

The business as at present constructed was established in March 1907, prior to which date Mr. T. R. Pratt, as manager for Messrs. Davidson & Co., in Northern India, represented in Calcutta: Messrs. Babcock and Wilcox; Samuel Osborn & Co., Ltd., Clyde Steel Works, Sheffield; Messrs. G. and J. Weir, Ltd., Cathcart, Glasgow; the Automatic Telephone Manufacturing Company, Ltd., Liverpool; Messrs. D. H. and G. Haggie, Ltd., Sunderland, and other firms, whose representation (excepting the first named) he still holds, together with the Turbon Patent Fan Company, Ltd., Llanmore, Llanelly, South Wales; the Daimler Motor Company, Coventry; the Sunbeam Motor Company, Wolverhampton; the Standard Motor Car Company, Ltd., Coventry; the Talbot Motor Car Company, London; Messrs. A. Darracq & Co., London; the Perry Motor Company, Ltd., Birmingham; the Commercial Cars, Ltd., Luton; and the Willys-Overland, Incorporated, Toledo, Ohio, U.S.A.

Mr. Pratt is an engineer and machinery merchant, and the scope of the business is varied and comprehensive. Many notable contracts have been entrusted to him and have been successfully carried through. The Government of India purchased from him 333 tons of copper wire for aerial lighting wires at the Imperial Durbar at Delhi in 1911, and he was responsible for the supply and upkeep of 64 motor-cars for the Imperial Camp at Delhi and Nepal for His Majesty King George V, the Nepal *shikar* party, and H.H. Sir Chandra Shamsher Jang, G.C.B., G.C.S.I., G.C.V.O., Prime Minister and Marshal.

The automatic telephone installation at Simla in 1911 was an enterprise attended with a considerable amount of anxiety, and as it was the first equipment of its kind in India its success was imperative. The erection, when completed, found instant favour, and the standard of efficiency achieved vindicated the striking claims made on behalf of the "Automatic." The service, as now provided in Simla, has resulted in other large contracts being placed for similar installations.

From a small nucleus in the motor-car industry, this branch of the business has gone forward with unerring speed. Mr. Pratt realized the potentialities of the motor in India, and the agencies which his enterprise secured have been ample reward for his perspicacity. The branches of the firm at Delhi and Dhanbad have contributed their quota, both as regards motor-cars and the engineering side of the business. The well-known "Overland" car is chiefly responsible for the wonderful increase and development of the motor-car department. The Overland Company were among the first (if not the original firm) to produce a reliable car with electric starting and lighting sets, together with complete equipment, at an almost incredibly low price, and the energy resulting from the concentration of massed organization to produce such a car has justified itself in the eminence in which it stands in the world to-day.

The agency for "Commer" cars was one which the firm did well to obtain. This vehicle is one of commercial utility, and is one of the leading transport lorries yet produced. It is entirely British, a triumph of British material and workmanship. The "Commer" has manifested its supremacy in no uncertain way during the present war, and its use in this country has demonstrated how practical and economical motor transport is as compared with the slow and unsatisfactory service provided by indigenous methods of conveyance.

The workshop department has also

T. R. PRATT.

1. HEAD OFFICE AND GARAGE. 2. PART OF INTERIOR OF GARAGE. 3. CORNER OF MACHINE SHOPS, LOWER CIRCULAR ROAD 4. CORNER OF THE WAREHOUSE IN MISSION ROW.

advanced in concert with others, and the accommodation of the premises now occupied not allowing of further extension, the works are being transferred to a more extensive site. The work, turned out under skilled management, has reflected highly on the supervision and upon the workmen employed.

Messrs. D. H. and G. Haggie, Ltd., Sunderland: The ropes manufactured by this firm have always been more or less known throughout the coalfields. The quality of material used and the reliable service they invariably provide have undeniably maintained the reputation they have always enjoyed, and have secured for them a popularity throughout the Indian coalfields which must be intensely gratifying both to the makers and to the local agent.

Samuel Osborn & Co., Ltd., Sheffield: Space does not permit a record in detail of the activities of this firm, as the ramifications of their business are so numerous that reference can only be made to a limited conspectus. They were the original makers of "Mushet" high-speed steel, which at the time of its inception caused such a sensation in the engineering world. "Mushet," though somewhat changed in formula, has held its own against more recent productions, and invariably asserts an ascendancy over similar materials against which it is demonstrated. "Mushet" high-speed drills are also commonly used, and their supremacy has also been well maintained. Mr. Pratt has been zealous in his claims on behalf of Osborn's products, the high-grade materials supplied having substantiated all assertions as to their superiority, and have established them throughout the country on an unassailable footing.

The Turbon Patent Fan Company, Ltd., Llanelly: Mr. Pratt has only recently acquired this agency, which, combined with the numerous other agencies he possesses, should turn to good account. The "Turbon" fan follows the latest developments in mining-fan construction, one special feature being the facility with which a damaged blade can be extracted and replaced. Radially the blades are narrow, and axially run the whole width of the fan, while the cubic discharge and pressure capacity of the latter are unsurpassed by any other in existence.

G. and J. Weir, Ltd., Cathcart, Glasgow: Every engineer is familiar with a "Weir" auxiliary. Weir's best-known products are boiler feed pumps, air pumps, hydraulic pumps, locomotive feed pumps, oil-fuel pumps, evaporators and distilling plants, and circulating pumps and condensers. The concentration of expert, technical, and scientific efforts specialized and devoted to definite lines of research, the comparison and analysis of results drawn from an ever-increasing range of examples, have all contributed to make Weir's auxiliary machinery the best and most reliable in the world. The latest and most up-to-date equipment and manufacturing facilities, a closely systematized industrial and commercial organization, a generous conception of duty to their *clientèle*, and a high ideal of quality and character in their products, are also factors which have obtained for Weir's products the reputation which they enjoy.

The Vaughan Pulley Company: This is one of the foremost firms in Great Britain engaged in the production of pulleys, shafting, gearing, and high efficiency power transmission. The considerable experience which this firm has accumulated is at the disposal of those interested in the question of power transmission, and they are always pleased to diagnose any special requirements, and to assist in settling such problems as may arise in planning mechanical and electrical power distributions. The Vaughan Pulley Company maintain a high degree of accuracy and unrivalled quality in materials and workmanship, factors which have earned for their goods an enviable distinction.

Mr. Pratt has been resident in India for the past 33 years, and, like most successful commercial men, has many and varied activities. He is keenly interested in sport, and is a familiar figure in racing, motoring, and golfing circles. Mr. Pratt devotes a good deal of his leisure to riding, and those of the old school who were familiar with the turf in the late eighties will still remember him as a prominent gentleman rider. He now owns a few promising horses.

Mr. Pratt also takes a lively interest in municipal affairs, and is one of the four members of the Bengal Chamber of Commerce elected by that body as representatives on the Corporation. He has held this honour for the past 13 years.

PYNE, HUGHMAN & CO., LTD.

It is not often that a firm with a life of only some half a dozen years can boast such a record of progress and important work accomplished as that of Messrs. Pyne, Hughman & Co., Ltd., of Grosvenor House, Old Court House Street, in the city of Calcutta.

The firm was established in London in 1910 by Mr. C. A. B. Pyne and Mr. E. M. Hughman (under the name of Pyne, Hughman & Co.), and in the same year they commenced business in Calcutta at 4 Lyons Range. The founders possessed sound, practical experience, and such boundless energy was manifested by them that a most remarkable development of their interests was noticeable even in the first year of their existence, and they are now (1916) well known throughout the length and breadth of India. They have erected more than a hundred electric lifts in various parts of the country, and have carried out upwards of a hundred installations in northern districts, among which were those at Government Houses at Ranchi, Bankipore, and Chittagong. Many contracts for lighting, involving the expenditure of considerable sums of money, have been executed in Calcutta, and chief among these are for work done at the new offices of Messrs. Graham & Co., the Planters' Stores and Agency Company, Ltd., the Allahabad and National Banks, and the Dharma Samavaya Mansions in Corporation Street, the last named being the largest building of its kind in India.

At the present time the firm are engaged in the erection of thirty 2-ton electric goods lifts and fifty-nine 2-ton electric travelling cranes for the new docks now in course of construction at Garden Reach for the Commissioners of the Port of Calcutta. These are the largest orders for lifts and cranes ever placed with any individual firm of engineering contractors in India.

Designs for a new bridge to replace the pontoon which spans the Hooghly River between Calcutta and Howrah were invited recently, and the plan submitted by Messrs. Pyne, Hughman & Co., as agents for a large firm, was, with a few slight variations, accepted by the Port Commissioners of Calcutta, who awarded a prize of £3,000 for the work.

Messrs. Pyne, Hughman & Co. competed at the Allahabad Exhibition in 1911 and obtained numerous gold, silver, and bronze medals for their exhibits, and as agents for the Aster Engineering Company, Ltd., they were awarded the gold medal for the famous "Aster" engine, which also received the Grand Prix at the Brussels Exhibition in 1910.

PYNE, HUGHMAN & CO., LTD.

1. Pyne, Hughman & Co., Ltd. (Head Office). 2. Harrington Mansions. 3. The Allahabad Bank, Ltd. 4. Oriental Life Insurance Buildings.

PYNE, HUGHMAN & CO., LTD.

1. Graham & Co.'s Offices. 2. New Telegraph Office, Calcutta. 3. National Bank, Ltd., Calcutta. 4. Port Commissioners' Transit Shed.

SHAW, WALLACE & CO.

1. Shaw, Wallace & Co.'s Office, 4 Bankshall Street. 2. The Hooghly Flour Mill. 3. Sterilized Animal Meal Factory, Dhappa. 4. Landing a Shipment of Nitrolin.

Photo Bourne & Shepherd

The business continued to grow to such an extent that early in the year 1916 a limited liability company was formed, with the object of providing for a still further expansion. Messrs. Gladstone, Wyllie & Co. one of the leading firms in Calcutta were appointed managing agents, and the directors of the company are the Hon. Sir F. H. Stewart, C.I.E. (of Messrs. Gladstone, Wyllie & Co.), chairman; Messrs. Gerald Stapledon (of Messrs. Morgan & Co.), C. A. B. Pyne, and E. M. Hughman.

L. E. SALSICCIONI.

1. A CORNER OF THE MARBLE YARD. 2. MARBLE STAIRCASE AND RAILS AT GALSTAUN'S PARK.

New workshops and godowns have recently been erected at 1 British Indian Street, under the name of "Porcupine Buildings," and the present offices in Grosvenor House are situated in a handsome new building in the centre of the commercial life of Calcutta.

L. E. SALSICCIONI

It is claimed that the godowns and warehouses at 205 Old China Bazar Street, Calcutta, belonging to Mr. L. E. Salsiccioni, contain the largest and most varied stock of marble, ceramic, and flooring and glazed wall-tiles in the Province of Bengal.

The business was established in the year 1902, and it has expanded with great rapidity owing to the most satisfactory manner in which the proprietor has carried out a large number of important works. Special mention may be made of marble columns and balustrade supplied for the staircase in Galstaun's Park; a marble balustrade and dado for staircase at the new Palace of the Nawab of Murshidabad; marble balustrade for verandas in the Viziaram Palace of the Maharaja of Vizianagram at Korukonda; marble balustrade and handrail for staircase of the Maharaja of Panchkote's New Palace at Kashipur, Manbhum; marble for the new Council House Room at Delhi; marble altars for St. James's, St. Teresa's, and other churches in Calcutta; and three massive marble staircases at Esplanade Mansions, in Calcutta, etc. The list of Mr. Salsiccioni's patrons is a long one, and it includes practically all the railway systems in India, rulers of the principal native States, the leading contractors' and merchants' firms, and a great many notable people in the country.

Flooring and other tiles, as well as marble, are imported monthly from Italy, while glazed wall-tiles are obtained from English factories; and between 100,000 and 200,000 square feet of marble and a large quantity of manufactured goods are usually kept on the premises.

SAXBY & FARMER (INDIA), LTD.

This company (incorporated in England) have their registered offices at 53 Victoria Street, Westminster, London, S.W., and they are well known throughout the world as engineers in connection with signalling upon railways.

Their works and offices in Calcutta are situated at 17 Convent Road, Entally, and their telegraphic address is "Interlock," Calcutta.

SHAW, WALLACE & CO.

There are several commercial houses in Calcutta whose history is a striking illustration of success obtained by capable and energetic men in a comparatively short period of time, and among the most prominent of these firms is Messrs. Shaw, Wallace & Co., of Bankshall Street, Calcutta, who occupy "Wallace House," one of the finest blocks of office buildings in the city.

Their business was established in an unpretentious manner in 1886 when they took over some of the interests of Messrs. Shaw, Finlayson & Co., and it has now become one of the largest of the great firms of East India merchants and agents established in Calcutta.

The founders were Mr. David Shaw and Mr. C. W. Wallace, and at the outset they were concerned chiefly in the management of the large tea interests of Mr. R. Gordon Shaw.

It was not long before a commencement was made with the importation of Manchester piece goods, and the firm is today one of the most prominent importers of cotton textile goods in India. The next substantial addition was the absorption of the firm of Messrs. Mitchell, Reid & Co., and with it was obtained the important agency of the Burma Oil Company. The firm have since that date been intimately concerned with the phenomenally rapid growth of that great enterprise, and they have, further, recently acquired the agency of the Anglo-Persian Oil Company. Considerable extension of the firm's operations took place between the years 1902 and 1908, when branch offices were opened in Bombay, Madras, Karachi, Cochin, Mormugao, Coconada, and Tuticorin, and, a year or two later, in Colombo. Side by side with this widening of its scope, the business activities of the firm increased with great rapidity, and each succeeding year witnessed some fresh and important development.

The gradual development of Indian industries has presented great opportunities, which this enterprising business house has been quick to embrace, and in addition to the large interests referred to above, Messrs. Shaw, Wallace & Co. are managing agents of a flourishing cotton mill in the Central Provinces, of two large and successful flour mills in Calcutta, of numerous collieries in Bengal and the Central Provinces, and a chemical factory in Bombay which is the largest of its kind in India.

The firm are large importers of piece goods, sugar, salt, machinery, pumps, rock drills, chemical fertilizers, aerial ropeways, wire ropes, timber and various metals; whilst they are exporters of gunnies, jute, rice, wheat, and all other descriptions of food grains, linseed, flour, hemp, hides, coal, copra, and almost every variety of the produce of India.

Among their other activities, they are bunkering contractors on a large scale; they control a diamond-drilling syndicate upon whom great demands have been made for the exploration of metalliferous lands; and they are the largest manufacturers and suppliers of chemical fertilizers in India.

Insurance business, too, is an important branch which deserves mention. The firm are agents for the Royal Insurance Company, the Liverpool, London, and Globe Insurance Company, Ltd., the Sun Life Insurance Company of Canada, the Union Marine Insurance Company, the British Dominions Insurance Company, L'Union Fire Insurance Company, Ltd., Paris, the General Accident Assurance Corporation, the Excess Insurance Company, Ltd., and, in Madras, the Queensland Insurance Company, all of which are first-class companies of world-wide reputation. Insurances are effected in connection with fire, life, marine, accident, loss of profits, motor-car, horse, jewellery, burglary, fidelity, earthquake, and storm.

Messrs. Shaw, Wallace & Co. are also in a position to arrange insurances at Lloyds Shipping Offices in London. Their corresponding firm in London is Messrs. R. G. Shaw & Co., of Winchester House, Old Broad Street, E.C.

F. A. SHEEHAN & CO.

Only twelve years have elapsed since Mr. F. A. Sheehan, late engineer officer of the Royal Indian Marine, commenced business as a mechanical engineer and contractor, by establishing the Albert Iron Works at 25 South Road, Entally, a most centrally situated suburb of Calcutta, but that period has sufficed to bring his establishment into a prominent position among the industrial enterprises of Eastern Bengal. His sound practical experience soon caused him to be recognized as a leading figure in commercial circles, with the result that he is to-day the sole proprietor of an exceedingly flourishing concern. Trade is carried on under the style of F. A. Sheehan & Co., and the firm are now manufacturers of light railway rolling stock, iron and brass founders, tin and copper smiths, and structural iron workers, while a large staff of skilled artisans, supervised by highly qualified Europeans, are engaged in effecting repairs to all kinds of machinery.

Mr. Sheehan is, however, in the proud position of being the inventor and patentee of metal water tanks, or *pakhals*, which have been adopted for military purposes on instructions from the Army Headquarters in India. A regular supply of pure water to troops in barracks, on a line of march, or in actual warfare, is one of the most difficult problems with which commanding officers are confronted, and the Sheehan pattern for pack-mule carriage has been found to be more suitable than any other kind hitherto used. The chief features of these tanks are their portability and lightness in weight, while their specially devised patent draw-out flush-cocks are exceedingly simple in construction, and cannot possibly get out of order. Another distinct advantage is that they are strapped in such a position on the backs of transport animals that the latter have absolute freedom in action, and are thereby kept in healthy condition.

The weight of a pair of empty tanks is 26 lb., full ones turn the scale at 190 lb., and the capacity of the two is 16¾ gallons.

Major-General Kitson, Quartermaster-General in India, addressed a circular letter from the Army Headquarters at Simla, in October 1909, to the generals commanding divisions at Peshawar, Rawal Pindi, Lahore, Quetta, Mhow, Poona, Meerut, Lucknow, Secunderabad, and Burma, and the Derajat, Kohat, Bannu, and Aden Brigades, in which he said: "It has been decided to adopt a metal water tank for pack-mule carriage, manufactured by Messrs. F. A. Sheehan & Co., engineers, Calcutta, in place of the present pattern. I am to request that, as the stocks of the latter become unserviceable, they may be replaced by the tanks of the 'Sheehan' pattern."

Since the commencement of the European war Mr. Sheehan has been engaged wholly in the manufacture of military stores and equipment, including water tanks, which are being made at the rate of at least seventy-five daily.

The workshops cover a very large area of ground, and they are well equipped with the latest type of machinery and plant, which is driven by electric power.

THE SOUTH BRITISH INSURANCE COMPANY, LTD.

Notwithstanding the increasing competition among insurance offices throughout the world, the South British Company has continued to make steady progress in India and the Far East since its establishment in Calcutta in the year 1885, and it has justly earned a very high reputation for the prompt and liberal manner in which claims are dealt with. Thirty years ago one small room and a couple of Europeans, assisted by a few Indian clerks, sufficed for the conduct of the business, whereas to-day the company has its own palatial premises in the heart of the commercial centre of Calcutta, and within a stone's-throw of the principal banks and mercantile houses. Branches or agencies have been opened in nearly all the principal towns in the Far East, as well as in South Africa and Australasia.

Mr. Victor Murray, who is the manager for the Far East, and controls all the company's affairs from Calcutta as far as Yokohama, has had a lifelong experience in insurance matters, and his enterprising spirit has contributed very largely to the successful position the South British Company now holds. Mr. Murray has taken a leading part in the affairs of the Calcutta Marine Insurance Association, and has been its chairman for many years, and is one of the most popular figures in business circles in Calcutta. Mr. Murray has been very ably supported by his assistant manager, Mr. G. F. Ross, who has been associated with the company for very many years, of which over twenty-one have been spent in the Eastern service of the company. Mr. Ross also has been closely identified with the Marine Insurance Association, and was chairman in 1915.

The capital of the company is £2,000,000 (of which £1,000,000 is subscribed), while the large amount of reserve funds is a striking proof of its stability as a business concern.

The home office of the company is at Jerusalem Chambers, 2 Cowper's Court, Cornhill, London, E.C.

F. A. SHEEHAN & CO.

1. General View of Workshops. 2. A Corner of the Open Yard. 3. Interior of Tin and Coppersmiths' Shop. 4. Interior of Machine Shop. 5. Blacksmiths' Shop and Foundry.

SOUTH BRITISH INSURANCE COMPANY, LTD.

1. Exterior. 2. Part of Manager's Office. 3 Eastern Department. 4. Outer Office.

THE STANDARD LIFE ASSURANCE COMPANY

It is not surprising that the country to the north of the Tweed should be regarded as the home of life assurance, seeing that the fellow-countrymen of Burns are proverbially thrifty, and have always been conspicuous for the ability which they have displayed in the management of public as well as private financial undertakings. They were not slow in realizing the necessity for making provision for themselves and their families, and the possibilities of effecting this by means of a policy of insurance appealed to them with considerable force. The "Standard" is one of many institutions in Scotland which deal only in life business in its various forms, and as it does not accept marine, fire, or accident risks, the large amount of its accumulated funds is available for fulfilling contracts in the only branch in which it is interested.

The company was formed in Edinburgh in the year 1825 under the name of the Life Insurance Company of Scotland, but this title was changed to the "Standard" in 1832, a special Act of Parliament being passed in that year to confirm the rules and regulations. The statute sets forth that the objects of the company are "to effect or make insurances on lives and survivorships, to make or effect all such other insurances connected with life, to grant, purchase, and sell annuities for lives or otherwise, to grant endowments for children or other persons, and to purchase and sell reversionary rights, and to receive investments of money for accumulation."

The "Standard" was not only established and conducted on sound economic principles, but its rates of premium were so reasonable, and its manner of settling claims was so prompt and generous, that a very rapid growth of the business took place. About twenty years after the inception of the company the directors had reasonable grounds for believing that India and the Colonies might be permitted to share in the benefits of life assurance, provided that special rates were charged in order to meet naturally greater risks.

The Colonial Life Assurance Company was therefore formed in 1846 for the express purpose of undertaking foreign and colonial business, and it made most satisfactory progress for a period of nineteen years, the policy-holders sharing in the very large profits which were made. Permission to travel or to reside abroad was extended to insurers, and the amount of annual premium was based upon reliable statistics of mortality in India, which had been carefully tabulated by expert officials of the company. In the year 1865, however, it was found that the interests of the two companies were practically identical, and that as the managers of each comprised the same individuals, it was considered that it would be to the advantage of all concerned if an amalgamation took place, and this proposed union became an accomplished fact on March 19, 1866, the original name of the Standard Life Assurance Company, Ltd., being retained. A number of insurance offices have, through various causes, been absorbed by the Standard Company, and these include the York and North of England (transferred in 1844), the Commercial (No. 1) in 1846, the Commercial (No. 2) in the same year, the Colonial and General in 1847, the Experience in 1850, the Minerva in 1864, the Victoria in the following year, and the Legal and Commercial and the London and Provincial in 1865. The following figures may be given to illustrate the progress of the company: Between the years 1850 and 1855 the number of new policies was 4,608, with £2,492,988 representing the sums assured; from 1880 to 1885 the respective totals were 11,925 and £6,714,260; while the period from 1905 to 1910 showed 22,055 and £10,658,889.

The annual reports and statements of accounts mark the steady growth and the enormous wealth of the company, and the subjoined extracts have been culled from the latest returns: Amount of assurances proposed during the year 1914 (3,630 proposals), £2,356,633; assurances accepted, 3,095, policies for £1,900,333; annual premium on new policies, £78,555; amount received in purchase of annuities, £53,268; claims by death during the year, £746,964; claims under endowment assurances matured during the year, £249,213; and subsisting assurances, £29,351,193. The annual revenue was £1,591,071, and the accumulated funds amounted at the end of the year to £13,735,374.

It will be readily understood that the investment of such huge sums of money demands financial skill of no ordinary character, and it redounds to the credit of the directors, managers, and other officials that the stability of the company is vouched for by the leading actuaries of the present day.

Branches and agencies have been established throughout the United Kingdom and India, and in China, Ceylon, Mauritius, the Straits Settlements, Canada, South Africa, Egypt, West Indies, Belgium, Hungary, Spain, Denmark, Norway, Sweden, Argentina and Uruguay, while the Calcutta office controls the work in Bengal, Assam, Orissa, the Punjab, Burma, the United Provinces of Agra, Oudh, the North-Western Frontier Provinces, the Central Provinces, Central India, and Rajputana.

The Calcutta offices are situated in a very handsome building at 32 Dalhousie Square, which was erected in the year 1895, and Mr. W. E. Hill is the local secretary.

STEUART & CO.

It is exceedingly improbable that there is any commercial firm in India which can boast of having been established for 140 years with the exception of that of Messrs. Steuart & Co., of 3 Mangoe Lane, Calcutta. Special interest is taken by partners in business concerns to-day in tracing the history of their firms from the date of foundation, and in noticing the remarkable changes which have taken place, not merely in the manner of conducting transactions, but in comparing the style, design, and quality of manufactured goods of earlier days with those which are in vogue now. It is within the knowledge of the present partners of Messrs. Steuart & Co. that correct records were actually kept of pioneering experiences, but they, in common with legions of others, have to deplore the fact that these interesting documents are not available for inspection now. In some instances they have been ruthlessly destroyed, but it is particularly annoying to the oldest firm in India that its valuable literary heirlooms have suffered destruction by white ants, those insidious pests of the East. There is evidence that tabulated statements showing the various changes in the *personnel* of the firm were carefully prepared from the very first, and although these were deposited in an iron safe, the key was, unfortunately, subsequently lost. When Mr. Walter Bushby, uncle of Mr. Frank E. Bushby, the present senior partner, joined the firm in the year 1885, the safe was opened by force, and it was discovered that the interior was coated with

THE STANDARD LIFE ASSURANCE COMPANY.

STANDARD LIFE OFFICE BUILDINGS, CALCUTTA.

STEUART & CO.

1. VARNISHING ROOM. 2. REPAIR SHOP. 3. EXTERIOR OF THE PREMISES. 4 WARRANT OF APPOINTMENT TO H.M. THE KING-EMPEROR.

rust, and that white ants had destroyed every vestige of the papers, only a heap of dust remaining of those priceless records. Notwithstanding this misfortune, however, it is known that a coach-builder's business was started by Mr. A. Steuart in 1775 at 8 Old Court House Corner, and that these premises were retained until the year 1907, when a move was made into Mangoe Lane.

Mr. Frank Bushby made strenuous efforts to discover traces of any other documents, but the earliest authentic ones found by him commenced with the year 1824, when the partners were Messrs. Robert, James, and John Hastie, who landed in India in 1807, 1811, and 1818 respectively. Following the Hasties came (among others) Mr. Burkinyoung in 1841, who was master of the Trades Association in Calcutta for two years, and who appears to have been a partner until 1860; Mr. W. Roberts, who after some years' service retired to Europe; Mr. T. C. Carter, who was made partner in 1860; Mr. R. Allardice, Junior, and Mr. Kilgour from 1868 to 1879; Messrs. Kilgour and Hay from 1881 to 1885; Mr. Walter Bushby and Mr. A. W. Westrop from 1886 to 1893; Mr. W. Bushby as sole partner from 1894 to 1901; and Messrs. W. Bushby and R. E. Josland in the following six years. Mr. Walter Bushby retired to Europe in 1907, leaving Mr. Josland, Mr. A. H. Martin, and Mr. Frank Bushby as partners. In 1911 Mr. Josland retired, when Mr. Frank E. Bushby became senior partner, his colleagues being Mr. G. Berridge-Page, M.I.A.E., and Mr. W. Shenton.

Some old leases relating to the original property of the firm are still in existence, and they contain the names of Captain Robert Steuart and Lady Mary Steuart, who in all probability were descendants of the founder of the business.

Early methods of conveying individuals and their chattels or merchandise take us back to the days when roads were conspicuous by their absence, and when pack-horses were more in evidence than they are to-day; then there was the palanquin, a hideous monstrosity for civilized countries; the sedan-chair (dearly loved by courtiers and their ladies) was produced early in the seventeenth century; and a few years later a form of carriage or hackney coach made its appearance. But the lumbering springless vehicles of those days soon underwent improvement, and those ant-consumed documents could throw no little light upon this interesting question if they had been forthcoming.

Wagons, roughly built and clumsy—of which we can gain some idea from the famous trek-wagons of South Africa—but capable of holding all the belongings of an entire household, were then made, and the transition from them to the luxuriant comfort of modern buggies or Ralli carts, mail phaetons, broughams, victorias, landaus, barouches, and State coaches has been gradual but complete.

There has not been a single vehicle on the roads within the last 150 years which has not had its type in the workshops of Messrs. Steuart & Co., and they have not only built carts and carriages for every-day use, but they have been entrusted with commissions for elegant State coaches largely composed of gold, silver, and precious stones, and fitted with the most costly appointments. Among these special mention should be made of a State howdah for the use of the late King Edward in 1876; about two years later they constructed a carriage for the Maharajah of Jind, which was enriched by no less than 25,000 *tolahs* (*tolah*=7 dwts. 12 grains troy) of silver; in 1882 and subsequent years gorgeous vehicles were supplied to the Nawab of Bhawalpore, the Commander-in-Chief of Nepal, and the Amir of Kabul; a solid silver elephant howdah was dispatched by the firm to the Durbar held by Lord Curzon in 1902; no fewer than twenty-two landaus and eighteen victorias were supplied for the Viceroy's personal guests; they supplied a most ornate carriage for His Majesty the King-Emperor when, as Prince of Wales, he visited India in 1906; and another of an exceedingly handsome description in 1911, after his accession to the throne. Many State and other carriages were built by Messrs. Steuart & Co. for ruling chiefs, princes, and other notable persons for the imposing ceremonies associated with the Royal visit, and it should be added that they have held special appointments to all the Viceroys of India up to the present time, and have enjoyed the patronage of nearly every ruling chief in the country.

The advent of the motor-car naturally made considerable difference to all builders of carriages, and the enterprising spirit of the partners was manifested when, realizing that a new page had been opened in connection with vehicular traffic, they quickly put themselves in a position to meet the changed requirements of customers by obtaining agencies from leading manufacturers in England and by establishing a factory for building their own cars. Chassis are imported but the whole of the body work is built in Calcutta with indigenous timber, which naturally is more suited to the Indian climate than European wood. Further than this, Messrs. Steuart & Co. have special knowledge of the requirements of local patrons, and they are thus in a position to guarantee their work to be equal in quality to any which is done by London tradesmen.

The firm are representatives in India for the famous Napier, Austin, Renault, Calcott, and Swift cars, and innumerable letters have been received by Messrs. Steuart & Co. testifying to the almost unparalleled qualities of these vehicles. Visitors to the firm's workshops may see the bodies in the course of construction from the bare skeleton to the finished articles, and a very important provision is made that bodies can be constructed and fittings supplied in conformity with the designs of prospective purchasers. The workshops have been very considerably enlarged owing to the rapid expansion of business, and there is now ample accommodation for carrying out alterations or repairs of all descriptions, for storing motor accessories and spare parts, including tyres and petrol, and for a large garage. Fully competent workmen are employed in each branch, but the sound, practical experience of the partners ensures, not a perfunctory, but a thorough, supervision of every detail of work.

STEWARTS AND LLOYDS, LTD.

There is probably no industry which does not in some part of working or development depend upon iron and steel tubes, and the requirements in this line are fully met by the enterprise of the firm of Messrs. Stewarts and Lloyds, Ltd., who have a world-wide reputation for the class of goods they manufacture.

This firm was among the first British manufacturers to recognize the potentialities of the Indian market and the necessity for being directly represented in order that engineers, contractors, and others could have the benefit of expert advice, and it is fully nine years since they opened an office in Calcutta, from which all information relative to the multitudinous uses of iron and steel tubes could be readily obtained.

This step was more than justified, as the Indian business of the firm increased with a rapidity beyond expectations. They were fully satisfied, however, that the limit had not been reached, and with the view of overcoming delays in obtaining supplies from Great Britain the firm leased ground on the Howrah foreshore, on which extensive warehouses connected with road, rail, and river communications have been built.

Railway companies, jute mills, collieries, tea gardens, and other industries can consequently have all their wants immediately met, as large stocks of all the necessary tubes and accessories for various purposes are kept; and special requirements can be fully attended to, as a well-equipped machine-shop and smithy is attached to the warehouse.

In India, as in nearly all other countries, agriculture is the principal industry, but in large tracts the failure of the rains is often the cause of famine. Irrigation has been resorted to as a means of meeting this deficiency, and although the Indian Government has spent large sums in this direction, there are still great expanses of agricultural ground awaiting development where water is obtainable. Subsoil water is prolific in most parts, and this is obtainable by sinking wells; but how few, if any, travellers in their journeyings throughout the length and breadth of the Indian Empire can have failed to notice the number of wells of costly and primitive designs, with their original methods for raising water!

In recent years a great advance has been made in sinking wells by means of tubes, and this method is much less costly than by digging and building up with brick or stone, as was formerly done. After the well has been sunk and water reached, the most up-to-date plan is to install Ashford's "Patent Well Screen" (the licensed manufacturers being Messrs. Stewarts and Lloyds, Ltd.), with a few feet of suction pipe and a reliable pump, as large tracts of rich soil have in this manner been irrigated. The Government having given their approval of this method of obtaining water for irrigation, it follows that the business of well-sinking will probably before long reach immense proportions. The procedure just described has also been recognized as being most suitable for obtaining water for village supplies, the water coming from such wells being potable and the nature of the well preventing contamination from the surface. Good water supplies for domestic and sanitary purposes are essential for the welfare and health of all people—and particularly of the inhabitants of India—and the wells described above seem to be the solution of a problem that has troubled the authorities for a long time.

The manufacture of steel tubes for water distribution mains is a branch of the industry to which Messrs. Stewarts and Lloyds have paid particular attention. These are much lighter than the heavy cast-iron pipes formerly used; they are made in long lengths up to 40 feet, in any diameter up to 6 feet; they are unbreakable, and they combine all the essentials for India, being cheaper in first cost, easier to handle, and having fewer joints to be made than is the case with cast-iron pipes. The numerous water-supply schemes throughout India in which they have been installed testify to their efficiency. High-pressure mains for hydro-electric power installations are also a

STEWARTS AND LLOYDS, LTD.

1. TUBE WAREHOUSE. 2. OFFICE, SHOWING TUBULAR CONSTRUCTION.

special feature of the firm's manufactures. Tubes are more commonly identified with water, gas, and steam installations, but Messrs. Stewarts and Lloyds have shown that they can be used for a great many other purposes, and in architectural work they are an improvement on the massive brick pillars or unsightly steel sections which are much too common in buildings. In the " City of Palaces " there are buildings in which tubular steel columns have been used, and as it is generally agreed behind those of other countries in obtaining up-to-date fittings.

Steel plates for boilers, and for use in the building of ships, bridges, tanks, and wagons, as well as iron and steel castings, are made by the firm; and although the manufacture of iron and steel tubes, with the allied trades to which reference has been made, have not yet become local industries, the enterprise of Messrs. Stewarts and Lloyds, Ltd., may be looked upon as an essential adjunct to the many The founder died in 1854, and he was succeeded by Mr. Thomas Teil, who in 1860 opened a branch establishment at Ballygunge under the name of Tomlin & Co. Six years later Mr. Teil admitted into partnership Messrs. R. S. Erskine and T. C. Barlow; in 1870 Mr. Teil died, and Mr. Erskine retired from the firm, leaving Mr. Barlow in sole possession until the latter's death in 1894, when Mr. R. W. Barlow accepted full responsibility for the whole concern.

JOHN TEIL & CO.

1. INTERIOR. 2 AND 3. VIEWS OF THE BUILDINGS.

that the appearance of the structures has been improved by the innovation, it follows that, in a city which prides itself on the beauty of its edifices, the use of similar columns will be greatly extended.

In districts far removed from modern means of transit, and where skilled labour is scarce, tubular steel trusses could be used with advantage for roofs of sheds and huts. Steel tubes are equally suitable for tramway, electric light, telephone, and telegraph poles. Ships' davits, derricks, and masts are also manufactured by the firm, and when shipbuilding becomes a fully established Indian industry the enterprise will not be industries of Bengal and Assam, or of any other province in India.

The local offices of Messrs. Stewarts and Lloyds, Ltd., are in Clive Buildings, 8 Clive Street, Calcutta, but they have other offices and works in Bombay, London, Birmingham, and Glasgow.

JOHN TEIL & CO.

This firm of tanners, curriers, and leather merchants was established in the year 1795 by Mr. John Teil, and the business is now carried on at 15 Watgunge Street, Kidderpore, near Calcutta, by the proprietor, Mr. R. W. Barlow.

The principal feature of the business is the tanning of cow-hides in a thoroughly effective manner, and the process is so well carried out that the firm meet with an exceedingly brisk demand for their produce in the London market. These leathers are used chiefly in the manufacture of bags, uppers for boots, football covers, and, when enamelled, for the hoods of motor-cars and carriages.

Messrs. Teil & Co. in earlier days held important contracts with the Government of India, among them being the making of accoutrements for the troops during the Burmese War; but since the Government tanneries were opened at Cawnpore, orders for the Imperial military service have been sent to that place.

The principal materials used in tanning are the bark of the babool (*acacia arabica*) tree and Mara *bolams*.

A bronze medal was awarded to the firm for the excellence of their goods at the Calcutta Exhibition held in 1882, and a gold one was obtained at Gwalior in 1913.

The telegraphic address is "Jonteil, Calcutta."

TURNBULLS (GLASGOW), LTD.

A most marked advance has been made in India in industrial enterprises of various kinds during the past fifty years, and this improvement is particularly noticeable in the coal, iron, and steel trades, as it is upon the products of these concerns that the majority of other branches of business depend so largely for the means of carrying on their mills and factories. The extension of railways has caused great demands for sleepers, bolts, nuts, spikes, and other appliances; bridges have been needed for the crossing of rivers and *nullahs*; new machinery has been required for mills; and steel beams and joists have been ordered for structural work in all parts of the country.

Foremost among Calcutta firms who have contributed brains as well as good workmanship to important undertakings of this character is that of Messrs. Turnbulls (Glasgow), Ltd., which was incorporated on December 14, 1911, and carries on business as agents, merchants, structural engineers, manufacturers of bolts, nuts, rivets, and spikes, and as mining engineers. In their capacity as general merchants they hold large stocks of iron and steel products, cement, paints, asbestos goods, and general hardware.

The firm are managing agents of the Kutra Iron Works at Kidderpore, near Calcutta, where are manufactured suspension and other bridges and the component parts of steel buildings of all kinds such as railway stations, bungalows, tea and other factories, sheds, stores, colliery pit-head frames, coolie lines, coal wagons, and a very large quantity of general mechanical appliances. These works comprise an extensive foundry together with forge, mechanical, fitting, tinsmiths', blacksmiths', and other shops, and they occupy an area of 90,000 square feet. About five hundred men are employed constantly.

The firm are, further, managing agents of The North British Bolt and Rivet Company., This is a branch of industry which is comparatively new to India, and only a few years ago engineers, contractors, and others had to import all bolts, nuts, rivets, and dog and chair spikes required in the building or repairing of practically every description of vessel, building, machinery, bridge, or railway rolling stock. The average monthly output of this factory is approximately 150 tons.

The East India Ruby Mica Company, Ltd., whose registered offices are at 10 Strand Road, Calcutta, opened mica mines in the State of Dhenkanal in the division of Orissa in the year 1915, and they placed the managing agency of them in the hands of the firm now under notice.

The mining of this mineral has been attended with much better results since the comparatively recent introduction of improved machinery and of methods of working. The Ruby Company have benefited by coming into line with up-to-date practices, with the result that steady development of their interests is being maintained.

The firm are also managing agents for the Raneedih Colliery Company, in the famous Jherria coal-field, in the district of Manbhum, in the Province of Behar and Orissa, for the Damagurria Coal Company, Ltd., whose property is situated near Sitarampur, in the district of Burdwan, in the Bengal Presidency, and for the Diamond Drill Association, who engage in prospecting and boring work in all parts of India.

The local offices of Turnbulls (Glasgow), Ltd., are at 10 Strand Road, Calcutta; their iron works, paint and oil godowns and metal yards are at Kidderpore and Howrah respectively, and the head offices are at 163 Hope Street and 156 St. Vincent Street, Glasgow.

TURNER, MORRISON & CO., LTD.

When one reads the history of the development of commercial enterprises in India, but particularly in Calcutta, one is struck by the fact that the founders of the majority of the leading business houses came originally from large trading centres in the northern counties of England, or from the country beyond the Tweed. Those pioneers were declared to be hard-headed, shrewd, and capable men of business, and upon reflection it will be readily conceded that it was only by making use of their hardly earned practical experience, by manifesting a spirit of determination, and by working on a strictly economical basis, that the well-known concerns of to-day are such substantial memorials of the insignificant beginnings from which they sprung.

There are several companies and firms in Calcutta at the present time whose records tally with what has been said above, and one need only refer to Messrs. Turner, Morrison & Co., Ltd., in proof of those assertions.

The business was established at 1 Lyons Range, Calcutta, in the middle of the nineteenth century, by Mr. Alfred Turner, of Liverpool, whose son, Mr. A. M. Turner, is still head of the firm. The original designation of the firm was Turner, Cadogan & Co., but it was subsequently changed to Turner, Morrison & Co.

Owing to the very rapid development of the business, and the consequent necessity for increased accommodation, the firm in the year 1868 removed to 6 Lyons Range, but since that date they have been compelled to secure additional premises, viz. Nos. 5½ and 7 in the same block.

The past two or three decades have witnessed a remarkable advance in industries of a general character in almost every part of India, and Messrs. Turner, Morrison & Co., in 1887, realized that the enlarged horizon of their commercial activities would be safeguarded to a greater extent by the opening of a branch in Bombay, where they are now established at 40 Church Gate Street.

While the Bombay house of the firm was concerned largely in extensive shipping transactions with Great Britain and other western countries and in meeting the coal requirements of customers in western India, and while the headquarters at Calcutta were engaged in the conduct of the firm's interests in a general manner, a new field of enterprise had sprung up which called for the opening of another branch which would be in closer connection with the north-eastern portion of Bengal and the Province of Assam. In order to supply this need the firm established themselves at Chittagong in the year 1904.

With such important centres as these in India, and being in communication, through their London and Liverpool houses, with the principal trading marts of the Western world, the firm's business continued to expand with remarkable rapidity, and reference may now be made

TURNBULLS (GLASGOW), LTD.

1. Calcutta Office. 2. A Corner of the Iron Foundry, Kutra Ironworks. 3. Part of the Fitting-shop, Kutra Ironworks. 4. Kuji-Daina Bridge, Carron. 5. Jainti Bridge, Cooch Behar.

TURNER, MORRISON & CO., LTD.

1. THE CALCUTTA OFFICES. 2. THE SHALIMAR WORKS, LTD. 3. THE SHALIMAR PAINT WORKS.

to some of the principal branches of business in which they are engaged.

They have one of the largest shipping connections in Calcutta, and a walk along the banks of the Hooghly from the Howrah bridge to the docks at Kidderpore will reveal a large number of vessels, under their control, during the periods of loading or discharging cargo. A very large amount of chartering business is done in Calcutta, and a glance at the principal morning newspapers of the city reveals a long list of names of arriving or departing ships, while in another column, parallel with such names, are the letters "T., M. & Co.," signifying that Messrs. Turner, Morrison & Co. are concerned in the control of their voyages. They also berth steamers from Bombay destined for the United Kingdom and Continental ports.

The firm are the managing agents of the Asiatic Steam Navigation Company, Ltd., which trades round the coast of India, to Burma and Java; also for the Bombay and Persia Steam Navigation Company, and the Arab Steamers, Ltd., whose headquarters are in Bombay, and whose trade is principally from Bombay and Calcutta to the Red Sea and the Persian Gulf.

They are sole agents for Messrs. Andrew Weir & Co.'s steamers to the River Plate and the West Coast of South America, the Venice Line running between Calcutta, Trieste, and Venice, and the Northern Steamship Company, Ltd., which is a Russian line trading between Calcutta and Vladivostock.

A joint agency is also held for the Anchor-Brocklebank Line, which runs from Calcutta to London, Dundee, and Liverpool, and also for Messrs. Andrew Weir & Co.'s service of steamers to the United States of America.

Salt.—The firm are the largest importers of salt in Calcutta, and they are the sole agents for the Salt Union of Liverpool, and the Italian Salt Company, at Massowah, while they have ninety-three up-country depots and out-agencies for the sale of that commodity.

Shalimar Works.—These engineering works were commenced in the year 1895 by Messrs. Turner, Morrison & Co. at Shalimar Point on the River Hooghly, opposite the docks at Kidderpore. The industry was an extremely insignificant concern at the time of its inception, and it is a fine illustration of rapid development of engineering works in Calcutta. A comparatively few hands were amply sufficient in number to cope with the business of twenty years ago, but to-day may be seen one of the busiest shipbuilding yards and engineering works on the Hooghly. All kinds of launches, barges, flats, and other boats are built by skilled mechanics under European supervision, and there are extensive shops and yards, immediately at the entrance to the docks, in which ironwork and repairs of all kinds are promptly carried out by a large staff of qualified workmen. A special feature is made of marine engineering work, and of repairs to machinery and plant in ships, and in jute, flour, and other mills. Included in the works are the foundry, which is able to turn out iron castings up to ten tons in weight; the machine-shop, well equipped with modern machinery and tools; the smithy, which is continuously employed in forgings of all kinds and sizes; the saw-mills, in which logs are cut into various sizes; and the angle-smith's shop, which is engaged in the construction of ribs for river-going craft.

The Shalimar Works have also an electric-welding plant which has been installed upon a barge that can be moored alongside ships for purposes of repairs to boilers or other steel parts, or it can be floated near to mills in which break-downs of plant have occurred.

The Shalimar Paint, Colour, and Varnish Company.—This company was founded by Messrs. Turner, Morrison & Co. in the year 1902, and they manufacture every description of paints, varnishes, and other similar products, which are sold in considerable quantities to private mercantile firms, and also under contracts with Governments in India and with several of the leading railway companies. The works are situated on the bank of the Hooghly at Goabaria, a few miles distant from Calcutta.

Shellac.—The firm are managing agents for Messrs. Angelo Brothers, who are, without exception, the largest manufacturers of shellac in India. The factory is situated at Cossipore, about three miles distant from Calcutta, and a very considerable quantity of orange and garnet lac is produced.

The Cossipore Sugar Works—for which the firm are managing agents—are built upon a bank of the River Hooghly at Cossipore, and every kind of sugar, ranging from the finest white crystals to "yellows" and "greys," is manufactured there, this being one of the largest sugar refineries in the country.

The Retriever Flotilla Company own a fleet of barges, together with a number of launches on the Hooghly, and they are engaged in the transport of bunker coal, jute, and other produce. They also are owners of several sea-going launches which run from Chittagong to Cox's Bazaar and the Naaf River, carrying cargo, passengers, and mails. Messrs. Turner, Morrison & Co., Ltd., are managing agents.

A very busy department of the firm is that in which insurances are effected in life, fire, and marine business, and agencies are held for the Scottish Union and National Insurance Company, the Union Insurance Society of Canton, Ltd., the Thames and Mersey Marine Insurance Company, Ltd., the Sea Insurance Company, Ltd., and the Queensland Insurance Company, Ltd.

The firm have for a considerable time represented the Vacuum Oil Company, and in addition to all the above important branches of enterprise they carry on an extensive export business of a general character, the principal commodities dealt with being gunnies, saltpetre, and country produce of various kinds.

Coal.—In 1896 the firm inaugurated the Lodna Colliery Company, Ltd., for the purchase and development of coal lands, but particular reference to the colliery is made elsewhere. The firm do a large bunkering business in Calcutta. They have a depot on the river bank opposite Prinsep's Ghat, in Strand Road, and they place the bunker coal alongside steamers in specially built iron barges.

The following is an interesting illustration of the comprehensive scale of Messrs. Turner, Morrison & Co.'s business. Let it be imagined that a steamer, having met with an accident, arrives in a damaged state in Calcutta; the owners avail themselves of the services of Messrs. Turner, Morrison & Co. as agents; the latter can discharge the ship, repair her, paint her inside and out, engage the requisite cargo for her return voyage, load her, insure her hull and cargo if necessary, supply her with bunker coal and stores, and dispatch her, without having to go outside of the concerns which they control, and it may be added that they are the only firm in Calcutta who can do this.

The partnership of Messrs. Turner, Morrison & Co. was turned into a private limited liability company in the year 1913, the first directors being Messrs. Cuthbert Radcliffe and F. W. Carter, the local directors consisting of Mr. R. M. W.

Smyth and Mr. W. S. J. Willson, Calcutta and Chittagong, and Mr. J. S. W. Milne at Bombay.

The correspondents of the company in England are Messrs. Turner & Co., of 6 Dale Street, Liverpool, and Messrs. Turner & Co., of 46 St. Mary Axe, London, E.C.

D. WALDIE & CO.

The late Dr. David Waldie, L.R.C.S., of Edinburgh, Scotland, surgeon and chemist, had not only the honour accredited to him of being a benefactor to suffering humanity by bringing chloroform to the notice of Sir J. Simpson and suggesting its use for the production of anæsthesia in surgical operations, but also of possessing the acumen to foresee the value of an indigenous production of chemical substances in the growing industrial activity of India. Being essentially a practical man, he founded in 1852 the well-known firm of Messrs. D. Waldie & Co., who were the pioneers of chemical industry in India, and undoubtedly the largest chemical manufacturers in the country.

The business was originally started at Dukinsore, and its rapid growth soon rendered it advisable to remove to Cossipore, but the further expansion of activities necessitated the choice of a yet larger and more favourable site, whence the rapid transit of the firm's products by rail, road, or river could be effected. A site fulfilling the needed requirements was secured at Konnagar, about nine miles north of Howrah Bridge, Calcutta, on the western bank of the Hooghly, where extensive plant was erected for the manufacture, on a far larger scale than had hitherto been attempted, of all the principal acids used in commerce as well as of heavy and fine chemicals.

The firm removed to the new premises in 1890, but as further accommodation became indispensable, five years later a branch factory was erected at Nawabgunge, Cawnpore, designed to cope with the volume of business with which the firm had to deal from Central India, but this did not mean the end of the capability of the firm for extension, as a third factory has recently been opened at Giridih.

Some idea of the large amount of chemicals manufactured may be inferred from the fact that of one line alone, sulphuric acid, about 3,500 tons are made per annum, while some 6,000 odd tons of raw materials, finished chemicals, and fertilizers are handled and transported, mainly by river and rail, in the course of a year at the Konnagar works alone.

One large department deals with the preparation of fertilizers, essential to the planter and agriculturist, by blending them on scientific principles, based on the deficiencies of soils and the needs of particular crops such as tea, rubber, coffee, tobacco, and various other kinds. Another department supplies the demands for disinfectants which modern science has shown to be necessary for the maintenance of hygienic conditions, while a third makes and issues that indispensable adjunct of surgery, ether; but the list could, without difficulty, be prolonged to an almost indefinite length.

The close association of a distillery in connection with the chemical works at Konnagar greatly facilitates the manufacture of all those products which require the use of alcohol, which is kept, duty free, under bond, and thus provides a ready means for the output of various galenical preparations as well as for the extraction of vegetable alkaloids.

It is not erroneous to assume that the firm are unique in their position as manufacturers in not combining any retail business with wholesale, by applying themselves entirely to the exploitation of manufactured chemical products on a scale suited to the demand of other industries dependent on such products for their upkeep.

The Calcutta offices of Messrs. Waldie & Co. are situated at 1 Royal Exchange Place, and their telegraphic address is "Waldie," Konnagar.

THE WATERLOO MOTOR WORKS

The advent of the motor-car was not accompanied by any outburst of enthusiasm on the part of the travelling public, and especially of those resident in the East, but since cars, cycles, boats, and other means of conveyance (driven by this force) are now a permanent institution, motor agencies or building and repairing works, are met with in nearly every street in every town in the world, and one might say that there is scarcely a village of any importance which does not boast of a resident who can at least supply petrol, tyres, or other accessories.

The Waterloo Motor Works at 8 Waterloo Street, Calcutta, are the property of Mr. M. Bouffe, who is known to motorists in the city as an expert mechanician, and whose experience has enabled him to secure the patronage of a large number of the leading inhabitants.

Mr. Bouffe arrived in India in the year 1905; for three years he was associated with the French Motor Car Company, and subsequently he was assistant manager and engineer for another firm, from whom he eventually—in 1914—purchased their business.

The owner has a staff of thoroughly competent workmen, but his own practical experience is the guiding power in his stores and shops, in which he keeps for sale a stock of new and second-hand cars, cycles, and accessories, and where he has, further, spare parts and requisites for repairs to all kinds of motor vehicles, motor boats, and boat motors.

Mr. Bouffe's telegraphic address is "Watlomo."

A. H. WHEELER & CO.

Communications from any part of the world addressed "Bookstall, India," would under normal conditions assuredly be correctly delivered to Messrs. A. H. Wheeler & Co., Calcutta, Allahabad, or Bombay, whose fame as bookstall proprietors and railway advertisement contractors in India has extended throughout the limits of the British Empire. The name of the firm is a household word in India, just as that of Messrs. W. H. Smith & Sons is in England.

Their stalls at all the principal railway termini, and at an increasingly large number of wayside stations, are filled with English and local newspapers, novels, periodicals, and journals, and travellers over the thousands of miles of Indian railways are able to obtain literature to relieve the monotony which is invariably associated with long journeys.

A great want has been met by the establishment of these stalls, and if no other reason than this, the firm of Messrs. A. H. Wheeler & Co. would deserve recognition, but in 1914 they directed their attention to the motor trade, which has brought them into still greater prominence.

The Indian interests of the Metallurgique, Calthorpe, and Briscoe cars, Calthorpe Jap motor cycles, and the Bengal agency of Hallford lorries were placed under their care when the outbreak of war, and the consequent cessation of export of English and Belgian cars, diverted their attention solely to the American market.

In the Briscoe car Messrs. A. H.

D. WALDIE & CO.

1. General View. 2. Works from River, showing Jetty. 3. Acid Retorts. 4. Nitric-Acid Shed.

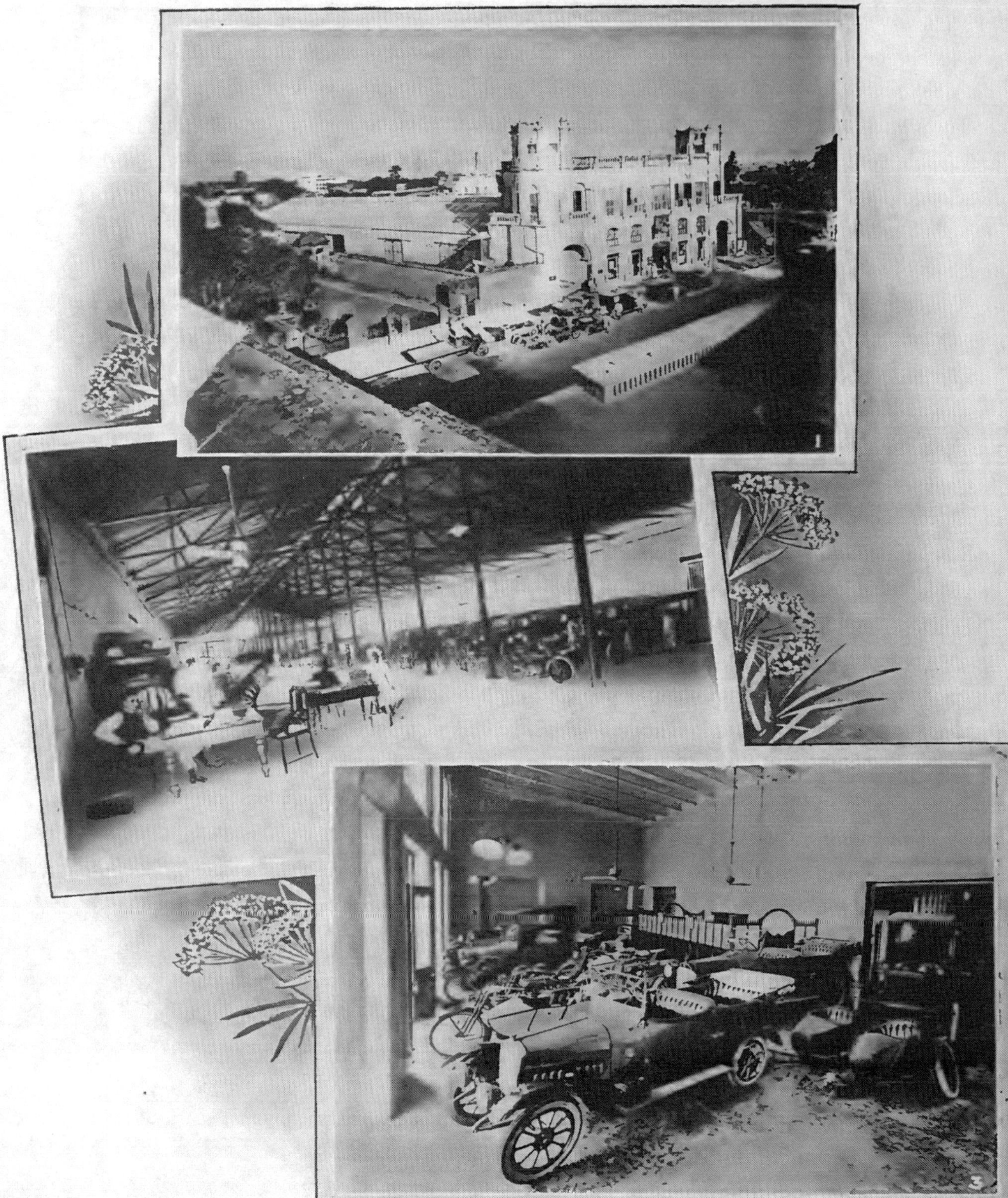

A. H. WHEELER & CO.

1. General View of Showrooms and Garage at 117-19 Park Street, Calcutta. 2. Interior of Garage. 3. Interior of Showroom.

Wheeler & Co. placed their faith nearly three years ago, and it has more than justified their early favourable impressions, which are now fully shared by the many Briscoe owners in India. The demand for motor cycles next attracted the attention of this firm, and as an outcome, one of the most famous of the motor cycle productions in America was secured in the Harley-Davidson "Silent Grey" machine.

The garage is certainly one of the largest in Calcutta, perhaps in the whole of India, and it is well equipped with plant and tools. In this direction Messrs. Wheeler & Co. have quite recently laid down additional machinery with a view to extending their repair department on a large scale.

The business connection of the firm through the medium of their advertising agency has brought them into close relationship with various aspects of the commercial world, and with new opportunities for development recently made possible, they have extended the field of their activities, and in addition to the agencies already referred to, they have now become general merchants and exporters of a variety of commodities.

The firm's head office is in Allahabad, and their motor department is controlled by their Calcutta office in Chartered Bank Buildings, Clive Street, while they also have offices in London and Bombay.

WILKINSON & CO.

The firm of Messrs. Wilkinson & Co., of 12 Dalhousie Square, Calcutta, have for a number of years been in the forefront, not only as dealers in all kinds of indigenous timber, but also as practically the only importers of North Japan and Manchurian oak and ash, which is supplied in the form of sleepers to the principal railways in India, and for the construction of carriages and wagons on the various systems.

Another special feature in the business of this enterprising firm is the very extensive connection which they have built up in supplying fancy woods, such as Honduras and Indian mahogany, rosewood or blackwood, satin-wood, and padouk, together with oak and ash planks, the last two being kiln-dried, for the manufacture of household furniture.

The firm keep in stock considerable quantities of Burma and Travancore teak, Moulmein-Eng, and Jarool in all standard sizes, but any timber can be machine-sawn according to the requirements of purchasers.

Messrs. Wilkinson & Co. are representatives in India, Burma, and Ceylon of the Japan and Eastern Trading Company, Ltd., which is a purely British company, with registered offices at Hamilton House, 155 Bishopsgate, London, E.C., and with branch establishments at Nagasaki and Otaru in Japan. Several important forest concessions and saw-mills in Northern Japan and Manchuria are held by the company, whose directors in London are Colonel G. T. B. Cobbett and Mr. Owen Percy.

The firm are, further, agents for Messrs. Holme, Ringer & Co., of Nagasaki and Shimonoseki, in Japan, for the sale of their well-known "Bridge" cement, creosote oil, and similar other goods, and also for the Beldam Tyre Company, Ltd., of London, who are manufacturers of high-grade motor tyres and all classes of rubber goods.

The managing partner in India is Mr. H. R. Wilkinson, and the telegraphic address of the firm is "Timberwilk," Calcutta.

WILKINSON & CO.

1. Stacking Sleepers at Depot. 2. Portion of Timber-yard.

GILLANDERS, ARBUTHNOT & CO.

Among the old-established firms of merchants in Calcutta is that of Messrs. Gillanders, Arbuthnot & Co., merchants, bankers, and commission agents, of 8 Clive Street.

In addition to the ordinary banking business of the firm, Messrs. Gillanders, Arbuthnot & Co., are managing agents of the Hooghly Mills Company, Ltd., one of the largest jute factories in Bengal, the Betjam Tea Company, Ltd., the Jutlibaree Tea Company, Ltd., and the Manipur Tea Estate, and agents for the Millars Timber and Trading Company, Ltd., the Nobel's (Glasgow) Explosives Company, Ltd., whose products have been used in the construction of all the principal railways, roads, and dock works in India, Burma, and Ceylon, Messrs. H. Dear & Co., Ltd., timber merchants and proprietors of saw-mills in the division of Patna in the Province of Behar and Orissa, the Asiatic Petroleum Co. (India), Ltd., La Société Générale Industrielle de Chandernagore, Sir W. G. Armstrong, Whitworth & Co., Ltd., Messrs. Vickers, Ltd., Messrs. Pinchin, Johnson & Co., Ltd., Messrs. Brown, Lenox & Co., Ltd., and the East Ferry Road Engineering Works, the Singlo Tea Company, Ltd., and the Empire of India and Ceylon Tea Company, Ltd. They are also managing agents for the Hardwar-Dehra Branch Railway Company, Ltd., the Darjeeling-Himalayan Railway Extensions Company, Ltd., the Hoshiarpur-Doab Branch Railway, Co., Ltd., and the Mymensingh-Bhairab Bazar Railway Company, Ltd., and agents for His Majesty's Ceylon Government, the British North Borneo Government, and the Darjeeling-Himalayan Railway Company, Ltd.

In connection with life assurance the firm issue policies on accepted proposals through the London Assurance Corporation, Ltd., which has been established for more than a hundred and ninety years, and also on behalf of the Scottish Provident Institution and the Royal Insurance Company, Ltd. They represent leading British fire insurance companies, who not only give security against damage to buildings but also to cover losses of profits, standing charges, and increased cost of working owing to the same cause. Risks against personal accidents are undertaken, and the firm issue the only policy in India which covers every form of sickness, protection against loss of jewellery, plate, and other valuables as a result of burglary, housebreaking, or theft by servants, is granted at low rates of premium; fidelity bonds, as substitutes for cash securities, are issued to guard merchants and others against loss through the dishonesty of their employees, and marine policies are issued on remarkably favourable terms. As sole agents for the South British Insurance Company, Ltd., the firm issue policies covering every conceivable contingency, and they are officially authorized to issue the special policy for members of the Automobile Association of Bengal. In short, all classes of insurances are effected at the lowest possible rates and without vexatious conditions or restrictions.

SUNSET ON THE HOOGHLY, CALCUTTA.

Photo by T. P. Sen.

PANORAMA OF DACCA, SHOWING THE RUINS OF THE FORT AND PALACE OF THE NAWABS OF DACCA CALLED LALL BAG.

Illustration from "Oriental Scenery," by Thomas Daniell (1795).

COMMERCE AND INDUSTRIES

BY J. A. SANDBROOK, EDITOR OF THE "ENGLISHMAN"

ALTHOUGH for administrative purposes the area covered by Bengal, Behar and Orissa, and Assam is divided into three Provinces, it is economically a single unit, whose commercial and industrial life may be said to centre in the great port of Calcutta. Nature has richly endowed these Provinces of North-Eastern India, which together cover 257,392 square miles and sustain in comfort a population of 92,000,000 souls. Generously watered by great rivers, which provide also a cheap and convenient means of transport, the soil is rich in crops of many varieties. Within the boundaries flourish the prosperous monopoly of jute and the successful manufacture of richly flavoured teas. Bengal is the principal producer of rice, the staple food crop of India. Its moist climate and assured rainfall produce at least two crops of rice yearly, and in some favoured places as many as five.[1] Bengal provides the largest crop of oil-seeds in India, and contributes in abundance many other agricultural products of prime importance. Between them, Bengal and Behar account for 95 per cent. of the coal output of India. They are the only Provinces of India in which iron ore is mined for smelting by European methods, providing 95·6 per cent. of the total quantity raised in the peninsula. The ground is rich in other minerals waiting to be won, but already the mineral output of the Provinces, the variety of manufactures, and the richness of the agricultural products make of Bengal, Behar and Orissa, and Assam the most important area, industrially, in the whole of India.

The rise of commerce in Bengal is one of the great romances of the British Empire. A province so richly endowed by Nature has always attracted the trader, and from the earliest times North-Eastern India has been noted for its productiveness and its skill in handicraft. Time was when Bengal was the common storehouse of cotton and silk, "not of Hindostan or the Empire of the Great Mogul only, but of all the neighbouring kingdoms and even of Europe."[2] The delicate beauty of Dacca muslins and embroidered fabrics had achieved a world-wide fame. They penetrated the mysterious recesses of Mecca; they were found from China in the East to Syria and Arabia, Ethiopia and Persia, and to the markets of Provence, Italy, and Spain. They held every market in Europe until the beginning of the nineteenth century, when the cheaper piece goods of Manchester brought about their downfall. It was not only in these stuffs, "extremely fine and delicate, coloured for their own use, and white for trade to all parts," that the merchants of mediæval Bengal traded. Eighteenth-century travellers have left us records of the commercial genius of the traders who congregated in Bengal on account of the country being "very fertile and of a temperate character." In the main, the produce they dealt with in mediæval times was the same as that dealt with by the traders of to-day, save for the introduction of jute and tea, and the passing of the wondrous beauty of those Dacca silks and muslins. And the means of transport that filled the early travellers with a joyous delight—though they were much nearer to the primitive scheme of things—can still be seen in the waterways of Bengal: the lazy country-boat,

[1] An important feature of the Bengal rice crop is the fact that a large portion of the area bears two or more crops a year, a circumstance that has led to the expression of a "vertical" as compared with a "horizontal" area. In fact, it has been pointed out that a proprietor of an estate with a fairly mixed soil might have three, four, or even five harvests of rice every twelve months: (1) *Aus*, from July to August; (2) *chotan aman*, from October to November; (3) *boron aman*, from December to January; (4) *buo*, from April to May; and (5) *raida*, from September to October.—"The Commercial Products of India," Sir George Watt.

[2] "Berniers' Travels."

tied up in a narrow creek, waiting hours and hours for the tide; the budgerows slowly toiling against the stream, driven by the patient, rhythmical oarsmen who crowd the deck.

But these signs of ancient commerce exist side by side with the bustle of the age of steel, and it is with the latter age that this article is more concerned. The English brought the age of steel and iron to Bengal. The transition period has seen the decay of the ancient arts of white silk manufacture and hand-loom weaving, but it has seen also an industrial development that contains infinite promise for the future of India and Bengal. The purpose of the present article is to give the reader some idea of the industrial progress and importance of Bengal and the adjoining Provinces.

The maritime trade of Bengal is the best indication of the increasing prosperity of the Province. This trade is concentrated in Calcutta. Here are imported and exported the produce not only of the three Provinces with which this article is directly concerned, but also of other Provinces as well. The progress of Calcutta is an index to the progress of its hinterland, and few ports in the world can show so great an improvement in the volume and the value of the tonnage handled. In 50 years the gross registered tonnage of vessels entering the port rose from 668,311 to 7,074,830 in 1912-13. The ratio of increase was greatest in the last decade of this period, when the value of merchandise, exclusive of treasure and minerals, imported into Calcutta by all routes, increased from £66,720,920 to £114,789,236, and the value of exports rose from £67,876,668 to £121,298,581. This means an annual average increase of £11,276,692, or nearly a million pounds sterling every single month. The tonnage of merchandise, on the same basis, increased during the same period from 7,586,988 to 12,646,337 for imports, and 5,503,987 to 8,801,935 for exports.

This rapid and phenomenal growth of the trade of the principal port led to congested conditions, which caused inconvenience and anxiety both to the docks and the railway companies serving the port. The situation was taken boldly in hand, and large new docks and extensive railway sidings are now in course of construction. The years of the Great War which followed immediately the period of phenomenal increase naturally checked the rapidly rising trade, but it is practically certain that with the return of normal conditions the trade of Calcutta will again resume its upward march, possibly with even greater rapidity; and the new docks and railways, although they are not likely to be completed for some years after the war is over, will enable the trade to be handled more expeditiously and cheaply.

The dislocation caused by the war, the difficulties of obtaining tonnage, and the large demand and exceptional prices for war material have produced somewhat abnormal conditions at the time this article is being written. In order, therefore, to obtain a fair idea of the trade of Bengal in normal times, it is necessary to take pre-war figures, and the year 1913-14, which, ending in March, was unaffected by the war, or the prospect of war, provides the latest and the best standard.

The sea-borne trade of the Province of Bengal in 1913-14 is set out in the following table :—

	Rs.	Rs.
Foreign trade—		
Imports ...	81,81,82,128	
Exports ...	103,41,99,849	
		1,85,23,81,977
Coasting trade—		
Imports ...	15,35,42,495	
Exports ...	14,26,23,848	
		29,61,66,343
Grand total of trade...	...	2,14,85,48,320

or £143,236,564 sterling.

The average yearly trade for the five preceding years, 1907-8 to 1911-12, was Rs. 1,61,12,17,491 (or £107,414,499), so that the total for 1913-14 is an increase over the average of Bengal's most prosperous period of Rs. 53,73,30,829, or £35,822,051.

As to the distribution of this trade, more than half the commerce of Calcutta is done with the United Kingdom, which does 44 per cent. of the total, and British possessions, which, apart from the United Kingdom, do 10·49 per cent. Australia is the largest individual customer amongst British possessions, taking 4·30 per cent. of Calcutta's exports and sending 3·06 of her imports. This is largely due to the Australian demand for jute manufactures in order to transport her crops. Amongst European countries, Germany used to be the largest customer, taking large quantities of raw jute and hides and sending in return railway material, cotton and woollen goods, and machinery. Her percentage of the total trade in 1913-14 was 8·64, the percentage of all European foreign countries being 19·98. The United States percentage of the total trade was 11·81, made up chiefly of raw jute and jute manufactures. Of Asiatic countries, Java, by reason of her large exports of sugar to Calcutta, occupies a prominent place, with a percentage of 4·19 of the total.

The growth of Japanese competition in the Indian markets has lately been attracting great attention, and although the total trade between Calcutta and Japan is small as yet (2·49 per cent. of the total in 1913-14), the successful manufacture by Japan of cotton hosiery, matches, beer, and a variety of small articles formerly supplied from Europe, even motor tyres, gives a special interest and importance to her future commercial connection with India. Japan, more than any country in the East or the West, seized the opportunity of the war to push her goods on the Indian market, but the retention of the trade will depend on the quality of the goods, which is not up to the standard set by Japan's competitors.

The following table gives the distribution of Calcutta trade for 1913-14 :—

	Imports.	Exports.	Total.
United Kingdom ...	68·45	25·50	44·00
Other British Possessions	6·47	13·53	10·49
Foreign countries—			
Europe	10·51	27·14	19·98
Asia...	11·79	8·49	9·90
Africa	·22	1·00	·70
America	2·56	24·00	14·77
Oceania	—	·28	·16

So far as the imports are concerned, 42·19 per cent. of the total trade consists of cotton goods, and, incidentally, this shows the enormous importance of Bengal as a market for Lancashire goods, for by far the greater portion of these imports comes from England. Next to cotton goods, metals and ores cover the largest item of import, sugar coming third, with railway plant and rolling-stock and machinery and millwork next. All these may be called articles of necessity. Articles of food and clothing are the essentials of industrial development. Here and there in the list of imports are to be found items that suggest the increasing wealth of Bengal, as well as the gradual change of Eastern opinion towards Western methods of life. The importation of motor-cars, for instance, is growing enormously year by year. Although the roads of Bengal leave much to be desired, the country offers a remarkable scope for the development of the motor industry.

COMMERCE AND INDUSTRIES

The exports from Calcutta—and, of course, Behar and Orissa are included in the totals—are made up, so far as value goes, to the extent of more than 50 per cent. of raw jute and jute manufactures, the percentage of each being 28·72 and 28·90 respectively. Tea forms the next great staple export, amounting to 10·82 per cent. of the total; and hides and skins form 8·86 per cent., grain, pulse, and flour 7·03 per cent., seeds 3·67 per cent., and so on.

1. AN ABANDONED MINE. 2, 3. VIEWS IN THE KODARMA MICA DISTRICT.

Photos by R. O. Podger.

The figures so far quoted do not, of course, include the frontier trade of Bengal, which is a much smaller but none the less a considerable total. From Sikkim Bengal draws living animals, grain and pulse, metals of various kinds, *ghee* and spices, of the aggregate value of Rs. 30,89,466, exporting in return cotton manufactures of Indian origin, provisions, sugar, and tobacco, of the aggregate value of Rs. 16,00,520. From Nepal were received animals, fruits, vegetables, nuts, and provisions valued at Rs. 29,58,925, and goods of the value of Rs. 36,23,131 were exported. Raw wool constitutes the main staple of import from Tibet, together with musk and yak's tails. The total imports from Tibet were Rs. 18,29,418, and in return Bengal exported cotton piece goods, woollen and silk manufactures, earthenware, porcelain, etc., to the value of Rs. 14,28,660. The trade with Bhutan was very much less, amounting in the aggregate to Rs. 5,03,974. Behar and Orissa do a large trade with Nepal, and Assam is dealing to an even larger extent with Bhutan, and the several tribes, notably the Abors and Mishmis, on her frontier, just emerging from the primitive state.

The transport of trade in Bengal and the adjoining Provinces is greatly facilitated by the spacious waterways with which Nature has endowed the Gangetic plains. Two great rivers, the Ganges and Brahmaputra, fed by many tributaries, drop slowly from the Himalayas to the Bay of Bengal. In the flat plains their streams have split into the countless waterways of the Bengal Delta. They flood and fertilize the plains in the rainy season, and when the crops are garnered they carry them to markets far removed and widely scattered.

The best has not been made of these countless waterways, many of which have fallen into decay and disuse by official neglect to counteract the changes of the flood and keep the course of the river steady and clear. To control accurately these erratic, wandering waterways, however, would require large capital. It is estimated that the river-bound commerce between Bengal and Behar and Orissa, Assam, and the United Provinces amounts to Rs. 13,01,00,000 (£8,673,000) in value, and that, of course, does not include the trade within the Province of Bengal itself. Besides giving to the Province the inestimable advantage of wide waterways, Nature has so constructed Bengal that, in spite of the heavy expenditure involved in bridges and repairing banks, railways can be worked on the flat plains at a very small cost, compared with the railways that have to reach the west coast across the western *ghats*; and if it were not for the Government of India supporting the western lines by the imposition of minimum rates the traffic freights to Calcutta could be reduced considerably, attracting to the port the produce and manufactures of the greater part of India. This is a subject of controversy that is not within the province of this article, but it is worthy of mention here as showing the extraordinary facilities for cheap railway traffic which the Bengal delta enjoys by reason of its flat and gradientless railways, as well as by reason of its unrivalled waterways.

It will be seen from the nature of the exports that in Bengal, as in many other Provinces of India, agriculture is the staple industry. This must be so for generations to come. The methods of husbandry are in many—in fact, in most—places of the most primitive kind, but gradually improvements are being introduced. Modern agricultural machinery, such as steam ploughs, for instance, will be long in making its impression felt on the simple cultivator whose wants are amply supplied by the primitive plough and a pair of oxen; but the possibilities of development are unlimited, and with the progress of co-operation and the gradual enlightenment of the cultivator the yield per acre of the agricultural crops of Bengal is bound to increase, bringing wealth to every class of the community. Rice is by far the principal crop of Bengal, Behar and Orissa, and, indeed, of all India. Of the 76,000,000 acres of India under this crop, as many as 40,500,000 acres are to be found in these Provinces, yielding from 13,000,000 to 15,000,000 tons annually, or in especially favourable seasons as much as 21,000,000 tons. No less than 54 per cent. of the net cropped area of the three Provinces is under rice crops. This is not surprising when it is remembered that rice is essentially a crop of damp tropical or semi-tropical climates. In Bengal it is a domestic crop, in that it provides the staple food of the people; but rice is put to many uses besides. A kind of beer (*pachwai*) is made from it. A dye is manufactured from the husk, and the straw may be used in papermaking; whilst the coarse varieties of rice, especially those from Burma, are exported for distillation and conversion into starch. The exports of rice, husked and unhusked, from Calcutta average something like 8,000,000 cwt. in a year, the greater part of the crop being consumed locally.

Next to rice, the principal crop of Bengal, Behar and Orissa, and Assam is that of oil-seeds—namely, linseed, sesamum, rape, and mustard; ground-nuts, etc.; and the three Provinces together account for, roughly, 21 per cent. of the acreage under these crops in India. The export of oil-seeds amounts to nearly 5,000,000 cwts. annually. The economic value of this export has always been questioned, for it goes without saying that it is economically and industrially unsound for any country to export oil-seeds in large quantities instead of manufacturing the oils and oil-cake itself. If the manufacturing industry were in India, not only would the manufacturers' profits be retained in the country, but, which is more important, comparatively, the country would not be deprived of so important a cattle food and manure. Before the European War the oil-seed output of India was exported largely to European countries, and it may be hoped that with the restoration of normal times the manufacture of the oil may be undertaken in India itself.

The products that have given to Bengal its prominent position in the foreign trade of the world are, however, jute, tea, hides, and skins. It is not necessary to deal in detail here with the first two of these industries, since they are treated in other pages of this book, but a survey of the trade of Bengal would be incomplete without pointing out their preponderance in the value of exports and their importance in the industrial development of Bengal. The capital invested in the Bengal jute-mill companies is upwards of Rs. 7,50,00,000 at par value, and war-time prosperity must have inflated the value by anything from 300 to 500 per cent. Between them, jute, tea, hides, and skins, including jute manufactures, represent in normal times something like 77 per cent. of the value of the export trade. In war-time they assumed, jute especially, an added importance, and in 1915-16 the proportion to the total export trade of Bengal rose to 84 per cent. During the years of the war the demand for jute bags for the trenches and for the carriage of grain brought to the jute mills on the banks of the Hooghly an unprecedented prosperity. The effects of the war on the trade, as set out in the report of the Collector of Customs for Calcutta for 1915-16, are worth placing on record here :—

"Throughout the year the export of jute and jute manufactures has been under restriction to one country or another, and the control of Government on these commodities becomes stricter and stricter. But, nevertheless, the year has been one of abundant prosperity to the industry. Blessed with cheap raw material, an insatiable demand from nearly all countries not at war with us, and a Government demand which has appropriated a considerable percentage of the looms, the local mills have made profits undreamt of in the years of peaceful progress. The increase was 26 per cent., with a record output; and although the total value was less than in 1913-14 (when the raw material controlled a very high range of prices), it was greater than in any other year, and exceeded the previous year by 40 per cent. With the stoppage of the mid-European demand, raw jute has gone away in smaller quantities than in previous years, but compared with 1914-15 the tonnage was larger by 23 per cent. and the value by 26 per cent. But when the shipments of bags and cloth are scrutinized, both have reached a summit never before approached : the former, in number, are better than in the previous year by 100 per cent., and the latter, in yardage, by 13 per cent. ; values are higher by 60 and 35 per cent. respectively ; combined, the increased value represents 47 per cent. Even 'other' manufactures (twist, yarn, and twine) are larger by 30 per cent. In 1914-15 the jute trade represented 53 per cent. of Calcutta's exports; in the past year it has risen to 60 per cent. . . .

"Last year it was remarked that neither the local mills nor the jute trade had been so prosperous in 1914-15 as in the previous year. The year under report has been a remarkable illustration of unexampled prosperity. Jute manufactures have risen in value from Rs. 25.77 to Rs. 37.90 crores, or by 47 per cent., attaining an altitude never before recorded. Both gunny bags and gunny cloth have been phenomenal in their expansion, the former increasing in volume by 100 per cent. and in value by 60 per cent. Cloth has advanced by 13 and 35 per cent. respectively. Throughout the year the mills worked full time and overtime for the purposes of military requirements. Restrictive ordinances controlled the export throughout the year. There was a constant and ever-increasing demand. . . .

"The local mills, in their great prosperity, have surpassed the records of any previous year, and have earned in net profits in 1915 the stupendous sum of Rs. 4.43 crores, of which Rs. 2.93 crores appertained to the second half of the year. In the two previous years the net profits were Rs. 2.45 crores and Rs. 96.18 lakhs respectively. Debit balances have been liquidated, large sums placed to reserve, and equally large sums distributed amongst shareholders. One mill declared 110 per cent. dividend, one 70, one 60, twelve between 30 and 55, and seventeen between 10 and 26 per cent."

Tea also prospered by the large demand during the war period. For many years past the Indian tea trade has been steadily expanding, and the exports from Calcutta by sea and land in 1913-14 were 217,987,401 lb. In 1915-16 the quantity had increased to 265,350,000 lb. The capital invested in tea companies in Assam and Bengal is upwards of Rs. 4,00,00,000 at par value, but as many of the companies pay handsome dividends there has been a considerable appreciation in the value of these securities, the best of which it is practically impossible to obtain in the open market, so highly are they prized as an investment.

For hides and skins the best customers of Bengal in normal times were Germany, Austria-Hungary, and the United States; and the closing of the Teutonic markets brought about a temporary crisis, the more serious because the trade in Calcutta had practically fallen into the hands of German and Austrian firms. The needs of the war, however, led to its re-organization under British control, and although the pre-war level had not been reached in 1915-16, the trade, nevertheless, was expanding and prosperous.

Indigo is dealt with elsewhere in this volume, and it need be referred to only briefly here. A quarter of a century ago indigo was one of the most prosperous industries in India. The planters of Behar were a large and wealthy community. Then came the German chemist and his synthetic dye, and the acreage in India under indigo, which was as much as 1,688,000 acres in 1894-5, dwindled to 169,221 in 1913-14. In this decline Behar was the greatest sufferer. But the war and the consequent shutting out of the German chemical dyes has brought a new spell of prosperity—albeit it may be a short one—to the industry.

The acreage under indigo increased in 1915-16 to 314,300 acres. Unfortunately, adverse climatic conditions reduced the yield per acre, but exports from Calcutta rose from 8,752 cwts. in 1913-14 to 13,147 cwts. in 1915-16. The average value of the maund, which was Rs. 149 before the war, touched Rs. 516 in 1914-15, was Rs. 419 in 1915-16, and good Behar indigo has risen at times to as much as Rs. 750 per factory maund. Advantage has been taken of the present prosperous conditions to make further efforts to place the industry on a sound commercial basis, and, by scientific research, to produce natural indigo in such a form that after the war it will be able to compete on a footing of equality with synthetic products.

Next to the United Provinces, Bengal, with Behar and Orissa and Assam, constitutes the largest sugar-producing area in British India; but considering the fact that India was probably the original home of the sugar-cane, the industry does not at present occupy the position which the demands of the country and the facilities for the growth of the sugar-cane alike demand that it ought to occupy. Of the total area of 2,708,000 acres under sugar-cane in British India more than half is in the United Provinces, 19 per cent. in Bengal, Behar and Orissa, and 16 per cent. in the Punjab. The other sugar-yielding plants—namely, the date-palm and the Palmyra palm—occupy a total area of 166,000 acres, of which 47 per cent. is in Madras and 36 per cent. in Bengal. Cultivation of sugar in India during the last thirty years has shown a declining tendency, and the explanation is to be found partly in the absence of scientific and up-to-date methods of cultivation and manufacture, and partly in the large importation of beet-sugar from Germany and Austria, and foreign cane-sugar from Java and Mauritius. The decline in local cultivation has been most marked in Behar and Bengal. The knowledge of the possibilities of India as a sugar-growing country, however, has recently led the Government of India to devote special attention to the industry. Experimental farms and factories have been established. Many reports have been issued, and these all go to prove that sugar-cane can be produced more economically in India than in any other country in the world. Few industries have been subjected so much to fiscal influences, such as cartels, bounties, and countervailing duties, and first beet-sugar and then the cane products of Java and Mauritius seriously competed with home-grown sugar in India. Hence it comes about that India, which once exported sugar to Europe, has become herself a field for European commercial enterprise in the possession of cheap refined sugar. Calcutta imports annually sugar to the value of between 6 and 7 lakhs. In the near future, however, it is quite possible that attempts will be made to completely revive the indigenous industry, and these attempts may not be limited to the encouragement of improved and scientific methods of cultivation and refining. In the Budget for 1916-17 the Finance Member of the Viceroy's Council announced a significant departure from the fiscal policy of India. There were a number of increases in the rate of duty, raising the general import tariff from 5 per cent. to $7\frac{1}{2}$ per cent. In the case of sugar, however, it was raised to 10 per cent., avowedly for the purpose of encouraging the Indian industry. Whether this measure of protection, added to the efforts of Government to improve cultivation, will restore the sugar trade of India to such a position that it will be able to provide the needs of the country and export the surplus remains to be seen, but the departure is a very significant one.

In the industrial development of India, which has already begun, and which must make much greater progress in the near future, Bengal, Behar and Orissa, and Assam are destined to play a predominant part. We have already seen that, in the matter of jute especially, the agricultural products of these Provinces are of great value to manufacturing industries. But it is to the vast mineral wealth that we must look for industrial development on a large and profitable scale. The Provinces are favoured in an exceptional degree with mineral deposits of the most important kind. Of the total output of minerals in India, valued in 1913 at $12\frac{1}{2}$ per cent., the greater part is derived from Bengal, and Behar and Orissa, whose coal output, valued at something like 5 crores, is 95 per cent. of the Indian production. This great store of coal gives Bengal and Behar exceptional industrial advantages, and the presence of other allied minerals in large quantities is leading to the establishment, slowly as yet, of important industries.

Next to the United Kingdom, India occupies the first place in the British Empire as a coal-producer. The total output in 1913 was 16,208,000 tons, of which Bengal produced 4,649,985 tons, Behar and Orissa 10,227,557 tons, and Assam 270,000 tons. The mines employ daily some 150,000 persons, and the capital of companies working coal in Bengal and Behar is Rs. 5,69,40,000. India herself consumes the greater part of the coal produced—as much as 94 per cent.—and the market for home consumption is steadily growing, leaving little for export. Indian coal exported amounted to 759,155 tons in 1912, the principal customers being Ceylon, the Straits Settlements, and Sumatra.

Coal is quite a modern industry in India. Although the occurrence of the mineral must have been known from time immemorial, it is only in recent times that European enterprise has developed the industry. Even now coal is very little used by the natives of India in indigenous industries, whilst for domestic purposes it is scarcely used at all. The increasing demand in India for indigenous coal comes, therefore, from the railways and from the numerous industries of large importance that are springing up—the jute and cotton mills, the iron and steel works, foundries, and other concerns. The first analytical reports of Indian coal were so unfavourable that attempts made to develop the industry in the early part of the nineteenth century met with failure. The prejudice that so long insisted on importing English coal because the local mineral was deemed inferior—on analyses taken of the deposits near the surface—was gradually broken down, but it was not until the rise of the jute-manufacturing industry that real vitality was given to coal-mining. Fifty years ago the annual output of coal was under half a million tons. To-day it is over 16,000,000 tons.

Bengal coal has the advantage of being by far the cheapest coal in the world, and the average value has not fluctuated very much in recent years. In 1909 the average value per ton at the pit-mouth was 4s. 8d. It fell to 3s. 11d. in 1911—a year of depression in coal—but in 1913 it was again 4s. 8d., and that figure will probably represent the normal average price of coal at the pit's mouth in India. A comparison with the pit-mouth value of other countries for the five years 1908-12 shows how great is the advantage that India enjoys in cheap fuel :—

	Per Ton. s.	d.
India	4	8
United States... ...	5	10¾
Australia	7	6
Japan...	7	8¾
United Kingdom ...	8	5¾
Germany	10	4¼
France	12	7

The cheapness of Bengal coal is not due to any marked inferiority of the mineral as compared with the fuels of other countries. On the contrary, laboratory analysis and practical experiments have shown that the finest Indian coals are little inferior to the best English and Welsh. Whilst labour for working the mines is fairly plentiful and cheap in India, it is also very inefficient relatively to the mine labour of other countries. Thus the coal raised per person employed in the rest of the British Empire is 266·2 tons, whilst in India it is only 109·4. In the mines outside India, however, machinery is used on a much larger scale than has hitherto been necessary for the shallow mining operations of India. Latterly the use of electricity in the Bengal coal mines has become an important factor in the efficiency of the mines, but expensive labour-saving devices, such as coal-cutting machinery, have not been extensively adopted because of the cheapness of labour. During the boom period, when the prices were high and the labour supply insufficient to give the output needed, some colliery proprietors put down coal-cutting machinery at high cost, but as the price of coal fell and labour conditions became easier, these machines passed gradually out of use. The time for them will come again, no doubt, when the demand for coal exceeds the capacity of the present labour force.

With coal, of course, goes iron ore, and it is in the iron and steel trades that many hope to see in time some remarkable developments in Bengal and Behar. As has been said already, these are the only Provinces in India in which iron ore is mined for smelting by European methods. From the very dawn of history iron-smelting must have been practised by the people of Bengal. Weapons used in ancient warfare show that a certain standard of manufacture, doubtless excellent in its day, had been achieved; but with the introduction of superior articles of Western make the indigenous industry declined, and although it is continued to this day, it is wasteful in its methods, and its achievements are only a poor imitation of goods of European manufacture. Bengal is more concerned, therefore, with the modern developments of the industry, and the enterprise of the Bengal Iron and Steel Company (of which Messrs. Martin & Co. are the managing agents) and of the Tata Iron and Steel Company, who have built great works at Barakar and Sakchi respectively, are fraught with immense possibilities. The Barakar works in 1913 used upwards of 96,000 tons of iron ore, chiefly derived from Manharpur, and they have produced iron of a quality which is said to be superior to any imported from Europe. The company employs upwards of 5,000 persons daily. The Tata enterprise is of a later date, and, partly under the direction of American experts, the works have been erected on modern lines. Although considerable difficulties were at first experienced in the manufacture of steel, the Tata Company, which employs a daily average of nearly 9,000 persons, is now producing a large quantity, and the Government of India, who maintain a testing laboratory at Sakchi, have placed a large standing order. It is needless to say that the war proved of great benefit to the iron and steel works in Bengal. The shutting down of enemy competition and the extraordinary rise in freights had a protective effect on the local industry, and much of the excellent iron and steel used for the manufacture of munitions in India was locally produced. Naturally, the operations of these two companies have made an enormous difference in the mining of iron ore in recent years. In 1909 Bengal and Behar and Orissa raised together only 72,000 tons, of the total value of £13,000. In 1913 the raisings had increased to 353,813 tons, valued at £35,000. This represented by far the greater part of the total output for India, which amounted to only 370,845 tons. How far this industry will develop in the future is purely a matter for speculation, but when it is borne in mind that India imports annually iron and steel materials of the value of between nineteen and twenty millions sterling on an average, it will be realized that there is a great scope for Indian manufactures of cutlery and hardware, railway plant, iron and steel beams, sheets, bars, and so on. There is also the prospect of an export trade in iron and steel. Japan is already taking large quantities of the Tata steel for shipbuilding purposes.

In the production of manganese ore, India competes with Russia for the first place in the world, but of India's total output of 800,000 statute tons Behar contributes a comparatively small portion.

Of the Indian production of mica, which amounted to 45,422 cwts. in 1913, or, roughly, 70 per cent. of the world's total, Behar and Orissa produce over 71 per cent. As this important industry is dealt with separately, however, it need only be mentioned here.

These are the principal minerals at present mined in these provinces. Assam has some encouraging oil-springs. Ideal climatic and other conditions make Behar easily the largest producer of saltpetre in India. Behar gives a modest yield of copper ore—modest, but still by far the largest in India. Prospecting is still going on and new deposits are being discovered. Of these it is impossible yet to speak with certainty, and their development may be a matter of years. A recent Administration Report of the Province, which refers to the encouraging results of prospecting for pitch-blende in the Gaya district, claims that the pitch-blende found is one of the richest in radium content in the world.

We have dealt so far, mainly, with the major industries of the Provinces which have been established by European enterprise, largely financed with European capital, and conducted by European managers. In these industries purely Indian enterprise and Indian capital have so far played an unimportant part, and the management is centred in the great firms of European managing agents which have been established in Calcutta for generations past. Indigenous enterprise, however, is making itself felt. Indians are opening up tea gardens and coal mines and cotton mills; but, so far as indigenous industries of the old-fashioned type are concerned, they have nowhere recovered the position that India once held as a manufacturing nation and lost because her craftsmen, working by hand, without capital, or organization, or enterprise, were unable to withstand the competition of the highly organized industries and superior manufactures of the West. Attempts have recently been made to revive these indigenous industries, and the growth of co-operation has given a new hope to the Indian craftsman, the handloom weaver, the metalworker, and the potter. Some of the work that these craftsmen produce is of a high standard of artistic beauty and quality, but, generally speaking, the arts and crafts of Bengal have not yet acquired a position of sufficient importance to justify treatment at any great length. The crafts are numerous, but in proportion the population engaged in them is negligible. The great majority of the people ($35\frac{1}{3}$ millions, or 78 per cent. in Bengal; 30 millions, or 81 per cent., in Behar and Orissa, according to the last census, which was taken before the new division of the province) are dependent on agriculture and cognate pursuits. Industry claimed at the last census but $3\frac{1}{2}$ million people in Bengal and 3 millions in Behar and Orissa. The big jute mills take a large number of these workers, and when the

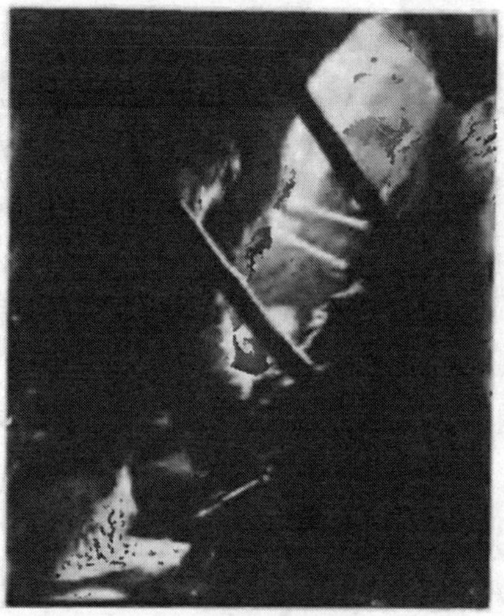

AN OLD MINE.
Photo by R. O. Podger.

balance is distributed amongst the silkweavers, the tanners, carpenters, metalworkers, and potters, it will easily be understood that these occupations claim but a small percentage of the population of these Provinces. A new desire for a revival of the indigenous industries has sprung up during the war, and it was hoped to take advantage of the elimination of German and Austrian competition —once very serious in the bazaars—to establish Indian manufacturing industries on a firm financial basis. It must be many years, however, before any revival of the cottage industries and the indigenous crafts of Bengal can materially affect the industrial outlook of the Province. Future progress is mapped out on well-defined lines where success has already been won. To the jute industry there is no limit of expansion. It was once thought foolish to build mills on the Hooghly, but in a quarter of a century they have grown in number from a dozen to fifty or more, and the profits of late have been fabulous. The output of Bengal and Behar and Orissa coal was under 2,000,000 tons in the 'eighties. It was over 15,000,000 tons in 1913. There is practically no limit to the expansion of these major industries, and the mineral wealth of the Gangetic Provinces has scarcely yet been touched. The rate of development must depend upon the availability of capital and the making of railway communications. Indian capital is shy. In spite of the large speculative dealings on the stock and share markets of Calcutta and Bombay, a comparatively small proportion of Indian capital is invested direct in industrial undertakings. But the well-established industries, like jute, cotton, coal, and tea, are impressing the Indian investor more and more, and in recent years the success of light railways under good management, with a guaranteed dividend, has succeeded in attracting capital in a larger degree. The outlook is improving year by year, and when the accumulating wealth of India is devoted to her industrial development, the Provinces of Bengal, Behar and Orissa, and Assam offer a field for enterprise second to none in the world.

THE MICA INDUSTRY

BY J. F. PODGER, Assoc.Inst.M.M.

WHEN the word "mica" is used outside the company of those connected with the industry, one is immediately asked: "What is mica?" and, "Is mica the same as talc?" It would seem advisable, therefore, to give an answer to these questions at the beginning of this article.

Firstly, then, mica is composed mainly of silica, alumina, and potash. There are many varieties, and all contain other constituents in greater or less percentages, but the composition is mainly silica and alumina; while talc, also of many kinds, is composed mainly of silica and magnesia. There is this difference between the two substances, that whereas mica is flexible and elastic, talc is sometimes flexible but never elastic.

It is doubtful when mica was first discovered, but it has been used in India for decorative and medicinal purposes from time immemorial. The medicine, a sort of patent cure-all, is made by reducing mica to a powder (biotite mica is usually employed), which is mixed with cow's urine and baked, this damping and baking process being repeated several times. The resulting medicine, rather like fine brickdust, is expensive, and is possibly as efficacious as some other patent powders. Mica has been found in the wrappings of ancient Egyptian mummies, and Thales, the Greek, knew of it some time before 550 B.C. It is related, too, that Columbus had his ships' lanterns fitted with it when setting out on his search for America.

The "Memoirs of the Geological Survey of India," vol. xxxiv, part 2, contain the following legend: "In ancient times, or Sat Yoga, it is supposed that in order to kill the enemy of the gods, Baratur (Vitra), Indra lifted his thunderbolt vajra, and a flash of lightning spread throughout the length and breadth of the sky, while the sparks which fell on the mountains were preserved in the form of mica."

Locally, many of the coolies believe that it grows, this idea being probably due to the fact that nearly all new outcrops are discovered during the first days of the rains, which wash away fallen leaves and dead grass, and so expose the surface of the ground more clearly than at other times of the year.

Mica is a constituent of all granites, although it only reaches commercial size in the giant granites, commonly referred to as granite pegmatite or simply pegmatite. Any consideration of the origin of mica resolves itself into a question of the origin of granite pegmatite, than which there have been few subjects more discussed or more controversial. The generally accepted theory is that these rocks originated by the crystallization of fluid magnas which have been forced from greater depth to fill the faults and fissures of the country rock into which they were thus forcibly intruded. It is not proposed to attempt to argue the question here, but it is relevant to remark that this theory appears to be well borne out as more knowledge of the physical conditions of the pegmatites and country becomes available. This doctrine is not entirely incompatible with that of precipitation from solution, as Nature, like the Mother of Parliaments, can arrive at a workable compromise.

It would be correct to say that mica is found in almost every known country of the world, but, from a commercial point of view, the following are the countries in which it is found: India, Canada, the United States, East Africa, South Africa, Ceylon, Brazil, Argentina, Peru, Guatemala, Labrador, Norway, Iceland, Russia, Japan, and Australia. Of these countries the greatest producers are India, Canada, and the United States, although there are possibilities that East Africa also may become one of the important producing centres. The earliest workings were in India, the Hindus raising mica for ornamental purposes in the neighbourhood of Delhi very many centuries ago.

The first shipments of Bengal mica are recorded as being made in 1863, but it was not until its unrivalled properties as an electrical insulator became known that the industry began to expand and assume some considerable importance in the mining and industrial world.

The whole of the Bengal mica area, extending through the districts of Hazaribagh, Gya, and Monghyr, comprises, roughly, 750 square miles, and was almost entirely the property of native Rajas and Zemindars. The chief outside area was the Kodarma Forest, a tract of about 50 square miles lying on the north of the Hazaribagh district, on the borders of Gya.

In or about the year 1872 the Government leased the mica-mining rights throughout the whole of this forest to a gentleman who had already acquired similar privileges over most of the Zemindari property. The rent accepted for the forest was about Rs. 270 annually. As practically the whole of the mica-producing area was then in the hands of one owner, there were no difficulties regarding mining or fears of theft. All visible mica belonged to the same proprietor, and the method of working was to send coolies into the jungles to dig and roughly trim it, and subsequently carry it to central godowns, the coolies being paid *pro rata*, according to size and weight.

It was not until about 1896 that Government asked for an enhanced rent, and, failing to get it, demarcated the several workings and put them up for sale by auction, the term of possession being for one year only. This system of annual auctions lasted until about 1902, and as much as Rs. 10,000 were obtained for the rent of one deposit in some years.

There need be no hesitation in saying that this system of annual auctions was the direct cause of the spoliation of the deposits and the consequent lack of mining methods, and it ought to have been obvious to any one that the result of such a policy would be the ruin of the workings. The lessees, having twelve months in which to recover their money, took out every ounce of mica they could get; they cut out all pillars, made no attempt to support any of their excavations, and formulated no plan of development or of permanent working for their mines. The better the prospects of the deposit the more it cost the lessee, and the less likely he would be able to retain it at the expiration of his lease.

Owing to the intervention of Mr. (now Sir) Thomas Holland and the interest of the then Viceroy (Lord Curzon of Kedleston) in industrial work, a new form of lease was drawn up about the year 1902, which gave mining rights for a term of thirty years over minimum areas of 40 acres.

Would that we had Sir Thomas back again! Government has reverted to its Gilbert and Sullivan methods, and, although it retains the thirty years' term, it adds such rules and conditions to the lease as make it impossible to work profitably. Apparently Government is obsessed with the idea that mica and coal are synonymous terms for the same mineral. Unhappy managers of mica mines have to put up with visits, suggestions, and orders of inspectors who have never in their lives worked, even if they have ever seen *in situ*, any other mineral than coal.

The distribution of the mica through the pegmatite is generally admitted to be entirely irregular or "pockety," and following no imaginable rule of occurrence, but it is possible that it does conform to certain rules which have not yet been recognized. Be that as it may, it is a fact that most of the workings, until recent years, were carried out by the simple process of following the strings of mica crystals through the pegmatite in irregular workings, and necessitated the employment of large numbers of women to keep the mines clear of water and débris. The usual procedure was to have two rows of women from the working face to the surface of the ground; one row passed down empty baskets and water-jars, which were filled at the bottom and then sent along to the other women to be thrown out at the surface. This system is still carried on to a large extent, but more mining-like methods are now coming into general practice.

In a paper on "The Mining, Preparation, and Uses of Mica," read in London in February 1913, it is stated that explosives are seldom used, and that the tools employed in the mines are of a primitive nature and are usually made locally. If the author of that paper had ever experienced a visit from the Inspector of Explosive Magazines he would have written differently, as Nobels' dynamite is used throughout the mica-field, and the consumption of it runs into many hundreds of cases annually. It is neither necessary nor desirable that the mining methods now employed by the most important companies in this Province should be expounded, as they are dealt with elsewhere in the descriptions of the mines.

One of the greatest difficulties the management of mica concerns has to contend with is the question of theft. It is doubtful if any mining company secures the whole of its output, and the higher police officials, in conversation, have given it as their opinion that a quantity equivalent to a lakh of rupees in value, up to half the output of the mines, is stolen annually.

The Kodarma Mica Mining Association took up the matter strongly, and the Lieutenant-Governor of the Province was good enough to visit Kodarma and discuss the matter with the Association. A draft Bill for the "prevention of mica theft" was submitted to the local Government, but the latter decided that the matter had better be postponed for a time, and the Association has accepted this decision as a temporary one only.

One might give numberless instances showing the absolute impunity with which thefts of mica are carried out, but mention of two cases will suffice for the purpose of demonstrating the insufficiency of the protection afforded by the local police authorities.

A bullock-cart was discovered at half-past ten at night outside a godown at Debour, 10 miles from Kodarma, and coolies were seen to bring sacks of mica and to place them in the cart. The driver and his cart were apprehended and taken to the police-station, where the man's defence was that he went to sleep, and that while he slept some evilly-disposed persons must have loaded his cart. He was a Kodarma cartman, but he did not know why he had gone to Debour, and he plaintively added that he was a poor man ! The police kept the mica, and there was an end of *that* case.

On the night of February 28, 1915, part of a large crystal of mica was cut out of a pillar in a level driven from a shaft at a depth of 60 feet from the surface, and on the following morning the manager of the mine concerned discovered the theft. He had a shrewd notion as to the culprit, and went straight to the godown of the person suspected and there found a part of a large crystal of mica. He waited at the mine until the suspected man arrived, and then returned with him to Kodarma, where he handed him over to the police, giving full details of the case and a request that the Sub-Inspector would visit the mine, fit the portion of crystal from the godown into the mica left in the pillar, and thus procure irrefutable evidence as to the identity of the stolen piece. The police undertook to do this without any delay. They, however, took no steps at all for more than twenty-four hours; then they visited the mine, but did not then or at any subsequent time enter it, contenting themselves by sending coolies down to remove from the pillar that part of the crystal which remained. Therefore they not only deliberately refrained from obtaining evidence themselves, but they took it out of the power of any other person to do so subsequently. The case was lost for lack of evidence, and the police kept the mica !

The opponents of the Bill put forward by the Association stated that it would ruin their businesses; and possibly it would, for, as one of them rather quaintly complained in a letter to a Calcutta newspaper, there are thousands of mica traders, while the Bill was brought forward by an insignificant body of miners of that substance.

During the year 1913 the shipments from Calcutta amounted to 49,949 cwts., although the total output from the mines of the whole Province, according to the official Report of the Inspector of Mines, amounted to only 31,239 cwts.

It is extremely rarely that a perfect mica crystal, unbroken and undistorted, is found, and the writer of these notes has not yet seen one during seventeen years' experience. The crystals are all broken and distorted *in situ*, are striated, bent, and frequently cut up into strips, triangles, and quadrilaterals by minor cleavage planes, and it is these triangles and quadrilaterals which are frequently mistaken for the perfect crystal.

MICA SORTERS AT WORK.

At the end of the day's work the rough mica from the mines is brought to the surface and split into sheets about one-eighth of an inch in thickness, the latter being subsequently tied in bundles of about 40 lb. each and carried into the company's godowns.

The course of preparation of this rough mica consists in trimming, sorting, grading, and splitting. It is split by the cutters into convenient thicknesses for trimming with a sickle (this means a thickness of about a thirty-second part of an inch), and all rough and cracked edges are cut off with as little waste as possible. This method of trimming leaves a sound plate of curvilinear configuration, containing the greatest possible area of sound mica that could be secured from the rough piece. This is certainly a less wasteful plan than that employed in Madras, Argentina, and Brazil, where the rough mica is cut into approximate rectangles by guillotine shears. These trimmed curvilinear plates are known as slab mica, and are sorted into sizes, "Special" and "No. 1" to "No. 6," these sizes being based on the area of the largest rectangle of sound mica that could be cut from each slab.

The areas of the standard sizes are as follows: No. 6, not less than 1 square inch; No. 5, under 6 square inches and not less than 3 square inches; No. 4, under 10 square inches and not less than 6 square inches; No. 3, under 15 square inches and not less than 10 square inches; No. 2, under 24 square inches and not less than 15 square inches; and No. 1, under 36 square inches and not less than 24 square inches; while for the "Special" size, all areas not less than 36 square inches are included.

In addition to these recognized sizes, some firms produce a small No. 5, consisting of slabs of 2½ square inches only; A1 size, intermediate between No. 1 and Special; and an Extra Special size, containing slabs of not less than 48 square inches.

The No. 6 size is graded into two qualities—clear and stained; black-spotted No. 6 is not usually brought from the mines, the value being nominal; all other sizes are graded into the qualities—clear, slightly stained, stained, densely stained, spotted, and densely spotted.

The No. 5 and No. 6 stained qualities are converted into splittings. The other grades are packed in cases containing about 56 lb. net, and it is most desirable that two sizes or qualities should never be packed in the same case, as buyers of one kind may have no use for the other.

The splitting of the No. 5 and No. 6 slabs into films suitable for the manufacture of micanite is done by women and children. Special knives are used for the purpose, and a skilled labourer is able to split to a given thinness—say, one twelve-hundredth part of an inch—with an extraordinary degree of uniformity.

As the value of the films depends on their being uniformly thin and free from torn or cracked pieces, it is evident that close supervision is required at all splitting factories, as there may be upwards of 5,000 films in a pound, and even a comparatively few thick films in a case will seriously affect the value. The work of splitting is carried on by contract, the operatives receiving a fixed rate per seer, according to the quality manufactured.

OLD METHOD OF RAISING WATER AND DÉBRIS.

Photo by R. O. Podger.

The first exports of Bengal mica, in 1863, amounted to about 67 cwts.; the average yearly export for the period 1904-8 was 23,624 cwts.; and although the increase was maintained until 1912, when 51,646 cwts. were exported, there has been a falling off since then, the figures being 49,949 cwts. for 1913 and 29,124 cwts. for 1914.

The Annual Report of the Chief Inspector of Mines gives a total of 12,314 persons employed daily in the Bengal (now Behar and Orissa) mica mines, but this figure does not include those employed in godowns and factories. The factory labour, it should be observed, is considerably in excess of that employed actually on the mines.

The principal use of mica is in the manufacture of electrical machinery. The invention of micanite, a sort of cardboard made of splittings, built up with a shellac cement, and consolidated under pressure, put a value on all the smaller sizes of mica, which had hitherto been discarded as valueless. Micanite can be moulded into any desired form, and is therefore capable of being used in a greater variety of forms than the slabs in their natural state.

A very considerable quantity of clear slab mica is used in the condensers of wireless telegraphy installations, for stove windows, incandescent gas chimneys, gramophone diaphragms, compass cards, and other purposes.

A small quantity of waste mica is pulverized, and the resulting powder is used as a lubricant; other portions are converted into efficient boiler-packing, and lagging for steam-pipes, but the supply very greatly exceeds the demand. The Canadian Phlogopite mica is superior to the Bengal product for the manufacture of powder, and that country having the advantage of cheaper freight to the European market, and possessing practically unlimited supplies of waste mica, it is unlikely that this Province will be able to enter into serious competition with the Dominion.

ADDITIONAL NOTES ON MICA

BY F. F. CHRESTIEN

SCIENTIFICALLY, mica comprises a group of rock-forming minerals, found in most parts of the world. The principal members of the family are Muscovite, Biotite, Phlogopite, and Lepidolite, all of them showing, in varying degrees, a marked tendency to cleave in a single direction. Confining our remarks to Behar, the two varieties of this monoclinic crystal which are found are Muscovite and Biotite. Only the former has any commercial value, and occurs in crystals of many colours—ruby, green, yellow, and white—frequently with black spots and splashes, due to the presence of iron and other foreign matter. Commercially, it may be said the ruby colour is preferred, especially when free from stains and spots.

Not much is known about mica, as, geologically, it has not been closely

F. F. CHRESTIEN & CO., LTD.

1. Managing Director's Bungalow at Domchanch. 2. Offices and Factory, Domchanch. 3. Lokai Offices and Factory. 4. Tisri Offices and Factory. 5. Bungalow at Tisri.

F. F. CHRESTIEN & CO., LTD.

1. Sickle-dressing Mica. 2. Sorting and Grading Mica. 3. Splitting Mica at Lokai Factory. 4. Knife-cutting and Examining Mica.

F. F. CHRESTIEN & CO., LTD.

1. Dispatching a Consignment. 2. Main Incline and Haulage Gear, Jhagriah Mine. 3. Main Incline and New Vertical Shaft (under construction), Buriah Mine. 4. Part of the Mica Dumps at Tisri.

studied; nor is it a mineral that obeys any very specific rules of occurrence. In Behar it is most commonly found, perhaps, in coarse pegmatite veins having a barren quartz core, and with foot and hanging walls of mica schist, the mica itself occurring at the contacts of the pegmatite with either the schist or quartz.

Such a vein may vary in thickness from a few inches to 50 feet and more, measuring from foot to hanging wall; may have a "strike" of a few feet to a mile, and on the dip may go down to a depth unknown, though several deposits appear to be very superficial.

The richness of any vein varies largely in different places, both along the strike and the dip. This, added to the general uncertainty of occurrence and the enormous wastage, makes mica-mining a very hazardous and speculative industry.

While in America mines have been taken to nearly 1,000 feet of depth, owing to primitive methods heretofore employed in Behar a mine has to be exceptionally rich to exceed 150 feet on the vertical, while the very deepest can scarcely exceed 300 feet, which is the depth to which the Bunderchua mine of Messrs. Chrestien & Co. was taken before work was stopped.

Once the vein has got below the level of surface influence, and where it can be affected by the infiltration of water and mud, depth in itself does not appear to have any influence on the quality of the mica. Mica is a most wasteful mineral to mine, scarcely 5 per cent. of the actual mica contents of any vein being of value. The mineral occurs in crystals known commonly as "books," from their inclination to split into sheets like the pages of a book.

These books vary much in size and in weight, from the fraction of an ounce to as much as half a ton, while crystals weighing from 100 lb. to 200 lb. are of daily occurrence. The value of mica, however, does not depend on the original size of the book, but on how that book has made up, i.e. on its freedom from cross grain or twining and from cracks. The books when found are dislodged by boring and blasting, and are then brought to the surface and split up into large and thick pieces. Such pieces as are obviously useless are thrown away on the mine, while the rest is sent to be dressed. After this the mica goes to the central factory of the mine-owner to be prepared for market.

The mica field of Behar and Orissa is the chief mica field in India, and covers a belt of some 600 square miles, where the districts of Hazaribagh, Gya, and Monghyr meet, though the lion's share of the mines lies in the first-named district.

The mica belt consists of a tangle of low hills, dying away into a flat tableland some 1,000 feet above the sea, and covered with a jungle of *sal* trees. In this jungle are to be found a few tigers, sometimes of marked man-eating propensities, leopards, the sloth bear, and the big woodland deer the sambhur.

Splittings are exported to the manufacturers of "micanite." Though micanite has now become almost a dictionary word, like "tabloid," it is really the trade-mark name of an American firm who were the first to manufacture micanite at Shenectady, U.S.A.

Artificial plates made from splittings and shellac are then subjected to great heat and pressure to remove the surplus shellac and the resultant micanite, which gives out a metallic ring when struck, can be cut into convenient sizes and used for electrical insulation. Year by year the consumption of mica by the three great buyers has increased. These three buyers were London, Hamburg, and New York. The Great War, by removing the custom of Germany, has naturally had a depressing effect on the industry, which, it is to be hoped, will only be temporary.

The principal mica concern in Behar—and, in fact, in the world—is Messrs. F. F. Christien & Co., Ltd. This company was formed in 1911 to take over the long-established business privately owned by Mr. F. F. Chrestien, who pioneered the industry as long ago as 1871, practically every mine in the mica belt of Behar having been worked by him at some time or another.

At present the company, besides controlling large areas and many mines in Behar, works mines in the Madras mica field of Nellore. The company, which has its registered offices at Domchanch, via Kodarma, East Indian Railway, has its most important mines in the Government forest of Kodarma and in several private estates, of which the principal is Gawan, an estate in itself as large as the whole Kodarma Forest. The company maintains some 16 factories to deal with the mica it produces or buys, the chief of which are at Domchanch, Lokai, and Tisri.

In normal times some four or five Europeans are engaged and a staff of over 100 babus to control the 8,000 coolies employed in the mines and factories. As the mines and factories of the company are dotted over some 600 square miles where railway facilities are very small, the company has to maintain motor-cars and several horses as means of locomotion.

The annual expenditure of the company in Behar only amounts to about 8 lakhs of rupees.

Owing to the heavy rains that take place between June and September, the company, like others, has found difficulty in keeping the mines sufficiently dry to work by the primitive method of hand-baling formerly in vogue. The company has now begun to tackle this particular difficulty by the use of steam-pumping and hoisting, and hopes within a year or two to have some 30 mines, each equipped with the necessary installation of boilers, pumps, and hoists.

SHELLAC

THE lac industry is one of the most ancient of the minor industries of India. Lac is a resinous incrustation produced by insects known as *Tachardia Lacca*, which swarm over the twigs of certain trees, suck up the sap, and give out an excretion which solidifies on contact with the air, and a scale is gradually formed round their bodies. This process continues until the twigs are encased by the incrustation. In this form it is collected by the villagers and sold in the local country markets as "sticklac," from which the product known as "shellac" is manufactured. Another substance known as "lacdye" is also obtained from sticklac, and formerly there was a large demand for it, but since the introduction of synthetic dyes the demand has disappeared. The chief districts in which sticklac is found are Behar and Orissa,

SHELLAC.

1. Crushing Stick-Lac. 2. Assorting Shellac. 3. Washing Crushed Lac.

SHELLAC.

1. Manufacturing Shellac from Seed Lac. 2. Washing Crushed Stick-lac. 3. Drying Crushed Lac.

the Central Provinces, the United Provinces, the Punjab, Assam, and Burma. There are many qualities of sticklac which vary according to the district and the kinds of trees on which it is grown.

The manufacture of shellac is largely in the hands of the natives of India, and their methods are primitive and practically the same now as they were hundreds of years ago. Several factories worked by machinery have been started, but with few exceptions none of them have so far been a success.

The process of the manufacture of shellac by the country hand-made method is as follows: The sticklac is broken up and granulated and the dye is then washed out. This is done by soaking the grain in water and rubbing it with the hands and feet, in stone vessels, and rinsing with water until free of dye. The washed grain is then known as "seedlac" and is ready to be made into "shellac." This operation requires considerable skill. The grain after being mixed with a small quantity of arsenic, so as to give the shellac a lighter and better appearance, is put into long sausage-shaped bags, one end of which is held by a man in front of a charcoal fire, and the other end being slowly twisted by an assistant. The pressure produced by twisting and the heat of the fire causes the lac to melt out through the cloth. The melted lac is then scraped off the bag by the man holding the end nearest the fire, and after sufficient is collected he places it, while hot, on to a cylindrical glazed earthenware vessel, over which it is spread into a thin sheet by another assistant, who quickly picks up the sheet, warms it at the fire, and by holding the bottom corners with his toes, the top corners with his hands, and the centre with his teeth, gradually extends himself until the sheet is sufficiently stretched and the right thickness obtained. The sheet, when cold, is broken up into flakes.

There are many qualities of shellac, but the standard article of commerce is known as "T N," the quality depending on the kind of sticklac from which it is made. The principal manufactures in which shellac is used are varnishes, hats, electrical appliances, and gramophone records as well as other goods in a less degree.

Previous to 1907 the average yearly production in India of shellac amounted to 145,000 chests, or 213,616 cwt., but during the past ten years it has risen to 250,000 chests or 386,335 cwt. The market has always been a very speculative one, and subject to violent fluctuations, the average yearly price having varied from 60 shillings to 215 shillings per cwt.

AGABEG BROTHERS

The Chief Inspector of Mines in India stated in a recent Report that the coal industry appeared to be in a remarkably healthy condition, and he certainly had good grounds for this assertion, seeing that the output has been increasing gradually for several years, although there was a slight set-back in 1909 owing to the inundation of several mines. The railway companies are by far the largest purchasers of coal, although there is a growing demand for steamships, jute, and cotton mills, iron and brass foundries, and other commercial concerns.

The Provinces of Bengal and Behar and Orissa yield approximately 90 per cent. of the total quantity raised in the course of a year, and the Jherria fields, in which the coal estate of Jogta, near Sijua, belonging to Messrs. Agabeg Brothers, is situated, are the richest in India. Mining operations commenced in Jherria in 1893, and it was in the same year that Messrs. E. C. and A. A. Agabeg began to develop their property, which covers an area of about 190 acres. There are five seams of solid coal, measuring fully 100 ft. in thickness, and it is estimated that fully 25,000,000 tons will eventually be obtained. Six inclines (the longest of which is 1,700 ft.) and one shaft of a depth of 300 ft. are being worked, and an average monthly yield of 24,000 tons can be secured. The beds consist of hard coal of first-class quality, containing from 10 to 12 per cent. of ash, and the product is brought to the surface by a number of steam engines, which are capable of raising a load of about 5 tons in weight.

The firm have a loading-up wharf of considerable length (which, by the way, can be used throughout the night, as it is illuminated by electricity), and as many as ninety wagons can be accommodated on the sidings and filled in the course of a day. A very large amount of the coal is exported to various places throughout the world, and, while the railways in India take an appreciable quantity, it is satisfactory to observe that the demand for industrial and domestic purposes is growing steadily. Messrs. Agabeg Brothers are fortunate in possessing a colliery which is so singularly free from the dire effects of too much water that the amount registered during wet seasons does not exceed 10,000 gallons an hour, while in dry weather there is scarcely any necessity whatever for pumping operations being carried on.

The manufacture of coke is part of the pioneer work undertaken by the firm, and up-to-date ovens have been erected, which are now turning out a considerable quantity, equal in quality to the imported fuel.

The arrangements for the supply of water for general use are most complete in every respect, as a sufficient amount for all purposes is forced by a pump through pipes, which are laid from a tank (holding 2,000,000 gallons) to all portions of the property.

The Province of Behar is decidedly in the van with regard to the possession of beautiful residences surrounded by well-kept grounds, and the estate now under notice is a notable illustration of this fact. The bungalows are substantially yet artistically built; they are fitted with modern improvements, including electric light; and they are charmingly situated among a wealth of flowering trees, shrubs, and plants. The East Indian Railway system has a station on the property, and a double-line private siding is attached to the colliery. Among the principal buildings are a Government Lecture Hall, post and telegraph offices, garage, manager's quarters, and coolie lines, constructed of brick, and the majority of these are connected by telephone and have electric lighting installations. Two European assistants are employed under the general manager, Mr. W. R. Lascelles, in the supervision of about 1,400 Indians, many of the latter being engaged in the workshops, in which all kinds of repairs for the mining machinery are undertaken.

The partners are Messrs. E. C. and A. A. Agabeg (the latter being the managing director), and they have invested in their mining concern no less a sum than nine lakhs of rupees. These gentlemen have had nearly forty years' experience in mining matters in India, and they have rendered most valuable assistance, both by precept and practice, in placing the coal industry on a sound commercial basis.

MESSRS. ANGELO BROS., LTD.

The manufacture of shellac in India can be traced back for several generations, but the methods of preparation were, until about sixty years ago, of a very primitive character. Notes upon this

AGABEG BROTHERS.

1. Depot with Wagons. 2. A General View. 3. No. 5 Incline. 4. Office and Power-house.

AGABEG BROTHERS.

1. MANAGER'S BUNGALOW. 2 JOGTA HOUSE—PROPRIETOR'S RESIDENCE.

ANGELO BROS.

1. Main Gate and Office. 2. Drying and Working Yard.

JOYRAMPORE COLLIERY (M. V. APCAR & CO.).

1. Manager's Bungalow. 2. General View of Loading Wharf. 3. No. 7 Inclined Shaft. 4. Colliery Office.

industry will be found on another page of this volume.

Early in the fifties of last century Mr. M. K. Angelo, of Calcutta, became greatly interested in the production of shellac. He was particularly struck by the fact that no attempt had been made to prepare it in any other manner than by, the old native hand method. He gave serious attention to the question, and after a number of experiments had been conducted, he established a factory at Cossipore, near Calcutta, in the year 1855.

The earliest output of machine-made shellac from the factory consisted of the now widely known Garnet Lac AC and for a considerable number of years that was the only machine-made lac. Mr. Angelo continued his investigations, however, and he eventually discovered a process by which he was able to make orange lac, and the now well-known mark A B TN was put on the market.

The output of the factory increased steadily year by year, and in 1907 the concern was reconstructed, and a limited liability company, known as Angelo Brothers, Ltd., was formed.

That event led to further experiments being made, and in 1915 an improved method of making various kinds of orange shellac was adopted, and "Angelos T.N." is now becoming familiar throughout the shellac world.

A well-equipped laboratory has recently been added to the factory, and scientific research has enabled the company to improve their methods continually. They now manufacture many grades of orange, garnet, and button shellac, and make a special study of the kind suitable for the various trades receiving it, and are always glad to give advice to buyers.

The registered offices of the company are situated at 6 Lyons Range, Calcutta, and the managing agents are Messrs. Turner, Morrison & Co., Ltd.

M. V. APCAR & CO.

The commercial world in Calcutta lost an honoured business colleague, and the Armenian community a cherished adherent of strong personality and genial nature, on the death, in the year 1914, of Mr. Minas Vertannes Apcar, the founder of the firm of Messrs. M. V. Apcar & Co., of 6 Fancy Lane. That gentleman was born at Julfa, Ispahan, in Persia, in November 1862, and such were the misfortunes under which he laboured—and through no fault of his parents or himself—that when he arrived in India at the age of fourteen years, his belongings consisted only of a small quantity of personal clothing. Truly this was an unenviable predicament for a boy, but Mr. Aleck Apcar sent him to St. Xavier's and the Armenian Colleges for only one and a half years (one year of which was spent at the latter and six months at the former), where he soon proved the metal of which he was formed. When the time arrived for the youth to make a start in business life he entered the important firm of Messrs. Burn & Co., but he shortly afterwards found employment with Messrs. Apcar and Demetrius, where he worked for a short period. Fired with a laudable ambition, young Apcar took a bold forward movement, and with "Excelsior" as his motto he commenced business on his own account, holding jute agencies, then becoming successively a Zemindar and a colliery owner.

Mr. Apcar's energy and strict integrity were strong features in his everyday transactions, and these characteristic traits had undoubtedly much to do with the magnitude and importance which the business had assumed at the time of his death. His son, Mr. John Minas Apcar, was associated in the management of the concern, and he and his brother, Mr. Thomas Minas Apcar, are now sole partners; and they are, further, the owners of several valuable properties in Calcutta, which they inherited from their late father.

They are proprietors of jute presses at Chaora Hat, Dewan Hat, Baneswar, Balarampur, Kakina, Haitbanda, Baura, Gauripur, and Dhubri. They purchase the raw material in up-country districts, and after it has been pressed and baled it is consigned to mills in Calcutta, where the private mark or brand of the firm is accepted as a guarantee of quality.

Messrs. M. V. Apcar & Co. are, further, proprietors of the M. V. A. coal concern at Joyrampore, in the famous Jherriah field; and they are also agents for the Seang line of steamers, plying between Chinese and Indian ports.

The telegraphic address of the company is "Minascar."

BANERJEE & CO.

The sole proprietor of this well-known firm is Mr. W. C. Banerjee, who has worked his way, by dint of sheer energy and honesty of purpose, to the position of one of the leading commercial men in Calcutta. He belongs to an honoured middle-class family, and he has carved his own way without having had at the outset any of the special advantages which have been enjoyed by so many others at the commencement of their careers. Mr. Banerjee passed an examination for a Government clerkship, in addition to another in accountancy, and his first step in public life was taken in the Political Department of the Government of Bengal; but, finding promotion too slow, he entered the service of the East Indian Railway Company, where he was employed in a branch of the agent's office dealing with the transport of coal, and he was thus brought into close relationship with colliery owners and dealers in that commodity. He engaged in coal brokerage for a time, and after three years' engagement with Messrs. Grindlay & Co., bankers, Mr. Banerjee commenced business on his own account as a coal broker and merchant, taking up selling agencies for collieries on a commission basis. He subsequently financed a number of concerns, charging interest on advances, plus a fixed commission on the annual output of each mine; but when a boom in coal occurred in India, in the year 1907, he promoted a few limited companies, under the management of European firms, and by these means obtained capital to enable him to purchase collieries on his own account.

The following particulars relate to half a dozen collieries owned by Messrs. Banerjee & Co.

The Poniati Coal Concern and the Poniati Coal Company comprise 250 bighas of land in the important Raneegunge field, in the district of Burdwan. Poniati coal, mined in the villages of Furridpur and Domohani, is hard, lumpy, and smokeless, and burns steadily, leaving very little ash and absolutely no clinkers. It is an excellent coal for locomotives, and is used largely on several railways, and in jute mills, Government factories, and in a number of steamships. The average annual output from the two mines is 48,000 tons.

The area of the Joogidih Coal Concern is about 330 bighas, and seams Nos. 10, 11, and 12 of Jherria good second-class coal are worked. The normal yield is some 48,000 tons yearly, but owing to a temporarily unsatisfactory market the

BANERJEE & CO.

1. Poniati Coal Concern: No. A Pit. 2. No. 1 Pit, Engine-house, Boilers, and Headgear, South Baraboni Colliery.
3. No. 2 Pit, Engine-house and Headgear, New Baraboni Colliery. 4. Jambad Coal Concern, No. 2 Pit. 5. No. 4 Incline, New Kusunda Colliery.
6. Peepratand Coal Concern's Inclines. 7. Mr. W. C. Banerjee.

BANERJEE & CO.

1. R. B. Sircar & Sons' Kirkend Colliery. 2. R. B. Sircar & Sons' Kirkend Colliery—2 Pits.
3. R. B. Sircar & Sons' Kirkend Colliery—Loading and Unloading Arrangements.

output has been restricted recently to 12,000 tons.

The Sinidih Colliery is about three miles distant from Katrasgarh Station, on the East Indian Railway system, and comprises 150 bighas of land. The annual raisings are about 24,000 tons.

The Jambad Colliery has an area of about 900 bighas in the Raneegunge district, and the product is particularly suitable for locomotives and steamers, although it is credited with yielding the best soft coke in Western Bengal. About 18,000 tons of coal have hitherto been brought to the surface annually, but when six prospective pits have been developed it is expected that this quantity will be increased to 100,000 tons.

Not more than a mile distant from Mohuda Station, on the Bengal-Nagpur Railway, is the Peepratand colliery, which possesses excellent seams of gas coal of high illuminating power. It strongly resembles English coal, and is a favourite in gasworks, factories, and mills which require gas-producing fuel. The present return of 18,000 tons will, it is confidently expected, be increased to nearly 50,000 tons in course of time.

These properties are now styled the South Baraboni Coal Concern and the New Baraboni Coal Concern. Messrs. Banerjee & Co. have recently purchased from the South Baraboni Coal Company and the New Baraboni Coal Company two collieries near the Baraboni Station, on the East Indian Railway. The product of these mines is unexcelled in quality (being obtained from the bottom or Dishergarh seam), and the demand for railways, mills, and steamships has become so great that orders cannot at all times be executed. Rather more than 40,000 tons are brought to the surface annually.

A sub-lease has, further, been obtained of Messrs. E. Meyer & Co.'s Neemcha colliery, 1,100 bighas in extent, with three pits of first-class Raneegunge coal, which is particularly suitable for use in mills and industrial factories generally. The annual output is about 48,000 tons.

The following collieries are controlled by Messrs. Banerjee & Co. as managing Agents :—

The New Kusunda Coal Company, Ltd., formed, in October 1908, with an authorized capital of Rs. 104,000, is the owner of 150 bighas of coal-bearing land in Mouzah Kusunda, in the district of Manbhum, in the Jherria field. An average annual quantity of 48,000 tons of coal was obtained up to the year 1914, when this mine—in common with others in the same neighbourhood—suffered considerable damage owing to floods; but at the time of preparing these notes it was hoped that the mischief done would be quickly repaired, and that the directors would be able to declare the customary dividend of 10 per cent. per annum. Local railway authorities speak highly of this coal, as it burns brightly without being rapidly consumed, and many years ago Mr. F. R. Hughes, F.R.G.S., published a fine testimony in its favour in the Memoirs of the Geological Survey of India.

Messrs. R. B. Sircar and Sons' Kirkend collieries are situated near Parbad and Kusunda, on the Bengal-Nagpur and East Indian Railways respectively, and they consist of about 200 bighas of land, from which the very best coal for locomotive purposes is obtained. Nearly all the railway systems in India receive supplies from these mines, while country mills, especially in the Presidency of Bombay and in the Punjab, are very large purchasers. About 100,000 tons of coal are produced annually.

The Tentulia colliery, owned by the Central Tentulia Coal Company, and situated about three miles from Katrasgarh, on the East Indian Railway, and the Angrapathra colliery, not more than a mile from the same station, comprise seams Nos. 11, 12, 13, and 15 of Jherria coal, and the major portion of the output is taken for railway and milling purposes. Hard coke, prepared out of machine-screened dust, finds a ready sale among foundry owners.

First-class anthracite coal, of the well-known Salanpur seam, is obtained from the Siriskanali colliery, about a mile distant from Salanpur Station, on the East Indian Railway; while the Ramnagar seam, in the same colliery, produces shining bituminous coal, which is used largely for the making of hard coke. These two workings belong to the Salanpur Coal Concern.

The Central Kendah Coal Company has a colliery near Toposi Station, on the East Indian Railway, and it yields about 18,000 tons of second-class Raneegunge coal, suitable for household purposes.

Selling agencies are held by the firm for the following colliery companies : Laik's Neamutpur and Hathnol collieries, in which the famous Dishergarh and Sanctoria seams are worked; the Jeenagarah colliery, comprising Nos. 11 and 12 Jherria seams, and producing coal adapted for railways, cotton mills, and ginning factories; Khora Ramjis Khas Jherria collieries, situated at the Jherria Station of the East Indian Railway; the Gareria collieries, at Bansjora Station, on the same railway system, working No. 10 Jherria seam; and the Kujama colliery, near Jherria Station, whose products are purchased chiefly by mill and factory owners.

Messrs. Banerjee & Co. have coal depots at Shalimar and Howrah, on the Hooghly River, where they keep a large stock of coal for bunkering purposes; they have another at Ultadanga, whence coal is supplied to oil and flour mills in Calcutta; and another at Bhadreshwar Ghat, for the delivery of coal to jute mills and brick manufacturers.

The firm are, further, largely interested in iron, hardware, and metal of all kinds, supplying considerable quantities to municipalities, railways, the Royal Indian Marine, ordnance factories, arsenals, tea gardens, collieries, and jute mills; they are agents for piece goods for Mr. Arthur Davy, of Bradford, and are sub-agents for the Burma Oil Company, Ltd.

Mr. W. C. Banerjee is a director of several coal companies in Calcutta. He founded the Indian Mining Federation, under the Bengal National Chamber of Commerce; and in earlier days he led the way in agitating for the right of Indians to be given contracts for the supply of coal to State and company owned railways in India.

The offices of the firm are at 7 Swallow Lane, Calcutta, and their telegraphic address is "Joogidih."

THE BENGAL COAL COMPANY, LTD.

Coal was discovered in Bengal in or about the year 1770, but very little mining was carried on until the East Indian Railway Company extended its system in 1854 to Raneegunge, in the very heart of the most important coal-producing centres in India. Prior to the opening of the line coal had to be conveyed to boats on the Damuda River, but as this stream was not navigable for more than four months in the year it will be understood that there was little inducement to capitalists to invest money in commercial enterprises which would be so seriously handicapped in the disposal of their products.

The Bengal Coal Company, usually referred to as "the premier coal company of India," was formed in 1843, the present registered offices being at 8 Clive Row, Calcutta.

Rights were obtained by the company over about 80,000 acres of land, but the area in which coal deposits are situated covers about 50,000 acres in the Raneegunge, Giridih, Jherria, and Palamow fields. The collieries now being worked are known as Seetalpore, Sanctoria, Sodepore, Banksimulia, Damudarpore, Koilhi, Bhatdee, Murulidih, Chanch, Dumarkunda, Dhobidih, and Raneegunge.

The coal is unrivalled in India for railway, navigation, factory, mill, household, and other purposes, but a word or two should be added about the nature of some of the seams in pits.

Excellent coal of a gaseous nature is raised chiefly at Bhatdee, and large quantities have been supplied to the gas companies of Calcutta, Bombay, and Colombo, while the Committee of the Allahabad Exhibition reported that "this was found to be a coal very suitable for gas-making in producers as it does not clinker, and this is a most important point. It burns with a remarkable freedom from smoke, a feature which may be greatly in its favour."

Another large consumer wrote: "I have subjected the coal sample to a very drastic test with regard to its non-caking character, and have no hesitation in stating that it is a most suitable fuel for suction gas plants constructed on the semi-bituminous principle. Another great feature in its favour is that it showed no disposition to clinker, and its utility for the above-named purposes should find it a ready market." Hard, clean-burning, and non-clinkering locomotive coal is obtained from the famous Kurhurbari, Seebpore, and Chanch seams of the Barraker series, and it is held in high esteem by owners of factories and steamers having plenty of draught. The Mohoda coal has a bright and shiny appearance, and breaks with a sharp cleavage, while it is regarded by consumers as one of the best products of the Jherria field. The company have received numerous letters from chief officers of steamers and others who have had practical experience of the value of the Deshergur coal for raising and maintaining a sufficient pressure of steam during a series of voyages, and there is in these testimonials a general consensus of opinion that this is one of the best on the Calcutta market.

It is only to be expected that, as more than seventy years have elapsed since the formation of the company, very great improvements should have been effected upon the whole estate, but the most important developments have been in connection with the raising and transport of coal, in providing modern machinery and plant, together with electric power for lighting, pumping, and other purposes, and also in the establishment of an overseas trade with Ceylon, Burma, the Straits Settlements, and other places.

The total output of the mines for the year 1905 was 596,966 tons, while at the end of 1915 the quantity had risen to more than a million tons per annum, and employment was being found for about 6,000 persons.

A glance at a recent balance sheet and statement of accounts shows that the capital of the company is Rs. 30,00,000; a sum of more than Rs. 80,000 is received annually from properties leased to other companies or individuals and from royalties; large sums are set aside annually for depreciation; and dividends during the past decade have ranged from 16 to as much as 70 per cent. per annum, while the average for that period has been rather more than 35 per cent.

The managing agents of the company are Messrs. Andrew Yule & Co., of 8 Clive Row, Calcutta.

MESSRS. BIRD & CO.'S COAL DEPARTMENT.

From the various collieries controlled by Messrs. Bird & Co. is derived an annual output of 1,500,000 tons, and employment is given to about 12,000 hands. These collieries are electrically equipped and installed with modern machinery for the preparation and screening of coal, and are situated as follows: Loyabad, Mudidih, Teetunmuri, Budroochuck, Katras, Choytoodih, and Jumoni, in the Jerriah field; and Saltore, Lutchipore, Hatgoori, Bhaskajuri, Charanpur, Burelia, Bankola, Kantapahari, Jamgram, and Joba, in the Raneegunge field.

F. W. HEILGERS & CO. (COAL DEPARTMENT).

The development of industrial concerns throughout India was exceedingly slow until about three or four decades ago, when the extension of railways made it possible for raw material produced in fertile districts in Provinces and States to be transferred quickly from inland regions to manufacturing centres, and the facilities thus granted have been the means of linking together the agriculturists of the villages on the one hand and of capitalists in cities on the other.

Coal was known to exist in untold quantity, but mining was not undertaken seriously, as the necessity for the use of this mineral as fuel had never been realized. The railways of the country burned timber, which was readily procured, for the firing of their engines, and there were scarcely any industries which required other than manual power. But an enormous change has taken place since the importation of Welsh coal for the bunkering of steamers, as the eyes of financiers and merchants were at once turned to the vast wealth of the coalfields of India, but more particularly of the Bengal Presidency and the Province of Behar and Orissa, which now yield about 95 per cent. of the total quantity raised to the surface in the whole of the country.

The railways alone consume fully one-third of the coal production of India, but large consignments are secured for cotton and jute mills, brick and tile works, iron and brass foundries, ocean and river steamers, and for industrial and domestic requirements.

Messrs. F. W. Heilgers & Co., of the Chartered Bank Buildings, Calcutta, were among the first merchants to seize the opportunities presented by the new state of affairs, and their enterprising spirit has placed them in nearly the leading position in India of those who handle large quantities of coal. They are managing agents for the following colliery and coal companies, namely: the Borrea Coal Company, Ltd., the Bhulanbararee Coal Company, Ltd., the Govindpur Coal Company, Ltd., the Khas Jherriah Colliery Company, Ltd., the Sendra Coal Company, Ltd., and the Standard Coal Company, Ltd., with mines of first-class coal in the famous Jherriah fields in the district of Manbhum, in the Province of Behar and Orissa, together with the Ondal Coal Company, Ltd., whose works are in the Raneegunge coal area, in the district of Burdwan, in the Bengal Presidency.

These companies have a total authorized capital of Rs. 40,25,000, and the majority of them have, during the past two or three years, been paying very satisfactory dividends, the Khas Jherriah Company alone having declared 170, 200, and 180 per cent. per annum for 1913, 1914, and 1915.

Nearly 1,000,000 tons of coal are now

BIRD & CO.'S COAL AGENCIES.

1. No. 3 Pit, Saltore. 2. No. 2 Pit, Saltore. 3 Power-house under Construction. 4. Aerial Ropeway.

STANDARD AND BHULANBARAREE COLLIERIES.

1. Generating Station Standard Colliery. 2. No. 10 Pit Headgear, Standard Colliery. 3. No. 7 Incline at Bhulanbararee. 4 Central Pit, Bhulanbararee.

raised annually from the various mines, and in normal times a considerable portion of this quantity (which is about one-fifteenth of the total quantity produced in India) is exported to the Straits Settlements, Ceylon, and ports in India.

The machinery at each colliery is quite up-to-date in every respect, and it is driven by steam excepting at the Standard and Bhulanbararee mines, where largely electric power is used.

From 10,000 to 12,000 hands are employed on the properties.

KILBURN & CO.

The most valuable deposits of coal in India are found in the Provinces of Bengal, and Behar and Orissa, chiefly in the districts of Chota-Nagpur and Burdwan, the seams running along the valleys formed by the Barrakur and Damudar rivers. The climate of India, and in earlier days the quantity of forest timber available for fuel, are responsible for the fact that the necessity for developing a mining industry was not apparent, but a glance at Government statistics of exports shows that, as wood became more and more scarce, there was a corresponding increase in the output of the older mines and a disposition on the part of investors to open up other coal-bearing areas. One might illustrate this by giving the quantity of coal produced in Bengal at the close of the three decades between the years 1879 and 1914. In the former year the amount was 891,047 tons; ten years later 1,541,356 tons were raised; in 1899 the production reached 4,035,265 tons; and in 1914 no fewer than 15,727,631 tons were brought to the surface.

The Raneegunge Coal Association, Ltd., for whom Messrs. Kilburn & Co., of Fairlie Place, Calcutta, are Managing Agents, was formed in 1873 by taking over from Messrs. E. D. Kilburn and others the lands known as Lot Jamgram and Bansra, in the district of Burdwan; but other properties have been acquired from time to time with the result that the Association is now (1916) in possession of thirty-four separate villages, having a total measurement of 39,586 bighas. Nearly 37,000 bighas have been leased for periods ranging from 99 to 999 years, at an annual rent of about Rs. 44,368.

The principal colliery, Kustore, is situated in the Jherria field, and covers an area of 2,428 bighas. It is divided into three parts, known as Kustore North, Kustore South, and Alkusa District (including Gundudih and part of Keska), and each of these is managed by a European holding a first-class certificate of competency, while the colliery as a whole is supervised by a General Manager.

According to the geological survey, there are fifteen separate seams, at various depths, in Kustore Mouzah, and fourteen separate seams in Alkusa Mouzah. Numbers 10, 11, 12, 13, 14, and 15 seams have been opened out. The method of working in the early stages of development was by means of inclines along the outcrops, but eventually the sinking of shafts was adopted. There are now seven shafts fully equipped and raising coal, the deepest shaft being 550 ft. Each shaft is fitted with steel pit-head frames connected with coupled and direct-winding engines, steam being supplied from Lancashire and Babcock and Wilcox boilers.

The pumping plant installed at the colliery is of the three-throw motor type and turbo sets, the capacity varying from 6,000 to 45,000 gallons per hour for each pump. The electrical power plant consists of one turbo k.w. set of 750 h.p. by the British Thomson-Houston Company, Ltd., and 200 and 400 k.w. sets of the Bellis and Morcom high-speed compound engines. The switchboard and motors at the colliery are of the British Thomson-Houston make.

The colliery is fully equipped with loading sidings and depôts connected with the East Indian and Bengal-Nagpur Railway systems. Each siding is fitted up with mechanical screening and loading plant, which classifies the coal in four different sizes—namely, steam, rubble, smithy, and dust.

The accommodation for the labour consists of masonry dowrahs with jack-arched roofs, each room being 10 ft. by 10 ft. The workmen have a good supply of filtered water, supplied through pressure filters by the Jewell Filter Company, the colliery being served throughout by a complete system of pipes and water-taps.

The European bungalows are fitted throughout with electric lights and fans.

The quantity of coal dispatched since the opening out of the colliery is 3,774,190 tons, to the end of March 1916, and it is estimated that approximately 74,494,828 tons are still to be mined.

The ordinary capital consists of Rs. 9,00,000, in 90,000 shares of Rs. 10 each. Accounts are made up half-yearly, for periods ending March and September, and dividends are declared at meetings of shareholders in June and December.

THE INDIAN COLLIERIES SYNDICATE, LTD.

The Indian Collieries Syndicate, Ltd., was registered in London in the year 1902, with an authorized capital of £100,000, of which £90,000 has been issued—namely, £15,000 of 7 per cent. preference and £75,000 of ordinary shares, together with a debenture issue amounting to £64,110. Messrs. Kilburn & Co., of 4 Fairlie Place, Calcutta, are Managing Agents.

The properties of the company consist of five mouzahs, in the district of Manbhum and villages, having a total area of 10,551 bighas, or 3,014¾ acres, equivalent to an area of rather more than 4½ square miles; and they comprise (1) Mouzah Jamadoba, consisting of 1,162 bighas, leased from the Raneegunge Coal Association, Ltd.; (2) Mouzah Jorapukhur, 4,750 bighas, leased from the Central Jherria Coal Company, Ltd.; (3) and (4) Mouzahs Doongri and Puttya, 4,536 bighas, leased from the Rajah of Jherria; (5) Mouzah Kapurgoria, 103 bighas, leased from the Raneegunge Coal Association, Ltd. The whole estate is commonly known by the single name of the Jamadoba Colliery.

The seams now being worked by the company are in the Jherria coal district—namely, Nos. 17 and 18, and the estimated contents of these respectively are 5,000,000 and 6,000,000 tons.

From a geological point of view, there is nothing of a remarkable nature, but it is noticed that "the greater portion of the property lies in a basin, the proved lines of outcrops of seams 17 and 18 forming a semi-circle, dipping to a point within the property itself, the dip being approximately 1 in 10 from the north-east, increasing to 1 in 2½ in the opposite directions following the outcrop." An analysis of a sample of coal extracted from seam 17 gave the following results: Fixed carbon, 64·22 per cent.; volatile carbonaceous matter, 26 per cent.; ash, 8·20 per cent.; moisture, 1·58 per cent.; specific gravity, 1·3130 per cent. The Jamadoba and a portion of the Jorapukhur workings were opened prior to the year 1908, and they comprise a number of inclines in Nos. 17 and 18 seams, which are mechanically

KILBURN & CO.'S COAL AGENCIES.

1. Shafts Nos. 6 and 7, Alkusa. 2. Shafts Nos. 10 and 11, Kustore. 3. Shafts Nos. 4 and 5 Kustore South. 4. Generating Station, Kustore South.

KILBURN & CO.'S COAL AGENCIES.

1. Workshops, Power Station, and Filter Houses, Jamadoba Colliery. 2. No. 1 Incline Bank. Jamadoba Colliery.
3. Electrica Coal-sorting and Screening Plant. 4. Pits Nos. 2 and 3, Division No 2, Jamadoba Colliery.

equipped with endless-rope haulage or with the usual main haulage system.

According to the geological survey, there are seventeen separate seams, at various depths, in Jamadoba, Doongri, Puttya, and Kapurgoria, and eighteen separate seams in Jorapukhur mouzah. Developments have only been made in Nos. 17 and 18 seams.

In the early stages of development of the Company's property the seams of coal were opened out by means of inclines along the outcrop, but eventually it was found necessary to sink shafts to improve the raisings and workings. There are three shafts fully equipped and fitted with steel pit-head frames direct-winding engines, Lancashire boilers, and Weirs feed-pumps.

The water underground is conveyed to the surface by means of 3-throw and turbo pumps, all of which are electrically driven. Steam pumps are also utilized at certain centres.

The colliery is provided with sidings and connected with the Bengal-Nagpur Railway system, each siding being equipped with a mechanical screening and loading plant which classifies the coal in four different sizes, viz. steam coal, rubble, smithy, and dust.

The electrical installation consists of 150 and 250 k.w. sets of the Bellis and Morcom high-speed compound engines, connected with Babcock and Wilcox boilers.

The labour is housed in comfortable dowrahs with arched roofs and verandas. Each block is made up of twenty rooms, each room being about 10 ft. square.

An excellent supply of water from the Damuda River is maintained, and filtered through two 10-ft. Jewell gravity filters, and from an elevated reservoir situated at a high part of the colliery the water is distributed throughout the colliery villages.

A certain number of the European bungalows are fitted with electric lights and fans.

The total quantity of coal dispatched since the opening out of the colliery is 2,75,959 tons, but as the Company is yet in its infancy, as far as development is concerned, a greatly increased output is anticipated. The colliery is at present equipped with plant capable of raising 35,000 tons monthly.

THE BANSRA COAL COMPANY, LTD.

This concern was registered in 1908, with Messrs. Kilburn & Co., of 4 Fairlie Place, Calcutta, as Managing Agents. The Company's properties are situated in the Raneegunge coal-field, and are connected with the East Indian Railway system. They consist of 2,834 bighas, in Mouzahs Bansra, Toposi, Dhusal, and Bajapti.

The only property at present worked is Toposi. This concern has been proved by bore-holes in the centre of the colliery, four seams of coal being proved, viz. Toposi, Chowkadanga, Dhusal, and Nandi.

The upper, or Toposi, seam is being worked by means of inclines and shafts, but recently the Chowkadanga seam has been opened out, at a depth of 290 ft. There are two shafts for working the Toposi seam, and two shafts for the working of the Chowkadanga seam, but the opening out of the latter is a new undertaking, and only one shaft has cut through the seam of coal.

The capital is Rs. 3,00,000, in shares of Rs. 10 each, of which Rs. 2,69,730 has been paid up. The accounts of the Company are made up annually, for the period ending March 31st, and meetings of shareholders are held in May or June.

THE LODNA COLLIERY COMPANY, LTD. (TURNER, MORRISON & CO., LTD.)

Reference is made elsewhere in this volume to the rise and subsequent development of the coal industry in the Bengal Presidency and in the Province of Behar and Orissa. It has been shown that in the year 1880 the total quantity of coal produced in the whole of India was less than a million tons, and although it was evident that the extent of workable coalfields was almost unlimited, practically little or no real mining work had been undertaken. That indifference arose principally from the fact that there was no appreciable demand for this mineral, seeing that wood was being used as fuel for household purposes and for railway and other engines, and further, that industrial enterprises, in which steam was required, were still in their infancy. In addition to these reasons there was another important one, namely, that ocean-going steamers arriving at Bombay or Calcutta did not require coal as they had invariably filled their bunkers with the product of the Welsh mines before leaving England.

A few far-seeing capitalists, however, realized the immense possibilities of mining in India, colliery after colliery being opened, and as analysis proved that the product was, generally, of first-class quality, the industry grew so quickly that thirty years later the quantity raised to the surface in twelve months was about twelve million tons. Such was the commencement of an industry which has affected every branch of commercial and social life, and the influence which it has had upon the financial progress of the country is incalculable.

The Lodna Colliery Company, Ltd., formed in 1896, are owners of mines in Mouza Lodna, Puttiadih, Mankanali Chuck, and Madhuba, all of which are situated in the famous Jherria coal-fields in the district of Manbhum, in the Province of Behar and Orissa, and they subsequently acquired the Chasnalla property, about five miles distant from Lodna.

In 1913 an extensive coal-bearing tract of land was purchased at Sripur in the well-known Raneegunge area, pits being sunk to a depth of 1,000 feet, and about a year later they obtained from the Jherria Coal Company the property known as Bhaga, which adjoins the Lodna colliery.

During the year 1916 the company completed the erection of a by-product recovery plant of the the latest approved type, and in addition to the manufacture of about 3,000 tons of coke monthly, corresponding quantities of coal tar and sulphate of ammonia are produced.

Messrs. Turner, Morrison & Co., Ltd., of 6 Lyons Range, Calcutta, are managing agents of the company.

MCLEOD & CO. (COLLIERIES)

The first coal property taken over by Messrs. McLeod & Co., of 31 Dalhousie Square, Calcutta, was the Singaran River colliery, in 1895, which is situated in the Raneegunge district, the first coal-bearing area in Bengal to be exploited. The acquisition of this colliery was followed in 1901 by the purchase of the Gopalichuck and Marine collieries, in the Jherriah district, and in 1907 the Bansjora colliery was taken over. The Sodeeh colliery was also acquired and floated as a joint-stock company in 1907, and this property includes the Sudi seam, better known as "Desherghur," one of the finest quality seams of coal in India. All these collieries are the property of joint-stock companies, having a total capital of Rs. 29,00,000, including debentures, and their total output of coal is about 3,00,000 tons annually.

The Jherriah collieries work first-class quality coal, viz. seams numbered 13, 14,

TURNER, MORRISON & CO, LTD.

1 and 2. By-product Recovery Plant, Lodna Colliery Company, Ltd., Jharia. 3. Pit-heads, Sripore Colliery, Assonsol.

MCLEOD & CO.'S COLLIERY AGENCIES.

1 AND 2. VIEWS OF THE GOPALICHUCK COAL COMPANY'S COLLIERIES.

MCLEOD & CO.'S COLLIERY AGENCIES.

1. SUPERINTENDENT'S BUNGALOW, PANSJORA. 2. THE HEAD COLLIERY (GOPALICHUCK COAL COMPANY).

and 15, which vary in thickness from 12 to 20 feet. Where the seams outcrop on a property, the coal was won by means of inclines, but as the workings gradually extended pits had to be sunk, and some of the shafts vary from 250 to 400 feet in depth.

The collieries have a ready demand for their coal, particularly Gopalichuck and Marine, which for years past have supplied large quantities to the various Indian railways, and to jute, cotton, and other mills. The export of Bengal coal from Calcutta averages about 3,000,000 tons annually, and during recent years Messrs. McLeod & Co. have sent regular supplies of this mineral to Rangoon, Colombo, Bombay, Singapore, and Karachi.

The employees at the various collieries comprise 13 Europeans and about 2,000 Indians.

MACNEILL & CO.'S COLLIERY AGENCIES

The coal deposits in India are of such vast proportions, and labour is so cheap compared with other countries, that the question has frequently arisen as to the causes which have operated against the development of the mining industry, which would eventually bring almost untold wealth to the promoters, and would give employment to hundreds of thousands of hands at remunerative wages.

Wood is generally used for fuel for domestic purposes in this part of the world, but as the supply of timber is becoming exceedingly scarce, its price has risen to a very considerable extent during the past few years, and it is evident that coal mining must, even if that were the only reason, be taken up much more seriously in the future.

Owing to the high price and scarcity of wood in many districts, coal in the form of "soft coke" is finding favour with the Indians for domestic use. This soft coke is made from inferior grades of Bengal coal, usually obtained from quarries or shallow mines. It is manufactured by piling coal in fairly large heaps, containing about twenty tons, and setting fire to it. When nearly all the free volatile matter is driven off the heap is quenched, leaving what is termed soft coke.

The railway companies are by far the largest purchasers of Indian coal at the present time, the annual consumption being about 4,000,000 tons out of a total production of 12,000,000 tons. Ocean steamers are next on the list; cotton mills are but a few points lower; then jute mills, iron and brass foundries, inland steamers, and various agricultural and industrial concerns follow in the order named.

The total exports of coal from this country in 1900 was 490,000 tons, and after alternating increases and decreases for the next ten years, the quantity shipped from these shores was about 988,000 tons in 1910, the principal destinations being Ceylon, the Straits Settlements, and Sumatra.

Several reasons might be given for the comparatively slow progress which has been made, but it is probable that the chief cause was the general depression in trade and agriculture throughout the world, which resulted in impoverished railway and shipping returns, adverse influences which tended to limit the opening-up of new lines and to bring about the crippling of certain industries.

Notwithstanding the difficulties of the past, however, investors will not fail to notice that the output was doubled during the decade from 1900 to 1910, and that since that date there has been further steady progress.

Messrs. Macneill & Co., of 2 Clive Ghat Street, Calcutta, are interested in a variety of industries, and one of the most important of these is the managing agency which they hold for five collieries in the Raneegunge and Jherria fields—namely, the Equitable Coal Company, Ltd.; the Aldih Coal Company, Ltd.; the Hurriladih Coal Company, Ltd.; the Nodiha Coal Company, Ltd.; and the Mundulpoor Coal Company, Ltd.

The equitable Company was registered in the year 1863, and there are five collieries in full working order, particulars of which are as follows: In the Raneegunge field there is the Dishergarh Colliery, 2,000 biggahs [1] in extent; Jamuria, with an area of 5,588 biggahs; Bejdih, 1,983 biggahs; Chowrassie, 3,533 biggahs; and Hurriladih, in the Jherria field, consisting of 950 biggahs.

Taking these collieries in the order named, it may be observed that mining is carried on at Dishergarh from four pits and one incline, and the seams of coal of first-class quality—14 to 20 feet in thickness, at an angle of 10 degrees—are yielding about 225,000 tons annually, although the raising of steam and stock coal during twelve months from July 1914 was 240,200 tons. The pits vary in depth from 202 feet to 487 feet, but two others are now being sunk which will descend to about 1,100 feet. No royalty is levied upon this property, but the company pays an annual rent of Rs. 11,472; and there are 2,375 male and female adults in daily employment above and below ground, together with 30 children under 12 years of age who are on the surface.

The Jamuria colliery is represented by eight pits (from four of which coal is raised), varying in depth from 157 feet to 463 feet; they have a 14-feet bed lying at a grade of 3 degrees; the yearly output is 145,000 tons; and the rental is fixed at Rs. 860, without royalty. The adult employees are 774 in number.

The 14-feet seam of best Dishergarh seam coal at Bejdih runs through two pits, which range in depth from 873 feet to 1,097 feet. The workings are yet in the development stage, but when completed they are estimated to produce 140,000 tons per annum and find employment for 1,000 head of labour.

There are six inclines at Chowrassie, containing 9-feet seams of good second-class coal, lying at an angle of 16 degrees, upon which there is a rental of Rs. 1,948, together with a royalty of 4 annas per ton on steam coal, rubble, and coke, and 1 anna 6 pies per ton on dust. This mine has been closed since October 1913, when a fire occurred; but about half of the mine has since been recovered, and will be capable of producing 150,000 tons per annum. The Hurriladih mine has two pits and three inclines, with two seams of coal at an inclination of 6 degrees. One of these, No. 16, contains 8 feet of second-class coal, but it has not been worked to its fullest extent in consequence of arrangements now in progress for sinking the pits to No. 14 seam, 26 feet in thickness, which consists of a first class bed at a depth of 475 feet. A royalty is payable here of 5 annas per ton on steam coal and rubble and 10 annas on coke, together with 3 annas on dust.

It is estimated that there are yet some hundreds of millions of tons of first-quality coal which can be raised from these five collieries, and with even a greater output than exists at present, the life of these pits must inevitably be a long one.

The capital of the company consists of Rs. 400,000, in 6 per cent. cumulative preference shares divided into 4,000 shares at Rs. 100. together with

[1] A biggah is equivalent to 1,600 square yards, i.e. $3\frac{1}{40}$ biggahs to an acre.

Rs. 20,00,000 in ordinary shares, divided into 200,000 shares each of Rs. 10. The dividends paid on ordinary capital during the past ten years give an average annual amount of 24 per cent.

Another of the managing agencies held by Messrs. Macneill & Co. is that of the Nodiha Coal Company, which was registered in 1907, with an ordinary capital of Rs. 400,000, divided into 40,000 shares of Rs. 10. It is estimated that the beds of coal will eventually yield some 6,000,000 tons, although the present yearly output is only some 50,000 tons. The property, which is called Nodiha, is situated in the Raneegunge field, and comprises 1,427 biggahs.

A 7-foot seam of second-class Dishergarh coal, lying at an angle of 22 degrees, is worked from three inclines by 431 men and women, but no children are employed upon any part of the works. The royalties are 7 annas on steam and rubble coal, 4 annas on dust, and 10 annas on coke. Several causes have militated against a really satisfactory development of the mine up to the present time, and dividends paid average only 1½ per cent. per annum since the company's inception.

The Aldih Coal Company, registered in 1901, with an ordinary capital of Rs. 800,000, divided into 8,000 shares of Rs. 100, and debentures amounting to Rs. 3,27,000, are owners of the Aldih and Bhutguria collieries, consisting of 1,530 and 1,000 biggahs respectively, which are situated in the Raneegunge and Jherria fields. The coal at Aldih is of first-class quality, known as "Dishergarh," and it is worked from two pits —570 feet in depth—from a seam which is 14 feet in thickness. A royalty of 7 annas a ton is paid on all steam coal, coke, and rubble, and the total annual gross yield of 100,000 tons is obtained by 710 hands. There are no fewer than 790 male and female workpeople employed in the Bhutguria colliery, which produces about 100,000 tons of best coal yearly. No. 17 seam, measuring 7 feet 6 inches, is found in two pits, which are 226 feet in depth, and the annual rent is Rs. 7,702. An amount equivalent to an average of 11 per cent. per annum on ordinary capital has been paid in dividends since the year 1904.

The Hurriladih Coal Company was formed in 1901 with the object of acquiring coal-bearing properties in the Raneegunge and Jherria fields, and eventually they obtained the Ackalpore and Kenwadi collieries, comprising 2,430 and 1,322 biggahs respectively. The seams in the two mines vary in thickness from 4 feet 8 inches to 14 feet, and best first-class coal is obtained from six pits, which run from 209 feet to 240 feet in depth. These pits have an annual output of about 190,000 tons, and some 1,053 male and female hands are required constantly.

The ordinary capital of the company is Rs. 800,000, divided into 8,000 shares of Rs. 100, while the debentures amount to Rs. 375,000. Interest on ordinary capital has averaged 3½ per cent. per annum during the past ten years.

There is no debit for royalty at Ackalpore, but the yearly rent is Rs. 18,750; while at Kenwadih the rent is Rs. 2,615, in respect of a plot of 300 bigahs, plus a royalty of 4 annas a ton on all steam coal, coke, and rubble in respect of raisings from the 1,022 biggahs plot.

The authorized capital in the Mundulpoor Company is Rs. 850,000, representing 3,700 fully paid shares of Rs. 100, together with 8,000 shares of Rs. 100, of which Rs. 60 have been called up. There are four pits on this property, which are from 113 feet to 240 feet in depth, and a 6-foot bed of coal of first-class quality is already returning some 50,000 tons a year, although the mine has only been partially developed. The property comprises 2,430 biggahs, and some difficulty has been experienced owing to an unusually large quantity of water having been met with in the workings. About 320 hands are employed at present, but this number is being increased in proportion to the progress made in the further opening of the mine. Royalties are levied as follows: 6 annas on steam coal, 8 annas on coke, 3 annas on rubble, and 1½ anna on dust.

TATA, SONS & CO. (MICA MINES)

There is abundant evidence that the mica-mining industry in India is now being conducted under more scientific conditions than has ever been the case in the past. This is especially noticeable with regard to the use of both hand and power machinery and the systematic work of development being carried on by Messrs. Tata, Sons & Co.

This firm are owners of an estate of 2,500 acres at Kodarma, in the Province of Behar and Orissa, which province produces about 70 per cent. of the whole of the mica output from India.

The property comprises some twenty mines of importance as well as innumerable prospect workings. A description of one of the mines will suffice for these notes, as all now working are being developed on similar lines, subject, of course, to such modifications as the particular conditions of each may require.

The Thorna Mine is included in an area of about 160 acres, and comprises one main outcrop, having a strike of some 2,500 ft. by varying thicknesses up to 50 ft. There is also a second and parallel strike, rather less well defined. The main strike is being worked by a system of shafts, cross-cuts, and levels, blocking out large stoppages for future work. There are four shafts, the deepest being about 200 ft., and one main incline of 250 ft. The total amount of underground sinking and driving already aggregates 1,000 ft., and it is anticipated that this number will be very greatly increased in the near future.

As the steam power on this mine is 28 h.p., the principal prime movers being a large hauling engine, two small winches, and three pumping sets, there is, of course, no longer any question of permitting the productive mines to be flooded during the rainy season. Dynamite is used exclusively for blasting in the mine.

The rough mica crystals won are brought to the surface every morning and evening, and there split into sheets of about one-eighth of an inch in thickness and made up into bundles of 30 to 40 lb. in weight. These bundles are carried, under the charge of an armed guard, into the central godown at Kodarma, where the rough mica is further split into a convenient thinness for trimming, and this process is carried out by mica-cutters using sickles. The slab mica thus prepared is sorted and graded according to the standard sizes and qualities recognized by the industry, the smaller grades being sent on to the splitting factories.

The splitting of the small sizes into untorn films of uniform and excessive thinness is a process which demands the closest and most careful supervision, and Messrs. Tata, Sons & Co.'s "Pan" films are, perhaps, the finest of all manufactured ones.

Some 1,200 hands, engaged on piece-work and daily pay, are employed constantly on the mines, godowns, and splitting factories.

The staff consists of six Babus, five *mistris* and *classis*, and several Nepalese guards, while the general manager is Mr. J. F. Podger, Assoc.Inst.M.M., who is ably assisted by his brother, Mr. R. O. Podger.

TATA, SONS & CO.

1. Rough Mica from Thorna Mine. 2. Cutting Rough Mica 3. Making Pan Splittings. 4. Loading Carts for Shipment.

TATA, SONS & CO.

1. Headquarters, Bungalow, and Godowns. 2. No. 1 Shaft, Thorna Mine. 3. No. 2 Shaft, Thorna Mine. 4. Hauling-gear, Main Incline, Thorna Mine.

THE TATA IRON AND STEEL COMPANY, LTD.

Startling proposals have always been received with great reticence—such is the natural conservatism of the human race—and there has been no revolution in modern days in India which has had a greater effect upon the commercial world than that which has taken place since iron and steel became such important factors in the civilization of every-day life. The number of industries in this country in which these two substances are required in some shape or form is increasing at a very rapid rate, and one has only to notice the huge foundries, working at full speed, to understand that capitalists are taking their full share in the activities which are everywhere apparent.

An industry destined to become world-wide in importance is that recently started by the Tata Iron and Steel Company, Ltd., at Sakchi, near Kalimati station, on the Bengal-Nagpur railway system, about a hundred and fifty miles distant from Calcutta. The land selected for the site of the works is about twenty-three and a half square miles in extent, and in addition to the enormous shops and sheds which have been erected, the company have provided bungalows for officials, cottages for workmen, coolie lines, business offices, club and reading-rooms, schools, and a hospital with wards and dispensary.

There were five determining factors which the originators of the company set themselves to solve, namely: (1) supply of ore; (2) supply of coal; (3) supply of labour; (4) markets; and (5) means of transportation.

A number of very valuable and large deposits of iron ore have been found in the Mourbhanj State of Orissa, and as it was highly desirable that the company should not be dependent upon a fluctuating market for its fuel, about 4,600 acres of coal-producing land were obtained in the heart of the famous Jherria field. A further area of about 800 acres in the Raneegunge field has been acquired more recently. Limestone and dolomite quarries, and manganese mines have also been secured, and it is not too much to say that nearly all necessary raw materials are now derived from the properties of the company.

The immense buildings include foundries; machine and other shops; all of which are equipped with an enormous plant comprising (*inter alia*) coke ovens; blast furnaces; steel plant; heating pits; rail, blooming, and bar mills; electrical machinery; hydraulic, condensing, and filtering services; power house; the mechanical department, and many others.

The capital of the company is Rs. 2,31,75,000, and the directors are the following well-known public men: Sir D. J. Tata, Kt., special director; Sir Sassoon David, Bart., chairman; Sir Cowasjee Jehangir, Bart., Sir Vithaldas Damodar Thackersey, Kt., Mr. Gorhandas Khattau, the Hon. Sir Fazulbhoy Currimbhoy, Kt., Mr. Narotium Morajee Goculdas, Mr. M. A. Tata, Mr. C. V. Mehta, Sir Shapurji B. Broacha, Kt., Mr. Ratan Tata, and Mr. A. J. Bilimoria.

VIEW TAKEN ON THE ESPLANADE, CALCUTTA.
Illustration from "Oriental Scenery," by Thomas Daniell (1795).

KINCHENJUNGA RANGE.

Photo by M. Sain, Darjeeling.

DARJEELING

WHEN that portion of the Province of Bengal now known as the district of Darjeeling was added, in the early years of the nineteenth century, to the area then under British supremacy, an epoch was reached which virtually completed the history of the establishment of the British Empire in India, which may be said to have commenced with the defeat by Clive of Suraj-ud-Dowlah, the Nawab of Bengal, at the battle of Plassey in the year 1757. Darjeeling, as it then was, had the native State of Sikkim on its northern boundary, and the warlike Gurkhas had filched from the Raja of that State the Morang *tarai*, or level land of the district of Darjeeling as it is now constituted. A number of wars followed in 1814-16, and on the conclusion of hostilities a treaty was signed in which there was a clause to the effect that the strip of territory so appropriated should be given up to the British, who forthwith returned it to its former owner. In 1835, during the Governor-Generalship of Lord William Bentinck, the altitude and the bracing air of Darjeeling was recognized, and it is recorded that in the same year "the sanatorium of Darjeeling, with some of the surrounding hills—a territory comprising about 140 square miles—was purchased from the Raja of British Sikkim in consideration of an allowance of Rs. 3,000, which was afterwards increased to Rs. 12,000 per annum."

Possessing a remarkably pure atmosphere, and a climate calculated by its normally cool temperature to put new vigour into persons of indifferent health, it is not surprising that Darjeeling became a recuperating station for European troops, and, shortly afterwards, a summer residence of the Government of Bengal and its principal officials.

In 1849 Sir Joseph Hooker and Dr. Campbell (Superintendent of the Darjeeling district), with the approval of the British Government and the permission of the Raja, paid a visit to the State of Sikkim on a purely private and peaceful mission, but they were treacherously seized and imprisoned with the full knowledge, if not actually at the instigation of, the Raja himself.

As such an insult could not be allowed to be overlooked, a military expedition was sent to rescue the prisoners and to teach the Raja a much-needed lesson, and the result was that the chief's yearly allowance was discontinued, that the Sikkim *tarai* at the foot of the hills was annexed, and that British territory was also extended to mountainous regions in other directions. This newly acquired land comprised about 640 square miles, and in 1866 about 480 square miles of hilly country, which had been obtained from Bhutan in the previous year, were also added; and thus the district of Darjeeling, as it is known to-day, was finally constituted.

It forms the northern portion of the division of Rajshahi in Bengal; it is bounded on the east by Bhutan, the independent Hindu State of Nepal lies on the western side, and the State of Sikkim is on the north.

The district, which has an area of about 1,230 square miles, has two distinct natural divisions — namely, the deep valleys and ridges of the Lower Himalayas and the level country at their base. The ridges rise abruptly from the plains

A VIEW FROM THE MALL.
Photo by M. Sain, Darjeeling.

to heights varying from 6,000 feet to 10,000 feet above sea-level, and the majority of them are clothed with dense forests even to their summits.

The scenery in this neighbourhood is so magnificent that it must be seen to be appreciated, as a mere description must fail to give an adequate idea of its extreme beauty. A writer in the "Encyclopædia of India" (1908) says: "A spectator in Darjeeling town stands on the stage of a vast amphitheatre of mountains, which in the springtime form a continuous snowy barrier extending over 150 degrees of the horizon, from Gipmochi on his right hand to Sandakhphu on the left. The sides of the amphitheatre are formed by the Singalila chain, 20 miles to the west, and by the loftier Chola range, 40 miles to the east. In front of him, at a distance of 45 miles, the great twin peaks of Kinchinjunga, in the Himalaya range (28,146 feet), tower above the titanic group of snow-clad mountains which fill the northern horizon. The rising sun sheds a golden radiance on the eastern slopes, which turn to dazzling whiteness as the day wears on. At evening the western flanks catch all the rosy glow of sunset, and as the sun sinks behind the hills the crimson hue fades away, only to reappear in a delicate afterglow. At last even this disappears, but if the moon be near the full its light streams down upon the snows, outlining their contours with an awesome purity."

In the far distance one sees the backbone of the lofty Himalayas, while the Singalila range marks the boundary-line between the States of Nepal and Sikkim, and also between the district of Darjeeling and Nepal. The highest peaks of the Singalila range are: Senchal, 8,163 feet; Tanglu, 10,074 feet; Phalut, 11,811 feet; Sabargam, 11,636 feet; and Sandakphu, 11,930 feet.

The Himalayan range, however, may be said to comprise three distinct portions—namely, the vast range of snow-clad peaks the principal of which are Kinchinjunga and Mount Everest (28,994 feet); secondly, the lower Himalayas; and thirdly, the sub-Himalayan zone, which consists of ridges separated from the last-named region by fertile valleys.

The Darjeeling district belongs to the area of the lower Himalayas, and it is rendered conspicuous by the number of ranges which extend from north to south, the town of Darjeeling itself being situated at an altitude of 7,346 feet above the level of the sea.

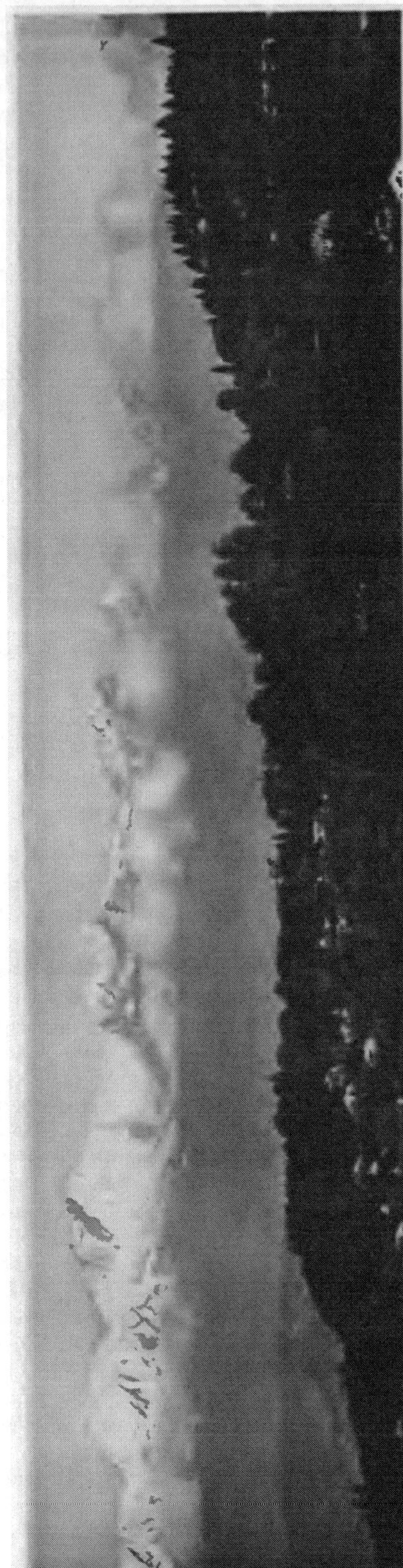

A VIEW FROM AUCKLAND ROAD.
Photo by M. Sain, Darjeeling.

Reserved forests include those portions of the mountains which are more than 6,000 feet in height, and of valleys below 3,000 feet ; while the intervening area lying to the east of the Teesta River is set apart chiefly for cultivation by natives, and the greater portion on the western side of the river is devoted to the production of tea.

Mountain slopes, which are yet untilled, are covered with tropical forest trees, while the undergrowth on the ridges, up to an elevation of some 2,000 feet, is very dense and luxuriant with choice ferns, the most delicately formed orchids, and mosses of every variety.

The lover of nature in its multitudinous aspects, however, will take pleasure in observing many types of beasts and birds, whose peaceful abode—until ruthlessly disturbed by wood-cutter or hunter—is in the jungly lairs or thickly leafed branches of this primeval forest. Elephants, tigers, wild hog, and several species of deer may be found on comparatively low land; bears are met with anywhere between 3,000 feet and 11,000 feet; leopards are still fairly common at all altitudes; and goats and antelopes, although somewhat rare, are seen in rocky fastnesses above 10,000 feet.

Government authorities divide the district of Darjeeling, for agricultural purposes, into three separate units—namely, (1) the mountains to the west of the Teesta River, (2) the Kalimpong area, and (3) the *tarai*. The staple industry is the growing and manufacture of tea, in which the proprietors of about 80 estates or gardens are concerned. The introduction of this plant into Darjeeling was due to the Government of Bengal, who were induced to obtain samples of seed from China for distribution among suitable persons in the district who were willing to experiment with them. The results of these trials were highly satisfactory, and in the year 1856 the first tea gardens were established at Alubari, Pandam, and Steinthal. The industry has progressed at a very rapid rate, and Darjeeling tea now commands high prices owing to its particularly fine flavour. The yield in this mountainous country may not be as great as in the plains, but the superior quality and better values more than counterbalance any deficiency in quantity. It may be mentioned that the majority of the gardens in this district are financed by British capital and are owned or managed by Englishmen.

Planters have recognized the necessity for the use of prime selected seed, and their efforts to obtain that standard have been warmly supported by the Government of Bengal, who have on various occasions imported fresh supplies for distribution.

Rice, maize (chiefly of American kinds), wheat, and other cereals are grown on suitable land, and fruits of choice varieties are to be seen in a large number of well-managed orchards.

Reserved forests, to the extent of about 400 square miles, are controlled by the Forest Department of the Government, and are under the supervision of a Deputy Commissioner. This district is noted for

1. MOUNT EVEREST (29,000 FT.) FROM SANDAKPHOO.
Photo by Himalayan Art Studio.

2. VIEW FROM TIGER HILL, DARJEELING.
Photo by M. Sain.

3. A VIEW FROM SANDAKPHOO.
Photo by Himalayan Art Studio.

the great variety of its trees, but the principal kinds are chestnut, silver fir, maple, magnolia, oak, birch, alder, and laurel.

General commercial trading is carried on to a large extent with many places, but the major portion of the transactions are with Calcutta merchants, the principal exports comprising tea, jute, and gunny-bags, while imports include Manchester piece goods, kerosene oil, and salt.

There is a plentiful supply of good labourers, and it is satisfactory to learn that these men are apt pupils in becoming acquainted with the intricate parts of the modern machinery and plant in tea and other factories.

Particular reference must now be made, however, to the town and neighbourhood of Darjeeling, as it is from that vantage-ground that one can behold the glories of the Himalayas, the richly clad slopes of the lower ranges, and the fertility of the cultivated land below.

On another page of this volume a description is given of the luxurious mail train which is run daily by the Eastern Bengal Railway Company from Sealdah Station, Calcutta, to Siliguri, its northern terminus. On arrival of the train at the latter station all comfort is at an end, as the northern passengers then travel by the 2-ft. gauge line of the **Darjeeling-Himalayan Railway** Company. The ruling gradient of the greater part of this line is about 1 in 25, from Sukhna to Ghum (the highest point on this section), and thence to Darjeeling there is a length of about three-quarters of a mile on grades of 1 in $22\frac{1}{2}$ to 1 in 23. Construction was commenced by Mr. Franklin Prestage in the year 1880, and the whole work to Darjeeling bazar was completed five years later.

Prior to the opening of this line, Darjeeling was practically inaccessible to tourists from Calcutta unless they had time and money to spare for a tedious journey, first by rail on the East Indian section to Sahebgunge, and thence by steam ferry and bullock cart, and the trip, which then occupied five or six days, can now be made in about twenty hours.

After the first half-dozen miles there is a steep gradient for the remainder of the journey, but in places where the ascent is at the sharpest gradient, engineering difficulties have been overcome by causing the permanent way to curve round mountain-sides in a most curious fashion. The keenest enjoyment is experienced as the higher regions are approached, and the stifling atmosphere of the plains, where the thermometer shows a temperature ranging from 85° to 95° Fahr., is succeeded by an exhilarating air which is at least 20° or 30° lower. It may be observed here that the mean temperature in Darjeeling during the cold and warm months is 41° and 60° respectively.

Views of striking beauty are continually being presented as the ascent is made, the huge mountain peaks in the distance vividly contrasting with the plains down below, which stretch away to the far-off horizon.

The name Darjeeling signifies "the place of the dorje," or the mystic thunderbolt of the Lamaist religion. The town, with the cantonments of Darjeeling and Leebong (which was constituted a municipality in the year 1850), had

1. VICTORIA FALL AND BRIDGE. *Photo by M. Sain.*

2. SUNDAY MARKET, DARJEELING. *Photo by Vanderlowen.*

3. THE RAILWAY STATION, DARJEELING. *Photo by M. Sain.*

a population of nearly 17,000 inhabitants at the census of 1911. It is situated upon a long ridge, upon which the major portion of the residences of Europeans are constructed on terraces one above another, and the highest and lowest points within the municipal area are respectively 6,000 to 7,800 feet above sea-level.

SUNRISE, DARJEELING, FROM TIGER HILL.

Photo by M. Sain.

Darjeeling is not a trading centre in the ordinary sense of the term, as its commercial activities are practically restricted to supplying the requirements of the tea-planters, and of the crowds of European inhabitants and visitors of the summer season.

The month of April in each year is marked by the exodus of H.E. the Governor of Bengal, of Government officials, and of a great many of Calcutta's influential citizens who are in the fortunate position of being able to turn their backs upon the torrid heat of streets in that busy port, and literally to revel in the enjoyment of a deliciously cool atmosphere and of some of the sublimest panoramic views in the world. It is not, of course, possible at all times of the year for the snowy summits of the giant Himalayas to be seen, as they are frequently entirely or partly obscured by mists ; but the months in which visitors are most likely to have their desires gratified are November, December, and January. It is then that the mountains stand out clearly on the skyline, and the fifty miles or thereabouts of intervening space are apparently reduced to a minimum owing to the remarkably clear atmosphere.

Numerous writers have made attempts to give descriptions of the glorious beauty of this enchanting scene, but all have failed to give an adequate representation of it.

VIEW FROM BIRCH HILL, DARJEELING.

Photo by M. Sain.

The Himalayas present a variety of scenery according to the locality from which it is viewed. One may take an easy walk to Observatory Hill, from which a remarkably fine picture of the everlasting snows is obtained on a favourable day; but the scene presented to the sightseer on this hill by the rays of the rising or setting sun touching the glistening peaks with colourings both delicate and rare is so gorgeous that the most artistic effects of the painter's brush would sink into insignificance in comparison with the original.

Senchal, seven miles in a south-easterly direction from Darjeeling, is another favourite resort for tourists ; but Tiger Hill (about 8,500 feet in height), if visited just before daybreak on a clear morning, probably affords the finest picture in a kaleidoscope of ever-changing beauties.

A word or two may be added here about Observatory Hill, which has been a sacred place for ages because of the presence of Mahapal Baba, who is worshipped by Buddhists and Hindus as a divine manifestation, and because its summit was once the site of one of their monasteries, which was destroyed by Gurkhas many centuries ago.

Visitors to this spot can scarcely be expected to obtain full enjoyment of the glorious surrounding scenery, as pious pilgrims engage in chanting, the ringing of bells, and in worshipping at a shrine enclosed by vertical poles, to which are attached flags that are believed to waft away to the gods the many prayers of the devout.

Several hundred feet below the summit of this hill is a monastery which contains a large number of idols, a library of sacred books, and mural paintings which certainly do not represent subjects calculated to uplift the thoughts of worshippers.

These places of interest are given merely as samples of the many show-places in the neighbourhood of Darjeeling, to which one may drive or walk in the certainty that entirely new effects may be witnessed daily owing to the varying conditions of sun and atmosphere.

The town not only contains the summer residence of H.E. the Governor of Bengal and the official quarters of heads of Departments, but it can boast of a number of excellent hotels, boarding-houses, private houses, a club, and several fine churches and schools, together with barracks at Kalapahar, Jalpahai, and Lebong.

St. Paul's School—founded in Calcutta in 1864 and shortly afterwards removed to Darjeeling—is built on an eminence

COOLIES, DARJEELING.
Photo by Himalayan Art Studio.

whence enchanting views are obtained, and Sir Joseph Hooker, referring to the site, said: "It is one quite unparalleled for the scenery it embraces, commanding the confessedly grandest known landscape of snowy mountains in the Himalayas, and hence in the world."

The club stands in an advantageous position in the town, and contains a large number of apartments for members, including reading, writing, smoking, and billiard-rooms, together with extensive stabling and motor garage. The Darjeeling Club, Ltd., was formed in 1908, but it was originally known as the Planters' Club.

The Secretariat is a fine three-storied building constructed of gneiss, locally obtained, and it contains the offices of the Chief Secretary to the Government, the Under-Secretary for the Political and Appointment Departments, and the Secretaries for Revenue; while other structures comprise the Imperial General Hospital, the Municipal offices, St. Andrew's Church, St. Paul's and other schools.

The only other places of any importance in the district are Kurseong, Kalimpong, and Tindharia.

Kurseong has in recent years come into some prominence as a growing hill

1. "MORNING LIGHT" FROM GOVERNMENT HOUSE, DARJEELING.
Photo by Himalayan Art Studio.

2. A BHUTIA BEGGAR, DARJEELING.
Photo by M. Sain.

3. SHRINE OF MAHAKAL, OBSERVATORY HILL, DARJEELING.
Photo by M. Sain.

station and sanitorium, and it is preferred by many visitors to whom a comparatively mild climate, consequent upon an altitude of only 4,860 feet above sea-level, is more beneficial than the higher elevation and keener atmosphere of Darjeeling. The town is the headquarters of a subdivision in the *terai*, and was constituted a municipality in the year 1879.

It possesses a club, the usual public offices, a Jesuits' Training College, and workshops of the Darjeeling-Himalayan Railway Company are situated at Tindharia. Shareholders in this company are receiving very satisfactory dividends upon their capital, but this is not surprising when the excessive passenger fares and freights are taken into consideration.

The line is undoubtedly all that it should be from an investor's point of view, but it is very far from being a real benefactor to the tea and other industries.

A VIEW FROM MACKENZIE ROAD.
Photo by Himalayan Art Studio.

good schools for both boys and girls. Kurseong has a station on the Darjeeling-Himalayan Railway, from which large quantities of tea are forwarded annually, and it is about twenty miles distant in a southerly direction from Darjeeling.

Kalimpong is a thriving village situated in a very healthy portion of the district, and is noted chiefly on account of a large annual fair at which consignments of agricultural produce and live stock are exchanged for English poultry and selected seeds of cereals. It is, further, the recognized market for the sale of Tibetan wool, and its agricultural show is second to none in importance in Bengal. The

RUNGNEET ESTATE

This estate of 400 acres, situated at an altitude of between 5,000 and 6,000 ft., and about one mile distant from Darjeeling, is one of the most attractive properties even in that wonderfully beautiful district, where the everlasting snows glistening in the sunlight on the summit of the mountains form such a magnificent contrast to the sombre yet variegated shades of the well-wooded slopes of the surrounding hills. Rungneet was acquired by the owner, Captain J. Oswald Little, in the year 1910, but the 190 acres of tea were then in full bearing, the first tea having been planted nearly half a century ago. The present proprietor devotes very great personal attention to the management of the estate; up-to-date methods of cultivation are practised; all vacancies are filled by vigorous and healthy young plants; and thus it happens that the yield of tea on this estate is noted particularly for its delicacy of flavour.

Quality and not quantity is the point kept in view by the owner, but the returns during an average season are about 3½ maunds to the acre. The factory contains the usual plant required in connection with the manufacture of tea, such as the machinery for rolling, sifting, and packing, together with a down-draught sirocco drier.

A water-power turbine is used for motive purposes, but as additional power is required during the season of heaviest work a steam engine has been fixed to meet such a contingency.

The "made" tea is packed in chests of various sizes on the premises, and the latter are consigned, principally in response to private orders, to many hotels,

RUNGNEET ESTATE.

1. Bungalow. 2 View of Tea Garden 3. Coolies Plucking Tea. 4. Factory.

THE VICTORIAN BREWERY.

1. The Bungalow. 2. Malt-House. 3. Bottling Plant. 4. General View of Brewery.

clubs, and regimental messes in India, as well as to customers in England and other parts of the world.

Captain Little occupies a charming bungalow, surrounded by terraced gardens containing the choicest English flowers and vegetables, and his residence is fitted with electric light and has telephonic communication with the town of Darjeeling. He takes a very keen interest in local affairs, and at the time of writing he has just been called upon, in view of his previous experience as a cavalry officer, to assume the Adjutancy of the North Bengal Mounted Rifles.

About two hundred coolies are generally employed on the garden, although in busy times this number may be exceeded.

The Calcutta agents of the estate are Messrs. Gillanders, Arbuthnot & Co., of Clive Street.

THE VICTORIA BREWERY

This brewery was erected in the year 1885 by the well-known firm of Messrs. Meakin & Co., but it was acquired in 1914 by Mr. H. J. Craddock, who purchased it as a going concern. It is situated at Sonada, near Darjeeling, and consists chiefly of a three-storied building of a pretentious character, together with brew-house, malting stores, bottling shed, warehouses, and offices standing upon two acres of freehold land, although the total extent of the land is rather more than 17 acres.

The first essential for the making of good beer is an abundance of pure water, and in this respect Mr. Craddock is fortunate in having an excellent supply from the hills in the neighbourhood of the brewery. The second point of importance is the absolute necessity for both barley and hops to be of undoubted quality, and here again the "Victoria" is in an advantageous position, as it obtains its grain from the district of Rewari, near Delhi (a corn centre unsurpassed in India), while the hops are from the best English and Pacific gardens.

Mr. Craddock had practical experience in five English breweries before he arrived in India in 1893, and he is now carrying on his Sonada business according to methods prevailing in the Old Country. The brewery premises contain a modern Pasteurizing plant, which enables the proprietor to ensure absolute purity, and analyses made from time to time by the Excise authorites show that both beer and stout are entirely free from arsenic or other deleterious ingredient. The principal brewings comprise pale ale, XX ale, XXX ale, and XXX stout; and the owner's godowns at Sonada are able to accommodate five hundred hogsheads.

The machinery is driven by an 8-h.p. steam engine, and about thirty-two hands are constantly employed in the brewery, cooperage, bottling, and other sheds.

Mr. Craddock has a large sale for beer and stout in local regimental and other messes, and consignments are also sent to all parts of Bengal and Assam, and even to certain places in Southern India.

M. SAIN

Several photographs bearing upon the literary matter in this volume have been obtained from the studio of Mr. M. Sain, of 22 Mackenzie Street, Darjeeling, and he has kindly allowed them to be reproduced here.

Mr. Sain was formerly connected in business with Mr. Thomas Paar, a well-known photographic artist at Darjeeling, but for the past two years he has been employed on his own account entirely. That he has been very successful in his studies of Nature and art is evidenced by the high-class character of the brush and camera productions which have had their birth in his studio, and he has reason to be proud of the fact that he has been awarded medals and certificates at various Arts Exhibitions in India on account of their excellence.

Mr. Sain's studio at the present time contains paintings and photographs of the exquisitely beautiful scenery of the district and town of Darjeeling, and of the grand Himalaya Mountains, with the vegetation of their lower slopes, and it is certain that a visit to it will mean a morning well spent.

GENERAL VIEW OF DARJEELING.
Photo by Himalayan Art Studio.

PANORAMIC VIEW OF DACCA, SHOWING SOME RESIDENCES OF PROMINENT EUROPEANS, WITH ST. THOMAS'S CHURCH IN THE DISTANCE

From Panorama of Old City of Dacca, published about 1847.

INDIGO IN BEHAR

By D. J. REID.

THE chief indigo districts in Behar lie to the north of the Ganges River, and comprise Muzaffarpur, Durbhanga, Champarun, and Chupra. Indigo is also cultivated in the districts, on the south of the river, Purneah, Monghyr, and Bhagalpur, but only to a very small extent as compared with the northern area. The first record of indigo being grown by Europeans in Behar is dated about 1778. The chief pioneer of the industry appears to have been a Mr. Alexander Noel (afterwards Noel & Co.); and it is also on record that Mr. Grand, a servant of the East India Company, whose widow subsequently married Talleyrand, was interested in indigo in Behar. The first European factories to be built were chiefly in the district now called Muzaffarpur, and among the oldest ones were Contai, dating back to 1778, Dooria 1780, and Singhia 1791. The last-named was perhaps the first concern in the Province to be owned by a European, as it appears to have originated as a saltpetre factory of the Dutch East India Company. It seems to be clear that there were about 12 European indigo concerns in existence in the Muzaffarpur district towards the end of the eighteenth century, while in Durbhanga, Champarun, and Chupra the first factories were not erected before the beginning of the nineteenth century. A very good criterion of the age of an indigo factory is in the size of the manager's bungalow, all the older factories having huge residences generally built on the most elementary architectural lines, giving the maximum of space with the minimum of accommodation or comfort. It is very evident that when these bungalows were built bricks and mortar were cheap. Throughout the nineteenth century the concerns in Behar steadily increased, and in 1896, the year preceding the advent of synthetic indigo, there were about 112 working, with a total output of about 80,000 maunds in a good season. In 1845, however, several large indigo concerns appear to have abandoned this plant in favour of sugar-cane, but the experiment did not last long, as in 1850 these concerns again reverted to indigo.

During the first part of the nineteenth century indigo was a most popular crop with the cultivator, and one of the greatest punishments possible was for an indigo factory to refuse to allow a cultivator to grow indigo for the factory. The reason for this may probably be found in the fact that in those early days money was scarce, and indigo was one of the few crops which could be turned into ready cash.

That the industry has been a real boon, especially to the landlord, in Behar is undeniable, as it brought a large flow of outside capital into the Province, and many a landowner has been saved from beggary, due to the ruinous practices of the *mahajans*, by the timely advances of large sums of money at reasonable interest from a neighbouring indigo concern.

An indigo concern consists of a number of factories grouped under the supervision of one manager, with usually a European assistant at each factory, or outwork, as it is termed. Some concerns consist of as many as seven or eight outworks, but the average is about three or four.

This system of grouping a number of factories under one manager is economical in working, but it has its limitations, and it is doubtful whether a single manager can efficiently supervise more than three or four. The concerns in Behar are privately owned, and the shares in these companies are calculated on the anna system, which means that a concern consists of sixteen "One Anna Shares," which are sometimes subdivided into "Pie Shares."

Indigo is cultivated under two systems, one of which is by direct cultivation of land held by the factory and known by the vernacular name of *Zerat*, while the other is called *Assamiwar*, and under it the tenants contract to sow a certain area of their holdings in indigo, and the factory contracts to pay a fixed price per acre irrespective of the condition of the crop. A modification of the *Assamiwar* system is known as *khuski*, whereby the cultivator contracts to sow a certain area with indigo, and to sell the green plants from this area at a fixed price per maund to the factory. Theoretically this system is the best, but in practice it is found that, owing to the very large number of small plots dealt with, it is impossible to give proper supervision and to check the weights of green plant.

Only a small proportion of the lands cultivated are directly owned by indigo factories in Behar. One of the reasons for this may perhaps be traced to the fact that in the old days, under the East India Company, it was not lawful for a European to be the direct owner of land in that Province. The remainder of the lands are held under several forms of tenure, the most common being an ordinary lease granted by local Indian landlords for a stated number of years.

Indigo factories can, however, under the Bengal Tenancy Act, acquire occupancy rights over certain lands, and a considerable area is held under this form of tenure. There is also a form of lease known in the vernacular as *makurry*, which is a lease in perpetuity and cannot under any circumstances be broken, although the holder can be sold up for default of rent. This document is very common in Behar, especially in the Champarun district, where many concerns hold large areas from the Bettiah Raj under this tenure. It is also a common practice for factories to acquire possession of lands by advancing moneys on mortgage.

Up to the end of the nineteenth century the only variety of indigo cultivated in Behar was *Indigofera sumatrana*, which was introduced into the Province some 150 years ago.

The cultivation and preparation of the lands for sowing are conducted from October to the end of February, the lands being hoed and cross-ploughed many times, all clods being thoroughly pulverized. In March the indigo is sown, and it is ready for manufacture by the end of June or the beginning of July. Two cuttings are generally obtained from the plant, and these are taken from July to the end of September, the yield of finished indigo being greatly affected by the character of the monsoon, a heavy monsoon being unfavourable to the production of indigotin, and also to the growth of the second cuttings. The heaviest yield is obtained from the first cuttings, and in good years, when the monsoon is light, 50 per cent. of the amount obtained from the first yield may be expected from the second cuttings, but in unfavourable years of heavy rainfall the latter are often a complete failure. The seed of *Indigofera sumatrana* used in Behar has always been obtained from the United Provinces, the best kind coming from the districts in the neighbourhood of Cawnpore, the reason for this being that although the indigo plant can be grown to produce seed in Behar, yet the germination of such seed is always defective owing to a hard outer coating, and it was found that seed grown on the irrigated lands of the United Provinces is free from this objection.

In 1904 a new variety of indigo was introduced from Java, known as *Indigofera arrecta*. This type came originally from Natal, and is really an improved variety of the wild indigo of that country; but owing to the difficulty in obtaining seed its cultivation was extended rather slowly, and it was not until 1906 or 1907 that it was grown to any extent in Behar. The superiority of the Natal over the Sumatrana type was very marked when first introduced, and in many instances yields of 100 per cent. greater than those of the older variety were obtained; but it was unfortunate that, in common with many newly imported varieties, the plant was attacked by disease. The most disastrous effect of this is the restriction of seed production, and although the plant was at first found to seed freely in Behar, the supply subsequently decreased so enormously that in latter years it became unobtainable in any quantity, and many concerns had to revert to the old Sumatrana variety. This problem, however, is now being investigated by Mr. Howard, the Imperial Economist Botanist at Pusa, and there are hopes that a way has been discovered of growing *Indigofera arrecta* for seed in Behar.

Notwithstanding the disease and shortage of seed supply, average yields of more than 20 seers of finished indigo to the acre have in many instances been obtained, and in selected fields returns of fully 1 maund have been known. When it is considered that the old Sumatrana variety only yields an average of about 8 seers per acre, the advantages of the Arrecta variety are obvious; and it is quite possible that when a better knowledge of the plant is acquired it may prove a profitable crop, despite the competition of the synthetic article.

The methods employed for extracting the finished indigo from the green plant are very simple and also very ancient. In the old days the manufacture was performed by hand labour alone, but in more modern times machinery has been introduced, although the actual process remains the same. The machinery employed in the factory is simple, and consists of two or three pumps and an engine for working the paddle-wheel in the oxidizing vats. The green plant, when brought from the fields, is placed in the steeping vats, and the latter are then filled with water, the dimensions of the vats varying somewhat, but the usual size being about 1,500 cubic feet. Between 120 and 150 maunds of green plant are "loaded" into 1,000 cubic feet of vat room, but this amount varies according to the state of the plant and to the ideas of different planters with regard to heavy or light loading. The correct steeping of the plant is one of the most important operations in the manufacture of indigo, and the time usually allowed is about 12 hours; the actual period, however, is regulated by the temperature of the vat. Extensive experiments were carried out in this line by Mr. Rawson, F.I.C., from 1898 to 1903; and while his inquiries failed to show any important results, he considered that under optimum conditions there was very little room for improvement on the present methods of steeping. In order to carry out this process efficiently, it is necessary for all indigo factories to have a good supply of pure water, as its purity has a great effect on the quality of the indigo produced. In this respect Mr. Rawson reported that the mineral matter present in water was of very little consequence as a determining factor, but that much depends on the presence or absence of organic matter, especially of minute living forms.

After the steeping operation is completed the liquid is run off into another vat, known as the "beating vat," and there it is oxidized by the simple process of agitating the liquid so as to mix it with air. This agitation was in former days performed by hand-beating with wooden paddles, but in modern days a paddle-wheel is revolved in the vat by machinery. Oxidization generally occupies about 1½ hours, after which time the liquid turns from a bright green to a dark blue colour with a purple or reddish tinge. It is then allowed to settle, and the indigo *fæculæ* precipitate to the bottom of the vat; the top water is then drawn off, and the indigo is collected and pumped into large boilers.

The boiled indigo is then run on to a straining table, and when nearly all of the water has been strained off the residue is collected and put into presses and the remaining fluid pressed out. The hard slab of indigo is then removed from the press and cut into cubes of 3 inches square, which are placed on racks to dry, the final drying operation occupying about three months. The *Indigotera arrecta* variety is treated more or less in the same manner, with the exception that it has been found to be better to steep it in warm water, which is heated by steam as it runs into the steeping vat.

After the cakes are dry they are packed in large wooden chests, each containing about $3\frac{3}{4}$ maunds of indigo. The weight of this product, however, varies greatly, as superfine indigo will not scale more than $2\frac{3}{4}$ maunds to the chest, while very poor samples will weigh as much as 5 maunds for a chest of the same size, this difference being due to the large amount of impurities contained in the inferior kind. The largest market in the world for indigo has always been Calcutta, where a very large proportion of the produce of Behar factories is sold, although a few planters vary this procedure by sometimes shipping direct to London. Prior to the coming of synthetic indigo, the Calcutta sales were roughly distributed as follows: Great Britain, 30 per cent.; Europe, 50 per cent.; America, 16 per cent.; Suez, 4 per cent. In latter years, however, since synthetic was available, the Arabs have become the best customers, and now take about 35 per cent. of the crop. In former days indigo was sold according to its appearance, and fancy prices were often paid for favourite marks; but in the present day all consignments are analysed, and subsequently disposed of on the basis of such tests of the indigotin contained in them.

The amount of finished indigo recovered from a given quantity of green plant varies to an extraordinary extent, from 300 to 400 per cent. being a common occurrence. Cold and rainy weather is detrimental to good produce, but often, from no apparent reason, produce will be low in quantity. It is obvious, therefore, that the efficiency of extraction is dependent on a multiplication of causes, such as the water supply used for steeping, the temperature of the air, and the condition of the plant itself. From *Indigotera sumatrana* 12 to 14 seers of finished indigo per 100 maunds of green plant is considered a good return at most factories, while the Arrecta kind often yields as much as 18 to 20 seers per 100 mounds of plant. The average yield per acre from these two types is respectively about 8 seers, and 12 to 14 seers finished indigo.

In 1877 the Behar Planters' Association was formed, and in 1878 Mr. W. B. Hudson (afterwards Sir William Hudson) became secretary. The duties of the Association were to control the relations between the planter and the cultivator, and the past history of Behar speaks well for the manner in which the Association has performed its obligations. In 1897 came the great crisis in the indigo industry, as in that year the synthetic product was first put on the market; and the effect on the natural produce was instantaneous, seeing that prices for the latter, during the three succeeding years 1897 to 1899, dropped to Rs. 152/- per maund, as compared with an average price of Rs. 234/- per maund obtained in the three preceding years 1894-6, while in 1904 ordinary consuming indigo was selling as low as Rs. 100/- per maund. This enormous fall in values had the inevitable effect of reducing the cultivation of indigo, and in 1914, when the Great European War began, there were only 59 concerns still growing indigo, with very reduced cultivations, and producing about 7,000 maunds, as against about 112 concerns, with an average production of more than 65,000 maunds, that were working before the synthetic indigo was invented. The effect of the war, however, with its consequent shutting off of all supplies of dye from Germany, was extraordinary. Prices for ordinary indigo in Calcutta leapt from Rs. 155/- to Rs. 675/- per maund, and those concerns which had still remained true to the old dye reaped a good harvest. These very high figures had the natural effect of stimulating cultivation, and in 1915 a considerably larger area was sown; but, unfortunately, the previous depression of the industry had greatly curtailed the supply of seed. Indigo is not a crop in which the finished product can be also utilized as seed, as the plant has either to be kept for seed or turned into dye—"You cannot eat your cake and have it." The boom in 1914 came too late to save any extra plant for seed, with the result that the latter, for any great increase of cultivation, was unobtainable for 1915. It followed that a good deal of very inferior seed was sown, and this, coupled with an unfavourable monsoon, restricted the produce, with the result that the total output for Behar in 1915 was not very much larger than for the previous year. Referring to the competition of the synthetic indigo, it is very often stated by chemists and other scientists (whose knowledge of the practical side of any question is generally limited) that the success of the synthetic product over natural indigo is greatly due to the lassitude and indifference of the planter, who, when he was in possession of a monopoly, neglected to fortify himself against any possible competition by research into methods of improving his existing processes. That no such attempt was ever made is true, but whether the whole onus of this neglect can be laid at the door of the planter is another matter. If the position of the indigo industry of British India be considered, it will be seen that it would have been unreasonable to expect any private individuals, either singly or in groups, to have borne the cost of research in methods of manufacture. Indigo was produced in practically every Province throughout the length and breadth of India by all sorts and conditions of people, and the result of any research in the improvement of manufacture would have become public property. The position of the indigo industry in India, spread as it was over such a wide area, therefore absolutely excluded any hope of organized research being undertaken, unless initiated by some central authority, with power to distribute the cost of such proceedings on all producers. Such a central authority was obviously the Government of India, and the entire blame for the lack of foresight in instituting inquiries (as regards manufacture, at least) is due to that authority. There is one impeachment, however, which can justly be laid at the door of the Behar indigo-planter, and that is his neglect to make any efforts to improve or guarantee the purity of his seed supply. As might have been anticipated, this neglect resulted in a marked deterioration of the *Indigotera sumatrana* plant. The Behar planter bought his seed from the United Provinces, his object being to grow a plant full of leaf, as that is the only portion of the plant from which indigo is extracted; while the seed-grower's object, on the other hand, was to grow a plant that yielded plenty of seed, and he was indifferent about leaf.

As there was no supervision exercised to see that the seed supplied was obtained from suitable plants, the indigo in later years in Behar showed a marked tendency to early flowering and seeding, which was very prejudicial to the yield of indigotin, as the percentage of the latter in the leaf during those periods is greatly reduced. Quite recently efforts have been made to secure a pure supply of seed of the

Indigofera sumatrana, but they were too late to be of any material assistance to the industry. It is possible, however, that had proper attention been paid to improvement of the plant the position of the industry to-day in Behar might have been very different, as it is an undeniable fact that crops are greatly improved by a scientific selection of seed, but no such attempt at improvement was ever made until recent years.

After the appearance of synthetic indigo in 1897, the Indian Government awoke to its responsibility on the subject, and an annual grant in aid of research was sanctioned, such amount being further supplemented from the Behar Planters' Association's funds. In 1898 Mr. C. Rawson, one of the most prominent chemists connected with the dyeing industry in England, was engaged to conduct researches into the manufacture of indigo. Mr. Rawson worked on this matter up to 1903, when he was succeeded by Mr. Bergtheil; and, after exhaustive experiments, both these gentlemen reported finally that, as a commercial process, the old method of manufacture could not be improved upon. Their results showed that under normal conditions 85 per cent. of the indigotin in the plant was extracted, and that the cost of recovering the remaining 15 per cent. would be prohibitive. These conclusions have, however, been challenged by Mr. Bloxham, another chemist, who is of the opinion that only 60 per cent. of the dye is recovered under existing methods of manufacture. However this may be, it was decided in 1909 to abandon any further experiments in manufacture, and to devote all attention to the botanical side of the question with the view of producing a plant with an increased indigotin content. Mr. Parnell, a botanist, was then engaged, and he, in conjunction with Mr. Bergtheil, carried on scientific work in this direction. It was subsequently found, however, that the Research Station at Sirsia, in the Muzaffarpur district, was not suitable for a botanical station, as, owing to its liability to periodical flooding, a great deal of the work was lost, and in 1913 it was decided to abandon the experiment at that place. Research work has, however, been taken over by the Imperial Government and placed under the direction of Mr. Howard, the Imperial Economic Botanist at Pusa. About 8 lakhs of rupees were spent on research work by the Behar Planters' Association, aided by the Government.

Although Messrs. Rawson and Bergtheil did not succeed in obtaining any important results, yet their labours have in some way guided the industry in its efforts to reduce the cost of production. It was Mr. Rawson who first pointed out that the indigo refuse (or *seeth*, as it is known as) could be much more profitably employed in manuring other crops than indigo, and it is by utilizing this *seeth* as a valuable by-product that it has been made possible to continue the cultivation of indigo to the limited extent that now exists. It has been shown that very heavy returns can be obtained from such crops as tobacco and wheat if manured with indigo refuse, and the result is that most concerns have adopted a system of rotation, and by judiciously combining the crops a fair profit can be secured. The combination of indigo with other crops has also, from a financial aspect, improved the methods of working the indigo industry. In former days, when indigo alone was grown, a very large working capital was necessary, and the fact that this large outlay was almost entirely at the mercy of the vagaries of the monsoon made the industry very speculative. The average outlay per acre in Behar was usually about Rs. 30/-, and as the average return of finished indigo per acre was only about 8 seers, it follows that the manufacture of 1 maund cost about Rs. 150/-. The greater part of this outlay of Rs. 30/- per acre was expended before the monsoon set in and before the crop was ready to cut, the heaviest expenses being in the rents of the lands, cultivation, and seed. If there was an early and abnormally heavy monsoon, followed by the usual flood, it often happened that a large portion of the crop was absolutely destroyed, while the yield from the remainder would be very disappointing. In years, therefore, of this description it might happen that the cost per maund of made indigo was very nearly Rs. 350/-. Now, as the average price of Behar indigo in the Calcutta market for the ten years 1888 to 1897 was Rs. 230/, it can be realized that in some seasons very heavy losses had to be faced independently of interest on the outlay. The indigo financial year usually commenced in October, but as the proceeds were not realized until January or February of the following year, the money spent in October had to carry interest for 15 to 16 months before it was repaid. It is these difficulties which probably account for the fact that when the crisis with the synthetic product came so many of the Behar concerns were found to be heavily mortgaged. Unless a planter had the necessary capital at his back to tide over the bad years, it was practically impossible for him to steer clear of debt.

It remains to be seen what the future has in store for the indigo industry of Behar, as it is possible that for many years to come the Germans will not be in a position to produce synthetic indigo at the very low rate which obtained before the war. For the ten years preceding hostilities ordinary Behar indigo sold at an average price of about Rs. 140/- per maund, and, unit for unit, this was some 35 per cent. higher than the rates obtained for synthetic dye. If on the conclusion of the war Rs. 175/- per maund could be obtained for any length of time, it is possible that the cultivation will be considerably increased ; and if Mr. Howard, at Pusa, can master the difficulties of the cultivation of *Indigofera arrecta*, such a price, combined with the increased yield of the latter variety, should show a very fair profit. It is, however, an undoubted fact that for indigo to recapture its lost position in the dyeing world it must, irrespective of price, be offered to the dyers in a more standardized form than at present. What the dyeing trade requires is a paste or powder which could be guaranteed to contain a stated amount of indigotin. This question was discussed at an indigo conference called by the Imperial Government of India, at Delhi, in February 1915, when the Behar Planters' Association, through their representatives, asked for the addition of a chemist to the Pusa establishment to investigate the possibility of turning indigo into a standard paste or powder, but up to date, however, the matter is still under discussion.

If a cheap and practicable way of turning out natural indigo in a standardized paste can be arrived at, there is no doubt that dyers would give preference to such a preparation over synthetic, provided that prices were more or less equal. It remains, however, to be seen what the Germans can do after the war, and if their cost of production is appreciably increased it is possible that the natural indigo will yet regain some of its lost markets.

Most of the principal indigo estates will be found fully described and illustrated in another section of this volume.

SONEPORE MALA FESTIVAL.

BEHAR AND ORISSA—EARLY HISTORY

By ARNOLD WRIGHT

BEHAR AND ORISSA, which have been constituted into a single administrative unit under the recent scheme of territorial reorganization in Eastern India, are regions which in the past have played a great part in Indian life. As, however, their history is closely interwoven with that of Bengal proper, which has been dealt with in the general historical survey at the commencement of the volume, it is unnecessary to do more here than briefly touch upon some of the distinctive features of their record. Dealing first with Behar, it is to be noted that this famous subdivision of the old Bengal Presidency has figured very extensively in Indian history. The principal town, named after the old subdivision, is supposed to have been the capital of the ancient kingdom of Majadha. Extensive Buddhist remains at various places, and notably at Nalanda, a famous seat of learning in the days of the Pal kings, attest the great antiquity and historical importance of the locality.

In regard to Orissa, as Sir W. W. Hunter observes in his well-known work, no part of India has attracted less notice from the historians than this Province. "The tempests of conquest and the tidal waves of nations that have swept across the rest of India, rarely overtopped the ridges which wall out these shores. Sanskrit literature, in its prehistoric panorama of the upper valleys of the Ganges, reaches the last of the slow-moving scenes far to the north of Orissa. . . . The great epic itself, with its bright nucleus in Hindustan, and its broad, comet-like tail curving downwards in streams of light to the farthest point of the peninsula, shed not a momentary flicker over Orissa."

The early Buddhist remains to be found in Orissa are of an extremely interesting character, and attest the great antiquity of the Province. They date, it has been surmised, as far back as the third century before the Christian era, and give evidence of the presence of extensive Buddhist colonies in that remote period. Orissa Buddhism is of interest from the fact that it is believed to have been from these colonies that Java was colonized in or about the first century after Christ.

The history of Orissa subsequent to this period differs very little from that of a very large part of the territory now under British rule in Eastern and Southern India. The Province was originally a part of the Kalinga kingdom, and shared in the vicissitudes of the powerful dynasty that reigned over that great country which stretched from the Ganges to the Godavery. On the decline of the Kalinga power in the first centuries of the Christian era, Orissa appears to have become independent. In the seventh century records show it to have been separately under the authority of Sasanka, King of Majadha, and Harshavardhana of Kananj. Considerably later, in the tenth and eleventh centuries, the Kesari kings held sway, and to them is attributed the building of the Saiva temples at Bhubaneswar and most of the ruins in the Alti hills. After the Kesari kings came the dynasty founded by Chora Ganga of Kalinganajar, who built the famous temple of Jaganath at Puri and the black pagoda of Konarak. Mahommedan influence commenced seriously to assert itself in the fourteenth century, when Firoz Shah conducted in person an expedition into Orissa. With varying fortunes lines of Hindoo kings, however, continued to reign until 1568, when Mukund Deo, the last of the race, was overthrown by Kala Pahar, the general of Sulaiman Kararani, the Afghan chief. The hold of the conquerors on the Province was not a substantial one, and in 1592 the territory was annexed to the Mogul empire by Akbar.

Orissa remained under the Moguls until 1751, when Ali Vardi Khan ceded the Province to the Mahrattas—the Bhonslas of Nagpur. The new owners, after the manner of their people, treated their possession with great harshness, harrying and oppressing the people and wasting their lands. In the circumstances it must have been with a sense of relief that the unfortunate inhabitants were transferred to British power as a result of the successful campaigns against the Mahrattas in 1803. At the outset the British administration in the Province was vested in a board of two Commissioners, but this arrangement quickly gave place to a more settled scheme, by which the territory, under the designation of the District of Cuttack, was placed in charge of a Collector, Judge, and Magistrate. In 1828 there was a further change, the Province being split up into three regulation districts of Cuttack, Balasore, and Puri, and the non-regulation tributary States. These arrangements continued until the recent changes gave the division a more dignified status in the Indian administration.

A word in conclusion as to the derivation of the name of the Province. Orissa is so called from Odra or Ntkala, the name given to the northern Kalinga kingdom. Why this nomenclature was used has long been a matter of controversy. Hindus have suggested that the word is associated with *unda* ("dirt"), and that Orissa was the filthy land in aboriginal times. "The orthodox," says Hunter, "insist that it means the 'glorious country'; lexicographers suggest that it may only be the land of the bird killers; and an admirable student of the modern Aryan tongues interprets it as the 'outlying strip.'" There is, therefore, as Hunter well says, a large choice for the reader to make his selection from.

THE PROVINCE OF BEHAR AND ORISSA

THE Province had no independent history as far as civil administration was concerned until the year 1912, as it had up to that time been included in the Province of Bengal. The district of Assam was also included in the same administration. The Governor-General of India, by Act of Parliament in 1834, became also Governor, without Council, of Bengal, and this arrangement as to territorial jurisdiction was, with a few slight changes, continued until 1874.

A TEMPLE AT GAYA.

In that year it was considered that the control of the Province of Assam pressed unduly upon the administration of Bengal, and therefore Assam, together with the districts of Sylhet, Cachar, and Garo Hills, was detached from Bengal and became a separate administration under a Chief Commissioner.

In 1903, when the area of Bengal comprised about 196,408 square miles, with a population of some 78,493,300 persons, a movement began for a drastic rearrangement of territorial areas in that part of India. Several minor alterations took place, but it was ultimately decided to divide Bengal, and attach the eastern portion of it, including the Dacca, Chittagong, Rajshahi, and other commissionerships of Assam, and thus form a new Province to be known as "Eastern Bengal and Assam." This proposal was carried into effect under the Governorship of Lord Curzon on October 16, 1905.

Under the new arrangement Bengal was left with an area of 148,592 square miles, and about 54,662,529 inhabitants. Grave discontent arose in consequence of the partition, which was felt by many Bengalis to be a blow to their racial interests and unity. Their grievances were taken up in England by leading men in political life, and a powerful movement, ultimately successful, was launched to secure a reconsideration of the arrangements for the revision of the administration of the Province.

At the Coronation Durbar of His Majesty the King-Emperor George V at Delhi in 1911, the Royal assent was given to a new scheme providing for the reunion of Bengal, on lines which were generally acceptable to Indians. The proposals took formal shape in a proclamation issued on March 22, 1912. This rescript reconstituted the Province of Bengal, elevating it to the status of a Presidency Government, and provided for the union of the divisions of Behar and Orissa, and their constitution into a separate province under a Lieutenant-Governor, while Assam took its place in the new system as a Province under a Chief Commissioner.

The Province of Behar and Orissa now comprises five divisions (under Commissioners), in which there are 21 districts, together with the Feudatory States of Orissa.

The Patna division contains the districts of Patna, Gaya, and Shahabad.

The Tirhut division consists of the districts of Saran, Champarun, Muzaffarpur, and Darbhanga.

The Bhagalpur division embraces the districts of Monghyr, Bhagalpur, Purnea, and Sonthal-Perganas.

The Orissa division includes the districts of Cuttack, Balasore, Angul, Puri, and Sambalpur.

The Chota-Nagpur division comprises the districts of Hazaribagh, Ranchi, Palamau, Manbhum, and Singhbhum.

The Province is bounded on the north by the independent State of Nepal, and the district of Darjeeling in Bengal; on the east by the Presidency of Bengal; on the south by the Bay of Bengal and the Presidency of Madras; and on the west by the United Provinces of Agra and Oudh, and the Central Provinces.

It comprises about 111,829 square miles of land (including the Feudatory States) and is in reality divided into two parts by the River Ganges, which traverses it from west to east.

The northern portion, called Behar, consists very largely of an extensive fertile plain which slopes down gradually from the foot of the Himalaya range of mountains towards the River Ganges, where the elevation is somewhat higher. The greater portion of the soil is of a yellowish clay colour, but in some parts the land has been defaced by the numerous rivers and streams which rush down from the Himalayas and have carried with them a considerable quantity of silt and sand.

On the southern side of the Ganges the effects of the Himalayan effluents are not so apparent as in the northern portion, especially towards the eastern boundary, where the undulating and sometimes hilly section of the Chota-Nagpur division defeats the action of the fluvial torrents.

The Orissa portion of the Province—stretching from the south of Behar to the west, is, generally speaking, a vast alluvial plain, of which the southern and central parts comprise the delta of the great Mahanadi River, while the northern area has been largely formed by deposits washed down from the Chota-Nagpur plateau. Farther to the south of this plain are the rocky ranges of the Feudatory States.

The principal rivers are the Ganges, which flows into the Province from the United Provinces, and which during its course in an easterly direction to Bengal receives the Gogra, the Sone, and the Gandak, all of these being important waterways; the Mahanadi, a magnificent river of great breadth and depth which is navigable for large flat-bottomed boats through the Feudatory States and as far north as Sambalpur; and the Baitarani, navigable only for small boats.

The forests of Behar and Orissa under Government control are about 3,700 square miles in extent (exclusive of vast areas in the Feudatory States), and these are supervised by a conservator and four Imperial and eight Provincial officers whose appointments were sanctioned by the Government of India.

Agricultural pursuits occupy a most prominent position among the industries of the whole Province, and the principal crops are rice, jute, cotton, indigo, wheat, barley, maize, oil-seeds, sugar-cane, tobacco, and a number of indigenous food-stuffs. The total area under various kinds of *bhadoi* non-food crops, such as jute, indigo, early cotton, and others, is about 793,600 acres in extent, while that under cultivation for *rabi* crops comprises about 9,344,000 acres.

Rice has from time immemorial been the staple food-crop of the native inhabitants of India; in fact, the grain is generally known by the name of *dhan* or *dhanya*, the latter word in Sanskrit signifying "the supporter or nourisher of mankind."

Government statistics for the year 1911 showed that the Province contained approximately about 53,200,000 acres; further, that the total cultivated area comprised some 27,400,000 acres; and that the ricefields were about 17,200,000 acres in extent. From these figures it will be seen that rice covered 32 per cent. of the gross area, and about 63 per cent. of the actual cropped area.

The most important district for the growing of jute is Purnea, which yields fully 85 per cent. of the total crop of that plant in the Province, but the fibre is not so good in quality as that which is exported from Bengal.

The district of Ranchi is famous for its splendid crops of cotton—especially the early species—and the annual yield of early and late kinds grown in the Province is about 20,000 bales, and one half of this quantity is obtained from this district.

Although wheat and barley are essential for food purposes, it is found that the annual returns vary to a very considerable degree, but these differences in yield are due less to the nature of the soil than to the manner of its cultivation. Such

CARVINGS ON THE GATEWAY OF A TEMPLE IN ORISSA

primary conditions as the cleaning of the land, deep ploughing, irrigation (where necessary), and the application of manures are either ignored or are not understood, and therefore it is not surprising that the average yields do not exceed five and a half *maunds* per acre for wheat and about ten *maunds* for barley. These two products are cultivated to the extent of 1,200,000 acres and 1,428,200 acres respectively.

Maize is growing in importance, and its area of cultivation is being extended very considerably.

Indigo concerns are found chiefly in Northern Behar, in the Champaran, Muzaffarpur, Darbhanga, Saran, Purnea, Monghyr, Bhagalpur, and Shahabad districts.

Methods of agriculture in all parts of the Province are, as a rule, practised in an exceedingly primitive manner, the great majority of the smallholders not caring to deviate from the hoary customs which have been handed down from generation to generation. Sons cultivate as their fathers and grandfathers did; why should they adopt new-fangled operations? Why should they pay attention to reports of heavier crops gained by improved tillage, of increased value of yields, or of a greater return for capital expended? This, in a word, describes the state of affairs which the Agricultural Department of the Province is seeking to remedy by practical demonstrations on experimental farms and by theoretical teaching in colleges, and even in village schools.

Agricultural stations have been established at Cuttack, Bankipore, Sabour, and Dumraon, at which work of an experimental character is carried on, while there are also two small demonstration farms at Angul and Sambalpur. Interesting and instructive experiments are being conducted by Government experts at Sabur, in the district of Bagalpur, with regard to different varieties of sugar-cane, on the character and quality of their fibres, and the effect of certain manures upon the time of ripening of the cane. Investigations are also being made at some or all of the stations into matters relating to the types of wheat, barley, rice, and other cereals which should be selected for various districts. The colleges furnish instruction in practical agriculture, chemistry, botany, mycology, entomology, bacteriology, and other similar subjects.

Divisional agricultural associations render efficient help to the Government of the Province by reporting upon the particular types of seeds and manures which are most suitable for their areas, and, further, upon such questions as rainfall, irrigation, yields and prices of crops, and by giving information as to the labour market in each district.

The most important mineral industry in the Province is the mining of coal, which is assuming immense proportions in the Jherria, Giridih, Hazaribagh, Palamau, and other colliery areas. These fields were practically undeveloped until railway companies extended their systems into those areas, when a remarkable demand sprang up for locally produced coal for fuel for locomotives, factories, mills, steamers, and household purposes. Minor industries in the five divisions may be referred to briefly as follows: Patna division—there are comparatively few evidences of any important advance having been made in recent years, although occupation is found for a large number of inhabitants in the manufacture of saltpetre, carpets, *dhurries*, copper and brass utensils, woollen blankets, palanquins, *ekkas*, boots, glass, wooden furniture, and gold and silver embroidery and cloth.

Sugar-refining is carried on at Sasaram and Buxar in the district of Shahabad, and in the first-mentioned place there is considerable activity in the quarrying of limestone and the burning of lime. The latest statistics show that 44,138 tons of limestone, 2,050 tons of ballast, and 1,649 tons of lime were exported in one year. There are also large flour and oil-pressing mills at Dinapore.

The division of Tirhut is noted chiefly for a very large increase in the area devoted to the cultivation of sugar-cane and in the number of refineries, and it is evident that the manufacture of sugar is taking the place of indigo concerns in many of the districts. Railway sleepers are made in the districts of Champaran and Darbhanga. In the division of Bhagalpur the industries include the manufacture of country cigarettes (known as *biris*), indican, silk and cotton cloths, bricks, steel trunks, guns, and sugar, while the smelting of iron is carried on by the Kols at Deogharh and Godda, the metal being used in the manufacture of spades, padlocks, ploughshares, and domestic articles. Filigree silver work manufactured in the division of Orissa is recognized throughout India for its artistic beauty, while the making of tassar and cotton cloths, fine muslins, and brass and bellmetal utensils and ornaments gives employment to a very large number of people.

Coal mining is the most important industry in the division of Chota-Nagpur, and the annual output from the district of Manbhum alone exceeds the quantity produced in the whole of the remaining portion of British India. Tea is produced in the district of Hazaribagh; tassar cloths in Manbhum; shellac, coarse cotton cloths, and brass articles in all districts; and granite and limestone quarries are worked in several commercial centres. Industrial concerns of comparatively recent establishment, but employing large numbers of hands, include the extensive works of the Tata Iron and Steel Company, Ltd., at Sakchi, the mining operations of the Cape Copper Company, Ltd., at Matigará, and the Bengal Iron and Steel Company, Ltd., at Dina and Turramdih.

The frontier trade of the Province is carried on exclusively with Nepal, the principal imports being rice and other food grains, livestock, hides, skins, jute, and oil-seeds, while the exports include cotton yarn, piece goods of foreign manufacture, and metals of all kinds.

In connection with educational matters it must not be forgotten that in very early days there were throughout the whole of India numerous seats of learning, and many Hindu *pundits* and Mahommedan *maulvis*, but the instruction then given was connected almost entirely with religious training, and was thereby cramped and narrowed into restricted channels by caste and social prejudices. It is generally admitted that the first attempt to give instruction in schools which were unconnected with racial or traditional barriers took place about a hundred years ago, when European missionaries began to teach in the vernacular, and, further, made a beginning with studies in the English language.

Some results of those first steps in education are to be seen to-day in several towns in Behar and Orissa, but, taking the Province as a whole, this most important question has only come to the front in comparatively recent years.

The efforts of the Government to foster education have met with a gratifying recognition by a very large proportion of the inhabitants of the various districts, and in proof of this one need only refer to figures published in the Administration Report of the Province in 1914. That report shows that, at the date of issue, there were 30,219 educational institutions with 847,244 pupils, this being an increase over the numbers for the previous years of 756 schools, and 42,586 scholars, but it is still a matter of controversy and opinion whether this class of education is of real advantage to the development of the country.

There are not many good roads in the Province, owing partly to the difficulty of construction upon alluvial soil and partly because a sufficient supply of suitable metal is rarely available in places where it is required, but competent engineers such as Mr. L. R. Broome, of Muzaffarpur and Mr. G. A. Ostler, of Motihari, are gradually improving the highways.

Excellent means of communication are, however, provided by rivers and canals, and by railways which are under the direct control and administration of the Railway Board of the Government of India.

The open mileage of railways in the Province was recently shown to be approximately: standard gauge, 1,750 miles; metre gauge, 1,150 miles; and 2 feet 6 inches in width, 250 miles.

The following towns are in the division of Patna:—

Arrah.—The terrible days of the mutiny of 1857 will long live historically in the annals of the town of Arrah, as one of the most stirring episodes in the rebellion occurred there. On July 27th in that year when news reached Arrah that about two thousand Sepoys and between seven and eight thousand armed villagers were marching upon the town, steps were at once taken to secure the safety of the women and children by removing them to another place. Some fifteen or sixteen Englishmen, however, were determined to defend themselves to the utmost of their ability, and they accordingly placed themselves under the leadership of a Mr. Vicars Boyle, an engineer employed in the construction of a section of the East Indian Railway. This gentleman barricaded the windows of the smaller of two houses which he then occupied, and, further, laid in a stock of provisions, doing his utmost to prevent his miniature fortress from being compelled to surrender. After the mutineers had released the prisoners from the jail and had plundered the Treasury, they turned their attention to Boyle and his companions, who were then supported by some fifty Sikhs supplied by the Commissioner of Patna, and commanded by the magistrate of the district. The invaders took possession of the large house belonging to Boyle, and from windows they continued to fire upon the besieged party until August 2nd, when the gallant garrison was relieved by the opportune appearance of Major Vincent Eyre and a hundred and fifty men of the 5th Regiment of Fusiliers and about thirty artillerymen. Eyre dispersed the rebels so efficiently that they never recovered from the blow.

Arrah is an important station on the East Indian Railway, and is 368 miles distant from Calcutta.

Bankipore, an important commercial town delightfully situated on the southern bank of the Ganges, is a junction station on the East Indian Railway system, and 338 miles distant from Calcutta.

The Province of Behar and Orissa is frequently referred to as the "Garden of India," and one can well imagine that such a flattering description might have been given after the author of it had made an inspection of the extremely fine European residences standing in trim gardens and grounds which slope to the very brink of the river at Bankipore.

The majority of the public edifices are of modern construction, and they include Government offices, court houses, and post and telegraph and other buildings.

Behar, known in history as being the capital in the ninth century of the Pala kings, is situated on the Panchana River, and it now resembles a long, narrow street with a number of lanes branching therefrom. The town possesses some of the most interesting structural remains in the whole of the Province.

Foremost among these is a sandstone pillar, 14 feet in height, upon which are two inscriptions of the period of the Gupta dynasty, bearing date between the years 413 and 480. The fort, of which ruins are still visible, was 2,800 feet in length from north to south, and 2,100 feet from east to west in width, and was surrounded by a wall about 20 feet in height.

Although *Gaya*, the chief town of the district of the same name, has a population of about 50,000 inhabitants, it has few industries of any importance, but as the centre of a thriving agricultural area its commercial activities are worthy of mention.

Gaya is the headquarters of ancient Buddhism, and Buddha himself is believed to have lived in the jungle near to the town during the time that he was preparing for his future work as a teacher of the law.

Mokameh is a busy town with nearly 14,000 inhabitants in the district of Patna, with a station on the East Indian Railway system, some 283 miles distant from Calcutta. It is connected by a branch line with Mokameh Ghat, and thence with the Bengal and North Western Railway, and therefore the passenger traffic through the town is occasionally very large. It derives much of its importance from its being a receiving and forwarding depot for agricultural produce and general merchandise from Patna and other districts.

It is more than probable that *Patna* is built upon the site of Pataliputra, which was founded in the fifth century B.C., and became the metropolis of India between the years 321-297 B.C.

Modern Patna, the largest city in the Province, extends for a distance of nearly nine miles along a bank of the Ganges River, and it is mainly a long, straggling place of little architectural beauty, although some of the buildings which have been erected in recent years have pretensions to distinction. Among the latter is the Patna College, founded in 1862, occupying a reconstructed building which was formerly the private residence of a wealthy Indian gentleman. The Patna Oriental Library, too, is a fine structure containing a number of beautiful Arabic and Persian manuscripts, some very rare specimens of Oriental calligraphy, and about four thousand volumes of Arabic and Persian books, and some three thousand European works. The city has a population of about 135,000 souls.

Sasaram.—The name of this town signifies "one thousand toys," and its derivation is locally ascribed to the fact that a certain Asura, or demon, who is said to have lived here, had a thousand arms, in each of which he held a separate plaything. Many visitors are attracted for the purpose of seeing the tomb of the Afghan Sher Shah, who defeated Humayun and subsequently became Emperor of Delhi. The tomb is in the form of an octagonal hall, which is surrounded by an arcade or gallery, while the roof is supported by four Gothic arches.

The town has a very large municipal market from which a considerable revenue is derived, and its population comprises about 23,000 persons.

The following places are in the division of Tirhut:—

Bettiah is by far the most important centre of trade in the district of Champaran, which produces very large crops of rice, a considerable quantity of indigo, and a fair annual yield of barley, oats, wheat, maize, gram, oil-seeds of various kinds, tobacco, and sugar-cane. There are few prettier towns in Northern Behar than Bettiah. Its streets are clean and well kept, and there is an atmosphere of prosperity which has been greatly developed, not by its inhabitants alone, but by the munificence of the Bettiah Raj which is situated within its borders. The beautiful snow-capped hills of Nepal make an exceedingly pretty background, and in the hottest weather one can enjoy the invigorating cool breezes which seem to be wafted from them across the intervening space. All colours of the rainbow are represented in the beautiful flowers and verdant foliage which are seen on every hand, and the efforts of a very active municipal council to secure conformity and artistic style in the construction of public buildings, as well as private residences, have been conspicuously successful. The palace of the Rajas of Bettiah is the chief attraction for visitors, but it is by no means disgraced by being in the company of the handsomely designed and well-equipped King Edward Memorial Hospital, facing the *maidan*, which is one of the most up-to-date institutions of its kind in the Province. This home of healing has been built, fitted throughout with the latest scientific appliances and apparatus, and endowed by the Bettiah Raj. The new town hall, high school, and other buildings are also worthy of inspection.

It may be added that the hospital was opened by Sir Charles Steuart-Bayley, Lieutenant-Governor of the Province, on March 16, 1915.

Chapra, the headquarters of the district of Saran, is situated on the left bank of the River Gogra.

Early in the eighteenth century the English, French, Portuguese, and Dutch had factories there, but the commercial activities of the town were seriously affected by the deflection first of the Ganges, and subsequently of the Gogra, rivers. An outbreak of plague occurred in the year 1900, and again in 1902 and 1903, and many panic-stricken people left the town and district. Confidence has been restored to some extent, however, and at the present time a considerable trade is carried on in the export of linseed, raw sugar, shellac, saltpetre, and opium.

The district of Darbhanga has a large export trade in rice, indigo, wheat, grain, pulses, fruit, vegetables, and oil-seeds, and its chief town, bearing the same name, has excellent means of communication with Calcutta and other places, not only by means of railways, but also by boats which ply upon the Baghmati River.

Darbhanga the town—extends for a distance of nearly six miles along the east bank of the above-named river, which is spanned by two iron bridges constructed by a rich banker of the town and by one of the Maharajas of Darbhanga. Some very fine tanks are distinctive features of the place, three of these—constructed in a line—having a total length of 6,000 feet, while others range from 1,600 feet to 2,400 feet, with a breadth of 1,000 ft.

The Maharajas of Darbhanga have had their residence here since the year 1762.

Hajipur, in the district of Muzaffarpur, is interested largely in trading in the rich agricultural products produced in surrounding villages, consisting of indigo, cotton, pulses, rice, grain, copper and brass vessels, linseed, tobacco, saltpetre, fruit, and vegetables. Several temples and mosques are to be seen, not only in the town but also in neighbouring villages.

Motihari.—This town occupies an attractive position on the eastern side of a pretty lake, and has a population of about 14,000 inhabitants.

As the chief town of the district of Champaran, which consists of an area of highly cultivated and productive land, it is naturally a busy centre for the disposal of agricultural produce, but many of its inhabitants are also engaged in oil-pressing, the weaving of *dhurries*, and the making of strong money bags and mats.

Muzaffarpur, situated on the Chota Gandak River, and about 337 miles distant from Calcutta, was founded by Muzaffar Khan, and is the headquarters of the district of the same name. It enjoys a very considerable trade in exporting agricultural produce, including cereals, indigo, hides, linseed, cotton, and saltpetre, and in importing different kinds of merchandise, and the greater portion of this traffic is carried on by means of boats upon the River Gandak, which is navigable for many miles during the rainy season. Daily markets are held in the bazars. The streets of the town are broad and well-kept, while many of its buildings are of a superior character, such as the collectorate, court houses, a dispensary, and several schools, some of which are supported by the Behar Scientific Society.

Samastipur is a very large trading centre in the district of Darbhanga, and the town on the south bank of the Burhi Gandak River is an important junction on the Bengal and North-Western Railway systems, in whose workshops more than a thousand hands are employed.

Municipal government was granted to it in the year 1897, and its inhabitants at a recent census were nearly 10,000 in number.

Sitamarhi.—A curious old legend is in existence to the effect that the lovely Janaki, or Sita, whose life is described in the "Ramayana," sprang to life at Sitamarhi out of an earthen vessel into which Raja Janak had driven his ploughshare. Apart from this story, however, the town is worthy of notice as one of the leading commercial centres of the district of Muzaffarpur, the chief produce in trading being rice, oil-seeds, hides, saltpetre, sacred threads, and pottery. It has a large bazar in which markets are held daily.

Sonepore.—It is tolerably certain that there is not a single sportsman connected with the turf in India who has not heard of the delightful racing fixtures and the festivities which were formerly held annually at Sonepore in the district of Saran.

The village is situated at the junction of the Ganges and Gandak Rivers, and its charming surroundings present a most pleasing contrast to the "canvas town" which came into existence when visitors from all parts of the Provinces of Bengal and Behar and Orissa—and even from far distant places—formerly pitched their tents for these delightful gatherings. The native fair is still one of the largest and most interesting in India.

The following towns are in the division of Bhagalpur:—

The "largest locomotive workshops in India" are those belonging to the East Indian Railway Company at *Jamalpur*, a municipal town in the district of Monghyr, and 297 miles distant from Calcutta. Nearly ten thousand hands are employed in the shops, which contain the most approved types of machinery for the construction of locomotives, and the manufacture of appliances requisite for the maintenance of the permanent way of the company's system.

The Kurruckpore range of hills, which have an average altitude of about 200 feet, form a pretty background to the well-kept roads and neat bungalows of the town, which, at the census of 1911, had a population of about 20,000 persons.

Six miles distant from Jamalpur, and connected therewith by a branch line of the East Indian Railway Company, is *Monghyr*, a municipal town with an area of three square miles and situated about 208 miles distant from Calcutta. The chief attraction of the place is a fort with walls 4,000 feet in length and 3,000 feet in width, which surround a high mound, the site of a citadel in earlier days.

A really go-ahead town in this neighbourhood is *Bhagalpur*, which has progressed at a remarkably rapid rate during the past few years owing to the greatly increasing export trade in agricultural produce and to the establishment of a number of local industries such as the manufacture of ropes, carpets, blankets, the grinding of grain, and the making of household furniture. In order to meet this commercial expansion, the East Indian Railway Company have erected a second goods station with the view of coping with the enormous traffic.

Sultangunge, in the district of Bhagalpur, and 280 miles distant from Calcutta, is a flourishing mart whence produce from the surrounding productive neighbourhood is carried by boats on the River Ganges to Calcutta and other important trade centres. There are a number of Buddhist monasteries near to the railway station, together with a famous Sivaite temple

I, 3. SONEPORE MALA FESTIVAL. 2. ELEPHANTS AT THE SONEPORE MALA FESTIVAL.
4. STOCK AT THE SONEPORE MALA FESTIVAL. 5. BRIDGE AT SONEPORE.

Photo by L. R. Broome.

standing on a rock in the middle of the Ganges.

The following are in the district of Orissa:—

About ten miles distant in a south-westerly direction is *Balasore*, on the right bank of the Burrabulang River and about six miles distant from the sea-coast. This is a busy commercial town, but it is coming more and more into prominence owing to an influx of visitors during the summer months, who take up their residence there with the view of enjoying a holiday within easy reach of the shores of the Bay of Bengal.

The chief attraction in Balasore is, however, the temple of Mahadev, which, according to local tradition, sprang directly from the ground, or, like the immortal Topsy, has "growed."

The headquarters for administrative purposes of the division of Orissa are at *Cuttack*, a pleasantly situated town on the Mahanadi River, in the district of Cuttack, and 253 miles distant from Calcutta on the Bengal-Nagpur Railway system. The town has an area of about four square miles, and extends from the Mahanadi on the north to the Katjuri River on the south. A writer, speaking of the picturesque appearance of Cuttack, says: "the horizon is bounded by a forest of beautiful trees, which extend as far as the eye can reach, and line the bottom and sides of a chain of high mountains that seem to reach to the very sky; and this charming prospect with its triple circle of beauties is enjoyed by the inhabitants all the year round."

The majority of the public buildings are of an imposing character and include the offices of the Bengal-Nagpur Railway Company, the general hospital, the court offices, and a number of educational establishments.

Cuttack is excellently served by railway, road, and river communications with places in the district, and with many of the principal commercial centres in the Province.

A legend, inscribed on palm-leaf records in the Jagannath temple says that the town was founded by Nrupakesari between the years 953 and 961, and that, as the site chosen was at a point where the Mahanadi is divided into several small streams, massive stone embankments were constructed to prevent damage accruing to the buildings by periodical overflows of water.

It is tolerably clear that Cuttack was strongly fortified in early days; its name even is believed to be connected with the word "kataka," signifying a fort, and at the present time visitors may see the remains of a very old citadel.

In the same district of Cuttack is *Jajpur*, historically a very interesting town built on the banks of the sacred River Bhaitarani. Near to this river may be seen temples dedicated to Jagannath and Kali, but the latter has special attractions for visitors, as a gallery on its eastern side contains seven life-sized monolith statues of the mothers in Hindu mythology, namely, Indrani, Varahi, Vaishnavi, Kumari, Yarna Matri, Kali, and Rudrani, together with one of the incarnation of Vishnu.

Puri.—It is barely twenty years since the Bengal-Nagpur Railway Company, impressed by the invigorating climate and the health-giving breezes of the sea at Puri, on the shores of the Bay of Bengal, extended their system by a branch line, 27 miles in length, from Khurda Road. The opening of the line resulted in such a marked development of the town that it is to-day visited by a large number of persons from Bengal and other portions of India. Hotels and boarding houses have been opened, and the numerous handsome villa-residences in the neighbourhood of the beach are evidence of the growing popularity of the place.

Puri is, however, famous primarily as the place of the venerated shrine of Jagannath, visited annually by some 300,000 pilgrims, and for the yearly car festival of that deity, which is attended by no fewer than 100,000 persons. A sacred enclosure, about 652 feet in height, has within it about a hundred temples, but the one dedicated to Jagannath is by far the most attractive one. The ceremonies connected with the car festival are described in a cyclopædia of India (1905) as follows: "A good broad road, about a mile and a half in length, leads from the temple of Jagannath to a place called Inderdumna, where the deity is supposed to spend eight days during the Rath Jatra festival. The Jagannath temple, called 'Sri Mundir,' is the largest, and the entrance to it is called the 'lion gate,' two stone lions keeping guard as it were on either side. In the courtyard of the temple pilgrims assemble at special times during the day and night to get a view of the images of Jagannath, and Bolaram his brother, and Subhadra his sister, which stand on an altar called the 'Rutna Bedi,' or jewel seat.

"The figures are decked with fine jewellery and gaudy dresses, and a large diamond glitters on the forehead of Jagannath. The dresses are changed several times during the twenty-four hours. 'Bhog,' or *prosad*, is offered to the god several times during the day; it is piled up before the deity; a large portion is distributed to the pilgrims who pay for it; and the rest is sent to Anandbazar, a place within the compound of the temple, for sale to the public. A fortnight before the Rath Jatra festival, the Snan Jatra, or bathing festival, takes place. Jagannath is bathed, and then remains indisposed for two weeks afterwards, during which time the doors of the temple are kept closed, although his car, with sixteen wheels, and the smaller ones of his brother and sister, are being made ready. On the auspicious day the three sacred images are placed on their respective cars amid great shoutings and rejoicings, accompanied by the beating of drums and the clashing of cymbals. Thousands of pilgrims prostrate themselves before the cars, and vast numbers catch hold of the towing ropes and commence hauling them to Jagannath's garden at Janakpur, a distance of nearly a mile, where the god remains for ten days."

About 133 miles distant from Calcutta is *Rupsa* junction, on the Bengal-Nagpur Railway system, which is connected with *Baripada*, the headquarters of Mayurbhanj (the largest and wealthiest of the Feudatory States of Orissa) by a branch narrow gauge line—33 miles in length—constructed by the State. This means of communication has resulted in a large development of trade in the district in paddy, firewood, and railway sleepers, and the permanent settlement of a considerable number of persons who are engaged in the reclamation of jungle land for agricultural purposes.

The town of *Sambalpur*, created a municipality in 1867, is the terminus of a branch line starting from Jharsuguda junction on the Bengal-Nagpur Railway system. It is the principal town of the district of the same name, and is 350 miles distant from Calcutta.

In the neighbourhood of many of the vast waterways of India one may be constantly charmed with the ever-varying freshness of riparian vegetation, and the picturesque surroundings of the countless number of private bungalows which peep out from the luxuriant foliage of tropical trees, and a good illustration of this is seen in the neighbourhood of the Mahanadi

River, upon whose banks the town of Sambalpur is built.

Sambalpur is a great centre of commerce, dealing largely with agricultural produce drawn from its surrounding villages and from the districts of Sonepur, Patna, and Rairakhol. Industries are few in number, although the weaving of tassar silk and cotton cloth is carried on by a number of the inhabitants.

The following towns are in the division of Chota-Nagpur:—

Chaibassa, the municipal town in the district of Singhbhum, is prettily situated on the River Roro, and its name, which means " a dwelling place of rest," is richly deserved. Its principal street has the appearance of a peaceful, old-world English village thoroughfare, in which dwelling houses and shops are irregularly but charmingly built among a profusion of grand old trees, but there seems to be little in the way of industrial or commercial enterprise excepting on Tuesday in each week, when crowds of people from the surrounding neighbourhood flock into the town to dispose of their wares in the busy bazar. The town is 184 miles distant from Calcutta.

Chulia, about two miles distant in an easterly direction from Ranchi, is a delightfully interesting place for archæologists as it contains fine ruins of a once dome-shaped building. Another special feature is the annual fair, at which an exceedingly large number of animals are offered for sale, these comprising almost every type of four-footed beast (excepting *feræ naturæ*) from massive elephants to the domestic goats.

Very little attention was paid to the value of the mineral wealth of the Province until about the middle of the nineteenth century, but rapid strides have been taken since that time in opening up coal and other mines, with the result that a very large industry, employing thousands of workers, has now been firmly established. Since the East Indian Railway Company extended their system to the district of Palamau, the coal fields in the neighbourhood of *Daltonganj* (422 miles distant from Calcutta) which were known to contain most valuable deposits, have been opened up by a number of companies, and the total annual output is increasing very considerably. Lime, too, has been discovered, and it is certain that the town, which now contains a population of about 8,000 persons, will soon be an important manufacturing centre.

The station at *Giridih*, on the East Indian Railway Company's system, is the terminal point of a branch line, 23 miles in length, running from the junction at Madhupur, and the town, which has a population of about 11,000 inhabitants, is the headquarters of a subdivision of the district of Hazaribagh. The Kurhurbaree coalfields—from whose mines the East Indian Railway Company draw the major portion of their coal—are quite near to Giridih, and it is these collieries which account for nearly the whole of the very heavy goods traffic on the railway.

1. A TEMPLE AT MUZAFFARPUR. 2. GOVERNMENT SCHOOL, MUZAFFARPUR.

Picturesquely situated among hills covered with dense forests, is the town of *Hazaribagh*, which is near to the station of Hazaribagh Road on the East Indian Railway system, and about 215 miles distant from Calcutta.

The town, by reason of its bracing climate at an altitude of 2,000 feet above the level of the sea, is regarded as a most desirable sanatorium by the inhabitants of the Province of Behar and Orissa. The name of Hazaribagh is said to be derived from a grove of mango-trees, about a thousand in number, and the village, as it then was, eventually grew into a township which is locally referred to as " the garden of a thousand trees." The district furnishes many attractions for sportsmen as it is well stocked with tigers.

A station of considerable importance on the northern section of the Bengal-Nagpur Railway is *Purulia*, the junction of a 2 feet 6 inch gauge branch line to Ranchi, which—together with Bankipore is the headquarters of the Government of Behar and Orissa. There are a number of industries in the town, such as the pressing of oilseeds, the pounding of aloes, weaving, gardening, and the making of cane and basket ware.

Purulia is the headquarters of the district of Manbhum, and is about 200 miles distant from Calcutta.

The town of *Ranchi* is most picturesquely situated on a plateau, some 2,000 feet in height, and enjoying commanding views of fertile plains, which are interspersed by rocky promontories, with the long, low range of the Ramgarh Hills in the distance. This elevation, coupled with the fact that any excessive rains disappear quickly down the sides of the plateau, give the town a remarkably healthy and invigorating climate, and a comparatively low temperature enables the occupiers of the many pretty private residences to cultivate a wealth of beautiful flowers, which give visitors the idea that they have been suddenly transported to English gardens. Bungalows inhabited by the Commissioner of the district of Ranchi, and of other prominent residents, are very charmingly situated amid a profusion of foliage near to the Ranchi Lake, which is a very fine piece of water about 50 acres in extent. The business portion of the town comprises native bazars, thronged by villagers of the neighbourhood, who carry on a brisk trade in agricultural and general produce. The principal buildings are the

Government offices and a strikingly handsome cathedral, surmounted by a graceful spire which can be seen from a great distance.

On the shores of the lake is a Hindu temple dedicated to Siva, and about three miles distant is the military cantonment of Doranda.

The station of the Bengal-Nagpur Railway Company at Ranchi is 273 miles distant from the terminus at Howrah. A motor-car service has been established from Hazaribagh Road station on the East Indian Railway to Bagoda, the town of Hazaribagh, and thence to Ranchi.

The Feudatory States of Orissa are twenty-four in number, the names of which are: Athgarh, Athmallia, Bamra, Baramba, Baud, Bonai, Daspalla, Dhenkanal, Gangpur, Hindol, Kalahandi, Keonjhar, Khandpara, Mayurbhanj, Narsinghpur, Nayagarh, Nilgiri, Pal Lohara, Patna, Rairakhol, Ranpur, Sonpur, Talchar, and Tigiria.

These States are attached to the division of Orissa, and have an area of 28,125 square miles, and are inhabited by a population of more than 3,000,000 persons.

Mr. L. E. B. Cobden-Ramsay, I.C.S., in the "Bengal Gazetteer" (1910) writes as follows: "The States have no connected or authentic history. Comprising, as they do, the western and hilly portion of Orissa, they were never brought under the Central Government, but from the earliest times consisted of numerous petty principalities, which were more or less independent of one another.

"They were first inhabited by aboriginal races, chiefly Bhuiyas, Savars, Gonds, and Khonds, who were divided into innumerable communal or tribal groups, each under its own chief or headman.

"They carried on incessant warfare with their neighbours on the one hand and the denizens of the forest on the other. In course of time their hill retreats were penetrated by Aryan adventurers, who, by reason of their superior powers and intelligence, gradually overthrew the tribal chiefs and established themselves in their place.

"Tradition relates how these daring interlopers, most of whom were Rajputs from the north, came to Puri on pilgrimage and remained behind to found kingdoms and dynasties."

The States consist of a succession of ranges of hills (from which noble peaks ascend to heights varying from 2,000 feet to nearly 5,000 feet), dense forests, and well-watered valleys of highly cultivated land, but the outstanding feature is the remarkably pleasing effect produced by the contrast between rugged grey rocks and the brilliant green foliage of the luxuriant vegetation.

It is the variety in the scenery which is so charming, for the eye may rest upon the freshness of growing crops of rice, mustard, sesamum, wheat, barley, or cotton, while the hills with their beautiful verdure are not a whit less pleasing, and a never-failing source of delight is furnished by the crystal rivers which flow along the plains, or rush from higher lands through narrow gorges, plunging over precipitous rocky mountains with a sheer drop of more than 2,000 feet.

It will be readily understood that the almost impenetrable jungle and the more sparsely populated portions of the States are well stocked with the large species of wild game. Elephants are still numerous in several of the States; bison are usually found in the same districts; and tigers and panthers are met with everywhere; while the smaller animals, which are plentiful, comprise bears, various kinds of deer, pigs, wild dogs, and jackals.

Fully two-thirds of the population obtain a livelihood from agricultural pursuits, and the majority of them belong to peaceable law-abiding tribes, among whom are the Khonds, Hos, Bhuiyas, Bhumijes, Oraons, Santals, Kharias, Savars, and others.

Local industries are comparatively few in number, and are not in any way remarkable. They comprise the manufacture of brass utensils, silver articles, tasser and cotton cloth, and a variety of iron implements for agricultural and domestic purposes.

Very little progress has been made with regard to education, but primary and secondary schools have been erected in the majority of the States in recent years, and already there are signs of a greater interest being manifested in this most important matter.

THE BEHAR PLANTERS' ASSOCIATION, LTD.

By the Hon. T. R. FILGATE, C.I.E.

INDIGO was a product of North Behar long before the advent of the British, but its cultivation by European methods appears to have been started by François Grand, the first Collector of Tirhut. Writing in 1785, three years after his appointment as Collector, he claims to have been the pioneer of the industry, and says:—

"I introduced the manufacturing of indigo after the European manner, encouraged the establishment of indigo works and plantations, and erected three at my own expense." It is at least from this time that the manufacture of indigo began to develop into an industry and to attract European enterprise. In 1788 there were five Europeans in possession of indigo works; in 1793 the number of factories had increased to nine, situated at Daudpur, Saraiya, Dhuli, Ottur (Athar), Shahpur, Kanti, Motipur, Deoria, and Banaria; and by the year 1803 altogether twenty-five factories had been established in Tirhut. During these early days the industry was directly fostered by the East India Company, and special permission had to be obtained by Europeans wishing to engage in it. In 1802, however, the Board of Directors passed orders that no further advances or pecuniary encouragement should be given to planters, as the large profits obtained from the sale of the product made such aid unnecessary. Indigo accordingly became an independent and self-supporting industry, the pioneer planting industry in Bengal.

Its progress in Tirhut during the next few years was rapid, though there appear to have been many failures, probably owing to over-production. In a report submitted in 1810, the Collector stated that, taking one year with another, the district seldom sent less than 10,000 maunds of indigo to Calcutta for export to Europe; that 30,000 to 50,000 souls received their principal support from the factories; and that on the average each factory disbursed from Rs. 25,000 to Rs. 30,000 per annum in hard cash to the labourers and cultivators for some miles round the various concerns. He estimated that in this way not less that six or seven lakhs of rupees were circulated every year by the planters in Tirhut, and urged that the advantages of the industry to the labouring classes were so great that Government should encourage it in every possible way. "Let the speculator win or lose," he wrote, "acquire a princely fortune or die a pauper, the district is equally benefited by his industry, and his struggles for prosperity do rarely succeed. Some of the planters succeed, but the majority of them fail." Difficulties appear to have arisen later through the competition of rival concerns, and in 1828 the Collector represented that indigo cultivation had extended so greatly that some restriction upon it was desirable for the benefit of the district. "From the misunderstanding," he wrote, "which has prevailed and still prevails among the European planters, disputes with one another are of very frequent occurrence; disputes have, however, of late occurred through descendants of Europeans embarking in indigo cultivation, worked chiefly, if not entirely, by native agency. For the peace of the district and welfare of the established planters, it therefore appears highly desirable that the Government restrictions regarding the erection of factories by Europeans should be extended to the descendants of Europeans, and power be vested in the magistrate to prevent engagements for the cultivation of indigo plant by other than the proprietor or proprietors of one established factory."

In 1850 there were no less than 86 factories in Tirhut, several of which were used for the manufacture of sugar, but about this time sugar was finally superseded by indigo as the European industry of the district, and many refineries were converted into indigo concerns. Difficulties were at one time threatened by the feeling of tension between the *ryots* and the factories, produced by certain abuses which had crept into the system of cultivation; but the danger was averted by the planters themselves, who, in 1877, formed the Behar Planters' Association in order to put matters on a satisfactory footing.

The Behar Planters' Association, as far as can be ascertained, is the senior association in the Province of Behar and Orissa. As there evidently was an association of some sort in 1801, certain by-laws were framed and agreed to on the 22nd of February in the same year, while on the 4th of June, 1837, another code was drawn up to be observed by planters. The Indigo Commission in Lower Bengal in the year 1860 were evidently of opinion that indigo planting in Behar was carried on satisfactorily, as paragraph 135 of that report says: "We should recommend the planters to consider seriously whether a system on the basis of that existent in Tirhut be not feasible, i.e. the crop should be valued on the ground and paid for on an estimate there and then made upon classification of the crop." In the early seventies constant complaints were lodged in the Criminal and Civil Courts, and the leading planters of that time were determined to do their best to remove the abuses and blots on the system, and after consultation with the Bengal Government, the Behar Indigo Planters' Association

JHERRIAH CLUB.

was formed, the constitution being a paid general secretary, an honorary general committee, consisting of four members each from the districts of Mozufferpore, Chumparun, Durbhanga, and Sarun, a district committee of nine members for each of the four districts (one who acted as hon. secretary), and the Calcutta Committee.

The Government of Bengal in their letter No. 3,987, dated August 29, 1877, to the Government of India, in paragraph 12, state: "In reference to the final paragraph of your letter I am to say that as long as the Association show their present willingness to meet the Lieutenant-Governor's views and get rid of the obvious blots on the system, the Lieutenant-Governor has no intention of interfering in any way or of doing anything which can hamper the planters in the conduct of their business. All he desires is that the law should be strictly obeyed, and that indigo planting should be carried on like other commercial enterprises without such frequent complaints over the necessity for executive interference which have hitherto characterized it."

The Government of India, replying to the Government of Bengal, in their letter No. 321, dated December 17, 1877, said: "In reply I am to say that the Lieutenant-Governor's action in reference to this question appears to the Governor-General-in-Council to have been very judicious, and will, His Excellency-in-Council hopes, prove successful in putting a stop to, or at all events greatly diminishing the abuses which have prevailed in the system heretofore in force in Behar. His Excellency-in-Council also cordially acknowledges the praiseworthy efforts made by the leading planters in the direction of reform, and concurs with the expression of the Lieutenant-Governor's satisfaction herewith quoted in paragraph 12 of your letter."

The Association has loyally adhered to its bond made with Government, and whenever complaints were brought to its notice with reference to any member's dealings with his *mallicks, ryots,* or brother planters, which were not in accordance with the Association rules and by-laws, matters were immediately put right, and it has been recorded over and over again in Government Reports that the Behar Planters' Association has been of considerable help in the administration of North Behar. In the general survey and settlement Report of the Mozufferpore district, paragraph 907, page 354, the following words appear: "The agricultural classes, however, have the more tangible advantage of knowing the ordinary indigo planter to be a good, considerate landlord, and it is an axiom of the Association that the successful cultivator is one on good terms with his tenants. The general tone in this respect is thoroughly sound and good, and the Government, the indigo community itself, and the cultivators, are largely indebted to the Indigo Planters' Association for its introduction, as well as for the cordial relations that exist between indigo managers and the local administration. The peace and contentment now existing is in strong contrast with the relations which prevailed before the Association was founded." In the Bengal Annual Report of 1871-2 we read: "During the Lieutenant-Governor's visit to North Behar he was in some places met by crowds making complaints regarding indigo cultivation in a way that had not occurred to him in other districts, but almost all these complaints had reference to one somewhat overgrown factory. The whole subject is one which requires careful management, as very little action, or even a few words, might cause great complication on one side or other. On the one hand the Lieutenant-Governor would be very unwilling to injure one of the most prosperous and profitable industries in the country, and on the other hand he is inclined to think indigo has already occupied as large a proportion of certain descriptions of soil in the densely populated district of North Behar as is desirable."

This extract and similar ones which might be produced from the reports of the following years indicate a degree of tension between the factories and their

JHERRIAH TOWNSHIP.

ryots, yet the area under indigo has very largely increased since Sir George Campbell published the remarks above quoted. Indigo planters of younger generations would do well to remember that it was their Association which accomplished these results.

"Paragraph 908.—My general conclusions then are that the indigo industry confers a very natural benefit on the district, it has saved many a proprietor from inevitable ruin; it has brought immense profits to the poorest and most depressed portion of the population, and the political and administrative advantages that occurred to the Government cannot admit of question." In the final report of the survey and settlement of the Chumparan District 1893 to 1899, para. 624, it is recorded that, "outside the department, Mr. Macnaghten, the secretary of the Behar Indigo Planters' Association, deserves our special acknowledgments for advice and co-operation." The final Report of the survey and settlement operations in the district of Monghyr-North (1906), para. 341, has the following: "It was not to the planters' interest to enhance rents or harass the tenants in any other way, and hence here as everywhere in Behar the indigo planter as *thikada* has been, as a general rule, a most considerate landlord."

On April 1, 1905, the Viceroy, Lord Curzon, in reply to an address of welcome at Pusa from the Behar Planters' Association said: "One needs but small acquaintance with Indian history to know that the indigo planter here represents the oldest British industry in rural Bengal, that the enterprise has given employment to hundreds of thousands of inhabitants of the country, and that their famous and traditional loyalty has for nearly half a century presented to the Government one of the finest volunteer regiments in India, by some of whose members I had the honour of being escorted to-day, and who carried the name of Behar and of its Light Horse to glory on the battlefields of the Empire."

The Viceroy, Lord Minto, in reply to an address of welcome from the Behar Planters' Association at Bankipore on February 7, 1906, said: "Perhaps you will allow me to say I have heard of the planters before this; I have heard of them as country gentlemen of the right sort, and good men of business, and I think they will not object to my saying as hard riders and good sportsmen also."

"You may well be proud of the contingent you sent to South Africa which did so well there, and material such as that of which you are composed, drawn from men accustomed to the every-day experience of an outdoor life, will in my opinion always be invaluable to the leader of mounted troops." In reply to an address of welcome from the Behar Planters' Association to His Excellency the Viceroy, at Bankipore, on December 1, 1913, Lord Hardinge said: "You have played an important part in making Behar, and specially Tirhut, the prosperous country it is"; and again: "By working as members of local and district boards and giving your time to the 'Punchayats' in the *chowkidari* union you are contributing to the progress and well-being of the people among whom you live, and are identifying yourself with their interests, while those among you who are helping on the furtherance of the system of co-operative credit are rendering great services to the agricultural classes by showing them the way to shake themselves free from debt and lift the condition of their life to a higher plane."

In closing a conference held at Darjeeling on May 9th and 11th, 1910, His Honour the Lieutenant-Governor, the late Sir Edward Baker said: "The present conference had again brought out the value of the Behar Indigo Planters' Association to the industry in Behar, without whose assistance it would have been difficult, if not impossible, for Government to have arrived at an arrangement in a satisfactory manner to all parties. Confidence had been reposed in the planters who in the recent disturbances had behaved exceedingly well in spite of the danger in which they were placed, and His Honour desired to express again his hearty appreciation of the forbearance, self-restraint, and good temper which they had exhibited in circumstances of difficulty and even danger."

In 1897 the placing of synthetic indigo on the markets of the world was a veritable bolt from the blue on the indigo planter of Behar. The Association at once took up the question of research, and nothing has been left undone in their endeavours to save the industry. The financial portion of the work has been heavy, as from June 1898 to November 1915 a sum of Rs. 8,04,119 has been spent, including a

Government grant of Rs. 4,72,661. The highest award possible was granted for this display of indigo at the British-Japanese Exhibition at Shepherd's Bush in 1910, while a similar honour was received at the Coronation Exhibition in London in 1911. The Behar planter, with true British grit and determination, though doing all in his power and straining every nerve for the preservation of the indigo industry, has turned his attention to sugar, tobacco, flax, and other crops, and the planter of to-day is more of a general farmer than a specialist in indigo only. The Association, keeping its primary and main object in view, has however, changed its constitution in order to meet new conditions and so as to bring into membership not only indigo planters but those who produce sugar or other crops. In February 1905 the Behar Indigo Planters' Association became the Behar Planters' Association and a limited liability company was formed; directors appointed in proportion to the total votes of each district (but not to exceed sixteen in number), taking the place of a general committee, and district directors superseding district committees. The annual general meeting elects the general secretary, who is paid an annual salary, while the directors elect their chairman and vice-chairman every year. There are standing committees for "legal subjects," "indigo," "sugar," and "other crops," and each of these deals with its own particular subject, and also elects its chairman and secretary. Under Lord Morley's scheme of enlarged legislative councils the Secretary of State allotted one seat to representatives of indigo or tea, and at the first Bengal Council the seat was taken by a tea-planter. The Behar planters, however, had one of their number on the Council, who was unanimously elected by the District Boards of the Tirhut Division to represent them, and as the majority of the members of district boards are Indians, it is a proof of the confidence of the *mallicks* and *ryots* of North Behar in the Association that they returned their general secretary. When the new Province of Behar and Orissa was created, a seat was allotted to the Behar planters, and their present general secretary represents them on the Council. In consideration of the stake they hold in the country of their adoption, the Behar planters asked for a seat on the Imperial Legislative Council, but this request has not yet been granted. Several of the estates are now managed by the third and fourth generation of descendants of pioneers, and tenants fly to the factory manager with all their troubles in times of stress, or for medicine for themselves, their families, or their cattle. The planter settles innumerable differences between them; he is in thorough touch and sympathy with the people among whom he spends his life, and in times of natural calamities such as famine, floods, or out-breaks of cholera and other fell diseases, his help is most valuable, not only to the people themselves, but to the Government, in seeing that there is no waste of public money and that funds are properly distributed. He has, previously to the establishment of the

PILLAR OF ASOKA, CHAMPARAN

large councils, studiously held himself aloof from politics, and now only takes part in them that his voice may be heard in connection with any measures calculated to raise the status of the people, or to advance the interests of the Province, and to support with all his power the supremacy of the British *Raj* and loyalty to the King-Emperor. In no part of India are there more cordial relations existing between Europeans and their Indian neighbours of all classes, and the agitator has signally failed to stir up racial ill-feeling between them. The best British traditions are still existent in North Behar, and in proof of this it may be observed that when the election of the District Board representative took place for the Behar and Orissa Council in 1912 the planters of Behar did not put forward a candidate but gave their full support to an Indian who had been a member of the Bengal Council and who was eventually returned unopposed. Individual planters can and have done much, but had it not been for the existence of the Behar Planters' Association and the members thereof working in a body as fair-dealing English gentlemen, the planting community of Behar would not hold such an exalted position as it does in the esteem of the people and the Government of the country.

In the year 1877 no fewer than sixty-eight concerns were represented in the list of members, and in 1914, despite the hard times the industry had to face, the number was sixty-six.

The late (afterwards Sir) William Hudson, K.C.I.E., was general secretary from May 15, 1878, to February 3, 1890, when he resigned, and the late Mr. E. R. Macnaghten held office from the last-mentioned date to January 28, 1905, when he died.

Mr. T. R. Filgate, C.I.E., was appointed to the vacant position on April 27, 1905, and he still holds the reins of office. The late Messrs. W. A. Cox and C. R. Macdonald occupied the chair of the Association from 1905 to 1914, and the present holder of the office is Mr. D. J. Reid.

BARRAH ESTATES, LTD., AND CHAMPARAN SUGAR COMPANY, LTD.

Many of the indigo and other planters in Behar hold a similar position to that formerly occupied by owners of cotton concerns in the Southern States of America, as they have plenary powers of jurisdiction in disputes between Indians, but in many instances these honorary magistrates, as they may be termed, act in a friendly manner as arbitrators rather than as strict adherents to the letter and not the spirit of common-law procedure. Mr. G. R. Macdonald, the manager of the Barrah Estates, Ltd., and of the Champaran Sugar Company, Ltd., has, through his long experience of Indians and their ways, gained the confidence of the inhabitants of a very wide area, and his assistance in the settlement of matters is accepted with the greatest respect.

The area of the Barrah Estates—that is, the total sphere of the manager's control—is about 60,000 acres, but the part cultivated by the company directly consists of 3,000 acres of indigo, 2,000 acres of sugar, and about 1,000 acres of wheat, oats, barley, and tobacco. The balance of the land is let out to *ryots*. The property is only a quarter of a mile distant from the post and telegraph offices at Bara-Chakia, and a quarter of a mile from the railway station at Chakia.

In regard to the early history of the estate, according to local tradition a factory was built by a Mr. Stewart about the year 1820, and estate documents are still existent which show that indigo was in cultivation in the year 1828. The managers in the earliest days of the concern included Messrs. Stewart, Moran Henry Hill, Captain Hickey, Henry and Joseph Hill and H. L. Hollway. Mr. A. S. Urquhart was in power in 1857-8, and he was followed by Messrs. W. Gibbon, J. N. Macqueen, James Begg, F. J. Nicolay, E. A. Hickey, A. D. Bolton, John C. Gale from 1880 to 1892, D. R. Crawford from 1895 to 1903, and in November of that year Mr. Macdonald took up the reins of office.

The outworks are Jagoulia, Mohowah, Russelpore, and Gowandrah, and the average annual yield of indigo is about 6½ seers of the Sumatrana type and 10 seers for that emanating from Java. There are very large pressing and drying houses on the concern, and the total vat capacity is about 70,000 cub. ft. Samples of the manufactured product are sent to London and Calcutta, and the bulk is sold in whichever place the best market prices can be obtained.

The crushing of sugar was commenced in the year 1906, although it is known that a factory was erected between the years 1840 and 1850. The machinery in the mill at the present time is up to date in every respect, and it includes a crushing plant by Harvey & Co., of Glasgow.

Manufacture is done by what is called the carbonation process. Limestone is placed in a kiln with coke, in the proportion of ten to one, and then burned, the carbonic gas being forced direct from the kiln through the tanks, this being the latest method of manufacture.

The mill is able to deal daily for 100 days in the year with 300 tons of cane, which gives an average return of 8 per cent. of sugar to cane. There is a great demand for the sugar made, as caste prejudices are scrupulously observed in the processes of manufacture. Nearly the whole of the output is disposed of locally and to the Native States in the Punjab.

Cereals are grown on well-manured land, and the yields of the various crops are: wheat 18 to 20 maunds to the acre, and oats 15 maunds. Tobacco is only grown upon lands which are sub-let to tenants.

The bungalow is a substantially built, handsome, and commodious structure, containing forty-four rooms, and it is surrounded by a large number of very fine old trees and neatly kept grounds.

There are three European assistants employed in connection with indigo, and about 200 native hands are required constantly, although the number engaged on piece-work or daily pay brings the total to about 1,500, while at the sugar factory there are two European assistants and 350 coolies during the crushing season.

BEHAR MOTOR WORKS

India has not been so much of a sealed book to Europeans who arrive at Bombay or Calcutta on a pleasure trip as it was three, or even two, decades ago, as places of interest can now be reached comfortably and with little loss of time owing to the greatly increased means of inter-communication. Railways have been opened in every possible direction. They wind along in serpentine fashion, scaling mountains of intense beauty, and they span rivers which in earlier days were practically insuperable barriers; but it is to motor-cars and cycles that the tourist of to-day owes so much. The *gharries* and bullock-carts of township and village were absolutely useless for sight-seeing in many districts, as distances were too great or the country was too broken, but now, thanks to modern progress, the traveller in his speedy and comfortable motor-car thinks nothing of a spin of 150 or 200 miles, or of hills which it would be too much to expect any horse to climb.

This latest method of getting about is now rendered more practicable from the fact that in every town of any size—and, indeed, in many villages—there are motor agencies in which repairs to cars can be quickly executed, and in which accessories and spare parts of all kinds may be procured. One of these invaluable establishments is situated at Muzaffurpur, in the district of Tirhut, and is known as the Behar Motor Works.

It was established by the proprietor, Mr. H. W. Crane, in the year 1908, and the business has extended so rapidly since that date that considerable enlargement of the premises has recently been necessary. Agencies are held for many of the leading cars now on the market, and the London representatives of Mr. Crane are ever on the alert to recommend and supply any improved car or fittings. Repairs are undertaken, under the supervision of the proprietor, by skilled workmen, but constant employment is also found for about twenty Indian labourers.

BELSUND CONCERN

Indigo is one of the most valuable products of some of the districts in the Province of Behar, but authentic records as to the earliest date when it was cultivated by Europeans are not available. There is no doubt that it is the product of an indigenous Indian plant (*Indigofera tinctoria*), and a reference to it as "Indicum" by Pliny, who lived more than eighteen hundred years ago, proves that it was not unknown to early Roman writers. It is stated definitely in Indian history that when the Government of the year 1788 compiled a list of Europeans who were not occupying official positions in the district of Tirhut, in Behar, it was found that of twelve persons thus scheduled no fewer than ten were engaged in the planting of indigo.

Mr. Minden Wilson in his most interesting handbook on the "History of Behar Indigo Factories" (1908) says: "In Germany in the seventeenth century indigo was denominated 'the devil's dye,' and by an Imperial edict its use was prohibited in A.D. 1654, as it appears to have caused a considerable decrease in the sale of wood, and Mr. Bancroft tells us that the Nurembergers exacted every year a solemn oath from the dyers to the effect that they would never have recourse to indigo as a dye. So little was the nature of indigo known at the time in Europe that the Elector of Saxony denounced it as a corrosive substance not fit for man or devil."

The Belsund Indigo Concern, situated about thirty miles distant from Muzaffurpur, in the district of Muzaffurpur, Tirhut, is interesting from the fact that the Makurry lease of its factory is dated 1794, and was given by Rajah Mustaffa Khan. Outworks were built at Bagwanpore, Sukereah, and Boijnathpore in the year 1846, and at Belai in 1861, but the second and third named have since been abandoned.

The estate at present comprises 4,500 acres of cultivated land, consisting at the present time of 3,000 acres of indigo, 1,000 acres of wheat, oats, and barley, and 500 acres of rice, although agricultural operations were commenced in 1794 with indigo and sugar-cane alone.

Mr. D. J. Reid became manager of the estate in the year 1903, but he sub-

BARRAH ESTATES, LTD., AND CHAMPARAN SUGAR COMPANY, LTD.

1. Bungalow. 2. Indigo Factory. 3. Sugar Factory. 4. Evaporating Plant.

BELSUND CONCERN.

1 AND 2. WHEAT CROP AT BELSUND. 3. MANAGER'S BUNGALOW. 4. FACTORY BUILDINGS.

sequently purchased a share in the concern, and since that time has been managing proprietor. Proof of the thoroughly systematic and careful manner in which the property has been managed is shown in the complete records disclosed by cash, ledger, and other books, from which some interesting particulars have been obtained.

Owing to the competition of the synthetic product many indigo concerns in Tirhut have had to abandon the cultivation of indigo, but by the combination of indigo with the cultivation of cereals Belsund Concern has managed to weather the storm, and even in the worst of years has always managed to show a fair profit. In former days the estate had about 6,000 acres under indigo, and although the area now has been reduced by half, the actual production of dye has not been proportionately affected, owing to the fact that in 1905 a new variety of indigo was introduced from Java. This variety of indigo was found to be particularly well suited to the kind of soil found in the Belsund estate, with the result that the return of dye per acre was increased by fully 50 per cent. During recent years also the quality of the indigo manufactured on the estate has been enormously improved, and from being one of the worst marks in the province it now ranks among the best.

As is universally the case in Behar, the soil on the Belsund estate varies greatly. The best lands, of course, are always selected for wheat, and an average yield of about 16 maunds (1,280 lb.) is obtained. Oats, which are generally sown on the poorer soils, average about 12 maunds to the acre, and rice, which is all hand-planted, yields from 16 to 25 maunds per acre.

The bungalow at Belsund is an exceptionally fine building, being built in the usual palatial style of most of the old factories in Behar. The nearest railway station is at Sitamarhi, thirteen miles distant, and there is a post and telegraph office at Belsund itself. One of the features of the estate is an ample supply of water, which is a great blessing in years of drought, as it enables irrigation to be conducted over a large proportion of the cultivation.

Two European assistants and some three hundred Indians are regularly employed on the estate, although the latter are greatly increased when necessary.

BELWA CONCERN

There is no more fertile soil in Behar and Orissa than that in the district of Champarun, but during recent years agriculturists and villagers alike have suffered enormous damage owing to terrible river floods, and the Belwa estate, in that district, affords a striking instance of the overwhelming force of disadvantageous conditions over which the owners have no control.

Mr. A. C. Amman, the managing proprietor of Belwa, has a sad tale to tell of the exceedingly severe losses which fell upon him and upon the inhabitants of many of the eighty villages under his control which are comprised within the area of the above estate. He points out that a considerable portion of the land between the Dwarda and Pandayi Rivers has always been subject to floods from the overflowing of these streams, but the waters have subsided in due course, and very little damage has been done. In October 1915, however, a most disastrous flood occurred, which swept away villages and live-stock, destroyed harvested crops, rotted growing ones, and completely buried in sand some 75 or 100 acres of rich agricultural land, and Mr. Amman maintains that "this was caused by the action of the Trebeni Canal and the Bengal and North-Western Railway embankments upon the volume of water discharged into the Belwa *dehat* (or neighbourhood) by an abnormal rainfall." This canal, says Mr. Amman, "appears to be designed against all preconceived ideas. A canal is usually aligned to flow along the natural line of drainage of the country which it is required to drain or irrigate, and therefore it ordinarily runs parallel to the course of adjacent main rivers, with which it interferes as little as possible; but the Trebeni one cuts across the watershed of the Nepal *tarai*, intersecting, almost invariably at right angles, the innumerable hill streams and rivers which at intervals of distances of three miles form a network on the Champarun frontier, and constitute the natural drainage of the country. The recent frequency of floods in North Champarun is due to the canal embankment (10 ft. in height), which dams up every petty rainfall until it accumulates, breaches the embankment, and, escaping as a flood, forms a huge lake, extending up the slope of the country for a third of a mile, submerging and rotting the crops and destroying homesteads. The railway embankment, too, crosses the natural course of the water-flow, diverting it and causing the ruin of villages and lands on the western side of the line." Mr. Amman estimated the damage done to eight or ten of his villages at Rs. 65,000, and the loss at his own bungalow, buildings, and bazaar at Rs. 15,000.

The boundaries of the estate, including the villages, are the River Uriya, some twelve miles distant from the bungalow on the east, and the Masan stream, twelve miles to the west, while the north and south limits are respectively nine and four miles distant.

About three hundred acres are cultivated on behalf of the proprietors, and the principal crops are rice, Indian corn, yellow mustard, wheat, barley, and gram, while a quantity of indigo is grown for the purpose of obtaining good seed, which at the present time is in very great request throughout the Province of Behar and Orissa.

Rice, which is the chief product, frequently gives a return of 35 maunds to the acre, but a fair average yield for the whole crop is 17 maunds. A mill has been erected at Bhiroganj, adjoining the railway station, and its eight hulling machines, driven by two steam engines (by Marshall, Sons & Co.), are able to deal each day with 800 maunds of rice. This factory is known as the B.B.A. Rice Mills, and is owned by Messrs. Bion, Broncke, and Amman, while Mr. R. S. Bion is managing proprietor.

All cereals give fair average returns, especially oats, which yield 17 maunds to the acre, and the bulk of these crops are grown chiefly for home consumption.

Dealing in hides has in recent years been established as a branch business, but transactions are limited to local purchases and sales.

Two bungalows, substantially constructed of brick in the years 1901 and 1910 respectively, are most conveniently situated almost in the centre of the estate, and not more than a quarter of a mile distant from the post and telegraph offices and railway station at Amolwa, while the outbuildings, consisting of stables, warehouses, and sheds for the housing of implements and the storage of general produce, are of a very superior character.

Lessees on this estate pay annual rents at the rate of four rupees to the *bigha*, and their expenses of cultivation amount to Rs. 25, but the preparation of new or previously uncropped lands would cost fully Rs. 40 for the same area. The

BELWA CONCERN.

1. The Snows above the Ramnagar Hills. 2. Belwa House. 3. View from Top of Bungalow.

BELWA CONCERN.

1. RICE MILL AT BHAIROGANG. 2. INTERIOR OF RICE MILL.

bigha is not a fixed standard of measurement in the district of Champarun, as it varies very considerably in size, ranging from 0·51 of an acre in the south, and increasing gradually in a northerly direction, until at Belwa it represents about 2½ English acres.

About thirty pairs of bullocks and five elephants are required for general work in the fields.

Mr. Amman retains the management of the entire estate in his own hands, and he usually employs about fifty Indian labourers.

BENIPORE

The lease of this concern, dated 1834, was given to a Mr. Henderson, then manager of the Hatte-Oustee factory, whose right to build was challenged by Mr. John Gale, of Pundoul, as the latter gentleman claimed that Benipore was within the borders of his *dehat*. The dispute was settled by the two places being worked together until the year 1890, when Mr. G. N. Wyatt, who had become the owner of the whole concern, disposed of the Benipore portion to Mr. Percy Jones and others. At the present time (1916) the owners of Benipore are Mr. W. K. Dunsford (temporary managing proprietor), Mr. Percy Jones, and certain members of the latter's family, who cultivate about 2,000 bighas for their own use, while the area of the estate over which they have control measures six miles in length by about four miles in width. The productive portion consists of 100 bighas of sugar, 1,000 bighas of indigo, 150 bighas of wheat, 150 bighas of oats, and about 600 bighas of paddy.

Indigo of the Java and Sumatrana types gives an average yield of about eight seers to the bigha, and the harvested crop is sent to the factory, which has a vat capacity of about 24,000 cubic feet. About 200 maunds of indigo are manufactured yearly, and the whole of this quantity is either shipped direct to London or sold in Calcutta.

There is a small sugar-mill at Benipore, which is capable of crushing 400 maunds of cane daily. The boiling process is carried out in open pans by means of six boilers, and after the product has been allowed to settle in tanks for a couple of weeks it is passed on to two centrifugal manufacturing machines. Non-granulated brown sugar is also made, and a very satisfactory price is obtained for it in local markets. The milling machinery includes a very fine boiler —using crushed cane as fuel—and it has a well-built chimney which is particularly noticeable.

A steam threshing machine is used for wheat, oats, and paddy, and an abundant supply of water for all purposes is derived from an adjacent river, upon which the owners possess riparian rights.

The proprietors have about twenty-eight pairs of bullocks on the concern, but the ploughing and other agricultural work on the estate requires the use of a far larger number of oxen, and the latter are hired from the tenants. A good bull is kept by the owners for stud purposes.

A small market is held every Tuesday upon the property, which is twelve miles distant from the post office and railway station at Sakri.

Practically all manufacturing is done at the outwork of Hursingpore, which is some four miles distant from the principal bungalow.

Mr. Dunsford, who has one European assistant, usually employs about a hundred hands.

THE BENGAL PRESERVING COMPANY

The varieties of fruits grown in the district of Muzaffurpur are not so numerous as in some other divisions of Behar, and market reports show clearly that the quantity produced annually is considerably below the actual demand. This shortage is not only the experience of ordinary consumers of freshly-plucked fruit, but it is a somewhat serious matter for industrial concerns like the Bengal Preserving Company, who are unable at present to obtain a sufficient supply for manufacturing purposes.

The business of this company was established by the proprietor, Mr. B. C. Sinha, of Muzaffurpur, in the year 1910 for preserving fruit, the principal kinds being mango, lichi, pineapple, and pear. The factory premises, covering about an acre of land, adjoin the owner's private residence at the above-named town, where he practises as a pleader, and they are equipped with modern machinery, obtained from New York, all of which, including the sterilization plant, is driven by steam. The annual output is about one hundred thousand bottles and tins, and large stocks of all kinds of preserves are kept in a very fine storeroom. An overhead tank holds a sufficient quantity of water for use throughout the factory, and the utmost cleanliness is observable in every branch of work. Tins to contain jam are made on the premises, and are packed for dispatch in boxes, each containing two dozen.

Calcutta is the principal market for these goods, although a considerable quantity has been exported to London and the Continent of Europe, while still more recently consignments have been sent to the United States of America.

The preserving season continues during the months of May, June, July, and

THE BENGAL PRESERVING COMPANY.
DISPLAY OF PRESERVES.

BENIPORE CONCERN.

1. BENIPORE BUNGALOW. 2. GENERAL VIEW OF FACTORY. 3. CATTLE. 4. CANE-CRUSHING MILL.

August, and about seventy hands are required during this portion of the year.

A branch has been opened in Calcutta for the sale of jams, jellies, chutneys, and condiments of all kinds.

BYREAH CONCERN

The total area of land comprised in the Byreah Concern in the district of Chumparun is about 22,000 acres, and the portion cultivated direct from the factory consists of 1,200 acres of indigo, 600 acres of oats, 200 acres of barley, sugar-cane, and native produce, together with 70 acres of tobacco grown upon land which is leased to native tenants.

It is ascertained from early historical records that the factory was erected in 1884 by Mr. C. F. Carlton, who was manager from that year until 1890, and again from 1891 to 1894, when it was sold to Mr. H. Hudson, who placed Mr. W. A. Cox in charge. Mr. H. E. Hudson, the present proprietor and son of Mr. H. Hudson, managed the concern in 1905, and Mr. H. C. M. Gale has had control of the concern since 1911.

BYREAH CONCERN.

1. Bungalow. 2. Bamboo Avenue. 3. Factory.

The original bungalow was built about the year 1885, but it was destroyed by fire, and another was erected in 1887. Adjoining it are an exceedingly pretty garden and ornamental grounds, in addition to a large area planted with vegetables, and the fine outbuildings include nice offices, a cake-house capable of holding 1,000 maunds of indigo, and stables, built on arches, for fourteen horses.

The whole of the land on the concern, including the outwork at Nowton, four miles distant, consists of first-class soil, upon which irrigation is unnecessary, and the average yields of all crops are most satisfactory.

Java indigo is grown at Byreah, as it has been found to be more suitable than the Sumatrana variety, and a return of about 14 seers to the acre may usually be relied upon. An ample supply of water is pumped from a lake to the factory, in which steam power is used, and the manufactured produce is either shipped direct to England or is disposed of in Calcutta. The total capacity of the vats at the two places is 36,000 cub. ft. Other crops, with the exception of oats, which are sent to Calcutta, are sold locally.

Byreah is situated in that portion of the district of Champarun known as the "old river country," which, prior to the construction of embankments, was frequently flooded, and low-caste Indians of the fisherman class, attracted thither for the purpose of earning livelihoods, are now employed as coolies by planters. Mr. Hudson finds constant work for about 250 of these under the supervision of Mr. Gale and one European assistant.

Some sixty-five pairs of bullocks are kept for cultivation of the land, and the modern farming machinery and implements, including a steam threshing machine, are kept in good working order by labourers attached to the carpentering and repairing shops on the concern.

Byreah is six miles distant from the railway station and post and telegraph offices at Bettiah.

BHICANPORE AND JAPAHA CONCERNS

Permission was given by the East India Company for the erection of an

BHICANPORE AND JAPAHA CONCERN.

1. Bhicanpore Bungalow. 2. Sugar Factory. 3. Vats at the Japaha Indigo Factory. 4. Manager's Bungalow, Japaha.

BHICANPORE AND JAPAHA CONCERN.

1. Steam Plough Engine. 2. Cane Crop. 3. Evaporating Pans. 4. 8-roller Cane Crushing Mill.

indigo factory at Bhicanpore, in the district of Tirhut, in the year 1819, and the letter addressed by the Commissioners of the Company to a Mr. Cahill authorized him "to hold 50 *bighas* of land" required by him for that purpose. The property now comprises 5,000 acres, the productive portion consisting of 2,000 acres of sugar-cane, 1,500 acres of indigo, and 1,500 acres of wheat, barley, oats, mustard, and other crops.

The land has been thoroughly well ploughed with steam tackle, and enriched by being manured with a crop of green flax turned in, with the result that the concern verifies the truth of the adage that there is nothing in the world more grateful for good treatment than the soil.

Dealing first of all with sugar, which occupies the largest area of the concern, it is observed that the cane is sent in carts to the cane carrier and conveyed to the splitting, crushing, and roller-mills, the refuse being elevated to boilers and subsequently used as fuel for raising steam.

The juice is pumped through boxes of sulphur fumes prior to being heated, and it is subsequently passed on to the defication plant, from which the clarified juice is transferred to eliminators for the removal of more impurities, the latter under pressure being passed through press filters. Following upon these measures the product is pumped into settling tanks, from which the juice is filtered through Taylor's filters and then through Harvey's "Triple" evaporator, leaving those as a clarified syrup, which is boiled in the vacuum pans and converted into sugar. The syrup leaves the pans as a mixture of sugar and molasses, going into a receiver with agitators which keep it in motion, and from there it is charged into the centrifugal machines, when the molasses is separated from the sugar. The latter is then conveyed by the use of elevators to the sugar floor, and after passing through a drier it is either crushed or kept as grained sugar, according to the demand, and is then packed in double gunny bags containing 200 lb.

A considerable quantity of the output is sold locally, but the greater portion is consigned to the Punjab and the North-Western Districts.

The season for crushing cane extends from December to April, and the average yield of sugar is 1 ton to 14 or 15 tons of cane.

The sugar factory and an excellent sugar store (which cover eight acres of land, and are erected on the banks of a beautiful lake, from which a good supply of water for all purposes can be obtained) are commodious buildings, constructed of brick, and equipped with excellent machinery, which is able to crush about three hundred tons of cane in a day of twenty-four hours.

The head indigo factory is at Bhicanpore, where there is a very fine bungalow, charmingly situated in a nice garden, and occupied by Mr. G. L. Richardson, the managing proprietor. There are also four out-factories (indigo), managed by European assistants, and sugar-cane and indigo grown at these places and at the head factory are sent by cart to the sugar factory.

CHITWARRAH CONCERN

The Chitwarrah concern is a portion of an estate in the district of Muzaffarpur, belonging to an old indigo company whose headquarters were at Shahpore Mircha the *mokararie pottah* being dated in the year 1799, but it became a separate property about forty-five years ago, having been purchased by the present manager's father and other partners. The property now belongs to the estate of G. D. Blake, deceased, and is under the control of Mr. G. C. Blake, and is, roughly, about nine miles by four miles in extent, the greater portion of the land being now a Zemindary, the *ryots* of the forty or more villages being tenants of the proprietor.

The cultivation of indigo has always been the staple industry of the concern, but the factory was closed in 1912 owing to unsatisfactory prices prevailing for the manufactured product. During the season of 1915, however, a small quantity of indigo was again sown, and in the present year (1916) about 850 *bighas* have been planted, the whole of the remainder of the estate being cropped by natives with country produce.

There are three old graves in the garden near the principal bungalow, one of them undated, but the other two bearing inscriptions showing the burials to have taken place in the years 1812 and 1838.

Chitwarrah is about two miles distant from the post office at Mahuwa, nine miles from the telegraph office and railway station at Bhagwanpore, and twenty-six miles from Muzaffarpur.

The management of the whole estate is under the personal supervision of Mr. Blake.

CHOWTURWA CONCERN

One has to look back to the early seventies of last century to obtain particulars of the property which was the first portion to be purchased of the very extensive estate of Chowturwa, in the district of Champaran, now in the hands of Messrs. Broucke Brothers, as *thikkadars* in the Bettiah Raj. The late Mr. W. J. Broucke secured a considerable quantity of land at Bhurpurwa, in the district of Gorakpur, and other tracts have been obtained from time to time, until now, in 1916, the area comprises a large stretch of country on the northern bank of the Naranie River, together with an area seven square miles in extent—known as Mudhbunny—situated on the western side of the Naranie River and running in a westerly direction to the Gorakpur border.

The principal crops grown at Chowturwa for a considerable number of years were sugar-cane, and various kinds of country produce, chiefly rice, oats, wheat, barley, maize, and *huldi*, were in evidence at Mudhbunny; but the cultivation of cane has been discontinued in favour of indigo. Sugar was manufactured under what is known as the "country" system until 1915, but the factory at Chowturwa has now been altered and equipped with machinery and plant to meet the new order of things.

About 1,000 acres of the estate were planted with indigo during the season 1915-16, and, if the present favourable prices for the product are maintained, the area under this crop will be very considerably extended. A new factory, designed on modern principles and equipped with up-to-date machinery, is now being erected at Mudhbunny.

The question of the steps to be taken for the improvement of the various breeds of cattle in Bengal has been under the consideration of the Government of the province for the past twenty years, and although valuable suggestions on the subject have been made in a Report by the Director of Agriculture of Bengal in 1915, the matter is one which must be eventually solved by individual breeders possessed of sound, practical common sense, who are prepared to spend both time and money in attaining the object in view.

Messrs. Broucke take a deep interest

CHOWTURWA CONCERNS.

1. Chowturwa Bungalow. 2. Elephants. 3. Mudhbunny Bungalow. 4. Elephants.

1. BAND AND GUARD. 2. POLO PONIES. 3. MADAN MOHAN TEMPLE.

and other important buildings. The Bairagidighi tank was considerably enlarged in the year 1897, and it is now 446 feet in length, 440 feet in breadth, and has an average depth of 289 feet.

The town is symmetrically and picturesquely laid out by means of straight and broad roads, which intersect one another at right angles, and they are planted with palm, *sisu*, mango, and other trees. On every hand is seen a wealth of luxuriant verdure, and as one alights from the train at the railway station an exceedingly pretty view of the town is obtained. Green woods and pastures abound, and away to the north and north-west are the blue-grey summits of the Bhutan Hills, and the peaks of the Himalayas in the far distance.

The Maharaja's Palace is a large and magnificent structure, beautifully classical in design and workmanship. It covers an area of 51,309 square feet, it is 393 feet in length, and 296 feet in breadth. The Durbar Hall, 72 feet by 65 feet, is on the ground floor, and the central portion is covered by an elegantly shaped metal dome surmounted by a lantern, the top of which is 124 feet 10 inches above the ground. Other apartments include a large number of bed or dressing-rooms, dining and drawing-rooms, a billiard room, four *Toshakhana* rooms, eleven bathrooms, and ladies' gallery and vestibule.

This fine mansion, decorated and furnished in the most sumptuous manner very largely according to English ideas, is situated in the south-western portion of an extensive park, and is surrounded by tastefully laid out and well-kept gardens. Within a short distance are stables, coach-houses, motor garages, and quarters for servants, while on the north side of the palace are spacious lawn tennis courts, covered tennis and racket courts, and a skating rink. The State library, which must not be overlooked, was established by Colonel Haughton in the year 1870, and one historian has expressed the opinion that "the little State of Cooch Behar on the borders of Assam can boast of a library richer than any to be found in Bengal outside Calcutta." It contains about nine thousand volumes, chiefly in English, although there are works in Bengali, Sanskrit, Urdu, Persian, and other languages. The library is now accommodated in Lansdowne Hall, which was erected in honour of the visit to Cooch Behar of the Earl of Lansdowne, Viceroy of India in the year 1892.

During the minority of His Highness Maharaja Sir Nripendra Narayan, the Government assumed control of administration, the State being governed by a Commissioner, but on attaining his majority he was given full powers, and from that time the Estates have been controlled by a Memorandum of Administration issued by him.

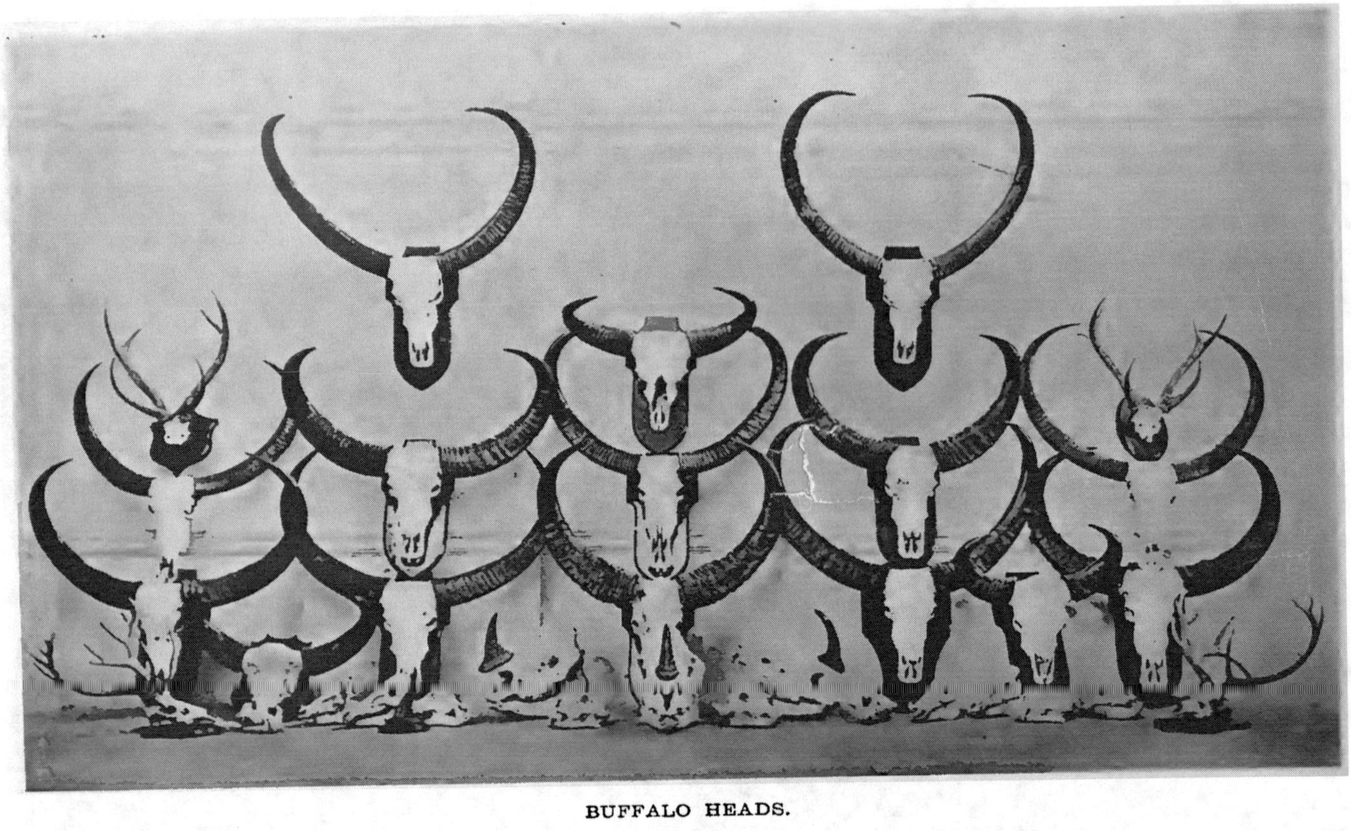

BUFFALO HEADS.

The functions of the State Council are three-fold, viz.: legislative, executive, and judicial. The Vice-President of the State Council is the head of the General Department, which has branches relating to education, public works, agriculture, forests, and other subjects; the Dewan is the head of the Revenue, Settlement, and *Dabutter* Department, and the Civil and Sessions Judge presides over the judicial department.

The inhabitants of Cooch Behar have for a considerable number of years enjoyed the advantages of being ruled by wise administrators, who have taken a deep personal interest in all State affairs, and have encouraged the people to raise themselves in moral, social, intellectual, educational and other problems.

The present Maharaja is greatly respected throughout the State, and his geniality and kindliness of heart have become household words.

His Highness is now causing the town of Cooch Behar to be greatly improved in general appearance by the opening up of new roads, the planting of trees, the installation of electric light for general use, and by the construction of a complete system of waterworks. Particular attention is being devoted to the class or style of architecture of the principal buildings now being erected, and English and Indian designs are occasionally blended with very pleasing effects.

In connection with Freemasonry it may be added that His Highness was, in the year 1905, initiated by special dispensation, and at the present time he is District Grand Warden of Bengal.

BERTRAM'S RHINO.

BENGAL AND ASSAM, BEHAR AND ORISSA

THE TRIPURA (HILL TIPPERA) STATE

By E. F. SANDYS

THE antiquity of an Indian Raj can only be determined by looking into the ancient history of India, so fully recorded in the old books handed down to us, together with the inscriptions on old monuments and coins revealed to modern times chiefly by European research. That history is a record of thirty-two centuries, and divides itself into five distinct epochs, each of which equals the entire history of most modern peoples. The greatest Sanskrit scholars have come to the conclusion that the first Aryan settlement of India was made in the Indus valley about 2000 B.C.

When the Aryans came to the Sutlej, having occupied all the land of the Punjab, they naturally crossed over and entered into the Gangetic Valley, or the Doab. During the course of the next four hundred years, down to 1000 B.C., the Hindus (by whom are meant the Indo-Aryans), spread down the Doab and founded powerful kingdoms and nationalities, who cultivated science and literature, and developed new forms of religion and civilization wholly different from the Vedic period. Among the nations who flourished in the Gangetic Valley the most renowned have left their names in the literature of Hindu India. The Kurus established their kingdom round about their capital, Hastinapur, near the site of modern Delhi. The Panchalas settled round about modern Kanauj, and called their capital Indraprasthra, to the south-east of Delhi, and the Kosalas occupied the country between the Ganges and the Gunduck, including modern Oude. The Vaidehis lived to the east of the Gunduck in what is now known as Tirhut. The Kasis settled round their capital Kasi, the modern Benares. Continuing farther east, and occupying what is now known as Bengal Proper and the Province of Assam, were to be found the kingdoms of the Angas, Bangas (whose name has survived in the name of Bangadesh or Bengal), Karoli, Mrittikavati, Mohana, Pattana, Tripura, and Kosala. Besides these in Northern India there were numerous great and small kingdoms in Central and Southern India.

It is unnecessary to describe the great war in detail, but a brief account is necessary to show what connection the Tripura Raj had with this ancient episode. Turning to the "Mahabharat," we find that Yudhisthira sent forth to conquer and bring to tribute the lesser kings. In the "Sabha Parva," Chapter XXXI, the sixtieth verse, it is found that Shahadeva, the younger brother of Yudhisthira, among others, conquered the "immeasurably effulgent Tripura." This epithet "immeasurably effulgent" clearly proves that Tripura was a Kshatriya, as only such ever had this designation applied to them.

After the departure of the Pandu brothers into forest exile (*vanavas*), Duryodhana became king and determined to have himself declared *samrat* or emperor. He therefore sent forth armies under various commanders, one of whom, Karna, as related in verses nine to eleven of Chapter CCLIII of Vana Parva of the "Mahabharat," after conquering various kingdoms, came to the Batsabhumi or grazing country, and subjugated Keroli, Mrittikavati, Mohana and Pattana, Tripura and Kosala, and made them all pay tribute.

In the great battle of Kurukshetra all the kings of the Lunar race ranged either on the side of Duryodhana or on that of Yudhisthira. Bhisma, the *senapati* or commander-in-chief of the Kuru (Duryodhana's) army, had under his command a number of subordinate generals. Three of these are mentioned in the Bhisma Parva, Chapter LXXXXIV, in the eighth and ninth verses, and are Drona, Bhagadatta, and Vrihatbala, the king of Kosalas. The last named had in his division the kinds of Melaka, Tripura, and Chichila.

From the foregoing facts and quotations it is indisputable:—

Firstly. That whenever the great war of the "Mahabharat" took place, or whether it took place at all, or is merely a Lunar myth, collected by Vyasa, yet the kingdom of Tripura did exist before Vyasa's time, that is, before 600 B.C., otherwise he could not have mentioned it in his list of kings.

The Tripura Raj, therefore, was considered a kingdom of sufficient importance to have been invaded and made to pay tribute to Yudhisthira and to Duryodhana, the *samrats* of India, and to have taken part in the great battle of Kurukshetra.

Secondly. That the Tripura, mentioned in the extracts from the "Mahabharat," was in eastern India below the Himalayas in the neighbourhood of Banga, or what we now call Bengal, that is where the present Raj of Tripura is now situated, even in its present shrunken dimensions. Furthermore, as there is no other *raj* or country or king to be found anywhere or at any time during the whole Hindu domination of India elsewhere, other than the Tripura Raj in question, it cannot be said that the Tripura of the "Mahabharat" is other than the Tripura now under notice.

Thirdly. That the use of the expression "immeasurably effulgent" applied to Tripura shows beyond dispute or cavil that the King of Tripura was a recognized Kshatriya of the Royal Warrior Caste in Vyasa's time, and at least six hundred years before the Christian era.

Fourthly. That the Rajput princes, though popularly considered the most ancient and honourable of all reigning feudatory rulers in India, only came into power as rulers about A.D. 750 to 950, or almost twelve hundred years after the Tripura kings are cited in at least three distinct, and far apart, verses of the "Mahabharat" by Vyasa two thousand five hundred years ago.

The Tripura Raj is mentioned in the list of kingdoms on the Emperor Asokas's pillar in the Fort of Allahabad, and is now after a lapse of over two thousand two hundred years, the only one State in existence of all those mentioned, another proof of its incomparable antiquity.

The third paragraph of the inscription on the Asoka *Lat* or Pillar, at present in the Fort of Allahabad, built by the Mogul Emperor Akbar in 1557, mentions Tripura among the frontier kingdoms, but this pillar was originally set up at Kausambi, because it bears, in addition to other records, an order of Asoka addressed to the officials of Kausambi, one of the most celebrated cities of ancient India, which probably stood on the sites of the present villages of Kosam Inam and Kosam Khiraj in the Manghampur *tahsil* of the Allahabad district, on the bank of the Jumma. The most recent location, however, is at Gurgi in the State of Rewah. "Whose imperious commands were fully gratified by the payment of taxes and the execution of his orders by the frontier kings (Pratyanta Nripati) or Sanatata, Davaka, Kamaruya, Napala, Kartripura, and other countries; and by the Matavas, Arjunda-

HER EXCELLENCY LADY CARMICHAEL, H.H. MAHARAJA BIRENDRAKISHOR MANIKYA, H.E. LORD CARMICHAEL.

yanas, Yaudheyans, Madrakas, Abhiras, Prajunas, Sanakanikas, Kakas, Kharaparikas, and other tribes."

We gather from the Purans that Pururavas was the first of the Chandravansa or Lunar line of kings. Fourth in descent from Pururavas was Gritsamada, whose son was Saunaka. His second cousin once removed was Dirghatamas, who is said to have begotten by the wife of Bali, the sixteenth in descent from Pururavas, five sons, named Anga, Banga, Kalinga, Sumbha, and Pundra, from whom the five countries of East Behar, East Bengal, Orissa, Tripura, and North Bengal, are named.

The Rajas of Tripura are Chandravansa Kshtriyas, and their ancestor Tripur was descended from Pururavas.

Chittrayudh was the "immeasurably effulgent," or the Kshatriya Rajah of Tripura, who was subjugated by Sahadeva, the Pandu general sent forth with the white horse by his eldest brother Yudhisthira, the rival of his cousin Duryadhana the Kuru. The subjugation of Chittrayudh has been related in the twenty-first chapter of the Digvijaya of the Sabha Parva of the "Mahabharata." Whenever a Kshatriya Raja of ancient times wished to have himself acknowledged as *samrat* (emperor) by contemporary rulers, he sent forth a white horse to wander at will over the dominions of his neighbours for the space of a year. Should any ruler oppose the progress of the white horse, he had to fight the accompanying army, sent for the purpose of subjugating refractory neighbours. When the wanderings of the white horse had been completed the animal was sacrificed with most imposing religious ceremonies at an *Asvamedha* (*asv* = horse, and *medha* = sacrifice). This sacrifice preceded the *rajasuya* or coronation of the raja as *samrat*. The coronation ceremony (described in the Aitareya Brahmana, Chapter VIII, verse 39) was attended by all the rajas who owned allegiance, and to them were allotted all the great offices of ceremonial as superintendents in various departments. At the close of the ceremony various honours were bestowed by the *samrat* on each of the rajas before they returned to their dominions. Chitrayudh attended the *rajasuya* of Yudhisthira, when, according to the Kanva text, the priests addressed the assembly and said:—

"This is your King, O ye Kurus, O ye Panchallas!"

The honour, or as it would now be called, the *khillat*, bestowed on Chittrayudh by the Emperor Yudisthira, was the *Svetachattra* (*svet* = white, and *chattra* = umbrella) or royal white umbrella, which to this day is the chief insignia of the rajas of Tripura, and is unfurled when they ascend the throne on their installation by direction of the Emperor of India, who also bestows a *khillat* of nine articles.

Era.

It should be noted that the Tripura is the only ruling dynasty that has an Era of its own. It dates from A.D. 590, when Raja Birraj, from whom the present raja is the hundred and seventeenth in descent, extended his conquests beyond the Ganges. The months of the Tripura year are the same as those generally prevailing in Bengal.

The following corresponding dates illustrate the various eras clearly: 1st September, 1915, Christian era; 15th Bhadra, 1322, Bengali; 15th Bhadra, 1325, Tripura; 8th Bhadra, 1322, Fasli; 8th Bhadra Budi, 1972, Samvat; 15th Bhadra, 1837, Saka; and 20th Showal, 1333, Hijri.

The Rajamala.

The origin and history of the Tripura Raj is given in the Rajamala (literally meaning the "Garland of Kings") or Chronicles of Tripura. It is the oldest specimen of Bengali composition extant. It is in verse, and was in a detached form, but was collected and written in sequence by the Brahmin officials of Raja Dharma Manikya, the hundred and second raja, who ascended the Tripura *gadi* in A.D. 1407. His successors have continued the task year by year until we have now one of the oldest continuous chronicles of any Indian reigning family.

Making every allowance for poetic fancy, Brahminical love of the supernatural, and courtly flattery, there is a written record stretching back to the Aryans in the Epic period, or three thousand years ago, when Druhya, the second son of the *Samrat* or Emperor Yayati, a Kshatriya of the Lunar Race, was exiled, together with his elder and two younger brothers, as is related in the "Mahabharat" (in Chapter LXXXIV of the Shambhava Parva of the Adi Parva), wherein it is described how the aged emperor called upon his five sons, each in order of his age, to take upon himself his old age and give him his youth for a time. The eldest Yadu, then Druhya, followed by his two next brothers, Turvasu and Anu, refused, and were cursed by their father with various penalties and sent into exile.

The curse upon Druhya is given in the twentieth, twenty-first, and twenty-second verses of the above-mentioned chapter. It is to the effect that he should go into exile and spend his days in a pathless country where the only means of conveyance was by rafts and floats. Consequently Druhya retired with his companions to the eastern parts of the empire, where the floods of the Brahmaputra submerged the surrounding country and necessitated water carriage.

Druhya's descendant Tripura settled on the banks of the Kapila, a confluent of the Brahmaputra, and founded the city of Tribeg ("the place where three streams meet") as the capital of his kingdom, which became known thenceforth to this day as Tripura, after its founder, who lived over three thousand years ago.

According to the legend, Tripur was the grandson of Chitrayudh, who had attended the *rajasya* or imperial assemblage of the *Samrat* Yudhisthira and had been granted the *Svetachattra* or white royal umbrella as his insignia by the emperor, as already mentioned. Tripur is said to have been a passionate, tyrannical ruler, who neglected the due worship of Siva. His subjects were in great distress and appealed to the Raja of Hidamba (Cachar), which in those days was in the valley of the Brahmaputra, from which its raja and people were driven by the oppression of more powerful princes. Under the ancestors of their Raja Govinda Deo, who ruled in the first half of the thirteenth century, they migrated to the valley of the Barak, which now forms the district of Cachar. The Raja of Hidamba could not or would not render the Tripuras any assistance, and, as Tripur became more and more tyrannical and godless, they cried to Siva, who, when sufficiently provoked by Tripur shooting arrows at the *lingam*, the emblem of Siva, and thus bringing his worship into contempt, slew Tripur in wrath. Tripur had left no son to succeed him, but his widow was pregnant. Great was the grief of the innocent and disconsolate rani, and her entreaties, joined to the prayers of the Tripuras, allayed the wrath of Siva, who promised that the rani's unborn child should be a son, who would be the recipient of his godship's favour. And, as a sign, he should have on his forehead the mark of the third or central eye, a distinguishing feature of Siva. In due course Tripur's widowed rani gave birth to a posthumous son, who bore Siva's

HIS HIGHNESS THE LATE MAHARAJA RADHAKISHOR MANIKYA.

HIS HIGHNESS BIRENDRAKISHOR ENTHRONED.

promised token and was accordingly named Trilochana (three-eyed) in compliment to the god, one of whose names is Tryambaka, having the same meaning. So that Tripur founded his capital Tribeg and was succeeded by his son Trilochana, a trio of trinities! Ancient history is usually veiled in myths and related in legends, but facts in almost every case form the foundation of these stories.

Trilochana was placed on the throne amidst the rejoicings of the people, and was distinguished for wisdom and piety at an early age. Neighbouring chiefs paid him homage, and the Raja of Hidamba (Cachar) offered Trilochana his daughter in marriage. The nuptials were celebrated with great rejoicings, and twelve sons were born of this union.

On the death of the sonless Raja of Hidamba a dispute arose as to which of his grandsons was to occupy the vacant throne. To solve the difficulty peacefully Trilochana sent messengers to the venerated shrine of Siva on Sagar Island, to request the priests to come and solve the difficulty. The name "Sagar" means the sea, and situated as it is at the point where the holy Ganges once mingled its waters with the bay, the island is regarded as peculiarly sacred. Thousands of pilgrims from all parts of India visit it annually to wash away their sins in the Bengali month of Magh. In ancient times there were on Sagar Island a famous *tol* or Sanskrit college for Pandits and a shrine of Siva, erected by the Rajas of Tripura when their dominions spread far more westward than they do now. The temple and *tol* were diluviated in 1842. The *Dandis*, as Siva's priests were called, remembering the persecutions of the godless Tripura, were afraid to send any *Pandits* to Tripura until they learnt of Trilochana's piety and peaceful habits. Some of the *Dandis* returned with the messengers, settled the question of the succession to Hidamba, and returned rejoicing with many gifts from Trilochana.

The cult of Siva still continues to be the State religion of Tripura, but the rajas are now personally Vishnavas, probably since Chaitanya's time, in 1485. It should be noted that when Siva promised Tripur's widowed rani a son he stipulated that Surya and Chandra, or the sun and moon, as well as the Chaudadevtas, should be duly and regularly worshipped. These gods are to this day so worshipped, and their temples and priests duly provided for by the State. These gods are: (1) Hara or Siva, the destroyer in the Hindu trinity; (2) Uma or Durga, the consort of Siva; (3) Hari or Vishnu, the preserver in the Hindu trinity; (4) Ma or Lakshmi, the consort of Vishnu, and the goddess of prosperity; (5) Bani or Saraswati, goddess of knowledge; (6) most sacred river of the Hindus; (12) Sekhi or Agni, the god of fire; (13) Kama, the god of love; and (14) Himadri, the Himalaya mountains.

The images of these Chaudadevatas are made of *Astadhatu*, an alloy of the eight

HIS HIGHNESS THE MAHARAJA BIRCHANDRA MANIKYA.

Kumara or Kartikeya, the god of war and the commander-in-chief of the gods; (7) Ganapa or Ganesha, the god of wisdom; (8) Bidhu or Chandra, the moon; (9) Ka or Brahma, the creator in the Hindu trinity; (10) Abdhi, the god of the ocean or water; (11) Ganga, the (sacred) metals, viz. gold, silver, lead, tin, copper, iron, antimony, and zinc. Originally the figures were about half life size, but now for some reason there are only the heads, with a portion of the neck.

The sacrificial worship of these *Devatas* is duly maintained, but goats are now sacrificed instead of human beings as in olden days. The priests are a special class known as *Chuntais,* and the chief Chuntai, according to a very ancient custom, wears a golden sacred thread (*poita* or *janeo*) and rules for three days in the year. This period is called the *Ker*, during which he and his priests or *Galims* are supreme, but now only symbolically.

Though the limits of the Tripura Raj have been altered, enlarged, and reduced, as is only natural through the thirty centuries of storm and stress of the Hindu, Mahommedan, and British dominations in India, yet this ancient Aryan Raj still survives in its present diminished territories, now bounded by the districts of Sylhet and Cachar on the north, Lushailand on the east, the Hill Tracts and Chittagong on the south, and by the districts of Noakhali and Tippera on the west. But so late as the sixteenth century the Raj stretched from Kamrup in Assam to the north, to Arakan in the south, from the empire of Burma on the east to the then densely populated Sunderbans on the west.

The capital was gradually moved from Tribeg, on the Brahmaputra on the north, to Udaipur, on the Gumti, on the south, and then back again to Agartala, on the Haura, where the present Raja has his seat of Government.

The early history of Cachar, or Hidamba, as it was anciently called, is obscure, but it appears that it formerly belonged to the kingdom of Tripura. It is, however, certain that the last native king of Cachar was the descendant of a line of princes who originally came from the Assam valley. The Cachar kings were forced, by the aggressions of the Ahoms on the north and of the Angami Nagas on the south, to remove and take up their abode on the Mahar River. While settled there, about the beginning or middle of the seventeenth century, the Cachari king married a daughter of the Tripura Raja who received the valley of Cachar as her dowry, and the capital was transferred to Kampur between 1700 and 1750. Govinda Chandra, the last Raja of Cachar, was assassinated in 1830, and as he left no heir, natural or adopted, the country was annexed by the British Government on August 14, 1832.

Mahommedan Period.

It is unnecessary to go through the detailed chronicles of the Rajamala until the first occasion of the Tripura Raj coming into hostile contact with the Mogul domination of Northern India which succeeded the Hindu rulers.

About A.D. 1270, a Hindu Chaudhuri passing through the Tripura Raj, on his way to the Court of the Mogul Subadar at Gour, complained that he had been robbed while passing through the Tripura Raj, but had not been able to obtain justice at the hands of the Tripura officials. The Subadar was only too glad to have an excuse for interfering, and he invaded Tripura with a large army, but was repulsed.

Hari, the ninety-seventh Raja, had eighteen sons, of whom Ratna, though one of the youngest, was considered the most intelligent, and he was sent by his father to travel abroad and gain experience. He visited and resided at the court of the Mogul Subadar, during which stay the Raja Hari died and an elder son ascended. Ratna asked Togral Khan, the Subadar of the Emperor Balban of Delhi, to help him gain the Raj. This request afforded the Subadar an excellent opportunity for retrieving the before-mentioned defeat of the Mogul army. As Stewart relates on page 70 of his "History of Bengal": "In the year 678 Hijri (A.D. 1279) he assembled a very numerous army and invaded the country of Jajnagar. After having defeated the Raja in a general engagement, he plundered the inhabitants, and brought away with him immense wealth and one hundred elephants."

Why Tripura should have been called "Jajnagar" by the Mahommedans is not clear, though the historian Farishta mentions a "Jajnagar" to the east of the Brahmaputra, and perhaps meant Tripura.

The following is a list of the rajas who ruled in Tripura from the year 1279:—

Ratna Manikya	1279—1323
Pratap, Manikya, Mukinda Manikya, and Maha Manikya...	1323—1407
Dharmma Manikya ...	1407—1458
Interregnum	1458—1490
Dhanya Manikya	1490—1520
Deva Manikya	1520—1535
Indra Manikya	1535
Bujaya Manikya	1535—1583
Ananta Manikya	1583—1585
Uday Manikya	1585—1596
Jai Manikya	1596—1597
Amar Manikya	1597—1611
Rajdhar Manikya	1611—1613
Jashadhar Manikya ...	1613—1623
Interregnum	1623—1625
Kalyan Manikya	1625—1659
Govinda Manikya	1659—1660
Chhattra Manikya	1660—1666
Govinda Manikya (for the second time)	1666—1669
Ram Manikya	1669—1682
Ratna Manikya II	1682
Narendra Manikya... ...	1682—1684
Ratna Manikya (for the second time)	1684—1712
Mahendra Manikya ...	1712—1714
Dharmma Manikya ...	1714—1732
Jagat Manikya	1732—1733
Dharmma Manikya (for the second time)	1733
Mukunda Manikya... ...	1733—1737
Jai Manikya	1737—1739
Indra Manikya	1739—1743
Bijai Manikya	Uncertain
Krishna Manikya	1760—1783
Jahnabi Mahadevi... ...	1783—1785
Rajdhar Manikya	1785—1804
Durga Manikya	1804—1813
Ramganga Manikya ...	1813—1826
Kasichandra Manikya ...	1826—1830
Krishnakishor Manikya ...	1830—1849
Isanchandra Manikya ...	1849—1862
Birchandra Manikya ...	1862—1896
Radhakishor Manikya ...	1896—1909
Birendrakishor Manikya (the present raja)	1909—

Ratna (1279—1323) having, by the help of the Mogul army, defeated his brother, beheaded him, and ascended the *gadi* as raja in A.D. 1279. Having presented the Subadar with a valuable ruby, the title of "Manikya" was bestowed on him. *Manikya* means a perfect ruby of a certain size and shape, and this title has been borne by the Rajas of Tripura ever since.

Ratna Manikya died in A.D. 1323, and was succeeded by his son Pratab Manikya, who was defeated by Sultan Iliya Shah, the ruler of Bengal. Pratab Manikya was succeeded by his younger brother Mokut Makunda, who in turn was succeeded by his son Maha Manikya, who died in 1407 and was succeeded by his son.

Dharma Manikya (1407-58). Meanwhile Sultan Fakiruddin Sikandar, having made himself independent of the Emperor of Delhi, became king of Bengal, and removed his seat of government to Sonargaon, south of Dacca. Fakiruddin was taken prisoner by Ali Mobarak, an imperial official, after a short reign of 2 years and 5 months. Ali Mobarak was assassinated after 1 year and 5 months by his foster brother Haji, who assumed the title of Shamsuddin and made himself King of Bengal.

After establishing his authority, Shamsuddin invaded the dominions of the Raja of Tripura and compelled him to pay a great sum of money and to give him a number of valuable elephants, with which he returned in triumph to his capital. Dharma Manikya in turn attacked and defeated the King of Bengal, Sultan Ahmad Shah, and plundered his capital at Sonargaon. This Raja had the "Dharma Sagar" excavated at Comilla, and he also reduced the great number of human sacrifices to a very small minimum. Dharma Manikya died in 1458.

An interregnum occurred till 1490, when Dhanya Manikya (1490–1520), the brother of Pratab Manikya, ascended the *gadi*. The Tripura Raj was at its zenith during Manikya's reign. In 1512 the Raja sent his general, Chuchug Rai, to attack the important Mogul garrison at Chittagong, or, as it was named by the Mogul, Islamabad (the abode of the Faith), and that expedition proved to be entirely successful. To avenge this disgrace Dhanya Manikya was attacked three times by the Moguls. Hussan Shah, the King of Jaunpur had contested the empire with the Emperor Sultan Beloli, and had, on being defeated, taken refuge at the Court of Allauddin, King of Bengal. Hussan Shah was sent at the head of a vast army gathered from the twelve provinces of Bengal to invade Tripura. He captured the fort at Meharkul, near Comilla, and proceeded up the Gumti River to attack the capital at Udaipur, but the Tripuras dammed up the river at Sonamora, where it debouches into the plains, and suddenly cutting the dyke at night, the Mogul encampment was swept away and most of the soldiers drowned. Shortly after this disastrous failure the Moguls again invaded Tripura under Haitan Khan and attempted to attack Udaipur, but they were similarly drowned by an artificial flood created in the narrow valley below Debtamora. A third invasion was defeated at Kasba.

Finding the Mogul horsemen such excellent cavalry, and having none of his own, the Raja of Tripura engaged a large number of Mogul sawars. When a thousand of them mutinied for arrears of pay and marched on Chittagong, then a Tripura garrison, the mutineers were overtaken and defeated, and those of them who were captured alive were beheaded at the temple of the Chaudadebta at Udaipur. To avenge this wholesale sacrificial slaughter the Mogul King sent a force of three thousand cavalry and six thousand infantry, under Mahammad Khan. At first he was successful, and the Tripuras lost their commander, but shortly after the Moguls were defeated and their general captured. He, too, was sent in a cage to the temple and sacrificed to the Chaudadevatas.

I. ARRIVAL OF HIS HONOUR THE LIEUTENANT-GOVERNOR AT THE PALACE, AGARTALA.
2. HIS HIGHNESS THE MAHARAJA RECEIVING THE LIEUTENANT-GOVERNOR AT THE PALACE.

Dhanya Manikya died in 1520, and was succeeded by his son—

Deva Manikya (1520-35). This Raja was defeated at Islamabad (Chittagong) by the Moguls under Sultan Nasrath Shah. On Deva Manikya's death the Chuntai (high priest) set up the late raja's nephew, Panchkauri Thakur, as—

Indra Manikya, but both were killed by the military party within the year.

2 K

Bijai Manikya (1535-83), the son of Deb Manikya, succeeded, and was a powerful ruler. He defeated the Mughs at Chittagong. He also regained what are now the British districts of Sylhet, Tippera, and Noakhali. He also had a canal excavated between the Hills and Kasba, known as the Bejai Naddi. Collecting an army of twenty-six thousand infantry and five thousand cavalry, the Raja conveyed them over the Megna in five thousand boats to Sonargaon, the Mogul capital of Bengal, but contented himself with laying waste the country. Crossing the Brahmaputra (then flowing in its old channel round the Garo Hills and through the modern district of Mymensingh) into Sylhet, he dug a large number of great tanks for the supply of good drinking water, this being intended as an act of piety.

Ananta Manikya (1583-85), the son of Bijai Manikya, declared war against the Mugh Raja Sikandar Shah (the Mugh rulers gave themselves Mohammedan names), but was repulsed, owing to the assistance of Portuguese gunners whom the Mugh Raja engaged. The Portuguese, under the leadership of Sebastian Gonsalez, were mutinous sailors who had killed their officers, and going off with their ships and driving away the Mogul Fouzdar, made their headquarters in the Island of Sandip, off the coasts of Chittagong and Noakhali at the head of the Bay of Bengal. Having built a fort and firmly established themselves, the Portuguese became pirates and preyed upon the coasts from the mouth of the Hooghly River along the Sunderbans, the mouths of the Ganges, Megna, Feni, Karnafuli, and Naaf Rivers, and from thence southwards along the coasts of Aracan. Being excellent gunners, and having armed ships at their command, these Portuguese took a large and deciding part in the politics and history of Eastern Bengal, including Aracan. They entered the service of the Mugh Rajas, then of the Rajas of Tripura, fighting for and against these potentates, and impartially plundering every trader they came across. The Raja of Tripura engaged eight of these Portuguese gunners, and their debased descendants, by low women of the country, still inhabit Miriamnaggar, between Old and New Agartala.

Having been repulsed by the Mugh Raja, Sikander Shah Ananta Manikya sent a larger army under the command of his three sons. One of the sons was killed by a wounded elephant, and the Tripuras were repulsed. The Mughs followed up their victory, marched on Rangamati and sacked the capital. Gopi Prasad, the Tripura commander-in-chief, strangled his son-in-law, Ananta Manikya, and set himself up as—

Udai Manikya (1585-96), and changed the name of the capital from Rangamati to Udaipur, after himself, and it is still known by that name. He was succeeded by his son, Jai Manikya (1596-7), who in turn was succeeded by the brother of Bijai Manikya, named Amar Manikya (1597—1611), who fought the Mughs and was defeated. The Mughs subsequently took Chittagong and plundered Udaipur. The Zemindar of Tarat in Sylhet refused to supply labourers to dig tanks, and being attacked by twelve thousand Tripura troops, was taken prisoner and brought in a cage to Udaipur. The tank at Udaipur was excavated by this raja and named after himself, Amar Sagar. He was succeeded by his son, Rajdhar Manikya I (1611-13). The Moguls attacked the Tripuras, but were defeated. This raja was accidentally drowned in the River Gumti, on which Udaipur is situated.

Jasadhar Manikya (1613-23), the son of Rajdhar Manikya I, succeeded, and was at constant war with the Moguls. The Emperor of Delhi, Jahangir, required his generals to procure elephants and a large army of Moguls under Nawab Futteh Jung, invaded Tripura in 1620. After long and severe fighting the Raja was defeated and taken captive, and, together with a large booty and numerous elephants, was sent to the Emperor at Delhi. Here the Raja was offered his freedom and restoration on condition of agreeing to pay an annual tribute of elephants. This the Raja declined to do and retired to Brindaban, where he died in his seventy-second year.

Brindaban is peculiarly sacred to the followers of Vishnu, among whom the Rajas of Tripura rank very high. The descendants of Nityananda, whose name is associated with the great Vishnuvite revivalist, Chaitanya, are settled at the Court of Tripura, and are the Raja's *gurus* or spiritual guides.

Meanwhile the Raj was wasted by the Moguls, and Sarkar Udaipur was formed and governed by Mogul Governors between 1623-5, during which there was an interregnum. It should be noted that, to avoid the attacks of the Portuguese pirates, who sailed up the Megna River, the Moguls had moved their capital, or seat of the *Subadar*, from Sonargaon to Dacca, situated on the Buriganga, a narrower and shallower river than the mighty Megna on which Sonargaon was situated. Sebastian Gonsalez, the leader of the pirates and founder of their fortified settlement in the Island of Sandip, had married a daughter of the Mugh Raja of Aracan, and had driven out the Mogul Fouzdar from Sandip. This naturally enraged the Mogul Subadar, and he determined to crush the Portuguese and punish all the rajas who had either employed or sheltered them. Hence the fierce onslaught on Tripura and ultimate defeat and captivity of Jasadhar Manikya. Another and more frequent reason for invading Tripura was that the Emperor of Delhi required a great and regular supply of elephants for State and war purposes, and the Hills of Tripura abounding then, as now, with great numbers of these animals, tempted frequent Mogul invasions and demands for them as tribute.

Kalyan Manikya (1625-59), a relative, or *Gyanti Bhrata*, of the childless Jasadhar Manikya, was elected by the Tripuras to be raja. Kalyan Manikya defied the Moguls and refused to pay any tribute. During his reign of twenty-four years there was incessant conflict with the increasing Mogul power, and towards the end these persistent efforts succeeded, and Kalyan Manikya had to submit to Sultan Suja Khan. The great tank at Kasba named Kalyan Sagar was excavated in this reign.

It may be noted here that the present Raja is descended from Kalyan Manikya through his eldest son Govinda Manikya.

Govinda Manikya (1659-60, and again from 1666-69) was the eldest son and Juvaraj of Kalyan Manikya. He was defeated and dethroned by his half-brother, Nakshatra Rai, who usurped the *gadi* as Chattra Manikya (1660-6). Chatrakhila, near Comilla is most probably named after Chattra Manikya. The French traveller Tavernier (1605-89) visited the Raj during this reign, and this fact is referred to in his "Travels" (between 1661 and 1668), in which he also gives an illustration of one of Chattra Manikya's coins.

On the death of Chattra Manikya, Govinda Manikya, the rightful Raja, regained the *gadi*, and during his second reign of three years had the waste lands of Pargana Maherkul in Chakla Roshunabad brought under cultivation, and also had the great tank in Jajiara excavated and named "Gun Sagar," after his Rani Gunavati Mahadevi. On the death of Govinda Manikya his eldest son and Juvaraj—

1. PALACE AT AGARTALA. 2. RESIDENCE OF HIS HIGHNESS, AT AGARTALA.
3. ANOTHER VIEW OF THE PALACE.

Ram Manikya (1669-82) ascended the *gadi* and caused the great tank in Maijkhara, called "Ram Sagar," to be excavated. He was succeeded by his eldest son and Juvaraj—

Ratna Manikya (1682). During his minority his uncle Narendra, the second son of Govinda Manikya, seized the throne.

Narendra Manikya (1682-4) after a usurpation of two years was displaced by the Nawab Nazim of Bengal to whom Ratna had appealed for assistance.

1708—during the reign of Ratna Manikya—and the government of the Nawab Nazim Mahomed Murshid Kuli Khan, the greatest of the Mogul *Subadars* of Bengal, Behar and Orissa, and the founder of Murshidabad, the last seat of the Mogul government in Bengal, it is recorded that "the rajas of Tripura, Cooch Behar, and Assam, whose countries, although they had been overrun by the Mahommedan arms, had never been perfectly subdued, and who therefore continued to spread the um-

Ghaneshyam Thakur, the second son of Ram Manikya and next brother of Ratna Manikya, murdered the Raja and usurped the *gadi* as Mahendra Manikya from 1712 to 1714, when Durjaya Deb as Dharma Manikya (1714-33), the next younger brother of Ram Manikya, and the Juvaraj appointed by him, succeeded.

During this reign, in 1730, Jegat Ram, the great grandson of Chattra Manikya and grand nephew of Govinda Manikya, and according to the Hindu custom of re-

1. KUKI SOLDIERS.

2. THE BINANDIAS, OR TRIPURA MILITIA.

Ratna Manikya (1684–1712) regained the *gadi*, and had the great temple of Jaggernath, called "Sattra Ratna," built in the neighbourhood of Comilla in Pargana Maherkul, Chakla Roshunabad. Towards the end of the seventeenth century Ratna Manikya shook off the Mogul yoke. Stewart in his "History of Bengal" (page 372), based upon, if not translated and arranged from, the best fourteen Mahommedan historians of the Mogul period, thus describes the relationship that existed between the Emperors of Delhi and the Rajas of Tripura, during the long-continued efforts made by various Mogul kings and governors to bring the Tripura Raj under the Mogul yoke. Writing of

brella of independence and to stamp the coins in their own names, were so impressed with the idea of the power and abilities of Mahomed Kuli Khan, that they forwarded to him valuable presents consisting of elephants, wrought and unwrought ivory, musk, amber, and various other articles in token of their submission, in return for which the Nawab sent them *khilats* or honorary dresses, by the receipt and putting on of which they acknowledged his superiority. This interchange of presents and compliments became an annual custom during the whole time of his government without either party attempting to recede from or advance beyond the implied line of conduct."

lationship, nephew of Dharma Manikya, displeased his uncle (Dharma Manikya) and was banished from the country. Jagat Ram took refuge with a Mahommedan Zemindar named Aka Sadik and entreated his assistance in recovering the *gadi* usurped by his great grandfather Chattra Manikya, or Nakshattra Rai, the second son of Kalyan Manikya. The Zemindar being intimately acquainted with Mir Habbib, the Dewan of the Naib Nazim at Dacca, recommended the cause of Jagat Ram to the Dewan and pointed out the favourable opportunity it would offer of subjecting Tripura to the Moguls. Mir Habbib having represented the circumstances to the Naib Nazim, obtained permission to proceed with all the troops that were in the vicinity of Dacca to effect this object. The Mogul troops crossed the Brahmaputra (which then flowed in its old course to the east of Dacca and joined the Megna, the western boundary of the Raj) and entered Tripura under the guidance of Jagat Ram before the Raja was aware of their intention. The Moguls reached the capital before the Raja could make any preparations to oppose them, and he fled to the hills, and Jagat Ram was raised to the *gadi* as—

Jagat Manikya (1732-3) upon the condition that he paid a large portion of the revenue to the Nawab Nazim. The whole country in the plain quietly submitted, and thus the Province of Tripura, which from time immemorial had been an independent kingdom, became annexed to the Mogul Empire. Although the northern and western portions of the Tripura plains, or the modern British districts of Sylhet, Tippera, and Noakhali, had been included by Raja Todar Mall, the famous finance Minister, in the Emperor Akbar's rent roll (*tauji*) in 1582, yet they were not conquered and brought into subjection by the British till long afterwards, as will be related in due course. However, the Naib Nazim was much pleased at Mir Habbib's success, and changed the name of Tripura to Roshunabad, or the "abode of light," probably because it was the eastern limit of the Empire where the sun first rose on the Mogul dominions. In order to support the young usurper, Jagat Manikya, against Dharma Manikya, and at the same time to secure his fealty, a considerable number of Mahommedan troops were left in the country under the command of Aka Sadik, the Zemindar who had first befriended Jagat Ram, and who was nominated Fouzdar. However, in 1733 the usurper was displaced from the *gadi* by order of the Nawab Nazim, whose ear Dharma Manikya reached through the great banker Jagat Seth of Azimganj, near Murshidabad.

Dharma Manikya (1733), ascended the *gadi* for the second time. The great tank of Kasba called the "Dharma Sagar" was excavated by this raja, who appointed his younger brother Juvaraj. In due course Chandramaani Juvaraj became Raja as Makunda Manikya (1733-7), and after a short reign was displaced by Rudramani Thakur, a great-great-grandson of Kalyan Manikya by his fourth son Rajballah Thakur, who ascended the *gadi* as Jai Manikya (1737-9) and named the Pargana Maherkul, of Chakla Roshunabad, after himself as "Jainagar." After an equally short usurpation Jai Manikya was displaced by the assistance of the Naib Nazim at Dacca in favour of Panchkouri Thakur, a son of Makunda Manikya, and who ascended the *gadi* as Indra Manikya (1739-43). The country was rent between the followers of Jai Manikya and Indra Manikya, and the former again received the *sanad* of the Naib Nazim, but Gadadhar Thakur, the son of Dharma Manikya, managed to secure the favour of the Nawab Nazim and ruled for a short time as Udai Manikya, but was displaced by Jai Manikya (for the second time), who in his turn was deposed by the assistance of Ali Verdi Khan, Nawab Nazim of Bengal.

Indra Manikya returned to the *gadi* for the second time, and in turn was displaced by Jai Manikya, who ascended for the third time, when Haridhan Thakur, his youngest brother, deposed Jai Manikya and usurped the position as Bejaya

1. RAPIDS ON RIVER GUMTI, ABOVE UDAIPUR. 2. VIEW OF THE COUNTRY NEAR AGARTALA.

Manikya, and received a *sanad* from the Nawab, but falling into arrears of revenue was sent as a prisoner to Delhi.

Shamsher Gazi, a notorious Mussulman plunderer in the districts of Tippera, Noakhali, and Chittagong, having obtained authority in Pargana Dakhinsik, proclaimed himself ruler of Roshunabad and agreed to pay revenue to the Moguls. He caused great tanks to be excavated in Dakhinsik, his native Pargana, and named them after himself. Shamsher was at the same time generous with his plunder to both Hindus and Mahommedans.

KUKI WOMEN.

Shamsher Gazi set up Banamali Thakur, the elder son of Gadadhar Thakur (the usurper Udai Manikya), the son of Dharma Manikya as Raja with the title of Lakshan Manikya, but the Tripuras would not accept him as Raja or follow his standard. His many cruelties and oppressions caused the Nawab to have Shamsher Gazi arrested, sent to Dacca, and then blown from a cannon after twelve years of lawlessness.

Meanwhile the Emperor of Delhi in 1740 conferred on Nawazish Khan, the nephew and eldest son-in-law of Nawab Nazim Ali Verdi Khan (1740-56) the titles of Shahamat Junj (Stewart, pages 440-7), "and that these titles should be supported with proper dignity the Nawab (Ali Verdi Khan) conferred on Nawazish Khan the Government of Dacca, to which he annexed the districts of Sylhet, Tippera, and Chittagong, with permission to perform the office (of Naib Nazim) by deputy."

After Shamsher Gazi's arrest and execution at Dacca, Krishnamani Thakur, brother of Indra Manikya and grandson of Makunda Manikya, ascended the *gadi* as Krishna Manikya (1760-83). A year after this raja's accession in 1761, the English East India Company appeared on the scene, being invoked by the Moguls under the following circumstances: A treaty, dated February 7, 1759, had been entered into between the Nawab Nazim Siraj-ud-Daula (the grandson and successor of Nawab Nazim Ali Verdi Khan, who died in 1756) and the East India Company. Circumstances with which this history has no concern led to the downfall of Siraj-ud-Daula and the putting of his brother-in-law, Mir Jafer in the *Nizamat*. A treaty was subsequently entered into with Mir Jafer confirming the one made with Siraj-ud-Daula. Article II of this treaty recites "that the enemies of the English are my enemies whether they be Indians or Europeans." And by an additional Article XIII, the English Company agreed as follows: "And, further, that we shall assist him to the utmost against all his enemies whatsoever, as soon as he calls upon us for that end."

It was this addition of Article XIII that led to the English Company interfering with Tripura affairs in a most high-handed and unscrupulous manner in 1761.

Chittagong was one of the first districts of Bengal which passed into the possession of the East India Company. In 1760 the Company deposed Mir Jafer and elevated his son-in-law, Mir Kasim Ali, to the *Nizamat*. By an article of a treaty, dated September 27, 1760, concluded with Mir Kasim Ali, the districts of Burdwan, Midnapore, and Chittagong, were ceded to the Company by the Nizam, and this cession was finally confirmed by the Emperor Shah Alam by a *firman* dated August 12, 1765, granting the Dewani of the three *subas* to the English Company.

The outlying and remote position of Chittagong led the Company to give a strong local government to Chittagong. On November 8, 1760, Mr. Verelst was appointed Chief of Chittagong, and, together with a Council, managed the Company's affairs on the spot.

English Period.

On January 20, 1761, Governor Vansittart wrote from Calcutta to the President and Council of the factory at Islamabad (Chittagong) as follows:

"With regard to the Tippera Raja, as the Nawab's Foujdar has been obliged from his ill behaviour to take up arms against him, we desire that you will use your endeavours to reduce him to his due state of obedience to the Government of Islamabad, acquainting us then what advantages may accrue to the Company from the possession of that country, and we will answer any representations the Nawab (the Nizam) may make on the subject."

This frank declaration of greed for their neighbour's property, which alone seemed to guide the action of the Company's representatives, and the calm assumption that because the Nizam had ceded "the Thanna of Chittagong" to the Company, the Government of Islamabad became the lords of the whole of Eastern Bengal, and required to reduce him (the independent Raja of Tripura) to his due obedience to the Company, not to the Nawab Nazim, was as astounding as it was shameless. There never could be any dispute about what the Nizam granted to the Company as the "Thanna of Islamabad or Chittagong" by a *sanad* (see Aitchison, vol. i. page 48). The River Feni had been its northern boundary from time immemorial, separating it from the Tripura Raj and the rest of Eastern Bengal. Further, the concluding words quoted, "and we will answer any representations the Nawab may make on the subject," clearly show that a guilty idea was at the back of Governor Vansittart's mind.

"In accordance with this order, Mr. Verelst, the chief at Islamabad, dispatched Lieutenant Mathew with two hundred sepoys and two guns to Tippera, where he found the Nawab's Dewan was already operating with Mahommedan troops. The Dewan had reported that he had obliged the Raja to take to the mountains, and had got possession of every fort in the country. On the arrival of our troops the Raja at once put himself in their hands."

No doubt, trusting to the notions of English honour and honesty, as contrasted with that of the Moguls, Krishna Manikya expected to get fair treatment, but found that he had only escaped from the claws of the Mogul tiger to fall into the jaws of the English lion!

"A Collector of Revenue was despatched from Chittagong with instructions to inquire into the resources of the country and demand payment of the expenses of the expedition. The Collector, finding the province desolated by the Nawab's troops, was compelled to take payment by instalments, 'as the Raja was very low in cash.' The revenue for the first year was fixed at one lakh and one sicca rupees."

This callous disregard of the crudest ideas of honesty by a trading Company's servants, shown in the above quotations from Mackenzie (pages 271-2), is followed by two paragraphs, showing how even a high official of the Crown had become infected with no higher ideas, and his sentiments are those of one who would appear to have suffered a personal loss through the Rajas of Tripura being allowed to retain even a scrap of their immemorial Raj after the Moguls had robbed them of the fairest and greatest portions, and the English Company had put forward, under the guise of respecting "a mere scrap of paper," the treaty with the Nizam of Bengal, and had robbed the robbers!

The unfortunate Krishna Manikya had in 1761 been forced by the Moguls into the hills, and the English had deprived him of the plains, and being thus restricted in territory, subjects, and revenue, the Raja had next to contend against Balaram Thakur, the son of the usurper Jagat Manikya, who collected a considerable following of Hill tribes and ousted him and proclaimed himself Balaram Manikya in 1776, but he only ruled for about a year when he in turn was deposed by the rightful Raja.

Krishna Manikya (1777 to 1783) having refused to settle with the English for his plains territory, of which the Company had deprived him, these were "attached" and placed under the direct control of the Company's local officer, who took all the revenue and doled out a pittance to the Raja! A tank, named after his consort, "Rani Dighi," was excavated in Comilla, and the Raja died childless leaving his widow, the Rani Jahnabi Mahadevi, and a nephew, Rajdharmani Thakur. Several claimants came forward for the vacant throne, each putting forward a different, and in his own estimation, a better title than his rivals. The Company's Resident, however, took the view that no one could deny that the widow was the Rani, and he recommended her being placed on the disputed throne. The Rani, as a pious Hindu widow, wished to be cremated with her husband, but acceding to the prayers of her subjects, who had just grounds for fearing that the Company would have an excuse for taking the kingless Hills (as they had taken the plains territory), she unwillingly agreed to occupy the vacant *gadi* until a male occupant was found. Meanwhile she had the *chita* or funeral pyre kept alight in order to be cremated when left in peace to follow her Hindu wifely wish, and she actually became a *sati* in 1785.

Jahnabi Mahadevi reigned from 1783 to 1785, and with a woman's common sense and regard for justice and equity, requested the Company to accept Rajdharmani Thakur, her childless husband's nephew and successor, as selected by himself, as the Raja, and Durgamani Thakur, son of Lakhan Manikya (who had been pitchforked on to the throne by Shamsher Gazi) as Juvaraj, so that both the principal claimants should be satisfied. The Company accepted the Rani's suggestion, and consequently—

Rajdhar Manikya (1785 1804), as Rajdharmani Thakur called himself, ascended the vacant throne, but had hardly seated himself thereon when he was accused by the Company's officials of "harbouring dacoits," and was deported to Chittagong, while the plains territory was again promptly "attached." Thus the unfortunate Raja was deprived of his *gadi* and of his plains territory as well until 1792, when by some miracle of right dealing his liberty and territories were restored. But not until the Raja had perforce entered into a "settlement" whereby he had to pay an annual revenue for Chakla Roshanabad, as, in the words of Mackenzie, "the Company sought

MURSUNGA, ONE OF THE TRIBUTARY KUKI RAJAS.

rupees, not elephants, and so the hills were left to their native rulers! "

A Rajbati and Tehsil Cutchery were built at Mugra in Pargana Meharkul, Chakla Roshanabad, and the bazar attached was named "Radharganj." In 1800 the Raja empowered his son Ramganga to exercise full authority, but this act of paternal affection led to very serious trouble on Rajdhar Manikya's death in 1804, when instead of allowing the recognized Juvaraj, Durgamani, to succeed, Ramganga formulated the doctrine that the Raja's son as such was the rightful successor, and that the title of Juvaraj was merely an honorary one. Being in possession of Chakla Roshanabad, from which the main income of the Raj was derived, Ramganga paid the Company's Collector the revenue and was acknowledged by that official as the *de facto* Raja, but the Company's Judge, having a judicial way of viewing such questions, took a legal rather than a pecuniary view of Durgamani's Juvarajship and championed his cause. The higher officials, representing the Company of Traders, "sought rupees, not elephants," and consequently they took a very benevolent view of Ramganga's doctrine, since he was the one who gave them the coveted rupees. Durgamani Juvaraj, the legal-minded judge's *de jure protégé*, was therefore referred to the Civil Court to prove his claims to the Revenue-paying Chakla Roshanabad, and he was promised recognition as Raja if the Courts declared him to be the person legally responsible for the revenue.

The Company was as yet only the Emperor Shah Alam's revenue-collecting Dewan, by virtue of the *Firman* of August 12, 1765, granted by His Majesty in gratitude for the Company defeating the rebellious Wazir of Oudh and restoring to him the districts of Allahabad and Kora and contributing 26 lakhs of rupees a year to the Imperial purse from the revenues of Bengal, Behar and Orissa. They were essentially traders seeking rupees, or that which produced them. Consequently the ideas of justice, equity, and fair dealing with Indian rajas and other rulers found no place in the mercantile and pecuniary minds of its officials, who shuffled out of the difficulty of inquiring in an impartial manner whether the Juvaraj was the rightful successor to the vacant throne, or whether he who bluntly stated that a raja's son was the raja's successor, and further strengthened his argument by paying the necessary rupees to the Company, should be given the position.

On Rajdhar Manikya's death, as has been stated, Ramganga seized the throne, having had possession of the Zemindari during his late father's reign. Had he been able to seize Durgamani Juvaraj as well he would speedily have made himself *de jure* as well as *de facto* raja. Durgamani, however, escaped, and lost no time in gathering together men and means for the expulsion of the usurper, and all the feelings of the people were in favour of the anointed Juvaraj. Ramganga was disliked for the sacrilege of his conduct and the tyranny and suspicion which he so frequently evinced. Durgamani was soon able to advance with his expedition, but the British officials interfered and insisted on his bringing a suit to establish his right to the Zemindari, promising to postpone recognition of the raja until the case was concluded. Durgamani therefore had to acquiesce in this decision, and Ramganga remained in possession of Chakla Roshanabad. The evidence of the principal officials of the Raj was entirely in Durgamani's favour. At length, on March 24, 1809, the Sadar Dewani Adalat, the highest Court in India, as its successor the High Court is now, gave judgment in Durgamani Juvaraj's favour, declaring the "Zemindari of Chakla Roshanabad to be an integral portion of an impartible Raj to which he, as nominated Juvaraj, should succeed." The Company accordingly invested him with the insignia of kingship as regards the Hill territory, while the Civil Court gave him possession of the lands in the plains. As Mr. Mackenzie remarked: "Years of misery might have been avoided had the Company assumed the paramount position which the application for recognition had virtually recognized. The Raj and the Zemindari being treated as impartible the Company might well have decided at once whom it would accept as heir."

During the years Ramganga had been in possession of the Chakla he erected several houses and a temple, and excavated the great tank named "Ganga Sagar" after himself at Mugra, completing what his father Rajdhar Manikya had begun.

Durga Manikya (1809-13), the son of Lakhan Manikya, the Juvaraj nominated by Krishna Manikya and his consort, Rani Jahnabi Mahadevi, was a peaceful and pious raja, and named the bazar at Sib Sagar, "Mahadayaganj," after his mother. Being childless he went on a pilgrimage to Kasi (Benares), and died *en route* of cholera, at Patna on the Ganges. He had made no appointment of a Juvaraj, hoping for a son, but had left Ramganga in charge of the Raj during his absence.

Ramganga Manikya (1813-26) naturally asked for recognition and investiture from the Company, but the poison of litigation having once entered the Raj there were several claimants to the throne, and Ramganga's title was disputed by Arjunmani Thakur and others. But so strong appears to have been the reverence entertained by the people for the customs of the Raj, that Ramganga had now no difficulty in securing their allegiance, as he was the son of Rajdhar Manikya, the Raja before Durga Manikya, who died childless and had made no appointment of a successor. Arjunmani Thakur, however, among others, claimed the vacant throne.

In order to understand Arjunmani's claim one must go back to Haramani Juvaraj, the son of Mukunda Manikya (1733-7). Haramani died during his Juvaraji, leaving two sons, Kanthamani and Rajdharmani. The former and elder son was born lame, and therefore, according to Hindu law and custom, could not become a Hindu raja. Consequently the younger brother Rajdharmani was selected as successor by Krishna Manikya and also by his Rani, Jahnabi Mahadevi. But Kanthamani Thakur had a son, Arjunmani, the first cousin of Ramganga, therefore when Durga Manikya died childless, and not having nominated any one as a successor, Arjunmani, of the elder branch, claimed the throne as preferential to Ramganga of the younger branch. But as Ramganga was in possession, having been left in charge by Durga Manikya, and had been paying the revenue of Chakla Roshanabad to the Company, and no doubt also owing to his being Rajdhar Manikya's son and *de facto* Zemindar, the Company's officials continued to accept the revenue from Ramganga, and as before, referred the claimant Arjunmani to the Sadar Dewani Adalat (Select Reports for 1815, vol. ii. page 177, Urjun Munik Thakur and others *versus* Ramganga Deo), which decided that Ramganga had the preferential right to the Zemindari. However, as this decision of the Sadar Adalat was only a summary one in Ramganga's favour, the unsuccessful claimants filed three regular suits, which were not finally decided till 1821, when the Company formally invested Ramganga as the Raja. Ramganga Manikya then formally appointed his younger half-brother as the Juvaraj and his own son Krishnakishore as Bara Thakur. This latter dignity, as will be seen later on, was the cause of an immense

1. ROCK TEMPLE AT UN KUTI, KOILASHAHAR.
2. FOREST SCENE NEAR UDAIPUR.
3. RUINS OF SIVA'S TEMPLE, UDAIPUR.
4. RUINS OF VISHNU'S TEMPLE, UDAIPUR.

amount of litigation, trouble, and expense. Ramganga Manikya was a very peaceful man who practically left the conduct of affairs to his younger half-brother Kasichandra. During this reign a great injustice was committed by the Company's local officials against the Tripura Raj by lopping off a large portion of the territory in the northern portion of the State south of the Kusiyara River, which formed for centuries the northern boundary of the State and the southern boundary of the district of Sylhet. It will be necessary to go back for several centuries to understand how the Kusiyara River became at length the northern boundary (in part) of the Tripura Raj.

Previous to the Mogul occupation of portions of India to the east of the Brahmaputra, that river flowed round the western end of the Garo Hills and then nearly due south, through the British district of Mymensigh, and then curved west and flowed into the Megna, and thus formed the western boundary of the Tripura Raj. In A.D. 590 Raja Biraj extended his conquests beyond the Ganges, which also then flowed in a south-easterly course, and through the districts of Faridpur and Bakargunj, before entering the Bay of Bengal, and the Tripura Raj comprised the present British districts of Chittagong, Noakhali, Tippera, Sylhet, Cachar, the Garo-Khasia and Jaintia Hills, Lushailand, and the Chittagong Hill Tracts. Consequently the district of Sylhet formed a part of the Raj. Subsequently "the district (Sylhet) was at one time divided into at least three petty kingdoms: Gor, or Sylhet proper, Laur, and Jaintia; and the country south of the Kusiyara seems to have been under the control of the Raja of Hill Tippera." (See page 191, Vol. XXIII, "Imperial Gazetteer of India"): "Gor was conquered by the Mahommedans in 1348, the last Hindu king, Gour Govind, being overcome more by the magic of the *Fakir*, Shah Jalal, than by the prowess of the officer in command of the expedition, Sikandar Ghazi. After the death of Shah Jalal, Gor was included in the kingdom of Bengal and placed in charge of a Nawab. In the reign of Akbar (Emperor of Delhi) it passed with the rest of Bengal into the hands of the Moguls; and, in the time of this Emperor, Laur was also conquered, though its rulers were for some time entrusted with the charge of the frontier, and were exempt from the payment of land revenue." However, the district of Sylhet was not finally lost to the Tripura Raj till the *Nizamat* of Nawab Ali Verdi Khan, who in 1740 conferred on his son-in-law, Nawzish Khan, the Government of Dacca, to which he annexed the districts of Sylhet, Tippera, and Chittagong (see Stewart's "History of Bengal," page 447). Gor (Sylhet) and Laur were included in Bengal when the British obtained the Dewani of that Province in 1765. Jaintia was never conquered by the Mahommedans, and retained its independence until 1835, when it was annexed by the British Government as no satisfaction could be obtained for the murder of three British subjects who had been kidnapped and sacrificed to the goddess Kali. During the early days of British rule, Sylhet, lying on the outskirts of the Company's territories, was much

MARRIAGE BEDI.

neglected; the population was turbulent, means of communication were difficult. The savage tribes living in the north and south of the valley disturbed the peace of the plains, and there were continual disputes as to the boundary between British territory and the Native State of Hill Tippera (the Tripura Raj).

In 1820, Lieutenant Fisher of the Survey Department, being deputed to ascertain the boundaries of Sylhet, sent in a report and a map through the Magistrate of Sylhet. Although, as appears from the quotation above made (from the "Imperial Gazetteer of India," Vol. XXIII), the country south of the Kusiyara (river) seems to have been under the control of the Raja of Hill Tippera, yet by a process of reasoning and action peculiar to the Company's officials, and in spite of this well-known fact of the Tripura Raj extending north to the Kusiyara River, Lieutenant Fisher traced boundaries, which being accepted by the various higher officials, calmly lopped off hundreds of square miles of most valuable agricultural land, as well as an equal or greater area of hill land on which there are now all the tea gardens of South Sylhet with their thousands of acres of the finest land for that plant, both areas worth crores of rupees, the revenues and rents of which are enjoyed by the Company's successors.

This robbery of territory on the Tripura-Sylhet border did not stop there, for when the neighbouring district of Cachar came into the Company's possession by the assassination of the last and heirless Raja, Govind Chandra, in 1830, in the reign of Kasichandra Manikya, the same procedure, but if anything on a larger scale, was adopted.

Kasichandra Manikya (1826-30) appointed his own son Krishnachandra, the Bara Thakur, but he pre-deceased his father, and Krishnakishor, the son and Bara Thakur of Ramganga Manikya, was appointed Juvaraj by his uncle, then sonless. Kasichandra Manikya began building a palace on the eastern bank of the "Amar Sagar," the great tank at Udaipur, but removed his residence to Agartala. The origin of this name, that of the present capital of the Tripura Raj, is obscure, but the most probable derivation is from the name of a respectable landholder, one Agar Mahammad, whose descendants are still living and in the employ of the Raj. It may be mentioned that the original Agartala, or Puranhaveli ("old residence") as it is popularly called, is some four miles east up the Haura River, and that the Notunhaveli ("new residence"), or what is now officially known as Agartala, and the residence of the late and present Raja, is lower down the Haura River. About the only important event of this reign was the offer made to the Company by Sambhuchandra Thakur (the grandson of Bijai Manikya (Haridan Thakur), the youngest brother of Jai Manikya, both father and son being usurpers during the troublous times from 1737 to 1760, when six members of the Tripura Raj family and the notorious Shamsher Gazi in turn usurped the throne or power of the Raj, chiefly through the machinations and assistance of the Moguls) to farm, as an *ijaradar* or *thikadar* (farmer), the Hill territory at an annual rental of Rs. 25,000. As Mackenzie explains: "This offer was rejected as they had been so long unassessed and had come to be looked upon as independent territory." This was not the first example of such arrogance directly encouraged by the behaviour of the Trading Company's officials towards the Rajas of Tripura. The former instance happened when Ramganga was trying to oust Durgamani Juvaraj. At Ramganga's request the local officers lent him troops and police, and but for this assistance he would have been expelled, for the whole country was hostile to him and his claims. Durgamani Juvaraj had obtained the assistance of the Poitu Kukis, whom Ramganga had oppressed, to help him enforce his right to succession as the Juvaraj. When the Company's troops and police confronted the Kukis, these hillmen did not understand the Company's action, and boldly charged its officials with inconsistency, for they had been told some years before that the Company had no concern with the Tripura territory. On this Mackenzie remarks in a footnote to page 274 of his "North-east Frontier of Bengal":

"How much doubt as to our (the Company's) position existed is seen from the fact that in 1800 (during Rajdhar Manikya's troublous reign) offers were made to the Board (of Revenue) for a farm of the mountains of Tippera." In rejecting this the Board say that "they conclude that the mountains form a part of the estate (not State, be it noticed) of the Raja of Tippera (Rajdhar Manikya), and that they are included in his existing engagements executed by him for the general settlement of his *Zemindari*." In reply to this the Collector reports that "on a reference to the *tahood* executed by the Raja for the general settlement of his *Zemindari* (in 1792, while he was a deportee at Chittagong, on a trumped-up charge of harbouring dacoits) it does not appear that the mountains of Tippera were included, but they always have been considered as constituting his property; neither does it appear from the records that he ever paid any revenue to Government for them for the last twenty-two years (since the time of Mr. Campbell)." It has been mentioned in the previous reign of Ramganga Manikya, that the Raj was deprived by Lieutenant Fisher's survey of large tracts of agricultural and tea lands to the south of the Kusiyara River and that the same process of spoliation was adopted in this reign.

It should be noted that the River Barak flows westwards out of the Manipur Raj, through the district of Cachar, and then bifurcates at Badarpur. The northern branch, the Surma, curves round the northern portion of the district of Sylhet, and the southern branch, the Kusiyara, pursues a similar course along the southern parts of Sylhet.

Fisher's survey of the Sylhet boundary was laid far south of the Kusiyara, as already stated, and he was appointed to the newly acquired district of Cachar in 1830, or thereabouts, as Superintendent, subordinate to the Governor-General's Agent in Assam.

The southern boundary of Sylhet had ended at the Chattanhura peak, some 2,069 feet in height, and formed the trijunction of the three boundaries of Tripura, Sylhet, and Cachar. Starting from this trijunction, by some clever juggling, another block of several hundreds of square miles of hills and valleys, as well as some more agricultural and tea lands, were lopped off from the Tripura Raj. There can be no contesting this or any other statement similarly made. Chapter and verse from Government publications have been given, and will now be quoted to prove the fact.

INSIGNIA OF THE RAJAS OF TRIPURA.

In Pemberton's report, dated 1835, it is shown that all the Lushai country, situated directly south of Cachar, belonged to the Tripura Raj. Mackenzie on page 286 in his "North-eastern Frontier of Bengal" writes with regard to the south-eastern and southern boundaries of Cachar, Tripura, and Manipur, as follows:

"In Pemberton's report we find that all the Lushai country east to Manipur was once considered to belong to Tippera. The south-eastern and southern boundaries of each are thus given by Pemberton in 1835:—

"'From the source of the Juree River along the western bank to its confluence with the Borak; then south to the western bank of the latter river to the mouth of the Chekoo (or Tipai) *nullah* which marks the triple boundary of Manipur, Cachar, and Tippera.'

"The southern extremity of the Suddashur Hills was the south-east corner of Cachar. It would appear from this that the narrow hilly tract running down between Hill Tippera and Manipur, and represented in our most recent maps as part of Cachar, was in Pemberton's considered to be part of Hill Tippera."

If there is any meaning in the above quotations from an Official Report, and statements in books published under authority, such as are the "Imperial Gazetteer" and Mackenzie's "North-east Frontier of Bengal," it must be that the River Kusiyara (tracing upstream) formed the northern boundary of the Tripura Raj (in a general direction from west to east) till its junction with the Surma at Badarpur; then the Barak (or combined streams of the Kusiyara and Surma) from Badarpur to the Manipur frontier.

This was the boundary when the Company took possession of the districts of Sylhet and Cachar, and not a single argument except the ***argumentum baculinum*** and ***argumentum ad crumenam*** to support the "might is right" procedure, was adopted by the Company's officials when dealing with the Raja of Tripura's territories, whether on the south, west, or north.

As to the hills and valleys on the east, it will hereafter be seen how they were divorced from the Raj in the reign of Maharaja Birchandra Manikya (1862-96), and the "Eastern Boundary" question arose and has been dragging along for fifty years or so, and is yet unsettled.

However, to return to Kasichandra Manikya—as already stated, Krishnakishor, the son and Bara Thakur of Ramganga Manikya, had been appointed Juvaraj by his uncle, therefore when Kasichandra died in 1830 he was succeeded by—

Krishna Kishor Manikya (1830-49). It was during this reign that Mr. Dampier, the Commissioner of Chittagong, to which division the district of British Tippera belongs, made an attempt to prove that the Raja of Tripura was merely a

Zemindar with no independent Raj whatsoever. This matter is very lucidly and at considerable length set out in a letter No. 121, dated December 27, 1838, from the Secretary to the Government of Bengal, acting under the orders of Lord Auckland, the Deputy-Governor of Bengal and Governor-General of India from 1836 to 1842, and addressed to the then Commissioner, Mr. Harvey, from which the following quotations of the most prominent points of the controversy have been taken.

This voluminous correspondence began with Mr. Dampier's letter, dated October 10, 1836, in which complaint was made of the Raja of Tippera levying "*sayerat* duties within his *Zemindary* on cotton and other produce, although at the time of the perpetual settlement" (made with Raja Rajdhar Manikya in 1792) "a remission to a large amount was granted on the *jumma* of his estate as a compensation for the abolition of the *sayer mehal*, and the collection of such duties has been expressly prohibited by law."

(Para. 5). "But it was remarked the Raja has two capacities, one as *Zemindar* within the pale of the Permanent Settlement, the other that of an independent prince in his own Hill territory, and it was clear, from a petition presented by his attorney (Mr. Bignell), that the Raja now claimed to levy transit duty on produce *within* his own territory, it being stated to be his only source of revenue."

(Para. 71). "To conclude, therefore, His Honour decides that the Raja has an independent hill territory; that your propositions for its resumption are totally inadmissible; that the Raja has a full right within his hill territory to levy any duties he pleases; and that there is no ground at present for setting on foot an inquiry into supposed encroachments by the Raja on the Company's territory."

No doubt the above-quoted very important State document—for such it is—though in the form of a Secretary's letter to a Commissioner, was one of the chief documentary proofs of the very explicit statement already quoted, that—

"Independent Tippera is not held by gift from the British Government or its predecessors or under any title derived from it or them, never having been subjected by the Mogul."

So the question, so often raised and argued, generally to the disadvantage of the Raja, as to the independence of any portion of the former kingdom left by the rapacity of the Company's officials, may be said to have been finally settled, and the delimitation of the Hill from the Plains Territory taken up, as usual to the disadvantage of the Raj. However, it must be admitted in all fairness that the rajas were badly served by their employés, who resorted to questionable methods to try and protect the Raj from the constant encroachments of its all-powerful neighbour's officials. But it was the usual conflict between the weak and the strong, of cunning and deceit against might. Had the Company's officials been less rapacious the Raja's employés would have been encouraged to be more straightforward. However, it is of little practical use deploring the morality of the methods employed by either party in days when India was in the melting-pot and Eastern Bengal not yet recovered from Mogul days and ways. The Company was grabbing an Empire, and the native rulers were trying by every means to withstand an overpowering dragon from swallowing them up and their territories completely. To make the constant complaints that Mackenzie does against the rajas and their employés reminds one of the fable of the wolf and the lamb, or of the burglar complaining that the householder attempted, by every artifice he could invent, to prevent himself from being completely robbed of all his valuables. Mackenzie's invective on page 272, when he himself gives the above-mentioned letter in full as Appendix D, on pages 405 to 414, is utterly absurd: "Not a word is found in these old papers recognizing the independence of the Raja in any part of his dominions. In fact, no reference is made to the hills in connection with the arrangements. The officers of the Company had more regard to substantial advantages than to theoretical symmetry. The paying part of Tippera lay on the plains, and appeared in the Mahommedan revenue roll as *pergunnah* Roshanabad. For this, of course, a settlement was made. We found it a *zemindari*, and as such we treated it. But of the barren hills that fenced it on the east we took no cognizance. Covered with jungle and inhabited by tribes of whom nothing was known, save that they were uncouth in speech, and not particular as to clothing, the hills were looked upon as something apart. The Raja claimed to exercise authority within them, but did not, as it seemed, derive much profit from them. Accordingly the hills became 'independent Tippera,' and the Raja, who is an ordinary Bengali *zemindar* on the plains, reigns as an independent prince over three thousand square miles of upland, and was for many years a more absolute monarch than Scindia or Patiala—owning no law but his sovereign will, bound by no treaty, subject to no control, safe in his obscurity from criticism or reform. And yet nothing can be more certain than the fact that the Mogul Government, through whom our paramount title comes, would have recognized no such vital distinction between the highlands and lowlands of the Tippera State. It may be true that they never carried their armies in victorious march through the bamboo thickets of the hills, or harried with fire and sword the wattled wigwams of the Kookie tribes; but when they appointed whom they would as raja, both hill and plain passed with the one *sanad* they gave. They would have scoffed at the idea of independence of any fragment of the entity they conveyed. Indeed, the chief object of their invasion having been to secure horses and elephants for purposes of State or war, to have excluded the hills from the periphery of their conquest would have cut them off from the very source of these supplies. The Company sought rupees, not elephants, and so the hills were left to their native ruler, and no misgiving seems to have cropped up that trouble would hereafter result from such a course. Trouble did result, not so much from the actual independence of the Raja as from a want of definitiveness in our relations to him, from the absence of any means of knowing what went on in his territory, and from the denial of that salutary control and advice without which our best feudatories come to certain grief."

The above is the most damning proof of the contempt and utter want of consideration shown to the Rajas of Tippera. Mackenzie cynically admits that "the barren hills" were allowed "to become independent Tippera" because "the Company sought rupees, not elephants, and so the hills were left to their native ruler," and every acre of rupee-producing land, whether in the west, in Tippera, or in the north, in Sylhet and Cachar, was systematically filched from the Raja, right up to the "barren hills."

Having accomplished a good deal of this landgrabbing by main force, a more refined method was adopted by the Company's officials, by standing upon boundaries thus laid down, not warranted even by Government records, already quoted, and then "informing the Raja that although he could not himself be sued in the courts of Sylhet, yet he was at liberty to sue the Government and the *zemindars* jointly in these courts, if he thought he could establish his claim to any lands outside the line laid down by Lieutenant Fisher between 1820 and 1822 in Ramganga Manikya's reign, and Government would honour the decision of its own tribunal and make over to him any lands he might prove to be his." To show how fruitlessly harassing such a procedure was (and it is incredible that the Company's officials were ignorant of such an inevitable result), it is sufficient to mention that after years of expensive litigation "the question of jurisdiction was then taken up by a full Bench" (of the Sadar Dewani Adalat at Calcutta) "which ruled, on September 19, 1848, that questions affecting the boundary of two independent Powers were not properly cognizable in Municipal Courts and the Raja's suits were dismissed after pending for sixteen years."

It is easy to see from the above, among many other instances, that the Company's officials were arrogantly and unjustly treating the Rajas of Tripura as anything but independent rulers, and that the Supreme Court of Calcutta, presided over by independent judges from England, who were not subservient to the Company in its search after rupees, declared the Raja to be an "independent Power" just as much as the Company, whose officials never seemed to be able to clear their minds of the simple fact that the Raja of Tripura was just as much, politically, if not as powerful, an independent sovereign as was the King of England, and certainly much more so than a company of traders, seeking rupees, by fair means or otherwise, under the Royal Charter to trade in India. This arrogance is justified by Mackenzie when he writes on page 272, "and yet nothing can be more certain than the fact that the Mogul Government, through whom our paramount title comes" (but which was robbed of its intended Tripura booty by the instructions issued by Governor Vansittart to President Verelst in 1761, as already mentioned in Krishna Manikya's reign), "would have recognized no such vital distinction between the highlands and lowlands of the Tippera State" (not estate, be it noted). "They would have scoffed at the idea of independence in any fragment of the entity they conveyed." This Mogul idea of political morality is what Mackenzie adopts and tries to justify the trading Company's officials adopting towards the Raja of Tripura.

Even Mr. Mackenzie, although he was in "immediate charge of the political correspondence of the Bengal Government" (see Preface to his book, "The North-east Frontier of Bengal"), yet, had he any glimmerings of *political* knowledge, he could never have written in the arrogant and contemptuous tone which blemishes his lucubrations regarding Tripura. And considering that he rose to be Sir Alexander Mackenzie, the Lieutenant-Governor of Bengal, he must be considered to have been above the average Agents and Residents should ever come into contact with ruling Chiefs, if their welfare and that of their Raj subjects is desired. But in the trading Company's days there was no such thing as politics and political training.

Krishna Kishor Manikya appointed his eldest son, Isanchandra, the Juvaraj, to succeed him.

Isanchandra Manikya (1849-62). It has been alleged that Isanchandra promised their father, Krishna Kishor Manikya, that he would appoint Nilkrishna, then a young

E. F. SANDYS.

Bengal civilian, serving the Crown, and not a trading company. It is just this want of the rudiments of *political* training and knowledge that has been the bane hitherto of the Tripura Raj when in contact with the local district magistrate and Divisional Commissioners, who have all their official lives been in contact and dealing with mere *zemindars, talukdars, ijaradars, et hoc genus* in the "*Jo hukm*" and "*Ji huzur*" style they usually adopt, generally through the medium of their *Amla*. None but officials trained in the political department of the Imperial Government of India to be political

boy and the son of the *Patrani*, or senior Rani, as his successor, as by that time he would be old enough to manage affairs. But, for some reason or other, this appointment was not made, and Nilkrishna left Agartala and lived in Comilla, the headquarters of the district of (British) Tippera.

Isanchandra Manikya, who was an exceedingly devout Hindu, devoting himself almost exclusively to religious affairs, left the conduct of the Raj almost entirely in the hands of his *Guru* (spiritual guide) Banwarilal Goshwami. For some time before his death Isanchandra became paralytic. As the Raja's end approached he was urged to appoint a successor, but he put it off till a day or two before his death, Nilkrishna was sent for from Comilla. But the latter delayed his departure, and as the Raja's end was very near, a *Rubakari*, or Proceeding, was drawn up by which Birchandra, the Raja's own younger brother, was appointed Juvaraj, while his own elder son, Brajendrachandra, was appointed Bara Thakur, and a younger son, Navadipchandra, the *Barakarta*, thus adding a third eventual claimant to the throne.

It appears that the unsettled state of things during the latter period of the Mogul rule made it necessary to take greater precaution in the appointment of the Yuvaraja for the purpose of preventing a break in the continuity of government and in order to avoid disputes with regard to succession in case the Yuvaraj died shortly before the death of the Raja or under circumstances in which a fresh appointment could not be made to fill the vacancy thus caused in the office of Yuvaraj. The Rajas of Tripura therefore created a new office and introduced the innovation of appointing what was called a Bara Thakur, who was to succeed to the throne in case the Yuvaraj predeceased the Raja, and if the latter could not or did not appoint any other person as Yuvaraj.

The succession *Sanad* granted by the Government of India on June 21, 1904, however, puts the succession on a simple and definite basis. It is as follows:—

"To His Highness the Raja of Hill Tippera.

"Whereas, with a view to continuing the representation of the ruling house and dignity of the State of Hill Tippera, it is desirable to remove all doubts as to the rule of succession to the Chiefship of the said State and the ownership of the *Zemindaries* and the property in British India which appertain thereto and are held therewith, it is hereby declared:—

"(1) That the Chiefship of the said State is and ever shall be hereditary in the Deb Burman family of Hill Tippera, of which His Highness Radhakishor Manikya, the present Chief of the said State, is now the lawful and acknowledged Head.

"(2) That the Chief of the said State, for the time being, may from time to time and at any time, nominate and constitute any male ancestor of his to be Juvaraj or successor to the said Chiefship.

"(3) That in the event of His Highness Radhakishor Manikya or any succeeding Chief of the said State dying without having nominated and constituted a Juvaraj, or successor, his nearest male descendant descended through males, according to the rule of lineal primogeniture, and in default of such descendant, his nearest male heir descended through males from any ancestor of his, according to the said rule, shall succeed to the said Chiefship, preference in either case being given to those of the whole blood over those of the half blood.

"(4) That in matters relating to the appointment of a successor and the succession to the said Chiefship not heretofore expressly provided for, the usages of the said Raj family shall prevail.

"(5) That every succession to the said Chiefship shall, as heretofore, require the recognition of the Government of India.

"(6) Raja Radhakishor Manikya may rest assured that nothing shall disturb the operation of this *Sanad* so long as he and his heirs are loyal to the Crown and faithful to the British Government.

(Signed) "AMPTHILL,
"Viceroy and Governor-General
of India.

"SIMLA,
"June 21, 1904."

It is now necessary to revert to the death of Isanchandra Manikya in 1862 and to what occurred thereafter: Nilkrishna, a younger son of Krishna Kishor Manikya, had been sent for from Comilla by Isanchandra Manikya, as already related, but he did not return. To avoid any mishap attending a vacant throne, to which no successor had been duly nominated, the *Rubakari*, or Proceeding, had been drawn up by order of Isanchandra Manikya nominating Birchandra, his younger brother, as Juvaraj, and his sons, Brajendrachandra and Navadipchandra respectively as Bara Thakur and Karta.

The British officials were duly notified of these appointments, and Birchandra Juvaraj took possession of the Raj. Nilkrishna protested and impugned the genuineness of the *Rubakari*. Instead of the Government immediately assuming the paramount position, which the application for investiture by the Rajas since 1804 had implied, and deciding, in its political capacity, as to the rightful successor to the Raj among the claimants, its officials, in their usual political purblindness, followed the former mischievous precedent and referred Nilkrishna, as they had previously directed Rajdharmani in 1804, to the Municipal Courts, to ascertain whether he was entitled to succeed to Chakla Roshanabad, the revenue-paying portion of the Raj in British Tippera. All the officials seemed to care about were the rupees from the assessed portion in the plains, apparently not caring a jot for the Raj *per se*, and thus Birchandra Juvaraj was acknowledged to be in possession and to be the revenue payer.

Nilkrishna lost all his money, and died during litigation proceedings; then Navadwipchandra (Brajendrachandra his elder brother having died) took up the legal burden, and thus litigation was prolonged for eight years in all, until 1870, when Birchandra Juvaraj was acknowledged the rightful successor and was duly invested as Raja.

Birchandra Manikya (1862-96). During the pending litigation, as has been mentioned, Brajendrachandra, the elder son and nominated Bara Thakur of Isanchandra Manikya, had died. Consequently Navadwipchandra, as nominated Karta, claimed to succeed to his deceased brother's office of Bara Thakur, and when Birchandra Juvaraj became Raja, Navadwipchandra claimed to be the Juvaraj. The Privy Council dismissed his suit, and when Birchandra Manikya appointed his eldest son Radhakishor to be the Juvaraj, Navadwipchandra sued to be declared the lawful successor to Chakla Roshanabad on the Raja's demise.

At length the High Court of Calcutta threw out the suit, on the common-sense ground that it had no jurisdiction, being a Municipal Court, to decide the succession to the throne of a Sovereign State in a roundabout way, by being asked to declare a certain person the lawful successor *to an integral portion of an impartible Raj*.

Legal peace therefore followed for the remainder of Birchandra Manikya's reign, until it was broken again in his successor's time by exactly a similar declaratory suit being filed.

Reference must now be made to other and more turbulent peacebreakers of the Tripura Raj, commonly known as the Kukis, or more correctly as the Lushais, living to the east of the State. A great deal of ingenuity has been employed to define and derive the name Kuki. The simplest, and apparently the correct derivation, is that from the Persian word *Koh* (a hill or mountain) and *Ki* (of). The word should therefore be *Kokhi* (of the mountain), that is, mountaineers or highlanders, who seem the world over to be naturally truculent marauders. The Persian Kokhi of the Moguls has been vulgarized by the Bengali-speaking inhabitants of neighbouring districts into *Kuki*, meaning the savages from the hills generally.

The derivation of Lushai, or more correctly Lusai, is from *Lu* (the head) and *sai* (to lop off), so that Lushais or Lusais mean the head-loppers, the fiercest of all the Kuki or Hill tribes.

reducing Lusailand to a peaceful frontier district.

That happy conclusion as usual ended in depriving the Tripura Raj of a large tract of territory all along its eastern frontier.

Birchandra Manikya, having been duly recognized and installed as Raja in 1870, appointed his eldest son Radhakishor as Juvaraj, and some years later his fourth son Shamarendrachandra as Bara Thakur. This second appointment, as might have been expected, led to trouble and litigation, when the Juvaraj became Raja and in his turn appointed his own son as Juvaraj, instead of promoting his half-brother from Bara Thakur to Juvaraj.

The Political Agency, as a separate post, was afterwards abolished, and the Magistrate of the adjoining district of British Tippera was appointed *ex officio* Political Agent, while an Indian Deputy Magistrate, Umakanta Das, was stationed at Agartala as Assistant Political Agent. In March 1890 the Maharaja selected Rai Umakanta Das Bahadur as Minister, and all duties in connection with the Political Agency were transferred to the *ex-officio* Political Agent at Comilla, the head-quarters of the district of British Tippera.

1. CARVED ROCKS AT UN KUTI, KOILASHAHAR. 2. RUINED TEMPLE OF SIVA, UDAIPUR.

Of these tribes, Colonel Lister in 1853 enumerates as the principal the Chilu, the Tadoes or Tewtangs, the Poitu Kukis, the Rankhal, the Tangue, and the Chansen. These tribes were stated by Lister to reside both "within our boundaries (Cachar), to the south and south-east, in the Independent Tippera Hills and in the Manipur territories."

It would take up an undue amount of space to enlarge on these Hill tribes. Suffice it to say that the Government of India ordered the Lushai expedition on July 11, 1871, and that successful campaign resulted in thoroughly subduing these formerly troublesome savages and

A Political Agent was about this time appointed to reside at Agartalla, the Raja's capital.

The main object of the appointment was the protection of British interests on the eastern frontiers, which were in special danger from Lushai raids. It was explained to the Raja that the Government of India, in sending an Agent to Agartala, had no intention of adopting a policy which would interfere with the exercise of authority with his State.

It may be added here that the appointment of a Resident Political Agent was again revived in the year 1910 with the view of ensuring direct friendly co-operation between the State and the Imperial Government.

One of the results of a Political Agency was the extradition of criminals escaping into British territory according to the general law and rules on the subject for trial in the Tripura Courts. Offenders escaping from British territory into the State are similarly surrendered to the British Courts, through the Political Agent.

The practice of *Sati* in Tripura was forbidden in 1888, while the abolition of slavery had been declared many years previously by the Raja, and both prohibitions are still in force in the State.

As already mentioned, serious raids were committed on Tripura, Sylhet, and Cachar by the Lushais, and especially by the two cognate tribes of Sailus and Howlongs, and a strong British force, in two columns, was directed against the offending tribes, the Raja supplying transport for the northern column. The tribes of powerful chiefs were reduced to submission; the fines imposed were paid; captives were recovered; and verbal agreements were taken from the Chiefs to live amicably with all British subjects between Manipur and Arracan, and to allow free access to their country. The expedition produced for a time the desired effect, as it showed the Lushais that their recesses were not inaccessible and that their inroads into British territory or into allied States would be duly punished. Since that time no raids have been made into Tripura. During Birchandra Manikya's reign a regular military force was organized by the assistance of the Political Agent, Captain Lillingston. Several frontier and sub-divisional guards are maintained, and a body of armed and drilled troops are kept at Agartala. Courts of Civil, Criminal, and Revenue jurisdiction, presided over by trained officers, were established, and a jail was built which is superintended by the State physician. Civil, criminal, and revenue laws have been framed and are administered at the Headquarters and Sub-Divisional Courts of First Instance and Appeal. A final appeal lies in all cases to the Raja, whose sanction is required before sentence of death passed by the Sessions Court can be executed.

During this reign Her Majesty Queen Victoria was pleased to assume the Imperial Crown as *Kaisar-i-Hind*, or Empress of India, at an Imperial Assemblage, the first of three great Darbars held respectively in 1877, 1903, and 1911. The Ruling Chiefs of India attended and received various honours, dignities, titles, salutes, and banners. Among them, Birchandra Manikya received the title of Maharaja as a personal distinction, and was granted a salute of thirteen guns and banner.

After a reign of thirty-four years Maharaja Birchandra Manikya died at Kalighat, and a *samadhi* was erected over the *chita*, near to that of the Maharaja of Mysore, who had also died at the same city in 1894.

Radhakishor Manikya (1896-1909), the duly appointed Juvaraj of his father, Birchandra Manikya, was duly installed on the throne on March 5, 1897. On June 12th, an earthquake reduced the palaces and other masonry buildings of Agartala, with one or two exceptions, to a heap of ruins in a few seconds. The catastrophe entailed enormous expenditure on the State, but on the other hand gave the Raja an opportunity of erecting a more dignified and suitable Palace and other public buildings than his predecessors had been able to provide. Naturally all the buildings required could not be erected during his comparatively short reign, but the present Raja is continuing the policy of his revered father in this and several other respects. In addition to the Palace and commodious family quarters, the Victoria Memorial Hospital, the Temple of Jaggarnath, a school and museum were built, and the jail was removed and reconstructed on a more suitable site. Administration buildings were commenced, and a technical school was established.

Radhakishor Manikya presented a handsome donation towards the Victoria Memorial at Calcutta, besides giving munificently to deserving institutions and helping scientists and scholars and the cause of education generally.

It has already been mentioned that in the previous reign, Birchandra Manikya, while appointing his eldest son Radhakishor as Juvaraj, also nominated his fourth son, Samarendrachandra, as Bara Thakur, and trouble was thus caused when Radhakishor Manikya naturally desired to nominate a successor and to appoint his son Birendrakishor as Juvaraj. Persisting in the claim that when the Juvaraj became Raja, the Bara Thakur became *ipso facto* the Juvaraj or next successor, Bara Thakur Samarendrachandra, petitioned the Government, claiming to be recognized as Juvaraj.

After the fullest consideration the Government rejected the claim of Samarendrachandra Bara Thakur to be declared the Juvaraj, and on February 8, 1899, Radhakishor Manikya appointed his son, Birendrakishor, the Juvaraj. Considering that due cause of action had arisen, the Bara Thakur Samarendrachandra filed a suit for a declaratory decree, in the Court of the Subordinate Judge of Alipur, that he should be declared the proprietor of Chakla Roshanabad and all other State property in British India on the demise of Radhakishor Manikya. Accepting the precedent of the High Court, when appealed to in the suit of Navadwipchandra, for a similar decree, the Subordinate Judge decided that his court had no jurisdiction in virtually declaring the plaintiff to be successor to the throne, and he therefore dismissed the suit.

Radhakishor Manikya performed pilgrimages to Tribeni, near Prayag (Allahabad), Brindaban, Gaya, and Kasi (Benares), and it was during this last pilgrimage, and on the very last day of his stay, that a most regrettable motor-car accident caused His Highness's death on March 12, 1909. The Raja's remains were cremated at a *ghat* on the banks of the holy Gunga.

Only a few days before his lamented death, a conference of *Pandits* from many lands assembled at Kasi, and conferred a title on the Raja in recognition of his piety and benevolence.

Radhakishor Manikya was an exceedingly kind-hearted and generous character. No needy hand was withdrawn empty, and no cry of distress went unheard. Though personally a pious Hindu, and a staunch follower of Vishnu, yet holders of all creeds received his unprejudiced benevolence and generosity, and all truly pious persons with whom he came in contact received his respect and reverence. True piety, need, and unselfishness received his full sympathy, and any place of worship, consecrated ground, or mausoleum was accorded as much respect as his own sacred temples. His tastes and dress were simplicity itself and marked him out in any assembly. Scientific facts and artistic objects always excited his interest and admiration. Radhakishor Manikya was in every sense of the word a thorough gentleman, detesting everything mean, vulgar, and deceitful, and his memory will be revered and loved for many a year by his people and those who had the honour and pleasure of knowing him.

The Maharaja was succeeded by the present ruler, His Highness the Bisana Samara Bijoyi Mahamahodaya Pancha Srijukta Raja Birendra Kishore Dev Burman Manikya Bahadur. His Highness was installed on the throne (*singhasana*) by His Honour Sir Lancelot Hare, the Lieutenant-Governor of Eastern Bengal and Assam, on behalf of His Excellency the Viceroy and Governor-General of India on November 25, 1909.

His Highness the Raja of Manipur honoured the installation ceremony with his presence, and His Highness Birendra

Kishor Manikya paid Manipur a return visit, thus continuing a friendship begun in Radhakishor Manikya's reign between the two rulers. It may be mentioned that several thousands of Manipuris settled in Tripura in the last century.

His Highness appointed his eldest son, Birbikramkishor, as Juvaraj immediately after his own installation, on November 25, 1909.

In former times, owing to remoteness and want of convenient means of communication, the Tripura Rajas were compelled to seek marriage alliances with the Kshatriyas of Manipur, as intermarriages in Tripura itself had come within prohibited degrees according to Hindu law. But with modern amenities of travel the field has been enlarged, and His Highness has been able to form alliances with Kshatriya families of Upper India and Nepal.

The State of Hill Tippera (Tripura) presents no physical features of special importance. There are six ranges of hills stretching from north to south, with peaks ranging from 1,400 feet to more than 3,000 feet in height, and the major portion of these is covered with fairly dense bamboo jungle. The western part of the State consists of broken ground made up of hillocks, which are utilized as sites for homesteads, and of marshy plains and valleys, which are cultivated for crops of several kinds, chiefly, however, of rice.

There is only one municipality, Agartala, the capital of the State, and the inhabitants live in that town and in some fourteen hundred villages.

More than 90 per cent. of the people depend for their livelihood upon agricultural resources, but the methods of cultivation are almost entirely of the *jhum* type, which consists of cutting down a forest on the sides of hills and of burning the timber as soon as it is dry, and of sowing seeds of various kinds when good rains fall. This process is repeated for two or three seasons until the land is impoverished by the absence of recuperative crops or fertilizers, when the happy-go-lucky agriculturist packs up his traps and selects another area of forest land.

The principal crop is rice, but others include cotton, jute, tobacco, mustard, onions, chillies, and sugar-cane. The forests on the hills contain *sal*, bamboos, and cane, together with mahogany, teak, rubber, and other trees in reserved areas.

There are practically no manufactures or industries, as the only product is coarse cotton cloth made by Manipuri and Tippera women.

Goods exported include timber, cotton, bamboo, cane, sesamum, and thatching grass, while imports comprise kerosene oil, tobacco, European piece goods, salt, and other commodities.

The question of education had been so much neglected that at the commencement of the twentieth century only 2·3 per cent. of the population were able to read and write; even in 1903 there were not more than about three thousand boys and a hundred girls being taught in schools; but shortly after that date the State provided an Arts College, a high school, as well as a number of primary and secondary institutions, and is now expending an annual sum of nearly Rs. 100,000 in order to provide free instruction for all children.

The State has an area of about 4,000 square miles, and the Raja is not only ruler of that territory, but he is also owner of an estate of about 570 square miles in extent in the districts of Tippera, Sylhet, and Noakhali.

A military force with a strength of about three hundred men is maintained by the State, and the Treasury is also responsible for the maintenance of ten charitable dispensaries.

RIVER HAURA, NEAR AGARTALA.

1. H.H. THE RAJA CHURA CHAND SINGH, OF MANIPUR. 2. THE GOLDEN TEMPLE OF GOVINDJI.
3. THE PALACE, IMPHAL.

THE NATIVE STATE OF MANIPUR

THE Native State of Manipur lies in the mountainous country between the Assam valley and Burma. It is bounded on the north by the Naga Hills, on the west by the Naga and North Cachar Hills and Cachar, on the south by the Lushai and Chin Hills, and on the east by the Upper Chindwin district of Burma, the little Shan State of Thaungdut, and unadministered hill tracts. The State consists of a broad valley intersected by lines of low hills, nearly 700 square miles in area, surrounded by some 8,000 square miles of hills.

The Manipuris call themselves Meitei or Mitei, and their country Manipur or Meitei leipak. The Burmese name for Manipur is Kathe, while the Shans call it Kase. The Ahom conquerors of Assam called it Mekheli, the Assamese Moglau, the Kacharis Magli, and the Bengalis Moglai.

The valley of Manipur lies at an elevation of 2,600 feet above the sea, and the climate is consequently cool and pleasant, healthy and equable. The average rainfall is about 52 inches in Imphal, the capital of the State. The greatest altitude in the hilly portion of the State is reached in the extreme north, where a peak on the border of the Naga Hills attains a height of nearly 10,000 feet. Numerous peaks in the eastern hills are over 9,000 feet.

The principal rivers are the Barak and the Imphal, the former with its tributaries draining the northern and western hills, and flowing through Cachar and the Surma valley into the lower Brahmaputra. The Imphal River, with its tributaries, drains the valley, the hills immediately surrounding it, and the southern hills, and flows through the Chin Hills and the Kale valley into the Chindwin River of Burma. The eastern hills are drained by a number of comparatively small streams flowing into the Yu and the Tuzu, tributaries of the Chindwin.

The valley, especially in the southern portion, is dotted with lakes and marshes, of which, however, all but two or three dry up completely during the hot weather preceding the rainy season. The largest is the Logtak Lake in the south-west of the valley. This varies considerably in size with the seasons, but at its largest it is about 8 miles in length and 5 in breadth.

Apart from tracks across the hills there are only three roads into the State. The chief is the Manipur-Dinapur cart road, which leaves the Assam-Bengal railway at Manipur Road Station. It is metalled the whole of its length, which is 134 miles. After passing through Kohima, the headquarters of the Naga Hills, it enters the State at Mao Thana, 67 miles from both Imphal and the railway. This is the highest point on the road, 5,762 feet above sea-level. The other two roads are only bridle-paths. One passes through the western hills into Cachar, the headquarters of which, Silchar, is 125 miles from Imphal. The State boundary is crossed at the Jiri River, 24 miles from Silchar. The other leads through the south-eastern hills into Burma, the frontier station,

1. A MANIPUR DURBAR AT THE NEW DURBAR HALL.
2. THE RAJA AND STATE ATTENDANTS RETURNING FROM A DURBAR.

Tamu, being 53 miles from Imphal and 2 miles from the border of the State. Through Tamu the road passes on to Sittaung on the Chindwin River.

The internal communications of the valley consist solely of unmetalled roads on raised earth embankments passable for carts. There are about 250 miles of this kind of road, usually bad in the rains, but good in the cold weather. Throughout the hills there are no roads, but merely tracks, though two bridle-paths are now in course of construction.

Completely surrounded as it is by mountains, the valley of Manipur is one of the most beautiful spots in a province which nature has dowered plentifully with magnificent scenery, and is the Kashmir of Eastern India. The description given by Mr. B. C. Allen, I.C.S., in the "Gazetteer" cannot be bettered. He says:—

"The traveller who enters Manipur by the Cachar Road obtains a magnificent view of the valley from the summit of the Laimatol hill. For several days his path has lain across range after range of mountains, covered with forest so dense that it is seldom that he can see as much as a quarter of a mile before him. Suddenly all is changed. The eastern face of the hill, as it slopes down before him to the valley, is covered with short grass, and rolling downs take the place of the dense tropical forest that lies concealed on the western side of the ridge. The valley lies before him like a map. At the northern end, some twenty miles away, are the dark-green groves that conceal the town of Imphal. Elsewhere are level rice-fields, and land covered with grass, about which are dotted the clumps of trees that mark the villages. These villages are much more scattered than they are in the densely populated portions of Assam. They do not stretch in one long continuous line, but stand out here and there, clear and well defined, and there is many a square mile of land without a trace of human habitation. Low ridges of hills stand up above the alluvium, and sheets of water gleam in the shallow depressions on the plain. To the south, the Logtak sparkles in the sun, and on every side the view is bounded by hills. But unlike the mountains that shut in the two great valleys of Assam, they are almost destitute of trees, and nowhere in the valley is there that rank growth of vegetation which is so distinguishing a characteristic of the British Province."

The upper slopes of the hills are invariably well wooded, but serious ravages have been made among the forests on the lower slopes by the wasteful method of cultivation known as *jhuming*, which is practised by the majority of the hill tribes. This consists of cutting down the jungle, burning it when dry, and planting rice and other crop in the ashes. After two or three years the *jhum* is abandoned, and reverts to grass and scrub, and another portion of the forest is selected for the same process of destruction. In the virgin forests many valuable varieties of timber abound. Teak grows on the lower slopes of hills bordering on Burma, many of the eastern and southern ranges are covered with pine forests, several varieties of oak are found, and the western hills are full of other useful kinds of timber, which form the chief supply of the district of Cachar, no less than twenty-four kinds being exported. Many wild varieties of

HIS HIGHNESS'S DOUBLE COMPANY OF MANIPURIS, ATTACHED TO 39TH GARWHALI RIFLES, FOR TRAINING FOR THE FRONT.

1. OLD MANIPUR, THE CORONATION HALL AND DRAGONS. 2. OLD MANIPUR. 3. OLD MANIPUR.

1. These latter were blown up after the Rising of 1891. 2. Group taken after the Relief of Kohima by the Maharaja Chandrakirti Singh and Col. Sir James Johnstone. 3. Entrance-gate to the old fort, now occupied as a Cantonment.

bamboo are plentiful. Wild fruits abound, including the chestnut, walnut, raspberry, strawberry, apple, and plum. Cultivated fruits include the orange, lemon, banana, pineapple, papaya, pomegranate, mango, guava, peach, and other less known varieties. The hills are covered with many beautiful kinds of orchids and flowering trees and plants, including the wild rose, azalea, bohinea, begonia, balsam, and various lilies, and, on the higher slopes, red and white rhododendron. English flowers and vegetables grow well, and experiments are now being made with English fruits, especially apples. Tea is indigenous in the hills.

The State is not, so far as is at present known, rich in minerals; there are deposits of copper ore on the borders of the Kabaw valley of Burma, salt wells are plentiful, both in the valley and in the hills, and coarse potters' clay is found in sufficient quantities to supply the needs of the people. Small deposits of iron in the valley were worked in former days, but have fallen into disuse with the advent of cheaper and better imported iron. Limestone is found in several places.

The larger kinds of fauna are less plentiful than would be expected in consideration of the sparse population of the greater portion of the State, especially the hills. The hill tribes are keen and uncontrolled hunters, and the former prevalence of muzzle-loading guns has had much to do with the disappearance of big game. Elephants are found but rarely, and are mere visitors from the herds of the Dhansiri valley of Assam and the Kabaw valley of Burma. The bison (*Bos gaurus*) and the tsaing (*Bos sondaicus*) occasionally cross the eastern border from the Kabaw valley, where they are common. The wild buffalo, plentiful in Assam, is not found or recorded. Several kinds of deer occur in fair numbers, e.g. the Malay sambar (*Cervus unicolor equinus*), and the barking deer (*Cervulus muntjac*) are found throughout the hills and on the fringes of the valley, the latter also occurring in the low ridges that intersect the valley itself, while the hog deer (*Cervus porcinus*) frequents the marshes and water meadows bordering the lakes. Peculiar to Manipur is the Manipuri deer (*Cervus Eldi cornipes*), which lives in the swamps and bogs in the south of the valley. This race differs from the other races of Eld's deer in Burma, Malay, Siam, and Hainan, in that its habitat is in wet ground, whereas its cousins prefer dry country. Leopards are fairly common both in the hills and in the valley, black specimens occurring rarely. Tigers are found in the hills, occasionally visiting the valley. The clouded leopard is not uncommon. The Himalayan black bear and the Malay bear are plentiful in the hills. The goral and the serao are to be met with in the rocky and precipitous ranges. Wild cats of many varieties, wild pigs, otters, many kinds of monkeys and rats are common, and wild dogs are not rare. The jackal is infrequently met with, being an immigrant from Assam, but it is increasing in numbers, an unpleasant legacy of the cart road. Domestic animals include the buffalo and a hardy little breed of cattle, also a small but strong and sturdy breed of pony. The hillmen keep pigs, goats, mithuns (*Bos frontalis*), and dogs, the latter being utilized both for hunting and culinary ends.

Manipur is a paradise of small game. The grey-leg goose is extraordinarily plentiful on the Logtak, and two other varieties of wild geese have been recorded. Large bags of duck and teal can be made in the cold weather, no fewer than twenty-two different kinds having been recorded. Snipe (six varieties) abound in the marshes, and seven varieties of quail can be obtained, though not in very large numbers. The black partridge is common, and three or four other kinds occur. Plover, woodcock, pigeon, jungle fowl, and four or five varieties of pheasant are also found, but are generally difficult to bag. Countless varieties of non-game birds occur.

Domestic birds include the fowl, the pigeon, the duck, and the goose, of which the two last named are not common.

Many species of freshwater fish abound in the valley, in spite of the relentless pursuit of the Manipuris, who, being Hindus of the Vaisnav persuasion, abstain from flesh and fowl and subsist on a diet of fish and vegetables only. The larger hill streams are well stocked with mahseer.

Cobras and most poisonous snakes are rarely found, but pythons and harmless snakes are not uncommon. Many varieties of lizards occur, and in the lower course of the Barak there are a few gharial, or fish-eating alligators.

The People.—Manipur is inhabited by a medley of tribes. The population of the State in 1911 was 346,323, made up approximately as follows: Manipuri Hindus, 198,000; Manipuri Mussulmans, 14,500; Indians, 3,750; Kukis (17 tribes), 63,500; Nagas (8 tribes), 66,500. The three first-named classes inhabit the valley and the last two the hills. The origin of the Manipuris and the other tribes inhabiting the State will always be doubtful, though they are, from their appearance and linguistic affinities, undoubtedly of Mongolian extraction. The Manipuris themselves do not seem very certain of their remote ancestry. Some claim a Hindu descent, and, identifying Manipur with the Manipur of the Mahabharat, assert that they are the offspring of Arjun by a Naga woman, but this is obviously the result of the conversion of the whole people to Hinduism some two centuries ago. They claim a clearly baseless affinity with the Rajputs of India. Other legends attribute a Chinese origin to the race, and Captain Pemberton, in his report of the eastern frontier, says "we may safely conclude them to be descendants from a Tartar colony from China." Later authorities have rejected this theory and agree that the Manipuris are sprung from various tribes which descended upon the fertile valley from the surrounding hills. Where these tribes, and the tribes at present inhabiting the hills, originated is not, and never will be known, but they all belong to the Tibeto-Burman family, and probably represent, with the Chins, Lushais, Nagas, and various peoples of Burma, successive waves of immigration from western China and eastern Tibet. The Kukis are obviously close relatives of the Chin and Lushai tribes, while the Naga tribes of Manipur are more or less closely connected with the tribes of the neighbouring Naga Hills. The Manipuris present affinities with both.

Religion.—The bulk of the population of the valley are Hindus. The early eighteenth century saw the advent of the first Hindu missionaries from India, and Gharib Nawaz, or Pamheiba, who came to the throne in 1714 and reigned for about forty years, was the first raja of that faith. The Manipuris are Vaisnavites, and worship Krishna under the name of Govindji. There are 8,000 Brahmans in the valley and 171,000 Kshattriyas. The latter include the not inconsiderable caste of Raj Kumars, or descendants in the male line of the royal family. The law that the raja may possess three principal and one hundred and eight subsidiary wives affords scope for a large family. The privilege is not often availed of, but a raja who occupied the throne for a few months in 1851 succeeded in amassing no fewer than ninety-six! The Raj Kumar is often an insignificant person, but he is not allowed

1. THE OLD RESIDENCY, BURNT IN THE RISING OF 1891. 2. THE PRESENT RESIDENCY, FROM THE DRIVE. 3. BACK OF PRESENT RESIDENCY.

1. KABUI MAGA DANCE. 2. STATE BOATMEN. 3. MOIRANG LAI HARAOBA. MEN IN BOATING-DRESS.

by custom to do agricultural labour. The raja is not permitted by custom to marry a Raj Kumari. There are also 18,000 Lois (tributaries), the descendants of subject communities, which in former times performed various menial services for the rajas, and were, in fact, practically slaves. They manufactured iron, silk, salt, and rice liquor, and provided grass, timber, fish, fruit, and earthenware pots. They possibly represent the aboriginal inhabitants of the valley, but their numbers were supplemented by Manipuris, who were frequently degraded to Loi as a punishment. They were originally animists, but the majority have now adopted the Hindu religion, though certain villages adhere to the animist cult of their forefathers. The Manipuri Mussulmans, to the number of 14,500, are the descendants of immigrants and captives from the Surma valley who married Manipuri women. There are two villages of Haris, or sweepers, who are animists. The hill tribes are all animists, with the exception of an inconsiderable number of Christian converts made by the American Baptist Missionaries in the eastern hills, and an offshoot of a Lushai Mission in the south-west. Previous to their conversion to Hinduism, the Manipuris themselves were animists, and, as in Burma, the old religion still survives side by side with the new, every house having its "Imung lai" or lares and penates, and every village its "Lam lai" or "Umang Lai," god or goddess of the countryside and jungle, which has been incorporated in the Hindu pantheon and is worshipped either under its own name or under a borrowed Hindu one. Relics of the old ritual survive in the "Lai Haraoba," or pleasing of the god, an annual ceremony in which each village propitiates its own particular "lai." The valley and hills abound in "laiphams," or god's seats, which are the abiding places of Lam and Umang Lais, and are reverenced accordingly. The ritual of the hill tribes consists solely of propitiation of the spirits of the stream and jungle, all of whom are malevolent in varying degrees. Both they and the Manipuris are extremely superstitious.

The recency of the Manipuri's conversion to Hinduism has rendered him strict in certain observances to the point of bigotry. Thus the mere contact of a European or Mahommedan with a Manipuri house is sufficient to defile it to such a degree that it is necessary to demolish and rebuild it. Hillmen, however, who, presumably owing to their race connection with the Manipuris, are permitted to embrace Hinduism, may enter the veranda of the house. In other matters they are more lax, for example, they permit the remarriage of widows—doubtless a survival of pre-Hindu days.

The life of the Manipuri is full of religious ceremonies apart from the ordinary ceremonial of his religious worship. At his birth the usual Hindu ritual is observed, together with a ceremony in honour of the Imung Lai, or god of the house. Another ceremony is performed at the giving of the first rice and another at the assumption of the sacred thread worn by all Manipuris. There is usually a ceremony at marriage, which can be contracted in several forms, the simplest being elopement and cohabitation, without any ceremony whatever. The dead are disposed of by cremation, with the exception of very young children, who are buried. There are various funeral ceremonies, extending over a period of thirteen days, though the cremation takes place

1. MANIPURIS FISHING.

2. SHOOTING CAMP ON THE LOGTAK LAKE.

a few hours after death. The frontal bone of the deceased is preserved and is taken at a later date by some member of the family going on pilgrimage, and after visits usually to Navadvip and Benares, is thrown into the Ganges at Radhakund. An annual ceremony is held in commemoration of the deceased.

The hill tribes also have their ceremonies, in propitiation of the malevolent spirits who constitute their gods. There are ceremonies at births, marriages, and deaths, during illness, in memorial of the dead, and at every important period of the year, such as the cutting of the *jhums*, the burning of the *jhums*, and the planting and reaping of the crops. These ceremonies are invariably attended with the sacrifice of some domestic animal, from a mithun down to a fowl, and with libations of liquor. The hillmen and the Mahommedans bury their dead, as the Manipuris did before their conversion to Hinduism.

Appearance and Dress.—The Manipuris and hill tribes alike, are fair, well-built, and muscular. The Mongolian type is predominant, but many possess regular features, which appear to indicate a different origin. The dress of the Manipuri man consists of a *dhuti* (shirt), and at night or in cold weather, a coat and a *chaddar* or shawl. *Pagris* are worn in full dress and on ceremonial occasions. The working dress consists of a *dhuti* or a scanty loin cloth round the waist. They all wear the sacred thread of their religion. More elaborate dresses, based upon the old national types, are worn by those taking part in polo, wrestling, boat races, "lai haraobas," and other State and religious ceremonies. The women, among whom the *purdah* is unknown, wear a *phanek* or skirt, folded across the breast under the armpits and tucked in at the side. For ordinary purposes this is made of white or green cotton material, but on high days and holidays striped *phaneks* of various colours are worn, made of silk and cotton and embroidered at the upper or lower edges with silk. A shawl is worn over the head or shoulders, on ordinary occasions of the same material as the *phanek*, but on great occasions of thin white muslin. Mahommedan men dress much the same as the Hindus, sometimes wearing a loose skirt instead of a *dhuti*, but the Mahommedan women wear a coloured cotton sash and *pagri* in addition to the dress worn by Hindu women. In the winter both Hindu and Mahommedan, women wear a tight fitting bodice with long sleeves, usually of black, green, or red velvet. The women tie their hair in a knot at the back. Unmarried Hindu girls and the girls of some of the hill tribes cut their hair in a fringe over the forehead. Kuki women do their hair in two plaits, tied together on the top of the head. Some Naga tribes crop the hair of the unmarried girls. In others the women wear the hair tied in two large knots hanging over the ears.

MANIPURI GIRL SPINNING.

Manipuri men cut their hair short with a sacred tuft at the crown of the head. Some of the older men wear their hair long and tied in a knot at the back of the head, as do the Kukis and some Nagas. Others among the Nagas cut the hair round the sides, leaving a pendulous mop on the top of the head. The Tangkhuls are known by shaving the sides of their heads, leaving the hair on the top sticking straight up like a cockatoo's crest. One tribe of Nagas tie their hair in a tight knot over the forehead, pierced with an iron pin and bound round with strings of beads.

Many men and most women wear plain gold earrings. Women when dressed in their best wear more ornate earrings, rings, necklaces, and bracelets of gold. Ankle ornaments and nose rings are not worn.

Among the hill tribes, the men of the Kuki clans wear a *dhuti, pagri,* and a wrapper of thick home-made cloth or blanket. The Tangkhuls, a Naga tribe of 27,000 persons inhabiting the eastern hills, wear a narrow strip of cloth, tied in a knot, with the ends hanging down in front, and a striped cotton wrapper. When working they are accustomed to remove all their clothing. The other Naga tribes wear a short kilt, like the Angamis in the Naga Hills. The women of all the hill tribes wear skirts of various colours, according to their tribes. The skirt is arranged like the *phanek* of the Manipuri women. The women of the Kabuis, a Naga tribe of 18,000 souls in the western hills, wear *pagris*, as do some of the Tangkhul women. Tattooing is practised by some of the Tangkhul women only.

Earrings of various shapes, sizes, and materials are practically universal among the hillmen, men, and women. The Tangkhuls prefer them of brass, frequently enclosing the brass ends of two 12-bore cartridges. The northern Naga tribes affect coloured cotton or wool or brass wire; many Kuki men wear cornelian beads, and the women, rings of brass or silver, distending the lobe of the ear. Kabui women wear large brass rings, dependent from the lobe. Bracelets of brass are worn by many Tangkhul men, but the women of the hill tribes as a rule only wear bracelets until they are married. Necklaces are largely worn by men and women. The Kuki women wear necklaces of cornelian and other beads. The men of the Tangkhul and northern Naga tribes wear row upon row of marvellous necklaces made of bone and shell and various coloured beads, which are often of great value.

The inhabitants of the valley, Hindu and Mahommedan, are extremely cleanly in their persons, and except when working wear spotlessly white clothing. The hillmen, on the other hand, are dirty, both in their persons and clothing, a wash being indulged in only when they happen to cross a river on a warm day.

Food and Drink.—As stated above, the Manipuri Hindu, being a Vaisnavite, eats the flesh of neither animal nor fowl, but confines himself to a fish and vegetable diet. Eggs and intoxicants are "taboo," but these rules are relaxed in favour of children, who may eat eggs and flesh without losing caste. In pre-Hindu days, of course, the Manipuris ate what the hill tribes eat to this day, nothing being forbidden except milk, which the hill men regard as an unclean article of diet. Various hill tribes still have their own particular "taboos." Thus, no hill man will eat the flesh of the tiger and leopard; some will eat monkeys and some not; dwellers in a large village in the north of the State do not keep or eat pigs, though most tribes prize them as an article of diet. The hillman is not particular as to the mode of death of the animals which he eats, with the result that cattle that have died of old age or disease always find some one to take pity on them. The non-Hindu Lois and the hillmen brew several varieties of not unpleasant beer from rice, millet, maize, and other food grains, the most palatable of which greatly resembles slightly sour cider. A raw and disgusting spirit distilled from this beer is greatly appreciated, and is drunk undiluted. It has been aptly described as tasting of candlegrease and methylated spirit.

The Manipuris smoke tobacco in *hukas* made of coco-nut shells, and are also extremely partial to cigarettes. Among the hillmen the *huka* is confined to the women of the Kuki tribes. The men either smoke pipes, chew tobacco, or sip and contain in the mouth water saturated with tobacco juice from the *hukas* of their lady friends and relatives. Betel leaf and nut are extensively chewed by the Manipuris, and to a less extent by some of the hill tribes. Opium and ganja smoking is practically unknown.

Agriculture, Manufactures, and Trade.—The agricultural produce of the country consists chiefly of rice, which is the staple food of the population. It grows abundantly and is of excellent quality, especially in the fertile alluvial soil of the valley. The central and lower portions of the valley are watered by inundation, but the land near the foot of the hills is irrigated, without difficulty, by channels from the many streams that have their sources in the ranges bordering the valley. Rice is sown in seed beds in the spring, and the seedlings are transplanted by hand in the early summer. Ploughing is done with a primitive wooden plough with a small share, drawn by a buffalo or a pair of bullocks, and is not at all deep, merely consisting of churning the wet surface of the fields into liquid mud. Weeding is done with a wooden harrow, consisting of a toothed bar of wood, like a rake, upon which a man stands and is drawn over the field by a buffalo. Rice and weeds are pressed into the mud indiscriminately, the latter dying and the former rearing its head again and surviving. The rice is reaped with sickles, from September to December, according to the variety, and is threshed in the field with a flail. The straw is mostly burnt, and the unhusked rice is carried to the cultivator's granary and stored there. The carting is usually done in baskets on a *kangpot*– a rough wooden sledge, drawn by a buffalo.

Other crops grown in the valley are wheat, mustard, pulses, sugar-cane, tobacco, potatoes, vegetables, and various kinds of oil-seeds, and a little jute. But these crops are almost entirely grown for local consumption and are not extensive.

The staple crop of the hills is also rice. It is chiefly grown in *jhums*, as described above, but in the north and east of the State, where the valleys are more open and the lower slopes of the hills more gradual, cultivation consists entirely of irrigated terraces. Rice in the hills, however, is largely supplemented by other food grains, such as millet, maize, and Job's tears. Other crops grown in the hills are cotton, potatoes, tobacco, and various kinds of tubers and vegetables. The chief of these is cotton, which is sufficient to supply the whole State and leave a margin for export. No cotton is grown in the valley, but experiments are being made with foreign varieties, which may grow in well-drained land near the foot of the hills.

NAGA GIRL FISHING.

The manufactures of the country, except for local needs, are practically *nil*. Every housewife is an expert at spinning and weaving the cotton cloths required by her family, of which an inconsiderable quantity is exported. Silk cloths are made in those Loi villages in which the silk industry is hereditary. The Loi potter

1. MANIPURI BOYS DANCING. 2. MANIPURI DANCE: KRISHNA AND THE MILKMAIDS.
3. MANIPURI DANCE : KRISHNA KILLING THE CRANE.

1. MANIPURI POLO-PLAYER.

2. MANIPURI GIRLS' DANCE.

3. ARROW THROWER.

The arrows are carried in a quiver on the pony, and consist of a heavy iron head attached to a feather streamer. Formidable weapons, they are the favourite arm of the famous Manipuri cavalry which is reputed to have raided into Burma, as far as Mandalay.

villagers make earthenware pots for local use, but by a laborious method, the use of the potter's wheel being unknown and attempts to introduce it have hitherto proved abortive. In other Loi villages, four or five in number, salt is made by evaporating brine from the salt wells on the eastern fringe of the valley. The brine is drawn in a closely woven basket from a well, the shaft of which consists of the hollowed trunks of trees. It is evaporated in shallow iron pans over a wood fire, and is sold in thin round cakes. Many wells exist throughout the hills and are the source of a thriving trade. In former times, certain Loi villagers possessed the art of smelting iron and preparing spears, *daos*, ploughshares, axes, hoes, and other primitive instruments. But this art is now extinct, having been killed by the competition of cheaper and better imported iron and steel. In the same way, imported cloth and salt are serious rivals of the local products, although conservative people still prefer the home-made article.

The Manipuri as a craftsman is found at his best in the work of the smith and the carpenter. He is capable of turning out first-class work and is ingenious and clever at imitating even the most intricate articles. There is a sewing machine in use in Imphal which has been copied in detail by Manipuri workmen from a European model. There is also an old silver and brass worker and watch mender who has evolved a set of false teeth for himself out of some ivory, lac, and silver wire.

Gold, silver, and brass workers make for the local market only. No export trade is done in these articles, and the smiths do not exhibit any extraordinary talent.

1. VIEW OF THE ANGAMI NAGA VILLAGE OF MAO.
One of the stages on the cart road at the boundary of the Manipur State.

The Manipuris do not paint badly, and there is a State artist, who with two or three others in Imphal, turns out very creditable pictures. At copying a photograph in colour they are really wonderful.

The chief articles of export from the State are rice and timber. Many tons of the latter commodity are annually floated down the Barak River into Cachar, and periodically teak is extracted in the foothills of the Kabaw valley and exported to Burma. No figures, however, are available. Rice practically monopolizes the remainder of the export trade, the amount exported by the Manipur—Dinapur cart road in a year being in the neighbourhood of 200,000 maunds (1 ton = 27·22 maunds). The last figures available are for 1914-15, when the exports were: Rice, 1,61,795 maunds; cloth and yarns, 207 maunds; *ghi*, 413 maunds; hides, 369 maunds; wheat, 109 maunds; molasses, 224 maunds; chillies, 158 maunds; mustard oil, 77 maunds. There is also a considerable export trade in cattle and ponies, and a transport trade in cattle and tea seed from Burma to Cachar and Sylhet.

The chief imports are salt, betel-nuts, and kerosene oil. The figures for 1914-15 of the quantity introduced by the Dinapur cart road, are as follows: Salt, 26,234 maunds; betel-nuts, 21,090 maunds; kerosine, 14,313 maunds; piece goods and yarns, 4,541 maunds; dried fish, 3,427 maunds; wheat and flour, 2,671 maunds; hardware, 3,147 maunds; sheet iron, 1,164 maunds; pulses, 578 maunds; sugar 487 maunds; books and stationery, 387 maunds; ammunition, 252 maunds; glass-ware, 187 maunds. The export and import trade by the other two roads leading out of the State, into Cachar and the Kabaw valley of Burma, is inconsiderable and is not recorded. These two roads are merely bridle-paths through the hills, and all trade passing over them has to be carried on the backs of coolies. Practically all the export and import trade of Manipur is in the hands of foreigners, chiefly Marwaris, as the Manipuris have little or no commercial enterprise, and lack capital.

A prominent feature of the internal trade and social life of the valley are the daily bazaars or markets, which usually take place in the late afternoon and evening. The vendors are women, and men do not often attend, even as purchasers. The chief one is the Imphal bazaar, in which four or five thousand women offer their wares daily. In this market, custom lays down that men are permitted to sell cigarettes and *hukas* only, and to change money. But even the dealers in these commodities are not allowed into the precincts of the bazaar proper, but are obliged to sit on the outskirts. There are ten or a dozen lesser bazaars in Imphal, and about twenty others throughout the valley.

The only coin originally recognized in Manipur was a bell-metal coin, weighing about 16 grains. The usual variation of its exchange value is from 450 to 500 for the rupee. This coin is said by the Manipuris to have been first struck by Pakhangba, the legendary progenitor of the royal family, who had the power of turning himself into a snake, and still reappears as such. Colonel McCulloch, who was Political Agent in Manipur in the middle of the last century, credits Khakamba, who reigned during the first half of the seventeenth century, with first introducing bell-metal coinage. There is evidence that a square silver rupee was coined by Chaurjit Singh in 1815, but there is no record of silver coinage by other rajas or of any gold coinage whatever. Indian coins have now almost entirely ousted the *sel*, as the bell-metal coins are called, but the latter are still current in some bazaars in the valley.

History.—The court chronicler keeps a record of events which purports to go back to the thirtieth year of the Christian era. The early portion, however, is unreliable, and has probably been committed to writing in comparatively recent times. The writings are in the dead language, and in an almost obsolete character which has been replaced in modern times by the Bengali character. Our certain knowledge of early times is confined to the fact that Manipur was tributary to the kings of Pong, the great Shan kingdom of Upper Burma. In 1475 we find the united forces of Pong and Manipur conquering Khumbat, with the result that the Kabaw valley was annexed to Manipur.

From 1714, the accession of Pamheiba, or Gharib Nawaz, the narrative is fairly continuous and authentic. His reign and those of his successors up to the First Burmese War are a long record of struggles between the Manipuris and the Burmese, with varying fortunes. Gharib Nawaz actually reached the walls of Ava, the Burmese capital, but patched up a peace and returned to Manipur owing to the alarm wrought in his suspicious mind by the fall of his standard in a gale. Subsequently, however, the Burmese were almost uniformly successful and made periodical invasions of the valley. It is said that on their final withdrawal from the State in 1824, the adult male population did not exceed three thousand souls.

The eighteenth century was also marked by revolting and treacherous internal wars. Previous to the reign of Gharib Nawaz, himself a younger son concealed by his mother, who came to the throne owing to the principal rani being barren, it had been the pleasant custom of the royal house to kill all sons born to the raja by his minor wives. Gharib Nawaz abolished this custom, with disastrous results to himself, as he and his eldest son were surprised and killed, while operating in Burma, by a force sent by a younger son who had cast covetous eyes on the throne. The remainder of the century is one long record of pretenders, civil war, and murder in the royal house, brother killing brother, father destroying son, and son the father, without the least compunction. The rajas of the nineteenth century, supported as they were by the British Government, and assisted with grants of guns and money, were stronger and more secure, and though this period was not without its pretenders, they were all overthrown.

The relations of the Manipur State with the British Government date from 1762, when a treaty was concluded whereby the Government undertook to assist the Raja Jai Singh against the Burmese. A force was dispatched from Chittagong, but disease and difficulties of transport prevented it from penetrating beyond Cachar. In 1823 Government opened communications with Raja Gambhir Singh, helping him with guns, ammunition, and money. the raja in his turn supplying a contingent to co-operate with the British troops in Cachar against the Burmese. In 1833 the Manipur Levy, which since 1825 had been commanded by British officers, and armed, accoutred, and paid by Government, was discontinued, but arms and ammunition for the reduction of refractory hill tribes were supplied to the raja. In 1833 a treaty was concluded between the raja and the Government, defining the boundary between Cachar and Manipur, agreeing on mutual alliance and assistance in the event of another war against Burma, and arranging for trade between Manipur and British territory. In 1834 another treaty was signed by which the raja ceded the Kabaw valley to the Burmese in return for an annual grant from Government of Rs. 6,270. In 1835 a Political Agent was placed in Manipur by the Government for "the preservation of a friendly intercourse and as a medium of communication with the Manipur Government, and, as occasion may require, with the Burmese frontier, and more especially to prevent border feuds and disturbances which might lead to hostilities between the Manipurians and the Burmese" (Lord William Bentinck's Minute, dated February 7, 1835).

For the next fifty-six years the relations of Manipur with the Government are uneventful, save for the participation of a Manipur contingent in the first expedition against the Lushais in 1871 and the relief of Kohima by a Manipuri force under the Political Agent, Colonel Johnstone, in 1879, when that station was besieged by Angami Nagas, subsequent to the murder of the Deputy Commissioner, Mr. Damant, at Khonoma. In 1891 the treacherous murder of the Chief Commissioner of Assam, Mr. Quinton, together with the Political Agent and three other officers and of two telegraph officers, was a blot on the modern history of the State. Five years previously Raja Sir Chandra Singh had died after a reign of fifty-two years. His eldest son and successor, who was deposed by his younger brothers in

A FINE STONE THREE-ARCH BRIDGE

Across one of the mountain gorges on the cart road, which was opened after the military expedition of 1891.

1890, applied to the Government for assistance in the recovery of his throne, and to deport the Senapati, another brother, who had been the leading spirit in the revolution. The Chief Commissioner accordingly proceeded to Manipur with an escort of four hundred rifles, and was received with every show of respect, but the Senapati failed to attend the Durbar at which the decision of the Government was to have been promulgated. After some negotiations a force was sent to seize the Senapati, but it was resisted, and Lieutenant Brackenbury was mortally wounded. The Manipuris then attacked the Residency, but in the evening a message was sent to the effect that the Senapati desired to confer with the Chief Commissioner. The latter and his party accordingly left the Residency and entered the fortified Palace precincts. They were never seen again, but it appears that, after a fruitless discussion, they were returning to the gate of the fort when one of the mob speared the Political Agent. He died shortly after from the wound, and the Manipuris, considering that nothing was to be gained by abstaining from further treachery, beheaded the other members of the party. The two telegraph officers who had left Imphal for Dinapur the previous day were pursued and wantonly murdered thirty-four miles out of Imphal.

Columns converged on Manipur from Cachar, Assam, and Burma, and it was quickly subdued. The raja and his brothers were deported, the Senapati and two others were hanged, and the Government of India declared that the Manipur State was forfeited to the Crown, but decided to regrant it to a scion of a junior branch. The present raja, His Highness Chura Chand Singh, was thereupon selected. He is the youngest of five brothers, great grandsons of Raja Nar Singh, through his fifth son. His Highness was only six years old in 1891, and Manipur passed through a long regency under the Political Agent as Superintendent of the State, until his Highness was installed on the *Gadi* in 1908, since which time he has administered the State, with the assistance of a Durbar presided over by an officer of the Assam Commission, lent to the State for the purpose by Government.

His Highness has shown himself a wise and benevolent ruler. The period of his administration has heralded the abolition of abuses and irksome institutions, together with the introduction of reforms and useful schemes for the future. The British regency was marked by the discontinuance of the system by which every inhabitant of the valley was obliged to do ten days' labour in every forty for the raja. His Highness has also abolished the system of keeping up roads, and local schoolhouses by forced labour, and of each village providing carriers for the baggage of officials on tour within the village boundaries, and of supplying them with food, and grain and grass for their ponies without payment. Other ancient dues and duties performed by the people were either abolished or regularized, and clearly defined. Recently an installation of pipes has been laid down to convey filtered water to Imphal from the hills ten miles to the west. The scheme benefits about 50,000 people in Imphal, where the water supply was exceedingly bad. His Highness has recently reformed the judicial system of the State, and has instituted the registration of documents. Projected improvements include the building of a large

1. MANIPURI BOY ON BUFFALO 2. MANIPURI MAHOMMEDAN WEDDING.

1 TONGKHUL NAGA IN WAR-PAINT.
Observe the red-hair tail.

2. TONGKHUL NAGAS IN WAR-PAINT 3–6. NAGA TYPES. 7. MAO NAGAS IN WAR-PAINT.

1 OFFICERS' QUARTERS. 2. OFFICERS' MESS. 3. MILITARY HOSPITAL.
4. A TYPICAL REST-HOUSE, ON THE MANIPUR-KOHIM CART-ROAD.

At one of the stages of the journey of 134 miles.

hospital on modern lines, a State printing press, and a residential high school four miles distant from Imphal. As soon as suitable officers are available, the forest and medical departments will be re-organized under European supervision. Meanwhile scholarships have been freely granted to Manipuri boys to continue their studies outside of the State with a view to their employment in the higher posts of the State service, many of which have which Government had to refuse owing to the lack of training officers. He has accordingly recruited a double company of Manipuri infantry for active service, and has offered a non-combatant corps of hill-men for manual labour in France. His Highness's great ambition is to be permitted to go on active service with his men.

Games and Sports.—The national game of Manipur is polo, which was introduced secured under the chin. The bridle and reins are of cotton rope, and the bridle is adorned with large balls of coloured cotton. The saddle carries large curved shields of lacquered leather on each side to protect the legs. These doubtless had their origin in war, in the days when the Kathe horse, armed with their peacock-feather-shafted darts, were a terror to the Burmese. The Burman is a poor rider, whereas most Manipuris are good horsemen.

1. VIEW OF A BOAT-RACE.

The boats are long dug-outs some 50 feet long, manned by 50 or 60 boatmen. Fouling is part of the game, and the endeavours to upset an adversary cause the greatest enthusiasm. Large crowds assemble to watch these events, and in their excitement men will plunge into the river to assist their partisans.

2. ANOTHER VIEW.

hitherto been held by Indian immigrants.

His Highness the Raja has, since the outbreak of war, rendered to the Imperial Government every assistance that the resources of the State could afford. He has presented four motor ambulances and an aeroplane, and has invested Rs. 34,000 of the State Reserve Fund in the Indian War Loan. He has imposed taxes upon carts plying on the Manipur-Dinapur road, and upon cattle transported through the State, the proceeds to be devoted to war purposes. He proposed raising a company of sappers and miners, an offer into India from Manipur more than fifty years ago. It has been played in the State for two or three hundred years. There is always an odd number of players on each side, usually seven, and they play for a fixed number of goals, the whole end of the field being the goal. There are no rules against crossing and fouling, and if the ponies were not small and extremely handy, accidents would be common.

The costume worn consists of a tightly tucked up *dhuti*, coloured cloth gaiters, a tight jacket, often made of velvet, and a *pagri* tied in the old fashion manner, and

Three varieties of hockey on foot are also played, one with a rope of twisted grass and a hard wild fruit of the lemon variety, another with a short polo stick and polo ball, and a third with a knobby cane, and a seed from the jungle, or a polo ball. Under certain circumstances, tackling is allowed, whether the player is in possession of the ball or not.

Foot racing used to be very common in Manipur, and the winner of the annual race was excused from all forced labour for life. This sport has now fallen into disuse.

Wrestling is a common sport. The

contact of any part of the body, except the foot, with the ground, constitutes defeat. The costume consists of a very tightly tied and tucked up *dhuti* and a *pagri* similar to that worn for polo.

In September and on great occasions there are boat races. The boats belong to His Highness the Raja, and, like all boats in the State, are hollowed out of a single tree, being about 70 feet in length. They are manned by about fifty rowers, two or three steersmen and a captain, who stands on a platform in the bow of the boat and urges on his crew by raising his paddle and stamping at intervals with his foot. The boats are generally manned by representatives of the four *paunas* of the valley, two by two. The *pannas* were probably originally military organizations, but are now revenue divisions of the valley. The main object is, of course, to pass the winning-post first, but there are no fouls, so this object is usually attained by the boat which gets off ahead running its nose across the rival boat and boring it into the bank. By this manœuvre one side of the hinder boat is prevented from using its paddles, and the greatest efforts of the crew merely succeed in pushing the leading boat towards the winning post. The partisans of each crew run along the river bank and dash into the water, attempting to push their boat away from the bank and to give it every assistance in their power. The races are run in two heats, and in the event of each boat winning a heat, the winner of the first heat is considered the winner. But the results are carried on from year to year. In the good old days, in the infrequent event of one boat being sunk, the captain became the slave of the other boat, and was compelled to ransom himself at a fixed price. The dress of the captains consists of a *dhuti*, waistcloth, and sash with a gay crimson pattern and border, a green velvet jacket, a *pagri* similar to the polo *pagri*, ornamented with a plume of pheasant and peacock feathers, and with sprays of orchid, and gold bracelets and armlets. The steersmen are slightly less ornately dressed, and the rowers wear only white *dhutis* and *pagris*.

The Manipuris are very fond of chess, of which they have a peculiar form of their own, and they also play many games of cards. They have other indoor games of the fox and geese and pitch and toss variety, and others played with dice. Pigeon fighting was formerly a common amusement, but the Manipuris are reckless gamblers, and thefts, which are usually committed by men who have lost their all, became so common that it was stopped by a royal edict. Other indoor amusements are reading, tale telling, and singing parties, in which sacred songs and stories, and the national ballads and folklore are declaimed. The singing is frequently accompanied by a monotonous chant played on a violin made out of half a coconut, fitted with a single string, or rather bunch of strings, and adorned with bells. The players of this instrument sing in the dead language of Manipur, the language of the chronicles.

Horse racing is not uncommon, consisting solely of matches between two owners, the stakes being either the pony or a considerable sum of money. The *venue* is always a road.

The hill tribes have few sports and games. Among the Kabuis on certain occasions, the young men of the village have a long-jumping competition, which takes place in the presence of a critical audience, the old men, as is their wont, lamenting that the present generation cannot jump nearly as far as the experts of their day. All the hill tribes play the fox and geese and pitch and toss games of the Manipuris.

Dancing among the Manipuris is alike an amusement and a religious ceremony. They have four dances, one performed by boys alone, the others by boys and unmarried girls. The music is supplied by a kind of guitar and drums, and by the voices of the dancers and orchestra. The most picturesque dance is a scena of events from the story of Krishna and Radha, the costume of Krishna, Radha, and the chorus, male and female, being gorgeous in the extreme. The dances are entirely free from the sensuous characteristics of Indian dancing.

Dancing among the majority of the hill tribes is confined to men, and is of the nature of a war dance. These dances are of little or no æsthetic interest, but the Marrings, a Naga tribe, have a pretty dance in which women take part. The Kabuis, another tribe of Nagas, have a series of dances, executed by the unmarried men and girls, which are artistic in form, and the music of which goes with a swing and is more in accordance with European ideas of melody than most Indian music.

Fishing and Hunting.—Being the sole animal diet of the Manipuris, fish are ardently pursued by every imaginable method both by men and women. Weirs, fishing baskets, traps, spears, drag nets, cast nets and lines, are all used. Poison was formerly used, especially by the hill tribes, but a recent order has put a stop to this wasteful and destructive method. Fishing by explosives is also forbidden, as well as by weirs and drag nets in the hill streams, which are largely the nurseries of the fish supply. There are about twenty-five different kinds of fish in the State, all of which are eaten by the Manipuris. Eels of a red colour are not eaten by the Manipuris, but are esteemed as a delicacy by the Nagas, who catch them with spears with three or four prongs.

The Manipuri, not being a flesh eater, abstains from hunting, but the Manipuri Mahommedan is a keen sportsman, those who have guns shoot duck and geese on the lakes, and also the deer that are found in the valley, but as they shoot regardless of sex, season, or maturity, it has recently been laid down that no deer shall be killed in the valley without a permit. The Mahommedans also kill black partridges by running them down with dogs. The birds are marked down and pursued every time they rise, and after the third flight they are usually so tired and mesmerized with fright that they refuse to rise and can be caught by the dogs. But the most sporting method of hunting indulged in by the Mahommedans is that by which they kill the hog-deer. In the late spring, when the lakes and marshes have mostly dried up, ten or fifteen men mounted on ponies, usually barebacked, and armed with polo-sticks, and accompanied by a mob of men armed with spears and sticks, and having dogs, proceed to the haunts of the deer. They beat the grass, and when a deer is put up it is pursued across country by the riders, who endeavour to hit it on the head with their polo sticks, or to drive it towards the foot people, who despatch it with their weapons. The going is usually very moderate, and tosses are not infrequent, but very seldom serious.

The hillmen, too, are keen and indefatigable hunters, and their persistent efforts have greatly reduced the stock of game in the hills. Certain kinds of game, such as bison and elephant, have been completely killed or banished by them. The Kukis are special offenders in this line, using the guns with which former rajas used to arm them as a first line of defence against marauding outsiders, such as the Burmese, Chins, and Angamis. Much has been done in the way of disarming the hill tribes, a certain number of guns being licensed and returned to them, but the mischief has been done, and it is doubtful whether the hills will ever be stocked with game as they were years ago. In addition to firearms, the hillmen use traps, snares, bows and arrows, and spears to kill all sorts and sizes of animals and birds. They are excellent trackers, and can follow wounded animals for long distances.

Administration.—The raja is the head of the State and has the ultimate word in all important matters. He is assisted and advised by a Darbar of seven members, presided over by a member of the Assam Commission lent to the State by the Government. The various departments of the administration are controlled by members of the Darbar, His Highness the Raja retaining the Medical and State Works (roads and buildings) departments in his own hands. All revenue matters and all revenue-producing departments are controlled by the President of the Darbar, who is also in charge of the hill tribes. There are nine local benches of five magistrates each, who try petty criminal and civil cases. In Imphal there are two benches of six magistrates each, one of which tries petty and the other more important cases. The Darbar is the supreme court of the State. Cases in which hillmen are concerned are tried by the resident of the Darbar, and when British subjects or other foreigners are parties they come under the jurisdiction of the Political Agent.

Modern punishments are the same as those in force in British India, with the addition of punitive labour for offences committed by whole villages in the hills, such as rioting or flagrant disobedience of orders. The punishments of the old régime were more brutal and picturesque. It was the custom to put a murderer to death in the same way as he had killed his victim, and it was only about thirty years ago that the raja, at the instance of the Political Agent, substituted decapitation after a particularly brutal murder. Members of the Royal Family were executed by being tied in a sack and thrown into a river at some place where another river meets it. Brahmans and women were exempt from capital punishment. In the case of the latter, a punishment known as "parading the villages" was substituted. This is described as follows in the Chronicles: "She is made thoroughly naked, only a small piece of cloth being tied round her waist; her hair is shaved, and her bare head and face are painted with lime, ink, and turmeric; broomsticks and a drum are tied on her back; a man in front drags her by a piece of rope tied round her neck; while a large crowd gathers behind, beating the drum; her crime is meanwhile proclaimed to the public, and thus she is made to walk through the several streets and bazaars." Flogging was a common punishment for theft, and on a second conviction the thief was liable to have his right hand cut off. A punishment commonly employed was banishment to a Loi village, entailing permanent social degradation. We read that in 1881 the raja, disagreeing with the court of justice, which acquitted the offender, banished his fourth son to a Loi village for a year for killing one of his servants.

Crimes of violence are rare in Manipur, but cattle theft and burglary are exceedingly prevalent and are difficult to detect.

NAGA HEADMEN OF MAO.

Education is entirely voluntary, and primary education is free. There are 71 lower primary schools, three upper primary schools, and three middle English schools. Higher and technical education is provided by scholarships tenable at schools and colleges in British India. But the institution of a high school in the near future is contemplated, the foundation stone of the building having been laid by the Chief Commissioner of Assam on the occasion of his last visit.

Western medical science does not greatly commend itself to the Manipuris, who prefer to rely on their own *maibas* and *maibis*, a class of men and women who combine the most elementary and extraordinary ideas of medicine and midwifery with soothsaying and prophecy. Two European remedies, however, are thoroughly popular, namely, vaccination and quinine. Statistics show that the central hospital in Imphal and the four dispensaries in the valley and hills are gradually gaining in popularity, and the State has now several students under training in a medical school in Assam.

Finances.—It is only in comparatively recent years that the State of Manipur has possessed any money revenue worth speaking of. In the old days a very large proportion of the revenue was paid to the raja in kind—rice, salt, cloth, fish, fruit, iron, timber, and other goods. Colonel McCulloch, the Political Agent in 1859, estimated the cash revenue at that time at from Rs. 12,000 to Rs. 15,000. By 1892-3, however, it had risen to Rs. 2,15,000, in 1900-1 it was Rs. 3,88,000, in 1910-11 Rs. 4,95,000, and in 1915-16 it reached Rs. 6,51,000. By far the largest source of revenue is the land. All land in the valley is assessed at the rate of Rs. 2-6-3 per acre, producing about Rs. 4,10,000. The next largest item is hill house-tax, which, assessed at Rs. 3 per house, produces about Rs. 75,000. Fisheries yield about Rs. 70,000, and forests about Rs. 25,000, with occasional windfalls from teak. Other less profitable sources are foreigners' tax, ferries, salt, tea-seed, law and justice, jail, excise, income tax and trading licences, water rate, Kabaw valley compensation, and miscellaneous items.

The chief spending department is that of State Works, with a present expenditure of about Rs. 1,60,00. The raja's civil list accounts for Rs. 1,25,000, administration Rs. 50,000, education for Rs. 30,000, military police for Rs. 37,000, and land revenue for Rs. 30,000. A tribute of Rs. 50,000 is paid to the Government of India. Smaller amounts are expended upon hill tribes, salt, forests, law and justice, civil police, jail, medical, postal, expeditions and tours, tea-seed, miscellaneous institutions, veterinary, waterworks and repayment of loan. The State is indebted to the Government to the amount of about Rs. 1,20,000, being the unliquidated balance of a loan of Rs. 1,75,000, contracted in order to construct the Imphal waterworks. Disastrous floods during October 1915, which surpassed any floods in the memory of man, did immense damage to the roads and bridges, and destroyed about half the rice crop of the valley, rendering it necessary to apply to Government for a further loan of Rs. 3,25,000.

A STATE OFFICIAL AND BODYGUARD.

THE AUL RAJ

The Aul Raj Estate is in the district of Cuttack and the Orissa division of the Province of Behar and Orissa.

The numerous waves of political and religious movements which in early days passed over Orissa, and the invasions and conquests which took place alternately in that country, naturally had an effect upon the Province of Aul, and therefore the history of the Raj is very closely connected with that of the area of which it was an integral part.

According to ancient tradition in Orissa, the whole of India was at one time under a sovereign who ruled at Hastinapur, the ancient name of Delhi. This king appointed four Maharajas, who, in turn, selected a number of petty rajas to assist in the government of his territory; one of these, known as Gajapati, ruled over the eastern portion of the kingdom, which included the then Province of Orissa. Each Maharaja had seven kinds of insignia, those in Orissa being named Deo, Dev, Rao, Ram, Chandol, Hazari, and Sinha, and some of these names, together with a number of coins issued in the year 1180, are still in existence.

In A.D. 774, Jajati Kesari drove from Orissa the Mohammedans who had been established in the country for a hundred and forty-six years, and forthwith set up his capital at Jajpur, in the district of Cuttack, becoming the founder of the Kesari dynasty. There is nothing much of importance to chronicle during the reigns of several succeeding Maharajas —excepting frequent internal struggles— until the year 1175, when Ananga Bhima Deva ascended the throne. This ruler became impressed with the idea that he had observed bad omens at Jajpur, and he thereupon changed his capital to Cuttack, where he built the fort of Barabati, various temples, palaces, roads, wells, and tanks, and founded 460 Brahman *sasans*. In 1197 he built the temple of Jaggannath at Puri at a cost of 40 lakhs of rupees.

Prominent among his administrative actions was a settlement of the kingdom, which was carried out with the help of his two ministers, Damodar Barapanda and Iswar Pattanaik. The territory over which he reigned at that time extended from Sonepur, in the present division of Tirhut, in the Province of Behar and Orissa, to the sea, and from the Hooghly River to the Godavari, in the Madras Presidency. Many important works of construction were undertaken during the reigns of kings in the next two centuries, among them being the famous Kanarka temple, and a fine bridge, with eighteen spans, at Puri.

In the year 1504 Protap Rudra Dev ascended the throne, and it is recorded of him that he was a firm believer in the teachings of Buddha until one Chaitanua Dev visited Orissa and displayed such acquaintance with occult matters in the name of religion that the Maharaja regarded him as an incarnation of Bishnu, becoming a Baishnab himself and converting the majority of his subjects to the same faith. While Protap Rudra Dev was away from his kingdom laying siege to the fort of Bijaynagar, the Pathans attacked Orissa with a very large army, and they plundered Cuttack and advanced towards Puri. The worshippers of Jagannath hid the image on the south-western side of Lake Chilka, as they feared that the Pathans might destroy it. Protap Rudra Dev returned, gave battle to the invaders, but, being worsted, was compelled to submit to terms of peace dictated by the conquerors.

Upon the death of Protap Rudra Dev in the year 1625 the independence of Orissa was partially destroyed, as the kingdom had been considerably weakened by repeated attacks by the Pathans and Deccanese.

This ruler was succeeded by his eldest son, who was assassinated by his powerful minister, Govind Bidyadhar; the second son shared a similar fate after a reign of only twelve months; then the remaining thirty sons of Protap Rudra Dev were killed; Govind Dev assumed power, and soon found himself involved in a war of retribution brought against him by Mukunda Harichandan and Janardan Bidyadhar, who were ultimately appointed respectively to the viceroyalty of Cuttack and the chief ministership of Orissa.

Mukunda Harichandan ascended the throne in 1551 with the title of Tailanga Mukunda Dev, and was the last independent King of Orissa. He founded many Brahman *sasans*, built several palaces, temples, and tanks, and defined the northern boundary of his kingdom by constructing the Tribeni Ghat on the sacred waters of the Ganges in Bengal.

Shortly after this, Suleman, the *subedar* of Bengal, made several attempts to subdue Orissa, but his plans were frustrated, and he attributed his want of success to the fact that the Lord Jagannath was established at Puri. Suleman then made grants of land to several of his favoured supporters, and to Kanai Lal, one of the principal of these adherents, he gave permission to make an attack upon Orissa.

The success which attended the raids of Kanai, or Kalapahar, as he subsequently styled himself, was so great that Mukunda Dev took refuge in flight, hiding himself in a number of forts between the Tribeni Ghat and Rajmuhandry in the district of Godavari, in the Madras Presidency. Kalapahar searched the villages for the runaway; he scoured the forests and climbed the hills of Orissa, he destroyed all the idols that could be found, oppressed Hindus, and, in a word, he aimed at rooting out the Hindu religion from Orissa. His determination to attack the temple and secure the idol of Jagannath was frustrated as the *Pandas* floated the image on the sea near Puri and thus preserved it from the ruthless grasp of the marauder. Mortified, possibly, by the failure of many of his cherished dreams, Kalapahar left the seashore and proceeded inland, where he plundered districts and towns as far in a southerly direction as Sambalpur.

After Mukunda Dev was dethroned, Orissa was ruled by two petty kings, but they were killed in the course of battle and the country was then the scene of anarchical disturbances for a period of about twenty-one years. The hiding-place of Mukunda Dev not having been discovered, his chief minister placed his own son upon the throne with the title of Gajapati Ramchandra Dev, and he was the founder of the Bhoi dynasty. The two sons of Mukunda Dev—Tailanga Ramchandra Dev and Chhakari Bhramarbar—attacked Puri, but after their defeat by Gajapati Ramchandra Dev they appealed to the Emperor Akbar, who deputed Todal Mall and Raja Mana Singh to make arrangements regarding rents and to commence a survey of the country.

The estates of Khurda, Puri, and others were given as *jaigir* to Raja Ramchandra Dev, together with power to rule over 129 *killas* of Orissa; to Tailanga Ramchandra Dev was granted Aul and 23 other *killas*; and Chhakari Bhramarbar received the fort of Saranggarh.

Aul at that time (1582) consisted of 23 *killas* and 42 *zemindaris*, the *killas* being Kanika, Rynta, Kojang, Kolla-Dip, Harispur, Marichpur, Bishunpur, Jamkurrera, Chhedra, Darpan, Dholtang, Daljora, Chatter, Amjera, Balpupur, Alemgir, Nattaigree, Kaluparah, Bhunia-Bhadrak, Noundih, Barmatree, Alumpedda, and Kaljang.

The Aul *killa* is now—January 1917—

THE AUL RAJ.

1. Raja of Aul in the Lions' Cage. 2. Raja and a "Favourite." 3. Raja seated upon a Leopard placed upon the Back of an Elephant.

THE AUL RAJ.

1. The Raja with the Heir-Apparent. 2. Raja on Horseback. 3. The Raja on His Throne.

situated in a north-easterly direction from the town of Cuttack, and is divided into three *pergannas*, namely, Utihar, Kutabsahi, and Dera-Barimul, with an area of about 134 square miles. The rivers Brahmini and Kharasrota form the four boundaries of the *killa*, and enormous embankments have been constructed in order to protect the land from periodical floods, which have in times past caused immense damage.

After Tailanga Ramchandra Dev received this *killa* from Mana Singh he defeated the petty local zemindars and became Raja in the year 1567. He also conquered Basu Kalpataru, the *Jogi* Raja of Derabisi, and proceeded to occupy the country, securing the *mahantship* of a small *math*, together with power over the inhabitants of the Baishnab caste. The last two-named privileges are enjoyed at the present time.

A lengthy period of peace and prosperity ensued during the reigns of Nilakantha Dev, Balabhadra Dev, Gopinath Dev, and of Trilochan Dev, who took a great interest in furthering trading relationships with various places in India as well as with other countries.

He equipped a fleet of about two hundred sailing vessels, which visited Bombay, Burma, Borneo, Java, and Sumatra, and they were not withdrawn from service until competition by steamers belonging to a number of shipping companies rendered their continuance unnecessary.

Succeeding Rajas included Kishori Dev, Nilakantha Dev (who constructed a beautiful temple and gave a *zilla* of Rs. 8,000 for the maintenance of worship), Gopinath Dev, and Ramkrishna Dev, who received authority from the Mahratta Government at Nagpur to be called the Moha Raja of Aul, in place of Gopinath Dev, and was invested with the royal insignia and given authority to keep five hundred cavalry.

During the reign of Ramkrishna, in 1803, Orissa was conquered by the British and an agreement was concluded under which a *peshkus* was permanently fixed, and all the powers of a *Killajat* Raja were conferred upon the ruler. One of the provisions of the agreement then entered into was that the Raja was required to pay an annual sum of 113,436 *kahans* of cowries, four *kahans* of which were equivalent to one rupee. Ramkrishna was a great warrior, and after his army had rendered assistance to General Harcourt in December 1803, in a battle at Kendrapara, he received from the Government of India a letter of acknowledgment of his services. He was succeeded by his son, Pratap Rudra Dev, who became insane, and the estate passed into the management of the Government Court of Wards, this control being continued until 1847, when Padmanabh Dev attained his majority and ascended the throne.

Orissa was in his time (1866) visited by such a terrible famine that the flesh of human beings was partaken of by the starving crowds of people, and the surviving subjects were reduced to a most abject state of misery. Padmanabh Dev was extremely pious, and introduced into his country many high caste Brahmans, Kshattriyas, and Karans, at the same time bestowing upon them lands for their maintenence. He reigned for forty-seven years and died in 1888.

His second son, Jadunath Dev, became the next Raja, and during his reign the last settlement of the district of Cuttack was completed. Jadunath was a man of strong religious tendencies, a considerable portion of his income being spent in building temples, in constructing tanks and wells, and in the establishment of a deity named Jadukulachandra, and the gift of property of the value of Rs. 2,000 for its maintenance. He ruled his subjects with firmness, tempered with justice, and did all in his power to promote their happiness. He, further, held a great festival annually, and for a whole week he, at a cost of several thousands of rupees, provided ample food for Brahmans, Baishnabs, and the needy poor of his territory. He died while worshipping in the temple of Lakshmi-Baraha-Jeo in the year 1900. He left three sons, the eldest of whom, Pitambar Dev, became Raja of Aul after his father's death. He had, however, only reigned for about five years when the steam launch in which he was returning from a hunting expedition, encountered a violent storm and sank beneath the waters of the river Kharasrota, carrying with it the Raja and all his attendants.

As Pitambar Dev died without an heir, and the second brother had been adopted by the Raja of Kanika, he was succeeded as Raja by his youngest brother, Braja Sunder Dev, who appears to have inherited all the praiseworthy qualities of his predecessors in office; he is wise in administration, devoted to music and religious pursuits, protecting upright men and punishing evil doers; he contributes liberally to the maintenance of temples, and the cause of education has in him a warm supporter, he having from his private purse founded Sanskrit and upper primary schools at Aul, and provided for assistance being rendered to poor students residing at a distance from his *killa*.

The Raja's estate has been considerably increased by the purchase of a portion of the Marichpur *killa*, together with some zemindaries in the neighbourhood of Aul, but he never seems to tire of spending the wealth derived from his properties in alleviating the distress of the poor, or in contributing to the support of educational, charitable, and religious institutions.

The Raja has from his youth indulged in all kinds of manly sports, and as an expert with rifle or gun he has few equals. His hunting expeditions led him to take a deep interest in the habits of wild beasts, and his great courage—which is one of the most noticeable features in his character —together with the knowledge of his power over those animals, doubtless caused him to become a *shikari* in real earnest.

There is probably no other occupant of a throne who has captured and trained wild animals, and the success of the Raja in that direction resulted in the formation of a travelling circus, of which he is the controlling spirit. Lions, tigers, bears, and other ferocious inhabitants of the jungle seem to be as harmless as the domestic cat when they are brought face to face with him, and the marvellous manner in which he compels submission to his will is a striking proof of the power of the man.

The Raja has, of course, his own methods of training, but he is invariably successful in the end, as his skill in subduing an animal is no less than the wonderful patience which he exhibits.

The "Aul Raj" circus is known throughout India and Burma, and numerous letters as to the high-class character of the performances have been received at Ranchi, Purulia, Bankipore, Ramnagore, Vizagapatam, and other places, while in 1916 His Excellency Lord Carmichael, Governor of Bengal, presented a testimonial to the Raja in recognition of his extraordinary courage. Medals have been received at the Delhi Coronation Durbar in 1911, at the Cuttack Coronation Durbar in the same year, and from many maharajas, rajas, and prominent Europeans at Calcutta.

THE DUDHORIA RAJ FAMILY OF AZIMGANJ

The hereditary chroniclers of ancient princely families in India have played a most important part in recording genealogies and in giving readers of twentieth century history most valuable and interesting information as to the soul-stirring episodes which occurred hundreds of years ago when kingdoms and dynasties were established or overthrown, when kings and princes entered into possession of vast territories, only to be deposed by other factions more powerful than themselves, and when wise rulers reigning over peaceful communities were very few in number. And among these curious old documents, and still more through the medium of carefully preserved traditions, one is able occasionally to get glimpses of a noble house whose lengthy list of princes contains the names of men who were in every way worthy of the honourable positions which they occupied.

An interesting illustration of one of these is found in the chronicles of the Dudhoria Raj family of Azimganj, in the district of Murshidabad in the Province of Bengal. One Raja Chaban, ruler of Ajmer (an extensive territory in Rajputana) between the years 135 B.C. and 110 B.C., was the first of the princely line from which the Dudhorias trace their descent, and there was a direct succession of Princes until the time of Raja Dudhor Rao (A.D. 165), who renounced the ancestral orthodox Vedic (or Saiva) faith in favour of Jainism, and it was from this time that the name "Dudhoria" was given to the descendants of the Raja who became converts to the new creed. Dudhoria means literally "the family belonging to Raja Dudhor."

RAJA BIJOY SING DUDHORIA OF AZIMGANJ.

1. Azimganj Rajbati. 2. Raja Bijoy Sing Dudhoria of Azimganj.

"The Jains," says Major Tull Walsh, I.M.S., F.L.S., in his "History of Murshidabad," "are a dissenting sect of Hindus, having, however, the same distinctions of caste. They regard life as sacred, and will not knowingly kill any living thing. They sweep the place on which they are going to sit, and sometimes even the ground on which they walk. They prefer to eat by daylight, lest, eating at night, they should swallow an insect, and no orthodox Jain may touch animal food or drink alcohol in any form. The highest respect and worship are given to holy men, or saints, their chief authority being the Yoga. Their beliefs include the eternity of matter, transmigration of the soul, and, in fact, just those things which are evident to the senses."

The Dudhorias, after their conversion to Jainism, engaged in various business occupations, migrating from place to place, until about the year 1774 they moved from Bikanir in Rajputana to Azimganj in the district of Murshidabad, in Bengal, where Harjimal Dudhoria and two sons commenced trading in country-made cloths. A certain amount of success was gained, but the real beginning of prosperity for the family began with Babu Harek Chand Dudhoria, who became a leading merchant, and, further, opened a money-lending business in Calcutta, Sirajganj, Azimganj, Jangipur, and Mymensingh. He died in 1862, leaving two sons, Babu Budh Singh and Babu Bissen Chand, who succeeded their late father in the flourishing concern which he had established. The new partners gained the entire confidence of their customers, and extended their operations by investing money in landed property, ultimately becoming Zemindars owning land in the districts of Mymensingh, Murshidabad, Birbhum, Faridpur, Nadia, Purnea, and Rajshahi.

In 1877, however, the brothers agreed to divide the colossal business into two equal parts, and from that time the establishments have been carried on under separate names. About twelve years later an incident occurred which led to very serious trouble, not only for the Dudhoria family but also for the Jain community to which they belonged. It appears that Rai Budh Singh Bahadur had a son, Babu Indra Chand, who, during the time that he was receiving an English education in India, succumbed to an overpowering desire to visit England and the continent of Europe, and accordingly he undertook the journey without the knowledge or consent of his father or uncle. "The Jains, like the Hindus, are an orthodox community, and not only discountenance sea voyages, but also excommunicate those who undertake them. Indra Chand's journey to Europe therefore created an unprecedented *furore* in this community, which resulted in splitting it up into two powerful factions, and creating much bad blood between them." The matter was subsequently taken to the High Court of Judicature in Calcutta, and some time elapsed before anything approaching peace was noticeable.

The controversy was as sad as it was serious, and the cause of it—Babu Indra Chand—died in 1899, leaving two sons who were minors.

Rai Bissen Chand—the father of the present Raja—died after a short illness in 1894, leaving his only son and heir, Babu Bijoy Singh—a promising youth of about fourteen years of age. The management of the estates and business inherited by the minor was taken in hand by his uncle, Rai Budh Singh Bahadur, who also gave a sound and liberal education to his ward under the tuition of Babu Abinas Chandra Das, M.A., B.L. When Bijoy Singh attained his majority in 1900, he took over the direct control of his estates, and of the banking and other business to which he had succeeded, and even at this early period of life he manifested strong common sense and keen shrewdness in commercial matters, and those with whom he came in contact recognized that he was following closely in the footsteps of his father in exhibiting a sound practical acquaintance with the duties of a landlord and as the controlling power over huge commercial concerns.

It was not likely that a young nobleman of great wealth and "with superb qualities of head and heart" would be left for long without his being invited to enter into public life, and thus it is noticed that in 1903 he was nominated by the Government as a Commissioner of the Azimganj Municipality.

An all-India Jain conference was held at Baroda in December 1904, at which Rai Budh Singh Dudhoria was appointed President and his nephew, Bijoy Singh, vice-president. The latter evinced great interest in municipal questions, and in 1906 he, as a candidate for the chairmanship, succeeded after a keen contest in defeating a rival candidate who had held the office for nine successive years. In January 1907 he was appointed an honorary magistrate of the independent Bench at Lalbagh, and in June in the following year, on the birthday celebration of the late King Edward VII, the title of Raja was conferred upon him by Lord Minto, the then Viceroy of India, in recognition of his public services, his liberality, and his high personal character. The *sanad* and *Khillut* of the new position were formally handed to the Raja at a Durbar held at Belvedere in Calcutta on November 14, 1908, by the Hon. Sir Andrew Fraser, K.C.S.I., then Lieutenant-Governor of Bengal. Public addresses—in some instances accompanied by silver caskets—were presented to the Raja from numerous public bodies, and his replies proved that he desired to show his deep appreciation of the honour conferred upon him by devoting himself still more fully to the welfare of the community at large, particularly in the form of educational and charitable institutions.

In January 1909 the Raja was re-elected chairman of the Azimganj Municipality, and in August of the same year he was the recipient of the highest praise and warmest thanks tendered on behalf of the Government by the Hon. Sir Norman Baker, K.C.S.I., when opening a new school building at Jiaganj, constructed by the Raja at a cost of about Rs. 20,000.

The Raja cannot have had many spare hours to himself since his majority, as in addition to functions already mentioned he has acted as member of the District Board of Murshidabad, was a member of the Executive Committees of the Imperial League, the King Edward Memorial Fund, and of the British Indian Association of Calcutta, of which he was a vice-president in 1915.

The Raja is an indefatigable worker, and gives personal attention to details in all departments, and this notwithstanding the fact that he has a large staff of capable officials.

Although keen in all business questions, the Raja is generous with his wealth, and no really deserving object brought to his notice fails to receive his hearty support.

The liberality of the Dudhoria family is well known, as they have founded *dharamsalas*, charitable dispensaries, hospitals, and schools, and since he attained his majority the present Raja has contributed Rs. 100,000 to Lady Minto's fête in aid of the Nursing Association; he gave about Rs. 20,000 for the construction of the Jiaganj Edward VII Coronation Institution; a sum of Rs. 4,000 was contributed to the Krishnagar College; Rs. 10,000 were given to the Imperial War Relief Fund; during a partial famine in 1906-7 he expended a very large sum in providing rice for needy poor people; and he subscribes to a number of private charities, and practically supports very many of his impoverished fellow Jains.

The Raja was married in February 1894 —when fourteen years of age—to the youngest daughter of the late Rai Dhanpat Singh Bahadur of Baluchar, and he has an only daughter, who was married to Babu Srichand Nahata, also of Baluchar.

This young nobleman—barely in the prime of life—has won the affections of his people by his upright conduct and his unostentatious kindliness of spirit to all with whom he comes into contact, and it has been well said that "goodwill towards all living creatures, kindness, and human fraternity, the three principal tenets of his religion, are well illustrated in the Raja's life."

The family residence of the Raja, situated on the right bank of the Bhagirathi River at Azimganj, is a stately structure, richly furnished, and containing a rich and rare collection of jewellery, and it is frequently the scene of elaborate festivities, to which the élite of the district are invited.

BAMRA STATE

There are twenty-four dependent territories attached to the division of Orissa, in the Province of Behar and Orissa, and they are about 28,125 square miles in extent. The general appearance of the country is exceedingly fine; there are vast ranges of forest interspersed with mountains, hills, and highly cultivated plains, while the Mahanadi, the Brahmani, and

BAMRA STATE.

1. Raja S. Tribhuban Deb and Rani. 2. Raja D. Sudhal Deb and Rani. 3. View of Deogarh, showing the Palace.

other navigable rivers present a pleasing contrast to the deep green foliage which abounds so luxuriously on every hand.

The Bamra State has an area of about 1,988 square miles, and it comprises some 930 villages, and one township, Deogarh, which has a population of 5,700 inhabitants. The present Chief, Raja Tribhuban, who succeeded his father, Sir Basudeo Sudhal Dev, K.C.I.E., in the year 1903, administers the State with the assistance of three *tahsildars*, who are receivers of land revenues in their respective subdivisions. These officials and other honorary magistrates dispose of criminal cases, but the Chief, although supreme in the State, is compelled to have any sentences of death confirmed by the Commissioner of the division of Orissa. The relationship between the State and the British Government was defined and regulations were promulgated by a *Sanad* in 1867, under which the Raja was recognized as a feudatory chief, and the annual tribute, which is liable to revision, but which was annexed in 1909 for thirty years —payable from the State Exchequer– is Rs. 7,500.

The various departments of the State are controlled by able officials, and special attention is devoted to the preservation of village forests, which in the past have been recklessly destroyed by inhabitants. The State jungle includes ten species of protected trees, and permission to fell these must be obtained from the Chief Officer of the Forest Department.

No assessment is levied upon vendors of merchandise in the majority of the markets or bazars, but local storekeepers pay a small charge, which is levied *pro ratâ* upon the value of the goods sold. The people, therefore, are not unduly harassed by taxation, and it is significant that the average annual number of civil suits in the Courts does not exceed 400 for the whole State, and about 11 per cent. of these plaints are for sums of less than Rs. 100. The principal industrial centre is at the jail at Deogarh, where prisoners are subjected to definite regulations regarding labour, and are taught weaving under modern methods, brick-making, oil-pressing, lime burning, and other useful and profitable trades.

The Raja is deeply interested in the question of giving sound education to boys and girls, and the State maintains more than thirty schools, in addition to giving substantial assistance to a considerable number of private establishments.

The soil is chiefly of light and sandy character, and the principal crops are rice, oil-seeds, cotton, and sugar-cane, and the Chief, who is progressive in this as in other matters, has established a model farm of his own, upon which one sees modern agricultural machinery, and steam engines and up-to-date plant in factories and mills. Experiments are carried on at this place, and every opportunity is given to villagers to acquire practical instruction in the problem of making the land as productive and as profitable as possible. Nearly 75 per cent. of the population are engaged in agricultural pursuits, while employment is found for a very large number of persons in saw-mills at Sirid, a village between Deogarh and Bamra.

The principal exports are iron, oil-seeds, timber, pulses, and general forest produce (including lac, silk, resin, honey, and beeswax), and the imports include mill-spun piece goods, salt, sugar, spices, and brass vessels.

There are State dispensaries at Deogarh, Kuchinda, and Barkut, and each one is in charge of a qualified medical officer, who attends to about six or seven thousand cases annually.

The opening of the Bengal-Nagpur Railway had a very marked effect on trade generally, large areas of undeveloped land were brought into cultivation, agriculturists found new openings for the sale of their crops, and a new era of prosperity dawned over the whole State. Other means of communication are afforded by several good roads, and especially the one between Bamra railway station and Deogarh, a distance of more than fifty miles, and by the Brahmani River, which is navigable for small open boats.

Telegraph and telephone facilities are available at the principal places in the State, while the Imperial postal service has provided letter-boxes in the school-houses in all of the large villages.

Deogarh, the headquarters of the State, is, according to an officially published Gazetteer, neatly laid out with a small park in the centre, the town is lighted by electricity, and a waterfall near at hand has been utilized to supply the town with a regular supply of water. The surrounding hills make a really charming background to a thriving centre whose population has increased rapidly during the past few years. A weekly paper is published, and a high school, affiliated to the Calcutta University, with a chemical and physical laboratory, is maintained by the State. There are several public buildings of an imposing character, including a masonry jail, police station, dispensary, and public courts and offices.

Bamra, the principal railway station, is a depot for the export of a considerable number of sleepers from the State forests, and is, further, the residency of a large number of commercial and industrial firms.

THE BANAILI RAJ

The Banaili Raj, which is now represented by Raja Kalanand Sinha and the Honourable Raja Kirtyanand Sinha, is an extensive estate in Behar, yielding an annual income of more than sixteen lakhs of rupees, comprising properties in the Districts of Bhagalpore, Monghyr, Sonthal, Pergannas, Purneah, Maldah, and Darbhanga. The founder of the family was Raja Dular Sinha Chaudhry Bahadur, who was originally a wealthy Maithil Brahmin Zemindar, residing in the district of Purnea. He helped the Government in its war against Nepal, and was consequently decorated with the title of Raja Bahadur about the year 1825. In the time of his successor, Raja Bedanand Sinha Bahadur, the extensive portion of the estate known as Mahalat Kharakpore, which was once a principality under the Mogul Emperors of Delhi, was acquired in revenue sale in the year 1840. Raja Bedanand Sinha Bahadur was succeeded by his son Raja Leelanand Sinha Bahadur, father of the present holders of the estate. Rajah Leelanand Sinha Bahadur, owing to his extremely generous attitude towards his *ryots* and the needy, is still remembered affectionately by the people of the Bhagalpore division. Raja Padmanand Sinha Bahadur succeeded his father, Raja Leelanand Sinha Bahadur, and during his time litigation was commenced between himself and his infant stepbrothers Kumar (now Raja) Kalanand Sinha and Kumar (now Raja) Kirtyanand Sinha, which led to the partition of the estate into nine-annas and seven-annas shares under a compromise decree. The seven-annas share was again subdivided into halves in a suit between Raja Padmanand Sinha Bahadur and his son Kumar Chandranand Sinha, and latterly the former sold all his interest to his son who held the seven-annas share, which is now represented by his widow, Rani Chandrabati, a ward of the Court. Raja Kalanand Sinha and his brother have lent a large amount of money to their co-sharer, and they hold the seven-annas

THE BANAILI RAJ.

1. RAJA KALANAND SINHA, BAHADUR. 2. THE HON. RAJA KIRTYANAND SINHA, BAHADUR.
3. THE RAJA SAHIBS WITH OFFICERS AND STAFF. 4. THE HON. RAJA KIRTYANAND SINHA ON HIS FAVOURITE HORSE.

THE BANAILI RAJ.

1. The Raja's Palace. 2. The Temple. 3. The Rajkumars with their Cousins. 4. The Palace Drawing-room.

THE BANAILI RAJ.

1. The Durbar Elephants in Full State. 2. Some Tiger and Leopard Skins. 3. Shikar Trophies. 4 A Boating Scene.

THE BANAILI RAJ.

1. THE EUROPEAN GUEST-HOUSE. 2. VIEW OF THE GARDEN. 3. ELECTRICAL POWER-HOUSE. 4. RUINS OF "BANAILI."

share under a lease from the Court of Wards.

Raja Kalanand Sinha and his talented brother, the Honourable Raja Kirtyanand Sinha, since they assumed the management of their estate, about the year 1904, have been generous supporters of public charities, the most notable gift being one of about seven lakhs of rupees to the Tej Narain Jubilee College, Bhagalpore, which but for their support would long ago have been abolished ; and further, the carrying on of the daily paper *Beharee*, published from Bankipore, which is the exponent of public opinion in Behar. It would occupy too much space to mention all the public charities helped and financed by these brothers, whose names as public benefactors have become a household word in the Province. The younger of them, Raja Kirtyanand Sinha, who is a graduate of the Allahabad University, is a member of the Behar Legislative Council as a representative of the landholders of his Province. He has been for three years a member of the Council of Bengal, upon which he has been doing very good work, and all measures of public utility have his heartiest support. His services have been recognized from time to time by the Government. He is the President of the Behar and Orissa Provincial Co-operative Bank, Ltd., and is also the President of the committee which is working in Patna for the establishment of a library of Sanskrit and Hindi manuscripts and books, to be called the "Rupkala Bhagwan Library."

The Hon. Raja is a nobleman of varied talents. He is a first-rate mechanic, electrician, and motorist, and is a devoted student of current English and Oriental literature. He has a passion for jungle sport, notably tiger-shooting, and for many other forms of popular games, e.g. football, polo, lawn-tennis, billiards, and yachting, and this is his distinguishing characteristic. He has written a book on *shikar*, in which he beautifully describes his chequered experiences with the carnivora in the jungles of Purnea. Himself a writer of no mean order, he stands as an acknowledged patron of letters. Several distinguished authors and literary men of the day are patronized by him. Apart from this, he has an intimate knowledge of Indian music, and is himself a musician. In short, the Hon. Raja enjoys a unique position among the Behar landholders, and stands for all that is good and progressive in modern Behar.

THE BETTIAH RAJ

The history of the Bettiah Raj may be traced back as far as the year 1244 A.D., when Raja Gungeswar Deo left Nimkhar Misiri, in Lucknow, and established himself at Jaithur, in the district of Saran, in the Tirhut division of the Province of Behar and Orissa. Authenticated records of the Raj begin with Raja Guj Singh, son of Raja Ugra Sen Singh, the ninth descendant of Raj Gungeswar Deo, who received the title of Raja from the Emperor Shah Jehan. He had six sons, namely, Raja Dullip Singh and Raj Kumars Kanak Singh, Kirat Singh, Anup Singh, Prithi Singh, and Chatrajit Singh. On the death of Raja Guj Singh in 1694 his eldest son, Raja Dullip Singh, succeeded him as Raja of Sirkar Champaran. The latter had five sons, the eldest of whom, Dhrub Singh, became Raja in 1715, about the time that the powers of the Emperors of Delhi had become nominal and the Rajas of Bettiah had declared themselves to be independent. Raja Dhrup Singh had only a daughter, whose son, Raja Joogole Kishore Singh, is said to have been adopted, and who "entered into the possession of Sirkar Champaran at the date when the East India Company assumed the government of the Province in 1764." During Raja Dhrup Singh's time Ali Verdi Khan, with the aid of an Afghan chief, Abdul Karim Khan, led an expedition against Bettiah, and being victorious he entered into an agreement with the Raja as to the amount of tribute to be paid by the latter. In 1748 Ali Verdi Khan, who was then Nawab of Bengal, was forced to return to Champaran in consequence of the rebellion of his former allies, the Afghans of Darbhanga, who, after their defeat, took shelter at Bettiah. The Raja of Bettiah sent a message to the Nawab stating that he was ready to pay three lakhs of rupees if he (the Nawab) would agree to forgo the surrender of the Afghan chiefs. The Nawab, however, refused the offer and advanced towards Bettiah, whereupon the Raja gave up the wife and daughters of Shum Sher Khan, who were subsequently treated with courtesy by the Nawab.

In 1716, Karim Hossein Khan, the Governor of Purnea, marched to join the forces of the Emperor Shah Alam, but he was defeated by Captain Knox and fled towards Bettiah. Shortly after this Major Cailland and Miran (son of Mir Jaffur Khan) set out in pursuit of Hossein Khan and defeated him on June 25th, his army being scattered in the hills. Miran was struck by lightning while sleeping in his tent near Bettiah, and on his death Major Cailland abandoned the campaign. The latter had moved his army up to the Fort of Bettiah, and after receiving the submission of the Raj (Dhrup Singh) he marched back to Patna.

Raja Dhrup Singh's term of office was also marked by the establishment of the first Mission at Bettiah, in December 1745, by the Rev. Father Joseph Mary Deibernini, an Italian Capuchin cleric. The Raja made the acquaintance of the Reverend Father, and was medically treated by him at Patna, and at a later date the priest was invited to visit Bettiah, where he cured the Rani of a serious illness. The Raja was so impressed by his skill that he requested the Reverend Father to remain at Bettiah, and when permission had been obtained from Rome, the latter journeyed back from Nepal on December 7, 1745, and the Raja assigned him a house and garden near his palace, allowed him to preach and make converts, and granted him 60 *bighas* of land near the fort, which is the modern Christian Tolli, and 200 *bighas* of land near Bettiah for the support of himself and his converts.

Raja Dhrup Singh again rebelled, and in 1762 Mir Kasim Ali sent an expedition against him. "The command of it," says the author of "Sair-ul Mutakharin," "was given to Bahadur Ali Khan, who had been for a long time grand master of artillery to Ali Verdi Khan. He had with him several commanders with their corps with some pieces of cannon in the English fashion, and some regiments of Talingas disciplined by Gurgan Khan. His orders were to take the fortress of that name and to chastise the Zemindar of that country who had proved unruly." The expedition proved entirely successful. Bahadur Ali sent Raja Dhrup Singh and Joogole Kishore Singh to the Nawab, but the former died, and the latter returned as Raja on his undertaking to pay the revenue and *Nazarana*. He, however, failed to redeem his promises and fled towards Nepal in order to save his life. The Nawab availed himself of this opportunity for an expedition against Nepal, and Gurgun Khan took command, being followed by the main body of troops under Mir Kasim Ali, who pitched his camp at Bettiah. Gurgan Khan commenced the ascent of a pass through the hills, and at first he was successful in driving off the Gurkhas, but his army pushed on to the summit, and halting for the night it was

BETTIAH RAJ.

1. Doorga Bagh Temple. 2. Palace. 3. Old Gate.

BETTIAH RAJ.

1. Manager's House. 2. Drawing-room, Manager's House. 3. Manager's House, the Hall.

BETTIAH RAJ.

1. The Guest House. 2. Assistant-Manager's House. 3. Forest Officer's House.

BETTIAH RAJ.

1. Hospital, Operating-room. 2. Hospital, Ward-room. 3. Ranee's Palace.

attacked by the Nepalis as soon as it was dark, and was compelled to fall back in disorder on the main camp at Bettiah. The Nawab with his troops then marched back to Patna, where matters were taking a serious turn. Nawab Kasim Ali arranged to have the revenue of Sirkar Champaran collected through his *amlas*, and Raj Kumar Babu Srikissoon Singh (who in the absence of Joogole Kishore Singh represented himself to be the Raja) with Raj Kumar Babu Abdhut Singh, and other sons of Satrajit Singh, began to carry on the affairs of the Zemindari in conjunction with the *amlas*. In 1764, Champaran, with the rest of Bengal, passed under British rule after the battle of Buxar. A *purwanah* dated January 24, 1764, was issued to Raja Srikissoon Singh, in the absence of Raja Joogole Kishore Singh, directing him to execute an agreement to pay rent at an enhanced rate, but owing to the desolate state of the country as a result of war, the question of assessment was left pending. In the meantime Raja Joogole Kishore, having received the news of the flight of Kasim Ali Khan, returned to Bettiah, but when Sir Robert Barker, with a detachment of troops, moved from Bankipore to Bettiah in 1766, he fled to Bundelkhund. Collections of revenue were then ordered to be made direct, and on January 8, 1771, the company issued a *puttah*, fixing two lakhs and one rupee as *jumma* in the name of Raja Srikissoon Singh and Raj Kumar Babu Abdhut Singh. The *puttah*, however, never came into force. Owing to famine and the desolate state of the country the revenue declined considerably, and eventually the Council at Patna, on the report of Mr. Golding, restored Raja Joogole Kishore Singh to his estate. It was settled that Raja Joogole Kishore Singh should retain the Perganna of Semra and Majhawa, while those of Maisi and Babra were to be settled between Raja Srikissoon Singh and Raj Kumar Abdhut Singh, and for these grants the recipients were to execute agreements with the Government. Raja Srikissoon Singh, however, refused to sign any document, and the Raja Joogole Kishore, although he signed his acceptance of the terms, failed to pay the revenue. The entire Sirkar Champaran then passed into the possession of the Government, and was held by farmers of revenue on temporary settlements extending over several years. Raja Joogole Kishore Singh received an allowance for maintenance from the Government, and died in 1783. On October 10, 1789, Mr. Montgomery, the Collector of Saran, addressed a letter to the Revenue Board asking for advice, and further mentioned that Srikissoon Singh, and Bir Kishore Singh, son of Joogole Kishore Singh, were competitors for the Zemindari. The Governor-General in Council directed that a decennial settlement was to be concluded with Raja Bir Kishore Singh for the Pergannas of Majhawa and Semraon, and with Raja Srikissoon Singh and Raj Kumar Abdhut Singh for the Pergannas of Maisi and Babra. Both parties were dissatisfied at this decision, as each one claimed the entire Sirkar Champaran, but on Mr. Montgomery's advice, they took possession of the Pergannas, settled in their own names, and made separate *dowl* settlements of Government revenue on the *Mahals* of the Pergannas. In the year 1808 Raja Gunga Prasad Singh, son of Raja Srikissoon Singh, commenced an action in the Provincial Court of Patna against Raja Bir Kishore Singh to recover possession of Pargannas Semraon and Majhawa, but the suit was dismissed on the ground that the cause of action was barred by limitation. From that time until after the death of Maharaja Sir Harendra Kishore Singh there was no dispute between the two branches of the families.

The Raja Bir Kishore Singh was succeeded in 1811 by Anand Kishore Singh, who was created Maharaja Bahadur owing to the valuable assistance with men and money rendered by him to the British Government during the Nepal War.

Maharaja Bahadur Anand Kishore Singh had no issue, and was succeeded by his younger brother, Newal Kishore Singh, who died in 1855. The latter was followed by his eldest son, Maharaja Rajendra Kishore Singh, "who gave at the time of the Mutiny praiseworthy aid and support to the Government during the whole of the rebellion," and who was, in turn, succeeded by his son, Maharaja Harendra Kishore Singh, who was made a K.C.I.E. In order to pay off debts which the Raj had incurred, a debenture loan of about 60 lakhs of rupees was in 1885 negotiated in London, bearing 5 per cent. interest and payable in thirty-five years. Maharaja Harendra Kishore Singh was a member of the Provincial Legislative Council for some time, and on his death in 1893 he was succeeded by his senior Maharani, who died in 1896. The estate passed to the junior Maharani in 1897. Owing to bad management of the Raj the Court of Wards then took charge of the estate. The Maharani's title has been disputed by the Babus of Sheohur and Madhuban, who are descendants of Raja Srikissoon Singh and Raj Kumar Abdhut Kishore Singh, but their claims have been disallowed by the High Court and the Privy Council in London.

The Court of Wards assumed charge of the Bettiah estate in the year 1897, and in 1898, when the administration was commenced, the annual income was Rs. 17,00,000.

Vast improvements have been effected within these twenty years, and all minor debts left by Maharaja Harendra Kishore Singh have been paid. The property of Bhoputpur was acquired in Maharaja Harendra Kishore's time by raising another debenture loan, but the debt was paid off in full during the period of control of the Court of Wards. A new palace for the present Maharani has been constructed, old ones have been rebuilt, and extensive office buildings have been erected for the management. A first-class modern hospital, which is acknowledged to be the best in the whole Province in point of architecture and equipment, has also been built, and it has been named after his late Majesty King Edward VII. In connection with this remarkably fine hospital it may be said that, on the death of King Edward, Babu Sidh Narayan Singh, the guardian of the Maharani Saheba, requested Mr. J. R. Lowis, then manager of the estate, to suggest some form of memorial whereby his late Majesty's name would be perpetuated in Bettiah. This hospital was suggested, and the foundation stone was laid on August 12, 1912, by Mr. H. C. Streatfeild, who was Commissioner of the Tirhut division at the time. It is a double-storied building, 210 feet in length and 49 feet in width, with a frontal projecting block 52 feet by 32 feet, and two wings at the back 28 feet by 16 feet. The ground floor contains two general wards, two eye wards, two godowns, and a staircase room; the frontal projection consists of a covered porch, emergency room, offices, and museum; the two wings contain bathing and other necessary rooms; and on the upper floor are various wards, microscopic, sterilizing, anæsthetic, recovery, surgical instruments, and store and other rooms. The style of architecture is English Renaissance, and the building is constructed of red bricks and white plaster.

A splendid supply of surgical and ophthalmic instruments has been purchased, at a cost of nearly Rs. 25,000, from the well-known Holborn Surgical

Instruments Company, and Messrs. John Weiss & Co., of London, and a complete antiseptic installation has been put in by Messrs. Incell and Silk, of Calcutta, who have, further, been responsible for a supply of hot and cold water to all parts of the building. Immediately adjoining the hospital are an out-door dispensary, quarters for surgeons, a matron, nurses, compounders, dressers, and a large staff of servants, and these structures, as well as the hospital, are situated opposite the *maidan*, a wide stretch of excellent turf on which games of all kinds are played. The cost of this handsome block of buildings, and its equipment, has been most generously borne by the Bettiah Raj, and Mr. Lowis, in his address at the opening ceremony in March 1915, stated that the Raj had further endowed the institution with a sum of money which would provide sufficient income for its future maintenance.

A "Dufferin" hospital for women was completed by Maharaja Harendra Kishore Singh, and considerable additions and improvements to it have been made by the Court of Wards, while minor hospitals have been constructed for the benefit of the tenantry. An English High School, with a commodious hostel and a Sanskrit school attached to it, has also been provided. Several upper primary schools have been opened in the interior of the district, and a large up-to-date market, constructed on sanitary principles, has been established in the town.

Comfortable quarters and inspection bungalows have been provided for officers of the estate, and a large number of old temples which were falling into ruins have been thoroughly renovated. An electric installation supplies power for lights and fans in the Raj houses and in some of the main streets of the town. Telephonic communications have been established between all offices, palace buildings, railway stations, and residential houses. Tanks have been re-excavated, numerous wells have been sunk, and irrigation channels in many villages have been supplied. A cattle-breeding farm, veterinary hospital, and an experimental agricultural farm are some of many other innovations introduced. No attempt has been made to unduly enhance the rent roll, and the *ryots* and leaseholders of the estate have been always treated with great consideration, but as a natural result of better management under the Court of Wards the rent roll of the estate has been increased by more than two lakhs of rupees, and is now considerably more than Rs. 19,00,000. The greater part of this revenue is derived from villages leased to European and Indian occupiers. The majority of the Europeans were originally indigo planters, but with the decline of this industry in recent years they have been compelled to devote their energies to the cultivation of other crops, and to the development of rice mills and sugar factories. Mr. J. R. Lowis has, with short intervals, been general manager of the estate during the whole period of control by the Court of Wards, and it was during his incumbency that the estate progressed from a condition of comparative indigence to its present state of security and prosperity and that these numerous works of improvement were undertaken. He has recently resigned owing to ill-health, and his place has been taken by Mr. J. T. Whitty, C.I.E., of the Indian Civil Service.

Mr. J. E. Rutherfoord and Mr. P. B. Hudson are the European assistant managers, and Babu Gopi Nath Sanyal and Babu Hazari Lal Sahu are their Indian colleagues. Mr. C. G. Lowe was appointed as executive engineer to the estate three years ago, but his predecessor, Babu Purna Chandra Mukerjee, had been in charge of that department for more than twenty-seven years. Babu Moti Lal Basu is superintendent of survey.

In addition to the many wars in which the Rajas of Bettiah were concerned during the period of their history covered by these notes, there were two most important events, namely, the Nepal War and the Indian Mutiny, which called forth a manifestation of that loyalty to British interests which the rulers of the Bettiah Raj have invariably shown.

The following details regarding circumstances which led to the Nepal War may now be given:—

"The Raja of Bettiah had for a long time been at war with the Raja of Mukwanpur for possession of a portion of the Semraon Perganna. In 1743 the latter granted the tenure of two *tuppas* to one Abdullah Beg, and this act was confirmed by the then Nawab of Bengal. The Raja of Bettiah, who was then in possession of these lands, resisted, but finally he also gave a *sanad* to Abdullah. Twenty years later Prithi Narayan of Nepal subdued the Mukwanpur Raja and claimed authority to avail himself of the grant, but Abdullah fled to the English authorities, and this was one of the pretexts for the declaration of war against Nepal. In 1767 the Raja of Katmundu, being hard pressed by the Gurkhas, appealed for help to Mr. Golding, the commercial agent at Bettiah, and Major Kurloch advanced with his troops, but having failed in October of that year to penetrate the hills owing to the unfavourable climate, he occupied the *terai*, or low lands. Abdullah then asserted his claim to the original grant, but this was opposed by the Bettiah Raj. In 1781 Warren Hastings finally decided to restore Abdullah's *jaigir*, but the twenty-two villages occupied by Prithi Narayan and subsequently taken back by Major Kurloch in 1768 formed part of Champaran and were settled upon Raja Bir Kishore Singh, with whom they remained until 1810. When in 1811 Luksman Gir, the Gurkha Governor, crossed the frontier and began to plunder the villages, the Raja of Bettiah's people resisted, and in an affray that followed, Luksman Gir was killed. The British Government directed the Assistant to the Magistrate of Saran to make an inquiry, and Commissioners were thereupon appointed by both Governments. Major Bradshaw, the British Commissioner, insisted on the restitution of the villages as a preliminary to the inquiry, and after much evasion the Nepal Commissioner suddenly returned to Katmundu, and war was declared in 1814. General Marley, sent to help Major Bradshaw, arrived at the frontier in December, but in the meantime General Ouchterlony was successful, and a treaty was signed at Sugauli in November 1815, the ratification of which was withheld by the Nepal Durbar in order to try the result of a second campaign. General Ouchterlony established his headquarters at Sugauli, whence he sent out four brigades to Nepal. This invasion was successful, and in December 1816 the treaty of Sugauli was finally signed, the whole *terai* falling into the hands of the British Government. It is needless to mention that during the whole of this war the Bettiah Raja helped the British Government in every possible way, and Lord William Bentinck, the Viceroy at the time, conferred the title of Maharaja Bahadur upon the then ruler in recognition of his services."

The Mutiny of 1857, which was a most formidable menace to British supremacy, affected many houses of Indian notabilities, but the Bettiah Raj—as in the case of the Nepal War—never flinched so much as the breadth of a single hair from its allegiance to the Throne and from its generous support of the forces which eventually crushed the rebellion. Major Holmes was in com-

BETTIAH RAJ.

1. St. Paul's Church. 2. Bettiah, from the Palace.

BETTIAH RAJ.

1, ELECTRIC POWER-HOUSE. 2, 3, TIMBER-YARDS.

mand of the 12th Irregular Cavalry in 1857 at the Sugauli Cantonment, 14 miles from Bettiah, and as danger began to threaten he took stern repressive measures to prevent the spread of mutiny, but these were nullified by the action of the local Government. On July 26th the regiment rose in rebellion, murdered the European civil and military officers, together with their wives and children, and, after plundering the treasury, marched to Siwan. Martial law was proclaimed on July 30th, but when two Gurkha regiments came to the help of the British, the confidence of the people was restored. An attempt was made by the rebels at Bagaha Ghat, thirty-two miles from Bettiah, to effect a further insurrection, but it was frustrated by the Gurkhas. Towards the end of December, the Maharaja Jung Bahadur, Prime Minister, and Commander-in-Chief of Nepal, arrived with his forces at Bettiah, and on December 26th fought a battle with the mutineers at Sahebgunge, on the River Gandak, and completely defeated them. From that time forward there has not been any disturbance upon the Bettiah estate.

THE BURDWAN RAJ ESTATE

One of the largest Zemindaries in the Province of Bengal is that of the Burdwan Raj Estate, of which the present owner is the Honourable Maharajadhiraja Bahadur Sir Bijay Chand Mahtab, K.C.S.I., K.C.I.E., I.O.M., Maharaja of Burdwan, and there are in existence most interesting records showing the history of the family practically from its commencement.

It appears that in the sixteenth century, Sangam Rai, a Kapur Kshattriya of Kolti Mahalla, in Lahore, one of a band of pilgrims who, after visiting the shrine of Jaggannath in Orissa, were returning to their homes, was so much attracted by the great fertility of the soil and the luxuriance of the crops in that portion of the province now known as the District of Burdwan, that he established a home and commenced business at a place called Baikunthapore, where he succeeded so well that he had amassed a large fortune at the time of his death. He was succeeded by his son, Banku Behari Rai, who was in due course followed by Abu Rai, who, according to the records, "was the real founder of the Burdwan house. In the year 1657 the latter was appointed by the Mogul Government to be Chaudhuri and Kotwal of Rekabi Bazar, in the town of Burdwan, and his son, Babu Rai, who owned Pargana Burdwan and three other estates, succeeded to the Chaudhuri and removed from Baikunthapore to Burdwan, since which time the family has been settled there." His son, Ghana Shyam Rai, left a consolidated estate for Krishna Ram Rai, who acquired other properties and was the recipient of a *Firman* (1694 A.D.) from the Mogul Emperor Aurangzeb, confirming him as Zemindar and Chaudhuri of Parganas Burdwan and other lands. The two subsequent successors, Jagat Ram Rai (1696-1702) and Kirti Chand Rai (1702-40), enriched the original estate by further additions. It may be interesting to know that Kirti Chand not only obtained from the Mogul Emperor the Zemindari of Bishnupur, but he won by his sword the estates of the Rajas of Chandrakona and Bardha, as well as of the Balghara Raj, in the Hooghly district, and added to the parent estate the pārganas, *inter alia*, of Chitwa, Bhursut, and Mānoharsahi.

THE HON. SIR BIJAY CHAND MAHTAB, MAHARAJADHIRAJA BAHADUR OF BURDWAN, K.C.S.I., K.C.I.E.

Chitra Sen Rai (1740-44) was the recipient of the title of Raja in the family, and he added the parganas of Mandalghat, Arsha, and Chandrakona. The owner of the Burdwan Raj was now a recognized dignitary of the Mogul Court, and his cousin and successor, Tilak Chand (1744-71), was created successively a Raja Bahadur and a Maharajadhiraja. Further honours and privileges were bestowed upon Tilak Chand, who was styled by the Mogul Emperor "Fidvi Khas"; and he was eventually made a "Panch Hazari Zat"—that is, Commander of 5,000 infantry, with permission to keep 3,000 cavalry—and was permitted to have guns, bands, and *nakarae*. After his death, Tej Chand (1771-1832), his son, was confirmed in all the honours of his father, and the Burdwan Raj was meanwhile treated more or less as a semi-independent State, and the owner wielded the power of administering the internal affairs of the estate independently. It was during Tej Chand's time, however, that the vast estates of the Burdwan Raj were brought under the operation of Regulation No. I of 1793, the basis of the Permanent Settlement of Bengal. Tej Chand's son, Pratap Chand, was instrumental in bringing up Regulation VIII. He died during the lifetime of his father.

The proprietor of the Raj had now become an important personage in the ranks of the Indian nobility, and Mahtab Chand (1832-79) was recognized by the British Government as Maharajadhiraja Bahadur, and in 1864 was "appointed an Additional Member of the Viceregal Legislative Council, being the first nobleman in Bengal to be thus honoured." Further honours were showered upon this potentate, as in 1868 he obtained for himself and his successors the Royal Licence to bear "Arms and Supporters," and nine years later the privilege was granted to him of receiving a personal salute of thirteen guns. Mahtab Chand was succeeded by Aftab Chand Mahtab, who died on March 25, 1885, leaving a widow but no heir. The Maharani Adhirani, in pursuance of authority given to her by her husband, adopted the son of Raja Ban Bihari Kapur Bahadur, who received the name of Bijay Chand Mahtab, and he is the present Maharajadhiraja Bahadur.

Born on October 19, 1881, the installation ceremony of Bijay Chand Mahtab (which had been postponed in November 1902 owing to the death of Sir John Woodburn, the Lieutenant-Governor) was conducted by the acting Lieutenant-Governor on February 10, 1903. On this occasion he was presented with two *Sanads*, signed by the Viceroy (Lord Curzon)—one conferring upon him as "Zemindar of Burdwan the hereditary title of Maharajadhiraja to be attached to the Estate," and the other the high personal title of Maharajadhiraja Bahadur. The whole title of Maharajadhiraja Bahadur was subsequently, in 1909, made hereditary and attachable to the estate by a *Sanad* received under the signature of Lord Minto. In February 1909 Maharajadhiraja Bijay Chand Mahtab Bahadur was created a Knight Commander of the Most Eminent Order of the Indian Empire, and at the same time was admitted into the Third Class of the Civil Division of the Indian Order of Merit "in recognition of the act of bravery of the Maharajadhiraja Bahadur for conspicuous courage displayed by him at the Overtoun Hall, Calcutta, on November 7, 1908, in connection with the attempt upon the life of Sir Andrew Fraser, the Lieutenant - Governor of Bengal." Sir Bijay Chand Mahtab was gazetted a Knight Commander of the Most Exalted Order of the Star of India on December 12, 1912, and was personally invested with the Star and Collar of the Order by His Majesty the King-Emperor at a Royal Chapter held on the occasion of the Great Durbar at Delhi.

The Raj estate is more than 4,000 square miles in extent, and the greater portion of this area is highly cultivated. The revenue that the Burdwan Raj pays to the Government is larger in amount than that of any other landholder in India.

THE CHOTA NAGPUR RAJ.

There is something very quaint in many of the traditional accounts of the origin of the kingdoms and States of India, and also of mythological statements as to the remarkable manner in which ruling chiefs and other notable personages are connected, through a lengthy genealogical tree, with some planet, animal, or bird, or even with some episode in the history of one of the prominent Hindu deities.

One of the most curious of these old legends is associated with the family of the Maharaja Pertab Udai Nath Shah Deo of the Chota Nagpur Raj in the division of Ranchi in the Province of Behar and Orissa. Dalton, in his "Descriptive Ethnology of Bengal," speaks of an old tradition relating to the origin of this family, and it appears that they claim descent from the great serpent, which is king of hell, that is to say, the devil, and this is considered to be a very ancient and honourable connection.

The current belief is that the Mundas were the first people to clear the jungle and subsequently cultivate the land in this district, colonizing some twenty or twenty-five villages. The question of the appointment of a Raja was a continual source of disagreement among the villagers, and an ancestor of the present Maharaja was eventually approved by the whole tribe.

Tradition is responsible for the following: One of the Rajas, named Janamejaya, in revenge for the death of his father, determined upon the destruction of the whole of the "Nag" or serpent race, but one Punderika was saved. The latter adopted the customs and dress of a Brahman and proceeded to Benares to the house of a Brahman, under whose tuition he desired to perfect his knowledge of the sacred books. The pupil was so diligent in his studies, and delighted his instructor so much that the latter gave his beautiful daughter Parvati as wife to the Nag; but it is said that Punderika could not rid himself of his serpent-like or double tongue, and this so exasperated Parvati that she rose into open rebellion against her husband. Some consolation to the offended wife was, however, afforded when she was taken by her husband to Puri, on the sea-coast near Cuttack, in the Province of Behar and Orissa (now one of the most fashionable holiday resorts on the eastern littoral), where she enjoyed herself so thoroughly that the objectionable features of her husband were forgotten. On returning from Puri the couple halted by the side of a lake of water, and Parvati, who had again become embittered against Punderika, gave birth to a son, and was so overwhelmed with sorrow that she prepared a funeral pyre and became *sati*. Another Brahman who passed near the lake at this juncture heard the cries of a child and discovered the newly born babe lying in a sheltered place and guarded by a large hooded snake. This was Punderika, in the form of a serpent, protecting his child, and the Brahman thereupon prophesied that the boy would become Raja of the country to be called Nagpur. The infant was taken to the house of a neighbouring Raja, who took charge of and educated him until he was fourteen years of age, when at a meeting of Rajas of adjoining territories it was decided that the youth should be named Phani Mukuta Raya, and that he should be proclaimed Raja of Chota Nagpur. In connection with this tradition it may be mentioned that the official seal and coat-of-arms of the Raja and his family show as a crest a cobra with a human face under its expanded head surrounded by all the insignia of royalty.

Chota-Nagpur—as part of Behar and Orissa—was ceded to the British Government in the year 1765, but the earliest arrangement with a Raja of which record can be found was in 1772, when it is stated that the chief appeared before Captain Camac, commanding a force in Palamau, and after exchange of turbans with the Government's representative, he duly acknowledged himself a vassal of the great Power, and further agreed to pay tribute. An interesting sidelight is given in connection with this interview, as it is said that Captain Camac solemnly assured the Raja that it was customary in England for the parties to an agreement to exchange head-wear in order to give validity to the proceedings, but the humorous side of the

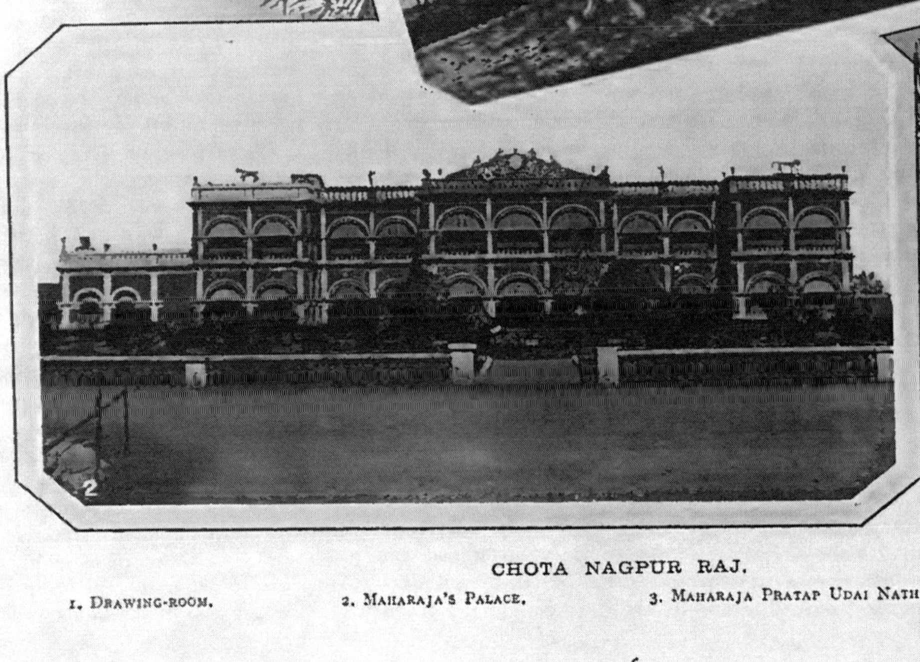

CHOTA NAGPUR RAJ.

1. Drawing-room. 2. Maharaja's Palace. 3. Maharaja Pratap Udai Nath Shah Deo, of Chota Nagpur.

CHOTA NAGPUR RAJ.

1. Ratu Lake, constructed in the Famine Year of 1897. 2. Manager's Bungalow, Ratu.
3. Jaggernathpur Temple, erected in Sambat 1742 (A.D. 1685). 4. Chutia Temple, erected by Harnath Bramchari, in Sambat 1742 (A.D. 1685).

matter appears only when it is added that the Raja's turban was literally studded with valuable precious stones, whereas that belonging to the captain was of a very ordinary description!

For many years the Raja was permitted to administer the territory as the chief of a tributary *makal*, but he was deprived of magisterial powers, and the estate was placed under the control of the magistrate of Ramgarh.

The new form of administration did not suit the people at all, and they soon gave expression to grievances of various kinds, the difficulties being mainly concerned with rights to hold lands. Disturbances arose in 1811, and it became necessary to call up a force of soldiers before the trouble was quelled. More serious conflicts with the authorities occurred in 1820, and very stringent measures had to be adopted. In 1831 the Kol insurrection broke out with the suddenness and fierceness of a forest fire, and raids on villages, involving considerable loss of life and destruction of property were participated in by large bodies of malcontents. The armed forces sent to quell the disturbances were not able to secure peace in the country until more than a year had elapsed.

The experiences of the past few years led the Government to make radical changes in the administration of the territory, the principal one being the organization of the disturbed districts as a "non-regulation Province under the name of the South-Western Frontier Agency." A system of zemindary was adopted, and for the future protection of the law-abiding portion of the inhabitants the Chota-Nagpur police force was established.

THE DARBHANGA RAJ.

The history of the Darbhanga Raj dates from the early portion of the sixteenth century, when Akbar, the Mogul Emperor of Delhi, granted certain estates to Sriman Mahamahopadhyaya Thakur Mahesh, the ancestor of the present Maharaja. A predecessor of Thakur Mahesh Mahamahopadhyaya Gangadhar Jha flourished some seven centuries ago, and one of his descendants, Swami Sankarashan Thakur, received some grants of land in Khandwa in the Central Provinces, together with the title of Thakur, and since that time the title has remained in the family. It is recorded that the lands and honour thus conferred were granted on account of the piety, intellectual abilities, and high social position of the recipient, and the Emperor agreed to the continuance of them so long as the Rajas ruled wisely and made it one of the chief objects of their lives to promote the material and moral well-being of the people.

These admirable qualifications appear to have been hereditary traits in the characters of succeeding chiefs, and the present Maharaja—to whom reference will be made hereafter—has not been surpassed by any of his predecessors in his loyalty to the conditions imposed by the Emperor.

This grant by the Emperor Akbar was further augmented by another from the Emperor Shah Alam, who gave a *parganna* in the Purnea district to Raja Ragho Singh and bestowed upon him the hereditary title of Raja Bahadur. Maharaja Chhatra Singh received a similar honour for his splendid services in the Nepalese War, and that distinction has continued in the family, without interruption, thus making it practically hereditary.

The estates originally extended from the Ganges to the Nepal mountains, and from the Gunduck River to Kosi, and comprised the present districts of Darbhanga, Muzaffarpur, and Champaran in the Tirhut division of the Province of Behar and Orissa, together with portions of the district of Bhagalpur and Purnea. The Raj now consists of properties in the districts of Darbhanga, Muzaffarpur, Monghyr, Bhagalpur, Purnea, Gaya, and Patna, together with palaces at Rajnagar, Darbhanga, Bankipore, Darjeeling, Simla, Allahabad, Calcutta, Purnea, Benares, Muzaffarpur, and other places.

The magnificent and stately pile of buildings at Darbhanga, which is the principal home of the Maharaja is famous throughout India. It is most sumptuously furnished, possessing collections of objects of art of the greatest beauty and value.

The extensive gardens and grounds, superbly kept under the management of an expert, are a wonderful manifestation of the art of horticulture. A considerable portion of the grounds bears a striking resemblance to those beautiful parks which are seen in every county in England, but there are also avenues of graceful tropical palms, shady walks, and flower-beds, glorious in their profusion of hundreds of flowers emitting the most delicate perfumes.

The present Maharaja, His Highness Sir Rameshwara Singh Bahadur, K.C.I.E., G.C.I.E., the youngest of the three sons of Maharaja Maheshwara Singh Bahadur, was born at Darbhanga in January 1860. The eldest son predeceased his father, who died while the other two brothers were still minors, and the Raj was consequently placed under the management of the Court of Wards. The youths were educated at Darbhanga, Muzaffarpur, and Queen's College, Benares, and they subsequently enjoyed private tuition under Mr. Chester Macnaughten, who afterwards became principal of the Raj-Kumar College, at Rajkot. The elder of the brothers, His Highness Sir Lakshmeshwara Singh, G.C.I.E., ascended the *gadi* on attaining his majority, while the younger received *Bachuar* in the district of Darbhanga as *Babuana Parganna*.

The latter exhibited great scholarly attainments, but he also manifested keen business qualifications which fitted him to undertake the personal management of his estates. With the view of obtaining further insight into official life he entered the Bengal Statutory Civil Service in 1878 and became joint-magistrate at Darbhanga, Chappra, and Bhagalpur, his ability in mastering details of evidence, his untiring patience, and his sound judgments earning for him the warm approval of Government and the goodwill of the public generally. He was appointed a member of the Bengal Legislative Council in 1885, and the title of Raja Bahadur was conferred on him in 1886, while other honours, including exemption from attendance in civil courts, and the allowance of a personal following of twenty-five armed men, followed in quick succession.

He succeeded to the *gadi* of the Darbhanga Raj on the death of Sir Lakshmeshwara Singh in 1898, and from that date to the present time he has exhibited all the qualifications of a wise administrator, and has been the generous supporter of a very large number of philanthropic movements, exclusive of the immense sums of money which he has given to private charities.

One of the most noticeable features in the character of the Maharaja is that he is a Hindu of the Hindus, strictly orthodox of the most orthodox type, but his catholicity of spirit is so remarkable that he is continually persevering in his efforts to promote cordial relations between Mahommedans and the holders of his own creed. He is credited with originating the idea of establishing the All-India Hindu Association, which has three special objects, viz. (1) to promote and protect Hindu interests, (2) to foster friendly relations between Hindus and other communities, and (3) to instil principles of loyalty to the King and Government.

The Maharaja is well versed in the

THE DARBHANGA RAJ.

1. The Ananda Bhag Palace. 2. The Rajnagar Palace.

THE DARBHANGA RAJ.

1. The Kankali Temple. 2. The Juran Chappra, Muzaffarpur. 3. Darbhanga House, Middleton Street, Calcutta.

THE DARBHANGA RAJ.

1. THE MAHARAJA'S DRAG-AND-FOUR, WITH THE GUARD. 2. THE MAHARAJA'S STUD. 3. THE DARBHANGA "TWINS."

sacred lore of Hinduism, and he is recognized as an authority upon customs, rites, and ceremonies of all kinds, and as head of the Maithil Brahman community, his decision in disputes, particularly with regard to caste problems, is always final. His acquaintance with the spiritual tenets of the Hindus is probably unique, and he scrupulously observes strict Hindu rites and ceremonies, even to the performance of penances and the observation of fasts. Under the presidency of the Maharaja the Sree Bharat Dharma Mahamandal, an all-Hindu religious association, has done good work in publishing books, training preachers, and arousing interest in the religion taught by ancient Rishis, the ancestors of the Hindus. His Highness has presided over several conferences at Calcutta, Allahabad, and elsewhere, including the All-India Brahmana Conference held at Lahore in 1902, and more recently at Hardwar and Muttra, when Hindu leaders of all sects from all parts of India assembled to further the interests of their cult. On two occasions he presided over the conference at which professors of all faiths met together in a friendly spirit and expounded the tenets of their respective creeds. He once led a deputation of Hindu leaders from all parts of India which waited upon Lord Minto on behalf of the Hindus, and he has also presided over an industrial conference at Lahore.

It would be impossible to find in India a more consistent supporter of the cause of education than the Maharaja of Darbhanga. He has endowed elementary and higher schools for instruction in English, Sanskrit, and the vernacular tongues; he maintains an English High School at Darbhanga; Sanskrit colleges at Darbhanga and Benares; he is sole trustee of the Mahakalee Pathsala, which was the first institution in Bengal to impart religious and moral instruction to Hindu girls, and from its foundation he has liberally supplied it with funds.

Two and a half lakhs of rupees have been given to the University of Calcutta for the building of a library; a magnificent grant of five lakhs was made to the Hindu University, of which he was the president before its incorporation, and on whose behalf His Highness has devoted an enormous amount of time and much of his tireless energy. He has, further, undertaken long tours to collect donations for the same, and as illustrating the broadmindedness of the Maharaja it may be said that he presented Rs. 20,000 to the proposed Muslim University.

That the munificent donations of the Darbhanga princely house have not by any means been confined to purely religious or educational purposes the following facts will show: He gave to the Victoria Memorial Hospital, Muzaffarpur, Rs. 34,000; to the Famine Relief Fund (1900), 1¼ lakhs of rupees; the Queen Victoria Memorial Fund, 1 lakh; the Calcutta University, 2½ lakhs; the Bharat Dharma Mahamandal, Rs. 25,000; King Edward Memorial Fund (Bengal), 1 lakh; the Patna Municipality, Rs. 25,000; the investment for Anathalaya, Rs. 1,00,243; and to the Muzaffarpur Waterworks, Rs. 75,000.

The Maharaja has, further, constructed temples in several places in the district of Darbhanga, also at Bankipore, Benares, Kamakhya, Kharagpore, and other places, and he has restored others which were partially destroyed by earthquake in the Kamakhya, Sylhet, and Khangra valleys. The marble temple built by him at Rajnagar is a standing monument of his deep devotion and piety. Within his own State he maintains a large general hospital, a hospital for women, and a number of dispensaries in various parts of his territory.

His Highness has always been a prominent figure in functions of a public character, and his election on five occasions by the non-official members of the Bengal Legislative Council to represent them on the supreme legislative body of India, proved that he had at that comparatively early stage in his career become a leader among men.

He is Life-President of the Bharat Dharma Mahamandal, of the Behar Landholders' Association, and the Maithil Mahasabha. On four occasions he has been elected president of the British Indian Association, the premier landholders' association in Bengal. The Maharaja was a most efficient chairman of the reception committee in connection with the visit of Their Majesties, the King Emperor and the Queen Empress, when, as Their Royal Highnesses the Prince and Princess of Wales, they visited Calcutta in 1906, and in commemoration of the event he offered one lakh of rupees to be devoted to such charitable objects as Their Royal Highnesses might approve. The money was subsequently apportioned between the Medical College Hospital, Calcutta, and the Lady Dufferin Hospital fund. On the occasion of the lamented death of His Majesty the King-Emperor, Edward VII, the Maharaja organized and led a mourning demonstration consisting of a vast concourse of Hindus, who marched from the City of Calcutta to the *maidan*, where His Highness read his historic speech, in which he voiced the feelings of hundreds of thousands of Hindus when he expressed their profound sorrow at the loss of their beloved ruler.

When the Coronation Durbar was held at Delhi in 1911 the Maharaja, acting on the suggestion of His Honour the Lieutenant-Governor of the Punjab, organized a grand procession of Hindus, who offered prayers for the long life and prosperity of Their Majesties, and he subsequently led a deputation of leaders of different Indian religions and sects which was presented to Their Majesties.

His Highness is very highly respected in all parts of the country, but he is beloved most by those who know him best, ample evidence of the sterling worth of this popular ruler.

His library at Darbhanga is one of the finest in India, and it contains very many valuable works, principally in English and Sanskrit, but the Maharaja is conversant with English, Sanskrit, Persian, Urdu, Hindi, and Bengalee. His favourite pastime is reading, but he also takes the deepest interest in the management of his estate, and he personally supervises the whole work of his numerous staff.

In the year 1912, when Behar and Orissa were separated from Bengal and formed into a new Province, the Maharaja Bahadur was appointed member of the first Executive Council, and during his service of the full term he has displayed a diplomatic statesmanship which has gone very far to accentuate the mutual understanding between the Government and the people. The rulers look to him for sage counsel, and for important and timely suggestions of policy, and the ruled look up to him for the sympathetic representation of their multifarious concerns. It can be safely asserted that it is only the Maharaja Bahadur who could have combined, adjusted, and reconciled all varying interests in such a harmonious fashion.

During his Executive membership, his activities in other directions have been no less remarkable. He is the originator and author of the idea of the Common Formula of Prayer for the long life and prosperity of Their Imperial Majesties, and for the triumphant victory of the allied forces. The form of the prayer is not yet definitely settled, but it has naturally enlisted the support of the entire Hindu India, and the Viceroy's Government have also approved the idea. In this connection he made an all-India tour, which was the most successful of its kind, and the ovation accorded to him in all places, from Kashmir to Rameshwaram, and from Peshawar to Puri, is eloquent testimony of his universal popularity. The rapt attention with which thousands of hearers would listen to his fervid and masterly exposition of the secrets and glories of the Hindu religion bespeaks the veneration in which he is held, while the emphatic and thorough approbation with which the entire population of the Hindus in India received the common prayer, testifies to the deep-rooted loyalty of the Hindus, of whom the Maharaja is so worthy a member and so great a leader.

The Maharajah was awarded the Kaisar-i-Hind Gold Medal in the year 1900; he served as a member of the Police Commission, travelling all over India, in 1902; he was created Knight Commander of the most eminent Order of the Indian Empire in 1907; he received the hereditary title of Maharaja Bahadur in 1907; and more recently he was invested with the honour of G.C.I.E.

His Highness has three children, namely, the Maharaj Kumari, born in 1905; the senior Maharaja Kumar, the heir-apparent, Maharaj Kumar Kameshwara Sing, born in 1907; and Maharaj Kumar Vishweshwara Singh, born in 1908.

THE DINAJPUR RAJ

The district of Dinajpur, in the division of Rajshahi in Eastern Bengal, has an area of about 3,900 square miles, and although it cannot be said to possess great natural physical attractions, it enjoys considerable fame on account of its antiquities. In addition to very fine temples at Kantanagore and Gopalganj, there are a number of ruins, as well as ancient buildings, which are traditionally connected with some important historical events.

Closely associated with this district is the Dinajpur Raj, which was founded about the middle of the fourteenth century by the celebrated Raja Ganesh, a " Hindu and Hakim of Dynwaj," who was a tributary chief under the kings of Gour. In the sixteenth century the Raj was in the possession of Srimanta Dutta Chowdhury, who was succeeded by his son Harishchandra. As the latter died without issue, the property, which at that time comprised ninety-three parganas, passed in the year 1644 to Raja Sookdeb Ray, the son of Srimanta's daughter. Sookdeb died in 1681, and was followed in succession by his three sons, Ramdeb, Jaydeb, and Prannath, the last-named ascending the *gadi* in 1687. He considerably increased the area of the Raj, and was honoured by the Imperial Court of Delhi with the hereditary title of Maharaja Bahadur. He commenced the building of a beautiful terra-cotta temple at Kantanagore with the intention of dedicating it to the god Kantaji, which he got at Brindaban, on his way back from Delhi, but he died in 1719, and the structure was completed and the god installed by his successor, his adopted son, Maharaja Ramnath Roy Bahadur. It was during the rule of the latter that the Raj attained its highest prosperity and glory, as the Maharaja had the oversight of 126 parganas, and was the recipient of high honours from the Emperor of Delhi. He maintained a regular military force, and fortified the original town of Dinajpur with moats and ramparts. He died in the year 1760, and was succeeded by his son Maharaja Baidyanath Roy Bahadur, who alienated not a small portion of his property by the creation of *Brahmatta* tenures and other endowments. He died without issue in the year 1780, and his widow, Maharani Saraswati, adopted Maharaja Radhanath Roy Bahadur. On payment of a fee of seven hundred and thirty gold mohurs he was declared successor to Maharaja Baidyanath Roy Bahadur, and was granted a *sanad* from the Emperor Shah Alam, which was countersigned by Warren Hastings on July 17, 1780. Maharaja Radhanath Roy Bahadur died in 1801, while still young, and as he did not leave issue he was succeeded by Maharaja Gobinda Nath Roy Bahadur, who was adopted by his widow. Maharaja Gobindanath died in 1841, and the Raj devolved on his son Maharaja Taraknath Roy Bahadur, who died in the year 1865, and whose widow, Maharani Syammohini, adopted Maharaja Sir Girija Nath Roy Bahadur, K.C.I.E., who now represents the historical house of Dinajpur.

Maharaja Girija Nath Roy Bahadur was born in 1862, and was adopted at the early age of four years and ten months. His early education was obtained at Queen's College, Benares, under the direct supervision of Maharani Syammohini, but his studies were completed at home under the guidance of distinguished teachers. While the present Maharaja Bahadur was a minor, the estate came under the management of the Maharani, who was assisted by her son-in-law, Raja Bahadur Khettra Mohan Sinha. The services of the latter were rewarded by the bestowal of the title of Raja by the Government of Lord Lytton. The title of Maharani, conferred upon the present Maharaja's mother, Syammohini, was given for her great services during the distressing time of the famine of 1873-74, when her liberal assistance enabled the *rayats* of Dinajpur to tide over the crisis. Since attaining his legal majority, Maharaja Girija Nath Roy Bahadur has taken a very active part in the administration of the district. He was Chairman of the Dinajpur Municipality for six years, and at present holds that office; he is also a member of the District Board, and an Honorary Magistrate. As a member of the Legislative Council of the Lieutenant-Governor of the late Province of Eastern Bengal and Assam, his services were of great value and were duly recognized by the Government. His wide knowledge and ripe experience have enabled him to give useful aid to the authorities, and he has always been foremost in forwarding the public movements of the day, by showing himself willing to assist with his purse, time, and labour, in all measures promoted for the welfare of the people. His public gifts, too, have been most generous. He founded the Diamond Jubilee and weaving schools, together with the Sanskrit Tol, and also two charitable dispensaries. At the expense of the Maharaja's estate, the Ghagra and Thomson canals (the latter named after Sir Rivers Thomson, formerly Lieutenant-Governor of Bengal) were built at Dinajpur, and they have greatly benefited that town by improving the means of sanitation. The title of Maharaja Bahadur was bestowed, by a *sanad*, upon the Maharaja in 1907, at a public Durbar at Dacca, when the Lieutenant-Governor, in making the presentation, spoke as follows in appreciation of the Maharaja's character and services: " By your unswerving loyalty, high character, and readiness to give your time and labour to promote all useful public objects, you have gained the high esteem of your countrymen and the grateful recognition of the Government. It is very gratifying to me to be able to express, by the ceremony of to-day, the satisfaction with which the Government has viewed your career." The Maharaja was chairman of the Reception Committee of the All-India Kayastha Conference held in Calcutta in December 1912, and was President of the Conference held in Allahabad in 1914.

He received the decoration of K.C.I.E.

DINAJPUR RAJ.

1. Serpent Gate in the Raj Palace. 2. Black Stone Gate. 3. A Pillar of Siva's Temple, built A.D. 966. 4. A Buddhist Chaitya, or Stupa. 5. Temple at Kantanagar.

DINAJPUR RAJ.

1. Maharaja Sir Girija Nath Roy, Bahadur, K.C.I.E., of Dinajpur. 2. Maharaja Kumar Jagadish Nath Roy. 3. Front View of the Palace.

on the birthday of His Majesty the King-Emperor in the year 1914.

The Maharaja is an orthodox Hindu, and he not only has taste for music, but is himself well versed in the art. In his early life he was fond of outdoor games, and was known in the locality as a keen sportsman.

Being without issue the Maharaja in the year 1900 adopted as his heir the Maharaj Kumar Jagadish Nath Roy.

THE DHENKANAL FEUDATORY STATE

Dhenkanal, one of the Feudatory States of Orissa (styled "the Gurjat mehals"), is situated between 20-30° and 21-12° north latitude and 85-15° and 86-5° east longitude. It is bounded on the north by the Pal Lahera and Keonjhar Feudatory States, and the Sukinda Zemindari in the Cuttack district; on the west by the district of Angul, and the States of Talcher and Hindol; on the south by the Baramba, Tigiriah, and Athgurh States, and by the Balarampur, Madhupur, Darpan, Kalkala, and Dalijorá Zemindaries, in the Cuttack district, on the east. In addition to the above, there are two detached villages, called Kabatbundh and Galiamuhapatna, which lie beyond the boundary of the State, within the district of Cuttack. The area of the State, which stands third in position among the Feudatory States of Orissa, is 1,463 square miles in extent. According to the census of 1911, the population consisted of 269,853 souls, of whom 131,240 are males and 138,613 females.

The State is divided into two natural divisions, viz. the North Brahmani and the South Brahmani, these being created by the Brahmani River flowing in an easterly direction from one extremity of the State to the other.

Dhenkanal is politically divided into two subdivisions for administrative purposes, viz. (1) the headquarter subdivision, comprising 15 bisos (parganas) with 656 villages, and (2) the Bysingha subdivision, consisting of 9 bisos (parganas) with 438 villages.

The State is interspersed with hills and forests, chiefly towards the north and south-east, and, although other parts have been opened out, they contain a certain number of wooded sections.

The most important hills are as follows: (1) Kapilas, 2,239 feet in height, in the south-eastern part of the State, is widely known throughout and beyond Orissa as a place of pilgrimage, owing to the existence of the Temple of Chandra Sakhar Jew and many other ancient architectural constructions since the time of Pratap Rudra Deb, the Maharaja of Orissa, whose name is associated with the establishment of this famous resort of devotees. A large *melá* (fair) is held here annually on the "Sivaratree" day by pilgrims who come from all directions. There is a perennial spring of health-giving water in the middle of this hill, where the temple stands. (2) Satsajia, 1,981 feet in height, is situated in the south-west portion of the State. Here is also a permanent spring running down from the top of the hill.

The River Brahmani, as stated above, passes through the middle of the State, dividing it into two equal parts; and other waterways, tributaries of this river and of the Mahanaddy, are the Ramial, Lingara, and Sapwa.

There are 175 miles of road in the State, the important ones being: from Cuttack to Angul, 37 miles in length, connecting Dhenkanal with the districts of Cuttack and Angul; the Tangi road, 22 miles, uniting the headquarters of Dhenkanal with Kapilas, and also with the Kapilas Road Station of the Bengal-Nagpur Railway at Tangi; Bhuban road, 17 miles, between the headquarters and Bhuban on the Brahmani, an important centre of trade; and the Sankarpur, Baramba, Palasuni, Aluajharan-Murhi, the Noagan, and other roads.

Mining and manufactures have not been greatly developed, but iron is smelted by Lohará-Kamárs in Palasuni, Parjang, and Jenadesh Bisos; gold is found in small particles, which are obtained by washing the sand of the Ramial rivulet; mica (black and white) is found in Kapilas and many other places, and a mine is now being worked at Dhobabahali; coal is found in occasional places; and bauxite is obtained near headquarters and in other parts.

Bell-metal and brass utensils are manufactured at Bhuban, Indipore, Oakhama, and in other villages. Tassar cloth is manufactured from the cocoons produced in the State forests, lac is obtained from kusum-trees, and cotton cloth is woven in the Bhuban and Siminai villages.

The present ruler of the State, Raja Sura Pratap Mahindra Bahadur, is the sixteenth ruler since the foundation of the State, and the eldest son and heir-apparent is Yubaraj Sankar Pratap Rai Sinha Bhramarabara Rai.

Before the predecessors of the present Raja occupied the Gadi of the State as ruling chiefs, and prior to the formation of the present compact area, a stretch of land to the south of the Brahmani River was subdivided into small principalities (comprising strips of lands and jungles), ruled over by semi-independent chiefs of Hindoo and aboriginal descent. At that time certain other land in and around the present headquarters of the State, comprising an area of one *kosh* (equivalent to two square miles), was ruled over by a chieftain named Dhenká, a member of the Savar tribe of the aboriginal class.

A similar area towards the west, called Gar-Besália, was at that time ruled by a chieftain of the Bhanja clan, named Sreedhar Bhanja (known as Samanta Singhar). Sreedhar killed Dhenká in an affray, and it is said that Dhenká, on his death-bed, asked Sreedhar Bhanja that, as the latter had mortally injured him and had intended to take possession of his favourite place, he should, in order to maintain his memory, name his territory after his (Dhenká's) own name, and that he would preserve and worship a relic of his own, representing his head. Sreedhar Bhanja was succeeded by Nilakantha and Sadasiva Samanta-Sinhars, the last chiefs of the Bhanja family. The name therefore owes its origin to the territory of Dhenká Savar, which was styled after him.

The genealogy of the line of the present ruling chiefs originates from Raja Hari Singh (afterwards Hari-Singh Bidyadhar), who came to Puri from the Paschim (Rajputana States), in company with his two brothers, Govinda Singh and Janardan Singh. These three brothers were Kshattriya descendants of the Yadubansa (dynasty of Yadus) family. They came to Puri in the time of Maharaja Protáp Rudra Deb of Orissa, and took shelter under Jagannath Mahaprobhu, and it is said that, according to the command of the Mahaprobhu in a dream, they served the then Maharaja as *Bhois*, or collectors of land revenue, having taken the *Sarhi* (office) as *Patras* (officers). Their family title was Sinha, but subsequently all were styled Bidyadhar Mahapatra. In recognition of their meritorious services, Govinda Bidyadhar rose to the office of Prime Minister, Janardan Bidyadhar was appointed Financial Minister, and Hari Bidyadhar became Commander of the Army.

The eldest, Govinda Bidyadhar, became the Maharaja of Orissa, after the death of Maharaja Protáp Rudra Deb. Hari

THE DHENKANAL FEUDATORY STATE.

1. The Five Rajkumars of Dhenkanal Raj. 2. Raja Sura Pratap Mahindra, Bahadur, Feudatory Chief of Dhenkanal. 3. The Late Raja Dinabandhu Mahindra, Bahadur, Present Chief's Father. 4. The Late Maharaja Bhagiratha Mahindra, Bahadur, Present Chief's Grandfather.

THE DHENKANAL FEUDATORY STATE.

1. The Palace, Dhenkanal. 2. Interior of Durbar Hall. 3. Baldev Jew's Temple, Dhenkanal. 4. The Dhamsa, Chadaknali, and Nishan.

THE DHENKANAL FEUDATORY STATE.

1. The State Jail. 2. The State H.E. School. 3. View in the Eastern Part of Dhenkanal. 4. Temple of Chandra Sakhar Jew.

Bidyadhar accompanied the Maharaja in his expedition to Southern India, who, having won victories in several campaigns, was able to vanquish a chief from whom the *minaketan katâri* and *minaketan pugree* (dagger and headgear marked with "Minaketan") were wrested for the Maharaja. The Maharaja offered him, as *jagir*, a strip of land called the Karamol-Patna or Singha-Rai-Khole (now called Karamol Patna and Singhari-kholá of Dhenkanal), comprising seven *kosh* (one kosh being equivalent to two miles) in the Jharkhanda, and made him a Raja of Jharkhanda, and also made him a present of the minaketan katari and minaketan pugree, to use as his *santak*, or family insignia. He was then styled the Raja of Karamol Patna in the Jharkhand. As a brother and a favourite of the Orissa Maharaja, Hari Bidyadhar was very ambitious, and in attempting to extend his possessions he overthrew the last Bhanja chieftain, Sadasiv Bhanja, and then added his territory to his own. He, at the request of the last Bhanja chieftain, and in honour of the last wish of Dhenká Savar, styled his territory "Dhenkanal," in place of "Jharkhanda Karamol Patna," with the permission of the Puri Maharaja, Ram Chandra Dev. After establishing his capital, and with an extended territory which he obtained through the co-operation of Lokenath Chainee and Murari Patnaik, both of whom accompanied him from Puri, Hari Bidyadhar went to the Gajapati Maharaja of Puri to do homage. The Maharaja received him cordially, as a kinsman of his own, and honoured him, as a faithful general and dependent, with the hereditary title of Raisingha Bhramarabar Ray, and styled him "Jharkhanda Padisha." He further allowed, in recognition of his relationship, some special concessions and privileges in the Jagannath Temple (Sree Mandir of Puri) for *darshan* to the deity, and also permitted him the proud privilege of full enjoyment of all the time-honoured customs and usages prevalent in the royal family, to be hereditarily held in the Dhenkanal Raj family, and it may be added that they are still enjoyed by them. Hari Bidyadhar ruled from 1529 to 1584.

Lokhnath Rai Singh Bhramarbar, chief between the years 1585 and 1606, was son of Hari Singh Bidyadhar, and when he succeeded his father he maintained the order and peace in the territory which had been established by his predecessor. The long period of his rule was very peaceful, and in pursuance of a progressive policy he laid the foundation of the Baldev Jew's temple at headquarters, which is at present the most important shrine in Dhenkanal. An old poetical work on a palm-leaf, entitled "Balbhadra Boli," gives an account of how the deity (Baldev Jew) was brought from Angul, Hindol, and other places by the Maharaja Ananga Bhim Deb of Puri, while on his way from Bhim Nagari to Puri, and how he happened to remain at Dhenkanal. Along with the history of Baldev Jew, the poem contains a contemporary account of the line of the ruling chiefs of Dhenkanal, commencing from the founder. This has been handed down by the people of Dhenkanal from generation to generation, and it inspires them to hold the Thakur in high reverence as the Protector of Dhenkanal.

The Dhenkanal State has endowed extensive landed properties for the Seba and Bhog of this Thakur, and the *biso* (pergana) "Balrampur," where these lands exist has been named after the deity. It was during the time of Lokhnath Bhramarabar that the proposal for the large temple to locate Baldev Jew was made, and he had only laid the foundation of the building when he was succeeded by his son, Balabhadra Rai Singh Bhramarabar Rai.

As the Dhenkanal territory was inhabited chiefly by low-class Hindoos and aboriginal tribes, the Rajas of the State, with the view of setting before them good examples of high morals, peaceful citizenship, and religious life, after the example of Puri Rajas, established Brahmin Sasans (colonies of Brahmins) by immigration from Puri and other noted places. Grants of brahmottar, or rent-free Lakhraj lands, for their homestead and for cultivation, was also made, and the chief established Lokenathpur Sasan in his own name.

Balabhadra Rai Singh Bhramarabar Rai, who ruled in 1606-32, succeeded his father in the former year, and he annexed a portion of the adjoining Talchar State and founded the Mundailo Balabhadrapur Sasan, after his own title.

The rule of Raja Nilakantha Rai Singh Bhramarabar Rai, from 1632 to 1652, was a very peaceful one, and he established the Nilakanthapur Sasan.

The rule of Nrusinha Rai Singh Bhramarabar Rai, son of Nilakantha Rai Singh Brahmarabar Rai, is the most important chapter in the history of Dhenkanal. The name of this chivalrous chief (during the long period between 1652 and 1694) is still proverbial among the people of the State. There is an old poem, called the "Madhupur Koily," which depicts the valour and skill of this warrior chief in defeating the Raja of Madhupur and in annexing a part of his estate. He further extended the area of Dhenkanal by attaching to it portions from Keonjhar, Athgurh, Tigria, Madhupur, and Sukinda, and he completed the temple of Baldev Jew and set up the idol in it. Up to the time of Nrusinha Bhramarabar the capital town of Dhenkanal had been at Karamol Gurh and Hadgurh, but this ruler founded the present one, where he spent a certain period in each year. He also established the Rai Nrusinhapur Sasan.

Kunja Behari Rai Singh Bhramarabar Rai, the next in succession (1694-1720), annexed the Gotmara Biso from Angul and established the Kunja Beharipur Sasan and the Mandir of Sambhu Gopal Jew at headquarters, while Braja Behari Rai Singh Bhramarabar Rai (1720-44) was responsible for the Braja Beharipur Sasan and the Mandir of Joygopal Jew.

Nothing of importance can be traced in the time of Damodar Rai Singh Bhramarabar Rai, who ruled from 1744 to 1746.

Trilochan Mahindra Bahadur (1746-88), who was a valiant warrior chief, fell out with the Mahratta Rajas of Nagpur, who had been establishing their supremacy in Orissa, owing to some disagreement in the payment of *pesh kush* (tribute). It appears that Rajaram Pandit, who demanded double *pesh kush*, sent troops to Dhenkanal, who were defeated at Motori (at present called the "Motori Gurh" in Dhenkanal). The Subadar then appealed to the Bhonsla Raja of Nagpur, and, in response to a requisition for fresh troops, a large army, led by Chimna Jea Babu, was sent to subdue Dhenkanal. A closely fought battle ensued, in 1781, which terminated in a treaty entered into by the parties, under which half of the tribute demanded was remitted. The *dhansa* (big drum) and the *chadak-nali* (matchlock) were the trophies that the Raja received from the Mahratta force. The Maharajas of Puri conferred on the Raja the hereditary title of Mahindra Bahadur, reserving that of Rai Singh Bhramarbar Rai to be enjoyed by the *Yubarajas* (heirs-apparent). A contemporary poet, named Braja Nath Badajena, has depicted the battle in his work called the "Samarataranga" ("Waves of the Battle"). The Raja also annexed a part of Keonjhar, and strengthened the borders of his State by the construction of well-defended forts and by stationing militia within the walls. Dayanidhy Mahindra Bahadur (1788-98), son of Trilochan Mahindra Bahadur, had a peaceful rule, and was followed by Ram Chandra Mahindra Bahadur, who formed the Sasan of Ramchandrapur.

The next rulers were Krishna Chandra Mahindra Bahadur (1812-22) and Syam Sundar Mahindra Bahadur (1822-32), and the latter was succeeded by Maharaja Bhagirath Mahindra Bahadur (1832-77). This period is a very important one in the annals of Dhenkanal, as it introduced an entirely new era. Maharaja Bhagirath, a profound scholar of high Sanskrit learning, an able administrator, a patron of learning and industrial improvements, a man of rare intellect, high morals, exemplary character, and of liberal views, restored all administrative reforms and secured order by settling the tenure of the State and by introducing working methods and the keeping of accounts in the various departments. The establishment of all public institutions, such as schools, dispensaries, jails, and courts, was undertaken by him; he built the present palace, and by virtue of his successful rulership he was created Maharaja by the British Government. His substantial donations towards the establishment of public institutions abroad, such as the Ravenshaw College of Cuttack, the Cuttack Printing Company, and medical schools, and to several pundits and scholars, who surrounded him from all quarters, his charity to the poor and the needy, and his impartial and even-handed justice, testify to his liberal-mindedness and to his sympathetic heart. He was a successful sportsman and a keen shot, and he killed no fewer than 352 tigers during his lifetime. The aboriginal classes of "leaf-wearers" (the Juangs) had a superstition that they would be eaten up by tigers if they wore clothes. But the Maharaja's high moral personality induced them to adopt proper costumes, for which purpose he made a free distribution of apparel among them. His highly talented, able, and far-sighted Dewan, Baba Banomaly Singh, a local man of high birth and rare intellect, and a true loyal benefactor of the Raj whose memory is ever green in the mind of the people of this State, enjoyed a long life, and died as recently as the year 1912.

Maharaja Bhagirath, having no issue of his own, adopted as his heir Raja Dinabandhu Mahindra Bahadur, the youngest brother of the late Chief of Boad, who came of a distinguished Kshattriya family. Dinabandhu was a minor when he died in 1885, the State having been under the management of the Court of Wards since the death of the late Maharaja, and he left an only son—a babe six months old (the present ruler) and his widowed Rani, the daughter of the old Chief of Banai, who is widely known as the "Rajarshi" (the most pious and orthodox ruler).

Sura Protap Mahindra Bahadur, the present chief, was born in 1885, and he took charge of the State in 1906, after completing his twenty-first year, up to which time the Court of Wards' management had been continued. The State, therefore, had remained under Government management for the long period of about thirty years. During his minority the chief was carefully educated for his high and responsible office by the Government at the Ravenshaw Collegiate School, under the direct guardianship and control of his Mother, the Dowager-Rani, whose piety is proverbial. This noble lady has been, since her widowhood, leading a life of austerity as a religious devotee, and she has fully dedicated herself to works of public good and to ameliorating the cause of suffering humanity. The large Narayan temple at Kapilas, the vast water reservoirs constructed by her orders, orchards planted at her own cost, and many other acts for the benefit of the public, will serve as lasting monuments to immortalize her name; and it was the noble example of such a virtuous mother which moulded the life of the present ruler. He has married the highly accomplished and well-educated granddaughter of the present Chief (Raja Bahadur) of Seraikella, whose high literary attainments and religious sentiments are manifested in the pages of his voluminous literary works, and who is a Kshyattriya of high order, being a member of the eminent Sinha Bansa. A treatise on music for beginners, compiled by her in the Uriya language, is now of great use to beginners of both sexes in Orissa. The Chief has five Kumars, the eldest of whom, Yubaraj Sankar Protap Rai Sinha Bhramarbar Rai, is the heir-apparent.

The Raja, since his installation to the *gadi*, has reserved forests by introducing forest laws, improved the working of the same by appointing qualified officers, reclaimed jungle lands by leasing them out on easy terms, executed irrigation works on important lines for facilitating agriculture, encouraged the breeding of cows and horses by the free distribution of good bulls and stallions, developed various kinds of arts and industries, such as weaving, carpentry, works in fine arts filigree, horn, and ivory; has sent candidates abroad for technical education; erected magnificent buildings for the English High School in commemoration of his illustrious grandfather; founded the George Primary School; started large orchards; erected *pucca* granaries for the storage of paddy and grain for people during famine; improved the town by the construction of fine buildings; encouraged people by grants of loans and gifts of timbers; made nice roads and streets; strengthened the police force by qualified officers; settled the *Pans* (professional robbers) by giving work and land and by starting Pan schools; worked the mica mines; constructed a masonry stockade in a convenient position in the hills, where elephants can resort throughout the year; controlled education by placing it upon a satisfactory and permanent footing by the introduction of an education *cess*; and supplemented the Courts of Justice by creating additional magistrates for the speedy disposal of cases. Further, for the protection of old and infirm cows from the grasp of butchers, and to shelter and give them proper attention, he started an asylum, the "Sankarasrama," so styled after the name of the Yubaraj Sankara Protap Rai Sinha Bhramarabar Rai. Aiming at the social amelioration and with the view of improving the education of Brahmins, he opened a *Samittee* of the Brahmins in every Brahmin village. During the famine of 1908-9 the Chief expended a sum of Rs. 60,000, three-fourths of which were spent in gratuitous relief by giving rice from kitchens started throughout the State; and, in addition to opening the reserve forests and lending money to shopkeepers to enable them to sell paddy and rice at cost prices, and by meeting the cartage thereof from the State Exchequer, he induced the Mahajans and rich people to advance cash and paddy on the security of the State. Such Mahajans were, for their benevolent act, rewarded with gold and silver medals, certificates, and titles of honour in a public State Durbar, at which the Political Agent of the Orissa Feudatory States distributed the rewards at the request of the Chief. With similar precautionary measures and help, he assisted the people to avert the pangs of scarcity during the years 1915-16.

Loans in cash and paddy were given from the State, as well as from the *Amars* of the Rani Saheba and Rajmata, and thousands of maunds of imported rice and paddy from the latter's granaries were sold at much lower rates than the existing market prices, and thus a threatened famine was avoided. Suspension of rent also was granted to deserving villages. Besides the judicious precautionary measures stated above, the Raja opened a State bank, from which *tuccavi* (agricultural and other loans) were made to the people at nominal interest. As permanent measures against scarcity of food, he started big irrigation schemes by damming up streams and rivulets, which irrigate many miles of adjoining land, and thereby saved his people from the effects of drought. The large lake at headquarters, called the Annapurna Sarobar, was excavated, at the expense of the Dowager-Rani, as a relief work during the strenuous portions of the past two years. The nice stone temple with marble pavements, dedicated to Lord Sreekrishna, has been constructed, with all up-to-date improvements and designs, upon a hill which overlooks the Annapurna Sarobar; and the temple in the town, dedicated to the goddess Kamana Devi, has been built by the Rani Saheba with the same object of affording relief. The new guest-house on the hill, with the new temple by its side and the extensive Sarobar underneath it, are located among the many mango groves planted by the Chief, by his late father and grandfather, and by the present Rani and Dowager-Rani. The above structures, combined with the High English School, the hostel, and the Circuit-house, situated upon hills overlooking each other, present a picturesque sight and afford a panorama of enchanting views in the eastern portion of the headquarters. The addition of a magnificent Darbar hall, called the Rangmahal, tho Devi mandir in front of the palace, and the Dhenkanal Castle at Puri, called the Annapurnalaya, after the name of the Chief's mother, do credit to the skill of the late State engineer, Rai Dwarkanath Sircar Bahadur, whose valuable services were employed to complete these important works. Rai Bankun Chandra Majumdar Saheb, a very able and skilful officer with vast experience, has succeeded the late Rai Bahadur and taken up all important projects, including irrigation works of the nature stated above.

The land revenue settlement of the State, started by the Chief on an improved method of measurement, is nearing completion under the control of the tactful and experienced Dewan Babu Raj Kishore Tripathy.

As already mentioned, the Chief took the reins of administration of his State into his hands in 1906, with the customary full powers of a Feudatory Chief, but he was invested by Government in 1909 with Sessions power in recognition of his sound and effective rulership on progressive lines.

It may be added that the Chief was an invited guest at the Coronation Durbar at Delhi in 1911, and that he was honoured by having a prominent position in the procession of nobilities who passed before the Royal Party.

THE DUMRAON RAJ.

The Dumraon Raj estates are situated in the district of Shahabad, in the Province of Behar and Orissa. The ancestral domain of the Maharaja is situated near to the town of Dumraon, which is about four hundred miles distant from Calcutta.

The present chief, the Maharaja Kesho Prasad Singh, claims descent from the ancient family of the Raja Vikramadait of Ujjain in the district of Malwa, but authentic records of early history are difficult to obtain. During the Indian Mutiny of 1857, the then Maharaja rendered very valuable assistance to the British troops in quelling disturbances, and his services were duly acknowledged by the Government.

THE GANGPUR STATE

The Feudatory States of Orissa—of which the Gangpur State is one of the largest—form a succession of ranges of forest-clad mountains and hills, with well-watered valleys, in which a productive soil yields bountiful harvests of rice, pulses, oil-seeds, and other crops. The majority of the people are almost wholly dependent upon agriculture, and the remainder may be classed as blacksmiths, potters, barbers, washermen, and a few carvers, while nearly every village has its own weaver of cotton cloths.

The Gangpur State was ceded to the British Government in the year 1826, and in 1905 it was transferred from the division of Chota-Nagpur to Orissa. It has an area of about 2,500 square miles, and consists chiefly of an undulating tableland, some 700 feet above the level of the sea, while in several parts there are ranges of hills with peaks rising to a height of more than 2,200 feet.

The present Chief, the Maharaja Raghunath Sikhar Deo, came into power in the year 1858 while still a minor, and his relations with the British Government are regulated by a *Sanad* granted nearly twenty years ago, and renewed, with certain alterations, in 1905. The Maharaja assumed control of State affairs in 1871, and he has been untiring in his efforts to promote the well-being of his people, especially with regard to education, which was in a very backward condition until a few years ago.

The Chief has subscribed handsomely to the various war funds. The title of Raja Bahadur was conferred on him by the Government on the occasion of the visit of their Imperial Majesties to India in the year 1911, and the title of Maharaja was granted as personal distinction in the year 1915. The State was recently visited by His Excellency Sir Edward Albert Gait, K.C.S.I., Lieutenant-Governor of Behar and Orissa, when the magnificent newly constructed Court buildings at Sundargarh were formally opened.

The inhabitants have increased rapidly in number since a portion of the Bengal-Nagpur Railway system passed through the south-eastern portion of the State and provided additional means of communication and facilities for transport of produce. In the year 1872 it was estimated that the population consisted of about 70,000 persons, but at the census of 1911 the number had risen to 303,829 inhabitants, of 1,132 villages. The principal races are the Oraons, the Gonds, the Bhuiyas, and the Agarias, the majority of whom are skilled agriculturists; but it must be added that, notwithstanding the encouragements of the Chief and his able Diwan, Mr. J. A. Craven, there is still a large proportion of the people who manifest a disinclination to occupy and cultivate land on their own account. It is a somewhat curious fact that in Gangpur—as in every other State—one can observe an intelligent and systematic course of husbandry in certain areas practically side by side with tracts which are subjected to the most primitive methods of tillage.

It is probable that agriculturists are the most conservative people in the world, and it is a common experience in India to hear the remark that the system of cultivation practised two or three generations ago is quite good enough for

THE DUMRAON RAJ.

1. MAHARAJ KUMAR RAMA RANABEJAI PRASAD SINGH. 2. MAHARAJA KESHAVA PRASAD SINGH, BAHADUR.

Photo by Johnston & Hoffmann.

THE DUMRAON RAJ.

1. Nowratlan. 2. Manager's Bungalow.

THE DUMRAON RAJ.

1. BEHARIJEE'S TEMPLE. 2. KAKIJEE'S TEMPLE.

THE GANGPUR FEUDATORY STATE.

1. General View of Sundargarh. 2. The Ib River at Sundargarh.
3. The Junction of the Koel and Sankh Rivers, forming the Brahmani River at Panposh, the Birthplace of the Sage Vidyas.

THE GANGPUR FEUDATORY STATE.

1. The Boys' School, Sundargarh. 2. The Victoria Memorial Hospital at Sundargarh. 3. The Court Buildings,

present-day requirements. This spirit of *laissez-faire* is discouraging to all who, by example or precept, are endeavouring to teach men to grow two blades of grass in places where only one had previously been produced. The Governments of Provinces and States in India have in recent years spent very large sums of money in giving practical demonstrations and instruction in arable and pastoral farming, but there are still vast tracts of land tilled or grazed in a haphazard fashion, which can only result in unsatisfactory crops or ill-conditioned strains of half-starved cattle.

The soil in the southern portion of Gangpur is rich in plant-forming constituents, and the clever Agarias make the most of their agricultural knowledge, and as a result they reap heavy crops of first-class quality. This success has not been attained without an intelligent application of such essential principles as thorough cultivation and cleaning of the land, a knowledge of the nature of the soil, and an ability to supply suitable manures for its sustenance, a judicious rotation of crops, and the selection of sound seeds.

The Agarias understand the value of co-operation, and they have wisely acted in conjunction not only with one another, but also with their headmen in carrying through schemes of irrigation or drainage on dry and wet lands respectively. The cultivators in the northern portion of Gangpur are certainly at a disadvantage in having to deal with soil somewhat inferior in composition, but their comparative lack of success is partly the result of ignorance coupled with absence of energy.

The general condition of the total population, however, is one of prosperity, and as it is extremely difficult to obtain a sufficient supply of labourers in farming and in various trades, such as masons, carpenters, and the like, it follows that wages are based upon a fairly liberal scale.

About 85 per cent. of the people are engaged in agricultural pursuits, and about 10 per cent. are employed in industrial work of various kinds.

Rice, sugar-cane, oil-seeds, and tobacco are the chief crops, although extensive areas are cultivated for grain, pulses, and millets.

Coal, limestone, gold, and iron are found in the State, and the mining of manganese is now a most important industry. There are sawmills at Raurkela and Kalunga, but it is unlikely that any real advance will be made in the timber trade for some years to come, as the forests were ruthlessly denuded of nearly all serviceable trees prior to the promulgation of Regulations regarding felling, and before the appointment of properly trained Forest Officers, who are directly responsible to the Head of the State.

The principal exports are cotton, sesamum, arrowroot, catechu, wax, and honey, while imported articles include piece goods, salt, sugar, spices, and kerosene oil.

The Bengal-Nagpur Railway system extends for a considerable distance within the borders of the territory. There is a good road connecting the principal town of Sundargarh with the railway-station at Jharsuguda, and during recent years several others of importance, spanned by masonry and iron bridges, have been constructed or are at the present time being made.

The rivers include the Ib, the Sankh, and the South Koel, the last two-mentioned streams uniting in the eastern portion of the State and forming the Brahmani, which flows in a southwardly direction into the plains of Orissa. Cobden-Ramsay, in his Gazetteer of the "Feudatory States of Orissa," says: "The confluence of the Koel and Sankh is one of the prettiest sights in Gangpur, and it is said by local tradition to be the scene of the *amour* of the sage Parasara with the fisherman's daughter Matsya Gandha, the offspring of which was Vyasa, the reputed compiler of the Vedas and the Mahabharata." Here an important "Mela" is held once a year, and is attended by a large number of pilgrims.

The Chief of the State is responsible for the general administration of affairs, but he has "advice from the Commissioner of Orissa on important matters relating to the settlement and collection of land revenue, the imposition of taxes, the administration of justice, arrangements connected with excise, salt, opium, and disputes in which other States are concerned."

The cause of education is one in which the Maharaja takes a deep personal interest, and although the percentage of literates is still exceedingly small, it is satisfactory to note that steady progress is being made, and that State Inspectors have been appointed to supervise methods of teaching and to induce parents as well as scholars to realize the vast importance of training the young.

Some reference should be made now to the system of administration—especially with regard to land revenue—prevailing in the villages. The latter, in the State of Gangpur, says Sir W. Hunter, in his "Statistical Account of Districts," "are held either on feudal tenure or on farming leases. The feudal tenures date back to early times when the vassals of the Chief received grants of land in consideration of rendering military service and making certain payments in kind. These payments were gradually commuted to a quit rent in money, but the service conditions were rigidly enforced. When the Raja went on a journey his military fief-holders were obliged to accompany him with their *naiks*, or headmen in charge of villages, and *paiks*, or foot-soldiers." A time arrived, however, when the payments made to the State were insufficient to meet the growing demands of the Treasury, and a cess, or tax, which was regarded by headmen and *paiks* alike as being entirely distinct from ordinary rent, was levied on behalf of the Chief. The employment of *paiks* as State militia has now been discontinued in Gangpur. Certain villages are held under leases for five years by small farmers, called *gaontias*, who pay an annual rent, and when the term is extended a bonus is demanded from the occupier. The principal officials in *Gaontia* villages are the headman, the priest, and the watchman, the latter being also an assistant to the first named, who is, *ex-officio*, a police officer, in the detection of crime. The first regular survey and settlement of all cultivated lands in the State was concluded in the year 1910 for a ten-year period, and a uniform assessment was made at fair and equitable rates. This has been the means of inducing immigrants from adjoining States and Districts to settle in the State, and upon reclaimed jungle areas which have been thrown open to cultivation.

The village headmen, it will be seen, have obtained a very prominent position in the administration of the land in Gangpur, and many of these officials are occupiers of extensive areas whose productiveness has rendered them unusually wealthy men. There are, too, vast tracts of uplands handed over for cultivation to occupiers from whom no rent is required, but who, in return for their holdings, render free service to the State.

The entire area of the State is highly mineralized. On the east the Bisra Stone Lime Company have their manufacturing works and headquarters at Bisra, on the Bengal-Nagpur Railway, which is connected by a system of light railways with

THE GANGPUR FEUDATORY STATE.

1. The Rajbari. 2. Some Man-eating Tigers and some Leopards shot by Mr. Craven. 3. The Dewan's House.

the limestone quarries. The company, of which Messrs. Bird & Co., of Calcutta, are the managing agents, have lately acquired further large concessions from the State, and contemplate the construction of a broad-gauge line from Panposh, on the Bengal-Nagpur system, northwards to Raipura, on the border of the district of Ranchi, where the most valuable deposits have been located.

The Tata Iron and Steel Company hold the lease of valuable dolomite quarries near Panposh, which yield an annual output of about 75,000 tons, which are conveyed to Sakchi for utilization in the company's iron and steel works there. Manganese occurs throughout the State, but the most valuable deposits are at a village called Gariajore, about 10 miles south-east of Sundargarh. The lease of these mines is held by a Nagpur syndicate. The annual output exceeds 50,000 tons, and arrangements are in progress to double this figure. The mines are connected by a light railway with Dharuadih Station on the Bengal-Nagpur Railway.

Coal has been found in the Hemgir Zemindary, in the western portion of the State, and a mining lease for the same is held by the Hemgir-Rampur Coal Company, but work has not yet commenced.

Mica has lately been discovered in the Sarapgarh Zemindary of the State, and negotiations for a lease are in progress.

The fauna in the Feudatory States are of a diversified character, the principal carnivora being the tiger, panther, hyena, wild dog, jackal, and fox. Wild buffaloes are now nearly extinct, and bison are found in the denser portions of forests in nearly all of the States, while the tiger is frequently met with. Many of the last named are notorious "man-eaters," and Mr. Craven has relieved the Gangpur State of some of these terrors to mankind, which have been responsible for the killing of about 130 natives.

Sundargarh, the headquarters of the State, is a small town of about 3,000 inhabitants, and is situated on the Ib River, which traverses the district from north to south and finally joins the Mahanadi in the district of Sambalpur. It contains the residence of the Chief, post and telegraph offices, a court-house, a large English school, a dispensary, and other buildings of a public as well as private character.

THE HUTWA RAJ

Shakespeare, in "The Merchant of Venice," wrote that "it is a wise father who knows his own child," but with apologies to the shades of the Bard of Avon one might be tempted to paraphrase those words by saying that he must be a happy man who can trace his descent in an unbroken line for many hundreds of years through a succession of eminent men, the majority of whom have—according to the spirit of the age in which they lived—exerted a beneficial influence upon those by whom they were surrounded.

It must be remembered that in India—a country of great antiquity—traditions have played an important part in its history, but these legends have been handed down most carefully from father to son by poets or bards who held special appointments as such in the houses of nobles of the land.

Generation has followed generation and kings and other rulers have arisen and have passed away, yet a number of Rajas of to-day are proud of the fact that amid all the wars, rebellions, and political upheavals of Governments, their possessions have remained practically intact.

In a "Brief History of the Hutwa Raj," compiled in 1909 by Bebendra Nath Dutta, Diwan of the estate, the writer says that in the Province of Bengal and Behar there are many ancient Rajs which pay revenue under the Permanent Settlement, and that "of these ancient and aristocratic houses Hutwa is one of the most eminent, its pedigree is one of the oldest in the land, the family has a stirring and somewhat romantic history, and traces its chronology back to remote antiquity."

The Hutwa family belongs to the caste known as Trikarma Brahmins, or, in popular phraseology, Bhuinhar Brahmins, a name which has been bestowed upon those who disregard the last three of the customary duties of a Brahmin, which are: (*a*) performing sacrifices, (*b*) giving of alms, (*c*) acquiring knowledge, (*d*) officiating as priests at the time of sacrifices, (*e*) taking of alms, and (*f*) teaching others.

The Diwan above referred to is confident that the earliest historical records of the Hutwa Raj were either destroyed or improperly removed, but tradition speaks of a Raja Birsen, from whom the present Maharaja is 103rd in the line of descent. An actual date regarding this ruler's accession cannot, unfortunately, be given, but by allowing twenty-five years as a moderate estimate for the life of each Raja, it would appear that he must have been in power about 600 years before the Christian Era. There are evidences, apart from manuscripts, that Raja Kaleyan Mull, the 86th in descent, was the first to receive the title of Maharaja, and that his successor, Raja Khemkaran Sahi, obtained the two titles of Maharaja Bahadur and Sahi from the Emperor of Delhi, but the earliest authentic records commence with the time of Fateh Sahi, the 99th Maharaja.

The history of this ruler is one of the darkest pages in the Hutwa annals. Cruelties and acts of violence were common; even murders were attributed to him; and he crowned his infamous practices by assisting in an attempt to overthrow British power. Though courageous to a degree, he was controlled by unworthy ambitions which caused him to make alliances with other potentates who were inveterate opponents of British authority, and who ultimately led him into open rebellion. Buoyed up by the plausible and tempting overtures of these rulers, he not only refused to pay revenue to the East India Company (who had obtained administrative powers in Behar), but he took up arms against the Company's forces, and the latter had considerable difficulty in overcoming him.

Fateh Sahi then fled into the jungle, whence he had easy access to the dominions of an independent prince, where the British troops could not touch him; and he forthwith commenced a series of freebooting excursions with the object of plundering villages and preventing the collection of revenue. The Hutwa estates were, about the year 1774, taken into direct management by the Government for a year, when they were let to one Babu Basant Sahi, cousin of the Maharaja, and Mir Jumla was appointed Superintendent of Government Revenue. In May of the following year these two officials were killed by Fateh Sahi during a night attack upon them at Jadopore, on the bank of the Gundak River. Several attempts were made to arrest the Maharaja, but he always managed to escape into friendly territories, and the object of the troops was rendered all the more difficult by reason of the fact that the Hutwa people were attached to their ruler and gave him such protection as was in their power to bestow.

Matters had not improved in 1786, when, with the Maharaja still at large and the country in a state of terror, the Government was approached with the

THE HUTWA RAJ.

1. Interior of Durbar Hall. 2. Residential Palace.

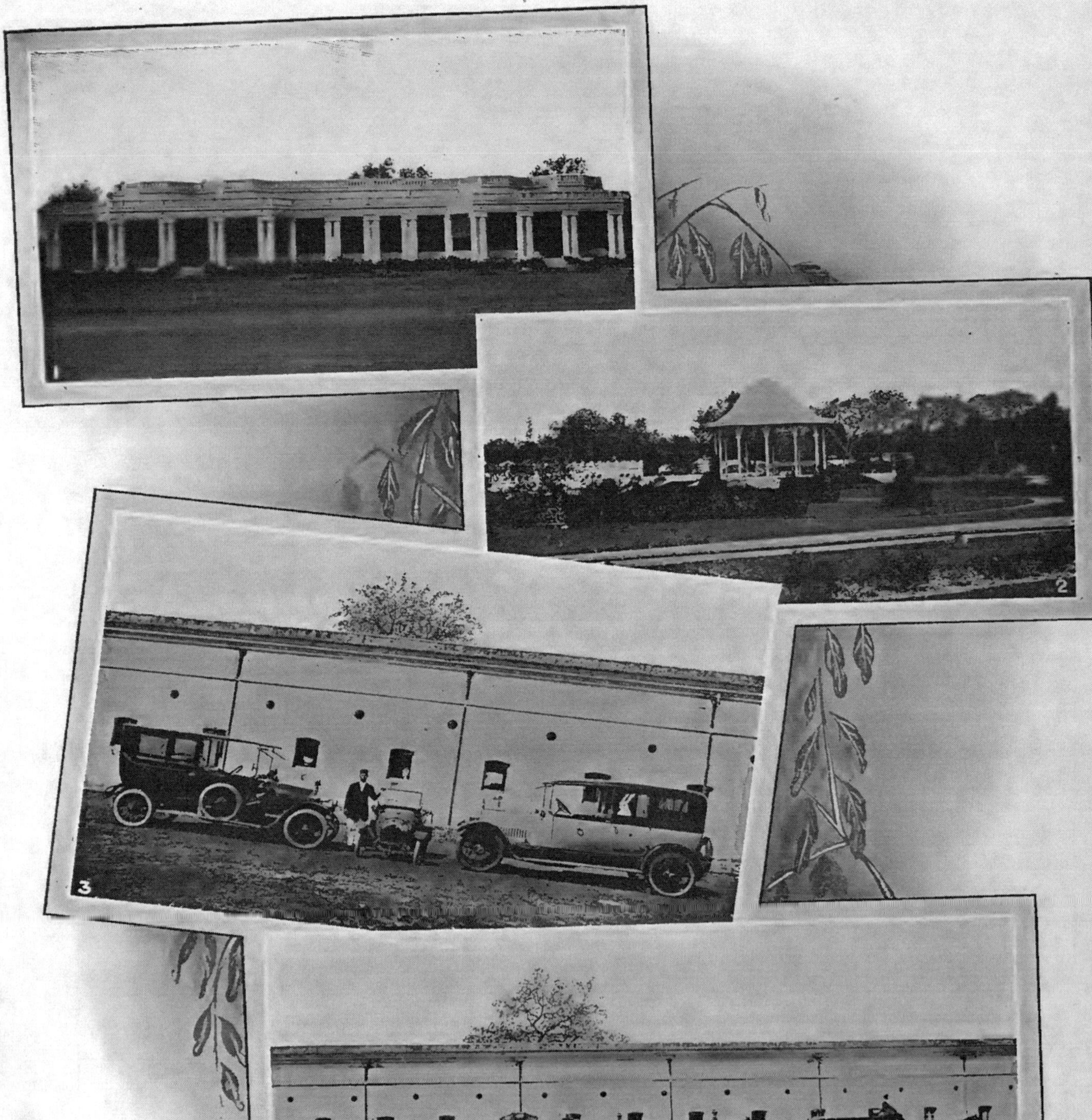

THE HUTWA RAJ.

1. Manager's Bungalow. 2. Kaserbagh Gardens. 3. Motor-Cars. 4. Carriages.

THE HUTWA RAJ.

1. OLD FORT AND PALACE. 2. VICTORIA HOSPITAL. 3. INTERIOR OF OPERATING-ROOM. 4. EDEN SCHOOL.

view of securing the deposition of the rebel and the subsequent appointment of his successor; but it was felt that the time had not arrived when it would be politic to accede to the request.

Shortly after this date Fateh Sahi went to reside on a portion of his property, in the district of Goruckpore, wisely abandoning his lawless acts; and he does not appear to have taken any steps—even if he had the desire—to be reinstated, as in the year 1808 he renounced this estate in favour of his family and became a *fakir*.

Such was the end of the career of a man whose abilities were misapplied, and who, though courageous against foes, was weak enough to be lured into the commission of crimes of the deepest dye.

During the retirement of Fateh Sahi the Government of Lord Cornwallis, the Viceroy, bestowed the Hutwa estates upon Chhattradhari Sahi, but as the latter was at that time only five years of age the property was placed in the management of the Court of Wards. The appointee attained his majority in the year 1802, and one of his first acts was "to found the seat of Hutwa, where he built his palace and fort, surrounding them by moats." The British Government did not feel able to recognize the new ruler in a formal manner as Maharaja, as Fateh Sahi was still living and had not been deprived of the title; but in 1837 representations were made by the Commissioner of Patna that "he could confidently assert that the general character and circumstances of the Maharaja were such that this honour might be conferred upon him with propriety, without fear of lowering the value of the distinction in the public estimation. His family is well known, as an individual he is highly respectable and respected, of commanding wealth and proportionate influence." The title was therefore conferred by the Government of Lord Auckland on September 10, 1837, Fateh Sahi having died in the meantime.

If there was one trait in the character of Chhattradhari Sahi which seemed to outshine all others, it was that of loyalty and whole-hearted devotion of his resources to British authority, and conspicuous examples of his services were manifested during the Sonthal rebellion in 1854 and in the Mutiny, which occurred three years later. At the time of the last-named outbreak, the Maharaja, who was then about seventy years of age, adopted such measures for the maintenance of peace in his Raj that not a single case of disaffection occurred, although the adjoining districts of Goruckpore and Shahabad were seething with rebellion. Further than that, he kept the Government well informed of movements of rebels; he subsequently collected a large body of armed men for guarding the river *ghats* and the private residences of Government officials; and he finally succeeded in inflicting a crushing blow on the rebels.

The Maharaja was the recipient of many congratulatory letters from public officials, and Sir Frederick James Halliday, then Lieutenant-Governor of Bengal, wrote as follows: "I have to offer my acknowledgment for the loyalty and good-feeling evinced by you towards the Government. I have noticed with great satisfaction the willing assistance you have rendered to the local officers in the district of Saran and the measures you have taken for the apprehension of any mutineers who may attempt to take shelter in your Zemindary."

The strain of the Mutiny had a serious effect upon the constitution of the Maharaja, and he died at Hutwa on March 16, 1858, beloved by his subjects, honoured by all with whom he came into contact, and enjoying the complete confidence of the British Government.

Writing to the great-grandson and successor of the late Maharaja, the Secretary to the Government of India said: "I have known him since the year 1837, when I was an Assistant at Chapra, and I always entertained a high respect for him, especially for the exemplary way in which he discharged his duties as a landlord and as a loyal subject of the British Government. The manner in which he behaved, from the first breaking-out of these unhappy mutinies until the day of his death, was such as to command the admiration of all his friends, and to entitle him to a high place in the estimation of the rulers of the country."

The Maharaja was devoted to intellectual pursuits, and as the patron of Sanskrit learning "he opened a Sanskrit school, under the supervision of the renowned Ramnijaram Swami (the greatest savant in India of that age), wherein nearly a thousand students from all parts of India received free education and food."

The late Maharaja's two sons predeceased their father; but each of them left two sons, and Rajendra Protap Sahi, the eldest-born of Ugra Pratap Sahi (heir in right of primogeniture, but who waived his claim), was the favourite great-grandchild of the late ruler, and he was eventually recognized by the Government, with the title of Maharaja Bahadur. The young Maharaja, on his accession to power, gave abundant proof of the confidence which his great-grandfather had reposed in him, as he rendered invaluable aid to the Government in suppressing the Mutiny, and his personal example of devotion to the Throne was a great inspiration to his subjects. The Commissioner of Patna gave a must favourable report upon this matter to the Government, and the latter forwarded a letter in reply, saying: "You will be so good as to express his Honour's acknowledgment to the great-grandson of the late Raja of Hutwa for his ready and cordial co-operation with the authorities, and assure him that his loyal behaviour will not be lost sight of."

The Government redeemed its promise in the year 1860, when His Excellency the Viceroy (Lord Mayo) "authorized the Lieutenant-Governor of Bengal to confer on the Maharaja the propriety right in confiscated villages in Shahabad yielding a gross rental of Rs. 20,000; in the following year the Maharaja was allowed to retain a gun in the Fort of Hutwa, and in 1869 was granted the privilege of private entrée to Government House."

These honours conferred upon the Maharaja were a tribute to his rulership, and were highly appreciated by him; but other events were occurring which were a source of great trouble, and which illustrated Shakespeare's dictum that "uneasy lies the head that wears a crown." Shortly after his succession, two members of a branch of the family commenced legal proceedings with the view of upsetting the will of the previous Maharaja, and of having the Raj divided on the plea that it was an ordinary Zemindary. The case was argued successively before the District Judge of Sarun, the High Court of Judicature in Calcutta, and the Privy Council in London, the last-named court deciding that the Raj was impartible, and that the succession of Rajendra Pratap Sahi was strictly in accordance with the "Kulachar," or rules of inheritance prevalent in the family. The Maharaja's solicitude for the welfare of his people grew year by year until 1871, when, to the sincere regret of a very large number of friends—independently of his own people—he died at the early age of 33 years.

His only son, Krishen Pratap Sahi, was a minor of fifteen, and the management of the estates was placed in the hands of the Court of Wards for a period of three years, until 1874, when he attained his majority and received the titles of Maharaja Bahadur. The Maharaja exercised a keen personal interest in the management of the Raj, and many reforms tending to the welfare of the *ryots* were instituted by him. He caused many beautiful buildings to be erected, chief among them being a new palace, containing the magnificently furnished and decorated Durbar Hall, which is referred to in another portion of these notes.

The Maharaja, as a landowner and an enthusiast in political and economic questions, was held in high esteem by the Government, and he was on several occasions offered a seat in the Legislative Council, although an inherent retiring disposition caused him to decline the honour. He possessed a thorough knowledge of the English language, and edited or translated many important works into Sanskrit, while his services and gifts to religious and educational institutions were of a remarkably generous character. A number of free primary and secondary schools were established by him, and he maintained a high-class English school at Hutwa, with scholarships for advanced education. A recognition of his public and private benefactions was bestowed upon him in 1889, when he was created a Knight Commander of the Most Eminent Order of the Indian Empire.

During the year 1896 the Maharaja was attacked by a very serious illness, and after six months of intense suffering he passed away on October 20th, when forty years of age, leaving a son aged four years, together with an infant daughter. The Raj was again managed by the Court of Wards, but the children found a most devoted mother and teacher in the person of Her Highness the present Maharani Sahiba of Hutwa. The latter's guardianship of her young son was of a very onerous character owing to family troubles.

The present ruler, Guru Mahadeo Asram Prasad Sahi, was born in the year 1893. He came of age in July 1914, the title of Maharaja Bahadur having been conferred upon him some months earlier. The installation ceremony was performed by Sir Charles Stewart Bayley, the Lieutenant-Governor of Behar and Orissa, at a Grand Durbar held at Hutwa on December 2, 1914; and the religious ceremonies of the *guddi* followed some months later amid great rejoicings and festivities, which continued for more than a month on a lavish scale commensurate with the wealth and dignity of the Hutwa House. When in his teens the present Maharaja Bahadur developed the most noble qualities of head and heart, and he was described as "most amiable and intelligent, particularly gentlemanly in his manner, and a thorough English scholar"; and it may be added that he has fully maintained the promise of his youth. He is noted for his hospitality, and keeps an open house for European residents in the district, who gather weekly at Hutwa for games of polo, while the yearly festivities at Hutwa during the Dusserah is a great event in Behar. The Maharaja is a most devoted son to his mother, the venerable Maharani Sahiba, and most considerate to his tenants and the officers of his Raj. He is extremely pious and whole-heartedly loyal to the British Throne, and on the breaking out of the Great European War, he and his mother most promptly made a handsome donation of Rs. 1,00,000 to the Indian War Relief Fund.

The Hutwa Raj estate—one of the largest in Eastern India—covers an area of about 800 square miles (512,000 acres), and it is distributed over the districts of Saran, Champaran, Muzaffarpur, Patna, Shahabad, Darjeeling, and Calcutta in Bengal, and Benares and Goruckpore in the United Provinces of Agra and Oudh. Nearly all of the land is in a high state of cultivation, and this accounts for the fact that there is a consequent lack of good pastoral ground for improving the breeds of horses and cattle. A stud farm of 500 acres has, however, been started at Siripore—twelve miles distant from Hutwa—and this is now producing fodder crops for the rearing of buffaloes and other cattle under the management of a European superintendent. Taking the estate as a whole, it is noticed that the principal crops are rice, wheat, barley, oats, maize, beans, peas, sweet potatoes, cotton, hemp, and flax, together with a small quantity of tobacco, sugar-cane, indigo, and opium, which is grown under Government licence.

Very little of the original jungle now remains, the only portions which can be designated even as small forests being situated at Thawe, Husseypore, and Charkia, in which there are wolves, jackals, wild pigs, porcupines, and nilghai. The principal timber trees include mango, red cotton, tamarind, jack, banyan, and palms, while a number of mahogany, *sal*, teak, and fir trees have been planted around the town of Hutwa.

The Raj is very densely populated, its inhabitants being about 600,000 in numbers, or rather more than 700 persons to the square mile; and the annual rent-roll exceeds thirteen lakhs of rupees.

The town of Hutwa, said to be "one of the cleanest and most picturesque places in the Province of Behar," is situated about three miles distant from the railway-station of Hathua, on the Siwan-Thawe branch of the Bengal and North Western Railway system. The country surrounding Hutwa is remarkably well wooded, and its park-like appearance, with towers of palaces and temples rising above the foliage of the trees, is not the least of its many charms.

The Maharajas of the Raj have resided here since the beginning of the nineteenth century, and the palace is an exceedingly beautiful building containing a large number of rooms, which have been fitted and furnished with exquisite appointments at a cost of large sums of money. The floors of many of the apartments are of solid marble, and the decorative work throughout is of that peculiarly handsome character which is only seen in Oriental mansions.

It may be mentioned that one room contains a bedstead made of gold and silver, and this is only a solitary instance of the magnificence of the interior of the whole palace. The banqueting-hall, library, and billiard-room are also fine examples in architectural and upholstering work. The Durbar-hall, situated on the western side of the courtyard of the palace, was completed in the year 1896. It was designed by Diwan Debendra Nath Dutt, and a description of the building may be extracted from his History of the Raj already referred to. He says: "It is a lofty building of brick, and faced with fine white plaster stucco resembling marble. At the four corners are towers in the Egyptian style of architecture. It has a portico of majestic proportions, and marble steps leading to a vestibule, with staircases to right and left leading to the upper story. This entrance is quite French-like, and it opens directly on to the lofty Durbar-hall, which is furnished according to the period of Louis XV. The upholstery of the gilded chairs is of rich brocaded damask silk, which harmonizes beautifully with the delicate tapestry-like painted walls. The state

THE HUTWA RAJ.

1. Gopalmandir Temple. 2. Durbar Hall and Palace. 3. Thawe Temple. 4. Thawe House.

THE HUTWA RAJ.

1. Elephant Lines. 2. Sripore Farm Cattle. 3, 4. Cattle.

chairs and couches at the southern end are of gold and silver and upholstered in rich crimson velvet. Enormous Venetian mirrors reflect in endless variety the beauties of the room, and wonderful glass chandeliers hang from the ceiling, which is decorated with rectangular *alto relievo* panels of polished teak in the Queen Anne style. The wall at the southern end is adorned with a portrait of Her Majesty the late Queen Victoria, while facing it at the northern end is one of the late Maharaja Bahadur. The side walls are embellished with oil-paintings of Their Majesties the present King and Queen (when Prince and Princess of Wales), the late Czar of Russia, the King of Spain, and Royal personages, together with others of Presidents of Republics and noted statesmen. Suites of apartments on the upper story are decorated in different colours, such as the red, green, and other rooms, and the artistic work on the panels of the doors is very effective in its representations of many leading Shakespearean characters. When the annual Dusserah festival is held in this hall, the Maharaja receives a large number of officials and European guests, and he then wears "a tunic embroidered with gold and pearls, and dons a richly ornamented sword; while his neck and arms, the front of his tunic, and turban are resplendent with jewels of great value, forming part of the priceless collection left him by his father, and which comprise the accumulations of many generations of wealthy ancestors." There are many other very imposing structures in the vicinity of the Durbar-hall, and one of the first to be noticed is the residential palace of the late Maharaja, known as "Rajendra Bhaban," in which may be seen a very fine collection of works of art and a number of sacred, mythical, and allegorical pictures relating to Hinduism. Another one, called the Manager's House, is a very handsome and commodious building, with ample accommodation for thirty guests, is situated in a finely wooded park, and the pleasing picture presented to the visitor brings to the mind very forcibly those "stately homes of England" concerning which so much has been written. Not far from this house is the Eden School, opened in 1881, which was built by the late Maharaja, and adjoining it is a library which contains a valuable collection of historical and fictional works. An extensive enclosure on the south-western side of the gardens contains a fort, which was in earlier years the residence of Maharajas, but which now embraces the Raj Treasury and other official buildings. A huge vault of solid masonry walls and iron girders sunk in the ground to a depth of 10 feet, which might be fairly described as being as safe as "the old lady of Threadneedle Street," has been the receptacle for a number of years of about 60 lakhs of rupees, each lakh being enclosed in a separate box.

The Great Temple of the Gopalji is a very fine structure situated in the western portion of the town of Hutwa, and its treasures include images of Radha and Krishna and a number of ancient oil-paintings, together with a library of valuable Sanskrit works.

One of the most cherished desires of the late Maharaja was that he might be able to construct a hospital worthy of being associated with the name of Her late Majesty Queen Victoria; but his premature death prevented the realization of his scheme, and the present Maharani Sahiba has made it a part of her life-work to give effect to the wishes of her late husband. The foundation-stone was laid in 1899 by Sir John Woodburn, K.C.S.I., then Lieutenant-Governor of Bengal, and about four years later the hospital was opened for the reception of patients. It is a magnificent building, in which there are eighty beds, separate wards for infectious cases, two fine operating-rooms, a complete plant for sterilizing purposes, a dark-room for ophthalmic work, and a dispensary for the relief of suffering and needy poor persons. The medical staff comprises three practitioners, one of whom is a lady.

The Maharaja has a very beautiful country seat at Thawe, which is one of the most densely wooded and picturesque portions of the Hutwa Raj, and in it may be seen interesting relics of an old fortress. Other mansions belonging to this young ruler are situated at Chapra, Patna, Benares, Calcutta, and Kurseong.

The Raj stables are substantially built of brick, and they contain about 100 houses for harness and saddle, while the adjoining coach-houses are filled with a considerable number of state and other equipages. It should be mentioned here that the horses include eight English-bred animals, which were brought to India for the use of Their Majesties the King and Queen at the Delhi Durbar, together with several pure white ones which are trained for dancing at festivals.

The motor-garage is occupied by a dozen or more cars of a most costly description, one of them, a "Cadillac," fitted with electric gearing and all latest improvements, being valued at no less than Rs. 25,000.

A recreation-ground comprising 300 acres is devoted to all kinds of sports, of which the Maharaja is a warm supporter, and polo and other manly games are provided for the occupants of the palaces.

The Maharaja has inherited many lovable features of character from Her Highness the Maharani Sahiba, and it is her diligent training and teaching which have instilled into the young ruler a keen and affectionate interest in the welfare of the Hutwa people, and which manifests itself in the many benevolent actions which stand to his credit.

On the authority of Diwan Devendra Nath Dutt's History of Huttwa, we give the following figures relating to the various amounts paid from the Raj Treasury for educational, medical, and other institutions showing the average sums expended in ten recent years:—

The Raj pays annually—

	Rs.
As Government revenue ...	2,00,075
As road, public works, and embankment cesses ...	78,545
For education	19,138
For medical relief	24,112
For agricultural and sanitary improvements	41,073
For Sripore Experimental Farm	30,000
For religious purposes ...	31,462
For charities and donations	61,153

THE KANDI AND PAIKPARA RAJ.

The Kandi and Paikpara Raj family, generally known in the Presidency of Bengal as "Lala Babu's family," belong to the "Uttarrardhi" class of Kayasthas, and their origin is traced from Anadibar Sinha, who settled in Bengal in the ninth century during the flourishing reign of King Adisur of Gour.

It is a matter for regret that the early history of many noble families of India is shrouded in so much obscurity, and that authentic literary documents are not forthcoming, but it is some satisfaction that local traditions have in numerous instances been so faithfully handed down from generation to generation that substantially reliable particulars concerning these ancestors can be obtained.

THE KANDI AND PAIKPARA RAJ.

BELGACHIA VILLA, SOUTHERN VIEW.

THE KANDI AND PAIKPARA RAJ.

Belcachia Villa, Northern View.

THE KANDI AND PAIKPARA RAJ.

THE RECEPTION HALL, BELGACHIA VILLA.

In connection with the Raj now under notice it is clearly established by traditional accounts that Rana Madan Sinha and Raja Laksmidhar, the fifth and eighth in descent, were great feudal lords to the Hindu Kings of Bengal, and that the ninth in succession, Vyas Sinha, a devoted minister of King Ballal Sen, suffered a martyr's death for the sake of his religion. From the same source it is learned that Raja Binayaka Sinha and Raja Laksmidhar II, the twelfth and thirteenth descendants, were feudal lords to the Pathan Kings of Delhi, rendering immense services to them in the internal administration of the empire, and, further, that the brothers, the Rajas Jibadhara and Pravakara, were noted for their strict adherence to religious practices and their munificent charitable donations, they being regarded as heads of their community, a distinction, by the way, which is enjoyed by the family even to this day.

Really authenticated history commences with the time of Harekrishna Sinha, who first settled in Kandi, in the district of Murshidabad, where he carried on an extensive business as banker and silk merchant, but he subsequently removed to Boalia, a village in the district of Rajshahi, which, together with others, was acquired from the Nawab of Murshidabad.

Harekrishna, a zealous Vaishnava, left a son named Murlidhar, whose second son, Gouranga Sunder, amassed great wealth and became possessor of a number of *mahals*, *taluqs*, and *lakhiraj* lands. The latter obtained from Shah Alum II, Emperor of Delhi, a *sanad* in perpetuity in order to enable him to endow the shrine of Thakur Sri Sri Radhaballav Jiu, and also received from the same source the title of *Mazumdar*. He adopted as his successor his nephew Radha Kanta Sinha, who held office under the "Bangadhikaris," and who rendered exceedingly valuable services to the British Government at the time of the establishment of the *Diwani* of Bengal, Behar and Orissa, for which he was rewarded by the Government with the grant of a *sayar mahal*, together with the right of collecting octroi at Hughly. Radha Kanta Sinha further gave great assistance to the British forces when Suraj-ud-Daula attacked Calcutta in 1757, and after the memorable battle of Plassey in June of that year he was appointed to manage the Revenue Department of Mir Jafar, who had become Nawab of Bengal upon the authority of Lord Clive. He was subsequently installed as *Diwan* by Clive when he proposed the abolition of the dual form of Government set up by that general, which, in a word, gave the British the right to receive revenue and maintain the army, while criminal jurisdiction was vested in the Nawab of Bengal. Radha Kanta died in the year 1179 (Bengal style), and by a deed of appointment he entrusted the management of his estates, together with the control of all matters relating to the worship of their family deity, Thakur Sri Sri Radhaballav Jiu, to his two brothers, Radha Charan and Ganga Gobinda. The last-named was largely responsible for the abolition of the joint administration above referred to, and when that event took place he was appointed by Warren Hastings to the high office of *Diwan* of the Committee of Revenue. He was afterwards selected for the important post of Head Commissioner with power to make investigations with regard to the settlement of revenue, and it is recorded that he discharged his duties in a most exemplary manner. His high attainments and strength of character secured for him the confidence of the people, and he was frequently called upon to solve difficult problems in State administration, and to undertake missions which could only be entrusted to a person possessing sound judgment combined with great tact. Warren Hastings, on the eve of his departure from India, expressed in a public speech his high appreciation of Ganga Gobinda's tenure of the *diwani* of the Calcutta Committee of the Honourable The East India Company, and further referred at length to the exceptional ability and fidelity displayed by him in the execution of most responsible official duties.

It was at the instance of Ganga Gobinda that Warren Hastings made grants of land which had a rent roll of Rs. 2,38,061-12-1.

Ganga Gobinda was a staunch supporter of Hindu religious and other customs, and this trait in his character was exemplified in the imposing funeral rites on the death of his mother, and in the marvellous *Sradha* ceremony, when tens of thousands of people were present, exclusive of invited *pandits*, rajas, and noblemen from all parts of India. The guests were received in large *shamianas* erected for the purpose, and they were lavishly supplied with ghee, oil, rice, honey, milk, vegetables, and other food. The cost of this entertainment, amounting to 20 lakhs of rupees, given in days of "peace and prosperity," is evidence of the magnitude of the gathering. Other large sums of money were spent on several occasions, and Ganga Gobinda not only founded four temples, but also liberally supported pilgrims, *pandits*, scholars, and a large number of needy persons. He was a great advocate of Sanskrit learning, and contributed a considerable amount of money towards the advancement of that language. He died in the year 1206 (Bengal style), leaving a son, Pran Krishna Sinha, who, having been adopted by his uncle Radha Kanta Sinha, became heir to two estates and the recipient of the major portion of the wealth of the family.

Pran Krishna for a number of years held the office of Naib Diwan, and also increased the area of his estates, but as neither wealth nor honours was sought by him, he retired into private life, devoting his energies to the cause of religion. He died in the year 1215 (Bengal style), leaving an only son, Krishna Chandra Sinha, who proved to be an exceedingly pious man. His early training included a thorough grounding in the Persian, Sanskrit, and Arabic languages, but the most remarkable feature of his character was an intensely benevolent spirit, which was manifested while he was still young. It is related that, when seventeen years of age, a Brahman asked him to give a thousand rupees for the marriage expenses of his daughter, and Krishna Chandra at once instructed his father's cashier to pay the amount, but that official reported the matter to his employer, who ordered him to comply with the request on the understanding that Krishna Chandra should in future make all such gifts out of his personal earnings. The youth thereupon forsook his studies and went to Burdwan, where he became *Sharistadar*, and, in 1803, Diwan in charge of Settlement. During those years, however, he acquired a considerable amount of money, out of which he purchased a number of properties and *pergannas*, in addition to the *zemindary* of Bisalakshmipur. Krishna Chandra and his father never met again after the incident connected with the Brahman's visit, but when Pran Krishna Sinha died, his son celebrated the *Sradha* ceremonies with great splendour. Shortly after that date Krishna Chandra resided chiefly in Calcutta, spending much of his time in the company of learned Brahmans, acquiring a knowledge of the *Puranas* and other literature. He subsequently retired into private life, and after fully providing for his only son's education, and making arrangements for the management of his vast estates, he removed to Brindabun, in the division of Agra, in the United Provinces of Agra and Oudh, where he gave himself up entirely to religious exercises and the bestowal of charities.

Krishna Chandra took with him to Brindabun a sum of 20 lakhs of rupees, which he expended in gifts and in the erection of a magnificent temple in honour of Sri Sri Krishna Chandra Jiu. Sir Charles Metcalfe, who had been made acquainted with Krishna Chandra's ascetic life and his extraordinary benevolence, presented him to the Emperor of Delhi as one who had rendered meritorious services to the East India Company in positions of great responsibility, and acting upon a suggestion of the Resident, the Emperor desired to confer upon Krishna Chandra (then familiarly known as "Lalu Babu"), the title of Maharaja Bahadur, but this honour was respectfully declined.

After the construction and endowment of temples at Brindaban, Krishna Chandra decided to become a *Yogi*, and with this end in view he went to reside at Gobardhan in the division of Agra, where he became a disciple of Krishna Das Babaji. After his assumption of *sanyash* he never associated with worldly people of either sex, and when the Maharani of Gwalior insisted on making her obeisance to such a holy man, he attempted to avoid her and was accidentally trodden upon by one of the lady's horses. That sad event occurred in the forty-sixth year of his age.

Sri Narayan Sinha, the next in succession, was a minor on the death of his father Krishna Chandra, or "Lala Babu," and the management of the estates fell into the hands of his mother, the Rani Katyayani, but as the duties were too onerous for her the Revenue Board assumed full control, leaving the Rani free to act as guardian to her son.

Sri Narayan, whose youth was carefully fostered by his mother, gave early promise of becoming a worthy son of his illustrious father, and while his educational studies were of a comprehensive character he manifested a pronounced talent for musical and vocal accomplishments, but he was by no means neglectful of art and literature. Unfortunately, however, he died while still young, having previously given permission to his two wives to adopt sons after his death. This was done according to the tenets of Hindu law, and the Rajas Pratap Chandra and Iswara Chandra were in due course selected. The Rani Katyayani charged one of her large estates with the payment of an annual sum for the upkeep of the famous Thakurbati temple at Cossipore which she had previously founded, and she, further, expended Rs. 500,000 in *Anna meru* and *Tuladan* ceremonies.

The *Dev Seva* and the charity house established by her at Cossipore remain to this day as a lasting memorial to her benevolent nature.

The Rani appeared to be tireless in her devotion to charitable works, and after having spent a further sum of 16 lakhs of rupees in donations to needy institutions and persons, she passed away in the year 1268 (Bengal style).

Raja Pratap Chandra Sinha proved to be a worthy representative of this distinguished family, and he contributed liberally towards the erection of the Medical College Fever Hospital at Calcutta.

He was an enthusiastic supporter of education, establishing several primary and high schools, including the High English School at Kandi. He was further a strong advocate in favour of the movement for the remarriage of Hindu widows, to which fund he gave a quarter of a lakh of rupees. The Raja was Vice-President of the British Indian Association (which was originated by him), and of several other district societies, and he was the prime mover in the revival of Hindu drama. The free dispensary at the Paikpara Rajbati was founded by the Raja, and briefly, it may be said that he was a staunch patron of a host of other praiseworthy institutions.

Notwithstanding his great abilities and his enormous wealth, the Raja was unostentatious in manner and kindly in disposition; as a zemindar he was considerate to his tenants, evincing a real desire to promote their welfare; and, indeed, one might say that he appeared to live almost solely in order to benefit his fellow-men. In his more public life he was known to be a keen sportsman, and one who rendered most valuable help to the Government during the Mutiny of 1857.

His unselfish services were rewarded by his being made a Raja Bahadur in 1854, and by his appointment to a Companionship of the Star of India, an honour which was conferred by Lord Canning, then Viceroy of India. The Raja died in 1866 at the early age of thirty-nine, leaving his widow, Rani Padmamukhi, and four sons.

Kumar Sarat Chandra Sinha, the youngest son of Raja Pratap Chandra Sinha, was born in the year 1859, and his early education was received at the Metropolitan Institution in Calcutta, but he was subsequently instructed by eminent tutors in his own home. In later years he became an expert in the art of photography and in engineering, and he submitted his special knowledge of these subjects to a practical test by remodelling the Cossipore Thakurbati and the mansion at Belgachia, near Calcutta, which belongs to the family. That palatial building, surrounded by sparious and artistically laid out gardens, was visited by His late Majesty King Edward VII, when Prince of Wales, in 1875, and in 1882 by the Marquis of Ripon, when festivities on a grand scale were held.

The Kumar was a public-spirited man, taking a keen interest in matters which tended for the good, not only of his own people, but of the community at large. Mention might be made of his foundation of the "Uttar-rardhi Kayastha Sabha," an institution for the furtherance of the educational, social, and moral progress of his own people, of his liberal donations to the Victoria Memorial Hall now being erected in Calcutta, to the Jessore Water Works scheme, the establishment of a *dharamsala* at Muttra, the founding of two scholarships in the University of Calcutta, and a charitable dispensary at Kandi. He managed his own estates with the assistance of highly paid efficient employees, and his consideration for his staff and strictly honourable dealings with his tenants made him beloved by all who knew him, and he was succeeded by his only son Kumar Birendra Chandra Sinha, who is now (1917) the eldest representative of the princely house of Paikpara.

It has been truly said of some men that they are at a disadvantage by being the sons of their fathers, implying that their sires were particularly famous as statesmen, politicians, scholars, or as princes among merchants. True as this aphorism may be in thousands of instances, it certainly cannot be applied to Kumar Birendra Chandra Sinha, as he is as good a landlord, as keenly intellectual, and as munificent in his liberality as his predecessors.

The Kumar was born in December 1881, and his early scholastic training was received at the Metropolitan Institution at Calcutta, while his education was completed under the very efficient guidance of the learned pandit, Hari Mohan Bandyapadhyaya. He is a student in every sense of the word, being passionately

THE KANDI AND PAIKPARA RAJ.

THE KANDI AND PAIKPARA RAJ.

Kumar Birendra Chandra Sinha.

fond of literature, general history, philosophy, and the English and Sanskrit languages, and he has obtained a high degree of efficiency in photography, horticulture, and the decorative arts and sciences. Prominent among his personal characteristics are the virtues of thrift, perseverance, patience, and industry, and in the management of his extensive estates he is noted for his deeply rooted interest in the welfare of his tenants and for a due appreciation of the excellent assistance rendered by his large staff of employees.

The Kumar has made such improvements in the mansion at Belgachia that it is now recognized as one of the "show places" near Calcutta, and his studious nature has led him to make regular additions of standard works to an already well-stocked library. He may not be regarded as an orator—that, perhaps, is not an unmixed blessing in these days of super-abundant talking—but if his speeches be few, his kindly actions towards his fellowmen are worth far more than volumes of words uttered merely for the sake of speaking. The Kumar is therefore a man of action; he thinks intelligently; he arrives quickly at just decisions; and he is prompt in doing what he believes to be his duty. A warm-hearted and philanthropic man, he endeavours to do the greatest good to the greatest number, and even in religious matters he is no bitter sectarian, but is broad-minded in his views, showing great tolerance for all castes and creeds. His amiable and refined manners have endeared him to many highly placed Government officials, and even the members of the Government manifested their appreciation of his sterling merits by appointing him an Honorary First-class Magistrate for the Presidency of Bengal. He was further honoured in 1906 when he was selected as page to His Majesty the King (then the Prince of Wales) at a reception given during a visit to India in that year. The Kumar is a zealous custodian of the traditions of his noble and ancient family, and one of these—a reputation for liberality—is not in the slightest danger of being lowered by the present head of the house. His charitable activities are not by any means confined to donations to people of his own race as the following instances (*inter alia*) of his liberality will clearly prove. He made large grants in aid of persons who suffered from the effects of an earthquake in the Kangra Valley in 1905; he constructed a burning ghat at Cossipore; he gave Rs. 50,000 for the Tropical School of Medicine in the Calcutta Medical College; and he has subscribed most liberally to various relief funds during the course of the European War. The Kumar has always taken a leading part in public movements, and the success which attended the demonstrations in connection with the King Edward Memorial in the northern suburbs of Calcutta was largely attributable to the zeal manifested by him as a member of the committee. He is a prominent member of the British Indian Association, and is on the governing body of a number of societies and institutions throughout India.

THE KANIKA RAJ

Some time about A.D. 1200 a brother of the then Chief of Mayurbhanj, by name Bhujabal Bhanja, acquired by conquest a small territory in what is now known as Kanika. The place was then ruled by a Raja of low caste, and Bhujabal Bhanja, having subdued the Raja, set up a Government of his own and thus founded the Bhanja Raj of this Killa, the status of which was recognized by the Vishnuvite or Gajapati (Gangetic) dynasty of Orissa in the middle of the thirteenth century of the Christian era.

The Killa originally consisted of what is now known as Elaka Chhamuka, to which the portion lying in the District of Balasore, and called Panchmuka, was soon added. Elaka Kerara was some time after acquired, probably by conquest, the date of which cannot now be ascertained. The last Elaka Kaladwip, which until the close of the eighteenth century formed part of a separate Raj known as Harichandan, was acquired by matrimonial alliance with its last Raja, whose daughter was married to Raja Balabhadra Bhanja Bahadur, of Kanika. The Killa is situated along the seacoast on both sides of the estuary of Dhamra, extending about 20 miles inland, and contains an area of 440 square miles, with a population of 100,000 souls.

The seat of the Raj was originally at a place called Bajarpur, on the right bank of the Baitarani River, and was afterwards removed to Righagarh, on the right bank of the Brahmani River. The latter place having proved unhealthy, it has since been removed to Rajkanika, which is situated directly on the Cuttack-Chandbally road, about four miles to the south of the Chandbally Port. The place is easily accessible from Cuttack and Calcutta by steamer plying with the port of Chandbally, and by rail from Bhadrak, the nearest station on the Bengal-Nagpur Railway.

The heraldic emblem of the family is the figure of a peacock, from which is derived the name of the Feudatory State of Mayurbhanj, a brother of the Chief of which State, as mentioned above, founded the Bhanja Raj family in Kanika. The family has its origin in the Solar dynasty, being a branch of the Raj family of Jaipur in Rajputana.

The following is the succession list of the Chiefs of the Killa since its foundation down to the British occupation of the Province in 1803: (1) Bhujabal Bhanja, (2) Bishwanath Bhanja, (3) Trilochan Bhanja I, (4) Gopinath Bhanja I, (5) Paramananda Bhanja I, (6) Dibyasinha Bhanja I, (7) Narasinha Bhanja I, (8) Tribikram Bhanja I, (9) Gangadhar Bhanja, (10) Gopal Bhanja I, (11) Basudeb Bhanja I, (12) Raghunath Bhanja, (13) Lakshman Bhanja, (14) Bairagi Bhanja I, (15) Trilochan Bhanja II, (16) Gopinath Bhanja II, (17) Paramananda Bhanja II, (18) Sarbasinha Bhanja, (19) Basudeb Bhanja II, (20) Dibyasinha Bhanja II, (21) Narasinha Bhanja II, (22) Tribikram Bhanja II, (23) Gadadhar Bhanja, (24) Gopinath Bhanja III, (25) Dasurathi Bhanja, (26) Gopal Bhanja II, (27) Bairagi Bhanja II, (28) Balabhadra Bhanja.

The status of the Chiefs of the Killa down to 1803 was more or less that of a semi-independent ruler of a small principality. They were in possession of full sovereign right within the Killa, and their allegiance to the Kings of Orissa and subsequently to the Mahommedan and the Mahratta rulers of the Province was only nominal.

"Kunka (Kanika) is a town in the Province of Orissa, in the district of Cuttack 80 miles north-east from the town of Cuttack. This is the capital of one of the Tributary States in Cuttack (subject to the British regulations), the exact limits of which have never been ascertained, but which have been roughly estimated at 75 miles from north to south by 50 from east to west. Prior to the acquisition of Cuttack by the British, the Raja of Kunka, who possessed this inundated and unhealthy tract of country, had long baffled the Mahratta generals in all their attempts to subdue him. The Mahrattas had been accustomed to embark troops and artillery on large, unwieldy flat-bottomed boats, unmanageable in large

THE KANIKA RAJ.

1. The Hon. Raja Rajendra Narayan Bhanja Deo, Bahadur, of Kanika. 2. Rajkumar Sailendra Narayan Bhanja Deo, of Kanika (Heir-Apparent).
3. Shreemati Jema Kanaklata Devi, of Kanika.
4. Group showing the Hon. Raja Bahadur, Heir-Apparent, and Daughter, together with Officers of the Raj.

THE KANIKA RAJ.

1. Kanika Rajbati at Cuttack. 2. The Palace at Raj Kanika. 3. The Temple at Righagur, the Ancient Capital of the Raj. 4. One of the Rogue Elephants shot by the Raja Saheb, at Dhenkanal. 5. The Temple at Keraragarh.

streams or near the sea, in consequence of which their ill-constructed fleets always fell a prey to the Raja's light-armed vessels, which were long, narrow, with barricades to cover the men, and some of them having 100 paddles or oars. When these squadrons met, the Ooria boats moved quickly round the heavy Mahratta armada and picked off the men with their matchlocks, until the remainder were compelled to surrender, when they were carried into a captivity from whence they seldom returned, the pernicious atmosphere of these morasses permitting none to live but the aborigines." [1]

The following extracts from Government publications will throw a light on the status of the Killa and the history of this ancient Rajgee and Raj family :—

(*a*) "The ancestors of the present Raja of Kujang and Kanika were barons of the land, created by the Gajapati Kings of Orissa." [2]

(*b*) "Aul, Patamundai, and Tirtol were for centuries under the influence of native Chiefs, and the Rajas of Kujang, Kanika, and Aul long exercised considerable power in the south-eastern and north-eastern parts of the district." [3]

(*c*) "When the English conquered the Province they found a few landowners of a superior class, descendants of noble families or high officials to whom larger States had been assigned for maintenance, subject only to the payment of a quit rent. Such were the Rajas of Kanika and Kujang, who were originally members of the Royal Family of Mayurbhanj, and were established in their possession about the thirteenth century, A.D." [4]

On the British occupation of the Province in 1803, treaty engagements were exchanged between the then representatives of the British Government appointed by the Marquis of Wellesley and the then Chief of Kanika.[5] Both of these documents are reproduced below :—

XCVII.

"Treaty Engagement executed by the Raja of Killa Kanika, a Tributary Mahal, subordinate to Cuttack, to the Honourable East India Company's Special Commissioners for the Soobah of Orissa, Messrs. Harcourt and Melville, 1803.

I, Raja Balabhadra Bhanja, Raja of Killa Kanika, in the Soobah of Orissa, engage faithfully and correctly to abide by this engagement, entered into by me with the Honourable East India Company, as contained in the following clauses, to wit :—

Clause 1. I will always hold myself in submission and loyal obedience to the Honourable East India Company aforesaid.

Clause 2. I will continue to pay, without demur, to the said Government, as my annual *peshkus* or tribute, 84,840 *kahans* of cowries, in three instalments, as specified herein below.

Clause 3. I will, on demand to that effect, cause any person who is an inhabitant of the Soobah appertaining to the Honourable Company aforesaid, and who may have fled and come into my territory, to be forthwith arrested and delivered over to the Government.

Clause 4. Should any person, who is a resident in my territories, commit a crime within the limits of the *Mogulbundi*, I hereby engage, on demand to that effect, to cause such person to be arrested and delivered over for trial to the Government Authority. Moreover, I further bind myself, in cases where I may possess any claim or demand on one who is an inhabitant of the *Mogulbundi*, not of my own authority to enforce such claim; but I will notify the same to the constituted authority and will act in accordance with such orders as may issue from him.

Clause 5. I engage that whenever the troops of the Honourable Company's Government shall pass through my territories, I will direct the people of my Killa to supply, to the extent of their capability, all *russud* and supplies, which shall be sold at fair prices. Further, I will, on no manner of pretext whatever, ever stop, or detain, or offer any let or hindrance to, any subject of the Honourable Company's Government, or to any other person whatever, who may be proceeding by land or water, with goods or orders, or with any *perwannah* on the part of the Government, through my boundaries, and will rather take care that no loss or mischief shall befall such parties in life or goods.

Clause 6. In case any neighbouring Raja or any other person whatever shall disobey the said Government, I engage, on demand and without demur, to depute a contingent force of my own troops with the forces of Government for the purpose of rebuking and chastising such rebel and bringing him under the subjection of the aforesaid Government. Such contingent to receive only rations agreeably to the previously current practice, so long as they shall be present.

These shall be the instalments of my *peshkus*, to be paid :—

In the month of Cheyt, *kahans* 28,840; Jeyt, 28,000; and Ashar, 28,000; total, 84,840.

Dated the 22nd November, 1803. Saban 6th, 1211.

UMLEE."

XCVIII.

"*Kaool-Namah* granted by the Honourable East India Company's Commissioners for the Soobah of Cuttack to Rajah Balabhadra Bhanja, Raja of Kanika, 1803 :—

We, Lieutenant-Colonel George Harcourt, commanding the victorious troops of the Honourable East India Company and Commissioner of the Soobah of Orissa, and John Melville, Commissioner of the same, appointed by the Most Noble the Marquis of Wellesley, Governor-General, for the settlement and pacification of the said Soobah, do, on behalf of the East India Company, execute this acknowledgment as set forth in the following paras., to Raja Balabhadra Bhanja, Raja of Killa Kanika, in the said Soobah of Orissa :—

Clause 1. The annual *peshkus* payable by the Raja for his Rajgee of the said Killa, is fixed in perpetuity at 84,840 *kahans*.

Clause 2. No further demand, however small, shall be made on the said Raja or received from him, as *nuzzur*, supplies, or otherwise.

Clause 3. The Government of the Honourable East India Company, it is well known, is ever gracious to those Rajas who are always loyal and obedient to them, and constant in the impartial administration of justice to all its subjects alike, and therefore in like manner extends the same impartiality to the Rajas, such as have been indicated above, and seeks always their prosperity and peace. Therefore any just representation or complaints made to the Government by the said Raja of Kanika will meet with a decision in accord with justice.

Dated 22nd November, 1803. Saban 6th, 1211.

(*Signed*)

G. HARCOURT (Lieut.-Colonel),
J. MELVILLE,
Commissioners."

[1] "Orissa," pp. 38–9. By Andrew Sterling, Esq., Persian Secretary to the Bengal Government. Edited by James Peggs, 1846.

[2] "Statistical Account," vol. xviii., p. 125. By W. W. Hunter.

[3] "Bengal District Gazetteer, Cuttack," p. 54.

[4] Ibid., p. 161.

[5] Vide pp. 314–16 of Part III. of Vol. I. of Aitchison's "Collections of Treaties, Engagements, and Sanads."

The following is the succession list of the Rajas of the Killa since the British occupation of the Province, i.e. after Raja Balabhadra Bhanja: (1) Jagannath Bhanja, (2) Harihar Bhanja, (3) Benayak Bhanja, (4) Tribikram Bhanja III, (5) Padmanabh Bhanja, (6) Nripendra Nath Bhanja (died minor), and (7) Rajendra Narayan Bhanja Deo (the present Rajah).

The Honourable Raja Rajendra Narayan Bhanja Deo, the present proprietor of the Estate, is the second son of the Raja of the adjoining Killa Aul. He was born in 1881 and adopted into the Kanika family in 1896. During his minority the Estate was under the management of the Court of Wards. He was educated at the Government Collegiate School and College, Cuttack. He married in 1899 a daughter of the late Chief of Nayagarh. He assumed management of the Estate from the Court of Wards on attaining majority in 1902. In December 1906 he presided over the Utkal Conference held at Berhampore, in the Ganjam District. In 1907 he visited England and travelled in other parts of Europe. In 1908 he was nominated a member of the Bengal Advisory Fishery Board, and in the following year he was elected as the representative of the Landholders of Orissa and Chota-Nagpur to the Bengal Council.

In 1910 he visited England again, joining Lincoln's Inn, and in 1911 he attended the Coronation ceremony of their Imperial Majesties at Westminster Abbey, in London. On his return to India, in December in the same year, he attended the Imperial Coronation Durbar at Delhi, and on the creation of the new Province of Behar and Orissa in 1912 he was elected to the Provincial Council as the representative of the Landholders of Orissa. He was again elected to the Council of Behar and Orissa by the same constituency in 1916. He has since been elected as an additional member of the Council of the Viceroy and Governor-General of India to represent the landholders of the entire Province of Behar and Orissa.

Raja Rajendra Narayan has always taken an active part in all matters before the Council, especially those relating to the interest of his constituents. The most important measure affecting their interests, before both the Bengal and the Behar and Orissa Provincial Councils, during his term of office was the Orissa Tenancy Bill. He vigorously opposed the passing of the measure, doing his best to protect the interests of the landlords, and although the Bill was eventually passed into law, he was no doubt able to secure certain rights and privileges for them.

The Raja has always taken a lively interest in every matter of public concern. He is President of the Orissa Landholders' Association and one of the Vice-Presidents of the Bengal and the Behar Landholders' Associations. He is also a member of the Royal Asiatic Society, London.

The Raja signalized the assumption of management of his Estate from the Court of Wards by providing the handsome "Lady Woodburn Female Ward," which supplied a long-felt want in the General Hospital, Cuttack. On several occasions he spent large amounts in relieving distress among his tenantry, and his services in this respect were always recognized by Government. In connection with the famine relief measures of 1913, the Hon. Mr. McPherson, Chief Secretary to the Government, thus spoke at the Council Meeting on August 29, 1913: "Local relief funds have been opened, and in this connection Government desire to record their appreciation of the generosity of the Hon. Raja Rajendra Narayan Bhanja Deo of Kanika, who has contributed very largely to the fund and has taken effective steps to assist the tenantry of his estate."

In reference to the same subject, at the Durbar held at Cuttack on November 28, 1913, His Excellency the Viceroy and Governor-General of India thus observed: "I am happy to think that on this occasion there was no loss of life in your district, and I trust that the prompt advances made by Government and the organization of relief funds, to which the Raja of Kanika so generously contributed, together with the repair of the irrigation channels, have done all that is humanly possible to minimize your losses, while some consolation is to be found in the anticipation of bumper *rabi* crops as the résult of seasonable rainfall and the unusual amount of silt deposits."

The Raja has always taken great interest in the cause of education. He was a member of the Patna University Committee, and is at present a member of the Governing Body of the Ravenshaw College, as well as of the Managing Committee of the Ravenshaw Girls' High English School, Cuttack. He has made provision for boys' and girls' schools on his estate, besides contributing liberally towards institutions outside. He maintains a High English School and several Upper and Lower Primary Schools, and there are, further, six *tols* to teach Sanskrit for the Oriental Titles.

The Raja maintains four charitable dispensaries within the estate, for free medical treatment of the tenantry as well as of the outside public. The Raja is an expert at billiards, tennis, and badminton, and is a great shikari and an admirable shot. In short, he possesses all the qualities and qualifications necessary for a refined nobleman of high and eminent order.

Titayet Sailendra Narayan Bhanja Deo, born on September 29, 1908, is the son and heir of the Raja. He is a fine and fair-looking lad, and is being brought up in a manner consistent with his position in life.

The usual places of residence of the Raj family are Cuttack and Raj Kanika, and at each of these places there are suitable palatial buildings. The one at Cuttack, with its spacious lawns and large tank, is quite imposing, being the best in the town, while the ideal palace at Raj Kanika, richly fitted and furnished, with its beautiful and spacious compound finely laid out, is considered to be the best structure in Orissa.

THE KASIMBAZAR RAJ.

The founder of the ancient and illustrious house of Kasimbazar was Dewan Krishna Kanta Nandy, who flourished during the days of Warren Hastings, the first Governor-General of India. When the latter was Commercial Resident of the East India Company at Kasimbazar, Seraj-ud-Dowla, then Nawab Nazim of Bengal, failing to extort money from him, sent him as a prisoner to Mushidabad and ordered him to be put to death. It was at that juncture that Babu Krishna Kanta Nandy went to the rescue of Warren Hastings by giving him shelter under his roof, and subsequently helped him to escape, thereby saving his life. This good deed was never forgotten, for in 1772, when Warren Hastings was appointed Governor-General, he made Krishna Kanta his Dewan and confidential agent. Krishna Kanta was at the time in affluent circumstances, having been employed as an English clerk in the Residency at Kasimbazar, and having also carried on business as a silk and rice merchant. Hastings subsequently conferred on him a *jaigir* in Ghazipur, and obtained for his son, Lokenath, the title of

THE KASIMBAZAR RAJ.

1. Kasimbazar Rajbari. 2. The Calcutta Garden House. 3. The Hon. Maharaja Sir Manindra Chandra Nandy, K.C.I.E.

Maharaja from the Nawab Nazim of Bengal. Before his death, in 1778, Kanta Babu, in addition to his ownership of the *jaigir* in Ghazipur, was possessed of immense property in the districts of Rangpur, Dinajpur, Burdwan, Bogra, and the 24 Parganas, Rajshahi, Maldah, Birbhum, and Murshidabad. Though he had not the advantage of being thoroughly acquainted with the English language, he had a good knowledge of it, as well as of Persian and Bengali, and was highly spoken of for his business capacity, administrative experience, and knowledge of the world. His son, Maharaja Lokenath Rai Bahadur, who was subject to an incurable malady, died in 1804, leaving a minor son, Kumar Harinath.

When the latter came of age, he maintained the reputation of the family by his charity and upright conduct, and Lord Amherst (then Governor-General of India), in appreciation of his beneficence, conferred on him the title of Raja Bahadur. The impetus given by him to the teaching of Sanskrit drew students from far and near, and many who became proficient in that language came into prominence during his lifetime. He was very fond of music and athletics, and maintained a gymnasium to encourage wrestling and sword-play. He passed away in 1832, when his minor son, Krishnanath, succeeded to the estate.

Krishnanath was a good scholar, and as he spoke and wrote English well, he was always in the company of his European friends, mixing freely with them. During the administration of Lord Auckland he won the distinction of Raja Bahadur. He was a great huntsman, and his shooting excursions were literally moving camps, but he frittered away the surplus that had accumulated during his minority, spending nearly half a crore of rupees within the short period of four years. It should be said to his credit, however, that he liberally supported every movement of public utility, and the officials of his staff, whom he believed had his welfare at heart, enjoyed his bounty. On October 31, 1848, he brought himself to an untimely grave by committing suicide while in a state of temporary insanity. A day before his tragic end he left a will bequeathing his estates for educational purposes, reserving only a grant to his wife, Rani Surnomoyee, of a paltry sum of Rs. 1,500 a month for her maintenance.

Maharani Surnomoyee was born in the year 1827 at Bhatakul, a village in the district of Burdwan, and in 1838 she married Raja Krishnanath Rai Bahadur. They had no son, and the Raja Bahadur had in his will unfortunately withheld from her the right of adoption. Rani Surnomoyee commenced an action at law, and it was ultimately proved that, at the time of the execution of the will, the Raja was of unsound mind, and accordingly the case was decided in her favour. In 1871 the Government of India recognized her beneficence and loyalty by granting her the personal distinction of Maharani, and a promise was at the same time held out to her that the title of Maharaja would be confirmed on her nephew and heir, Manindra Chandra Nandy. The valuable services rendered by her during the terrible famine of 1874 were greatly appreciated by the Government of India, and they affirmed again that the distinction of Maharaja would be extended to her successor. In 1878 Her Majesty the Queen-Empress Victoria was graciously pleased to admit the Maharani to the Order of the Crown of India. At the Durbar held to invest her with the insignia, the Divisional Commissioner, while enumerating her charitable acts, brought to the notice of his hearers that up to that date the Maharani had spent the munificent sum of eleven lakhs of rupees, and further observed: "Your appointment to the Order is in recognition of the public spirit as well as of the munificent charity you have at all times and in so many ways displayed. There are doubtless many who hear me to-day who are far better acquainted than I am, not only with your good deeds, but with the manner in which your vast estates are managed, but there may be some who are not so well informed on those points, and who, while knowing your reputation for charity, have no idea of its scope or of its nature. Under these circumstances it will not, I think, be out of place if I mention a few of those acts of benevolence and liberality which have procured for you this signal mark of the approbation of Her Majesty the Empress. It would not be difficult for me to recount the doings of your long past years which have, with those that have followed, made your life one long act of charity. In this country we are accustomed to see a good deal of what I may call spasmodic money-giving, where large sums are frequently given to purposes no doubt very good and very useful, but which are aided not so much because they are so, as because the donors hope to bring their names before the public, or obtain some future reward. This has not been your case. You have not been content to wait till you were asked to give, but have taken steps to ensure worthy objects for assistance being brought to your notice and have then given liberally, hoping for nothing in return. In a word, your charity has been such as springs from a simple unostentatious desire to do good, when the left hand knoweth not what the right hand doeth, which is as admirable as, I fear, it is uncommon. Of the management of your large estates, lying in no less than ten districts in Bengal and the North-Western Provinces, I need say but little. In this you have always taken an active part and have manifested an acquaintance with detail and an aptitude for business generally, almost, if not quite, without parallel among persons of your sex in this country. The consequence is that, aided by your able adviser, Babu Rajib Lochan Roy, you have, while securing the rents to which you are justly entitled, done so without harassing or oppressing your *ryots*, and have thus escaped those difficulties and complications into which so many landowners have of late years fallen. For myself I need not say that the duty which I am called upon to perform to-day is one that gives me great pleasure, for both as Magistrate of the Twenty-four Parganas and as Commissioner of the Dacca Division, I have had on more than one occasion reason to thank you for assistance freely and liberally given to projects which I had in view, and I cannot let this opportunity pass without thanking you for the aid you afforded to the sufferers from that fearful calamity which, on October 31, 1876, swept over the southern portion of the District of Backergunj, carrying death and destruction with it, and leaving behind it distress and misery from which it will be long before the sufferers fully recover. It only remains for me, Maharani, to hand to you the insignia of the Order to which Her Majesty has been pleased to appoint you, with the congratulatory letters of His Excellency the Viceroy, and His Honour the Lieutenant-Governor of Bengal, and to express the hope that you may live long in all prosperity to enjoy the honour you have now attained and which you have worthily deserved."

The hostel for the lady students attending the Calcutta Medical College was one of her gifts; she inaugurated the water works (called after her) at Berhampore at a cost of three lakhs; she paid annually twenty thousand rupees towards the maintenance of the Berhampore College; she distributed clothes to poor Brahmins, mendicants, and others; and fed a large

THE KASIMBAZAR RAJ.

1. Gola Bari. 2. Saidabad Palace. 3. Banjetia House.

number of people on festival days. Her name was a household word in Bengal, and even to-day it is venerated. This noble and philanthropic lady passed away on August 25, 1897. The estate then reverted to her mother-in-law, Rani Harasundari, a recluse at Benares, who relinquished her right in favour of the reversionary heir, Manindra Chandra Nandy, her grandson by her daughter Gobinda Sundari. An honorarium of nine lakhs and a monthly allowance of ten thousand rupees was settled on her during her lifetime.

Maharaja Manindra Chandra Nandy was born in the year 1860. A chain of misfortunes befell him while very young, for he lost his mother when he was barely two years of age, his father died when he was twelve, and his elder brother passed away in his thirteenth year. Illness of a virulent type, at the comparatively young age of fourteen, stood in his way of obtaining school education, but when change of air and skilful medical treatment recruited his health, he improved his knowledge by private study. Pursuant to the promise held out to Maharani Surnomoyee, the Government of India conferred the title of Maharaja upon him on May 30, 1898. He is a great benefactor to his country in his generous support of the cause of education. He maintains a first-grade college at Berhampore, called the "Berhampore Krishnath College," at an annual expense of Rs. 45,000, and he maintains all the boarding establishments and messes attached to the college and college school at an annual expense of Rs. 15,000. Owing to a large influx of students from various parts of Bengal, additions had to be made to his old college building at an enormous cost. For the accommodation of the college school students the Maharaja spent about Rs. 150,000 upon a large building which was constructed on the site which had been transferred by the Government, free of revenue, to the college authorities. He has further been corresponding with the Government of Bengal for the establishment of a thoroughly equipped technical college. At Mathrun, his ancestral village, he has established an English high school, with a hostel attached to it, at a cost of half a lakh of rupees; he maintains high schools at Saktipur, Ethora, Beldanga, Jabagram, Saidabad, and Ulipur, where the children of his tenants receive education at a nominal fee. At his own expense he has sent out students to England, Japan, America, Austria, and other parts of the world to obtain experience in industrial concerns. The Association for the Scientific and Industrial Education of Indians, the National College, the Bengal Technical Institution, the Deaf and Dumb School, the School for Blind Children, the Mahakali Pathshala in Calcutta and at Berhampore, and the Mohula Ramkrishna Asram count him among their patrons. He pays the fees of fifty pupils attending the Sanskrit College, and more than Rs. 2,000 every year to the poor students sitting for University examinations, while more than a hundred and fifty others are provided with free board and lodging at Berhampore, Mathrun, and Calcutta. For the encouragement of artisans and agriculturists, he holds an annual exhibition at the Banjetia Gardens, Kasimbazar, the major portion of the expenses being borne by him. He is the foremost patron of Bengali literature: he has engaged Pandit Rash Behari Sankhatirtha to edit the great Vaishnab *Granthas*, he has commissioned Babu Jageswar Banerjee to prepare a most valuable work on the history of the civilization of the world, and he has appointed Babu Lalit Mohan Banerjee and Babu Radhakamal Mukherjee to be editors respectively of the Vaishnab magazine *Gouranga Shebak* and a magazine of a general character called *Upasana*. The sites on which the Bungya Sahitya Parishad building stands, and on which the Ramesh Bhaban is to be built, are a free gift by the Maharaja. The Sahitya Sammilan, for promoting the advancement of the Bengali language and literature, was first held in 1910 under his auspices at the Kasimbazar Rajbari. For educational progress alone he spends a lakh and a half annually, two lakhs are given for other charitable purposes, and he expends annually about Rs. 1,500 towards the maintenance of Sanskrit Toles. He contributed Rs. 15,000 in the construction of the Albert Victor Hospital at Belgachia, Rs. 5,000 for Daulatpur College, Rs. 5,000 for a library at Navadwip, Rs. 50,000 for Rangpur College, and Rs. 5,000 for the Puri Ved Bidyalaya. He contributed a lump sum towards the building fund of the charitable dispensary, and, further, makes donations to the maintenance of that institution whenever he is called upon to do so. He established the Curzon Charitable Hospital at Kasimbazar, he maintains similar institutions at Ulipore, Rajshahi, and Ballia, which were founded by his aunt and predecessor, Maharani Surnomoyee, and the water works at Berhampore, inaugurated by her, were completed by him. He carefully manages his estates, which are scattered over thirteen districts of Bengal and the United Provinces, as well as the six trust estates in Sribati, Matiari in the Katwa subdivision, Berhampore, the city of Murshidabad, and at Gaya. Prompted by his generous nature, the Maharaja took over the management of these heavily encumbered estates with the view of relieving their proprietors from their embarrassment, and he supplied funds from his own treasury for the liquidation of their respective debts. He has been Chairman of the Berhampore municipality for more than fifteen years, and has held important offices in such influential bodies as the British Indian Association, the Bengal Landholders' Association, the Bengal National Chamber of Commerce, and the Murshidabad Association. When the right of nominating a representative to the Bengal Council was conferred on the British Indian Association the Maharaja had the honour of being nominated for the position, and since then has been re-elected. In 1912 he was elected to the Imperial Council as representative of Bengal landholders, and he was again returned in the year 1915. During the year 1914 he contributed Rs. 5,000 towards the Medical College and Hospital for Women and the Nurses' Training Institution at Delhi in memory of the late Lady Hardinge, who initiated the scheme.

When His Majesty the King-Emperor conferred Birthday Honours in June 1915, the Maharaja received the well-merited distinction of K.C.I.E.

Numerous acts of munificence and usefulness distinguish the career of the Maharaja, and in leading an exemplary life he is in every way worthy of the trust reposed in him by the Government, as well as by the people.

THE MAYURBHANJ STATE

Mayurbhanj State, the largest and wealthiest of the Feudatory States of Orissa, is a good illustration of a territory which for several generations has enjoyed the advantage of being ruled by Chiefs possessing initiative, energy, and administrative ability. Their personal acquaintance with their country, and readiness to distinguish and accept practical suggestions for development have resulted in the establishment of sound commercial prosperity.

The greater portion of these States consists of forests of considerable extent,

THE MAYURBHANJ FEUDATORY STATE.

1. Maharaja Purna Chandra Singh Bhanj Deo. 2. Rantrai Sahib Sridam Chandra Singh Bhanj Deo.

THE MAYURBHANJ FEUDATORY STATE.

1. General View of Baripada, the Capital. 2. Hariballadeb Temple and Tank. 3. Superintendent's Bungalow, Belgaria.

THE MAYURBHANJ FEUDATORY STATE.

1. Talbandh, Terminus of Railway Extension. 2. Baldiha Irrigation Dam. 3. Tata Company's Iron-ore Mines at Gurumukisai. 4. Falls on the Burrabalang River, at Baripada.

interspersed with extensive ranges of mountains and cultivated plains; and it is a common experience in India, Africa, and other countries that the aboriginal natives who first inhabited hill fastnesses were of a very warlike character, and that they invariably quarrelled not only among themselves, but also with their neighbours. This appears to have been precisely what occurred in the district now known as the Feudatory States, as it is related that the petty Chiefs of numerous tribes or groups warred against each other until they in turn were ousted by enemies more powerful than themselves.

When the conquest of Orissa by the British took place in 1803-4, several of the States—including Mayurbhanj—were ceded with the remainder of Orissa, and treaties were entered into whereby the Rulers undertook, among other things, to preserve loyalty and to pay certain sums as tribute money.

At the time of the cession of the Mayurbhanj State, the position of Ruler was held by Rani Sumitra Dei Bhanj, and in 1812, during the Chieftainship of her successor, the annual tribute to be paid by the State was fixed at the sum of Rs. 1,001.

The grandfather of the present Chief—Maharaja Krishna Chandra Bhanj Deva—was an exceedingly able and wise Ruler, not only in administrative work, but also in his encouragement of the people to develop manufactures and industries. His death in 1882 was greatly mourned throughout the State, and in 1890 his son, Sriram Chandra Bhanj Deva, attained his majority and took over the management of the State, which for eight years previously had been controlled by the Government. This was another well-educated and enlightened chief, who followed in the footsteps of his late father by the exercise of great liberality and by giving assiduous attention to all State matters. The title of Maharaja was bestowed as a mark of personal distinction at the Imperial Durbar held at Delhi in January 1903, when he was also the recipient of a gold medal. In 1910 Lord Minto, in a Durbar, conferred upon the ruling Chief the dignity of Maharaja as a hereditary family title.

Once again the State came under the direct control of the Government, as on the death of the Maharaja, in February 1912, the heir to the *gadi* was still under age.

The majority of the young Maharaja, Purna Chandra Bhanj Deo, will not take place until the year 1920. He is meantime being educated in the Mayo College for Chiefs, Ajmere, where he has made his mark as scholar, prefect, and captain of the College cricket XI. He is also a keen polo player, and both he and his younger brother are fine horsemen and keen sportsmen.

Mayurbhanj is essentially an agricultural State, and fully 95 per cent. of the population are wholly or partly dependent upon the products of the land. This has been accorded a growing and intelligent recognition by recent rulers. An experimental farm has been established in charge of a trained agriculturist; many canals, dams, and other irrigation works have been carried out or are down for future construction ; and experiments with fruit trees and some new staple crops are slowly overcoming the prejudices of local conservatism.

The principal crops grown are rice, maize, millet, and oil-seeds, and various kinds of vegetables.

Irrigation is necessary in several portions of Mayurbhanj, and this process is carried on with water obtained almost wholly from the rainfall. The water for the main irrigation system is conserved in two storage dams. The present scheme, however, is incomplete, and as it is dependent almost entirely upon somewhat uncertain sources for its successful working, a much more pretentious one is now contemplated.

Extensive surveys have already been made, and it is proposed to utilize the water to be obtained by the construction of a dam across the Burrabalang River, a perennial stream and the largest in the State. It is anticipated that a quantity will thus be available sufficient to irrigate the greater part of the area of the Sadar subdivision, and it is expected that the extreme length of the distributories will be not less than 80 miles. The total cost of the proposed new works is about 50 lakhs of rupees.

It will be seen from the above that the State authorities are doing all in their power to prove to the people that agriculture is a science, and that the application of this science, supported by sound practical experience, is the only method by which the best results can be obtained.

There is considerable mineral wealth, especially in iron ores, in the State, and in 1909, shortly before the death of the late Maharaja, negotiations were commenced with the Tata Iron and Steel Company, Ltd., for the lease of iron-ore deposits in the Gurumasaiani Hill, in the northern subdivision of the State, and the result was that the company shortly afterwards obtained rights over an area about $5\frac{1}{2}$ square miles in extent. The mining of the ore proved to be so successful that arrangements are now (1916) in progress under which it is proposed that a further area of about $14\frac{1}{2}$ square miles shall be granted to the company under similar conditions. The ore is transported to the Tata works at Sakchi by means of a branch railway running between the mines and the main line to Bombay.

The Tata company raised about three lakhs of tons of iron during the year 1915, and upon this quantity a tonnage royalty was paid to the revenue of the State.

There is now afoot a scheme to quadruple the output of the Tata works. If this materializes, the works will employ some 12,000 to 15,000 hands and export 10 to 12 lakhs of tons of iron ore. The scheme involves an extension of the broad-gauge Bengal-Nagpur Railway into the heart of the State to tap new rich deposits found there.

A geological survey of a considerable portion of India was made some years ago, and since that time it has been left to individual enterprises to ascertain the mineral wealth of certain districts. A survey was undertaken in Mayurbhanj recently, when it was discovered that, among the valuable deposits, iron ore was undoubtedly the richest—in fact, it was stated that in all probability there were not more extensive or richer fields in India. Gold, too, is found in various parts, but hitherto not in paying quantities. A few native workers earned a scanty livelihood by washing river deposits. There are extensive granite quarries leased at present to the Bengal Granite Company, and soapstone quarries near Lubang turn out quantities of pots and dishes, which find a ready sale. The reserved and protected forests, about 1,700 square miles in extent, are found both on the hills and on a portion of the plains, but up to about twenty years ago felling was carried on by persons who, in the absence of any State regulations, cut down selected trees in districts favoured by having comparatively satisfactory facilities for removal. A Forest Department was subsequently established, and full control over the timber purchasers has now been fully secured.

The first real aid to the opening up of the country on a more generous scale by

THE MAYURBHANJ FEUDATORY STATE.

1. The Leper Asylum. 2. Chahalla Forest Bungalow, in Reserve. 3. Mahadev Mandir at Kiching.

the reclamation of jungles, thus giving increased opportunities for obtaining greater productiveness from the land, was the construction of the Mayurbhanj State Railway ; but the further possibilities which presented themselves for a much larger and more systematic trade in timber caused the formation of the Mayurbhanj Light Railway Syndicate, who are extending the line from Baripada, the chief town in the State, to Talbandh, a distance of 32 miles. The necessary earthworks have already been completed, and progress in other directions is being made. It is expected that the extension will be open for traffic by the year 1917.

The timber industry has now been established on a firm basis, and by far the greater portion of it is in the hands of Messrs. B. Borooah & Co., of 5 Royal Exchange Place, Calcutta, who (under the direct supervision of the State Forest Department) are engaged chiefly in manufacturing railway sleepers for *Sal* (*Shorea robusta*). Nearly all of these are taken by the Bengal-Nagpur Railway Company, but timber goods of various descriptions are being supplied in increasing quantities to contractors and others.

It has been shown that, as nearly all of the inhabitants are engaged in some form of agricultural pursuits, it follows that there has been very little development of manufacturing or industrial concerns, although it should be added that a considerable number of aboriginals are employed in the weaving of coarse cloths and the production of tusser cocoons and lac. Statistics show that the volume of trade in the State has increased to a remarkable extent during recent years, and while the output of forest produce shows the greatest advance, the exports of rice, millets, hemp fibre, and oil seeds are by no means inconsiderable.

There is a large supply of nux vomica, used for manufacturing strychnine, for which Messrs. Smith, Stainstreet & Co., of Calcutta, hold a lease; and the State forests supply myrabolams, and other tanning products to which the war has given a greatly enhanced value and a consequently accelerated development.

What looks like becoming one of the most valuable side-products is Sabai grass, from which an excellent quality of paper can be made. The Titaghur Paper Mills are at present negotiating for huge supplies of this from the State.

While the social and economic conditions of the people have been greatly improved under the beneficent rulership of enlightened chiefs, that important essential in the true prosperity of a country—namely, education—has received its full share of recognition. New schools are being opened yearly, and there is now a large number of teaching establishments for boys and girls under the supervision of an Educational Officer specially appointed for the Feudatory States.

There are unusually good means of communication, not only within the State, but also from its borders, to important centres in other districts; and in addition to the railway facilities already referred to there are about 150 miles of gravelled and 350 miles of unmetalled roads, while felled timber is floated down the Burrabalang River.

Baripada, the headquarters, is situated in the north-eastern portion of the State. It was constituted a Municipality in 1905, and is administered by a chairman, vice-chairman, and 15 commissioners.

The ruins of an ancient city were discovered at Kiching a few years ago, and excavations have revealed the presence of a large number of most interesting relics, including a Mandir of Mahadev, with beautifully carved frescoes and *bas-relief* panelling, and a number of more or less intact figures sculptured in a peculiar hard black stone. Further excavations will be undertaken, and it is hoped to be able to reconstruct the temples on their original sites.

THE MURSHIDABAD SERKAR ALI (HOUSE OF MURSHIDABAD)

The real history of Murshidabad commences in the year 1704, when Murshid Kuli Khan, Dewan of Bengal and Orissa, made that place the capital of Bengal. In 1713 the Dewan was appointed Subadar and Nawab Nazim of Bengal and Orissa by the then Emperor of Delhi. He was independent and very powerful, and it is an undoubted fact that he was the greatest and most energetic ruler in Bengal since the days of Sher Shah. His son-in-law, Suja-ud-Din Khan, the good Nawab, succeeded in 1725 to the Subadari of Bengal and Orissa, to which Bihar was afterwards added. He proved to be a capable and wise administrator, and he was succeeded in 1739 by his son Sarfaraz Khan, who was killed by Ali Verdi Khan at the battle of Giria Nala in 1740.

Ali Verdi Khan therefore became Nawab Nazim of Bengal, Bihar and Orissa, in 1740, and for sixteen years he proved himself to be an able ruler, possessing great military talent. During his reign the interests of England advanced very considerably.

Ali Verdi Khan was succeeded by his grandson, Seraj-ud-Dowla, in the year 1756. The latter unhappily turned out to be a cruel, unprincipled, and despicable ruler. His people became gradually alienated from him, exasperated by his inordinate rapacity, insolence, and profligacy. When they found that their life and liberty, property and honour were at the mercy of so self-willed and arbitrary a ruler, they formed a conspiracy to bring about the downfall of the tyrant. Then was fought the great and decisive battle of Plassey on June 23, 1757, between the East India Company and Seraj-ud-Dowla. It took place on an assurance given by Meer Jaffer to Lord Clive that he would withhold the troops under his command and not interfere in any way on behalf of Seraj-ud-Dowla, as the latter had by his infamous treatment of Meer Jaffer rendered himself despicable alike to him (Meer Jaffer) and to his subjects, who were therefore in favour of Meer Jaffer ascending the throne of Murshidabad as Subadar of Bengal, Behar and Orissa, in place of Seraj-ud-Dowla, Meer Jaffer being a prince, a general, a leading statesman of the kingdom, possessing great wealth and power and holding large territorial property, and who, in the words of Lord Clive, "was as much esteemed as the other was detested."

As the power of the Great Mogul began to decline, the Nawabs Nazim became virtually independent rulers of Bengal, Behar and Orissa, and although Mir Quassim came to the throne in 1760, Meer Jaffer was reinstated in 1763. Meer Jaffer was succeeded by his son, Nujmud Dowla, in 1765, at the age of twenty years. During the reign of Nujmud Dowla, the revenue of Bengal, Behar and Orissa, together with *Nizamut Zygirs* (freeholds), the income of which was about 16 lakhs, was made over to the East India Company for a stipend of Rs. 53,86,131. This was done after the grant of Dewani by Shah Alum with the consent of the Nawab Nazim. In August 1765 Lord Clive obtained the *diwani*, or financial administration, of Bengal, Behar and Orissa with the nominal sanction of the Emperor Shah Alum. In 1766 the Nawab sat as Nazim, with Lord Clive on his left, as Diwan, and he opened the ceremony of commencing the annual collection of revenue

THE MURSHIDABAD SERKAR ALI.

1. His Highness the Hon. Nawab Bahadur of Murshidabad, Amir-ul-Omra, K.C.S.I., K.C.V.O.
2. The Heir-Apparent, Murshid Zada Asif Jah Saiyid Wares Ali Mirza.
3. The Nawab Bahadur on Venus.

Photo by Bourne & Shepherd, India.

THE MURSHIDABAD SERKAR ALI.

1. The Palace. 2. The New Palace, or Wasif Manzil 3. The Drawing-room of the New Palace.

THE MURSHIDABAD SERKAR ALI.

1. The New Palace. 2. The Palace from the Farther Side of the Bhagirathi. 3. The Landscape Garden.

in full Durbar. Nujmud Dowla died on May 8th in that year. During the régime of the next ruler, Saifud Dowla, a reduction of the stipend stipulated to be paid to the Nizamut at the time of the transfer of the revenue collection to the English took place. The Nawab died of small-pox on March 10, 1770, and was succeeded by his younger brother, Mobaruk-ud-Dowla, whose pension was fixed at the sum of Rs. 3,181,991; two years later this amount was reduced to Rs. 1,600,000. The civil and criminal Courts were transferred from Murshidabad to Calcutta in 1790. Nawab Mobaruk-ud-Dowla died in 1793 and was succeeded by Babar Jung Nasir-ul-Mulk, Zynuddin Ali (or Ali Jah), Wala Jah, and Humayun Jah respectively. The building of the palace of the Nawab was commenced in 1829 and completed in 1838, at a cost of over Rs. 1,600,000.

Humayun Jah died in 1838 and was succeeded by his son Munsur Ali Khan, who visited England about the year 1869 for the purpose of conferring with the Home Government on questions relating to his position and dignity as a sovereign prince, and also with regard to the amount which should be paid annually to him. He, however, resigned his title and position on November 1, 1880, and was succeeded by his eldest son, His Highness Nawab Ali Kudr Syed Sir Hussan Ali Meerza Bahadur, G.C.I.E., in February 1882, when he was honoured with the hereditary title of the Nawab Bahadur of Murshidabad, Rais-ud-Dowla, Amir-ul-Omra, and whose family still continue to occupy the *gadi*.

The Nawab was the eldest of a very large family, and his education, which was entrusted to English tutors, was well calculated to fit him for the exalted position which he held, but side by side with his literary studies he entered with zest into games of all kinds, becoming an expert athlete, a fine horseman, a good shot, and an excellent pig-sticker. When quite a boy the conduct of the young Nawab was marked by steadiness of purpose, great amiability, and a high moral tone, traits which, in the opinion of his tutors, were inherited from his mother.

At nineteen years of age the Nawab and two of his younger brothers visited England in the care of Colonel Herbert, and there is no doubt that his experiences gained in conversing with men of position in the old country, in seeing large and busy cities with their factories, railway centres, harbours, museums, and art galleries, and by an intelligent observation of the habits and customs of Western people, were of incalculable benefit to him in the high office to which he succeeded.

The travellers broke their journey at Cairo and Alexandria, and having disembarked at Southampton, made their way to London, where they took up their residence at South Kensington. While the trip was in itself of great educational value, it should be mentioned that purely literary studies were not neglected, as a specially qualified tutor was then engaged to look after that portion of their training.

The party arrived in London during the most favourable portion of the year, as the first city in the world is dressed in its fresh spring costume from April to June; its streets are closely packed with pedestrians and vehicles of all descriptions, its shops are more than usually attractive, and there is a ceaseless activity on all hands which must inevitably make a lasting impression upon the mind of one brought up in the East.

The stately dignity of the magnificent buildings appealed to the sightseers, while diversion of a lighter character was found in visits to picture galleries, museums, parks, races, theatres, and other places where innocent pleasures could be obtained.

It is related that in the Natural History Section of the British Museum, when the youths were deeply interested in inspecting the beautiful collection of birds, one of them exclaimed in surprise: "I always understood that the Almighty made ten thousand birds of all kinds, but how many more are here?"

The trio received the greatest kindness from distinguished persons, who vied with one another in providing excursions and amusements for their pleasure; but they never forgot the *levée* held by his late Majesty King Edward VII, when Prince of Wales, to which they were by virtue of their high rank granted a private entrance.

Among a number of notable persons whom they met was Lady Williams, a granddaughter of Clive, who remarked upon the fact that she, a descendant of one who had played such an important part in the settlement of Bengal, should have met youths one of whose ancestors, Meer Jaffer, had, along with Lord Clive, been chiefly instrumental in laying the foundation of the British Empire in India.

After "doing" the metropolis thoroughly the party left for Sandgate (for Dover Castle), Southsea, Portsmouth, and other places in the southern and western counties of England, but before they left for the midland and northern cities they had the pleasure of seeing the yacht *Victoria and Albert*, belonging to her late Majesty Queen Victoria.

The large industrial centres claimed their attention next, and at Birmingham they witnessed the manufacture of glass, *papier-mâché*, brass bedsteads, steel pens, screws, and small arms; at Coventry they were shown the weaving of ribbons from silk, some of which had been imported from Murshidabad, the place of their birth; the weaving of carpets was seen at Kidderminster; and glove factories were visited at Worcester, while the Royal Porcelain Works, in the same city, held a peculiar charm for individuals who were accustomed to the artistic pottery work of India.

The summer was now advancing, but it was unthinkable that the northern counties should be entirely overlooked, and therefore they entrained for Manchester, the world's emporium of the cotton trade, where they beheld thousands of busy operatives at the numberless looms in that great city. A visit was also paid to Eaton Hall, the magnificent pile of buildings belonging to the Duke of Westminster, and to many other places of historical or commercial interest.

London was preparing for Christmas when the party again reached the banks of the Thames, but this added to, rather than detracted from, their enjoyment of a round of drawing-rooms, theatres, shops, and other amusements, which fully occupied their time until December 2nd, when they left England for the Continent of Europe. Opportunity was there found for flying visits to Paris, Bologna, Geneva, Florence, Leghorn, Rome, Naples, and Pompeii, and early in March they arrived in Calcutta, where they received a most cordial welcome from many relatives and friends.

The Nawab's subsequent life was marked by an intelligent use of the opportunities which so exalted a position conferred, and his transparently honourable dealings with all with whom he came in contact were an important factor in establishing the most friendly relationship with his people.

This Prince lived only for others. He was a glory to the Murshidabad *Musnud*, which he adorned with a credit few of the family equalled but none ever surpassed. His high character, his innate sense of justice, and his unbounded generosity towards all classes of people, without distinction of caste or creed, spread his fame far and wide as an able,

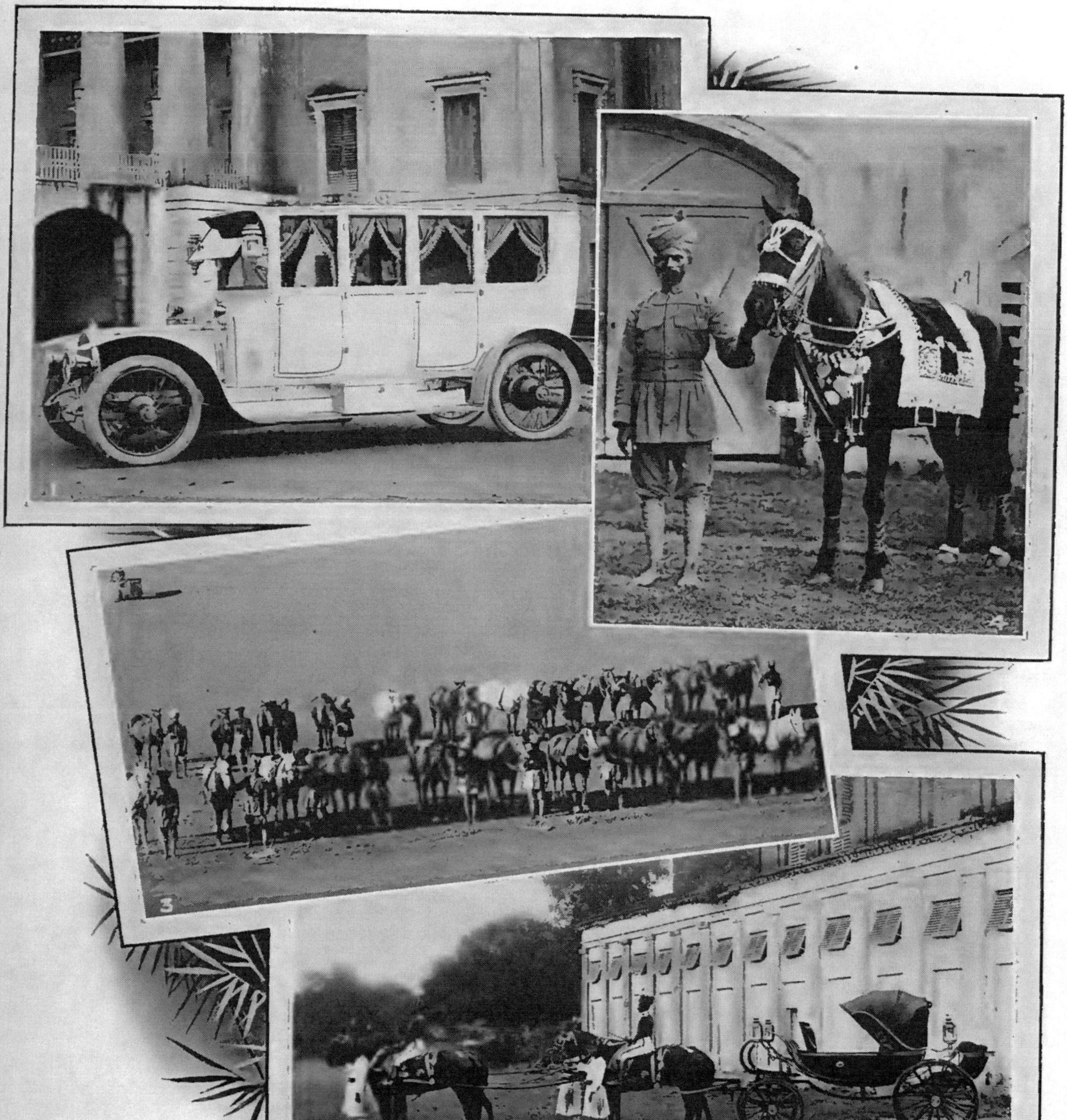

THE MURSHIDABAD SERKAR ALI.

1. The State Motor-car. 2. The State Carriage. 3. Group of Polo Ponies. 4. Polo Pony, Venus.

THE MURSHIDABAD SERKAR ALI.

1. The Imambarah 2. The Katra Musjid, built by Nawab Murshedkuli Khan. 3. Seraj-ud-Dowlah's Tomb. 4. The Jaffraganj Cemetery.

THE MURSHIDABAD SERKAR ALI.

1. MOTI MAHAL. 2. THE SOUTH GATE. 3. THE STABLES. 4. THE CLOCK TOWER.

just, and wise administrator. Government appreciated his inestimable character and large benefactions for public good by successively honouring him with the titles of K.C.I.E. and G.C.I.E., and other high distinctions.

His Highness held rank as the premier noble of the Province under the Governor of Bengal, with the hereditary title (in addition to that of Nawab Bahadur of Murshidabad) of Amir-ul-Omra, which means "chief of the nobles," and he was the only hereditary Nawab in Bengal.

The Nawab resided in a magnificent palace, proud of his allegiance to the King-Emperor, and resting in full enjoyment of privileges—especially of peace—to which the majority of his ancestors were strangers.

It may be added here that the esteem in which His Highness was held was manifested by the bestowal upon him of the following honourable titles: Ali Kadr, signifying "of first rank"; Ihitsham-ul-Mulk, "dignifier of the country"; Rais-ud-dowla, "premier of the State"; and Mahabat Jang, "horror in war."

His Highness the present Nawab, the Honourable Ihitsham-ul-Mulk, Rais-ud-dowlah, Amir-ul-Omra, Nawab Sir Asif Saiyid Wasif Ali Mirza, Khan Bahadur, Mahabatjang, K.C.V.O., K.C.S.I., the eldest son of the late Nawab Bahadur, was born in the year 1875, and at an early age he manifested a deeply intelligent mind and an ability to grasp the meaning of educational questions, a characteristic which is not frequently seen in one so young in years.

After a course of study at the Doveton College in Calcutta (where he obtained a good general knowledge of the English language) he proceeded to the Old Country and passed through the schools of Sherborne and Rugby and the University of Oxford. During this period of his life, however, he travelled over a considerable portion of the British Isles, the Continent of Europe, and Egypt, and it was his constant ambition to make himself acquainted with the habits and customs of the people whom he met, and the experiences then gained have been of incalculable benefit to him in the responsible position of acting on his father's behalf in the administration of domestic affairs, as well as in the larger matters of the Raj estates. He comes of a succession of potentates who learned to rule, not by force, but by a spirit of justice and kindly consideration of the needs of their people, and his counsel is eagerly sought by those who know the sterling worth of his character.

The business capabilities of His Highness were recognized when he became Chairman of the Municipal Council of Murshidabad; in 1901 he was nominated by Sir John Woodburn, K.C.S.I., Lieutenant-Governor of Bengal, to a seat on the Legislative Council of that Province; and in the following year he was chosen by Lord Curzon as representative of Bengal at the coronation of his late Majesty King Edward VII.

The Prince possesses charming and refined manners, and it has been truly said of him that he has all the attributes of an eastern prince with the bearing of a western gentleman. His noble appearance, beaming with intelligence, attracts the attention and admiration of every one with whom he comes in contact. His command of the English language and literature, and his knowledge of English manners, customs, and etiquette, acquired during a lengthy residence in England, are a theme of admiration everywhere. His wonderful presence of mind, his indomitable energy, and his buoyant habit of looking at the bright side of everything under all difficulties and adverse circumstance, are some of the most brilliant traits of his noble character.

He has always taken a deep interest in healthy outdoor pastimes, such as cricket, football, and tennis, and his love of sport has lured him on to the shooting of tigers and pig-sticking, while in polo—at which he is a crack player—he has usually captained a team whose colours are very rarely lowered.

There are many ancestral "palaces" or "mansions" in Europe, and India too, to which these terms may be applied in their rigid exclusiveness, but those to which the word "home," dignified by family ties and associations of the closest description, can be given are comparatively few in number. One of these highly favoured residences, the Nizamut Kila (or fort) or Hazar Dawari, to give it the name by which it is known to natives in Bengal, is the palace belonging to His Highness the Nawab Bahadur of Murshidabad. The construction of the building was commenced in the year 1829, and from the date when it was first occupied (1837) it has been inhabited by members of the same distinguished family.

It is 416 feet in length, 204 feet in width, and 85 feet in elevation, and it cost about 16½ lakhs of rupees, or £167,000 sterling. Surrounded by some of the most charming wooded scenery of Bengal, and standing on the east bank of the Bhagirathi River, it presents a noble aspect, and its well-kept lawns and drives, its graceful proportions, and the splendid dome of the adjoining *Imambara* (or "house of prayer") add to the general beauty of the picture.

This is one of the most historically and architecturally interesting mansions in India, as it is a veritable storehouse of magnificent paintings of Dutch, Flemish, French, and Italian schools, of works of art, priceless gems, and stately statuary, yet withal it is one around which are clustered such tender memories that its domestic life may, without challenge, be said to be one of its greatest attractions. The building follows the Doric style of architecture, and is approached by a noble flight of 36 steps, the bottom and top ones being 108 feet and 65 feet in width respectively. The portico is supported by Doric pillars, and the entrance, oval in form, is paved with polished grey marble which was imported from Italy for the purpose.

Immediately after entering, one notices the circular Durbar Hall, in which is the *gadi*, or throne, of the Nawab, constructed of marble, richly decorated with gold. A silver chair is used on State occasions, and there are other richly furnished seats for distinguished personages.

By passing through a door from this hall one enters a spacious dining-room 94 feet in length and 57 feet in width, but when State banquets are given sliding doors are opened, and smaller apartments on the eastern and western sides afford sitting accommodation for about 350 guests. On the walls are hung speaking portraits of her late Majesty Queen Victoria, H.R.H. the Prince Consort, the Duke of Wellington, and other notabilities of the early portion of the nineteenth century.

A visit must now be paid to several picture galleries, which contain priceless examples of many of the most famous masters, and one is perplexed to know which are to be left out in giving a brief description, but the following may suffice. There is an exceptionally fine painting by Schotel, named "A Sea View," and the artist with consummate skill appears to have put actual motion into the scurrying clouds and the surging waves of a tempestuous sea. Near to this one are others truly characteristic of the great genius of Raphael, Snyders, Rembrandt, and others, while in the grand *salon* is an original

THE MURSHIDABAD SERKAR ALI.

1. The Chowk Musjid. 2. The Changney Chowk, showing Tripolia Gate. 3. The Bakr-Id Procession from the Chowk Musjid.

THE MURSHIDABAD SERKAR ALI.

1. The Garden House, Mobarak Manzil. 2. Interior of the Power-house. 3. The Great Gun, Jahan Kosha. 4. The Motijhil Garden House.

life-size portrait of King William IV. This picture is very highly prized by the house of Murshidabad, as it was painted expressly at the King's command to be sent by him as a present to the Nawab Nazim Humayun Jah Bahadur, and it was accompanied by a personal letter from His Majesty. This was in September 1836. One must not overlook a famous painting by Sir Edwin Landseer, the world-renowned portrayer of animals, which is executed in the best style of the artist. There are probably thousands of engravings of the original picture, which is therefore, by description, well known among all classes of people. Who can forget the solemn dignity of a French poodle which occupies the judge's seat in a court of law, or the judicial manner in which he, with one paw on an open legal text-book, calmly surveys counsel, represented by a curious collection of dogs of various breeds? The scene is so well depicted that one is almost persuaded that a question, or a rebuke to an over-zealous advocate, is about to fall from the lips of the president of the court.

The furniture in the *salon* is of the Georgian period, but the most interesting objects are couches and chairs of exquisitely carved ivory, similar to the delicate lace-work for which the ancient city of Murshidabad was justly famed, together with ivory horses, camels, State elephants, carriages, gods, goddesses, and other subjects.

In the immediate vicinity of the *salon* is a State bedroom, 47 feet by 29 feet, and adjoining it is the family portrait gallery, containing a splendid collection of paintings of past and present members of the Nawab's family, including the Nawab Murshid Kuli Khan, the Nawab Mir Jaffar, two sons of the present Nawab, and a host of other historically interesting personages. The principal drawing-room, truly a restful apartment, is beautified by a large number of exceedingly fine water colours, while other rooms contain paintings, pictures, and works of art far too numerous to particularize. The magnificent ball-room is above, and of the same size as the banqueting-hall, but the large library is worthy of some notice. It contains about five thousand English volumes and nearly four thousand printed in several Oriental languages. Many illustrated books are of priceless value, but particular mention should be made of three volumes of the sacred *Koran*, beautifully illuminated in gold and dated 1277-1281, and 1724, respectively.

Very valuable illustrated editions may be seen of Shakespeare (1803), of Hogarth's drawings, Lewis's "English Scenery," and many works dear to the hearts of literary connoisseurs. It should be mentioned here that His Highness, with his large-hearted consideration for others, has presented several rare and costly volumes to the trustees of the Victoria Memorial Hall, now being erected in Calcutta, his reason for making the gift being that "he would rather they were viewed by thousands of interested persons than be displayed to a few visitors at the Palace."

One of the wonderful sights in the mansion, however, is the Toshakana, or treasure house, which contains a marvellous collection of armour, jewels, personal adornments for State ceremonies and other very valuable insignia of high rank. The eye will speedily be attracted by magnificent emeralds, measuring 2 inches by $1\frac{3}{4}$ inches, which are worn occasionally as armlets, or on the belt, or as part of an ornament for the head, when they are supported by beautiful diamonds. These were presented by a former Emperor of Delhi, and their value has never been appraised. There are jewelled swords to be seen, one of which was given by the late Queen Victoria to His Highness's father, and another one which formerly belonged to the Mogul Emperor, Humayun. In another portion of the wizard's cave is a Sedan chair of solid silver, and around the walls and standing in various corners are old cannon of Hindu, Mahommedan, English, and Dutch manufacture, swords, spears, muskets, and a curious assortment of weapons of different types.

Outside the fort and not more than half a mile from the Palace on the Berhampore road is an extensive range of stables for horses and elephants, together with coach-house for State and other carriages.

The manufacture of silk was one of the earliest of the industries in Murshidabad, and ancient records state that as far back as the year 1621 the East India Company, who had established a factory at Kasimbazar, "were forbidden to make further purchases of raw material." But the industry was not thereby killed, as it is known that about the year 1750 it was in a flourishing condition. The Company took a deep interest in the question, going so far as to offer to *ryots* waste lands for a period of two years provided that they undertook the cultivation of mulberry-trees.

THE NADIA RAJ

The district of Nadia, in the Presidency division of Bengal, is bounded on the north by the districts of Murshidabad, Rajshahi, and Pabna, on the east by the districts of Faridpur and Jessore, on the south by the district of 24 Parganas, and on the west by the districts of Hooghly, Burdwan, and Murshidabad.

The Nadia Raj family claim direct descent from Bhattanarayan, who was one of the five Brahmans selected by Adisur, King of Bengal, for the conduct of ceremonies of purification. It is one of the oldest and most respectable Hindu noble families in Bengal. The present Chief, the Maharaja Bahadur Kshaunish Chandra Ray, is thirty-sixth in the genealogical line, and it was at the time of the Coronation Durbar at Delhi in December 1911 that the title of "Maharaja" was bestowed on him. He was made a "Maharaja Bahadur" in January 1917, and he enjoys the privilege of a return visit from His Excellency the Governor of Bengal. Maharaja Bahadur Kshaunish Chandra Ray was born at the Palace, Krishnagar, on October 29, 1890. He married Maharani Jyotirmoyee Dabee, the youngest daughter of the late Raja Ashutosh Nath Ray, of Kasimbazar, in the district of Murshidabad. The Maharaja has one daughter, who was born in Calcutta on November 1, 1916.

The early history of the family is based to a very considerable extent on traditions, but according to such statements, and to certain Sanskrit writers, it appears that Bhattanarayan's estate comprised a number of villages which he had obtained by purchase or grant from Adisur. There are few legendary events of importance during the rule of several of the earliest Chiefs, but the estate of Kasinath—nineteenth in succession—was invaded by Mussulmans, who eventually captured and put him to death. His posthumous son, Ram, became a great scholar, and his property was enlarged by the devise of the kingdom of Harikrishna Samaddhar, he being subsequently known as Ram Samaddhar. Durgadas, *alias* Bhabananda, son of the last-named, received from the Delhi Emperor, Akbar, the title of *Majumdar*, and he inherited his father's estate and built a palace in Parghana Bagwan, which was the largest zemindary of the Nadia Raj in those days. Majumdar subsequently rendered valuable services to Raja Man Singh, Akbar's general, in the expedition against Pratapaditya, the Chief of Jessore. Man Singh took Majumdar

MAHARAJA KSHAUNISH CHANDRA RAY BAHADUR, OF NADIA.
Photo by Edna Lorenz.

to Delhi and presented him to the Emperor Jehangir, bringing to His Majesty's notice the services rendered by him. The Emperor restored him to his ancestor's (Kasinath's) Raj, and conferred on him the title of Maharaja. This was about the beginning of the seventeenth century.

Ram Krishna—twenty-seventh in succession—administered the affairs of the Nadia Raj for a long time, living happily at the new capital, Krishnagar, and he was also on terms of amity with the then Governor of the English settlement at Calcutta. The latter, in token of his regard for Ram Krishna, placed at his disposal a garrison of 2,500 soldiers. He was of a somewhat aggressive nature, and added land to his territory by the conquest of the Raja of Jessore, but he ultimately became a prisoner and died in confinement.

Bengal was passing through a most critical period during the rulership of Krishna Chandra, thirtieth in succession, but the latter assisted so loyally in the establishment of British power that Lord Clive bestowed upon him the title of "Rajendra Bahadur," and also presented him with twelve guns and a sword used at the battle of Plassey. These gifts may still be seen at the Palace at Krishnagar. Krishna Chandra lived to a good old age, and was followed by Siva Chandra, Iswar Chandra, Girish Chandra, Srish Chandra, Satish Chandra, and Kshitish Chandra, all of whom encouraged education and strenuously supported measures of reform tending to elevate the social condition of their subjects. The Government recognized and confirmed Srish Chandra's title of "Maharaja Bahadur" conferred by the Mahommedan rulers, and bestowed upon him the usual *khilat* and other honours appertaining thereto. The same title and honours have all along been enjoyed by the head of the family of the Nadia Raj for the past seventy years. Maharaja Bahadur Kshitish Chandra died in August 1910, and was succeeded by his only son, Kshaunish Chandra, who has already been referred to.

The family holds a unique position in Hindu society, having been the recognized patron of Sanskrit teaching in Navadwip, the "Oxford" of Bengal, for centuries past. Maharaja Krishna Chandra, the most famous man of his age, was known as *Nabadwipadhipati*, and the successive Maharajas have held the title since that time. He was universally considered the head of Hindu society, and the arbitrator on all questions of caste.

In works of munificence and public charity the family yield to none in the country. It is a well-known fact in Bengal that there is scarcely a house of learned Brahmans which does not enjoy a free gift of land from the Nadia Raj, and there have also been numerous grants of *Pirottar* lands to Mahommedans.

At one time the family property consisted of extensive zemindaries, and comprised 84 *pergannas*, but it is now reduced owing to the unlimited charity of the Maharajas from the time of Krishna Chandra. The family, however, maintains its position as one of the noblest in Bengal.

THE NASHIPUR RAJ.

The Hon. the Maharaja Ranjit Sinha, of Nashipur, son of the late Raja Kirti Chandra Sinha Bahadur, was born on June 9, 1865, and he has a most distinguished ancestry, the family history being traced to Maharaja Tarawah, who was the ruling chief of Bijapur, in the Deccan, in the fourteenth century. After the Maharaja Tarawah, his son Prince Madan Singh came into possession of the vast zemindary, and Rai Sambhunath, another of the present Maharaja's ancestry, was appointed by the Emperor of Delhi as Subadar and Nazim of the whole tract of country from Shahranpur to Meerut, and his brother, Rai Badrinath, took part in the battle of Shamli under Colonel Burn. But the credit of founding the Nashipur Raj belongs to the Maharaja Devi Sinha Bahadur, whose father Rai Dewali Sinha left Panipat in the beginning of the eighteenth century and arrived at Murshidabad, then the capital of Bengal. Devi Sinha entered the service of the Honourable East India Company in the Revenue Department, in which he held a high and responsible position in connection with the permanent settlement of Bengal. He farmed the revenues of Purnea, and of the districts of Rungpur, Dinajpur, and Edrakpura, and in the year 1773 became Steward or Secretary to the Provincial Council of Murshidabad. Having rendered important services to Lord Clive at the battle of Plassey he was honoured with the title of Maharaja Bahadur. Later on in the history of this family is found the name of Raja Udmunt Sinha Bahadur, who was widely known for his liberality, and it was during his time that the Thakoor *Bari*, which is not only picturesque but grand, was constructed.

The Maharaja Ranjit Sinha's father died when the former was very young, and consequently his extensive zemindary, situated in the districts of Birbhum, Murshidabad, Malda, Pabna, Bogra, and Rajshahi (of which the Government revenue is Rs. 3,32,000), was managed by the Court of Wards during his minority. The young Maharaja received his early education at the Berhampore College, Bengal, where he had a brilliant career, and he devoted himself specially to mathematics, in which branch of study he made considerable progress and in which he even now takes great interest. From his boyhood he was remarkable for punctuality and steady habits, and his high intelligence attracted the notice of his teachers and professors, all of whom were of opinion that this youth would in the future be a leader of men in his own country. On attaining his majority in the year 1886, he directed his attention to the management of his estate, establishing it on a firm and sure basis, but he was specially concerned in the improvement of the condition of his tenants, and in this respect he has proved himself a model zemindar. Unlike some zemindars he does not leave the management of his estate in the hands of subordinates, and he has introduced rules for its guidance which have proved so useful that they have been adopted by many of the leading landowners of Bengal. His book, named "The Rules for the Management of the Nashipur Raj Estate," though prepared with the chief object of controlling his own estate, is a model guide to zemindary matters, and it shows the close and comprehensive grasp which the author has of such questions. His officials are governed by those rules, and enjoy privileges, such as leave and pension, while everything is conducted in accordance with the strict rules and procedure laid down in the book above referred to.

The chief characteristic of the subject of this sketch is versatility. His varied talents are used with discretion, and whatever he takes in hand he does well. He is very regular and punctual in the discharge of his duties, attending his office regularly from 11 a.m. to 5 p.m. During the cold weather he tours the Mofussil, and he has gained such vast experience that he can enter into the details of his zemindary work with admirable precision and consideration.

The Maharaja's public career began in the year 1887, when he was appointed as an honorary magistrate of the Lalbag Independent Bench. In 1888 he was elected chairman of the Murshidabad municipality, and during his incumbency of that office he introduced many sanitary reforms which made him highly popular and earned for him the golden opinion of the local authorities. In the year 1889, when he was still chairman of municipality, the town of Murshidabad was heavily inundated, and many families were reduced to the brink of starvation and ruin, their houses having been swept away by floods. But the Maharaja, although a young man at the time, had the pluck to risk his own life in saving the lives and houses of many of these families, and for this benevolent and heroic act Sir Steuart Bailey, the then Lieutenant-Governor of Bengal, applauded his services very highly. On January 1, 1891, he was created Raja, and Sir Charles Elliot addressed him thus: "It is a very great pleasure to me to convey to you the *Sanad* of the title of Raja which the Viceroy has been pleased to confer upon you. The title is one which has been honourably borne by your family for many generations, and it is now committed to you to hold untarnished. One of your ancestors, Raja Devi Sinha, rendered very valuable services to Clive at Plassey, and the continued favour in which your family has been held and the honour which is today entrusted to you, is a proof that the Government of India is never slow to recognize and never forgets services rendered to it by the houses in this country. You have lately attained your majority and succeeded to your property. I trust you will manage your estate in a manner worthy of your ancestry, and that your career may compare favourably with that of other zemindars in the Province, and that it will be so distinguished that further honours will be conferred upon you, not on account of the good work of those who have gone before you, but as a reward for your own merit and exertions."

In 1894 he was invested with the powers of a magistrate of the second class, empowered to sit singly. In this capacity he displayed so much zeal and ability that the Government in appreciation of his services conferred upon him the powers of a magistrate of the first class on March 1, 1897, and entrusted him with powers to take cognizance of offences on complaints and reports of police. It was during that time that he was placed in entire charge of the Lalbag Bench, and he virtually discharged the duties of a Sub-Divisional Officer after the abolition of the Lalbag Sub-Division. In 1899, and again in 1903, he was re-elected as chairman of the Murshidabad municipality, and in that capacity he was at the helm of its administration for about ten years. In 1897 he was created Raja Bahadur, and when conferring that title upon him Sir Charles Stevens observed as follows: "Raja, you are a scion of a very ancient and respectable family, and as the proprietor of extensive zemindaries, have conducted yourself in a manner worthy of your origin and of your rank and responsibilities; you have the reputation of being a good and liberal landlord to your own *ryots*; but your desire to do good service to the public has led you to enter a more extended sphere of usefulness. As a municipal commissioner and an honorary magistrate you have rendered great assistance to the local authorities. It has been deemed just and proper that you should be raised to the dignity which your father enjoyed. You have therefore been created a Raja Bahadur, and it gives me great satisfaction to hand you the *Sanad* and

NASHIPUR RAJ.

1. The Hon. Maharaja Ranjit Sinha, of Nashipur. 2. The Palace, Nashipur. 3. The Nashipur Raj Temple.

the *Khilat* which mark your elevation to that rank."

On January 1, 1910, the title of Maharaja was conferred upon him by the Government on account of his manifold services of public utility, and Sir Edward Norman Baker, K.C.S.I., on the occasion of the presentation of the *Sanad* and *Khilat* to the Maharaja, said: "It is always a matter of gratification to me to be the instrument for conveying marks of public recognition to those who have deserved well of the State. That pleasure is much enhanced when the recipient of the honour is an old and valued friend of my own. In your case, our friendship dates back to the year 1898, when we were serving on the Bengal Council, and when I first learned to appreciate in you those qualities of rectitude, sincerity, straightforwardness, and moderation which have given you so high a place in my regard.

"The family of which you are the head is both old and distinguished, and one member of it enjoyed the title of Maharaja as long ago as the year 1800; more than a century ago. Twice already you yourself have received marks of the favour of Government, in 1892 and again in 1897; and it gives me peculiar pleasure now to hand you the *Sanad* of the still higher title of Maharaja, together with the *Khilat* which accompanies it.

"This honourable distinction you have worthily earned, not merely by service in a variety of public offices, as chairman of of the Murshidabad municipality, as an honorary magistrate, as member of the Legislative Council and the like; but still more by the loyal and devoted spirit which you have invariably displayed in times of difficulty and temptation, and by the influence which you have uniformly exerted to counteract the evil forces of sedition, and to further the cause of law, order, and good government. I am hopeful that influence will be further strengthened by the honourable preferment which you have now received, and which I earnestly hope you will live long to enjoy."

That the Government held him in high esteem is evidenced by his being appointed as a member of the Bengal Legislative Council in the year 1899. In that body he has played the part of an active and patriotic member, and his speech on the amendment of the Municipal Bill was recognized as a masterly performance. This memorable address made him highly popular with his own countrymen, and his name became a household word in every cultured family in Bengal. The Government also recognized in him a true councillor who fearlessly expressed his opinion in a very considerate and able manner, so as to justify his being classed as a truly wise statesman who might take place by the side of such distinguished leaders as the late Babu Krishtadas Paul and the Maharaja Sir Jotindra Mohan Tagore. He is not an impetuous politician, but a sound and sober statesman, who is never contented with merely taking a superficial view.

The superb mansion at Nashipur, in which the Maharaja generally resides with his family, is a palatial building constructed after the style of Government House in Calcutta. The Maharaja is always a kind patron and benefactor, particularly to the inhabitants of Nashipur, for whom he has sunk wells, founded schools, and established a charitable dispensary called the Nashipur Raj Charitable Dispensary, which is under the supervision of an able medical officer. The inhabitants of Nashipur are particularly grateful to him for the manifold acts of kindness which they receive at his hands, and, in fact, he might reasonably be called the uncrowned king of Nashipur.

There is no public institution in Bengal with which he is not connected; his charities are unbounded, and many thousands of rupees are systematically spent every year in benevolent donations.

The Nashipur Raj family has always been treated by Government with great honour on account of its loyalty, and it, indeed, reflects great credit upon the Maharaja that when the atmosphere of the country was surcharged with political discontent, he remained firmly loyal to the Government and never allowed his own men to be swayed by the empty vituperations of political anarchists. His keen insight has helped him rightly to understand the political condition of the country, and with the view of inducing the people to take an impartial view of the economic situation of India, he published an "appeal" to his countrymen, in English and Bengali, urging them to be firmly loyal to the Government, and at the same time respectfully to represent their legitimate political aspirations. He was the first among native princes who responded to the call of Government for aid in the suppression of anarchism in India. In his private life the Maharaja is a Hindu of the best type, and although moderate in his views, he is orthodox in all social and religious observances. He is endowed with an amiable disposition, and is uniformly courteous to all. He has a family of four sons and four daughters.

In recognition of his great services in the Council, the District and Local Board members of the Presidency Division elected him again as their representative in the Governor's Council in the election held on January 6, 1913. The Bengal Council elected him as an additional member of the Imperial Council, thus making him a member of both Councils, and since the separation of Behar from Bengal, the Honourable the Maharaja, though belonging to the aristocracy, and being himself a wealthy zemindar, has been elected to the Council as representative of the people. He therefore enjoys a unique position enjoyed by no other member of his class in Bengal. The Honourable Maharaja's services to both the Councils have been largely appreciated both by the Government and the people, mainly on account of his moderate views, and he has laid the inhabitants of Bengal under deep obligation for his strenuous efforts in moving both the Councils to adopt measures for the prevention of malaria and other epidemic diseases which have caused so much havoc among all classes. He has made education and sanitation special subjects, and by his advocacy has endeavoured to educate the public mind to realize the great importance of these questions; his versatility and thorough genius enable him to handle other important political and social matters with that keen penetration and deep insight which have made him so famous.

It is interesting to note that the eldest Maharaj Kumar Bhupendra Narayan Sinha successfully passed the I.A. examination in the first division in 1911; he took the B.A. degree at the Calcutta University in 1913; and is now a graduate preparing himself for both the M.A. and law examinations. The Maharaj Kumar has been nominated by the Government as a member of the District Board of Murshidabad, and as a Commissioner of the municipality of the same city. He has, further, been appointed as an honorary bench magistrate, and has already commenced his public career as such. This reflects great credit upon him, as sons of rich men in India seldom achieve such distinctions in the acquisition of knowledge, preferring rather to lead lives of ease and luxury. The second Maharaj Kumar Nripendra Narayan Sinha is preparing for the B.A. degree; the third

Maharaj Kumar Rajendra Narayan Sinha is studying for the I.A. examination; and the fourth Maharaj Kumar Birendra Narayan Sinha is still young in years. The Government has been pleased to declare that the title of Raja Bahadur shall be an hereditary one in the Nashipur family. The Dewan of the estate is Babu Devendranath Sen, M.A., B.L., who is known as a good and able officer.

THE STATE OF NAYARGARH

The Nayargarh Feudatory State of Orissa is bounded on the north by the States of Daspalia and Khandpara, on the east by the State of Ranpur, on the south by the Khurda subdivision of the district of Puri and by the district of Ganjam in the Madras residency, and on the west by the district of Ganjam.

It is 590 square miles in extent, and is divided into nine *zillas* or *perganas*, and three *mals* which are occupied by aboriginal Khonds. The State contains 710 villages, or about five villages to every four square miles of territory, and the inhabitants are about 151,293 in number. The physical aspects of the State present wonderfully divergent features, the south and south-eastern portions being too hilly to be cultivated, while elsewhere there are widespread tracts of highly cultivated lands. Ranges of hills of various altitudes are found in all parts of the State, and the Sulia range running through the centre has a number of peaks which are from 2,000 feet to 2,500 feet in height. The majority of the hills are covered with fine timber trees, and the whole of the western portion of the State bordering on the Ganjam boundary contains valuable forests which yield a handsome revenue. *Sal* and *piasal* sleepers, and minor forest products such as *kamalagundi* (a dye for colouring silk cloth), *kuchila* (nux vomica), myrabolam, and char seeds (for making sweetmeats), are exported to other States and districts from Khurda Road station on the Bengal-Nagpur system of railways. The forests are controlled by a ranger and two deputies, all of whom were trained for the purpose in the Kurseong School of Forestry.

There are five rivers in Nayargarh, but all are practically dry about the end of December, and not one is navigable even for a short distance. The State therefore enjoys complete immunity from danger of floods, although there are a sufficient number of natural springs to ensure an adequate supply of water for all practical purposes.

The means of communication are of an indifferent character; there is no railway within the State, and there is only one metalled road connecting the headquarters at Nayargarh with the village at Dighari, where it meets another road leading to Khurda Road station. The Nayargarh-Ranpur road—10 miles in length—passes through the State of Ranpur to the railway station at Kalupara, while another highway, from Nayargarh to Daspalla, is in course of construction and will probably be completed by the end of the year 1918.

The "Ramsay" bridge has been constructed on the Nayargarh-Bolgarb road at a cost of Rs. 56,839, and the "Madagni" bridge on the Nayargarh-Ranpur road cost Rs. 8,120.

About 60 per cent. of the population are dependent for a livelihood upon agricultural resources, but the methods of cultivation are of a very primitive character. Sugar-cane is the most profitable crop, but the absence of any permanent means of irrigation tends to prevent *ryots* from growing it; the soil throughout the State is admirably suited for rice, which is sown upon nearly 70 per cent. of the cultivated area; and cotton, wheat, jute, potatoes, and oil-seeds of various kinds are receiving more attention.

A number of irrigation *bundhs*, invaluable in times of drought, have been constructed, but many others are needed before agriculture can become the successful occupation that it ought to be.

Local manufactures and industries are of an insignificant character, the principal being the making of cotton fabrics, tusser cloth, wooden cups, brass and bell-metal utensils, ivory chains, buttons, sticks and ornaments, while the chief exports include timber, rice, cotton, oil-seeds, hides, and minor forest products.

Education is making steady progress in the State, there being 79 schools as follows: one middle English school and two Sanskrit *tols* at Nayargarh; one *maktab*; seven upper primary schools; and 68 lower primary institutions. There has been a notable increase in the number of special schools for Pans, Khonds, and other races, and there is a demonstration farm in charge of an agricultural expert, who gives weekly lessons on practical agriculture to a considerable number of boys. A joint sub-inspector has been appointed for Nayargarh and Daspalla States to supervise the work done in the upper and lower primary schools.

The State does not possess an unhealthy climate, but a considerable amount of sickness frequently takes place owing to a lack of energy on the part of the people with regard to the adoption of modern hygienic methods. Reforms in this direction have been introduced and great benefits have resulted from the opening of two dispensaries, which are under the control of a qualified sub-assistant surgeon.

There are also two indoor wards for patients, one at Nayargarh and the other at Orgaon, and a sub-assistant surgeon from the Cuttack Medical School is permanently employed in primary vaccinations and re-vaccinations of the people.

The principal buildings in the State are well constructed, and they comprise the *Rajbati*, Jagannath Jews' temple, Gopinath Jews' temple, the State offices, a dak bungalow for an inspecting officer, a middle-class English school and hostel, a dispensary, and wards for in-patients, together with a police station and quarters for officers and constables.

The relations between the State and the British Government are regulated by a *sanad* granted in 1908, and the amount payable annually as tribute is Rs. 5,525, while the income reaches Rs. 2,27,802.

The State is now under the management of the Government, and the present chief is Raja Narayan Singh Mandhata. The Jubaraj (heir-apparent) is aged six years and the San Deo (second Raj-Kumar) three years.

THE RAMGOPALPUR RAJ

Raja Jogendra Kishore Roy Chowdhury belongs to an ancient Zemindar family of Ramgopalpur, in the district of Mymensingh, Bengal. The family history commences from Srikrishna Chowdhury, the founder of the family. Raja Jogendra Kishore is the sixth descendant of him who obtained the Parganas Mymensingh and Jafarshahi from Nawab Murshidkuli Khan of Bengal in the early part of the eighteenth century. He was an inhabitant of Karai, a village in the district of Bogra. His daughter-in-law, Narayani Devi, gained the share of her ancestral property after several contested suits with her co-sharer, and she took possession of her share on the strength of a *sanad* granted to her on July 12, 1774, by Warren Hastings. Narayani Debi's great-grandson was the late Kashi Kishore Roy Chowdhury, the father of the present Raja. On Kashi Kishore Roy Chowdhury was conferred, for the first time in the district

NAYARGARH FEUDATORY STATE.

1. RAJA NARAYAN SINGH MANDHATA (PRESENT RAJA). 2. RAJA RAGHUNATH SINGH MANDHATA. 3. RAJA LADU KISHORE SINGH MANDHATA.
4. THE RAJA AND THE JUBARAJ.

NAYARGARH FEUDATORY STATE.

1. The New Rajbati, Nayargarh. 2. The Old Rajbati. 3. Jagganath Temple. 4. Office Building.

of Mymensingh, an Honorary Magistracy, and he exercised his powers for a period of twenty-two years with extraordinary ability and success, holding his court at his own residence at Ramgopalpur. Kashi Kishore Roy Chowdhury nicely managed and greatly increased his ancestral property by the purchase of new Zemindaries in the districts of Faridpur, Dacca, and Silhat. In recognition of his loyalty to the British Raj as a leading Zemindar in the district of Mymensingh, a certificate of honour was presented to him by the Government in the year 1877. Kashi Kishore Roy Chowdhury was an orthodox Hindu of exemplary character and scholarly attainments.

Raja Jogendra Kishore Roy Chowdhury was born in the month of January 1858. He has inherited all the qualities and virtues of his father, and, like him, he is trusted and regarded highly by the Government for his loyalty, munificence, and devotedness to the welfare of his tenants. Many Sanskrit scholars, hailing from different parts of the country, are welcomed by him every year, and they are encouraged with annual donations according to their merits. In 1897 a certificate of honour was presented to him in the following words :—

"By command of His Excellency the Viceroy and Governor-General in Council this certificate is presented in the name of Her Most Gracious Majesty Queen Victoria, the Empress of India, to Rai Jogendra Kishore Roy Chowdhury, Bahadur, son of Babu Kashi Kishore Roy Chowdhury, Zemindar, in recognition of his excellent management of his estate and public liberality.

"(*Signed*) A. MACKENZIE,
"Lieutenant-Governor of Bengal.
"*June* 20, 1897."

Raja Jogendra Kishore is known to the public for his liberality and high-mindedness. His charities are many-sided—a first-class charitable dispensary and a High School are supported by him at his own residence, and he has an *Atithshala* at Ramgopalpur, where thousands of travellers are sumptuously fed year after year. He has spent a large sum on the extension of education, and the Kashi Kishore Technical School at Mymensingh owes its existence to his donation of nearly Rs. 45,000. The Anandamohan College at Mymensingh is the outcome of his timely donation of Rs. 30,000, and it was proposed by the Government to name it after the donor; but the benevolent Raja, in order to commemorate the memory of the late Anandamohan Bose, requested the Government to connect the name of the latter gentleman with the college, and this was accordingly done. Raja Jogendra Kishore has since contributed Rs. 2,000 towards the college fund. His monthly subscriptions to many institutions and hospitals are still continued. Towards the excavation of tanks, wells, and the extension of waterworks at Mymensingh and Dacca he gave altogether nearly Rs. 20,000. Among his numerous donations the following deserve mention. He gave towards the Lady Dufferin's Fund the sum of Rs. 1,500; to the Darjeeling Sanatorium, Rs. 1,200 ; the Queen Victoria Memorial Fund, Rs. 1,200; the King Edward Memorial Fund, Rs. 2,000; the Mymensingh New Hospital Fund, Rs. 1,000; and the Mymensingh Old City College Fund, Rs. 1,000. Besides making these gifts he has lent his support to the Dacca Northbrook Hall, the Mymensingh Alexandria Girls' School, the boarding establishment in connection with the Eden School (Dacca), the Town Hall at Jamalpur, the Sir John Woodburn Memorial Fund, the Keshab Academy in Calcutta, the Kangra Valley Earthquake Fund, the Endowment Fund for a Hindoo Hostel at Mymensingh, Famine Relief Funds in several districts, the Dacca Mitford Hospital, the Pasteur Institution in Shillong, and towards the renovation of Barabanal Kunda at the Chandranath Shrine.

For his liberality and public spirit, the Government conferred upon him the title of Rai Bahadur in 1895, and in 1909 he was honoured with the title of Raja. At the time of the Investiture Durbar at Dacca, His Honour the Lieutenant-Governor of Eastern Bengal and Assam alluded to him as follows :—

RAJA JOGENDRA KISHORE ROY CHOWDHURY, OF RAMGOPALPUR.

"It is with much pleasure that, by the direction of the Government of India, I now confer upon you with this *Khilat* the title of Raja. As owner of a very extensive Zemindary, you have shown, by your residence on the estate and your careful regard to the requirements of your tenants, by your loyalty during the recent disturbance in your district, and by your unswerving support of the officers of

Government in their efforts to maintain order, eminent and distinguished services, which the Government are very pleased to acknowledge and reward. Your liberality has been conspicuous. Your charitable donations for public purposes amount to very large sums, including a contribution of Rs. 30,000 towards the Mymensingh College, and a promise of Rs. 30,000 towards the construction of a bridge over the Brahmaputra River. I trust and feel sure that you will continue in the same course of meritorious action in the future as you have in the past, and that your tenants and the public may look to you for support and assistance. I wish you long life to enjoy the honour which has now been conferred upon you."

TALCHER FEUDATORY STATE.

Talcher, a Feudatory State of Orissa, lies between 20° 52′ and 21° 18′ N., and 84° 54′ and 85° 16′ E., at a distance of nearly 60 miles from Cuttack, the capital of the Orissa Division of the Province of Behar and Orissa, and a station on the Bengal-Nagpur Railway. It is bounded on the north by the Bamra and the Pal-Lahara States, on the east by the Dhenkanal State, and on the south and west by the district of Angul. It covers an area of 399 square miles, and has a population of 66,206 persons scattered over five hundred villages. The net income of the State, from all sources, is nearly two lakhs of rupees, of which a sum of Rs. 1,039-10-5 is paid as tribute money to the British Government.

The State contains a workable coal-field, and the Brahmani River, which traverses the State, washes down small quantities of gold, while iron and limestone are found in nearly all parts.

The country is full of beautiful hills and dales situated on both sides of the Brahmani and on the spur of the great Indian tableland. Talcher has one of the finest climates in Orissa, and it may one day become an important sanatorium for the Province. The soil consists of sandy clay, disintegrated from rocky matter, and is highly productive.

It is said that at the end of the twelfth century four younger brothers of the Jaipur Rana Thakur family, who belonged to the ancient Surya Vansa (Solar Race), quarrelled with the eldest son and went to Puri to see the idol Jagannath. They were so proud of their Surya Vansa and Rana Thakur family that they did not properly salute the then Raja, and in consequence they were not allowed to see the idol. Two of them were killed and the other two fled to a place named Bhimanagari, in the State of Dhenkanal, where the eldest of them ruled up to his death. He built a temple near his fort and set up an idol named Ramchandi Devi. The place and the idol now belong to Dhenkanal.

The name of the elder of the two brothers was Narahari Sinha, while the other was called Udeykar Sinha. After the death of the former, his son Tej Bhanu Sinha became Raja of that place and conquered Parjang and Subalaya, now in the Dhenkanal State. His uncle, Udeykar Sinha, then went to Bonai, and became Raja of that State. Tej Bhanu's son and successor, Raja Govind Charan Routa Rai, was the first to assume the title of "Birbar Harichandan." Six generations followed. The last of these, Raja Padmanav Birbar Harichandan, left Subalaya, defeated by the Raja of Dhenkanal State, and crossed the Brahmani on an expedition of new conquest, during which the goddess Taleswari is said to have made him victorious over his enemy the Khondual Zemindar of Remwa. The deity Hingula Devi, according to tradition, also befriended him in a battle, appearing in the shape of a royal Bengal tiger, which became the State insignia. The Raja, in honour of Taleswari, then gave the name of Talcher to the place where the victory was won. Raja Chakradhar Birbar Harichandan was the next ruler, and his son Gopinath succeeded him in 1651.

Until 1803 the ruler of the State was a feudatory of the Mahrattas, but in November of that year he entered into a treaty with the British Government, whereby he engaged to be loyal and submissive to them.

Raja Dayanidhi Birbar Harichandan, the present Raja's grandfather, helped the British troops at the time of the rebellion of the Angul Raja in 1847, and was rewarded with the title of Mahendra Bahadur, and the gift of a *Khilat* and an elephant.

The present chief, Raja Kishore Chandra Birbar Harichandan, born on June 9, 1880, succeeded his father, Raja Ram Chandra Birbar Harichandan, in December 1891. During his minority the State was under the administration of the Government, and he was educated at the Cuttack Ravenshaw College. In very early days he was eager to learn and studied diligently; but he was not unmindful of his physical training, and entered heartily into all games and manly exercises and distinguished himself in athletics.

His formal installation took place on June 9, 1901, when he attained his legal majority. The State has prospered under the Raja's rule as he has initiated several reforms, among which may be mentioned the thorough reorganization of the revenue department and its establishment under a competent revenue officer. The method of levying the land tax has been improved, and protection has been, as far as possible, given to *ryots* against heavy and unjust assessments. The Raja is keenly interested in, and devotes much time and attention to, the construction of public works, and in recent years he has spent vast sums of money upon a number of fine buildings, four hundred miles of roads leading to every nook and corner of the State have been opened, and several dak-bungalows have been erected.

The Raja pays special attention to the subject of education, and there has been a marked progress during his rule. He raised the local M.V. school to the status of a Middle English school, and this again to a High English school, and there are now the following educational establishments in the State: namely, the Juvaraj High English School, the Sanskrit Tol, one upper primary girls' school, six upper primary schools, fifty-four lower primary schools, five lower primary girls' schools, one training school, and one low caste school.

In the matter of affording medical relief, the State has adopted standards which are generally approved at the present day. This department is controlled by a fully qualified medical officer, and the hospital is equipped with up-to-date medical appliances.

The Forest Department has also been considerably improved. Before the present chief came to the *gadi*, the forests were scanty and had been denuded of all the best timber trees, but now there are nearly 39 square miles (comprising 18 blocks) of reserved and 144 square miles of protected forests.

Wild animals, including elephants, bison, deer, sambur, bear, tiger, leopard and pig, are fairly numerous, and *keddahs* are constructed for the purpose of capturing wild elephants from the jungle.

Endeavours are being made to secure efficient conservancy and the planting of new trees, while the felling of forest trees which bear fruit for food of value to the poor and destitute is strictly prohibited. The department is under the charge of

TALCHER FEUDATORY STATE.

1. Raja Kishore Chandra Birbar Harichandan, Feudatory Chief of Talcher State. 2. Juvaraja Hridaya Chandra Dev. 3. Pataet Promoda Chandra Dev. 4. The Shikar Trophies of the Raja.

TALCHER FEUDATORY STATE.

1. Raja Ram Chandra Birbar Harichandan. 2. The Lion's Gate, Talcher State. 3. The Raj Palace, Talcher.
4. Raja Dayanidhi Birbar Harichandan Mahindra, Bahadur (Grandfather).

a forest officer and a trained staff of rangers.

The ruler of Talcher is most enthusiastic in the matter of improving his subjects, and experimental farms have been established in various places for the guidance of occupiers of land in modern methods of cultivation. Several channels and tanks have already been excavated in order to facilitate irrigation, and a considerable number in addition are now under construction. The chief is most energetic in his attempts to promote the industrial education of artisans, and for this purpose he has opened a school and workshop at Talcher, where various kinds of indigenous arts and trades are taught in a practical manner. It may be added that this school is the only one of its kind in Orissa.

The Raja is a profound believer in education, and with the view of providing a plentiful supply of cheap literature he has founded the Talcher Kishore Steam Press, in which the entire work of printing is carried out by local residents.

Further, the inauguration of the *Kishore Chandra Sahitya Samaj* for the literary advancement of the Talcher people denotes a marked advance in the path of progress. The chief is a man of high literary distinction, and in recognition of his merits in this direction the *Utkal Sahitya Shabha* of Orissa invited him to preside at their last annual conference held at Cuttack. He is enthusiastic in his encouragement of authors, and is always prepared to render financial assistance to them; while he is deeply interested in the annual examination held under the auspices of the *Utkal Sahitya Shabha* at Cuttack, when a medal for research work in the field of old Uriya literature is presented.

Patriotism is a distinctive feature in the Raja's character, and he is a loyal supporter of any movement devoted to the welfare of his motherland. In fact, it was in order to do honour to him for his deep attachment to his own country that he was unanimously elected as President of the third session of the Utkal Union Conference held at Balasore.

The inhabitants of Talcher are the special objects of the chief's love and care, and he gives much thought to the question of the improvement of their condition. Without the help of a *dewan* he controls all State affairs, and thus by coming into close relationship with his devoted people he is able to exercise special personal care over their interests.

In short, the Talcher people are contented and live peacefully under the rule of the chief, who may be regarded as the creator of modern Talcher.

For the purposes of administration the State is divided into five *zillas* and three police *thanas*. There are the first and the second class magistrates' courts, the revenue court, the *Dharmadhykohya's* court, the assistant session judge's court, and the sessions court, for administration of justice. All appeals from the lower courts are heard by the chief, who exercises full powers in both civil and criminal actions. Death sentences are, however, subject to the confirmation of the Commissioner of the Orissa Division of the Province. The Raja personally supervises the work of all departments and attends daily to all State correspondence.

In private life the Raja is a perfect gentleman, sociable, and courteous in behaviour, and he is simple in manners and habits. As a social reformer, his efforts to destroy several evil practices have been most successful. He takes great interest in the development of commerce, and his private enterprises in this direction are distinctly encouraging.

The Raja, with a keen eye for men of ability and character, has surrounded himself with very able and experienced officials, who co-operate with him, in every possible way, in the work of administration.

No more keen and enthusiastic sportsman than the Chief of Talcher can be found in the whole of Orissa, and his skill as a marksman is rarely at fault. He has bagged forty-seven tigers in addition to numerous other animals.

The chief married the fourth daughter of the late Maharaja Sir Basudeb Sudhal Deb, K.C.I.E., of Bamra, and has two sons and one daughter. The eldest prince was born on February 27, 1902, the second on September 12, 1903, and the princess, an accomplished girl, on December 10, 1900.

The Raj-*Kumars* are very amiable and accomplished, and give promise of being worthy sons of their worthy father. Their education, carried on under the personal supervision of the chief, is not a bit inferior to that given to any of their rank in Raj-Kumar colleges. They are very eager to learn and are diligent in their studies. Like their father they are even now brave riders, expert cyclists, good shots, and excellent motor-drivers. They take deep interest in all kinds of sports and pastimes, and it is through their enthusiasm that the Talcher Club, organized to cultivate the physical development of the young men of Talcher, has made such rapid progress in athletics.

Talcher, the headquarters of the State, and the residence of the Raja, is situated on the right bank of the Brahmani River, and has a population of nearly five thousand inhabitants. The town contains several main streets with masonry houses and shops of prosperous traders. There are also the State offices and courts, the *Sadar* police station, a commodious jail, the State hospital, the *Ayurvedic Hall*, the Juvaraj High English School, the girls' school, the training school, a resthouse, an imperial post and telegraph office.

Talcher is a mart of considerable importance.

The palace of the chief is a spacious and imposing edifice, superbly furnished and picturesque, being situated on the bank of the Brahmani River. The Talcher "lion's gate," unique in Orissa, is one of the finest examples of the magnificent architecture of India.

The conservancy and sanitation of the whole town are conducted by the Talcher municipality.

THE HON. RAJA RESHEE CASE LAW, C.I.E.

Many of the existing families in India, and notably in the Province of Bengal, are able to trace an honourable history through many generations, and the commercial and social spheres in which their predecessors moved have been raised to a higher level mainly through their instrumentality. Ancestors made their mark as merchants, or in some other calling, but their true memorial—namely, the respect and affection with which their names are cherished to-day—will last far longer than any masonry monument which may have been erected over their remains. The history of the Law family, widely known in Bengal, affords an excellent example of the manner in which leading men in Calcutta and elsewhere can look back with pride upon the records of their forefathers.

The founder of the well-known firm of Prawnkissen Law & Co., merchants, capitalists, and zemindars of Calcutta, was Prawnkissen Law, who was born at Chinsurah, about 23 miles from Howrah Station, on the East Indian Railway system, about the beginning of the nineteenth century. He was a man of shrewd common sense in business, and although he never attained a leading position as a merchant during the years that he traded in opium, salt, and other produce, he nevertheless laid the basis of a concern which is to-day one of the leading establishments in financial, mercantile, and land-holding circles in Calcutta.

Mr. Prawnkissen Law left three sons, the eldest of whom was the Maharaja Durga Charan Law, born at Chinsurah in November 1822. He received a sound general education in private schools and in the Hindu College, until he was seventeen years of age, when he became an assistant to his father, until the latter's death in 1853. He then assumed full control, and at once grasped the opportunity afforded him of displaying those natural business qualifications which he had inherited from his father, and which had been put into practice during his years of training.

It was recognized by those with whom he came into contact that he was a man of sterling integrity, and it was not long before positions of responsibility and honour were conferred upon him by the Government. He was made a Justice of the Peace and an Honorary Presidency Magistrate, and his opinions on important questions were so respected that he was frequently consulted by the Government of the Province upon various matters affecting administration. He has been a Port Commissioner since the foundation of the Port Trust about fifteen years ago.

Durga Charan Law was never one to thrust himself into prominent positions—he was too modest for that; and as his business capabilities could not be hidden from the general public, he was accordingly appointed Sheriff of Calcutta, a member of the Legislative Council of Bengal in 1874, and in 1882 and 1886 he occupied a seat on the Imperial Legislative Council of India. A Companionship of the Indian Empire was conferred upon him in 1884, he was elected President of the British Indian Association upon two occasions, he became a Raja in 1887, and only four years later he was raised to the dignity of a Maharaja.

The business of the firm continued to grow rapidly, as it was founded and conducted upon strictly honourable lines. While it was expanding, however, the Maharaja never lost sight of what he regarded as his duties towards his fellow-man, and his donations to public institutions and to private individuals were both numerous and generous. In order to illustrate this, reference may be made to his foundation of scholarships in several schools and colleges in Calcutta and Chinsurah by a gift of Rs. 50,000 to the Calcutta University, a donation of Rs. 24,000 to various charitable societies, and of Rs. 5,000 to the Mayo Hospital, in Calcutta, of which he was appointed a Governor in 1883.

Durga Charan did not take any active part in the working of the firm after about the year 1894, and he only ceased to be a partner thereof on his death in 1904. He retired after a most successful business career, and although he naturally was proud of the position which he had attained in the world of commerce, he appeared to value most of all the privileges which his wealth afforded him of benefiting others by his large-hearted support of educational and charitable institutions.

The strenuous life which he had led caused a considerable strain upon his physical vigour, and after a brief retirement of only about ten years he died, deeply regretted by a very wide circle of friends.

The present proprietors of the firm are Raja Kristo Dass Law, the Hon. Raja Reshee Case Law, C.I.E., Babu Chundy Charan Law, and Ambica Charan Law.

Prior to about twenty years ago the firm held banianships for various Calcutta firms, and were large exporters, and dealers in all kinds of imported goods and country produce, but its business is now confined to imports only from England.

The partners are owners of extensive zemindaries in various parts of Bengal and Orissa, and their properties in Calcutta comprise a large number of tenanted houses and private residences.

The mantle of Durga Charan Law has truly fallen upon the shoulders of his successors, and munificent gifts are continually being made by them to charitable and public objects. Among a number of charitable donations have been Rs. 80,000 towards the construction of waterworks for the Chinsurah and Hooghly Municipality, and Rs. 75,000 to the University at Benares; but it is unnecessary to prolong the list, as it is almost a daily occurrence for the partners—either collectively or individually—to assist some worthy cause or to render help in an unostentatious manner to private persons.

Raja Reshee Case Law is the younger of the two sons of Maharaja Durga Charan Law, C.I.E. He was educated in the Calcutta Hindu School and afterwards in the Presidency College of Calcutta. When he was about nineteen years of age he was taken by his father from the College and placed in the firm of Messrs. Kelly & Co., with the view of giving him a good commercial training in exports and, in a small way, in imports, and his quick intelligence enabled him shortly to understand thoroughly the intricacies of a mercantile concern. He stayed there for several years, but was afterwards transferred to his father's business, where he used to attend to not only the commercial but also the Zemindary branches of the concern. During the lifetime of his uncle, Babu Sham Charan Law, and after his death, the management of the extensive Zemindary property of the family devolved upon him, and though at first quite a novice in the work, he managed it to the satisfaction of his father and uncles. He has had a considerable experience of Zemindary work, covering a period of about thirty-five years, and he only retired from the management about two or three years ago, owing to ill-health and to pressure of public duties. He left the Zemindary on a firm footing, with a contented tenantry and as a profitable concern. After the death of his father he became, and still is, a partner in the firm of Messrs. Prawnkissen Law & Co. He is connected with almost all the well-known public bodies in Calcutta. He is an Honorary Presidency Magistrate of Calcutta, has been a member of the Calcutta Corporation for over ten years, was elected a member of the Calcutta Port Trust for the first time by the Bengal National Chamber of Commerce, and afterwards on four occasions by the Calcutta Corporation as their representative; and he has been a member of the Calcutta Improvement Trust as the representative of the Calcutta Corporation since its establishment and a member of the District Board of 24 Parganas for more than twenty-five years. As President of the Bengal National Chamber of commerce for over ten years, and as Secretary of the British Indian Association, his work has always been highly appreciated. He was also Vice-President of the latter association; he has been a member of the Local Consulting Committee of the East Indian Railway for several years; he is a Director of the Sara-Sarajgunge Railway, a member of the Advisory Board of the China Mutual Insurance Company, a member of the Bengal Chamber of Commerce, Secretary of the Imperial League, and a Governor of the "Refuge." He is a Vice-President and Trustee of the Ram Mohan Library,

HON. RAJA RESHEE CASE LAW, C.I.E.

1. RESIDENCE. 2. THE HON. RAJA RESHEE CASE LAW, C.I.E. 3. KUMAR SURENDRA NATH LAW. 4. KUMAR NARENDRA NATH LAW.

which was founded largely through his help and efforts, President of the Suvarnavanik Samaj for some years—an honour which has been placed upon him by his fellow caste-men—and he was elected as the President of the Conference of the Suvarnabanik of Bengal which was convened for the purpose of amalgamation of all the sections of the caste for the improvement of their education and for the removal of the abuses which have crept into their marriage system. He is also a member of the Suvarnabanik Charitable Association, a Joint Secretary of the Suvarnabanik Samiti (a charitable institution), Honorary Secretary of the Maharraj Mata Hindu Widows' and Brahmamoyi Hindu Orphans' Funds, President (Calcutta Branch) of Anathbhandar Ram Krisha Mission (a charitable institution), a Trustee and Honorary Treasurer of the Indian Museum, and a member of the Government Art Gallery. He is, further, a member of the Royal Society of Arts (England) and of the East India Association (England), a member of the Executive Committee of the Bengal Branch of the Imperial Indian Relief Fund; he has also served as a member of the Advisory Board of Fisheries, as a member of the Executive Committee of the King Edward Memorial Fund, of the Executive Committee of the Imperial Reception Committee, and of the Calcutta Military Tournament, and as a member and Trustee of the College of Physicians and Surgeons. He was recently elected by the Bengal National Chamber of Commerce to represent the Indian Commercial Community in the Ports Facilities Committee, which was appointed by Government to consider the question of the development of the Port of Calcutta; he was Joint Honorary Secretary of the Burdwan Division Flood Relief Fund (when he was highly praised for his efficient and economical work); he was also Joint Honorary Secretary in the Eastern Bengal Famine Fund, and has, in addition, held many minor posts which need not be recapitulated. He has been a member of the Bengal Legislative Council since December 1909, and although he was offered a seat in the Imperial Legislative Council, he was compelled for various reasons to decline the honour. He was appointed Sheriff of Calcutta for one year in December 1914.

The double honour of Raja and the Companionship of the Indian Empire was conferred upon him in recognition of his manifold services to the Government and the general public, while the interest which he takes in all public affairs and the whole-hearted way in which he discharges his public duties cannot escape attention.

There is, in fact, hardly any movement in Calcutta of a public nature with which he is not connected in some way or other. The Raja is a man of retiring disposition, and, like his illustrious father, he is too modest to thrust himself into prominent positions.

PRITHI CHAND LALL CHOUDHRY (ZEMINDAR OF NAZARGUNGE)

This wealthy Zemindar and banker of Purnea, in the division of Bhagalpur, in the Province of Behar and Orissa, was born in 1886, and during the lifetime of his father was educated at the Purnea Zilla School. After his father's death his education was continued privately under the supervision of Rev. A. H. Manning, a Cambridge graduate.

Prithi Chand Lall entered into possession of his splendid inheritance on his coming of age on March 3, 1906. He succeeded his father, Dharam Chand Lall Choudhry, in March 1899, and as the property had been managed during his minority in a most able manner by the executors of his father's will (one of whom was a European), Prithi Chand Lall had the felicity of inheriting a well-organized and systematically conducted estate. He is probably one of the richest men in the district, and certainly the wealthiest in the town of Purnea itself, and, like his father and grandfather before him, he is a philanthropist as well as a business man, and his splendid gifts to all charitable institutions are well known.

Babu Nackched Lall Choudhry, the grandfather of the present incumbent of the estate (known as the Nazargunge estate), was most public-spirited and liberal. He, among other charitable acts, subscribed Rs. 80,000, representing more than half the cost of the construction of the fine Sowra bridge over the River Sowra at Purnea, which now connects the civil station with the old city of Purnea.

Babu Dharam Chand Lall Choudhry succeeded his father, Nackched Lall Choudhry, when quite young, to what might be called rather a small estate, but having had a keen insight into both the zemindary and banking business, he increased the latter enormously by wise administration and careful investments, and although he died in the prime of life, he left a very large sum of money. He was intelligent and hardworking, and by personal supervision of his property he became one of the foremost zemindars of the district.

In public life he was equally hardworking, and was much respected as a honorary magistrate. Among his numerous charitable acts was a substantial contribution towards the establishment of the Lady Dufferin Hospital at Purnea. He died in 1899, much regretted by all who knew him, his death being regarded as a serious public loss.

Since his accession, Prithi Chand Lall Choudhry has personally managed the affairs of his State with great ability, thereby giving abundant evidence of the careful training he had received. He is very persevering and enterprising, and in proof of this introduced in his office a system of division of work with a responsible officer at the head of each department. Although that system worked well, he required more time to devote to the call of public duties, and in furtherance of that object he in 1911 entrusted his whole estate to the management of the Honourable Rai Bahadur Nishi Kanta Sen, B.L., F.R.S.A., a well-known man of exceptional ability and intelligence throughout the Province of Behar and Orissa. Under this new regime many reforms have been introduced, and the reputation of the estate has been firmly and wisely established.

Prithi Chand Lall is very popular with European officials and others, with whom he associates freely. He is the ruling energy of the Purnea Polo Club, keeping a large number of ponies; he has several good performers on the turf; he rides well, and is a volunteer in the Northern Bengal Mounted Rifles. He is an honorary magistrate of the Purnea Sudder independent bench, a member of the District Board, and vice-chairman of the Purnea municipality. He takes a keen interest in municipal affairs, devoting much of his time to them, and his work in a responsible position has been highly eulogized by the Government in its annual administration reports. His charities are numerous, and in addition to defraying the expenses of many poor boys at schools and colleges and subscribing liberally to educational establishments and hospitals, he has created a trust of Rs. 3,500 a year, chargeable on his property, of which the chairman of the District Board is trustee, for the following purposes:—

"1. That out of the Trust Fund the

ZEMINDAR OF NAZARGUNGE.

1. Jasmine Palace, Purnea City. 2. Zemindar of Nazargunge on Sultan. 3. Nazargunge Polo Team. 4. Zemindar of Nazargunge in State Costume.

trustee will pay Rs. 8 a month for a scholarship called the 'Prithi Chand Scholarship,' to be awarded to the student who stands first in order of merit in the matriculation examination from the Purnea Zilla School, but who fails to secure a Government scholarship, the scholarship to be tenable for two years, provided the student continues his study in any approved college and is of good conduct.

"2. That a gold medal called 'Bhagwanbati Choudhrain Medal,' Rs. 60 in value, shall be given annually to the leading student of the Purnea Zilla School in the matriculation examination.

"3. That Rs. 2,000, or an approximate sum which the trustee shall think sufficient, shall be paid annually to the Purnea Charitable Hospital to be utilized, in the first instance, for the maintenance of a surgical ward to be constructed by Babu Prithi Chand Lall in the Sadar Charitable Hospital compound, to be called the 'Dhuram Chand Surgical Ward,' and, further, for the general benefit and relief of poor patients confined in that hospital.

"4. That the sum of Rs. 1,200 a year shall be paid to the President of the Purnea City Dispensary Committee for the purpose of making provision for the supply of good and fresh drugs for medicines, and for engaging an efficient senior sub-assistant surgeon for the said dispensary. The Trustee shall be at liberty to fix the amount which will have to be paid out of the aforesaid sum on account of the extra remuneration to be paid to such surgeon who is to be engaged by the District Board."

In addition to the above Trust a sum of Rs. 20,000 has been promised by Mr. P. C. Lall for the construction of the above-named surgical ward in the Sadar Charitable Hospital. This splendid endowment has brought Mr. Lall to the front rank of public-spirited men in Behar and Orissa, and it will undoubtedly be a lasting monument to commemorate his memory. His liberal donations of Rs. 15,000 for the Hardinge Memorial Park at Bankipore and of Rs. 9,000 for a motor ambulance car as a contribution to the "Behar War Fund" have not passed unnoticed by the public. He is a liberal-minded young man of broad views, and never refuses when his helping hand is sought in furtherance of objects of public utility. He takes special interest in agriculture and in indigenous industries, and has established a model farm in the vicinity of the city of Purnea under his personal supervision. Attached to the annual Purnea city fair, of which he is the proprietor, an industrial and agricultural exhibition is held every year, and four gold and eight silver medals and money prizes are awarded by him to exhibitors gaining the highest distinctions. The cattle show is also an important function in connection with the agricultural section of the exhibition, and handsome money prizes are awarded to the owners and traders of the best animals. The Government Agricultural Department and the Purnea District Board render assistance by contributions towards these two exhibitions.

The building built by himself in Purnea is a palatial one, and it is exquisitely furnished and equipped with a complete electric installation.

Prithi Chand Lall Choudhry is a well-educated young man of temperate habits, affable, courteous, and pleasing in manners, and he is also a promoter of all kinds of healthy sports, while he personally is a keen sportsman and has accounted for a large number of big game.

THE RACECOURSE. CALCUTTA (VICEROY'S CUP DAY).

Photo by Johnston & Hoffmann.

SPORT

THE TURF

THE "sport of kings," as racing is usually termed, is a manifestation of that in-born spirit of emulation which is common to all races of mankind and to all species of the animal kingdom. In other words there is in a healthy body a natural desire to strive against some other man or animal, to overcome that opposing force, and to enjoy the sensation of being an easy first in the struggle.

Very interesting notes are given in *The India Sporting Review*, vol. i., March-June, 1845, regarding the origin and antiquity of horse-racing, and it is tolerably certain, from the earliest records of this sport, that games were held in patriarchal times, when horses, yoked to chariots, were driven by Romans or Greeks. "The first account of these races was given in connection with the festivities of Mithras, or the Sun, to whom Porphyry assures us the people paid their worship in a cavern." Persian monarchs celebrated the worship of Mithras with great pomp, and it is clear that horse-racing, to which they were greatly attached, was included in their programme of sports. This may be inferred from Holy Writ, where it is stated that on account of the idolatry of the King of Judah, some 2,550 years ago, or 633 years before the Christian era, King Josiah "took away the horses that the former had given to the sun, and he also burned their chariots." But the holding of these Mithraic festivities spread from Eastern to Western countries, as the ancient Greeks had their hippodromes, and the Sicilians had their Ludus Trojanus. Sculptures representing the sacrifices and symbols of Mithraic worship have been discovered in many cavernous places in the East, but in the year 1747 others were unearthed in the city of York, in England, proving that the Romans had introduced the festivities into Britain during the five centuries of their power in that country, that is, between 55 B.C. to A.D. 446. In a description of London, written by Fitzstephen in the reign of Henry II, a reference is made to horse-racing, and this sport was frequently indulged in during the reign of Charles I (1640) at Newmarket and other places. Charles II spent a considerable sum of money in the importation of high-class mares for breeding purposes, and from that time to the present there has been steady progress in the evolution of the horse.

Notwithstanding the above-mentioned facts, it may be taken for granted that horses began to compete against each other when in a wild state long before they were taken in hand by man and subsequently trained for sport. And after many long years we have secured the perfect symmetry, the courage, and the ability to endure which are so much to be admired in the thoroughbreds now seen on racecourses in all parts of the world.

The old question as to whether racing really tends to improve and encourage the breeding of horses has been answered so completely in the history of the turf, and by the experiences of owners of studs, during recent years, that it need not be considered in these notes.

The high standard of the racehorse of to-day is due in a very large measure to racing, hunting, and, in later years, polo. Winning sires and dams on the flat or o sticks, and hunters which have carried their riders without fault for long and tiring days are eagerly sought after for stud purposes, and even then the greatest care is taken in making a judicious selection of sires and dams in order that points of excellence may be maintained or strengthened, or, on the other hand, that any slight fault in conformation may be corrected.

The genealogy of the principal turf-winners of the present day can be traced to ancestors whose sterling worth was proved in many exceedingly keen contests, and proud indeed were those successful owners who in many instances not only rode their own horses but also bred them in their own stables, and trained them on their own private courses. But it must not be forgotten that we are now dealing with India and must refer to some aspects of racing in the Provinces of Bengal, Behar and Orissa, and Assam, in that vast country.

There is little doubt that this princely pastime was popular in far-off ages, and even with the comparatively few authoritative available records it is not difficult to learn that very great and rapid progress has been made in the quality both of horses and sport. The hardy, and in some instances remarkably well-bred, ponies provided an unusual amount of enjoyment at meetings, sometimes extending over a week, held in all parts of India, and it is a well-known fact that lovers of horse-flesh were in the habit of riding many a dozen miles in order to be present at some of these gatherings. And what gatherings they were too! One can easily picture a number of tents, forming almost a small town of canvas, pegged out among the most charming scenery, and occupied by well-to-do men who kept open house for all comers, in addition to acting as hosts for perhaps twenty or thirty invited guests. Grand stands, starting gates, and other adjuncts of present-day conditions were then unknown, but their absence did not appear to militate against successful meetings.

By the kindness of Mr. James Hutchison, the secretary of the Calcutta Turf Club, access has been had to some of the earliest available records of racing in India, and extracts therefrom are made in these notes. In the previously mentioned *Sporting Review* a prefatory note states that "the want of a journal to record sports in the East has been strongly felt," and that "the decision to publish one was only resolved upon at the repeated instigation of a number of sporting men."

Although racing was to have priority of place in the new publication, the table of contents of that volume includes articles on "The Osteology of the Elephant," "Elephant Hunting in Ceylon," "Review of the Calcutta Hunting Season," "Cricket," "A Glance at the Stage," and "The Dacca Turf," together with reports of fixtures at Calcutta, Dinapore, and elsewhere.

Particulars are given of the races at Calcutta for the meetings of 1844-5, and the principal feature of the fixture was the remarkably fine performances of the two maidens, Crab and Oranmore, belonging respectively to Mr. Petre and Mr. Alexander.

Crab won four times at the first and second meetings, while Oranmore accounted for six races. They ran three dead heats at the two meetings, the first two at equal weights of 8 stone 7 lb., while Oranmore was in receipt of 2 lb. in the

1. MONSOON RACES, CALCUTTA. 2. MAYFOWL, WINNER OF THE VICEROY'S CUP ON FOUR OCCASIONS. 3. FITZGRAFTON, WINNER OF THE VICEROY'S CUP IN 1906 AND 1907.

SOME OLD VIEWS OF INDIAN SPORTS.

(From "Oriental Field Sports," by Edward Orme, London, 1807.)

1. Hunting Jackals. 2. Shooting a Leopard. 3. Hunting an Old Buffalo. 4. Hunting a Kutlauss, or Civet Cat.

third contest. For the Bengal Club Cup (2 miles) Oranmore won his heat, covering the mile in 1 min. 52 sec., while in the dead heat the time was 1 min. 51½ sec.

There were thirty-four races; twenty-two horses were saddled; thirteen were winners; and of the nine who were beaten only two came out twice. The winners were Elepoo, seven times; Oranmore, six; Crab, four; Soldan, four; Rocket, four; Jack Cade, two; and Young Gazelle, Flibbertigibbet, Clem of the Clough, Selim, Chusan, Cashmere, and Marsaroni, one each. The famous Elepoo arrived in Calcutta in the hot weather of 1842, and his first appearance under silk was in the Derby in December 1843, and during that and the second meetings of the same season he ran eleven times in five days, winning the first Calcutta Derby, the Great Welter, the Calcutta Stakes, the Maiden Arab Purse, the Purse and Sweepstakes (2 miles), the Bengal Club Cup, the first Calcutta St. Leger, the Welter Sweepstakes, the Radamadub Banerjee's Purse, the Trades' Plate, and the Maiden Arab Sweepstakes. During the meetings of 1844-45 Elepoo won the Governor-General's Cup and a Handicap Purse, and "walked over" five times, thus making thirteen contested races without having been beaten once.

The next periodical to be noticed is *The Bengal Sporting Magazine*, dated October 1845. Its contents included articles on pig-sticking, fishing in Tirhut, races at Karachi, Simla, Meerut, Allahabad, Sonepur, and Umballah, together with notes on nominations and prospectuses for other meetings. It is observed that Calcutta is not mentioned in that list of fixtures, but in the racing season in 1845-6 nominations were invited for a cup presented by the Deputy-Governor of Bengal "for all maiden horses, English excepted," the race to be run in Calcutta. The names of leading owners at that date included Barker, Green, East, Petre, Jones, Abram, "The Squire," Robert, Sheik Ibrahim, and Newton, while well-known horses comprised Janbay, Sheriff, Banker, Burkra, Dacoit, Oberon, Flail, Camel, Merry Monarch, Oily Gammon, Energy, Farewell, and Queen Bee.

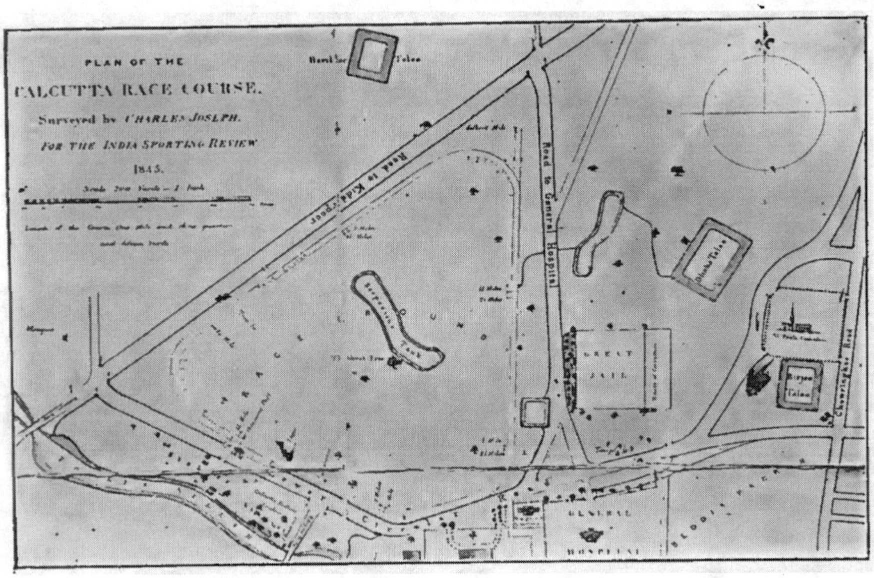

PLAN OF THE CALCUTTA RACECOURSE IN 1845.

An important event in sporting circles in Calcutta occurred on February 27, 1847, when a meeting of gentlemen interested in the turf was held at the Race Stand, the chairman being Mr. J. F. McKilligin.

A paper, signed by thirty-six gentlemen who were stewards, owners of horses, and others in favour of the formation of a sporting club, was presented, and after discussion, a comprehensive resolution, proposed by Mr. J. Staniforth and seconded by Mr. W. Grey, was carried unanimously to the effect "that the Calcutta Turf Club be constituted, and that the following gentlemen form the committee until the 1st of December next, on which date an election shall take place annually."

The names put before the meeting were: Messrs. J. Staniforth, J. Beckwith, W. Grey, W. F. Fergusson, and W. P. Grant. It was further resolved that one gold mohur should be charged as admission fee, and also for every annual subscription. Mr. James Hume was appointed secretary.

During the following half-dozen years racing was warmly supported, but in the *Sporting Review* for the latter portion of the year 1855 it is stated that "Calcutta is no longer the centre of a great and active sporting interest," and it was a sore disappointment to many that for the meeting in 1854-56 subscriptions had not been paid, and that there had been no racing worthy of the name, whereas in 1850 some 350 gold mohurs were subscribed, and twenty-nine races were pulled off at two meetings, the stakes amounting to nearly £8,000. The reason given for this failure was that owners ran horses for gambling only, and that the true sporting element had almost disappeared. It seems that this absence of real interest on the part of owners, as sportsmen, in Calcutta, was a kind of epidemic, as there are no records of meetings at Krishnagar, Berhampore, Jessore, and other well-known places. Many were the lamentations respecting this set-back, and, as troubles never come singly, the stewards in the early portion of the year 1856 were threatened with the possible breaking up of their racecourse and the conversion of it into market gardens. Captain Turnbull, who was secretary at the time, worked with a will to prevent such a desecration, and he ultimately succeeded in obtaining a fresh list of subscribers, and further secured considerable support for forthcoming meetings.

A revival set in, but it was checked by great unpleasantness occurring in connection with what was known as "The Dealers' Plate," and as to the admission of jockeys, stable-keepers, and dealers as owners of running horses.

The stewards therefore held a conference prior to the meetings in 1856-57, and it was unanimously decided "that no horse could start on the Calcutta course unless declared *bona-fide* the property of a gentleman subscriber, nor could any confederacy with dealers or jockeys European or native) be allowed."

It is believed that this decisive action on the part of the stewards had a most beneficial effect upon subsequent racing, but it is unfortunate that few particulars relating to turf matters in Calcutta can be obtained until the year 1870, when the *Oriental Sporting Magazine* took the place of the *Indian Sporting Review*. The stewards for the Calcutta first meeting

SOME OLD VIEWS OF INDIAN SPORTS.

(From "Oriental Field Sports," by Edward Orme, London, 1807.)

1. Death of the Bear. 2. A Tiger springing upon an Elephant. 3. Chasing a Tiger across a River.

held on December 17, 1870, and January 1, 1871, were the Hon. Major Bourke, Mr. J. A. Crawford, Colonel Raikes, Mr. T. M. Robinson, and Major Mylne. The clerk of the course was Mr. W. Pritchard; the judge, Mr. J. A. Crawford; and the secretary, Mr. Charles Hartley.

Racegoers of those days assert that the entries for the principal races were extremely good, but it was feared that, owing to continued heavy rains, which had impeded the training of horses, the success of the forthcoming meeting was somewhat doubtful.

It appears that Bombay horses were strongly in evidence for the Derby Stakes (so much so that only three Bengal entries were seriously mentioned in the money market), and the result of the race proved the correctness of public opinion, as The Earl, belonging to a Mr. Field, hailing from the Western Presidency, won with a length to spare from Mr. W. W. Grey's Warrior, who was a similar distance in front of Silvertail, belonging to H.H. Aga Khan.

A controversy sprang up about this date as to the advisability of holding racing fixtures during afternoons instead of mornings, and one sporting writer, in giving vent to his opinions on the subject, said: "Why races are held in the morning I cannot conceive. We do not leave the lottery room until after 2 a.m. to make arrangements for racing which is to commence at seven o'clock. It is nonsense to say that it is on account of the heat, as it is hotter with a rising sun at 9.30 than it is at 3.30. Nearly every one who is interested seems to prefer afternoon sport; the majority of owners, the jockeys to a man, and certainly all the ladies, would welcome the change. Why, then, should stewards persist in the antediluvian and barbarous custom of racing before breakfast? Up in the morning before daylight, out on the *maidan* in fog bad enough to produce phthisis in man and pleuro-pneumonia in horses, simply because stewards refuse to listen to the protests of owners and others."

The question was left in abeyance for a time, but it was ultimately decided that "out of a total of eight days' racing at two meetings, two days during the first fixture should be given up to afternoon racing, and the remaining six days should be devoted to early morning racing as heretofore."

Prior to the racing season of 1872-73 the stewards were compelled to re-model their prospectus as the Lieutenant-Governor of Bengal refused to allow the usual English Derby lottery to be held in Calcutta, and as the percentage upon tickets sold had for many years past provided the club funds with an annual sum ranging from Rs. 5,000 to Rs. 8,000, it became necessary to reduce the value of the purses, and further, to obtain gifts of special cups to meet the deficiency.

The baneful effect upon racing in India caused by the veto placed by the Sultan of Turkey upon the exportation of Arab horses was never more keenly realized than it was at the Calcutta Christmas meeting of 1873. The imported animals of previous years had been absorbed in various parts of the country, with the result that the entries for the forthcoming Derby were no more than eight in number, whereas between twenty and forty horses had hitherto been counted upon.

The season of 1875-76 will long be remembered for the visit to Calcutta of his late Majesty King Edward VII, when Prince of Wales, and the event proved to be a landmark in the history of the turf in India.

A specially attractive programme of events was prepared; purses of large amounts were promised; and the Viceroy and a number of Indian gentlemen offered cups with the object of inducing owners of the best horses in India to attend the meeting. Stewards and members of the club vied with one another in making arrangements, and a sum of Rs. 6,000 was expended in repairs, repainting, and refurnishing the grand stand, and a further amount of Rs. 2,000 was spent on the course. The grand stand was reserved for the royal party, the Viceroy, Government officials, and a number of chiefs from all parts of India, and the spectacle of the sombre garments of the West presented a fine contrast to the dazzling costumes and jewels of Eastern potentates.

The royal cortège, it is said, arrived upon the course in true Ascot fashion, and it was met by stewards at the two-mile post and at the foot of the steps of the grand stand.

Royal success attended a royal meeting, and the Prince of Wales, with his customary courtesy, expressed his great satisfaction at the manner in which the arrangements had been carried out.

A glance may now be taken at the results of some of the principal races held in Calcutta in recent years. Thirty years ago (1887) in the race for His Excellency the Viceroy's Cup ($1\frac{3}{4}$ miles), the bay Australian gelding Myall King, belonging to that fine sportsman, Lord William Beresford, won in 3 min. $9\frac{1}{2}$ sec.; and the same horse pulled off that event for his owner in the following year in two seconds less time and carrying a burden of 9 st., this being 6 lb. over the weight of the previous year. In 1890, Myall King was again saddled for the same race, and once more he brought a cup to swell the list of Lord William's trophies. Probably the chief feature of this event was the unparalleled success attained by Mr. (afterwards Sir) A. A. Apcar with his grand horse Mayfowl, who was stripped for the race in 1910 and who was first past the post with his weight of 9 st. 3 lb. in the remarkably good time of 3 min. 2 sec. In 1911, Mayfowl, again carrying 9 st. 3 lb., ran away with the Cup in 3 min. $1\frac{1}{2}$ sec. In the following year the same old horse was again sent to the post by Sir A. A. Apcar, and after a most exciting race, fought inch by inch with the English mare, Brogue, owned by Mr. M. Goculdas, the judge was unable to separate the pair, who were respectively ridden by the brothers C. and A. Hoyt, time 3 min. $3\frac{2}{5}$ sec. But Mayfowl was not done with yet, even for first-class performances, and in 1913 he again secured His Excellency's Cup in 3 min. $7\frac{1}{2}$ sec. He ran in that race for Mr. "R. R. S.," who won the same event in 1914 with Bachelor's Wedding in 3 min. 8 sec. There are few racegoers of to-day who do not remember with pleasure the splendid victory of that keen little horse, Kiltoi, who carried to the front the colours of General Nawabzada Obaidulla Khan in 1915.

His Majesty the King-Emperor when in India in 1911 presented a Cup to be competed for annually, and the first race took place in 1912, over a course 1 mile 5 fur. 58 yds., when first blood was drawn by Mr. J. C. Galstaun, of Calcutta, one of the staunchest supporters of the turf in India. In 1915 this event was won by Bachelor's Wedding, who, it will be remembered, had in the previous year secured the Viceroy's Cup for Mr. "R. R. S."

The Indian Grand National Steeplechase of three miles is one of the principal attractions of the year, and in 1895 and 1896 His Highness the Maharaja of Patiala was the winner with his horses, Prince Imperial and Wanderer, in the respective times of 6 min. 58 sec. and 7 min. $3\frac{3}{5}$ sec. This event has not been won twice in succession by any horse, but Mr. Straw took honours in 1897 and 1898; the Hon. Mr. A. A. Apcar in 1906

SOME OLD VIEWS OF INDIAN SPORTS.

(From "Oriental Field Sports," by Edward Orme, London, 1807.)

1. Beating Sugar-cane for a Hog. 2. The Chase after the Hog. 3. The Hog at Bay. 4. The Dead Hog.

and 1907; Mr. Curtis-Hayward led in his horse Pilot in 1914 after a journey covered in 6 min. 10 sec., and in the following year Mr. M. Goculdas was the proud owner of the winner, First Venture, who safely negotiated all obstacles and passed the flags in 6 min. 5⅗ sec.

Records show that "sky" meetings were held at various places in Bengal and Behar in the forties of last century, but they lapsed for several years and were revived again early in the twentieth century. One of the earliest in Calcutta was held in December 1844. The chief event was for a purse of Rs. 200, together with plate and a cup. The weights appear to have been most irregularly apportioned, but sheer good fun permeated the whole meeting. One horse, Monument, standing 16 hands 1 inch, was supposed to carry 13 st. 7 lb., but when the time came for weighing out not a single competitor could adjust his balance. Some one proposed that Monument should carry a man and a boy, as the jockey's normal weight was only 9 st., and others suggested the carrying of two saddles, but eventually an agreement was arrived at, and the first heat resulted in a win for Over-the-left, Monument, the favourite, having refused to leave the starting-post. In the second heat Monument's jockey won "hands down," with the others nowhere. The Earl of Mayo, during his viceroyalty, was a warm supporter of, and constantly attended race meetings in various parts of India, and he was always assured of an exceedingly warm welcome at the small but intensely enjoyable fixtures at Sonepore.

There are few sportsmen in India who have not heard of, even if they have not participated in the enjoyable annual fortnight spent in racing and general sports at Sonepore, in the district of Saran, in Behar. These festivities were established many years ago by planters who made these gatherings the occasion for entertaining friends in a princely fashion; races of all kinds were held daily, the evenings were devoted to dances and other amusements in which the ladies of the party were the leading spirits; and the fun and frolic which took place on those occasions was a thing to be remembered for many years afterwards. A meeting held in November 1844 may be specially mentioned, as it witnessed the striking success of a Captain Lovatt, who won seven out of nineteen events, and secured second honours on six occasions. The last race of that fixture was probably the most interesting event. It was open to all horses, with weights according to the Calcutta standard, which was for two-year-olds, feather-weight; three years, 7 st. 4 lb.; four years, 8 st. 4 lbs.; five years, 8 st. 13 lb.; six years, 9 st. 3 lb.; and aged, 9 st. 5 lb. Captain Lovatt was represented by his Cape horse, Napoleon, who was opposed by Ecarté, Gregor, Orville, and Minor. Gregor made the running, and was followed by Minor, but all competitors were bunched together at the end of a mile. At the turn for home Napoleon shot ahead and soon outpaced the others, cantering in an easy winner in front of Ecarté and Gregor.

At the fixture held in the month of November 1871, His Excellency Lord Mayo received Sir Jung Bahadur in open Durbar. The latter arrived with his *entourage*—in all the splendour of an Oriental potentate; he was received with a salute of artillery; and the proceedings were marked by great enthusiasm and delight among the crowd of visitors at this most enjoyable annual gathering. The visit of His Highness was returned by the Viceroy during the afternoon of the same day, when the latter reviewed and complimented the smart and soldierly appearance of Sir Jung's military escort.

Many years ago very enjoyable "sky" races were held at Dum Dum, a cantonment situated about four miles from Calcutta. The special interest attaching to these fixtures was that they were held in the "off" season as regards leading centres of racing, which corresponded with the time of year when the ordinary inhabitants and visitors in the chief city on the Hooghly had, as they expressed themselves, nothing to do by way of amusement. After a long interval these meetings were resumed on November 18, 1874, chiefly through the enterprising spirit of the 62nd Regiment (stationed at Dum Dum) and of military detachments from Calcutta. Success, written in capital letters, must be the historical verdict of the proceedings, as everything went with a swing from start to finish. Many first-class horses were saddled for cross-country events, and there was a general consensus of opinion that the majority of the performers (which belonged to non-professional racing men, and were piloted by gentlemen riders) were capable of acquitting themselves with credit upon any racecourse in India.

The fine sport afforded by the meeting just referred to was so greatly appreciated that early in the year 1875 energetic stewards were appointed to collect subscriptions and issue a prospectus for another one to be held in the month of November following. There was a very gratifying response both as regards money and horses, and long before the eventful day, November 6th, the Dum Dum Executive formed the opinion that future meetings would be the commencement of first-class fixtures. A sufficiently warm sun for an early winter day put gladness into the hearts of visitors, and with a well-filled card and the course in an excellent condition, there was every prospect of real enjoyment, provided, of course, that the unexpected did not happen, and that the vision of prospective winnings might not give place to a clouded horizon upon which banknotes were drifting farther and farther away.

As far as racing went, however, there was nothing left to be desired, as scratchings were remarkably few in number. In four events, for example, the starters comprised twelve, ten, ten, and six horses, while the other events were nearly as well supported.

POLO IN CALCUTTA

By PAT LOVETT

THE claim of Calcutta to be the nursery of the modern game of polo is indisputable; it would, indeed, be hardly an extravagance to contend that it was also its birthplace. It is true that before the Calcutta Polo Club was established there existed, for a year or a little more, a polo club at Cachar, the members of which were planters and Manipuris. It was formed by Colonel R. Stewart, the superintendent, who got the Manipuris to teach the game to the Europeans of the station. That was undoubtedly the germ of the sport which reached its full stature in the historic international encounter between England

and the United States of America at Long Island, New York, in June 1914, when Captain Barrett, 15th Hussars, who took a notable part in the jubilee celebration of the Calcutta Polo Club, led to victory the team which vindicated the primacy of England. The Cachar Club, however, was never more than a local institution which cannot be said to have had any part in the development of hockey on slow, diminutive tats, 12-2 hands in height, to modern polo on galloping ponies of 14 hands. It is a cherished tradition that the Manipur game was introduced into Calcutta by a well-known merchant, Mr. "Bobbie" Hills. He was a gallant sportsman and a most popular member of Calcutta Society, and to him belongs the glory of founding the Calcutta Polo Club in 1862. His portrait will be seen in the historic group accompanying this article. It is a remarkable coincidence that in the larger group, in the year of the jubilee of the club, there is also a Mr. Hills, who likewise did much to maintain the prestige of Calcutta in the world of polo.

To write a full account of the vicissitudes of polo in Calcutta and the heroic efforts of a few enthusiastic merchants to keep the game alive in spite of the most heart-breaking obstacles and discouragements, would take far more space than is at my disposal. At first things went with a bang. Hockey on tats was inexpensive and did not involve hard training. Matches were easily arranged between sides composed of members of the Club, or between Calcutta and Barrackpore. So many were the thrusters for glory that it was possible in 1874 to start a new polo club at Calcutta, for which, we read, "Mr. R. B. King, the first honorary

CALCUTTA POLO CLUB.

JUBILEE TOURNAMENT AND I.P.A. CHAMPIONSHIP, 1862-63—1912-13.

Photo by Bourne & Shepherd.

Back Row (standing).
Mr. G. E. Llewelyn (Behar Light Horse).
Mr. C. Ismay (Committee C.P.C.).
Mr. H. D. Cartwright (Committee C.P.C.).
Jemadar Sunda Singh (Patiala).
Capt. Gunda Singh (Patiala).
Major J. J. Richardson (Hon. Sec. I.P.A.).
Thakur Fateh Singh (Kishenghur).
Mr. R. G. Bates (Steward, C.P.C.).
Col W. McL. Campbell (2nd Batt. Black Watch).
Mr. R. E. Forrester (2nd Batt. Black Watch).
Mr. H. B. Turner (17th Lancers).
Capt. T. Nisbet (Behar Light Horse).
Capt. N. G. B. Henderson (2nd Batt. Black Watch).
Capt. R. Fergusson-Pollok (Old Fettesians).
Capt. J. Henderson (Old Fettesians).
Mr. E. Danby (Behar Light Horse).
Mr. W. H. Todd (Old Fettesians).

Front Row (standing).
Capt. Thakura Singh (Patiala).
Col. Jugendra Singh (Patiala).
General Saroop Singh (Patiala).
Capt. Juswant Singh (Patiala).
Prince Sirdar Singh (Kishenghur).
Col. Chunda Singh (Patiala).
Capt. T. P. Melville (17th Lancers).
Capt. F. St. J. Atkinson (Tigers).
Thakur Dhonkal Singh (Kishenghur).
Lt.-Gen. Sir B. Mahon, K.C.V.O., C.B. (Tigers; Steward, C.P.C.).
Count J. de Madre (Tigers).
Thakur Bane Singh (Kishenghur).
Capt. J. F. Todd (Old Fettesians).
Mr. D. C. Boles (17th Lancers).
Capt. R. B. Worgan (Calcutta).
Mr. F. Lyall, I.C.S. (Behar Light Horse).
Capt. D. Wood (H E. the Governor's Staff).

Back Row (seated).
Capt. A. C. Ross (Calcutta).
Mr. C. T. Hills (C.P.C.).
Mr. E. C. Apostolides (Steward, C.P.C.).
H.H. the Maharaja of Patiala (Patiala).
H.E. LORD CARMICHAEL, GOVERNOR OF BENGAL.
H.H. the Maharaja of Kishenghur (Kishenghur).
Sir Cecil Graham (Calcutta).
Capt. F. W. Barret (Tigers).
Capt. V. Lockett (17th Lancers).

Front Row (seated).
Mr. E. Smallwood (Calcutta B.).
Prince Hitendra of Cooch Behar (Calcutta B.).
I.P.A. Championship Challenge Cup.
Capt. W. Kenworthy (H.E. the Governor's Staff).
H.E. the Governor's Cup, presented for *The C.P.C. Jubilee Tournament.*
Capt. K. Robertson (Calcutta).
The Ezra Challenge Cup.
Mr. K. R. Gilroy (2nd Batt. Black Watch).

secretary, did eminent service." The second honorary secretary of this club was no less a personage than Mr. Henry Neville Gladstone, third son of the great commoner. Candour compels the admission that for many years after the institution of polo tournaments, namely in 1876, the standard of the game in Calcutta was what soldier players derisively call "bumblepuppy." The reason is not far to seek. Shortly after the spread of the game through Northern India by General Stewart and Lieutenant Sherer, polo became *par excellence* the sport of the cavalry. The British and Indian horse regiments produced the most famous exponents, who set the fashion in the increasing height of the ponies and the consequent intenser pace of the play. Calcutta has never been a cavalry station. A detachment of Indian cavalry at Ballygunge and the Viceroy's bodyguard in the cold weather were all the citizens ever saw of the aristocracy of the Army, except on the rare occasion of a royal visit, when a full *risala* would be imported from the Punjab to astonish the vulgar. There has always been a British infantry regiment in Fort William, and two native infantry regiments in the neighbourhood, but their support of polo has been fitful. Calcutta was thus out of the beaten track of first-class polo, which in the 'eighties found a much more genial atmosphere at Bombay.

Although the senior and junior clubs continued to eke out a separate existence, polo in Calcutta was at a low ebb in the 'eighties, when changes were being made at Meerut and Hurlingham which completely revolutionized the game. At the end of 1899 the two clubs were amalgamated, and we soon saw the dawn of a better day. The late Mr. J. D. West was then honorary secretary, in which office Mr. E. C. Apostolides was presently associated with him. "Peter" and "The Apostle" worked with a will to give the Calcutta Polo Club the best polo ground in the world, and to attract to the annual tournament the most famous teams in India. Their success was wonderful.

THE ORIGINAL POLO CLUB, CALCUTTA, 1864–65.

COLIN SMITH. DUNCAN STEWART. R. E. GOOLDEN. D. G. LANDALE.
R. S. HILLS. GEORGE MILLER. ELLIOTT ANGELO. JOHN THOMAS.
W. BLANDFORD. MONTAGUE CHAMPNEYS, I.C.S. LEWIS PUGH EVANS. CAPT. CROSS (52ND REGT.).
CAPT. SHOWERS, A.D.C.

Thanks to the liberality of the Calcutta Turf Club it was possible to spend large sums of money each year on the ground in the middle of the racecourse. The result was that teams in the very first flight were glad to journey from all parts of India for a game on a ground which had no equal in any other country.

The Calcutta tournament gained great distinction from the countenance of that magnificent Viceroy, Lord Curzon, whose Staff always included players of the highest order. Every year some native prince visited the Viceroy at Calcutta, and if he were a Rajput or Sikh, brought with him his polo team, which almost invariably was *pila lumba*.

But what gave Calcutta its biggest lift was the great tournament held during the visit of the Prince of Wales in 1905-6. The teams engaged were the most splendid in India. The Indian aristocracy was fully represented, and so was its greatest rival, the British cavalry. The cup was won by the Golconda team from Hyderabad, which displayed such perfection of skill and horsemanship as to fairly witch the spectators. This tournament gave the Indian Polo Association furiously to think, and it was not long before it came to the conclusion that Calcutta was the only proper and logical venue for the yearly discussion of the championship of India.

The Indian Championship Tournament of the Indian Polo Association was first played in Calcutta in 1907, and appropriately enough it was won by the Calcutta "A" Team, which beat the 12th Lancers in the final. This victory gave Calcutta polo *izzat* and standing in the great *mofussil* military and native teams, which were ever after most eager to come to the premier city of India to dispute the title of primacy. In 1909 and 1910 Calcutta again defeated all comers; but in the next year the coveted championship was wrested from the Calcutta Polo Club by the doughty 10th Hussars, the regimental champions of India. Just before the war Lord Hardinge's Staff won the title.

During the war there has not been a first-class tournament in Calcutta, but the game has not been allowed to die out, and the ground is still maintained in tip-top condition in the hope that when peace is restored Calcutta will once again become the Mecca of Indian polo-players.

This hasty sketch would be incomplete if mention were not made of the encouragement given by Lord Carmichael, the first Governor of Bengal. He presented a handsome cup for a handicap tournament to spread the sport among "small" men who could not afford to keep and train more than two ponies. It was a happy idea, and but for the war would have gained its whole object.

The present honorary secretary of the Calcutta Polo Club is Mr. Claude Ismay, who in his day was the most brilliant civilian player the club had ever produced. He keeps the sacred flame alight with wonderful resource and enthusiasm, and is admirably assisted by Mr. Ross Craik and the evergreen "Apostle," who has done more for polo in Calcutta than lovers of the game can possibly repay. A Calcutta Calendar of enthusiasts would include scores of distinguished men, but I doubt that any will be so honoured by posterity as Mr. J. D. West and Mr. E. C. Apostolides, who saved the cult in its worst crisis.

SPORT

ATHLETICS

THE climatic conditions of Bengal do not lend themselves to any appreciable extent to games such as hockey and Association and Rugby football, but nevertheless these games are played year in and year out by a large number of persons. The games are confined to the leading European, Anglo-Indian, and Indian (Native) clubs, the members of which display a keen interest in them, but none of the clubs has really good teams. Individual members of some of the European clubs are what would be called at Home first-class players, inasmuch as they have represented counties in the Old Country, and a noticeable feature of the game played in Bengal is the number of men who play for their clubs in all the various games. So far as Bengal is concerned, Calcutta is really the only place where these games are seriously played, and this is chiefly owing to the fact that the English have introduced the games and the native element has entered into it.

Rugby football was the first game played in earnest in this country, but the effect of the climatic conditions is realized to a greater extent in this game than in any other, as it can only be engaged in for a very limited period. It is a game which does not appeal to the native as he cannot understand it, and the physique and strength of the ordinary Bengali does not encourage him to play it. The Association game has therefore always been far more popular than Rugby, as physical strength is not such an important factor as cleverness and trickiness in controlling the ball. The Indian is an adept in the latter tactics, and it is a most noticeable feature that a large number of Indian teams have now taken up "Soccer," and that they have a much larger following than in either Rugby football or hockey. So far the professional element has not interfered with the game, but there are indications that this is coming into Indian football. The casual way in which players transfer their interests from one club to another is rather striking, but this is not done for the benefit of the club which a man proposes to join; it is rather for personal flattery and "kudos" that he so readily does this.

Hockey, as at Home, is only a new game and has only been in existence for about fifteen years. A number of Indian teams entered into it after the European community had started it and interest is gradually growing, but it is one in which Anglo-Indian teams display their best skill, as, generally speaking, they are fast and very clever with the sticks.

It would perhaps be as well to give a few details about these games. Hockey is played from the middle of February until about the middle of April, but there is not a great deal of interest displayed in it. The Calcutta Football Club hold the premier position, but all the local clubs play in a League competition, controlled by the Bengal Hockey Association. They play each other on the League system of so many points for a win. At the end of the season a knock-out tournament is held for the Beighton Cup, and all the local teams enter for this, one or two up-country teams frequently visiting Calcutta in order to participate. The Aligarh College team (United Provinces), composed of Mahommedan players, has always done well during the past two or three years. This is a game that British regiments stationed in Fort William have not been keen upon, and they have never entered for the League or Beighton Cup competitions. Native regiments play hockey to a certain extent, but they are practically beginners as far as Calcutta is concerned, although in other parts of India it is believed that there are regiments which have really good teams. Bengalis have never yet excelled at the game, but they are gradually improving players, and it will not, in all probability, be long before they are admitted into the first League.

The leading clubs are: Calcutta, Rangers, Dalhousie, Customs, and Sibpore College.

There are no players of any particular merit, but several of the men have in the past played for counties at Home, or their Universities, or in large trial matches in England before the war.

Mr. Cole, of the Chartered Bank, was perhaps the best player seen in Calcutta for many years, but he has now retired from the game, and Mr. A. L. Hosie is said to be the best exponent of the game in Calcutta at the present time.

Hockey does not attract a large crowd of Indians.

Association football may be regarded as the most popular game in Bengal, and it is probable that there are nearly a hundred and fifty Indian clubs in Calcutta and district. The standard of their play is, on the whole, good, but not good enough to compete with the leading military and civilian teams. "Soccer" has almost invariably been the great game of the British soldiers stationed in Calcutta, and many regiments, containing excellent teams, have played there, such as the Black Watch, the Gordon Highlanders, and others. The Calcutta team have always had good players, but the extra training of the soldiers has always told, and although Calcutta have occasionally won the League and Shield competitions, they have generally succumbed to the military. This game is more or less controlled by the Indian Football Association, composed of members of one or two European clubs and a very large number of Indian team representatives. Many competitions are played for from the middle of April until the second or third week in September. The grounds during April, May, and part of June are very hard and fast, but after the monsoon has broken they are soft and slippery, and this condition is detrimental to the play of Indian teams, as practically all of them play without boots or socks. This game is immensely popular, and during important matches in the Cup competition there are probably between 10,000 and 15,000 spectators. The most important league is controlled by the Indian Football Association, and is composed of the leading clubs, such as Calcutta, Dalhousie, Rangers, Customs, regiments stationed at Fort William, a few minor clubs, and one or two Indian teams, the most important of which is the Mohan Bagan. The last-named have secured the majority of the best-known Bengali players, owing to the fact that men who become really efficient seem to be always ready to forsake their own team in order to gain personal popularity. This is not a prevailing characteristic of English players, who remain with their own clubs for years although they may not be on the winning side. After the League fixtures at the end of June a Cup competition is held for which there are generally from twenty to twenty-five entries. Many up-country British regiments send representative teams to Calcutta, and some exceedingly good games are witnessed, but the refereeing at many of the matches leaves a great deal to be desired. During the season there are three and sometimes four large charity matches, such as Civil *versus* Military, or England *versus* Scotland, the proceeds

1. THE RACECOURSE, SHILLONG. 2. POLO GROUND, SHILLONG. 3. GOLF.
4. CRICKET AT SHILLONG. 5. KHASI ARROW-SHOOTING.

Photos by Ghoshal Bros.

of which are devoted to local charities. This game is also most popular amongst European players and others, but native regiments have not entered into it to any large extent.

Rugby football is only played during the monsoon period, when the ground is soft enough to permit of it. It commences as a rule at the end of July as soon as the sister game is finished, and it is continued until about the middle of September. Indian teams have never entered into the game as it is too strenuous for them, nor is it one which greatly attracts British soldiers, and it is seldom that Calcutta is visited by a regiment playing Rugby. Anglo-Indian teams also are not keen about it, and, although some of them have taken it up, their success has not been great, and they have eventually discontinued it. The game is virtually only just kept alive by the Calcutta Football Club, who play many inter-club games in order to get into practice for the tournament games. Formerly there was a Rugby League, but owing to the small number of entries, that has been abandoned, and the tournament contests are the chief games of the season. Until the war broke out the Presidency towns of Calcutta, Madras, and Bombay always had an annual meeting, and those events added considerable interest to the game, many successful tournaments having been held. The number of entries has, however, generally been small, not more than eight teams playing, of which three or more have been up-country regimental teams, the leading ones during recent years being the Welsh, the West Riding and the Leicester Regiments. The two former have on many occasions annexed the Cup, and although Calcutta has put up a good fight, the trophy has not been secured by the city team for several years past.

Perhaps the best-known player of recent years was the late Mr. H. W. Thomas, who played for Wales for two seasons, the class of football played by him being far superior to that of the ordinary players in Bengal.

Cricket is played in the cold weather from the beginning of November to the end of February. The class of cricket is on the whole fair, but it does not compare with even second or third-class form in England. The season is not only short, but it is seldom that the leading clubs get good games, as the only days on which they can play are on Saturday and Sunday, and the many counter attractions of Calcutta during the cold weather are largely responsible for men deserting cricket for racing or other sport. The premier club is the Calcutta Cricket Club (whose members are drawn almost entirely from the mercantile community in the city), who have by far and away the best ground at their disposal at the Eden Gardens in Calcutta, and they are one of the few clubs that are permitted to play on Sunday.

The majority of the other clubs have grounds on the *maidan*, but as they are not allowed to play there on Sunday, and only have Saturday afternoon for any play at all, it is impossible to raise enthusiastic support among either European or Indian teams for the game. The best cricket is played at Christmas time, when the Calcutta Cricket Club have all their important matches. In pre-war days a European team from Bombay, Colombo, or some other part of India visited Calcutta for ten days or so and played the two largest clubs, and possibly a Maharaja's team.

During the past few years several rajas have taken up this game, and, although they do not maintain regular teams, they manage to get the services of many well-known Indian players, generally from Bombay, to play for them for a month or two during the cold weather. The Maharajas of Cooch Behar, Nattore, and Mymensingh have all had teams, and in many instances they have also been able to obtain the services of a well-known English professional. The first two of these Maharajas have their own grounds in Calcutta. The leading clubs are the Calcutta, Ballygunge, Rangers, Customs, Dalhousie, Aryans, and the Town Club.

At intervals there have been a few well-known first-class players in Calcutta, and during recent years Mr. H. L. Simms and Mr. M. C. Bird are perhaps the best known.

The class of cricket played by these two gentlemen is very different from the style usually seen in Bengal, and the bowling of the former during the season of 1916-17 will long be remembered by the various batsmen playing against it. The Indian displays a certain amount of interest in this game, but the standard of play by the ordinary Bengali is poor.

Tennis is perhaps the most popular game in India, as it is one in which ladies and gentlemen can participate, and it is also a game that is perhaps more suited to this country than any of the games previously referred to in these notes. It can be played for about eight months of the year, from November until June, and there are many exceedingly good private courts in and about Calcutta. The standard of play is on the whole good, and compares favourably with that of an ordinary individual who plays the game at Home. It is not first-class, but the average man not only plays until he is more than fifty years of age, but he plays an exceedingly good, steady game, whereas in the Old Country it is generally found that a man considers himself too old at forty, and even then he is only a mediocre player. The conditions under which one plays tennis are more favourable, because during the eight months referred to above one can almost guarantee a fine day, although in April, May, and June it is too hot to be really pleasant. The comfort of the player is studied as far as possible, as there are boys who pick up stray balls, and every court has blue screens behind it. These conditions do not obtain in England, and perhaps it is the very existence of them in India which encourages men to continue playing to a greater age than they do in England.

The only important tournament is the Bengal Tennis Championship, which takes place at the Eden Gardens, Calcutta, towards the end of January or the beginning of February in each year. The entries are, as a rule, fairly good, but for many years past there has only been one really first-class player in Bengal, namely Mr. A. R. F. Kingscote, who played in, and easily won, the Championship in the year 1914. This tournament has always been won by Europeans except on three occasions: a Japanese player, Mr. Z. Shimidzu, has won it twice, and a Madrassi player has secured it on one occasion.

In recent years the Championship has been extended, and ladies are now allowed to enter for it. There are mixed double and ladies' single Championships.

Until very recently the Indian has displayed very little inclination for this game, but there are indications that he is taking it up more seriously and is likely to become a gradually improving player.

THE COUNCIL HOUSE, CALCUTTA.
Illustration from "Oriental Scenery," by Thomas Daniell (1795).

SUGAR

BY WYNNE SAYER, B.A., ASSISTANT TO THE AGRICULTURAL ADVISER TO THE GOVERNMENT OF INDIA.

IT is probable that the sugar-cane plant originally spread from the tropical islands of the East Indies, but whether this be so or not, it has existed for so long in this country that it is impossible to trace any record of its original importation. Some idea of the antiquity of its cultivation may be gathered from the fact that it is definitely mentioned in the *Institutes of Manu* and in the later Hindu medical works. The art of sugar manufacture has also been known in Bengal from that time, as in the same *Institutes* crystalline sugar and sweetness are mentioned.

There is a saying in Eastern Bengal and Assam which runs: "Unless a man has seven sons and twelve grandsons he should not cultivate sugar-cane." This, I think, shows more effectively than any other explanation the fact that sugar-cane as a crop requires more watching and irrigation than any other crop grown, and it is this fact, coupled with the labour and water difficulties which are continually arising, that limits its cultivation to a great extent among the people of these three Provinces.

In our discussion of the crop it will be, perhaps, best to divide it into the following heads: (1) General features of the three provinces, and the conditions of rainfall and climate; (2) area under cane, varieties of cane, methods of cultivation; (3) fungus diseases and pests attacking the crop; (4) jaggery and sugar-making, sugar factories; (5) the work done by the Agricultural Department in improving the crop; and (6) past history of sugar-making and the general outlook for the development of the industry in the three Provinces.

1. GENERAL FEATURES, RAINFALL, SOIL, AND CLIMATE.

(a) *General Features.*

We may, therefore, in the first place consider the nature of the soil, rainfall, and climate, and here we can do no better than summarize the information given in the *Imperial Gazetteer* of India.

Bengal.—Bengal proper sub-divides itself naturally into four distinct parts: West Bengal, Central Bengal, East Bengal, and North Bengal. West Bengal lies outside the true delta. The eastern portion of this tract is low and of alluvial formation, but farther west laterite begins to predominate. Central Bengal was formerly the Ganges delta, but it has gradually been raised above flood-level, and now no longer receives any fresh deposits of silt. East Bengal includes the present delta of the Ganges and Brahmaputra, and here the process of land formation is still going on; but in the south-east the hill range which divides Assam from Burma projects into it, while on the confines of Dacca and Mymensingh the Madhupur jungle, a tract of quasi-laterite, rises above the recent alluvium. North Bengal is mostly alluvial. In spite of its proximity to the hills, the general level of this alluvial country is very low, especially in Cooch Behar, Rangpur, and the central part of Rajshahi; and it also suffers from obstructed drainage, due to the silting up of the rivers and the general raising of their beds by this means.

Behar.—Behar is divided by the Ganges into two parts: north and south. North Bihar is a level plain falling very gradually from the foot of the Himalayas, and with a belt of fairly high land along the bank of the Ganges. Between these two extremes the general elevation is lower, and considerable areas are liable to damage by floods. The soil consists mostly of the older alluvium, or *bangar,* a yellowish clay with frequent deposits of *kankar*; but in many parts this has been cut away by the torrents that rush down from the Himalayas, and the low land through which these rivers have at one time or another found an exit to the Ganges is composed of more recent deposits of sand and silt brought down by them when in flood. In South Behar the effects of recent fluvial action are less marked, especially towards the east, on account of the outlying hills and undulations of the Chota Nagpur plateau.

Chota Nagpur and Orissa.—Chota Nagpur is a rugged tract of hill and jungle broken by deep ravines and river valleys. The greater part of Orissa belongs to the same formation as Chota Nagpur, but along the coast there is a narrow belt of alluvium formed from the silt deposited by the rivers which drain the hills as they find their sluggish way to the sea.

Assam.—The province of Assam falls into three natural divisions : the valley of the Surma, the valley of the Brahmaputra, or Assam proper, and the intervening range of hills. The Surma Valley is a flat plain, about 125 miles in length by 60 miles in width, shut in on three sides by ranges of hills. The Brahmaputra Valley is an alluvial plain, about 450 miles in length, with an average breadth of about 50 miles, enclosed by hills on every side except the west. In the centre of this valley the soil consists of a light layer of clay superimposed upon beds of sand. Farther back from the Brahmaputra the alluvium is more consolidated, and here and there are to be found the remains of an older alluvium of a closer and heavier texture, corresponding to the high land of the Gangetic plain. Outlines of gneissic rock from the Assam range are common between Goalpara and Gauhati, and are found as far east as Tezpur.

(b) *Climate and Rainfall.*

Although Bengal is situated almost entirely outside the tropical zone, its climate for about two-thirds of the year, i.e. from the Middle of March to the end of October, is of the kind usually described as tropical; it has a high temperature and humidity, and dry and wet seasons. During the other months the temperature is much lower, the humidity is slight or moderate, and the rainfall is generally scanty. Hence during these months fine dry weather prevails in all parts of the Province. Excluding the Darjeeling hills, the areas of greatest precipitation are in the south-east, where the rainfall ranges between 100 and 140 inches. In the remaining portion of East Bengal it is between 70 and 80 inches; but it again rises in North Bengal, to 84 inches in Rangpur and to between 100 and 130 inches in the sub-montane plains. In the coast districts of Central and West Bengal the annual fall is generally from 60 to 70 inches, but in places it is 80 inches. In the other districts of Bengal proper, where the influence of mountain ranges and cyclonic storms is less apparent, the rainfall is lighter and more uniform, being generally between 50 and 60 inches. Irrigation is necessary for cane mainly in Western Bengal, and in the laterite soil of Northern and Eastern Bengal from November to April.

In Orissa, where the effect of cyclonic storms from the Bay of Bengal is felt, the annual rainfall is generally from 60 to 70 inches. In the east of Behar, where the influence of mountain ranges and cyclonic storms is less apparent, the rainfall is lighter and more uniform, being generally between 50 and 60 inches. Farther west it diminishes to 45 inches in Chota Nagpur and 42 inches in South Behar. In the sub-montane tracts of North Behar the annual fall varies from 50 to 55 inches.

The climate of Assam is characterized by coolness and extreme humidity, resulting from its geographical situation. Its most distinguishing feature is the copious rainfall between March and May. The year is thus, roughly, divided into two seasons—the cold season and the rains, the hot season of the rest of India being completely absent. The total amount of rain which falls in Assam during the year is always abundant, and although it is sometimes unfavourably distributed, there have been no complete droughts affecting the general harvest to any serious extent. The Province has a decided advantage over nearly all other parts of India in regard to the cultivation of sugar-cane, as the need for irrigation, which adds greatly to the cost of cultivation elsewhere in India, is seldom felt here. The climate closely approaches that of the cane-growing countries in the tropics. The peculiar difficulty in Assam is the almost entire absence of a labouring class. In the Surma Valley, Kamrup, and Goalpara agricultural labourers are few in number, and in Central and Upper Assam they are practically non-existent. The climate of the country during the rains is not calculated to stimulate the inhabitants to prolonged physical exertion.

2. Area under Cane. Classes of Soil on which the Crop is Grown. Methods of Cultivation and Varieties of Cane.

In Bengal sugar-cane cultivation is undertaken wherever water is available. The normal area under this crop in this Province is 260,000 acres, of which the Dacca and the Rajshahi divisions account for nearly 150,000 acres. It is cultivated more or less in every plains district, but in the hill districts the crop is negligible. In the open well-cultivated parts of Eastern Bengal sugar-cane has a formidable rival in jute, but, on the other hand, the cultivation of sugar-cane has been rapidly increasing in those more backward tracts where jute does not thrive well. There can be no doubt that, with the sole exception of jute when grown in those portions of the country most suitable to its cultivation, there is no crop which pays the cultivator so well as sugar-cane—*always provided he can command the necessary labour.* The growing demand for "jaggery," which has been brought about by the increasing prosperity of the rural population, and the opening up of communications in the interior of the country has undoubtedly increased the profitable nature of the crop.

Nearly all kinds of soil—from the Sedentary Archæan strata of Chota Nagpur to the old alluvium of North Behar—are suitable for growing cane. In alluvial tracts the most suitable soils are good firm loams or light clays, but the irrigated crop adapts itself to any description of soil of fair depth if drainage is secured by a pervious subsoil or other similar process, as waterlogged soil is not favourable to successful cultivation. It is said that in Bengal the best canes grow at the junction of old and new alluvia on the sides of streams and rivulets where the soils are red clay loams, rich in mineral matter.

In the Province of Behar and Orissa the total area under this crop in 1914-15 was 270,300 acres, but the crop is of greatest importance from the point of view of white sugar manufacture, especially in North Behar, where it covers an area of nearly 100,000 acres in Saran and the adjoining districts of Muzaffarpur, Champaran, and Darbhanga. The sugar-cane industry is being revived there consequent upon the decline of indigo. Labour is comparatively cheap, and cane is grown in some parts without irrigation. The future of Behar seems to lie in the development of the sugar industry, and sugar factories now working in Behar are proving a financial success. Assam and Behar offer good openings for the establishment of central factories for the manufacture of white sugar direct from the cane; but Behar has an advantage over Assam in that the industry is already well established there and there are comparatively good communications in the shape of railways and roads, while in Assam land has to be reclaimed, roads made, and labour-saving appliances arranged for, as labour is both costly and scarce.

The area under sugar-cane in districts in Assam in 1914-15 was 37,620 acres, viz.: Cachar, 8,519 acres; Sylhet, 7,036; Goalpara, 1,474; Kamrup, 5,444; Darrang, 2,541; Nowgong, 1,938; Sibsagar, 7,005; and Lakhimpur, 3,663. The rapid development in Cachar and in Sylhet is said to be due to time-expired garden coolies opening up hilly land previously under jungle. In Lakhimpur and in the east of Sibsagar and Darrang cultivation is mainly in the hands of Nepalese, who plant the cane on virgin soil in forest clearings. The bulk of the crop is grown in small patches of one or two *bighas*. The soil is generally loam or clayey loam, while the old alluvium found in many parts of the Assam Valley, especially in Golaghat, is very popular. In Upper Assam and in the hilly tracts in the south of the Surma Valley this nomadic system of cultivation is practised by the Nepalese on land newly reclaimed from jungle, and as the soil is rich in humus it gives the best outturn. In the open thickly populated parts of East Bengal this crop is grown on alluvial land beyond the reach of floods, and as the soil is usually of a loamy character, and as it is seldom allowed to remain fallow, it is too poor as a rule to bear sugar-cane without manure. The crop is, therefore, invariably manured and cultivated with great care and attention. The varieties of sugar-cane usually grown in this class of land are the medium soft yellow, or white cane preferred for the manufacture of jaggery, and also used for chewing. In the deltaic districts of the Dacca and Rajshahi divisions, where alluvial land is annually submerged and enriched with silt, the thin and hardy kinds of cane which can bear submersion are favoured. The jaggery made is of inferior quality, and in many places where the inundation is heavy and of long duration, the crop droops prematurely as the result of prolonged waterlogging, and it has to be harvested as early as October.

Thin, hardy canes are also grown for preference in the old alluvium (*khiar* or *barind*) in the Rajshahi division, where the prevailing soil is a red or yellow clay, more difficult to work than new alluvial soil and liable to suffer from drought.

Methods of Cultivation.

It is important that the field selected for cane should receive a thorough preparation, the soil being carefully worked by ploughing, cross-ploughing, and laddering, until it is brought into a fine state of tilth. For this preparation of the land the implements used generally are the ordinary country plough and harrow (a ladder made of bamboo or a beam of wood). Hand-hoeing with the *kodali* is also done in many districts. The system of planting common among *ryots*—that is, on the plough furrow—not only requires more than three times the seed that is necessary under the ridge and furrow system, but the outturn per acre of *gur* in maunds is also lower. Further, the cost of cultivation in the local *ryot's* method is higher than in the trenching system. In some of the more advanced sugar districts in Bengal the *bunds*, or ridges, on which sugar-cane is planted are so arranged that they serve a double purpose, viz. to give facility for irrigation and to remove the rain-water from the field as speedily as possible. The Mauritius system of planting is not unknown in Bengal, but among planters in Behar the trenching system is commonly adopted, in which tops of sugar-canes and also parts of the stem (sets) are used. To a limited extent, in places where white ants are troublesome, the whole cane, without being cut, is sown in shallow trenches, the number of sets planted per acre varying from 12,000 to 30,000. The manures commonly used are from cows, pigs, and horses, sweepings, ashes, and mud from tanks, although sheep-folding is also practised in some parts. Cowdung is ordinarily put on at the rate of 100 maunds per acre. On land thus treated oil-cakes are generally used during earthing-up, and it is a common practice in Bengal to apply from 10 to 15 maunds at sowing-time, and the same amount again when the plants are from 1 to 3 feet in height. It has, however, been found on the Government Farms that 200 maunds of cowdung, plus 8 maunds of castor cake per acre, is the most economical for sugar-cane, but *seet*, or indigo refuse, is generally used as manure by planters in Behar. As a protection against high winds, ravages of wild animals, and other adverse influences, the practice of tying a number of plants together is in some places adopted where the canes are thick and tall. The time for harvesting is generally from December to February, and this is also the usual time for planting. The early varieties are planted in November and December, however, and are reaped about the same time the following year. The earlier the cane is planted the better it is, in order that it may be established before the hot weather sets in. When irrigation is poor, sowing in Bengal is generally left over until April. The crop does not as a rule occupy the ground for a longer period than twelve months.

In Behar sugar-cane is planted in February and reaped in January-March of the following year.

Sugar-cane is considered an exhaustive crop, and is therefore not grown on the same field twice consecutively; but it frequently follows *aus* paddy, and a rotation with pulse crops is also common.

Green-manuring is practically unknown in Bengal, but in Behar it has been found that indigo forms a good rotation with cane, while ratooning is practised to a limited extent with some varieties in the latter Province and in the deltaic areas. The planting season in Eastern Bengal and Assam extends from January to May. In moist alluvial soil planting takes place as a rule in the first three months of the year, but where the soil is liable to become dry during the hot weather this work is deferred until the spring showers of April and May have sufficiently moistened it, and in unfavourable years it may be continued up to the first fortnight of June. In the case of such late planting as this, the invariable custom is to put the sets in seed-beds, and then transplant them at a later date in the field. This appears to be the usual custom in most parts of the Assam Valley and in portions of the Surma Valley division.

The reaping season for jaggery-canes is governed largely by the exigencies of general agriculture. In Assam the reaping commences with ratoon-cane, which attains maturity in a shorter time than plant-cane; and where there is much of it crushing may commence as early as the middle of November—that is, as soon as the weather has become fair and settled. The bulk of the cane crop is reaped between the middle of January and the end of March, but in localities where it is largely cultivated reaping may continue to as late a period as the end of April. The period which elapses between planting and reaping may be said to vary from seven to twelve months.

Varieties of Cane.

It is probable that a considerable amount of deterioration has occurred in Indian canes, and this is due to the fact that in the majority of cases the Indian peasant is not in the habit of selecting his seed for replanting. It has been shown by Geerligs and Kobus, of Java, after lengthy experiments with many canes, that, in the main, cuttings from strong sweet canes give strong plants, and that in this way it is possible to improve the stock of cane both by field and chemical selection. In India until very recently nothing appears to have been done to improve the varieties existing in the country, or even to try if such a course were possible. The classifications of cane previously made rested upon the basis of some superficial characteristics, such as local names, and not upon fundamental properties such as early or late ripening, or hardness or softness of cane, which are physiological properties of the plant very unlikely to change. Differences in soil and climate produce great modifications in canes, and it is possible that the country canes of India, though all directly descended from a common stock, have developed to some extent such different characteristics that they are likely to be classified by ordinary observers as being of different races. Now that trained and skilled botanists are available in the Agricultural Departments, the systematic classification of canes, based upon chemical and botanical observations, is being taken in hand.

This is not a scientific treatise, and therefore, for purposes of convenience, the canes indigenous to Bengal and Behar have been classified here as thick canes with soft rinds and thin canes with hard rinds. Among the latter are the Khari, Ketari, Khelia, Khagri, Nargori, Mango, Shakar-Chinia, Maneria, Pansahi, Bunsa, Baraukha, Kevali, Buxaria, Ketar, Hemja, Chynia, Rheora, Lata, Paunri, Poraya, and Lewari.

The thick canes include the Bhuri, Poori, Pundi, Kajla, Dhalsunder, Shamshara, Bombai, Ruppa, Sukli, and Bangla.

In addition to these, striped Mauritius and Bourbon canes have also been introduced. A short description of some of the principal varieties is given here. Shamshara, a large-sized cane, is a great favourite in the deltaic area of Bengal, but pigs and jackals must be carefully excluded, as they do much damage. A plentiful supply of water is necessary throughout the early growing season. This variety produces a light-coloured *rab* which is much prized by confectioners. Poundia and Bangla are appreciated as chewing varieties, while Poori, or Koori, is said to be one of the richest in sugar of all the Bengal species; but it is liable to break, and hence is not much cultivated. Dhalsunder is not so easily damaged by waterlogging as other soft canes, and it is cultivated largely in East Bengal. Of the thin canes, Shoori, Poraich, Ikri, and Khagri grow in low lands and withstand waterlogging. Reora, though rich in sugar, is not suited to heavy soils, as it suffers from a superabundance of water. Khari is a thin but very hardy variety, withstanding drought and waterlogging remarkably well. Being very hard and thick-skinned, it resists attacks of animals and is not much harmed by white ants. It is very prolific, a good yielder, and produces a fine quality of *gur*.

In Behar, Mango is very popular; it resists drought, and although its percentage of sugar to juice is large, it is liable to damage by waterlogging. Khari and Shakar Chinia are early ripening varieties (the former being more fibrous than the latter), and both of these can be cut in January without serious loss. The dwarf canes, Buxaria, Poraya, Paunri, Rheora, Hemja, and Mango, ripen late, and have a medium content of a highly absorbent fibre. When properly grown they should never be cut before February, as they show a large increase in saccharose even up to March.

A collection of the canes of Bengal was made at Sabour in 1908, and an examination of the varieties and races of cane was taken up from a chemical and botanical standpoint. The results of the work have been published in Vol. VII, No. 2, Botanical Series, *Memoirs of the Department of Agriculture in India*.

3. Fungus Diseases and Insect Pests.

Fungus Diseases of the Stem.

The most serious disease the sugar-cane is subject to in these Provinces is that known as "red rot" (red smut), caused by the fungus *Colletotrichum falcatum*, Went. Red rot is capable of arising from wound infection of the stem of the cane, but this mode of attack is secondary in importance to infection through the unwounded shoot and "root eyes" at the nodes. In Northern India the disease generally comes from the planting of infected canes, and systematic and thorough selection of the sets used for planting has been found instrumental in greatly diminishing the incidence of the disease. In India the thin varieties of cane are, on the whole, found to be less susceptible than are the thick ones.

Smut caused by *Ustilago sacchari*, Rab., is the most easily recognized of the fungus diseases of sugar-cane. As a rule it does not cause much damage, since it is only prevalent in certain varieties of thin or reed-like canes.

Botryodiplodia theobromæ, Pat., is also found in Bengal. This species is one of the many which can live both as a parasite and as a saprophyte, i.e. on living or dead material; and as belonging to the latter family, Dr. Butler found it on canes that had been killed by red rot, and on others that had apparently withered naturally. As a parasite, its effects appear to be not unlike red rot; but it is not so common nor so virulent, and it is, in fact, at present of quite minor importance.

Wilt.—Another disease which causes distinct reddening of the cane pith has lately been found throughout North-Eastern India. It is due to *Cephalosporium sacchari*, Butl. This fungus can enter the cane through wounds, through the uninjured root eyes at the nodes, and through the planted sets. The control, therefore, should be much on the same lines as in true red rot. As, however, wound infection is very common, diseased clumps must be removed before they have time to rot and set free the spores.

Collar rot, caused by ***Hendersonina sacchari***, Butl., was found by Dr. Butler on the Jorhat Farm, in Assam, attacking several varieties of thick cane; it is found also at Samalkota and in Mysore. The last two diseases have been described in Vol. VI, No. 6, Botanical Series, *Memoirs of the Department of Agriculture in India*.

Fungus Diseases of the Leaf.

Among these is the brown-leaf spot caused by *Cercospora longipes*, Butl., which is responsible for heavy loss in the yield of sugar. It is exceedingly common in North and South Behar. Like smut, it chiefly occurs in the thin canes, and it attacks almost if not quite every variety of these; but it is sometimes found on thick canes as well. The disease, like several other of the leaf diseases of the sugar-cane, is confined to the leaf blade, and is not found on the sheath. It appears when the leaves are not yet fully grown, and it continues to show itself with increasing vigour until they fade.

Resembling the last disease in several respects is the ring spot caused by *Leptosphæria sacchari*, Br. d'H., but the damage done by it in these Provinces is comparatively slight.

Sooty Mould.—It is not uncommon to find leaves or even whole plants of sugar-cane turned black by the deposit of a superficial black mould, and such plants are always found to be infested by mealy-bugs. Though the fungus is entirely superficial, and not a parasite, its presence is harmful to the plant. The mould develops in a sugary excretion known as honey-dew, produced in considerable quantities by the insects which are the real cause of the disease. In Saran the disease is locally known as "Lahi," and is considered in some places to be the worst disease of sugar-cane, Treatment should be confined to getting rid of the insects, as the fungus cannot flourish in the absence of honey-dew. Excepting the red rot, none of these diseases cause losses approaching those experienced in other countries from cane diseases such as "Sereh," "Gummosis," and root disease, which have not yet reached India.

Insect Pests.

A detailed study of the insect pests affecting the sugar-cane in Bengal, Behar and Orissa, and Assam has not yet been completed, but the literature available for reference shows that those found to attack sugar-cane in these three Provinces are known, in ordinary phraseology, as leaf-eating, leaf-mining, boring, and sucking insects.

Of the leaf-eating insects *Cercospora trachypterus* is the most important. In particular years, more especially when there is no rainfall during May and June, the hoppers appear in large numbers and devour the tender leaves of the newly planted sugar-cane. They generally breed in grassy lands, and when such lands are near enough to sugar-cane plantations they move into the latter and do much damage. The best method of dealing with these pests is to bag them in the open with large field bags. *Marasmia trapezalis* occurs as a very minor pest during the rains, and is easily kept in check by plucking away the folded leaves within which the caterpillar feeds and ultimately pupates.

A small black beetle, *Phidodonta modesta*, with spines on its body, also attacks cane. The grubs tunnel into the leaves and form irregular, whitish patches on them; the pupa is within the tunnel, and the adult, after emergence, remains feeding on the leaves, making long, thin, membranous slits upon them. This is easily checked by bagging with hand-nets and cutting away the affected leaves.

The borers, taken together, play an important part in the economy of successful sugar-cane cultivation in these Provinces. The ordinary cultivator does not realize the gravity of the situation, and it will take some time before he is convinced of the necessity of adopting preventive and remedial measures to circumvent the loss annually brought about by them. Of these the moth borer, *Chilo simplex*, and the white moth borer, *Scirpophaga auriflua*, are the most important. The moth borer lays its eggs in two rows on the leaves and produces the characteristic dead hearts so often seen in infested fields. Systematic and persistent removal of the dead hearts as soon as they are seen in the fields, planting only healthy sets, planting maize as a trap crop, and destroying stubbles of *Andropogon sorghum* after the crop is harvested, have given good results in the past.

In some years the white moth borer does great damage in Behar. The infested cane ceases to grow, and has a general appearance of drying up owing to withering of the top shoots. The collection of egg-masses and the systematic and persistent removal of the dead hearts have been found effectual against the pest.

Of the other borers, two, *Sesamia inferens* and *Anerastia ablutella*, bore into the stem, and are occasionally bad in particular localities. *Polyocha saccharella*, though perhaps the most deadly of the cane-borers, attacks the roots, but it is not greatly in evidence.

The white ant, *Termes* sp., sometimes causes great loss in particular localities. Dipping the cane sets, before planting, in a strong solution of copper sulphate in cold water prevents them from being eaten up while under ground. Later on, charging the irrigation water with crude-oil emulsion, at 13 pints to an acre, has been found effective in driving away the ants and mitigating the damage.

Of the sucking insects, *Pyrilla aberrans*, *Repersia sacchari*, and *Aleurodes barodensis* are the most important. The first named, which is a leaf-hopper, sucks the juice of the leaves and then lowers the vitality of the plants. The second one occurs on the nodes below the sheathing leaves, and its presence is not easily detected. It occurs also on rice, and if the two crops are close to each other, transference takes place from one to the other. Planting only healthy sets, and dipping them in crude-oil emulsion after stripping the sheathing leaves, has been found effective. *A. barodensis* occasionally does considerable damage to cane in some places. Removal of the infested leaves in early stages of the development of the pest does much to check it, but if this is neglected the infested leaves turn pale yellow in colour, and the crop not only appears sickly in appearance but produces very inferior sugar.

4. Extraction of Juice and its Conversion into "Gur" or Sugar.

The old *Kolhu* and *chaki* have been generally supplanted by iron roller cane-crushing mills in Bengal, but the shallow evaporating-pan has not yet been adopted to any great extent. Cultivators as a rule do not take much care in the manufacture of *gur*, the juice being rarely strained and the scum not always wholly removed. Liming is sometimes resorted to in order to neutralize the acidity of the juice. Milk diluted with water is often added to the boiling juice to assist coagulation and to bring the scum to the surface.

In Lower Bengal, when the cultivation of cane and *gur*-making is done by hired labour, the cost per acre is about Rs. 224, while the outturn is Rs. 342. A net profit of Rs. 118 per acre is thus obtained under normal conditions.

Rab and *gur* are the two products obtained by cultivators out of the cane juice, *rab* being liquid and *gur* a solid mass, not liable to drainage.

Prior to the foundation of central factories, a large amount of sugar was refined by native manufacturers, either by the rough *sewari* method or by the more refined course of the hand centrifugal. The *sewari* method appears to be largely the same as the so-called claying of the early days of West Indian manufacture, and, further, to depend upon the washing of the sugar with a limited supply of water. To achieve this end the sugar is put into a basket and a layer of water weed is placed on the top of it; after a short time the weed is removed and the top layer, which is found to be whitened, is scraped away, leaving a surface of uncleansed sugar, on which a fresh layer of weed is placed.

Chini is made by refining and draining

the molasses contained in *rab* and *gur*. There are several classes of this drained sugar, of which "kuchcha" sugar is one. As the *rab* is not subjected to any refining process in the making of "kuchcha" sugar, the quality of the "chini" entirely depends upon that of the original *rab*. This "kuchcha" sugar is valued by confectioners for making different kinds of sweetmeats, and it is also consumed in the hot weather in the form of sherbet. In the Bengal districts both cane and date "kuchcha" sugars are highly valued for making *sandesh*, the best kind of bazaar sweetmeat made in Bengal. Mauritius sugar, beet sugar, and all other refined sugars are not adapted to the preparation of *sandesh* and *batasha*, simply because they do not contain sufficient molasses to produce adhesiveness between the sugar and the curd in native sweets.

Pakka chini is made by refining *rab* or *gur* by reboiling it, and with the assistance of defecants, and by draining off the molasses afterwards. *Pakka dolo* is an intermediate class of "chini" made in the date-growing districts by refining a mixture of *gur* and juice and then draining off the molasses. *Dowara chini* is double-refined "chini" and is so called from refining pakka, or dolo sugar, over again. *Doem chini* is a second crop of sugar obtained by reboiling the molasses separated in the manufacture of *kachcha* and *pakka chinis*.

Dowara sugar is the dearest in Bengal, and its use is limited to the preparation of the best kinds of native sweets. Statistics regarding the output of small native refineries where sugar is manufactured according to indigenous methods are not available. It may be mentioned that while an efficient factory run on European lines recovers 70 to 80 per cent. of the total possible sugar, the native methods extract probably not more than 40 per cent. of the total saccharose, the rest remaining in the molasses.

In Behar the cost of cultivation does not exceed Rs. 50 an acre, and the manufacture of *gur* costs about Rs. 20 more. The yield in *gur* per acre is 30 to 35 maunds, which is usually worth about Rs. 3 to Rs. 4 a maund. The quality of *gur* manufactured is inferior, and so the product is largely used for refining. In Bengal good outturns as obtained at the Agricultural Stations were 50 to 70 maunds per acre. The usual price per maund of *gur* is higher. It therefore pays cultivators in Bengal to convert their crop into *gur*. This, coupled with the fact that the crop is cultivated in small plots of land, explains to some extent the absence of factories manufacturing sugar direct from the cane. In Behar, as the price of *gur* is low, the cultivators are not averse to selling their crop to factories. Sugar-cane is grown in some parts of Behar, without irrigation, and labour is comparatively cheap; hence cane is available for factories at a price which leaves a margin of profit when working it up into sugar.

In Assam the iron mill has supplanted the old wooden one in Cachar, and amongst the Nepalis; but the latter is still used by the Assamese. *Gur* is very cheap in the Sadar sub-division of Lakhimpur and in the Langai and Singla Valleys of Sylhet, owing apparently in both districts to the planting of cane on virgin soil. Mr. Basu estimates the normal yield per acre to be 9 tons of cane in the Brahmaputra Valley and 2,200 lb. of *gur* for the Province. Mr. Basu's figures, given below, show that it should pay cultivators well to take up sugar-cane extensively on the virgin forest soil; but the great difficulty is the lack of enterprise and capital amongst the people, and also the labour difficulty: Lakhimpur (Dibrugarh average of three years)—cost of cultivation per acre, Rs. 40; cost of manufacture per acre, Rs. 48; total cost per acre, Rs. 88. Yield per acre, 42 maunds; value of yield per acre, Rs. 173. Net profit per acre, Rs. 90.

In Bengal sugar is also extracted from the date palm (*Phœnix sylvestris*) and the palmyra palm (*Borassus flabelliformis*). The cultivation of date palms is an important industry in Jessore; the other districts where it is carried on are Khulna, Nuddia, Faridpur, Backergunj, and 24 Parganas. The amount of palm sugar produced in Bengal alone is probably some 100,000 tons, worth well over £500,000 sterling; thus the industry is a source of profit to a large number of people. Palm *gur* and its products are largely consumed in the districts in which they are made, but in the Jessore district there are many refineries. Most of the sugar refined in Jessore goes to Calcutta, and is largely used for the preparation of native sweetmeats. Mr. H. E. Annett has investigated the condition of the date-sugar industry in Bengal and published the results in the *Memoirs of the Department of Agriculture in India*, Chemical Series, Vol. II, No. 6. The methods of sugar manufacture and refining carried out in the district are very crude, and are, in that author's opinion, capable of great improvement.

At present only 240 trees per acre are usually grown, giving a yield of 2·3 tons of *gur*; but by the regular planting of 350 trees per acre, an average of 3 tons of *gur* can be obtained. It has been found that the thickest trees are the largest yielders; hence the sowing of selected seed from such trees is well worth trying. The present method of refining by means of water-weed is an exceedingly slow process, and if centrifugals were introduced the process would be much quicker and the turnover much greater. The juice exuding from a freshly cut surface of the date-tree contains only sucrose, and inversion takes place afterwards while it is standing in the pot overnight. Mr. Annett recommends washing the cut surface of the tree with formalin once a week and the addition of a small quantity of formalin to the pots daily, and if treated in this way a very appreciable increase in yield of sugar per tree might be obtained. It was at first supposed that the use of dirty earthen pans in which the juice is boiled is to a large extent responsible for the dark colour of the date *gur*, and that with the substitution of iron pans jaggery of very fine quality could be produced. It has, however, been established that the substitution of metal pans for earthen jars does not produce a lighter coloured *gur*. The dark colour of the date *gur* is due to the inherent alkalinity of the palm juice, and by rendering the latter slightly acid *gur* of an excellent colour can be obtained. The fuel question is one of importance, as it adds considerably to the cost of preparation. A very large number of experiments have shown that 2 to 3 maunds of coal (costing 15 annas) or 7 to 9 maunds of fuel (costing Rs. 1.20) are required to produce 1 maund of *gur*. From this it would seem that there is a considerable future for coal fuel. The furnaces at present in use have no under-draught at all and are simply holes in the ground, and a cheap furnace which will burn coal is being evolved. At present the day juice in the palm groves is largely allowed to run to waste, but from heavy yielding trees it is collected and boiled in the evenings to a syrup. Owing to the high glucose ratio it does not crystallize, but by the use of lime or of formalin in the collecting pots this juice has been found capable of being manufactured into very good crystallized *gur*. Metal buckets are now being substituted for earthenwares for collecting the juice. In Mr. Annett's opinion, there seems no reason why, with careful seed selection, the amount of sugar in the juice should not be raised considerably, and under these circumstances there might be openings for large central factories. The same author calls attention to the long season which is possible when dealing with palm sugar. The date-palm yields its juice in the hot weather from April to September. There are many places where these palms would grow very well together, and thus a factory would be able to make its sugar-boiling season last over practically the whole year.

5. Work done by the Agricultural Department.

The Department of Agriculture, Bengal, has the cane crop under study at Dacca and Burdwan. Local varieties are being collected and tested with a view to find out the most suitable kind. Vandamakhi and White Tanna have proved their superiority at Rajshahi and Burdwan respectively, while at Dacca, of the five varieties tested—Dacca Ganderi, Yellow Tanna, Striped Tanna, B. 147, and B. 208—up to date B. 147 has been found the most promising. It has a richer juice, and yields far more heavily than the local Ganderi. It is a hard cane, and therefore not suitable for chewing purposes. B. 208 has the highest percentage of sugar in the juice, but it is rather too soft and too delicate for Dacca. Yellow Tanna, though not very rich, is very hardy and a good yielder. Striped Tanna is a thick cane with a luxuriant growth; but it has two defects—the impurity of its juice and the difficulty of crushing it. Sarethi of Aligarh promises to do extremely well. Ratoon canes of all the five varieties are found to be badly attacked both by red rot and the stem-borer. The advantage of the ridge and furrow system of planting and cultivation is being demonstrated, especially in places where irrigation is possible. The advantages of castor cake in combination with cowdung as a manure for sugar-cane are also being demonstrated. An experiment is also being made on the Dacca Farm to see whether any advantage will be gained by running off water from the soil.

In Assam the Agricultural Station at Jorhat, which was taken up in 1906, has been devoted mainly to the sugar-cane crop. Although owing to the exceeding poverty of the soil the sugar-cane experiments on this farm were at first unpromising, the work done there by Messrs. Meggitt and Birt is now beginning to yield results of great interest and value. The qualities of different local and imported canes have been carefully studied, and as a result it has been found that, in Assam, local varieties of cane are incapable of competing with exotic varieties. Barbadoes and Mauritius canes have proved their superiority in all ways, the average yields from these canes being 20 to 30 tons, which is a great advance on Mr. Basu's figures. Demonstrations have been given on cultivators' holdings alongside the local cane, and some 75,000 sets were distributed in the Assam Valley in the year 1915 of the three best varieties, viz. striped Mauritius, B. 147, and B. 376. Experiments on the study of the questions of tillage, manuring, and drainage in the light of local conditions, so as to increase the average outturn per acre, are being carried on at Jorhat.

At Sabour, in Behar, much useful work has been done by Messrs. Woodhouse and Taylor in connection with the botanical and chemical aspects of this crop.

As a result of experiments, it has been found that heavily manured canes ripen from a fortnight to a month later than lightly manured crops, and that variation in the date of planting does not alter the date of maturity. The Agricultural Department is demonstrating the superiority of Khari and Mango canes and the advantages of the ridge and furrow system in certain parts of Orissa and Bhagalpore.

6. Past History and General Outlook for the Development of the Sugar Industry in these Provinces.

There is an interesting note on the past history of the sugar-cane crop in Bengal, by Mr. C. S. Taylor, in the *Bengal Quarterly Journal*, vol. iii, Nos. 2 and 3, to which I am indebted for much of the information given in this section as regards past efforts in the direction of sugar-making in Bengal and Behar. The sugar trade from Bengal was, in the first half of the eighteenth century, a great source of profit to the merchants of Calcutta. Towards the latter half of the eighteenth century this trade was almost annihilated, partly on account of difficulties of transport and the preference given by England to the West Indies over all other sugar-producing countries, and partly on account of the rise in the price of native sugar, due to wasteful methods in native factories. Towards the end of the eighteenth century attempts were therefore made to establish the industry upon European lines by starting factories financed with European capital and run under European supervision. It was foreseen that the only arrangement by which a European could hope to succeed in cane cultivation would be by obtaining land at a low rate and with good irrigation facilities. The charges of cane cultivation by a European planter, however, are higher than when the crop is raised by the *ryots*; it was therefore thought that the cane-farming system would, in theory, pay both manufacturer and *ryot* better than the plantation system, provided steps were taken to ensure an absolutely certain crop within easy distance of every factory so as to ensure success. Small central factories located in a cane-growing tract and buying their cane from natives were advocated. Towards 1845 planters began to come over in large numbers from the West Indies, and as the price of indigo had fallen to Rs. 110 per maund at that time, the Behar planter thought of substituting sugar for indigo. To this end he was encouraged by the exceedingly good returns obtained in the first place by the planting of Otaheite cane on a small scale in particularly good land, and on these calculations from £700,000 to £1,000,000 were invested in the importation and setting up of expensive machinery from England. All kinds of land were put into cane, and no rotation of crops was followed, nor was manure applied in the majority of instances. The result was a falling off in yield, and sugar did not pay. Thus it was that about 32 distinct sugar concerns started between 1842 and 1850 closed down within a couple of years, and as the price of indigo rose at the same time sugar was rapidly abandoned for indigo. In the opinion of Mr. Taylor, the failure was due to erroneous calculations in the first place, followed by want of system afterwards. For fifty years after this great failure no attempt appears to have been made by Europeans to start the manufacture of refined sugar on a large scale, but in 1900, owing to the fall in the price of indigo, the sugar question again came into prominence. A Sugar Commission, appointed by Government to consider the question, came to several definite conclusions on the subject which led them to believe that success might be achieved by central factories alone. Large concerns sprang up soon after this report.

A modern factory fitted with plant capable of turning out a large quantity of vacuum-pan sugar demands such an outlay of capital that it must make large profits to pay the necessary interest. Unless such a factory is placed in the midst of a country almost devoted to cane-growing, so that the sugar is, as it were, at the very doors of the concern, endless delays and numerous stoppages must take place owing to the non-delivery of the raw material. A large factory in such a tract would, owing to its greater efficiency, be of greater use than a small one. In India, with the inefficient means of transport and a hot climate, the losses due to inversion and fermentation on the road, and storage in the event of stoppages, are very serious. It is sometimes suggested that all Indian sugar factories should act primarily as refineries taking the *gur* from the native manufacturer for the following reasons: *gur* is made very cheaply by the *ryot*, there is less trouble in carrying the manufactured article than the more bulky cane, and because the prices could be graduated by the quality of the *gur*. But this suggestion on trial in Behar has not met with much success owing to the great fluctuations in the supply and price of *gur*. Where the factory can rapidly obtain *gur* or raw sugar from outside its province, as is the case at Cossipur, it has naturally succeeded.

The majority of canes in Behar are grown by the *ryot* under contract, although some land is under the direct control of the factory. In this way the factory is dependent to a considerable extent on a supply of cane from land not under its direct control, and management becomes difficult. The *ryot*, whose sole object is to sell his crop, becomes careless, and very often restive in his desire to clear the land early and prepare it for the following crop. Sometimes an excessive quantity of cane will be received, and at others it will be insufficient to keep the factory at work; but another defect is that canes are bought by weight, without reference to their richness in sugar. The climate of Behar is not so favourable to cane as it is in Java, where the whole of the cultivation is done on a different plan. It is of the utmost importance in Behar that facilities for irrigation in the cane-growing tract should be obtained and that manuring on a liberal scale should be practised. As Mr. Taylor has pointed out, the lands are highly calcareous, giving every chance to the nitrifying organisms of the soil to supply every trace of applied nitrogen to the nitrogen-loving cane crop; and therefore by manuring properly, together with irrigation, extremely good results have been achieved. Unless the cane is continuously irrigated during the dry months there is every likelihood that the entire crop will be carried off by white ants.

It has been proved that substantial profits may be made by a man who has an estate and who will set up a small sugar-making plant and run it himself, but it is essential that the proprietor must not be afraid of working and that he must personally supervise the whole of the work, or the majority of the profits will be lost in paying the expenses of the staff.

There is great scope for improvement in Behar, both in the direction of better cultivation and in the introduction of canes of high purity to increase the weight of cane and sugar per acre. The usual weight of thin cane per acre is 12 to 15 tons and 20 to 25 tons for thick canes, and it requires from *16 to 18 tons to make 1 ton of sugar*. In other countries 30 to 40 tons of cane per acre is the usual outturn, and 10 tons of cane for a ton of sugar; and this brings us to the fact that while an acre of land in other countries will produce 3 to 4 tons of sugar, in Behar it will only yield three-quarters of a ton. It was principally with a view to ascertain whether this defect of low yield can be remedied that the Board of Agriculture in India recommended the establishment of a sugar-cane station in North Behar to act as a receiving station for the seedling canes produced by the sugar-cane specialist, Dr. Barber, at the cane-breeding station in Madras. This station would grow and test the seedling canes before they are given out to cultivators, and it will also be a centre for introducing improved methods of cultivation. It is certain that, with the introduction of improved canes evolved by Dr. Barber and some exotic canes tested by Mr. Clarke at Shahjahanpur, the sugar industry in Behar will be placed on a firmer footing.

At the present moment there are no fewer than 10 central factories in Behar, crushing approximately 3,000 tons of cane a day, and the addition of others is in contemplation. These factories are all working during the present time (1916) at very handsome profits, owing to the rise in prices brought about by the war; but even before the war, when the price of sugar dropped to a very low figure, the majority were giving excellent financial results. That the price will ever be as low again as it was before the war is highly improbable, and we are therefore safe in assuming that sugar factories in Behar have a good future before them, given that they are run on proper lines and do not fall into the errors which led to the downfall of indigo.

The cost of cane in the Behar factories varies a little according to quality and the distance it has to be brought, but it may be said to cost from 4 to 6 annas a maund at the factories, according to quality. As regards the size of central factories in Behar, it has been found that those having a capacity of 300 tons of cane per 24 hours answer the requirements of successful working. The smallest unit area to feed such a factory is one of 2,000 acres of cane, which postulates some 6,000 to 8,000 acres of land in order to allow free scope for rotation, and it is on obtaining this area that the future of a central factory must rest.

The cost of cane is a basic figure in calculating the success or otherwise of a central sugar factory. It can be safely said that wherever cane can be grown in a more or less compact area, and in sufficient quantities at from 4 to 6 annas a maund, according to the quality of the cane, the success of a factory is assured. There are large areas in Behar and Gorakhpur where cane can be grown and sold at this figure. The *gur* produced in these parts is of inferior quality, suitable only for refining purposes. The cultivators have therefore no objection to selling their canes direct to factories. In parts of North Behar cane is grown without irrigation, but if water be required it can be had at a low cost. Floods in Behar are not frequent, and do not last long enough to do any appreciable damage to the sugar-cane crop.

The heavy crops of cane on the Pusa Farm, where the soil is by no means of the most favourable type, but rather the reverse, show what can be done by improved cultural methods. Mr. Coventry is of opinion that by the introduction of an improved cane and the application of improved methods of cultivation in Behar we could raise the production of sugar per acre to a very much higher figure than it stands at present, and it is not too much to say that it could be easily doubled. At present there is no other part of India where the prospect of successfully introducing the central factory system is so promising as in Behar. Progress is at present slow owing to the fact that owners of indigo estates on which cane can be grown are unable to find the requisite capital.

There is no sugar factory in Assam which is equipped with modern machinery, if we leave out of consideration the few sugar-cane farms in Lakhimpur and Barpathar, where steam-power mills are said to be employed in crushing. The object of these two farms is, however, the production of *gur*. A ton of cane would seem to cost about Rs. 5 in Lakhimpur. The expense of cultivating forest land is so low that a few years ago *gur* was selling at Rs. 2.8 per maund in the Dibrugarh market. The cost can no doubt be reduced considerably by improved cultivation, and it may not be too sanguine to expect that, under favourable conditions, a *ryot* should be able to deliver cane at the factory door at about Rs. 4 per ton. If cane could be taken to a factory and disposed of there at a rate which would leave a fair margin of profit, it is probable that many persons, who are now deterred by the cost and trouble involved in the crushing of sugar-cane and the manufacture of jaggery, could be induced to cultivate this crop. The great majority of *ryots* keep barely enough capital to till their holdings, nor can they spare any for the crushing of cane. Central mills, where the cane would be crushed by steam power, are expected, therefore, to be popular when the *ryots* are persuaded to sell their crops instead of making jaggery for themselves. There are large unoccupied tracts of land in Goalpara, Kamrup, and Nowgong eminently suited to the growth of heavy crops of cane, and the climate, both as regards temperature, rainfall, and its distribution, is excellent. The apparent richness of the soil, its excellent conditions as regards moisture, and the facilities for irrigation would show that if these large blocks of land could be brought under cane cultivation they would probably yield very handsome returns. Assam thus offers a possible area for a large number of central factories.

Only the advent of the capitalist into Assam can put the sugar-cane industry on a proper footing. The growth alone of high-class canes for central factory work demands more care in cultivation, more capital, and more supervision than the *ryots* are at present prepared to give. The cost of machinery for manufacturing into sugar, the cost of land reclamation, and the labour provision all indicate the necessity for well-financed concerns. Nothing in the way of improvement or extension can be hoped for from the comparatively limited areas now under cane under the ordinary *ryot's* conditions. With a view to help capitalists to form a clear idea of the prospects of sugar in Assam, the Local Agricultural Department has opened a station at Kamrup, as recommended by the Board of Agriculture in India. The object of the experiment is to ascertain whether it is possible to produce, on sufficiently large and compact areas, crops of high-class cane at a low cost, ranging from 4 annas to 6 annas per maund of 82 lb. and averaging 25 to 30 tons per acre, so as to give a crushing season of at least 100 days per annum, and thus furnish the matrix of a properly controlled industry. The land on the above-named station has been reclaimed from waste and put under cane on a small scale, and it is intended to increase the area to 1,000 acres. After the cessation of the heavy rains the cane was found to make wonderful growth, and on the higher-lying areas it made a good crop. Tillering was extraordinarily good and the crop extremely healthy. In the light of experienced gained, there appears to be every prospect of success with earlier planting and a thorough scheme of drainage.

Labour in Assam is notoriously deficient, but this difficulty, it is thought, can be overcome by the use of steam tackle and labour-saving appliances. Experiments to this end are being made, and the results so far are full of promise. These are the districts where no tea is being grown, and there is already a fair indigenous native population, which, with the aid of steam tackle, will be found sufficient for the cultivation of sugar. In the areas in Lower Assam not likely to compete with the tea industry for labour, there is every probability of the Local Administration granting tracts of land on a 30 years' lease, in the first instance, for sugar-cane cultivation on terms as favourable as those for tea. If the present experiment proves that a plantation containing a factory is a sound investment, there is every hope that the lower districts of the Assam Valley will be opened up by the sugar industry just as the upper districts have been developed by the growth of tea.

This gives a view of the general conditions for producing cane and sugar in the three Provinces, and provided that the possibility of improving the output of sugar per acre becomes an established fact, and assuming that sufficient land to maintain a factory running full time can be obtained, there is certainly, under present conditions, a great future for sugar-cane, so great a future that there should be no difficulty as to getting the requisite capital necessary for launching out on a large and paying scale.

FAUNA

BY W. M. NUTTALL

ANIMAL life in the Bengal Presidency and in the Provinces of Behar and Orissa, and Assam, is exceedingly abundant, but it varies greatly in character according to the physical conditions prevailing in the several divisions. In regions where the rainfall is slight the fauna is of an inferior character to that found in those tracts where such soil is productive of a wealth of luxuriant vegetation.

It is true that some of the larger species of wild game are becoming extinct, and that many others have been driven from their homes in the fastnesses or forests and mountains by the ubiquitous hunter or by the agriculturist who has cleared away jungle for the cultivation of land. But the lordly elephant still roams in many forests, the beautiful tiger levies toll upon cattle, and even mankind, the agile leopard is a menace to goats, sheep, and cattle, ferocious buffaloes afford dangerous and exciting sport, and the comparatively small wild boar retains his title of the pluckiest of all wild animals in India.

It will be understood that space will permit reference to be made only to some of the principal fauna which are most commonly met with.

The elephant, the largest of the Ungulata family, haunts forests and wild-looking jungle in many parts of the Provinces, but particularly in the territory sloping northward towards the Himalayas, or in the dense vegetation to the north and south of the Ganges River, in Upper Assam, and in the central and north-eastern portions of the Feudatory States of Orissa. Their chief habitat in these States is in the exceedingly sparsely populated and forest-clad parts of the State of Mayurbhani; in fact, it is said that practically all the elephants in Orissa have at one time or other been domiciled in those fastnesses.

The height of an adult male at the shoulders varies from 9 feet to 9 feet 6 inches, while that of a fully grown female is about 8 feet, although in the Calcutta Museum there is the skeleton of a male which measured 11 feet 3 inches.

DUCK-SHOOTING AT TURKOULIA.

Two methods of capture are usually practised in India, namely, (1) by driving and impounding the animals in stockades, and (2) by hunting them on tame elephants and subsequently noosing them, or, as the natives say, "*mela shikar*." Impounding may be carried out by driving a herd into a strongly constructed stockade, but this practice frequently involves the hardships and disappointments of following and guiding a herd for several days, and of being compelled to camp out in all weathers, frequently in jungles, in order that sight of the quarry may not be lost. The plan more generally adopted is to build a *Keddah* at one of the outlets of a salt-lick or *poong*, where obtainable, which is voluntarily visited by elephants, and for native servants to be in readiness to secure all barriers as soon as the herd has entered the enclosure.

The noosing plan appeals with peculiar force to sportsmen of a true type who believe in giving an opponent what is known as "a fighting chance." Further than that, the sport requires sound nerves and good judgment, especially as hunted animals usually make for the densest jungle, full of thorns and cane, impassable as a rule to any beast but an elephant.

Medium-sized animals are caught in this manner, but stockades enclose young and old, of all ages. Fully grown elephants, with the whole of their lives spent in the enjoyment of liberty, naturally enough resent the encircling ropes which threaten them with captivity and obedience to man. Their struggles for continued freedom are frequently so severe that the ropes cut their flesh, and the subsequent process of training is thus delayed by reason of the time required for the healing up of wounds, and of the more or less surly temper of an enraged beast.

Young animals are easily and quickly trained, and therefore command a ready sale throughout India, but the education of an old one necessitates the constant attendance—and tuition too—of at least three huge *koonkies*, or tame elephants.

Tiger (*Felis tigris*).—This beautifully marked specimen of the feline family is found in almost every part of the Provinces, and the majority of them are killers of cattle and other game, while not a few are destructive to human life. Their tracks are regular "beats," several miles in length, and one native method of killing them is to set traps, in the form of a gigantic bow or arrow, on their well-defined paths. Tigers do not as a rule attack man, but Government statistics prove that very large numbers of cattle, goats, and other domestic animals are destroyed by them.

The rhinoceros belongs to the one-toed, or perissodactyle ungulates, and two varieties are met with. One of these (*R. sondaicus*) is found in Bengal—especially in the Sunderbunds—occasionally in Assam, throughout Burma, and as far as the Malay Peninsula. They differ slightly in colouring and in the folds of skin covering their bodies. They inhabit grass jungle in remote localities, delighting in swamps and mud holes, and they are frequently met with in flowing rivers. As their name implies, they have one horn which usually measures from 10 inches to 12 inches in length, although a few have been obtained which reached 16 inches. This horn is, in reality, a conglomeration of hairs, liable to be destroyed by injury or disease, whereupon another one grows in its place. The skin of the animal is remarkably thick; its colour is dusky black; its length of body is about 10½ feet; its tail measures 2½ feet; and its height at the shoulders varies from 5 feet 6 inches to more than 6 feet.

INDIAN RHINOCEROS, ZOOLOGICAL GARDENS, CALCUTTA.

Considering its huge bulk, great weight, and its awe inspiring and formidable head, the rhinoceros is naturally a timid beast, and will generally endeavour to escape from close quarters with human beings.

When, however, it is suddenly disturbed or wounded, it will make a series of most ferocious charges which result in death to any living creature with which it comes in contact. On the other hand it is easier to kill than many other wild animals, and is far less tenacious of life than the wild boar, which probably affords finer sport than any other inhabitant of the jungle.

The natives of Assam are very keen upon securing its flesh, as they have a profound belief in its medicinal properties, and as the species is becoming somewhat scarce in that Province the Government has provided reserved areas for its preservation.

Wild buffaloes (*Bos bubalus*) usually inhabit tracts of swampy jungle, such as are seen at the foot of the south-eastern portion of the Himalayan range, or in the deltaic areas of the Ganges and Mahanadi Rivers and in Assam.

It possesses a well-rounded body covered with a thin, dark-brown or blackish-grey coat of hair, it has white legs, and contrasts most favourably with the domesticated type, which is frequently of a lean and scraggy appearance.

Buffaloes are remarkably savage animals, an infuriated bull having on several occasions been known to charge a line of shooting elephants, and many a hunter in India has had nerve-racking experiences both in jungle and upon open ground.

The gaur (*Bos gaurus*) is generally designated by the name *mithan* in Assam, and by bison in other parts of India. They herd together in the denser portions of the forest, but they emerge into open places occasionally, but especially when young blades of grass are sprouting after the vegetation has been burned off the land. These temporary excursions are made in the early hours of the day, and at sunrise the animals seek the glades of the forest, where they remain hidden during the day. They are, further, frequently found grazing in close proximity to elephants. Some of these animals are 6 feet in height at the shoulder, and have massive forequarters and chest, small legs and hoofs, and rather poor hindquarters. They are nearly black in colour, with reddish lower parts, and white legs from hoofs to knees and hocks.

Grasses and creepers of various descriptions form their staple food, but as they lie *perdu* during the day one must be afoot early in the morning in order to bag one.

This animal must be distinguished from the gazal, or *Bos frontalis*, which is a slightly smaller animal of the same colour and having nearly straight horns. It lives in hilly tracts, and while it is occasionally kept in captivity, it has been found that even in its wild state it will inter-breed with tame cattle.

Sambur (*Cervus unicolor*), the largest member of the deer tribe in India, is fairly numerous in almost inaccessible heights, but as the females of the species appear to be surprisingly unable to realize when they are in danger, they and their calves are indiscriminately shot by native hunters, and thus the species is decreasing at a rapid rate. Although sambur prefer to roam among the hills, one may occasionally see a stray animal feeding upon open ground in the early morning, especially in Assam, where it is found upon numerous plains, but it is always within a short distance from its sheltered retreat where it rests during the greater part of the day.

It is of a fairly dark brown colour, with a whitish-yellow shade between the thighs, and the height of a fully grown stag is about 13½ hands. The males are much darker than the females.

The handsome spotted deer (*Cervus axis*) need not be sought in any place where there is not an abundant supply of good water for drinking purposes, as it suffers from an almost unquenchable thirst. It is generally found among jungle at the base of a range of hills, but occasionally it ascends to a height of about 3,000 feet.

Among the smaller species of this family is the barking deer (*Curvulus muntjac*) whose home is on thickly wooded hills. It is not more than about 20 inches in height, and its horns do not, as a rule, exceed 5 inches in length.

Other animals of the same species are the Indian antelope (*Antelope cervicapra*), found in nearly all districts where the jungle is not particularly dense; together with the handsome little mouse deer, which is not more than 10 inches or 12 inches in height at the withers. It is found chiefly on hill ranges at an elevation of about 1,500 feet.

The Leopard (*Felis pardus*).—The two varieties of this species in India are usually known as panthers and leopards, and they differ slightly both in colour and size. The former varies in length from 6 feet to nearly 8 feet, with skins of light yellow colour, while the latter rarely exceeds 6 feet, and has darker spots placed close together. It is said that black specimens are occasionally seen in the district of Cachar in the Surma Valley in Assam. Both types destroy and eat cattle, dogs, deer, pigs, monkeys, and other animals of a smaller size, and their boldness is manifested by their entering villages and carrying away their prey from the houses of natives. They are widely distributed, and are usually found in moderately open country near cultivated areas, but they frequently conceal themselves in trees.

Striped hyænas (*Hyena striata*) common in all parts of the Indian Peninsula, prowl fearlessly in the neighbourhood of native villages, where stray goats, dogs, and other domestic animals fall an easy prey to them, but in the absence of a living victim they are always ready to satisfy their hunger with carrion.

Other members of the feline family found in nearly every district of the three Provinces include the cheetah (or hunting leopard), the clouded leopard, the ounce, and the fishing cat.

The Indian wolf (*Canis pallipes*) is a determined hunter of various kinds of deer, as well as of sheep and goats, and natives have asserted that children have occasionally been carried off by a pack of these ferocious animals.

The Indian sloth bear (*Ursus labiatus*) has long and shaggy black hair, especially on the shoulders, together with white fur, in the shape of a horse's shoe, on the chest. It has indifferent eyesight, and when charging (as it invariably does when disturbed suddenly) it is guided chiefly by its sense of hearing and scent, both of which are unusually keen. This species of bear is common in the Provinces, being met with upon forest-clad ranges of hills where there are caves or recesses, from which it emerges to take its nocturnal rambles. In Assam it is in the habit of making small *machans* in trees—similar to, but stronger than, a stork's nest—in which it sleeps during the daytime. It is not generally known that sloth bears will eat carrion flesh, and a well-known hunter in Assam asserts that he has frequently shot them when feeding upon the carcases of sambur and other animals which have died several days previously. It searches during the night for food, which includes termites, or white ants, which the bear obtains from the ground by digging to a depth of from 3 feet to 6 feet.

The length of body and head varies from 4 feet 6 inches to 5 feet 8 inches; and the height at the shoulder ranges from 2 feet 2 inches to 2 feet 9 inches. .

The Malayan species, only rarely found in Upper Assam, is black in colour, with short hair, and an almost white muzzle.

HEAD OF RHINOCEROS, SHOT BY W. M. NUTTALL.

Sus Indicus, the Indian wild boar, is one of the best-known species of game in the Peninsula. It belongs to a family which has types in nearly every country of the civilized world. It was formerly common in England and France, and is still plentiful in Russia, Spain, and elsewhere in Europe. It is a remarkably courageous animal, and more than one historian has stated that a full-sized tusker will quench its thirst at a pool of water with a tiger drinking on either side of him. Colonel Heber Percy says that in several instances an old boar has beaten off a tiger and has subsequently killed him, while the writer, shooting from the back of an elephant, wounded one, which immediately charged and inflicted injuries to the legs and trunk of his mount.

Pig-sticking is possibly the most exciting and dangerous sport in which a man can engage, and many hunters will, to the end of their lives, carry indelible scars resulting from their adventures.

The boar is in the habit of making small but exceedingly strong houses of grass, leaves, and jungles; these are circular in form, with an entrance on one side, and they are used as shelters during the heavy rains of the monsoon period. It usually feeds upon roots, but it has been known to dig into the earth to obtain worms, while it is not averse to carrion. In certain districts there are trees which during the months of August and September are laden with nuts, similar in shape to but harder than walnuts, and when these fall to the ground one is certain to find a number of pigs feeding upon them.

The boar is from 2 feet 6 inches in height at the shoulder, and it will frequently turn the scale at 200 lb. to 300 lb., some even exceeding this weight.

Wild dogs (*Canis rutilans*), which are very numerous in well-wooded districts in each Province, are exceedingly destructive to small game. They usually hunt in packs, exhibiting considerable intelligence in following their quarry, and it is said that a number of them have been known to pull down and kill an Indian gaur.

The jackal is no stranger to any one who is acquainted with India. Its wailing howl, repeated three or four times and followed by as many sharp yelps, resounds through the stillness of the night as the animal emerges from its jungly haunts bent upon scavenging excursions in the neighbourhood of native villages.

It is impossible to refer here to many varieties of smaller animals, including weasels, martens, monkeys, polecats, and badgers; to birds, such as vultures, kites, falcons, parrots, cranes, wildfowl, and hundreds of other species; or even to alligators, crocodiles, snakes, lizards, and other unpleasant reptiles; and it need only be added that a special article on salt and fresh-water fish will be found on another page of this volume.

The eastern portion of India, to which these notes refer, is second to none as a hunter's paradise. The majority of the haunts of large and small game can at the present time be reached in comfort in luxurious railway carriages or well-fitted steamers, and guides and beaters are always available at the nearest town or village. Opportunities for obtaining "my first tiger," or a record trophy of one of the various antlered animals, are presented in such a manner that the traveller must be a listless hunter if he does not avail himself of them.

The city of Calcutta is an admirable place for headquarters, and all kinds of weapons, ammunition, and other equipment can be procured there at an exceedingly moderate cost.

The following notes relate to a few of the many exciting incidents which have been experienced by me during several years' enjoyment of big game shooting in the Province of Assam, and not at any great distance from my home on the Digultarung Tea Estate, Rungarara, Upper Assam:—

"An old Assamese *shikari* of mine was killed lately by following up a wounded tiger. He had fired at it at close quarters from a *machan*, and as he felt certain that it would be found lying dead in the vicinity, he collected a number of friends to assist him in the search. The brute had lost a good deal of strength, but he had sufficient left in him to make a charge at some of the party, and in the general scurry which took place a boy fell to the ground almost within reach of the tiger. The *shikari* returned to render help, but he himself was badly mauled, being bitten at the waist, and he succumbed to his injuries on the following day." The writer is confident that a tiger can exist for two or even three weeks without any flesh food, and he supports his opinion by the following incident: "I recently got information of a 'kill,' not far distant, and as the tiger which had been seen in the neighbourhood did not appear to be at all shy, I was urged to hurry along in the hope that I might bag him before darkness set in. The 'kill' could not be seen, as it had been placed in long grass at the bottom of a broad and deep *nullah* with a high bank on either side. I therefore sat on the ground in such a position that I could see the opposite bank and jungle from which it was expected the tiger would emerge on his way to the 'kill.' I had not waited long when, as the sun was sinking on the horizon, I caught sight of a magnificent tiger—truly a monarch—standing on the opposite bank and casting his keen eyes up and down the *nullah*. Just as his gaze fell upon me I levelled my rifle and fired; there was an awful roar as he bounded high in the air, and then, rolling down the bank, bounded off into a patch of long grass. Thence he dragged himself into a mass of terrible jungle and eventually crawled into low, broken, bogland covered with trees.

"I could at that time only obtain leave of absence on Sundays, so on the first available day I took native *shikaris* with me to endeavour to drive the tiger out of his lair on to higher and clearer ground. The land was very broken and boggy, so it will be understood that we were keenly on the alert to prevent a surprise.

"Trees were climbed in order to give us an opportunity of seeing what might be ahead, and after a long time, spent in arduous work, we eventually drove our game out, but why he did not charge us I cannot say.

"I then became nervous about the possible fate of the villagers and decided that I would follow him up on elephants and put an end to his career. We found his tracks which led in the direction of the village, and after making circuits around them, I soon afterwards succeeded in laying him low. This was a fine tiger, although very emaciated, and I am able to state confidently that he had been without meat food for more than three weeks. My opinion was that the monster was then on his way to secure easy prey as he was far too weak to hunt and kill game on his own account. In all probability this tiger would—owing to his parlous condition—have become a man-eater. My first bullet entered his mouth, carrying away one of his fangs, and I believe that it was thereby diverted, as, instead of penetrating the brain, it passed down the throat, and then shattered the shoulder.

"Monkeys, by giving utterance to a cry totally different from their usual chatter, have frequently informed me of the presence of a tiger, and my discovery of this was made when I was returning home with a dead one on the back of my elephant.

"Luck has a good deal to do with getting a glimpse of a tiger, but in a general way I may say that experience is necessary in order that one may observe tracks, or recent lairs, or some other unusual feature which would never be noticed by an uninitiated hunter.

"I have a perfect recollection of my first tiger! It was not the tedious tracking, or the long waiting for a shot, but it was the excitement of the moment when my bullet went home!

"In later days I was in the habit of walking in a circle round the 'kill,' and I invariably found that, when I approached the place where the beast was lying in a concealed spot, he would move away to a distance and again hide himself. I therefore tried the following method, and as it was so successful I have since that time always adopted the same plan when sitting in a *machan* over the 'kill.' I took elephants and men, and instructed the natives to arouse the tiger while I hid myself in a tree. At a given signal they were to assemble near the 'kill,' and then march away singing and shouting, when I expected the tiger would return to the bait. The beast did so, and found everything quiet, but still hearing the men, he followed them for some distance and once more made his way to the bait to enjoy his meal, but he never finished it, as I rolled him over while my servants were still singing. The tiger was strapped on an elephant within twenty minutes of our arrival.

"I was out one day with a friend when we picked up the tracks of a very fine tiger and followed them from morning to dusk, but as it became too dark to see clearly we decided to encamp for the night and endeavour to secure our prey on the morrow.

"As soon as it was light we went to a neighbouring village and were told that on the previous day a native had shot at and wounded a large cattle-killing tiger, whose tracks we had been following in the semi-darkness not many hours before. It was a great piece of luck that there was no accident. On another occasion I followed a tigress (which was stalking pig) and upon shooting her I found that she had only three legs, one of them having been broken off at the hock joint, where a hard pad had subsequently been formed.

"People have been heard to declare that elephants appear to be dense and devoid of understanding, but such an opinion can be held only by those who have never had anything to do with them.

"I remember on one occasion that a *mahout* unconsciously dropped his knife while riding his elephant, and when the animal suddenly stopped and refused to proceed, the man was unable to discover the reason until his loss was pointed out. A really well-trained animal would have picked up the knife and handed it up to the owner.

"On another occasion my servants were engaged in driving wild elephants towards a stockade, but on nearing the entrance they broke and fled in all directions. Our only course then was to return to our camping-place of the previous night and endeavour to collect the herd on the morrow. This proved to be a difficult matter, as the journey was a long one, and it became so dark that I could not see the driver sitting on the neck of my own elephant. One of the men shortly afterwards called out that his mount refused to proceed farther, and he suggested that we had probably arrived at the camp. I therefore struck a light and found that the unerring instinct of the so-called dense elephant had guided us to our destination!

"I have witnessed some striking incidents in noosing wild elephants. I remember seeing some *phandis* (noosing men) separate a very large female and her two daughters (one nearly full-grown and the other quite a youngster) from the herd. The mother charged the men as they approached her and actually put up a good fight with the tame elephants, but the young ones returned to the herd, the elder of the two commencing to charge while the mother and baby made themselves scarce. They relieved one another in this manner for a considerable time, in fact, until one of the daughters was captured.

"Elephants have remarkably keen scent, and I have frequently seen tame ones pointing, with their trunks high in the air, in the direction of a wild herd. They raise or lower the trunk according to the probable distance of the troop, and thus render most important assistance to the hunter.

"If a wild herd suspects danger ahead while being driven, no power on earth—not even the firing of a cannon—can make them proceed. They will wheel round and break off in a lateral direction, or return towards their pursuers, and Heaven protect the latter if they are in the course of flight.

"One day when suffering from fever I was returning along the bank of a river in the direction of my home and saw a fine male sambur standing in the stream. I felt too unwell to trouble about it, but as my *shikaris* required food for the larder I stopped for the purpose of securing him. I fired two shots without any apparent effect, but the third attempt caused him to make for the jungle. I followed a blood trail, and eventually found and killed the animal, when to my surprise I discovered that my first two shots had actually found their mark, although the sambur had remained perfectly still.

"Very fine sport can be had in shooting gaur. A friend of mine (J. W.) wounded one, but we did not succeed in bagging it until four days later, and this was only accomplished by waiting for it to return in its previous tracks.

"We sent men on elephants to follow it while we searched for convenient hiding-places for ourselves. Before I had secured a place, the beast came bounding along the track, and as he swung round a bend in the path I had barely time to step aside and get a rapid shot at him. On another occasion I crawled through an exceedingly dense patch of cane jungle, but when I was near the gaur I could only see a black shape and a switching tail. I fired, however, and he immediately turned and charged in my direction, when I managed to drop him. An examination of the place where I had come upon him showed that he had been standing in a *cul-de-sac*, caused by a fallen tree, and was therefore unable to go forward. He was nearly 6 feet 8 inches in height at the shoulder.

"I once shot what I thought was a full-grown bear resting in a tree, but I soon found that it was a large cub, and that its mother, though unseen at first, was near to it. The latter dropped from the tree and began to stalk me in the dense jungle. It moved about in a circle, gradually reducing the radius until she stood on her hind legs, towering above me, when I placed the muzzle of my gun upon her chest and fired. I have frequently noticed that bears drop or fall from great heights without any apparent ill effects.

"One of the most thrilling hunting experiences I ever had was when two friends (C. and H.) were shooting buffaloes in the jungle in Upper Assam. Mounted on elephants we left camp in the early morning, and, after proceeding for about two miles along the bed of the Kolopani River, came upon the tracks of a very large bull which had been previously seen by me and which possessed a pair of very fine horns. The ground was hard owing to the absence of rain, and this rendered it an exceedingly difficult matter to trace the spoor, but towards evening we discovered marks which had been recently made by the buffalo. It was then too late in the day, however, to pursue him further, therefore on the following morning we set off in confident hope of securing a fine trophy. Soon after we started I scented our quarry, and I at once signalled to that effect to my friends.

"It is an easy matter for an experienced hunter to tell when buffaloes are near, as they emit a very strong odour when they have been resting for a whole night. We moved along very cautiously, but suddenly there was a crash in the jungle and I caught a glimpse of the bull as he charged away from us without affording the slightest opportunity for a shot. My *mahout* then guided the elephant through

ELEPHANT CATCHING AND TRAINING.

Photos by W. M. Nuttall.

ELEPHANT CATCHING AND TRAINING.

Photos by W. M. Nutall.

the dense foliage and pointed out a huge female buffalo, which had evidently joined the male, and was lying down calmly chewing her cud. I saw her distinctly enough, but as I personally only wanted the bull, I tried to show C. where she was hiding. He advanced in the right direction, but the cow must have heard or scented him, as she rose quickly and charged in the direction of the elephant ridden by H. As the undergrowth was nearly as high as the elephants we were quite unable to see where the buffaloes had gone. I called a halt and explained to my friends that our only chance of securing them was to proceed on foot. They agreed to my proposal, and I led the way, my tracker behind me, then came my two friends, with the elephants in the rear. After we had been following the spoor for about an hour I heard the two animals in the jungle ahead, and at once sent my tracker to the remainder of the party, who had lagged behind, to caution them against a surprise rush. I then tried to get round the buffaloes with the view of making them break back towards C. and H., when there was a sudden crash of jungle and a charge of the two beasts in my direction. The bull tore off at an angle where I was standing, while the other turned back on her own tracks and nearly knocked over H., who had barely time to fire and then jump aside as she pursued her headlong flight. We subsequently found a trail of blood at the spot where the cow had been hit by H. I was very anxious to secure the bull on account of his exceedingly fine head, but as I did not wish to leave a wounded animal to succumb to its injuries, I determined to follow up the latter at the risk of losing her mate. My tracker and I therefore took the lead, and soon left my companions behind as the evening was fast approaching. The trail led us into the most impossible places, such as muddy pools where the cow had rolled in order to keep flies from her wound. This mud, thick upon the undergrowth, soon covered me from head to foot, and I became unrecognizable. On reaching a pool of water, however, we noticed that it was disturbed as if an animal had recently passed through it, and as we were thereby convinced that our quarry must be near, we crawled through exceedingly dense jungle, over fallen trees, and through pools of mud, but always on the alert, looking carefully into the thick foliage lest the wounded and infuriated beast should take us by surprise. As I was climbing over a fallen tree my tracker pulled me back saying that he could see the cow about twenty paces ahead of us, and as she moved I managed to let her have a bullet. Suddenly she broke through the jungle, leaving a track which showed that she was bleeding profusely. My friends—who had now joined me—were convulsed with laughter at my torn clothing and muddy appearance. It seemed to be madness to follow the cow in a waning light through such jungle, but I determined to have her if possible, and arranged with my tracker that he should lead the way and should immediately step out of the line of fire if he discerned any-

A TIGRESS WITH THREE TOES.

thing. The jungle now consisted of masses of thorns and brambles, which were continually tearing our hands and faces, but as we were ascending a slight incline, my servant called out, in Assamese, 'It's coming! it's coming!' and then ran behind me. There was a terrific crashing noise, and although I was unable to see any animal I suddenly found myself flying through space, eventually falling flat on my back, half stunned, but fortunately grasping my rifle. Never shall I forget the moment when I was conscious of my position, as the brute was standing over me! I had fallen upon the slope of the incline, and that piece of luck undoubtedly saved my life, as the buffalo began to horn me most savagely, cutting and bruising the side of my face. Another servant who carried my spare rifle would have shot, but he was afraid of hitting me. Oh, the horrors of those passing seconds! Thousands of thoughts passed through my mind: I pictured myself sitting comfortably in my bungalow; I wondered where my friends were, and why they did not come to my assistance! At last she ceased horning me and began to administer similar treatment to my tracker, who had also been knocked over. The cow then managed to get one of her horns between his back and his cartridge case, which was quickly torn off, and at the same time she inflicted a slight cut into his flesh. The buffalo then turned her attention to me again, horning me with renewed vigour, but on her hearing the approach of my friends upon their elephants she raised her head and snorted, thus giving me time for thought as to my course of action. I accordingly picked up my rifle, a ·577 bore, but in doing this I must have touched her, as she treated me to a kick with one of her hind feet, knocking the weapon out of my hands. I again secured the rifle, but owing to the undergrowth I did not see any chance of making use of it. Eventually I placed the butt end on the ground between my legs and took the best aim possible in that most dangerous position, as I felt certain that if I killed her she would probably fall upon and crush me, and that, if only wounded, she would become much more infuriated. Hopeless as either way seemed to be, I fired, and the brute in bounding forward damaged the muscles of my thigh. The cow was now standing slightly behind me, bellowing furiously, and as I was unable to move on account of the numbness in my leg, I pointed the rifle behind my head and discharged the second barrel, the bullet smashing the pelvis and causing her to collapse. The native servant with my spare gun saw me crawl away and at once fired at the buffalo, but probably from excitement he nearly shot me! As it was practically dark by this time we had to grope our way homewards, thinking possibly that we might be lost, but we suddenly found the bed of a river which was known to us, and after following this for a short distance, we saw our camp fires, which sent to us one of the most inviting welcomes that has ever fallen to our lot.

"I have had several exciting encounters with large game since that day, but keen as I am on sport, I have no desire to repeat the experience of lying almost helpless under a maddened Indian buffalo.

"Bad luck seems in some mysterious way to breed bad luck, as shortly after my encounter with the buffalo referred to I had two narrow escapes with my life. Information reached me one Saturday that two wild buffaloes had been visiting certain villages and were causing a great deal of trouble by annoying tame·herds belonging to natives, and by threatening and chasing their cowherds, who had attempted to drive away the intruders. On the following morning—a peaceful Sunday which seemed to promise anything but exciting adventures—I took three elephants, one being a very staunch animal which I rode myself, and soon picked up tracks leading across a river, through possibly owing to its extreme density, one of the pair could not force its way through and came full speed for me, and as I had only one barrel left I steadied the elephant and fired at the head of the brute when he was not more than 20 feet from me. He turned a complete somersault, and after attempting in his convulsions to stand on his head once or twice, he fell dead at the feet of my elephant. We then went in pursuit of the larger of the two few yards, and although a large fallen tree (over which my elephant scrambled) sent the buffalo to a point at a right angle to me, it was impossible to get a shot at him. Imagine my position! I could not release my hold of the rope in my right hand, my rifle was in my left hand, there I was upon a runaway elephant with an infuriated buffalo at its heels, the two spare elephants shrieking with fright, and tearing along in front of me, to say

1. LEOPARD SHOT BY W. M. NUTTALL. 2. SOLITARY BULL MITHAN, 20 HANDS HIGH, SHOT BY W. M. NUTTALL. 3. WILD BUFFALO SHOT IN OPEN COUNTRY THATCHLAND, NORTH BANK OF THE BRAHMAPUTRA.

which we had to swim. It was evident that the wild buffaloes had turned away from the villages in the direction of their natural haunts, but unfortunately the tame animals from the village had wandered with or after them, towards the jungle, which was very dense. After following up the spoor for a considerable time we came to an open glade, where I saw the two beasts enjoying themselves in a wallow. I was about to fire when my *mahout* stopped me by calling out that they were tame animals, but during this palaver the quarry bolted into the jungle, affording me only a 'snap-shot' at one of them. The two bulls were now indistinguishable in the thick undergrowth, but bulls by following the trails of blood which were fairly distinct, but every time we got near to him he plunged still deeper into the recesses of the forest. He apparently grew tired of these tactics, as he suddenly charged back on his tracks, snorting furiously, and this assault was so unexpected that the two spare elephants lost nerve, trumpeted, and bolted, while the one I was riding—although she had remained staunch and true in many tests—whisked round and followed her companions. What a ride we had, to be sure; it was uncertain whether we were to fall or be dragged off the elephant, be killed by the buffalo, or impaled on a branch of a tree. The bull was gaining ground every nothing of the forest jungle with every conceivable kind of thorn and creeper to arrest one's progress, or the uncomfortable nautical roll of an elephant travelling at its fastest speed.

"Once or twice I was nearly dragged off by creepers, or ran the risk of having my eyes torn out by bamboos, but my native servant behind me was not so fortunate, as some tendrils encircled his neck and hurled him to the ground while he still retained my spare rifle in his hand. The buffalo came on in his mad rush, nearly goring the native as he passed, yet in this most dangerous predicament in which I found myself, I could not help admiring the pluck of my pursuer. My *mahout* succeeded—at my urgent request—in stopping the elephant for a few seconds when I managed to get a one-handed shot just as the buffalo crashed into us. The next thing I remembered was that I was trying to raise myself, as when falling I had been struck on the head by the branch of a tree. My elephant had been knocked over and was attempting to get on his legs again, and the bull, a few feet away from me, was endeavouring to stand up. Fortunately my shot had had some effect, so I seized my rifle and fired the remaining bullet into the animal's face. I immediately opened the breech for the purpose of reloading when to my horror I found that the gun had exploded, that the two barrels were wide apart, that one was choked with earth, and the other had become shortened by about 2 inches. After a hurried council with my faithful old servant, the latter rushed towards some rising ground, while I made for the jungle, only to be promptly followed by the bull.

"Placing my useless rifle at the foot of a tree, I managed to raise myself a few feet from the ground, and although this was no place of safety I had the utmost satisfaction in seeing the wounded animal staggering along and passing me in his blind rage. We were now several miles from home, our elephants were lost, and we possessed two broken rifles. Truly our position was not an enviable one, but late at night we were met by a party of natives who had been sent in search of us. It appears that one of the *mahouts*, who was riding the elephant which had been the first to bolt, had been severely cut on the face by a sharp piece of bamboo and had fallen to the ground, but he managed to reach camp, when his blood-stained condition gave some verification of his highly imaginative story that the *Sahib's* elephant had been knocked over, and that every member of the party had been killed. The servants on the other elephant were thrown to the ground before they had travelled far, but they eventually reached home. On the day following the adventure we found the dead buffalo, but several days elapsed before we recaptured the lost elephants.

"After the mishap which had previously befallen me when I was lying beneath a buffalo, a sportsman with many years' experience advised me never to go on foot after large game in that awful jungle, and especially when animals have been wounded and the hunter is following them with light weapons. Buffaloes are, in my opinion, by far the most savage and dangerous of all our local wild animals.

"It will be admitted that the work of that eventful Sunday was an expensive item, but even that has not prevented me from occasionally engaging in a sport in which I take such a keen delight.

"Finally, it may be said that one's fascination for hunting dangerous large game does not arise so much from the mere fact of killing, but of tracking when it is extremely difficult to arrive at a definite conclusion as to the age of the trail marks or as to the probable distance between pursuer and pursued. It is also produced by the existence of other inhabitants of the jungle which have to be avoided, as they frequently give the alarm of danger from one to another.

"This curious method of signalling is sometimes helpful, however, as a hunter may by it be informed of the presence of the game for which he is searching, while on the other hand squirrels with their chattering, and wild fowl uttering their shrill cries, frequently dispose of all chances of a shot.

"The jungle is an open book, full of interest to those who understand it, and happy is the man who can read its secrets."

THE RACE-STANDS, CALCUTTA.

1. FULL-GROWN JUTE.

2. CUTTING JUTE.

JUTE

THE spinning and weaving by hand of fibrous plants in India have been practised from time immemorial, but it is not necessary in this brief review to penetrate into the history of the industrial occupations of the people farther back than the beginning of the nineteenth century, when the native inhabitants of the country were in the habit of weaving jute into cordage, and cloth for bedding, garments, sacking, and other purposes.

Dr. Forbes Royle, in his "Fibrous Plants of India," published in 1885, wrote: "The great trade and principal employment of jute is for the manufacture of gunny chuts or *chuttees*, i.e. lengths suitable for making bags. This industry forms the grand domestic manufacture of all the populous Eastern districts of Lower Bengal. It pervades all classes and penetrates into every household—men, women, and children finding occupation therein. Boatmen, in their spare moments, husbandmen, palankeen-carriers, and domestic servants—everybody, in fact, being Hindus (for Mussulmans spin cotton only) pass their leisure moments, distaff in hand, spinning gunny twist. Its preparation, together with the weaving into lengths, forms the never-failing resource of that most humble, patient, and despised of created beings the Hindu widow, saved by law from the pyre, but condemned by opinion and custom for the remainder of her days, literally, to sackcloth and ashes and the lowest domestic drudgery in the very household where once her will was law. There is, perhaps, no other article so universally diffused over the globe as the Indian gunny bag. All the finer and long-stapled jute is reserved for the export trade, in which it secures a comparatively high price. The short staple serves for the local manufactures, and it may be remarked that a given weight of gunny bag may be purchased at about the same price as a similar weight of raw material, leaving no apparent margin for spinning and weaving."

These hand-woven bags and cloth were exported to Great Britain in increasing quantities, and it was through such consignments that flax and hemp-spinners in Dundee had their attention directed to the valuable nature of Indian fibre. Several of them essayed the manufacture of this imported jute with the spinning machinery in their mills, but it is generally believed that the raw material with which experiments were made must have been of an inferior character, as the results were so unsatisfactory that Dundee merchants felt compelled to guarantee the output of their mills to be "free from Indian jute." It is related, however, that after further trials had been made it was clearly demonstrated that Indian jute was particularly suitable for sacking and wrappers for packing and other purposes, and this important discovery, together with the effects of the Crimean War, was the means of establishing an industry in Dundee which has added enormous wealth to that city and has given employment to thousands of its inhabitants.

Before reviewing the circumstances which led to the construction of jute mills in Lower Bengal, and to the marvellous progress which has been made in this branch of commerce, a few words should be said as to the nature of the jute plant and the method of cultivation, and a reference to the various processes of manufacture.

There are two species of jute in India from which fibre is obtained—namely, *Corchorus capsularis* and *C. colitorius*, and they are annual plants with a growth of from 5 feet to 10 feet in height. The stalks are cylindrical in form; their leaves are of a bright green colour, and flowers small in size and of a yellow shade. The leaves are valuable, as they are extensively used as pot-herbs, and it may be added that their employment in the domestic cuisine was centuries ago, and still is, a common practice not only in India but also with the Greeks and other people on the shores of the Mediterranean Sea. Jute is usually known by the name of *pat* in Eastern Bengal and Assam; in Orissa it is called *nalita*, and in Behar the word is *patna*. *Nalita*, however, is generally applied in all these Provinces to the leaves when used as edible vegetables.

It is believed that the word "jute" is derived from *jhot* or *jhout* (Sanskrit, *jhat*), this being the vernacular name in the district of Cuttack, where the East India Company had roperies about the year 1795.

The Province of Bengal, however, is the real home of the jute plant, as the climate, rainfall, and nature of the greater portion of the soil are extremely favourable for its cultivation. New alluvial soils, such as are seen in Eastern and Northern Bengal and in Northern Behar, are particularly suitable, and the enormous quantity of jute produced in these areas annually verified the truth of the saying that its fibre "occupies a position in the manufacturing scale inferior only to cotton and flax." The greatest danger to the young plant arises from water-logging; hence it is that a loam or sandy loam soil—through which rain can percolate—is infinitely better than clay, which cannot absorb or get rid of an abnormal quantity of water.

Thorough preparation of the land by four or five ploughings and weeding is absolutely essential to the successful cultivation of jute; large clods of earth must be broken by harrows or *kodalis*; and the surface must be thoroughly pulverized until a very fine tilth is obtained. From 8 lb. to 10 lb. of seed to the acre are sown broadcast during the season, which extends from the middle of February to the end of May; and it is a common practice for the sower to walk over the ground a second time in order to secure an even distribution of seed.

Jute grown on the same land year after year in succession is an exhausting crop, and the cultivator who looks for satisfactory results, unless he has applied a liberal dressing of manure, is doomed to disappointment. From experiments which have been made in recent years, it has been shown that cowdung is the best fertilizer, used alternately with castor-oil cake.

Jute is cut with a sickle shortly after the commencement of the flowering period, and the plants are then tied in bundles and kept under water for the steeping or "retting" process until the fibre can easily be separated from the woody portion of the stem. The time taken up by this treatment extends from five or ten days to even a month, the result depending upon the maturity of the plant and climatic and other conditions.

Professor Finlow (Jute Specialist in Bengal and Assam), writing of this process of separating the fibre, says: "This is brought about by fermentation, during which time the tissue in which the fibres are embedded is softened or dissolved. It is apparently the result of the work of a particular bacterial organism, and sterilized stems of jute inoculated with what are believed to be pure cultures of this organism ret rapidly."

The work of stripping the fibre from the stem should be completed within two or three days after retting has been completed, and the separated portion is then washed in clean water and subsequently placed on a bamboo frame to be dried, after which it is tied in bundles for transfer to the jute-pressing machine. The contents of these bundles are sorted into lots, according to the various qualities of fibre; and after these separate parcels have undergone immense hydraulic pressure, they reappear in the well-known form of bales of 400 lb. in weight.

A fair average return from a jute crop is about 15 maunds, and although 30 maunds have sometimes been obtained from plants grown on well-manured land, a yield of 20 to 24 maunds is by no means uncommon.

The various articles manufactured from jute in India and Europe include hessian cloth, gunny bags, paulins, corn sacks, wool sheets, nitrate and sugar bags, shirtings, curtains, carpets, rugs, sacking, string, rope, sails, paper, cord, and *kampa* (a net-like bag for carrying bundles on bullocks). Inferior fibre, known as "rejections" and "cuttings," can now be worked up in the mills, or it may be used in connection with the manufacture of paper, or in steam ropeworks in the preparation of cordage.

In the earlier portion of these notes it has been shown that Dundee spinners, manifesting their hereditary traits of caution and shrewdness, were in no hurry to accept Indian raw jute as a possible profitable factor in commerce; and, although they eventually realized very large pecuniary results from the products of the previously despised fibre, it was left to an Englishman to seize an opportunity which, in its far-reaching effects, has literally been the making of the city of Calcutta.

The Englishman just referred to, a Mr. George Acland, who in early life was in the employ of the East India Marine Service, arrived in Calcutta in the year 1853, and his keen business instincts led him to the conclusion that a very great saving would be effected if Indian jute could be manufactured in India, as such a course would obviate the heavy freightage to Europe; and, what was an even stronger argument in favour of his idea, the cost of labour would be immeasurably lower than the wages paid to mill hands in either Scotland or England. Here, then, was the opportunity and here was the man to grasp it. Acland proceeded to the Old Country in 1855 and became acquainted with Mr. John Kerr, a prominent figure in the machinery world in Dundee, who warmly advocated the shipment of a quantity of plant for a mill to be erected in some place near Calcutta which would be within a reasonable distance from the jute-growing centres of Bengal.

A plot of land was acquired on the western bank of the River Hooghly at Ischera (Rishra), near Serampore, which, by the way, was a portion of the property formerly belonging to Warren Hastings, and about 14 miles distant from Calcutta; and a factory was built under the superintendence of Mr. Acland, which was the forerunner of some 40 or 50 mills that have added enormous wealth to the city of Calcutta.

Jute yarns were therefore first spun by machinery in Bengal in 1855, and the original modest output, which was only 8 tons per day, has grown to about 1,000,000 tons, this being the total production of the mills for the year 1915.

There are always difficulties to contend with at the commencement of a business, in the flotation of a company, or in the foundation of an industry; but all originators of commercial concerns are not called upon to face a mutiny such as that which broke out in 1857 at Barrackpore (within two or three miles distance from the Ischera mill), and it is not surprising to learn from history that Mr. Acland applied to the military authorities for the grant of an armed guard for the protection of his property. Shortly after this time the mill buildings were considerably extended, and a limited liability company was formed under the name of the Ischera Twine and Yarn Mills Company, Ltd.. but this concern is now known as the Wellington Jute Mills.

The Borneo Jute Company was the first

to be registered in England, and the first to introduce power loom for jute cloth—this was in 1859—and the success which attended this venture was so great that the mill was, within half a dozen years from its erection, enlarged to fully twice its original size. In 1872 the concern became the Barnagore Jute Manufacturing Company, Ltd., and it then had more than 500 looms and a capital fund amounting to considerably more than the value of the property.

During the years 1861-2 the Gouripore and Serajgunge Companies were formed, and these were followed by the India Jute Mills erected at Serampore in 1866.

Up to this period there was practically no export trade, with the exception of gunny bags consigned to Burma; but, notwithstanding this fact, the five companies already mentioned found that their mills were veritable gold mines, owing to the remarkably extensive and profitable businesses in which they were engaged. A boom in jute products commenced about the year 1868; factories were enlarged, machinery was imported, and the 950 looms of a couple or more years previously were increased to 1,250 in number. One who was well-known in the manufacturing world at this time asserted that "it was only necessary to issue a prospectus of a jute mill to have all the shares snapped up in a forenoon."

So buoyant was the jute market at this period that during the years 1872-3 the Fort Gloster, Budge-Budge, and Seebpore mills were erected, two companies registered in England commenced operations in the following year, and from 1874 to 1876 no fewer than eight other factories had been built. With thirteen new companies thrust upon the market within the space of about five years, it is not surprising that the increased output had a most serious effect on the financial status of several of the concerns. In fact, the history of the jute trade during the succeeding decade may be summed up in the words "a struggle for existence"; but it is satisfactory to note that nearly all of the mills were able to keep open doors until outlets for manufactured goods were secured in other countries than Great Britain.

The events which led to this most serious depression were not calculated to encourage the opening of other factories, and thus it is found that only six were started between the years 1876 and 1894—namely, the Kamarhatty, Hooghly, Titaghur, Victoria, Kanknarrah mills, together with the Calcutta Twist mill.

The tide of events took a favourable turn about the year 1884, principally in hessian cloth destined for the United States of America, although outlets which have grown to very large dimensions were found in South America for nitrate bags and in Canada and Australia for wheat sacks.

At this juncture, however, with hessians showing a most appreciable advance in output, and in price too, and notwithstanding the opening up of other foreign markets, it cannot be said that the mills were giving satisfactory results to the shareholders. The demand for manufactured articles was not keeping pace with the supply from the mills, and several meetings of directors and managers were held with the object of reversing this state of affairs. Steps had been taken to limit production temporarily, but the absence of unanimity among the millowners prevented the achievement of the end in view. The question of a bona-fide combination then forced itself upon the attention of those interested, and an association of millowners was formed at a meeting held on November 10, 1884, at which it was arranged that managers should meet weekly to fix the prices of their manufactured goods. The output from the mills, however, continued to be larger than the quantity required to meet current orders, and the managers of all the mills excepting two agreed to work the machinery for a reduced number of hours, and this arrangement met with varying success until the early part of the year 1891.

In the year 1892 the price of raw jute increased to such an unusually high figure that several mills were closed temporarily, and others were compelled to curtail their already shortened working hours, but a general improvement of a most promising character was manifested in 1894.

Between the years 1885 and 1895 the companies in existence increased the number of their looms from 6,700 to nearly 10,000, but it is noted that the advance made during the following five years was still more marked, as no fewer than 20 mills were added to the list. In order to illustrate the growth of the jute industry the following figures may be given: In 1895 the mills on the Hooghly, numbering about 40, contained 9,700 looms and 203,522 spindles, and at the commencement of the year 1910 the numbers were 30,685 looms (comprising 12,950 for sacking and 17,735 for hessians) and 677,070 spindles. The employees too, in 1895, were 57,000 Indians and 180 Europeans, and in 1910 they had reached a total of nearly 200,000 Indians and some 450 Europeans.

Other statistics show that in 1901 North America (including Canada) imported 34,000,000 bags and 319,000,000 yards of cloth, and that in 1910 those countries took no less than 63,000,000 bags and 713,000,000 yards of hessians; while the total exports and the Indian consumption of jute fabrics during the same period increased from nearly 263,000,000 bags and 416,000,000 yards of cloth in 1901 to 465,000,000 bags and 1,006,000,000 yards of cloth in 1910. Japan, China, Africa, and other countries are increasing their imports at a fairly rapid rate, while the figures for Australia at the commencement and close respectively of the above-mentioned decade were 9,000,000 and 22,000,000 yards of cloth and 38,000,000 and 73,000,000 bags.

Reference has already been made to the unprecedented rise in the price of raw jute which had such a serious effect upon the trade in the early nineties. That depression was not of long duration, but the fluctuation of prices remained a baffling factor in the situation.

In connection with this matter, it may be mentioned that tabulated reports show that the average price of raw jute in bales of 400 lb. at Calcutta was Rs. 37 in the year 1900; it had risen to Rs. 47 in 1905; twelve months later it was Rs. 67; and in 1907 the sum of Rs. 97 was obtained. This abnormal increase naturally tended to retard the industry, as it placed a check on the purchasing market, which in turn caused a reduction in the quantity sent to the mills for manufacturing purposes. Again, one might point to the fact that with a larger number of mills springing into existence from time to time, there must necessarily be a greater demand for raw material, and enhanced prices had to be given in order to keep the mills going at all. Investigations go to prove that practically the only remedy for this state of affairs is the cultivation of jute on a larger area of land than has hitherto been the practice.

Every mill is now equipped with up-to-date machinery, and Calcutta has, by the high-class character of its products, succeeded in ousting Dundee from its former proud position as the jute manufacturing centre of the world.

True, there are other industries in Bengal and neighbouring Provinces, such as indigo, tea, and rice, but capitalists are always forthcoming when the prospectus of a new jute company is issued to the public. Dividends paid are a sure index of the profitable or unprofitable character of any commercial undertaking; and a glance at balance-sheets of jute mills recently published shows that, in the majority of instances, the percentage varies from 5 to 20, or even 25, upon invested capital.

At the commencement of the year 1916 the mills on the Hooghly contained 38,098 looms and 791,194 spindles.

The managing agents, secretaries, or proprietors of the jute mills in Bengal include such well-known firms in Calcutta as Messrs. Bird & Co., Thomas Duff & Co., Jardine, Skinner & Co., Gillanders, Arbuthnot & Co., Begg, Dunlop & Co., George Henderson & Co., Andrew Yule & Co., Macneill & Co., Mackinnon, Mackenzie & Co., McLeod & Co., F. W. Heilgers & Co., Barry & Co., Duncan Bros. & Co., James Finlay & Co. Ltd., Anderson, Wright & Co., Birkmyre Bros., and Kettlewell, Bullen & Co.; and a full description of several individual mills will be found elsewhere in this volume.

1. PEELING OFF THE JUTE FIBRE. 2. DRUMMING JUTE (FILLING THE DRUM)

Photos by Johnston & Hoffman.

CALCUTTA INDUSTRIES

THE most important factor in any consideration of the question of industrial activities in India is the inherent character of the people. Hindus have from time immemorial been looked upon as being skilful in certain arts, quiet in nature, contented with their positions, and devoted to religious rites and ceremonies.

The average Indian of earlier days was not distinguished for display of personal effort, but he has responded in no uncertain manner to the possibilities of trading on a large scale which have been made clear to him by the go-ahead example of European merchants.

In a country such as India, where climatic conditions are not conducive to the expenditure of vigorous strength for any protracted period there is quite naturally a tendency to take things as easily as possible, but a remarkable change has been manifested in recent years, and great progress has been made in the strengthening of old-established industries and the commencement of new ventures.

Again, the Hindu has been hampered by venerable religious and social customs which have kept him in certain prescribed grooves, and have placed a check upon any laudable desire to extend the horizon of his activities, but in this aspect of the question too, there has been an influence at work which has been permeating the whole brotherhood, and its effects are seen to-day in the removal of many barriers and the opening up of avenues of profitable service.

India has been noted for certain industries from time immemorial, and the "Rig-Veda" (1500 B.C.) refers particularly to certain arts which had been practised in very early days, special mention being made of weaving, and the manufacture of silk and other articles. History tells us of traders who in far-gone days visited India and took away with them muslin, cloth, gold and silver vessels and ornaments, and many beautiful temples and mosques speak silently but truly of the wonderfully skilful work of Indian masons and carvers.

Many of these industries have, however, been discontinued from various causes, and it is a matter of history that the East India Company in the eighteenth century favoured its shareholders rather than the Indian people, and that its policy tended in some directions to suppress local manufactures. It must also be remembered that the majority of the vast population of India is supported by agriculture in some shape or form, and that in practically every village there are artisans who make their own community self-supporting and entirely independent of outside influences. Ninety per cent. of the people of India lead isolated lives in villages almost entirely unaware of what is happening in the outer world, and this fact alone has forced the country to be a home of small industries.

The first sign of industrial evolution in India occurred shortly after the establishment of British rule, when more stable conditions of life, improved means of transport, and the growth of mutual confidence between the two races, made enterprise possible. The spread of education also had its influence on industrial conditions; and so it came about that the quiet and comparatively uneventful life of economic India was aroused, and a magnetic wave of pulsating Western industrialism spread over the whole country.

Industrial enterprises began to develop at a great pace, and the introduction of cotton spinning and weaving machinery, invented in England by Arkwright, Hargreaves, Crompton, and others, tended to put an end to many small industries which had for centuries been indigenous in India, but it caused employment to be found for hundreds of thousands of its population.

Then followed the building of jute, cotton, and flour mills, the opening of tea and other estates, and the development of coal fields, and all these industries have been manned by Indian workers, showing that under European leadership there is in this vast country an almost limitless supply of effective labour.

In due course of time the twentieth century has been marked by a steady and continuous growth of trade relations, not only between India and other countries, but also within her own borders, and Europeans and Indians alike are to-day reaping a rich harvest from the industrial agencies which were established only a few years ago.

The more recently established industrial concerns in Bengal, Behar and Orissa, and Assam, financed and managed almost wholly by Europeans, include bone-crushing mills, chemical works, cotton mills (12 in Bengal), flour mills (18 in Bengal), iron works (45 in Bengal and 3 in Behar and Orissa), jute mills (47 in Bengal), jute presses (45 in Bengal), potteries and brickyards, saw-mills (13 in Assam), shipbuilders' yards (12 in Bengal), coal companies or collieries (127 in Bengal and 224 in Behar and Orissa), and tea companies or estates (238 in Assam and a large number in various districts in Bengal).

The notes contained in the following pages will serve as an illustration of the growth of industrial activities of a few Hindu commercial houses.

ALECK APCAR, C.E.

For considerably more than a century the name of Apcar has been prominently connected with the commercial and industrial activities in the East, and the member of the family to whom these notes refer is the eldest grandson of Aratoon Apcar, the founder of the well-known firm of Apcar & Co.

ALECK APCAR, C.E.

Mr. Aleck Apcar, son of the late Apcar Aratoon Apcar, was born in India in 1848, and when he was still young in years he was sent to England to be educated at the fine old school of Harrow. He was a painstaking and successful scholar, yet at the same time he had a keen love of sport, in which field he was the winner of many handsome trophies.

It was Mr. Apcar's intention to join the Royal Engineers, but he was induced to return to India with a view of entering his father's office (Messrs. Apcar & Co.) in Calcutta, and although he held a position therein for a few years, he eventually left of his own accord, as the prospects did not seem to be sufficiently encouraging. He then obtained several small steamers and tugboats, and with these he became the pioneer in opening up trade relationships between Calcutta, Balasore, Ghatal, and Midnapore; but, unfortunately, this venture was not a success, and he was compelled to dispose of his vessels.

The difficulties experienced by Mr. Apcar in this early stage of his career did not daunt him, and he turned his attention to the jute trade, in which he gave assistance to his son, who had agencies in the Dacca and Mymensingh districts. Once again the fates were against him, but his innate energy caused him to make a bold stroke by starting business as a coal merchant, builder, and contractor, and his qualifications as a civil engineer, architect, and surveyor were a great aid to him in this matter.

The business has grown rapidly, and Mr. Apcar now has his own brickfields and *soorkey* mills in conection with his building and other workshops at 47 Baniapukur Road, Calcutta, and he is, further, the owner of several valuable properties in the city.

A man who had faced and overcome difficulties was not likely to be allowed to pursue the even tenor of his way without being invited to take a share in the local administrative work of Calcutta; but although he has on several occasions been asked to serve as a municipal councillor, or to take a seat on the board of managers of other important institutions, he has been compelled to decline all such honours, as he was unwilling to accept responsible positions unless he could afford the time to discharge his duties conscientiously.

Mr. Apcar's offices are at 27/7 Waterloo Street, and his telegraphic address is "Solace, Calcutta."

THE ARTISTIC GLASS WORKS

Art in India is as old as the country itself, and historical records attest the eminence attained in sculpture and painting, and afford evidence of the exceedingly fine workmanship in gold, silver, glass, and metals of various kinds which was displayed in bygone ages. But in recent years there has been a marked change in ideas, which may in some measure be due to the influence of Western example, though it is more probable that it is the natural result of the establishment of Schools of Arts throughout India. An illustration of the advance made by workers in glass is obtained by a visit to the Artistic Glass Works at 1-2 Tagore Castle Road, Calcutta.

The proprietor, Mr. S. N. Banerjee, was trained in the carriage and wagon workshops of the East Indian Railway Company at Lillooah, and in the year 1913 he established what he called a "cottage industry" for manufacturing silvered mirrors, and bevelled, frosted, stained, and decorated glass-ware of all descriptions. Only two years had elapsed, however, when orders for goods for military purposes, such as first-class reflectors, and heliograph and other glasses were pouring in upon Mr. Banerjee, and the diminutive concern of 1913 became one of the leading establishments of its kind in India. Since that date very little manufacturing of a private character has been performed as the works have been almost entirely engaged in meeting military requirements.

Mr. Banerjee has formulated many plans for the further expansion of his business, but he is utterly unable to carry them out until the conclusion of the European War.

J. C. BANERJEE

Mr. J. C. Banerjee, whom the Hon. Mr. Lyon (member of the Council of the Government of Bengal) in his speech in connection with the opening ceremony of the University Institute by His Excellency the Lord Carmichael, Governor of Bengal, complimented as "that prince of contractors," was born in September 1883. His early education was at the Metropolitan Institution, Balakhana Branch, founded by the late Pundit Isswar Chandra Vidyasagar, and subsequently he studied at the General Assembly's Institution in Calcutta (now the Scottish Churches College), whence he joined the Sibpur Engineering College. Leaving there in 1905, he, unlike most of his fellow students, never entertained the idea of entering official life, but started on his own account as an engineering contractor. His first undertakings, though not of considerable magnitude, involved a lot of technical knowledge and nicety of judgment, and the execution of works entrusted to him and carried out with almost clock-like precision naturally marked him as the coming man in his profession. It may be mentioned in passing that he owes his present success, not in a small degree, to the excellent discipline he underwent at home in his boyhood under his revered mother, whose loss in 1895 he mourns even now. Punctuality and honesty in all affairs have been his watchwords, traits which he has inherited from his father, Babu Narendra Nath Banerjee, late head assistant in the financial department in the Government of Bengal, and now a retired pensioner.

It is a pleasure to note here that all the sons of Mr. Banerjee, senior, are useful members of society in the truest sense of the term—the eldest, Dr. Satish Chandra, being the leading medical practitioner in Muzaffarpur, in Behar; the second son, Mr. Sarat Chandra Banerjee, a vakil of the High Court, with a well-known and extensive practice at Darjeeling; the third being Mr. J. C. Banerjee, the subject of these notes; and the fourth, Dr. C. C. Banerjee, an eminent physician and surgeon of Calcutta.

Mr. J. C. Banerjee's first large achievement was the completion of the Baker Laboratory (new physics laboratory attached to the Presidency College, Calcutta), at an estimated cost of Rs. 6,75,000. This was commenced in 1910 and finished in less than a year's time. Since 1912 Mr. Banerjee has been literally overwhelmed with work, such as the construction of the University College of Science, the University Institute, the Government salt golahs at Sulkea, and last, though not least, the new Royal Exchange building, and several hostels for the leading colleges of Calcutta. It is extremely gratifying to note in particular that Mr. Banerjee, within a comparatively short time, and in spite of his multifarious business engagements, has been able to start a new industry in the manufacture of bolts, nuts, rivets, and dogspikes, under the name of "The Standard Rivet, Bolt and Nut Works," which has supplied a long-felt want in this country. His extensive workshops at Ramkristopore, with the most up-to-date installation for manufacturing the above articles, are really worth a visit to any one interested in Indian industries and engineering works, and a brief account of them will be found in a separate notice.

THE ARTISTIC GLASS WORKS.
GLASSES READY FOR DISPATCH TO THE MILITARY DEPARTMENT.

THE STANDARD RIVET, BOLT, AND NUT WORKS

It was not until after the memorable battle of Plassey was fought, in June 1757, in which Lord Clive defeated Suraj-ud-daulah, Nawab of Bengal, and virtually gave Great Britain her Empire in India, that traders who had made their way to the shores of Bengal established business houses on permanent foundations at Kalikata, and thus consolidated the trade of Calcutta, which to-day occupies the proud position of "the second city in the Empire," and is recognized as one of the leading commercial ports in the East.

India is a rich agricultural and mineral country, it has untold potential wealth, many of its raw materials and much of its produce are calling for factories and mills, and the question of a sufficient supply of suitable labour should not be an insuperable difficulty.

J. C. BANERJEE.

1. The New Royal Exchange, 2. The Baker Laboratory, Presidency College. 3. The University Institute. 4. The University College of Science.

CALCUTTA INDUSTRIES

True, jute mills have been at work on the banks of the Hooghly for nearly seventy years and have proved to be a veritable gold mine for Calcutta; indigo, tea, and other products of the field are being exported in increasing quantities; and progress is noted in several other branches of industrial occupations, but development has been remarkably slow for a considerable number of years, and even now, in 1916, there are many important industries which are still in their infancy, while others have not yet been commenced. This fact leads one to refer to the Standard Rivet, Bolt and Nut Works, at Ramkristopore, near Calcutta, which have not been in existence for more than about half a dozen years, and are now the property of Mr. J. C. Banerjee, engineer, builder, and contractor, of 21 Canning Street, Calcutta.

Railway companies, shipbuilders, contractors, and others in daily need of bolts, nuts, and similar appliances, have until recently been compelled to rely upon importations from Great Britain, and although some firms in Calcutta are now manufacturing these necessaries solely for their own use, it has been left to Mr. Banerjee to become the sole proprietor of the only manufacturing works of this kind in Bengal whence supplies for general constructional purposes can be obtained. The works are situated on the western bank of the River Hooghly (immediately opposite Calcutta), and the Port Commissioners' railway, which is connected with the East Indian and Bengal-Nagpur systems respectively at Howrah and Shalimar, is within a distance of 12 ft. or 15 ft. from the main entrance to the shops.

The latter are extensive, but as they are not large enough for the greatly increasing demands made upon them, Mr. Banerjee has secured a more spacious area of land on the foreshore of the river, and adjacent to the present works, upon which new buildings will be erected and new machinery installed, and into which it is proposed to run a siding from the Commissioners' railway.

Iron bars and rods, round and square, are obtained from the Tata Iron and Steel Company, Ltd., of Sakchi, which is two and a half miles distant from Kalimati station, on the Bengal-Nagpur railway.

These are first intensely heated in furnaces, and then they are passed along a line of up-to-date machines in which the various processes of manufacture are carried out: they are cut to required lengths, the embryo rivets, spikes, and bolts are then forged and compressed to the necessary thickness, various dies being used for different diameters, and then follows the neatest possible work in pointing and placing heads upon them. The "worm" in bolts, screws, and nuts, which are suitable for household use on the one hand, or for joining plates on a huge ocean-going steamer on the other, for securing fishplates on railway sleepers, for the construction of bridges, or fixing joists on buildings, and for general structural work, is made by steel "chasers" of all sizes, which perform their work with the utmost precision.

The whole of the motive power is obtained from a 24-h.p. steam engine (by Garrett & Co.), and the manufacturing plant includes two "heading" machines by Samuel Platts, two others of similar character named respectively the "Acme" and "Horsfall," four screw machines, two others for pointing the ends of bolts and spikes, and three for shaping, shearing, and grinding, while the remainder comprises a number of lathes and the customary adjuncts usually met with in a well-equipped foundry.

A dynamo has been installed by Mr. Banerjee for the supply of electricity for the lighting of all the buildings. Works so unique in character as the "Standard" have naturally so great a demand made upon them that the sixty hands now employed experience considerable difficulty, although they are frequently retained for overtime service, in executing the large number of orders for specialities in foundry products for which the name of Banerjee has now become so famous.

Orders from Government Departments throughout India, from railway companies, owners and builders of ships, the establishments of the Port Commissioners of Calcutta, contractors, and others, are continually pouring in, and, were it not for the projected extension of the works, the proprietor might have doubts as to his ability to execute them within a reasonable time.

A large stock of iron bars, rods, joists for buildings, and pillars, together with manufactured products such as bolts, nuts, and spikes, is always kept on hand, and it would have to be an unusually large and comprehensive contract which Mr. Banerjee would be unable to undertake.

The proprietor's telegraphic address is "Boltnut," Calcutta.

UNIVERSITY COLLEGE OF SCIENCE, CALCUTTA

In the construction of this college Mr. J. C. Banerjee has set permanently before the public view an example of what might be termed the "free classic" style of building, and this is all the more interesting as it has been designed by a Bengalee architect.

The building consists of three stories, arranged with a main block, parallel to the road, with a long projecting wing at each end. The plan is a simple one, consisting as it does of a south verandah to each back wing, from which access is obtained to the various rooms, and it therefore follows that each of the latter has a north light, which is particularly suitable for all work of a scientific character. These verandahs lead to the front block, with its corridor and main staircase and lift, and also to the lavatory block joined on to the main building in the centre.

This huge building, in common with the majority of the structures in Calcutta, is finished in plaster, concealing brickwork; the floors are supported on transverse steel beams, and the partitions have been constructed of light 5-inch reinforced brickwork, resting in most cases on the steel beams. The accommodation consists of numerous laboratories, lecture-rooms, a library, museum, and workshops for all scientific occupations, the larger rooms being on the top floor. There are three floors, connected by one central main staircase and lift, with subsidiary staircases towards the extremities of each wing, and these have been constructed in concrete steel, in the use of which material this contractor has had so much experience.

Mr. Banerjee has, as usual, faithfully given expression to the wishes of the architect in all matters connected with this building.

The new University College of Science building in Circular Road, Calcutta, is a lasting monument to the princely liberality of the late Sir Taraknath Palit and of Sir Rashvihari Ghosh. Sir Taraknath made a gift of the entire magnificent site, about 11 *bighas* in extent, and facing a public square, to the University authorities, with the object of founding and conducting a college in order to encourage higher research work in the various branches of science—a feature of education which was sadly wanted in that part of India.

The building, which is in the "free classic" style of architecture, was designed by Mr. A. C. Mukerjee, B.A.C.E., the consulting engineer and architect to the Calcutta University, is a three-storied one, the main façade of which measures 200 feet in length, while the dimensions of each of the two side wings are 288 feet in length, and between them is a lawn measuring 160 feet by 109 feet.

The height of the plinth is 4 feet, and that of the upper stories 17 feet 6 inches, 18 feet 6 inches, and 19 feet 6 inches respectively. Each of the three blocks has a splendid staircase of its own, with Chunar stone-paved steps on encased joist stringers with moulded plaster panels to the flights and landing.

The ground floor accommodates the laboratory for higher research work; on the first floor are the lecture theatres and demonstration rooms; and the second floor contains the library and museum; the total floor area being over 60,000 square feet.

A corridor, 12 feet in width, runs along the front block with large arch openings, while a continuous verandah, 8 feet in width, runs along the rear and the two side wings.

A notable feature of the buildings is the provision of exceptionally large door and window openings, and fume pipes embedded in the walls, for effective ventilation. Made-up earth was met with in several sections of the foundations, and 9-inch tarred *Sal bulla* piles were driven in these to an average depth of 22 feet below the level of the bottom of the trench. The width of the foundation trenches for the several walls varied from 7 feet to 13 feet, and the depth of the excavation was 6 feet below the general ground level.

Mr. J. C. Banerjee is to be congratulated on his successful completion of the University College of Science within about a year, and the building bears eloquent testimony to Mr. Banerjee's resources and ability, especially in view of the war having broken out before the works were well in hand.

THE NEW ROYAL EXCHANGE, CALCUTTA

This structure, upon which Mr. Banerjee is engaged at the time of writing, is in the "Corinthian classic" style, and has been designed by the architects, a well-known Bombay firm, with a view of preserving in a semi-public building of this nature all those attributes which exist in the Royal Exchanges of other cities of the world, particularly in London and Paris. Bearing this in mind, it will be seen that Mr. Banerjee has before him a task of the first importance, necessitating the utmost application on his part, for he must not only reproduce the architects' requirements to an exactitude, but he must interpret them in such a way that there is no room for a feeling of incompleteness in the mind of the observer as he gazes on the huge structure of brick and plaster. And this faithful attention to details is all the more necessary in this instance as the exigencies of building work in Calcutta make it impossible for the Exchange to be erected in stone.

The structure measures roughly 165 feet by 122 feet, and it is nearly 70 feet in height to the top of the four floors. The chief external features are the magnificent loggias, the one on the

J. C. BANERJEE.

1. The Standard Rivet, Bolt, and Nut Works (Exterior). 2. Interior, Standard Rivet, Bolt, and Nut Works.

principal front being 107 feet in length and 15 feet in width, with ten columns which are being skilfully constructed in reinforced concrete, and measure 3 feet 4 inches in diameter, and nearly 38 feet in height. There are two loggias in the other important elevation, and each of these has two columns of similar dimensions.

These columns, and the huge architrave; 3 feet square, which will be constructed across their tops, are in reinforced concrete. This material is comparatively new to India, and it certainly is quite a new departure in building methods in Calcutta, but Mr. Banerjee has been most successful in this direction in other parts of the building, especially in the flooring, all of which has been laid in this substance, 4 inches in thickness. The method of construction is a combination of brick walls and steel stanchions and beams, necessitated by the large open spans which are required.

The Exchange Hall, which will be finished in plaster in a nearly "pure classic" style, will be a magnificent room rising to a height of 30 feet, with a floor space measuring 80 feet by 60 feet. Here will be seen the advantage of the mixed method of construction, where steel stanchions stand some 6 feet away from each side wall and still leave a clear floor space of 48 feet between them. That space forms the body of the hall, but at the same time the long surfaces of the walls are pleasingly broken up into recesses containing arched and panelled openings. Other additions to the hall are a wide gallery at the west end, and a narrow one on each side between the columns, together with the lintelled openings at the "mezzanine" floor level, whence members will be able to look from corridor or restaurant upon the busy throng on the ground floor.

Numerous large rooms, including a post office, arbitration rooms, and a large public hall, are also provided.

Mr. Banerjee has accepted a most responsible task in producing a building which will be second to none in the world for convenience, excellent construction, and pleasing aspect.

BAKER LABORATORY, PRESIDENCY COLLEGE, CALCUTTA

This laboratory was designed by Mr. H. A. Crouch, F.R.I.B.A., Government architect for Bengal, and with his unerring taste, and Mr. Banerjee's never-failing adaptability, the building was erected, and now stands as a scholastic adjunct to the great University of Calcutta. The design is in the "severe classic" style, so easily conformable to Eastern conditions, and as the main front faces in a southerly direction, the long connecting corridors have been formed as verandahs, with plastered columns and piers and a well-designed iron railing between them.

As the building is intended for scientific purposes, many interesting problems as regards light, sight, hearing, and ventilation called for solution, and these have been carried out successfully by Mr. Banerjee, under the direction of the architect. The main building consists of two floors, but the central portion, enclosed by end pavilions, rises to three stories in a similar manner to portions at the back of the side wings. It is 171 feet in length, and each of the side portions is 107 feet in length, making a total of 383 feet for the whole building, with a depth of 80 feet. The height in the centre is 56 feet, and at the ends 40 feet.

The accommodation provided is adapted for several scientific purposes, and includes many laboratories and other rooms, together with large and small lecture theatres.

Mr. Banerjee has followed his customary practice by a free use of concrete and steel, and this method is chiefly apparent in the staircase, the sloping seating accommodation, and the galleries in the theatres.

NEW POLICE OFFICES FOR CALCUTTA

The new offices of the Commissioner of Police will be built a little to the south of the former site, with a frontage upon Lall Bazar Street. It will be a four-storied structure, brick pointed, with Porebunder columns, facings, and balustrades repeated from story to story. The building has been designed by Mr. Henry Crouch, architect to the Government of Bengal, and the work of erection has been entrusted to Mr. J. C. Banerjee.

The ground floor will provide ample accommodation for the motor-car pass office, the lost property office, the stamp and accounts departments, the treasury, and *Malkhana*. There will be a lift and three staircases. From the imposing-looking porch at the rear of the building, entrance will be given to the main staircase, which is intended for officers, while the other two staircases will be for litigants, clerks, and the general public who have business there.

On the first floor there will be offices for the Commissioner, the Assistant and Deputy Commissioners, Inspectors, report and record rooms, and several waiting-rooms for the various branches. On the second floor will be located the Deputy Commissioner's offices, the central reserve office, and rooms for inspectors and sub-inspectors, in addition to accommodation for stationery and other departments. The third floor will consist of two comfortable suites of apartments for residential purposes, and on the fourth floor there will be the servants' quarters, kitchen, and a room for the lift machinery.

The plinth of the building, running from east to west, will be treated with a Mirzapore stone superstructure on brick pointing, and the ornamentation will be strikingly handsome. There will be thirteen arches on the Lall Bazar Street frontage; the three in the centre will give entrance to the corridor on the ground floor, and the five on each side will be closed up with ornamental railings. Over this will be Porebunder stone columns, repeated from floor to floor, with handsome balustrades of the same material. The arches over every door and window will have reinforced concrete ornamentations. At each of the four corners there will be a turret of Porebunder stone, and a royal coat-of-arms worked out in the same material will be put on the centre panel.

It may be added that Mr. Banerjee has quite recently been entrusted with the construction of the Hongkong and Shanghai Banking Corporation building, which is for one of the premier banks in India.

DR. K. C. BOSE

A laboratory was established in Amherst Street, Calcutta, in the year 1909 by Dr. Kartick Chandra Bose, M.B., for the purpose of carrying on research in indigenous drugs and of manufacturing efficient and high-class pharmaceutical preparations. Labour and money have been freely expended in making the laboratory thoroughly complete and up-to-date, and Dr. Bose's vast experience in this line of his profession, as well as in the treatment of diseases, has helped him to equip the laboratory with the latest chemical and scientific apparatus.

The preparations turned out by this laboratory are made from the very best ingredients, and the latest methods are

DR. K. C. BOSE.

1. Dr. K. C. Bose, M.B. 2. A Portion of the Sale-room. 3. Dr. Bose's Laboratory (Head Office).
4. Distillery Building, for Manufacturing Tinctures and Extracts under Bond.

employed in their manufacture. All preparations are scrupulously tasted and standardized by expert chemists and physiologists before being sent out, and thus they can be always safely depended upon for their efficacy.

Dr. Bose's laboratory consists of four departments — namely, (1) Pharmaceutical, (2) Chemical, (3) Bacteriological, and (4) Dispensing.

1. Pharmaceutical Department: This is fitted with a grinding machine for drugs, percolators, tincture presses, tablet machines, vacuum pan steam drying chamber, and a boiler. Solid and liquid extracts are prepared from indigenous drugs, and many of the preparations are put up in tablet form, for which a speciality is claimed by the proprietor.

2. The Chemical Department is very thoroughly equipped, and is in charge of expert chemists. Original investigations on the nature and constituents of indigenous drugs, standardizations, and the assay of active principles and determination of their physiological and other properties, are conducted, and analyses of foodstuffs, milk, water, wax, and urine are undertaken.

3. The Bacteriological Department is well supplied with incubators, autoclave, vaccine baths, and electric centrifuge; and the laboratory not only supplies vaccines made from the patient's own infecting organisms, but it also keeps a stock of recognized vaccines. Examination of sputum, blood, and other pathological fluids is made with the utmost care and precision. Lactic acid therapy has now gained a prominent place in medical treatment, and Dr. Bose claims that he is the only bacteriologist in India who is manufacturing fresh cultures of *Streptothrix dadhi* (local strain of the Bulgarian bacillus), the efficacy of which in intestinal troubles is now being widely recognized.

4. Dispensing Department: In order that the products of Dr. Bose's laboratory may be within easy reach of the public and medical profession, a well-fitted dispensary, styled the Standard Drug Stores, has been attached to the laboratory.

The dispensary is well stocked with pharmaceutical preparations, patent medicines, druggists' sundries, surgical instruments, and other goods, and it is attended during the day and night by qualified medical men, so that professional help is always available. Dr. Kartick Chandra Bose personally attends outdoor patients morning and evening, and this department is fully equipped with all kinds of instruments and apparatus for treatment of every variety of diseases; but special arrangements are made for dealing with affections of eye, ear, nose, and throat. Prescriptions are dispensed throughout the day and night.

The Union Distillery warehouse, for the manufacture of high-class rectified spirit and alcoholic pharmaceutical preparations in bond, under the control of the Excise authorities, is situated at 28 Bahir Mirzapur Road, in Calcutta.

THE BENGAL NATIONAL BANK, LTD.

This institution (incorporated under the Indian Companies Act) was established in the year 1907 with the object of meeting a long-felt want, namely, the commencement of a bank with Indian capital to foster and encourage Indian trade and industries.

Offices were originally opened at 22 Canning Street, Calcutta, but the growth of business caused the directors to remove in the year 1913 to more commodious premises at 11 Clive Street, which is practically the centre of the leading Indian as well as European commercial houses of the city.

All descriptions of ordinary banking business are carried on, such as the purchase and collection of bills of exchange, dividends or interest, the granting of drafts, and the issue of letters of credit. Current accounts are opened with minimum amounts of Rs. 200, and interest is allowed at current rates upon daily balances from Rs. 200 to Rs. 1,00,000.

Savings bank accounts, too, are opened, and interest is allowed at the rate of 3 per cent. per annum. Credits are granted on approved securities, and the directors further undertake, on behalf of their constituents, the safe custody of shares, title deeds, and other securities.

THE BENGAL NATIONAL BANK, LTD.
1. PORTION OF THE INTERIOR. 2. EXTERIOR VIEW.

Fixed deposits are received and interest is allowed at the following rates: 4 per cent. for a six months' deposit; 4½ per cent. for twelve months; and 5 per cent. for a term of two years; but special rates are arranged for shorter or longer periods and for large amounts.

The authorized capital of the company is Rs. 50,00,000, made up of 50,000 shares of Rs. 100 each, the capital issued amounts to Rs. 16,00,000, the amount paid up is Rs. 8,00,000.

The directors are Messrs. B. Chakravarti, P. L. Roy, Upendra Nath Sen, Mangla Prasad, Jogendra Nath Roy, Hirendra Nath Datta, W. C. Banerjee, and R. Mukerjee, managing director.

The Bank has correspondents in London and in all the principal towns in India.

B. BROTHERS & CO.

1. Premises (Cycle Department). 2. Cycle Show-room. 3. Show-room with Manager and Clerks. 4. Group of Staff. 5. Steel Trunk Department.

CALCUTTA INDUSTRIES

B. BROTHERS & CO.

This firm makes a speciality of the manufacture of steel trunks and of the importation of all kinds of bicycles, and they are in the proud position of being able to say that by placing upon the market high-class goods at a uniformly low price, by efficient management, and by the manifestation of the greatest courtesy to customers, their business has flourished to such an extent that their books and records contain the names of a larger number of customers than any other firm in Calcutta trading on similar lines.

The late Mr. Abinash Chandra Bhattacharyya, the founder of the establishment, commenced business in 1904 under the style of B. Brothers & Co., with premises at 14/4 Old China Bazaar Street, and he began by importing steel trunks, cash and dispatch boxes, leather portmanteaux, handbags, and rugs, in addition to a large variety of other travelling requisites.

A sound footing having been obtained among business concerns in the city, the firm felt warranted in 1905 in opening a branch shop, but this step had only just been taken when the *Swadeshi* movement, which gave to country-made articles a preference over foreign manufactures, was started in India. This radical change placed such an incubus upon imported goods that it became necessary, in 1906, to open a factory for the manufacture of steel trunks, and this building was fitted with thoroughly modern machinery. A supplying and forwarding department, dealing with inquiries from the Mofussil, was established, and it was soon found that—particularly from old customers and Government officials—mail orders had increased fully tenfold.

The very great demand for cycles necessitated the commencement of a separate branch for all classes of these machines and accessories, and suitable premises at Dhurrumtollah Street, Calcutta, were secured, Mr. S. R. Bhattacharyya being placed in sole charge. Wholesale and retail orders for cycles flowed in from the Mofussil, Burma, the Madras Presidency, Hyderabad, the Central and United Provinces, and the Punjab, and the resources of the forwarding staff were taxed to their utmost extent in attending to the mass of increased business. Further accommodation for this branch soon became necessary, and the entire cycle department was removed to a desirable and commodious building at 36 Harrison Road, Calcutta, wherein are located main offices, showrooms, repairing shops, and godowns.

An irreparable loss was sustained by the firm in 1912 owing to the sudden death of its founder, Mr. Abinash Chandra Bhattacharyya, but the sound business principles inculcated by him were not lost upon his fellow-workers, who, with commendable energy, undertook the task of maintaining the very high reputation which had been gained.

The reconstituted firm succeeded in making rapid advancement, and opportunity was found for the opening of yet another branch of business by the importation of all kinds of musical instruments, but chiefly organs and harmoniums.

Messrs. B. Brothers & Co., in common with other mercantile firms, have felt the disastrous effects of the European War, but their indomitable courage, supported by the strictest attention to details, has enabled them not only to face these difficulties with composure, but also to make even further headway in every branch of their large establishment.

The telegraphic address of the firm is "Unity, Calcutta."

BUKHSH ELLAHIE & CO.

The honour of being the largest purveyors of tobacco and cigarettes to the military forces in India belongs to the above-named firm, of which Haji Bukhsh Ellahie is managing proprietor. This gentleman is descended from a family of merchants who have for a very long period carried on an extensive business in Delhi, and in the year 1878, when quite a young man, he visited Calcutta and became an assistant with a Mahommedan merchant in that city. It was not long before he manifested such a natural aptitude for a commercial life that his elder brother, Haji Karam Ellahie, decided in 1885 to open a business with the view of dealing in tea, tobacco, and other merchandise, under the name of Bukhsh Ellahie & Co., but under the directorship of the promising young recruit from Delhi.

The latter held progressive ideas, and his determination to follow some line of business which had not at that time become overcrowded led him to take up imported tobacco as the special object of his attention. He subsequently entered into communication with some of the largest manufacturers in America, and with Messrs. W. D. and H. O. Wills, of Bristol, in England, and that step resulted in a very considerable development of the tobacco trade in India.

In 1901, on the eve of the tobacco war between England and America, Haji Bukhsh Ellahie, accompanied by his secretary, Mr. A. Azeez, proceeded to England at the invitation of Messrs. Wills, and since the conference which then took place Messrs. Bukhsh Ellahie & Co. have been dealing in tobacco imported from British sources to the exclusion of consignments from any other portion of the world, an arrangement which has made them the chief agents in India of the Imperial Tobacco Company. The firm have branches at Delhi, Karachi, and many other important centres, and they are the medium through whom a very large quantity of tobacco manufactured in England is distributed throughout the markets of India.

As a citizen of Calcutta, Haji Bukhsh Ellahie has distinguished himself by his careful attention to the needs of his own community, while at the same time he has not overlooked the claims of the other citizens of the city of his adoption. Evidences of his forethought and benevolence are seen in the Mosafirkhana, or rest-house, situated on the Chitpore Road, in Calcutta, and, in a particular manner, in the formation of the Mahommedan Burial Association, which provides for the interment of unclaimed Mahommedan bodies with all the ceremonies prescribed by Islamic law.

Reference may also be made to the following, among many other, instances of the generous nature of this honoured citizen. On the occasion of the King-Emperor's Durbar at Delhi, 500,000 cigarettes were sent to His Excellency the Commander-in-Chief for British soldiers, and a dozen silver challenge cups were given by way of encouraging sports competitions among the various divisions of the Army in India. Many years previously—during the Boer War, as a matter of fact—large quantities of tobacco and cigarettes were presented to the British troops in South Africa.

Haji Bukhsh Ellahie is a member of the Chamber of Commerce of Bengal and the Punjab, of the Calcutta Mahommedan Orphanage Committee, the Calcutta District Charitable Society, the Central National Mahommedan Association, and the Calcutta Mahommedan Burial Board, and it may be said briefly that he is ever ready to give the most generous support to all movements calculated to promote

BUKHSH ELLAHIE & CO.

1. Mr. Abdur Rahim, Managing Director. 2. Group of Assistants, 3. Premises.

the well-being of the public generally. It was in recognition of his services to the public that the Government of India decorated him with the distinguished honour of C.I.E. and the Oriental title of Khan Sahib. He has three sons, who have been educated and trained to assist their father in his many-sided activities, the second in age of these, Mr. Abdur Rahum Bukhsh Ellahie, being the managing partner of the firm in Calcutta.

A few words must be added to show the broad-minded interest taken by the Haji in public matters. He organized a splendid entertainment, consisting of an afternoon party and a treat for school-boys of all denominations in Calcutta on the occasion of the Coronation of His Majesty the King in England in June 1911. The function was held in the Town Hall, which had been beautifully decorated, and it was attended by many of the leading inhabitants of the city, who expressed delight at the manner in which provision had been made with music, toys, and refreshments for the enjoyment of the children.

About 750 scholars were present from the Catholic Male Orphanage, St. Joseph's Free School, the Calcutta Free School, the Mahommedan Orphanage, the Madrassah, and the Martin Institution.

DR. S. K. BURMAN

The medicinal treatment of diseases is probably the oldest science in existence. Primitive man was as susceptible to the countless ills of the flesh as is the individual of to-day, and ancient records and traditions show that even in those far-away ages his remedies or potions were the result of practical trials of the herbs of the field. The physician of the twentieth century works upon similar lines, although he has incomparably greater and more efficacious stocks of ingredients in his pharmacopœia, and there are now specialists in every country in the world who have been true benefactors to the human race by the discoveries which they have made.

One of these practitioners—Dr. S. K. Burman—established a Medical Hall at 4, 5, and 6 Tarachand Dutt's Street, Calcutta, in the year 1884, and his name has become popular throughout India on account of the valuable medicinal preparations which have been issued to the public. More than forty specifics for the treatment of various diseases have been prepared, but special mention should be made of three which are widely used throughout India.

The first of these is an essence of pure camphor, which the proprietor regards as the best preventive of cholera or choleric diarrhœa that has ever been discovered. Hundreds of thousands of phials are being sold in India, Burma, and Ceylon every year, and thousands of unsolicited testimonials as to its curative properties have been received. The second one to be noticed is a cure for asthma, which was not manufactured until after Dr. Burman had spent several years in a careful study of this distressing malady. It is said that a couple of doses are sufficient to check the trouble, and that by continuing the medicine the disease is absolutely cured.

Practically every district in India is a hotbed of malaria and ague, but these recurrent scourges appear to be swiftly overcome by the use of Dr. Burman's specifics, which are said to kill the germs, create new blood-cells, and restore a healthy tone to the system.

A certificate of honour was presented to Dr. Burman in recognition of his liberality by His Honour the Lieutenant-Governor of Bengal, in the name of His Majesty King Edward VII, then Emperor of India, by command of His Excellency the Viceroy and Governor-General in Council on January 1, 1903.

Surgical and optical instruments are always kept in stock at the Medical Hall, and the present proprietor—Mr. C. L. Burman, a son of the founder of the practice—is a constant importer of fresh drugs and chemicals from the leading manufacturers of Europe.

DR. S. K. BURMAN.

1. "CAMPHOR HOUSE," OFFICE OF S. K. BURMAN.

THE CAPITAL ENGINEERING COMPANY

The construction of places of business, as well as of private residences, designed to suit a tropical climate but combining modern improvements suggested by Western styles of architecture, is now a prominent feature with contractors in India, and one has only to witness works now in progress in Calcutta to obtain abundant proof of this statement.

Old-established firms have recognized the necessity for remodelling their plans, but architects and others who have commenced business in recent years have readily adopted the new procedure. The Capital Engineering Company, by way of example, have already gained considerable reputation for the excellent manner in which they have carried out works entrusted to them.

Their offices are at 7 Old Post Office Street, Calcutta, and they have also extensive workshops and godowns at 120 Upper Circular Road, in the same city. The proprietors are consulting engineers, and their thorough training in this branch enables them to give sound advice upon all matters relating to structural work.

The company have earned high com-

THE CAPITAL ENGINEERING COMPANY.

1. Kamarhatty "A" Mill Extension. 2. Premises of Mr. L. B. Dutt, 120/2 Upper Circular Road.

mendation from the superintendent of the Kamarhatty Jute Mills for extensive alterations to those premises, and the manager of the Kinnison Jute Mills, in a letter dated September 1, 1915, said that the firm gave great satisfaction in the carrying out of various building contracts; but these are merely a sample of numerous testimonials of a similar character.

A branch establishment has been opened at Bankipore, where a Training College and Hostel are now being built under instructions from the Public Works Department of the Government of Behar and Orissa.

DAS & CO.

If the making of household vessels and ornaments of brass and other metals and weaving and spinning done by hand in villages are excepted, there were practically no industries in India worth mentioning at the beginning of the nineteenth century, and this seems to be a particularly strange fact when one reflects that many hundreds of years ago this country was carrying on an extensive trade not only within its own borders, but with several European nations. A great change has, however, taken place, and among the numerous successful industrial concerns which have been established on European lines is one in which the firm of Messrs. Das. & Co. are

DAS & CO.

1, 2. Views of the Building. 3. "Noorjahan Safe. 4. W. N. Das, Proprietor.

engaged in manufacturing patent locks, safes, boxes, trunks, and scales and weights at the "Abba" manufactory at 12, 13, 14, and 14/1 Cossipore Road, Chitpore, a northern suburb of the city of Calcutta.

The firm was founded by Babu Krishna Lal Das, who commenced business life in one of the Government offices, but who, finding that his aspirations would never be realized in a purely clerical position, looked to the commercial and industrial world to provide him with the opening upon which he had set his heart. Selecting as a promising field for enterprise the manufacture of locks for safes and boxes of various kinds, he managed to induce the late Kumar Indra Chandra Sinha Bahadur, of the Paikpara Raj, to take an interest in his scheme, with the result that the latter rendered substantial financial assistance in furtherance of the project and a workshop was opened in 1879.

It is said that "money talks," but money only in this instance was not able to uproot the ultra-conservative prejudices of smiths obtained by Das Babu from neighbouring villages, who flatly refused to adopt new methods of work. This was a disappointing beginning, but, after exercising great patience and perseverance, young boys, tempted by liberal allowances, were obtained and trained by the Babu personally. This procedure naturally occupied some considerable time, but the proprietor was subsequently rewarded by the excellent work done by these new hands; and after his "safety" principle had been patented and then added to the mechanism of locks, the Babu received numbers of orders from heads of Government departments. The business then progressed rapidly, and a further impetus was given by a circular letter, in which the then Viceroy, Lord Ripon, directed all Government officers "to use goods of Indian manufacture wherever practicable."

The Babu, about that time, appointed a European firm in Calcutta as agents for the sale of his manufactured articles in order that he might devote greater attention to perfecting the various goods then being manufactured in his shops, and for this purpose he imported a large quantity of modern machine tools.

Onerous duties, frequently carried on under discouraging circumstances, affected the Babu's health so seriously that, after giving a preliminary training to his nephew, Babu Woopendra Nath Das, in September 1891 he transferred the whole concern to him as a gift and retired from active life.

The new proprietor had to face an organized opposition from workmen who had prospered under the old régime, but who, with base ingratitude for the satisfactory position they had attained, refused to carry out the orders of a younger man, who, they ignorantly believed, knew nothing of the business to which he had succeeded. "Everything comes to him who waits," however, and Babu Woopendra Nath Das soon came to be recognized by the obstructionists as a man of experience and of undoubted ability, and they began to obey him and carry out his orders. The firm's business continued to grow, and in order to meet the wishes of customers they added carpenter's and tinsmith's departments and general engineering works to the business.

A reference to price-lists shows that the firm have a grand selection of safes, cash chests, and patented "safety" locks and boxes, together with a great variety of iron and brass fittings, for the safe keeping of personal effects of all kinds, ranging from the most valuable diamonds to the ordinary things of daily use.

The sole agents in Burma are Messrs. S. Oppenheimer & Co., Ltd., Rangoon.

Communications to the firm are addressed to their head office, 14 Cossipore Road, Calcutta (telephone 416 Calcutta), or by telegram to their registered address, "Safeguard, Calcutta."

S. M. DEY & CO.

One of the oldest and largest direct importers of builders' materials, hardware, indiarubber goods, paints, cements, rolled steel girders, angles, bars, plates, galvanized iron sheets, copper ingots, bolts, nuts, rivets, wire nails, shovels, and all kinds of mill, factory, mining, and other miscellaneous stores and requisites, is that of Messrs. S. M. Dey & Co., engineers, merchants' agents, and Government contractors, of 41 Strand Road, Calcutta.

S. M. DEY & CO.

1. Proprietor and Son. 2. Assistants and a Display of Filters.

The firm was established in the year 1882 by Mr. Soorendra Mohun Dey, the sole proprietor, who is enabled to carry on a large and prosperous business by regular importations of goods, which, by reason of their reliability, have found favour with a very large circle of customers.

A special feature is made of the agency for the Pasteur-Chamberland Filter Company, of 5 White Street, Finsbury, London, E.C., whose filters are the only ones in the world authorized by the famous scientist to bear his name. Medical research has proved conclusively that certain diseases, such as typhoid fever, dysentery, and cholera, frequently result

DINSHAW & SORABJEE.

1. Restaurant Car, Calcutta-Darjeeling Mail Service. 2. Refreshment Room, Eastern Bengal State Railway, Sealdah Terminus.
3. Duty Paid Stores. 4. Front View of Premises.

from the drinking of impure water, and although the germs of these plagues may to some extent be combated by distillation, boiling, and sterilization, it is an undoubted fact that all bacteria can be strained out by passing the water through a genuine Pasteur-Chamberland filter.

These receptacles are made in a variety of shapes and sizes to suit all requirements, being serviceable alike for the pocket or for large installations for town reservoirs, and they have been recognized as standard filters in the laboratories of the Royal College of Physicians (London) and Surgeons (England). Monsieur Pasteur wrote many years ago in answer to inquirers that "the filter was invented and tested in my laboratory, and was rewarded by one of the prizes of the Academy of Sciences, and I have willingly and deliberately authorized Dr. Chamberland to add the words 'Systeme Pasteur' to the title filtre Chamberland."

Messrs. Dey & Co. always carry a large stock of these filters and all spare parts, and a special feature is made in their works of giving immediate attention to any repairs which may be needed.

DINSHAW AND SORABJEE

This is one of the best-known business houses in Calcutta, the firm having extensive connections throughout Bengal, the United Provinces, Behar and Orissa, Assam, and the Central Provinces. Their wonderful growth from a small beginning in 1885 is a tribute to the business acumen of the original partners, namely, Mr. Sorabjee C. Colah and the late Mr. Dinshaw B. Bamjee, who commenced trading at Bogoola, on the Eastern Bengal Railway, and two years later obtained their first contract as caterers on board the ferry-steamers plying between Damukdia and Saraghat, on the northern section of the railway. Owing to the success with which they controlled this service, and to the recognition by the railway authorities of the business capabilities of the partners, they were offered, and accepted, the entire management and control of the refreshment-rooms throughout the Eastern Bengal Railway systems. The business from now onwards showed rapid extension, until in 1896 it necessitated the opening of wholesale warehouses at 12 Esplanade East, Calcutta. In the following year the firm obtained the catering contract on the Darjeeling-Himalayan Railway, and in 1905 they were asked to take over the refreshment-rooms on the North-Western Railway. These responsible positions were filled with marked success, until in 1911, when they found it almost impossible to control the enormous trade over such great distances, and were reluctantly compelled, owing to the exigencies of their Bengal enterprises and the demand made on the time of the two partners, to relinquish their connection with the North-Western Railway, and thus to concentrate their efforts upon their own business, where a greater field for their activities existed. Previous to this, in the year 1899, to be exact, they found that their large warehouses at 12 Esplanade East were far too small for their business, and they were compelled to acquire more commodious and central premises at 8 Dhurrumtollah Street, but with a view to serve the public and afford greater business facilities and conveniences to their numerous clients they opened a branch at 17 Chowringhee Road.

The volume of trade continued to expand in a marvellous manner, and again the acquisition of a large number of additional warehouses or godowns became necessary, and in 1908 the increased space acquired was no less than 20,000 sq. ft. In 1909 the firm suffered an irreparable loss in the death of Mr. Dinshaw Bamjee, whose genius and organizing powers meant so much to the business, but fortunately the firm possessed in Mr. J. Dinshaw Bamjee, his eldest son, one who inherited his father's great powers.

The establishment had now attained such huge proportions that the partners felt compelled to institute closer control over the multitudinous departments in which their business was carried on, and at this time Mr. R. S. Colah, Mr. P. Bamjee, and Mr. K. S. Colah were brought into the concern, which thus consisted of one of the original partners and the sons of both. The fine reputation which this firm had built up for itself by careful attention to details, by innate honesty, punctual services, and courtesy, is exemplified in their being appointed caterers to Lord Curzon, Viceroy and Governor-General of India in 1904, Earl Kitchener, a former Commander-in-Chief, and the Governor of Bengal, in addition to which they practically monopolized the supplies to a number of messes and clubs throughout India. It is of interest to see that Mr. Sorabjee C. Colah, at the age of seventy, still takes the greatest interest in the business, his great personal gifts being directed towards the higher control of the firm's trade, while commercial details are looked after by the younger partners.

Messrs. Dinshaw and Sorabjee hold a number of valuable agencies, among which are those of Messrs. J. and R. Tennent, D. and J. McCallum, Robert Brown, Ltd., William Teacher & Sons, Bisquit Dubouche & Co., Courvoisier & Co., James Keiller & Son, Ltd., Spratt's, Ltd., and Chivers & Sons, Ltd. The remarkable evidence of the continued prosperity of this firm is exemplified by the busy hives of employees constantly engaged in packing wines, spirits, stores, and provisions for up-country constituents, many of whom reside from two to three thousand miles distance from the firm's head office in Calcutta.

P. N. DUTT & CO.

The proprietors of this firm were the first to introduce into India the manufacture of galvanized buckets, baths, drums, and many other receptacles of a similar character. There are four partners, all of whom take an active share in management—namely, Messrs. S. N. Dutt, B. B. Dutt, P. N. Dutt, and G. C. Dutt, and the senior partner, Mr. S. N. Dutt, has on more than one occasion visited factories in Europe, in which he became thoroughly acquainted with Western methods of galvanizing. This led to the establishment in 1906 of the Bengal Galvanizing works, at 43 Musjidbaree Street, Calcutta, and, commencing with a daily production of five dozen buckets by hand-power, the firm now have a factory, constructed on modern lines and fully equipped with the most up-to-date machinery and plant capable of making in a working day some 200 dozens of buckets, together with a considerable number of baths, drums, and other sheet-metal goods.

A large quantity of acid being required in the galvanizing process in the factory, the partners started in 1912 "the Bengal Acid Manufacturing Company" at Ultadanga, and they are now able to meet their own requirements and to furnish supplies to a large circle of private customers.

The firm are sole agents for the Union Electric Company, Ltd., of London, and they are selling-agents at their Ramkristopore Steel Yard for the Tata Iron and Steel Company, Ltd.

The progress made by this firm is an

excellent illustration of a thoroughly successful *Swadeshi* concern in India, and an industry, started by the Messrs. Dutt, is likely to become a most important one in a country in which such enterprises are sadly too few.

P. N. DUTT & CO.

1. Partners of the Firm. 2. Bengal Galvanizing Works, Interior of Bucket Shop.

The telegraphic address is "Galvanize, Calcutta."

DWARKIN & SON

What a dismal world this would be without the uplifting strains of music, which is the first of the arts to be developed in childhood! It is the welcome of the birds to each newborn day, it is an inspiration to the tired body and the depressed mind, it puts new life into the soldier as he swings along on his weary march, it is suitable for palace or cottage or king or peasant, and the man or woman who is unmoved by it is one to be shunned. Does not Shakespeare in the "Merchant of Venice" say :—

The man that hath no music in himself,
Nor is not mov'd with concord of sweet sounds,
Is fit for treasons, stratagems, and spoils.

These words spring unbidden to the mind as one enters any of those establishments in which are seen grand collections of musical instruments of all kinds, together with copies of the works of some of the brilliant composers of this and many preceding generations.

One of the leading firms in this particular line of business is Messrs. Dwarkin & Son, of Dalhousie Square and Bowbazar Street, Calcutta.

Mr. Dwarkanath Ghose, the founder and present head of the firm, originally started as a piano-tuner and repairer of musical instruments, under the name and style of D. Ghose & Son, and he had a small shop in 6 Lower Chitpore Road. In those days Western musical instruments were not used by Indians generally, and business could only be done among the few European residents. Bengali gentlemen, however, appreciated European instruments, and a few of them commenced to give expositions of Indian music on European instruments, and to sing Bengali songs to the accompaniment of harmoniums by Alexandre of Paris. Mr. Dwarkanath foresaw the great possibilities of the musical instrument trade in India, and in 1878 he established the firm of Dwarkin & Son, and commenced importing instruments of all kinds from England, France, and Germany, as well as America, and soon succeeded in creating a demand for them among the Indian people. The enterprise succeeded to such an extent that he was soon compelled to remove to larger premises in 2 Lower Chitpore Road. In 1887 Mr. Dwarkanath invented, and began manufacturing, a small hand harmonium, which was specially suitable for Indian music, and which could be sold so cheaply as to bring it within the reach of the poorest. This invention popularized music in India, and gave a great impetus to the harmonium trade. The firm's business went up by leaps and bounds, and more extended accommodation becoming necessary, they, in the year 1895, removed to spacious premises in 267 Bowbazar Street, where they now have their workshop, stores, and packing departments, and in 1903 they opened their splendid showrooms in Dalhousie Square.

Messrs. Dwarkin & Son import violins and accessories from Germany and France, orchestral and band instruments from England and France, pianos from England, Japan, and Germany, and harmoniums and organs from France, America, and Japan. They are sole agents in India for Putnam American Organs of Staunton, United States, and of Messrs. the Nippon Piano and Organ Company of Japan.

This firm keep a stock of orchestral instruments of various descriptions in their warehouses, and cabinets and shelves, almost without end in number, in their shop are packed with violins, mandolins, guitars, banjoes, accordeons, concertinas, musical-boxes, gramophones, flutes, and sundry other articles. The immense stock of harmoniums and organs carried shows what a large business they do in these special lines. The Indians are no longer content with their *setars* and *vennas*, and to-day there are few homes that do not possess a Dwarkin's organ or harmonium. The use of these instruments has perhaps altered the character of Indian music, but it is not denied that music is now more easily learnt and is more popular than when people had to depend on purely Indian instruments.

The book and sheet music department is up to date in every respect, as the London agents of the firm are exceedingly prompt in sending to India any composition of merit which makes its appearance in London or any other important musical centre.

Messrs. Dwarkin are the largest importers in India of reeds and other harmonium and organ fittings, and the progress that the harmonium industry has made in India recently is largely due to the efforts of this firm in securing materials from all parts of the world and in selling them at a very small profit.

Messrs. Dwarkin & Son possess a large clientele among the Europeans in India, with whom they do a brisk trade in music and small goods, but their special study

DWARKIN & SON.

1. Dalhousie Square Show-room. 2. Branch and Godowns at Bowbazar Street.

is to meet the requirements for Indians and Indian music, and in this branch of business they have practically no competitors.

A unique feature of this firm's business lies in the fact that they have published several music books in Bengalee.

Mr. Dwarkanath does not now take any active part in the business, the management being entirely in the hands of his eldest son, Mr. Kiron Chunder Ghose.

THE EAST INDIA CIGARETTE MANUFACTURING COMPANY, LTD., DUM-DUM.

THE EAST INDIA CIGARETTE MANUFACTURING COMPANY, LTD.

This is an Indian company, financed by Indian capital, and depending almost entirely upon Indian customers for its support. It was formed in the year 1908 to acquire, carry on, and extend the cigarette manufacturing business of the East India Cigarette Manufacturing Company, which had been established and worked successfully for some years previously by Mr. Mahomed Omari, the present managing director. It was incorporated under the Indian Companies Acts with a capital of Rs. 30,00,000, of which Rs. 10,00,000 were issued and fully paid. A reserve fund of no less than Rs. 6,50,000 accumulated and was used in the business, and of this amount Rs. 5,00,000 have recently been capitalized, and 50,000 fully paid ordinary shares have been distributed as a bonus among the shareholders.

There has been a growing demand among Indians for these cigarettes, and some twenty brands—including the favourites known as "Holy," "Crown," and "Ram Ram"—are being manufactured. A large factory has been erected at Dum Dum Road, Cossipore, near Calcutta, and it is equipped with modern machinery of an approved type, which is capable of turning out about 8,000,000 cigarettes daily. Packets and boxes are made on the premises, and printing presses for the preparation of labels have been installed.

The company have excellent godowns for the storage of tobacco leaf and other materials, and more than Rs. 6,70,000 have been expended during the past six years on the erection and equipment of the factory and other works.

The turnover in the business is increasing rapidly, and the temporary depression alluded to above will soon be a matter of past history.

The directors are Messrs. Mahomed Omari (managing director), A. C. Bannerjee, and Mirza Ahmed Ally.

The registered offices of the company are at 104 Canning Street, Calcutta.

D. GOOPTU & CO.

The firm of Messrs. D. Gooptu & Co., which was named after its founder, was established in 1840 by the late Dr. Dwarkanath Gooptu, G.M.C.B., one of the successful candidates of the first lot of students who qualified in the Medical College of Bengal. He was born in the year 1818 of respected parents, who had considerable landed properties in and about Calcutta. He was one of the favourite students of David Hare, being educated under his care at the Hare School in Calcutta, and on the establishment of the Medical College of Bengal, in June 1835, he was admitted as one of the foundation students. Having passed his final examination in March 1839, he was appointed by the Honourable East India Company as medical officer in one of the north-western towns, but as he was inclined for independent practice he

D. GOOPTU & CO. & F. N. GOOPTU & CO.

1. Head Office, D. Gooptu & Co., Upper Chitpore Road. 2. Interior of Sale-room, Upper Chitpore Road. 3. Residence of G. C. Gooptu. 4. Interior of F. N. Gooptu & Co.'s Workshop. 5. F. N. Gooptu & Co.'s Workshop. 6. The late Dr. D. Gooptu, G.M.C.B.

refused the post. He soon became family physician to Prince Dwarka Nath Tagore, who introduced him to all the Tagore and many other rich families of Calcutta, and thus at the age of twenty-two he began his career as a medical practitioner, becoming the chief medical adviser in all the Tagore households. In 1840 the first indent of Messrs. D. Gooptu & Co. was written by Sir William Brook O'Shaughnessy, the then professor of chemistry of the Medical College, and it is worthy of note that this firm owned the first dispensary of English drugs in India which was started by a Bengalee doctor. The business grew rapidly in succeeding years, and in 1871 Dr. D. Gooptu became the sole proprietor of the firm, carrying it on until 1882, when he died, leaving the business in the hands of his sons, Mr. Gopal Chandra Gooptu, the late Mr. Ram Ch. Gooptu, and Mr. Nando Lall Gooptu, who conducted it until 1913, when Mr. R. C. Gooptu died, leaving his sons as his heirs and executors. At present the firm consists of Mr. G. C. Gooptu, Mr. N. L. Gooptu, and the executors of the late Mr. R. C. Gooptu, and business is transacted at their premises at 369 Upper Chitpore Road and 13 Esplanade Row East, Calcutta.

A speciality is made by Messrs. D. Gooptu & Co. of their anti-periodic mixture, commonly known as "D. Gooptu," which is the specific for all kinds of malarial fever, and it has perhaps one of the largest sales among patent medicines in India, being held in high esteem by all who have used it. In addition to the antiperiodic mixture, there are several other very good and efficacious proprietary medicines of the firm, the names of which are (1) antiperiodic mixture "Falena Parichiyata"; (2) spleen and liver ointment; (3) special liver mixture for all kinds of disorders of that organ; (4) diarrhœa and dysentery pills, a specific for all kinds of bowel complaints; (5) antiperiodic pills for adults and boys; (6) liver-purging pills; and (7) essence of Jamaica sarsaparilla.

Dr. Dwijendra Nath Gooptu, B.A., L.M.S. Gold Medalist, the eldest son of Mr. G. C. Gooptu, is now the consulting physician.

F N. GOOPTU & CO.

Mr. G. C. Gooptu entertained the idea a few years ago of starting a new industry in Calcutta, and he accordingly trained his youngest son, Mr. F. N. Gooptu, in all departments necessary for the carrying on of a manufacturing business. In 1905 the latter started the firm of Messrs. F. N. Gooptu & Co., for manufacturing penholders for the first time in India. Quite a modest beginning was made at 5 Middleton Street, the residence of Mr. G. C. Gooptu, and the proprietor at once secured the service of a European expert from England, and himself studied the secrets of the trade, together with the methods followed in the Western world in a manufacturing business. His enterprise met with unprecedented success, and through the good offices of the Hon. Mr. K. C. De, C.I.E., I.C.S., at present Commissioner of Chittagong, and Mr. M. J. Cogswell, Controller of Printing, Stationery, and Stamps, he secured the active support of the Government of India in the shape of a standing yearly order. In 1910 the factory was enlarged, and the present commodious workshop was constructed at 12 Beliaghatta Road, on six bighas of land, at a cost of more than two and a half lakhs of rupees. All the machinery has been imported from England, and the whole concern is now being carried on under the management and supervision of the founder, Mr. F. N. Gooptu. This firm has secured the whole of the orders from the Government of India for penholders, pens, and pencils, which have, further, commanded a large sale all over the country. Mr. J. A. L. Swan, I.C.S., visited the factory as a deputation from the Government of Bengal and expressed great satisfaction with what he saw there (vide Mr. Swan's report on the "Development of Industries in Bengal," 1915). Owing to the extreme difficulty—if not the impossibility—of obtaining pens, pencils, and penholders from European countries (which have hitherto been exporters of large quantities, but are now engaged in war), Messrs. Gooptu & Co. have secured a practical monopoly for manufacturing and supplying these articles throughout the whole of India.

THE HINDUSTHAN CO-OPERATIVE INSURANCE SOCIETY, LTD.

The Hindusthan Insurance Society was founded in May 1907 on the co-operative plan, and registered as a joint stock company with limited liability.

Its establishment was an attempt to create for the whole of India, firstly, an accumulating and investing centre in which periodic savings, placed by way of calls paid on shares in its capital, or premiums on its life policies, would remain safe, and grow to the best advantage. As a means to this end the respective rights of shareholders and policy-holders were clearly defined and safeguarded in the constitution of the society so as to prevent any danger of combined exploitation; the shareholders were further enabled, under certain conditions, to take life policies in lieu of profits, and the policy-holders were given every opportunity to acquire shares, in order to afford every scope for a mutualizing of the business to any desired extent. The principle of "one man, one vote" was adopted, with the view of preventing power being usurped by any group of wealthy shareholders; and, lastly, the different provinces of India, being entitled to have their own provincial boards, and having the fullest possible facilities for representation by proxies or delegates at the general meetings of the society, were enabled to feel that they could have a hand in shaping the policy and working of the society's administration.

Secondly, the "accumulating machine" being thus created, and started fairly working, the society's programme included the co-operative feature of investing these accumulations in ways which would, so far as possible, directly or indirectly conduce to the benefit of the contributing locality. This it was proposed to do by financing, in conjunction with municipal or other corporations, or public-spirited individuals of wealth and position, such progressive schemes as drainage, waterworks, building societies, and electric power installations at reasonable rates of interest, and on adequate security being furnished.

Judging by the progress made by the society, it may be reasonably expected that, with the completion of its first decade on April 30, 1917, it will have been soundly and firmly established so far as the first part of its programme is concerned. It already has an insurance business of about one crore and fifty-five lakhs (Rs. 1,55,00,000) on its books, with life funds totalling more than twenty-three lakhs (Rs. 23,00,000), which are more than fully covered by real assets invested at a good average rate of interest. It has branches and agencies throughout India, Burma, and Ceylon, and it is also represented in the Indian

HINDUSTHAN CO-OPERATIVE INSURANCE SOCIETY, LTD.

1. Hindusthan Buildings, North View. 2. Hindusthan Buildings, South View.

communities in Africa, the Straits, and the Federated Malay Settlements.

A commencement has also been made with the next part of its policy, namely, regulating the investment of its accumulating capital in the interest of its contributories. Schemes are under consideration and preparation for (1) an up-to-date nursing home with the co-operation of certain leading medical practitioners of Bombay, (2) electric power installations for several small towns, and (3) building societies in the suburbs of Madras and Calcutta. The present European War, with its world-wide disturbing effects, may retard the progress of the society for a while, but, based as its programme is on the permanent foundation of the alleviation of common wants by self-help and mutual aid, the society's activities must, in the end, redound to the economic development of the localities which are far-sighted and enterprising enough to join whole-heartedly in, and thereby contribute to, the strength of its organization.

The Hindusthan Buildings in Corporation Street, Calcutta, in which the head offices of the society are located, represent an investment yielding a guaranteed net rent of 7 per cent. per annum on an outlay of about Rs. 10,00,000.

HAJEE ALLABUX AND HAJEE MAHAMMED JAN

This enterprising firm was established in the year 1863 by the above-named partners, who, from the very commencement of their career, determined that the guiding principle of their business creed should be that all transactions must be conducted with the most scrupulous regard for dealing in a strictly honourable manner with regard to the quality and price of their goods.

They opened a store at 3 Rathu Sircar's Lane, Colootollah, in Calcutta, trading in stationery, hosiery, matches, fancy goods, cutlery, soap, cigarettes, and sundry other articles; but soon discovering that these premises were too small for their rapidly increasing business, they removed to 11 Colootollah Street. This building served their purpose for a time, but a further expansion of trade caused them to secure greater accommodation at their present address, No. 80 in the same street.

Further assistance in carrying on the concern became necessary, and they admitted some of the workers of their own firm into partnership; and the firm now (1916) consists of Hajee Allabux, Hajee Mahammed Jan, Hajee Mahammed Ismail, Munsi Mahammed Amin, Hafez Mahammed Amin, and Ubaidur Rahman.

It is the boast of the firm that when they have secured customers they retain them, because the latter have had reason to place unbounded confidence in the partners, and to be completely satisfied with the manner in which their orders have been executed. A similar bond exists between the firm and the manufacturers from whom they purchase goods, and proof of this was given in 1915, when a representative visited Japan and found that manufacturers and agents in that country who had supplied various goods in former years were most anxious to continue business relationships.

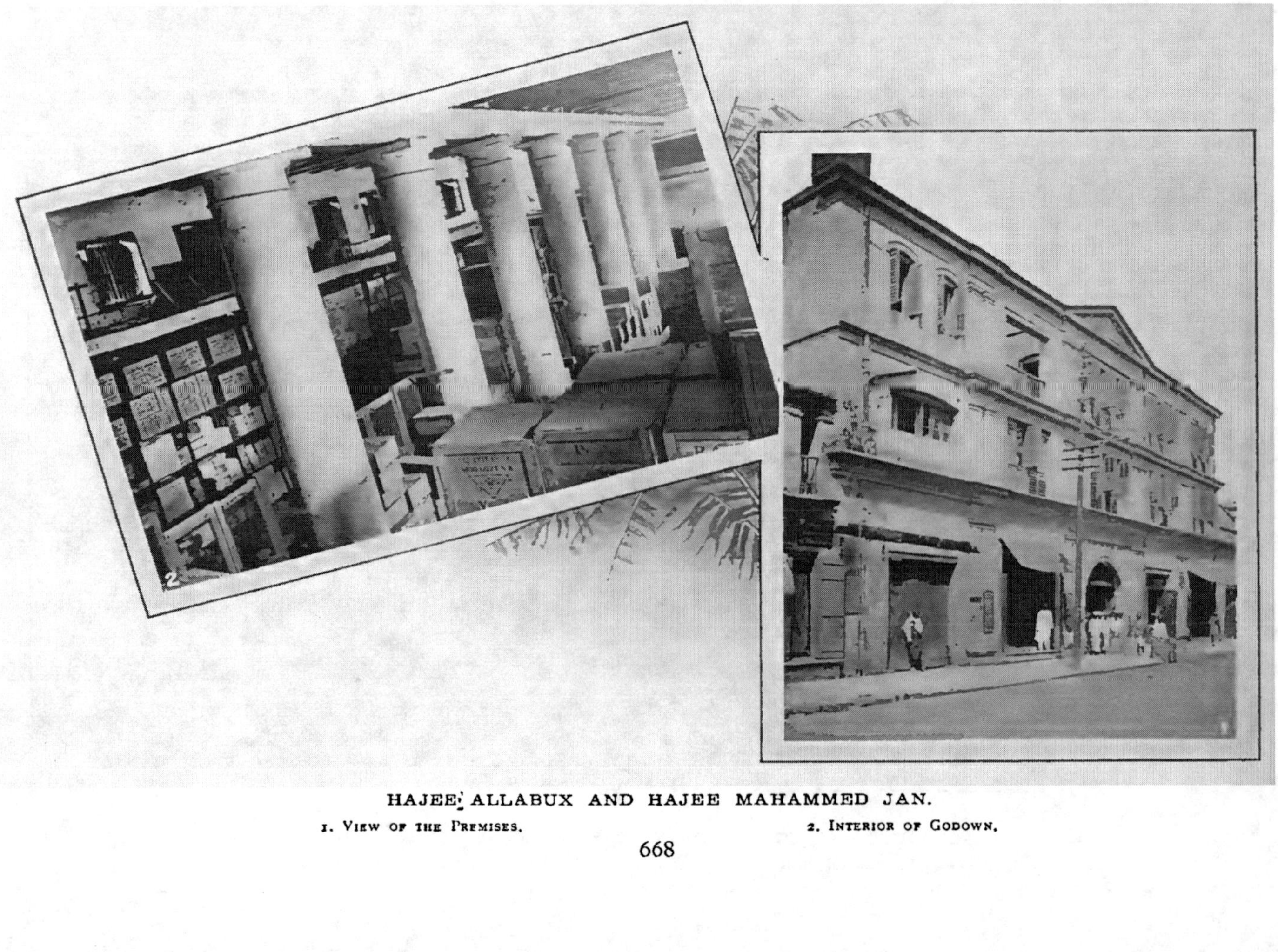

HAJEE ALLABUX AND HAJEE MAHAMMED JAN.

1. VIEW OF THE PREMISES. 2. INTERIOR OF GODOWN.

M. M ISPAHANI & SONS.

1. Office Premises at 51 Ezra Street. 2. Hide Store, Kidderpore. 3. Interior of Hide Store. 4. Press House for Baling Hides and Skins. 5. Tea Blending Room.

The firm are now manufacturers of soaps for laundry purposes, under the style and name of the Salim Soap Company, the principal kinds being "Elephant" brand (in qualities Nos. 1, 2, and 3), bar, carbolic, and other varieties. The raw materials, with the exception of grease, are imported from Europe, and the factory is equipped with the latest type of machinery and plant. The firm are sole agents in Bengal for Goodwin's Soaps and the Imperial Tobacco Company's cigarettes.

Messrs. Hajee Allabux and Hajee Mahammed Jan now import the major portion of their goods from foreign countries, through Messrs. Mohamed Ismail Mohamed Rafee, who carry on their business in the same premises, 80 Colootollah Street.

JEEWANLALL & CO.

1. Premises. 2. Show-room and Assistants.

M. M. ISPAHANI & SONS

Messrs. M. M. Ispahani & Sons, of 51 Ezra Street, Calcutta, and of Popham's Broadway, Madras, are Indian produce merchants, but they are more than that, as they have for a number of years specialized in certain lines, which have been so satisfactorily managed that they now occupy a very honourable position among traders in the East.

It is nearly fifty years since the firm was established in Madras, and prominence was at that time given to supplying indigo to Europe and other countries, but as this dye was purchased largely in the Province of Bengal, it became necessary to establish a temporary office in Calcutta. It was shortly after this time that German *Badishe*, or synthetic indigo, was placed on the Indian market, and the firm then realized that if they were to retain their trade in the natural dye it was necessary that a permanent office should be opened in Calcutta, and this further accommodation was secured about the year 1900.

The general business of the firm has expanded very rapidly indeed, and while the partners are, in every sense of the word, Indian produce merchants, they may be described concisely as general merchants, commission agents, and exporters of tea, indigo, hides, cotton, skins (raw and tanned), gunnies, and other merchandise. The firm's branch in Madras deals in and exports very large quantities of indigo, ground-nuts, oil seeds of various kinds, condiments, and hides and skins; while buying agencies have been established at Malabar and Cannanore, in Southern India, for the purchase of all kinds of Indian produce. Skins and hides are either sold in the raw state or are tanned for consignment to Europe, Japan, and America.

The turnover of the firm in the above-mentioned articles is very considerable, but it is in the buying and selling of tea that Messrs. Ispahani & Sons hold one of the leading positions among Calcutta merchants. They purchase large quantities at the auction sales in Calcutta, and in normal years the amount exported by them from these sales is not exceeded by more than two or three other firms in the city.

Godowns and stores in Calcutta and at Kidderpore are available for the storage of skins, hides, tea, and other goods, and the firm's bright, airy, and commodious offices in Ezra Street are within a couple of minutes' walk of the Royal Exchange and other centres where business men are in the habit of congregating. The Madras premises are admirably adapted for trade purposes, and they are not more than about 300 yards distant from the harbour and the joint station of the Madras and Southern Mahratta and the Southern Indian Railway systems.

There are three partners in the firm: Mr. M. H. Ispahani is in charge of the London offices at 21 Mincing Lane, E.C., Mr. M. M. Ispahani is supreme in Calcutta, and Mr. M. A. Ispahani looks after the Madras establishment.

Several hundred labourers are constantly employed under the direction of three European assistants.

JEEWANLALL & CO.

Comparatively few years have elapsed since aluminium ware of all kinds for domestic and other purposes became a recognized feature in the markets of the world, and, like other novelties, it was subjected to a considerable amount of keen criticism and even prejudice, not alone from cutlers, ironmongers, chinaware dealers, and others who had goods to sell, but from private individuals as well. The inherent qualities of the metal have, however, been fully recognized, and the extent to which it has replaced other substances, especially in connection with culinary and other utensils of a similar character, is strong evidence of its claims to superiority.

Messrs. Jeewanlall & Co., of 55 Canning Street, Calcutta, are sole agents in Bengal for the "Crown" brand aluminium wares manufactured by the Indian Alumininum Company, Ltd., of Madras, who produce goods from British aluminium of a guaranteed purity of more than 99 per cent. Their business was commenced in an unassuming manner in the year 1910, the partners, Messrs. Jeewanlall Motichand, Durlabhdas Ramjee, Ramjee Hunsraj, and Harakchand Motichand, dealing in aluminium ware, with the purchase and sale of rice as a branch department.

The proprietors determined at the commencement of their commercial life in Calcutta that they would have nothing whatever to do with any other aluminium goods than those manufactured from superior metal imported from England, and this is undoubtedly the secret of the successful enterprise which is now established on so firm a basis. In strolling through the Cannon Street stores or the branch shop at C 53 in the Stewart Hogg Market, one notices *degchies*, saucepans, stewpans, trays of various descriptions, tumblers, ice-pails, pie and butter dishes, milk-cans, teapots, kettles, cups, saucers, tiffin-carriers, basins, jugs, hot-water bottles, knives, forks, spoons, and a host of other useful articles. The firm have, by their consistent dealing in thoroughly reliable goods, built up a large connection in Calcutta, while the Mofussil trade, which is extending rapidly, is in the hands of Mr. D. P. Desai, travelling agent and assistant to the manager.

Tenders have been submitted by the firm for the supply of aluminium articles, and contracts have subsequently been entered into with naval and regimental messes, hospitals, public institutions of a charitable or reformatory order, gun and shell factories, and railway and navigation companies and others, and the partners have been gratified by the receipt of numerous unsolicited testimonials as to the satisfaction given.

A large stock is kept on hand in godowns in Canning Street and at 32 and 43 Ezra Street, and from fifteen to twenty assistants are employed under the supervision of Mr. Jeewanlall Motichand, who is general manager.

The firm are, further, agents for the well-known "Elephant" brand of aluminium wares manufactured by Messrs. Walter N. Cresswell & Co., of Bombay.

Messrs. Jeewanlall & Co. are now importing aluminium goods from England, America, and Japan, and they are about to undertake other agencies for foreign merchants.

KAR & CO.

This firm of engineers and contractors was established in the year 1906 by Mr. Upendra Nath Kar, M.A., B.E., the present managing proprietor, who had a very brilliant career as a student in general and engineering subjects. He obtained several open scholarships, studied for three sessions at the Engineering College, Sibpur, and subsequently obtained degrees, medals, and further scholarships, which enabled him to prosecute researches in electrical engineering.

Mr. Kar served as executive engineer in the Holkar State, where his services were highly appreciated by the Indore Durbar. His work in the decoration and lighting arrangements for the reception of His Highness the Prince of Wales at Indore was fully recognized by Major Daly, the then agent to the Governor-General of Central India. During this service Mr. Kar very successfully designed and executed a flat bridge of reinforced concrete.

Business was commenced in 1906 with works and offices at Canning House, 137 Canning Street, Calcutta, and since that time the firm have been engaged in contracts for many very important works, chief among which are drainage works at Baraset, Barnagar, Kamarhatty, Gya, Monghyr, and the Corporation of Calcutta; waterworks at Naihati and Gya; the erection of railway buildings at Kanchrapara and Gangnapur; the construction of an institute, manager's quarters, schools, and bungalows for the Tata Iron and Steel Company, Sakchi; the erection of gaol works at Monghyr; police buildings at Sakchi; post-offices at the same place and at Gya; and the building of godowns, boiler-house, coolie lines, engine-house, and other structures for the Reliance and Kamarhatty Jute Mills.

Special reference might be made to the Gya Waterworks scheme, the principal feature of which was the construction of two reinforced concrete reservoirs on the Mangla Gouri Hills at a height of 139 ft. above the level of the town. Each reservoir has an inside diameter of 65 ft., and contains 400,000 gallons of water, and it should be added that these two were the first of their kind and size to be put up in India.

The general manager of the Tata Iron and Steel Company, Ltd., writing on January 25, 1916, said that Messrs. Kar & Co. had done a considerable amount of very satisfactory building work for the company, and, further, that the erection of the "Mrs. Perin Memorial School" building was a noteworthy example of their energy, as they completed the first story from the foundation in one month, in order to have the building in shape to be formally opened by His Excellency the Lieutenant-Governor of Behar and Orissa during his visit to Sakchi in April 1915. The officiating sanitary engineer of Bengal, in a letter dated September 1, 1913, certified that Messrs. Kar & Co. had been engaged under the Government Drainage and Waterworks Department on the construction of waterworks and sewerage schemes for the Gya Municipality for the previous two years, and that the scheme was completed to his satisfaction. The total cost of the works was about Rs. 300,000.

Very extensive repairs and renewals were completed by this firm at the General Hospital, Howrah, a few years ago, and Lieutenant-Colonel A. H. Nott, I.M.S., secretary and superintendent, stated in writing on May 14, 1910, that "the supervising authorities were well satisfied with the character of the work." Extracts could be given from hundreds of other testimonials received acknowledging the excellent work of this firm, but, after all, the most valuable tribute is the fact that these buildings and water and other schemes are bearing witness to-day to the skill and the conscientious service of the contractors.

Messrs. Kar & Co. have several important contracts in hand at the present time, and reference may be made to (1) the building of a college at Pabna, the foundation stone of which was laid early this year (1916) by Mr. H. F. Samman, I.C.S., Commissioner of the division of Rajshahi; (2) drainage works at Katwa; (3) the erection of Zilla School at Balasore; (4) new roads for the Calcutta Corporation; and (5) road and other works to the Tata Iron and Steel Company.

The firm have brickfields at Gangnapur, via Ranaghat, on the Eastern Bengal Railway, and at Kalimati, Bengal-Nagpur Railway, together with a *soorkee* mill at Gangnapur, while their wood manufacturing concern is also established at Kalimati.

The assistant manager is Mr. A. Dass Gupta, B.E., formerly district engineer of Chaibasi, in the district of Singbhum.

The telegraphic address of the firm is "Karcompy," Calcutta.

L. H. LILLARAM & CO.

One frequently reads in books, or hears in conversation, of the wealth of India.

KAR & CO.

1. Pumping Station, Gaya Waterworks. 2. Tata Iron & Steel Company's Institute, Sakchi. 3. Reinforced Concrete Reservoir, Gaya. 4. School Building, Tata Iron & Steel Company. 5. Manager's Quarters, Tata Iron & Steel Company, Sakchi. 6. Foundation Ceremony, Reservoir, Gaya Waterworks.

L. H. LILLARAM & CO.

1. Workshop. 2 Exterior of Show-room. 3. Interior. 4. Mr. Lillaram's Sons.

The wealth of this country could never be reduced to plain figures; it is too fabulous and too rich in variety. Many hundreds of years ago classical authors wrote of the magnificence of its precious stones and metals, and the heirlooms of diamonds, pearls, rubies, and other brilliants which are to-day in the possession of a large number of rulers of independent States bear abundant testimony to the truth of this. And now in the twentieth century every city and town has its goldsmiths and silversmiths. Calcutta has a due proportion of these, and foremost among them is the well-known firm of Messrs. L. H. Lillaram & Co., of 6 and 7 Park Street.

The business was established about the year 1875, on a somewhat small scale, at No. 6 in the same street, but as those premises were required for the extension of a building belonging to other merchants, possession was obtained of the present building, in which the shop and warehouses, covering a large area of ground, have a very extensive frontage on a thoroughfare which is in the most fashionable centre of the city.

The eye is almost dazzled on entering the spacious showrooms, where cabinet after cabinet is stocked with a marvellous assortment of valuable goods, among which are necklaces, pendants, bracelets, rings, brooches, ear-rings, and pins, set with diamonds, rubies, pearls, sapphires, opals, emeralds, and amethysts; silver caskets, rose-bowls, dishes, trays, tea-sets, presentation cups, smokers' requisites, writing-desk articles, mirrors, brushes, toilet and scent jars, liqueur stands, photograph frames, and a host of other beautiful things.

The Oriental and general department contains a fine selection of Indian, Japanese, and Chinese embroideries; Rampur, Kashmir, and other shawls; Indian, Maltese, and Ceylonese laces; high-class Bukhora, Persian, Indian, and Turkish silk carpets; brassware; finely carved goods from Japan, Thibet, Jeypore, Moradabad, and Benares; and Indian carved wood furniture; together with antique and modern curios from Burma and other countries.

Intending purchasers of jewellery or art treasures would be exceedingly difficult to please if they were unable to obtain exactly what they required in this establishment; but Messrs. Lilaram & Co. do more than keep a stock of manufactured goods, as they are always prepared to make jewellery, caskets, mugs, bracelets, and many other articles according to special designs submitted by their patrons. Diamonds of the highest possible quality are obtained from Native States of India, but others, together with certain kinds of jewellery, are imported from Europe. A very large stock of every variety of precious stones, valued at between five and six lakhs of rupees, is kept by the firm, whose customers include Indian and European notabilities hailing from every part of the country.

Highly skilled workers in gold and silver are employed in the manufacture of special articles, while the regular staff consists of about 200 persons.

The firm bestow the greatest care in connection with orders received through the post, and goods sent on approval, on deposit of their approximate value, or to well-known correspondents, are effectively insured before dispatch.

Mr. Lilaram is assisted in the management of the business by his two sons and Mr. S. Edwards.

J. F. MADAN

Prominent in the ranks of those who have achieved success in the commercial world in Calcutta is Mr. J. F. Madan, of 5 Dhurrumtollah Street, who was the pioneer of picture palaces in that city, and who has, further, established one of the largest wholesale and retail purveyor's businesses in Bengal. This gentleman's early educational career was terminated abruptly by reason of the very serious financial losses of his father owing to the failure of the Bombay Land Reclamation Bank, but this catastrophe did not turn out to be a misfortune for young Madan, as it threw him upon his own resources, and brought to the front latent qualifications which he was not slow in turning to good account. He began by securing a minor position, at a small salary, with a theatrical company, and here he gradually worked his way upwards until he was offered a partnership in the year 1875 in conjunction with Dr. N. N. Parekh, Mr. Sakloth, and Mr. D. M. Wacha. Six years later he—without entirely severing his connection with the stage—began to visit cities and towns in India for the purpose of buying up stocks of merchandise which were advertised for public competition, and his sound judgment and keen insight enabled him to acquire a very considerable amount of profit.

These transactions paved the way for the establishment of a mercantile partnership between Mr. Sakloth and himself, which continued for two years until 1885, when Mr. Madan opened a place of business on his own account at 5 Dhurrumtollah Street.

All kinds of provisions and household requisites of all descriptions were imported regularly, and he soon established a reputation for supplying goods of first-class quality at reasonable rates. The business grew very rapidly, and the requirements of customers in even remote parts of India were met with that promptitude in dispatch which has ever been one of the chief characteristics of Mr. Madan, who can with confidence claim that he is the largest importer in Bengal of household goods and consumable stores. He publishes a voluminous price list monthly, which gives full particulars of the many articles he sells.

Mr. Madan is purveyor to regimental messes, depots, restaurants, co-operative stores, leading clubs, steamship companies, and to the trade generally, and he has been instrumental in the opening of shops in numerous places in Bengal and the United Provinces. Branches have been established at 35 Park Street, 52 Garden Reach Circular Road, and 3 Store Road, Ballygunge, all in or near Calcutta; at Piroj Villa, Post Office Road, and the Stores, Chowrasta, both in Darjeeling; at the Exchange Building, in Lucknow; and in the Mall, at Delhi. He is one of the largest and most reliable contractors for the supply of nearly all sorts of goods to the supply and transport corps, and he is also sole agent for the Asiatic Petroleum Company, Ltd., in Bareilly, Pilibhit, Shahjahanpur, Haldwani, Lucknow, Chandausi, Sitapur, Cawnpore, Delhi, and Darjeeling. Mr. Madan is now dealing largely in all kinds of gram, ghee, and other produce, and the business in these lines has grown to such an extent that he has been compelled to make use of several godowns in native commercial quarters.

Thousands of testimonials have been received from commanding officers, superintendents of Army dry canteens, and private individuals, and all of these letters speak in terms of highest praise as to the excellent quality of Mr. Madan's goods, and as to the unexampled manner in which large or small orders are executed. Special significance, however, is attached to a letter dated April 11, 1913, from the Controller of the Household of His Excellency the Right Hon. Baron

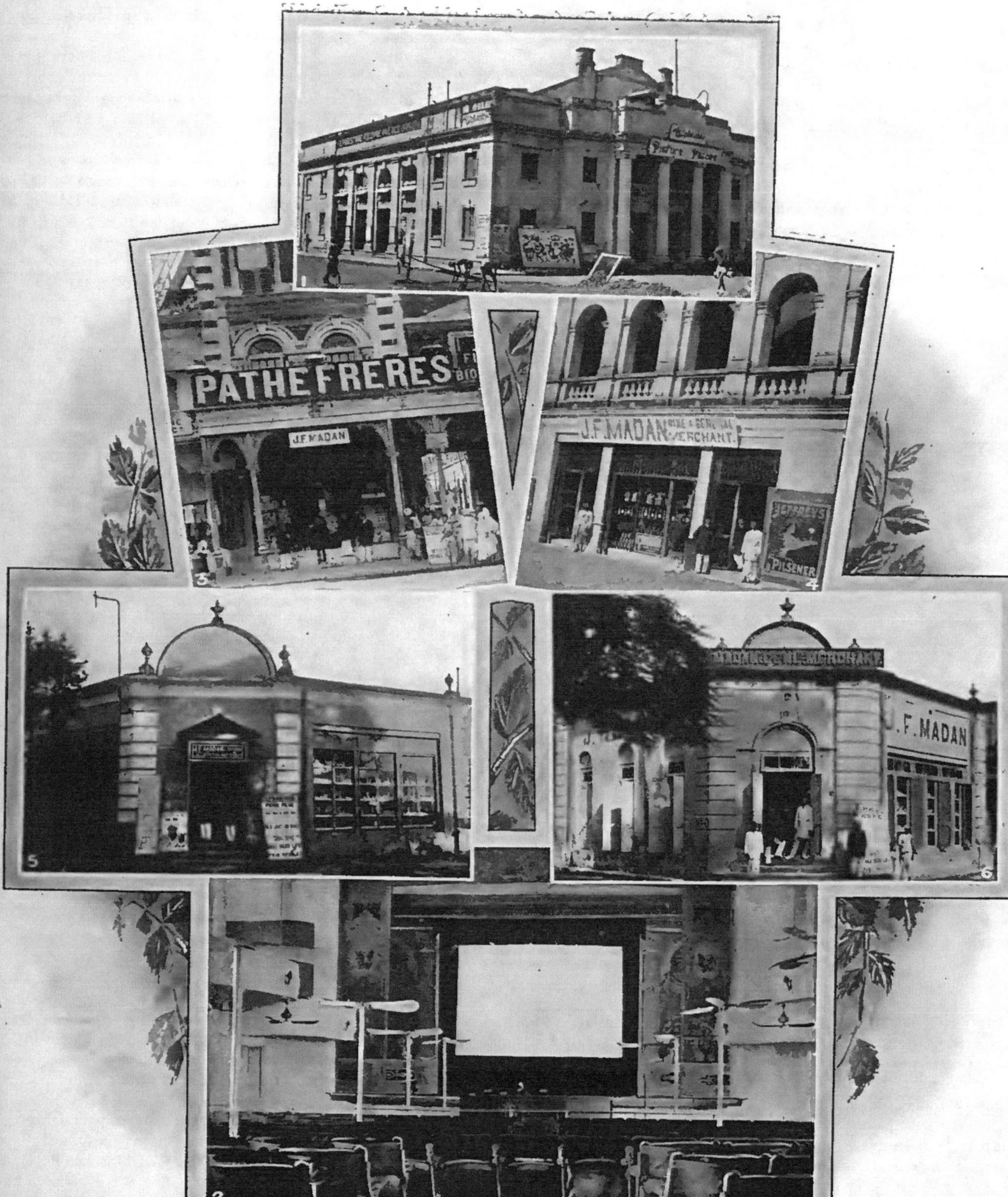

J. F. MADAN.

1. The Elphinstone Picture Palace. 2. Interior of the Elphinstone Picture Palace. 3. Head Office, 5 Dhurrumtollah Street. 4. Branch at 35 Park Street. 5. Kidderpore Branch. 6. Branch at 3 Store Road, Ballygunge

Hardinge of Penshurst, the late Viceroy, in which Mr. Madan is appointed purveyor of wines and oilman's stores; and to another communication from the Military Secretary to His Excellency the Right Hon. Baron Carmichael of Skirling, Governor of Bengal, wherein "His Excellency is pleased to appoint Mr. J. F. Madan, of Calcutta, to be purveyor in ordinary, and he is authorized to style himself purveyor in ordinary accordingly."

Reference has already been made to Mr. Madan's pioneer work in connection with picture palaces, and it will be of interest to note that he is the sole proprietor of the Elphinstone Picture Palace in Chowringee Place, Calcutta. This fine building, surrounded by the leading hotels, clubs, and residential mansion suites, has separate chair accommodation for two thousand persons, together with twelve private boxes, two Zenana boxes, and an exceedingly comfortable gallery. Two performances are given daily in this hall, and the crowds of people who attend are certain of witnessing the very latest productions in the picture world, as Mr. Madan has secured exclusive rights from film-producing firms of the highest repute. Two other picture palaces in Calcutta cater entirely for the Indian population, and, during the winter months, another entertainment is provided in a tent on the Maidan, which is close to Government House. Mr. Madan is also the owner of the Elphinstone Picture Palace in Rangoon (which is practically a copy of the one of the same name in Calcutta), and he is at the present time constructing a similar place of amusement in Mount Road, Madras, while his representatives are touring throughout India with up-to-date machinery, apparatus, and films.

Mr. Madan was an exhibitor of pictures by Royal command before their Majesties the King and Queen at Government House, Calcutta, during the Coronation Durbar in 1911, and the Controller of the Viceroy's Household, writing on February 2, 1912, said that "the exhibition was much appreciated by their Majesties."

The "Kok" drawing-room cinematograph, which is said to be the most perfect and the safest apparatus for home entertainment, is supplied, together with all accessories, by Mr. Madan.

Engagements to give bioscope performances at *nautch*, marriage, and private evening parties are undertaken at the shortest notice, and in this way Mr. Madan is affording enjoyment to hundreds of persons who, possibly, never have the opportunity of attending public entertainments.

P. C. MITTER & CO.

1. Sand Filters under Construction for Howrah Municipality at Serampore.
2. Tumbling Weirs and Settling Tanks under Construction for Howrah Municipality.
3. Laying 24-in. Steel Main for Howrah Municipality in the Grand Trunk Road.
4. Façade of Rai Bahadur T. N. Sadhu's Residence, Calcutta.

P. C. MITTER & CO.

One of the most promising of the younger firms in the mercantile world in Calcutta is that of Messrs. P. C. Mitter & Co., of 98 Clive Street, whose business as civil, sanitary, and waterworks engineers, architects, iron founders, brick manufacturers, and quarrying and general contractors was in the year 1908 founded by Mr. P. C. Mitter, B.E., who threw into the concern the full weight of his previous practical experience in engineering and other work gained during his connection with some of the leading firms in the city.

The firm have completed many large schemes in sanitary, drainage, and construction work, and reference may be made to a few of these important undertakings. They provided the Municipality of Jessore with a waterworks system which included the intake and distributing arrangements, together with the building of a clear-water reservoir; they were responsible for the Howrah Waterworks Improvement Scheme, constructing settling tanks, filters, and laying 24-in. steel main pipes for a distance of more than twelve miles (costing about four lakhs of rupees); they erected the "Orion" soap factory at Paikpara, and the Raja Bazaar market, off Upper Circular Road in Calcutta; blocks were also constructed for warehouses at Barra Bazaar, and residential houses of an imposing character have been built for Ray Bahadur Tarak Nath Sadhu, Babu Nagendra Nath Palit, and many other leading citizens.

A major portion of the Government buildings and ironworks designed for Monghyr Central Jail, estimated to cost about forty lakhs of rupees, was entrusted to them, but the contract was suspended while the works were in progress owing to the project being abandoned in consequence of the separation of the Governments of Bengal and Behar.

Messrs. Mitter & Co. quarried and supplied about 20,00,000 cubic feet of standard pitching boulders for the famous Hardinge Bridge—more than a mile in length—which spans the Lower Ganges River at Sara and connects the broad-gauge system of the Eastern Bengal Railway south of the Ganges with the railways to the north of that river.

The firm have carried out several drainage, sanitation, and waterworks systems for municipalities and village boards throughout the Province of Bengal, and they employ from 300 to 500 labourers, according to the extent of works on hand. Their iron foundry and workshops are situated at Salkeah, near Calcutta, and they import from England a considerable quantity of construction materials and sanitary and other appliances.

Mr. P. Mitter has supreme control over every branch of work, and he is assisted by eight or ten supervisors and clerks. The telegraphic address of the firm is "Eximpeer, Calcutta."

K. P. MOOKERJEE & CO.

This firm is credited with the honour of being the oldest established engravers in the city of Calcutta, and they make a speciality of engraving on presentation articles, as well as on all kinds of metals, wood, brass, brass and silver stamps and badges, and upon half-tone, line, and tri-colour blocks. The manufacture of rubber stamps is another leading feature of the firm's industries.

Mr. Kally Prasanna Mookerjee, the proprietor of the firm, started business life in 1868 by entering the engraving shop of his father, the late Babu Durga Das Mookerjee, who had inherited the property from his maternal uncle, H. C. Gangooly, who left Calcutta in 1857 in order to illustrate the *Comus* newspaper, then being edited by one Captain Moore, and he died at Delhi.

Mr. K. P. Mookerjee named the firm H. C. Gangooly & Co. to perpetuate the name of his grand-uncle (who, by the way, had opened the engraving shop in the year 1833), and he conducted the business for twenty-two years with great success, drawing to it many of the most prominent persons of India. He then retired in favour of his younger brothers, and commenced trading on his own account as K. P. Mookerjee & Co.

KALLY PRASANNA MOOKERJEE,
Proprietor of K. P. Mookerjee & Co.

The firm have commodious premises at 7 Waterloo Street, in the very heart of the city, and they are described as stationers, printers, and dealers in fancy goods, perfumery, jewellery, pictures, mouldings, and miscellaneous goods, the majority of which are imported from England. The printing press is engaged in artistic and general jobbing, and in turning out books of all descriptions.

Messrs. Mookerjee & Co. also undertake painting in oils, the enlarging and colouring of photographs, and the framing of pictures. The commission agency department is being extended very rapidly, and goods of all kinds are regularly imported for customers, while their wide circle of patrons and friends includes residents in England, France, Italy, and other European countries.

S. C. MOOKERJEE & CO.

A builder's and contractor's business was established in Calcutta in the year 1891 by the late Mr. Shama Charan Mookerjee, who made a special feature of supplying the Bengal Government Public Works Department, railway systems, and jute and other mills with wood and iron works, and constructing entire jute-mills, flour-mills, etc.

The founder's practical experience gained him the support of a large number of patrons, and his sons, Messrs. Amrita Lal Mookerjee and Chuni Lal Mookerjee, who are now joint proprietors, have not merely succeeded their father in a business venture which has been particularly successful, but they have, in the management of it, fully maintained the high reputation which attached to it on their taking up the reins of government.

The firm have excellent offices and godowns at 10 Sukea's Lane, off Radha Bazar Street, together with a foundry, timber-yard, and works at 267 Grand Trunk Road, Sibpur, near Calcutta.

S. C. MOOKERJEE & CO.
WORKSHOPS.

BUTTO KRISTO PAUL & CO.

"Calcutta can at least boast of one pharmacy organized and financed solely by Indian brain and capital, which, only through unstinted honesty of purpose and dogged perseverance of its founder-proprietor, has fully won the confidence and esteem of even the Western world." This quotation from the *Indian Medical Record* of October 1909 has reference to the business of the highly-respected firm of Butto Kristo Paul & Co., at 7 Bonfield's Lane and other addresses in the city of Calcutta.

About the middle of the nineteenth century a small single-storied shop in Khengraputty Street, Calcutta, was occupied by Mr. Butto Kristo Paul, who was a dealer in miscellaneous goods, usually denominated "smalls," but his keen observation led him to see that European medicines and Western methods of treatment in sickness and disease must eventually supersede indigenous drugs and Indian systems of applying them. At the same time he realized that, without substantial capital, he would be compelled to purchase his stocks of chemicals from local merchants, and, further, that he would have to contend with a natural prejudice on the part of Indians to foreign goods; but he had the courage of his convictions, and "by honesty of purpose and dogged perseverance" (as the above quotation says) he succeeded in placing upon the market drugs and medicines at the lowest possible prices consistent with purity and freshness.

The firm of B. K. Paul & Co. was then established, and, as the founder of the business had by this time so far improved his financial position that arrangements could be made for direct importations, the new management forthwith indented for a large quantity of genuine drugs, chemicals, proprietary medicines, surgical instruments, and other goods to be supplied by well-known and reliable manufacturers in England.

In the year 1882 Mr. Bhut Nath Paul joined his father, and he at once took upon himself the task of establishing the European connection of the firm on a sound commercial basis, with the result that he secured for the firm a monopoly in the East for the sale of many patent medicines of proved efficacy. Shortly after this time the firm secured a commodious building at 7 Bonfield's Lane, to which a very large proportion of the business was transferred; but notwithstanding these additions there was still a real need for more room, and in 1902 very extensive premises were erected at 12 Bonfield's Lane, in which a homœopathic department has been carried on with considerable success.

The next advance made by the firm was the establishment of a laboratory, which is fitted with up-to-date scientific instruments and apparatus for manufacturing, analytical, and bacteriological work. This department is in the care of two highly-qualified chemists.

Still forging ahead, the firm subsequently opened an optical department for supplying spectacles (after examination by competent ophthalmists), artificial eyes, magnifying and opera glasses, microscopes, and other scientific instruments. In 1907 the Ayurvedic, or Hindu indigenous, method of treatment was taken in hand, and a well-equipped dispensary was placed under the charge of an experienced and capable *kabiraj*.

These brief particulars will suffice to show that the insignificant little business in Khengraputty Street has developed into an enormous concern, and the unpretentious shop—perhaps 10 by 12 ft.—has been superseded by the following extensive buildings: 120 and 121 Khengraputty Street, with a floor area of 448 sq. ft.; 7 Bonfield's Lane, 13.920, 48,276, and 46,818 ft.; 16 and 17 China Bazar Lane, 20,640 ft.; 30 Sova Bazar Street, 17,700 ft.; and 18 Soshi Bhusan

B. K. PAUL & CO.

1, 2. Exterior of Main Premises. 3. Interior Second Floor Store-room.
4. Interior of Store-room and Sale Department (Second Floor). 5. Godown.

Soor's Lane, 6,600 ft.; making a total of 154,402 sq. ft.

It may be mentioned here that on the occasion of the visit of their Majesties the King and Queen to Calcutta in 1911, Messrs. Paul & Co. were selected by the Imperial Reception Committee to establish a fully equipped camp dispensary and hospital for the gratuitous supply of medicines and for rendering free medical aid to retainers who took part in the pageant, as well as to any of the vast concourse of persons who attended the ceremony.

Mr. Edmund White, President of the Pharmaceutical Society of Great Britain, after a visit to the various places of business of this firm, wrote on October 28, 1914:—

"During my stay in India I had many opportunities of studying the conditions under which pharmacy was practised in the East. The firm of Butto Kristo Paul & Co. is well known in England, but until I saw their establishments in Calcutta I had no conception of the magnitude of the business carried on by this deservedly successful firm. I was indebted to the courtesy of Mr. H. D. Nag for many interesting explanations of the methods of business in the East, and this gentleman also conducted me over the numerous premises controlled by this firm. . . . The chief features which arrested my attention were the overflowing stream of customers, the scientific and progressive organization of the business, the activity in the dispatch department, and the systematic handling of the dispensing of physician's prescriptions. . . . I feel that my visit to India would not have been complete without this entertaining visit, which showed how much could be done by combining Indian and English methods of business, and adapting them both to the needs of progressive Indian pharmacy."

Messrs. Paul & Co. are chemists and druggists by appointment to His Excellency the Right Hon. Baron Hardinge of Penshurst, ex-Viceroy of India, and His Excellency Baron Carmichael of Skirling, the Governor of Bengal, and their regular and distinguished clients include the Presidency General Hospital, the Medical College Hospital, the Campbell Hospital, the Police and Albert Victor Hospital, all in Calcutta; Colonial Governments, civil surgeons, District Boards, Municipalities, and Government offices, together with a number of native princes, nobles, and other dignitaries. One might add that in the year 1906 the firm were appointed chemists and druggists to the Right Hon. the Earl of Minto, then Viceroy and Governor-General, and this honourable distinction had never previously been conferred upon an Indian firm engaged in a similar kind of business.

Mr. Bhut Nath Paul, the present head of the firm, is assisted by his two brothers, Messrs. Hari Sankar Paul and Hari Mohal Paul, and constant work is found for between five and six hundred employees.

RAHIMBUX & MOHAMMED IBRAHIM.

1. Exterior of New Premises. 2. Old Premises, Ruttoo Sircar's Lane. 3. S. Fazal Ellahi.

RAHIMBUX & MOHAMMED IBRAHIM

A strict attention to business is invariably accompanied by success, and in Calcutta and other cities in India there are numberless instances of extensive profitable trading enterprises which have been developed from very small beginnings.

In the year 1887 Messrs. Haji Ahmed Jan, Rahimbux, Jewanbux, and Khodabux, established themselves as partners under the title of Messrs. Rahimbux and Mohammed Ibrahim (the son of Mr. Jewanbux), dealing in oilman's stores, which they imported from the United Kingdom.

The capital with which the business was commenced proved to be somewhat inadequate for a concern which began to grow rapidly almost from the time of its foundation, but the deficiency in finances was to some extent counterbalanced by the indefatigable energy of Mr. Haji Ahmed Jan, who, as managing proprietor, devoted himself whole-heartedly to the interests of the firm. Strictly straightforward conduct was conspicuous in all transactions, and in order to meet the increasing demands of customers the firm extended the scope of their activities by adding to their stock large quantities of perfumes, patent medicines, toilet requisites, cigarettes, and other articles of every day use.

Haji Ahmed Jan gave thirty years of the best portion of his life for the good of the firm, and on his retirement from active service, his son, Mr. Fazal Ellahi, who had inherited keen business qualifications, stepped into the vacant position.

As very large quantities of all kinds of goods have to be imported, owing to the enlarged business connections of the firm, the partners are able to obtain rebate on most favourable terms, and therefore they are in a position to offer their commodities at a cheaper rate than they could do if they were only purchasing limited supplies.

Mr. Khodabux died in the year 1913, and his share in the partnership was handed over to his legal heirs.

The firm occupy a shop at 49/1 Rattu Sirkar's Lane, in Calcutta, in addition to new buildings recently opened at 4 Ram Mohan Ghose's Lane, which are used as a godown and dispatching department.

M. RITA & CO.

Not more than five years have elapsed since Messrs. Rita & Co. commenced business at 9 Hastings Street, Calcutta, as agents for the sale of the "Royal" typewriter and as importers and dealers in rebuilt second-hand typewriter machines and their accessories, but the practical experience of the partners and the energy which they have displayed have secured for them a reputation equal to that of any other firm of a similar character in Eastern India.

Further accommodation soon became necessary owing to the very rapid expansion of the business, and they were fortunate enough to secure a commodious workshop at 8/2 Hastings Street, in the same city. The firm have obtained up-to-date machinery for effecting all kinds of repairs, and it would be a difficult matter to hand over to them a typewriter so much out of order that they would be unable to return it in a completely renovated state.

Messrs. Rita & Co. are now sole agents for machines manufactured by Messrs. L. C. Smith & Brothers, and they are sole importers of general stationery and other goods, all of which are known by the name of "Ritaco," and these include ribbon and carbon papers, clipless paper fasteners, and fountain and stylo-pens. They are also commission agents, exporters of Indian produce, and importers of general merchandise, and they deal largely in articles made by the Caribonum Company, Ltd.

Branches or agencies have been established at Bombay, Srinagore, Bankipore, Muzaffarpur, Cocanada, and, in fact, nearly all of the principal cities and towns in India, and their representatives travel throughout the Provinces of Bengal and Behar and Orissa.

The proprietors are Messrs. S. Mukerjee & Brothers, and their telegraphic address is "Ritaco, Calcutta."

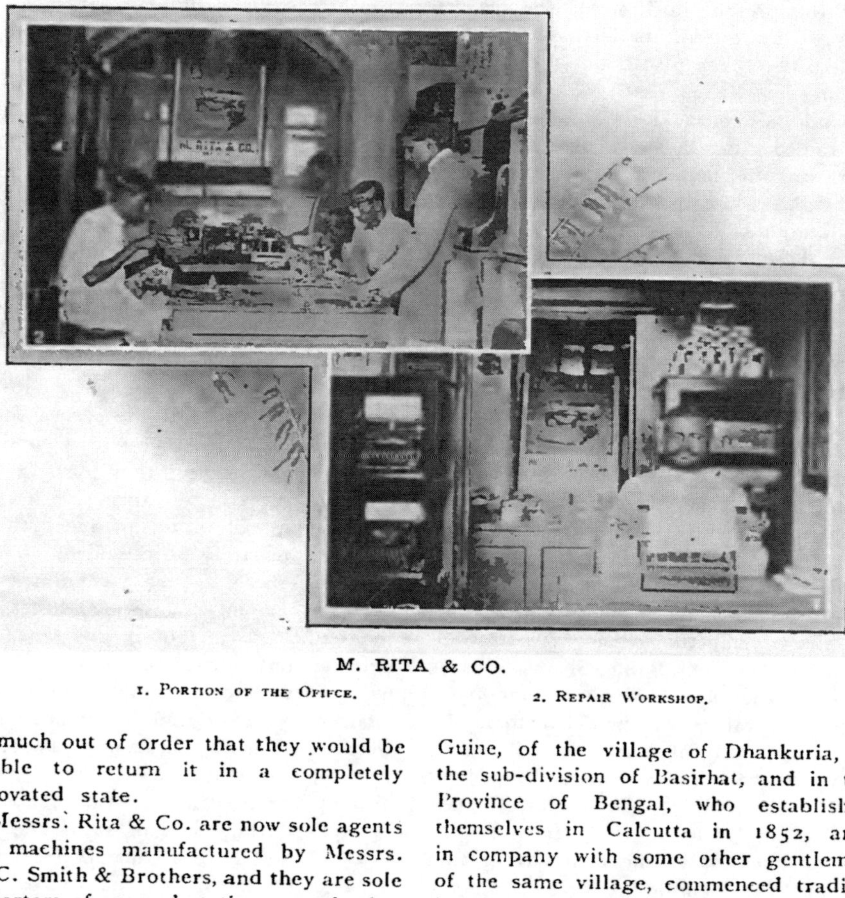

M. RITA & CO.

1. Portion of the Office. 2. Repair Workshop.

P. C. AND W. SAWOO

The extensive business of this firm owes its origin to the untiring energy and honest industry of the late Babus Patit Chandra Sawoo and Gobindo Chandra Guine, of the village of Dhankuria, in the sub-division of Basirhat, and in the Province of Bengal, who established themselves in Calcutta in 1852, and, in company with some other gentlemen of the same village, commenced trading in *ghee*, flour, and country sugar with a nominal capital. A few years later, as the business prospered, they included seeds, and afterwards jute, which was commencing to be an important commodity at the time. About the year 1865 Babu Shama Charan Ballav, the son-in-law of Patit Chandra Sawoo, was admitted into the concern, and some years after the other co-sharers left the firm except Patit Babu, Govindo Babu, and Shama Babu. Owing to the subsequent deaths of Babus Govindo Chandra and Patit Chandra the entire management devolved upon Babu Shama Charan Ballav, who had already displayed a remarkable aptitude for business, and then the company was reconstituted under the name and style of Messrs. P. G. and W. Sawoo, with Babus Patit Chandra Sawoo, Govindo Chandra Guine, and Shama Charan Ballav as partners. Babu Nafar Chandra Guine, the second son of Govindo Babu, was also admitted at this time, and most actively co-operated with him as a working partner. It was to the exceptional genius and ceaseless activity of Babu Shama Charan Ballav that the present position of the firm is mainly due, and if its business may be said to have been placed on a solid foundation by Babus Patit Chandra and Govindo Chandra, it was Babu Shama Charan to whom must be given the credit of raising the immense superstructure to a height scarcely anticipated by his predecessors.

In the early days of the jute industry the original partners of the firm realized its great commercial possibilities. Babu Shama Charan was among those who took advantage of the new enterprise, and, being advised by him, the partners began by hiring the Golabari Press from Messrs. Finlay, Muir & Co., of Calcutta. Several other presses were subsequently, and from time to time, hired by the partners. Numerous agencies for purchasing jute direct from the cultivators and local traders were established in almost all the jute-producing districts of Bengal, and, to give an impetus to the extensive cultivation of jute, Babu Shama Charan adopted the system of giving out *dadan* (money advances) to the cultivators. He introduced several marks for the bales, of which the "Ballav," which headed the list, still occupies the foremost place among the group in the market.

The business of the firm having thus attained considerable proportions, Messrs. P. G. and W. Sawoo in the year 1891 purchased the Jheel Press at Cossipore, on the east bank of the Hooghly, and not more than two miles distant from Calcutta. There were five Nasmith patent pressing machines in the building at the time of purchase, but the partners subsequently discarded one of these and secured two of a more up-to-date character, known by the name of "Watson's Patent Press," and, as the accommodation on the Jheel property was quite inadequate for the firm's increasing business, they utilized adjoining land, and erected godowns (with room for 12,000 bales) and other premises in order that they might be able to meet the exigencies of expanding trade. The press was originally only able to turn out about 800 bales of fibre daily, but with enlarged buildings the presses can now deal with some 2,000 bales in the same period. A private jetty on the river enables the firm to secure quick transport of raw jute from up-country boats to the factory, and special facilities are obtained by the firm having their own launch and cargo boat for conveying bales to ocean-going steamers and to mills up and down the river.

In 1896 Babu Nafar Chandra Guine died, and Babu Aukshoy Kumar Guine, the youngest son of Babu Govindo Chandra Guine, joined the firm to assist Shama Charan Babu in working the concern. The death of Babu Shama Charan, which followed three years after, came as a great shock; but Rai Bahadoor Woopendra Nath Sawoo (the son of Patit Babu), along with Babu Mahendra Nath Guine (the third son of Govinda Babu), took up the charge of managing the business, and with their joint efforts and activity, carried on upon the lines of their enterprising predecessors, maintained the business with continued success; and in 1903 they purchased the Ashcroft Press, by the side of the Hooghly at Chitpore, to meet the increasing demands of the firm.

The Ashcroft Press contained two Watson's patent presses, and although the buildings, including godowns, were unfortunately burned to the ground about five years later, premises of a more modern character and of greater extent were subsequently erected. These two presses, which are now in constant use, are capable of dealing with 1,000 bales in every working day of 12 hours. The new godowns have a capacity for storing about 8,000 bales. The packed bales are carted from the press to the bank of the river, where they are placed on cargo lighters, or flats, whence they are distributed in a similar manner to that which obtains at the Jheel premises, and also by wagons to the Kidderpore Docks and loaded direct on ocean-going steamers.

The Jheel and Ashcroft Presses are fitted throughout with electric light and telephonic connections, and when the baling of jute is at its busiest season of the year, about four and five hundred hands are employed constantly at the respective places.

In 1910, Rai Bahadoor Woopendra Nath Sawoo having retired owing to illness (which afterwards resulted in his death in 1915), Rai Bahadoor Debendra Nath Ballav (the eldest son of Babu Shama Charan) joined the firm to relieve him. The business of the firm is at present under the management of the partners Babus Mahendra Nath Guine, Aukshoy Kumar Guine, and Rai Bahadoor Debendra Nath Ballav, the proprietorship being confined to the families of Rai Bahadoors Woopendra Nath Sawoo and Debendra Nath Ballav, and of Babus Mahendra Nath Guine and Aukshoy Kumar Guine as before.

THE SHAM SUNDAR RICE MILL

The members of the firm of Messrs. P. G. and W. Sawoo have individually as well as collectively shown an intelligent interest and keen ability in commercial enterprises, and as a further illustration of these qualifications reference may be made to the Sham Sundar rice-mill, situated at Tollygunge, on the bank of the Addi Ganges River, which was purchased in 1914 by Babu Mohendra Nath Guine and Aukshoy Kumar Guine, who are sole proprietors.

Paddy is milled on account of the proprietors themselves and on behalf of other persons, and it is conveyed to the mill in carts or boats from the various centres in which it is grown. The processes include husking, cleaning, and polishing, and there are eight hullers, which have a daily output capacity of rice of 450 maunds. The building is equipped with modern machinery, and the whole of the plant is driven by a 30-h.p. engine by Marshall, Sons & Co., which is fitted with a fire-box specially designed for the consumption of paddy husks as fuel. The boiler, of 25 h.p., is by the same makers. The godowns are unusually extensive, and storage accommodation is easily found for 30,000 maunds of the milled product. All the buildings, in fact, are replete with modern fittings, which include telephonic connection with the Central Telephone Exchange. During the busy season of the year some 225 hands are employed.

H. N. BALAUB & CO.

In 1914 a partnership was entered into between Debendra Nath Balaub and H. N. Balaub (trading as H. N. Balaub & Co.), and in the following year the firm purchased a rice-mill on the bank of the New Cut Canal, and it practically adjoins the Ultadanghi Station on the

P. G. & W. SAWOO.

1. Mohendra Nath Guine. 2. Aukhoy Kumar Guine. 3. Front View of Jheel Press. 4. Jheel Press. 5. Ashcroft Press. 6. Assorting Godown.

Eastern Bengal Railway system. Paddy is boiled before being milled; it is then cleaned and polished, the eight hullers being worked by a plant driven by a 100-h.p. motor engine, the current being obtained from the General Electric Supply Company.

The mill—in conformity with the practice prevailing in Eastern Bengal—is worked for twelve consecutive hours, commencing at 6 a.m., and no fewer than 500 maunds of rice are passed through the machines daily on the account of the partners alone. Paddy is purchased in various parts of Bengal, and is conveyed in carts or canal boats to the factory, whence it is forwarded to local markets for sale. The employees are about 225 in number.

T. P. SEN

Calcutta is not by any means short of photographers, but of artists in photography, of men who really understand the science of their work, of operators who can judge distances to a nicety, can balance lights and shades, and who, above all, can reproduce a really creditable picture, she has a remarkably small number.

Situated in Waterloo Street, a somewhat secluded yet not unimportant thoroughfare, is the studio of Mr. T. P. Sen, which was established twenty-two years ago and which is still carried on under the same name, although the founder has been dead for some years.

Mr. Sen belonged to a very respectable Baidya family, and even as a young man was an exceedingly clever photographer, being well grounded both in theory and practice. Prior to his death, the founder had been assisted by his brother, Mr. R. L. Sen, who had proved himself to be thoroughly well versed in every branch of the business, and when the regrettable separation occurred, the latter took up the management of the concern with the help of his younger brother, Mr. H. D. Sen, whose all-round work in photography, but particularly in connection with illustrations in newspapers and magazines, has secured for the firm widespread fame in England as well as in India.

These two brothers made the best possible use of the helpful advice and instruction given by their late brother, and the enviable reputation gained by them is very largely due to their own diligent and persevering efforts to carry on the business upon the lines originally mapped out by the founder.

Personal photographs, as well as artistic scenic views, sent out from Sen's studio speak for themselves, but the proprietor naturally feels proud of the fact that he has received unsolicited patronage from His Excellency Lord Carmichael, Governor of Bengal, and that a large number of the nobility and gentry of India have shown their keen appreciation of the manner in which their orders have been executed.

C. K. SEN & CO., LTD.

The system of the Ayurvedic treatment of diseases in India, which in other words means the application of medicines prepared from indigenous drugs and herbs, may be "as old as the hills," but it is only within the past thirty or forty years that it has come into prominence as a formidable competitor with Western ideas.

It was the proud boast of ancient India that the pharmacology of her physicians contained reliable prescriptions for the cure of nearly all diseases to which the human body is subject, and it is claimed to-day by the successors of those early practitioners that present methods of treatment of ailments are just as efficacious as they were in bygone ages. There is no other firm in the East which has done so much to popularize the Ayurvedic system as Messrs. C. K. Sen & Co., Ltd., of 29 Colootollah Street, Calcutta, whose pharmacy and training school for students have become renowned institutions in the world of medical science.

The firm was established in the year 1874 by the late Mr. C. K. Sen, who was at that time the leading *Kaviraj*, or Ayurvedic medical practitioner, in India, and he was consulting physician to the majority of the Independent Chiefs of this vast country. The business developed very rapidly indeed, and it had attained an exceedingly sound position when the founder unfortunately died in 1892.

A limited company was then formed, the shares being taken up by members of the family only, with the second son, Mr. U. N. Sen, as managing director.

It may be interesting to note that the principles upon which the late Mr. Sen started and conducted the business were as follows: (1) to diagnose diseases according to Ayurvedic science, i.e. in accordance with the directions of the ancient *rishis*; (2) to ensure the efficacy and genuineness of the medicines and drugs by direct and unremitting personal supervision; (3) to sell genuine medicines at the lowest possible rates for the special benefit of the general public; and (4) to be strictly honest in all dealings.

The extent to which this establishment has been patronized may be gathered from the fact that the head office of the company has been built in the heart of Calcutta at a cost of more than two lakhs of rupees, and a large three-storied house on the opposite side of the street, secured for about a lakh of rupees, is now used as a storehouse of medical preparations and as the residence of students who are gratuitously taught the Ayurvedic system.

The large hall in the principal building is thronged daily with patients to whom free advice is given, but the company have an increasing *clientèle* in the Mofussil, from the Himalayas to Cape Comorin, as well as in Ceylon, Burma, Java, Arabia, Egypt, Mauritius, Africa, and England.

It would be impossible to enumerate a tithe of the diseases and ailments for which specifics are prepared and sold by this company, but they include such troublesome complaints as ague, anæmia, asthma, bronchitis, cholera, cancer, cataract, diabetes, eczema, elephantiasis, gout, heart disease, jaundice, malaria, ophthalmia, paralysis, phthisis, skin troubles, ulcers, and many other equally well-known complaints.

The laboratory is in charge of a competent official, and all preparations are conducted under the immediate supervision of Mr. Upendra Nath Sen, who is assisted by a large staff of fully qualified men.

The company are chemists and druggists to several of the ruling chiefs of India, including His Highness the Nizam of Hyderabad, and their Highnesses the Maharajas of Mysore, Baroda, Travancore, Indore, Kashmir, Jodhpur, and Patiala.

The company have received thousands of unsolicited testimonials from patients who gratefully acknowledge the great benefits which they have derived from the advice and treatment given either at personal interviews or by correspondence.

Some very old treatises and prescriptions, originally written on palm-leaves, relating to Ayurvedic treatment have been translated into Bengali by Kaviraj Devendra Nath Sen and Kaviraj Upendra Nath Sen, and the new volumes are now published in the private printing-press of the company in Colootollah Street. Notes

C. K. SEN & CO.

1. Upendra Nath Sen. 2. Exterior View of Premises. 3. Compounders. 4. Show-room. 5. Staff. 6. Residence.

have been added by the translators, and the works include: Rasa Ratna Samuchyaya, Ayurvedic Sangraha, Charak Sanhita, Susruta Sanhita, Chakradatta, Rasendrasar, Sangraha, Bhaboprokash, Madhabnidan, Sarangadhar, Baidak Sabdasindhu, Drabya Guna, Ayurveda Pradip, Pachan Sangraha, Nari-Prokash, Nari-Bijnap, Paribhasa Pradip, Palmirghantu, and Astanga Hridaya, Sanhita or Bhagbhat.

SIKDAR & CO.

This happens to be one of the few purely Indian manufacturing concerns which have been holding their own against imported articles for the sufficiently long period of nearly thirty-seven years, thus justifying their being regarded as well established, and recognized—as, indeed, they are—as the premier manufacturers of cast-iron rain-water pipes.

Four young men, namely, Messrs. K. N. Sikdar, P. K. Sen, J. C. Mukherjee, and H. C. Paul, with characteristic juvenile zeal, commenced business as "E. and H. Union" as far back as 1879, but the firm acquired its present style of Sikdar & Co. in the year 1885, and has since been reckoned as one of the leading Indian firms of importance. Unlike firms of their kind, limiting themselves to execution of orders and works, Messrs. Sikdar & Co. have always been busy with experiments, designs, and specialities, which ultimately resulted in their manufacturing "C.I." hand printing presses, rice bowls, and pipes. For these they have obtained a number of certificates and medals at several exhibitions, a record of which any firm may well be proud of possessing.

They have now specialized in their castings, especially cast-iron rain-water pipes, which they are turning out and selling daily in considerable quantities. Their process of manufacture is entirely their own, being with plant worked under compressed air appliances designed and placed upon a working basis by their late engineer and partner, Mr. Prosonna Kumar Sen, L.C.E., to whom the firm owes a great deal. Messrs. Sikdar & Co. are now on the Government list, enjoying the patronage of the Public Works Department, Municipalities, District Boards, and several bodies and corporations, in addition to leading firms of engineers and contractors all over India, Burma, and Ceylon, and their pipes are now generally recognized as the best obtainable, having regard to considerations of quality, price, and promptitude in delivery.

They enjoy the confidence of the public also in the matter of structural steel works and castings, which for beauty and effect of design, and in price, are known to excel articles and works of local manufacture, and they possess the record of some of the best undertakings of the country.

Having their office in 5 Hastings Street, Calcutta, near the High Court, and with workshops at 135/3 Manicktola Main Road, in the same city, situated on the eastern bank of the canal known as Tolly's Nulla, the entire business is now managed and controlled by Mr. N. K. Sarkar, engineer and contractor, Calcutta, Howrah, and Bankipore, who carries on his own business of fourteen years' standing, he having large establishments in various places.

The firm is, to a very appreciable extent, indebted to the present management for the satisfactory position attained by it; and Mr. N. K. Sarkar's latest attempt at improvement is the opening of a London office for the better control of the securing of raw materials for structures of all kinds, a duty which has been entrusted to, and is being organized by, one of the assistants of Mr. N. K. Sarkar, namely, Mr. K. C. Bannerjee, M.I.M.C.E., M.R.San.I., who was formerly sanitary engineer of the Province of Behar, and engineer to the Calcutta Improvement Trust, but who is now in London. Between Mr. Sarkar and Messrs. Sikdar & Co. the firm have in view the successful handling of agencies for articles of European manufacture, and it is practically certain that the arrangements now in progress will enable these to be secured.

SITALPRASAD KHARAGPRASAD

This firm of bankers, mill-owners, and merchants was established about the year 1833 at 30 Burtolla Street, Calcutta, where, at present, they still engage in their vast business of private banking. The firm's other banking houses are situated at Benares, Azmatgarh (district Azamgarh), Azamgarh proper, Barhalganj (district Gorakhpur), and Fyzabad, all in the United Provinces of Agra and Oudh.

The business at Azmatgarh is carried on under the name of Messrs. Ratan Chand Lallu Mal, and that at Benares, established immediately after the dark days of the Indian Mutiny in 1857, under the name of Messrs. Balkrishna Das Bisheshwar Prasad.

The firm is a joint family concern, and the present members are: The Hon. Babu Motichand Saheb, C.I.E., Benares; Babu Gokul Chand Saheb and Babu Mangla Prasad Saheb, Calcutta; Babu Shiva Prasad Gupta Saheb, Benares; Babu Harakh Chand Saheb, Azamgarh; and Babu Makund Lal Saheb, Azmatgarh; and they are landlords of extensive properties in the districts of Benares, Jaunpur, Ballia, Gorakhpur, and Azamgarh in the Province of Agra; Fyzabad and Gonda in Oudh; and Arrah, Saran, and Bhagalpur in the Province of Behar and Orissa.

The resident members in Calcutta are Babu Gokul Chand Saheb and Babu Mangla Prasad Saheb.

The firm is one of the largest and most influential among private Indian banking concerns, the partners enjoying the reputation of being great financiers; but the firm are also interested in the import of piece-goods of all descriptions, both of European and Japanese manufacture.

About the year 1833, when the firm opened their business in Calcutta railways were unknown, and merchandise had for many years to be brought to Calcutta by river craft; and besides attending to the financial part of the business, they insured goods against loss or damage in course of transit from the interior and until safely delivered into the consignee's godowns in Calcutta. This underwriting of cargo formed an important part of the firm's business in its day. But with the advent of steam and railways in India the hitherto universal method of transportation of merchandise by river slowly declined until the volume of business passing became so meagre that insurance ceased to be a necessity, and consequently the firm discontinued the practice.

In the year 1908 the firm purchased the Bharat Abhyuday cotton mills, with buildings covering an area of 15 *bighas* of land, and situated on the western bank of the River Hoochly, at Salkia, in the district of Howrah. The mills then contained 16,160 mule and ring spindles, but as the machinery in general was old it was being replaced by up-to-date plant. In February 1915 a fire unfortunately occurred in the spinning department of the mills, and the whole of this structure was destroyed, together with portions of other departments. Owing to the war considerable difficulties in the reconstruction of

SIKDAR & CO.

1. Exhibition Certificate, 1906. 2. Exhibition Certificate, 1900. 3. Exhibition Certificate, 1897. 4. Port Commissioners' Certificate. 5. Mr. N. K. Sarker.

the mills had to be contended with, but by the year 1916 they had been rebuilt and fitted out with the latest and most up-to-date machinery. The main building of the mills contains 26,356 mule and ring spindles for spinning cotton into yarn in counts from 6's. to 50's., but higher counts can be spun if necessary; while the grade of cotton used is solely Indian. It is partly two and partly three stories in height, and is of fireproof construction. All the buildings, including mills and outhouses, are fitted with "sprinklers" and the latest up-to-date fire appliances.

Adjacent to the main building there is a three storeyed building in which the reeling, bundling, and baling of the yarn is effected.

To the north of the main building there is a ginning block which contains 15 single gins and also plant for cleaning "kapas." Situated near to the ginning block there is another building which contains a complete plant for the preparing and weaving of lamp wicks, bed tape, cotton listing, and twine and cotton cord of various degrees.

The full product of the mills is consumed locally.

The mills in the hands of the present proprietors have been a success, and in eight years the power of production has been increased by about 65 per cent. in order to meet the ever-growing demand for yarns and other goods.

The staff, including the manager, are Indians, and they attend to the erection, repairing, working, and maintenance of all the machinery, while they also have to supervise eight hundred workers daily.

The machinery in the mills was supplied by the following British concerns: Boilers by Messrs. Thomas Beeley & Sons; engine, Messrs. Yates and Thom; and cotton machinery, Messrs. Platt Brothers, Messrs. Asa Lees & Co., Messrs. Brooks and Doxey, Messrs. Howard and Bullough, Messrs. John Hetherington & Sons, and Messrs. William Tatham & Co.

The family trace their ancestry back for several generations to Babu Nilkanth, Agraval Vaishyas of the Punjab, and they appear to have migrated from that territory to the United Provinces, first of all residing at Nagpura in Ballia, and subsequently at Azmatgarh, where they still have large residential houses. They have always been noted for their loyalty and devotion to the Crown, and for their consistent support of the British Government. During the dark days of the Indian sepoy mutiny of 1857, one of the leaders of the rebels, Kuar Singh, encamped near Azmatgarh and demanded to be supplied with provisions, but the demand being met with a refusal, the family incurred the enmity of the sepoys who forthwith proceeded to attack the firm's business premises. Information as to the treasure contained in the buildings was imparted to the rebels by one Gogo Halwai, and it is estimated that goods and money to the value of several lakhs of rupees were plundered. The family at Azmatgarh rendered yeoman service to the Government during that troublous period, and the latter entrusted to their custody for safe keeping a vast amount of Government treasure. When order was restored, the Government, in appreciation of the family's loyalty, and also to recompense them for the loss sustained when their premises were raided by the rebels, gave to the family the confiscated property of Goga Halwai, and the then head of the house, Babu Beni Prasad, was exempted from the operations of the Arms Act, and also received other privileges in recognition of the valuable services rendered to the Government.

As in the past, so in the present, do the family place their services entirely at the disposal of the Government, as witness the splendid record rendered through their head, the Hon. Babu Moti Chand, C.I.E., of Benares, towards the conduct of the European war.

A contribution of Rs. 2,000 was made to the Imperial Indian Relief Fund, and to the St. John Ambulance Fund the sum of Rs. 400, in addition to gifts of articles of clothing, metal utensils, and other goods, for which thanks were received from Lady Meston, the wife of the present Lieutenant-Governor of the United Provinces. Two subscription lists were opened amongst Indian ladies for the St. John Ambulance Fund, and a third in aid of the British Women's Hospital for disabled soldiers and sailors at Richmond, England. Soldiers when leaving for field service have been entertained, and the wants of the wounded provided for on their return from the front. A contribution to the Officers' Families' Fund, Berkeley Square, London, was suitably acknowledged by Lady Hope, the hon. secretary.

At an early period of the war a fully equipped motor ambulance, costing Rs. 15,000, was presented to the Government of India, for which an acknowledgment, together with the thanks of the Government, of the Army Department, and of the Local Government, was received, as the following excerpts of letters will show.

On October 29, 1914, to the Hon. Babu Moti Chand, Mr. Hopkins, the Commissioner of Benares Division, wrote "to express His Honour's (the Lieutenant-Governor) appreciation of your patriotic offer of a sum of £900 for a motor ambulance and an additional £100 for the fittings," and on November 18th in the same year, the Under-Secretary to the Government of the United Provinces wrote to the Commissioner "to convey the warmest thanks of the Government of India to the Hon. Babu Moti Chand of Benares for his most generous offer of £1,000 for a motor ambulance and fittings, which has been gratefully accepted by the Government of India." On December 18th, also in 1914, Colonel H. Holloway, Secretary to the Army Department of the Government of India, wrote to the Chief Secretary of the Government of the United Provinces to request "that you will inform the Hon. Babu Moti Chand of Benares that a suitable motor car has now been purchased and is being adapted as a motor ambulance in the conveyance from the railway station to hospitals of the sick and wounded Indian troops from the forces overseas, and it cannot fail to be of the greatest value in this respect. I am to add that H.E. the Commander-in-Chief and Army Member, is very grateful to the Hon. Babu Moti Chand for his most valuable and generous gift to the troops." Then, on June 30, 1916, the Under-Secretary to the Government of the United Provinces wrote, "I am to add that the Government of India intimate that this ambulance has proved of the greatest value in lessening the discomfort entailed in the carriage of the sick and wounded."

As the prices of foodstuffs were increasing, whereby the poorer classes were being put to great hardship, the Hon. Babu Moti Chand organized a grain relief fund and thus rendered valuable aid.

In order to stimulate recruiting, and to show his appreciation of the action of those who were prepared to leave hearth and home and give their lives in the service of their King and country, the Hon. Babu Moti Chand issued a notification on March 18, 1915, to all his estate officials and tenants to the effect that the rents of those tenants who had gone, or would thereafter go, to the front, would be remitted for the duration of the war, and that the dependents of those killed in action, of those who returned maimed or seriously injured, and of those who gained

THE BHARAT-ABHYUDAY COTTON MILLS.

1, 2, The Charat-Abhyuday Cotton Mills. 3. Howrah. 4. The Hon. Babu Moti Chand, C.I.E. 5. Babu Gokul Chand Saheb. 6. Babu Mangla Prasad Saheb.

Photos by Bourne & Shepherd, India.

distinction in the form of the Victoria Cross or other decoration for deeds of valour in the field, would receive still further consideration. The effect which this notification had on other *taluqdars* in following suit in regard to their own estates, and on the sepoys who were at the front, and also upon stimulating recruiting, is ascertainable by the following extracts of letters sent to the Hon. Babu Moti Chand. Mr. Lambert, the District Officer of Benares, on March 23, 1915, wrote, "I think it is an excellent move, and I wish landlords would adopt the same line generally. It must be a great relief to soldiers on service to know that their families at home are adequately provided for." On the same date the District Officer of Jaunpur wrote, "Your action seems to be highly commendable and such as might well be followed by other estates." On March 26th, the Deputy Commissioner of Gonda, which is one of the best recruiting districts of the United Provinces wrote, "I can imagine no more patriotic action than that which you propose to take. I have every hope that it will do much to stimulate recruiting for the army in the Gonda district." On April 3rd, Mr. Hopkins, Commissioner of Benares, wrote, "The Lieutenant-Governor desires me to acknowledge your action with gratitude, and to convey to you the thanks of Government." Again on May 20th, Mr. Hopkins wrote, "I am desired to convey to you the thanks of the Government and to inform you that it appreciates the feelings of loyalty which prompted your action."

On May 22, 1915, the Adjutant-General wrote from Simla, "His Excellency the Commander-in-Chief has asked me to convey to you his great appreciation of the loyalty and generosity which has prompted you to make these concessions. A remission of rent is a form of generosity which is greatly esteemed by soldiers, and it is very gratifying to know that you are taking such keen interest in the welfare of those who are serving their country at the front."

On October 4, 1915, the officer commanding the 9th Behar Infantry wrote from Bushire to the Under-Secretary to the Government of the United Provinces, "Would you please convey my thanks to the Hon. Babu Moti Chand for his kindness, which is greatly appreciated by the sepoys."

On April 23, 1916, Mr. Hopkins wrote, "I am glad to hear that your public-spirited action has attracted public attention." On June 27th, Mr. R. Burn, C.I.E., Chief Secretary to the Government of the United Provinces, writing from Nainital, said, "Your noble example in the treatment of your tenants who have gone to war has been imitated by quite a number of landlords."

The Belgian Relief Fund did not escape attention, as the Hon. Babu Moti Chand contributed to it the sum of Rs. 500, and in its behalf issued three appeals for it to be loyally supported; these actions were suitably acknowledged by the Hon. Secretary and the Hon. Treasurer of the Fund for the United Provinces. Mr. Smith, the Hon. Treasurer, wrote from Cawnpore on July 29, 1915, to the Hon. Babu Moti Chand, "I am very pleased to see from to-day's *Leader* that you are interesting yourself on behalf of the Belgian Relief Fund, and I am glad to see that you have already secured some substantial subscriptions." On August 4, 1915, Mr. J. G. Ryan, Hon. Secretary, wrote from Cawnpore, "I am again to thank you for your successful efforts on behalf of the Belgians."

In connection with the United Provinces special War Fund, the Hon. Babu Moti Chand contributed Rs. 7,500 for the purchase of a motor ambulance car, and he raised for the fund the sum of Rs. 500 from among the estate tenants in the Gonda district.

Babu Gokul Chand Saheb, Calcutta, contributed Rs. 2,000 to the Marwari War Fund, Rs. 1,500 to the Y.M.C.A. Relief Fund, and Rs. 500 to the Bengalee Battalion Patriotic Fund, besides undertaking the maintenance and upkeep of some of the men who have joined the battalion.

One of the most pressing needs of the campaign was the full provision of munitions, and to ensure an adequate and continuous supply the Lieut.-Governor of the United Provinces appointed a committee under the presidency of Sir Verney Lovett, K.C.S.I., which was called the Munitions Committee, on which the Hon. Babu Moti Chand was invited by His Honour to serve. In that capacity he furnished nearly one-fourth of the number of lathes supplied in the Provinces, and he would have provided more had the necessity for them arisen. There was further a paucity of skilled workmen at the munition works, and here again the Hon. Babu Moti Chand rose to the occasion and furnished all the skilled labour required. There was also a dearth of unskilled labour, and the deficiency was filled by him. In this connection Mr. T. Gregson, the Locomotive Superintendent, on May 25, 1916, wrote, "It is very gratifying to know that you take such a keen interest in the matter and your generous assistance in both machines and labour has been of great service to Government."

Sir Verney Lovett, President of the Committee, in a letter to the Government dated May 10, 1916, wrote, "I have much pleasure in acknowledging . . . the energetic and persistent efforts of the Hon. Babu Moti Chand, C.I.E., of Benares. He has done us exceptional service." In acknowledging the final report of the President, the Government, in a resolution dated January 10, 1917, published in the United Provinces Government *Gazette* of January 13, 1917, said, "His Honour also desires to thank the members of the Munition Committee for their useful work, and more especially the Hon. Sir Verney Lovett, K.C.S.I., and the Hon. Babu Moti Chand, C.I.E., . . . for the energy displayed by them in making the scheme a complete success."

Just as in March 1915 certain concessions were offered to tenants on the estates as an inducement to join the army, so again in March 1916 was a similar notification issued to all estate officials and tenants by the Hon. Babu Moti Chand, but this time the notification was specially directed to stimulate the recruitment of camp followers. Apparently this procedure had the desired effect, as Mr. W. S. Cassels, Deputy Commissioner of Gonda, in his letter dated March 28, 1916, wrote, "I am very glad to find you are encouraging the recruitment of coolies for the war, and are offering inducements to those who will enlist." On May 16, 1916, Mr. Lambert, Collector of Benares, wrote, "Your generosity places us under yet another obligation."

In order to carry on recruiting a regular organization was instituted at the end of May 1916, and by the second week in July ninety recruits were made over to the military authorities at Lucknow. Lieut. Simmonds, officer in charge of supplies in that city, writing to the *Leader*, an Allahabad daily newspaper, in its issue of July 12, 1916, said, "I am very pleased with his services which he has so kindly lent to the Government in this war time, and it would give one greater pleasure if other *taluqdars* would come forward as the Hon. Babu Moti Chand, C.I.E., has done and help the Government in like manner." On July 21, 1916, the Officer Commanding Followers' Camp, Lucknow, wrote to the *Leader*, "In continuation of my previous letter, will you kindly notify the following in your columns: I have very great pleasure in announcing that the Hon. Babu Moti Chand, C.I.E., of Benares, has given a further batch of forty-seven useful followers to the Officer Commanding Followers' Camp at Lucknow. He has also continued his treat of refreshments to the men at the railway stations, which have been gratefully enjoyed. His magnificent support to the Government in the matter of supplies of men deserves every praise, and has been highly appreciated. He has got his own organization for enlistment, and the amount of trouble and expense involved in recruiting must be very great. The military authorities are much obliged to the Hon. Babu Moti Chand for all that he is doing, and hope that other *taluqdars* will also follow his noble example."

In August 1916 the military authorities, finding it necessary to raise two bullock corps for field service, and they were in urgent need of a thousand or more drivers, within a couple of months after the matter had been brought to his notice the Hon. Babu Moti Chand supplied more than four hundred, or 40 per cent. of the number; the other 60 per cent. being recruited by the district officers, maharajas, rajas, and other *taluqdars*. The military authorities, to show how highly they valued the service rendered, and as a mark of their appreciation of the same, named a troop in each corps the "Moti Chand Troop." Touching this matter, Lieut.-Colonel G. Sanders, Assistant Director of Supplies and Transport, 8th Lucknow Division, on October 9, 1916, wrote, "The General Officer Commanding has been pleased to allow a troop of No. 1 B.C. to be called after you. . . . I am very grateful to you for your help in procuring bullock drivers; but for your assistance No. 1 Bullock Corps could not be ready to leave at an early date. The bullock corps at Cawnpore is still very short of drivers. I hope you will continue to send in men."

The Officer Commanding the Lucknow bullock corps on November 2, 1916, wrote to the *Leader* of Allahabad, "The first bullock corps is now ready and is starting immediately for field service. But before going I must acknowledge with thanks the very great help which I have received from the Hon. Babu Moti Chand, C.I.E., of Benares, in raising the corps. But for his magnificent aid we would not have been able to complete our corps so easily. At a time when we were hard pressed for bullock drivers and when the civil authorities were at their wits' ends where and how to get them, it was wonderful to see how Babu Moti Chand kept on supplying the men by dozens every day, with the result that in but a short time he gave us as many as 224 of them, and he would have given more if we had required them. Our demands have been finished but his supplies are going on as briskly as before, and men are now being given over to form another corps at Cawnpore. Besides this, Babu Moti Chand was always ready to give us any other help that we required. I wish other noblemen of these provinces would have helped as much as he has done and is doing. . . . I may also observe that Babu Moti Chand did not charge the Government any expenses which he must have incurred in getting and collecting these men, and these expenses we are sure must have been very great."

On November 2, 1916, the Under-Secretary to the Government of the United Provinces, wrote, "I am desired to convey to you the best thanks of Government for your valuable assistance in the matter of the recruitment of camp followers and bullock drivers for the war."

On November 17, 1916, His Honour Sir James Meston, K.C.S.I., Lieutenant-Governor of the United Provinces, speaking at a Durbar at Allahabad, was pleased to remark, "In many parts of the Province, zemindars have come forward to collect followers and labourers needed for transport and similar work. Among them I would mention particularly the Hon. Babu Moti Chand, C.I.E., of Benares, both for his untiring zeal in the matter, and for his assistance in munition work." Again, at a Durbar held at Lucknow on January 10, 1917, His Honour the Lieutenant-Governor again graciously observed, "You will further be interested to learn that some of the best work done in Northern India, both in the provision of followers and in ammunition work, stands to the credit of a gentleman who is a member of the British Indian Association, the Hon. Babu Moti Chand, C.I.E., of Benares."

Special Hindu prayers and *pujas* for the victory of the British arms have been organized on different occasions.

The Hon. Babu Moti Chand, C.I.E., is a member of the Executive Committee of the United Provinces Special War Fund, of the United Provinces Munitions Committee, and of the War League started by Mr. Webb, of Karachi.

This gentleman has been the chairman of the Board of Directors of the Benares Bank, Ltd., Benares, for the last ten years or more; he was the first non-official chairman of the Benares Municipal Board, and he represents the zemindars (landlords) of the Province of Agra in the Legislative Council of the United Provinces.

With regard to the philanthropy of the family, the following benefactions, among many others, are briefly noted: A donation of one lakh of rupees to the Benares Hindu University, and Rs. 33,000 to the King Edward memorial. The family defrayed the full cost of, and maintain, a free dispensary at Benares, a vernacular school at Benares with a model agricultural farm and boarding house attached to it, an English school at Azmatgarh, a *pathshala* at Ayodhya, and many primary schools in different villages on the estate. A *pucca* public road, two miles in length, has been constructed by them at considerable cost in the Azamgarh district, and it is named after a former Lieutenant-Governor, Sir John Digges la Touche.

The firm have subscribed Rs. 2,25,000 towards the Indian War Loan.

The Benares residency of the family is known as the Azmatgarh Palace.

1. PLOUGHING WITH BULLOCKS IN ASSAM.
Photo by D. C. Ghoshal.
2. BUSH APPLE-TREE AT THE SHILLONG FRUIT EXPERIMENTAL STATION.
3. APPLES GROWN AT THE SHILLONG FRUIT EXPERIMENTAL STATION.

THE AGRICULTURAL RESEARCH INSTITUTE AND COLLEGE, PUSA

BY WYNNE SAYER, B.A., ASSISTANT TO THE AGRICULTURAL ADVISER TO THE GOVERNMENT OF INDIA

AGRICULTURE is India and India is agriculture. These words may sound too drastic, but the truth is all too evident to those who really know India.

Other trades, other industries may loom larger to the outside eye, but behind them, silent and unseen, is the source of all the real wealth of India, the land and the wealth of the land—agriculture. To finance, railways, and export trade agriculture gives all the sinews of life. The word "famine" spells loss to them, and even to law courts, for a famine alone can deprive the Indian of his favourite recreation—going to law. This short introduction may give the reader a slight idea of the vast importance of agriculture in India. It is in this field of work that the slightest improvement gives a return of *crores*, and there is no industry more in need of improvement. Agriculture gives India all its wealth; yet India supports agricultural improvement with an infinitesimal amount, compared with the sums spent in all other civilized countries.

The American, who represents 6 per cent. of the human race, raises one-fifth of the wheat of the world, one-half of the cotton, and three-fourths of the corn. Where is India in comparison with these figures? Is there not here food for thought and an opportunity to realize where real improvement can be made? Could the present yearly income of the ryot be raised by one-fourth, the sum would pay many a national debt. Where else can one see an industry which will repay money spent upon it like agriculture? Truly it has been said that one cannot educate a hungry man, and this proverb should be well remembered in connection with agriculture. First improve agriculture and the social conditions will follow.

GENERAL DESCRIPTION OF THE INSTITUTE.

The Agricultural Research Institute at Pusa, the subject of the present article, was founded on April 1, 1904; and during the 12 years of its existence it has achieved practical results which are of far-reaching importance to Indian agriculture, while the scientific work turned out during this brief period has won for it recognition throughout the scientific world. It is a "Central Research Institute" where investigations are made into the higher problems dealing with soil fertility and kindred subjects, which are of general application to the whole of India. It was founded in response to an insistent demand for the prosecution of research in agriculture, which is the most important industry in the country, maintaining as it does about 70 per cent. of the total population of India. In a backward country like this, where the development of agriculture affords the surest way of improving the material condition of a very large mass of the population, the necessity for a Research Institute like this cannot be overestimated. The great importance of research in unravelling the principles underlying agricultural practices, and crop production, and in improving imperfect methods and material, is now thoroughly appreciated throughout the world, and Institutes such as Pusa, started with a view to promote and improve the productive capacity of a country, are considered, and rightly so, to be good national investments. The work done by the Rothamsted Experiment Station in England is a case in point.

The Pusa Research Institute challenges comparison with any similar establishment in the East. It attracts annually increasing numbers of visitors. It has been well said by Mr. Mackenna that "no visitor to India who is interested in scientific agriculture should leave the country without seeing Pusa." The Institute is located in the district of Darbhanga, on an estate of over 1,300 acres, bounded on three sides by a loop of the Chota Gandak River, on the bank of which the Institute stands. It is six miles distant from the Pusa Road Station on the Bengal and North-Western Railway, with which it is connected by a good road. It is situated in a tract of country with a comparatively good climate, where the heat is not so severe as it is higher up on the Gangetic plain.

The soil is deep alluvial, and is capable of growing successfully nearly every "rains" crop which can be produced in the plains of India; and with irrigation from wells or from the river, it can grow successfully the majority of the more important garden crops. Provision has accordingly been made for all necessary means of irrigation from the river and from wells. The rainfall of Pusa and of Behar generally is secure a fact proved by its population, averaging 950 to the square mile. Pusa is situated in the heart of an intensive agricultural district, which is largely controlled by a community of indigo-planters. And as a result, agricultural improvements, through their influence, can be brought to the notice of ordinary cultivators in a manner which is unparalleled in other parts of India. This was one of the reasons why Pusa was selected as the Central Research Station, and Mr. Coventry, an experienced indigo-planter and an extensive experimenter in agricultural problems, was selected as the first Director.

The work of the Institute and College is apportioned under the following sections: (1) General Administration; (2) College; (3) Farm; (4) Chemistry; (5) Botany and Plant Improvement; (6) Bacteriology; (7) Plant Pathology; (8) Entomology; (9) Pathological Entomology.

Officers of mature experience and standing have been appointed to the various divisions, in addition to supernumerary officers to act as assistants, and as reserves in cases of leave of absence from duty. The chiefs of the sections (1) of Botany and Plant Improvement, and (2) of Plant Pathology, have also a colleague under the designation of Second Imperial Economic Botanist and Second Imperial Mycologist. A higher and lower subordinate staff has also been appointed.

There is at Pusa the Phipps' Laboratory, a two-storied building, magnificently equipped with a laboratory for each branch of agricultural science; and there is, in addition, a physical laboratory. The main building also includes museums for the various sections herbaria and lecture-rooms. There is also a library, containing the best and latest literature on all branches of agriculture and its allied science, numbering over 21,000 volumes, which are available for workers in the Provinces as well as at Pusa. Pot-culture houses and small outside laboratories have also been provided. There is an Insectary for rearing insects and studying their life history, together with a house for carrying out experiments in connection with the rearing of silkworms and the reeling of silk. The Institute is served with water power and has a gas and electric installation. Comfortable quarters have been constructed both for the Indian and European staffs; and there is also a hostel with accommodation for 70 students and a rest-house for visitors, together with a well-equipped hospital and dispensary. The farm has more than 500 acres under arable, and some 200 acres in grass for cattle-breeding. The fruit orchards and the botanical area are very attractive features of the Institute. A large vegetable garden is maintained, and beautiful lawns, laid out around the College building, have been planted with trees and ornamental shrubs. These lawns are irrigated from the river, as are also the vegetable and botanical gardens, the pumping being done by electricity.

Among the most noticeable of the features of the estate are the existing fine teak, shishum, bamboo, and mahogany avenues, which are an object-lesson to many parts of India. Endeavours are, further, being made to improve the attractiveness of the estate by planting and protecting young trees in the pasture areas, along the frontage of the river and the avenues; while the proper preservation of the existing magnificent avenues is carefully looked after, decayed trees being cut down and all gaps filled up.

Before proceeding to a detailed description of the work done by each section of the Institute, it would perhaps be well to give a brief retrospect of its history. The post of the Inspector-General of Agriculture in India was created in 1901, and its duties were, broadly speaking, defined as those of an "adviser in agricultural matters" both to the Government of India and Local Governments. This central expert authority was appointed with a view to stimulate agricultural research and to guide and co-ordinate the efforts of those engaged in agricultural experiments in different parts of India. This was an essential step towards the more active prosecution of that policy of scientific and practical inquiry and experiment in agricultural matters on which so much stress had been laid by the Famine Commission of 1878, and the necessity for which was again emphasized by Dr. Voelcker, who was deputed in 1890 to advise on the best course to be adopted in order to effect improvements in Indian agriculture. To enable the Inspector General of Agriculture to perform the task entrusted to him, a Cryptogamic Botanist and an Entomologist were added to his staff, in addition to the Agricultural Chemist whose services were already at his disposal. The provision of a fully equipped research laboratory, in which the agricultural experts could pursue their various inquiries, was under the consideration of the Government of India when

Mr. Henry Phipps, an American gentleman, came forward with his munificent donation of £20,000 (subsequently raised to £30,000), to be devoted to whatever object of public utility (if possible in the direction of scientific research) His Excellency Lord Curzon, then Viceroy and Governor-General of India, might prefer. Part of the donation was devoted to the construction of a "Pasteur Institute" at Coonoor, in Southern India, and it was decided that the balance should be utilized in erecting a laboratory for agricultural research. The Government of India originally intended to locate the laboratory at Dehra Dun, where the Agricultural Chemist and Cryptogamic Botanist were already stationed; but at Dehra it was found impossible to have a farm at hand where practical and scientific work could be carried out, and where the crops which are of most importance and require the closest investigation could be grown in the immediate neighbourhood. Some other suitable locality was being sought when the Bengal Government submitted a scheme for the establishment of an agricultural station and experimental farm on the Government estate of Pusa, in the district of Darbhanga. This estate, first acquired by Government in the year 1796, was used as a stud farm until 1874, when for certain reasons horse-breeding operations were abandoned and a part of the property was utilized as an experimental farm, special attention being paid to the growth and curing of tobacco. In 1877 it was leased to Messrs. Begg, Dunlop & Co., of Calcutta, as a tobacco estate and factory; but they abandoned the enterprise in 1897, when the Bengal Government again took over the property. It was then proposed by the Bengal Government to start a cattle-breeding and dairy farm on this estate, and a scheme for this purpose was drawn up in 1899. Meanwhile, however, the question of agricultural research in Bengal had come into prominence. Accordingly, proposals for establishing an Agricultural Research Station and College were added to the original scheme. The Bengal Government wished the Institute to remain under the management of the Provincial Agricultural Department, but they expressed a hope that, having regard to the general benefit likely to result to agriculture in Northern India from the work of the Institute, some contribution towards the cost of its establishment and maintenance would be made by the Imperial Government and the Government of the United Provinces. The Government of India, on the receipt of these proposals, thought that such a station might be suitable for the Imperial Laboratory of Agricultural Research which they intended to establish. They therefore caused the relative merits of Pusa and Dehra to be examined by a strongly constituted committee, and the opinion of that body was unanimously in favour of Pusa. With the full concurrence of the Government of Bengal, it was therefore decided to make Pusa the headquarters of the Imperial Agricultural Department, and to establish there the laboratories required by the experts, combining with them an experimental farm, an agricultural college, and a cattle farm for the improvement of the local breeds of cattle. The Institution was thus made an Imperial one, under the general supervision and control of the Inspector-General of Agriculture in India, who is now the Agricultural Adviser to the Government of India. Lord Curzon utilized the greater part of Mr. Phipps' donation in the establishment of this Institute, and the main building, the foundation-stone of which was laid by the Viceroy on April 1, 1905, is called after its donor, the Phipps Laboratories at Pusa.

The scheme for the Pusa Institute, as originally sanctioned, comprised: (1) an experimental farm; (2) a cattle-breeding farm; (3) a garden for working out the problems of economic botany; (4) a research institute; and (5) an agricultural college.

Pusa Farm.

The farm was placed in the charge of an expert agriculturist from England, and it was intended that it should serve as a model for similar institutions in the Provinces. On it would be initiated lines of inquiry which would be tested before being recommended for trial under local conditions on provincial experimental farms. It would also test, under different conditions and with more highly skilled supervision, results reported from provincial farms, and, in particular, would secure continuity for any experiments which might have been tried and then discontinued on a provincial farm. The programme was an ambitious one, and it has not been found possible to work up to it in all respects. The capacity of the farm is limited by the conditions of climate and soil. The Pusa estate, like other parts of Behar, is liable to be suddenly flooded owing to heavy continuous rain, and it has therefore been found necessary to throw up embankments. A power-driven pump has been provided to deal with excess water accumulating on the estate, and this pump is worked by steam-tackle engines to prevent flooding in the experimental areas.

Reference may now be made to the important work done on the farm. The maintenance of soil fertility under a double-cropping system (i.e. two crops per annum) by the use of manures is being investigated, but perhaps amongst the most useful work carried out on the farm is that relating to the preservation of fodder. In a country like India, where cattle-food supplies are subject to the vicissitudes of an uncertain climate, this subject is of the utmost importance, and the production of ensilage on the American principle has been found the most satisfactory method of preservation. Maize has been found to give the most nutritious food when thus prepared, but in point of yield per acre sorghum gives more weight, and is therefore more economical. An objection to the American system of making ensilage in this country is the expense of constructing the silo. This has been overcome, and instead of a masonry silo a simple pit has been found to answer the purpose quite satisfactorily, even in the moist soil of Pusa.

Among the labour-saving implements and machinery tested on the farm may be mentioned steam threshers and a Fowler's double-engine steam cultivation tackle with a disc plough, cultivator, harrow, and roller. The farm was not an ideal one for steam cultivation, being intersected by roads which cut it up into irregularly shaped fields; but by taking the whole available area, squaring up some of the fields, and abandoning odd corners a sufficient area has been made available to employ the steam tackle to the limit of its capacity. The result of two years' working shows that it is of particular value at Pusa, with its large area under crop, in lightening the work of the supervising staff and allowing of more concentration on experimental work and necessary improvements. Trials with a new type of motor-plough have shown that some modifications of the engine are necessary to suit the Indian climate, and these are being introduced.

Sheep-breeding experiments were begun in 1909, when 80 Bikaner ewes—a white-fleeced breed with a high reputation for yield and quality of wool—were obtained,

THE AGRICULTURAL RESEARCH INSTITUTE, PUSA.

1. The Agricultural Research Institute. 2. A Corner of the Chemical Laboratory.

but they did not do well. The change from the arid conditions of the Bikaner desert to the moist climate of Behar caused a breakdown in their constitution. In their place a flock of Gorakhpur ewes, which are good specimens of the local breed, was substituted. A cross between them and the *Dumba* ram has been successfully effected, and the advantage of this crossing for the production of mutton has been fully demonstrated. An attempt is now being made to improve the wool of these sheep by crossing them with Merino rams.

Poultry-breeding experiments were carried out on a large scale at Pusa during the years 1908-13, with a view to supply at reasonable prices fresh blood of imported strains to provincial agricultural farms and private individuals who are unable to afford the risk and expense of direct importation. Out of 31 breeds imported and put under trial, the following three were found most suitable for the country and for crossing purposes: (1) Buff Orpingtons, (2) White Wyandottes, and (3) Mammoth Bronze Turkeys; while Indian breeds, Chittagongs, and Lahha game have proved useful. These breeds were therefore distributed. Nowadays there are such clear indications of a growing general interest in poultry-keeping in the Provinces that it has been decided to limit the functions of Pusa to the importation of pure-bred birds to maintain the breeds kept on provincial farms. Besides this, Pusa will keep in view the possibilities of the introduction and successful acclimatization of fresh strains.

Perhaps the most important line of work in the agricultural section at Pusa is in connection with the breeding and rearing of farm live-stock. A carefully selected herd of Montgomery cattle, one of the best milk-breeds of India, is maintained. The high milking qualities of these animals are becoming more appreciated year by year, and dealers from different parts of India carry off large numbers from the half-yearly fairs at Amritsar. The Report of the Imperial Agriculturist for 1907-9 states that out of the then Pusa herd of 39 cows 16 gave over 4,000 lb. each of milk during their last lactation period (under a year in each case), and of these five gave over 5,000 lb. each; one gave 6,300 lb., and the record of another was slightly under 6,000 lb. When it is remembered that the average yield of milk in some of the best dairying districts in England is said to be under 5,000 lb. per cow, with a considerably lower percentage of butter fat than is found in the milk of the Montgomery breed, it is possible to realize what a valuable asset India has in the latter, especially as the extent to which improvement is possible is not yet in sight.

A large and remunerative export trade in Indian cattle has already arisen. Probably no Indian breed will meet the requirements of this foreign demand better than Montgomery cattle. They are useful for milk, for work, and for beef; and in South Africa, the Southern States of America, and in the Straits Settlements—to quote only three of the principal export centres—they should prove very useful, as pure and half-bred Indian cattle have been found to thrive well in these parts, as they are not affected by flies and ticks in the same disastrous way as are the local cattle.

At Pusa a record of the milk yield of each cow is kept, with a view to raise the milking standard (which is now very high) by selection on the basis of these records. The breeding operations have, since 1912, been based entirely on these milk records of the cows, and the initial steps have been completed for the building up of a milk pedigree, which is such an infallible guide. The poorest milkers in this breed are being crossed with an Ayrshire bull, as it has been demonstrated on the Military Dairies in Northern India that the product of this cross is exceedingly useful, the heifers giving milk in amounts comparable with those given by Ayrshire cows; while the bullocks carrying the free forehand of the Ayrshire make excellent work-cattle, being both fast and strong. Two herds are therefore being maintained at Pusa—one of selected milkers of the Montgomery breed, the other a herd of cross-bred Ayrshire-Montgomery cattle.

The results of Dr. Leather's work on the yield and quality of milk of the Montgomery herd at Pusa, and the numerical value of the errors accompanying milk tests, have been published in the *Chemical Memoir*, vol. iii, No. 6. The data obtained showed that the yield of milk of most of the cows laid between 10 lb. to 14 lb. a day, and that there was little difference in the yield from two sides of the udder, or of the morning and evening milk, although in point of fat percentage the morning milk was always richer. The mean percentage of fat in the milk of individual animals varied from 3·5 to 5·0. Dr. Leather's experiments have confirmed the value of the freezing-point of milk as a means of detecting added water in it. The test was applied to a large number of milk samples at dairy farms, and although the variation of freezing-point among milks of Indian cattle is greater than has been found elsewhere, the method has been found to form a much more delicate test for added water than any other method.

The cattle-breeding farm of this Institute was originally intended to serve the needs of Bengal and Behar with regard to the supply of best local pure-bred draught and milch cattle; about 50 cows and one bull were therefore purchased in the Shahabad and Ballia *diaras*, and breeding operations were continued until 1909. By that time it was found that the resources of the Institute were overtaxed in maintaining this herd as well as the Montgomery herd. The *deshi* herd, then amounting to 92 head of cattle, after rigid selection of young stock, was made over to the Bengal Department, who transferred it to the Bettiah Raj Estate, under the management of the Court of Wards. The herd is doing well, and the bulls have proved of great value to the tenants of the Raj.

AGRICULTURAL CHEMISTRY.

This section was until recently in the charge of Dr. J. Walter Leather. On his retirement from service Mr. J. Sen, M.A., F.C.S., Supernumerary Agricultural Chemist, was appointed Officiating Imperial Agricultural Chemist. This section has not only a well-equipped chemical laboratory, but also a house for experiments on plants and soils by pot-culture methods. For a detailed description of this, reference is invited to *Memoirs of the Imperial Department of Agriculture, Chemical Series*, vol. i, No. 3, 1907. Four drain gauges have been constructed for the investigation of the chemical and other effects of the passage of water through the soil, under Indian conditions, on the lines of the Rothamsted experiments.

Meteorological records are also kept in this section. At Pusa experiments regarding the availability of various items of plant food have shown the economical use of phosphatic manures on a large range of Indian soils. Valuable work has also been done on *usar* or alkali land, and the question whether this alkaline condition is increased by irrigation has also been investigated. An examination of the water requirements of some Indian crops has been taken up, and the transpiration

THE AGRICULTURAL RESEARCH INSTITUTE, PUSA.

1. HARVESTING OATS. 2. ONE OF THE AVENUES AT PUSA.

ratio of plants at different stages of their growth, and also the amount of water required by them at these periods, has been studied. The interesting and important discovery has been made that practically all the water assimilated by a crop is obtained within the root range —from 6 to 8 feet and that the great stores below this depth are of no real service to the plant. Interesting results have also been obtained from drain gauges at Cawnpore and Pusa as to the rate of evaporation of water from fallow and from cropped land, and as to the formation and movement of nitrates in the soil. A large number of samples of Indian food grains have been analysed to determine their comparative value, and the results are published in *Agricultural Ledgers*. The amount of oil contained in different varieties of oil-seeds, collected from all parts of India, has been determined, with the result that large variations were found in the oil-content of samples of oil-seeds received from different parts, more particularly of ground-nut, sesamum, mustard, and safflower. Vol. i, No. 2 of the *Chemical Series of Memoirs* records these results. Important work has also been done in the saltpetre industry, and an improved method of refining crude saltpetre, devised by Dr. Leather, has been described in *Pusa Bulletin* No. 24. A study of soil gases in relation to other constituents in the soil was taken up by Dr. Leather, and the results have been published in *Chemical Memoir*, vol. iv, No. 3.

Observations on the evaporation from a plain water surface at Pusa, Lyallpur, and Madras, published by the Imperial Agricultural Chemist in the form of a Memoir, are of practical interest in connection with problems of irrigation and the storage of water. Dr. Leather's work on sugar at the Tarnab Farm reveals the capabilities of the Peshawar Valley for its production. It has been ascertained that sugar-cane can be preserved in "clamps" over the months of February and March, and that sugar-beet of good manufacturing quality can be grown there to perfection and in such quantity as to keep a factory running from the middle of March until the end of June.

An examination of the proportion of starch in some of the Indian starch-producing crops is being made, and their possible utility from the manufacturing standpoint is under investigation. One of the results of the war has been to cut off some of the usual sources of manufactured starch, and this has caused greatly enhanced prices. Hence the inquiry is of considerable economic importance.

Botanical Section.

Mr. A. Howard, C.I.E., M.A., took charge of the office of the Imperial Economic Botanist in 1905. He has under his control at Pusa a large area of land, which is used partly for growing many varieties of fruits and partly as a botanical garden chiefly devoted to economic plants. The rest is really a field laboratory, in which varieties of some important Indian crops are tested in small plots, from which botanical descriptions and other data are obtained. Those chiefly dealt with are wheat, indigo, tobacco, fruit, fibre crops, and oil-seeds.

The most important work which Mr. and Mrs. Howard have done is in connection with wheat. They undertook a complete survey of Indian wheats, and separated type specimens of almost every Indian variety. The results of the botanical survey of these are given in the book entitled "Wheat in India," which deals in a complete manner with production, varieties, and methods of improvement of Indian wheat. From the wheats of the Punjab 25 types were isolated. These yielded, as pure types, enormously increased outturns, although great variations in yield were found, but none of them indicated any strength in milling. These pure types had also another defect, viz. weak straw. The Howards also found in all Indian wheats a great liability to rust, and in some varieties a great tendency to shatter. Finally, varieties differ in yield, although good cultivation increases production. The Howards set themselves to work with a view to eliminate the defects and obtain the qualities which are essential in a good wheat. As the Indian wheat season is a short one they have avoided all high-yielding varieties with any tendency to lateness and confined their attention to those sorts which ripen well within the available growth period. So far as strength of flour was concerned, rapid progress was made by selection from existing varieties and their propagation as pure types. For characteristics such as strength of straw, experiments on Mendelian lines have been conducted and are in progress. As a result, a very wide range of wheats likely to be useful over a large area in India have been evolved. Heavy yielding, strong white wheats have been produced; these have been successfully grown by the cultivators in other Provinces and in a new environment. One of these, Pusa No. 12, has the power of retaining the quality that gives stability to the dough to an unusual extent under varying conditions. This wheat has invariably given satisfactory returns (over a ton of grain), both as regards yield and milling and baking quality, in almost every district from Gurdaspur in the Punjab and through the United Provinces to Bhagalpur in Behar. It is a white wheat with smooth red chaff and long ears, which are without awns. In the field it is an attractive-looking wheat, and the typical red ears and smooth shining straw at once distinguish it from other kinds. It has stood the test of adverse seasons, and has been taken up for cultivation on a large scale by cultivators in Behar, the United Provinces, the Punjab, and the Central Provinces. A trial consignment of this wheat was sent to England in 1915 and also in 1916, with a view of bringing it to the notice of home millers, and it is hoped further to organize the work in such a manner that some of the local markets will be able to supply it to the shippers. Besides Pusa No. 12, two other new wheats, No. 4 and No. 6, are proving useful. Pusa No. 4 is suitable where the supply of soil moisture is limited, and where the general conditions require a rapidly maturing wheat, e.g. in Bundelkhand. This variety possesses strong straw and good grain, and is also practically immune against yellow rust. It is also useful as a cover crop for Java indigo in Behar. Pusa No. 6, as a separate crop, however, appears to be more suitable for Behar, as it is practically immune to both the common rusts in Behar, and it thrives even under adverse conditions.

The Pusa wheats have been subjected to milling and baking tests in England and placed above all other Indian types. They have even been ranked by some of the trade with Manitoba Spring wheats, which are in greatest demand for breadmaking in England and which command the highest prices. The Indian consumer also has expressed a preference for the varieties which are finding favour on the English market. Work still goes on to improve the best of the Pusa wheats in standing power, rust resistance, and general hardiness. For this purpose crosses between Indian wheats of good grain quality and various English and American varieties were made in England in 1910. These new wheats are now in

THE AGRICULTURAL RESEARCH INSTITUTE, PUSA.

1. MONTGOMERY COW. 2. MONTGOMERY BULL.

the fifth generation and are practically fixed.

It has been calculated that a safe estimate of the gain to Indian wheat-growers, if the crop were replaced by varieties like Pusa No. 12, would be Rs. 15 per acre per year. The rate at which extension will take place must depend on the efficiency of provincial organization for seed distribution. So far as one can predict, the future seems full of promise.

The investigations on indigo carried out by the Howards at Pusa, to whom this work was entrusted after the closing of the Sirsiah Research Station in 1913, are reported to have yielded interesting results. The diseased condition of Java indigo, known locally as "wilt," which principally brought about the reduction in the area under this variety in Behar from 70,000 bighas in 1910 to 15,000 bighas in 1913, and to which the non-success of the Sirsiah experiments with Java indigo has been attributed, has been said by them to be due to a long-continued wet condition of the soil, which destroys the feeding roots. The Howards also maintain that if Java indigo is sown for seed early in August on well-drained land in good heart, the diseased condition is avoided, good crops of well-developed seed having been produced; and it may be added that these results are reported to have been successfully repeated under estate conditions. Besides the seed supply, other aspects of improvement in the cultivation of indigo have also been investigated and some results of practical interest already obtained. These are described in *Pusa Bulletins* No. 51 and No. 54, and in the reports of the Imperial Economic Botanist for 1913-14 and 1914-15.

The progress which has already been made in the indigo investigations indicates that the prospects of resuscitating the industry are very favourable. The competition of synthetic indigo having been for the time removed, a period of high prices has set in, which will afford an opportunity of re-establishing confidence and of putting into order those estates which are still growing indigo, prior to the introduction of new and improved methods of cultivation and manufacture. The Government of India have also decided to supplement the work done by the Howards by the employment of a chemist to continue the investigation of the chemical problems in manufacture.

Much excellent work has also been done at Pusa on the tobacco crop. A number of the American varieties, suitable for cigarettes, and tried at Pusa, having been found unsuitable, attention has been mainly concentrated on the indigenous varieties, and a type (No. 28) has been discovered, of light colour, fine product, and good texture, which has been favourably reported on by the trade as suitable for the above purpose. On a large scale, under estate conditions, it has done exceedingly well, and a great demand for seed has arisen, not only in Behar but in other parts of India. The cultivation of the plant has also been studied, and it has been found that *sann* hemp as a green manure is most successful. In the existing rough methods of cultivation many of the seedlings die and are lost. This loss, it has been found, can be prevented by making fires on the seed beds and so sterilizing them. Some progress has also been made in the curing process, and, by a slight modification of existing methods, it has been found possible to preserve the colour better. Selected seed has been distributed to planters, and it now rests with the factories to assure a steady supply by offering prices commensurate with the extra trouble involved.

Mrs. Howard has studied this crop on the purely botanical side, and has published her work on the inheritance of characters in tobacco as *Botanical Memoir*, vol. vi, No. 3. It has been found that the possibility of obtaining better tobacco by breeding is certain, and several promising varieties have been isolated during the progress of the work. It now remains, on Mendelian lines, to isolate and fix the qualities most desired by the trade.

The fruit experiments at Pusa have already yielded results of considerable practical value, and they have proved the suitability of the soil and climate in Behar for growing certain important varieties. The results are published in *Pusa Bulletins* Nos. 4 and 61. A method has also been devised and successfully tested for sending peaches and other fruit over long distances by rail in India.

Among fibre crops studied in the botanical section, the most important are *sann* hemp (*Crotalaria juncea*) and Deccan hemp (*Hibiscus cannabinus*). In connection with the latter, after selecting a suitable type (No. 3), a system of removing heterozygotes during the seedling stage was adopted in order to minimize the effect of natural crossing. This proved successful, and when a supply of pure seed was obtained a sample of fibre, carefully retted and cleaned in clear river water, was sent home for valuation. It was valued at £18 per ton, as against £8 for ordinarily cleaned fibre. The type is being grown on some estates in Behar with a view to discovering whether it can be grown on a commercial scale.

Investigations now in progress on some important Indian oil-seeds, such as safflower, *rai*, and linseed, point to the necessity of selection in these crops, as some crossing takes place and because the range of "form" is very great. Form separation conducted on a broad basis is likely to lead to the isolation of a desired type, which could then be multiplied and issued to cultivators. The work done is recorded in the *Botanical Memoirs*, vol. ii, Nos. 6 and 7. Practical results of value have also been obtained from the work done on soil ventilation and drainage. The surface drainage method devised by Mr. Howard is now being adopted with success on several estates in Behar, and the practical application of the conclusions reached regarding soil ventilation seems likely to lead to a great increase in the productive capacity of the alluvial soil in Upper India.

MYCOLOGY.

Mycology is the science which deals with fungal diseases of plants; the work is highly specialized, and there is wide scope for research. But the workers are few, there being only three or four trained European Mycologists in the Agricultural Department of the whole of India, two of whom are at Pusa—Dr. E. J. Butler, Imperial Mycologist, and Mr. F. J. F. Shaw, Second Imperial Mycologist. The field is unlimited, the problems new. Samples of unknown diseases are being constantly received, and in each case the disease has to be diagnosed, the cause studied, and remedies tried and proved. In spite of the complexity of the subjects, results of great practical value have, however, already been obtained.

The first step was a preliminary survey of the important fungus diseases of Indian crops, and the formation of a collection of types as a basis for the identification of further specimens. Next, the more important diseases, many of which were new or but little known, had to be submitted to detailed investigation in order to ascertain their cause, the life history of the parasites, and the effects on the plant. Not until these are known can measures to check them be ordinarily recommended. There are various ways of dealing with

THE AGRICULTURAL RESEARCH INSTITUTE, PUSA.

1. Some of the Montgomery Milch Herd. 2. Young Ayrshire-Montgomery Cross-bred Stock.

fungus diseases, and the treatment is in many cases drastic. Spraying is not likely to be taken up in India except with garden or other equally valuable crops, e.g. potatoes, which are sprayed against blight in the Khasia Hills, and areca-nut in Mysore and South Canara, where the disease locally called Koleroga, caused by *Phytophthora omnivora*, var. *arecæ*, is being successfully controlled by this practice. The destruction of diseased parts of plants or the whole of the crop by burning is in many cases the only effective treatment, but it is not always possible to get the cultivator to agree. Smuts which are conveyed in the seed may be killed by disinfection, while the use of thoroughly healthy seed is another and a very effective way of preventing an increase of certain forms of disease. General measures of plant sanitation, such as control of drainage, avoidance of excessive shade or overcrowding and the like, are valuable in many cases. Finally, for many diseases the introduction of resistant varieties is the only certain method to avoid epidemics.

Dr. Butler has already studied in this manner the rusts of wheat and other crops, diseases of sugar-cane, the wilt of *arhar*, several diseases of palms, mulberries, and rice, and the *tikka* disease of ground-nut; but these are only a few of the many investigations that have been carried out. Mr. Shaw has studied the various *Rhizoctonias* in India, a sclerotial disease of rice, also the *tokra* disease, caused by *Orobanche*, on various crops such as tobacco and cabbage, and some allied diseases caused by flowering parasites. A serious disease attacking *sal* (*Shorea robusta*) in the forests of the Buxar Duars Division is also being investigated by him. Useful work on the potato blight, which is present in the hills in India, has been done by Mr. Dastur, senior Assistant to the Imperial Mycologist. It has been shown that the disease cannot long survive the heat of the Indian plains. If potatoes are imported from the hills for seed purposes, they should be obtained in time to allow them to pass a part of the summer on the plains in order to kill the fungus in the diseased tubers. The "black thread disease" of *Hevea brasiliensis* in Burma, caused by a *Phytophthora*, is also under study.

Among the achievements of directly practical value may be mentioned an elaborate campaign against the bud-rot disease of palms in the Godaveri delta. An organized scheme to prevent the spread of the disease, and to stamp it out in the affected area in the Godaveri and Kistna districts, was started in 1907. The parasite attacks the crown of the palm only, killing the tree by destroying the growing point. The only practicable method of checking the spread of infection was to burn the diseased tops before spores had time to form. A large staff was employed by the Madras Government to carry out this work, and over half a million palms were cut out. In Godaveri the disease has been confined to the area originally affected, and it is hoped that its spread to other areas has been checked. Madras values the work at a saving, roughly, of 20 lakhs of rupees annually.

An important discovery recently made by Dr. Butler is that an eelworm is the cause of the disease called *ufra* in paddy, and experiments to combat it are being carried out by the Imperial Mycologist, in conjunction with the Bengal Department. The losses caused by this pest are enormous, and its spread must be checked. The most hopeful method of attack appears to be the destruction by burning, or clean cultivation, of the stubble of diseased fields; and experiments having proved this to be correct on a small scale, the remedy is now being tried on larger areas. The treatment is simple and easy of application, and this investigation occupies a foremost place in the programme of this section.

To obviate the risk of the introduction into British India of any insect, fungus, or other pest which is or may be destructive to crops, both the Imperial Mycologist and the Imperial Entomologist strongly advocated the expediency of legislative measures, and the Destructive Insects and Pests Act, 1914 (11 of 1914), was passed into law. Disinfection, fumigation, quarantine, prohibition, and destruction are the powers with which the law is invested.

Entomology.

India teems with insect life, some useful, but the majority the reverse, and the scope for entomological work in India is unlimited. But there are only three posts for trained European entomologists in India, two of whom are at Pusa. The Entomological section, when first started, was in the able hands of Mr. H. Maxwell-Lefroy, and since his resignation in 1912 Mr. T. Bainbrigge Fletcher has been in charge.

The application of remedies in India is exceedingly difficult. It is only when attacks are concentrated and when wholesale damage has been done that public attention is attracted. The early attacks are not noticed, but their efforts are cumulative, and it is only when they assume large dimensions that the danger is realized. Prompt remedies are expected, though in many cases prevention would probably be better than cure. Again, in many parts of the country there are prejudices against the only method of cure, which is destruction.

The Department was fortunate in securing the services of Mr. H. Maxwell-Lefroy as its first Economic Entomologist, who, with his past experience in the West Indies, started and organized the work in such a way that within the fourteen years that the work has been in progress sufficient men have been trained to study the pests that levy a heavy toll on the country's yearly produce, and to devise and put into practice efficient means of dealing with them successfully. A fairly large collection, representative of the varying fauna of the different parts of the country, has been made and classified, life histories of most of the destructive pests have been worked out in detail, coloured plates illustrating different stages of the pests have been drawn and are available for distribution, with appropriate explanations. A large number of observations of economic and biological interest have been made. These have been incorporated in Memoirs and Bulletins, and are thus available for reference to the provincial assistants working in close touch with Pusa, as well as other workers in India and elsewhere. Much useful work has been done in connection with the industries dependent on the products of insects, viz. eri and mulberry silk culture, lac culture, and apiculture. Several Bulletins have been issued on these subjects, and short courses are given to students. Among these publications may be mentioned the following: Bulletin No. 28, on lac culture, by Mr. C. S. Misra; Bulletin No. 39, on sericulture, by Mr. M. N. De; and Bulletin No. 46, on apiculture, by Mr. C. C. Ghosh. These contain simple and practical instructions, and their usefulness has been widely appreciated. The Bulletins on lac and silk have also been translated into the vernacular with a view to make them useful to the people in those parts where the two industries chiefly flourish. The issue of the textbooks "Indian Insect Life," "Indian Insect Pests," and "Some South Indian Insects" has removed the long-felt want of standard books of reference specially dealing with Indian insects. In fact, within the short space of time during which the work has been in progress so much material has been accumulated that it has paved the way for effectively dealing with the insect pests which break out every year in one or other part of the country, and, along with the accumulation of information, the training of men who have to grapple with the difficulties created by the outbreak of pests has not been lost sight of. Every Province now possesses from two to three, or even more, trained Indian assistants and fieldmen, but there is no European entomologist except in Madras. These officials visit places where a pest has broken out and advise the cultivators about the remedial measures to be adopted. It is with such an organization that marked success has been achieved in the case of the potato moth (*Pthorimæa operculella*, Zell.). The recommendation made by the Department to store seed potatoes in sand has saved the country an annual loss of 14 lakhs of rupees. Extensive operations have been conducted in the past to deal with the greasy cut worm (*Agrotis ypsilon*, Rott.) in Behar and Orissa by catching the moths in "Andre Maire" traps, and by picking off the first broods of caterpillars. Investigations regarding the cotton boll worm have revealed the presence of parasites which destroy the worms. Recent operations against the rice leaf-hoppers (*Nephotettix bipunctatis*, Fabr., and *N. apicalis*, Motsch.) conducted by the Department of Agriculture, Central Provinces, with the help of the Imperial Entomologist, are likely to be of far-reaching economic importance to eastern rice-growing tracts of the Province. With the ever-increasing interest that is shown by the people towards the development of the sugar industry in India, the study of insect pests of this crop is assuming greater importance. Investigations have revealed the presence of borers and other sucking insects, which annually lessen the outturn to a considerable extent; and as these inquiries proceed it is possible that pests which have not hitherto been reported to occur in the country will be found to be present in fairly large numbers in certain parts of India, especially in the tracts in which sugar-cane is cultivated.

The object of the entomological work has been to obtain a comprehensive survey of the economic pests of the country, and to devise and recommend such measures, by means of bulletins, leaflets, popular lectures, and lantern-slide exhibitions, as would be readily accepted and adopted by the people. It will thus be seen that a great amount of spade work has been done by Mr. Lefroy and his successor, Mr. Bainbrigge Fletcher, but no great success can be achieved in this direction until the number of entomological workers, both European and Indian, is largely increased.

PATHOLOGICAL ENTOMOLOGY.

For a brief description of the work done in this section of Pathological Entomology, and of the lines of inquiry followed by Mr. Howlett, who is in charge, I can do no better than reproduce *in toto* the very popular account given by Mr. James Mackenna in his pamphlet on "Agriculture in India":—

"A fascinating branch of entomological work is under the direction of Mr. Howlett. He starts from the standpoint that agricultural, veterinary, and medical entomology has reached a stage at which methods based merely on a general knowledge of life histories, combined with a more or less superficial study of habits, have been to a great extent worked out. This has been done by men possessed of ingenuity and ability, and in most cases it is difficult to see how their recommendations are to be improved upon with the knowledge at present at our disposal.

"For example, the chief anti-mosquito measures now advocated are the destruction of breeding-places by oiling or drainage, the destruction of larvæ by fish, and the use of mosquito nets—*all measures well known long before the definite connection of mosquitoes and malaria was established*. Similarly, the only practical preventive of several animal parasites (practically all the 'external' ones) is to wash, spray, or dip the animal in one of the few well-known mixtures, such as lime-sulphur or crude-oil emulsion, while spraying the crop with these or similar mixtures is also recognized as the only method of destroying a large number of plant-feeding insects.

"There are thus a number of stock methods which are quite familiar to professional entomologists, veterinary officers, and medical men. In some cases these methods can be effectively used at comparatively small cost, but frequently the expense makes it difficult to recommend them unless the crops or animals to be treated are specially valuable and unless a cure can be guaranteed.

"Particularly is this the case in India, where, perhaps, more than in any other country it is *cheap* methods that are required for general use.

"Economy and efficiency can be attained only by more accurate knowledge in certain directions, and Mr. Howlett is attempting to ascertain the factors which influence the more practically important activities of insects, such as pairing, egg-laying, blood-sucking, and the choice of food plants.

"He advocates the principle of what he terms 'control-breeding' for the reduction of noxious and parasitic insects, the idea being to encourage breeding by the provision of breeding-places, as far as possible ideal, in areas which can be easily controlled.

"It is a method which economizes energy to a marked extent, and will, it is hoped, have a wide application when more precise knowledge is available as to the factors which influence the choice of breeding-places. Partly with the object of furthering knowledge in this direction, Mr. Howlett is paying special attention to chemical influences, and he has succeeded in isolating the actual compounds which exert a remarkable attractive influence on male fruit-flies. This, it is believed, is the first instance of the kind in which the chemical nature of such substances has been ascertained, and the discovery opens up a wide field of research, which it is hoped to pursue with the ultimate object of introducing more efficient and economic methods of dealing with insect pests, particularly those concerned in the conveyance of animal disease."

The three main lines of inquiry engaging attention are: (1) A thorough investigation of disease-carrying insects; (2) chemotactic reactions of fruit-flies and chemotropism in general; and (3) general bionomics of mosquitoes, especially with regard to ovulation, æstivation, and hibernation, and the physiology of their respiration and digestion. With regard to (1), a large series of observations have been made on the bionomics of many of the Indian blood-suckers, and these have been recorded in manuscripts. An article on the Indian species of *Phlebotomus* has already appeared in the *Bulletin of Entomological Research*. Papers bearing on inquiry No. 2 have been published in *Transactions of the Entomological Society* and the *Bulletin of Entomological Research*. The work done on (3) has been published in the form of an illustrated article on "Respiration of Culicidæ" in the *Indian Journal of Medical Research.*

AGRICULTURAL BACTERIOLOGY.

Bacteria play a large part in vegetable as they do in animal life, and agricultural bacteriology concerns itself with their action. The subject falls into two main branches—soil bacteriology and plant pathology.

Much of the earlier work done by Mr. C. M. Hutchinson, who is in charge of this section, has been of a preliminary nature, and confined largely to trial and selection of the bacteriological methods best adapted for dealing with special conditions of soil and climate in India.

The biological analysis of a soil involves a determination of the number and kinds of bacteria contained in it, and more particularly the measurement of the physiological activity of the soil organisms. In this kind of analysis are also included investigations having for their aim the discovery of how such useful bacterial functions as make for fertility may be encouraged and harmful ones checked in the ordinary operations of agricultural practice. Hence the main lines of work of this section have been aimed at determining under what conditions various soils will best serve as culture media for those beneficial bacteria naturally present in them.

Samples of soils taken from several places have been analysed bacteriologically, pure cultures of bacteria found have been made and their physiological functions examined. The systematic investigation of the distribution, physiological characters, and functions of soil bacteria in these soils is a huge task, and the complete results are not capable of being published immediately; but organisms interesting or new to science which have been noticed so far are described in *Memoirs of the Department of Agriculture, India,* Bacteriological Series.

A special study has been made of the effect of hot-weather ploughing on the bacteriological content of the soil, and the possibility of a bacteriological explanation of the undoubted increase in fertility resulting therefrom. It was found that the net result is an extremely rapid formation of ammonia, part of which becomes available to plants and part of which is lost. Depletion of soil nitrogen is a necessary consequence, and the maintenance of fertility must depend on the restoration of this by green manure or some other nitrogenous manure.

The chief forms of nitrogenous manures easily available to the Indian cultivator are, however, of an organic nature only; and when large quantities of nitrogenous organic matter are turned into the soil and put under intensive cultivation, much nitrogen may be lost in the form of ammonia, under the high soil temperature conditions prevailing in India. Accordingly, methods of biological analysis have been applied to different soils to find out the capabilities of different bacterial flora of dealing successfully with the organic matter supplied to them. Hence, also, the supply of available nitrogen by the biolysis of such substances as green manures and root residues has received careful attention, from a bacteriological point of view. The

1. REARING MUGA (SILK) WORMS ON GUM-TREES, IN ASSAM.
2. REELING OF PAT (MULBERRY) WORMS IN ASSAM. 3. SPINNING COCOONS ON SCREEN.
Photos by D. C. Ghoshal, Jorhat.

experiments conducted in the laboratory and in the field have led to a special modified method of dealing with a green-manure crop. It consists in hastening the initial stages of decomposition by steeping the cut crop in water and then fermenting it in heaps, the fermented material being then used in the same way as farmyard manure. The advantages of this method, in addition to the principal one of eliminating the uncertainty of the rainfall as a factor in decomposing the buried green material, include the possibility of supplying the fermented manure at the best rate per acre, and at the best time for producing its maximum manurial effects.

An investigation of natural conditions under which nitrogen is taken from the air and added to the soil in this country has also been taken up. It is, perhaps, unnecessary to emphasize the importance of the question of the fixation of nitrogen, but it may be pointed out that, in this country, where cultivators do not generally purchase adequate supplies from external sources, and where bones and hides, which represent nitrogen, collected from very extensive areas of land are exported, the introduction of intensive cultivation, leading to a more rapid conversion of non-available plant food, especially nitrogen, into the available condition, renders the study of nitrogen-fixing members of soil flora such as *Phlebotomos radicicola azotobacter*, and *Clostridium* of very great importance.

The results of the preliminary investigation on nitrogen fixation by *Azotobacter* are recorded in a Memoir of the Department, Bacteriological Series, vol. i, No. 4, by J. H. Walton.

The action of bacteria upon the organic matter of soils may result in the formation, amongst other decomposition products, of toxic substances which lead to infertility. It has been shown at Pusa that such toxins are readily formed in waterlogged soils, and produce infertility either by direct action upon the crop if present in large quantities, or indirectly by interfering with the normal processes of nitrification upon which the nitrogen supply of the growing plant depends. Certain classes of soil bacteria have been shown to produce these toxins in large amounts, and they flourish in soils in which excess of water and consequent lack of air are found. These toxins are for the most part readily destroyed by oxidation, so that the ordinary methods of cultivation and tillage not only tend to inhibit their formation, but serve to destroy them.

In the domain of plant pathology, the wilt of tobacco in Rangpur and the rot of potato tubers have been investigated. The wilt was found to be caused by a strain of *Bacillus solanacearum*, an organism known to cause disease in several cultivated crops such as potato, brinjal, and tomato. The Rangpur strain differs slightly in some of its physiological characters from those described in America and Japan.

ELEPHANTS REMOVING TIMBER.

In connection with the rot of potato, two kinds of bacteria (rot-producers) were found to be invariably present, and these are normally present in Indian soils. It was found that rotting could take place in presence of these bacteria if the dry tubers suffered mechanical injury, or if the uninjured tuber were kept under conditions in which its surface could remain moist for a few hours. Tubers stored in sand to keep out potato moth can be attacked if the rotting organisms are present either through bruising due to careless handling, or by reason of the sand not being perfectly dry, or by contact between a rotting potato exuding moisture and a sound one; hence this latter possibility necessitates the frequent examination of stored tubers and the picking out of rotten ones. Two per cent. of copper sulphate used as a wash to the tubers was found to give very good results. An account of the work done has been published by Messrs. Hutchinson and Joshi in *Bacteriological Memoir*, vol. i, No. 5.

Agricultural bacteriology in the wider sense, including bacteriology of industries dependent on agriculture, has made great strides in recent years, and development in practical application of this branch of agricultural science in the tropics is certain of conferring benefits on those engaged in such industries. The Bacteriological section at Pusa has carried out investigations on fermentation organisms, whereby decided improvements in the yield of alcohol from such fermentable materials as were utilized in Indian distilleries have been secured. In another direction work has been carried out with a view to the possible improvement and extension of the indigenous saltpetre industry, and it has been shown possible to increase greatly the output and purity of this raw material by the introduction of controlled methods.

Agricultural College.

The idea of attaching to the Research Station an agricultural college really grew out of the necessities of Bengal. The Agricultural College at Sibpur was not successful, its situation being entirely unsuited to its purpose. There was no place in Bengal where a new college could be started with the advantage of an experimental farm in its neighbourhood, the only farm belonging to Government being then at Chittagong. The Bengal scheme for the utilization of Pusa therefore contemplated the transfer of this college to Pusa. When, therefore, the Pusa scheme was taken over by the Government of India, it appeared essential that Pusa should include a college to provide for Bengal, even though admission should not be confined to that Province. This, though one of the objects, was not the chief reason for the establishment of a Central Imperial College. It was necessary to provide for the extension and completion of provincial educational facilities, and also to arrange for the training of the teachers of the future and of specialists in the various branches of science connected with agriculture, so that India might ultimately be able to meet her own requirements as regards a higher agricultural staff. In short, Pusa was intended to serve as a model for and raise the standard of agricultural colleges in other Provinces, and provide for a more complete and efficient agricultural education than was then possible in any of the existing institutions.

On the educational side the aim at the outset was twofold. In the first place, it was intended to train students who could not attend any of the provincial colleges or schools, and, in the second place, to provide a higher course of training to those who had studied at provincial institutions, and who desired to qualify themselves for professorships, research work, or for posts requiring special scientific attainments. The complete course of instruction at Pusa was intended to be one of five years. It was anticipated that the college would be ready about the end of 1907, but, pending the opening, some provincial candidates were taken up in 1904-5 for training in practical agriculture and entomology, in order to qualify them for posts in Provincial Departments. This start met with such success, and the necessity of securing quickly the nucleus of a staff of trained assistants in each Province was so great, that arrangements were subsequently made to train similar candidates in practical agriculture, agricultural chemistry, mycology, and entomology.

In the scheme for the expansion of the Agricultural Department prepared in 1905, great stress was laid on the establishment in each important Province of an agricultural college, with a competent teaching staff and fully equipped laboratories. It was held that these colleges should be located on principal experimental and instruction farms, which would also be central research stations. The superior staff proposed was an Expert Agriculturist, an Agricultural Chemist, an Economic Botanist, an Entomologist, and a Mycologist, one of the members of the staff discharging the duties of Principal of the College. The staff was to combine teaching with research. It was held that research work would ordinarily be more active and better sustained if associated with lecturing, as this would check any tendency to the investigation of problems unlikely to lead to practical results. To enable the experts to carry on research and to tour, an adequate number of assistants and demonstrators was to be provided. They would also assist in teaching, so that the time of experts might not be wasted in elementary tuition. The course of instruction was to last three years, after which it was hoped that a few of the best students would proceed to Pusa for a further post-graduate course of two years in order to fit them to fill the higher appointments. This part of the scheme, with the omission of an Entomologist and a Mycologist, was sanctioned, and accordingly agricultural colleges providing a three years' course were established at Sabour, Cawnpore, Lyallpur, Nagpur, Poona, and Coimbatore. It has therefore been definitely decided that Pusa shall only be chiefly a higher teaching Institution with post-graduate studies, and that it shall be specially open for admission to selected graduates of Provincial Agricultural Colleges and distinguished science graduates of Indian Universities. The arrangement is in every way satisfactory. It has placed the staff in a position which enables them to give their undivided attention to important investigations, and it provides means for acquiring that knowledge which is a condition precedent to training others. The graduate who has completed his general agricultural education, and is undergoing specialization in one branch, has the advantage of the personal supervision of an expert in his subject and every facility in the way of laboratories and libraries.

Arrangements have also been made at Pusa, for the time being, to give instruction in short practical courses in agriculture, fruit, silk, lac, cattle-breeding, and other subjects.

If we take into account not only the students who have undergone training in post-graduate courses, and probationers trained for special posts in Provincial Agricultural Departments, but also short-course students and casual workers in the laboratories, their number already comes to more than 230.

Not the least important work of the Institute consists in the publication of the results of scientific research done by the officers. Pusa has, in fact, become the central bureau of information on Indian agricultural matters. The Imperial Department of Agriculture in India issues quarterly an agricultural journal which contains popular articles intended for educated Indian agriculturists and general readers interested in agriculture, while papers of a more scientific or technical nature are published as Memoirs. These are issued from time to time under Botanical, Chemical, Entomological, Bacteriological, and Veterinary Series. The Institute also issues a series of Bulletins, which are more of practical than scientific interest, and these are widely distributed in India and to learned societies and interested individuals in all countries. The exchange in publications is considerable, and the Institute corresponds with some 150 to 200 important societies at home and abroad, most of which have entered into exchange relations.

Already over 110 Memoirs, 60 Bulletins, and 44 issues of the *Agricultural Journal of India* have been published, to which may be added three important books on Indian Insect Life, Indian Insect Pests, and Wheat in India.

The above gives but a meagre description of the work done and of the activities of the Institute, but space does not permit of any further enlargement. It may, however, be remarked in conclusion that the results already obtained by the Institute are of far-reaching and great practical value, and that even greater results may be contemplated for the future than have been obtained in the past; and that, with an increased staff and wider range of activities, the Agricultural Department, furnished as it will be in the near future with a large number of experiments of proved value to Indian agriculture, will go on from strength to strength, paying tribute to the wisdom of the policy which led to its establishment from the first on a basis of research followed by demonstration, the only true way to promote improvements which are to be of any lasting value to the country for which they are undertaken.

CLEARING A PADDY-FIELD IN EASTERN BENGAL.

Photo by D. C. Goshal.

KIDDERPORE DOCKS, CALCUTTA.

THE PORT OF CALCUTTA

COMPILED FROM NOTES SUPPLIED BY THE PORT COMMISSIONERS, CALCUTTA

MORE than one literary critic has ventured to question the wisdom of Job Charnock's selection of the site of Calcutta, but those cavillers appear to have entirely overlooked the fact that a position at the mouth of the Gangetic valley, and a connection, by means of the Ganges and Brahmaputra Rivers and their affluents, with an enormous territory of fertile land inhabited by more than 60 millions of people, appealed with considerable force to the astute Charnock, who regarded the objections that the locality was unhealthy as meriting little or no consideration, in view of the vast potential wealth which, in his opinion, would ultimately be brought to the projected port.

There were others who held that a seaport, to be of any real value to a country, must be at the outlet of a large river; but it has been pointed out that, long before Charnock made his choice, in the year 1690, Portuguese traders from the west coast of India moored their ships, built stores for merchandise, and even erected a temporary town practically on the very spot where Calcutta's palatial offices and mercantile houses now seethe with activities. The French and Dutch were pioneers among European traders, and they, too, established factories not only within a few miles to the north of Calcutta, but at other places at much greater distances from the coast.

When the East India Company came upon the scene, their servants extended their business centres from Calcutta to Dacca, Murshidabad, Berhampur, Patna, and other towns, and their ships, which brought goods of European manufacture, returned with cargoes of country produce such as silk, cotton, rice, and saltpetre.

Shipping facilities for the growing town were at first obtained by the erection of a quay along the western front of the original Fort William, which occupied the site of the present Custom House and the thoroughfares now known as Fairlie Place and Koila Ghat Street.

Government records show that in May 1758 Clive informed a Select Committee that "Admiral Pocock, at his departure, represented to him the necessity of having a dock in Bengal for the reception of His Majesty's ships in case the squadron should winter here; and as he thinks that the expense of making such a dock would be greatly overbalanced by the advantages resulting from having the squadron refit at Bengal instead at Bombay, by which means they would have it in their power to return much earlier to the coast, he hopes, therefore, the Committee will immediately order a survey to be made of the spot most proper to make a dock at, and give directions for its being begun and completed as soon as it possibly can be done."

It appears from records still in existence that wet and dry docks and a marine yard for repairing vessels of war and merchantmen were established at Kidderpore in 1780 by Colonel Henry Watson, who acted as "second" to Sir Philip Francis in his historic duel with Warren Hastings at Belvedere House, Alipore. The building of vessels was forthwith commenced by Watson, and in the following year the frigate *Nonsuch*, with 36 guns, was launched, while the *Surprise* frigate, of 36 guns, was completed about seven years later. Shortly after this date the dockyard was taken over by two sons of Captain Kyd, who was the Chief Engineer on the establishment of the East India Company; and between the years 1781 and 1821 more than 230 vessels were constructed at a cost of more than £2,000,000.

At Fort Gloucester, near Calcutta, where there are now flourishing jute mills, there was a dockyard, where nearly 30 vessels were launched between the years 1811 and 1828, and at Titaghur (12 miles distant from Calcutta) a vessel of 1,445 tons burthen, the *Countess of Sutherland*, was built in 1801.

These shipbuilding yards and places of anchorage were of little practical value to the growth of a port, and while it was generally agreed that the construction of docks was an absolute necessity to meet the ever-growing shipping trade of Calcutta, there was at the same time a great diversity of opinion respecting the most suitable site for them.

The project of constructing at Diamond Harbour was under consideration prior to a report on the subject by Captain Boileau in 1839, and between the years 1844 and 1847 a thorough investigation took place with regard to means of improving the trade facilities of Calcutta. A committee reported in May 1846 in favour of wet docks at Kidderpore, while in 1847 Mr. F. W. Simms, C.E., examined very fully the proposals of a "Calcutta and Diamond Harbour Dock and Railway Company," coming to the conclusion, as between Diamond Harbour and Kidderpore, that "one site possessed no great advantage over the other." Lord Dalhousie, Viceroy of India at the time, in a Minute dated April 20, 1853, emphatically condemned the project of railway communication with Diamond Harbour in these words: "I do not believe that the formation of a railway to Diamond Harbour would be of the slightest benefit to the fine steamships of the Peninsular and Oriental Company, the large mail steamers of the Screw Company, or the heavily armed steam frigates of the Indian Navy, which perpetually traverse the channel without difficulty or danger; it would not induce any one of them to anchor there or to depart from their usual plan of proceeding direct to Calcutta, with the advantages of proximity to their cargo and agents, of accessibility to their passengers, and manifold other conveniences, both for those who belong to the ships and for those ashore."

It should be observed here that the trade had increased to such an extent by the year 1858 that Lord Canning, the Viceroy of India at the time, made representations to the Secretary of State with the view of obtaining sanction from the India Office for the expenditure of 100 lakhs of rupees in the construction of wet docks at Calcutta. Jetties had been constructed on the banks of the river, but they were totally insufficient to meet the then existing needs of the port, and it was further found that direct control by the Government of shipping affairs was not conducive to the best interests of Calcutta.

An Act of Parliament was therefore passed in the year 1866 under which management was placed in the hands of the Municipal authorities, who were Justices of the Peace, but this plan proved in practice to be unworkable.

Very valuable reports were about this time prepared by Mr. Leonard, engineer of the port, relating to the burning question of control, and these were followed in 1870 by an Act of Parliament which gave the then Lieutenant-Governor of Bengal power to appoint nine Commissioners, to whom authority was given to construct wharves, quays, jetties, and landing-places, tramways, and warehouses, and to undertake other works of improvement. This was the beginning of the Port Trust as now constituted.

The Commissioners proceeded to spend very large sums of money in reproductive works, but still the lack of proper dock accommodation had become greatly intensified, and at their request a Committee was appointed by Sir Ashley Eden, the then Lieutenant-Governor, "to confer upon a proposal to construct docks at Diamond Harbour." The majority of the members of the Committee were in favour of the scheme, but there was considerable opposition from leading merchants, who urged, as one of their main reasons, that they would be compelled to keep a staff of officials at Diamond Harbour as well as at Calcutta.

Very little progress appears to have been made, however, until the Diamond Harbour scheme was revived in 1881, but in the intervening years various schemes were launched for wet docks in the suburbs of Calcutta—namely, at Howrah, at the Botanical Gardens, Chitpore, Sealdah, Akra, and Kidderpore.

On February 23, 1883, a Memorandum was addressed by the Joint Secretary to the Government of Bengal, Public Works Department, to the Vice-Chairman of the Port Commissioners, in which he stated that Sir Rivers Thompson (who had succeeded Sir Ashley Eden) had decided that "before any action is taken upon the proposals of the Committee, the question as to the further capabilities of the extension of the port should receive a fuller and closer investigation than has yet been attempted. I am therefore to request that the Port Commissioners will, in communication with the Chamber of Commerce, institute an inquiry, and submit a report as to the measures which it is possible to take for the extension of the present accommodation of the port, and the cost at which any changes which may be recommended can be carried out."

The report of the Committee—dated September 3, 1883—recommended, *inter alia*: (1) That the accommodation for the trade of the port requires immediate extension; (2) that extra wharves should be provided; (3) that there is room for a considerable number of additional jetties, but for general convenience they consider wet docks to be preferable; and (4) the immediate construction of wet docks at Kidderpore, with an entrance through the Government Dockyard. In connection with the last-mentioned recommendation (in preference to the Diamond Harbour scheme), the Committee urged that the docks, if constructed upon the site suggested by them, "should be placed in direct communication with the eastern canals and rivers round Calcutta, and cargo coming into port by those means of carriage for ultimate shipment could be stored in warehouses in connection with the docks." In a dispatch dated March 6, 1884, by the Rt. Hon. the Earl of Kimberley, Her Majesty's Secretary of State for India, the following words occur: "I affirm the conclusion of the Government of India in selecting Calcutta as the place for the future docks, and in adopting the Kidderpore site for them. Pending the completion of the docks, it is, however, obvious that such steps as are possible should be taken for increasing the accommodation of the export trade, and the proposals that these should comprise the organization of a suitable cargo-boat service, the extension of boat-wharves on the Howrah side of the river, and other improvements have my approval."

Several years were then occupied in the preparation and consideration of plans and with inquiries into the effects of the proposed works upon the sanitation of the neighbourhood in question, and eventually the sanction of the Government of India was obtained for the commencement of construction according to designs prepared by Mr. W. Duff Bruce, M.I.C.E.

These docks consist of a basin, entered from the River Hooghly by two entrances —one, a lock pointing upstream at an angle of about 20 degrees with the flood tide, and the other, a single entrance by which the basin is entered direct from the river. The basin entrance may thus be used as a large lock, and from it entrance is given on the east side of two dry docks, and at the south end by a double passage to Wet Dock No. 1, which dock is connected by a single passage with Wet Dock No. 2.

A dry dock and a slipway for small craft between the two lock entrances are entered direct from the river.

The numerical particulars contained in the following paragraphs have been kindly supplied by the Port Commissioners :—

Length of lock, 520 feet ; width of lock, 60 feet; width of tidal entrance, 80 feet; depth of water over entrance sills at mean high water, 34 feet, low water, 23 feet; mean rise of tide, 11 feet.

Tidal Basin.—Length of basin, 600 feet; width, 680 feet; area, 9½ acres ; quayage of basin, west side, accommodating one vessel, 600 feet.

Dock No. 1.—Width of entrance to tidal basin, 60 and 80 feet; length, 2,700 feet; width, 600 feet; depth of water, 30 feet; water area, 33 acres; quayage, 5,400 feet; 12 single-storied cargo-sheds with an area of 542,500 superficial feet; 9 hydraulic cranes to lift each 5 tons; 69 hydraulic cranes to lift each 35 cwts.; and sheers to lift 100 tons.

Dock No. 2.—Width of entrance from Dock No. 1, 80 feet; length, 4,500 feet; average width, 400 feet; depth of water, 30 feet; quayage, east side (9 berths), 4,320 feet, west side (6 berths), 2,616 feet; and 5 double-storied sheds (at produce berths), with a floor area of 492,400 superficial feet.

Each of these berths is provided with 5 35-cwt. hydraulic cranes, and each shed with 5 35-cwt. electric cranes. One of the coal berths on the west is fitted with mechanical appliances (Beckett's patent) for loading, while another one has been fitted with a belt-conveyor plant.

There are 33 sheds, with an area of 1,081,990 square feet, for the storage of wheat and seeds, 2 double-storied sheds on the river bank where tea is received from inland vessels pending shipment, and a four-storied warehouse, 670 feet by 120 feet, in which sales of tea take place. A second four-storied warehouse, 600 feet by 120 feet, is under construction.

The export trade in hides and skins is provided for with 357,595 square feet of warehouse floorage, with drying grounds attached, the total area occupied being 25 acres.

Water-level in docks is maintained by pumping higher than the level of high water in the river, and the docks are in railway communication with the jetties and the Indian broad-gauge railways. Quays and cargo-sheds are lit by electricity.

The construction of four riverside berths, built on screw piles, with 4 double-storied transit-sheds, with a frontage of 2,630 feet, is in hand, and a riverside coaling berth has been recently brought into commission. The Port Commissioners' jetties are 4,735 feet in length, and can berth 9 large steamers. The depth of water alongside the jetties is maintained by dredging, and in the reconstruction of the older jetties, as well as in the new ones, a depth of 30 feet at lowest low water is provided.

The jetties are in railway communication with the Indian broad-gauge railways and the Kidderpore Docks, and the Commissioners' line of railway extends along both banks of the river throughout the port. The jetties are equipped with 56 hydraulic cranes, each to lift 35 cwt.; 1 hydraulic crane to lift 5 tons, 2 floating cranes to lift 30 tons, 2 electric cranes to lift 1 ton, 11 electric cranes to lift 35 cwt., and 1 electric 30-ton "Goliath" cantilever crane.

The Commissioners have provided accommodation at Budge-Budge, 12 miles down the river, for all petroleum brought to the port. There are 5 jetties, with pontoons, to afford facilities to vessels bringing either case or bulk oil, and the arrangement of storage and factory sheds, as well as that of tanks for the storage of oil, has been remodelled so as to minimize all fire risks. This depot, in addition to 278,000 square feet of covered area for the storage of oil in tins, has a tank storage capacity of 23,614,773 gallons for bulk oil.

Moorings are laid for the accommodation of a large number of vessels in the stream, and much of the trade of the port is dealt with at these anchorages.

The lighters employed in carrying cargo are accommodated at wharves known as the Indian vessels' wharves, which extend for many miles along both banks of the river, and are in communication with the Indian broad-gauge railways.

The docks are in direct railway communication with the import jetties, the city of Calcutta, the East Indian, the Eastern Bengal, the Bengal-Nagpur Railway systems, and by the Commissioners' lines of railway on each bank of the river.

The Commissioners have their own rolling stock, consisting of 58 locomotives and 1,736 wagons, for terminal purposes and for the carriage of goods between the jetties, the docks, and the busy junctions with which other lines of railways are connected, the length of the Commissioners' own railway track being 135 miles of 5 feet 6 inch gauge.

A ferry service on the Hooghly, with a fleet of 13 steamers, was started in 1907, and landing-stages have been erected at various places on the river above and below the Howrah bridge. The number of first and second-class passengers carried declined—owing to the utilization of some of the vessels by the Government on account of the European War—from 10,248,752 during the year ended March 31, 1915, to 9,795,699 persons in the corresponding period between 1915 and 1916.

It is generally admitted that the Hooghly presents as many, if not more, obstacles to successful navigation as any other river in the world, but the duties of surveying channels, the erection of lighthouses and lightships, and the fixing of buoys have been undertaken in such a thoroughly capable and scientific manner that the normal draught of water is exceedingly satisfactory. It is learned from the office of the Port Commissioners that the surveying of the Hooghly proceeds without intermission throughout the year, a staff of from 15 to 20 specially qualified officials having been appointed for this duty.

Plans are then lithographed and printed for distribution to pilots, who have tremendous responsibilities placed upon them in conducting ships either up or down the river.

The patrolling officers make daily surveys of anchorages, channels, lights, buoys, bars, and the famous James and Mary shoal situated between the mouths of the Damudar and Rupnarain Rivers, which flow into the Hooghly. This shoal received its name from a ship called the *Royal James and Mary*, which was wrecked there in the year 1694.

Various schemes for the improvement of the channels of the river have been proposed from time to time, but the most important one adopted by the Commissioners was the purchase, in 1907, of the powerful sand-pump dredger *Sandpiper*, which has accomplished such good results that ocean-going steamers drawing as much as 28 feet 3 inches of water are able to navigate the river in safety. The dredger *Balari* has since been secured,

THE PORT OF CALCUTTA

and a greater depth of water in the channel is now obtained.

The control of the port is vested in an authority known as the Commissioners for the Port of Calcutta, and incorporation was granted in the year 1870. The Chairman is usually the senior member of the Board of Revenue of the Bengal Government. Both he and the Vice-Chairman, who is the administrative head of the port, are appointed by the Government of Bengal, who also nominate seven Commissioners; two other members are elected by the Calcutta Trades Association, one by the Bengal National Chamber of Commerce, and another by the Corporation of Calcutta. The Executive consists of four departments—namely, the Audit and Accounts Department, the Chief Engineer's Department, the Deputy Conservator's Department, and the Traffic Department; while the Medical Officer is Lieutenant-Colonel R. Bird, C.I.E., M.V.O., I.M.S. Mr. J. Angus, M.Inst.C.E., is Consulting Engineer and London Agent, and Mr. S. C. Williams is Secretary.

The following particulars are extracted from the Administration Report of the Commissioners for the year ending March 31, 1916. The income of the Trust during the year 1915-16 amounted to Rs. 1,59,35,456, against an expenditure on Revenue Account of Rs. 1,49,07,001, showing a credit balance on the year's working of Rs. 10,28,455. The year, however, opened with a debit balance on Revenue Account of Rs. 10,88,490, the result of restricted trade during the previous financial year throughout the eight months of the European War from August 1914 to March 1915, which had only been partially met by the special war surcharges imposed with effect from February 1, 1915. The net deficit at the close of the year under review was therefore Rs. 60,035.

For the purposes of comparison, it may be observed that the net tonnage of the port during the three financial years 1913-14, 1914-15, and 1915-16 was respectively 4,256,987 tons, 3,705,160 tons, and 2,967,798 tons. During the past year 1,150 vessels arrived in the port, with an aggregate gross tonnage of 4,848,961 tons, as compared with 1,428 ships, with a tonnage of 5,997,639, in 1914-15.

The following figures, relating to some of the imports and exports landed and shipped over the dock quays, may be read with interest. Imports during the years 1914-15 and 1915-16 respectively: general, 41,526 tons and 13,064 tons; sugar, 193,267 tons and 229,663 tons; salt, 3,936 tons and 6 tons; rice, 417,024 tons and 324,491 tons; and railway-sleepers, 41,735 tons and 3,263 tons. Exports: wheat, 272,937 tons and 200,603 tons; jute, 294,778 tons and 378,696 tons; tea, 104,710 tons and 119,347 tons; coal, 2,633,805 tons and 1,610,645 tons; cotton, 8,957 tons and 13,126 tons; and gunny bags, 25,354 tons and 81,528 tons respectively.

These particulars show, in the clearest possible manner, how the war has affected the trade of the port, and, indeed, of the whole of that portion of India for which Calcutta is the natural outlet. The extension of railways is for the time being practically at a standstill, and therefore the import of railway material and other accessories has been enormously restricted; while the demand for jute fabrics, cotton goods, and gunny bags, to be used for sandbags in trenches and for packing purposes, has increased to a very considerable extent. Although the past year's working shows an actual deficit, the Commissioners are confident that many of the extensions and improvements at the docks which are temporarily delayed will ultimately be completed in a satisfactory manner.

These proposals for extensions have been before the Commissioners for a number of years, and the works which are projected will, in all probability, cover a period of 35 or 40 years. The scheme, in brief, involves the acquisition of 1,843 acres of land; the making of three large additional modern docks, and the equipment of them with sheds, quayage, cranes, and other facilities for the quick handling of cargoes; the making of new roads, and of termini for the various railway companies whose lines will be connected with the docks; and the erection of suitable accommodation for the officials of the Commissioners.

It is anticipated that the entire cost of these works will not be less than five millions sterling.

Notwithstanding the adverse conditions which have so seriously affected international trade during the past couple of years, the Commissioners have the satisfaction of knowing that the balance to the credit of the Revenue Reserve Fund at the close of the last financial year was no less than Rs. 21,75,321—a very satisfactory record under the circumstances.

THE PORT OF CHITTAGONG

CHITTAGONG, the chief port in the eastern portion of the Bengal Presidency, is situated on the Karnafuli River, and in the north-eastern extremity of the Bay of Bengal.

History tells that the Afghans were in supreme power in Bengal between the thirteenth and sixteenth centuries, and that when their reigning king received an embassy from the Viceroy of Goa, he had suspicions regarding the bona-fides of the members of the mission, and forthwith seized them, together with the crew of their ship, which had anchored at the mouth of the Karnafuli. The Portuguese, in return for this treatment of their emissaries, sent a powerful expedition, which captured the town and port of Chittagong.

Some years later the Mahommedans took possession of the place, but it was afterwards held by Rajas of the Arracan Province of Burma until the year 1666, when it became attached to the Delhi Empire. Chittagong was subsequently the headquarters of a number of marauders who had fled from justice in Goa, Cochin, and elsewhere, who became pirates and raided a large number of villages in the estuaries of the Ganges and Brahmaputra Rivers.

The English made their appearance in Chittagong about the year 1685, when the East India Company had troubles with the Emperor Aurungzebe; and as trade had been hampered very considerably by the Governor of Bengal, Job Charnock was ordered to take warships for the purpose of seizing and fortifying Chittagong. Matters seemed to get from bad to worse up to the time of the Mutiny, when Chittagong again suffered at the hands of pirates.

During the whole of this period the natural harbour at Chittagong had been constantly used by ships trading between various ports in the East, but nothing had been done in the formation of quays, landing-stages, or berthing-places. The inhabitants of the town—or rather village—of those days were not able to set up commercial establishments owing to periodical visits of bands of plunderers.

In the year 1887 an Act of Parliament was passed to provide for the management of the port of Chittagong and to appoint Commissioners, but it was not until the completion of the Assam-Bengal Railway in 1904 that definite steps were taken to provide accommodation for loading and unloading ships, or to erect warehouses and sheds for the storage of merchandise and other goods.

The Act stipulated that there should be nine Commissioners, of whom six should be appointed by the Government of Bengal and three others by firms engaged in commerce in the port. These officials were authorized, *inter alia*, to construct wharves, quays, jetties, piers, warehouses, sheds, engines, and other necessary appliances; to reclaim or enclose any part of the bank or bed of the river within the limits of the port; and to carry out all such other works as might, in the opinion of the Commissioners, be necessary for giving effect to the provisions of the Act, with the reservation, however, that all acts and proceedings of the Commissioners should be subject to the approval of the Government.

The Government of Bengal, in 1905, appointed Messrs. Dumayne and Palmer, Vice-Chairman and Chief Engineer of the Calcutta Port Commissioners, to inquire and report upon the needs of the port and upon the best way of meeting them, and shortly after that date extensive works were taken in hand with the view of providing jetties, sheds, and general equipment to facilitate the berthing of ships and the handling of cargoes.

In February 1914 the Chairman of the Commissioners for the port invited the Hon. Sir Francis Spring, K.C.I.E., M.Inst.C.E., the Engineer-Chairman of the Madras Port Trust, to report upon the conditions and prospects of the Port of Chittagong in matters of finance, administration, railway development, and other allied questions, and in the following month a most comprehensive and valuable memorandum was issued.

It is unnecessary to refer in detail to this Report, but it may be said that Sir Francis Spring dealt most fully with the following, among other, subjects: the port's area of influence, the Assam-Bengal Railway in relation to the port, the arguments for and against the port becoming a section of the railway, the development of the trade of the port, and other questions upon financial administration. Commander B. H. Jones, R.I.M., the present Port Officer at Chittagong, has furnished particulars for the following notes upon the port.

There are two bars, known as the Outer and the Inner, at the entrance to the River Karnafuli; and each of these is covered with from 22 feet to 24 feet of water at high-water ordinary spring tides. The latter rise from 13 feet to 15 feet, and neaps from 7 feet to 10 feet, while night tides are higher than those occurring during the day between the months of September and March and lower between March and September. Vessels drawing from 23 feet to 25 feet of water can enter the port at spring tides between May and September, but during the dry season the draught must not exceed 18 feet to 20 feet.

There are four jetties, under the management of the Assam-Bengal Railway Company, for the berthing of four large steamers, which are respectively 420 feet, 510 feet, 450 feet, and 600 feet in length, with depths at low water of 21 feet, 20 feet, 17 feet, and 24 feet, but there are no graving or dry docks. Lines of railway are laid alongside the jetties, thus greatly facilitating the transfer of cargo in bulk direct from steamers into wagons. Twenty-one hydraulic cranes have been erected upon the jetties; each one of 17 of these is capable of lifting 35 cwts., and 4 can raise 5 tons at full rake and 10 tons at half-rake; while there are also sheds in which about 30,000 tons of cargo can be stored.

Messrs. Turner, Morrison & Co., Ltd., of Calcutta, have a pontoon for the landing and shipping of goods from and into vessels belonging to the Asiatic Steam Navigation Company.

Dredging operations have been carried on since the year 1907 with the object of clearing the bars, and in November 1915 the latter showed a depth of 10 feet at lowest water during ordinary spring tides. Cargoes are loaded in the stream, and are discharged into lighters, ordinary cargo boats, and country brigs.

The moorings in the stream now available are as follows: double moorings with three berths, 520 feet, 580 feet, and 520 feet in length respectively, with draughts at low water of 10, 11, and 10 feet.

There is one swinging mooring of 210 feet in length and three of 300 feet respectively, with draughts at low water of 12 feet, 11 feet, 17 feet, and 12 feet.

There is a mail service between Chittagong and Burma by regular weekly and bi-weekly coasting steamers, and another between the port and inland places by railway and other agencies.

The export trade of the port consists chiefly of consignments of tea, jute, hides, cotton, kapas, rice, paddy, eggs, poultry, and live stock; while imports include salt, mineral oil, machinery, railway materials, tea-garden stores, rice, coal, and general goods.

Pilotage is optional on the part of masters of vessels, but a cutter with pilots on board is always stationed at the mouth of the river. Full instructions for the guidance of pilots, together with a scale of fees chargeable for their services, were promulgated by a Notification of the Government of Bengal, dated October 31, 1884, and amended by Notification 35 (Marine) on March 18, 1889. The following dues have also been sanctioned by the Government of Bengal: Port dues, 4 annas per registered ton; hospital dues, ½ anna per registered ton; Harbour Master's charges, Rs. 8 up or down the river; mooring and unmooring in fixed berths, Rs. 32 each time, and in swinging berths, Rs. 16; shifting vessel's berth, Rs. 16; and a berth alongside railway jetty, Rs. 30 a day or part of a day. River dues of 2 annas a ton are levied on all goods landed from or shipped into sea-going vessels. Customs duty on raw jute is charged at the rate of 2 annas a bale of 400 lb., while 12 annas are claimed for a ton (2,240 lb.) of manufactured jute. It should be added, however, that river dues were temporarily increased from April 1, 1915—owing to the European War—from 2 to 4 annas a ton, while the cost of hauling vessels in and out of moorings has been raised 25 per cent. The Commissioners have a powerful tug for towing vessels.

COX'S SHIPPING AGENCY, LTD.

This agency was established on November 1, 1911, with the primary object of undertaking shipping, passage, and agency business of every description, including the import and export of cargo and baggage, together with the storage of personal effects and general merchandise, on behalf of the numerous clients of the Army Banking Institution of Messrs. Cox & Co., of 16 Charing

COX'S SHIPPING AGENCY, LTD.

1. Cargo Barges on the Hooghly containing 16-ton Drums of Cable for Messrs. Glover, of Manchester.

2. 3-4 Ton Motor Lorries for General Contracting Work.

3. Overhead Tank for Water Supply of Calcutta City. All the ironwork (some 8,500 tons) in this structure was moved from steamer to site by Cox's Shipping Agency, Ltd.

4. Furniture and General Warehouse Opposite Import Jetties.

Cross, London, whose offices in Calcutta are at 5 Bankshall Street. The last-named company has been in existence since the year 1758, and while transacting all classes of ordinary banking business, including the issue of letters of credit and drafts, is known more particularly as the chief pay agency of the British Army.

The Shipping Agency is therefore a most valuable adjunct to the banking concern, for whose clients it takes full control of all shipping and agency matters. In Calcutta it is the successor to the Eastern Landing, Clearing, and Forwarding Company, Ltd. (whose business they purchased in 1911), which had been established for about fourteen years, and branches have already been opened in nearly every city in which the bank is represented.

The large staff of employees consists of men trained in shipping work generally, experts in dealing with the Customs regulations, and accustomed to the handling of all kinds of goods, and ample warehousing accommodation for household furniture and other goods is provided in an exceptionally fine, new four-storied building at the corner of Strand Road and Hastings Street. This is an admirable position, as the site practically adjoins the wharves on the east side of the Hooghly River, and is literally within a few yards distance from the leading banks, merchants' warehouses, the General Post Office, and other important centres of commercial activities. The floor space is about 40,000 sq. ft. in extent. The structure has an imposing appearance, and is thoroughly up to date in every respect. Each floor is served by two 2-ton electric lifts, and the lighting and other arrangements leave nothing to be desired.

The company were, practically, pioneers in motor-lorry traction in Calcutta, and as they own three 4-ton wagons of that kind, and also possess a fleet of barges for service on the River Hooghly, they are particularly well fitted to undertake the removal by land or water of any kind of heavy or light merchandise or personal effects.

Many very large contracts in this direction have been entered into with leading firms, but special mention may be made of a contract made with Messrs. W. T. Glover & Co., of Manchester, which involved the unloading from steamer and the delivery to an appointed place of 6,500 tons of electrical material and drums of cable. Another important undertaking by the Agency was the removal from ship to site of 8,500 tons of structural ironwork and machinery for Messrs. Clayton & Co., Ltd., of Leeds, who held the contract for the erection of the overhead tank for the water supply of Calcutta.

Branch offices have been opened at Southampton, in England; at Bombay, Karachi, Rawalpindi, Murree, and Srinagar, in India; at Cairo, Port Said, and Alexandria in Egypt; and, since the opening of Messrs. Cox & Co. (France), Ltd., bankers, at Paris, Rouen, and Boulogne, Messrs. Cox's French Forwarding Agency, Ltd., of Marseilles (an affiliated company), have opened branches in these towns also.

In addition to general shipping business, the agency arranges passages upon all shipping lines, and reliable information as to dates of sailing and other particulars is always obtainable at any of the offices. Railway tickets, too, are issued for circular tours, and intending passengers can arrange through Messrs. Cox & Co. for letters of credit to meet them at any part or place in the world.

The head offices of the Agency are at 16 Charing Cross, London, and the telegraphic address for the head office and all branches is "Coxia."

THE INDIA GENERAL NAVIGATION AND RAILWAY COMPANY, LTD.

BY ALFRED DRAME,

Marine Superintendent

The history of this company, the oldest of those engaged in the inland water transport of India, may be briefly told as follows.

In the days before steamers and railways made their appearance in India, the principal means of transport in Bengal and the province of Hindustan was by boats, laboriously towed or sailed over the magnificent waterways of the Ganges and its affluents. Tedious indeed must have been the conditions of travel in days when it took one month to reach Monghyr, two months to Buxar, and three months to Allahabad, the passenger being cooped up in pinnaces and budgerows, and deprived of the amenities of life as we know them in the shape of electric fans, ice, and other luxuries.

A steamer service on the Ganges was inaugurated in 1834, under the direct control of the Honourable East India Company, and was a vast step in advance of previous means of locomotion. The steamers were few and ran at long intervals, with the result that rates were high and bookings uncertain. Some far-seeing merchants of Calcutta conceived the idea that if private enterprise was allowed to enter into the field it would conduce to better results for the trade of the province, and they accordingly waited upon the Governor-General of that day, Lord Ellenborough, with their proposals that a private company might be permitted to provide steamers to meet the demands of the merchants of Calcutta, leaving the Government steamers to deal with the Honourable East India Company's requirements.

Lord Ellenborough was a more than usually enlightened man, and, instead of sternly warning them off the Government's preserves, he encouraged the idea, and even went so far as to promise that when private enterprise had sufficiently advanced so as to meet the legitimate demands of trade, the Government steamers would be withdrawn from competition. Emboldened by this, the promoters of the scheme started the India General Steam Navigation Company, in March 1844, with a capital of Rs. 20,00,000, and ordered a couple of steamers from Europe. As considerable time must elapse before these vessels would be ready, they purchased three steamers locally and commenced to ply on the Ganges, the name of the first of these early steamers being the *Assam*, prophetic in view of subsequent events. In the following year the two steamers built in England were sent out in sections, and were subsequently erected in Calcutta. The company, in common with all new ventures, made mistakes, and had its periods of ups-and-downs during its early years; but it grew steadily, and in 1854 possessed six steamers and eight flat-bottomed boats, eventually called "flats."

The Indian Mutiny of 1857 brought continuous and exacting work to the steamer company, as the East Indian Railway had only advanced to a distance of 160 miles from Calcutta, and was therefore useless for the conveyance of troops and munitions of war to the scene of the great struggle which centred at Delhi, Agra, Lucknow, and Cawnpore. The entire fleet was taken up by Government, and rendered invaluable service in the transport of men and material as far as Allahabad, from which place they were taken by road to the fighting-line.

THE INDIA GENERAL NAVIGATION AND RAILWAY COMPANY, LTD. (KILBURN & CO.).

1. Main Steamer "Burdwan" with Flats in Tow. 2. Assam Dispatch Steamer "Matu." 3. Steamer under Construction at Rajbagan Dockyard

BENGAL AND ASSAM, BEHAR AND ORISSA

Prior to 1860 the steamer company had confined its operations to the Ganges, but by that date the railway had been advanced to Patna, running parallel to the river, tapping the principal marts of trade. The competition was so keen as to compel the steamer company to look elsewhere for an outlet for its energy. The province of Assam was at this period coming into prominence on account of the nascent tea industry, and the India General Company undertook, with considerable misgivings, to send one steamer every six weeks to Assam as an experiment. That country was at that time being developed for tea cultivation, and the steamer service was so successful that by 1862 the six-weekly service was changed into a four-weekly one. In 1863 the district of Cachar, included in the Province of Assam, but watered by an entirely different river system, was invaded by steam, and from this time forward the Ganges trade slowly declined, and Assam and Cachar absorbed more and more of the attention of the company. The East Indian Railway had advanced to Allahabad by 1864, but it was not until 1874 that the steamer company finally abandoned its original hunting-ground and closed its Ganges service.

Although the block of the company had increased to 16 steamers and 34 flats by the year 1870, the carriage of jute from the districts of Eastern Bengal commenced to engage serious attention, and between 1870 and 1880 considerable additions were made to the fleet, to meet the demands of a rapidly expanding trade. In 1882 the company took over the transport of goods previously carried by the Eastern Bengal State Railway flotilla, and in the same year a sea-going steamer service was opened to the coast ports of Orissa. The record of the company was not one of unchallenged prosperity, as at various times rival concerns were started, flourished for a season, like the traditional green bay-tree, and were bought up or amalgamated with, or succumbed to, the energies of the older company.

In 1889 the India General Company entered into an arrangement with the River Steam Navigation Company, by which the work of passenger and goods transport was equally divided, each company remaining a distinct entity.

In 1890 the fleet consisted of 66 steamers and 72 flats—a marked increase on the previous decade.

In 1896 the India General Steam Navigation Company obtained sanction to construct a railway connecting Mymensingh with the Brahmaputra River, and in 1899 it was considered expedient to transfer the headquarters of the company to London, the name being altered at the same time to that of the India General Navigation and Railway Company, Ltd. The history of the company since that date has been one of steady progress, and at the present date its fleet consists of 136 steamers, 185 flats, and 182 barges.

The Rivers of the Plains.

As has been related in the previous section, the waterway on which the India General Company commenced its career was the mighty Ganges, which rises in the high plateau of the Himalayas, its source being not far distant from that of the Brahmaputra, Sutlej, and Indus, rivers which run in totally different directions. It traverses India in a south-easterly course through a densely populated and historic country, and mingles its waters with the Bay of Bengal, forming an innumerable number of channels, only one of which, the Hooghly, is navigable to ocean craft. Vessels of shallow draught ply on the Ganges to considerable distances, and when the India General Company commenced its operations the upper terminus of the journey was Allahabad, 800 miles distant by water from Calcutta, although during the Mutiny an India General steamer reached Cawnpore with men and munitions of war, another 150 miles beyond Allahabad. The volume of trade was immense, Manchester piece goods, ironware, salt, and manufactured articles being the principal items of carriage upward, while opium, indigo, seeds, hides, and general produce formed the leading downward staples. These latter cargoes were especially valuable, and on one occasion the sinking of a flat and loss of its cargo swallowed up the entire profits of the half-year. Bhagalpur, Patna, Buxar, Ghazipur, Benares, and Allahabad were large and busy trade centres, and from the last-named place goods were transhipped from steamers to light country craft for further transport to Upper India.

In the course of time the railways made their appearance, and their original alignment being parallel to the river, they competed strongly with the steamers which had hitherto held the field.

Another factor of a disturbing nature appeared in the shape of the irrigation works of the Indian Public Works Department on the upper reaches of the Ganges. During the dry season, which lasts from November to June, the natural channels of the river shrink to meagre proportions, and navigation had always been difficult. The Irrigation Department deflected, from the headwaters of the river, all the water that came down and sent it into their canals, thus leaving the scantiest supply for navigation, and river transport suffered in consequence. Railway competition and a depleted water supply caused the steamer company to look elsewhere for a living, and, as we have seen, they turned their attention to the Brahmaputra River and the Province of Assam. The Ganges again heard the sound of steamers' paddles in the year 1886, when the India General Company reopened a service to Dinapore, which is still continued, and steamers maintain a daily connection for passengers and goods between Goalundo and the Patna district; but the importance of the Ganges trade is overshadowed by the steadily expanding Assam, Cachar, and Delta lines.

The Brahmaputra is one of the great rivers of India and has a romantic history. It rises in the plateau of the Himalayan regions (which gives birth to all the huge rivers of Northern India), and for 1,000 miles it runs eastward under the name of the Sanpo, cutting through the main chain of the Himalayas by gorges which no traveller has yet traced, and debouching into a wide valley below Sudiya. For many years geographers debated whether the Sanpo ultimately became the Irrawadi or the Brahmaputra, and it is only within the present generation that this question has been solved. From Sudiya it then flows in a westwardly direction, and enters the plains of Bengal at Dhubri; from here its course is nearly due south until it joins its waters with the Ganges at Goalundo, and eventually it finds its way to the sea after a course of 2,100 miles.

At the time when the India General Company sent their first steamer up the Brahmaputra in 1860, Assam was the most backward province of the Indian Empire. It was not in the direct route to any place of importance, it was sparsely populated, it possessed no towns of any size, and its communications, apart from the Brahmaputra, were unspeakably bad. The cultivation of tea was then commencing, and this proved to be the salvation of the province. "The history

THE INDIA GENERAL NAVIGATION AND RAILWAY COMPANY, LTD. (KILBURN & CO.).

1. Discharging Tea at the Garden Reach Warehouse. 2. Assam Dispatch Steamer Loading at Jagarnath Ghat. 3. Steamers in Dock at Rajbagan Dockyard.

of Assam is the history of tea," and although coal and mineral oil have since been discovered and exploited, and a certain amount of seed is exported, tea still remains the backbone of the Assam trade. The upward cargoes consist of foodstuffs (as Assam is not self-supporting in the main staples of food), salt, kerosene oil, garden stores, piece goods, and machinery. The principal towns on the Brahmaputra are Dhubri, Goalpara, Gauhati, Tezpur, and Debrugarh, at the last of which general navigation ceases, although a steamer service is run to Sadiya, the farthest outpost of the British Empire and of civilization on the North-East Frontier.

The Surma valley, although politically in Assam, is divided from the Brahmaputra valley by the range of the Khasia and Jyntia Hills, and it comprises the districts of Cachar and Sylhet. The Surma River, with its tributaries, traverses these populous districts, rising in the Manipuri Hills and flowing westward until it joins the united waters of the Ganges and Brahmaputra at Chandpur. The leading exports are tea and limestone, the latter being found in great quantities on the southern slope of the Khasia Hills. The imports are much the same as pertain to Assam.

The great jute-producing districts are principally situated in the low-lying lands formed by the delta of the three great rivers, Ganges, Brahmaputra, and Surma, and they centre round Narainganj, Serajganj, Madaripur, Chandpur, and a number of smaller places contiguous to these busy marts.

Jute is the largest, although not the most valuable, commodity dealt with by the steamer company, but it is a comparatively new staple, the earliest mention of its carriage by the company being in 1873. Its development has been enormous, and during the season, which runs from August to December, a very large proportion of the company's vessels is engaged in its transport. Owing to the nearness of the jute districts to Calcutta, a vast quantity of this commodity is annually poured into that city, and it is either worked up in the numerous mills on the banks of the Hooghly or is exported to foreign countries.

No survey of the steamer company's field of operations would be complete without a reference to the Sunderbunds, that marvellous network of rivers lying between the combined main streams of the Ganges, the Brahmaputra, and the Hooghly. The greater portion of the company's fleet traverses this labyrinth in their journeys to and from Calcutta. A large part of the Sunderbunds is dense jungle, the home of the tiger and deer, but it is slowly being brought under cultivation. Its intricate navigation may be appreciated when we find that between Calcutta and Chandpur 52 distinct rivers are traversed in a distance of 450 miles.

The Floating Craft.

When the India General Company commenced its operations on the Ganges in 1844, it followed the practice of the Honourable East India Company by carrying cargo on steamers and devoting the attendant flat-bottomed boat, called an "accommodation boat," to the conveyance of passengers. This boat was divided into cubicles, shared by two passengers, but they messed at the captain's table on the steamer. The accommodation boat was towed astern of the steamer, a broad gangway plank affording communication between the vessels. In the early fifties it was found desirable to alter this arrangement and to carry passengers on the steamer only, the "boat" carrying cargo and the name being altered from "accommodation boat" to "cargo flat." The steamers were about 160 feet in length, with low-pressure engines which consumed considerable quantities of coal. Another change was made about this time, the flat being towed alongside or abreast the steamer instead of astern. The enterprising skipper who introduced this practice was solemnly censured by the directors for needlessly imperilling the safety of the company's property; but, nevertheless, the advantage of "towing abreast" was so apparent that it became general, and is universally adopted in all Indian waters. Both steamers and flats carried masts and yards, and sail was set when a favourable wind prevailed.

The general features of both steamer and flat remained unchanged while engaged on the Ganges, but when the venue was changed to Assam masts and sails were done away with, owing to the absence of "prevailing winds" in the Assam valley. In or about the year 1872 the compound engine was introduced into the fleet, resulting in a considerable economy in the consumption of coal and enabling steamers to carry larger cargoes. A steady advance in the size of steamers took place during the seventies, reaching a maximum in the case of the *Sudiya* (1878)—280 feet in length and 40 feet beam. This has not been exceeded in later years. Flats were also advanced in size until they reached the dimensions of 220 feet by 32 feet in 1882, and they remained at that size for several years. The depth of both steamers and flats of the main services has remained the same for fifty years, and it is not likely to be changed. Six feet is considered the maximum draft for the rivers of Bengal and Assam, and no vessel is built to exceed that depth, although for special services in very shallow waters a light-draft fleet has been provided.

Up to 1882 the passenger traffic of the Assam Province was catered for by steamers carrying cargo and towing flats. It was usual for a trip to Debrugarh to take about eighteen days, even when the railway was available as far as Goalundo. A service of small passenger steamers, under a contract with the Assam Government for the carriage of mails, was started by the River Steam Navigation Company in 1883, and this was the commencement of the parting of the ways between cargo and passenger transport. A period of keen competition prevailed between the India General and the river companies for the passenger trade on the Brahmaputra, but in 1889 all differences were harmonized, and the river carrying trade of the province was equally shared. From this date forward the older main-line steamers dropped their passenger-carrying character and became towing steamers only, and they remain much the same up to the present day.

The dispatch steamers advanced in size, speed, and accommodation year by year. In 1883 the first of these was 145 feet in length and carried 60 tons. In 1888 they had advanced to 190 feet and 200 tons respectively, while in 1902 the figures were 240 feet and 470 tons, and at the present day there are 13 steamers of 253 feet, each carrying 700 tons. In passenger accommodation they have advanced from 400 in 1883 to 2,200 in 1915 in each steamer.

The dispatch steamers of the present day are commodious, double-decked vessels, the lower deck being principally utilized for cargo and the upper deck devoted to passengers. The first-class cabins are supplied with electric lights and fans, and a trip on Indian rivers is now a pursuit of pleasure instead of being, as in olden days, a period of penance. Apart from the main-line towing steamer commanded by Europeans, there is an intermediate class of similar steamers commanded by Indians; these are increasing in size and power, and in time will be very close competitors with the larger ones.

For the various services in which the company is engaged, a varied class of vessel is provided; stern-wheel steamers, some of which are of large size, will be found on the shallow-watered Ganges; twin-screw steamers are used for the Chittagong sea service, and for certain special services when that type of craft is found suitable; but the paddle remains pre-eminent for general inland work.

The cargo-carrying flats of the company deserve special notice. They gradually increased in capacity from 250 tons in 1850 to 1,000 tons in 1894, when they reached their maximum. A reaction set in, and there has been a general feeling against such large carriers which has been prompted by various reasons. The present-day flat is about 500 to 600 tons burthen, and it is found easier to handle, to load, and to discharge, and, in the event of a disaster from fire or "snagging," there is less value at stake.

Considering the intricate nature of the Sunderbund navigation, through rivers so narrow that one could jump ashore on either side, and the shoal and tortuous channels of Assam and Cachar, accidents are rare in proportion to the volume of trade and the risks run. Still, accidents do and will happen, either from fire in connection with such a highly inflammable cargo as jute, or from grounding and straining in tidal rivers, or from contact with snags in the narrow Sunderbund rivers. Cyclones, too, occasionally visit inland waters and do considerable damage, the Goalundo cyclone of 1909 sinking 19 vessels (steamers and flats) of the India General and river companies' fleets.

In addition to steamers and flats, the company owns a large fleet of cargo boats and barges, principally engaged in the transport of jute from the running flats to the various jute mills scattered along the banks of the Hooghly over a distance of 30 miles.

The total block of the company in 1915 stood as under: Towing steamers, 26; dispatch, 90; tugs and launches, 20; making a total of 136. Flats of all classes, 185; and cargo boats and barges, 182.

The Dockyard.

The existence of a fleet naturally demands a dockyard where building and repair operations can be carried on. Usually the fleet comes first and the dockyard afterwards, but the India General Company obtained possession of a dockyard before the fleet made its appearance, thus reversing the general order. Their first holding was a piece of land purchased from the Prinsep family, conveniently situated, with an excellent river frontage at the upper end of Garden Reach adjoining the Government dockyard. Originally this site was used for other purposes than that of a dockyard, cargo godowns, offices, and loading berths of the steamers being situated here. A year's experience showed that it was more convenient to carry on cargo operations nearer to the business part of the city, and the godowns and offices were therefore removed to the Strand Road, in Calcutta. The premises were thenceforward used exclusively for the building and repairing of the company's vessels, and were known colloquially as "Carr Company ka Bankshall," owing to the fact that Messrs. Carr, Tagore & Co. were the previous holders of the place; and one might reflect here that names die hard in India.

The first steamers of the company were built in England, shipped out in sections, and put together in India—a tedious and costly undertaking, as voyages were long and freights were high in those days; but the company conceived the idea that it would be cheaper for them to import the plain iron plates and angles from England and build the vessels themselves *ab initio*. The first vessel built entirely in India by the company's own engineers was the *Calcutta*, in 1855, and since that date the bulk of the block, both steamers and flats, has been designed and built in India. Engines and boilers are invariably constructed at Home, but experience has shown that hulls can be built in India quite as satisfactorily and cheaper in cost. The largest steamer, the *Sudiya* (1878), and the largest flats, of the *Gunga* class (1894), were designed and constructed entirely by the company's officers at their own dockyard. From 1844 until 1880 all the building and repair work of the company was undertaken at Garden Reach, one single slipway sufficing for repairs. The fleet was about this time undergoing a rapid increase and, as it outgrew the facilities of the Garden Reach yard, a large piece of land comprising 10 acres was acquired four miles lower down the river at a place called Rajabagan, and this was laid out as an auxiliary to the head yard. It was used at first only as a repairing yard; a mud dock was excavated, and a slipway laid down; and it may be here explained that in the case of a mud dock, the vessel is floated into the dock at high water, a mud *bund*, or dam, is built across the mouth, and the enclosed water is either drained or pumped out. A slipway has rails laid down on a gradient into the water, and the vessel is placed on a carriage or cradle which runs on wheels and is hauled up to above high-water level.

Year by year Rajabagan increased in importance, and it became a building as well as a repairing yard, the first vessel to be laid down here being the flat *Kullung*, in 1882. More land was taken up, machinery shops were erected, and additional docks and a slipway were provided. This was found necessary, not only on account of the increase of the fleet, but also owing to the knowledge that the Garden Reach property would at some future time be needed for the Kidderpore Dock scheme, then in course of extension. In 1898 the final move was made, the Garden Reach yard was closed, and all work was transferred to Rajabagan. A further acquisition of land was made in 1910 by the purchase of 6 acres with riverside frontage, bringing up the total area to about 24 acres. The Rajabagan property now represents a valuable site with excellent river frontage, and is quite an up-to-date establishment with modern appliances for the building and repairing of a large fleet. There is docking accommodation for seven vessels, independently of the building slips, which can provide space for the construction of another five vessels. Thus twelve vessels can be built or repaired simultaneously.

There is a large staff of European engineers, shipwrights, and artificers controlling the work of the yard, and during a busy time about 2,000 Indian and Chinese workmen are engaged. Indians are expert in ironwork, and Calcutta has for generations been a shipbuilding centre, both in wood and iron. English visitors have frequently expressed their astonishment at seeing Indians, without any apparent supervision, engaged in construction work which they had previously considered was the prerogative of the Clyde, Tyne, or Tees.

In the year 1913, 13 vessels, steamers and flats, were built, and 87 vessels were docked and repaired at the Rajabagan establishment.

Cargo Transport and Storage.

As previously mentioned, the earliest warehouses—or godowns, as they are termed in India—of the company were at the dockyard in Garden Reach, but as this situation was found to be too far from the business part of the town to be convenient, warehouses were rented on the Strand Road for many years, vessels berthing alongside the river bank, abreast of the godowns, communication being maintained by pontoon stages.

About 1870 the Port Commissioners of Calcutta commenced building jetties for ocean traffic along the Strand bank, and the inland steam companies had to find quarters elsewhere. These were found at Nimtolla, about a mile higher up the River Hooghly. The site was a convenient one, as it was near the Indian quarter of the city, from which part the greater share of the business is done; but when the Howrah floating bridge was built in 1874, this formed a serious obstacle to inland trade, as the bridge was only opened twice a week, Tuesday and Friday, for the passage of vessels to or from the inland steamer wharves. Nimtolla remained, and still remains, the principal place for the company's cargo operations as conducted by their main-line steamers and flats, and several commodious godowns are situated close by, where goods are received and delivered.

The dispatch services are accommodated at other points. The Cachar Sunderbund dispatch steamers are berthed at Armenian Ghat, immediately below the Howrah bridge; while the Assam Sunderbund vessels work from Jagarnath Ghat, above the bridge, where an immense godown has recently been constructed by the Port authorities to meet the demands of a steadily increasing trade. Tea imports are dealt with at special godowns at Garden Reach, on the site of the original dockyard of the India General Company. Tea and jute intended for export are received here, and are railed alongside ocean steamers in the Kidderpore Docks. Mineral oil (kerosene) is not handled in Calcutta, but is shipped on board inland vessels at Budj-Budj, twelve miles to the south of Calcutta. Salt is loaded from the Government bonded warehouse at Howrah, on the opposite side of the river from Calcutta, although in many cases it is received direct into the company's vessels from ocean steamers; and coal is loaded from the depots at Shalimar, where the East Indian and Bengal-Nagpur Railways have extensive sidings. A very large amount of jute imported into Calcutta is not handled within port limits, but is conveyed direct in the carrying vessel to the various mills and presses which line the banks of the Hooghly for 30 miles, both above and below the city. It will thus be seen that the operations of the company are scattered over a large area instead of being concentrated in one or two centres, and this necessitates the maintenance of a considerable fleet of harbour launches to attend to the movements of craft within the larger limits of the port.

The Howrah floating bridge is now opened every night for the passage of vessels, and, aided by the electric search-light, a considerable number of vessels are moved up or down the river.

At all the various centres where cargo is handled, and in spite of the vast strides that machinery has made in supplanting manual labour, the method employed is exactly the same as adopted by Captain Noah in the good ship *Ark*. Human labour in India is cheap, plentiful, and adaptable. In a full swing of work, a stream of coolies, resembling a line of ants, connects the godown with the vessel by an endless chain; each man carries his load on his head, deposits it at the appointed place, and hurries back for another load. It is needless to say that this bustle is only observant where "piece-work" prices rule, as no living person ever saw an Indian coolie hurry over anything if paid a daily wage. From time to time mechanical appliances have been suggested and considered, but in every case a return has been made to the coolie, who is the basic principle of India and its industries.

As far as imports are concerned, jute is easily first in quantity; tea comes next, and is the staple of the greatest value; then follow limestone, seeds, hides, and miscellaneous Indian products.

Exports are extremely varied, but piece goods, coal, salt, mineral oil, ironware, manufactured goods, vegetable oils, and foodstuffs predominate. In many cases specially constructed flats are detailed to deal with particular commodities.

Capital and Management.

The company started with a capital of 20 lakhs of rupees, or £20,000, as in those happy, far-away days the rupee stood at the par value of 2s., and the original shares were of the value of Rs. 1,000, or £100 each.

From time to time as the company's property increased in value, the capital was augmented as follows:—

			Rs.
1856	...	...	13,00,000
1859	...	...	15,60,000
1862	...	...	20,28,000
1868	...	...	29,00,000
1879	...	...	33,00,000
1882	...	...	55,00,000

In 1883 the shares, which had been valued at Rs. 1,000/- since the commencement of the company's operations, were divided into shares of Rs. 100/- each in order to bring them more in unison with the general value of commercial stock. In 1885 the capital was advanced to Rs. 70,00,000; in 1890 the company was reconstructed in order to enable its stock to be divided into ordinary and preference shares; and in 1895 the capital was increased to Rs. 100,00,000 (100 lakhs); and it is now (1915) £1,000,000, in addition to which there have also been issued 5 per cent. debentures amounting to £200,000.

The fleet, as valued at present, represents £1,080,788, in addition to which freehold property to the value of £105,450 is held. The company have other assets, such as the Jaggarnathganj-Mymensingh Branch Railway, of which it is sole proprietor, and the Sylhet Lime Company, of which it is half-owner.

During the early years of the company the management was vested in a secretary, acting under a board of directors. In 1873 Messrs. Schoene, Kilburn & Co. became managing agents in conjunction with the directors, and although the title of the firm was altered to Messrs. Kilburn & Co. in 1889, this in no way disturbed the position of this firm.

In 1899 the company was transferred to London, the name being altered to that of India General Navigation and Railway Company, Ltd., and the capital was based on a sterling basis. Business is controlled by secretaries and a board of directors in London, with managing agents in India.

JOHN KING & CO., LTD.

A historian of undoubted veracity has it on record that an English countrywoman, when paying her first visit to the metropolis of the world, remarked, with all the seriousness of a philosopher, that "it is most fortunate for London that the River Thames happens to flow so

JOHN KING & CO., LTD.

1. Engine for SS. "Victoria." 2. The Shipbuilding Yard, Howrah. 3. The Head Office at Howrah.

JOHN KING & CO., LTD.

1. Steam Tug "Victoria." 2. Steam Tug "Buckleto." 3. Twin-screw Motor Launch "Mithila."

near to the huge warehouses and the busy centres of the great city" ! She entirely overlooked the fact that the turbid old waterway pursued its tortuous course from the Cotswolds to the shores of Essex and Kent long before the idea of building even a market town of moderate size was ever contemplated. But the pioneers of those days realized the commercial value of the site where London now stands, and they looked with confidence to the results which might be expected to follow the establishment of a trading centre on the banks of that stream and within a very short distance of the continent of Europe. As it was in the West, so it has been in the East. The keynote of the growth of Calcutta is "trade"; trade depends upon facilities for transport; and long before the network of railways had come into existence, and when roads were merely jungle tracks, the villages on the Hooghly—then known as Govindpur, Kallikatta, and Sutanuti Hat—were selected as the base of operations for the transfer of merchandise upon the Ganges, Brahmaputra, and other rivers. This was the beginning of Calcutta, now the second city in the British Empire in population; and the history of its rapid progress as a seaport and city is bound up with that of business companies and firms whose descendants are to-day reaping the benefits which are inseparable from the exercise of foresight, intelligence, energy, and straightforward dealings in commercial enterprise.

Fifty years ago—that was in the year 1865—the well-known firm of Messrs. John King & Co., Ltd., of Howrah and Calcutta, was formed by the late Mr. John King, who was born and educated in the famous industrial town of Paisley, in Scotland. The company had a small beginning, perhaps, but it was a promising one, as the founder was a native of the "land o' cakes," whose sons are imbued with that dogged persistency and shrewdness which are the greatest assets in a business career.

Mr. King was an engineer by profession, and he had the good fortune to arrive in India at a time when a new era was dawning in connection with the development of railways, the bridging of rivers, the construction of piers, jetties, and pontoons, and the building of steamers and other vessels and boats. He found that he must march with the times or be left hopelessly in the lurch, and, setting his mind to the task before him, he developed the business to a remarkable extent, but his death in 1890 unfortunately took place before his sanguine expectations had been fully realized.

A limited liability company was then formed, and Mr. John Clarke, who had been associated with the late Mr. King, became managing agent. Since that time the firm has succeeded in establishing one of the largest engineering businesses in India, which includes shipbuilding, and brass founding, general engineering, contracting, and large repairing shops at the Kidderpore Docks. The work undertaken by Messrs. King & Co. is of a very varied character, and includes the turning out of steamers, launches, barges, ferry-boats, and pontoons, as well as jetties, bridges, roofs, engines, and castings up to 15 tons. Up to the year 1915 the firm had constructed more than 700 vessels, and at the present moment the hands in the yards are fully employed. The majority of the steam-launches made by the company are fitted with engines designed and built in their workshops at Howrah, and it is believed that this is a feature which few, if any, other firms in the East are in a position to emulate. Cargo boats and pleasure craft launched from the Howrah yards are found on the Hooghly and on rivers and canals in the interior of Bengal and other provinces; and princes and other notabilities in India have on many occasions favoured the firm with orders for house-boats, yachts, and pleasure steamers, several of which have been furnished and fitted throughout in the most luxurious manner.

It was not long after the company came into existence that, owing to the exceedingly rapid manner in which the business had grown, branch works were opened near to the dry dock at Kidderpore, where Messrs. King & Co. have for many years past secured a large share of the work of overhauling and repairing vessels of all kinds, and commanders and engineers have nothing but unstinted praise for the extremely satisfactory way in which the firm have discharged such work. These works had a record turnover during the past year (1914-15), notwithstanding the dislocation in the commercial world caused by the European War, and the reputation of the firm has been considerably enhanced by the expeditious and thorough manner in which they fitted out no fewer than 12 transports.

The company's machinery and stores department, at 40 Strand Road, Calcutta, carries considerable stocks of mill and colliery requirements, machine tools, vertical and Lancashire boilers, engines and pumps of all descriptions, wire ropes, chains, anchors, and machines of various kinds, together with a huge quantity of sundry appliances necessary for the proper conduct of large shipping and general engineering yards and works.

Messrs. King & Co. hold agencies in India for several English manufacturing firms whose productions are noted throughout the world for their excellence. These include Messrs. N. Hingley and Sons, Ltd., manufacturers of "Netherton" iron and chains; Messrs. Thomas and William Smith, Ltd., of Newcastle, for steel wire ropes; Messrs. W. B. Haigh, Gruban & Co., Ltd., of Keighley, for wood-working machinery; the Penberthy Injector Company; the Graphite Products, Ltd.; and the Henry Wells Oil Company, of Manchester, who are makers of special engine and cylinder oils. The firm are, further, sole representatives for Bengal and Assam of Messrs. J. W. Brooke & Co., of Lowestoft, builders of the famous "Brooke" marine motors; and they hold a similar agency for the British Steel Piling Company, makers of "Universal" and "Simplex" steel sheet piling.

Two sons of the late Mr. John King—namely, Mr. Millar M. King and Mr. George A. King—are now on the directorate of the company, and it is particularly gratifying to them that the jubilee of the firm, which is being celebrated this year (1915), will be marked by the completion of considerable alterations and additions to their property, an occurrence which will commemorate the occasion in a permanent and progressive form.

THE RIVERS STEAM NAVIGATION COMPANY, LTD.

The Rivers Steam Navigation Company, Ltd., was formed in the year 1862 under the name of the New River Steam Company, but it was reconstructed in 1873 and converted into a limited liability company, with a capital of £100,000, which sum, by the way, has now been increased to £500,000. The fleet consisted originally of three steamers and three flats, but at the commencement of the present year (1915) it had reached a total of 417 vessels, of which 141 were steamers or launches and 185 were flats,

MACNEILL & CO.

1. River Steam Navigation Company's Yard, Garden Reach. 2. Steamer with Flats. 3. Godowns on Jagarnath Ghat.
4. R.S.N. Co.'s Dispatch Steamer "Kohistani."

together with 91 of a miscellaneous character, but including 16 vessels owned jointly with the India General Navigation and Railway Company, Ltd.

Messrs. Macneill & Co., of 2 Clive Ghat Street, Calcutta, are agents of the Rivers Company, and they have for a considerable number of years interested themselves largely in connection with the passenger and freight traffic between that city and Assam, Cachar, and other places. This firm have been pioneers in reducing the cost of transport of goods, in securing greater regularity in the time-table, and in providing better accommodation for passengers.

The waterways traversed by the vessels of the Rivers Steam Navigation Company extend through the Province of Bengal, Assam, the United Provinces, and of Behar and Orissa, and the mileage of the rivers navigated is 4,642. The traffic (excluding coaching) handled during the year 1913 amounted to 523,14,955 maunds, and the number of passengers carried during the same period was 76,06,748, while at the present there are no fewer than 612 stations on the rivers, which are available for passengers or goods. This company and the India General Navigation and Railway Company have conjointly established a fast daily service between Goalundo and Dibrugarh, and between the former place and Gauhati and Chandpur, working in connection with the Eastern Bengal State and the Assam-Bengal Railway systems. Further than this, they have special steamers or flats for conveying raw jute to the mills on the Hooghly River. The average number of employees of the Rivers Company (and of the India Company where they unite their forces) is about 13,200, exclusive of those who are engaged in handling cargo.

The principal dockyard of the Rivers Steam Navigation Company is about 21 acres in extent, and is situated at Garden Reach, near to Calcutta. It contains two dry docks, three shipways, including two transverse grids which are capable of accommodating from three to five vessels at the same time. There are also three building slips and extensive workshops, in which all kinds of construction and repairing work is carried on, and some 2,000 labourers are constantly employed. Workshops—owned jointly with the India General Navigation Company—have been opened at several of the chief up-country stations, and very extensive warehouses for dealing with the immense traffic in merchandise are to be found at Juggernathghat, Kidderpore, Armenian Ghat, Nimtollah, Chitpore, and other places in the neighbourhood of the river in Calcutta.

THE NIPPON YUSEN KABUSHIKI KAISHA

The Nippon Yusen Kabushiki Kaisha, or Japan Mail Steamship Company, Ltd. (incorporated in Japan), which owns at present a fleet of 101 vessels with a gross tonnage of 500,000 tons, came into being in the year 1885 as the result of the amalgamation of two rival companies which then existed.

At that time the company confined itself to Japanese coastwise trade, but it gradually extended its sphere of work to Vladivostock, North China, and Korea, with regular sailings to those ports, and occasional voyages to both Australia and Hawaii with emigrants and cargo. During that period, the company received a yearly subsidy from the Government provided that it not only maintained several mail routes, but also held itself in readiness to place its entire fleet, if required, at the Government's immediate disposal for use as transports and other purposes. The wisdom of the Japanese Government in financially supporting and fostering the company's marine was soon put to a severe test. War broke out in 1894 between China and Japan, and nearly every vessel in the company's fleet was required for service as a transport, or an armed cruiser, or a hospital ship. The Nippon Yusen Kaisha was able to meet the Government's needs, sacrificing its own commercial interests in so doing. It then became necessary for the company to purchase more steamers to carry on its business and fulfil its mail contracts which had been temporarily interrupted or delayed by the withdrawal of so many ships from the regular service. This placed the efficiency of the company beyond question and firmly established its reputation. But it did more than this; it showed the world at large that Japan had a mercantile marine of her own which could be depended upon to supply the Government's wants if required.

After the close of the war, the Nippon Yusen Kaisha determined to extend its foreign lines and fly its flag in all parts of the world. In order to do this it inaugurated, in 1896, three monthly mail and passenger services, namely, a European, an American, and an Australian line.

These three well-established passenger services are too familiar to the travelling public to call for comment here beyond this, that travellers from India to London can take one of these European Line steamers from Colombo, while others wishing to reach Victoria, B.C., Seattle, San Francisco, or in fact, any part of America or Canada, or even Europe, via America, may avail themselves of the American service from Hongkong. The following particulars in respect of services of more recent origin and in direct touch with India will not be found out of place.

The Calcutta-Japan Line of the Nippon Yusen Kaisha, which runs between Yokohama, Japan, and Calcutta, calling at Kobe, Moji, Hongkong, Singapore, Penang, and Rangoon on the way to Calcutta, and stopping at Rangoon, Penang, Singapore, Hongkong, Shanghai, Kobe, and Yokohama on the return voyage from Calcutta, began operations in 1911, and there is now a fortnightly service in which six large steamers are engaged, principally for the transport of cargo. The Calcutta-Japan Line, unlike the majority of others of the Nippon Yusen Kaisha, has no connection with the Japanese Government, and receives no subsidy. It carries the Japan mail, however, for which service a charge is made against the Japanese Post Office Department. This line is for the carriage of freight, cargoes from Japan being of a general nature, while those from India consist chiefly of cotton, seeds, and gunnies.

The Bombay-Japan Line of the Nippon Yusen Kaisha, which connects Kobe and Bombay, calling at Moji, Hongkong, Singapore, Malacca, and Colombo on the way to Bombay, and stopping at Tuticorin or Colombo, Singapore, Hongkong, Shanghai, Moji, and Kobe, on returning to Japan, was established in 1893, and was this company's pioneer service to India. Fine large steamers are engaged on this run and thus prompt transport of cargo is assured. Like its sister line to Calcutta, it has no connection with the Japan Government and receives no subsidy, depending for the main portion of its revenue upon the carrying of freight. The distance of both runs is about 5,000 miles, and the voyage occupies about thirty days.

The Japan-New York Line of the Nippon Yusen Kaisha is its most recently inaugurated enterprise, and is in keeping with the company's ambition to fly its flag on all routes and in all countries. Steamers on

NIPPON YUSEN KAISHA (JAPAN STEAMSHIP COMPANY).

1. Steamer. 2. Suite of Rooms, Bedroom. 3. Smcking-room. 4. Drawing-room. 5. Dining-room.

this service began to run about the middle of the year 1916, and there are now six vessels, each of about 7,000 tons gross, running every four weeks from Japan. Before steamers sail from Japan for New York they usually make a round trip to Philippine Island ports, and on returning to Japan, they call at Moji, Kobe, Yokkaichi or Nagoya (occasionally), Yokohama, and proceed thence to New York via Panama, calling at San Francisco *en route*. The return journey is made by the same route to Kobe and Yokohama, after calling generally at Vladivostock. Shippers in India having merchandise for any of the above ports will do well to remember that transport can be made economically and safely, as well as quickly, by consigning the goods via Nippon Yusen Kaisha from either Calcutta or Bombay for transhipment at Hongkong or Kobe. There is no accommodation for passengers on this line, the service being devoted entirely to the handling of freight of a general nature. The distance travelled is nearly 15,000 miles.

In addition to the lines above mentioned the company maintains various other regular lines in foreign as well as in home waters, a complete list being as follows: European Line, fortnightly; European Line (auxiliary service), fortnightly; New York Far East Line (via Panama), every four weeks; American Line (Hongkong-Seattle service), every three weeks; American Line (Kobe-Seattle service), fortnightly; Australian Line, monthly; Bombay Line, fortnightly; Calcutta Line, fortnightly; Yokohama-Shanghai Line, semi-weekly; Osaka, Kobe, Shanghai Line, weekly; Osaka-Tsingtau Line, twice a week; Yokohama-North China Line, three times a month; Kobe-North China Line, every six days; Kobe-Vladivostock Line, twice every three weeks; Kobe-Keelung Line, weekly; Yokohama-Formosa Line, four times a month; Kobe-Otaru Line, thirteen times a month; Saghalien Line, six times a month; Hakodate-Yetrofu Line, six to eight times a month; Otaru-Wakanai Line, four to five times a month.

The company employs 750 officials in its head offices and branches, and the staff afloat is more than 6,000 in number, comprising officers, engineers, and others serving on board its steamers. The capital of the company is Y44,000,000, this being equivalent to about Rs. 6,70,00,000.

Passenger and cargo rates, as well as other information can be obtained from the company's offices and agents in India, Burma, and Ceylon, namely: Nippon Yusen Kaisha, 2-3 Clive Row, Calcutta; Nippon Yusen Kaisha, Hornby Road, Bombay; Messrs. Andrew Yule & Co., 8 Clive Row, Calcutta; Messrs. The Arracan Company, Ltd., Rangoon; The Bombay Company, Madras; The Carson Company, Ltd., Colombo.

The head office of the company is in Tokyo, Japan, and the branch offices are at London (4 Lloyds Avenue, E.C.), Bombay, Calcutta, Hongkong, Shanghai, Tientsin, Keelung, Nagasaki, Moji, Kobe, Osaka, Yokohama, Hakodate, Otaru, Seattle, and New York, while its agents are to be found in all parts of the world.

1. SAUGOR LIGHTHOUSE. 2 HOOGHLY PILOT BRIG.
3 SHIPPING ON THE HOOGHLY IN THE NINETIES.

THE PRESS

"CAPITAL," LIMITED

THE weekly financial and commercial paper known as *Capital* was started in Calcutta in November 1888 by Mr. Shirley Tremearne and the late Mr. W. H. Targett. The former was very successful in the editorial chair, and the journal grew rapidly in favour with the leading banking concerns, stockbrokers, and business houses throughout Bengal. Mr. Tremearne became sole proprietor in 1896, and his capable conduct of the paper greatly increased its reputation until the year 1905, when he converted the business into a private limited liability company with a capital of Rs. 3,00,000, of which Rs. 1,00,000 and Rs. 2,00,000 represented ordinary and debenture shares respectively, the latter bearing interest at the rate of 7 per cent. per annum.

The revenue continued to increase steadily, and annual dividends have, for some years past, reached more than 30 per cent.

In 1912 Mr. Tremearne retired from the editorship, and was succeeded by Mr. Pat Lovett, under whose guidance the paper has attained an imperial position, and has found support in every important commercial centre in India.

Although *Capital* is primarily a financial review, its pages are crammed with good readable articles on political, social, trading, and other items of general interest.

In a comparatively recent issue, taken promiscuously from the file, the following brief particulars of its contents have been obtained. The paper opens with a trenchant leading article on India's foreign trade, in which comparison is drawn between exports and imports at that date, and in July 1914, prior to the outbreak of the European war. This is followed by "The Week Abroad," wherein the writer gives some straight talk on events connected with the war, upon politics at Westminster as they appear to Britons in India, and upon important social events in various parts of the world.

Next in order comes the usual weekly "Diary of a Ditcher," which contains crisp, and sometimes caustic criticisms of men, women, and things as they are seen by the editor from the window of his *sanctum*, or as they are revealed to him by "persons in the know." On succeeding pages one sees contributions from Bombay, Madras, the Assam tea valleys, and other places, all of which deal in an interesting manner with affairs of a general character. "The Money Market" is a most exhaustive review of bank and other securities, of the balance of trade, of exchange quotations, of the movements of gold and silver, and other kindred subjects. Then follow: Stock Exchange notes, agricultural and commercial prospects and reports, scientific miscellany, general notes on Indian products, and references to annual reports of a large number of public and private companies, together with market, and stock and share lists.

This paper was never more influential and powerful than it is to-day, and there is no paper published in India which is so well known in other countries as *Capital*, or which can give greater facilities for advertisements relating to financial and commercial concerns.

Mr. T. F. Tremearne, the son of the founder, is manager in Calcutta, and the correspondents in London are Messrs. A. H. Wheeler & Co., of Temple Chambers, Temple Avenue, E.C.

"THE ENGLISHMAN"

The Englishman was founded in the year 1821 under the title of *John Bull*, and the first editor was a Mr. James Mackenzie, who in his introductory address proclaimed that the paper would be "the supporter of Church and King, the contemner of private scandals, the counterpoise of the pernicious influence of other journals." Mr. Mackenzie, however, did not last very long, and *John Bull* was edited from 1822 to 1825 by Mr. Greenlaw, a naval officer, who seems to have combined with his editorial duties those of the Coroner of Calcutta and of Secretary to the Marine Board. He finally resigned in order to make room for a Dr. James Bryce, who was the first chaplain of the Calcutta Scotch Kirk. This was the Bryce who made Bishop Middleton very unhappy in the old far-off days by theological disputations. It is stated it was he who placed the gilt cock on the top of the steeple of the kirk in order that the kirk might crow for ever over the Established Church. As might be supposed Bryce was not to be controlled in the editorial chair. He seems finally

CAPITAL

THE INDIAN FINANCIAL REVIEW

BANK OF BENGAL

Manchester Assurance Co.

IMPORTS CLEARED

ANGLO-INDIAN CARRYING CO.

BANK OF RANGOON LD.

NEW ZEALAND INSURANCE CO. LD.

FIRE & MARINE

THE SOUTH BRITISH INSURANCE CO. LD.

STANDARD

1. THE "STATESMAN" OFFICES, CALCUTTA. 2. "THE ENGLISHMAN" OFFICES, CALCUTTA. 3. "CAPITAL."

to have bought the paper, and then he began a series of attacks upon everybody, whether a Tory or no. Finally the East India Company told him either to discontinue the paper or leave their service. Bryce then, in 1829, sold it to an agency house in Calcutta, Messrs. Cruttenden & Co., who appointed Captain Robert Adair Macnaughton as editor.

In 1832 the firm of Cruttenden & Co. failed, and the assignee decided to sell the paper. In 1833 a purchaser was found in the person of Joachim Hayward Stocqueler, a remarkable personality under whose able editorship the journal flourished exceedingly. Among his earliest contributors was Charles Makepeace Thackeray, an uncle of the novelist, and the following passage occurs in one of Stocqueler's diaries:—

"I found a suitable henchman in Charles Thackeray, barrister by profession, nothing particular in practice. Bacchus claimed him, and he had long yielded to the seductive influence of the rosy deity. In a word, he was drunk every day of his life, and consequently, never was employed by attorneys. He despised briefs and adored brandy. Sending for him I proposed that he should join the staff and do the 'grievance" business. The terms were ten rupees and a bottle of claret for each leading article, long or short. Every day at eleven he came to the office only half-gone from the effects of the matutinal 'pick-me-up.' I put him into a room with a sheet of foolscap, pen, ink, and the bottle of claret. By 1 p.m. the article was written, the bottle emptied, and the ten rupees sacked. Thackeray staggered home. The editorials were vigorous home thrusts. *In vino veritas.*"

But apart from the literary ability with which the paper was conducted, there was another reason for Stocqueler's success. To his personal beauty he added a great charm of manner. In those days the average newspaper man was a frowsy kind of individual with no footing in society. Stocqueler altered all that. He was intimate with persons who would not have allowed his predecessors across their thresholds. Lord William Bentinck was quite fond of him and supplied him with all kinds of information of the most precious kind. Other officials followed suit, particularly the military, and presently the paper came to be known throughout India as the best-informed and most reliable of all the daily organs, a position which it has never lost.

In 1843 Stocqueler sold the paper to William Cobb Hurry. For twelve years he managed its affairs with success, and then came his great opportunity.

In 1857 the Mutiny broke out, and in the course of a few weeks *The Englishman* was recognized as the one exponent of British feeling about the event. Owing to the many military correspondents *The Englishman* had all over India, its news about the progress of the tremendous calamity was fuller than that of any other paper, and Hurry at his desk was able to collate, comment, and criticize in a way that drew everybody to subscribe.

By the time the Mutiny was over Hurry had made for himself and for *The Englishman* a great name. The more peaceful days that followed the hunting down of the last rebel Hurry found somewhat dull after the stimulation of Delhi and Lucknow, and having lost interest in India he sought to dispose of *The Englishman,* now become, of course, a very valuable property. People were, naturally, only too anxious to have a share in it, and Hurry was soon able to arrange to sell the greater part of the paper to Mr. J. O'B. Saunders and a somewhat extraordinary individual known as "Walter Brett." Hurry kept a small share for himself. He died in England in 1862.

Mr. Saunders remained at the manager's desk till 1867. Then, the finances of the paper being firmly established he went home for two years. But the ruling passion was so strong in him that he started a political newspaper called *The Day* in London. It did not last long, however, for the writers concerned in it were not journalists or literary men but very selfish politicians. In 1869 Saunders returned to India. He found *The Englishman* so well established in the popular favour that it was hardly necessary for him to retain any of the duties of management, and he went home again very shortly afterwards. He paid one more visit to India in 1876, and died at Kensington, in London, on June 7, 1879, leaving his son, the late Mr. J. O'B. Saunders, a chief proprietor of *The Englishman.*

Mr. J. O'B. Saunders, the second, was in active charge down to the year 1904, and under his rule the paper continued to exert a great influence.

In 1903, on the occasion of Lord Curzon's great Durbar, Mr. Saunders was decorated with the C.I.E. He was twice married, first to the daughter of the late Mr. Justice Barrow, and his only son, Mr. J. O'B. Saunders (the third) is now managing director of *The Englishman.* His second marriage was with the widow of the late Mr. W. Brown, advocate. He died at Naples in 1905 after a lingering illness, which he bore with great patience.

For nearly a hundred years the paper has been established in the affection and respect of the British community in India as the faithful exponent of the British point of view and the frank and fearless critic of the Government. In pursuance of that tradition it has vigorously opposed any agitation from the outside, or any policy on the part of the Government that might tend to destroy or weaken the British character of the administration in India.

Mr. J. A. Sandbrook is the present capable editor.

THE FOREIGN AND COLONIAL COMPILING AND PUBLISHING COMPANY

THE main purpose of these volumes is to arouse in the English-speaking peoples an intelligent and enduring interest in the King's Dominions and Colonies beyond the seas, and at the same time to give such an accurate picture of each section of the Empire as shall make them standard works of reference for all who desire a fuller knowledge of the enormous resources and commercial possibilities of each Colony. To this end the compilers and editors have kept in view the Rt. Hon. Joseph Chamberlain's words, spoken when he held office as Secretary of State for the Colonies, and after he had returned from his colonial tour. "Books," said Mr. Chamberlain, "were required on the Colonies both for use within themselves and at home and abroad; books giving the history, commerce, industries, and resources of each country; to prove what industrial enterprise could attain under new and sometimes hard conditions."

Mr. Somerset Playne, F.R.G.S., founder of the Foreign and Colonial Compiling and Publishing Company, who is the compiler of these volumes, has now been associated with this class of publication for several years. The books themselves are compiled from information gathered by personal calls on planters, merchants, and industrial concerns, the country journeys involving many thousands of miles of travel and the expenditure of a large amount of money, and the information thus gained together with any opinions expressed by the person interviewed, is entered in the work under that person's name. It is confidently believed that the first-hand information thus carefully collected, and presented in sumptuous and attractive form, with all the aid that lavish and artistic photographic illustration can give, will not only place the country before the world in a clearer and more favourable light, and in truer perspective than ever before, by fully revealing the general grandeur of its scenery and the magnificence of its resources, but will *ipso facto* render most material aid in its social and industrial progress and development.

Volumes have been graciously accepted by His late Majesty King Edward VII, His Majesty King George V, and H.R.H. the Duke of Connaught; while the Colonial and Foreign Offices, as well as the Governments of the various Colonies and Possessions, have invariably taken a keen interest in these books, having assisted by granting free railway passes and by the purchase of numerous copies of the works for libraries and general distribution.

The Foreign and Colonial Compiling and Publishing Company was started by Mr. Playne in 1908 for the purpose of compiling a standard work of reference on British East Africa. This volume was practically "off his own bat," but later works were produced with the very able assistance of Mr. F. Holderness Gale, who collaborated as Editor until his lamented death in 1914, when the services of Mr. Arnold Wright, our present Editor and Historian, were secured. "East Africa," which received the highest encomiums from the London and Colonial Press, was followed in 1910 by "Cape Colony," which is a volume of some 800 pages, illustrated with upwards of 2,000 photographs. At this period Mr. J. W. Bond joined the staff as a compiler, and Mr. R. Vintcent Solomon was appointed to the post of chief clerk and secretary, while later the literary department was strengthened by the addition of Mr. J. W. Kiddall. The services of Capt. H. H. F. Stockley, F.R.G.S., were then secured as another compiler for the "Orange Free State" volume, and as soon as this was completed the whole staff sailed for New Zealand, via Australia, and thence to India.

A few words regarding the mode of travelling in the various countries which were visited may be of interest. As far as the volume on East Africa was concerned, the whole of the work of compilation was done by Mr. Playne, not in a luxurious saloon railway car, nor even in a comfortable motor-car, but upon the back of a mediocre mule. The photographers, too, had to rely on this not too comfortable beast of burden, or, in the alternative, they had to make use of the ordinary "push-bike." Many adventures with lions and rhinos were recorded, and long journeys over native tracks through the bush frequently involved a night in the open without food, and also with grave doubts as to one's whereabouts.

Numerous hardships were experienced by the staff in Cape Colony and in the Orange Free State; nights had to be spent on the bleak hills, in unsavoury sheep sheds, or under the Cape cart (which, however, is the most satisfactory method of transit in those parts); and one photographer was snowed up for a week on the mountains above Cathcart, without any means of communication. In negotiating the treacherous *drifts* across rivers serious dangers were encountered, and on more than one occasion it was a case of stripping off one's clothing and of taking to the water in order to turn the frightened horses and bring the outfit safely to the opposite bank. Many breakdowns occurred to the Cape carts and horses, owing mainly to the abominable state of the mountain roads; but when it is realized that members of the staff covered some 15,000 miles, it will be considered singularly fortunate that mishaps were unattended by any serious results. New Zealand supplied a new set of experiences and extended travelling under novel conditions was again the lot of the compilers; but thanks to the generous hospitality and freely tendered assistance of the warm-hearted inhabitants of the Dominion, rough paths were smoothed out and the work in hand was carried out under the pleasantest conditions. Southern India was the next field of operations, and here a tour of over 7,000 miles was done in a motor-car by Mr. Somerset Playne throughout the Anamalais, Nilgiris, Wynaad, and the West Coast, Coorg, and Mysore; while Mr. J. W. Bond and other members of the staff motor-cycled throughout Cochin, Travancore, and most parts of the Madras Presidency.

The life of the compilers, and to a certain extent that of the photographers, is one of constant change and excitement. Many a bad spill, resulting in a long walk, has occurred; many a tyre has had to be repaired in pelting rain or in excessive heat; and it will be admitted that motoring on unknown, and frequently bad, roads at night when flocks of sheep or herds of cattle are lying about, must occasionally be attended by disaster. To suddenly round a corner and your headlights to show a wild elephant evidently contemplating whether to take your car as a personal insult, or to retire into the jungle, is far from being a pleasant experience; and yet this happened on more than one occasion, but luckily the jungle was in each case favoured. But, after all, these misfortunes, though distressing at the time, are usually a source of amusement subsequently.

SOMERSET PLAYNE, F.R.G.S.

The compiler of works of the magnitude of "East Africa," "Cape Colony," "Orange Free State," "New Zealand," "Southern India," and "Bengal and Assam: Behar and Orissa: their History, People, Commerce, and Industrial Resources," must of necessity have had considerable experience of the world, and Mr. Somerset Playne has had a more varied career and can boast of a wider acquaintance with the Britains beyond the Seas than most men. He was educated at Clifton College, and at St. Edward's School, Oxford. At the age of nineteen he paid his first visit to the United States, spending most of his time in the West, and indulging for some months in the joys of ranching and cowboy-life. He was called home to England, but the spirit of adventure reasserted itself, and Mr. Playne sailed for South Africa, where he spent some time on Angora goat and ostrich farms. The Matabele Rebellion was then a very recent memory, and

Francistown was still the terminus of the railway; but Mr. Playne went up-country to the then new Rhodesia, and at Inyati took a hand in big-game shooting, store-keeping, and trading.

After having travelled in every part of Africa south of the Zambesi, Mr. Playne took part, in 1899, in an expedition into German East Africa, and on his return from this trip he made the acquaintance for the first time of British East Africa, travelling over the Uganda Railway from Mombasa to Voi, which was then the terminus of the line.

SOMERSET PLAYNE, F.R.G.S.,

COMPILER OF "EAST AFRICA," "CAPE COLONY," "NEW ZEALAND," "SOUTHERN INDIA," "BENGAL AND ASSAM, BEHAR AND ORISSA," ETC.

Another visit to the Old Country took place, and then Mr. Playne tempted fortune for the second time in South Africa, meeting with experiences not infrequently the lot of those who venture in "new" countries. Later he joined a firm which was engaged on the compilation of an encyclopædic work on Natal, and on the completion of the task in that colony he returned to England to superintend the passing of the volume through the press.

For the same firm Mr. Playne later supervised the compilation of books on Ceylon, the Federated Malay States, Hong Kong and Shanghai, and visited Java, Labuan, Borneo, and Formosa. Then, having meanwhile severed his connection with the business which had carried him to the Far East, he travelled through India, and, sailing from Bombay, arrived in British East Africa in November 1908, on which country he then compiled his now well-known standard work.

A trip to Europe via Cairo followed; thence he sailed to Cape Colony, where he arrived in March 1910. Returning to England in 1911, the "Cape Colony" work was subsequently passed through the press. Having previously started on the "Orange Free State" volume, which had been carried on during his absence, another trip to South Africa was necessary; and after a stay of a few months he sailed, in 1912, for Australia, and later proceeded to New Zealand in order to compile his well-known work on that Dominion. From there he journeyed, in September 1913, to South India, where he covered over 7,000 miles in one tour by motor-car for compilation purposes. In 1914 a short period of two weeks was spent in England, and in the following year he proceeded to the scene of his recent labours in Bengal, Behar, Orissa, and Assam, practically every part of which he has toured, mostly by road; whilst in 1916, in order to join the ranks of the benedicts, he again visited New Zealand for a short period.

Mr. Somerset Playne is a Fellow of the Royal Geographical Society, a Freemason, and a member of the Royal Societies and Sports Clubs.

THE STERN-WHEEL STEAMER "KITTY."
Belonging to the Fishery Department, Bengal and Behar and Orissa.
Photo by Mondul, Indian Museum.

THE FISHERIES OF BENGAL AND BEHAR AND ORISSA

By T. SOUTHWELL, A.R.C.Sc. (London), F.Z.S., National Scholar 1902; Deputy Director of Fisheries Bengal and Behar and Orissa; Honorary Assistant, Indian Museum; Late Scientific Adviser and Inspector of Pearl Banks to the Ceylon Company of Pearl Fishers.

IN Bengal the staple article of food is rice. Next in importance is fish, which takes the same place in the dietary of Bengalees as does meat in the dietary of Europeans. It is estimated that not less than 80 per cent. of the entire population consume fish as a regular article of food. During recent years, owing to a variety of causes, the supply of fish throughout the Province has undoubtedly been insufficient. Consequently the price has risen everywhere. Many Indians believe that the diminished consumption of fish, particularly among the poorer classes, has resulted in the physical deterioration of this section of the community.

In certain parts of Behar and Assam, wheat, maize, and other grains are preferred to rice. It is well known that fish is more commonly eaten with rice than with grain. Fish, therefore, is not so extensively consumed in Behar and parts of Assam, its place being taken by meat. It is possible that the general or entire absence of fish in many parts of Behar and Assam has necessitated this change in the two principal foodstuffs.

The first investigations into the fisheries of Bengal were initiated by Dr. Buchanan, who joined the East India Company's service in 1794. He at once commenced inquiries into the "Fishes of the Ganges," and published his report thereon in the year 1822. About the year 1840 Dr. M'Clelland contributed an excellent account on "Indian Carps," and did useful work on the Salt Lake Fisheries situated near Calcutta. Some years later Edward Blythe, who was Curator of the Asiatic Society of Bengal from 1841 to 1862, published an account of the ray, or skate fishery.

In 1868 the Government of India deputed Surgeon-Major Francis Day to investigate the effects of the anicuts or weirs on the fisheries in the Madras Presidency. The inquiry was subsequently generalized and extended to Orissa and Lower Bengal, and eventually over the whole of the Indian Empire. The monumental work of Dr. Day represents the first serious attempt made in India towards the improvement of the fisheries. The work continued until the death of Dr. Day, in the year 1889. So far as the Provinces of Bengal and Behar and Orissa are concerned, no further work was done on the fisheries until the year 1906.

During this interval, however, very great additions to our knowledge of the deep-sea fishes in the Bay of Bengal were made by Colonel Alcock, I.M.S., Surgeon Naturalist to the Indian Marine Survey, and, later, Superintendent of the Indian Museum.

In 1906 Mr. K. G. Gupta, C.S.I., I.C.S. (now Sir K. G. Gupta), a senior member of the Board of Revenue, Bengal, was placed on special duty by the Government of Bengal in order to inquire into the fisheries of this Province and its fish supply, and his final reports were placed before Government in 1908. As a result, a steam trawler was purchased with the object of surveying the marine fisheries in the Bay of Bengal. Dr. Jenkins, of the

BENGAL AND ASSAM, BEHAR AND ORISSA

Lancashire Sea Fisheries, conducted the inquiry, which extended over the greater part of two years. On the return of Dr. Jenkins to England in 1910, the Department of Fisheries was amalgamated with the Department of Agriculture. The Director of Agriculture thus became Director of Fisheries. The present Deputy-Director of Fisheries assumed charge of the Department in December 1911, and is assisted by two Superintendents of Fisheries (who have had some training in Europe and America) and a temporary officer with the title of Zoological Assistant. It is now proposed to separate the Department of Fisheries from the Department of Agriculture, and to create a new and special post of Director of Fisheries.

The work of the Department extends over the two Provinces of Bengal and Behar and Orissa. A special stern-wheel steamer has been provided for work in the shallow rivers and in the delta of the Ganges.

Until quite recently the Fisheries of Bengal were entirely neglected, owing principally to the fact that their value was not appreciated. The establishment of a Fishery Department may be taken as an indication that Government have at last recognized the economic importance of the fishery resources of the Province. Excluding Assam, the area over which the Department works, together with the population according to the census of 1911, is given in the following table:—

Locality.	Number of Districts.	Area in Square Miles.	Population.
Bengal ...	27	84,092	46,305,642
Behar and Orissa	21	111,829	38,740,935
Total ...	48	195,921	85,046,577

In addition, the potential marine fisheries cover an area of over 40,000 square miles.

The area covered by the British Isles is, roughly, 121,000 square miles, and the population, in 1911, was about 45,141,000 persons. It will thus be seen that the area covered by the Provinces of Bengal and Behar and Orissa is more than one and a half times that of the British Isles, and the population is almost double.

We have no means of estimating the total quantity of fish caught per annum in the Province. Calcutta is the great fish emporium, and practically all the catches from the larger fishing centres are sent to Calcutta for disposal. The quantity of fish imported into Calcutta from all sources and by all routes (railways, roads, and boats) for the year ending March 31, 1916, amounted to 8,822 tons. The following table serves to show the general inadequacy of the supply:—

It will be obvious that, with the enormous fishery areas just named, a shortage in the fish supply indicates a lamentable mismanagement of the potential resources of the Province. That the supply is inadequate is admitted. Many causes have contributed to bring about this unfortunate state of affairs. In the first

	Population.	Total Quantity available per Annum.	Value	Average Quantity available per Head per Annum.
		Maunds.	Rs.	
England and Wales ...	35,000,000	21,966,720	10,009,900	0·63 md. = 50 lb.
Calcutta	900,000	240,143	4,802,860	0·27 md. = 21 lb.

It is thus clear that, other things being equal, the supply of fish in Calcutta is, roughly, three-sevenths of what is available over the whole of England and Wales. Outside Calcutta (that is, in the Province generally) the supply falls much below the figure for the city above. Yet Bengal is rich in waterways, as are also the Provinces of Assam and Behar and Orissa, and the potentialities are enormous. The coast-line of Orissa, from the mouth of the Chilka Lake to Contai, is, roughly, 250 miles in length, while that of Bengal is about 400 miles, measured in a straight line drawn east from Contai to Chittagong. The Sunderbuns area comprises 5,700 square miles. In the dry season the river area of both Provinces is not less than 3,300 square miles, and during the rains the area is very much greater. The Chilka Lake covers an area of 344 square miles. It is difficult to estimate the area occupied by *jheels*, irrigation canals, and other waterways, but it is considerable. Finally, it should be remembered that in Bengal there are not less than 100,000 tanks in which fish are cultivated to a greater or less extent. Until quite recently it was considered a religious duty for every well-to-do Hindu or Mahommedan in Lower Bengal to dig a tank for the benefit of man and beast, but latterly the practice has fallen into desuetude, and even existing tanks are badly neglected. In some districts it is impossible to construct a house, except perhaps on the bank of a river, without first digging a tank and utilizing the earth for elevating the site. Hence it is that tanks are so numerous. The tanks are usually square or rectangular. If excavated by a Hindu, the longer side runs from north to south, while if excavated by a Mahommedan, the longer side is from east to west.

place, it should be remembered that, until a few years ago, no official interest was taken in the fisheries beyond the realization of revenue. There are practically no fishery regulations operative in Bengal. The Bengal Act No. II of 1882 relates to laws regarding embankments and water-courses, and is of no direct importance so far as the fisheries are concerned. Act No. IV of 1897 applies to the whole of India except Burma. This Act merely prohibits the dynamiting and poisoning of waters in order to kill fish, but it empowers Local Governments under certain conditions to frame rules with reference to the following points: (*a*) The erection and use of fixed engines, (*b*) the construction of weirs, (*c*) kinds of nets to be used and the methods of using them, and (*d*) prohibiting all fishing in any specified water area for a period which may not exceed two years.

Unfortunately, up to the present no rules have been framed under this Act either in Bengal or Behar and Orissa.

It will be observed that this Act does not provide for close seasons for any species of fish, nor are any regulations laid down designed to prevent the indiscriminate capture and sale of fry or brood fish.

The absence of suitable administration has resulted not only in a serious deterioration of the fisheries, but also in Government having lost control over considerable fishery areas, particularly in the Sunderbuns, owing to the establishment of prescriptive rights. In consequence of the Permanent Settlement Act, further extensive river fisheries are now owned by Zemindars. The river fisheries at present owned and controlled by Government probably do not represent more than one-fifth of the total fishery area. Further, the irrigation schemes of the

THE FISHERIES OF BENGAL AND BEHAR AND ORISSA

Province, initiated for the benefit of cultivators, have had a most disastrous effect on the fisheries; for, during the rains, when the principal food-fish of the Province breed, their eggs and fry are carried in immense numbers into the paddy-fields, where they are lost. Lastly, the absence of fishery laws has left unchecked the ravages of men. Undoubtedly there are other minor contributory causes, but they need not be detailed here.

1. FISHING ON LAKE CHILKA.   2. HILSA FISHING WITH CAST-NETS IN THE MAHANADI, NEAR CUTTACK.

Photo by Southwell.

Unfortunately, in Bengal the occupation of fishing or dealing in fish is looked upon as a business to be carried on exclusively by the lower classes. There are about twenty castes of Hindus and nine social groups of Mahommedans engaged in the trade. The whole industry is thus left in the hands of people with no capital, no education, no initiative, and no business capacity. Under such circumstances, it is hardly to be wondered at that the fisheries of the Province are undeveloped and the supply scanty.

The various fisheries in the Province, whether belonging to Government or to private individuals, are leased out for varying periods. The right to fish may be sold by public auction, or a private treaty may be concluded. The lessee of the fishery, practically in every case, sublets at a large profit, and this process is carried on through several stages, until the fishery right comes to be owned in small lots. The last lessee, as a rule, compels the fishermen to pay him a nominal sum per month for the privilege of fishing; and, in addition, it frequently happens that the fisherman is obliged to sell his catches to the lessee at no more than one-fourth of their face value. Fish is usually bought from the fishermen at from Rs. 3 to Rs. 5 per maund, and sold wholesale at Rs. 20 per maund, while retail the fish usually realizes Rs. 30 per maund. This has the effect of keeping the fishermen extremely poor, as a result of which they are unable to procure suitable boats and nets. Consequently, many fishermen have forsaken their calling and have taken up agricultural pursuits. In addition, this system of re-leasing keeps the price of fish high and the pockets of the middlemen full. A common Bengali proverb is that *Nikarir Kane sona, Jaliar parane tena* ("A middleman wears gold ear-rings, but a fisherman wears rags").

Calcutta is the principal fish market of the Province, and to this centre fish arrives daily from nearly all parts of Bengal, and also from certain places in Behar and Orissa. The price of fish can be gathered from the following statement, which shows the retail prices in the Sir Stuart Hogg Market, Calcutta, on August 1, 1916:—

Fish.			Rs.	as.		Rs.	as.
Bhetkes (Jhill)	...	per seer	1	2	to	1	4
„ (cut pieces)		„	1	6	„	1	8
„ (salt-water)		„	1	6	„	1	8
„ (salt-water, cut pieces)	...	„	1	12	„	2	0
Butter fish ...	...	„		14	„	1	0
Crab ...		per lot of 4		2	„		3
Cutla ...	...	per seer		8	„		12
Hilsa (Padma)	...	each		4	„		12
„ (Ganges)	...	„		8	„	1	4
Meergal ...	...	per seer		8	„		12
Mullet ...	...	„		10	„		12
Pangash ...	...	„		12	„		14
Pomfret ...	...	„		12	„	1	2
Prawns ...	...	„		8	„		10
„ (Bagda)	...	„		10	„		12
Rohu ...	...	„		8	„		12
Sea fish ...	...	„		8	„		12

Large quantities of hilsa (*Clupea ilisha*) arrive in Calcutta, during the rains, from Goalundo, Khulna, Sara Ghat, Daulatpur,

Kusthea, Belgachi, and other stations on the Eastern Bengal Railway; as well as from Uluberia and Kolaghat, on the Bengal-Nagpur Railway; and Sahebgunge, Rajmehal, Monghyr, and other places on the East Indian Railway. Bhetki (*Lates calcarifer*) and topsi or mangoe-fish (*Polynemus paradiseus*) come from Diamond Harbour, Magrahat, Canning, Dhappa, Khulna, Daulatpur, Budge-Budge, Huruoa Khal, Chingrighatta, the Chilka Lake, and from certain canals.

Carp generally, panagash (*Pangash buchanani*), *Silundia gangeticas* (Silond), and other species are exported from Ashuganj, Goalundo, Daulatpur, Khulna, Paksey, Dacca, Narayanganj, Patna, Rajmehal, Bhagalpur, Sahebgunj, Lalgola Ghat, and Murshidabad. Prawns, lobsters, and crabs are imported to Calcutta from Khulna, Chingrihatta, Ashuganj, and the canals generally. Mullet, pomfret, sole, and other sea fish come from Puri, Balasore, the Chilka Lake, and certain canals, and are also imported into Calcutta at certain times of the year in considerable quantities.

Oysters are available in small quantities all along the Orissa coast and in the Chilka Lake, but experiments made to place these on the Calcutta markets indicates that there is little or no demand for them.

The fish most favoured by the Indian population comprise the various carp, all of which are fresh-water species. Among the European population carp are seldom eaten, but bhetki, topsi, and hilsa are in great demand. The hilsa is a marine species which ascends the various rivers to breed during the rains. It occurs only on the east coast, and has not yet been recorded from the west.

Mr. Kemp, of the Zoological Survey of India, says that the shrimps commonly brought into the Calcutta markets for sale belong to two families and to two different tribes, the *Palæmonidæ* of the tribe *Caridea*, and the *Penæidæ* of the tribe *Penæidea*.

The most abundant species in the former of these families is *Palæmon carcinus*, Faber, a common fresh-water form. Other species of the same genus are doubtless offered for sale, the most important being *P. malcolmsoni*, Milne-Edwards, while even the much smaller *P. lemarrei*, Milne-Edwards, is probably eaten in large numbers. *Leander styliferus*, Milne-Edwards, a marine form that appears to migrate into brackish water at the close of the monsoon, is sometimes to be found on sale.

Of the *Penæidæ*, by far the most important is *Penæus carinatus*, Dana (*P. semisulcatus* of Alcock's memoir); but many other species, such as *Penæus indicus*, Milne-Edwards, *Metapenæus monoceros*, Fabr., and *M. brevicornis*, Milne-Edwards, are also sold. Little is known of the life-history of the *Penæidæ*. The different varieties are only found in brackish water, and are probably migratory, travelling to the sea at the breeding season, which takes place in the cold weather.

Various species of terrapins and mud-turtles are fished in Lower Bengal, and at Rajmehal, in Behar.

The principal among these are: (1) *Trionychidæ*—(*a*) *Trionyx hurum*, Gray; (*b*) *Trionyx gangeticus*, Cuvier; (*c*) *Chitra indica*, Gray; (*d*) *Emyda granosa*, Schœpff. (2) *Testudinidæ*—(*a*) *Hardelli thurgii*, Gray; (*b*) *Hardelli lineata*, Gray; (*c*) *Kachuga dhonagoka*, Gray; (*d*) *Kachuga smithii*, Gray; (*e*) *Kachuga tectum*, Gray.

In many cases the flesh is eaten locally, but considerable numbers are exported to Calcutta, where the retail price is about 4d. per lb., or 8 annas per *seer*. The catches in Lower Bengal alone amount to no less than 100,000 per annum.

Several species of mussels are also fished extensively, both in Lower Bengal and in the Motihari district in Behar.

The shells principally used in the manufacture of buttons and ornaments in Bengal and Behar belong to two genera, viz. *Parreysis* and *Lamellidens* (family *Unionidæ*). Representatives of the genus *Lamellidens* have shells which usually are not very massive. Members of the genus *Parresyia*, Conrad, 1853, have shells more rounded in appearance and more massive than is the case in the genus *Lamellidens*.

The following are the species most commonly used for button-making: *Parreysia corrugata* (Muller); *Parreysia favidens* (Benson); *Parreysia daccænsis* (Preston); *Lamellidens marginalis*, var. *corrianus*, Lea; *Lamellidens narainporensis*, Preston.

There are a large number of varieties both of *P. corrugata* and *L. marginallis* in Bengal, and in all probability many of these varieties are also used; but up to the present a full and specific list has not been prepared. In olden days the shells were utilized for the manufacture of pearl buttons and other ornaments. In Bengal this business is strictly a cottage industry, but in Behar button-making machinery has been imported. In the Murshidabad district of Bengal mussels are fished specially for pearls, but the industry is a very small one, while in Lower Bengal pearls of considerable value are obtained. Throughout both Provinces there is a great scarcity of good shell, due in large measure to indiscriminate and unrestricted fishing. The deterioration of the fisheries has also contributed to a diminished supply, inasmuch as the larval mussels cannot complete their life-cycle in the absence of certain species of fish. Hence a diminished fish supply reacts directly on the supply of mussels.

In the Dacca, Pabna, Dinajpur, Rungpur, Nadia, and Chittagong districts bangles and other ornaments are manufactured in considerable quantities from the chank-shell (*Turbinella pyrum*), practically all of which is imported from Southern India. The industry is of great antiquity. The value of the shell imported to Calcutta during recent years is shown in the following table:—

			Rs.
1905-6	...	...	1,85,385
1906-7	...	...	2,39,067
1907-8	...	...	95,519
1908-9	...	...	2,38,769
1909-10	...	...	2,38,877

The number of shells imported per annum is, roughly, 2,000,000, of which number

Ceylon furnishes...		1,650.000 shells
Tuticorin	...	250,000 „
Other sources	...	50,000 „
Total	...	1,950,000 „

"At the present time the industry enjoys considerable prosperity. The demand for bangles suitable for low-caste Hindu women and for the hill tribes is a stable one, influenced by no fluctuations of fashion and dependent only upon the general well-being of the Province" (Hornell, "Chank Bangle Industry," Mem. A.S., B. vol. iii. No. 7. Calcutta, 1913).

The various methods of fishing practised in Bengal and Behar and Orissa are too numerous to describe in any great detail. They are all surprisingly effective, even if primitive. These methods of fishing are to-day similar to those practised a century ago, and no appreciable improvement is perceptible.

The cast-net is found throughout both Provinces. Drag-nets, often provided with a purse, are plentiful, and are utilized for the capture of carp in the main rivers. Gill-nets are also numerous.

Purse-nets (*sutyal*) are remarkably common, but perhaps the most interesting net is the Kona Jal, or *Labyrinth* net, utilized for catching hilsa in the Madhumati River. It is really a drift-net fitted with a large purse and two side walls of net. The net is kept in position by means of bamboo poles.

For catching hilsa two kinds of nets are principally used. The poorer fishermen have a net called the *sangla jal*. It is elliptical in shape, and is controlled by two pieces of split bamboo sticks; a rope is attached to the lower piece, and by means of this rope the fishermen can feel when a fish enters the net. The boat, with the *sangla* net forward, drifts downstream, and the hilsa, migrating upstream, enter the net and are caught one at a time.

The other net employed in hilsa-fishing is the *burra jal*, or big net. This is an enormous drag-net, cast between two boats and drifted downstream between them. When hauling, the two boats approach the same point on shore, gathering in their net on the way. Occasionally 200 hilsa are caught in this net.

In the River Mahanadi at Cuttack cast-nets are used by hilsa-fishermen in the vicinity of the anicut. Poles about 10 feet in length are firmly fixed into the mud in an upright position. On the top of the pole, and at right angles to it, a piece of wood about 1 foot square is fixed, and on this the fisherman sits throughout the hot day ready to cast his net when a fish is sighted. It is a common occurrence to see the fishermen coiled up asleep on the seat, while beneath them the river flows swift and deep.

1, 2. FISHING-BOATS ON LAKE CHILKA. 3. JHANS IN THE CHILKA LAKE. 4. JHANS.

Photos by permission of the Director, Zoological Survey of India.

There are numerous other forms of nets, but they need not be considered here. Fixed engines, or traps, are in use everywhere in both Provinces—from the seaface to the smallest pool of water. They are usually made from split bamboos, and are frequently employed with various forms of nets.

The *jhan* in use on the Chilka Lake is an example of another method of capturing fish. At certain times of the year fishermen are specially deputed to watch for shoals of fish entering a cul-de-sac in search of food. When the migration is complete, a bamboo structure (known locally as a *jhan*) is thrown across the entry, and the enclosure is then ruthlessly fished. Mullet and pomfret are caught in large quantities by this method in the Chilka Lake. Other bamboo structures for the capture of prawns are extremely numerous and varied.

In certain parts of Bengal and Behar spearing fish is also practised, especially at night. A torch is placed on the bow of a dugout, and fish, attracted by the light, are speared alongside the boat. The bow and arrow is said to be utilized occasionally in the clear water of the Gandak River. In the dry weather, when tanks are frequently empty, certain *Siluroidea* bury themselves in the mud, and it is a common sight to see the poorer people digging in order to capture the burrowing fish.

Mussels are fished by naked divers, and turtles are frequently caught in large drag-nets.

A peculiar method of catching turtles is, however, practised near Khulna, but only one species—viz. *Trionyx gangeticus* (Khalu Kachim), which is a very gross feeder—is caught by this method. The Deputy Director of Fisheries, Bengal, has seen this species feeding on the highly putrid carcass of a buffalo, and the fact that certain turtles are fond of eating human corpses, left partly burnt in Hindu cremation grounds, is well known among fishermen, who actually utilize this fact in capturing them. The method is as follows: A man is covered from head to foot with a white sheet, and is placed at a short distance from the water, and a trench being dug between them. The party of fishermen then cry out, "Hari bol"—a phrase usual when the dead body of a Hindu is brought for cremation. At this cry the turtles come out of the water, and, in their attempt to get at the supposed dead body, fall into the trench and are taken by the fishermen.

Another method of fishing for turtles in beels is common in Eastern Bengal. During the rains, and for some time subsequently, these beels are connected to the main river or rivers by a series of narrow, shallow, and tortuous channels. As the rains recede, the turtles follow these channels in order to reach the main rivers. The turtle-fishermen select a place along the course of such a channel where there is a sudden bend, and a small excavation is made in order that the water may have a fall of about 1 foot. The turtles migrate to the rivers during the night, and on account of the narrowness of the channel at the site selected, they are obliged to travel in single file. The method of fishing is as follows: A fisherman stands in the water close to the "fall"; his hands are outstretched in such a manner that any turtle moving downstream falls into his hands. When caught, the fisherman immediately makes over his catch to a second fisherman, who is waiting near by: and after a time the latter is relieved by another fisherman, the catches being placed in the hold of a boat which is kept in readiness. The success of this method depends on everything being done quietly, so as not to frighten other turtles in the rear. It is said that by this method as many as 600 turtles have been caught in one night at one place, but the average catch is usually about 100. It is further stated that only Kali Kattua (*Hardelli thurgii*) is caught in this manner, and this species is docile when caught.

The transport of the fish from the various fishing centres to the principal markets is effected in a variety of ways, and in this connection there is room for vast improvement. It should be remembered that among the Indian population fish which has been gutted and cleaned is not saleable. It must be intact and whole, just as obtained from the river.

Many of the bigger fishing centres, such as Goalundo, Khulna, Saraghat, Monghyr, Bhagalpur, Rajmehal, Balasore, Puri, the Chilka Lake, Kolaghat, and others, have excellent railway facilities for disposing of their fish. The East Indian Railway taps the valley of the Ganges; the Bengal-Nagpur Railway offers facilities for transport from the coast of Orissa, Balasore, and Cuttack; and the Eastern Bengal Railway embraces large areas in Eastern Bengal where the most productive fisheries exist. Large quantities of live fish and turtles are brought by boat during the cold weather from Eastern Bengal to Calcutta, through the canals, the journey occupying from four to eight days. The following statistics show the quantities of fish imported to Calcutta for the year ending March 31, 1916, by the means indicated:—

Names of Places from which Exported.	Maunds.	Seers.	Weight.		
			Tons.	Cwt.	Lb.
Railways—					
Assam-Bengal	242	10	8	17	108
Baraset-Basirhat Light	6,364	—	233	15	66
Bengal and North-Western	5,534	16	203	6	8
Bengal-Nagpur	22,207	36	815	15	110
Eastern Bengal	145,705	38	5,352	9	17
East Indian	9,025	39	331	11	35
Howrah-Amta Light	1,069	—	39	5	43
Howrah-Sheakhala Light	4	—	—	2	105
Total by Railways	190,153	19	6,985	4	44
Steamers—					
Calcutta Steam Navigation Company ...	2,732	30	100	7	79
Country Boats—					
Calcutta Canals	31,542	—	1,158	13	79
By Road	15,715	8	557	5	95
Grand Total of Imports by all routes ...	240,143	17	8,801	11	73

Fish is very seldom exported in ice, because in many cases ice is not available, and even where it is obtainable the cost is very high. No care is taken to keep the fish fresh. It has already been noted that the fish is never gutted, but, in addition, it is often knocked about considerably and exposed to the hot tropical sun. It is not surprising, therefore, that large quantities of fish are landed in Calcutta in a semi-rotten condition, particularly in the hot weather. The railways do not always pass close to the fishing grounds, as in very many instances the fisheries are situated several miles away. In these cases the fish is carried by coolies from the fishing grounds to the railways, and during this time the fish is exposed to the hot sun.

There are many important fisheries, however, which are situated at a great distance from the railway. In these cases no means of transport exist at present. Frequently there are no roads, or, even where they exist, they are impassable in the rainy season.

The Dhamra fisheries are situated 50 miles from the nearest railway-station, and the journey by boat to Calcutta occupies well over a day. The same is true of many of the larger *jheels*. In these instances it is clear that the development and improvement of the fisheries concerned depends on the initiation of suitable methods of transport. At present the fish is cured at such places and exported as dried fish.

The estuarine fisheries rank next in importance to the fresh-water fisheries, and of these the Sunderbuns, comprising the delta of the Ganges, and situated in the districts of Khulna and the Twenty-four Parganas, are by far the most important. The Sunderbuns comprises an area of 5,700 square miles, made up of forest, swamp, estuary, islands, and a multitude of rivers which communicate with each other by innumerable channels. This enormous tract of potential fishing ground is, however, comparatively unexploited, owing to the general absence of suitable transport facilities. Although fast steamers (belonging to the India General Steam Navigation Company) pass through the Sunderbuns on their way to and from Calcutta and Khulna, Goalundo and other towns, they are seldom made use of. This circumstance arises from the fact that the service is somewhat irregular; the steamers frequently do not call anywhere *en route*, and even if they did, the fishermen, having no agents, are compelled to dispose of their fish personally, and this is not possible unless they bring the fish to Calcutta themselves. Hence in these cases the present steamer facilities are of little account. For the development of these fisheries, suitable, capacious, but light-draught steamers will be necessary, and centres will have to be established where the fish caught can be collected. As the fishermen found a ready sale for their fish, they would acquire better boats and more suitable nets.

It has been pointed out that, as a result of the representations made by Sir K. G. Gupta in his report dated January 27, 1908 (where he urged the necessity for a systematic fishery survey in the bay), a steam trawler was obtained by Government without loss of time, and within six months was at work in the Bay. This trawler, the *Golden Crown*, started on her first trip on June 13, 1908, and completed her last voyage on December 17, 1909. The investigations made by that vessel in the Bay of Bengal, and by the steam launch *Ila* in the Sunderbuns, were carried out by Dr. J. Travis Jenkins, of the Lancashire Sea Fisheries, whose services had been specially engaged by the Government of Bengal. The primary object of the investigations in the Bay of Bengal was not to supply the market with fish, or merely to attempt to prove that trawling operations in the bay could be made commercially successful, but to locate and chart the principal fishing grounds, to ascertain what kinds and quantities of fish were obtainable, and where they were to be found at particular seasons. The results obtained by Dr. Jenkins are of great importance, and in particular he showed that trawling could be carried on successfully right through the monsoon. Twenty-eight voyages were made between June 1908 and December 1909. The kinds of fish obtained during each voyage were determined in very great detail and tabulated; the quantity was also noted, and a comparison made between the weight of the average daily catches of the *Golden Crown* and those of other trawlers working in Iceland, the White Sea, Rockall, Faroe, Bay of Biscay, North Sea, Irish Sea, English Channel, Portugal and Morocco, West of Scotland, and off the coasts of Scotland and Ireland; and he showed that the results obtained by the *Golden Crown* compared very favourably with the results obtained by the first-class steam trawlers in England.

Dr. Jenkins also located some of the best fishing grounds, and prepared a chart showing the area which had been trawled over, the nature of the bottom, and what results had been obtained. He further proved that sea fish could be landed in a fresh condition in Calcutta from places as distant as Akyab and Santapillai.

It will therefore be seen that the Provinces of Bengal and Behar and Orissa rely for their supply on the fresh-water fisheries, supplemented by catches from the estuaries and small consignments from the foreshore fisheries. The deterioration of the fresh-water fisheries has been very marked during recent years, and the factors which have conduced to bring about this result are numerous. Reference has been made to the bad effects which the various irrigation schemes have on the fisheries. Throughout India agriculture has been developed at the expense of the inland fisheries without even a passing thought for their well-being, and in this country it is hardly possible for these two industries to develop side by side. In order to understand how the irrigation schemes re-act on the fisheries, it is necessary to state that the eggs of carp (the principal food-fish of the people of Bengal) float near the surface of the water. The fish breed in the rains, and at that time the Province is flooded, the result being that the eggs escape into the paddy-fields, through the irrigation channels, where they are exterminated by the *ryots*. The anicuts over the Rivers Cossye, Sone, and Mahanadi have an equally disastrous effect. In the case of the Cossye, the eggs and fry are carried over the anicut into an area which practically dries up six months later. The same is the case with the Sone River, except that there

PRAWN TRAPS.

Photo by permission of the Director, Zoological Survey of India.

It has been ascertained that the area covered by the potential marine fisheries is, roughly, 40,000 square miles, and it will be obvious that over such a vast area the supply must be wellnigh inexhaustible. Foreshore fishing is practically confined to Balasore, Puri, and Dhamra. No further direct work on marine fisheries has been possible since Dr. Jenkins concluded his observations, as no steamer was available. It is very unfortunate that, although six years have elapsed since Government published the results of these inquiries, capitalists in Calcutta have not yet taken up these fisheries, which therefore remain totally unexploited; and it is improbable that they will ever be in a thoroughly satisfactory condition until the marine resources have been opened out.

the eggs and fry have a reasonable chance of entering the River Ganges before the dry weather sets in. In the case of the Mahanadi, the fry are carried into brackish water about 60 miles below. In all these cases the upper reaches of the river are being rapidly depleted, since practically no fish going upstream ever succeed in passing the anicut. In these large rivers it is not too much to say that the anicuts have practically ruined the fisheries. Another factor tending to deplete the fresh-water fisheries is at work in such of the small rivers as flow into the sea, or which open into larger rivers in close proximity to the sea.

The case furnished by the Damudar River is a typical one. This river is a comparatively short one, and during the rains the current flows at a rate of about five miles an hour. The eggs of carp are carried into the estuaries and destroyed long before they are capable of any appreciable movement. That such is the case is indicated by the fact that at places like Amta and Champadanga, situated on the banks of this river, just beyond the tide limit, millions of carp-fry are actually removed year by year for the purpose of stocking tanks. It is clearly impossible to prevent the escape of eggs or fry from the rivers to the paddy-fields, or to prevent them from being carried into brackish water and lost ; but it will be obvious that this extensive drain on the resources of both the large and small rivers re-acts extremely adversely on the fish supply of the Provinces. Further, it is important to note that the fisheries are entirely unprotected, and the ravages of rapacious man proceed unchecked.

The cultivation of fish in tanks is carried on very extensively in Bengal. The fish cultivated are Rohu (*Labeo rohita*), Catla (*Catla buchanani*), Mirgal (*Cirrhina mirgala*), and Calbasu (*Labeo calbasu*). These fish do not breed in tanks, but the eggs and fry are obtained from the main rivers during the rains, and are sold retail by itinerant vendors throughout the Province. During July and August the Department of Fisheries, Bengal and Behar and Orissa, supplied to applicants seven lakhs of fry for cultivation in tanks. Usually, however, the cultivation of the above species of fish in tanks is not so productive as one might expect, the reason being that the eggs and fry sold are not exclusively those of carp. There is a large admixture of predatory fish such as *Silundia gangeticus*, *Notopterus chitala*, various species of *Ophiocephalus*, *Saccobranchus fossilus*, *Clarius magur*, *Wallago attu*, and several species of *Macrones*. In addition, many of the fry sold as carp-fry consist of small species which never grow more than a few inches in length. The result is that the predatory fish previously introduced into the tanks devour the new fry put in year by year, while the small species, even if not devoured, never attain a marketable size.

In some parts of Bengal the cultivation is carried out in a more logical manner. The fry are allowed to develop until the species can be recognized; predatory fish are then thrown away, and the carp, often 4 inches in length, are sold for cultivation in tanks. The latter method has the advantage of stopping the introduction of predatory fish into tanks, and further, the carp-fry are placed in the tank in such a condition that they can escape the pursuits of predatory species.

The price of the small mixed fry is about Rs. $\frac{1}{8}$/- per 1,000, while that of pure carp, 2 to 4 inches in length, is about Rs. 6/- to Rs. 8/-. These fry are only available from the middle of July until about the first week of September.

Something of the nature of the work before the Department of Fisheries will be evident from what has been written. To increase the fish supply, action must be taken to prevent wanton, wilful, and unnecessary loss ; and further, artificial cultivation of the principal marketable species must be undertaken. Before this can be done a knowledge must be acquired of breeding-habits and means suitable for artificially cultivating them must be discovered. With this knowledge, simple laws for protecting them can then be designed.

With reference to the fishing industry generally, steps are being taken to exclude middlemen as far as possible. Where practicable, Government fisheries are leased to fishermen as co-operative bodies, and up to the present nine such societies have been formed in Bengal. These societies are, for the present, still more or less dependent on the middlemen for the disposal of their catches, but there can be no doubt that in due time the societies will dispose of their own catches and arrange their own transport. The movement is growing. Until these societies were formed the Fishery Department had no control over any fisheries in the Province, but now the Department is taking over the administration of Government Fisheries where possible. The movement has the further effect of enabling the Department to get in touch with the fishermen.

Progress is slow, but this is largely because the staff is very limited and the area so enormous.

MAHSEER WEIGHING 28 LB., CAUGHT ON A LIGHT 14-FT. FLY ROD BY W. M. NUTTALL IN ASSAM.

Photo by N. E. W.

PRIMITIVE METHOD OF TRAVEL.

THE BENGAL PRESIDENCY

THE geographical area of that portion of India known during the past two or three hundred years as Bengal has varied very considerably, owing to numerous wars which resulted in the acquisition or loss of territory, and also to those re-arrangements for administrative purposes which the governing authorities from time to time considered advisable. The early history, therefore, of the Province, as it is constituted to-day, naturally relates in some measure to integral portions of surrounding countries or States.

Speaking in a general way, however, one may say that the earliest European traders were Portuguese who, about the year 1530, were found at Chittagong, in the extreme eastern portion of Bengal, and at Satgaon, near Hooghly, some 24 miles distant from Calcutta. But their power was wrested from them by the Dutch, who, towards the close of the seventeenth century, were the greatest European force in Asia. Holland's loss, shortly after this date, of much of her prestige in Europe seriously affected her position in the East, and thus the English and French were left as the dominating commercial factors in India.

The East India Company, about the year 1650, established factories at Hooghly, Kasimbazar, Murshidabad, and other places for the manufacture of silk and muslins, and for trading in salt, saltpetre, and other commodities.

Their proceedings were greatly hampered by disputes with the Nawab of Bengal, and frequent conflicts took place between the troops of that ruler and the forces of the Company, and in one of these the factory at Kasimbazar was utterly wrecked. These disturbances were caused by interference with the Company's boats as they voyaged up and down the Hooghly, and by personal grievances between the servants of the rivals. But while these troubles were continually occurring in a comparatively limited area, neighbouring powers, including Mahrattas and others, were invading Bengal, with the result that the country was in a continual state of turmoil; rulers were being deposed and others appointed, and the form of government which then existed was entirely unable to grapple with the difficulties of the situation.

The terrors of the reign of Suraj-ud-dowlah, the Nawab of Bengal, which led to the tragedy of the "Black Hole" in Calcutta in 1756, have been too vividly described by various writers to need repetition; and it need only be added that invasions from without and disorders within the Province, were of constant occurrence until 1766, when Clive left Bengal in, as he described it, a state of peace.

With the view of obtaining some definite method of administration—including the collection of revenue—Warren Hastings appointed collectors in various districts of the Province, and this step was rendered necessary, as the East India Company were only willing to sit at the receipt of custom without undertaking any responsibilities of government. During the Governor-Generalship of Lord Cornwallis in 1786 the collectors were made Civil judges and magistrates, and the administration of 1916 is the gradual outcome of the arrangement then made.

The partition of Bengal into two administrative areas, little more than a decade ago, was productive of widespread dissatisfaction, not only in India but also in England, and a dispatch from the Government of India to the Secretary of State contained these momentous words: "There was reason to fear that, instead of dying down, the bitterness of feeling would become more and more acute." The reunion of Bengal, coupled with the creation of a new Province elevated to the status of a Presidency Government, was confirmed by His Majesty the King-Emperor at the Coronation Durbar at Delhi in 1911, and the pronouncement, thus royally made amid a fanfare of trumpets and the thundering of guns, produced a feeling of intense joy throughout Bengal, as it foreshadowed a more democratic form of government; and, to quote Lord Hardinge, the Viceroy of India at that time, "it is certain that in the course of time the just demand of Indians for a larger share in the government of the country will have been satisfied, and that at last India will consist of a number of administrations, autonomous in all provincial affairs, with the Government of India above them all, and possessing power to interfere in cases of misgovernment, but ordinarily restricting their functions to matters of Imperial concern."

Bengal is bounded on the north by Bhután and the native State of Sikkim, on the east by Burma and the Province of Assam, on the west by the Province of Behar and Orissa, and on the south by the Bay of Bengal. The greater portion of its area, possessing a fertile soil enriched by copious rains, is primarily an agricultural country, and abundant employment is found for its dense population in pursuits connected with the cultivation of the land. The great waterways are met with chiefly in the eastern and central parts of the Province, and hence it follows that the land through which they pass is subject to frequent floods, and is therefore peculiarly suitable for crops of rice and jute, which are grown to perfection. The western portion is more hilly; irrigation is necessary when the rainfall is slight; but rice (the principal product), barley, maize, wheat, oil-seeds, and gram are cultivated on an extensive scale.

Food crops represent about 85 per cent. of the total area cropped, oil-seeds yield from 4 to 5 per cent., and then follow cereals, tobacco, and pulses. There are about 140 varieties of rice, but those kinds most in favour in Bengal are three in number. Winter rice is grown on low land from seedlings planted after the rains of July and August; early rice, sown in April or May, either broadcast or by transplants; and spring rice, from seedlings planted on banks of rivers or other moist ground in November, and harvested in the months of March and April following. It is said that the northern and eastern districts of Bengal are the largest jute-growing areas in the world. Certainly it is a most valuable crop for the cultivator, and the processes of pressing and manufacture in the 40 or 45 mills on the Hooghly, near Calcutta, give constant employment to thousands of hands whose earnings contribute largely to the wealth of the city. Maize is a very valuable food crop, and it is somewhat extensively grown, but it is more productive in Darjeeling than in any other district.

The cultivation of oil-seeds has increased in recent years, but the value of the oil expressed by machinery, and, indeed, of the residuum too, has not yet been fully realized.

Probably few agriculturists in India have had more diversified experiences than the planters of indigo. They have witnessed times of steady progress for a number of years, they have seen the flotation and subsequent collapse of company concerns which ought never to have been started, and the introduction of synthetic dyes from Europe deprived scores of them of a payable market for their produce; but they have once again come into enjoyment of a greatly increased demand—at good prices—for indican produced on Bengal estates. The cultivation of indigo is the subject of lengthy notes on another page. Tea is grown chiefly in the districts of Darjeeling, Chittagong, and Jalpaiguri, and while prices remain steady at a moderately profitable figure, improved methods of cultivation have increased the average annual yield per acre.

Cultivated fruits include mango, jack-fruit, guavas, custard-apples, and several varieties of figs and melons; while vegetables, grown in garden plots or in larger areas near towns, comprise potatoes, radishes, onions, carrots, cabbages, and cauliflowers.

The Government of Bengal is taking very active measures to improve agricultural knowledge in schools by practical demonstrations by experts, and by the establishment of experimental farms, upon which tests are made of various kinds of seeds, and instruction is given upon the highly important questions of the soil and its constituents, and the necessity for and the proper use of various kinds of manures.

The cattle of the Province are as a rule small in stature and of indifferent milk-producing capabilities. Recent action by the Department of Agriculture has resulted in the crossing of cows in Bengal with bulls obtained from the United Provinces, and this has led to the production of larger animals and to an increase in the yield of milk. Horses, with the exception of imported animals or their descendants, would be more correctly described as weedy ponies of stunted growth—the result of indiscriminate mating and an insufficiency of food in their early days.

Indigenous forests are a valuable asset, but it is sad to reflect that during the time of the East India Company many of them were depleted for the sake of the value of timber alone, without a thought for the indiscriminate manner in which this destruction was carried out. Further damage was done by natives who practised the system of cultivation of the land by what is called in Bengal the "jhum" process. This consisted, in plain words, in making as much profit as possible out of certain areas with a minimum of trouble or expense, and in leaving the cropped land in an impoverished state for future occupiers. These men were in the habit of selecting a portion of forest on the side of a hill where the soil was productive; they would fell and then burn the trees, and subsequently sow seeds in holes in the ground. When they had reaped their harvests they would pack up their belongings and proceed to another site and repeat the operation.

The chief industry in Bengal is the mining of coal, but the output at the present time is exceedingly small when compared with the vast potential wealth of this mineral, not only in the fields now being worked, but also in the areas which are as yet untouched. Two or three reasons might be advanced in explanation of the fact that coal mining is only yet in its infancy. One is that from time immemorial there has been an abundant supply of timber for fuel, and that until quite a recent period the necessity for any other substance had not arisen. Again, steamships visiting the ports of India were in the habit of using Welsh coal and industrial development had scarcely commenced.

Thirty-five years ago the whole of India produced less than a million tons of coal, but since that date the railway companies have greatly increased the length of their several systems, and mills, factories, and private houses have become consumers of coal obtained locally. The total quantity now raised to the surface annually is about 15,000,000 tons, nearly 90 per cent. of which is derived from the mines in Bengal and Behar and Orissa. Other minerals in the Presidency include mica, gold, copper, tin, limestone, and granite and other rocks.

Any history of Bengal would have to be an exceedingly ancient book if it did not refer to home industries of various kinds. Going back no more than two or three centuries, one finds that practically every village had its weaver, its worker in gold, copper, brass, and other metals, and some of the products of those days are evidences of the artistic skill of the people.

Cotton goods were in such demand in Europe very early in the eighteenth century as it is on record that, with the view of increasing the quantity for exportation, steps were taken in 1706 to induce weavers to settle in the neighbourhood of Calcutta.

The cities of Dacca and Santipur were famous for their muslins, and the beautiful silk produced at Murshidabad, Kasimbazar, and other places was known throughout the world, but the introduction of machinery into factories in Europe has almost entirely put these industries outside of the list of payable concerns.

Public interest in the manufacture of silk has, however, been considerably aroused in recent years. The Government of Bengal has established sericultural schools, has employed a silk expert to introduce improved methods of rearing silkworms, of reeling, dyeing, and weaving silk, and has in other ways given incomparable opportunities to companies, or to single individuals, to become profitably employed in the production of silk.

Jute is worked into cloth for gunny-bags, sails, quilts, and other articles, or it is twisted into twine for the making of ropes. It is not necessary to refer here at any length to the present-day weaving of woollen and cotton goods, the pressing of jute and oil-seeds, the ginning of cotton, the manufacture of earthenware vessels, and to a large number of other industries which are referred to elsewhere, but one might just remark that the manufacture of brass and copper utensils appears to be the only indigenous industry which has not been affected by foreign competition.

Bengal is well supplied with efficient railway facilities, chiefly by the Bengal-Nagpur, Eastern Bengal, and East Indian Railway Companies; steamers belonging to many of the leading shipping companies connect Calcutta with the principal ports of the world; and a really excellent service for passengers and cargo is provided by small steamers, flats, and boats upon the waters of the Brahmaputra, Ganges, Mahanadi, Padma, and other rivers.

The great rivers of Bengal—the Ganges and Brahmaputra—with their affluents and distributaries, provide excellent yet economical means of transport for passengers and cargo; they contain a practically inexhaustible supply of fish; and they carry down towards the coast an immense quantity of fertilizing silt, which is deposited on the surface of the soil in their respective deltaic areas.

The Ganges enters the Presidency on its western boundary, and during its easterly course its waters have occasionally—owing to the alteration of channels caused by shifting soil—merged with those of the Ichamati, Jalangi, and the Matabhanga Rivers, but it breaks forth again and continues its flow until it is met and stopped by the Brahmaputra. The river below the point at which the Bhagirathi leaves it is called Padma. The Brahmaputra has its source in the Himalaya range, and it passes through Tibet to the north of the eastern portion of the Province of Assam, then southwards through the Eastern Himalayas to the north-eastern boundary of Bengal, and finally discharges itself into the Bay of Bengal.

Good roads are by no means plentiful, as the alluvial soil found in so many parts of Bengal is, by itself, unsuitable; and as a supply of hard metal is only occasionally available, the difficulties of construction are very greatly increased.

Bengal, for administrative purposes, comprises five divisions, under Commissioners, containing 28 districts, and a number of subdivisions which are usually administered by magistrates.

The District Officer is the man at the helm in administration, as all other magisterial, revenue, and police officers within his area are subordinate to him. An Act of Parliament of 1885 provided, *inter alia*, for the appointment of district and local Boards, whose members are entrusted with the maintenance of roads, the control of dispensaries, pounds, ferries, sanitation in villages, the supervision of certain schools and other matters of a similar character.

A TEMPLE AT BISHNUPUR.
Upon the walls of which are inscribed the whole of the Ramayan, or Hindu Scriptures.
Photo by T. P. Sen.

The teaching of the English language in schools appears to have been undertaken primarily by missionaries, but Lord William Bentinck, Governor-General of India about the year 1830, strongly supported similar work being conducted in non-mission schools. Effect was given to the Viceroy's proposal in 1835, when it was decided to give instruction in higher educational establishments through the medium of the English language. A Council of Education was appointed, and arrangements were made for inspection of schools, the holding of examinations, and the granting of scholarships. Rapid development has taken place throughout the Presidency in the number of efficient educational establishments, and in the percentage of children who are regularly receiving instruction. The University of Calcutta was founded in the year 1857, when regulations were framed for the conduct of examinations and the granting of degrees, while technical and other colleges and schools are now affiliated with that Institution. The Department of Public Instruction is under the control of a Director, who is assisted by a competent staff of European and Indian Inspectors and other subordinates.

The Presidency comprises the following five divisions, in which there are 28 districts :—

1. The Burdwan division, in which there are the districts of Burdwan, Birbhum, Bankura, Midnapur, Hooghly, and Howrah.

2. The Presidency division, with the districts of Calcutta, the Twenty-four Perganas, Nadia, Murshidabad, Jessore, and Khulna.

3. The Dacca division, with the districts of Dacca, Mymensingh, Faridpur, and Backergunge.

4. The Chittagong division, having the districts of Chittagong, Noakhali, Tippera, and Chittagong Hill Tracts.

5. The Rajshahi division, comprising the districts of Rajshahi, Dinajpur, Jalpaiguri, Rungpur, Bogra, Pabna, Malda, and Darjeeling.

There are also two Native Principalities under the Government of Bengal—namely, the States of Cooch Behar and Hill Tippera.

Several towns and villages have been described in the notes of places situated upon or near to the railway systems which intersect Bengal, and a further reference to them is therefore unnecessary.

The Burdwan Division.

Burdwan, 67 miles distant from Calcutta, and the chief town and civil station of the district of Burdwan, is a thriving commercial centre on the East Indian Railway system, its principal industries comprising the weaving of cloth for Indian garments and the manufacture of brass vessels for household purposes, and of most artistic ornaments in gold and silver. The beautiful palace of the Maharaja and a group of more than 100 temples are worthy of a visit.

Asansol is an important junction on the East Indian and Bengal-Nagpur Railway systems, and as it is the centre of the Raneegunge coalfields it has drawn a large number of individuals from other portions of Bengal, with the result that an insignificant and almost unknown village has grown into a thriving town of nearly 20,000 inhabitants. Its locomotive engine-shed is believed to be one of the largest of its kind in the world. The railway-station is 132 miles distant from Calcutta, and is in the district and division of Burdwan.

Bankura.—This town is believed to have been named after an early settler named Banku Rai, and credence is generally given to this tradition as some direct descendants of his are living at Bankura at the present time. The manufacture of tassar silk is the chief industry, but a considerable trade is carried on in the export of rice, oil-seeds, lac, cotton, silk cloth, and silk cocoons, and in importing English soft piece goods, salt, spices, tobacco, cocoanuts, and pulses. The climate is dry and healthy, and the delightful position of the town on the north bank of the Dhalkisor River renders it a favourite place of residence.

Bishnupur was the ancient capital of the district of Bankura; but it was more than that, as, according to the records of native chroniclers, it was in very early days a more beautiful city than the beautiful house of "Indra in heaven." The city was strongly fortified, and its walls enclosed a citadel containing a palace; but at the present time one can only see extensive remains of these and of other buildings, as masses of jungle have assisted in the work of destruction. There is, however, an old iron gun, 10½ feet in length, which was given, according to tradition, by a deity to a Raja, in addition to the ruins of a number of temples, upon which may still be seen curious representations of birds and flowers.

The town is now a forwarding centre for large consignments of rice, oil-seeds, lac, silk cloth, cocoons, and cotton, and very many of its inhabitants are employed in the manufacture of tassar silk and silk scarves and shawls.

Raneegunge is the centre of the most important coal-producing area in Bengal, and the extensive mining of this mineral has led to the establishment of a number of other industries, chief among which are the manufacture of paper and of pottery ware, together with articles suitable for domestic use. The East Indian Railway system bisects this rich colliery area, and its station at Raneegunge has an exceedingly heavy traffic for coal, which is forwarded to nearly every part of India. The town has a population of more than 15,000 inhabitants, and is situated about 120 miles distant from Calcutta. There are about 130 coal or colliery companies with mines in the Province of Bengal.

Tamluk is situated on a tributary of the Hooghly, in the south-eastern portion of the district of Midnapur. Ancient Hindu history relates that it was a port of trade when it was visited by the Chinese pilgrim Fa Hian in the fifth century, and that 200 years later it was described by another pilgrim, Hiuen Tsiang, as an important harbour, with 10 Buddhist monasteries, 1,000 monks, and a pillar, erected by Osaka, 200 feet in height. It is further stated that there formerly existed a royal palace and grounds which covered an area of eight square miles, but the only traces of that building to-day are ruins which, owing to the lapse of years, are frequently discovered at a depth of from 18 feet to 20 feet below the surface of the ground. The present town has gained considerable importance as a forwarding station upon the Rupnarayan River for all kinds of produce. A very fine temple, dedicated to the goddess Barga Bhima, or Kali, may be seen on the bank of the river just referred to.

Almost immediately opposite Barrackpore, on the western bank of the Hooghly, are the townships of Hooghly, Chandernagore, Chinsurah, and Bandel.

Hooghly is about 25 miles distant from Calcutta, and was founded by the Portuguese in the year 1457; but nearly 200 years afterwards it became an English Settlement, when the East India Company opened a factory and made it one of their trading stations.

Chandernagore is a much-favoured riverside resort of week-end parties from Calcutta. It became a French Settlement in 1673, but during the wars of the eighteenth century, when Bengal was overrun by invaders from without and rebels from within, it passed into the possession of the British on two separate occasions, but it was finally handed over to the French in the year of Waterloo.

Chinsurah is visited chiefly on account of some quaint old Dutch architecture which is still in existence, although some of it dates from the closing years of the seventeenth century.

Bandel, about 25 miles distant from Howrah Station, was in the hands of the Portuguese about the year 1596, when they built a fine monastery and church. That building was destroyed about 50 years later, and was succeeded by the imposing structure which is the principal attraction of the town.

Howrah.—The name Howrah is usually associated with the city of that name, which extends for a distance of nearly seven miles along the western bank of the Hooghly, and is connected with Calcutta by a floating bridge.

The district of Howrah comprises about 510 square miles, and the soil, rendered fertile by the silt deposited by the Gaighata, Bakshi, Khal and other rivers, produces excellent crops of rice, wheat, barley, maize, mustard, and jute. The city participates to some extent in this wealth of agricultural produce, but its real interests lie in the 50 or 60 factories which are situated either upon or near to the banks of the Hooghly. These include jute, flour, and paper mills, railway workshops, engineering and iron works, shipbuilding and dock yards, in all of which considerably more than 50,000 persons find constant employment.

Howrah became a municipal town in 1862, and it has progressed at a very rapid rate in the making of new streets and in supplying the citizens with a plentiful quantity of filtered water for household purposes.

Its principal buildings are the terminus station of the Bengal-Nagpur and East Indian Railway Companies, magistrates' offices, civil courts, district board and municipal offices, and the Howrah General Hospital.

The inhabitants at the census of 1911 were nearly 200,000 in number.

Ballabpur, a suburb of Serampore, is about 12 miles distant from Calcutta, and may be reached from that city by train on the East Indian Railway, or by one of the comfortable steamers which ply daily on the Hooghly. Two very important festivals are held annually, the first being the *Snan Jatra,* or bathing festival, and the second the *Rath Jatra,* or car festival, which is held six weeks later.

The god Jagannath is removed from his temple at Mahesh, an adjoining village, and placed in the temple of another idol at Ballabpur, and after eight days the car is returned to Mahesh. A fair, held during the last-named festival, is continued for eight days, and no fewer than 100,000 persons assemble for religious ceremonies, and for the sale or purchase of agricultural and other produce.

Ulubaria, 20 miles distant from Calcutta on the Bengal-Nagpur Railway system, is known in history as the place where Job Charnock lived for some time prior to his selection of the site of Calcutta. It has a daily service of steamers to Calcutta and Ghatal, and is the starting-point of a canal leading to Midnapur. There were about 5,300 inhabitants at the latest census.

A FESTIVAL AT PURI.

Photo by T. P. Sen.

THE PRESIDENCY DIVISION.

Alipore, the headquarters of the district of Twenty-four Perganas, is a southern suburb of Calcutta and within the municipal limits of that city. Reference is made elsewhere to Belvedere House and Hastings House, which are so intimately connected with the political life of Warren Hastings, but the village is now a very popular residential quarter for Europeans who are engaged in business in Calcutta. It has also a very large and well-supplied general market at Orphanganj; a reformatory in which more than 200 boys can be taught carpentering, canework, painting, turning, polishing, bookbinding, tailoring, gardening, and other trades of a similar character; and a jail capable of accommodating about 1,800 prisoners, whose period of detention is occupied in manufacturing gunny-bags, cloth, and jute twine. There are no industries of any importance, but a very considerable amount of business is carried on in the native bazars.

Diamond Harbour.—The sub-division, of which the village of Diamond Harbour is the principal commercial centre, comprises about 1,280 square miles of land, 900 square miles of which are in the Sundarbans, a low-lying area through which the outlets of the River Ganges wend their way to the sea. In earlier days many ships belonging to the East India Company were wont to anchor at Diamond Harbour; and although the village and harbour suffered very considerably through the severe cyclone of 1864, a harbour-master and customs officials are still stationed there for the purpose of inspecting vessels proceeding up the Hooghly River. Calcutta, about 30 miles distant, can be reached by the Eastern Bengal Railway system, or by cart along a well-made road. Quarantine accommodation for pilgrims arriving from Mecca has been provided here.

Barrackpore.—One of the most charming drives in the neighbourhood of Calcutta is along the splendid grand trunk road to Barrackpore, on the eastern bank of the River Hooghly, and distant about 14 miles from the city. It can also be reached by rail on the Eastern Bengal system and by ferry steamers. On entering the spacious park of 250 acres, beautifully timbered with fine old trees, one notices the country residence of His Excellency the Viceroy and Governor-General of India. The construction of the mansion was commenced during the Viceroyalty of the Earl of Minto in 1812, but it was considerably enlarged by the Marquis of Hastings. About 100 yards from the house is a very fine Memorial Hall in the Corinthian style of architecture, which was built by Lord Minto in 1813 in honour of men who fell during the capture of the Islands of Mauritius and Java in 1810-11. The cantonment, on the northern side of the park, is usually occupied by British regiments. Barrackpore was the scene of a rising among Sepoy troops in the year 1824, and the mutiny of 1857 may be said to have broken out there, when disaffected native infantry were sent from Berhampore to be disbanded. The men openly defied their commanding officers, set fire to barracks, officers' quarters, and telegraph station; but they were eventually subdued, and were stripped of their accoutrements and marched out of the cantonment.

There is a fine club-house with splendid tennis-grounds, while many of the riverside bungalows are extremely picturesque.

Krishnagar City is near Krishnagar Road Station, on the Eastern Bengal Railway system, and about 62 miles distant from Calcutta. It was a thriving and populous city in the days when Bengal was enduring the bitter experiences of the wars of the eighteenth century, but it has now a reputation for important industries, among which are the manufacture of mustard-oil and the making of mats, bricks, and other goods. Many of its buildings are handsome structures, but special mention should be made of a Government College, which is affiliated with the University of Calcutta.

Santipur, in the district of Nadia, is one of many unfortunate towns which have lost much of their former prosperity owing to outside influences. A century and a half ago it possessed silk-weaving factories belonging to the East India Company, and its muslins were well known throughout Europe; but the introduction of machinery into mills in England administered so severe a blow to those industries, and the terrible earthquake of 1897 destroyed such a large number of the principal buildings, that this last-named catastrophe, falling upon people whose pockets had already been lightened by the decline of their chief trade, made it impossible for a large number of them to reconstruct their premises and to regain their former prosperity. The town, however, is the centre of a prosperous district, and therefore a considerable trade is carried on in agricultural and general produce. The inhabitants of Santipur at the latest census were about 27,000 in number.

Berhampore's place in comparatively recent history arises from the fact that some of the first indications of a rising which eventually led to the mutiny in 1857 occurred there. Very few British troops were in the town at the time, and the trouble began among Sepoy soldiers who had been maliciously told that substances insulting to the religious faith of Mahommedans were used in the preparation of a portion of their food, but prompt action by the officer in charge sufficed to quell the disaffection. Another trouble occurred about two years later among recently arrived English troops, and matters became so serious that officers were threatened and fires were kindled in the barracks, but a hasty summoning from Barrackpore of a loyal regiment caused the mutineers to desist.

The fearful earthquake of 1897 did extensive damage to Government and other buildings, the loss being estimated at about Rs. 60,000.

The only industries in the town are the pounding of *surki*, the weaving of *daris*, carpentering, and the making of bamboo and cane furniture and other articles.

A very fine college, founded by the Government in 1853, a large library managed by a board of trustees, and the hospital, containing 36 beds, should not be overlooked by visitors. The town is situated on the left bank of the Bharirathi River in the district of Murshidabad.

The old city of *Murshidabad* probably figures more largely in the history of the establishment of British supremacy in Bengal than any other town in the whole of the Province, and an extended account of its rise and decline are referred to fully on another page. Suffice it to say that it became the capital of Bengal in the year 1706, but the transference of power did not protect it from assaults by the Mahrattas and other warlike tribes, as it was frequently attacked and a large number of its handsome palaces and other residences were razed to the ground. This city was formerly known throughout Europe as the chief place in India in connection with the manufacture of silk, but since machinery was introduced into England a very serious check was placed upon this industry.

Very little now remains of the ancient city, although the ruins which are still visible are forcible reminders of the architectural splendour of the majority of its buildings. There are, however, many places of interest to be seen at the present day, among them being the magnificent palace of the Nawab of Murshidabad, and a mosque, built in the year 1723, in the courtyard of which are a number of cells occupied in former days by some 600 or 700 students who attended there for daily reading of the Koran.

Plassey.—This name will recall to the mind the cruel tragedies which were enacted during the period when Suraj-ud-daula was Nawab of Bengal, for it was at that place that Clive, in 1757, inflicted a crushing defeat upon the Nawab's forces, just twelve months after that tyrant had been the instigator of the awful devilry connected with the "Black Hole" of Calcutta.

This victory practically put an end to a series of wars in Bengal which had been almost continuous for very many years, and it virtually proclaimed the establishment of British supremacy in India.

Azimganj, in the district of Murshidabad, derives much of its reputation as a busy centre for the import and export of agricultural and general produce from the fact that it has excellent railway and shipping facilities for the forwarding of merchandise to Calcutta and other markets. The town, which has a population of about 14,000 inhabitants, is situated on the right bank of the Bhagirathi River, and it is connected by river steamers with Berhampore, the chief city of the district, and with Lalhagh, Jiagunge, Dhulian, and other places in the neighbourhood. Jain merchants, who are numerous, have erected temples, as well as a number of really well-built houses, in which they reside.

Kandi, in the district of Murshidabad, would not be such an important place if it did not contain the residence of the Rajas of Paikpara. The founder of the family—who, by the way, are devout and wealthy Hindus—was Ganga Gobind Singh, who amassed a very large sum of money as *banian* for Warren Hastings, and who spent a very large portion of it in the erection of shrines and images of Krishna.

Municipal government was granted to Kandi in 1896, and it has a considerable number of the usual official buildings.

Jessore, the chief town in the district of Jessore, practically consists of five villages, which were amalgamated and formed the municipality under the single name of Jessore. It is a busy station on the Eastern Bengal Railway, as the surrounding district produces and exports large quantities of bricks, cane and bamboo goods, coir mats, and jute string.

One of the villages above referred to was known as Chanchra, and remains are still visible of the palace of former Rajas of Chanchra, and of the rampart and fossé by which the building was surrounded.

Khulna, about 107 miles distant from Calcutta, is the southern terminus of the central section of the Eastern Bengal railway, and for a hundred years or more it has been a receiving depot for large quantities of rice, sugar, betel-nuts, and other produce grown in the neighbourhood. It is on the verge of the Sundarbans, and in a northerly direction it has a service of steamers to Narayanganj, Madaripur, Muhammadpur, and other places.

1. NEW GOVERNMENT HOUSE, DACCA. 2. NEW GOVERNMENT SECRETARIAT.

Photos by Dr. S. C. Banerji.

THE DACCA DIVISION.

Narayanganj is a railway-station on the Dacca section of the Eastern Bengal Railway Company, and there is also a regular steam ferry service between the town and Goalundo. Very large quantities of tea, jute, and other produce are forwarded from Narayanganj to all parts of Bengal, and it now holds the position of chief river port in the Province.

Dacca, in the district and division of the same name, situated on the northern bank of the Burigunga River, and about 187 miles distant from Calcutta, was the capital of Bengal in the year 1706, when Murshid Kuli Khan (Diwan of the Province) transferred the Courts of Law, the Mint, and other public buildings to Muxsudabad, which was thereafter known as Murshidabad. The city at that time contained a number of such imposing buildings of beautiful architectural designs that it was frequently referred to as the "Athens of Bengal." There was the Great Kuttra, believed to have been erected about the year 1645, which, according to tradition, was built as a palace for Muhammad Suja, and an inscription in Persian on one of its walls may perhaps tend to confirm this legend. A translation of the words is as follows: "Sultan Shah Suja was employed in the performance of charitable acts. Therefore Aboo-ul-Kasim Tubba Hosseine Ulsummanee, in hopes of mercy of God, erected this building, of auspicious structure, together with 22 shops adjoining, to the end that the profits arising from them be solely appropriated by the Agents and Overseers to their repairs, and the necessities of the indigent, who, on their arrival, are to be accommodated with lodgings free of expense. And this condition is not to be violated, lest on the day of retribution the violator be punished." A fort was constructed in 1690, and although there were formerly many buildings within its walls, there are now only ruins, with the exception of the jail, which is a modern building.

Dacca still possesses many signs of its old-time greatness, although the great earthquake of 1897 caused a tremendous amount of damage. Nowadays one may see the handsome Ahsun Munzul, the palace of the Nawab of Dacca, many beautiful mansions belonging to wealthy Hindu Zemindars, as well as the Court Houses of the District Commissioner, judges, and magistrates, and the Northbrook Hall.

Excellent provision for educational facilities has been made, but the principal establishment is the Dacca Government College. The Chowk, or market-place, for merchants and traders from various places in the division is a centre where a large trade is done in agricultural and other produce.

Mymensingh, in the division of Dacca, is situated in a rich rice-growing district on the banks of the Brahmaputra River, and it is one of those towns which have grown considerably in importance since the extension of the Eastern Bengal Railway and the establishment of ferry services on the waterways of Bengal provided a larger number of outlets for the marketing of merchandise grown or produced in that Province.

Kishorganj, in the district of Mymensingh, was formerly noted for the manufacture of muslins, and for the silk factory owned by the East India Company; but its chief importance at the present day centres in a large festival, which lasts for a whole month, held in honour of Krishna. The town is about 13 miles distant from the Brahmaputra, with which it is connected by the Kunduli Khal River, upon whose bank it is built.

Faridpur, on the bank of the Mara (Dead) Padma River, is connected with the immense waterways of Bengal, which are of incalculable value in linking the city of Calcutta with towns and villages in the interior of the Province. The district, bearing the same name, produces large quantities of jute, rice, and oil-seeds; and among the industries of the town are the pressing of jute and oil, the manufacture of gold and silver jewellery, brass and copper utensils, and the making of cane furniture.

Madaripur is a rapidly growing town in the district of Faridpur, with two markets in which extensive trading takes place in all kinds of agricultural produce, but chiefly in jute. Steamers run to the Khulna terminus of the Eastern Bengal Railway, and to Goalundo, Barisal, and other places.

The Chittagong Division.

The port of Chittagong is five miles from the mouth of Karnafuli River, which flows into the north-eastern extremity of the Bay of Bengal. The town is more than a mile farther inland, while the district of Chittagong has an area of about 2,560 square miles, its boundaries being: on the north by Tippera, on the south by Arakan, on the east by the Hill Tracts of Chittagong, and on the west by the Bay of Bengal.

About twenty years ago Chittagong was the outlet for a very small quantity of tea grown in Assam, or of produce from the eastern portion of Bengal; in fact, by far the bulk of the merchandise was exported by means of boats upon the Brahmaputra River. A new era dawned, however, when the Assam-Bengal Railway, commenced in the year 1892, drew traffic from a large number of inland towns and villages, and such statistics as are available show that the trade of the port began to increase simultaneously with the extension of the line, until at the present time the value of the trade is fully four times as great as it was prior to about the year 1890.

The port, and town too, at the latter date manifested few activities, and the people themselves appeared to be indifferent to the possibilities of the local situation. With the completion of the railway in 1904, it was found that additional tea gardens had been opened by enterprising companies, and that up-country traders were only too glad to avail themselves of improved communications for the import as well as the export of merchandise. The consumption of salt, sugar, oil, and piece goods—just to mention some of the imports—has grown rapidly in the past ten or fifteen years, while the figures showing the export of tea and jute in 1900 bear no comparison with those of to-day.

There is, therefore, the prospect of a much greater trade being carried on through the port, provided that—as expert opinion says—the authorities improve not only the approaches, but also landing and shipping facilities, in order that there may be inducements for shippers to make far more use of it.

An important memorandum on the conditions and prospects of the Port of Chittagong in matters of finance, administration, and railway development (excluding engineering problems) was prepared in 1914 by the Hon. Sir Francis F. E. Spring, K.C.I.E., at the request of the Chairman of the Commissioners of the Port; and in that document the writer dealt in an exhaustive manner with the port's area of influence, the Assam-Bengal Railway in relation to the port, the development of trade, and financial and other questions; and he finally submitted a series of suggestions which, in his opinion, would, if carried out, result in making the port and the Assam-Bengal Railway (which is primarily interested in the development of the trade of the port) sound undertakings of a profitable character. Several jetties have been constructed, and the handling of cargo is greatly facilitated by hydraulic cranes of a modern type; railway lines are laid alongside the sheds on the wharves, and a complete system of electric lighting enables a pressure of work to be dealt with during the night.

The principal building in the town is the railway-station, a fine red-brick structure, ornamented at each end by minarets; and its really handsome appearance is intensified by its background of dark green foliage of palms, cacti, creepers, and other trees and plants.

Chittagong is the seat of a Commissioner, District Magistrate, and Session Judges; and while it has a number of large warehouses and commercial houses, it also possesses several bazars, which are not the healthiest and cleanest places in Bengal.

The town still shows signs of its possession, in the early days of the sixteenth century, by Portuguese, as there is a ruined fort in existence which was doubtless once the home of pirates who infested the seas in that portion of the Bay of Bengal.

Cox's Bazar, it is said, received its name from Lieutenant Cox, who was appointed to control the arrangements made for the support of Arakanese fugitives who sought shelter in British territory after their defeat by the Burmans in 1799.

The weaving of silk *lungis*, or kilts, is the chief industry carried on by these people, but the demand for these goods does not appear to be making any headway.

Comilla is the headquarters town of the district of Tippera, and is situated on the main road between Chittagong and Dacca. It suffered in earlier days from the flooding of the Gumti River, but is now protected by an embankment, which is maintained by the Raja of Hill Tippera. The town possesses a large tank, with a circumference of about a mile, which was constructed in the fifteenth century.

Much has been done in providing educational facilities, among which may be mentioned an Arts College, and a school for artisans which is attached to the Engineering College at Sibpur, near Calcutta.

The Rajshahi Division.

Rampur Boalia, or Rajshahi, is the principal town in the district of Rajshahi, and as it is not many miles distant from the towns of Murshidabad and Berhampore, which were, in the prosperous days of the East India Company, noted for their manufacture of silk, it is not surprising that a similar industry has been carried on here for nearly 150 years. The present town, situated on the north bank of the Padma River, is of comparatively modern growth, but it has a population of about 21,000 persons. Among the principal buildings is the Rajshahi College, which imparts an excellent education up to the Master of Arts standard, and a school for the study of law and Oriental languages.

Dinajpore is the centre of an exceedingly fertile district in which large quantities of rice are grown, and it is, further, a busy mart for the disposal of all kinds of agricultural produce. The town is situated on the east bank of the Purnabhaba River.

Rungpur, in the district of the same name, is one of those many towns in Bengal which underwent spoliation, and even capture, at the hands of ruthless invaders, as it is recorded that a king of Afghanistan compelled surrender of it at the close of the fifteenth century. With the supremacy of the British power, however, it has regained a position of commercial importance as the centre of a fertile district in which agricultural produce of all kinds is extensively grown. Its industries are not numerous, but they include the making of bamboo and cane furniture, carpentering, the husking of paddy and wheat, and the pressing of oil-seeds. Not far from the town are the ruins of an old fort, constructed, it is believed, by Nilambar, the last of the Khan Rajas, and a shrine said to have been erected over the staff of Muhammud Saint Ismail Ghazi, Governor of Choraghat.

Bogra.—This town, and Sherpur, are centres of commercial activity in the fertile district of Bogra. Remarkably fine crops of jute, rice, sugar-cane, and oil-seeds are grown; and the majority of the people are in a prosperous condition, chiefly owing to the wealth of agricultural products, although a considerable number are engaged in minor industries, such as the making of bamboo furniture and mats.

Pabna is a thriving town with about 18,000 inhabitants, the majority of whom are employed in connection with the export to Calcutta of large quantities of jute, rice, pulses, and oil-seeds. This is conveyed either by river boats through the Sundarbans or by steamer to Goalundo and thence by the Eastern Bengal Railway. Pabna is the headquarters of the district of Pabna.

Serajgunj.—This town, of about 23,000 persons, possesses one of the chief jute-pressing industries in Bengal. The raw material is collected from the districts of Pabna (in which Serajgunj is situated), Mymensingh, Bogra, and Rangpur, and the bales are forwarded to factories at Calcutta. Agricultural produce, too, of every description is forwarded from Pabna and adjoining districts for transference to Calcutta and other markets in Bengal.

THE "PUSH-PUSH."

Photo by T. P. Sen.

English Bazar.—Somewhere about the year 1675 the East India Company had a silk factory at this place, situated in the district of Malda, and 207 miles distant from Calcutta on the Eastern Bengal Railway. It is recorded that the Company's factory attained such importance as a commercial centre during the latter portion of the seventeenth century that its "Diaries and Consultations" from 1685 to 1693 are preserved in the India Office under the title of "Malda and Englesavada." The Bazar consists of a number of trading villages, which have a population of about 14,000 inhabitants.

At the present time the town is interested chiefly in the sale of grain, which is grown extensively in the surrounding district.

Darjeeling.—People in England and other European countries may take up an encyclopædia or a volume of travels in India and read of the huge range of the Himalayan mountains; they marvel at the description of the wondrous scenery, comprising towering peaks, glistening snow, fertile plains, and luxuriant vegetation, but anything approaching a realistic conception of the transcendent beauties of the picture cannot be given in cold print.

Darjeeling is situated at an elevation of about 7,000 feet above the level of the sea, and the bracing air, swept from snowy summits about 50 miles distant, gives new life and increased energy to individuals whose daily work is carried on in the humid and depressing atmosphere of Calcutta and other cities.

The Governor of Bengal and many Government officials, as well as private persons, migrate from Calcutta to Darjeeling at the commencement of the summer months, and the town now enjoys a well-deserved reputation as an ideal place for a holiday or as a sanatorium for overworked or invalid persons.

Further reference to Darjeeling will be found on another page in this book.

Native States under the Government of Bengal.

The Cooch Behar Native State is in political relationship with the Government of Bengal, and it is bounded on the north by the Western Dooars of Jalpaiguri, on the south by the district of Rungpur, on the east by the districts of Rungpur and Goalpara, and on the west by the districts of Rungpur and Jalpaiguri. It has an area of about 1,307 square miles; its greatest length is 64 miles, and it is 33 miles in breadth; and the inhabitants, at the census of 1911, numbered nearly 600,000 persons.

The State was originally a portion of the ancient Kamrup kingdom, but it was recognized as a separate country in 1502. It is not by any means clear when the Kamrup dynasty was a power in India, but it is tolerably certain that Bhugadatta, one of its kings, reigned during the twelfth century before the Christian era, and Hindu traditions lead one to believe that its foundation took place quite twelve centuries before Bhugadatta began to reign.

The Kamrup country was governed successively by Naraki, Pala, and Khen kings, but troubles arose by reason of a successful invasion by Mussulmans, who in their turn were expelled by Assamese, and by a subsequent period of anarchy, which resulted in the kingdom being split up into a number of small principalities.

Chiefs of the great Koch tribe were paramount in some of these divided territories, and it is from one of these Rulers, who was King of Chikna about the year A.D. 1510, that the Cooch Behar family can trace its descent.

Cooch Behar, one of the divided areas, consisted, at the last-mentioned date, of a very large area of Bengal, but envious eyes prompted invasions by the Mahommedan Governors of Gaur and Chittagong, and by Mir Jumla, Governor of Bengal, who deposed the reigning king, destroyed Hindu temples, and created great unrest among the people. Bitterness among the inhabitants, caused by intolerant government, followed until the year 1788, when a Commission was appointed to inquire into the causes and effects of maladministration. The inquiry resulted in the appointment in 1822 by the Governor of an agent whose headquarters were on the north-eastern frontier of the Province, whose duty it was to act as the medium between the Government of Bengal and Cooch Behar.

Coming to later years, it is found that the title of Maharaja was subsequently conferred upon the Ruling Chiefs, who, successively, took a deep interest in the prosperity of their country and in the welfare of its people. The Maharaja Sir Nripendra Narayan Bhup Bahadur, G.C.I.E., C.B., A.D.C., was born in the year 1826, and he succeeded the Maharaja Narendra Narayan Bhup Bahadur in the following year. The early portion of his life was spent in Cooch Behar, but he afterwards prosecuted his studies under accomplished tutors in Benares, and ultimately in Europe, where he visited England, France, Belgium, and other countries. He paid frequent visits to Cooch Behar, however, where he gratified his natural inclination for indulging in manly exercises of all kinds. He became an expert shot, and it is probable that he had a unique experience in bagging a tiger when only ten years of age.

The Maharaja attained his majority in October 1883, and was formally installed in his high position on the 8th of the following month by Sir Rivers Thompson, then Lieutenant-Governor of Bengal. His marriage, in 1878, with Suniti Bala Devi, eldest daughter of Keshub Chunder Sen, the founder of the New Dispensation Church, evidently caused him to establish, in 1888, the Somaja, or the Reformed Church of the State.

The Maharaja, accompanied by the Maharani and their children, visited England on the occasion of the Jubilee of Queen Victoria in 1887, and he was then personally invested with the honour of G.C.I.E., while his consort was decorated by Her late Majesty with the Imperial Order of the Crown of India.

The present Ruler is His Highness the Maharaja Jitendra Narayan Bhup Bahadur.

The majority of the inhabitants of the State are connected in some way or other with agricultural pursuits, and very large areas are devoted to the cultivation of sugar-cane, tea, oats, tobacco, and jute. Ordinary industries are therefore few in number and do not command much attention, but mention may be made of the weaving of silk and cotton cloths, the manufacture of pottery, gold and silver ornaments, bamboo cots and chairs, mats, *hookahs*, fans, and sandals.

The town of Cooch Behar is situated on the western bank of the River Torsha, and a very pleasing prospect meets one's eye on emerging from the railway-station, as in the immediate neighbourhood are luxuriant pasture lands backed up by the steely-grey slopes of the Bhutan range, while the towering heights of the Himalayas are visible in the far distance.

Roads and streets, running at right angles, have an abundance of welcome shade afforded by avenues of palm, mango, and other trees, while glimpses of domes and spires of temples and remarkably pretty private residences are obtained through the verdant foliage. The palace of the Maharaja and the public buildings of the State are clustered around the Sagai Dighi Square, in which there is an extensive sheet of water, 945 feet in length and 536 feet in breadth, constructed in the year 1812. Other fine structures include a hospital, dispensary, a Gothic Court of Justice, and Lansdowne House, erected in honour of the visit to the State of the Marquis of Lansdowne, a former Viceroy of India.

The old palace of the Maharajas was superseded in 1828 by a magnificent building, described by the architect as follows: "The Cooch Behar Palace is designed after the classical style of architecture. It is, in the main, with the exception of the three pavilions on the roof and the basement of the dome, a well-defined two-storied building, raised 4 feet 9 inches from the ground, with an area of 1,309 square feet; its length is 393 feet and its breadth is 296 feet."

The interior is luxuriously furnished, almost entirely in accordance with English tastes, but the Durbar Hall is Oriental in character. When the Maharaja ascends the *gadi* on special occasions a brilliant and impressive scene is witnessed, in which the rich costumes of the East, studded with priceless jewels of all kinds, form a picture of bewildering beauty.

The palace stands in a magnificent park, in which there are grounds for tennis, racquets, and cricket, while the lovely flower gardens are the envy of all beholders.

Hill Tippera is a Native State in the northern portion of the division of Chittagong, and has an area of about 4,086 square miles, with a population of 230,000 inhabitants.

History shows that the ancient kingdom of Tippera had a much larger area than the State has at the present time, that its people were almost continually embroiled in conflicts with their neighbours, that the Mahommedans and others raided the country in the year 1279, and at intervals during the succeeding four centuries, in which period the extent of the kingdom very materially decreased in size. When the East India Company obtained the *dewani* of Bengal, they placed a Raja in power, and during the past 100 years each Ruler has received investiture from the Government of India, the present Raja, His Highness the Bisama Samara Bijoyee Mahamahadaya Pancha Srijukta, Raja Birendra Kishore Dev Burman Manikyam Bahadur, succeeding to the title in 1879.

Primitive methods of preparing and cultivating land are still in vogue throughout the greater portion of the State, and these consist chiefly in the felling and burning of trees and the sowing of seeds in roughly made holes as soon as rain falls. The principal crops are rice, tobacco, cotton, chilies, mustard, sugar-cane, and onions, and a considerable quantity of these are exported; while the imports comprise European goods of various kinds, kerosene oil, and salt.

Manufactures and industries are almost non-existent, although cotton cloth is made by Tippera and Manipuri women; and schools have been started, in many of which carpentering and working in iron and other metals are taught.

The capital of the State, Agartala, situated on the right and left banks of the River Haora, is unimportant, excepting that it contains the palace of the Raja.

Near to the mansion is a temple regarded as sacred by the Tipperas, as it contains fourteen heads (made in gold and other metals) of their tutelary deities.

The vast tract of forests and swamps forming the lower portion of the delta of the Ganges River, known as the Sundarbans, comprises the districts of Twenty-four Perganas, Khulna, in the Presidency division, and Backergunge, in the division of Dacca, but its physical features are so distinct from the remainder of Bengal that it may be advisable to treat it here as a separate entity. The area is about 6,526 square miles in extent, and it stretches for 170 miles along the shores of the Bay of Bengal and for 60 to 80 miles in an inland direction. It is intersected by estuaries of the Ganges, the chief of which are the Hooghly, Matla, Raimangal, Haringhata, and Meghna. It is, in fact, a network of streams and rivers, among which are a large number of islands, varying from time to time in size and shape, according to the action of the watercourses. Land is being reclaimed for cultivation purposes, not only from the swamps but also from the islands, upon many of which there are dense forests and jungle.

This alluvial soil is exceedingly rich in productive constituents, and very heavy crops of rice are grown, chiefly in the northern portion; but good returns are also obtained from sugar-cane and betel-nuts. There are about 2,080 square miles of reserved forests within the district of Khulna, from which immense quantities of good timber, firewood, and thatching and other similar materials are derived; while in the protected forests in the Twenty-four Perganas (which about the year 1910 were about 1,600 square miles in extent) have in recent years been thrown open for cultivation, and have consequently been considerably reduced in size.

The principal exports are timber, rice,

1. A HINDU HOME, BENGAL. 2. HINDU OFFERING FRUIT AND SWEETMEAT TO THE SACRED RIVER, GANGES.

Photos by T. P. Sen.

3. VILLAGE BOAT IN EASTERN ASSAM.

Photo by D. C. Ghosha.

and betel-nuts, together with pottery, made by inhabitants from black clay.

Port Canning, situated on the Matla River, and in the north-western portion of the Sundarbans, is connected by rail with Calcutta, but the only other means of communication with that city and other business centres in Bengal are obtained by steamers and various kinds of country boats, which are used for the transport of passengers as well as cargo.

The dense jungle on the islands is still the home of a considerable number of wild animals, which include tigers, buffaloes, and spotted and other deer. The rivers are infested with crocodiles, dangerous to man and beast, and the cobra, python, and other species of snakes are far too plentiful; while geese, ducks, and other waterfowl may always be relied upon to provide the enjoyment of a day's good shooting.

There does not appear to be any historic account of this deltaic plain until about the middle of the fifteenth century, when a Mahommedan, named Khan Jahan, received permission from the King of Gaur to clear jungle in the area now known as the district of Khulna.

The Sundarbans are now visited by tourists, who find much to interest them in the pleasant trip down the Hooghly from Calcutta, in witnessing the work of reclamation of land from swamps, in the methods of agriculture, and in the habits and customs of the people. Archæologists will endeavour to inspect the tomb of Khan Jahan; the ruins of Iswaripur, an ancient capital of a Raj granted by an Emperor of Delhi to a chief Minister of Daud, King of Bengal; and the remains of the temple of Navaratna, all of which are near Khaliganj, in the district of Khulna.

Traces are still visible also of the Jhatar Dad temple in the district of the Twenty-four Perganas.

THE ASANSOL DISTILLERY

This distillery was erected by Messrs. Carew & Co., Ltd., in 1905-6, in order to fulfil contracts entered into with the Government of Bengal for the supply of spirit to various districts under their contract system; but, unfortunately, the quantity called for was considerably curtailed by the partition of Bengal. The distillery is well equipped with the most modern plant, and turns out spirit of the highest quality. It also produces a certain amount of high-strength alcohol for medical and industrial purposes, and, with a view of extending the business, plant is being erected for the purification of crude alcohol, producing a spirit equal to the high standard demanded by pharmaceutical chemists. It also manufactures methylated spirit.

The raw materials used are Mowha flowers and molasses. The former are procured from various districts in Bengal, Behar and Orissa, and the Central Provinces, the best quality being obtained from the last-named district.

The distillery is a good example of the ability of India to produce, within her own confines, articles which she normally imports from outside.

Asansol is a large town, 132 miles distant from Calcutta, with a station on the East Indian Railway system, and it is situated in the centre of the famous Raneegunge coal fields in the district of Burdwan, in Bengal.

THE BENGAL PAPER MILL COMPANY, LTD.

This company was registered in the year 1889, and the mill, which is situated on the bank of the Damoodar River at Raneegunge, in the district of Burdwan, is about 120 miles distant by rail from Calcutta. The manufacture of paper was commenced there in the year 1891.

The whole of the property extends to about 173 acres, the mill and adjoining premises alone covering more than four acres. The cost of the erection of the buildings was approximately Rs. 2,1,60,000.

For several years after formation the company made little or no headway, owing to the keen competition of other Indian mills and the importation of cheap papers from Europe.

Reconstruction of the company took place in 1903, and the capital now stands at Rs. 6,00,000, in 16,000 ordinary shares of Rs. 25 each and 4,000 preference shares of Rs. 50 each, fully paid up, together with debentures amounting to Rs. 5,07,700. The directors of the company are Messrs. C. W. Foley, R. J. G. Ballantyne, and H. W. Carr. The managing agents are Messrs. Balmer, Lawrie & Co., of 103 Clive Street, Calcutta, whose offices are the registered address of the company.

There are three paper-making machines in the mill, and one of these is 120 inches in width and is the largest in India. The mill steam boiler installation consists of a battery of ten Lancashire boilers, for supplying steam for the main engine of 1,300 h.p. and auxiliary plant, and also for that which is required for boiling grass and other raw material used in the process of manufacture.

The chief productions of the mill are white printing and writing papers, and Badami and brown wrapping papers made from grass, wood pulp, rags, and jute. The whole of the raw material required is found in India, with the exception of wood pulp, which, together with all chemicals, has to be imported from Europe, and suitable grass is obtained from the Nagpur, Sahebgunge, and Nepal Hill districts.

The raw material is first carefully dusted, then well boiled, and again similarly treated until all the dirt has been removed, after which it is pulped and bleached to the required whiteness, chloride of lime being used in the latter process. The mills are equipped with an up-to-date plant, to which additions are being made whenever improvements are discovered.

One of the most important phases of the manufacturing process is carried out in the beating engines (of which there are a large number), and it is here that the sizing, loading, and colouring matters are added to the half-prepared raw material. When beating and mixing have been completed the material is ready to be made into paper on the paper-making machines, and it is then run into a large stuff chest placed at the end of each machine. The arrangement of the buildings and plant is so complete that no wastage of water takes place, as the latter is pumped back again to storage tanks for further use. The wet pulp is run through the paper-making machine at the required thickness, and it is gradually dried by a large number of steam-heated cylinders, the necessary finish being placed on the paper by means of callender rolls situated at the extreme end of the paper-machine. The paper is then cut to the required size and conveyed to the finishing-houses, where it is sorted and packed for dispatch.

The average monthly output of the mill is about 570 tons, a considerable portion of this quantity being supplied under contracts to the Government of India and to railway authorities. Water for all purposes is derived from the Damoodar River.

The mill and bungalows are lighted by electricity generated by the company's

NURSAMOODA DISTILLERY.

1. Distilling Yard. 2. Fermentation House. 3. Distillery from the North. 4. Manager's Bungalow.

THE BENGAL PAPER MILLS COMPANY, LTD.

1. No. 2 Finishing-room. 2. The Mill from the North. 3. The Mill from the West. 4. South View.

THE BENGAL PAPER MILLS COMPANY, LTD.

1. Paper Cutters. 2. No. 1 Beater House. 3. No. 2 Machine. 4. No. 3 Machine.

own electric plant, and protection against fire is secured as far as possible by an elaborate hydrant service, which is placed in conspicuous positions in every portion of the buildings. Large warehouse accommodation for raw material is also available, and the mill is equipped with the most up-to-date plant in its soda-water factory, and there are also necessary engineering workshops for new work and general repairs.

Mr. Horsburgh, the manager of the mill, resides at Raneegunge, and he is assisted by twelve Europeans, for whom furnished bungalows are provided, while the average number of the Indian staff employed is about 1,000 daily.

KUMARDHUBI ENGINEERING WORKS, LTD.

These works, of modern and electrical equipment, are situated at Barakar, in the midst of the coal and iron districts. They are devoted to the manufacture of mining machinery, hauling and winding engines for steam, air, and electric power, head-gears, coal screening and preparing machinery, roofs, bridges, aerial rope-ways, etc. The establishment comprises a large up-to-date foundry capable of turning out 1,500 tons of finished iron and brass castings monthly. The company is one of a large group of industrial concerns controlled by Messrs. Bird & Co., Calcutta.

KUMARDHUBI FIRECLAY AND SILICA WORKS, LTD.

This concern is controlled by Messrs. Bird & Co., Calcutta, and is in close proximity to Kumardhubi Engineering Works. It manufactures fireclay, magnesite, silica, and chrome bricks, and refractory goods generally for iron, steel, ordnance, railway, and gas and industrial works, as well as glazed stoneware pipes and similar material.

THE RANEEGUNGE POTTERY WORKS

There is no doubt that India possesses a practically inexhaustible supply of clays of various grades, ranging from low-class substances, which for generations have been made into sun-dried bricks, to a high-class composition for the manufacture of earthenware and ornamental pottery. Every Hindu village has its potter, who makes small vessels for cooking and other purposes, and larger ones for the storage of grain, water, and other commodities, but in recent years large enterprises have been established on modern lines, one of the foremost of which may be seen at Raneegunge.

These works were established in the year 1866 by a Mr. George Macdonald, son of a Caithness (Scotland) minister, who had previously practised for a number of years in Calcutta as a civil engineer, and on his retirement they were acquired by Messrs. Burn & Co.

There are several varieties of clay within a radius of a few miles from the Raneegunge Works, and supplies of these are conveyed to the yards by bullock-carts. In the workshops one can witness the various operations which convert masses of earth into small pipes for household purposes, larger ones for drainage and sewerage works (some of the latter being 24 in. in diameter and weighing more than 250 lb.), roofing and floor tiles, building bricks, glazed stone-ware, and sundry other articles, and pottery of the highest grade of ceramics. Modern machinery is employed in nearly all processes of manufacture. The clay is first of all ground or crushed to powder by rollers $2\frac{3}{4}$ tons in weight; it is then elevated to a screen, through which it is passed. After being mixed with water it is thoroughly worked in pug mills; then it is forced through a die of the required diameter. The length of pipe is then determined by means of a piece of thin wire, and finally the completed pipes are automatically turned out by the plant. Hand trolleys are used for the conveyance of the "made" pipes to the drying tunnel, or shed, which is 110 ft. in length and has a floor space of 45,000 sq. ft. In this building, which is heated by steam and kept at a regular temperature, the pipes are remedied where practicable, but those containing serious flaws or which are broken in any way are returned to be re-ground. When the pipes are sufficiently dry they are transferred to the kilns to be burned and glazed. There are sixty-five kilns in use at the present time. The pipes manufactured at these works in the course of a year would, if placed in a line, cover a distance of more than 130 miles, and the immense stock kept in the yards covers an area of not less than 7 acres in extent. These pipes are well known throughout the whole of India, and large quantities are shipped to Burma, the Straits Settlements, and Aden and other distant places.

An excellent supply of water is obtained from a tank 18 ft. in depth and $3\frac{1}{2}$ acres in extent. This water is also available for the large boilers and engines of over 200 h.p. which have been constructed by the company at their Howrah Ironworks.

For testing purposes several pipes are taken from each burning, and their strength is ascertained by subjecting them to a pressure of 30 lb. to the square inch. This is merely a private test, sufficient for all practical purposes, but a few years ago trials were conducted in the presence of a committee appointed by the Government of India, and the results proved that the Raneegunge pipes were superior to those manufactured in England. For example, six Raneegunge pipes of 9 in. diameter required an average internal pressure of 121·8 lb. to burst them, while those from England of the same dimensions withstood only 52·5 lb. Again, a similar number of pipes were crushed by machines, with the following results: 9-in. ones from Raneegunge broke at an average weight of 4,037·3 lb., English ones gave way at 3,192 lb., while the figures for 12-in. pipes were respectively 5,069·5 lb. and 3,472 lb. From the point of view of strength alone a verdict would be given in favour of Raneegunge products, but a further recommendation is that whereas a 1,760 yards layer of pipes from the latter works costs Rs. 2,640, the charge for iron ones of the same diameter would be considerably more than Rs. 9,000.

Large sheds are fitted with up-to-date machinery, which is capable of turning out some thirty thousand firebricks daily. Enamelled bricks are made by hand, being prepared with white faces; they are then dried and burned to a "biscuit" colour, glazed, and subsequently re-burned. The large stock kept at the factory includes glazed bricks suitable for bath and other rooms, together with damp-proof bricks for stores and go-downs. Other buildings are occupied by workers who manufacture sanitary appliances of all kinds, water-filters, fireclay bricks and blocks for mills, collieries, ironworks, and tea factories. Roofing and flooring tiles are manufactured by the thousand every day of the week.

Something of a more artistic character is seen upon entering the terra-cotta department, in which all kinds of mouldings are stamped from iron moulds, while larger pieces are produced by hand from plaster moulds. Here may be noticed

THE BENGAL IRON AND STEEL COMPANY, LTD. (MARTIN & CO.).

1, 2. Coke Ovens, Charging Side. 3, 4. Views of the Bengal Iron and Steel Company's Works at Kulti, East Indian Railway.

(For letterpress, see p. 157.)

KUMARDHUBI ENGINEERING WORKS, LTD.

1. New Foundry and Blacksmith Shop under Construction. 2. Office and Constructional Yard. 3. Interior of Fitting Shop.

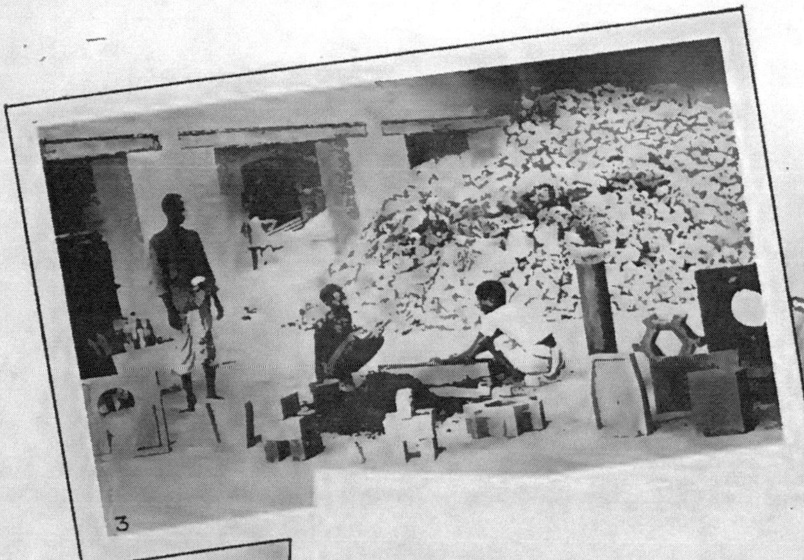

KUMARDHUBI FIRECLAY AND SILICA COMPANY, LTD.

1. GENERAL VIEW. 2. KILNS AND STACKS. 3. INTERIOR OF SILICA AND MAGNESITE MOULDING SHEDS.

THE RANEEGUNGE POTTERY WORKS.

1. General View of a Portion of the Raneegunge Potteries. 2. Stock Yard.

a choice selection of vases, capitals, cupolas, cornices, scrolls, linings, and beadings, while several statues and portico entablatures of considerable size have been executed with the greatest skill in these shops. Many of the finest buildings in India have been decorated with terra-cotta made at these works, which adds very considerably to their appearance, and among these structures in Calcutta are the Government Museum, the Serpent House at the Zoological Gardens, the boiler-house at the Government Docks, and shipping and other offices. Another building to claim notice is the one devoted to the production of indoor ceramics, and the visitor is struck by the marvellous and unique design of the various works of art in the process of being manufactured. One operative is busy over an ordinary household teapot, another displays, with some pride, a mural panel upon which a Hindu divinity is depicted, and, in fact, all the hands are employed in making choice specimens of vases, ornaments, trays, images, and a large number of other artistic wares, all of which are designed in the company's drawing offices at the works, or are made according to the expressed wishes of clients. Specimens of these articles have been exhibited from time to time, and several medals have been awarded for their excellent style and quality. About 100 tons of coal are required daily for the burning process, and this quantity is obtained from the firm's own mines on the estate, two shafts, each of 100 ft. in depth, having been sunk.

Messrs. Burn & Co. have erected very comfortable lines for their coolies employed at the Raneegunge Works, and further provision for the welfare of these hands has been made by the opening of a dispensary and the appointment of a fully qualified medical officer, who resides near the works.

TARPUR SUGAR WORKS, LTD.

1. The Tarpur Sugar Mill. 2. Factory Yard and Godown.

CONCLUDING NOTE

BEFORE taking final leave of this volume, the compiler finds pleasure in acknowledging the services of those who contributed so markedly to the successful outcome of the enterprise. To some extent a stranger in a strange land, he had no claim, other than his record of work done in other spheres, to any special consideration when he commenced his labours. But nothing could have been happier than the conditions under which he actually prosecuted his enterprise in Bengal and the adjoining Provinces. A kindly disposition to lighten the work of himself and his representatives went hand in hand with the most charming hospitality and a *camaraderie* which never failed under the most exacting conditions. But bright as the compiler's memories are of his Indian experiences, he would be conveying a wrong impression if he allowed it to be understood that the work was all plain sailing. The European War has raged throughout the whole period of compilation, causing inevitable serious delays; and it was always somewhat doubtful whether the valuable letterpress and photographs, dispatched week by week, would reach London in safety.

The general members of the staff actively engaged in Bengal rendered efficient and loyal service throughout the period in which the book was in process of production. Special thanks are due to Mr. R. Vintcent Solomon, who superintended the Calcutta office, and through whose hands the entire letterpress and photographs passed, and who also carried the management of the business on his shoulders during the compiler's absence in New Zealand and Ceylon; to Mr. J. W. Kiddall, to whose pen is due the various descriptive articles of the towns and districts, together with many valuable notes obtained by careful research; to Messrs. J. W. Bond and E. T. Mungavin for help in compilation; and to Babu G. C. Chatterjee for clerical assistance.

The compiler was especially fortunate in securing from expert authorities valuable monographs on the subjects with which they are acquainted. In this connection thanks are due and tendered to His Excellency the Right Hon. Baron Carmichael of Skirling, G.C.I.E., K.C.M.G., Governor of Bengal; the Hon. Mr. P. C. Lyon, C.S.I., I.C.S.; and the Hon. Mr. N. D. Beatson-Bell, C.S.I., C.I.E., I.C.S., Members of the Bengal Council; to Captain H. G. Vaux, Military Secretary to H.E. the Governor of Bengal; Captain Oswald Smith, of His Excellency's Bodyguard; the Hon. Mr. T. R. Filgate, C.I.E.; Mr. C. B. Bayley, C.V.O., of the Bengal Public Works Department; and to Mr. McGlashan, M.Inst.C.E., of the Port Commissioners Trust, Calcutta, for their advice and kindly co-operation. Grateful acknowledgments are also due to the following gentlemen for the articles against their names: To Mr. L. S. S. O'Malley, I.C.S., of the Bengal Secretariat (Native Races); Mr. J. A. Sandbrook, editor of the *Englishman* (Commerce); Mr. T. Southwell, A.R.C.Sc. (Lond.), F.Z.S., Director of Fisheries, Bengal, Behar and Orissa (Fisheries); Mr. Walter Nuttall, of Digultarung Estate, Assam (Fauna); Mr. Wynne Sayer, B.A., Assistant to the Agricultural Adviser, Government of India (Sugar and Agriculture); Mr. G. D. Hope, B.Sc., Ph.D., Scientific Officer, Indian Tea Association (Tea); Mr. J. F. Podger and Mr. F. F. Chrestien (Mica); Mr. D. J. Reid (Indigo); and Mr. Humphrey G. Carter, M.B., Ch.B., Officiating Director, Botanical Survey of India (Flora); and Mr. A. B. Morrison. Thanks, too, must be given to Messrs. Shirley Tremearne and Pat. Lovett, of *Capital*; Mr. James Hutchinson, Secretary of the Royal Calcutta Turf Club; Captain Alfred Brame; the Registrar, Assam Secretariat; Mr. C. H. Gordon, of Moorla Indigo Concern; Mr. C. Ismay, of the Bengal-Nagpur Railway Company, Calcutta; and Mr. J. A. M. Wilson, of the Behar Planters' Association.

This is the second volume for which I have been fortunate enough to secure the services of Mr. Arnold Wright as Editor. Mr. Wright is an author whose books and articles are well known throughout the world, and who also served many years in India.

Thanks are also due to Messrs. J. F.

CONCLUDING NOTE

Peters and W. Van der Lowen, of the general staff, for the majority of the photographs in the volume; and to the following for permission to reproduce various illustrated photographs: Messrs. Johnston and Hoffmann, Calcutta ; the Himalayan Art Studio and Mr. M. Sain, of Darjeeling ; Mr. T. P. Sen, of Calcutta; Messrs. Ghosal Bros., of Shillong; Mr. D. C. Ghosal, of Jorhat ; the Director, Zoological Survey of India; Commander la Touche, R.I.M.; and Messrs. W. M. Nuttall and R. O. Podger.

My sincere thanks are also tendered to Messrs. Unwin Bros., Ltd., printers, of Pilgrim Street, London, E.C., for the great care and attention which they have, as heretofore, devoted to the preparation of the book for publication under conditions of serious embarrassment owing to the heavy military calls made upon their staff.

Somerset Playne

The Foreign and Colonial Compiling and Publishing Company

GLOSSARY

Anna. One sixteenth of a rupee : equivalent to a penny.

Bahádur. Under the Mahommedan Government a title of honour given to the nobles of the Court. At the present day a distinction conferred upon Indian officers in the service of the Government, usually in association with an additional title as Khan Bahádur.

Banian. A Hindu trader, shopkeeper, or moneylender. In Bengal it is commonly applied to the Indian cashier or man of business in the service of European firms.

Bhadra-lok. Indian gentleman.

Chaddar. A sheet or cloth ; also used to describe a shawl.

Chowkidar. A watchman.

Crore. Ten millions, a hundred lakhs or hundred thousands.

Dák Bungalow. A travellers' rest-house maintained by the Government.

Dehát. Villages collectively belonging to the same proprietor ; the whole of an estate.

Dewan. The chief executive officer of a ruling chief.

Dharamsálá. A rest-house for Indian travellers.

Dhoti. A scanty loin-cloth worn by men.

Dhurries. Cotton carpets.

Farashes. Cloths.

Farman. A mandate, an order, a command, a patent.

Gadi. The seat of rank or royalty ; a throne.

Gharry. A carriage of any description.

Ghát. A landing-place, steps on the banks of a river, a quay, a wharf ; also a pass through mountains.

Ghee. Clarified butter.

Gur. Molasses, treacle, raw sugar, the produce of the first inspissation of the juice of the cane.

Hooka. A pipe.

Jemadar. A headman.

Juming. Wasteful cultivation of land by devastation of forests for the production of one crop.

Kumar. The eldest son of a Raja.

Kumari. The eldest daughter of a Raja.

Kutchery. A court, a hall, an office. The place where any public business is transacted.

Lakh. One hundred thousand.

Lota. An earthen vessel.

Luggy. A pole : a measuring rod.

Mali. A gardener.

Mallick. An owner.

Mantras. Prayers.

Maund. 80 lb.

Mauza. A village.

Nalita. Jute leaf.

Nazarana. Succession fees.

Pagri. A turban.

Panchayat. A court of arbitration consisting of five or more members.

Pat. Jute.

Pathsala. An aided private school.

Peon. The term commonly used by Europeans for the Hindustani *piada*, a footman, a foot soldier ; an inferior officer of police, a personal messenger or servant.

Perganna. A district, a province, a tract of country containing many villages, a fiscal division.

Peshkosh. Tax, tribute—literally, what is first drawn ; fine, quit rent ; a fine or present to the ruling power on receiving an appointment.

Pice. A quarter of an anna : equivalent to one farthing.

Pottah. An ordinary lease.

Pujá. Ceremonial worship.

Punkah. An overhead fan.

Purdah. A veil, a screen, a curtain especially one which excludes the women of a family from the gaze of men.

Purdah-nisheen. Literally seated behind a curtain. An Indian lady who observes the rules of exclusion.

Rabi. A winter crop.

Raj. The estate of a Raja.

Rani. The wife of a Raja.

Ryot. A cultivator, a farmer, a peasant.

Sanad. A grant, a diploma, a charter, a patent ; a document defining the status and rights of an Indian ruler under the British Government.

Saree. A long cloth worn by Indian women, wrapped round the body and passed over the head.

Shikari. A hunter.

Swadeshi. Refers chiefly to goods manufactured by Indians for Indians ; a swadeshi industry is one exclusively financed and worked by Indians.

Tahsildar. A Government receiver of revenue.

Talug. A dependency, a district, a division of a province, a part of a Zemindari.

Terai. Plains or flat land.

Zemindar. A landlord.

Zemindary. An estate.

INDEX

The black figures indicate the principal notices in this work.

INDEX

INDEX

INDEX